LITERATURE
FOR OUR TIME

THIRD EDITION

LITERATURE FOR OUR TIME

An Anthology for College Students

THIRD EDITION

Edited by

HARLOW O. WAITE
Syracuse University

BENJAMIN P. ATKINSON
Hobart and William Smith Colleges

HENRY HOLT AND COMPANY · NEW YORK

COPYRIGHT, 1947, 1953, © 1958, BY
HENRY HOLT AND COMPANY, INC.
LIBRARY OF CONGRESS CATALOG CARD NUMBER: 58-6315

29175-0418

PRINTED IN THE UNITED STATES OF AMERICA

PREFACE TO THE THIRD EDITION

IN THIS THIRD EDITION we have again organized our selections from modern writing according to the types of literature they exemplify. To make room for many new readings we have eliminated those having a relatively limited appeal. In making these changes we have held to our standards for the first edition: to offer to the modern reader a selection of the best literature in drama, essay, poetry, short story—and through these and other art forms to stimulate interest in the significant ideas and attitudes of the twentieth century. As we wrote in 1946, "the problem of our time is how modern man can learn to live in harmony with his neighbors. He can more easily achieve that harmony if he understands his world, with all its political, social, moral, ethical, and spiritual puzzles. This book shows him how some of the writers of our time have endeavored to solve the puzzles." A good many of the additions we have made in the present revision were chosen to reflect an increasing concern with the assumptions and origins of this problem, as well as to illustrate the ways in which it is currently expressed.

We have made four major changes in the readings. The addition of Joseph Conrad's *Heart of Darkness* has enlarged the short story section and provided an example of the short novel. Two of the plays have been replaced by George Bernard Shaw's *Major Barbara* and Jean Giraudoux's *Tiger at the Gates* (in the Christopher Fry translation). Along with additions to the poems of Frost, Auden, and Thomas, which make possible a more thorough study of these three poets, we have added works of seven poets who have come to notice since 1950. Further additions to the anthology as a whole include short stories by Dylan Thomas and Mark Schorer, and essays by Herbert Gold, Carlton J. H. Hayes, John Kouwenhoven, Weller Embler, C. E. Montague, O. R. Frisch, and Peter Drucker. Among the new illustrations are drawings by Saul Steinberg as well as paintings by George Tooker, Stanley Spencer, Andrew Wyeth, and Ben Shahn.

Within each section of the anthology we have intended a particular purpose or plan, which selection and arrangement make clear. This is most apparent in Part I, where painter, poet, short story writer and essayist deal with the theme of "Coming-of-Age in Our Time" in their differing ways. This opening

Preface to the Third Edition

section is meant to suggest to the reader how the selections that follow may be used in exploring themes and viewpoints through various types of literature and art. Part II, "How Writing Is Written," presents the writer on his own art and emphasizes the sense of craft which the modern reader needs in order to share fully in literary experience. Here, for example, will be found Thomas Wolfe on the novel, Maugham on prose, Anderson on tragedy.

Parts III, IV, V, and VI bring together varying examples of the literary types—Story, Drama, Poetry, Prose. Within each of these Parts, the selections are arranged to help the reader, by taking him from the easy to the difficult (as in the story), or by offering him the older and more familiar as an introduction to the newer and more complex (as in the poetry), or by keeping his attention on a number of recurrent ideas (as in the prose). The Appendices include listings of modern novels and of recordings by contemporary poets, biographies of the authors, and an index of titles, first lines, and contributors.

We wish to express our thanks to Donald Dike of Syracuse University and John Lydenberg of Hobart and William Smith Colleges for their many suggestions.

Syracuse University   H. O. W.
Hobart and William Smith Colleges   B. P. A.
September 1, 1957

CONTENTS

PART I: COMING-OF-AGE IN OUR TIME

Prefatory note, 1
Walt Whitman: "Years of the Modern," 2
Shakespeare: from *As You Like It,* 3
E. E. Cummings: "in Just-spring," 3
Archibald MacLeish: "Eleven," 4
Picture: Picasso, "Youth," 5
John Steinbeck: "The Red Pony," Part I, 5
Picture: Ben Shahn, "Handball," 23
Aldous Huxley: "Young Archimedes," 24
James Joyce: "Araby," 46
Dylan Thomas: "Extraordinary Little Cough," 50
Thomas Wolfe: "The Lost Boy," 57
Shakespeare: "Polonius to Laertes," 79
F. Scott Fitzgerald: letter to his daughter, 80
W. B. Yeats: "A Prayer for My Daughter," 81
Carl Sandburg: "A father sees a son nearing manhood," 82
Kenneth Fearing: "Any Man's Advice to His Son," 83
Picture: Stanley Spencer, "The Nursery," 84
Herbert Gold: "The Age of Happy Problems," 85

PART II: HOW WRITING IS WRITTEN

Prefatory note, 93
Picture: Abner Dean, "Inspiration," 94-95
C. E. Montague, "Words, Words, Words," 96
W. Somerset Maugham: "Writing Prose," 100
Ben Jonson: from "Discoveries," 110
Joseph Conrad: "Preface" to *Nigger of the Narcissus,* 110
Randall Jarrell: "The Obscurity of the Poet," 113
S. T. Coleridge: from "On Style," 125
Picture: March Avery, line drawing, 126
William McFee: from *The Pattern-Makers,* 126
S. I. Hayakawa: "The Language of Reports," 127
George Orwell: "Politics and the English Language," 135

Contents

Thomas Wolfe: from *The Story of a Novel,* 144
Life: "Untragic America," 150
Maxwell Anderson: "The Essence of Tragedy," 153
Bonamy Dobrée: "The New Way of Writing," 158
Leo Stein: from *Appreciation,* 168
Picture: Harold Edgerton, speed photograph, 168
Picture: Picasso, detail from Guernica mural, 168
Gertrude Stein: "How Writing Is Written," 169
Picture: Saul Steinberg, line drawing, 176-177

Part III: STORIES

Prefatory note, 179
John Dos Passos: "The Campers at Kitty Hawk," 180
John Dos Passos: "Proteus," 183
Aldous Huxley: "Education in the World State," 185
Picture: George Tooker, "The Subway," 190
E. M. Forster: "The Machine Stops," 190
James Thurber: "The Day the Dam Broke," 211
Picture: Peter Blume, "Parade," 215
James Thurber: "The Secret Life of Walter Mitty," 215
Picture: James Thurber, "Home," 219
Mark Schorer: "The Face Within The Face," 220
Eudora Welty: "Death of a Travelling Salesman," 228
D. H. Lawrence: "The Rocking-Horse Winner," 236
Lionel Trilling: "Of This Time, Of That Place," 246
F. Scott Fitzgerald: "The Rich Boy," 271
William Faulkner: "The Bear," 295
Picture: photograph of Mt. Kilimanjaro, 306
Ernest Hemingway: "The Snows of Kilimanjaro," 307
Joseph Conrad: "Heart of Darkness," 322

The following stories will be found in Part I:
John Steinbeck: "The Red Pony"
Aldous Huxley: "Young Archimedes"
James Joyce: "Araby"
Dylan Thomas: "Extraordinary Little Cough"
Thomas Wolfe: "The Lost Boy"

[viii]

Contents

PART IV: DRAMA

Prefatory note, 383
George Bernard Shaw: *Preface to Major Barbara*, 384
       Major Barbara, 403
Philip Barry: *The Philadelphia Story*, 464
Eugene O'Neill: *The Hairy Ape*, 515
Tennessee Williams: *The Glass Menagerie*, 543
Picture: Andrew Wyeth, "Christina's World," 585
Jean Giraudoux: *Tiger at the Gates* (translated by Christopher Fry), 586

PART V: POETRY

Prefatory note, 629
Picture: Luigi Lucioni, "Lake Through the Locusts," 630
Ralph Waldo Emerson
 "The Rhodora," 631
 "Ode . . . to Channing," 631
 "Give all to love," 633
 "Days," 633
 "Brahma," 634
Picture: Chinese vase, 634
Emily Dickinson
 "This is my letter," 635
 "I never saw," 635
 "Elysium is as far," 635
 "Much madness," 635
 "There's a certain slant," 636
 "Success is counted," 636
 "The soul selects," 636
 "To fight aloud," 637
 "Although I put away," 637
 "My life closed twice," 638
 "Just lost," 638
Walt Whitman
 "One's-Self I Sing," 639
 "Song of Myself" (Parts 1, 3, 30, 52), 639
 "When lilacs last in the dooryard bloom'd," 642
 "When I heard the learn'd astronomer," 649

Contents

Thomas Hardy
   from "Preface" to *Late Lyrics and Earlier,* 649
   "Hap," 650
   "The Impercipient," 651
   "Ah, are you digging on my grave?" 652
   "In Tenebris, II," 652
   "To an Unborn Pauper Child," 653
   "The Oxen," 654
   "Afterwards," 655
A. E. Housman
   from *The Name and Nature of Poetry,* 656
   "Soldier from the wars returning," 657
   "The half-moon westers low, my love," 657
   "Think no more, lad," 658
   "The laws of God, the laws of man," 658
   "The chestnut casts his flambeaux," 658
   "Terence, this is stupid stuff," 659
   "When I was one-and-twenty," 661
   "Reveille," 661
   "Loveliest of trees," 661
Edwin Arlington Robinson
   from *Selected Letters,* 662
   "Credo," 662
   "Mr. Flood's Party," 663
   Sonnet: "Never Until Our Souls," 664
   "The Mill," 664
   "Richard Cory," 665
   "Flammonde," 665
   "The Master," 667
Picture: Marsden Hartley, "Weary of the Truth," 668
Robert Frost
   from "The Figure a Poem Makes," 669
   "Two Tramps in Mud Time," 669
   "The Lockless Door," 671
   "The Star-Splitter," 671
   "Departmental," 674
   "To a Thinker," 674
   "The Vantage Point," 675
   "A Drumlin Woodchuck," 676
   "Stopping by Woods on a Snowy Evening," 676

Contents

    "Neither Out Far Nor In Deep," 677
    "West-running Brook," 677
    "Fire and Ice," 679
    "Mending Wall," 680
    "There Are Roughly Zones," 681
    "Acquainted with the Night," 682
Picture: Edward Hopper, "Nighthawks," 682
Carl Sandburg
    The People, Yes (Part 57), 683
William Butler Yeats
    "The Rose of the World," 687
    "The Second Coming," 687
    "Leda and the Swan," 688
    Note on "Byzantium" from *A Vision*, 688
    "Sailing to Byzantium," 688
    "Byzantium," 689
Kimon Friar: A Note on "Byzantium," 691
T. S. Eliot
    from *Selected Essays*, 693
    "Animula," 694
    "The Love Song of J. Alfred Prufrock," 695
Picture: Mary Petty, "Promise you'll wait for me," 699
    "Portrait of a Lady," 700
    "The Hollow Men," 702
    "Journey of the Magi," 704
    "Triumphal March," 705
    "East Coker," 706
    "Macavity: The Mystery Cat," 712
Picture: James Thurber, "The Bloodhound and the Bug," 714-715
Robinson Jeffers
    from "Foreword" to *The Selected Poetry of Robinson Jeffers*, 716
    "Hurt Hawks," 717
    "To the Stone-Cutters," 718
    "Shine, Perishing Republic," 718
    "The Purse-Seine," 719
    "The Answer," 720
    "The Inquisitors," 721
Archibald MacLeish
    "You, Andrew Marvell," 723
    from *The Hamlet of A. MacLeish*, 723

Contents

"American Letter," 725
"Men," 728
"Speech to Those Who Say Comrade," 729
America Was Promises, 730
"Memorial Rain," 736
"Epistle to be Left in the Earth," 738
"Geography of This Time," 739

E. E. Cummings
"Space being curved," 740
"O sweet spontaneous," 741
Picture: Robert Day, "Well, it looks like a buttercup to me," 742
"nobody loses all the time," 743
"If you can't eat you got to," 744
"since feeling is first," 744
"anyone lived in a pretty how town," 744
"these children singing," 745
"love is more thicker," 746
"when serpents bargain," 746

Kenneth Fearing
"Travelogue in a Shooting-Gallery," 747
Picture: Abner Dean, "Return to Normal," 748
"Reception Good," 749
"No Credit," 750
"Portrait (2)," 750
"American Rhapsody (4)," 751
"Readings, Forecasts, Personal Guidance," 752
"Devil's Dream," 754

Stephen Spender
from "Foreword" to *The Still Centre,* 755
"The Express," 755
"Not palaces, an era's crown," 756
"The Landscape Near an Aerodrome," 757
"Ultima Ratio Regum," 758
from *Spiritual Explorations,* VI, 758
"I think continually," 759

W. H. Auden
from "Squares and Oblongs" in *Poets at Work,* 760
"Now through night's caressing grip," 761
from "Letter to Lord Byron," Part IV, 761
"Musée des Beaux Arts," 766

[xii]

Contents

"Law Like Love," 767
"Casino," 768
"Prime," 769
"Nones," 770
"Under Which Lyre," 772

Dylan Thomas
　from *Selected Writings*, 777
　"In my craft or sullen art," 777
　"The Hand That Signed the Paper Felled a City," 777
　"Poem in October," 778
　"In the White Giant's Thigh," 780
　"On No Work of Words," 782
　"Poem on His Birthday," 782
　"A Winter's Tale," 784
　"Do Not Go Gentle Into That Good Night," 788

Robert Conquest
　"Guided Missiles Experimental Range," 789
　"A Girl in the Snow," 789
　"A Level of Abstraction," 790
　"Epistemology of Poetry," 790
　"Humanities," 791

E. J. Scovell
　"Child Waking," 791

Picture: Eugene Harris, "Piper," 792

Geoffrey Hill
　"Genesis," 793

Iain Fletcher
　"Time and Motion Study," 794

Kingsley Amis
　"Masters," 795
　"The Sources of the Past," 796
　"A Dream of Fair Women," 796

Donald Hall
　"The World, the Times," 797

Richard Wilbur
　"Love Calls Us to the Things of This World," 798
　"Looking Into History," 799

[xiii]

Contents

PART VI: PROSE

Prefatory note, 801
William Faulkner: "Remarks upon Receiving the Nobel Prize," 803
Thomas Jefferson: "On Natural Aristocracy," 804
Thomas Babington Macaulay: "Letter to a Correspondent in America," 807
Walt Whitman: from "Preface" to 1855 Edition of *Leaves of Grass,* 809
Frederick Jackson Turner: "The Significance of the Frontier in American History," 816
Carlton J. H. Hayes: "The American Frontier—Frontier of What?" 833
John A. Kouwenhoven: "What's American about America?" 842
Morris R. Cohen: from "The Future of American Liberalism," 854
James Truslow Adams: "Our Changing Characteristics," 855
Picture: Mary Petty, "Has anybody ever thought . . ." 865
Lee Strout White: "Farewell, My Lovely," 866
Charles A. Beard: "Whither Mankind?" 871
Peter Drucker: "Coming Issues in American Politics," 878
Franklin D. Roosevelt: "The Four Freedoms," 889
Ruth Benedict and Gene Weltfish: "The Races of Mankind," 889
Walter Millis: from "The Faith of an American," 903
George Washington: from "Farewell Address," 904
Lincoln Barnett: *The Universe and Dr. Einstein,* Part I, 905
Picture: Nagasaki, Japan, under atomic bomb attack, 916
U. S. War Department Release on New Mexico Test, 917
Picture: Charles Addams, rocket-ship ark, 922
O. R. Frisch: "Unlocking the Storehouse of Energy," 923
José Ortega y Gasset: "The Primitive and the Technical," 932
James Thurber: "An Outline of Scientists," 938
John Donne: from *An Anatomie of the World:* "The First Anniversary," 941
Picture: Abner Dean, "The Bright Young Men," 942-943
J. W. N. Sullivan: "The Values of Science," 944
Picture: Charles Sheeler, "Earth and Sky," 962
Weller Embler: "Metaphor and Social Belief," 963
Matthew Arnold: "Dover Beach," 973
Walter Lippmann: "The Problem of Unbelief," 973
E. M. Forster: "What I Believe," 982

Appendices: 987
  Some Modern Novels, 987
  Recordings of Poems, 988
  Biographical Notes, 990
Index of Authors, Titles, and First Lines, 1005

PART I · COMING-OF-AGE IN OUR TIME

THIS IS an introductory section intended to show how various types of literature deal with a universal theme. Here, in poem, story, play, prose, and picture are some of our finest creative artists dealing with certain problems posed by coming of age.

We often forget that none of us is one individual; we are several or many, at different times and at different ages. One way of seeing this is to watch the individual grow up. The following selections proceed through several of the ages of man, from the bright springtime of his childhood, through the wondering awkwardness of adolescence, the worldly assurance of young manhood, and the uncertainties of maturity. The Cummings and MacLeish poems show us children who "belong," who feel themselves part of things; Wolfe's "lost boy" discovers that something he once clung to has gone from his life, and the advice that follows recognizes this as a condition of youth. In these and the other stories are presented the discovery of moral values, the reluctant acceptance of what has to be, and with this discovery and acceptance are developed the flexibilities which any being must possess to survive. As the characters become aware of their own fragility in a harsh natural and social world, they have glimpses—and sometimes experiences—of something unbreakable and immutable that may be theirs in time. And this is ultimately as true of the springtime in Cummings' poem and the summer of "Sophistication" as it is of Anderson's *Winterset*.

The last few selections in this section are concerned with what can and what cannot be said to the young in the form of advice; they suggest that there is more to a man's life than the process of existing through several stages of growth.

YEARS OF THE MODERN
by Walt Whitman

Years of the modern! years of the unperform'd!
Your horizon rises, I see it parting away for more august dramas,
I see not America only, not only Liberty's nation but other nations preparing,
I see tremendous entrances and exits, new combinations, the solidarity of races,
I see that force advancing with irresistible power on the world's stage,
(Have the old forces, the old wars, played their parts? are the acts suitable to them closed?)
I see Freedom, completely arm'd and victorious and very haughty, with Law on one side and Peace on the other,
A stupendous trio all issuing forth against the idea of caste;
What historic denouements are these we so rapidly approach?
I see men marching and countermarching by swift millions,
I see the frontiers and boundaries of the old aristocracies broken,
I see the landmarks of European kings removed,
I see this day the People beginning their landmarks, (all others give way);
Never were such sharp questions ask'd as this day,
Never was average man, his soul, more energetic, more like a God,
Lo, how he urges and urges, leaving the masses no rest!
His daring foot is on land and sea everywhere, he colonizes the Pacific, the archipelagoes,
With the steamship, the electric telegraph, the newspaper, the wholesale engines of war,
With these and the world-spreading factories he interlinks all geography, all lands;
What whispers are these O lands, running ahead of you, passing under the seas?
Are all nations communing? is there going to be but one heart to the globe?
Is humanity forming en-masse? for lo, tyrants tremble, crowns grow dim,
The earth, restive, confronts a new era, perhaps a general divine war,
No one knows what will happen next, such portents fill the days and nights;
Years prophetical! the space ahead as I walk, as I vainly try to pierce it, is full of phantoms,
Unborn deeds, things soon to be, project their shapes around me,
This incredible rush and heat, this strange ecstatic fever of dreams O years!
Your dreams O years, how they penetrate through me! (I know not whether I sleep or wake;)
The perform'd America and Europe grow dim, retiring in shadow behind me,
The unperform'd, more gigantic than ever, advance, advance, upon me.

From *Leaves of Grass* by Walt Whitman. With permission from Doubleday and Company, Inc

> *. . . all the men and women merely players:*
> *They have their exits and their entrances;*
> *And one man in his time plays many parts,*
> *His acts being seven ages.*
>   —As You Like It

IN JUST-SPRING

by E. E. Cummings

in Just-
spring when the world is mud-
luscious the little
lame balloonman

whistles far and wee

and eddieandbill come
running from marbles and
piracies and it's
spring

when the world is puddle-wonderful

the queer
old balloonman whistles
far and wee
and bettyandisabel come dancing

from hop-scotch and jump-rope and

it's
spring
and
  the

    goat-footed

balloonman whistles
far
and
wee

Copyright, 1923, by Thomas Seltzer, Inc. From: *Collected Poems,* published by Harcourt, Brace and Company, Inc.

ELEVEN
by Archibald MacLeish

And summer mornings the mute child, rebellious,
Stupid, hating the words, the meanings, hating
The Think now, Think, the O but Think! would leave
On tiptoe the three chairs on the verandah
And crossing tree by tree the empty lawn
Push back the shed door and upon the sill
Stand pressing out the sunlight from his eyes
And enter and with outstretched fingers feel
The grindstone and behind it the bare wall
And turn and in the corner on the cool
Hard earth sit listening. And one by one,
Out of the dazzled shadow in the room
The shapes would gather, the brown plowshare, spades,
Mattocks, the polished helves of picks, a scythe
Hung from the rafters, shovels, slender tines
Glinting across the curve of sickles—shapes
Older than men were, the wise tools, the iron
Friendly with earth. And sit there quiet, breathing
The harsh dry smell of withered bulbs, the faint
Odor of dung, the silence. And outside
Beyond the half-shut door the blind leaves
And the corn moving. And at noon would come,
Up from the garden, his hard crooked hands
Gentle with earth, his knees still earth-stained, smelling
Of sun, of summer, the old gardener, like
A priest, like an interpreter, and bend
Over his baskets.
                And they would not speak:
They would say nothing. And the child would sit there
Happy as though he had no name, as though
He had been no one: like a leaf, a stem,
Like a root growing—

The selection from Archibald MacLeish *Poems 1924-1933* is used by permission of the publishers, Houghton Mifflin Company.

The Red Pony

Youth

Pablo Picasso. 1905

From the Collection of Edward M. M. Warburg, New York. Photograph, courtesy the Museum of Modern Art, New York.

THE RED PONY

by JOHN STEINBECK

Part I. The Gift

AT DAYBREAK Billy Buck emerged from the bunkhouse and stood for a moment on the porch looking up at the sky. He was a broad, bandy-legged little man with a walrus mustache, with square hands, puffed and muscled on the palms. His eyes were a contemplative, watery gray and the hair which protruded from under his Stetson hat was spiky and weathered. Billy was still stuffing his shirt into his

From *The Long Valley* by John Steinbeck. Copyright, 1937, 1938 by John Steinbeck. By permission of The Viking Press, Inc., New York.

Pony = a symbol of hope that all he has, that all things will be different after he has grown up, there can and they lived to suit themselves. This story is the destruction of that hope. of meaning in reality.

Coming-of-Age in Our Time

blue jeans as he stood on the porch. He unbuckled his belt and tightened it again. The belt showed, by the worn shiny places opposite each hole, the gradual increase of Billy's middle over a period of years. When he had seen to the weather, Billy cleared each nostril by holding its mate closed with his forefinger and blowing fiercely. Then he walked down to the barn, rubbing his hands together. He curried and brushed two saddle horses in the stalls, talking quietly to them all the time; and he had hardly finished when the iron triangle started ringing at the ranch house. Billy stuck the brush and currycomb together and laid them on the rail, and went up to breakfast. His action had been so deliberate and yet so wasteless of time that he came to the house while Mrs. Tiflin was still ringing the triangle. She nodded her gray head to him and withdrew into the kitchen. Billy Buck sat down on the steps, because he was a cow-hand, and it wouldn't be fitting that he should go first into the dining-room. He heard Mr. Tiflin in the house, stamping his feet into his boots.

The high jangling note of the triangle put the boy Jody in motion. He was only a little boy, ten years old, with hair like dusty yellow grass and with shy polite gray eyes, and with a mouth that worked when he thought. The triangle picked him up out of sleep. It didn't occur to him to disobey the harsh note. He never had: no one he knew ever had. He brushed the tangled hair out of his eyes and skinned his nightgown off. In a moment he was dressed—blue chambray shirt and overalls. It was late in the summer, so of course there were no shoes to bother with. In the kitchen he waited until his mother got from in front of the sink and went back to the stove. Then he washed himself and brushed back his wet hair with his fingers. His mother turned sharply on him as he left the sink. Jody looked shyly away.

"I've got to cut your hair before long," his mother said. "Breakfast's on the table. Go on in, so Billy can come."

Jody sat at the long table which was covered with white oilcloth washed through to the fabric in some places. The fried eggs lay in rows on their platter. Jody took three eggs on his plate and followed with three thick slices of crisp bacon. He carefully scraped a spot of blood from one of the egg yolks.

Billy Buck clumped in. "That won't hurt you," Billy explained. "That's only a sign the rooster leaves."

Jody's tall stern father came in then and Jody knew from the noise on the floor that he was wearing boots, but he looked under the table anyway, to make sure. His father turned off the oil lamp over the table, for plenty of morning light now came through the windows.

Jody did not ask where his father and Billy Buck were riding that day, but he wished he might go along. His father was a disciplinarian. Jody obeyed him in everything without questions of any kind. Now, Carl Tiflin sat down and reached for the egg platter.

"Got the cows ready to go, Billy?" he asked.

"In the lower corral," Billy said. "I could just as well take them in alone."

"Sure you could. But a man needs company. Besides your throat gets pretty dry." Carl Tiflin was jovial this morning.

Jody's mother put her head in the door. "What time do you think to be back, Carl?"

"I can't tell. I've got to see some men in Salinas. Might be gone till dark."

The eggs and coffee and big biscuits disappeared rapidly. Jody followed the

[6]

two men out of the house. He watched them mount their horses and drive six old milk cows out of the corral and start over the hill toward Salinas. They were going to sell the old cows to the butcher.

When they had disappeared over the crown of the ridge Jody walked up the hill in back of the house. The dogs trotted around the house corner hunching their shoulders and grinning horribly with pleasure. Jody patted their heads—Doubletree Mutt with the big thick tail and yellow eyes, and Smasher, the shepherd, who had killed a coyote and lost an ear in doing it. Smasher's one good ear stood up higher than a collie's ear should. Billy Buck said that always happened. After the frenzied greeting the dogs lowered their noses to the ground in a businesslike way and went ahead, looking back now and then to make sure that the boy was coming. They walked up through the chicken yard and saw the quail eating with the chickens. Smasher chased the chickens a little to keep in practice in case there should ever be sheep to herd. Jody continued on through the large vegetable patch where the green corn was higher than his head. The cow-pumpkins were green and small yet. He went on to the sagebrush line where the cold spring ran out of its pipe and fell into a round wooden tub. He leaned over and drank close to the green mossy wood where the water tasted best. Then he turned and looked back on the ranch, on the low, whitewashed house girded with red geraniums, and on the long bunkhouse by the cypress tree where Billy Buck lived alone. Jody could see the great black kettle under the cypress tree. That was where the pigs were scalded. The sun was coming over the ridge now, glaring on the whitewash of the houses and barns, making the wet grass blaze softly. Behind him, in the tall sagebrush, the birds were scampering on the ground, making a great noise among the dry leaves; the squirrels piped shrilly on the side-hills. Jody looked along at the farm buildings. He felt an uncertainty in the air, a feeling of change and of loss and of the gain of new and unfamiliar things. Over the hillside two big black buzzards sailed low to the ground and their shadows slipped smoothly and quickly ahead of them. Some animal had died in the vicinity. Jody knew it. It might be a cow or it might be the remains of a rabbit. The buzzards overlooked nothing. Jody hated them as all decent things hate them, but they could not be hurt because they made away with carrion.

After a while the boy sauntered down hill again. The dogs had long ago given him up and gone into the brush to do things in their own way. Back through the vegetable garden he went, and he paused for a moment to smash a green muskmelon with his heel, but he was not happy about it. It was a bad thing to do, he knew perfectly well. He kicked dirt over the ruined melon to conceal it.

Back at the house his mother bent over his rough hands, inspecting his fingers and nails. It did little good to start him clean to school for too many things could happen on the way. She sighed over the black cracks on his fingers, and then gave him his books and his lunch and started him on the mile walk to school. She noticed that his mouth was working a good deal this morning.

Jody started his journey. He filled his pockets with little pieces of white quartz that lay in the road, and every so often he took a shot at a bird or at some rabbit that had stayed sunning itself in the road too long. At the crossroads over the bridge he met two friends and the three of them walked to school together, making ridiculous strides and being rather silly. School had just opened two weeks before. There was still a spirit of revolt among the pupils.

It was four o'clock in the afternoon when Jody topped the hill and looked down on the ranch again. He looked for the saddle horses, but the corral was empty. His father was not back yet. He went slowly, then, toward the afternoon chores. At the ranch house, he found his mother sitting on the porch, mending socks.

"There's two doughnuts in the kitchen for you," she said. Jody slid to the kitchen, and returned with half of one of the doughnuts already eaten and his mouth full. His mother asked him what he had learned in school that day, but she didn't listen to his doughnut-muffled answer. She interrupted, "Jody, tonight see you fill the wood-box clear full. Last night you crossed the sticks and it wasn't only about half full. Lay the sticks flat tonight. And Jody, some of the hens are hiding eggs, or else the dogs are eating them. Look about in the grass and see if you can find any nests."

Jody, still eating, went out and did his chores. He saw the quail come down to eat with the chickens when he threw out the grain. For some reason his father was proud to have them come. He never allowed any shooting near the house for fear the quail might go away.

When the wood-box was full, Jody took his twenty-two rifle up to the cold spring at the brush line. He drank again and then aimed the gun at all manner of things, at rocks, at birds on the wing, at the big black pig kettle under the cypress tree, but he didn't shoot for he had no cartridges and wouldn't have until he was twelve. If his father had seen him aim the rifle in the direction of the house he would have put the cartridges off another year. Jody remembered this and did not point the rifle down the hill again. Two years was enough to wait for cartridges. Nearly all of his father's presents were given with reservations which hampered their value somewhat. It was good discipline.

The supper waited until dark for his father to return. When at last he came in with Billy Buck, Jody could smell the delicious brandy on their breaths. Inwardly he rejoiced, for his father sometimes talked to him when he smelled of brandy, sometimes even told things he had done in the wild days when he was a boy.

After supper, Jody sat by the fireplace and his shy polite eyes sought the room corners, and he waited for his father to tell what it was he contained, for Jody knew he had news of some sort. But he was disappointed. His father pointed a stern finger at him.

"You'd better go to bed, Jody. I'm going to need you in the morning."

That wasn't so bad. Jody liked to do the things he had to do as long as they weren't routine things. He looked at the floor and his mouth worked out a question before he spoke it. "What are we going to do in the morning, kill a pig?" he asked softly.

"Never you mind. You better get to bed."

When the door was closed behind him, Jody heard his father and Billy Buck chuckling and he knew it was a joke of some kind. And later, when he lay in bed, trying to make words out of the murmurs in the other room, he heard his father protest, "But, Ruth, I didn't give much for him."

Jody heard the hoot-owls hunting mice down by the barn, and he heard a fruit tree limb tap-tapping against the house. A cow was lowing when he went to sleep.

When the triangle sounded in the morning, Jody dressed more quickly even than usual. In the kitchen, while he washed his face and combed back his hair, his mother addressed him irritably. "Don't you go out until you get a good breakfast in you."

He went into the dining-room and sat at the long white table. He took a steaming hotcake from the platter, arranged two fried eggs on it, covered them with another hotcake and squashed the whole thing with his fork.

His father and Billy Buck came in. Jody knew from the sound on the floor that both of them were wearing flat-heeled shoes, but he peered under the table to make sure. His father turned off the oil lamp, for the day had arrived, and he looked stern and disciplinary, but Billy Buck didn't look at Jody at all. He avoided the shy questioning eyes of the boy and soaked a whole piece of toast in his coffee.

Carl Tiflin said crossly, "You come with us after breakfast!"

Jody had trouble with his food then, for he felt a kind of doom in the air. After Billy had tilted his saucer and drained the coffee which had slopped into it, and had wiped his hands on his jeans, the two men stood up from the table and went out into the morning light together, and Jody respectfully followed a little behind them. He tried to keep his mind from running ahead, tried to keep it absolutely motionless.

His mother called, "Carl! Don't you let it keep him from school."

They marched past the cypress, where a singletree hung from a limb to butcher the pigs on, and past the black iron kettle, so it was not a pig killing. The sun shone over the hill and threw long, dark shadows of the trees and buildings. They crossed a stubble-field to shortcut to the barn. Jody's father unhooked the door and they went in. They had been walking toward the sun on the way down. The barn was black as night in contrast and warm from the hay and from the beasts. Jody's father moved over toward the one box stall. "Come here!" he ordered. Jody could begin to see things now. He looked into the box stall and then stepped back quickly.

A red pony colt was looking at him out of the stall. Its tense ears were forward and a light of disobedience was in its eyes. Its coat was rough and thick as an airedale's fur and its mane was long and tangled. Jody's throat collapsed in on itself and cut his breath short.

"He needs a good currying," his father said, "and if I ever hear of you not feeding him or leaving his stall dirty, I'll sell him off in a minute."

Jody couldn't bear to look at the pony's eyes any more. He gazed down at his hands for a moment, and he asked very shyly, "Mine?" No one answered him. He put his hand out toward the pony. Its gray nose came close, sniffing loudly, and then the lips drew back and the strong teeth closed on Jody's fingers. The pony shook its head up and down and seemed to laugh with amusement. Jody regarded his bruised fingers. "Well," he said with pride—"Well, I guess he can bite all right." The two men laughed, somewhat in relief. Carl Tiflin went out of the barn and walked up a side-hill to be by himself, for he was embarrassed, but Billy Buck stayed. It was easier to talk to Billy Buck. Jody asked again—"Mine?"

Billy became professional in tone. "Sure! That is, if you look out for him and break him right. I'll show you how. He's just a colt. You can't ride him for some time."

Jody put out his bruised hand again, and this time the red pony let his nose be rubbed. "I ought to have a carrot," Jody said. "Where'd we get him, Billy?"

"Bought him at a sheriff's auction," Billy explained. "A show went broke in Salinas and had debts. The sheriff was selling off their stuff."

The pony stretched out his nose and shook the forelock from his wild eyes. Jody stroked the nose a little. He said softly, "There isn't a—saddle?"

Billy Buck laughed. "I'd forgot. Come along."

In the harness room he lifted down a little saddle of red morocco leather. "It's just a show saddle," Billy Buck said disparagingly. "It isn't practical for the brush, but it was cheap at the sale."

Jody couldn't trust himself to look at the saddle either, and he couldn't speak at all. He brushed the shining red leather with his fingertips, and after a long time he said, "It'll look pretty on him though." He thought of the grandest and prettiest things he knew. "If he hasn't a name already, I think I'll call him Gabilan Mountains," he said.

Billy Buck knew how he felt. "It's a pretty long name. Why don't you just call him Gabilan? That means hawk. That would be a fine name for him." Billy felt glad. "If you will collect tail hair, I might be able to make a hair rope for you sometime. You could use it for a hackamore."

Jody wanted to go back to the box stall. "Could I lead him to school, do you think —to show the kids?"

But Billy shook his head. "He's not even halter-broke yet. We had a time getting him here. Had to almost drag him. You better be starting for school though."

"I'll bring the kids to see him here this afternoon," Jody said.

Six boys came over the hill half an hour early that afternoon, running hard, their heads down, their forearms working, their breath whistling. They swept by the house and cut across the stubble-field to the barn. And then they stood self-consciously before the pony, and then they looked at Jody with eyes in which there was a new admiration and a new respect. Before today Jody had been a boy, dressed in overalls and a blue shirt—quieter than most, even suspected of being a little cowardly. And now he was different. Out of a thousand centuries they drew the ancient admiration of the footman for the horseman. They knew instinctively that a man on a horse is spiritually as well as physically bigger than a man on foot. They knew that Jody had been miraculously lifted out of equality with them, and had been placed over them. Gabilan put his head out of the stall and sniffed them.

"Why'n't you ride him?" the boys cried. "Why'n't you braid his tail with ribbons like in the fair?" "When you going to ride him?"

Jody's courage was up. He too felt the superiority of the horseman. "He's not old enough. Nobody can ride him for a long time. I'm going to train him on the long halter. Billy Buck is going to show me how."

"Well, can't we even lead him around a little?"

"He isn't even halter-broke," Jody said. He wanted to be completely alone when he took the pony out the first time. "Come and see the saddle."

They were speechless at the red morocco saddle, completely shocked out of comment. "It isn't much use in the brush," Jody explained. "It'll look pretty on him though. Maybe I'll ride bareback when I go into the brush."

"How you going to rope a cow without a saddle horn?"

"Maybe I'll get another saddle for every day. My father might want me to help him with the stock." He let them feel the red saddle, and showed them the brass chain throat-latch on the bridle and the big brass buttons at each temple where the headstall and brow band crossed. The whole thing was too wonderful. They had to go away after a little while, and each boy, in his mind, searched among his possessions for a bribe worthy of offering in return for a ride on the red pony when the time should come.

Jody was glad when they had gone. He took brush and currycomb from the wall, took down the barrier of the box stall and stepped cautiously in. The pony's eyes glittered, and he edged around into kicking position. But Jody touched him on the shoulder and rubbed his high arched neck as he had always seen Billy Buck do, and he crooned, "So-o-o Boy," in a deep voice. The pony gradually relaxed his tenseness. Jody curried and brushed until a pile of dead hair lay in the stall and until the pony's coat had taken on a deep red shine. Each time he finished he thought it might have been done better. He braided the mane into a dozen little pigtails, and he braided the forelock, and then he undid them and brushed the hair out straight again.

Jody did not hear his mother enter the barn. She was angry when she came, but when she looked in at the pony and at Jody working over him, she felt a curious pride rise up in her. "Have you forgot the wood-box?" she asked gently. "It's not far off from dark and there's not a stick of wood in the house, and the chickens aren't fed."

Jody quickly put up his tools. "I forgot, ma'am."

"Well, after this do your chores first. Then you won't forget. I expect you'll forget lots of things now if I don't keep an eye on you."

"Can I have carrots from the garden for him, ma'am?"

She had to think about that. "Oh—I guess so, if you only take the big tough ones."

"Carrots keep the coat good," he said, and again she felt the curious rush of pride.

Jody never waited for the triangle to get him out of bed after the coming of the pony. It became his habit to creep out of bed even before his mother was awake, to slip into his clothes and to go quietly down to the barn to see Gabilan. In the gray quiet mornings when the land and the brush and the houses and the trees were silver-gray and black like a photograph negative, he stole toward the barn, past the sleeping stones and the sleeping cypress tree. The turkeys, roosting in the tree out of coyotes' reach, clicked drowsily. The fields glowed with a gray frost-like light and in the dew the tracks of rabbits and of field mice stood out sharply. The good dogs came stiffly out of their little houses, hackles up and deep growls in their throats. Then they caught Jody's scent, and their stiff tails rose up and waved a greeting—Doubletree Mutt with the big thick tail, and Smasher, the incipient shepherd—then went lazily back to their warm beds.

It was a strange time and a mysterious journey, to Jody—an extension of a dream. When he first had the pony he liked to torture himself during the trip by thinking Gabilan would not be in his stall, and worse, would never have been there. And he had other delicious little self-induced pains. He thought how the rats had gnawed ragged holes in the red saddle, and how the mice had nibbled Gabilan's tail until it was stringy and thin. He usually ran the last little way to the barn. He unlatched the rusty hasp of the barn door and stepped in, and no matter how quietly he opened the door, Gabilan was always looking at him over the barrier of the box stall and Gabilan whinnied softly and stamped his front foot, and his eyes had big sparks of red fire in them like oakwood embers.

Sometimes, if the work horses were to be used that day, Jody found Billy Buck in the barn harnessing and currying. Billy stood with him and looked long at Gabilan and he told Jody a great many things about horses. He explained that they were terribly afraid for their feet, so that one must make a practice of lifting the legs and patting the hooves and ankles to remove their terror. He told Jody how horses love conversation. He must talk to the pony all the time, and tell him the reasons for everything. Billy wasn't sure a horse could understand everything that was said to him, but it was impossible to say how much was understood. A horse never kicked up a fuss if someone he liked explained things to him. Billy could give examples, too. He had known, for instance, a horse nearly dead beat with fatigue to perk up when told it was only a little farther to his destination. And he had known a horse paralyzed with fright to come out of it when his rider told him what it was that was frightening him. While he talked in the mornings, Billy Buck cut twenty or thirty straws into neat three-inch lengths and stuck them into his hatband. Then during the whole day, if he wanted to pick his teeth or merely to chew on something, he had only to reach up for one of them.

Jody listened carefully, for he knew and the whole country knew that Billy Buck was a fine hand with horses. Billy's own horse was a stringy cayuse with a hammer head, but he nearly always won the first prizes at the stock trials. Billy could rope a steer, take a double half-hitch about the horn with his riata, and dismount, and his horse would play the steer as an angler plays a fish, keeping a tight rope until the steer was down or beaten.

Every morning, after Jody had curried and brushed the pony, he let down the barrier of the stall, and Gabilan thrust past him and raced down the barn and into the corral. Around and around he galloped, and sometimes he jumped forward and landed on stiff legs. He stood quivering, stiff ears forward, eyes rolling so that the whites showed, pretending to be frightened. At last he walked snorting to the water-trough and buried his nose in the water up to the nostrils. Jody was proud then, for he knew that was the way to judge a horse. Poor horses only touched their lips to the water, but a fine spirited beast put his whole nose and mouth under, and only left room to breathe.

Then Jody stood and watched the pony, and he saw things he had never noticed about any other horse, the sleek, sliding flank muscles and the cords of the buttocks, which flexed like a closing fist, and the shine the sun put on the red coat. Having seen horses all his life, Jody had never looked at them very closely before. But now he noticed the moving ears which gave expression and even inflection of expression to the face. The pony talked with his ears. You could tell exactly how he felt about everything by the way his ears pointed. Sometimes they were stiff and upright and sometimes lax and sagging. They went back when he was angry or fearful, and forward when he was anxious and curious and pleased; and their exact position indicated which emotion he had.

Billy Buck kept his word. In the early fall the training began. First there was the halter-breaking, and that was the hardest because it was the first thing. Jody held a carrot and coaxed and promised and pulled on the rope. The pony set his feet like a burro when he felt the strain. But before long he learned. Jody walked all over the ranch leading him. Gradually he took to dropping the rope until the pony followed him unled wherever he went.

And then came the training on the long halter. That was slower work. Jody stood in the middle of a circle, holding the long halter. He clucked with his tongue and the pony started to walk in a big circle, held in by the long rope. He clucked again to make the pony trot, and again to make him gallop. Around and around Gabilan went thundering and enjoying it immensely. Then he called, "Whoa," and the pony stopped. It was not long until Gabilan was perfect at it. But in many ways he was a bad pony. He bit Jody in the pants and stomped on Jody's feet. Now and then his ears went back and he aimed a tremendous kick at the boy. Every time he did one of these bad things, Gabilan settled back and seemed to laugh to himself.

Billy Buck worked at the hair rope in the evenings before the fireplace. Jody collected tail hair in a bag, and he sat and watched Billy slowly constructing the rope, twisting a few hairs to make a string and rolling two strings together for a cord, and then braiding a number of cords to make the rope. Billy rolled the finished rope on the floor under his foot to make it round and hard.

The long halter work rapidly approached perfection. Jody's father, watching the pony stop and start and trot and gallop, was a little bothered by it.

"He's getting to be almost a trick pony," he complained. "I don't like trick horses. It takes all the—dignity out of a horse to make him do tricks. Why, a trick horse is kind of like an actor—no dignity, no character of his own." And his father said, "I guess you better be getting him used to the saddle pretty soon."

Jody rushed for the harness-room. For some time he had been riding the saddle on a sawhorse. He changed the stirrup length over and over, and could never get it just right. Sometimes, mounted on the sawhorse in the harness-room, with collars and hames and tugs hung all about him, Jody rode out beyond the room. He carried his rifle across the pommel. He saw the fields go flying by, and he heard the beat of the galloping hoofs.

It was a ticklish job, saddling the pony the first time. Gabilan hunched and reared and threw the saddle off before the cinch could be tightened. It had to be replaced again and again until at last the pony let it stay. And the cinching was difficult, too. Day by day Jody tightened the girth a little more until at last the pony didn't mind the saddle at all.

Then there was the bridle. Billy explained how to use a stick of licorice for a bit until Gabilan was used to having something in his mouth. Billy explained, "Of course we could force-break him to everything, but he wouldn't be as good a horse if we did. He'd always be a little bit afraid, and he wouldn't mind because he wanted to."

The first time the pony wore the bridle he whipped his head about and worked his tongue against the bit until the blood oozed from the corners of his mouth. He tried to rub the headstall off on the manger. His ears pivoted about and his eyes turned red with fear and with general rambunctiousness. Jody rejoiced, for he knew that only a mean-souled horse does not resent training.

And Jody trembled when he thought of the time when he would first sit in the saddle. The pony would probably throw him off. There was no disgrace in that. The disgrace would come if he did not get right up and mount again. Sometimes he dreamed that he lay in the dirt and cried and couldn't make himself mount again. The shame of the dream lasted until the middle of the day.

Gabilan was growing fast. Already he had lost the long-leggedness of the colt; his mane was getting longer and blacker. Under the constant currying and brushing his coat lay as smooth and gleaming as orange-red lacquer. Jody oiled the hoofs and kept them carefully trimmed so they would not crack.

The hair rope was nearly finished. Jody's father gave him an old pair of spurs and bent in the side bars and cut down the strap and took up the chainlets until they fitted. And then one day Carl Tiflin said:

"The pony's growing faster than I thought. I guess you can ride him by Thanksgiving. Think you can stick on?"

"I don't know," Jody said shyly. Thanksgiving was only three weeks off. He hoped it wouldn't rain, for rain would spot the red saddle.

Gabilan knew and liked Jody by now. He nickered when Jody came across the stubble-field, and in the pasture he came running when his master whistled for him. There was always a carrot for him every time.

Billy Buck gave him riding instructions over and over. "Now when you get up there, just grab tight with your knees and keep your hands away from the saddle, and if you get throwed, don't let that stop you. No matter how good a man is, there's always some horse can pitch him. You just climb up again before he gets to feeling smart about it. Pretty soon, he won't throw you no more, and pretty soon he *can't* throw you no more. That's the way to do it."

"I hope it don't rain before," Jody said.

"Why not? Don't want to get throwed in the mud?"

That was partly it, and also he was afraid that in the flurry of bucking Gabilan might slip and fall on him and break his leg or his hip. He had seen that happen to men before, had seen how they writhed on the ground like squashed bugs, and he was afraid of it.

He practiced on the sawhorse how he would hold the reins in his left hand and a hat in his right hand. If he kept his hands thus busy, he couldn't grab the horn if he felt himself going off. He didn't like to think of what would happen if he did grab the horn. Perhaps his father and Billy Buck would never speak to him again, they would be so ashamed. The news would get about and his mother would be ashamed too. And in the school yard—it was too awful to contemplate.

The Red Pony

He began putting his weight in a stirrup when Gabilan was saddled, but he didn't throw his leg over the pony's back. That was forbidden until Thanksgiving.

Every afternoon he put the red saddle on the pony and cinched it tight. The pony was learning already to fill his stomach out unnaturally large while the cinching was going on, and then to let it down when the straps were fixed. Sometimes Jody led him up to the brush line and let him drink from the round green tub, and sometimes he led him up through the stubble-field to the hilltop from which it was possible to see the white town of Salinas and the geometric fields of the great valley, and the oak trees clipped by the sheep. Now and then they broke through the brush and came to little cleared circles so hedged in that the world was gone and only the sky and the circle of brush were left from the old life. Gabilan liked these trips and showed it by keeping his head very high and by quivering his nostrils with interest. When the two came back from an expedition they smelled of the sweet sage they had forced through.

Time dragged on toward Thanksgiving, but winter came fast. The clouds swept down and hung all day over the land and brushed the hilltops, and the winds blew shrilly at night. All day the dry oak leaves drifted down from the trees until they covered the ground, and yet the trees were unchanged.

Jody had wished it might not rain before Thanksgiving, but it did. The brown earth turned dark and the trees glistened. The cut ends of the stubble turned black with mildew; the haystacks grayed from exposure to the damp, and on the roofs the moss, which had been all summer as gray as lizards, turned a brilliant yellow-green. During the week of rain, Jody kept the pony in the box stall out of the dampness, except for a little time after school when he took him out for exercise and to drink at the water-trough in the upper corral. Not once did Gabilan get wet.

The wet weather continued until little new grass appeared. Jody walked to school dressed in a slicker and short rubber boots. At length one morning the sun came out brightly. Jody, at his work in the box stall, said to Billy Buck, "Maybe I'll leave Gabilan in the corral when I go to school today."

"Be good for him to be out in the sun," Billy assured him. "No animal likes to be cooped up too long. Your father and me are going back on the hill to clean the leaves out of the spring." Billy nodded and picked his teeth with one of his little straws.

"If the rain comes, though—" Jody suggested.

"Not likely to rain today. She's rained herself out." Billy pulled up his sleeves and snapped his arm bands. "If it comes on to rain—why a little rain don't hurt a horse."

"Well, if it does come on to rain, you put him in, will you, Billy? I'm scared he might get cold so I couldn't ride him when the time comes."

"Oh sure! I'll watch out for him if we get back in time. But it won't rain today."

And so Jody, when he went to school left Gabilan standing out in the corral.

Billy Buck wasn't wrong about many things. He couldn't be. But he was wrong about the weather that day, for a little after noon the clouds pushed over the hills and the rain began to pour down. Jody heard it start on the schoolhouse roof. He considered holding up one finger for permission to go to the outhouse and, once outside, running for home to put the pony in. Punishment would be prompt both at school and at home. He gave it up and took ease from Billy's assurance that rain couldn't hurt a horse. When school was finally out, he hurried home through the dark rain. The banks at the sides of the road spouted little jets of muddy water. The rain slanted and swirled under a cold and gusty wind. Jody dog-trotted home, slopping through the gravelly mud of the road.

From the top of the ridge he could see Gabilan standing miserably in the corral. The red coat was almost black, and streaked with water. He stood head down with his rump to the rain and wind. Jody arrived running and threw open the barn door and led the wet pony in by his forelock. Then he found a gunny sack and rubbed the soaked hair and rubbed the legs and ankles. Gabilan stood patiently, but he trembled in gusts like the wind.

When he had dried the pony as well as he could, Jody went up to the house and brought hot water down to the barn and soaked the grain in it. Gabilan was not very hungry. He nibbled at the hot mash, but he was not very much interested in it, and he still shivered now and then. A little steam rose from his damp back.

It was almost dark when Billy Buck and Carl Tiflin came home. "When the rain started we put up at Ben Herche's place, and the rain never let up all afternoon," Carl Tiflin explained. Jody looked reproachfully at Billy Buck and Billy felt guilty.

"You said it wouldn't rain," Jody accused him.

Billy looked away. "It's hard to tell, this time of year," he said, but his excuse was lame. He had no right to be fallible, and he knew it.

"The pony got wet, got soaked through."

"Did you dry him off?"

"I rubbed him with a sack and I gave him hot grain."

Billy nodded in agreement.

"Do you think he'll take cold, Billy?"

"A little rain never hurt anything," Billy assured him.

Jody's father joined the conversation then and lectured the boy a little. "A horse," he said, "isn't any lap-dog kind of thing." Carl Tiflin hated weakness and sickness, and he held a violent contempt for helplessness.

Jody's mother put a platter of steaks on the table and boiled potatoes and boiled squash, which clouded the room with their steam. They sat down to eat. Carl Tiflin still grumbled about weakness put into animals and men by too much coddling.

Billy Buck felt bad about his mistake. "Did you blanket him?" he asked.

"No. I couldn't find any blanket. I laid some sacks over his back."

"We'll go down and cover him up after we eat, then." Billy felt better about it then. When Jody's father had gone in to the fire and his mother was washing dishes, Billy found and lighted a lantern. He and Jody walked through the mud to the barn. The barn was dark and warm and sweet. The horses still munched their evening hay. "You hold the lantern!" Billy ordered. And he felt the pony's legs and tested the heat of the flanks. He put his cheek against the pony's gray muzzle and then he rolled up the eyelids to look at the eyeballs and he lifted the lips to see the gums, and he put his fingers inside the ears. "He don't seem so chipper," Billy said. "I'll give him a rub-down."

Then Billy found a sack and rubbed the pony's legs violently and he rubbed the chest and the withers. Gabilan was strangely spiritless. He submitted patiently to the rubbing. At last Billy brought an old cotton comforter from the saddle-room, and threw it over the pony's back and tied it at neck and chest with string.

"Now he'll be all right in the morning," Billy said.

Jody's mother looked up when he got back to the house. "You're late up from bed," she said. She held his chin in her hard hand and brushed the tangled hair out of his eyes and she said, "Don't worry about the pony. He'll be all right. Billy's as good as any horse doctor in the country."

Jody hadn't known she could see his worry. He pulled gently away from her and knelt down in front of the fireplace until it burned his stomach. He scorched himself through and then went in to bed, but it was a hard thing to go to sleep. He awakened after what seemed a long time. The room was dark but there was a grayness in the window like that which precedes the dawn. He got up and found his overalls and searched for the legs, and then the clock in the other room struck two. He laid his clothes down and got back into bed. It was broad daylight when he awakened again. For the first time he had slept through the ringing of the triangle. He leaped up, flung on his clothes and went out of the door still buttoning his shirt. His mother looked after him for a moment and then went quietly back to her work. Her eyes were brooding and kind. Now and then her mouth smiled a little but without changing her eyes at all.

Jody ran on toward the barn. Halfway there he heard the sound he dreaded, the hollow rasping cough of a horse. He broke into a sprint then. In the barn he found Billy Buck with the pony. Billy was rubbing its legs with his strong thick hands. He looked up and smiled gaily. "He just took a little cold," Billy said. "We'll have him out of it in a couple of days."

Jody looked at the pony's face. The eyes were half closed and the lids thick and dry. In the eye corners a crust of hard mucus stuck. Gabilan's ears hung loosely sideways and his head was low. Jody put out his hand, but the pony did not move close to it. He coughed again and his whole body constricted with the effort. A little stream of thin fluid ran from his nostrils.

Jody looked back at Billy Buck. "He's awful sick, Billy."

"Just a little cold, like I said," Billy insisted. "You go get some breakfast and then go back to school. I'll take care of him."

"But you might have to do something else. You might leave him."

"No, I won't. I won't leave him at all. Tomorrow's Saturday. Then you can stay with him all day." Billy had failed again, and he felt badly about it. He had to cure the pony now.

Jody walked up to the house and took his place listlessly at the table. The eggs and bacon were cold and greasy, but he didn't notice it. He ate his usual amount. He didn't even ask to stay home from school. His mother pushed his hair back when she took his plate. "Billy'll take care of the pony," she assured him.

He moped through the whole day at school. He couldn't answer any questions nor read any words. He couldn't even tell anyone the pony was sick, for that might make him sicker. And when school was finally out he started home in dread. He walked slowly and let the other boys leave him. He wished he might continue walking and never arrive at the ranch.

Billy was in the barn, as he had promised, and the pony was worse. His eyes were almost closed now, and his breath whistled shrilly past an obstruction in his nose. A film covered that part of the eyes that was visible at all. It was doubtful whether the pony could see any more. Now and then he snorted, to clear his nose, and by the action seemed to plug it tighter. Jody looked dispiritedly at the pony's coat. The hair lay rough and unkempt and seemed to have lost all of its old luster. Billy stood quietly beside the stall. Jody hated to ask, but he had to know.

"Billy, is he—is he going to get well?"

Billy put his fingers between the bars under the pony's jaw and felt about. "Feel here," he said and he guided Jody's fingers to a large lump under the jaw. "When that gets bigger, I'll open it up and then he'll get better."

Jody looked quickly away, for he had heard about that lump. "What is it the matter with him?"

Billy didn't want to answer, but he had to. He couldn't be wrong three times. "Strangles," he said shortly, "but don't you worry about that. I'll pull him out of it. I've seen them get well when they were worse than Gabilan is. I'm going to steam him now. You can help."

"Yes," Jody said miserably. He followed Billy into the grain room and watched him make the steaming bag ready. It was a long canvas nose bag with straps to go over a horse's ears. Billy filled it one-third full of bran and then he added a couple of handfuls of dried hops. On top of the dry substance he poured a little carbolic acid and a little turpentine. "I'll be mixing it all up while you run to the house for a kettle of boiling water," Billy said.

When Jody came back with the steaming kettle, Billy buckled the straps over Gabilan's head and fitted the bag tightly around his nose. Then through a little hole in the side of the bag he poured the boiling water on the mixture. The pony started away as a cloud of strong steam rose up, but then the soothing fumes crept through his nose and into his lungs, and the sharp steam began to clear out the nasal passages. He breathed loudly. His legs trembled in an ague, and his eyes closed against the biting cloud. Billy poured in more water and kept the steam rising for fifteen minutes. At last he set down the kettle and took the bag from Gabilan's nose. The pony looked better. He breathed freely, and his eyes were open wider than they had been.

"See how good it makes him feel," Billy said. "Now we'll wrap him up in the blanket again. Maybe he'll be nearly well by morning."

"I'll stay with him tonight," Jody suggested.

"No. Don't you do it. I'll bring my blankets down here and put them in the hay. You can stay tomorrow and steam him if he needs it."

The evening was falling when they went to the house for their supper. Jody didn't even realize that someone else had fed the chickens and filled the wood-box. He walked up past the house to the dark brush line and took a drink of water from the tub. The spring water was so cold that it stung his mouth and drove a shiver through him. The sky above the hills was still light. He saw a hawk flying so high that it caught the sun on its breast and shone like a spark. Two blackbirds were driving him down the sky, glittering as they attacked their enemy. In the west, the clouds were moving in to rain again.

Jody's father didn't speak at all while the family ate supper, but after Billy Buck had taken his blankets and gone to sleep in the barn, Carl Tiflin built a high fire in the fireplace and told stories. He told about the wild man who ran naked through the country and had a tail and ears like a horse, and he told about the rabbit-cats of Moro Cojo that hopped into the trees for birds. He revived the famous Maxwell brothers who found a vein of gold and hid the traces of it so carefully that they could never find it again.

Jody sat with his chin in his hands; his mouth worked nervously, and his father gradually became aware that he wasn't listening very carefully. "Isn't that funny?" he asked.

Jody laughed politely and said, "Yes, sir." His father was angry and hurt, then. He didn't tell any more stories. After a while, Jody took a lantern and went down to the barn. Billy Buck was asleep in the hay, and, except that his breath rasped a little in his lungs, the pony seemed to be much better. Jody stayed a little while, running his fingers over the red rough coat, and then he took up the lantern and went back to the house. When he was in bed, his mother came into the room.

"Have you enough covers on? It's getting winter."

"Yes, ma'am."

"Well, get some rest tonight." She hesitated to go out, stood uncertainly. "The pony will be all right," she said.

Jody was tired. He went to sleep quickly and didn't awaken until dawn. The triangle sounded, and Billy Buck came up from the barn before Jody could get out of the house.

"How is he?" Jody demanded.

Billy always wolfed his breakfast. "Pretty good. I'm going to open that lump this morning. Then he'll be better maybe."

After breakfast, Billy got out his best knife, one with a needle point. He whetted the shining blade a long time on a little carborundum stone. He tried the point and the blade again and again on his calloused thumb-ball, and at last he tried it on his upper lip.

On the way to the barn, Jody noticed how the young grass was up and how the stubble was melting day by day into the new green crop of volunteer. It was a cold sunny morning.

As soon as he saw the pony, Jody knew he was worse. His eyes were closed and sealed shut with dried mucus. His head hung so low that his nose almost touched the straw of his bed. There was a little groan in each breath, a deep-seated, patient groan.

Billy lifted the weak head and made a quick slash with the knife. Jody saw the yellow pus run out. He held up the head while Billy swabbed out the wound with weak carbolic acid salve.

"Now he'll feel better," Billy assured him. "That yellow poison is what makes him sick."

Jody looked unbelieving at Billy Buck. "He's awful sick."

Billy thought a long time what to say. He nearly tossed off a careless assurance, but he saved himself in time. "Yes, he's pretty sick," he said at last. "I've seen worse ones get well. If he doesn't get pneumonia, we'll pull him through. You stay with him. If he gets worse, you can come and get me."

For a long time after Billy went away, Jody stood beside the pony, stroking him behind the ears. The pony didn't flip his head the way he had done when he was well. The groaning in his breathing was becoming more hollow.

Doubletree Mutt looked into the barn, his big tail waving provocatively, and Jody was so incensed at his health that he found a hard black clod on the floor and deliberately threw it. Doubletree Mutt went yelping away to nurse a bruised paw.

In the middle of the morning, Billy Buck came back and made another steam bag. Jody watched to see whether the pony improved this time as he had before. His breathing eased a little, but he did not raise his head.

The Saturday dragged on. Late in the afternoon Jody went to the house and brought his bedding down and made up a place to sleep in the hay. He didn't ask permission. He knew from the way his mother looked at him that she would let him do almost anything. That night he left a lantern burning on a wire over the box stall. Billy had told him to rub the pony's legs every little while.

At nine o'clock the wind sprang up and howled around the barn. And in spite of his worry, Jody grew sleepy. He got into his blankets and went to sleep, but the breathy groans of the pony sounded in his dreams. And in his sleep he heard a crashing noise which went on and on until it awakened him. The wind was rushing through the barn. He sprang up and looked down the lane of stalls. The barn door had blown open, and the pony was gone.

He caught the lantern and ran outside into the gale, and he saw Gabilan weakly shambling away into the darkness, head down, legs working slowly and mechanically. When Jody ran up and caught him by the forelock, he allowed himself to be led back and put into his stall. His groans were louder, and a fierce whistling came from his nose. Jody didn't sleep any more then. The hissing of the pony's breath grew louder and sharper.

He was glad when Billy Buck came in at dawn. Billy looked for a time at the pony as though he had never seen him before. He felt the ears and flanks. "Jody," he said, "I've got to do something you won't want to see. You run up to the house for a while."

Jody grabbed him fiercely by the forearm. "You're not going to shoot him?"

Billy patted his hand. "No. I'm going to open a little hole in his windpipe so he can breathe. His nose is filled up. When he gets well, we'll put a little brass button in the hole for him to breathe through."

Jody couldn't have gone away if he had wanted to. It was awful to see the red hide cut, but infinitely more terrible to know it was being cut and not to see it. "I'll stay right here," he said bitterly. "You sure you got to?"

"Yes. I'm sure. If you stay, you can hold his head. If it doesn't make you sick, that is."

The fine knife came out again and was whetted again just as carefully as it had been the first time. Jody held the pony's head up and the throat taut, while Billy felt up and down for the right place. Jody sobbed once as the bright knife point disappeared into the throat. The pony plunged weakly away and then stood still, trembling violently. The blood ran thickly out and up the knife and across Billy's hand and into his shirtsleeve. The sure square hand sawed out a round hole in the flesh, and the breath came bursting out of the hole, throwing a fine spray of blood. With the rush of oxygen, the pony took a sudden strength. He lashed out with his hind feet and tried to rear, but Jody held his head down while Billy mopped the new wound with carbolic salve. It was a good job. The blood stopped flowing and the air puffed out the hole and sucked it in regularly with a little bubbling noise.

The rain brought in by the night wind began to fall on the barn roof. Then the triangle rang for breakfast. "You go up and eat while I wait," Billy said. "We've got to keep this hole from plugging up."

Jody walked slowly out of the barn. He was too dispirited to tell Billy how the barn door had blown open and let the pony out. He emerged into the wet gray morning and sloshed up to the house, taking a perverse pleasure in splashing through all the puddles. His mother fed him and put dry clothes on. She didn't question him. She seemed to know he couldn't answer questions. But when he was ready to go back to the barn she brought him a pan of steaming meal. "Give him this," she said.

But Jody did not take the pan. He said, "He won't eat anything," and ran out of the house. At the barn, Billy showed him how to fix a ball of cotton on a stick, with which to swab out the breathing hole when it became clogged with mucus.

Jody's father walked into the barn and stood with them in front of the stall. At length he turned to the boy. "Hadn't you better come with me? I'm going to drive over the hill." Jody shook his head. "You better come on, out of this," his father insisted.

Billy turned on him angrily. "Let him alone. It's his pony, isn't it?"

Carl Tiflin walked away without saying another word. His feelings were badly hurt.

All morning Jody kept the wound open and the air passing in and out freely. At noon the pony lay wearily down on his side and stretched his nose out.

Billy came back. "If you're going to stay with him tonight, you better take a little nap," he said. Jody went absently out of the barn. The sky had cleared to a hard thin blue. Everywhere the birds were busy with worms that had come to the damp surface of the ground.

Jody walked to the brush line and sat on the edge of the mossy tub. He looked down at the house and at the old bunkhouse and at the dark cypress tree. The place was familiar, but curiously changed. It wasn't itself any more, but a frame for things that were happening. A cold wind blew out of the east now, signifying that the rain was over for a little while. At his feet Jody could see the little arms of new weeds spreading out over the ground. In the mud about the spring were thousands of quail tracks.

Doubletree Mutt came sideways and embarrassed up through the vegetable patch, and Jody, remembering how he had thrown the clod, put his arm about the dog's neck and kissed him on his wide black nose. Doubletree Mutt sat still, as though he knew some solemn thing was happening. His big tail slapped the ground gravely. Jody pulled a swollen tick out of Mutt's neck and popped it dead between his thumb-nails. It was a nasty thing. He washed his hands in the cold spring water.

Except for the steady swish of the wind, the farm was very quiet. Jody knew his mother wouldn't mind if he didn't go in to eat his lunch. After a little while he went slowly back to the barn. Mutt crept into his own little house and whined softly to himself for a long time.

Billy Buck stood up from the box and surrendered the cotton swab. The pony still lay on his side and the wound in his throat bellowsed in and out. When Jody saw how dry and dead the hair looked, he knew at last that there was no hope for the pony. He had seen the dead hair before on dogs and on cows, and it was a sure sign. He sat heavily on the box and let down the barrier of the box stall. For a long time he kept his eyes on the moving wound, and at last he dozed, and the afternoon passed quickly. Just before dark his mother brought a deep dish of stew and left it for him and went away. Jody ate a little of it, and, when it was dark, he set the lantern on the floor by the pony's head so he could watch the wound and keep it open. And he dozed again until the night chill awakened him. The wind was blowing fiercely, bringing the north cold with it. Jody brought a blanket from his bed in the hay and wrapped himself in it. Gabilan's breathing was quiet at last; the hole in his throat moved gently. The owls flew through the hayloft, shrieking and looking for mice. Jody put his hands down on his head and slept. In his sleep he was aware that the wind had increased. He heard it slamming about the barn.

It was daylight when he awakened. The barn door had swung open. The pony was gone. He sprang up and ran out into the morning light.

The pony's tracks were plain enough, dragging through the frostlike dew on the young grass, tired tracks with little lines between them where the hoofs had dragged. They headed for the brush line halfway up the ridge. Jody broke into a run and followed them. The sun shone on the sharp white quartz that stuck through the ground here and there. As he followed the plain trail, a shadow cut across in front of him. He looked up and saw a high circle of black buzzards, and the slowly revolving circle dropped lower and lower. The solemn birds soon disappeared over the ridge. Jody ran faster then, forced on by panic and rage. The trail entered the brush at last and followed a winding route among the tall sage bushes.

At the top of the ridge Jody was winded. He paused, puffing noisily. The blood pounded in his ears. Then he saw what he was looking for. Below, in one of the little clearings in the brush, lay the red pony. In the distance, Jody could see the legs moving slowly and convulsively. And in a circle around him stood the buzzards, waiting for the moment of death they know so well.

Jody leaped forward and plunged down the hill. The wet ground muffled his steps and the brush hid him. When he arrived, it was all over. The first buzzard sat on the pony's head and its beak had just risen dripping with dark eye fluid. Jody plunged into the circle like a cat. The black brotherhood arose in a cloud, but the big one on the pony's head was too late. As it hopped along to take off, Jody caught its wing tip and pulled it down. It was nearly as big as he was. The free wing crashed into his face with the force of a club, but he hung on. The claws fastened on his leg and the wing elbows battered his head on either side. Jody groped blindly with his free hand. His fingers found the neck of the struggling bird. The red eyes looked into his face, calm and fearless and fierce; the naked head turned from side to side. Then the beak opened and vomited a stream of putrefied fluid. Jody brought up his knee and fell on the great bird. He held the neck to the ground with one hand while his other found a piece of sharp white quartz. The first blow broke the

The tragedy is that he knows that the buzzard did not kill the pony. This is Jody's last rebellion against maturity

The Red Pony

beak sideways and black blood spurted from the twisted, leathery mouth corners. He struck again and missed. The red fearless eyes still looked at him, impersonal and unafraid and detached. He struck again and again, until the buzzard lay dead, until its head was a red pulp. He was still beating the dead bird when Billy Buck pulled him off and held him tightly to calm his shaking.

Carl Tiflin wiped the blood from the boy's face with a red bandana. Jody was limp and quiet now. His father moved the buzzard with his toe. "Jody," he explained, "the buzzard didn't kill the pony. Don't you know that?"

"I know it," Jody said wearily.

It was Billy Buck who was angry. He had lifted Jody in his arms, and had turned to carry him home. But he turned back on Carl Tiflin. " 'Course he knows it," Billy said furiously, "Jesus Christ! man, can't you see how he'd feel about it?"

Handball   Ben Shahn
Collection, Museum of Modern Art

[23]

YOUNG ARCHIMEDES

by Aldous Huxley

It was the view which finally made us take the place. True, the house had its disadvantages. It was a long way out of town and had no telephone. The rent was unduly high, the drainage system poor. On windy nights, when the ill-fitting panes were rattling so furiously in the window-frames that you could fancy yourself in an hotel omnibus, the electric light, for some mysterious reason, used invariably to go out and leave you in the noisy dark. There was a splendid bathroom; but the electric pump, which was supposed to send up water from the rain-water tanks in the terrace, did not work. Punctually every autumn the drinking well ran dry. And our landlady was a liar and a cheat.

But these are the little disadvantages of every hired house, all over the world. For Italy they were not really at all serious. I have seen plenty of houses which had them all and a hundred others, without possessing the compensating advantages of ours—the southward facing garden and terrace for the winter and spring, the large cool rooms against the midsummer heat, the hilltop air and freedom from mosquitoes, and finally the view.

And what a view it was! Or rather, what a succession of views. For it was different every day; and without stirring from the house one had the impression of an incessant change of scene: all the delights of travel without its fatigues. There were autumn days when all the valleys were filled with mist and the crests of the Apennines rose darkly out of a flat white lake. There were days when the mist invaded even our hilltop and we were enveloped in a soft vapor in which the mist-colored olive trees, that sloped away below our windows towards the valley, disappeared as though into their own spiritual essence; and the only firm and definite things in the small, dim world within which we found ourselves confined were the two tall black cypresses growing on a little projecting terrace a hundred feet down the hill. Black, sharp, and solid, they stood there, twin pillars of Hercules at the extremity of the known universe; and beyond them there was only pale cloud and round them only the cloudy olive trees.

These were the wintry days; but there were days of spring and autumn, days unchangingly cloudless, or—more lovely still—made various by the huge floating shapes of vapor that, snowy above the far-away snow-capped mountains, gradually unfolded, against the pale bright blue, enormous heroic gestures. And in the height of the sky the bellying draperies, the swans, the aerial marbles, hewed and left unfinished by gods grown tired of creation almost before they had begun, drifted sleeping along the wind, changing form as they moved. And the sun would come and go behind them; and now the town in the valley would fade and almost vanish in the shadow, and now, like an immense fretted jewel between the hills, it would glow as though by its own light. And looking across the nearer tributary

From *Young Archimedes and Other Stories*, by Aldous Huxley. Harper & Brothers. Copyright, 1924, by Aldous Huxley.

[24]

Young Archimedes

valley that wound from below our crest down towards the Arno, looking over the low dark shoulder of hill on whose extreme promontory stood the towered church of San Miniato, one saw the huge dome airily hanging on its ribs of masonry, the square campanile, the sharp spire of Santa Croce, and the canopied tower of the Signoria, rising above the intricate maze of houses, distinct and brilliant, like small treasures carved out of precious stones. For a moment only, and then their light would fade away once more, and the travelling beam would pick out, among the indigo hills beyond, a single golden crest.

There were days when the air was wet with passed or with approaching rain, and all the distances seemed miraculously near and clear. The olive trees detached themselves one from another on the distant slopes; the far-away villages were lovely and pathetic like the most exquisite small toys. There were days in summer-time, days of impending thunder when, bright and sunlit against huge bellying masses of black and purple, the hills and the white houses shone as it were precariously, in a dying splendour, on the brink of some fearful calamity.

How the hills changed and varied! Every day and every hour of the day, almost, they were different. There would be moments when, looking across the plain of Florence, one would see only a dark blue silhouette against the sky. The scene had no depth; there was only a hanging curtain painted flatly with the symbols of mountains. And then, suddenly almost, with the passing of a cloud, or when the sun had declined to a certain level in the sky, the flat scene transformed itself; and where there had been only a painted curtain, now there were ranges behind ranges of hills, graduated tone after tone from brown, or grey, or a green gold to far-away blue. Shapes that a moment before had been fused together indiscriminately into a single mass, now came apart into their constituents. Fiesole, which had seemed only a spur of Monte Morello, now revealed itself as the jutting headland of another system of hills, divided from the nearest bastions of its greater neighbor by a deep and shadowy valley.

At noon, during the heats of summer, the landscape became dim, powdery, vague, and almost colorless under the midday sun; the hills disappeared into the trembling fringes of the sky. But as the afternoon wore on the landscape emerged again, it dropped its anonymity, it climbed back out of nothingness into form and life. And its life, as the sun sank, and slowly sank through the long afternoon, grew richer, grew more intense with every moment. The level light, with its attendant long, dark shadows, laid bare, so to speak, the anatomy of the land; the hills—each western escarpment shining, and each slope averted from the sunlight profoundly shadowed—became massive, jutty, and solid. Little folds and dimples in the seemingly even ground revealed themselves. Eastward from our hilltop, across the plain of the Ema, a great bluff cast its ever-increasing shadow; in the surrounding brightness of the valley a whole town lay eclipsed within it. And as the sun expired on the horizon, the further hills flushed in its warm light, till their illumined flanks were the color of tawny roses; but the valleys were already filled with the blue mist of evening. And it mounted, mounted; the fire

[25]

went out of the western windows of the populous slopes; only the crests were still alight, and at last they too were all extinct. The mountains faded and fused together again into a flat painting of mountains against the pale evening sky. In a little while it was night; and if the moon were full, a ghost of the dead scene still haunted the horizons.

Changeful in its beauty, this wide landscape always preserved a quality of humanness and domestication which made it, to my mind at any rate, the best of all landscapes to live with. Day by day one travelled through its different beauties; but the journey, like our ancestors' Grand Tour, was always a journey through civilization. For all its mountains, its steep slopes and deep valleys, the Tuscan scene is dominated by its inhabitants. They have cultivated every rood of ground that can be cultivated; their houses are thickly scattered even over the hills, and the valleys are populous. Solitary on the hilltop, one is not alone in a wilderness. Man's traces are across the country, and already—one feels it with satisfaction as one looks out across it—for centuries, for thousands of years, it has been his, submissive, tamed, and humanized. The wide, blank moorlands, the sands, the forests of innumerable trees—these are places for occasional visitation, healthful to the spirit which submits itself to them for not too long. But fiendish influences as well as divine haunt these total solitudes. The vegetative life of plants and things is alien and hostile to the human. Men cannot live at ease except where they have mastered their surroundings and where their accumulated lives outnumber and outweigh the vegetative lives about them. Stripped of its dark woods, planted, terraced, and tilled almost to the mountain tops, the Tuscan landscape is humanized and safe. Sometimes upon those who live in the midst of it there comes a longing for some place that is solitary, inhuman, lifeless, or peopled only with alien life. But the longing is soon satisfied, and one is glad to return to the civilized and submissive scene.

I found that house on the hilltop the ideal dwelling-place. For there, safe in the midst of a humanized landscape, one was yet alone; one could be as solitary as one liked. Neighbors whom one never sees at close quarters are the ideal and perfect neighbors.

Our nearest neighbors, in terms of physical proximity, lived very near. We had two sets of them, as a matter of fact, almost in the same house with us. One was the peasant family, who lived in a long, low building, part dwelling-house, part stables, storerooms and cowsheds, adjoining the villa. Our other neighbors—intermittent neighbors, however, for they only ventured out of town every now and then, during the most flawless weather—were the owners of the villa, who had reserved for themselves the smaller wing of the huge L-shaped house—a mere dozen rooms or so—leaving the remaining eighteen or twenty to us.

They were a curious couple, our proprietors. An old husband, gray, listless, tottering, seventy at least; and a signora of about forty, short, very plump, with tiny fat hands and feet and a pair of very large, very dark black eyes, which she used with all the skill of a born comedian. Her vitality, if you could have harnessed it and made it do some useful work, would have supplied a whole town with electric light. The physicists talk of deriving energy from the atom; they would be more profitably employed nearer home—in discovering some way of tapping those enormous stores of vital energy which accumulate in unemployed women of sanguine temperament and which, in the present imperfect state of social and scientific organization, vent themselves in ways that are generally so deplorable: in interfering with other people's affairs, in working up emotional scenes, in thinking about love and making it, and in bothering men till they cannot get on with their work.

Signora Bondi got rid of her superfluous energy, among other ways, by "doing in" her tenants. The old gentleman, who was a retired merchant with a reputation for the most perfect rectitude, was allowed to have no dealings with us. When we came to see the house, it was the wife who showed us round. It was she who, with a lavish display of charm, with irresistible rollings of the eyes, expatiated on the merits of the place, sang the praises of the electric pump, glorified the bathroom (considering which, she insisted, the rent was remarkably moderate), and when we suggested calling in a surveyor to look over the house, earnestly begged us, as though our well-being were her only consideration, not to waste our money unnecessarily in doing anything so superfluous. "After all," she said, "we are honest people. I wouldn't dream of letting you the house except in perfect condition. Have confidence." And she looked at me with an appealing, pained expression in her magnificent eyes, as though begging me not to insult her by my coarse suspiciousness. And leaving us no time to pursue the subject of surveyors any further, she began assuring us that our little boy was the most beautiful angel she had ever seen. By the time our interview with Signora Bondi was at an end, we had definitely decided to take the house.

"Charming woman," I said, as we left the house. But I think that Elizabeth was not quite so certain of it as I.

Then the pump episode began.

On the evening of our arrival in the house we switched on the electricity. The pump made a very professional whirring noise; but no water came out of the taps in the bathroom. We looked at one another doubtfully.

"Charming woman?" Elizabeth raised her eyebrows.

We asked for interviews; but somehow the old gentleman could never see us, and the Signora was invariably out or indisposed. We left notes; they were never answered. In the end, we found that the only method of communicating with our landlords, who were living in the same house with us, was to go down into Florence and send a registered express letter to them. For this they had to sign two separate receipts and even, if we chose to pay forty centimes more, a third incriminating document, which was then returned to us. There could be no pretending, as there always was with ordinary letters or notes, that the communication had never been received. We began at last to get answers to our complaints. The Signora, who wrote all the letters, started by telling us that, naturally, the pump didn't work, as the cisterns were empty, owing to the long drought. I had to walk three miles to the post office in order to register my letter reminding her that there had been a violent thunderstorm only last Wednesday, and that the tanks were consequently more than half full. The answer came back: bath water had not been guaranteed in the contract; and if I wanted it, why hadn't I had the pump looked at before I took the house? Another walk into town to ask the Signora next door whether she remembered her adjurations to us to have confidence in her, and to inform her that the existence in a house of a bathroom was in itself an implicit guarantee of bath water. The reply to that was that the Signora couldn't continue to have communications with people who wrote so rudely to her. After that I put the matter into the hands of a lawyer. Two months later the pump was actually replaced. But we had to serve a writ on the lady before she gave in. And the costs were considerable.

One day, towards the end of the episode, I met the old gentleman in the road, taking his big maremman dog for a walk—or being taken, rather, for a walk by the dog. For where the dog pulled the old gentleman had perforce to follow. And when it stopped to smell, or scratch the ground, or leave against a gatepost its visiting-card or an offensive challenge, patiently, at his end of the leash, the old man had to wait. I passed him standing at the side of the road, a few hundred yards below our house. The dog was sniffing at the roots of one of the twin cypresses which grew one on either side of the entry to a farm; I heard the beast growling indignantly to itself, as though it scented an intolerable insult. Old Signor Bondi, leashed to his dog, was waiting. The knees inside the tubular gray trousers were slightly bent. Leaning on his cane, he stood gazing mournfully and vacantly at the view. The whites of his old eyes were discolored, like ancient billiard balls. In the gray, deeply wrinkled face, his nose was dyspeptically red. His white moustache, ragged and yellowing at the fringes, drooped in a melancholy curve. In his black tie he wore a very large diamond; perhaps that was what Signora Bondi had found so attractive about him.

I took off my hat as I approached. The old man stared at me absently, and it was only when I was already almost past him that he recollected who I was.

"Wait," he called after me, "wait!" And he hastened down the road in pursuit. Taken utterly by surprise and at a disadvantage—for it was engaged in retorting to the affront imprinted on the cypress roots—the dog permitted itself to be jerked after him. Too much astonished to be anything but obedient, it followed its master. "Wait!"

I waited.

"My dear sir," said the old gentleman, catching me by the lapel of my coat and blowing most disagreeably in my face, "I want to apologize." He looked around him, as though afraid that even here he might be overheard. "I want to apologize," he went on, "about that wretched pump business. I assure you that, if it had been only my affair, I'd have put the thing right as soon as you asked. You were quite right: a bathroom is an implicit guarantee of bath water. I saw from the first that we should have no chance if it came to court. And besides, I think one ought to treat one's tenants as handsomely as one can afford to. But my wife"—he lowered his voice—"the fact is that she likes this sort of thing, even when she knows that she's in the wrong and must lose. And besides, she hoped, I dare say, that you'd get tired of asking and have the job done yourself. I told her from the first that we ought to give in; but she wouldn't listen. You see, she enjoys it. Still, now she sees that it must be done. In the course of the next two or three days you'll be having your bath water. But I thought I'd just like to tell you how . . ." But the Maremmano, which had recovered by this time from its surprise of a moment since, suddenly bounded, growling, up the road. The old gentleman tried to hold the beast, strained at the leash, tottered unsteadily, then gave way and allowed himself to be dragged off. ". . . how sorry I am," he went on, as he receded from me, "that this little misunderstanding . . ." But it was no use. "Good-bye." He smiled politely, made a little deprecating gesture, as though he had suddenly remembered a pressing engagement, and had no time to explain what it was. "Good-bye." He took off his hat and abandoned himself completely to the dog.

A week later the water really did begin to flow, and the day after our first bath Signora Bondi, dressed in dove-gray satin and wearing all her pearls, came to call.

"Is it peace now?" she asked, with a charming frankness, as she shook hands.

We assured her that, so far as we were concerned, it certainly was.

"But why *did* you write me such dreadfully rude letters?" she said, turning on me a reproachful glance that ought to have moved the most ruthless malefactor to contrition. "And then that writ. How *could* you? To a lady . . ."

I mumbled something about the pump and our wanting baths.

"But how could you expect me to listen to you while you were in that mood? Why didn't you set about it differently—politely, charmingly?" She smiled at me and dropped her fluttering eyelids.

I thought it best to change the conversation. It is disagreeable, when one is in the right, to be made to appear in the wrong.

A few weeks later we had a letter—duly registered and by express messenger—in which the Signora asked us whether we proposed to renew our lease (which was only for six months), and notifying us that, if we did, the rent would be raised 25 per cent, in consideration of the improvements which had been carried out. We thought ourselves lucky, at the end of much bargaining, to get the lease renewed for a whole year with an increase in the rent of only 15 per cent.

It was chiefly for the sake of the view that we put up with these intolerable extortions. But we had found other reasons, after a few days' residence, for liking the house. Of these, the most cogent was that, in the peasant's youngest child, we had discovered what seemed the perfect playfellow for our own small boy. Between little Guido—for that was his name—and the youngest of his brothers and sisters there was a gap of six or seven years. His two elder brothers worked with their father in the fields; since the time of the mother's death, two or three years before we knew them, the eldest sister had ruled the house, and the younger, who had just left school, helped her and in betweenwhiles kept an eye on Guido, who by this time, however, needed very little looking after; for he was between six and seven years old and as precocious, self-assured, and responsible as the children of the poor, left as they are to themselves almost from the time they can walk, generally are.

Though fully two and a half years older than little Robin—and at that age thirty months are crammed with half a lifetime's experience—Guido took no undue advantage of his superior intelligence and strength. I have never seen a child more patient, tolerant, and untyrannical. He never laughed at Robin for his clumsy efforts to imitate his own prodigious feats; he did not tease or bully, but helped his small companion when he was in difficulties and explained when he could not understand. In return, Robin adored him, regarded him as the model and perfect Big Boy, and slavishly imitated him in every way he could.

These attempts of Robin's to imitate his companion were often exceedingly ludicrous. For by an obscure psychological law, words and actions in themselves quite serious become comic as soon as they are copied; and the more accurately, if the imitation is a deliberate parody, the funnier—for an overloaded imitation of someone we know does not make us laugh so much as one that is almost indistinguishably like the original. The bad imitation is only ludicrous when it is a piece of sincere and earnest flattery which does not quite come off. Robin's imitations were mostly of this kind. His heroic and unsuccessful attempts to perform the feats of strength and skill, which Guido could do with ease, were exquisitely comic. And his careful, long-drawn imitations of Guido's habits and mannerisms were no less amusing. Most ludicrous of all, because most earnestly undertaken and most incongruous in the imitator, were Robin's impersonations of Guido in the pensive mood. Guido was a thoughtful child, given to brooding and sudden abstractions. One would find him sitting in a corner by himself, chin in hand, elbow on knee, plunged, to all appearances, in the profoundest meditation. And sometimes, even in the midst of his play, he would suddenly break off, to stand, his hands behind his back, frowning and staring at the ground. When this happened Robin became overawed and a little disquieted. In a puzzled silence he looked at his companion. "Guido," he would say softly, "Guido." But Guido was generally too much preoccupied to answer; and Robin, not venturing to insist, would creep near him, and throwing himself as nearly as possible into Guido's attitude—standing Napoleonically, his hands clasped behind him, or sitting in the posture of Michelangelo's Lorenzo the Magnificent—would try to meditate too. Every few seconds he would turn his bright blue eyes towards the elder child to see whether he was doing it quite right. But at the end of a minute he began to grow impatient; meditation wasn't his strong point. "Guido," he called again and, louder, "Guido!" And he would take him by the hand and try to pull him away. Sometimes Guido roused himself from his reverie and went back to the interrupted game. Sometimes he paid no attention. Melancholy, perplexed, Robin had to take himself off to play by himself. And Guido would go on sitting or standing there, quite still; and his eyes, if one looked into them, were beautiful in their grave and pensive calm.

They were large eyes, set far apart and, what was strange in a dark-haired Italian child, of a luminous pale blue-gray color. They were not always grave and calm, as in these pensive moments. When he was playing, when he talked or laughed, they lit up; and the surface of those clear, pale lakes of thought seemed, as it were, to be shaken into brilliant sun-flashing ripples. Above those eyes was a beautiful forehead, high and steep and domed in a curve that was like the subtle curve of a rose petal. The nose was straight, the chin small and rather pointed, the mouth drooped a little sadly at the corners.

I have a snapshot of the two children sitting together on the parapet of the terrace. Guido sits almost facing the camera, but looking a little to one side and downwards; his hands are crossed in his lap and his expression, his attitude are thoughtful, grave, and meditative. It is Guido in one of those moods of abstraction into which he would pass even at the height of laughter and play—quite suddenly and completely, as though he had all at once taken it into his head to go away and had left the silent and beautiful body behind, like an empty house, to wait for his return. And by his side sits little Robin, turning to look up at him, his face half averted from the camera, but the curve of his cheek showing that he is laughing; one little raised hand is caught at the top of a gesture, the other clutches at Guido's sleeve as though he were urging him to come away and play. And the legs dangling from the parapet have been seen by the blinking instrument in the midst of an impatient wriggle; he is on the point of slipping down and running off to play hide-and-seek in the garden. All the essential characteristics of both the children are in that little snapshot.

"If Robin were not Robin," Elizabeth used to say, "I could almost wish he were Guido."

And even at that time, when I took no particular interest in the child, I agreed with her. Guido seemed to me one of the most charming little boys I had ever seen.

We were not alone in admiring him. Signora Bondi when, in those cordial intervals between our quarrels, she came to call, was constantly speaking of him. "Such a beautiful, beautiful child!" she would exclaim with enthusiasm. "It's really a waste that he should belong to peasants who can't afford to dress him properly. If he were mine, I should put him into black velvet; or little white knickers and a white knitted silk jersey with a red line at the collar and cuffs! or perhaps a white sailor suit would be pretty. And in winter a little fur coat, with a squirrel skin cap, and possibly Russian boots . . ." Her imagination was running away with her. "And I'd let his hair grow, like a page's, and have it just curled up a little at the tips. And a straight fringe across his forehead. Everyone would turn round and stare after us if I took him out with me in Via Tornabuoni."

What you want, I should have liked to tell her, is not a child; it's a clock-work doll or a performing monkey. But I did not say so—partly because I could not think of the Italian for a clock-work doll and partly because I did not want to risk having the rent raised another 15 per cent.

"Ah, if only I had a little boy like that!" She sighed and modestly dropped her eyelids. "I adore children. I sometimes think of adopting one—that is, if my husband would allow it."

I thought of the poor old gentleman being dragged along at the heels of his big white dog and inwardly smiled.

"But I don't know if he would," the Signora was continuing, "I don't know if he would." She was silent for a moment, as though considering a new idea.

A few days later, when we were sitting in the garden after luncheon, drinking our coffee, Guido's father, instead of passing with a nod and the usual cheerful good-day, halted in front of us and began to talk. He was a fine handsome man, not very tall, but well-proportioned, quick and elastic in his movements, and full of life. He had a thin brown face, featured like a Roman's and lit by a pair of the most intelligent-looking gray eyes I ever saw. They exhibited almost too much intelligence when, as not infrequently happened, he was trying, with an assumption of perfect frankness and a childlike innocence, to take one in or get something out of one. Delighting in itself, the intelligence shone there mischievously. The face might be ingenuous, impassive, almost imbecile in its expression; but the eyes on these occasions gave him completely away. One knew, when they glittered like that, that one would have to be careful.

Today, however, there was no dangerous light in them. He wanted nothing out of us, nothing of any value—only advice, which is a commodity, he knew, that most people are only too happy to part with. But he wanted advice on what was, for us, rather a delicate subject: on Signora Bondi. Carlo had often complained to us about her. The old man is good, he told us, very good and kind indeed. Which meant, I dare say, among other things, that he could easily be swindled. But his wife . . . Well, the woman was a beast. And he would tell us stories of her insatiable rapacity: she was always claiming more than the half of the produce which, by the laws of the metayage [1] system, was the proprietor's due. He complained of her suspiciousness: she was forever accusing him of sharp practices, of downright stealing—him, he struck his breast, the soul of honesty. He complained of her short-sighted avarice: she wouldn't spend enough on manure, wouldn't buy him another cow, wouldn't have electric light installed in the stables. And we had sympathized, but cautiously, without expressing too strong an opinion on the subject. The Italians are wonderfully noncommittal in their speech; they will give nothing away to an interested person until they are quite certain that it is right and necessary and, above all, safe to do so. We had lived long enough among them to imitate their caution. What we said to Carlo would be sure, sooner or later, to get back to Signora Bondi. There was nothing to be gained by unnecessarily embittering our relations with the lady—only another 15 per cent, very likely, to be lost.

Today he wasn't so much complaining as feeling perplexed. The Signora had sent for him, it seemed, and asked him how he would like it if she were to make an offer—it was all very hypothetical in the cautious Italian style—to adopt little Guido. Carlo's first instinct had been to say that he wouldn't like it at all. But an answer like that would have been too coarsely committal. He had preferred to say that he would think about it. And now he was asking for our advice.

Do what you think best, was what in effect we replied. But we gave it distantly but distinctly to be understood that we didn't think that Signora Bondi would make a very good foster-mother for the child. And Carlo was inclined to agree. Besides, he was very fond of the boy.

"But the thing is," he concluded rather gloomily, "that if she has really set her heart on getting hold of the child, there's nothing she won't do to get him—nothing."

He too, I could see, would have liked the physicists to start on unemployed childless women of sanguine temperament before they tried to tackle the atom. Still, I reflected, as I watched him striding away along the terrace, singing powerfully from a brazen gullet as he went, there was force there, there was life enough in those elastic limbs, behind those bright gray eyes, to put up a good fight even against the accumulated vital energies of Signora Bondi.

It was a few days after this that my gramophone and two or three boxes of records arrived from England. They were

[1] share-cropping.

[32]

a great comfort to us on the hilltop, providing as they did the only thing in which that spiritually fertile solitude—otherwise a perfect Swiss Family Robinson's island—was lacking: music. There is not much music to be heard nowadays in Florence. The times when Dr. Burney could tour through Italy, listening to an unending succession of new operas, symphonies, quartets, cantatas, are gone. Gone are the days when a learned musician, inferior only to the Reverend Father Martini of Bologna, could admire what the peasants sang and the strolling players thrummed and scraped on their instruments. I have traveled for weeks through the peninsula and hardly heard a note that was not "Salome" or the Fascists' song. Rich in nothing else that makes life agreeable or even supportable, the northern metropolises are rich in music. That is perhaps the only inducement that a reasonable man can find for living there. The other attractions—organized gaiety, people, miscellaneous conversation, the social pleasures—what are those, after all, but an expense of spirit that buys nothing in return? And then the cold, the darkness, the mouldering dirt, the damp and squalor. . . . No, where there is no necessity that retains, music can be the only inducement. And that, thanks to the ingenious Edison, can now be taken about in a box and unpacked in whatever solitude one chooses to visit. One can live at Benin, or Nuneaton, or Tozeur in the Sahara, and still hear Mozart quartets, and selections from the Well-Tempered Clavichord, and the Fifth Symphony, and the Brahms clarinet quintet, and motets by Palestrina.

Carlo, who had gone down to the station with his mule and cart to fetch the packing-case, was vastly interested in the machine.

"One will hear some music again," he said, as he watched me unpacking the gramophone and the disks. "It is difficult to do much oneself."

Still, I reflected, he managed to do a good deal. On warm nights we used to hear him, where he sat at the door of his house, playing his guitar and softly singing; the eldest boy shrilled out the melody on the mandolin, and sometimes the whole family would join in, and the darkness would be filled with their passionate, throaty singing. Piedigrotta[2] songs they mostly sang; and the voices drooped slurringly from note to note, lazily climbed or jerked themselves with sudden sobbing emphases from one tone to another. At a distance and under the stars the effect was not unpleasing.

"Before the war," he went on, "in normal times" (and Carlo had a hope, even a belief, that the normal times were coming back and that life would soon be as cheap and easy as it had been in the days before the flood), "I used to go and listen to the operas at the Politeama. Ah, they were magnificent. But it costs five lire now to get in."

"Too much," I agreed.

"Have you got *Trovatore?*" he asked.

I shook my head.

"*Rigoletto?*"

"I'm afraid not."

"*Bohème? Fanciulla del West? Pagliacci?*"

I had to go on disappointing him.

"Not even *Norma?* Or the *Barbiere?*"

I put on Battistini in "La ci darem" out of *Don Giovanni*. He agreed that the singing was good; but I could see that he

[2] popular songs of Naples.

didn't much like the music. Why not? He found it difficult to explain.

"It's not like *Pagliacci*," he said at last.

"Not palpitating?" I suggested, using a word with which I was sure he would be familiar; for it occurs in every Italian political speech and patriotic leading article.

"Not palpitating," he agreed.

And I reflected that it is precisely by the difference between *Pagliacci* and *Don Giovanni*, between the palpitating and the nonpalpitating, that modern musical taste is separated from the old. The corruption of the best, I thought, is the worst. Beethoven taught music to palpitate with his intellectual and spiritual passion. It has gone on palpitating ever since, but with the passion of inferior men. Indirectly, I thought, Beethoven is responsible for *Parsifal, Pagliacci,* and the *Poem of Fire;* still more indirectly for *Samson and Delilah* and "Ivy, cling to me." Mozart's melodies may be brilliant, memorable, infectious; but they don't palpitate, don't catch you between wind and water, don't send the listener off into erotic ecstasies.

Carlo and his elder children found my gramophone, I am afraid, rather a disappointment. They were too polite, however, to say so openly; they merely ceased, after the first day or two, to take any interest in the machine and the music it played. They preferred the guitar and their own singing.

Guido, on the other hand, was immensely interested. And he liked, not the cheerful dance tunes, to whose sharp rhythms our little Robin loved to go stamping round and round the room, pretending that he was a whole regiment of soldiers, but the genuine stuff. The first record he heard, I remember, was that of the slow movement of Bach's Concerto in D Minor for two violins. That was the disk I put on the turntable as soon as Carlo had left me. It seemed to me, so to speak, the most musical piece of music with which I could refresh my long-parched mind—the coolest and clearest of all draughts. The movement had just got under way and was beginning to unfold its pure and melancholy beauties in accordance with the laws of the most exacting intellectual logic, when the two children, Guido in front and little Robin breathlessly following, came clattering into the room from the loggia.

Guido came to a halt in front of the gramophone and stood there, motionless, listening. His pale blue-gray eyes opened themselves wide; making a little nervous gesture that I had often noticed in him before, he plucked at his lower lip with his thumb and forefinger. He must have taken a deep breath; for I noticed that, after listening for a few seconds, he sharply expired and drew in a fresh gulp of air. For an instant he looked at me—a questioning, astonished, rapturous look—gave a little laugh that ended in a kind of nervous shudder, and turned back towards the source of the incredible sounds. Slavishly imitating his elder comrade, Robin had also taken up his stand in front of the gramophone, and in exactly the same position, glancing at Guido from time to time to make sure that he was doing everything, down to plucking at his lip, in the correct way. But after a minute or so he became bored.

"Soldiers," he said, turning to me; "I want soldiers. Like in London." He remembered the rag-time and the jolly marches round and round the room.

I put my fingers to my lips. "Afterwards," I whispered.

Robin managed to remain silent and still for perhaps another twenty seconds.

Then he seized Guido by the arm, shouting, "Vieni, Guido! Soldiers. Soldati. Vieni giuocare soldati!"

It was then, for the first time, that I saw Guido impatient. "Vai!" he whispered angrily, slapped at Robin's clutching hand and pushed him roughly away. And he leaned a little closer to the instrument, as though to make up by yet intenser listening for what the interruption had caused him to miss.

Robin looked at him, astonished. Such a thing had never happened before. Then he burst out crying and came to me for consolation.

When the quarrel was made up—and Guido was sincerely repentant, was as nice as he knew how to be when the music had stopped and his mind was free to think of Robin once more—I asked him how he liked the music. He said he thought it was beautiful. But *bello* in Italian is too vague a word, too easily and frequently uttered, to mean very much.

"What did you like best?" I insisted. For he had seemed to enjoy it so much that I was curious to find out what had really impressed him.

He was silent for a moment, pensively frowning. "Well," he said at last, "I liked the bit that went like this." And he hummed a long phrase. "And then there's the other thing singing at the same time—but what are those things," he interrupted himself, "that sing like that?"

"They're called violins," I said.

"Violins." He nodded. "Well, the other violin goes like this." He hummed again. "Why can't one sing both at once? And what is in that box? What makes it make that noise?" The child poured out his questions.

I answered him as best I could, showing him the little spirals on the disk, the needle, the diaphragm. I told him to remember how the string of the guitar trembled when one plucked it; sound is a shaking in the air, I told him, and I tried to explain how those shakings get printed on the black disk. Guido listened to me very gravely, nodding from time to time. I had the impression that he understood perfectly well everything I was saying.

By this time, however, poor Robin was so dreadfully bored that in pity for him I had to send the two children out into the garden to play. Guido went obediently; but I could see that he would have preferred to stay indoors and listen to more music. A little while later, when I looked out, he was hiding in the dark recesses of the big bay tree, roaring like a lion, and Robin, laughing, but a little nervously, as though he were afraid that the horrible noise might possibly turn out, after all, to be the roaring of a real lion, was beating the bush with a stick, and shouting, "Come out, come out! I want to shoot you."

After lunch, when Robin had gone upstairs for his afternoon sleep, he reappeared. "May I listen to the music now?" he asked. And for an hour he sat there in front of the instrument, his head cocked slightly on one side, listening while I put on one disk after another.

Thenceforward he came every afternoon. Very soon he knew all my library of records, had his preferences and dislikes, and could ask for what he wanted by humming the principal theme.

"I don't like that one," he said of Strauss's *Till Eulenspiegel*. "It's like what we sing in our house. Not really like, you know. But somehow rather like, all the same. You understand?" He looked at us perplexedly and appealingly, as though begging us to understand what he meant and so save him from going on explaining. We nodded. Guido went on. "And then," he said, "the end doesn't seem to come properly out of the beginning. It's not like the one you played the first time." He hummed a bar or two from the slow movement of Bach's D Minor Concerto.

"It isn't," I suggested, "like saying: All little boys like playing. Guido is a little boy. Therefore Guido likes playing."

He frowned. "Yes, perhaps that's it," he said at last. "The one you played first is more like that. But, you know," he added, with an excessive regard for truth, "I don't like playing as much as Robin does."

Wagner was among his dislikes; so was Debussy. When I played the record of one of Debussy's Arabesques, he said, "Why does he say the same thing over and over again? He ought to say something new, or go on, or make the thing grow. Can't he think of anything different?" But he was less censorious about the "Après-Midi d'un Faune." "The things have beautiful voices," he said.

Mozart overwhelmed him with delight. The duet from *Don Giovanni,* which his father had found insufficiently palpitating, enchanted Guido. But he preferred the quartets and the orchestral pieces.

"I like music," he said, "better than singing."

Most people, I reflected, like singing better than music; are more interested in the executant than in what he executes, and find the impersonal orchestra less moving than the soloist. The touch of the pianist is the human touch, and the soprano's high C is the personal note. It is for the sake of this touch, that note, that audiences fill the concert halls.

Guido, however, preferred music. True, he liked "La ci darem"; he liked "Deh vieni alla finestra"; he thought "Che soave zefiretto" so lovely that almost all our concerts had to begin with it. But he preferred the other things. The *Figaro* overture was one of his favorites. There is a passage not far from the beginning of the piece, where the first violins suddenly go rocketing up into the heights of loveliness; as the music approached that point, I used always to see a smile developing and gradually brightening on Guido's face, and when, punctually, the thing happened, he clapped his hands and laughed aloud with pleasure.

On the other side of the same disk, it happened, was recorded Beethoven's *Egmont* overture. He liked that almost better than *Figaro*.

"It has more voices," he explained. And I was delighted by the acuteness of the criticism; for it is precisely in the richness of its orchestration that *Egmont* goes beyond *Figaro*.

But what stirred him almost more than anything was the *Coriolan* overture. The third movement of the Fifth Symphony, the second movement of the Seventh, the slow movement of the Emperor Concerto, —all these things ran it pretty close. But none excited him so much as *Coriolan*. One day he made me play it three or four times in succession; then he put it away.

"I don't think I want to hear that any more," he said.

"Why not?"

"It's too . . . too . . ." he hesitated, "too big," he said at last. "I don't really understand it. Play me the one that goes like this." He hummed the phrase from the D Minor Concerto.

"Do you like that one better?" I asked.

He shook his head. "No, it's not that exactly. But it's easier."

[36]

"Easier?" It seemed to me rather a queer word to apply to Bach.

"I understand it better."

One afternoon, while we were in the middle of our concert, Signora Bondi was ushered in. She began at once to be overwhelmingly affectionate towards the child; kissed him, patted his head, paid him the most outrageous compliments on his appearance. Guido edged away from her.

"And do you like music?" she asked.

The child nodded.

"I think he has a gift," I said. "At any rate, he has a wonderful ear and a power of listening and criticising such as I've never met with in a child of that age. We're thinking of hiring a piano for him to learn on."

A moment later I was cursing myself for my undue frankness in praising the boy. For Signora Bondi began immediately to protest that, if she could have the upbringing of the child, she would give him the best masters, bring out his talent, make an accomplished maestro of him—and, on the way, an infant prodigy. And at that moment, I am sure, she saw herself sitting maternally, in pearls and black satin, in the lee of the huge Steinway, while an angelic Guido, dressed like little Lord Fauntleroy, rattled out Liszt and Chopin, to the loud delight of a thronged auditorium. She saw the bouquets and all the elaborate floral tributes, heard the clapping and the few well-chosen words with which the veteran maestri, touched almost to tears, would hail the coming of the little genius. It became more than ever important for her to acquire the child.

"You've sent her away fairly ravening," said Elizabeth, when Signora Bondi had gone. "Better tell her next time that you made a mistake, and that the boy's got no musical talent whatever."

In due course, the piano arrived. After giving him the minimum of preliminary instruction, I let Guido loose on it. He began by picking out for himself the melodies he had heard, reconstructing the harmonies in which they were embedded. After a few lessons, he understood the rudiments of musical notation and could read a simple passage at sight, albeit very slowly. The whole process of reading was still strange to him; he had picked up his letters somehow, but nobody had yet taught him to read whole words and sentences.

I took occasion, next time I saw Signora Bondi, to assure her that Guido had disappointed me. There was nothing in his musical talent, really. She professed to be very sorry to hear it; but I could see that she didn't for a moment believe me. Probably she thought that we were after the child too, and wanted to bag the infant prodigy for ourselves, before she could get in her claim, thus depriving her of what she regarded almost as her feudal right. For, after all, weren't they her peasants? If anyone was to profit by adopting the child it ought to be herself.

Tactfully, diplomatically, she renewed her negotiations with Carlo. The boy, she put it to him, had genius. It was the foreign gentleman who had told her so, and he was the sort of man, clearly, who knew about such things. If Carlo would let her adopt the child, she'd have him trained. He'd become a great maestro and get engagements in the Argentine and the United States, in Paris and London. He'd earn millions and millions. Think of Caruso, for example. Part of the millions, she explained, would of course come to Carlo. But before they began to roll in, those millions, the boy would have to be trained. But training was very expensive.

In his own interest, as well as in that of his son, he ought to let her take charge of the child. Carlo said he would think it over, and again applied to us for advice. We suggested that it would be best in any case to wait a little and see what progress the boy made.

He made, in spite of my assertions to Signora Bondi, excellent progress. Every afternoon, while Robin was asleep, he came for his concert and his lesson. He was getting along famously with his reading; his small fingers were acquiring strength and agility. But what to me was more interesting was that he had begun to make up little pieces on his own account. A few of them I took down as he played them and I have them still. Most of them, strangely enough, as I thought then, are canons. He had a passion for canons. When I explained to him the principles of the form he was enchanted.

"It is beautiful," he said, with admiration. "Beautiful, beautiful. And so easy!"

Again the word surprised me. The canon is not, after all, so conspicuously simple. Thenceforward he spent most of his time at the piano in working out little canons for his own amusement. They were often remarkably ingenious. But in the invention of other kinds of music he did not show himself so fertile as I had hoped. He composed and harmonized one or two solemn little airs like hymn tunes, with a few sprightlier pieces in the spirit of the military march. They were extraordinary, of course, as being the inventions of a child. But a great many children can do extraordinary things; we are all geniuses up to the age of ten. But I had hoped that Guido was a child who was going to be a genius at forty; in which case what was extraordinary for an ordinary child was not extraordinary enough for him. "He's hardly a Mozart," we agreed, as we played his little pieces over. I felt, it must be confessed, almost aggrieved. Anything less than a Mozart, it seemed to me, was hardly worth thinking about.

He was not a Mozart. No. But he was somebody, as I was to find out, quite as extraordinary. It was one morning in the early summer that I made the discovery. I was sitting in the warm shade of our westward-facing balcony, working. Guido and Robin were playing in the little enclosed garden below. Absorbed in my work, it was only, I suppose, after the silence had prolonged itself a considerable time that I became aware that the children were making remarkably little noise. There was no shouting, no running about; only a quiet talking. Knowing by experience that when children are quiet it generally means that they are absorbed in some delicious mischief, I got up from my chair and looked over the balustrade to see what they were doing. I expected to catch them dabbling in water, making a bonfire, covering themselves with tar. But what I actually saw was Guido, with a burnt stick in his hand, demonstrating on the smooth paving-stones of the path, that the square on the hypotenuse of a right-angled triangle is equal to the sum of the squares on the other two sides.

Kneeling on the floor, he was drawing with the point of his blackened stick on the flagstones. And Robin, kneeling imitatively beside him, was growing, I could see, rather impatient with this very slow game.

"Guido," he said. But Guido paid no attention. Pensively frowning, he went on with his diagram. "Guido!" The younger child bent down and then craned round his neck so as to look up into Guido's face. "Why don't you draw a train?"

"Afterwards," said Guido. "But I just want to show you this first. It's *so* beautiful," he added cajolingly.

"But I want a train," Robin persisted.

"In a moment. Do just wait a moment." The tone was almost imploring. Robin armed himself with renewed patience. A minute later Guido had finished both his diagrams.

"There!" he said triumphantly, and straightened himself up to look at them. "Now I'll explain."

And he proceeded to prove the theorem of Pythagoras—not in Euclid's way, but by the simpler and more satisfying method which was, in all probability, employed by Pythagoras himself. He had drawn a square and dissected it, by a pair of crossed perpendiculars, into two squares and two equal rectangles. The equal rectangles he divided up by their diagonals into four equal right-angled triangles. The two squares are then seen to be the squares on the two sides of any one of these triangles other than the hypotenuse. So much for the first diagram. In the next he took the four right-angled triangles into which the rectangles had been divided and rearranged them round the original square so that their right angles filled the corners of the square, the hypotenuses looked inwards and the greater and less sides of the triangles were in continuation along the sides of the square (which are each equal to the sum of these sides). In this way the original square is redissected into four right-angled triangles and the square on the hypotenuse. The four triangles are equal to the two rectangles of the original dissection. Therefore the square on the hypotenuse is equal to the sum of the two squares—the squares on the other two sides—into which, with the rectangles, the original square was first dissected.

In very untechnical language, but clearly and with a relentless logic, Guido expounded his proof. Robin listened, with an expression on his bright, freckled face of perfect incomprehension.

"Treno," he repeated from time to time. "Treno. Make a train."

"In a moment," Guido implored. "Wait a moment. But do just look at this. *Do.*" He coaxed and cajoled. "It's so beautiful. It's so easy."

So easy.... The theorem of Pythagoras seemed to explain for me Guido's musical predilections. It was not an infant Mozart we had been cherishing; it was a little Archimedes with, like most of his kind, an incidental musical twist.

"Treno, treno!" shouted Robin, growing more and more restless as the exposition went on. And when Guido insisted on going on with his proof, he lost his temper. "Cattivo Guido," he shouted, and began to hit out at him with his fists.

"All right," said Guido resignedly. "I'll make a train." And with his stick of charcoal he began to scribble on the stones.

I looked on for a moment in silence. It was not a very good train. Guido might be able to invent for himself and prove the theorem of Pythagoras; but he was not much of a draughtsman.

"Guido!" I called. The two children turned and looked up. "Who taught you to draw those squares?" It was conceivable, of course, that somebody might have taught him.

"Nobody." He shook his head. Then, rather anxiously, as though he were afraid there might be something wrong about drawing squares, he went on to apologize and explain. "You see," he said, "it seemed

[39]

to me so beautiful. Because those squares"—he pointed at the two small squares in the first figure—"are just as big as this one." And, indicating the square on the hypotenuse in the second diagram, he looked up at me with a deprecating smile.

I nodded. "Yes, it's very beautiful," I said—"it's very beautiful indeed."

An expression of delighted relief appeared on his face; he laughed with pleasure. "You see, it's like this," he went on, eager to initiate me into the glorious secret he had discovered. "You cut these two long squares"—he meant the rectangles—"into two slices. And then there are four slices, all just the same, because, because—oh, I ought to have said that before—because these long squares are the same, because those lines, you see . . ."

"But I want a train," protested Robin.

Leaning on the rail of the balcony, I watched the children below. I thought of the extraordinary thing I had just seen and of what it meant.

I thought of the vast differences between human beings. We classify men by the color of their eyes and hair, the shape of their skulls. Would it not be more sensible to divide them up into intellectual species? There would be even wider gulfs between the extreme mental types than between a Bushman and a Scandinavian. This child, I thought, when he grows up, will be to me, intellectually, what a man is to a dog. And there are other men and women who are, perhaps, almost as dogs to me.

Perhaps the men of genius are the only true men. In all the history of the race there have been only a few thousand real men. And the rest of us—what are we? Teachable animals. Without the help of the real men, we should have found out almost nothing at all. Almost all the ideas with which we are familiar could never have occurred to minds like ours. Plant the seeds there and they will grow; but our minds could never spontaneously have generated them.

There have been whole nations of dogs, I thought; whole epochs in which no Man was born. From the dull Egyptians the Greeks took crude experience and rules of thumb and made sciences. More than a thousand years passed before Archimedes had a comparable successor. There has been only one Buddha, one Jesus, only one Bach that we know of, one Michelangelo.

Is it by a mere chance, I wondered, that a Man is born from time to time? What causes a whole constellation of them to come contemporaneously into being and from out of a single people? Taine thought that Leonardo, Michelangelo, and Raphael were born when they were because the time was ripe for great painters and the Italian scene congenial. In the mouth of a rationalizing nineteenth-century Frenchman the doctrine is strangely mystical; it may be none the less true for that. But what of those born out of time? Blake, for example. What of those?

This child, I thought, has had the fortune to be born at a time when he will be able to make good use of his capacities. He will find the most elaborate analytical methods lying ready to his hand; he will have a prodigious experience behind him. Suppose him born while Stonehenge was building; he might have spent a lifetime discovering the rudiments, guessing darkly where now he might have had a chance of proving. Born at the time of the Norman Conquest, he would have had to wrestle with all the preliminary difficulties created by an inadequate symbolism; it would have taken him long years, for example, to learn the art of dividing MMMCCCCLXXXVIII by MCMXIX. In five years, nowadays, he will learn what it took generations of Men to discover.

And I thought of the fate of all the men born so hopelessly out of time that they could achieve little or nothing of value. Beethoven born in Greece, I thought, would have had to be content to play thin melodies on the flute or lyre; in those intellectual surroundings it would hardly have been possible for him to imagine the nature of harmony.

From drawing trains, the children in the garden below had gone on to playing trains. They were trotting round and round; with blown round cheeks and pouting mouth, like the cherubic symbol of a wind, Robin puff-puffed, and Guido, holding the skirt of his smock, shuffled behind him, tooting. They ran forward, backed, stopped at imaginary stations, shunted, roared over bridges, crashed through tunnels, met with occasional collisions and derailments. The young Archimedes seemed to be just as happy as the little tow-headed barbarian. A few minutes ago he had been busy with the theorem of Pythagoras. Now, tooting indefatigably along imaginary rails, he was perfectly content to shuffle backwards and forwards among the flower-beds, between the pillars of the loggia, in and out of the dark tunnels of the laurel tree. The fact that one is going to be Archimedes does not prevent one from being an ordinary cheerful child meanwhile. I thought of this strange talent distinct and separate from the rest of the mind, independent, almost, of experience. The typical child-prodigies are musical and mathematical; the other talents ripen slowly under the influence of emotional experience and growth. Till he was thirty Balzac gave proof of nothing but ineptitude; but at four the young Mozart was already a musician, and some of Pascal's most brilliant work was done before he was out of his teens.

In the weeks that followed, I alternated the daily piano lessons with lessons in mathematics. Hints rather than lessons they were; for I only made suggestions, indicated methods, and left the child himself to work out the ideas in detail. Thus I introduced him to algebra by showing him another proof of the theorem of Pythagoras. In this proof one drops a perpendicular from the right angle on to the hypotenuse, and arguing from the fact that the two triangles thus created are similar to one another and to the original triangle, and that the proportions which their corresponding sides bear to one another are therefore equal, one can show in algebraical form that $c^2 + d^2$ (the squares on the other two sides) are equal to $a^2 + b^2$ (the squares on the two segments of the hypotenuse) $+ 2ab$; which last, it is easy to show geometrically, is equal to $(a + b)^2$, or the square on the hypotenuse. Guido was as much enchanted by the rudiments of algebra as he would have been if I had given him an engine worked by steam, with a methylated spirit lamp to heat the boiler; more enchanted, perhaps—for the engine would have got broken, and remaining always itself, would in any case have lost its charm, while the rudiments of algebra continued to grow and blossom in his mind with an unfailing luxuriance. Every day he made the discovery of something which seemed to him exquisitely beautiful; the new toy was inexhaustible in its potentialities.

In the intervals of applying algebra to the second book of Euclid, we experimented with circles; we stuck bamboos into the parched earth, measured their shadows at different hours of the day, and drew exciting conclusions from our observations. Sometimes, for fun, we cut and folded sheets of paper so as to make cubes and pyramids. One afternoon Guido arrived carrying carefully between his small and rather grubby hands a flimsy dodecahedron.

"E tanto bello!" he said, as he showed us his paper crystal; and when I asked him how he managed to make it, he merely smiled and said it had been so easy. I looked at Elizabeth and laughed. But it would have been more symbolically to the point, I felt, if I had gone down on all fours, wagged the spiritual outgrowth of my *os coccyx,* and barked my astonished admiration.

It was an uncommonly hot summer. By the beginning of July our little Robin, unaccustomed to these high temperatures, began to look pale and tired; he was listless, had lost his appetite and energy. The doctor advised mountain air. We decided to spend the next ten or twelve weeks in Switzerland. My parting gift to Guido was the first six books of Euclid in Italian. He turned over the pages, looked ecstatically at the figures.

"If only I knew how to read properly," he said. "I'm so stupid. But now I shall really try to learn."

From our hotel near Grindelwald we sent the child, in Robin's name, various post cards of cows, Alp-horns, Swiss chalets, edelweiss, and the like. We received no answers to these cards; but then we did not expect answers. Guido could not write, and there was no reason why his father or his sisters should take the trouble to write for him. No news, we took it, was good news. And then one day, early in September, there arrived at the hotel a strange letter. The manager had it stuck up on the glass-fronted notice-board in the hall, so that all the guests might see it, and whoever conscientiously thought that it belonged to him might claim it. Passing the board on the way in to lunch, Elizabeth stopped to look at it.

"But it must be from Guido," she said.

I came and looked at the envelope over her shoulder. It was unstamped and black with postmarks. Traced out in pencil, the big uncertain capital letters sprawled across its face. In the first line was written: AL BABBO DI ROBIN, and there followed a travestied version of the name of the hotel and the place. Round the address bewildered postal officials had scrawled suggested emendations. The letter had wandered for a fortnight at least, back and forth across the face of Europe.

"Al Babbo di Robin. To Robin's father." I laughed. "Pretty smart of the postmen to have got it here at all." I went to the manager's office, set forth the justice of my claim to the letter and, having paid the fifty-centime surcharge for the missing stamp, had the case unlocked and the letter given me. We went in to lunch.

"The writing's magnificent," we agreed, laughing, as we examined the address at close quarters. "Thanks to Euclid," I added. "That's what comes of pandering to the ruling passion."

But when I opened the envelope and looked at its contents I no longer laughed. The letter was brief and almost telegraphical in style. "SONO DALLA PADRONA," it ran, "NON MI PIACE HA RUBATO IL MIO LIBRO NON VOGLIO SUONARE PIU VOGLIO TORNARE A CASA VENGA SUBITO GUIDO." [3]

---

[3] I am at the Padrona's—I don't like it—she has stolen my book—I don't want to play [the piano] any more—I want to return home—come quickly—Guido.

Young Archimedes

"What is it?"

I handed Elizabeth the letter. "That blasted woman's got hold of him," I said.

Busts of men in Homburg hats, angels bathed in marble tears extinguishing torches, statues of little girls, cherubs, veiled figures, allegories and ruthless realisms—the strangest and most diverse idols beckoned and gesticulated as we passed. Printed indelibly on tin and embedded in the living rock, the brown photographs looked out, under glass, from the humbler crosses, headstones, and broken pillars. Dead ladies in the cubistic geometrical fashions of thirty years ago—two cones of black satin meeting point to point at the waist, and the arms: a sphere to the elbow, a polished cylinder below—smiled mournfully out of their marble frames; the smiling faces, the white hands, were the only recognizably human things that emerged from the solid geometry of their clothes. Men with black mustaches, men with white beards, young clean-shaven men, stared or averted their gaze to show a Roman profile. Children in their stiff best opened wide their eyes, smiled hopefully in anticipation of the little bird that was to issue from the camera's muzzle, smiled skeptically in the knowledge that it wouldn't, smiled laboriously and obediently because they had been told to. In spiky Gothic cottages of marble the richer dead privately reposed; through grilled doors one caught a glimpse of pale Inconsolables weeping, of distraught Geniuses guarding the secret of the tomb. The less prosperous sections of the majority slept in communities, close-crowded but elegantly housed under smooth continuous marble floors, whose every flagstone was the mouth of a separate grave.

These continental cemeteries, I thought, as Carlo and I made our way among the dead, are more frightful than ours, because these people pay more attention to their dead than we do. That primordial cult of corpses, that tender solicitude for their material well-being, which led the ancients to house their dead in stone, while they themselves lived between wattles and under thatch, still lingers here; persists, I thought, more vigorously than with us. There are a hundred gesticulating statues here for every one in an English graveyard. There are more family vaults, more "luxuriously appointed" (as they say of liners and hotels) than one would find at home. And embedded in every tombstone there are photographs to remind the powdered bones within what form they will have to resume on the Day of Judgment; beside each are little hanging lamps to burn optimistically on All Souls' Day. To the Man who built the Pyramids they are nearer, I thought, than we.

"If I had known," Carlo kept repeating, "if only I had known." His voice came to me through my reflections as though from a distance. "At the time he didn't mind at all. How should I have known that he would take it so much to heart afterwards? And she deceived me, she lied to me."

I assured him yet once more that it wasn't his fault. Though, of course, it was, in part. It was mine too, in part; I ought to have thought of the possibility and somehow guarded against it. And he shouldn't have let the child go, even temporarily and on trial, even though the woman was bringing pressure to bear on him. And the pressure had been considerable. They had worked on the same holding for more than a hundred years, the

[43]

men of Carlo's family; and now she had made the old man threaten to turn him out. It would be a dreadful thing to leave the place; and besides, another place wasn't so easy to find. It was made quite plain, however, that he could stay if he let her have the child. Only for a little to begin with; just to see how he got on. There would be no compulsion whatever on him to stay if he didn't like it. And it would be all to Guido's advantage; and to his father's, too, in the end. All that the Englishman had said about his not being such a good musician as he had thought at first was obviously untrue—mere jealousy and little-mindedness: the man wanted to take credit for Guido himself, that was all. And the boy, it was obvious, would learn nothing from him. What he needed was a real good professional master.

All the energy that, if the physicists had known their business, would have been driving dynamos, went into this campaign. It began the moment we were out of the house, intensively. She would have more chance of success, the Signora doubtless thought, if we weren't there. And besides, it was essential to take the opportunity when it offered itself and get hold of the child before we could make our bid—for it was obvious to her that we wanted Guido just as much as she did.

Day after day she renewed the assault. At the end of a week she sent her husband to complain about the state of the vines: they were in a shocking condition; he had decided, or very nearly decided, to give Carlo notice. Meekly, shamefacedly, in obedience to higher orders, the old gentleman uttered his threats. Next day Signora Bondi returned to the attack. The padrone, she declared, had been in a towering passion; but she'd do her best, her very best, to mollify him. And after a significant pause she went on to talk about Guido.

In the end Carlo gave in. The woman was too persistent and she held too many trump cards. The child could go and stay with her for a month or two on trial. After that, if he really expressed a desire to remain with her, she could formally adopt him.

At the idea of going for a holiday to the seaside—and it was to the seaside, Signora Bondi told him, that they were going—Guido was pleased and excited. He had heard a lot about the sea from Robin. "Tanta acqua!" It had sounded almost too good to be true. And now he was actually to go and see this marvel. It was very cheerfully that he parted from his family.

But after the holiday by the sea was over, and Signora Bondi had brought him back to her town house in Florence, he began to be homesick. The Signora, it was true, treated him exceedingly kindly, bought him new clothes, took him out to tea in the Via Tornabuoni and filled him up with cakes, iced strawberryade, whipped cream, and chocolates. But she made him practice the piano more than he liked, and what was worse, she took away his Euclid, on the score that he wasted too much time with it. And when he said that he wanted to go home, she put him off with promises and excuses and downright lies. She told him that she couldn't take him at once, but that next week, if he were good and worked hard at his piano meanwhile, next week . . . And when the time came she told him that his father didn't want him back. And she redoubled her petting, gave him expensive presents, and stuffed him with yet unhealthier foods. To no purpose. Guido didn't like his new life, didn't want to practice scales, pined for his book, and longed to be back with his brothers and sisters. Signora Bondi, meanwhile, continued to hope that time and chocolates would eventually make the child hers; and to keep his family at a distance, she wrote to Carlo every few days letters which still purported to come from the seaside (she took the trouble to send them to a friend, who posted them back again to Florence), and in which she painted the most charming picture of Guido's happiness.

It was then that Guido wrote his letter to me. Abandoned, as he supposed, by his family—for that they shouldn't take the trouble to come to see him when they were so near was only to be explained on the hypothesis that they really had given him up—he must have looked to me as his last and only hope. And the letter, with its fantastic address, had been nearly a fortnight on its way. A fortnight—it must have seemed hundreds of years; and as the centuries succeeded one another, gradually, no doubt, the poor child became convinced that I too had abandoned him. There was no hope left.

"Here we are," said Carlo.

I looked up and found myself confronted by an enormous monument. In a kind of grotto hollowed in the flanks of a monolith of gray sandstone, Sacred Love, in bronze, was embracing a funerary urn. And in bronze letters riveted into the stone was a long legend to the effect that the inconsolable Ernesto Bondi had raised this monument to the memory of his beloved wife, Annunziata, as a token of his undying love for one whom, snatched from him by a premature death, he hoped very soon to join beneath this stone. The first Signora Bondi had died in 1912. I thought of the old man leashed to his white dog; he must always, I reflected, have been a most uxorious husband.

"They buried him here."

We stood there for a long time in silence. I felt the tears coming into my eyes as I thought of the poor child lying there underground. I thought of those luminous grave eyes, and the curve of that beautiful forehead, the droop of the melancholy mouth, of the expression of delight which illumined his face when he learned of some new idea that pleased him, when he heard a piece of music that he liked. And this beautiful small being was dead; and the spirit that inhabited this form, the amazing spirit, that too had been destroyed almost before it had begun to exist.

And the unhappiness that must have preceded the final act, the child's despair, the conviction of his utter abandonment—those were terrible to think of, terrible.

"I think we had better come away now," I said at last, and touched Carlo on the arm. He was standing there like a blind man, his eyes shut, his face slightly lifted towards the light; from between his closed eyelids the tears welled out, hung for a moment, and trickled down his cheeks. His lips trembled and I could see that he was making an effort to keep them still. "Come away," I repeated.

The face which had been still in its sorrow, was suddenly convulsed; he opened his eyes, and through the tears they were bright with a violent anger. "I shall kill her," he said, "I shall kill her. When I think of him throwing himself out, falling through the air . . ." With his two hands he made a violent gesture, bringing them down from over his head and arresting them with a sudden jerk when they were on a level with his breast. "And then crash." He shuddered. "She's as much responsible as though she had pushed him down herself. I shall kill her." He clenched his teeth.

To be angry is easier than to be sad, less painful. It is comforting to think of revenge. "Don't talk like that," I said. "It's no good. It's stupid. And what would be the point?" He had had those fits before, when grief became too painful and he had tried to escape from it. Anger had been the easiest way of escape. I had had, before this, to persuade him back into the harder path of grief. "It's stupid to talk like that," I repeated, and I led him away through the ghastly labyrinth of tombs, where death seemed more terrible even than it is.

By the time we had left the cemetery, and were walking down from San Miniato towards the Piazzale Michelangelo below, he had become calmer. His anger had subsided again into sorrow from which it had derived all its strength and its bitterness. In the Piazzale we halted for a moment to look down at the city in the valley below us. It was a day of floating clouds—great shapes, white, golden, and gray; and between them patches of a thin, transparent blue. Its lantern level, almost, with our eyes, the dome of the cathedral revealed itself in all its grandiose lightness, its vastness and aerial strength. On the innumerable brown and rosy roofs of the city the afternoon sunlight lay softly, sumptuously, and the towers were as though varnished and enameled with an old gold. I thought of all the Men who had lived here and left the visible traces of their spirit and conceived extraordinary things, I thought of the dead child.

ARABY
by JAMES JOYCE

NORTH RICHMOND STREET, being blind, was a quiet street except at the hour when the Christian Brothers' School set the boys free. An uninhabited house of two stories stood at the blind end, detached from its neighbors in a square ground. The other houses of the street, conscious of decent lives within them, gazed at one another with brown imperturbable faces.

The former tenant of our house, a priest, had died in the back drawing room. Air, musty from having been long enclosed, hung in all the rooms, and the waste room behind the kitchen was littered with old useless papers. Among these I found a few paper-covered books, the pages of which were curled and damp: *The Abbot,* by Walter Scott, *The Devout Communicant,* and *The Memoirs of Vidocq.* I liked the last best because its leaves were yellow. The wild garden behind the house contained a central apple tree and a few straggling bushes under one of which I found the late tenant's rusty bicycle pump. He had been a very charitable priest; in his will he had left all his money to institutions and the furniture of his house to his sister.

When the short days of winter came dusk fell before we had well eaten our dinners. When we met in the street the houses had grown somber. The space of

From *Dubliners* by James Joyce. By permission of The Viking Press, Inc., New York.

Araby

sky above us was the color of ever-changing violet and towards it the lamps of the street lifted their feeble lanterns. The cold air stung us and we played till our bodies glowed. Our shouts echoed in the silent street. The career of our play brought us through the dark muddy lanes behind the houses where we ran the gauntlet of the rough tribes from the cottages, to the back doors of the dark dripping gardens where odors arose from the ashpits, to the dark odorous stables where a coachman smoothed and combed the horse or shook music from the buckled harness. When we returned to the street, light from the kitchen windows had filled the areas. If my uncle was seen turning the corner we hid in the shadow until we had seen him safely housed. Or if Mangan's sister came out on the doorstep to call her brother in to his tea we watched her from our shadow peer up and down the street. We waited to see whether she would remain or go in and, if she remained, we left our shadow and walked up to Mangan's steps resignedly. She was waiting for us, her figure defined by the light from the half-opened door. Her brother always teased her before he obeyed and I stood by the railings looking at her. Her dress swung as she moved her body and the soft rope of her hair tossed from side to side.

Every morning I lay on the floor in the front parlor watching her door. The blind was pulled down to within an inch of the sash so that I could not be seen. When she came out on the doorstep my heart leaped. I ran to the hall, seized my books and followed her. I kept her brown figure always in my eye and, when we came near the point at which our ways diverged, I quickened my pace and passed her. This happened morning after morning. I had never spoken to her, except for a few casual words, and yet her name was like a summons to all my foolish blood.

Her image accompanied me even in places the most hostile to romance. On Saturday evenings when my aunt went marketing I had to go to carry some of the parcels. We walked through the flaring streets, jostled by drunken men and bargaining women, amid the curses of laborers, the shrill litanies of shop boys who stood on guard by the barrels of pigs' cheeks, the nasal chanting of street singers, who sang a *come-all-you* about O'Donovan Rossa, or a ballad about the troubles in our native land. These noises converged in a single sensation of life for me: I imagined that I bore my chalice safely through a throng of foes. Her name sprang to my lips at moments in strange prayers and praises which I myself did not understand. My eyes were often full of tears (I could not tell why) and at times a flood from my heart seemed to pour itself out into my bosom. I thought little of the future. I did not know whether I would ever speak to her or not or, if I spoke to her, how I could tell her of my confused adoration. But my body was like a harp and her words and gestures were like fingers running upon the wires.

One evening I went into the back drawing room in which the priest had died. It was a dark rainy evening and there was no sound in the house. Through one of the broken panes I heard the rain impinge upon the earth, the fine incessant needles of water playing in the sodden beds. Some distant lamp or lighted window gleamed below me. I was thankful that I could see so little. All my senses seemed to desire to veil themselves and, feeling that I was

Coming-of-Age in Our Time

about to slip from them, I pressed the palms of my hands together until they trembled, murmuring: *"O love! O love!"* many times.

At last she spoke to me. When she addressed the first words to me I was so confused that I did not know what to answer. She asked me was I going to *Araby*. I forgot whether I answered yes or no. It would be a splendid bazaar, she said; she would love to go.

"And why can't you?" I asked.

While she spoke she turned a silver bracelet round and round her wrist. She could not go, she said, because there would be a retreat that week in her convent. Her brother and two other boys were fighting for their caps and I was alone at the railings. She held one of the spikes, bowing her head towards me. The light from the lamp opposite our door caught the white curve of her neck, lit up her hair that rested there and, falling, lit up the hand upon the railing. It fell over one side of her dress and caught the white border of a petticoat, just visible as she stood at ease.

"It's well for you," she said.

"If I go," I said, "I will bring you something."

What innumerable follies laid waste my waking and sleeping thoughts after that evening! I wished to annihilate the tedious intervening days. I chafed against the work of school. At night in my bedroom and by day in the classroom her image came between me and the page I strove to read. The syllables of the word *Araby* were called to me through the silence in which my soul luxuriated and cast an Eastern enchantment over me. I asked for leave to go to the bazaar on Saturday night. My aunt was surprised and hoped it was not some Freemason affair. I answered few questions in class. I watched my master's face pass from amiability to sternness; he hoped I was not beginning to idle. I could not call my wandering thoughts together. I had hardly any patience with the serious work of life which, now that it stood between me and my desire, seemed to me child's play, ugly monotonous child's play.

On Saturday morning I reminded my uncle that I wished to go to the bazaar in the evening. He was fussing at the hall stand, looking for the hat brush, and answered me curtly:

"Yes, boy, I know."

As he was in the hall I could not go into the front parlor and lie at the window. I left the house in bad humor and walked slowly towards the school. The air was pitilessly raw and already my heart misgave me.

When I came home to dinner my uncle had not yet been home. Still it was early. I sat staring at the clock for some time and, when its ticking began to irritate me, I left the room. I mounted the staircase and gained the upper part of the house. The high cold empty gloomy rooms liberated me and I went from room to room singing. From the front window I saw my companions playing below in the street. Their cries reached me weakened and indistinct and, leaning my forehead against the cool glass, I looked over at the dark house where she lived. I may have stood there for an hour, seeing nothing but the brown-clad figure cast by my imagination, touched discreetly by the lamplight at the curved neck, at the hand upon the railings and at the border below the dress.

When I came downstairs again I found Mrs. Mercer sitting at the fire. She was an

Araby

old garrulous woman, a pawnbroker's widow, who collected used stamps for some pious purpose. I had to endure the gossip of the tea table. The meal was prolonged beyond an hour and still my uncle did not come. Mrs. Mercer stood up to go: she was sorry she couldn't wait any longer, but it was after eight o'clock and she did not like to be out late, as the night air was bad for her. When she had gone I began to walk up and down the room, clenching my fists. My aunt said:

"I'm afraid you may put off your bazaar for this night of Our Lord."

At nine o'clock I heard my uncle's latchkey in the hall door. I heard him talking to himself and heard the hall stand rocking when it had received the weight of his overcoat. I could interpret these signs. When he was midway through his dinner I asked him to give me the money to go to the bazaar. He had forgotten.

"The people are in bed and after their first sleep now," he said.

I did not smile. My aunt said to him energetically:

"Can't you give him the money and let him go? You've kept him late enough as it is."

My uncle said he was very sorry he had forgotten. He said he believed in the old saying: "All work and no play makes Jack a dull boy." He asked me where I was going and, when I had told him a second time he asked me did I know *The Arab's Farewell to His Steed*. When I left the kitchen he was about to recite the opening lines of the piece to my aunt.

I held a florin tightly in my hand as I strode down Buckingham Street towards the station. The sight of the streets thronged with buyers and glaring with gas recalled to me the purpose of my journey. I took my seat in a third-class carriage of a deserted train. After an intolerable delay the train moved out of the station slowly. It crept onward among ruinous houses and over the twinkling river. At Westland Row Station a crowd of people pressed to the carriage doors; but the porters moved them back, saying that it was a special train for the bazaar. I remained alone in the bare carriage. In a few minutes the train drew up beside an improvised wooden platform. I passed out on to the road and saw by the lighted dial of a clock that it was ten minutes to ten. In front of me was a large building which displayed the magical name.

I could not find any sixpenny entrance and, fearing that the bazaar would be closed, I passed in quickly through a turnstile, handing a shilling to a weary-looking man. I found myself in a big hall girdled at half its height by a gallery. Nearly all the stalls were closed and the greater part of the hall was in darkness. I recognized a silence like that which pervades a church after a service. I walked into the center of the bazaar timidly. A few people were gathered about the stalls which were still open. Before a curtain, over which the words *Café Chantant* were written in colored lamps, two men were counting money on a salver. I listened to the fall of the coins.

Remembering with difficulty why I had come I went over to one of the stalls and examined porcelain vases and flowered tea sets. At the door of the stall a young lady was talking and laughing with two young gentlemen. I remarked their English accents and listened vaguely to their conversation.

"O, I never said such a thing!"

"O, but you did!"

"O, but I didn't!"
"Didn't she say that?"
"Yes. I heard her."
"O, there's a . . . fib!"

Observing me, the young lady came over and asked me did I wish to buy anything. The tone of her voice was not encouraging; she seemed to have spoken to me out of a sense of duty. I looked humbly at the great jars that stood like eastern guards at either side of the dark entrance to the stall and murmured:

"No, thank you."

The young lady changed the position of one of the vases and went back to the two young men. They began to talk of the same subject. Once or twice the young lady glanced at me over her shoulder.

I lingered before her stall, though I knew my stay was useless, to make my interest in her wares seem the more real. Then I turned away slowly and walked down the middle of the bazaar. I allowed the two pennies to fall against the sixpence in my pocket. I heard a voice call from one end of the gallery that the light was out. The upper part of the hall was now completely dark.

Gazing up into the darkness I saw myself as a creature driven and derided by vanity; and my eyes burned with anguish and anger.

EXTRAORDINARY LITTLE COUGH

by Dylan Thomas

One afternoon, in a particularly bright and glowing August, some years before I knew I was happy, George Hooping, whom we called Little Cough, Sidney Evans, Dan Davies, and I sat on the roof of a lorry travelling to the end of the Peninsula. It was a tall, six-wheeled lorry, from which we could spit on the roofs of the passing cars and throw our apple-stumps at women on the pavement. One stump caught a man on a bicycle in the middle of the back, he swerved across the road, for a moment we sat quiet and George Hooping's face grew pale. And if the lorry runs over him, I thought calmly as the man on the bicycle swayed towards the hedge, he'll get killed and I'll be sick on my trousers and perhaps on Sidney's too, and we'll all be arrested and hanged, except George Hooping who didn't have an apple.

But the lorry swept past; behind us, the bicycle drove into the hedge, the man stood up and waved his fist, and I waved my cap back at him.

"You shouldn't have waved your cap," said Sidney Evans, "he'll know what school we're in." He was clever, dark, and careful, and had a purse and a wallet.

"We're not in school now."

"Nobody can expel me," said Dan Davies. He was leaving next term to serve in his father's fruit shop for a salary.

We all wore haversacks, except George Hooping whose mother had given him a brown-paper parcel that kept coming undone, and carried a suitcase each. I had placed a coat over my suitcase because the initials on it were "N.T." and everybody would know that it belonged to my sister. Inside the lorry were two tents, a box of food, a packing-case of kettles and sauce-

Copyright 1940 by New Directions, reprinted by permission of New Directions.

pans and knives and forks, an oil-lamp, a primus stove, ground sheets and blankets, a gramophone with three records, and a table-cloth from George Hooping's mother.

We were going to camp for a fortnight in Rhossilli, in a field above the sweeping five-mile beach. Sidney and Dan had stayed there last year, coming back brown and swearing, full of stories of campers' dances round the fires at midnight, and elderly girls from the training college who sunbathed naked on ledges of rocks surrounded by laughing boys, and singing in bed that lasted until dawn. But George had never left home for more than a night; and then, he told me one half-holiday when it was raining and there was nothing to do but to stay in the washhouse racing his guinea-pigs giddily along the benches, it was only to stay in St. Thomas, three miles from his house, with an aunt who could see through the walls and who knew what a Mrs. Hoskin was doing in the kitchen.

"How much further?" asked George Hooping, clinging to his split parcel, trying in secret to push back socks and suspenders, enviously watching the solid green fields skim by as though the roof were a raft on an ocean with a motor in it. Anything upset his stomach, even liquorice and sherbet, but I alone knew that he wore long combinations in the summer with his name stitched in red on them.

"Miles and miles," Dan said.

"Thousands of miles," I said. "It's Rhossilli, U.S.A. We're going to camp on a bit of rock that wobbles in the wind."

"And we have to tie the rock on to a tree."

"Cough can use his suspenders," Sidney said.

The lorry roared round a corner— "Upsy-daisy! Did you feel it then, Cough? It was on one wheel"—and below us, beyond fields and farms, the sea, with a steamer puffing on its far edge, shimmered.

"Do you see the sea down there, it's shimmering, Dan," I said.

George Hooping pretended to forget the lurch of the slippery roof and, from that height, the frightening smallness of the sea. Gripping the rail of the roof, he said: "My father saw a killer whale." The conviction in his voice died quickly as he began. He beat against the wind with his cracked, treble voice, trying to make us believe. I knew he wanted to find a boast so big it would make our hair stand up and stop the wild lorry.

"Your father's a herbalist." But the smoke on the horizon was the white, curling fountain the whale blew through his nose, and its black nose was the bow of the poking ship.

"Where did he keep it, Cough, in the washhouse?"

"He saw it in Madagascar. It had tusks as long as from here to, from here to . . ."

"From here to Madagascar."

All at once the threat of a steep hill disturbed him. No longer bothered about the adventures of his father, a small, dusty, skull-capped and alpaca-coated man standing and mumbling all day in a shop full of herbs and curtained holes in the wall, where old men with backache and young girls in trouble waited for consultations in the half-dark, he stared at the hill swooping up and clung to Dan and me.

"She's doing fifty!"

"The brakes have gone, Cough!"

He twisted away from us, caught hard with both hands on the rail, pulled and trembled, pressed on a case behind him

Coming-of-Age in Our Time

with his foot, and steered the lorry to safety round a stone-walled corner and up a gentler hill to the gate of a battered farm-house.

Leading down from the gate, there was a lane to the first beach. It was high-tide, and we heard the sea dashing. Four boys on a roof—one tall, dark, regular-featured, precise of speech, in a good suit, a boy of the world; one squat, ungainly, red-haired, his red wrists fighting out of short, frayed sleeves; one heavily spectacled, small-paunched, with indoor shoulders and feet in always unlaced boots wanting to go different ways; one small, thin, indecisively active, quick to get dirty, curly—saw their field in front of them, a fortnight's new home that had thick, pricking hedges for walls, the sea for a front garden, a green gutter for a lavatory, and a wind-struck tree in the very middle.

I helped Dan unload the lorry while Sidney tipped the driver and George struggled with the farm-yard gate and looked at the ducks inside. The lorry drove away.

"Let's build our tents by the tree in the middle," said George.

"Pitch!" Sidney said, unlatching the gate for him.

We pitched our tents in a corner, out of the wind.

"One of us must light the primus," Sidney said, and, after George had burned his hand, we sat in a circle outside the sleeping-tent talking about motor cars, content to be in the country, lazily easy in each other's company, thinking to ourselves as we talked, knowing always that the sea dashed on the rocks not far below us and rolled out into the world, and that to-morrow we would bathe and throw a ball on the sands and stone a bottle on a rock and perhaps meet three girls. The oldest would be for Sidney, the plainest for Dan, and the youngest for me. George broke his spectacles when he spoke to girls; he had to walk off, blind as a bat, and the next morning he would say: "I'm sorry I had to leave you, but I remembered a message."

It was past five o'clock. My father and mother would have finished tea; the plates with famous castles on them were cleared from the table; father with a newspaper, mother with socks, were far away in the blue haze to the left, up a hill, in a villa, hearing from the park the faint cries of children drift over the public tennis court, and wondering where I was and what I was doing. I was alone with my friends in a field, with a blade of grass in my mouth, saying, "Dempsey would hit him cold," and thinking of the great whale that George's father never saw thrashing on the top of the sea, or plunging underneath, like a mountain.

"Bet you I can beat you to the end of the field."

Dan and I raced among the cowpads, George thumping at our heels.

"Let's go down to the beach."

Sidney led the way, running straight as a soldier in his khaki shorts, over a stile, down fields to another, into a wooded valley, up through heather on to a clearing near the edge of the cliff, where two broad boys were wrestling outside a tent. I saw one bite the other in the leg, they both struck expertly and savagely at the face, one struggled clear, and, with a leap, the other had him face to the ground. They were Brazell and Skully.

"Hullo, Brazell and Skully!" said Dan.

Skully had Brazell's arm in a policeman's grip; he gave it two quick twists and stood up, smiling.

Extraordinary Little Cough

"Hullo, boys! Hullo, Little Cough! How's your father?"

"He's very well, thank you."

Brazell, on the grass, felt for broken bones. "Hullo, boys! How are your fathers?"

They were the worst and biggest boys in school. Every day for a term they caught me before class began and wedged me in the waste-paper-basket and then put the basket on the master's desk. Sometimes I could get out and sometimes not. Brazell was lean, Skully was fat.

"We're camping in Button's field," said Sidney.

"We're taking a rest cure here," said Brazell. "And how is Little Cough these days? Father given him a pill?"

We wanted to run down to the beach, Dan and Sidney and George and I, to be alone together, to walk and shout by the sea in the country, throw stones at the waves, remember adventures and make more to remember.

"We'll come down to the beach with you," said Skully.

He linked arms with Brazell, and they strolled behind us, imitating George's wayward walk and slashing the grass with switches.

Dan said hopefully: "Are you camping here for long, Brazell and Skully?"

"For a whole nice fortnight, Davies and Thomas and Evans and Hooping."

When we reached Mewslade beach and flung ourselves down, as I scooped up sand and let it trickle grain by grain through my fingers, as George peered at the sea through his double lenses and Sidney and Dan heaped sand over his legs, Brazell and Skully sat behind us like two warders.

"We thought of going to Nice for a fortnight," said Brazell—he rhymed it with ice, dug Skully in the ribs—"but the air's nicer here for the complexion."

"It's as good as a herb," said Skully.

They shared an enormous joke, cuffing and biting and wrestling again, scattering sand in the eyes, until they fell back with laughter, and Brazell wiped the blood from his nose with a piece of picnic paper. George lay covered to the waist in sand. I watched the sea slipping out, with birds quarrelling over it, and the sun beginning to go down patiently.

"Look at Little Cough," said Brazell. "Isn't he extraordinary? He's growing out of the sand. Little Cough hasn't got any legs."

"Poor Little Cough," said Skully, "he's the most extraordinary boy in the world."

"Extraordinary Little Cough," they said together, "extraordinary, extraordinary, extraordinary." They made a song out of it, and both conducted with their switches.

"He can't swim."

"He can't run."

"He can't learn."

"He can't bowl."

"He can't bat."

"And I bet he can't make water."

George kicked the sand from his legs. "Yes, I can!"

"Can you swim?"

"Can you run?"

"Can you bowl?"

"Leave him alone," Dan said.

They shuffled nearer to us. The sea was racing out now. Brazell said in a serious voice, wagging his finger: "Now, quite truthfully, Cough, aren't you extraordinary? Very extraordinary? Say 'Yes' or 'No.'"

"Categorically, 'Yes' or 'No,'" said Skully.

"No," George said. "I can swim and

I can run and I can play cricket. I'm not frightened of anybody."

I said: "He was second in the form last term."

"Now isn't that extraordinary? If he can be second he can be first. But no, that's too ordinary. Little Cough must be second."

"The question is answered," said Skully. "Little Cough is extraordinary." They began to sing again.

"He's a very good runner," Dan said.

"Well, let him prove it. Skully and I ran the whole length of Rhossilli sands this morning, didn't we, Skull?"

"Every inch."

"Can Little Cough do it?"

"Yes," said George.

"Do it, then."

"I don't want to."

"Extraordinary Little Cough can't run," they sang, "can't run, can't run."

Three girls, all fair, came down the cliffside arm in arm, dressed in short, white trousers. Their arms and legs and throats were brown as berries; I could see when they laughed that their teeth were very white; they stepped on to the beach, and Brazell and Skully stopped singing. Sidney smoothed his hair back, rose casually, put his hands in his pockets, and walked towards the girls, who now stood close together, gold and brown, admiring the sunset with little attention, patting their scarves, turning smiles on each other. He stood in front of them, grinned, and saluted: "Hullo, Gwyneth! Do you remember me?"

"La-di-da!" whispered Dan at my side, and made a mock salute to George still peering at the retreating sea.

"Well, if this isn't a surprise!" said the tallest girl. With little studied movements of her hands, as though she were distributing flowers, she introduced Peggy and Jean.

Fat Peggy, I thought, too jolly for me, with hockey legs and tomboy crop, was the girl for Dan; Sidney's Gwyneth was a distinguished piece and quite sixteen, as immaculate and unapproachable as a girl in Ben Evan's stores; but Jean, shy and curly, with butter-coloured hair, was mine. Dan and I walked slowly to the girls.

I made up two remarks: "Fair's fair, Sidney, no bigamy abroad," and "Sorry we couldn't arrange to have the sea in when you came."

Jean smiled, wriggling her heel in the sand, and I raised my cap.

"Hullo!"

The cap dropped at her feet.

As I bent down, three lumps of sugar fell from my blazer pocket. "I've been feeding a horse," I said, and began to blush guiltily when all the girls laughed.

I could have swept the ground with my cap, kissed my hand gaily, called them señoritas, and made them smile without tolerance. Or I could have stayed at a distance, and this would have been better still, my hair blown in the wind, though there was no wind at all that evening, wrapped in mystery and staring at the sun, too aloof to speak to girls; but I knew that all the time my ears would have been burning, my stomach would have been as hollow and as full of voices as a shell. "Speak to them quickly, before they go away!" a voice would have said insistently over the dramatic silence, as I stood like Valentino on the edge of the bright, invisible bull-ring of the sands. "Isn't it lovely here!" I said.

I spoke to Jean alone; and this is love, I thought, as she nodded her head and swung her curls and said: "It's nicer than Porthcawl."

Brazell and Skully were two big bullies in a nightmare; I forgot them when Jean and I walked up the cliff, and, looking back to see if they were baiting George again or wrestling together, I saw that George had disappeared around the corner of the rocks and that they were talking at the foot of the cliff with Sidney and the two girls.

"What's your name?"

I told her.

"That's Welsh," she said.

"You've got a beautiful name."

"Oh! it's just ordinary."

"Shall I see you again?"

"If you want to."

"I want to alright! We can go and bathe in the morning. And we can try to get an eagle's egg. Did you know that there were eagles here?"

"No," she said. "Who was that handsome boy on the beach, the tall one with dirty trousers?"

"He's not handsome, that's Brazell. He never washes or combs his hair or anything. And he's a bully and he cheats."

"I think he's handsome."

We walked into Button's field, and I showed her inside the tents and gave her one of George's apples. "I'd like a cigarette," she said.

It was nearly dark when the others came. Brazell and Skully were with Gwyneth, one each side of her holding her arms. Sidney was with Peggy, and Dan walked, whistling, behind with his hands in his pockets.

"There's a pair," said Brazell, "they've been here all alone and they aren't even holding hands. You want a pill," he said to me.

"Build Britain's babies," said Skully.

"Go on!" Gwyneth said. She pushed him away from her, but she was laughing, and she said nothing when he put his arm around her waist.

"What about a bit of fire?" said Brazell.

Jean clapped her hands like an actress. Although I knew I loved her, I didn't like anything she said or did.

"Who's going to make it?"

"He's the best, I'm sure," she said, pointing to me.

Dan and I collected sticks, and by the time it was quite dark there was a fire crackling. Inside the sleeping-tent, Brazell and Jean sat close together; her golden head was on his shoulder; Skully, near them, whispered to Gwyneth; Sidney unhappily held Peggy's hand.

"Did you ever see such a sloppy lot?" I said, watching Jean smile in the fiery dark.

"Kiss me, Charley!" said Dan.

We sat by the fire in the corner of the field. The sea, far out, was still making a noise. We heard a few nightbirds— "'To-whit! to-whoo!' Listen! I don't like owls," Dan said, "they scratch your eyes out!"—and tried not to listen to the soft voices in the tent. Gwyneth's laughter floated out over the suddenly moonlit field, but Jean, with the beast, was smiling and silent in the covered warmth; I knew her little hand was in Brazell's hand.

"Women," I said.

Dan spat in the fire.

We were old and alone, sitting beyond desire in the middle of the night, when George appeared, like a ghost, in the firelight and stood there, trembling, until I said: "Where've you been? You've been gone hours. Why are you trembling like that?"

Brazell and Skully poked their heads out.

"Hullo, Cough my boy! How's your

father? What have you been up to tonight?"

George Hooping could hardly stand. I put my hand on his shoulder to steady him, but he pushed it away.

"I've been running on Rhossilli sands! I ran every bit of it! You said I couldn't, and I did! I've been running and running!"

Someone inside the tent put a record on the gramophone. It was a selection from *No, No, Nannette*.

"You've been running all the time in the dark, Little Cough?"

"And I bet I ran it quicker than you did, too!" George said.

"I bet you did," said Brazell.

"Do you think we'd run five miles?" said Skully.

Now the tune was *Tea for Two*.

"Did you ever hear anything so extraordinary? I told you Cough was extraordinary. Little Cough's been running all night."

"Extraordinary, extraordinary, extraordinary Little Cough," they said.

Laughing from the shelter of the tent into the darkness, they looked like a boy with two heads. And when I stared round at George again he was lying on his back fast asleep in the deep grass and his hair was touching the flames.

THE LOST BOY

by Thomas Wolfe

I

Light came and went and came again, the booming strokes of three o'clock beat out across the town in thronging bronze from the courthouse bell, light winds of April blew the fountain out in rainbow sheets, until the plume returned and pulsed, as Grover turned into the Square. He was a child, dark-eyed and grave, birthmarked upon his neck—a berry of warm brown—and with a gentle face, too quiet and too listening for his years. The scuffed boy's shoes, the thick-ribbed stockings gartered at the knees, the short knee pants cut straight with three small useless buttons at the side, the sailor blouse, the old cap battered out of shape, perched sideways up on top of the raven head, the old soiled canvas bag slung from the shoulder, empty now, but waiting for the crisp sheets of the afternoon—these friendly, shabby garments, shaped by Grover, uttered him. He turned and passed along the north side of the Square and in that moment saw the union of Forever and of Now.

Light came and went and came again, the great plume of the fountain pulsed and winds of April sheeted it across the Square in a rainbow gossamer of spray. The fire department horses drummed on the floors with wooden stomp, most casually, and with dry whiskings of their clean, coarse tails. The street cars ground into the Square from every portion of the compass and halted briefly like wound toys in their familiar quarter-hourly formula. A dray, hauled by a boneyard nag, rattled across the cobbles on the other side before his father's shop. The courthouse bell boomed out its solemn warning of immediate three, and everything was just the same as it had always been.

He saw that haggis of vexed shapes with quiet eyes—that hodgepodge of ill-sorted architectures that made up the Square, and he did not feel lost. For "Here," thought Grover, "here is the Square as it has always been—and papa's shop, the fire department and the City Hall, the fountain pulsing with its plume, the street cars coming in and halting at the quarter hour, the hardware store on the corner there, the row of old brick buildings on this side of the street, the people passing and the light that comes and changes and that always will come back again, and everything that comes and goes and changes in the Square, and yet will be the same again. And here," the boy thought, "is Grover with his paper bag. Here is old Grover, almost twelve years old. Here is the month of April, 1904. Here is the courthouse bell and three o'clock. Here is Grover on the Square that never changes. Here is Grover, caught upon this point of time."

It seemed to him that the Square, itself the accidental masonry of many years, the chance agglomeration of time and of disrupted strivings, was the center of the universe. It was for him, in his soul's picture, the earth's pivot, the granite core of changelessness, the eternal place where all things came and passed, and yet abode forever and would never change.

He passed the old shack on the corner —the wooden fire-trap where S. Goldberg

From *The Hills Beyond*, by Thomas Wolfe. Harper & Brothers. Copyright, 1937, by Maxwell Perkins as Executor.

ran his wiener stand. Then he passed the Singer place next door, with its gleaming display of new machines. He saw them and admired them, but he felt no joy. They brought back to him the busy hum of housework and of women sewing, the intricacy of stitch and weave, the mystery of style and pattern, the memory of women bending over flashing needles, the pedaled tread, the busy whir. It was women's work: it filled him with unknown associations of dullness and of vague depression. And always, also, with a moment's twinge of horror, for his dark eye would always travel toward that needle stitching up and down so fast the eye could never follow it. And then he would remember how his mother once had told him she had driven the needle through her finger, and always, when he passed this place, he would remember it and for a moment crane his neck and turn his head away.

He passed on then, but had to stop again next door before the music store. He always had to stop by places that had shining perfect things in them. He loved hardware stores and windows full of accurate geometric tools. He loved windows full of hammers, saws, and planing boards. He liked windows full of strong new rakes and hoes, with unworn handles, of white perfect wood, stamped hard and vivid with the maker's seal. He loved to see such things as these in the windows of hardware stores. And he would fairly gloat upon them and think that some day he would own a set himself.

Also, he always stopped before the music and piano store. It was a splendid store. And in the window was a small white dog upon his haunches, with head cocked gravely to one side, a small white dog that never moved, that never barked, that listened attentively at the flaring funnel of a horn to hear "His Master's Voice" —a horn forever silent, and a voice that never spoke. And within were many rich and shining shapes of great pianos, an air of splendor and of wealth.

And now, indeed, he *was* caught, held suspended. A waft of air, warm, chocolate-laden, filled his nostrils. He tried to pass the white front of the little eight-foot shop; he paused, struggling with conscience; he could not go on. It was the little candy shop run by old Crocker and his wife. And Grover could not pass.

"Old stingy Crockers!" he thought scornfully. "I'll not go there any more. But—" as the maddening fragrance of rich cooking chocolate touched him once again—"I'll just look in the window and see what they've got." He paused a moment, looking with his dark and quiet eyes into the window of the little candy shop. The window, spotlessly clean, was filled with trays of fresh-made candy. His eyes rested on a tray of chocolate drops. Unconsciously he licked his lips. Put one of them upon your tongue and it just melted there, like honeydew. And then the trays full of rich home-made fudge. He gazed longingly at the deep body of the chocolate fudge, reflectively at maple walnut, more critically, yet with longing, at the mints, the nougatines, and all the other dainties.

"Old stingy Crockers!" Grover muttered once again, and turned to go. "I wouldn't go in *there* again."

And yet he did not go away. "Old stingy Crockers" they might be; still, they did make the best candy in town, the best, in fact, that he had ever tasted.

He looked through the window back into the little shop and saw Mrs. Crocker there. A customer had gone in and had

The Lost Boy

made a purchase, and as Grover looked he saw Mrs. Crocker, with her little wrenny face, her pinched features, lean over and peer primly at the scales. She had a piece of fudge in her clean, bony, little fingers, and as Grover looked, she broke it, primly, in her little bony hands. She dropped a morsel down into the scales. They weighted down alarmingly, and her thin lips tightened. She snatched the piece of fudge out of the scales and broke it carefully once again. This time the scales wavered, went down very slowly, and came back again. Mrs. Crocker carefully put the reclaimed piece of fudge back in the tray, dumped the remainder in a paper bag, folded it and gave it to the customer, counted the money carefully and doled it out into the till, the pennies in one place, the nickels in another.

Grover stood there, looking scornfully. "Old stingy Crocker—afraid that she might give a crumb away!"

He grunted scornfully and again he turned to go. But now Mr. Crocker came out from the little partitioned place where they made all their candy, bearing a tray of fresh-made fudge in his skinny hands. Old Man Crocker rocked along the counter to the front and put it down. He really rocked along. He was a cripple. And like his wife, he was a wrenny, wizened little creature, with bony hands, thin lips, a pinched and meager face. One leg was inches shorter than the other, and on this leg there was an enormous thick-soled boot, with a kind of wooden, rocker-like arrangement, six inches high at least, to make up for the deficiency. On this wooden cradle Mr. Crocker rocked along, with a prim and apprehensive little smile, as if he were afraid he was going to lose something.

"Old stingy Crocker!" muttered Grover. "Humph! He wouldn't give you anything!"

And yet—he did not go away. He hung there curiously, peering through the window, with his dark and gentle face now focused and intent, alert and curious, flattening his nose against the glass. Unconsciously he scratched the thick-ribbed fabric of one stockinged leg with the scuffed and worn toe of his old shoe. The fresh, warm odor of the new-made fudge was delicious. It was a little maddening. Half consciously he began to fumble in one trouser pocket, and pulled out his purse, a shabby worn old black one with a twisted clasp. He opened it and prowled about inside.

What he found was not inspiring—a nickel and two pennies and—he had forgotten them—the stamps. He took the stamps out and unfolded them. There were five twos, eight ones, all that remained of the dollar-sixty-cents' worth which Reed, the pharmacist, had given him for running errands a week or two before.

"Old Crocker," Grover thought, and looked somberly at the grotesque little form as it rocked back into the shop again, around the counter, and up the other side. "Well—" again he looked indefinitely at the stamps in his hand—"he's had all the rest of them. He might as well take these."

So, soothing conscience with this sop of scorn, he went into the shop and stood looking at the trays in the glass case and finally decided. Pointing with a slightly grimy finger at the fresh-made tray of chocolate fudge, he said, "I'll take fifteen cents' worth of this, Mr. Crocker." He paused a moment, fighting with embarrassment, then he lifted his dark face and said quietly, "And please, I'll have to give you stamps again."

[59]

Mr. Crocker made no answer. He did not look at Grover. He pressed his lips together primly. He went rocking away and got the candy scoop, came back, slid open the door of the glass case, put fudge into the scoop, and, rocking to the scales, began to weigh the candy out. Grover watched him as he peered and squinted, he watched him purse and press his lips together, he saw him take a piece of fudge and break it in two parts. And then old Crocker broke two parts in two again. He weighed, he squinted, and he hovered, until it seemed to Grover that by calling *Mrs.* Crocker stingy he had been guilty of a rank injustice. But finally, to his vast relief, the job was over, the scales hung there, quivering apprehensively, upon the very hair-line of nervous balance, as if even the scales were afraid that one more move from Old Man Crocker and they would be undone.

Mr. Crocker took the candy then and dumped it in a paper bag and, rocking back along the counter toward the boy, he dryly said: "Where are the stamps?" Grover gave them to him. Mr. Crocker relinquished his claw-like hold upon the bag and set it down upon the counter. Grover took the bag and dropped it in his canvas sack, and then remembered. "Mr. Crocker—" again he felt the old embarrassment that was almost like strong pain—"I gave you too much," Grover said. "There were eighteen cents in stamps. You—you can just give me three ones back."

Mr. Crocker did not answer. He was busy with his bony little hands, unfolding the stamps and flattening them out on top of the glass counter. When he had done so, he peered at them sharply for a moment, thrusting his scrawny neck forward and running his eye up and down, like a bookkeeper who totes up rows of figures.

When he had finished, he said tartly: "I don't like this kind of business. If you want candy, you should have the money for it. I'm not a post office. The next time you come in here and want anything, you'll have to pay me money for it."

Hot anger rose in Grover's throat. His olive face suffused with angry color. His tarry eyes got black and bright. He was on the verge of saying: "Then why did you take my other stamps? Why do you tell me now, when you have taken all the stamps I had, that you don't want them?"

But he was a boy, a boy of eleven years, a quiet, gentle, gravely thoughtful boy, and he had been taught how to respect his elders. So he just stood there looking with his tar-black eyes. Old Man Crocker, pursing at the mouth a little, without meeting Grover's gaze, took the stamps up in his thin, parched fingers and, turning, rocked away with them down to the till.

He took the twos and folded them and laid them in one rounded scallop, then took the ones and folded them and put them in the one next to it. Then he closed the till and started to rock off, down toward the other end. Grover, his face now quiet and grave, kept looking at him, but Mr. Crocker did not look at Grover. Instead he began to take some stamped cardboard shapes and fold them into boxes.

In a moment Grover said, "Mr. Crocker, will you give me the three ones, please?"

Mr. Crocker did not answer. He kept folding boxes, and he compressed his thin lips quickly as he did so. But Mrs. Crocker, back turned to her spouse, also folding boxes with her birdlike hands, muttered: "Hm! *I'd* give him nothing!"

Mr. Crocker looked up, looked at

The Lost Boy

Grover, said, "What are you waiting for?"

"Will you give me the three ones, please?" Grover said.

"I'll give you nothing," Mr. Crocker said.

He left his work and came rocking forward along the counter. "Now you get out of here! Don't you come in here with any more of those stamps," said Mr. Crocker.

"I should like to know where he gets them—that's what *I* should like to know," said Mrs. Crocker.

She did not look up as she said these words. She inclined her head a little to the side, in Mr. Crocker's direction, and continued to fold the boxes with her bony fingers.

"You get out of here!" said Mr. Crocker. "And don't you come back here with any stamps. . . . Where did you get those stamps?" he said.

"That's just what *I've* been thinking," Mrs. Crocker said. *"I've* been thinking all along."

"You've been coming in here for the last two weeks with those stamps," said Mr. Crocker. "I don't like the look of it. Where did you get those stamps?" he said.

"That's what *I've* been thinking," said Mrs. Crocker, for a second time.

Grover had got white underneath his olive skin. His eyes had lost their luster. They looked like dull, stunned balls of tar. "From Mr. Reed," he said. "I got the stamps from Mr. Reed." Then he burst out desperately. "Mr. Crocker—Mr. Reed will tell you how I got the stamps. I did some work for Mr. Reed, he gave me those stamps two weeks ago."

"Mr. Reed," said Mrs. Crocker acidly. She did not turn her head. "I call it mighty funny."

"Mr. Crocker," Grover said, "if you'll just let me have three ones—"

"You get out of here!" cried Mr. Crocker, and he began rocking forward toward Grover. "Now don't you come in here again, boy! There's something funny about this whole business! I don't like the look of it," said Mr. Crocker. "If you can't pay as other people do, then I don't want your trade."

"Mr. Crocker," Grover said again, and underneath the olive skin his face was gray, "if you'll just let me have those three—"

"You get out of here!" Mr. Crocker cried, rocking down toward the counter's end. "If you don't get out, boy—"

"I'd call a policeman, that's what I'd do," Mrs. Crocker said.

Mr. Crocker rocked around the lower end of the counter. He came rocking up to Grover. "You get out," he said.

He took the boy and pushed him with his bony little hands, and Grover was sick and gray down to the hollow pit of his stomach.

"You've got to give me those three ones," he said.

"You get out of here!" shrilled Mr. Crocker. He seized the screen door, pulled it open, and pushed Grover out. "Don't you come back in here," he said, pausing for a moment, and working thinly at the lips. He turned and rocked back in the shop again. The screen door slammed behind him. Grover stood there on the pavement. And light came and went and came again into the Square.

The boy stood there, and a wagon rattled past. There were some people passing by, but Grover did not notice them. He stood there blindly, in the watches of the sun, feeling this was Time, this was the center of the universe, the granite core of

[61]

changelessness, and feeling, this is Grover, this the Square, this is Now.

But something had gone out of day. He felt the overwhelming, soul-sickening guilt that all the children, all the good men of the earth, have felt since Time began. And even anger had died down, had been drowned out, in this swelling tide of guilt, and "This is the Square"—thought Grover as before—"This is Now. There is my father's shop. And all of it is as it has always been—save I."

And the Square reeled drunkenly around him, light went in blind gray motes before his eyes, the fountain sheeted out to rainbow iridescence and returned to its proud, pulsing plume again. But all the brightness had gone out of day, and "Here is the Square, and here is permanence, and here is Time—and all of it the same as it has always been, save I."

The scuffed boots of the lost boy moved and stumbled blindly. The numb feet crossed the pavement—reached the cobbled street, reached the plotted central square—the grass plots, and the flower beds, so soon to be packed with red geraniums.

"I want to be alone," thought Grover, "where I cannot go near him.... Oh God, I hope he never hears, that no one ever tells him—"

The plume blew out, the iridescent sheet of spray blew over him. He passed through, found the other side and crossed the street, and— "Oh God, if papa ever hears!" thought Grover, as his numb feet started up the steps into his father's shop.

He found and felt the steps—the width and thickness of old lumber twenty feet in length. He saw it all—the iron columns on his father's porch, painted with the dull anomalous black-green that all such columns in this land and weather come to; two angels, fly-specked, and the waiting stones. Beyond and all around, in the stonecutter's shop, cold shapes of white and marble, rounded stone, the languid angel with strong marble hands of love.

He went on down the aisle, the white shapes stood around him. He went on to the back of the workroom. This he knew —the little cast-iron stove in left-hand corner, caked, brown, heat-blistered, and the elbow of the long stack running out across the shop; the high and dirty window looking down across the Market Square toward Niggertown; the rude old shelves, plank-boarded, thick, the wood not smooth but pulpy, like the strong hair of an animal; upon the shelves the chisels of all sizes and a layer of stone dust; an emery wheel with pump tread; and a door that let out on the alleyway, yet the alleyway twelve feet below. Here in the room, two trestles of this coarse spiked wood upon which rested gravestones, and at one, his father at work.

The boy looked, saw the name was Creasman: saw the carved analysis of John, the symmetry of the s, the fine sentiment that was being polished off beneath the name and date: "John Creasman, November 7, 1903."

Gant looked up. He was a man of fifty-three, gaunt-visaged, mustache cropped, immensely long and tall and gaunt. He wore good dark clothes—heavy, massive—save he had no coat. He worked in shirt-sleeves with his vest on, a strong watch chain stretching across his vest, wing collar and black tie, Adam's apple, bony forehead, bony nose, light eyes, gray-green, undeep and cold, and, somehow, lonely-looking, a striped apron going up around his shoulders and starched cuffs. And in one hand a tremendous rounded wooden

The Lost Boy

mallet like a butcher's bole; and in his other hand, a strong cold chisel.

"How are you, son?"

He did not look up as he spoke. He spoke quietly, absently. He worked upon the chisel and the wooden mallet, as a jeweler might work on a watch, except that in the man and in the wooden mallet there was power too.

"What is it, son?" he said.

He moved around the table from the head, started up on "J" once again.

"Papa, I never stole the stamps," said Grover.

Gant put down the mallet, laid the chisel down. He came around the trestle.

"What?" he said.

As Grover winked his tar-black eyes, they brightened, the hot tears shot out. "I never stole the stamps," he said.

"Hey? What is this?" his father said. "What stamps?"

"That Mr. Reed gave me, when the other boy was sick and I worked there for three days. . . . And Old Man Crocker," Grover said, "he took all the stamps. And I told him Mr. Reed had given them to me. And now he owes me three ones—and Old Man Crocker says he don't believe that they were mine. He says—he says—that I must have taken them somewhere," Grover blurted out.

"The stamps that Reed gave you—hey?" the stonecutter said. "The stamps you had—" He wet his thumb upon his lips, threw back his head and slowly swung his gaze around the ceiling, then turned and strode quickly from his workshop out into the storeroom.

Almost at once he came back again, and as he passed the old gray painted-board partition of his office he cleared his throat and wet his thumb and said, "Now, I tell you—"

Then he turned and strode up toward the front again and cleared his throat and said, "I tell you now—" He wheeled about and started back, and as he came along the aisle between the marshaled rows of gravestones he said beneath his breath, "By God, now—"

He took Grover by the hand and they went out flying. Down the aisle they went by all the gravestones, past the fly-specked angels waiting there, and down the wooden steps and across the Square. The fountain pulsed, the plume blew out in sheeted iridescence, and it swept across them; an old gray horse, with a peaceful look about his torn lips, swucked up the cool mountain water from the trough as Grover and his father went across the Square, but they did not notice it.

They crossed swiftly to the other side in a direct line to the candy shop. Gant was still dressed in his long striped apron, and he was still holding Grover by the hand. He opened the screen door and stepped inside.

"Give him the stamps," Gant said.

Mr. Crocker came rocking forward behind the counter, with the prim and careful look that now was somewhat like a smile. "It was just—" he said.

"Give him the stamps," Gant said, and threw some coins down on the counter.

Mr. Crocker rocked away and got the stamps. He came rocking back. "I just didn't know—" he said.

The stonecutter took the stamps and gave them to the boy. And Mr. Crocker took the coins.

"It was just that—" Mr. Crocker began again, and smiled.

Gant cleared his throat: "You never were a father," he said. "You never knew the feelings of a father, or understood the feelings of a child; and that is why you

Coming-of-Age in Our Time

acted as you did. But a judgment is upon you. God has cursed you. He has afflicted you. He has made you lame and childless as you are—and lame and childless, miserable as you are, you will go to your grave and be forgotten!"

And Crocker's wife kept kneading her bony little hands and said, imploringly, "Oh, no—oh don't say that, please don't say that."

The stonecutter, the breath still hoarse in him, left the store, still holding the boy tightly by the hand. Light came again into the day.

"Well, son," he said, and laid his hand on the boy's back. "Well, son," he said, "now don't you mind."

They walked across the Square, the sheeted spray of iridescent light swept out on them, the horse swizzled at the water-trough, and "Well, son," the stonecutter said.

And the old horse sloped down, ringing with his hoofs upon the cobblestones.

"Well, son," said the stonecutter once again, "be a good boy."

And he trod his own steps then with his great stride and went back again into his shop.

The lost boy stood upon the Square, hard by the porch of his father's shop.

"This is Time," thought Grover. "Here is the Square, here is my father's shop, and here am I."

And light came and went and came again—but now not quite the same as it had done before. The boy saw the pattern of familiar shapes and knew that they were just the same as they had always been. But something had gone out of day, and something had come in again. Out of the vision of those quiet eyes some brightness had gone, and into their vision had come some deeper color. He could not say, he did not know through what transforming shadows life had passed within that quarter hour. He only knew that something had been lost—something forever gained.

Just then a buggy curved out through the Square, and fastened to the rear end was a poster, and it said "St. Louis" and "Excursion" and "The Fair."

II—*The Mother*

As we went down through Indiana—you were too young, child, to remember it—but I always think of all of you the way you looked that morning, when we went down through Indiana, going to the Fair. All of the apple trees were coming out, and it was April; it was the beginning of spring in southern Indiana and everything was getting green. Of course we don't have farms at home like those in Indiana. The childern had never seen such farms as those, and I reckon, kidlike, they had to take it in.

So all of them kept running up and down the aisle—well, no, except for you and Grover. *You* were too young, Eugene. You were just three, I kept you with me. As for Grover—well, I'm going to tell you about that.

But the rest of them kept running up and down the aisle and from one window to another. They kept calling out and hollering to each other every time they saw something new. They kept trying to look out on all sides, in every way at once, as if they wished they had eyes at the back of their heads. It was the first time any of them had ever been in Indiana, and I reckon that it all seemed strange and new.

And so it seemed they couldn't get enough. It seemed they never could be still. They kept running up and down and back and forth, hollering and shouting to each other, until—"I'll vow! You childern! I never saw the beat of you!" I said. "The way that you keep running up and down and back and forth and never can be quiet for a minute beats all I ever saw," I said.

You see, they were excited about going to St. Louis, and so curious over everything they saw. They couldn't help it, and they wanted to see everything. But— "I'll vow!" I said. "If you childern don't sit down and rest you'll be worn to a frazzle before we ever get to see St. Louis and the Fair!"

Except for Grover! He—no, sir! not him. Now, boy, I want to tell you—I've raised the lot of you—and if I do say so, there wasn't a numbskull in the lot. But *Grover!* Well, you've all grown up now, all of you have gone away, and none of you are childern any more. . . . And of course, I hope that, as the fellow says, you have reached the dignity of man's estate. I suppose you have the judgment of grown men. . . . But *Grover! Grover* had it even then!

Oh, even as a child, you know—at a time when I was almost afraid to trust the rest of you out of my sight—I could depend on Grover. He could go anywhere, I could send him anywhere, and I'd always know he'd get back safe, and do exactly what I told him to!

Why, I didn't even have to tell him. You could send that child to market and tell him what you wanted, and he'd come home with *twice* as much as you could get yourself for the same money!

Now you know, I've always been considered a good trader. But *Grover!*—why, it got so finally that I wouldn't even tell him. Your papa said to me: "You'd be better off if you'd just tell him what you want and leave the rest to him. For," your papa says, "damned if I don't believe he's a better trader than you are. He gets more for the money than anyone I ever saw."

Well, I had to admit it, you know. I had to own up then. Grover, even as a child, was a far better trader than I was. . . . Why, yes, they told it on him all over town, you know. They said all of the market men, all of the farmers, knew him. They'd begin to laugh when they saw him coming—they'd say: "Look out! Here's Grover! Here's one trader you're not going to fool!"

And they were right! *That* child! I'd say, "Grover, suppose you run uptown and see if they've got anything good to *eat* today"—and I'd just wink at him, you know, but he'd know what I meant. I wouldn't let on that I *wanted* anything exactly, but I'd say, "Now it just occurs to me that some good fresh stuff may be coming in from the country, so suppose you take this dollar and just see what you can do with it."

Well, sir, that was all that was needed. The minute you told that child that you depended on his judgment, he'd have gone to the ends of the earth for you—and, let me tell you something, he wouldn't *miss,* either!

His eyes would get as black as coals—oh! the way that child would look at you, the intelligence and sense in his expression. He'd say: "Yes, *ma'am!* Now don't you worry, mama. You leave it all to me—and I'll do *good!*" said Grover.

And he'd be off like a streak of lightning and—oh Lord! As your father said to me, "I've been living in this town for

[65]

almost thirty years," he said—"I've seen it grow up from a crossroads village, and I thought I knew everything there was to know about it—but that child—" your papa says—"he knows places that I never heard of!" . . . Oh, he'd go right down there to that place below your papa's shop where the draymen and the country people used to park their wagons—or he'd go down there to those old lots on Concord Street where the farmers used to keep their wagons. And, child that he was, he'd go right in among them, sir—*Grover* would!—go right in and barter with them like a grown man!

And he'd come home with things he'd bought that would make your eyes stick out. . . . Here he comes one time with another boy, dragging a great bushel basket full of ripe termaters between them. "Why, Grover!" I says. "How on earth are we ever going to use them? Why they'll go bad on us before we're half way through with them." "Well, mama," he says, "I know—" oh, just as solemn as a judge— "but they were the last the man had," he says, "and he wanted to go home, and so I got them for ten cents," he says. "They were so cheap," said Grover, "I thought it was a shame to let 'em go, and I figgered that what we couldn't eat—why," says Grover, "you could *put up!*" Well, the way he said it—so earnest and so serious— I had to laugh. "But I'll vow!" I said. "If you don't beat all!" . . . But that was *Grover!*—the way he was in *those* days! As everyone said, boy that he was, he had the sense and judgment of a grown man. . . . Child, child, I've seen you all grow up, and all of you were bright enough. There were no half-wits in *my* family. But for all-round intelligence, judgment, and general ability, Grover surpassed the whole crowd. I've never seen his equal, and everyone who knew him as a child will say the same.

So that's what I tell them now when they ask me about all of you. I have to tell the truth. I always said that *you* were smart enough, Eugene—but when they come around and brag to me about you, and about how you have got on and have a kind of name—I don't let on, you know. I just sit there and let them talk. I don't brag on you—if *they* want to brag on you, that's *their* business. I never bragged on one of my own children in my life. When father raised us up, we were all brought up to believe that it was not good breeding to brag about your kin. "If the others want to do it," father said, "well, let *them* do it. Don't ever let on by a word or sign that you know what they are talking about. Just let *them* do the talking, and say nothing."

So when they come around and tell me all about the things *you've* done—I don't let on to them, I never say a word. Why yes!—why, here, you know—oh, along about a month or so ago, this feller comes —a well-dressed man, you know—he looked intelligent, a good substantial sort of person. He said he came from New Jersey, or somewhere up in that part of the country, and he began to ask me all sorts of questions—what you were like when you were a boy, and all such stuff as that.

I just pretended to study it all over and then I said, "Well, yes"—real serious-like, you know—"well, yes—I reckon I ought to know a little something about him. Eugene was my child, just the same as all the others were. I brought him up just the way I brought up all the others. And," I says—oh, just as solemn as you please—

The Lost Boy

"he wasn't a *bad* sort of a boy. Why," I says, "up to the time that he was twelve years old he was just about the same as any other boy—a good, average, normal sort of fellow."

"Oh," he says, "But didn't you notice something? Wasn't there something kind of strange?" he says—"something different from what you noticed in the other childern?"

I didn't let on, you know—I just took it all in and looked as solemn as an owl—I just pretended to study it all over, just as serious as you please.

"Why no," I says, real slow-like, after I'd studied it all over. "As I remember it, he was a good, ordinary, normal sort of boy, just like all the others."

"Yes," he says—oh, all excited-like, you know— "But didn't you notice how brilliant he was? Eugene must have been more brilliant than the rest!"

"Well, now," I says, and pretended to study that all over too. "Now let me see. . . . Yes," I says—I just looked him in the eye, as solemn as you please—"he did pretty well. . . . Well, yes," I says, "I guess he was a fairly bright sort of a boy. I never had no complaints to make of him on that score. He was bright enough," I says. "The only trouble with him was that he was lazy."

"Lazy!" he says—oh, you should have seen the look upon his face, you know—he jumped like someone had stuck a pin in him. "Lazy!" he says. "Why, you don't mean to tell me—"

"Yes," I says—oh, I never cracked a smile— "I was telling him the same thing myself the last time that I saw him. I told him it was a mighty lucky thing for him that he had the gift of gab. Of course, he went off to college and read a lot of books, and I reckon that's where he got this flow of language they say he has. But as I said to him the last time that I saw him: 'Now look a-here,' I said. 'If you can earn your living doing a light, easy class of work like this you do,' I says, 'you're mighty lucky, because none of the rest of your people,' I says, 'had any such luck as that. They had to work hard for a living.'"

Oh, I told him, you know. I came right out with it. I made no bones about it. And I tell you what—I wish you could have seen his face. It was a study.

"Well," he says, at last, "you've got to admit this, haven't you—he was the brightest boy you had, now wasn't he?"

I just looked at him a moment. I had to tell the truth. I couldn't fool him any longer. "No," I says. "He was a good, bright boy—I got no complaint to make about him on that score—but the brightest boy I had, the one that surpassed all the rest of them in sense, and understanding, and in judgment—the best boy I had—the smartest boy I ever saw—was—well, it wasn't Eugene," I said. "It was another one."

He looked at me a moment, then he said, "Which boy was that?"

Well, I just looked at him, and smiled. I shook my head, you know. I wouldn't tell him. "I never brag about my own," I said. "You'll have to find out for yourself."

But—I'll have to tell *you*—and you know yourself, I brought the whole crowd up, I knew you all. And you can take my word for it—the best one of the lot was—*Grover!*

And when I think of Grover as he was along about that time, I always see him sitting there, so grave and earnest-like, with his nose pressed to the window, as we went down through Indiana in the morning, to the Fair.

[67]

Coming-of-Age in Our Time

All through that morning we were going down along beside the Wabash River—the Wabash River flows through Indiana, it is the river that they wrote the song about—so all that morning we were going down along the river. And I sat with all you childern gathered about me as we went down through Indiana, going to St. Louis, to the Fair.

And Grover sat there, so still and earnest-like, looking out the window, and he didn't move. He sat there like a man. He was just eleven and a half years old, but he had more sense, more judgment, and more understanding than any child I ever saw.

So here he sat beside this gentleman and looked out the window. I never knew the man—I never asked his name—but I tell you what! He was certainly a fine-looking, well-dressed, good, substantial sort of man, and I could see that he had taken a great liking to Grover. And Grover sat there looking out, and then turned to this gentleman, as grave and earnest as a grown-up man, and says, "What kind of crops grow here, sir?" Well, this gentleman threw his head back and just hah-hahed. "Well, I'll see if I can tell you," says this gentleman, and then, you know, he talked to him, they talked together, and Grover took it all in, as solemn as you please, and asked this gentleman every sort of question—what the trees were, what was growing there, how big the farms were—all sorts of questions, which this gentleman would answer, until I said: "Why, I'll vow, Grover! You shouldn't ask so many questions. You'll bother the very life out of this gentleman."

The gentleman threw his head back and laughed right out. "Now you leave that boy alone. He's all right," he said. "He doesn't bother me a bit, and if I know the answers to his questions I will answer him. And if I don't know, why, then, I'll tell him so. But he's *all right*," he said, and put his arm round Grover's shoulders. "You leave him alone. He doesn't bother me a bit."

And I can still remember how he looked that morning, with his black eyes, his black hair, and with the birthmark on his neck—so grave, so serious, so earnest-like—as he sat by the train window and watched the apple trees, the farms, the barns, the houses, and the orchards, taking it all in, I reckon, because it was strange and new to him.

It was so long ago, but when I think of it, it all comes back, as if it happened yesterday. Now all of you have either died or grown up and gone away, and nothing is the same as it was then. But all of you were there with me that morning and I guess I should remember how the others looked, but somehow I don't. Yet I can still see Grover just the way he was, the way he looked that morning when we went down through Indiana, by the river, to the Fair.

III—*The Sister*

Can you remember, Eugene, how Grover used to look? I mean the birthmark, the black eyes, the olive skin. The birthmark always showed because of those open sailor blouses kids used to wear. But I guess you must have been too young when Grover died. . . . I was looking at that old photograph the other day. You know the one I mean—that picture showing mama and papa and all of us children

The Lost Boy

before the house on Woodson Street. *You* weren't there, Eugene. *You* didn't get in. *You* hadn't arrived when that was taken. . . . You remember how mad you used to get when we'd tell you that you were only a dishrag hanging out in Heaven when something happened?

You were the baby. That's what you get for being the baby. You don't get in the picture, do you? . . . I was looking at that old picture just the other day. There we were. And, my God, what is it all about? I mean, when you see the way we were—Daisy and Ben and Grover, Steve and all of us—and then how everyone either dies or grows up and goes away—and then—look at us now! Do you ever get to feeling funny? You know what I mean—do you ever get to feeling *queer*—when you try to figure these things out? You've been to college and you ought to know the answer—and I wish you'd tell me if you know.

My Lord, when I think sometimes of the way I used to be—the dreams I used to have. Playing the piano, practicing seven hours a day, thinking that some day I would be a great pianist. Taking singing lessons from Aunt Nell because I felt that some day I was going to have a great career in opera. . . . Can you beat it now? Can you imagine it? *Me!* In grand opera! . . . Now I want to ask you. I'd like to know.

My Lord! When I go uptown and walk down the street and see all these funny-looking little boys and girls hanging around the drug store—do you suppose any of them have ambitions the way we did? Do you suppose any of these funny-looking little girls are thinking about a big career in opera? . . . Didn't you ever see that picture of us? I was looking at it just the other day. It was made before the old house down on Woodson Street, with papa standing there in his swallow-tail, and mama there beside him—and Grover, and Ben, and Steve, and Daisy, and myself, with our feet upon our bicycles. Luke, poor kid, was only four or five. *He* didn't have a bicycle like us. But there he was. And there were all of us together.

Well, there I was, and my poor old skinny legs and long white dress, and two pigtails hanging down my back. And all the funny-looking clothes we wore, with the doo-lolley business on them. . . . But I guess you can't remember. You weren't born.

But, well, we were a right nice-looking set of people, if I do say so. And there was "86" the way it used to be, with the front porch, the grape vines, and the flower beds before the house—and "Miss Eliza" standing there by papa, with a watch charm pinned upon her waist. . . . I shouldn't laugh, but "Miss Eliza"—well, mama was a pretty woman then. Do you know what I mean? "Miss Eliza" was a right good-looking woman, and papa in his swallow-tail was a good-looking man. Do you remember how he used to get dressed up on Sunday? And how grand we thought he was? And how he let me take his money out and count it? And how rich we all thought he was? And how wonderful that dinkey little shop on the Square looked to us? . . . Can you beat it, now? Why we thought that papa was the biggest man in town and—oh, you can't tell me! You can't tell me! He had his faults, but papa was a wonderful man. You know he was!

And there was Steve and Ben and Grover, Daisy, Luke, and me lined up there before the house with one foot on our bicycles. And I got to thinking back about it all. It all came back.

[69]

Do you remember anything about St. Louis? You were only three or four years old then, but you must remember something. . . . Do you remember how you used to bawl when I would scrub you? How you'd bawl for Grover? Poor kid, you used to yell for Grover every time I'd get you in the tub. . . . He was a sweet kid and he was crazy about you—he almost brought you up.

That year Grover was working at the Inside Inn out on the Fair Grounds. Do you remember the old Inside Inn? That big old wooden thing inside the Fair? And how I used to take you there to wait for Grover when he got through working? And old fat Billy Pelham at the newsstand—how he always used to give you a stick of chewing gum?

They were all crazy about Grover. Everybody liked him. . . . And how proud Grover was of you! Don't you remember how he used to show you off? How he used to take you around and make you talk to Billy Pelham? And Mr. Curtis at the desk? And how Grover would try to make you talk and get you to say "Grover"? And you couldn't say it—you couldn't pronounce the "r." You'd say "Gova." Have you forgotten that? You shouldn't forget *that,* because—you were a *cute* kid, then—Ho-ho-ho-ho-ho—I don't know where it's gone to, but you were a big hit in those days. . . . I tell you, boy, you were Somebody back in those days.

And I was thinking of it all the other day when I was looking at that photograph. How we used to go and meet Grover there, and how he'd take us to the Midway. Do you remember the Midway? The Snake-Eater and the Living Skeleton, the Fat Woman and the Chute-the-chute, the Scenic Railway and the Ferris Wheel?

How you bawled the night we took you up on the Ferris Wheel? You yelled your head off—I tried to laugh it off, but I tell you, I was scared myself. Back in those days, that was Something. And how Grover laughed at us and told us there was no danger. . . . My Lord! poor little Grover. He wasn't quite twelve years old at the time, but he seemed so grown up to us. I was two years older, but I thought he knew it all.

It was always that way with him. Looking back now, it sometimes seems that it was Grover who brought us up. He was always looking after us, telling us what to do, bringing us something—some ice cream or some candy, something he had bought out of the poor little money he'd gotten at the Inn.

Then I got to thinking of the afternoon we sneaked away from home. Mama had gone out somewhere. And Grover and I got on the street car and went downtown. And my Lord, we thought that we were going Somewhere. In those days, that was what we called a *trip*. A ride in the street car was something to write home about in those days. . . . I hear that it's all built up around there now.

So we got on the car and rode the whole way down into the business section of St. Louis. We got out on Washington Street and walked up and down. And I tell you, boy, we thought that that was Something. Grover took me into a drug store and set me up to soda water. Then we came out and walked around some more, down to the Union Station and clear over to the river. And both of us half scared to death at what we'd done and wondering what mama would say if she found out.

We stayed down there till it was getting dark, and we passed by a lunchroom—an old one-armed joint with one-armed chairs and people sitting on stools and eating at the counter. We read all the signs to see what they had to eat and how much it cost, and I guess nothing on the menu was more than fifteen cents, but it couldn't have looked grander to us if it had been Delmonico's. So we stood there with our noses pressed against the window, looking in. Two skinny little kids, both of us scared half to death, getting the thrill of a lifetime out of it. You know what I mean? And smelling everything with all our might and thinking how good it all smelled.... Then Grover turned to me and whispered: "Come on, Helen. Let's go in. It says fifteen cents for pork and beans. And I've got the money," Grover said. "I've got sixty cents."

I was so scared I couldn't speak. I'd never been in a place like that before. But I kept thinking, "Oh Lord, if mama should find out!" I felt as if we were committing some big crime.... Don't you know how it is when you're a kid? It was the thrill of a lifetime.... I couldn't resist. So we both went in and sat down on those high stools before the counter and ordered pork and beans and a cup of coffee. I suppose we were too frightened at what we'd done really to enjoy anything. We just gobbled it all up in a hurry, and gulped our coffee down. And I don't know whether it was the excitement—I guess the poor kid was already sick when we came in there and didn't know it. But I turned and looked at him, and he was white as death.... And when I asked him what was the matter, he wouldn't tell me. He was too proud. He said he was all right, but I could see that he was sick as a dog. ... So he paid the bill. It came to forty cents—I'll never forget *that* as long as I live.... And sure enough, we no more than got out the door—he hardly had time to reach the curb—before it all came up.

And the poor kid was so scared and so ashamed. And what scared him so was not that he had gotten sick, but that he had spent all that money and it had come to nothing. And mama would find out.... Poor kid, he just stood there looking at me and he whispered: "Oh Helen, don't tell mama. She'll be mad if she finds out." Then we hurried home, and he was still white as a sheet when we got there.

Mama was waiting for us. She looked at us—you know how "Miss Eliza" looks at you when she thinks you've been doing something that you shouldn't. Mama said, "Why, where on earth have you two children been?" I guess she was all set to lay us out. Then she took one look at Grover's face. That was enough for her. She said, "Why, child, what in the world!" She was white as a sheet herself.... And all that Grover said was— "Mama, I feel sick."

He was sick as a dog. He fell over on the bed, and we undressed him and mama put her hand upon his forehead and came out in the hall—she was so white you could have made a black mark on her face with chalk—and whispered to me, "Go get the doctor quick, he's burning up."

And I went chasing up the street, my pigtails flying, to Dr. Packer's house. I brought him back with me. When he came out of Grover's room he told mama what to do but I don't know if she even heard him.

Her face was white as a sheet. She looked at me and looked right through me. She never saw me. And oh, my Lord, I'll never forget the way she looked, the way my heart stopped and came up in my throat. I was only a skinny little kid of fourteen. But she looked as if she was dying right before my eyes. And I knew that if anything happened to him, she'd never get over it if she lived to be a hundred.

Poor old mama. You know, he always was her eyeballs—you know that, don't you?—not the rest of us!—no, sir! I know what I'm talking about. It always has been Grover—she always thought more of him than she did of any of the others. And—poor kid!—he was a sweet kid. I can still see him lying there, and remember how sick he was, and how scared I was! I don't know why I was so scared. All we'd done had been to sneak away from home and go into a lunchroom—but I felt guilty about the whole thing, as if it was my fault.

It all came back to me the other day when I was looking at that picture, and I thought, my God, we were two kids together, and I was only two years older than Grover was, and now I'm forty-six. . . . Can you believe it? Can you figure it out—the way we grow up and change and go away? . . . And my Lord, Grover seemed so grown-up to me. He was such a quiet kid—I guess that's why he seemed older than the rest of us.

I wonder what Grover would say now if he could see that picture. All my hopes and dreams and big ambitions have come to nothing, and it's all so long ago, as if it happened in another world. Then it comes back, as if it happened yesterday. . . . Sometimes I lie awake at night and think of all the people who have come and gone, and how everything is different from the way we thought that it would be. Then I go out on the street next day and see the faces of the people that I pass. . . . Don't they look strange to you? Don't you see something funny in people's eyes, as if all of them were puzzled about something? As if they were wondering what had happened to them since they were kids? Wondering what it is that they have lost? . . . Now am I crazy, or do you know what I mean? You've been to college, Gene, and I want you to tell me if you know the answer. Now do they look that way to you? I never noticed that look in people's eyes when I was a kid—did you?

My God, I wish I knew the answer to these things. I'd like to find out what is wrong—what has changed since then—and if we have the same queer look in our eyes, too. Does it happen to us all, to everyone? . . . Grover and Ben, Steve, Daisy, Luke, and me—all standing there before that house on Woodson Street in Altamont—there we are, and you see the way we were—and how it all gets lost. What is it, anyway, that people lose?

How is it that nothing turns out the way we thought it would be? It all gets lost until it seems that it has never happened—that it is something we dreamed somewhere. . . . You see what I mean? . . . It seems that it must be something we heard somewhere—that it happened to someone else. And then it all comes back again.

And suddenly you remember just how it was, and see again those two funny, frightened, skinny little kids with their noses pressed against the dirty window of that lunchroom thirty years ago. You remember the way it felt, the way it smelled, even the strange smell in the old pantry in that house we lived in then. And the steps before the house, the way the rooms looked. And those two little boys in sailor suits who used to ride up and down before the house on tricycles. . . . And the birthmark on Grover's neck. . . . The Inside Inn. . . . St. Louis and the Fair.

It all comes back as if it happened yesterday. And then it goes away again, and seems farther off and stranger than if it happened in a dream.

The Lost Boy

IV—The Brother

"*This* is King's Highway," the man said.

And then Eugene looked and saw that it was just a street. There were some big new buildings, a large hotel, some restaurants and "bar-grill" places of the modern kind, the livid monotone of neon lights, the ceaseless traffic of motor cars—all this was new, but it was just a street. And he knew that it had always been just a street and nothing more—but somehow—well, he stood there looking at it, wondering what else he had expected to find.

The man kept looking at him with inquiry in his eyes, and Eugene asked him if the Fair had not been out this way.

"Sure, the Fair was out beyond here," the man said. "Out where the park is now. But this street you're looking for—don't you remember the name of it or nothing?" the man said.

Eugene said he thought the name of the street was Edgemont, but that he wasn't sure. Anyhow it was something like that. And he said the house was on the corner of that street and of another street.

Then the man said: "What was that other street?"

Eugene said he did not know, but that King's Highway was a block or so away, and that an interurban line ran past about half a block from where he once had lived.

"What line was this?" the man said, and stared at him.

"The interurban line," Eugene said.

Then the man stared at him again, and finally, "I don't know no interurban line," he said.

Eugene said it was a line that ran behind some houses, and that there were board fences there and grass beside the tracks. But somehow he could not say that it was summer in those days and that you could smell the ties, a wooden, tarry smell, and feel a kind of absence in the afternoon after the car had gone. He only said the interurban line was back behind somewhere between the backyards of some houses and some old board fences, and that King's Highway was a block or two away.

He did not say that King's Highway had not been a street in those days but a kind of road that wound from magic out of some dim and haunted land, and that along the way it had got mixed in with Tom the Piper's son, with hot cross buns, with all the light that came and went, and with coming down through Indiana in the morning, and the smell of engine smoke, the Union Station, and most of all with voices lost and far and long ago that said "King's Highway."

He did not say these things about King's Highway because he looked about him and he saw what King's Highway was. All he could say was that the street was near King's Highway, and was on the corner, and that the interurban trolley line was close to there. He said it was a stone house, and that there were stone steps before it, and a strip of grass. He said he thought the house had had a turret at one corner, he could not be sure.

The man looked at him again, and said, "This is King's Highway, but I never heard of any street like that."

Eugene left him then, and went on till he found the place. And so at last he turned into the street, finding the place where the two corners met, the huddled block, the turret, and the steps, and paused a moment, looking back, as if the street were Time.

[73]

For a moment he stood there, waiting—for a word, and for a door to open, for the child to come. He waited but no words were spoken; no one came.

Yet all of it was just as it had always been, except that the steps were lower, the porch less high, the strip of grass less wide, than he had thought. All the rest of it was as he had known it would be. A graystone front, three-storied, with a slant slate roof, the side red brick and windowed, still with the old arched entrance in the center for the doctor's use.

There was a tree in front, and a lamp post; and behind and to the side, more trees than he had known there would be. And all the slatey turret gables, all the slatey window gables, going into points, and the two arched windows, in strong stone, in the front room.

It was all so strong, so solid, and so ugly —and all so enduring and so good, the way he had remembered it, except he did not smell the tar, the hot and caulky dryness of the old cracked ties, the boards of backyard fences and the coarse and sultry grass, and absence in the afternoon when the street car had gone, and the twins, sharp-visaged in their sailor suits, pumping with furious shrillness on tricycles up and down before the house, and the feel of the hot afternoon, and the sense that everyone was absent at the Fair.

Except for this, it all was just the same; except for this and for King's Highway, which was now a street; except for this, and for the child that did not come.

It was a hot day. Darkness had come. The heat rose up and hung and sweltered like a sodden blanket in St. Louis. It was wet heat, and one knew that there would be no relief or coolness in the night. And when one tried to think of the time when the heat would go away, one said: "It cannot last. It's bound to go away," as we always say it in America. But one did not believe it when he said it. The heat soaked down and men sweltered in it; the faces of the people were pale and greasy with the heat. And in their faces was a patient wretchedness, and one felt the kind of desolation that one feels at the end of a hot day in a great city in America—when one's home is far away, across the continent, and he thinks of all that distance, all that heat, and feels, "Oh God! but it's a big country!"

And he feels nothing but absence, absence, and the desolation of America, the loneliness and sadness of the high, hot skies, and evening coming on across the Middle West, across the sweltering and heat-sunken land, across all the lonely little towns, the farms, the fields, the oven swelter of Ohio, Kansas, Iowa, and Indiana at the close of day, and voices, casual in the heat, voices at the little stations, quiet, casual, somehow faded into that enormous vacancy and weariness of heat, of space, and of the immense, the sorrowful, the most high and awful skies.

Then he hears the engine and the wheel again, the wailing whistle and the bell, the sound of shifting in the sweltering yard, and walks the street, and walks the street, beneath the clusters of hard lights, and by the people with sagged faces, and is drowned in desolation and in no belief.

He feels the way one feels when one comes back, and knows that he should not have come, and when he sees that, after all, King's Highway is—a street; and St. Louis—the enchanted name—a big, hot, common town upon the river, sweltering in wet, dreary heat, and not quite South, and nothing else enough to make it better.

It had not been like this before. He could remember how it would get hot, and how good the heat was, and how he would lie out in the backyard on an airing mattress, and how the mattress would get hot and dry and smell like a hot mattress full of sun, and how the sun would make him want to sleep, and how, sometimes, he would go down into the basement to feel coolness, and how the cellar smelled as cellars always smell—a cool, stale smell, the smell of cobwebs and of grimy bottles. And he could remember, when you opened the door upstairs, the smell of the cellar would come up to you —cool, musty, stale and dank and dark— and how the thought of the dark cellar always filled him with a kind of numb excitement, a kind of visceral expectancy.

He could remember how it got hot in the afternoons, and how he would feel a sense of absence and vague sadness in the afternoons, when everyone had gone away. The house would seem so lonely, and sometimes he would sit inside, on the second step of the hall stairs, and listen to the sound of silence and of absence in the afternoon. He could smell the oil upon the floor and on the stairs, and see the sliding doors with their brown varnish and the beady chains across the door, and thrust his hands among the beady chains, and gather them together in his arms, and let them clash, and swish with light beady swishings all around him. He could feel darkness, absence, varnished darkness, and stained light within the house, through the stained glass of the window on the stairs, through the small stained glasses by the door, stained light and absence, silence and the smell of floor oil and vague sadness in the house on a hot mid-afternoon. And all these things themselves would have a kind of life: would seem to wait attentively, to be most living and most still.

He would sit there and listen. He could hear the girl next door practice her piano lessons in the afternoon, and hear the street car coming by between the backyard fences, half a block away, and smell the dry and sultry smell of backyard fences, the smell of coarse hot grasses by the car tracks in the afternoon, the smell of tar, of dry caulked ties, the smell of bright worn flanges, and feel the loneliness of backyards in the afternoon and the sense of absence when the car was gone.

Then he would long for evening and return, the slant of light, and feet along the street, the sharp-faced twins in sailor suits upon their tricycles, the smell of supper and the sound of voices in the house again, and Grover coming from the Fair.

That is how it was when he came into the street, and found the place where the two corners met, and turned at last to see if Time was there. He passed the house: some lights were burning, the door was open, and a woman sat upon the porch. And presently he turned, came back, and stopped before the house again. The corner light fell blank upon the house. He stood looking at it, and put his foot upon the step.

Then he said to the woman who was sitting on the porch: "This house—excuse me—but could you tell me, please, who lives here in this house?"

He knew his words were strange and hollow, and he had not said what he wished to say. She stared at him a moment, puzzled.

Then she said: "I live here. Who are you looking for?"

He said, "Why, I am looking for—"

And then he stopped, because he knew he could not tell her what it was that he was looking for.

"There used to be a house—" he said.

The woman was now staring at him hard.

He said, "I think I used to live here."

She said nothing.

In a moment he continued, "I used to live here in this house," he said, "when I was a little boy."

She was silent, looking at him, then she said: "Oh. Are you sure this was the house? Do you remember the address?"

"I have forgotten the address," he said, "but it was Edgemont Street, and it was on the corner. And I know this is the house."

"This isn't Edgemont Street," the woman said. "The name is Bates."

"Well, then, they changed the name of the street," he said, "but this is the same house. It hasn't changed."

She was silent a moment, then she nodded: "Yes. They did change the name of the street. I remember when I was a child they called it something else," she said. "But that was a long time ago. When was it that you lived here?"

"In 1904."

Again she was silent, looking at him. Then presently: "Oh. That was the year of the Fair. You were here then?"

"Yes." He now spoke rapidly, with more confidence. "My mother had the house, and we were here for seven months. And the house belonged to Dr. Packer," he went on. "We rented it from him."

"Yes," the woman said, and nodded, "this was Dr. Packer's house. He's dead now, he's been dead for many years. But this was the Packer house, all right."

"That entrance on the side," he said, "where the steps go up, that was for Dr. Packer's patients. That was the entrance to his office."

"Oh," the woman said, "I didn't know that. I've often wondered what it was. I didn't know what it was for."

"And this big room in front here," he continued, "that was the office. And there were sliding doors, and next to it, a kind of alcove for his patients—"

"Yes, the alcove is still there, only all of it has been made into one room now—and I never knew just what the alcove was for."

"And there were sliding doors on this side, too, that opened on the hall—and a stairway going up upon this side. And halfway up the stairway, at the landing, a little window of colored glass—and across the sliding doors here in the hall, a kind of curtain made of strings of beads."

She nodded, smiling. "Yes, it's just the same—we still have the sliding doors and the stained glass window on the stairs. There's no bead curtain any more," she said, "but I remember when people had them. I know what you mean."

"When we were here," he said, "we used the doctor's office for a parlor—except later on—the last month or two—and then we used it for—a bedroom."

"It is a bedroom now," she said. "I run the house—I rent rooms—all of the rooms upstairs are rented—but I have two brothers and they sleep in this front room."

Both of them were silent for a moment, then Eugene said, "My brother stayed there too."

"In the front room?" the woman said.

He answered, "Yes."

She paused, then said: "Won't you come in? I don't believe it's changed much. Would you like to see?"

He thanked her and said he would, and he went up the steps. She opened the screen door to let him in.

Inside it was just the same—the stairs, the hallway, the sliding doors, the window of stained glass upon the stairs. And all of it was just the same, except for absence, the stained light of absence in the afternoon, and the child who once had sat there, waiting on the stairs.

The Lost Boy

It was all the same except that as a child he had sat there feeling things were *Somewhere*—and now he *knew*. He had sat there feeling that a vast and sultry river was somewhere—and now he knew! He had sat there wondering what King's Highway was, where it began, and where it ended—now he knew! He had sat there haunted by the magic word "downtown" —now he knew!—and by the street car, after it had gone—and by all things that came and went and came again, like the cloud shadows passing in a wood, that never could be captured.

And he felt that if he could only sit there on the stairs once more, in solitude and absence in the afternoon, he would be able to get it back again. Then would he be able to remember all that he had seen and been—the brief sum of himself, the universe of his four years, with all the light of Time upon it—that universe which was so short to measure, and yet so far, so endless, to remember. Then would he be able to see his own small face again, pooled in the dark mirror of the hall, and peer once more into the grave eyes of the child that he had been, and discover there in his quiet three-years' self the lone integrity of "I," knowing: "Here is the House, and here House listening; here is Absence, Absence in the afternoon; and here in this House, this Absence, is my core, my kernel—here am I!"

But as he thought it, he knew that even if he could sit here alone and get it back again, it would be gone as soon as seized, just as it had been then—first coming like the vast and drowsy rumors of the distant and enchanted Fair, then fading like cloud shadows on a hill, going like faces in a dream—coming, going, coming, possessed and held but never captured, like lost voices in the mountains long ago—and like the dark eyes and quiet face of the dark, lost boy, his brother, who, in the mysterious rhythms of his life and work, used to come into this house, then go, and return again.

The woman took Eugene back into the house and through the hall. He told her of the pantry, told her where it was and pointed to the place, but now it was no longer there. And he told her of the backyard, and of the old board fence around the yard. But the old board fence was gone. And he told her of the carriage house, and told her it was painted red. But now there was a small garage. And the backyard was still there, but smaller than he thought, and now there was a tree.

"I did not know there was a tree," he said. "I do not remember any tree."

"Perhaps it was not there," she said. "A tree could grow in thirty years." And then they came back through the house again and paused at the sliding doors.

"And could I see this room?" he said.

She slid the doors back. They slid open smoothly, with a rolling heaviness, as they used to do. And then he saw the room again. It was the same. There was a window at the side, the two arched windows at the front, the alcove and the sliding doors, the fireplace with the tiles of mottled green, the mantel of dark mission wood, the mantel posts, a dresser and a bed, just where the dresser and the bed had been so long ago.

"Is this the room?" the woman said. "It hasn't changed?"

He told her that it was the same.

"And your brother slept here where my brothers sleep?"

"This is his room," he said.

They were silent. He turned to go, and said, "Well, thank you. I appreciate your showing me."

She said that she was glad and that it was no trouble. "And when you see your family, you can tell them that you saw the house," she said. "My name is Mrs. Bell. You can tell your mother that a Mrs. Bell has the house now. And when you see your brother, you can tell him that you saw the room he slept in, and that you found it just the same."

He told her then that his brother was dead.

The woman was silent for a moment. Then she looked at him and said: "He died here, didn't he? In this room?"

He told her that it was so.

"Well, then," she said, "I knew it. I don't know how. But when you told me he was here, I knew it."

He said nothing. In a moment the woman said, "What did he die of?"

"Typhoid."

She looked shocked and troubled, and said involuntarily, "My two brothers—"

"That was a long time ago," he said. "I don't think you need to worry now."

"Oh, I wasn't thinking about that," she said. "It was just hearing that a little boy—your brother—was—was in this room that my two brothers sleep in now—"

"Well, maybe I shouldn't have told you then. But he was a good boy—and if you'd known him you wouldn't mind."

She said nothing, and he added quickly: "Besides, he didn't stay here long. This wasn't really his room—but the night he came back with my sister he was so sick—they didn't move him."

"Oh," the woman said, "I see." And then: "Are you going to tell your mother you were here?"

"I don't think so."

"I—I wonder how she feels about this room."

"I don't know. She never speaks of it."

"Oh. . . . How old was he?"

"He was twelve."

"You must have been pretty young yourself."

"I was not quite four."

"And—you just wanted to see the room, didn't you? That's why you came back."

"Yes."

"Well—" indefinitely—"I guess you've seen it now."

"Yes, thank you."

"I guess you don't remember much about him, do you? I shouldn't think you would."

"No, not much."

The years dropped off like fallen leaves: the face came back again—the soft dark oval, the dark eyes, the soft brown berry on the neck, the raven hair, all bending down, approaching—the whole appearing to him ghostwise, intent and instant.

"Now say it—*Grover!*"

"Gova."

"No—not Gova.—*Grover!* . . . Say it!"

"Gova."

"Ah-h—you didn't say it. You said Gova. *Grover*—now say it!"

"Gova."

"Look, I tell you what I'll do if you say it right. Would you like to go down to King's Highway? Would you like Grover to set you up? All right, then. If you say Grover and say it right, I'll take you to King's Highway and set you up to ice cream. Now say it right—*Grover!*"

"Gova."

"Ah-h, you-u. You're the craziest little old boy I ever did see. Can't you even say Grover?"

"Gova."

"Ah-h, you-u. Old Tongue-Tie, that's what you are. . . . Well, come on, then, I'll set you up anyway."

It all came back, and faded, and was

lost again. Eugene turned to go, and thanked the woman and said good-by.

"Well, then, good-by," the woman said, and they shook hands. "I'm glad if I could show you. I'm glad if—" She did not finish, and at length she said: "Well, then, that was a long time ago. You'll find everything changed now, I guess. It's all built up around here now—and way out beyond here, out beyond where the Fair Grounds used to be. I guess you'll find it changed."

They had nothing more to say. They just stood there for a moment on the steps, and then shook hands once more.

"Well, good-by."

And again he was in the street, and found the place where the corners met, and for the last time turned to see where Time had gone.

And he knew that he would never come again, and that lost magic would not come again. Lost now was all of it—the street, the heat, King's Highway, and Tom the Piper's son, all mixed in with the vast and drowsy murmur of the Fair, and with the sense of absence in the afternoon, and the house that waited, and the child that dreamed. And out of the enchanted wood, that thicket of man's memory, Eugene knew that the dark eye and the quiet face of his friend and brother—poor child, life's stranger, and life's exile, lost like all of us, a cipher in blind mazes, long ago—the lost boy was gone forever, and would not return.

POLONIUS TO LAERTES

Look thou character. Give thy thoughts no tongue,
Nor any unproportioned thought his act.
Be thou familiar, but by no means vulgar,
Those friends thou hast, and their adoption tried,
Grapple them to thy soul with hoops of steel,
But do not dull thy palm with entertainment
Of each new-hatch'd unfledged comrade. Beware
Of entrance to a quarrel; but being in,
Bear 't, that the opposed may beware of thee.
Give every man thy ear, but few thy voice:
Take each man's censure, but reserve thy judgement.
Costly thy habit as thy purse can buy,
But not expressed in fancy; rich, not gaudy:
For the apparel oft proclaims the man; . . . .
Neither a borrower nor a lender be:
For loan oft loses both itself and friend,
And borrowing dulls the edge of husbandry.
This above all: to thine own self be true,
And it must follow, as the night the day,
Thou canst not then be false to any man.
—Shakespeare, *Hamlet*

F. SCOTT FITZGERALD TO HIS DAUGHTER

August 8, 1933
La Paix, Rodgers' Forge,
Towson, Maryland

Dear Pie:

I feel very strongly about you doing duty. Would you give me a little more documentation about your reading in French? I am glad you are happy—but I never believe much in happiness. I never believe in misery either. Those are things you see on the stage or the screen or the printed page, they never really happen to you in life.

All I believe in in life is the rewards for virtue (according to your talents) and the *punishments* for not fulfilling your duties, which are doubly costly. If there is such a volume in the camp library, will you ask Mrs. Tyson to let you look up a sonnet of Shakespeare's in which the line occurs *Lilies that fester smell far worse than weeds.*

Have had no thoughts today, life seems composed of getting up a *Saturday Evening Post* story. I think of you, and always pleasantly; but if you call me "Pappy" again I am going to take the White Cat out and beat his bottom *hard, six times for every time you are impertinent.* Do you react to that?

I will arrange the camp bill.

Half-wit, I will conclude. Things to worry about:

Worry about courage
Worry about cleanliness
Worry about efficiency
Worry about horsemanship . . .

Things not to worry about:

Don't worry about popular opinion
Don't worry about dolls
Don't worry about the past
Don't worry about the future
Don't worry about growing up
Don't worry about anybody getting ahead of you
Don't worry about triumph
Don't worry about failure unless it comes through your own fault
Don't worry about mosquitoes
Don't worry about flies
Don't worry about insects in general
Don't worry about parents
Don't worry about boys
Don't worry about disappointments
Don't worry about pleasures
Don't worry about satisfactions

Things to think about:

What am I really aiming at?
How good am I really in comparison to my contemporaries in regard to:

(a) Scholarship
(b) Do I really understand about people and am I able to get along with them?
(c) Am I trying to make my body a useful instrument or am I neglecting it?

With dearest love,

Copyright 1945 by New Directions. Reprinted by permission of the estate of F. Scott Fitzgerald.

A PRAYER FOR MY DAUGHTER
by William Butler Yeats

Once more the storm is howling, and half hid
Under this cradle-hood and coverlid
My child sleeps on. There is no obstacle
But Gregory's wood and one bare hill
Whereby the haystack- and roof-leveling wind,
Bred on the Atlantic, can be stayed;
And for an hour I have walked and prayed
Because of the great gloom that is in my mind.

I have walked and prayed for this young child an hour
And heard the sea-wind scream upon the tower,
And under the arches of the bridge, and scream
In the elms above the flooded stream;
Imagining in excited reverie
That the future years had come,
Dancing to a frenzied drum,
Out of the murderous innocence of the sea.

May she be granted beauty, and yet not
Beauty to make a stranger's eye distraught,
Or hers before a looking-glass, for such,
Being made beautiful overmuch,
Consider beauty a sufficient end,
Lose natural kindness and maybe
The heart-revealing intimacy
That chooses right, and never find a friend.

Helen being chosen found life flat and dull
And later had much trouble from a fool,
While that great Queen, that rose out of the spray,
Being fatherless could have her way
Yet chose a bandy-leggèd smith for man.
It's certain that fine women eat
A crazy salad with their meat
Whereby the Horn of Plenty is undone.

In courtesy I'd have her chiefly learned;
Hearts are not had as a gift but hearts are earned
By those that are not entirely beautiful;
Yet many, that have played the fool
For beauty's very self, has charm made wise,
And many a poor man that has roved,
Loved and thought himself beloved,
From a glad kindness cannot take his eyes.

May she become a flourishing hidden tree
That all her thoughts may like the linnet be,
And have no business but dispensing round
Their magnanimities of sound,
Nor but in merriment begin a chase,
Nor but in merriment a quarrel.
Oh, may she live like some green laurel
Rooted in one dear perpetual place.

My mind, because the minds that I have loved,
The sort of beauty that I have approved,
Prosper but little, has dried up of late,
Yet knows that to be choked with hate
May well be of all evil chances chief.
If there's no hatred in a mind
Assault and battery of the wind
Can never tear the linnet from the leaf.

An intellectual hatred is the worst,
So let her think opinions are accursed.

From W. B. Yeats, *Collected Poems*. By permission of The Macmillan Company, publishers.

Have I not seen the loveliest woman born
Out of the mouth of Plenty's horn,
Because of her opinionated mind
Barter that horn and every good
By quiet natures understood
For an old bellows full of angry wind?

Considering that, all hatred driven hence,
The soul recovers radical innocence
And learns at last that it is self-delighting,
Self-appeasing, self-affrighting,
And that its own sweet will is Heaven's will;
She can, though every face should scowl
And every windy quarter howl
Or every bellows burst, be happy still.

And may her bridegroom bring her to a house
Where all's accustomed, ceremonious;
For arrogance and hatred are the wares
Peddled in the thoroughfares.
How but in custom and in ceremony
Are innocence and beauty born?
Ceremony's a name for the rich horn,
And custom for the spreading laurel tree

from THE PEOPLE, YES
by Carl Sandburg

9

A father sees a son nearing manhood.
What shall he tell that son?
"Life is hard; be steel; be a rock."
And this might stand him for the storms
and serve him for humdrum and monotony
and guide him amid sudden betrayals
and tighten him for slack moments.
"Life is a soft loam; be gentle; go easy."
And this too might serve him.
Brutes have been gentled where lashes failed.
The growth of a frail flower in a path up
has sometimes shattered and split a rock.
A tough will counts. So does desire.
So does a rich soft wanting.
Without rich wanting nothing arrives.
Tell him too much money has killed men
and left them dead years before burial:
the quest of lucre beyond a few easy needs
has twisted good enough men
sometimes into dry thwarted worms.
Tell him time as a stuff can be wasted.

From *The People, Yes* by Carl Sandburg. Copyright, 1936, by Harcourt, Brace and Company, Inc.

Any Man's Advice to His Son

Tell him to be a fool every so often
and to have no shame over having been a fool
yet learning something out of every folly
hoping to repeat none of the cheap follies
thus arriving at intimate understanding
of a world numbering many fools.
Tell him to be alone often and get at himself
and above all tell himself no lies about himself
whatever the white lies and protective fronts
he may use amongst other people.
Tell him solitude is creative if he is strong
and the final decisions are made in silent rooms.
Tell him to be different from other people
if it comes natural and easy being different.
Let him have lazy days seeking his deeper motives.
Let him seek deep for where he is a born natural.
    Then he may understand Shakespeare
    and the Wright brothers, Pasteur, Pavlov,
    Michael Faraday and free imaginations
bringing changes into a world resenting change.
    He will be lonely enough
    to have time for the work
    he knows as his own.

ANY MAN'S ADVICE TO HIS SON
by KENNETH FEARING

If you have lost the radio beam, then guide yourself by the sun or the stars.
(By the North Star at night, and in daytime by the compass and the sun.)
Should the sky be overcast and there are neither stars nor a sun, then steer by dead
    reckoning.
If the wind and direction and speed are not known, then trust to your wits and
    your luck.

Do you follow me? Do you understand? Or is this too difficult to learn?
But you must and you will, it is important that you do,
Because there may be troubles even greater than these that I have said.

Because, remember this: Trust no man fully.
Remember: If you must shoot at another man squeeze, do not jerk the trigger.
    Otherwise you may miss and die, yourself, at the hand of some other man's son.

From Kenneth Fearing, *Collected Poems*. Copyright, 1940, by Random House, Inc. Reprinted by permission of Random House, Inc. Originally appeared in *The New Yorker*.

Coming-of-Age in Our Time

And remember: In all this world there is nothing so easily squandered, or once gone,
   so completely lost as life.

I tell you this because I remember you when you were small,
And because I remember all your monstrous infant boasts and lies,
And the way you smiled, and how you ran and climbed, as no one else quite did,
   and how you fell and were bruised,
And because there is no other person, anywhere on earth, who remembers these
   things as clearly as I do now.

The Nursery — Stanley Spencer
Collection, The Museum of Modern Art, New York

THE AGE OF HAPPY PROBLEMS
by Herbert Gold

I

Recently I have had occasion to live again near my old college campus. I went into a hole-in-the-wall bakery where the proprietor recognized me after ten years. "You haven't changed a bit, son," he said, "but can you still digest my pumpernickel? The stomach gets older, no? Maybe you want something softer now—a nice little loaf I got here."

He had worn slightly. But for me the change was from twenty-two to thirty-two, and it is this ten-year time that I want to think about—the generation which came back from the war to finish college on the GI Bill and is now deep into its career. We are the generation which knew the Depression only through the exhilaration of the burgeoning New Deal and the stunned passion of war. I remember the bank crash because my mother wept and I said, "If we're poor now, can I wear corduroy pants?" For the most part, we were taken care of and never hopelessly hunted jobs. Now some of us say we are cool, say we are beat; but most of us are allrightniks—doing okay. We are successful. In the late forties and the fifties, it was hard to know economic struggle and want—and for the most part we didn't experience these traditional elements of youth—and it was hard for the skilled and the trained not to know success. We did not doubt overmuch. We have done well. How well?

"Money money money," as Theodore Roethke says.

I have married my hands to perpetual agitation,
I run, I run to the whistle of money.

Money money money
Water water water

I should like to take a look at some of the college idealists. The lawyer, fascinated by "the philosophy of law," now uses his study to put a smooth surface on his cleverness. Cardozo and Holmes? Very interesting, but let's find that loophole. The doctor who sent flowers to the first mother whose baby he delivered now specializes in "real-estate medicine"—his practice gives him capital for buying apartment houses. The architect who sat up all night haranguing his friends about Lewis Mumford and Frank Lloyd Wright now works for a mass builder who uses bulldozers to level trees and slopes, then puts up tri-level, semi-detached, twenty-year mortgaged, fundamentally identical dormitories for commuters. He admits that his designs make no decent sense, but they do have that trivial, all-important meaning: "It's what the market wants, man. You'd rather I taught city planning for six thousand a year?"

The actor becomes a disk jockey, the composer an arranger, the painter a designer; the writer does TV scripts in that new classic formula, "happy stories about happy people with happy problems." How hard it is to be used at our best! One of the moral issues of every age has been that of finding a way for men and women to test, reach, and overreach their best en-

Copyright 1957, by Herbert Gold. Reprinted by permission of James Brown Associates.

ergies. Society has always worked to level us. Socrates has always made it hot for the citizens in the market place. But there was usually room for the heroic—hemlock not a serious deterrent—and perhaps rarely so much room on all levels as in the frontier turbulence of the nineteenth and early twentieth century in America. Hands reached out like the squirming, grasping, struggling railroad networks; the open society existed; freedom had a desperate allure for the strongly ambitious, and men stepped up to take their chances—Abraham Lincoln and William James, Mark Twain and Melville, Edison and Rockefeller and Bet-a-Million Gates.

Allowing for a glitter of nostalgia on what we imagine about the past, still something has happened to change the old, movemented, free, open American society to something persuasive, plausible, comfortable, and much less open. We are prosperous, we get what we think we want, we have a relatively stable economy without totalitarian rule. "I'm not selling out," my friend the architect says, "I'm buying in." Without attempting a simple explanation of the causes of this age of happy problems, let us look at its consequences for the new post-war young people who should be in full action toward their ambitions and the surest, sturdiest signs of a civilization's health.

What are these personal symptoms? How is the vital individual human creature doing in his staff meetings, at his family's table, over the baby's bassinet, and with that distant secret self that he may sometimes meet at the water cooler? Well, for this man it is very hard to be exceptional. Talent apart, he has too much to do, too much on his mind, to give himself over to his best energies. Think, for example, of the writers in the advertising agencies, on TV, or in the colleges. They all wanted to write great books; they tend now to prefer "competence" as an ideal to greatness. Some of them are trying, but they risk the situation of the girl in the short-story writing class: "I can't be a creative writer, I can't, because I'm still a stupid virgin." She will take up going steady, she will take up marriage; she will be mildly disappointed; she will remain as she was, but aging—"adjusted," "integrated," virgin to danger, struggle, and the main chance of love and work.

In composite, in our thirties, we of this prosperous and successful generation are still in good health and rather fast at tennis (but practicing place shots which will eliminate the need to rush the net); hair receding but still attractive to college girls, or at least recent graduates; a slight heaviness at the middle which makes us fit our jackets with especial care (sullen jowls beginning, too) or, if not that, a skinniness of anxiety (etching around the mouth, dryness of lips). We go to an athletic club. We play handball in heavy shirts "to sweat it off."

The girls we marry are beautiful in wondrous ways. Savant make-up is no longer sufficient. Blemishes are scraped until the skin is pink and new; scars are grown away by cortisone injections—what reason to be marked in this world?; noses are remade, the same for mother and daughter, just like heredity. Money is spent much more gracefully than in those fantastic times when silver coins were put in ears and jewels in navels.

The old truth—"we must all come from someplace"—is amended in 1956. We can create ourselves in our own image. And what is our own image? The buttery face in the Pond's advertisement, the epicene face in the Marlboro publicity.

The Age of Happy Problems

The matters that we are told to worry about—and perhaps we think we worry about them—do not really trouble us. The prospect of war is like a vague headache, no worse. The memory of war is even dimmer. A depression is something which will reduce the value of our shares in the mutual fund, make us keep the old car another year. Radioactive fall-out and the slow destruction of the human species through cancerous mutation—well, what is so much bother to imagine cannot really come to pass. Who lets the newspaper interfere with a good meal?

2

Still, we are not blithe spirits; birds we are not. This generation is particularly distinguished by its worry about making its wives happy, about doing right by its kids (title of a hugely popular paperbound book: *How to Play with Your Child*), about acquiring enough leisure and symbols of leisure, which it hopes to cash in for moral comfort. *Fortune* reports a method used by salesmen to get the second room air conditioner to the couple which already has one in its bedroom. "The machine operates as expected? Fine! You sleep better with it? So do I, that's just dandy. But, friends, let me tell you how I sleep so much better now that I know my kiddies are cool and comfy, too."

This capitalizes on the child-oriented anxiety which the class known commercially as Young Marrieds has been taught to feel by modern psychiatry. Advertisements for *McCall's*, "The Magazine of Togetherness," demonstrate Togetherness in a brilliant summer scene. The man, wearing a white skirtlike apron and a proud simper, is bending to serve a steak to his wife (summer frock, spike heels), who will season it for them and for their happy gamboling children. The little boy and girl are peeking and smiling. The wife is lying in a garden chair. Togetherness consists in the husband's delighting his wife and kids by doing the cooking.

Actually, of course, most American women don't want to go this far. They are already equal with men. Women are usually too wise to define "equal" as "better than." It is not momism or any such simple psychological gimmick that tells this sad tale. The consumer culture—in which leisure is a menace to be met by anxious continual consuming—devours both the masculinity of men and the femininity of women. The life of consuming requires a neuter anxiety, and the pressure to conform, to watch for our cues, to consume, makes us all the same—we are customers—only with slightly different gadgets. Women have long bought men's shirts; men are buying colognes with "that exciting musky masculine tang."

Togetherness represents a curious effort by a woman's magazine to bring men back into the American family. Togetherness does not restore to the man a part of his old-time independence. It does not even indicate that he may be the provider with an independent role defined partly by ambitions outside his family. Instead, it suggests the joys of being a helpmate, a part of the woman's full life, and battens greedily on the contemporary male's anxiety about pleasing his wife. The Togetherness theme has been a great commercial success. A full-page advertisement by that canny old American institution, the New York Stock Exchange, shows a photograph of a harried young man pleading with a young woman on a parlor couch. She remains unconvinced, pouting, hands gloved and folded together, as brutal as the shocked beauties in the classical halitosis or B.O. tragedies. The caption reads: "Is the girl you want to marry reluctant to say Yes? Do you need to build character with your wife? Then just use the magic words: "I'LL START A MONTHLY INVESTMENT PLAN."

It used to be thought that answering economic needs was the main purpose of man's economic efforts. Now, however, an appeal to emotional insecurity about money—without crass financial trouble—can do good work for an advertiser. "Do you need to build character with your wife?" This is whimsey with a whammy in it. Money works symbolically to stimulate, then assuage male doubts.

> SHE: What can the stock do for our marriage?
> HE: It can help keep it sweet and jolly because when we own stock we are part-owners of the company.

In the image projected by this advertisement, the wife is prosecutor, judge, and jury. She may fall into a less exalted role, however, while her husband is downtown making the money which will go for food, clothing, shelter, and sound common stocks. That she too frets about keeping her marriage sweet and jolly is obvious. The popular media again point to trouble while pitching a new solution to her problems. One of the former soap operas is now sponsored by Sleepeze. Apparently almost everyone uses soap these days, but not everyone has caught on to the virtues of non-habit-forming sedatives. Want your husband to love you? This pill will help or your money back. "Ladies! Fall asleep without that unsightly twisting and turning."

It's time to mention Barbara. A tough wise creature of a girl, Barbara comes to this observation out of her marriage and love life: "Men worry too much about making the girl happy. We seem to scare them out of themselves. Let them really be pleased—that's what we want most of all—and then we'll be happy. Delighted. But really."

In other words, long live primary narcissism! And secondary. And tertiary. But let us call it by an older, better name—respect for the possibilities of the self. This includes the possibility of meaningful relationships with meaningful others.

3

Our wounds as a people in this time and place are not unique in kind, but the quality of difference makes this a marvelously disturbing period. The economic problem, no longer rooted in hunger for essential goods, food, housing, clothing, is an illustration of the difference. Sure, we are still busy over food—but packaged foods, luxury foods, goodies in small cans; housing—but the right house in the right neighborhood with the right furnishings and the right mortgage; clothing—but the cap with the strap in the back, Ivy League pants, charcoal gray last year and narrow lapels this year, and male fashions changing as fast as female.

It used to be thought that, given money, relative job security, and the short work week, culture would then bloom like the gardens in the suburbs and the individual spirit would roar with the driving power of a Thunderbird getting away after a red light.

Who could have predicted that we

would have to keep pace with a cultural assembly line in the leisure-time sweatshop? At least in the older sweatshop, you sighed, packed, and left the plant at last. Now we are forever harassed to give more, more, more. We no longer have to keep up with the Joneses; we must keep up with Clifton Fadiman. He is watching *you*. The steady pressure to consume, absorb, participate, receive, by eye, ear, mouth, and mail, involves a cruelty to intestines, blood pressure, and psyche unparalleled in history. The frontiersmen could build a stockade against the Indians, but what home is safe from Gilbert Highet? We are being killed with kindness. We are being stifled with cultural and material joys. Our wardrobes are full. What we really need is a new fabric that we don't have to wrinkle, spot, wash, iron, or wear. At a beautiful moment in *Walden,* Thoreau tells how he saw a beggar walking along with all his belongings in a single sack on his back. He wanted to weep for the poor man—because he still had that sack to carry.

The old-style sweatshop crippled mainly the working people. Now there are no workers left in America; we are almost all middle class as to income and expectations. Even the cultural elite labors among the latest in hi-fi equipment, trips to Acapulco and Paris, the right books in the sewn paper editions (Elizabeth Bowen, Arnold Toynbee, Jacques Barzun —these are the cultivated ones, remember), *Fortune* and the *Reporter,* art movies and the barbecue pit and the Salzburg music festival. It is too easy to keep up with the Joneses about cars and houses, but the Robert Shaw Chorale is a *challenge.* In the meantime, the man in the sweatshop is divorced or psychoanalyzed (these are perhaps remedies in a few cases); he raises adjusted children, or kills them trying; he practices Togetherness in a home with a wife who is frantic to be a woman and a non-woman at the same time; he broods about a job which does not ask the best that he can give. But it does give security; it is a good job. (In college this same man learned about the extreme, tragic instances of desire. Great men, great books. Now he reads Evelyn Waugh.)

In his later, philosophical transmogrification, David Riesman consoles the radar-flaunting other-directeds by holding out the reward of someday being "autonomous" if they are very, very good. Same thing, brother, same thing. When he describes the autonomous personality's "intelligent" distinctions among consumer products, exercising his creative imagination by figuring out why "High Noon" is a better western than a Gene Autry, well, then, in the words of Elvis Presley:—

Ah feel so lonely,
Ah feel so lo-oh-oh-lonely.

We're in Heartbreak Hotel where, as another singer, Yeats, put it:—

The ceremony of innocence is drowned;
The best lack all conviction, while the worst
Are filled with a passionate intensity.

Refusal to share to the fullest degree in the close amity of the leisure-time sweatshop is—for Mr. Riesman—a kind of ethical bohemianism. His autonomous consumer, sociable, trained, and in the know, is a critic of the distinctions between the Book-of-the-Month Club and the Reader's Subscription, Inc., marks the really good shows in his TV guide, buys educational comic books for his children, tastes the difference in fine after-dinner coffee, knows that the novel is a dead form and why. Bumper to bumper in the traffic home from work, or jammed into the commuter train, he has plenty of time to think. And he does think (thinking means worrying) while the radio blares "The House with the Stained Glass Window" or "The Magic of Believing," a little rock-and-roll philosophical number.

Does he have a moral problem, let's say, about leaving a changing neighborhood "for the sake of the children"? He is a liberal, of course, but after all, the Negroes who are moving in come from a different world and he should not inflict his principles on his children. Still, there is a certain discomfort. He discusses it with his analyst. *Why* does he suffer from this moral qualm? Does it have some link with the ever ambiguous relationship with parents? *What* moral problem? They are all psychological. Anxiety can be consumed like any product. And from his new, split-level, sapling-planted housing development he speeds into the city now ten miles further out.

We are a disappointed generation. We are a discontented people. Our manner of life says it aloud even if discreetly our public faces smile. The age of happy problems has brought us confusion and anxiety amid the greatest material comfort the world has ever seen. Culture has become a consolation for the sense of individual powerlessness in politics, work, and love. With gigantic organizations determining our movements, manipulating the dominion over self which alone makes meaningful communion with others possible, we ask leisure, culture, and recreation to return to us a sense of ease and authority. But work, love, and culture need to be connected. Otherwise we carry our powerlessness with us onto the aluminum garden furniture in the back yard. Power lawn mowers we can buy, of course.

The solution in our age of happy problems is not to install (on time) a central air-conditioning system and a color TV this year because the room air conditioner and the black-and-white TV last year did not change our lives in any important respect. The solution is not in stylish religious conversions or a new political party. The answer is not even that Panglossian fantasy about "the autonomous personality" which will naturally emerge out of the fatal meeting of the other-directed consumer with a subscription to the *Saturday Review*.

The ache of unfulfilled experience throbs within us. Our eyes hurt. Vicarious pleasures buzz in our heads. Isn't there something more, something more?

There is still awareness; there is still effort. "It should be every man's ambition to be his own doctor." This doesn't mean that he should not see a dentist when his tooth hurts, perhaps a psychoanalyst when his psyche hurts; but he must hold in mind the ideal maximum of humanity—the exercise of intelligence and desire within a context of active health. The Stoic philosophers had a great although impossible idea for these crowding times: cultivate your own garden. We cannot retreat from the world any more —we never really could—but we can look for our best gardens within the world's trouble. There we must give ourselves silence and space; we can see what the will wants; we can make decisions. Only then —having come to terms with our own particularities—can we give the world more than a graceless prefabricated commodity.

Hope? Some sweet Barbara is hope.

And a work we love. And the strength, O Lord, not to accept the easy pleasures (easy anxieties) which have pleased us (made us anxious) so far. And the strength, O Lord, you who reign undefined above the psychoanalysts and the sociologists, the market researchers and the advertising agencies, the vice presidents and the book clubs, to refuse the easy solutions which have becalmed us so far.

Then with good belly luck we will be able to digest strong, irregular, yeasty, black bread.

PART II · HOW WRITING IS WRITTEN

ALL WRITING, as Thomas Mann has said, is autobiographical. It is the work of the whole man, the way he takes himself becoming what is called his style. The selections which follow will show how the writer takes himself and afford a number of clues to why he writes the way he does. Some of them will give aid toward better writing and some toward improvement in reading.

The writer in our time has been faced with a number of difficulties, both technical and personal. He has often felt alone, at cross currents with the flow of the times, yet in his desire to put down what he sees he has also reflected the world in which he finds himself. He has often had to invent new manners and methods to express the strange, new and intractable experiences of his world, but he has also felt the need to arrange and clarify those experiences for his readers.

The writer is here posed as the representative individual, whose values lie in honesty to his knowledge and fidelity to his beliefs. The emphasis is on a man's need to know himself and his world before he can act.

If the writing itself is an act both enjoyable and meaningful, so much the better. Some of the writers here leave no doubt that it was so with them, and they echo the attitude Byron expressed in *Childe Harold's Pilgrimage:*

> 'T is to create, and in creating live
> A being more intense that we endow
> With form our fancy, gaining as we give
> The life we image, even as I do now.
> What am I? Nothing: but not so art thou,
> Soul of my thought! with whom I traverse earth,
> Invisible but gazing, as I glow
> Mix'd with thy spirit, blended with thy birth,
> And feeling still with thee in my crush'd feelings' dearth.
> —Canto III, Stanza VI

Inspiration

From It's a long way to Heaven, *copyright, 1945, by Abner Dean, and reproduced by permission of Rinehart & Company, Inc., Publishers.*

WORDS, WORDS, WORDS

by C. E. Montague

In youth you easily fall in love with words, written and spoken. You come, like other lovers, to feel an unreasoned sensuous thrill of joy at a word because it is just what it is—the sound of it and the look of it on a page—as a child's mind thrills at the touch of fur because it is sleek and at that of a file because it is not. Apart from the interest of their use in any particular place, such words as "burnish," "crozier," "lustre," "beatitude," "dawn" become enamouring objects, with glowing hearts of their own, like red wine or rubies.

A sculptor alone in his studio will fondly stroke a lump of unworked marble or bronze; he can dote on its qualities. A writer or a good reader will do much the same: his mind will finger single words and caress them, adoring the mellow fullness or granular hardness of their several sounds, the balance, undulation or trailing fall of their syllables, or the core of sunlike splendour in the broad, warm, central vowel of such a word as "auroral." Each word's evocative value or virtue, its individual power of touching springs in the mind and of initiating visions, becomes a treasure to revel in.

Besides this hold on affection a word may well have about it the glamorous prestige of high adventures in great company. Think of all that the plain word "dust" calls to mind. "Then shall the dust return to the earth as it was." "Dust hath closed Helen's eye." "All follow this and come to dust." "The way to dusty death." So, to the lover of words, each word may be not a precious stone only, but one that has shone on Solomon's temple or in Cleopatra's hair. Out of these illustrious atoms all the freakish pinnacles and cupolas of the world's wit were made, all the glow and intensity of its eloquence and the sweet poignancy of songs. All things in literature are born of them; into them all things will die, but the words themselves will remain, like the gases and salts into which we go back at our deaths; and each word is like some small parcel of earth that was once Caesar's brain and may yet make the brain of the next Christ that comes. Storied and ancient, it still has the freshness of youth; it lies, shiningly new, at the hand of every boy or girl who opens eager eyes upon life; it is as ready to enter into new melodies now as the single notes that were marshalled by Bach.

Thus, and with no qualification to his ecstasy, meditates the young, the unwedded wooer of words.

2

The happiest of wedded lives is a different thing from a wooing. It is a better state. But it is also a more open-eyed state. In it there may come a sense, not felt before, that married happiness is a thing to be kept only on certain conditions. The terms of the lease are not harsh; still, it is not fee-simple. To anyone who espouses the art of letters, and treats his bride fairly, there comes a somewhat similar recognition. He who weds words is tied, like the husband of the fairest lady, to one who has to carry about

From *A Writer's Notes on His Trade* by C. E. Montague. Reprinted by permission of Chatto and Windus Ltd.

her many other properties of earth besides the power, which he had already noted, of growing roses and lilies on her surface.

Like the sculptor, who never can fashion a hair or a thread in marble, the writer finds himself pulled up at many points by the nature of his material. Words, like marble, have their own chilling form of rigidity. Inspire and prompt as it may, in practice the beloved material is always imposing upon its lover some limitation or other, and there is no sentence in which a writer burning to charge his utterance with its utmost fill of significance does not feel that some words, at least, are mere structural necessities, not signal rockets but only the deadweight sticks that must attend them. The harder a writer tries to add beauty to clearness, the more surely does he feel himself to be held off from perfection by attributes of language which he did not make and cannot do away with; words that otherwise come near to expressing fully his personal sense of some enchanting thing may be found to hiss with sibilant letters, or scrunch and jolt with grinding lumps of harsh consonants, or dribble off into weak trickles of unaccounted syllables. At every turn he is faced with a demand for compromise; either the sensuous rightness of rhythm may have to forego a part of its dues, or the more austere beauty of precision and coherence must be marred. At moments the true wedded lover almost craves for a larger liberty—Oh for some yet undiscovered mode of notation! Why should not mind be able to pass on to mind its thrilled sense of a storm or a flower without having to knead up the air and fire of the delighted spirit with the earth of a current vocabulary?

So, in certain moods, the writer who loves words most truly may come near to thinking of them as "matter," the accursed thing, the ever-present incubus which obstructs and disables. Wooden, lumpish, perverse, they seem to head him off from the goal; they keep his work from being all that it seems as if it might be. Like "the flesh" or "the world," in the Biblical contrasts between these things and grace, they are that in which the divine agency of his art is destined to labour and which it has to transfigure or to redeem, but which never ceases to stand out frowardly for its now graceless ways. Objects, to him, of intense affection and of unquenchable hope, as the world was to Christ, words are the enemy too, the careless, unfeeling brute mass that will not respond; they may even crucify those who, like Flaubert, try the hardest to deliver them from their common poorness of significance.

3

In yet another light a writer may view the dear enemies, as old lovers in books used to say, of his repose. In words themselves he may see a kind of internal conflict. You can fancy the marble "David" of Michelangelo as existing before it was actually carved. Immured like some fossilized shell in the marble surrounding it, there it was, every grain of it, only awaiting release from the oppression of that encumbering bulk of gross matter. And yet the statue itself was matter as well as the rest of the block, and so it is now. It was, till liberated, a piece of matter kept out of its rights, debarred from being all that it had it in itself to be. When the sculptor had disengaged it from its prison, it was the same piece of matter that had lain "in cold obstruction" in the dark midst of a formless rock. Yet something momentous had befallen it. It had been charged with immediate power to stir mind and heart. It had attained so choice a measure of self-completion that, as long as it lasts, it will be as wonderfully different from any rough block of similar stone as Michelangelo himself was from a tall ape.

Still, we should go too fast or too far if we were to write off as "mere matter" or as "waste matter" all the rest of the block from which a "David" has been extricated. Relatively to the "David," no doubt it is waste matter. Relatively to something else it may be splendidly to the purpose. Every good-sized splinter of it must have held a fine statuette that some artist with the right power might have rescued from its particular dungeon. Relatively to some unachieved possibility of its own, every flake that is chipped off may be essential and organic. That it is so is the only safe working assumption; we may find least to abandon or to overhaul, as our thinking goes on, if we think now of all marble, all paint, all words, all the material in which any art works, as capable of transfiguration, as awaiting it, almost as attempting it and crying to artists for their help in this continual effort of self-emancipation, self-realization.

What, then, becomes of that lover's quarrel between the writer and his material? And of the brothers' quarrel between the marble that is taken and that which is left? These piques seem to dwindle in presence of a more momentous war in which all these, or the souls of all these, fight as allies. The rescue of matter from being mere matter, of marble from being mere flaky lumps of the crust of the earth, of language from being a buzz of crude signals and rudimentary chatter and no more—this is the divine event that beckons to both sculptors and writers and, in a sense, to matter itself, and the contribution of matter to its own deliverance is its evolution of special qualities conducive to the end in view, the choice loveliness of the textures of stone, its fissile quality, its gift of weathering; the brilliant lustre depth and diversity of paint and the inherent comeliness and melody of words to eye and ear, apart from their meanings, in the obvious sense of meaning. They find these sinews of war while the artists fight for them and with them.

4

The common adversary is less easily definable than these aspiring forces that are leagued against him. He is formlessness —a kind of lumpish and sluggish recalcitrance, a huggermugger fecklessness always ready to possess the world and ourselves, an inveterate halfness afflicting, if it can, the glories of our birth and state.

A man who writes, at the top of his powers, from a full mind, is always longing to be shorter than he is. Why, he feels, should not these symbols that he has to use be cut free from their baggage of lengthiness and their cumbrous rules of construction? Why should a glowing sentence have to be dulled with such lack-lustre dust as all the "it's" and "is" and "that" and "which" and "to" that clog it? When all is done that man can do, what a quantity of dull setting there has had to be for each gem that he has cut! At best, how much of matter to how little of form!

There is no coherent sentence in which you will not find, in some proportions or other, both matter and form. Even in a

[98]

song of Shakespeare's there are some words which, you may say, contribute nothing directly to the intoxicant glory of the whole. They are not vines; only props in the vineyard. And even in the frisking of the cheap humorists there is a kind of form; the old words do, at least, go through a kind of poor weary dance, like the Frenchman's chained bear. What differs is the extent to which, in each case, matter has been taken up into form, merged in it and become inseparable from it.

In the inarticulate exhaustiveness of an English dictionary you may see the huge range of living stone out of which have been quarried and modelled such treasures of art as

> the tide of pomp
> That beats upon the high shore of this world.

What has befallen those four common nouns, one common verb and one common adjective, dug out of the hill-side? First a triumphant survival, a retention of prestige, when each was tried, as it were, for its life, in the pitiless just court of a supreme artist seeking the perfect means to his end. One imagines Shakespeare writing the passage, perhaps, as long at first as one of his full-blown similes—King Richard's simile of the clock, or the Primate's of the bee-hive—and then asking himself, "Can I not by some ellipse, some crystallization of the value of all these words into a few granules of gleaming suggestiveness, make the whole mass of significance flash out at once instead of slowly blinking and twinkling its way into clearness?" And then the slaughter of a dozen lines and the reconcentration of all their sum of value on the twelve words left—to the mysterious enrichment of these, as if, like primitive man in his own imagination, they had taken into themselves the virtues of the rivals whom they had killed and devoured. Thus, at every step in the ascending scale of creative energy which brings such things to the birth, you see two interdependent processes at work. The thing which is coming to perfection is being drastically purged of words, more and more words, as if words were presumptively dross; and a diminishing residue of words are being impregnated and reimpregnated with a strange, super-normal glory and wonder of expressiveness and beauty.

Or is this enrichment not super-normal at all, but really normal, simply the release of the chosen words, for the moment, from an abnormal or subnormal dullness and plainness that afflict them at other times?

> She walks in beauty, like the night
> Of cloudless climes and starry skies.

All the words here are common enough; and one may feel either that kitchen coals have turned for a moment into diamonds, or else that a few diamonds have ceased for once to masquerade as kitchen coal. It all depends on what you take to be "par" in the scale of expressiveness—the faint significance of words like "ridge," "pine," "wild," "fledged," for a common dullard, or their evocative magic for a Keats, when writing of a wild ridge fledged with pine.

That, in turn, may depend on what you are inclined to think of the future of the race—whether mankind strikes you as resembling an adolescent, only on the threshold of a glorious adult life, or as a rose that already is overblown. You may like to think of any word that has colour and form as of Stratford or Haworth in the Middle Ages, waiting obscurely for a Shakespeare or Brontë to make it illustrious, or as one of the physical elements of which a living body, of special beauty, is presently to be composed.

5

One of the oldest of common antitheses is the one between the ideal and the thing that we have to put up with, an imaginable perfection and some moderate good which must serve. Nor is it a long step from thinking of something as distinguishable from the ideally good to thinking of it as bad. Hence the old friarly feuds against the common good things of life, the backing of spirit against flesh and of the Kingdom of God against this pleasant faulty world, and, in art, the setting of matter and form by the ears.

But, for all we can see, matter and form, like body and soul, are co-extensive and interdependent; each is a condition of the other's existence, and Shakespeare's art itself could no more decline to be yoked with that plodding Dobbin, the English speech that others had made before he arrived, than his spirit could go from Stratford to London without certain help from his legs. If form enables matter to rise to the highest achievable power of itself, matter is that in which, alone, form can find exercise for its own transfiguring faculty. In the most perfect picture or book there may be almost no mere matter left; but what has happened is not that matter, in the main, has been expelled; rather, that no considerable margin of matter remains unanimated by form. There is scarcely any mere paint in the Sistine Madonna, but there is plenty of paint.

Obvious analogies can be found in the fields of religion and of morals. The faith of the man who, whether he eats or drinks or does anything else, does it all to the glory of God, is an own sister to the form which marshals and inspirits matter of all sorts into beauty and nobility. And when the devout speak of "the beauty of holiness," or men of science speak of a "beautiful" or an "elegant" demonstration of some physical fact or law, you may feel how far the workings of form, in the sense known to art, extend beyond the tender contentions of artists in letters, marble or paint with the beloved and exasperating materials that they have espoused.

WRITING PROSE
by W. Somerset Maugham

I HAVE NEVER had more than two English lessons in my life, for though I wrote essays at school, I do not remember that I ever received any instruction on how to put sentences together. The two lessons I have had were given me so late in life that I am afraid I cannot hope greatly to profit by them. The first was only a few

From: *The Summing Up,* by W. Somerset Maugham, copyright, 1938, reprinted by permission of Doubleday and Company, Inc.

years ago. I was spending some weeks in London and had engaged as temporary secretary a young woman. She was shy, rather pretty, and absorbed in a love affair with a married man. I had written a book called *Cakes and Ale,* and, the typescript arriving one Saturday morning, I asked her if she would be good enough to take it home and correct it over the weekend. I meant her only to make a note of mistakes in spelling that the typist might have made and point out errors occasioned by a handwriting that is not always easy to decipher. But she was a conscientious young person and she took me more literally than I intended. When she brought back the typescript on Monday morning it was accompanied by four foolscap sheets of corrections. I must confess that at the first glance I was a trifle vexed; but then I thought that it would be silly of me not to profit, if I could, by the trouble she had taken and so sat me down to examine them. I suppose the young woman had taken a course at a secretarial college and she had gone through my novel in the same methodical way as her masters had gone through her essays. The remarks that filled the four neat pages of foolscap were incisive and severe. I could not but surmise that the professor of English at the secretarial college did not mince matters. He took a marked line, there could be no doubt about that; and he did not allow that there might be two opinions about anything. His apt pupil would have nothing to do with a preposition at the end of a sentence. A mark of exclamation betokened her disapproval of a colloquial phrase. She had a feeling that you must not use the same word twice on a page and she was ready every time with a synonym to put in its place. If I had indulged myself in the luxury of a sentence of ten lines, she wrote: "Clarify this. Better break it up into two or more periods." When I had availed myself of the pleasant pause that is indicated by a semicolon, she noted: "A full stop"; and if I had ventured upon a colon she remarked stingingly: "Obsolete." But the harshest stroke of all was her comment on what I thought was rather a good joke: "Are you sure of your facts?" Taking it all in all I am bound to conclude that the professor at her college would not have given me very high marks.

The second lesson I had was given me by a don, both intelligent and charming, who happened to be staying with me when I was myself correcting the typescript of another book. He was good enough to offer to read it. I hesitated, because I knew that he judged from a standpoint of excellence that is hard to attain; and though I was aware that he had a profound knowledge of Elizabethan literature, his inordinate admiration for *Esther Waters* made me doubtful of his discernment in the productions of our own day: no one could attach so great a value to that work who had an intimate knowledge of the French novel during the nineteenth century. But I was anxious to make my book as good as I could and I hoped to benefit by his criticisms. They were in point of fact lenient. They interested me peculiarly because I inferred that this was the way in which he dealt with the compositions of undergraduates. My don had, I think, a natural gift for language, which it has been his business to cultivate; his taste appeared to me faultless. I was much struck by his insistence on the force of individual words. He liked the stronger word rather than the euphonious. To give an example, I had written that a statue would be placed in a certain square and he suggested that I should write: the statue will stand. I had not done that because my ear was offended by the alliteration. I noticed also that he had a feeling that words should be used not only to balance a sentence but to balance an idea. This is sound, for an idea may lose its effect if it is delivered abruptly; but it is a matter of delicacy, since it may well lead to verbiage. Here a knowledge of stage dialogue should help. An actor will sometimes say to an author: "Couldn't you give me a word or two more in this speech? It seems to take away all the point of my line if I have nothing else to say." As I listened to my don's remarks I could not but think how much better I should write now if in my youth I had had the advantage of such sensible, broadminded and kindly advice.

As it is, I have had to teach myself. I have looked at the stories I wrote when I was very young in order to discover what natural aptitude I had, my original stock-in-trade, before I developed it by taking thought. The manner had a superciliousness that perhaps my years excused and an irascibility that was a defect of nature; but I am speaking now only of the way in which I expressed myself. It seems to me that I had a natural lucidity and a knack for writing easy dialogue.

When Henry Arthur Jones, then a well-known playwright, read my first novel, he told a friend that in due course I should be one of the most successful dramatists of the day. I suppose he saw in it directness and an effective way of presenting a scene that suggested a sense of the theater. My language was commonplace, my vocabulary limited, my grammar shaky, and my phrases hackneyed. But to write was an instinct that seemed as natural to me as to breathe, and I did not stop to consider if I wrote well or badly. It was not till some years later that it dawned upon me that it was a delicate art that must be painfully acquired. The discovery was forced upon me by the difficulty I found in getting my meaning down on paper. I wrote dialogue fluently, but when it came to a page of description I found myself entangled in all sorts of quandaries. I would struggle for a couple of hours over two or three sentences that I could in no way manage to straighten out. I made up my mind to teach myself how to write. Unfortunately I had no one to help me. I made many mistakes. If I had had someone to guide me like the charming don of whom I spoke just now, I might have been saved much time. Such a one might have told me that such gifts as I had lay in one direction and that they must be cultivated in that direction; it was useless to try to do something for which I had no aptitude. But at that time a florid prose was admired. Richness of texture was sought by means of a jeweled phrase and sentences stiff with exotic epithets; the ideal was a brocade so heavy with gold that it stood up by itself. The intelligent young read Walter Pater with enthusiasm. My common sense suggested to me that it was anemic stuff; behind those elaborate, gracious periods I was conscious of a tired, wan personality. I was young, lusty, and energetic; I wanted fresh air, action, violence, and I found it hard to breathe that dead, heavily scented atmosphere and sit in those hushed rooms in which it was indecorous to speak above a whisper. But I would not listen to my common sense. I persuaded myself that this was the height of culture and turned a scornful shoulder on the outside world where men shouted and swore, played the fool, wenched and got drunk. I read *Intentions* and *The Picture of Dorian Gray*. I was intoxicated by the color and rareness of the fantastic words that thickly stud the pages of *Salome*. Shocked by the poverty of my own vocabulary, I went to the British Museum with pencil and paper and noted down the names of curious jewels, the Byzantine hues of old enamels, the sensual feel of textiles, and made elaborate sentences to bring them in. Fortunately I could never find an opportunity to use them and they lie there yet in an old notebook ready for anyone who has a mind to write nonsense. It was generally thought then that the Authorized Version of the Bible was the greatest piece of prose that the English language has produced. I read it diligently, especially the Song of Solomon, jotting down for future use turns of phrase that struck me and making lists of unusual or beautiful words. I studied Jeremy Taylor's *Holy Dying*. In order to assimilate his style I copied out passages and then tried to write them down from memory.

The first fruit of this labor was a little book about Andalusia called *The Land of the Blessed Virgin*. I had occasion to read parts of it the other day. I know Andalusia a great deal better now than I knew it then, and I have changed my mind about a good many things of which I wrote. Since it has continued in America to have a small sale, it occurred to me that it might be worth while to revise it. I soon saw that this was impossible. The book was written by someone I have completely forgotten. It bored me to distraction. But what I am concerned with is the prose, for it was as an exercise in style that I wrote it. It is wistful, allusive, and elaborate. It has neither ease nor spontaneity. It smells of hothouse plants and Sunday dinner like the air in the greenhouse that leads out of the dining-room of a big house in Bayswater. There are a great many melodious adjectives. The vocabulary is sentimental. It does not remind one of an Italian brocade, with its rich pattern of gold, but of a curtain material designed by Burne-Jones and reproduced by Morris.

I do not know whether it was a subconscious feeling that this sort of writing was contrary to my bent or a naturally methodical cast of mind that led me then to turn my attention to the writers of the Augustan Period. The prose of Swift enchanted me. I made up my mind that this was the perfect way to write and I started to work on him in the same way as I had done with Jeremy Taylor. I chose *The Tale of a Tub*. It is said that when the Dean re-read it in his old age he cried: "What genius I had then!" To my mind his genius was better shown in other works. It is a tiresome allegory and the irony is facile. But the style is admirable. I cannot imagine that English can be better written. Here are no flowery periods, fantastic turns of phrase or high-flown images. It is a civilized prose, natural, discreet, and pointed. There is no attempt to surprise by an extravagant vocabulary. It looks as though Swift made do with the first word that came to hand, but since he had an acute and logical brain it was always the right one, and he put it in the right place. The strength and balance of his sentences are due to an exquisite taste. As I had done before I copied passages and then tried to write them out again from memory. I tried altering words or the order in which they were set. I found that the only possible words were those Swift had used and that the order in which he had placed them was the only possible order. It is an impeccable prose.

But perfection has one grave defect: it is apt to be dull. Swift's prose is like a French canal, bordered with poplars, that runs through a gracious and undulating country. Its tranquil charm fills you with satisfaction, but it neither excites the emotions nor stimulates the imagination. You go on and on and presently you are a trifle bored. So, much as you may admire Swift's wonderful lucidity, his terseness, his naturalness, his lack of affectation, you find your attention wandering after a while unless his matter peculiarly interests you. I think if I had my time over again I would give to the prose of Dryden the close study I gave to that of Swift. I did not come across it till I had lost the inclination to take so much pains. The prose of Dryden is delicious. It has not the perfection of Swift nor the easy elegance of Addison, but it has a springtime gaiety, a conversational ease, a blithe spontaneousness that are enchanting. Dryden was a very good poet, but it is not the general opinion that he had a lyrical quality; it is strange that it is just this that sings in his softly sparkling prose. Prose had never been written in England like that before; it has seldom been written like that since. Dryden flourished at a happy moment. He had in his bones the sonorous periods and the baroque massiveness of Jacobean language and under the influence of the nimble and well-bred felicity that he learnt from the French he turned it into an instrument that was fit not only for solemn themes but also to express the light thought of the passing moment. He was the first of the rococo artists. If Swift reminds you of a French canal Dryden recalls an English river winding its cheerful way round hills, through quietly busy towns and by nestling villages, pausing now in a noble reach and then running powerfully through a woodland country. It is alive, varied, windswept; and it has the pleasant open-air smell of England.

The work I did was certainly very good for me. I began to write better; I did not write well. I wrote stiffly and self-consciously. I tried to get a pattern into my sentences, but did not see that the pattern was evident. I took care how I placed my words, but did not reflect that an order that was natural at the beginning of the eighteenth century was most unnatural at the beginning of ours. My attempt to write in the manner of Swift made it impossible for me to achieve the effect of inevitable rightness that was just what I so much admired in him. I then wrote a number of plays and ceased to occupy myself with anything but dialogue. It was not till five years had passed that I set out again to write a novel. By then I no longer had any ambition to be a stylist; I put aside all thought of fine writing. I wanted to write without any frills of language, in as bare and unaffected a manner as I could. I had so much to say that I could afford to waste no words. I wanted merely to set down the facts. I began with the impossible aim of using no adjectives at all. I thought that if you could find the exact term a qualifying epithet could be dispensed with. As I saw it in my mind's eye my book would have the appearance of an immensely long telegram in which for economy's sake you had left out every word that was not necessary to make the sense clear. I have not read it since I corrected the proofs and do not know how near I came to doing what I tried. My impression is that it is written at least more naturally than anything I had written before; but I am sure that it is often slipshod and I daresay there are in it a good many mistakes in grammar.

Since then I have written many other books; and though ceasing my methodical study of the old masters (for though the spirit is willing, the flesh is weak), I have continued with increasing assiduity to try to write better. I discovered my limitations and it seemed to me that the only sensible thing was to aim at what excellence I could within them. I knew that I had no lyrical quality. I had a small vocabulary and no efforts that I could make to enlarge it much availed me. I had little gift of metaphor; the original and striking simile seldom occurred to me. Poetic flights and the great imaginative sweep were beyond my powers. I could admire them in others as I could admire their far-fetched tropes and the unusual but suggestive language in which they clothed their thoughts, but my own invention never presented me with such embellishments; and I was tired of trying to do what did not come easily to me. On the other hand, I had an acute power of observation and it seemed to me that I could see a great many things that other people missed. I could put down in clear terms what I saw. I had a logical sense, and if no great feeling for the richness and strangeness of words, at all events a lively appreciation of their sound. I knew that I should never write as well as I could wish, but I thought with pains I could arrive at writing as well as my natural defects allowed. On taking thought it seemed to me that I must aim at lucidity, simplicity and euphony. I have put these three qualities in the order of the importance I assigned to them.

I have never had much patience with the writers who claim from the reader an effort to understand their meaning. You have only to go to the great philosophers to see that it is possible to express with lucidity the most subtle reflections. You may find it difficult to understand the thought of Hume, and if you have no philosophical training its implications will doubtless escape you; but no one with any education at all can fail to understand exactly what the meaning of each sentence is. Few people have written English with more grace than Berkeley. There are two sorts of obscurity that you find in writers. One is due to negligence and the other to willfulness. People often write obscurely because they have never taken the trouble to learn to write clearly. This sort of obscurity you find too often in modern philosophers, in men of science, and even in literary critics. Here it is indeed strange. You would have thought that men who passed their lives in the study of the great masters of literature would be sufficiently sensitive to the beauty of language to write if not beautifully at least with perspicuity. Yet you will find in their works sentence after sentence that you must read twice to discover the sense. Often you can only guess at it, for the writers have evidently not said what they intended.

Another cause of obscurity is that the writer is himself not quite sure of his meaning. He has a vague impression of what he wants to say, but has not, either from lack of mental power or from laziness, exactly formulated it in his mind and it is natural enough that he should not find a precise expression for a confused idea. This is due largely to the fact that many writers think, not before, but as they write. The pen originates the thought. The disadvantage of this, and indeed it is a danger against which the author must be always on his guard, is that there is a sort of magic in the written word. The idea acquires substance by taking on a visible nature, and then stands in the way of its own clarification. But this sort of obscurity merges very easily into the willful. Some writers who do not think clearly are inclined to suppose that their thoughts have a significance greater than at first sight appears. It is flattering to believe that they are too profound to be expressed so clearly that all who run may read, and very naturally it does not occur to such writers that the fault is with their own minds which have not the faculty of precise reflection. Here again the magic of the written word obtains. It is very easy to persuade oneself that a phrase that one does not quite understand may mean a great deal more than one realizes. From this there is only a little way to go to fall into the habit of setting down one's impressions in all their original vagueness. Fools can always be found to discover a hidden sense in them. There is another form of willful obscurity that masquerades as aristocratic exclusiveness. The author wraps his meaning in mystery so that the vulgar shall not participate in it. His soul is a secret garden into which the elect may penetrate only after overcoming a number of perilous obstacles. But this kind of obscurity is not only pretentious; it is shortsighted. For time plays it an odd trick. If the sense is meager, time reduces it to a meaningless verbiage that no one thinks of reading. This is the fate that has befallen the lucubrations of those French writers who were seduced by the example of Guillaume Apollinaire. But occasionally it throws a sharp cold light on what had seemed profound and thus discloses the fact that these contortions of language disguised very commonplace notions. There are few of Mallarmé's poems now that are not clear; one cannot fail to notice that his thought singularly lacked originality. Some of his phrases were beautiful; the materials of his verse were the poetic platitudes of his day.

Simplicity is not such an obvious merit as lucidity. I have aimed at it because I have no gift for richness. Within limits I admire richness in others, though I find it difficult to digest in quantity. I can read one page of Ruskin with delight, but twenty only with weariness. The rolling period, the stately epithet, the noun rich in poetic associations, the subordinate clauses that give the sentence weight and magnificence, the grandeur like that of wave following wave in the open sea; there is no doubt that in all this there is something inspiring. Words thus strung together fall on the ear like music. The appeal is sensuous rather than intellectual, and the beauty of the sound leads you easily to conclude that you need not bother about the meaning. But words are tyrannical things, they exist for their meanings, and if you will not pay attention to these, you cannot pay attention at all. Your mind wanders. This kind of writing demands a subject that will suit it. It is surely out of place to write in the grand style of inconsiderable things. No one wrote in this manner with greater success than Sir Thomas Browne, but even he did not always escape this pitfall. In the last chapter of *Hydriotaphia* the matter, which is the destiny of man, wonderfully fits the baroque splendor of the language, and here the Norwich doctor produced a piece of prose that has never been surpassed in our literature; but when he describes the finding of his urns in the same splendid manner the effect (at least to my taste) is less happy.

But if richness needs gifts with which everyone is not endowed, simplicity by no means comes by nature. To achieve it needs rigid discipline. So far as I know ours is the only language in which it has been found necessary to give a name to the piece of prose which is described as the purple patch; it would not have been necessary to do so unless it were characteristic. English prose is elaborate rather than

Writing Prose

simple. It was not always so. Nothing could be more racy, straightforward and alive than the prose of Shakespeare; but it must be remembered that this was dialogue written to be spoken. We do not know how he would have written if like Corneille he had composed prefaces to his plays. It may be that they would have been as euphuistic as the letters of Queen Elizabeth. But earlier prose, the prose of Sir Thomas More, for instance, is neither ponderous, flowery nor oratorical. It smacks of the English soil. To my mind King James's Bible has been a very harmful influence on English prose. I am not so stupid as to deny its great beauty. It is majestical. But the Bible is an oriental book. Its alien imagery has nothing to do with us. Those hyperboles, those luscious metaphors, are foreign to our genius. I cannot but think that not the least of the misfortunes that the Secession from Rome brought upon the spiritual life of our country is that this work for so long a period became the daily, and with many the only, reading of our people. Those rhythms, that powerful vocabulary, that grandiloquence, became part and parcel of the national sensibility. The plain, honest English speech was overwhelmed with ornament. Blunt Englishmen twisted their tongues to speak like Hebrew prophets. There was evidently something in the English temper to which this was congenial, perhaps a native lack of precision in thought, perhaps a naive delight in fine words for their own sake, an innate eccentricity and love of embroidery, I do not know; but the fact remains that ever since, English prose has had to struggle against the tendency to luxuriance. When from time to time the spirit of the language has reasserted itself, as it did with Dryden and the writers of Queen Anne, it was only to be submerged once more by the pomposities of Gibbon and Dr. Johnson. When English prose recovered simplicity with Hazlitt, the Shelley of the letters, and Charles Lamb at his best, it lost it again with De Quincey, Carlyle, Meredith, and Walter Pater. It is obvious that the grand style is more striking than the plain. Indeed many people think that a style that does not attract notice is not style. They will admire Walter Pater's, but will read an essay by Matthew Arnold without giving a moment's attention to the elegance, distinction and sobriety with which he set down what he had to say.

The dictum that the style is the man is well known. It is one of those aphorisms that say too much to mean a great deal. Where is the man in Goethe, in his birdlike lyrics or in his clumsy prose? And Hazlitt? But I suppose that if a man has a confused mind he will write in a confused way, if his temper is capricious his prose will be fantastical, and if he has a quick, darting intelligence that is reminded by the matter in hand of a hundred things, he will, unless he has great self-control, load his pages with metaphor and simile. There is a great difference between the magniloquence of the Jacobean writers, who were intoxicated with the new wealth that had lately been brought into the language, and the turgidity of Gibbon and Dr. Johnson, who were the victims of bad theories. I can read every word that Dr. Johnson wrote with delight, for he had good sense, charm and wit. No one could have written better if he had not willfully set himself to write in the grand style. He knew good English when he saw it. No critic has praised Dryden's prose more aptly. He said of him that he appeared to have no art other than that of expressing with clearness what he thought with vigor. And one of his *Lives* he finished with the words: "Whoever wishes to attain an English style, familiar but not coarse, and elegant but not ostentatious, must give his days and nights to the volumes of Addison." But when he himself sat down to write, it was with a very different aim. He mistook the orotund for the dignified. He had not the good breeding to see that simplicity and naturalness are the truest marks of distinction.

Whether you ascribe importance to euphony, the last of the three characteristics that I mentioned, must depend on the sensitiveness of your ear. A great many readers, and many admirable writers, are devoid of this quality. Poets as we know have always made a great use of alliteration. They are persuaded that the repetition of a sound gives an effect of beauty. I do not think it does so in prose. It seems to me that in prose alliteration should be used only for a special reason; when used by accident it falls on the ear very disagreeably. But its accidental use is so common that one can only suppose that the sound of it is not universally offensive. Many writers without distress will put two rhyming words together, join a monstrous long adjective to a monstrous long noun, or between the end of one word and the beginning of another have a conjunction of consonants that almost breaks your jaw. These are trivial and obvious instances. I mention them only to prove that if careful writers can do such things, it is only because they have no ear. Words have weight, sound, and appearance; it is only by considering these that you can write a sentence that is good to look at and good to listen to.

If you could write lucidly, simply, euphoniously and yet with liveliness you would write perfectly: you would write like Voltaire. And yet we know how fatal the pursuit of liveliness may be: it may result in the tiresome acrobatics of Meredith. Macaulay and Carlyle were in their different ways arresting; but at the heavy cost of naturalness. Their flashy effects distract the mind. They destroy their persuasiveness; you would not believe a man was very intent on plowing a furrow if he carried a hoop with him and jumped through it at every other step. A good style should show no sign of effort. What is written should seem a happy accident. I think no one in France now writes more admirably than Colette, and such is the ease of her expression that you cannot bring yourself to believe that she takes any trouble over it. I am told that there are pianists who have a natural technique so that they can play in a manner that most executants can achieve only as the result of unremitting toil, and I am willing to believe that there are writers who are equally fortunate. Among them I was much inclined to place Colette. I asked her. I was exceedingly surprised to hear that she wrote everything over and over again. She told me that she would often spend a whole morning working upon a single page. But it does not matter how one gets the effect of ease. For my part, if I get it at all, it is only by strenuous effort. Nature seldom provides me with the word, the turn of phrase, that is appropriate without being far-fetched or commonplace.

I have read that Anatole France tried to use only the constructions and the vocabulary of the writers of the seventeenth century whom he so greatly admired. I do not know if it is true. If so, it may explain why there is some lack of vitality in his beautiful and simple French. But simplicity is false when you do not say a thing that you should say because you cannot say it in a certain way. One should write in the manner of one's period. The language is alive and constantly changing; to try to write like the authors of a distant past can only give rise to artificiality. I should not hesitate to use the common phrases of the day, knowing that their vogue was ephemeral, or slang, though aware that in ten years it might be incomprehensible, if they gave vividness and actuality. If the style has a classical form it can support the discreet use of a phraseology that has only a local and temporary aptness. I would sooner a writer were vulgar than mincing; for life is vulgar, and it is life he seeks.

I think that we English authors have much to learn from our fellow authors in America. For American writing has escaped the tyranny of King James's Bible and American writers have been less affected by the old masters whose mode of writing is part of our culture. They have formed their style, unconsciously perhaps, more directly from the living speech that surrounds them; and at its best it has a directness, a vitality, and a drive that give our more urbane manner an air of languor. It has been an advantage to American writers, many of whom at one time or another have been reporters, that their journalism has been written in a more trenchant, nervous, graphic English than ours. For we read the newspaper as our ancestors read the Bible. Not without profit either; for the newspaper, especially when it is of the popular sort, offers us a part of experience that we writers cannot afford to miss. It is raw material straight from the knacker's yard, and we are stupid if we turn up our noses because it smells of blood and sweat. We cannot, however willingly we would, escape the influence of this workaday prose. But the journalism of a period has very much the same style; it might all have been written by the same hand; it is impersonal. It is well to counteract its effect by reading of another kind. One can do this only by keeping constantly in touch with the writing of an age not too remote from one's own. So can one have a standard by which to test one's own style and an ideal which in one's modern way one can aim at. For my part the two writers I have found most useful to study for this purpose are Hazlitt and Cardinal Newman. I would try to imitate neither. Hazlitt can be unduly rhetorical; and sometimes his decoration is as fussy as Victorian Gothic. Newman can be a trifle flowery. But at their best both are admirable. Time has little touched their style; it is almost contemporary. Hazlitt is vivid, bracing, and energetic; he has strength and liveliness. You feel the man in his phrases, not the mean, querulous, disagreeable man that he appeared to the world that knew him, but the man within of his own ideal vision. (And the man within us is as true in reality as the man, pitiful and halting, of our outward seeming.) Newman had an exquisite grace, music, playful sometimes and sometimes grave, a woodland beauty of phrase, dignity and mellowness. Both wrote with extreme lucidity. Neither is quite as simple as the purest taste demands. Here I think Matthew Arnold excels them. Both had a wonderful balance of phrase and both knew how to write sentences pleasing to the eye. Both had an ear of extreme sensitiveness.

If anyone could combine their merits in the manner of writing of the present day, he would write as well as it is possible for anyone to write.

How Writing Is Written

Language most shows a man: Speak, that I may see thee. It springs out of the most retired and inmost parts of us, and is the image of the parent of it, the mind. No glass renders a man's form or likeness so true as his speech. Nay, it is likened to a man; and as we consider feature and composition in a man, so words in language; in the greatness, aptness, sound, structure, and harmony of it.

—Ben Jonson in *Timber, or Discoveries Made Upon Men and Matter*

Preface to NIGGER OF THE NARCISSUS
by JOSEPH CONRAD

A WORK that aspires, however humbly, to the condition of art should carry its justification in every line. And art itself may be defined as a single-minded attempt to render the highest kind of justice to the visible universe, by bringing to light the truth, manifold and one, underlying its every aspect. It is an attempt to find in its forms, in its colors, in its light, in its shadows, in the aspects of matter and in the facts of life what of each is fundamental, what is enduring and essential—their one illuminating and convincing quality —the very truth of their existence. The artist, then, like the thinker or the scientist, seeks the truth and makes his appeal. Impressed by the aspect of the world the thinker plunges into ideas, the scientist into facts—whence, presently, emerging they make their appeal to those qualities of our being that fit us best for the hazardous enterprise of living. They speak authoritatively to our common-sense, to our intelligence, to our desire of peace or to our desire of unrest; not seldom to our prejudices, sometimes to our fears, often to our egoism—but always to our credulity. And their words are heard with reverence, for their concern is with weighty matters: with the cultivation of our minds and the proper care of our bodies, with the attainment of our ambitions, with the perfection of the means and the glorification of our precious aims.

It is otherwise with the artist.

Confronted by the same enigmatical spectacle the artist descends within himself, and in that lonely region of stress and strife, if he be deserving and fortunate, he finds the terms of his appeal. His appeal is made to our less obvious capacities: to that part of our nature which, because of the warlike conditions of existence, is necessarily kept out of sight within the more resisting and hard qualities—like the vulnerable body within a steel armor. His appeal is less loud, more profound, less distinct, more stirring—and sooner forgotten. Yet its effect endures forever. The changing wisdom of successive generations

From: *Nigger of the Narcissus*, by Joseph Conrad, copyright 1914 by Doubleday and Company, Inc.

discards ideas, questions facts, demolishes theories. But the artist appeals to that part of our being which is not dependent on wisdom; to that in us which is a gift and not an acquisition—and, therefore, more permanently enduring. He speaks to our capacity for delight and wonder, to the sense of mystery surrounding our lives; to our sense of pity, and beauty, and pain; to the latent feeling of fellowship with all creation—and to the subtle but invincible conviction of solidarity that knits together the loneliness of innumerable hearts, to the solidarity in dreams, in joy, in sorrow, in aspirations, in illusions, in hope, in fear, which binds men to each other, which binds together all humanity—the dead to the living and the living to the unborn.

It is only some such train of thought, or rather of feeling, that can in a measure explain the aim of the attempt, made in the tale which follows, to present an unrestful episode in the obscure lives of a few individuals out of all the disregarded multitude of the bewildered, the simple and the voiceless. For, if any part of truth dwells in the belief confessed above, it becomes evident that there is not a place of splendor or a dark corner of the earth that does not deserve, if only a passing glance of wonder and pity. The motive then, may be held to justify the matter of the work; but this preface, which is simply an avowal of endeavor, cannot end here —for the avowal is not yet complete.

Fiction—if it at all aspires to be art— appeals to temperament. And in truth it must be, like painting, like music, like all art, the appeal of one temperament to all the other innumerable temperaments whose subtle and resistless power endows passing events with their true meaning, and creates the moral, the emotional atmosphere of the place and time. Such an appeal to be effective must be an impression conveyed through the senses; and, in fact, it cannot be made in any other way, because temperament, whether individual or collective, is not amenable to persuasion. All art, therefore, appeals primarily to the senses, and the artistic aim when expressing itself in written words must also make its appeal through the senses, if its high desire is to reach the secret spring of responsive emotions. It must strenuously aspire to the plasticity of sculpture, to the color of painting, and to the magic suggestiveness of music—which is the art of arts. And it is only through complete, unswerving devotion to the perfect blending of form and substance; it is only through an unremitting never-discouraged care for the shape and ring of sentences that an approach can be made to plasticity, to color, and that the light of magic suggestiveness may be brought to play for an evanescent instant over the commonplace surface of words: of the old, old words, worn thin, defaced by ages of careless usage.

The sincere endeavor to accomplish that creative task, to go as far on that road as his strength will carry him, to go undeterred by faltering, weariness or reproach, is the only valid justification for the worker in prose. And if his conscience is clear, his answer to those who in the fullness of a wisdom which looks for immediate profit, demand specifically to be edified, consoled, amused; who demand to be promptly improved, or encouraged, or frightened, or shocked, or charmed, must run thus:—My task which I am trying to achieve is, by the power of the written word to make you hear, to make you feel —it is, before all, to make you *see*. That —and no more, and it is everything. If I succeed, you shall find there according to your deserts: encouragement, consolation, fear, charm—all you demand—and, perhaps, also that glimpse of truth for which you have forgotten to ask.

To snatch in a moment of courage, from the remorseless rush of time, a passing phase of life, is only the beginning of the task. The task approached in tenderness and faith is to hold up unquestioningly, without choice and without fear, the rescued fragment before all eyes in the light of a sincere mood. It is to show its vibration, its color, its form; and through its movement, its form, and its color, reveal the substance of its truth—disclose its inspiring secret: the stress and passion within the core of each convincing moment. In a single-minded attempt of that kind, if one be deserving and fortunate, one may perchance attain to such clearness of sincerity that at last the presented vision of regret or pity, of terror or birth, shall awaken in the hearts of the beholders that feeling of unavoidable solidarity; of the solidarity in mysterious origin, in toil, in joy, in hope, in uncertain fate, which binds men to each other and all mankind to the visible world.

It is evident that he who, rightly or wrongly, holds by the convictions expressed above cannot be faithful to any one of the temporary formulas of his craft. The enduring part of them—the truth which each only imperfectly veils—should abide with him as the most precious of his possessions, but they all: Realism, Romanticism, Naturalism, even the unofficial sentimentalism (which like the poor, is exceedingly difficult to get rid of), all these gods must, after a short period of fellowship, abandon him—even on the very threshold of the temple—to the stammerings of his conscience and to the outspoken consciousness of the difficulties of his work. In that uneasy solitude the supreme cry of Art for Art itself, loses the exciting ring of its apparent immorality. It sounds far off. It has ceased to be a cry, and is heard only as a whisper, often incomprehensible, but at times and faintly encouraging.

Sometimes, stretched at ease in the shade of a roadside tree, we watch the motions of a laborer in a distant field, and after a time, begin to wonder languidly as to what the fellow may be at. We watch the movements of his body, the waving of his arms, we see him bend down, stand up, hesitate, begin again. It may add to the charm of an idle hour to be told the purpose of his exertions. If we know he is trying to lift a stone, to dig a ditch, to uproot a stump, we look with a more real interest at his efforts; we are disposed to condone the jar of his agitation upon the restfulness of the landscape; and even, if in a brotherly frame of mind, we may bring ourselves to forgive his failure. We understood his object, and, after all, the fellow has tried, and perhaps he had not the strength—and perhaps he had not the knowledge. We forgive, go on our way—and forget.

And so it is with the workman of art. Art is long and life is short, and success is very far off. And thus, doubtful of strength to travel so far, we talk a little about the aim—the aim of art, which, like life itself, is inspiring, difficult—obscured by mists. It is not in the clear logic of a triumphant conclusion; it is not in the unveiling of one of those heartless secrets which are called the Laws of Nature. It is not less great, but only more difficult.

To arrest, for the space of a breath, the hands busy about the work of the earth, and compel men entranced by the sight of distant goals to glance for a moment at the surrounding vision of form and color, of sunshine and shadows; to make them pause for a look, for a sigh, for a smile—such is the aim, difficult and evanescent, and reserved only for a few to achieve. But sometimes, by the deserving and the fortunate, even that task is accomplished. And when it is accomplished—behold!—all the truth of life is there: a moment of vision, a sigh, a smile—and the return to an eternal rest.

THE OBSCURITY OF THE POET
by RANDALL JARRELL

WHEN I WAS ASKED to talk about the Obscurity of the Modern Poet I was delighted, for I have suffered from this obscurity all my life. But then I realized that I was being asked to talk not about the fact that people don't read poetry, but about the fact that most of them wouldn't understand it if they did: about the difficulty, not the neglect, of contemporary poetry. And yet it is not just modern poetry, but poetry, that is today obscure. *Paradise Lost* is what it was; but the ordinary reader no longer makes the mistake of trying to read it—instead he glances at it, weighs it in his hand, shudders, and suddenly, his eyes shining, puts it on his list of the ten dullest books he has ever read, along with *Moby Dick, War and Peace, Faust,* and Boswell's *Life of Johnson.* But I am doing this ordinary reader an injustice: it was not the Public, nodding over its lunch-pail, but the educated reader, the reader the universities have trained, who a few weeks ago, to the Public's sympathetic delight, put together this list of the world's dullest books.

Since most people know about the modern poet only that he is *obscure*—i.e., that he is *difficult,* i.e., that he is *neglected*—they naturally make a causal connection between the two meanings of the word, and decide that he is unread because he is difficult. Some of the time this is true; some of the time the reverse is true: the poet seems difficult *because* he is not read, *because* the reader is not accustomed to reading his or any other poetry. But most of the time neither is a cause—both are no more than effects of that long-continued, world-overturning cultural and social revolution (seen at its most advanced stage here in the United States) which has made the poet difficult and the public unused to any poetry exactly as it has made poet and public divorce their wives, stay away from church, dislike bull-baiting, free the slaves, get insulin shots for diabetes, or do a hundred thousand other things, some bad, some good, and some indifferent. It is superficial to extract two parts from this world-high whole, and to say of them: "This one, here, is the cause of that one, there; and that's all there is to it."

If we were in the habit of reading poets their obscurity would not matter; and, once we are out of the habit, their clarity does not help. Matthew Arnold said, with plaintive respect, that there was hardly a sentence in *Lear* that he hadn't needed to read two or three times; and three other appreciable Victorian minds, Beetle, Stalky, and McTurk, were even

Reprinted from *Poetry and the Age* by Randall Jarrell, by permission of Alfred A. Knopf, Inc. Copyright 1951, 1953, by Randall Jarrell.

[113]

harder on it. They are in their study; Stalky reads:

Never any.

It pleased the king his master, very late,
To strike at me, upon his misconstruction,
When he, conjunct, and flattering in his displeasure,
Tripped me behind: being down, insulted, railed,
And put upon him such a deal of man
That worthy'd him, got praises of the King
For him attempting who was self-subdued;
And, in the fleshment of this dread exploit,
Drew me on here.

Stalky says: "Now, then, my impassioned bard, *construez!* That's Shakespeare"; and Beetle answers, "at the end of a blank half minute": "Give it up! He's drunk." If schoolboys were forced to read "The Phoenix and the Turtle," what *would* Beetle have said of these two stanzas?

Property was thus appalled
That the self was not the same;
Single nature's double name
Neither two nor one was called,

Reason, in itself confounded,
Saw division grow together;
To themselves yet either-neither,
Simple were so well compounded. . . .

You and I can afford to look at Stalky and Company, at Arnold, with dignified superiority; we know what those passages mean; we know that Shakespeare is never *obscure*, as if he were some modernist poet gleefully pasting puzzles together in his garret. Yet when we look at a variorum Shakespeare—with its line or two of text at the top of the page, its forty or fifty lines of wild surmise and quarrelsome conjecture at the bottom—we are troubled. When the Alexandrian poet Lycophron refers—and he is rarely so simple—to the *centipede, fair-faced, storkhued daughters of Phalacra,* and they turn out to be boats, one ascribes this to Alexandrian decadence; but then one remembers that Welsh and Irish and Norse poets, the poets of a hundred barbarous cultures, loved nothing so much as referring to the very dishes on the table by elaborate descriptive epithets—periphrases, kennings—which their hearers had to be specially educated to understand. (Loved nothing so much, that is, except riddles.) And just consider the amount of classical allusions that those polite readers, our ancestors, were expected to recognize—and did recognize. If I recite to you, *The brotherless Heliades/ Melt in such amber tears as these,* many of you will think, *Beautiful;* a good many will think, *Marvell;* but how many of you will know to whom Marvell is referring?

Yet the people of the past were not repelled by this obscurity (seemed, often, foolishly to treasure it); nor are those peoples of the present who are not so far removed from the past as we: who have preserved, along with the castles, the injustice, and the social discrimination of the past, a remnant of its passion for reading poetry. It is hard to be much more difficult than Mallarmé; yet when I went from bookstore to bookstore in Paris, hunting for one copy of Corbière, I began to feel a sort of mocking frustration at the poems by Mallarmé, letters by Mallarmé, letters to Mallarmé, biographies of, essays on, and homage to Mallarmé with which the shelves of those bookstores tantalized me. For how long now the French poet has been writing as if the French public did not exist—as if it were, at best, a swineherd dreaming of that faraway princess the poet; yet it looks at him with traditional awe, and reads in dozens of literary newspapers, scores of literary magazines, the details of his life, opinions, temperament, and appearance. And in the Germanic countries people still glance at one with attentive respect, as if they thought that one might at any moment be about to write a poem; I shall never forget hearing a German say, in an objective considering tone, as if I were an illustration in a book called *Silver Poets of the Americas:* "You know, he looks a little like Rilke." In several South American countries poetry has kept most of the popularity and respect it formerly enjoyed; in one country, I believe Venezuela, the president, the ambassador whom he is sending to Paris, and the waiter who serves their coffee will four out of five times be poets. "What sort of poetry do *these* poets write?" is a question of frightening moment for us poor Northern poets; if the answer is, "Nice simple stuff," we shall need to question half our ways. But these poets, these truly popular poets, seem to have taken as models for their verse neither the poems of Homer, of Shakespeare, nor of Racine, but those of Pablo Picasso: they are all surrealists.

Is Clarity the handmaiden of Popularity, as everybody automatically assumes? how much does it help to be immediately plain? In England today few poets are as popular as Dylan Thomas—his magical poems have corrupted a whole generation of English poets; yet he is surely one of the most obscure poets who ever lived. Or to take an opposite example: the poems of the students of Yvor Winters are quite as easy to understand as those which Longfellow used to read during the Children's Hour; yet they are about as popular as those other poems (of their own composition) which *grave Alice, and laughing Allegra, and Edith with golden hair* used to read to Longfellow during the Poet's Hour. If Dylan Thomas is obscurely famous, such poets as these are clearly unknown.

When someone says to me something I am not accustomed to hearing, or do not wish to hear, I say to him: *I do not understand you;* and we respond in just this way to poets. When critics first read Wordsworth's poetry they felt that it was silly, but many of them *said,* with Byron, that "he who understands it would be able/To add a story to the Tower of Babel." A few years before, a great critic praising the work of that plainest of poets, John Dryden, had remarked that he "delighted to tread on the brink where sense and nonsense mingle." Dryden himself had found Shakespeare's phrases "scarcely intelligible; and of those which we understand some are ungrammatical, others coarse; and his whole style is so pestered with figurative expressions that it is as affected as it is coarse." The reviewers of "The Love Song of J. Alfred Prufrock," even those who admired it most, found it almost impossible to understand; that it was hopelessly obscure seemed to them self-evident. Today, when college girls find it exactly as easy, exactly as hard, as "The Bishop Orders his Tomb at St. Praxed's," one is able to understand these critics' despairing or denunciatory misunderstanding only by remembering that the first generation of critics spoke of Browning's poem in just the terms that were later applied to Eliot's. How long it takes the world to catch up! Yet it really never "catches up," but is simply replaced by another world that does not need to catch up; so that when the old say to us, "What shall I do to understand Auden (or Dylan Thomas, or whoever the latest poet is)?" we can only reply: "You must be born again." An old gentleman at a party, talking to me about a poem we both admired, the *Rubaiyat*, was delighted to find that our tastes agreed so well, and asked me what modern poet I like best. Rather cutting my coat to his cloth, I answered: "Robert Frost." He looked at me with surprise, and said with gentle but undisguised finality: "I'm afraid he is a little after my time." This happened in 1950; yet surely in 1850 some old gentleman, fond of Gray and Cowper and Crabbe, must have uttered to the young Matthew Arnold the same words, but this time with reference to the poetry of William Wordsworth.

We cannot even be sure what people will find obscure; when I taught at Salzburg I found that my European students did not find "The Waste Land" half as hard as Frost's poetry, since one went with, and the other against, all their own cultural presuppositions; I had not simply to explain "Home-Burial" to them, I had to persuade them that it was a poem. And another example occurs to me: that of Robert Hillyer. In a review of *The Death of Captain Nemo* that I read, the reviewer's first complaint was that the poem is obscure. I felt as if I had seen Senator McCarthy denounced as an agent of the Kremlin; for how could Mr. Hillyer be obscure?

That the poet, the modern poet, is, understandably enough, for all sorts of good reasons, more obscure than even he has any imaginable right to be—this is one of those great elementary (or, as people say nowadays, *elemental*) attitudes about which it is hard to write anything that is not sensible and gloomily commonplace; one might as well talk on faith and works, on heredity and environment, or on that old question: why give the poor bath-tubs when they only use them to put coal in? Anyone knows enough to reply to this question: "They don't; and, even if they did, *that's* not the reason you don't want to help pay for the tubs." Similarly, when someone says, "I don't read modern poetry because it's all stuff that nobody on earth can understand," I know enough to be able to answer, though not aloud: "It isn't; and, even if it were, *that's* not the reason you don't read it." Any American poet under a certain age, a fairly advanced age—the age, one is tempted to say, of Bernard Shaw—has inherited a situation in which no one looks at him and in which, consequently, everyone complains that he is invisible: for that corner into which no one looks is always dark. And people who have inherited the custom of not reading poets justify it by referring to the obscurity of the poems they have never read —since most people decide that poets are obscure very much as legislators decide that books are pornographic: by glancing at a few fragments someone has strung together to disgust them. When a person says accusingly that he can't understand Eliot, his tone implies that most of his happiest hours are spent at the fireside among worn copies of the *Agamemnon*, *Phèdre*, and the Symbolic Books of William Blake; and it is melancholy to find, as one commonly will, that for months at a time he can be found pushing eagerly through the pages of *Gone with the Wind* or *Forever Amber*, where *with head, hands, wings, or feet* this poor fiend *pursues his way, and swims, or sinks, or wades, or creeps, or flies;* that all his happiest memories of Shakespeare seem to come from a high school production of *As You Like It* in which he played the wrestler Charles; and that he has, by some obscure process of free association, combined James Russell, Amy, and Robert Lowell into one majestic whole: a bearded cigar-smoking ambassador to the Vatican who, after accompanying Theodore Roosevelt on his first African expedition, came home to dictate on his deathbed the "Concord Hymn." Many a man, because Ezra Pound is too obscure for him, has shut forever the pages of *Paradise Lost;* or so one would gather, from the theory and practice such people combine.

The general public [in this lecture I hardly speak of the happy few, who grow fewer and unhappier day by day] has set up a criterion of its own, one by which every form of contemporary art is condemned. This criterion is, in the case of music, melody; in the case of painting, representation; in the case of poetry, clarity. In each case one simple aspect is made the test of a complicated whole, becomes a sort of loyalty oath for the work of art. Although judging by this method is almost as irrelevant as having the artist pronounce *shibboleth*, or swear that he is not a Know-Nothing, a Locofocoist, or a Bull Moose, it is as attractive, in exactly the same way, to the public that judges: instead of having to perceive, to enter, and to interpret those new worlds which new works of art are, the public can notice at a glance whether or not these pay lip-service to its own "principles," and can then praise or blame them accordingly. Most of the music of earlier centuries, of other continents, has nothing the public can consider a satisfactory melody; the tourist looking through the galleries of Europe very soon discovers that most of the Old Masters were not, representationally speaking, half so good as the painters who illustrate *Collier's Magazine;* how difficult and dull the inexperienced reader would find most of the great poetry of the past, if he could ever be induced to read it! Yet it is always in the name of the easy past that he condemns the difficult present.

Anyone who has spent much time finding out what people do when they read a poem, what poems actually mean for them, will have discovered that a surprising part of the difficulty they have comes from their almost systematic unreceptiveness, their queer unwillingness to pay attention even to the reference of pronouns, the meaning of the punctuation, which subject goes with which verb, and so on; "after all," they seem to feel, "I'm not reading *prose.*" You need to read good poetry with an attitude that is a mixture of sharp intelligence and of willing emotional empathy, at once penetrating and generous: as if you were listening to *The Marriage of Figaro*, not as if you were listening to *Tristan* or to Samuel Butler's Handelian oratorios; to read poetry—as so many readers do—like Mortimer Snerd pretending to be Dr. Johnson, or like Uncle Tom recollecting Eva, is hardly to read poetry at all. When you begin to read a poem you are entering a foreign country whose laws and language and life are a kind of translation of your own;

but to accept it because its stews taste exactly like your old mother's hash, or to reject it because the owl-headed goddess of wisdom in its temple is fatter than the Statue of Liberty, is an equal mark of that want of imagination, that inaccessibility to experience, of which each of us who dies a natural death will die.

That the poetry of the first half of this century often *was* too difficult—just as the poetry of the eighteenth century *was* full of antitheses, that of the metaphysicals full of conceits, that of the Elizabethan dramatists full of rant and quibbles—is a truism that it would be absurd to deny. How our poetry got this way—how romanticism was purified and exaggerated and "corrected" into modernism; how poets carried all possible tendencies to their limits, with more than scientific zeal; how the dramatic monologue, which once had depended for its effect upon being a departure from the norm of poetry, now became in one form or another the norm; how poet and public stared at each other with righteous indignation, till the poet said, "Since you won't read me, I'll make sure you can't"—is one of the most complicated and interesting of stories. But modernism was not "that lion's den from which no tracks return," but only a sort of canvas whale from which Jonah after Jonah, throughout the late '20's and early '30's, made a penitent return, back to rhyme and metre and plain broad Statement; how many young poets today are, if nothing else, plain! Yet how little posterity—if I may speak of that imaginary point where the poet and the public intersect—will care about all the tendencies of our age, all those good or bad intentions with which ordinary books are paved; and how much it will care for those few poems which, regardless of intention, manage at once to sum up, to repudiate, and to transcend both the age they appear in and the minds they are produced by. One judges an age, just as one judges a poet, by its best poems—after all, most of the others have disappeared; when posterity hears that our poems are obscure, it will smile indifferently—just as we do when we are told that the Victorians were sentimental, the Romantics extravagant, the Augustans conventional, the metaphysicals conceited, and the Elizabethans bombastic—and go back to its (and our) reading: to Hardy's "During Wind and Rain," to Wordsworth's story of the woman Margaret, to Pope's "Epistle to Dr. Arbuthnot," to Marvell's "Horatian Ode," to Shakespeare's *Antony and Cleopatra,* to Eliot's *Four Quartets,* and to all the rest of those ageless products of an age.

In this age, certainly, poetry persists under many disadvantages. Just as it has been cut off from most of the people who in another age would have read it, so it has been cut off from most of the people who in another age would have written it. Today poems, good poems, are written almost exclusively by "born poets." We have lost for good the poems that would have been written by the modern equivalents of Henry VIII or Bishop King or Samuel Johnson; born novelists, born theologians, born princes; minds with less of an innate interest in words and more of one in the world which produces words. We are accustomed to think of the poet, when we think of him at all, as someone Apart; yet was there—as so many poets and readers of poetry seem to think—*was* there in the Garden of Eden, along with Adam and Eve and the animals, a

The Obscurity of the Poet

Poet, the ultimate ancestor of Robert P. Tristram Coffin? . . . When I last read poems in New York City, a lady who, except for bangs, a magenta jersey blouse, and the expression of Palamède de Charlus, was indistinguishable from any other New Yorker, exclaimed to me about a poet whom the years have fattened for the slaughter: "He read like a young god." I felt that the next poet was going to be told that I read like the young Joaquin Miller; for this lady was less interested in those wonderful things poems than in those other things, poets—not realizing that it is their subordination to the poems they write that makes them admirable. She seemed to me someone who, because he has inherited a pearl necklace, can never again look at an oyster without a shudder of awe. And this reminds one that, today, many of the readers a poet would value most have hardly learned to read any poetry; and many of those who regularly read his poems have values so different from his that he is troubled by their praise, and vexed but reassured by their blame.

Tomorrow morning some poet may, like Byron, wake up to find himself famous—for having written a novel, for having killed his wife; it will not be for having written a poem. That is still logically, but no longer socially, possible. Let me illustrate with a story. I once met on a boat, travelling to Europe with his wife and daughter, a man with whom I played ping-pong. Having learned from a friend that I wrote poetry, he asked one day with uninterested politeness, "Who are the American poets you like best?" I said, "Oh, T. S. Eliot, Robert Frost." Then this man—this father who every night danced with his daughter with the well-taught, dated, decorous attractiveness of the hero of an old *Saturday Evening Post* serial by E. Phillips Oppenheim; who had had the best professional in Los Angeles teach his wife and daughter the tennis strokes he himself talked of with wearying authority; who never in his life had gone through a doorway before anyone over the age of seven—this well-dressed, well-mannered, travelled, urbane, educated gentleman said placidly: "I don't believe I've heard of them." For so far as literature, the arts, philosophy, and science were concerned, he might better have been the policeman on the corner. But he was perfectly correct in thinking—not that he had ever thought about it—that a knowledge of these things is not an essential requirement of the society of which he is a part. We belong to a culture whose old hierarchy of values—which demanded that a girl read Pope just as it demanded that she go to church and play the pianoforte—has virtually disappeared; a culture in which the great artist or scientist, in the relatively infrequent cases in which he has become widely known, has the status of Betty Grable or of the columnist who writes that, the night before, he met both these "celebrities" at the Stork Club.

When, a hundred and fifty years ago, a man had made his fortune, he found it necessary to provide himself with lace, carriages, servants, a wife of good family, a ballerina, a fencing master, a dancing master, a chaplain, a teacher of French, a string quartet perhaps, the editions of Pope and Steele and Addison through which he worked a laborious way on unoccupied evenings: there was so much for him to learn to *do,* there in his new station in life, that he must often have thought with nostalgia of the days in which all that he had to do was make his fortune. We have changed most of that: in our day the rich are expected not to do but to be; and those ties, tenuous, ambiguous, and immemorial, which bound to the Power of a state its Wisdom and its Grace, have at last been severed.

When Mill and Marx looked at a handful of workingmen making their slow firm way through the pages of Shelley or Herbert Spencer or *The Origin of Species,* they thought with confident longing, just as Jefferson and Lincoln had, of the days when every man would be literate, when an actual democracy would make its choices with as much wisdom as any imaginary state where the philosopher is king; and no gleam of prophetic insight came to show them those workingmen, two million strong, making their easy and pleasant way through the pages of the New York *Daily News.* The very speeches in which Jefferson and Lincoln spoke of their hope for the future are incomprehensible to most of the voters of that future, since the vocabulary and syntax of the speeches are more difficult—more obscure—than anything the voters have read or heard. For when you defeat me in an election simply because you were, as I was not, born and bred in a log cabin, it is only a question of time until you are beaten by someone whom the pigs brought up out in the yard. The truth that all men are politically equal, the recognition of the injustice of fictitious differences, becomes a belief in the fictitiousness of differences, a conviction that it is reaction or snobbishness or Fascism to believe that any individual differences of real importance can exist. We dislike having to believe in what Goethe called inborn or innate merits; yet—as a later writer more or less says—many waiters are born with the taste of duchesses, and most duchesses are born (and die) with the tastes of waiters: we can escape from the level of society, but not from the level of intelligence, to which we were born.

One of our universities recently made a survey of the reading habits of the American public; it decided that forty-eight percent of all Americans read, during a year, no book at all. I picture to myself that reader—non-reader, rather; one man out of every two—and I reflect, with shame: "Our poems are too hard for him." But so, too, are *Treasure Island, Peter Rabbit,* pornographic novels—any book whatsoever. The authors of the world have been engaged in a sort of conspiracy to drive this American away from books; have, in 77 million out of 160 million cases, succeeded. A sort of dream-situation often occurs to me in which I call to this imaginary figure, "Why don't you read books?"—and he always answers, after looking at me steadily for a long time: "Huh?"

If my tone is mocking, the tone of someone accustomed to helplessness, this is natural: the poet is a condemned man for whom the State will not even buy breakfast—and as someone said, "If you're going to hang me, you mustn't expect to be able to intimidate me into sparing your feelings during the execution." The poet lives in a world whose newspapers and magazines and books and motion pictures and radio stations and television stations have destroyed, in a great many people, even the capacity for understanding real poetry, real art of any kind. The man who monthly reads, with vacant relish, the carefully predigested sentences which

The Obscurity of the Poet

the *Reader's Digest* feeds to him as a mother pigeon feeds her squabs—this man *cannot* read the *Divine Comedy,* even if it should ever occur to him to try: it is too obscure. Yet one sort of clearness shows a complete contempt for the reader, just as one sort of obscurity shows a complete respect. Which patronizes and degrades the reader, the *Divine Comedy* with its four levels of meaning, or the *Reader's Digest* with its one level so low that it seems not a level but an abyss into which the reader consents to sink? The writer's real dishonesty is to give an easy paraphrase of the hard truth. Yet the average article in our magazines gives any subject whatsoever the same coat of easy, automatic, "human" interest; every year *Harper's Magazine* sounds more like *Life* and the *Saturday Evening Post*. Goethe said, "The author whom a lexicon can keep up with is worth nothing"; Somerset Maugham says that the finest compliment he ever received was a letter in which one of his readers said: "I read your novel without having to look up a single word in the dictionary." These writers, plainly, lived in different worlds.

Since the animal organism thinks, truly reasons, only when it is required to, thoughtfulness is gradually disappearing among readers; and popular writing has left nothing to the imagination for so long now that imagination too has begun to atrophy. Almost all the works of the past are beginning to seem to the ordinary reader flat and dull, because they do not supply the reader's response along with that to which he responds. Boys who have read only a few books in their lives, but a great many comic books, will tell one, so vividly that it is easy to sympathize: "I don't like books because they don't really show you things; they're too slow; you have to do all the work yourself." When, in a few years, one talks to boys who have read only a few comic books, but have looked at a great many television programs—what will *they* say?

On this subject of the obscurity of the poet, of the new world that is taking the place of the old, I have written you a poem—an obscure one. I once encountered, in a book, a house that had a formal garden, an English garden, a kitchen garden, and a cutting garden; through these gardens gentlemen walked in silk stockings, their calves padded like those of Mephistopheles; and I made that cutting garden, those padded calves, my symbols for the past. For the present and the future I had so many symbols I didn't know what to do: they came into the poem without knocking, judged it, and did not leave when they had judged; but the one that summed them all up—that had, for me, the sound of the Last Morning of Judgment—was a slogan from a wine-advertisement, one that I used to see every day in the New York subways. My poem is called "The Times Worsen":

If sixteen shadows flapping on the line
All sleek with bluing—a Last Morning's
  wash—
Whistle, "Now that was thoughty, Mrs.
  Bean,"
I tell myself, I try: A dream, a dream.
But my plaid spectacles are matt as
  gouache;
When, Sundays, I have finished all the
  funnies,
I have not finished all the funnies. Men
Walk in all day (to try me) without
  knocking—
My jurors: these just, vulgar, friendly
  shades.
The cutting garden of my grandmama,

My great-great-great-grandfather's padded calves
(Greeted, at cockcrow, with the soft small smile
Of Lilith, his first morganatic wife)
Are only a tale from E. T. W. Hoffmann.
When Art goes, what remains is Life.
The World of the Future does not work by halves:
Life is that "wine like Mother used to make—
So rich you can almost cut it with a knife."

The World of the Future! That world where vegetables are either frozen, canned, or growing in the fields; where little children, as they gaze into the television viewplate at the Babes dead under the heaped-up leaves of the Wood, ask pleadingly: "But where was their electric blanket?"; where old books, hollowed-out to hold fudge, grace every coffee-table; where cavemen in grammar school pageants, clad in pelts of raw cotton, are watched by families dressed entirely—except for the Neolite of their shoe-soles—in rayon, cellulose, and spun nylon; where, among the related radiances of a kitchen's white-enamelled electric stove, electric dish-washer, electric refrigerator, electric washing-machine, electric dryer, electric ironer, disposal unit, air conditioner, and Waring Blendor, the homemaker sits in the trim coveralls of her profession; where, above the concrete cavern that holds a General Staff, the rockets are invisible in the sky . . . Of this world I often think.

I do not know whether, at this point, any of my hearers will feel like saying to me, "But all this is Negative. What do you want us to *do* about all this?" If I have sounded certain about "all this," let me apologize: these are conclusions which I have come to slowly and reluctantly, as the world forced them on me. Would that I were one of those happy reactionaries, born with a Greek vocabulary as other children are born with birthmarks or incomes, who at the age of four refuse indignantly to waste on that "humanitarian phantasy of a sentimental liberalism, the Kindergarten," the hours they instead devote to memorizing their catechism! But I had a scientific education and a radical youth; am old-fashioned enough to believe, like Goethe, in Progress—the progress I see and the progress I wish for and do not see. So I say what I have said about the poet, the public, and their world angrily and unwillingly. If my hearers say, "But what should we do?" what else can I answer but "Nothing"? There is nothing to do different from what we already do: if poets write poems and readers read them, each as best they can—if they try to live not as soldiers or voters or intellectuals or economic men, but as human beings—they are doing all that can be done. But to expect them (by, say, reciting one-syllable poems over the radio) to bring back that Yesterday in which people stood on chairs to look at Lord Tennyson, is to believe that General Motors can bring back "the tradition of craftsmanship" by giving, as it does, prizes to Boy Scouts for their scale-models of Napoleonic coaches; to believe that the manners of the past can be restored by encouraging country-people to say *Grüss Gott* or *Howdy, stranger* to the tourists they meet along summer lanes.

Art matters not merely because it is the most magnificent ornament and the most nearly unfailing occupation of our lives, but because it is life itself. From Christ to Freud we have believed that, <u>if we know the truth, the truth will set us free</u>: art is indispensable because so much of this truth can be learned through works of art and through works of art alone—for which of us could have learned for himself what Proust and Chekhov, Hardy and Yeats and Rilke, Shakespeare and Homer learned for us? and in what other way could they have made us see the truths which they themselves saw, those differing and contradictory truths which seem nevertheless, to the mind which contains them, in some sense a single truth? And all these things, by their very nature, demand to be shared; if we are satisfied to know these things ourselves, and to look with superiority or indifference at those who do not have that knowledge, we have made a refusal that corrupts us as surely as anything can. If while most of our people (the descendants of those who, ordinarily, listened to Grimm's Tales and the ballads and the Bible; who, exceptionally, listened to Aeschylus and Shakespeare) listen not to simple or naive art, but to an elaborate and sophisticated substitute for art, an immediate and infallible synthetic as effective and terrifying as advertisements or the speeches of Hitler—if, knowing all this, we say: *Art has always been a matter of a few,* we are using a truism to hide a disaster. One of the oldest, deepest, and most nearly conclusive attractions of democracy is manifested in our feeling that through it not only material but also spiritual goods can be shared: that in a democracy bread and justice, education and art, will be accessible to everybody. If a democracy should offer its citizens a show of education, a sham art, a literacy more dangerous than their old illiteracy, then we should have to say that it is not a democracy at all, but one more variant of those "People's Democracies" which share with any true democracy little more than the name. Goethe said: <u>The only way in which we can come to terms with the great superiority of another person is love.</u> But we can also come to terms with superiority, with true Excellence, by denying that such a thing as Excellence can exist; and, in doing so, we help to destroy it and ourselves.

I was sorry to see this conference given its (quite traditional) name of The Defense of Poetry. Poetry does not need to be defended, any more than air or food needs to be defended; poetry—using the word in its widest sense, the only sense in which it is important—has been an indispensable part of any culture we know anything about. Human life without some form of poetry is not human life but animal existence. Our world today is not an impossible one for poets and poetry: poets can endure its disadvantages, and good poetry is still being written—Yeats, for instance, thought the first half of this century the greatest age of lyric poetry since the Elizabethan. But what will happen to the public—to that portion of it divorced from any real art even of the simplest kind—I do not know. Yet an analogy occurs to me.

One sees, in the shops of certain mountainous regions of Austria, bands of silver links, clasped like necklaces, which have at the front jeweled or enameled silver plates, sometimes quite large ones. These pieces of jewelry are called *goiter-bands*: they are ornaments which in the past were used to adorn a woman's diseased, enormously swollen neck. If the women who wore them could have been told that they had been made hideous by the lack of an infinitesimal proportion of iodine in the water of the mountain valley in which they lived, they would have laughed at the notion. They would have laughed even more heartily at the notion that their necks *were* hideous—and their lovers would have asked, as they looked greedily at the round flesh under the flaxen pigtails, how anyone could bear to caress the poor, thin, scrawny, chickenish necks of those other women they now and then saw, foreigners from that flatland which travellers call the world.

I have talked about the poet and his public; but who is his public, really? In a story by E. M. Forster called *The Machine Stops,* there is a conversation between a mother and her son. They are separated by half the circumference of the earth; they sit under the surface of the earth in rooms supplied with air, with food, and with warmth as automatically as everything else is supplied to these people of the far future. "Imagine," as Forster says, "a swaddled lump of flesh—a woman, about five feet high, with a face as white as a fungus." She has just refused to go to visit her son; she has no time. Her son replies:

"The air-ship barely takes two days to fly between me and you."

"I dislike air-ships."

"Why?"

"I dislike seeing the horrible brown earth, and the sea, and the stars when it is dark. I get no ideas in an air-ship."

"I do not get them anywhere else."

"What kind of ideas can the air give you?"

He paused for an instant.

"Do you not know four big stars that form an oblong, and three stars close together in the middle of the oblong, and hanging from these stars, three other stars?"

"No, I do not. I dislike the stars. But did they give you an idea? How interesting; tell me."

"I had an idea that they were like a man."

"I do not understand."

"The four big stars are the man's shoulders and his knees. The three stars in the middle are like the belts that men wore once, and the three stars hanging are like a sword."

"A sword?"

"Men carried swords about with them, to kill animals and other men."

"It does not strike me as a very good idea, but it is certainly original."

As long as these stars remain in this shape; as long as there is a man left to look at them and to discover that they are the being Orion: for at least this long the poet will have his public. And when this man too is gone, and neither the poems, the poet, nor the public exist any longer—and this possibility can no longer seem to us as strange as it would once have seemed—there is surely some order of the world, some level of being, at which they still subsist: an order in which the lost plays of Aeschylus are no different from those that have been preserved, an order in which the past, the present, and the future have in some sense the same reality. Or so—whether we think so or not—so we all feel. People always ask: *For whom does the poet write?* He needs only to answer, *For whom do you do good? Are you kind to your daughter because in the end someone will pay you for being?* . . . The poet writes his poem for its own sake, for the sake of that order of things in which the poem takes the place that has awaited it.

But this has been said, better than it is ever again likely to be said, by the greatest of the writers of this century, Marcel Proust; and I should like to finish this lecture by quoting his sentences:

"All that we can say is that everything is arranged in this life as though we entered it carrying the burden of obligations contracted in a former life; there is no reason inherent in the conditions of life on this earth that can make us consider ourselves obliged to do good, to be fastidious, to be polite even, nor make the talented artist consider himself obliged to begin over again a score of times a piece of work the admiration aroused by which will matter little to his body devoured by worms, like the patch of yellow wall painted with so much knowledge and skill by an artist who must for ever remain unknown and is barely identified under the name Vermeer. All these obligations which have not their sanction in our present life seem to belong to a different world, founded upon kindness, scrupulosity, self-sacrifice, a world entirely different from this, which we leave in order to be born into this world, before perhaps returning to the other to live once again beneath the sway of those unknown laws which we have obeyed because we bore their precepts in our hearts, knowing not whose hand had traced them there—those laws to which every profound work of the intellect brings us nearer and which are invisible only—and still!—to fools."

from ON STYLE
by S. T. COLERIDGE

In order to form a good style, the primary rule and condition is, not to attempt to express ourselves in language before we thoroughly know our own meaning:—when a man perfectly understands himself, appropriate diction will generally be at his command either in writing or speaking. In such cases the thoughts and the words are associated. In the next place preciseness in the use of terms is required, and the test is whether you can translate the phrase adequately into simpler terms, regard being had to the feeling of the whole passage. Try this upon Shakespeare, or Milton, and see if you can substitute other simpler words in any given passage without a violation of the meaning or tone. The source of bad writing is the desire to be something more than a man of sense,—the straining to be thought a genius; and it is just the same in speechmaking. If men would only say what they have to say in plain terms, how much more eloquent they would be! . . . And I cannot conclude this Lecture without insisting on the importance of accuracy of style as being near akin to veracity and truthful habits of mind; he who thinks loosely will write loosely, and, perhaps, there is some moral inconvenience in the common forms of our grammars which give our children so many obscure terms for material distinctions. Let me also exhort you to careful examination of what you read, if it be worth any perusal at all; such an examination will be a safeguard from fanaticism, the universal origin of which is in the contemplation of phemonena without investigation into their causes.

From The New Generation, *Summer 1952.*
The New Generation, Inc., Geneva, New York.

from THE PATTERN-MAKERS
by William McFee

The encouragement a young writer wants is mainly the inspiration of masterpieces, and when he learns a trade he can be forever bringing those masterpieces to the touchstone of reality. Better than any rumble-bumble of philosophy and theory is the ring of steel on an anvil, the clean finish of a finely made pattern. The pattern is a symbol of what he is to do in the future. For what a man writes is no more than a pattern fashioned in the workshop of his soul, and goes out thence to be cast and cunningly fashioned for the public eye. He must allow for shrinkage and the passage of time. He must make it so all parts fit truly yet will draw from the mold with ease and smoothness. Above all, he must take heed never to use words that have no meaning, any more than he would put fillets and beadings on a pattern no workman in the foundry could understand, and he will use clean, dry scantling, keeping his tools very sharp, so that part fits into part as I have shown, and his work will hold together, year after year, without shake or bind.

From: *Swallowing the Anchor,* by William McFee, copyright, 1921, 1925, reprinted by permission of Doubleday and Company, Inc.

THE LANGUAGE OF REPORTS
by S. I. Hayakawa

To put it briefly, in human speech, different sounds have different meanings. To study this co-ordination of certain sounds with certain meanings is to study language. This co-ordination makes it possible for man to interact with great precision. When we tell someone, for instance, the address of a house he has never seen, we are doing something which no animal can do.

LEONARD BLOOMFIELD

Vague and insignificant forms of speech, and abuse of language, have so long passed for mysteries of science; and hard or misapplied words with little or no meaning have, by prescription, such a right to be mistaken for deep learning and height of speculation, that it will not be easy to persuade either those who speak or those who hear them, that they are but the covers of ignorance and hindrance of true knowledge.

JOHN LOCKE

FOR THE PURPOSES of the interchange of information, the basic symbolic act is the *report* of what we have seen, heard, or felt: "There is a ditch on each side of the road." "You can get those at Smith's hardware store for $2.75." "There aren't any fish on that side of the lake, but there are on this side." Then there are reports of reports: "The longest waterfall in the world is Victoria Falls in Rhodesia." "The Battle of Hastings took place in 1066." "The papers say that there was a big smash-up on Highway 41 near Evansville." Reports adhere to the following rules: first, they are *capable of verification;* second, they *exclude,* as far as possible, *inferences* and *judgments.* (These terms will be defined later.)

Verifiability

Reports are verifiable. We may not always be able to verify them ourselves, since we cannot track down the evidence for every piece of history we know, nor can we all go to Evansville to see the remains of the smash-up before they are cleared away. But if we are roughly agreed on the names of things, on what constitutes a "foot," "yard," "bushel," and so on, and on how to measure time, there is relatively little danger of our misunderstanding each other. Even in a world such as we have today, in which everybody seems to be quarreling with everybody else, *we still to a surprising degree trust each other's reports.* We ask directions of total strangers when we are traveling. We follow directions on road signs without being suspicious of the people who put them up. We read books of information about science, mathematics, automotive engineering, travel, geography, the history of costume, and other such factual matters, and we usually assume that the author is doing his best to tell us as truly as he can what he knows. And we are safe in so assuming most of the time. With the emphasis that is being given today to the discussion of biased newspapers, propagandists, and the general untrustworthiness of many of the communications we receive, we are likely to forget that we still have an enormous amount of reliable information available and that deliberate misinformation, except in warfare, still is more the exception than the rule. The desire for self-preservation

From *Language in Thought and Action* by S. I. Hayakawa, copyright, 1941, 1949, by Harcourt, Brace and Company, Inc.

that compelled men to evolve means for the exchange of information also compels them to regard the giving of false information as profoundly reprehensible.

At its highest development, the langauge of reports is the language of science. By "highest development" we mean greatest general usefulness. Presbyterian and Catholic, workingman and capitalist, German and Englishman, *agree* on the meanings of such symbols as $2 \times 2 = 4$, $100°$ *C.*, HNO_3, *3:35 A.M., 1940 A.D., 5000 r.p.m., 1000 kilowatts, pulex irritans,* and so on. But how, it may be asked, can there be agreement about even this much among people who are at each other's throats about practically everything else: political philosophies, ethical ideas, religious beliefs, and the survival of my business *versus* the survival of yours? The answer is that circumstances *compel men to agree,* whether they wish to or not. If, for example, there were a dozen different religious sects in the United States, each insisting on its own way of naming the time of the day and the days of the year, the mere necessity of having a dozen different calendars, a dozen different kinds of watches, and a dozen sets of schedules for business hours, trains, and radio programs, to say nothing of the effort that would be required for translating terms from one nomenclature to another, would make life as we know it impossible.[1]

The language of reports, then, including the more accurate reports of science, is "map" language, and because it gives us reasonably accurate representations of the "territory," it enables us to get work done. Such language may often be what is commonly termed "dull" or "uninteresting" reading: one does not usually read logarithmic tables or telephone directories for entertainment. But we could not get along without it. There are numberless occasions in the talking and writing we do in everyday life that *require that we state things in such a way that everybody will agree with our formulation.*

Inferences

The reader will find that practice in writing reports is a quick means of increasing his linguistic awareness. It is an exercise which will constantly provide him with his own examples of the principles of language and interpretation under discussion. The reports should be about firsthand experience—scenes the reader has witnessed himself, meetings and social events he has taken part in, people he knows well. They should be of such a nature that they can be verified and agreed upon. For the purpose of this exercise, inferences will be excluded.

Not that inferences are not important— we rely in everyday life and in science as

---

[1] According to information supplied by the Association of American Railroads, "Before 1883 there were nearly 100 different time zones in the United States. It wasn't until November 18 of that year that . . . a system of standard time was adopted here and in Canada. Before then there was nothing but local or 'solar' time. . . . The Pennsylvania Railroad in the East used Philadelphia time, which was five minutes slower than New York time and five minutes faster than Baltimore time. The Baltimore & Ohio used Baltimore time for trains running out of Baltimore, Columbus time for Ohio, Vincennes (Indiana) time for those going out of Cincinnati. . . . When it was noon in Chicago, it was 12:31 in Pittsburgh; 12:24 in Cleveland; 12:17 in Toledo; 12:13 in Cincinnati; 12:09 in Louisville; 12:07 in Indianapolis; 11:50 in St. Louis; 11:48 in Dubuque; 11:39 in St. Paul, and 11:27 in Omaha. There were 27 local time zones in Michigan alone. . . . A person traveling from Eastport, Maine, to San Francisco, if he wanted always to have the right railroad time and get off at the right place, had to twist the hands of his watch 20 times en route." Chicago *Daily News,* September 29, 1948.

much on *inferences* as on reports—in some areas of thought, for example, geology, paleontology, and nuclear physics, reports are the foundations, but inferences (and inferences upon inferences) are the main body of the science. An inference, as we shall use the term, is *a statement about the unknown made on the basis of the known*. We may *infer* from the handsomeness of a woman's clothes her wealth or social position; we may *infer* from the character of the ruins the origin of the fire that destroyed the building; we may *infer* from a man's calloused hands the nature of his occupation; we may *infer* from a senator's vote on an armaments bill his attitude toward Russia; we may *infer* from the structure of the land the path of a prehistoric glacier; we may *infer* from a halo on an unexposed photographic plate that it has been in the vicinity of radioactive materials; we may *infer* from the noise an engine makes the condition of its connecting rods. Inferences may be carelessly or carefully made. They may be made on the basis of a great background of previous experience with the subject-matter, or no experience at all. For example, the inferences a good mechanic can make about the internal condition of a motor by listening to it are often startlingly accurate, while the inferences made by an amateur (if he tries to make any) may be entirely wrong. But the common characteristic of inferences is that they are statements about matters which are not directly known, made on the basis of what has been observed.

The avoidance of inferences in our suggested practice in report-writing requires that we make no guesses as to what is going on in other people's minds. When we say, "He was angry," we are not reporting; we are making an inference from such observable facts as the following: "He pounded his fist on the table; he swore; he threw the telephone directory at his stenographer." In this particular example, the inference appears to be fairly safe; nevertheless, it is important to remember, especially for the purposes of training oneself, that it is an inference. Such expressions as "He thought a lot of himself," "He was scared of girls," "He has an inferiority complex," made on the basis of casual social observation, and "What Russia really wants to do is to establish a world communist dictatorship," made on the basis of casual newspaper reading, are highly inferential. One should keep in mind their inferential character and, in our suggested exercises, should substitute for them such statements as "He rarely spoke to subordinates in the plant," I saw him at a party, and he never danced except when one of the girls asked him to," "He wouldn't apply for the scholarship although I believe he could have won it easily," and "The Russian delegation to the United Nations has asked for A, B, and C. Last year they voted against M and N, and voted for X and Y. On the basis of facts such as these, the newspaper I read makes the inference that what Russia really wants is to establish a world communist dictatorship. I tend to agree."

Judgments

In our suggested writing exercise, judgments are also to be excluded. By judgments, we shall mean *all expressions of the writer's approval or disapproval of the occurrences, persons, or objects he is describing*. For example, a report cannot say, "It was a wonderful car," but must say something like this: "It has been driven 50,000 miles and has never required any repairs." Again statements like "Jack lied to us" must be suppressed in favor of the more verifiable statement, "Jack told us he didn't have the keys to his car with him. However, when he pulled a handkerchief out of his pocket a few minutes later, a bunch of car keys fell out." Also a report may not say, "The senator was stubborn, defiant, and unco-operative," or "The senator courageously stood by his principles"; it must say instead, "The senator's vote was the only one against the bill."

Many people regard statements like the following as statements of "fact": "Jack *lied* to us," "Jerry is a *thief*," "Tommy is *clever*." As ordinarily employed, however, the word "lied" involves first an inference (that Jack knew otherwise and deliberately misstated the facts) and secondly a judgment (that the speaker disapproves of what he has inferred that Jack did). In the other two instances, we may substitute such expressions as, "Jerry was convicted of theft and served two years at Waupun," and "Tommy plays the violin, leads his class in school, and is captain of the debating team." After all, to say of a man that he is a "thief" is to say in effect, "He has stolen *and will steal again"*—which is more of a prediction than a report. Even to say, "He has stolen," is to make an inference (and simultaneously to pass a judgment) on an act about which there may be difference of opinion among those who have examined the evidence upon which the conviction was obtained. But to say that he was "convicted of theft" is to make a statement capable of being agreed upon through verification in court and prison records.

Scientific verifiability rests upon the external observation of facts, not upon the heaping up of judgments. If one person says, "Peter is a deadbeat," and another says, "I think so too," the statement has not been verified. In court cases, considerable trouble is sometimes caused by witnesses who cannot distinguish their judgments from the facts upon which those judgments are based. Cross-examinations under these circumstances go something like this:

WITNESS: That dirty double-crosser Jacobs ratted on me.
DEFENSE ATTORNEY: Your honor, I object.
JUDGE: Objection sustained. (Witness's remark is stricken from the record.) Now, try to tell the court exactly what happened.
WITNESS: He double-crossed me, the dirty, lying rat!
DEFENSE ATTORNEY: Your honor, I object!
JUDGE: Objection sustained. (Witness's remark is again stricken from the record.) Will the witness try to stick to the facts.
WITNESS: But I'm telling you the facts, your honor. He did double-cross me.

This can continue indefinitely unless the cross-examiner exercises some ingenuity in order to get at the facts behind the judgment. To the witness it is a "fact" that he was "double-crossed." Often hours of patient questioning are required before the factual bases of the judgment are revealed.

Many words, of course, simultaneously convey a report and a judgment on the fact reported, as will be discussed more fully in a later chapter. For the purposes of a report as here defined, these should be avoided. Instead of "sneaked in," one might say "entered quietly"; instead of "politicians," "congressmen," or "aldermen," or "candidates for office"; instead of "bureaucrat," "public official"; instead of "tramp," "homeless unemployed"; instead of "dictatorial set-up," "centralized authority"; instead of "crackpots," "holders of uncommon views." A newspaper reporter, for example, is not permitted to write, "A crowd of suckers came to listen to Senator Smith last evening in that rickety firetrap and ex-dive that disfigures the south edge of town." Instead he says, "Between seventy-five and a hundred people heard an address last evening by Senator Smith at the Evergreen Gardens near the South Side city limits."

Snarl-Words and Purr-Words

Throughout this book, it is important to remember that we are considering language not as an isolated phenomenon, but language in action—language in the full context of the nonlinguistic events which are its setting. The making of noises with the vocal organs is a muscular activity, and like other muscular activities, often involuntary. Our responses to powerful stimuli, such as to something that makes us very angry, are a complex of muscular and physiological events: the contracting of fighting muscles, the increase of blood pressure, change in body chemistry, clutching one's hair, and so on, *and* the making of noises, such as growls and snarls. We are a little too dignified, perhaps, to growl like dogs, but we do the next best thing and substitute series of words, such as "You dirty double-crosser!" "The filthy scum!" Similarly, if we are pleasurably agitated, we may, instead of purring or wagging the tail, say things like "She's the sweetest girl in all the world!"

Speeches such as these are, as direct expressions of approval or disapproval, judgments in their simplest form. They may be said to be human equivalents of snarling and purring. "She's the sweetest girl in all the world" is not a statement about the girl; it is a purr. This seems to be a fairly obvious fact; nevertheless, it is surprising how often, when such a statement is made, both the speaker and the hearer feel that something has been said about the girl. This error is especially common in the interpretation of utterances of orators and editorialists in some of their more excited denunciations of "Reds," "greedy monopolists," "Wall Street," "radicals," "foreign ideologies," and in their more fulsome dithyrambs about "our way of life." Constantly, because of the impressive sound of the words, the elaborate structure of the sentences, and the appearance of intellectual progression, we get the feeling that something is being said about something. On closer examination, however, we discover that these utterances merely say, "What I hate ('Reds,' 'Wall Street,' or whatever) I hate very, very much," and "What I like ('our way of life') I like very, very much." We may call such utterances "snarl-words" and "purr-words." They are not reports describing conditions in the extensional world in any way.

To call these judgments "snarl-words" and "purr-words" does not mean that we should simply shrug them off. It means that we should be careful to *allocate the meaning correctly*—placing such a statement as "She's the sweetest girl in the world" as a revelation of the speaker's state of mind, and not as a revelation of facts about the girl. If the "snarl-words" about "Reds," or "greedy monopolists" are accompanied by verifiable reports (which would also mean that we have previously agreed as to who, specifically, is meant by the terms "Reds" or "greedy monopolists"), we might find reason to be just as disturbed as the speaker. If the "purr-words" about the sweetest girl in the world are accompanied by verifiable reports about her appearance, manners, skill in cooking, and so on, we might find reason to admire her too. But "snarl-words" and "purr-words" as such, unaccompanied by reports, offer nothing further to discuss, except possibly the question, "Why do you feel as you do?"

It is usually fruitless to debate such questions as "Was President Roosevelt a great statesman or merely a skillful politician?" "Is the music of Wagner the greatest music of all time or is it merely hysterical screeching?" "Which is the finer sport, tennis or baseball?" "Could Joe Louis in his prime have licked Bob Fitzsimmons in his prime?" To take sides on such issues of conflicting judgments is to reduce oneself to the same level of stubborn imbecility as one's opponents. But to ask questions of the form, "Why do you like (or dislike) Roosevelt (or Wagner, or tennis, or Joe Louis)?" is to learn something about one's friends and neighbors. After listening to their opinions and their reasons for them, we may leave the discussion slightly wiser, slightly better informed, and perhaps slightly less one-sided than we were before the discussion began.

How Judgments Stop Thought

A judgment ("He is a fine boy," "It was a beautiful service," "Baseball is a healthful sport," "She is an awful bore") is a conclusion, summing up a large number of previously observed facts. The reader is probably familiar with the fact that students almost always have difficulty in writing themes of the required length because their ideas give out after a paragraph or two. The reason for this is that those early paragraphs contain so many judgments that there is little left to be said. When the conclusions are carefully excluded, however, and observed facts are given instead, there is never any trouble about the length of papers; in fact, they tend to become too long, since inexperienced writers, when told to give facts, often give far more than are necessary, because they lack discrimination between the important and the trivial.

Still another consequence of judgments early in the course of a written exercise —and this applies also to hasty judgments in everyday thought—is the temporary blindness they induce. When, for example, an essay starts with the words, "He was a real Wall Street executive," or "She was a typical cute little co-ed," if we continue writing at all, we must make all our later statements consistent with those judgments. The result is that all the individual characteristics of this particular "executive" or this particular "co-ed" are lost sight of entirely; and the rest of the essay is likely to deal not with observed facts, but with the writer's private notion (based on previously read stories, movies, pictures, and so forth) of what "Wall Street executives" or "typical co-eds" look like. The premature judgment, that is, often prevents us from seeing what is directly in front of us. Even if the writer feels sure at the beginning of a written exercise that the man he is describing is a "loafer" or that the scene he is describing is a "beautiful residential suburb," he will conscientiously keep such notions out of his head, lest his vision be obstructed.

Slanting

In the course of writing reports of personal experiences, it will be found that in spite of all endeavors to keep judgments out, some will creep in. An account of a man, for example, may go like this: "He had apparently not shaved for several days, and his face and hands were covered with grime. His shoes were torn, and his coat, which was several sizes too small for him, was spotted with dried clay." Now, in spite of the fact that no judgment has been stated, a very obvious one is implied. Let us contrast this with another description of the same man. "Although his face was bearded and neglected, his eyes were clear, and he looked straight ahead as he walked rapidly down the road. He looked very tall; perhaps the fact that his coat was too small for him emphasized that impression. He was carrying a book under his left arm, and a small terrier ran at his heels." In this example, the impression about the same man is considerably changed, simply by the inclusion of new details and the subordination of unfavorable ones. Even if explicit judgments are kept out of one's writing, implied judgments will get in.

How, then, can we ever give an impartial report? The answer is, of course, that we cannot attain complete impartiality while we use the language of everyday life. Even with the very impersonal language of science, the task is sometimes difficult. Nevertheless, we can, by being aware of the favorable or unfavorable feelings that certain words and facts can arouse, attain enough impartiality for practical purposes. Such awareness enables us to balance the implied favorable and unfavorable judgments against each other. To learn to do this, it is a good idea to write two essays at a time on the same subject, both strict reports, to be read side by side: the first to contain facts and details likely to prejudice the reader in favor of the subject, the second to contain those likely to prejudice the reader against it. For example:

FOR	AGAINST
He had white teeth.	His teeth were uneven.
His eyes were blue, his hair blond and abundant.	He rarely looked people straight in the eye.
He had on a clean blue shirt.	His shirt was frayed at the cuffs.
He often helped his wife with the dishes.	He rarely got through drying dishes without breaking a few.
His pastor spoke very highly of him.	His grocer said he was always slow about paying his bills.

Slanting Both Ways at Once

This process of selecting details favorable or unfavorable to the subject being described may be termed slanting. Slanting gives no explicit judgments, but it differs from reporting in that it deliberately makes certain judgments inescapable. The writer striving for impartiality will, therefore, take care to slant both for and against his subject, trying as conscientiously as he can to keep the balance even. The next stage of the exercise, then, should be to rewrite the parallel essays into a single coherent essay in which details on both sides are included.

His teeth were white, but uneven; his eyes were blue, his hair blond and abundant. He did not often look people straight in the eye. His shirt was slightly frayed at the cuffs, but it was clean. He frequently helped his wife with the dishes, but he broke many of them. Opinion about him in the community was divided. His grocer said he was slow about paying his bills, but his pastor spoke very highly of him.

This example is, of course, oversimplified and admittedly not very graceful. But practice in writing such essays will first of all help to prevent one from slipping unconsciously from observable facts to judgments; that is, from "He was a member of the Ku Klux Klan" to "the dirty scoundrel!" Next, it will reveal how little we really want to be impartial anyway, especially about our best friends, our parents, our alma mater, our own children, our country, the company we work for, the product we sell, our competitor's product, or anything else in which our interests are deeply involved. Finally, we will discover that, even if we have no wish to be impartial, we write more clearly, more forcefully, and more convincingly by this process of sticking as close as possible to observable facts. There will be, as someone once remarked, more horsepower and less exhaust.

A few weeks of practice in writing reports, slanted reports, and reports slanted both ways will improve powers of observation, as well as ability to recognize soundness of observation in the writings of others. A sharpened sense for the distinction between facts and judgments, facts and inferences, will reduce susceptibility to the flurries of frenzied public opinion which certain people find it to their interest to arouse. Alarming judgments and inferences can be made to appear inevitable by means of skillfully slanted reports. A reader who is aware of the technique of slanting, however, is relatively difficult to stampede by such methods. He knows too well that there may be other relevant facts which have been left out.

Discovering One's Bias

Here, however, a caution is necessary. When a newspaper tells a story in a way that we dislike, leaving out facts we think important and playing up unimportant facts in ways that we think unfair, we are often tempted to say, "Look how they've slanted the story! What a dirty trick!" In making such a statement we are, of course, making an inference about the newspaper's editors. We are assuming that what seems important or unimportant to us seems equally important or unimportant to them, and on the basis of that assumption we are inferring that the editors "deliberately" gave the story a misleading emphasis. Is this necessarily the case? Can the reader, as an outsider, say whether a story assumes a given form because the editors "deliberately slanted it that way" or because that was the way the events appeared to them?

The point is that, by the process of selection and abstraction imposed on us by our own interests and background, experience comes to all of us (including newspaper editors) already "slanted." If you happen to be pro-CIO, pro-Catholic, and a midget-auto racing fan, your ideas of what is important or unimportant will of necessity be different from those of a man who happens to be indifferent to all three of your favorite interests. If, then, some newspapers often seem to side with the big businessman on public issues, the reason is less a matter of "deliberate" slanting than the fact that publishers are often, in enterprises as large as modern urban newspapers, big businessmen themselves, accustomed both in work and in social life to associating with other big businessmen. Nevertheless, the best newspapers, whether owned by "big businessmen" or not, often do try to tell us as accurately as possible what is going on in the world, because they are run by newspapermen who conceive it to be part of their professional responsibility to present fairly the conflicting points of view in controversial issues. Such newspapermen are *reporters* indeed.

But to get back to our exercises—the importance of trying to "slant both ways" lies not in the hope of achieving a godlike impartiality in one's thinking and writing —which is manifestly an impossible goal. It lies in discovering what poor reporters most of us really are—in other words, how little we see of the world since we of necessity see it from our own point of view. To discover one's own biases is the beginning of wisdom.

If one man says, "Co-operatives will be the salvation of America," and another replies, "Co-operatives are un-American," they might as well stop talking right there. If, however, one says, "Co-operatives seem to me, *from where I sit,* to offer a solution to our problems," and the other says, *"From where I sit,* they look like a pretty vicious institution," the possibility of further communication between the two remains. "Whenever agreement or assent is arrived at in human affairs . . . this agreement is reached by linguistic processes, or else it is not reached." To be aware of one's own "slant" and to be able to make allowances for it is to remain capable of continuing those linguistic processes that may eventually lead to agreement.

POLITICS AND THE ENGLISH LANGUAGE
by GEORGE ORWELL

MOST PEOPLE who bother with the matter at all would admit that the English language is in a bad way, but it is generally assumed that we cannot by conscious action do anything about it. Our civilization is decadent, and our language—so the argument runs—must inevitably share in the general collapse. It follows that any struggle against the abuse of language is a sentimental archaism, like preferring candles to electric light or hansom cabs to aeroplanes. Underneath this lies the half-conscious belief that language is a natural growth and not an instrument which we shape for our own purposes.

Now, it is clear that the decline of a language must ultimately have political and economic causes: it is not due simply to the bad influence of this or that individual writer. But an effect can become a cause, reinforcing the original cause and producing the same effect in an intensified form, and so on indefinitely. A man may take to drink because he feels himself to be a failure, and then fail all the more completely because he drinks. It is rather the same thing that is happening to the English language. It becomes ugly and inaccurate because our thoughts are foolish, but the slovenliness of our language makes it easier for us to have foolish thoughts. The point is that the process is reversible. Modern English, especially written English, is full of bad habits which spread by imitation and which can be avoided if one is willing to take the necessary trouble. If one gets rid of these habits one can think more clearly, and to think clearly is a necessary first step towards political regeneration: so that the fight against bad English is not frivolous and is not the exclusive concern of professional writers. I will come back to this presently, and I hope that by that time the meaning of what I

From *Shooting An Elephant and Other Essays* by George Orwell, copyright, 1945, 1946, 1949, 1950, by Sonia Brownell Orwell. Reprinted by permission of Harcourt, Brace and Company, Inc.

have said here will have become clearer. Meanwhile, here are five specimens of the English language as it is now habitually written.

These five passages have not been picked out because they are especially bad—I could have quoted far worse if I had chosen—but because they illustrate various of the mental vices from which we now suffer. They are a little below the average, but are fairly representative samples. I number them so that I can refer back to them when necessary:

(1) I am not, indeed, sure whether it is not true to say that the Milton who once seemed not unlike a seventeenth-century Shelley had not become, out of an experience ever more bitter in each year, more alien (*sic*) to the founder of that Jesuit sect which nothing could induce him to tolerate.

PROFESSOR HAROLD LASKI
(Essay in *Freedom of Expression*).

(2) Above all, we cannot play ducks and drakes with a native battery of idioms which prescribes such egregious collocations of vocables as the Basic *put up with* for *tolerate* or *put at a loss* for *bewilder*.

PROFESSOR LANCELOT HOGBEN
(*Interglossa*).

(3) On the one side we have the free personality: by definition it is not neurotic, for it has neither conflict nor dream. Its desires, such as they are, are transparent, for they are just what institutional approval keeps in the forefront of consciousness; another institutional pattern would alter their number and intensity; there is little in them that is natural, irreducible, or culturally dangerous. But *on the other side,* the social bond itself is nothing but the mutual reflection of these self-secure integrities. Recall the definition of love. Is not this the very picture of a small academic? Where is there a place in this hall of mirrors for either personality or fraternity?

Essay on psychology
in *Politics* (New York).

(4) All the "best people" from the gentlemen's clubs, and all the frantic fascist captains, united in common hatred of Socialism and bestial horror of the rising tide of the mass revolutionary movement, have turned to acts of provocation, to foul incendiarism, to medieval legends of poisoned wells, to legalize their own destruction of proletarian organizations, and rouse the agitated petty-bourgeoisie to chauvinistic fervour on behalf of the fight against the revolutionary way out of the crisis.

Communist pamphlet.

(5) If a new spirit *is* to be infused into this old country, there is one thorny and contentious reform which must be tackled, and that is the humanization and galvanization of the B.B.C. Timidity here will bespeak canker and atrophy of the soul. The heart of Britain may be sound and of strong beat, for instance, but the British lion's roar at present is like that of Bottom in Shakespeare's *Midsummer Night's Dream*—as gentle as any sucking dove. A virile new Britain cannot continue indefinitely to be traduced in the eyes, or rather ears, of the world by the effete languors of Langham Place, brazenly masquerading as "standard English." When the Voice of Britain is heard at nine o'clock, better far and infinitely less ludicrous to hear aitches honestly dropped than the present priggish, inflated, inhibited, school-ma'amish arch braying of blameless bashful mewing maidens!

Letter in *Tribune*.

Each of these passages has faults of its own, but, quite apart from avoidable ugliness, two qualities are common to all of them. The first is staleness of imagery: the other is lack of precision. The writer either has a meaning and cannot express it, or he inadvertently says something else, or he is almost indifferent as to whether his words mean anything or not. This mixture of vagueness and sheer incompetence is the most marked characteristic of modern

English prose, and especially of any kind of political writing. As soon as certain topics are raised, the concrete melts into the abstract and no one seems able to think of turns of speech that are not hackneyed: prose consists less and less of *words* chosen for the sake of their meaning, and more and more of *phrases* tacked together like the sections of a prefabricated hen-house. I list below, with notes and examples, various of the tricks by means of which the work of prose-construction is habitually dodged:

Dying metaphors. A newly invented metaphor assists thought by evoking a visual image, while on the other hand a metaphor which is technically "dead" (e.g. *iron resolution*) has in effect reverted to being an ordinary word and can generally be used without loss of vividness. But in between these two classes there is a huge dump of worn-out metaphors which have lost all evocative power and are merely used because they save people the trouble of inventing phrases for themselves. Examples are: *Ring the changes on, take up the cudgels for, toe the line, ride roughshod over, stand shoulder to shoulder with, play into the hands of, no axe to grind, grist to the mill, fishing in troubled waters, on the order of the day, Achilles' heel, swan song, hotbed.* Many of these are used without knowledge of their meaning (what is a "rift," for instance?), and incompatible metaphors are frequently mixed, a sure sign that the writer is not interested in what he is saying. Some metaphors now current have been twisted out of their original meaning without those who use them even being aware of the fact. For example, *toe the line* is sometimes written *tow the line.* Another example is *the hammer and the anvil,* now always used with the implication that the anvil gets the worst of it. In real life it is always the anvil that breaks the hammer, never the other way about: a writer who stopped to think what he was saying would be aware of this, and would avoid perverting the original phrase.

Operators, or verbal false limbs. These save the trouble of picking out appropriate verbs and nouns, and at the same time pad each sentence with extra syllables which give it an appearance of symmetry. Characteristic phrases are: *render inoperative, militate against, prove unacceptable, make contact with, be subjected to, give rise to, give grounds for, have the effect of, play a leading part (role) in, make itself felt, take effect, exhibit a tendency to, serve the purpose of,* etc., etc. The keynote is the elimination of simple verbs. Instead of being a single word, such as *break, stop, spoil, mend, kill,* a verb becomes a *phrase,* made up of a noun or adjective tacked on to some general-purpose verb such as *prove, serve, form, play, render.* In addition, the passive voice is wherever possible used in preference to the active, and noun constructions are used instead of gerunds (*by examination of* instead of *by examining*). The range of verbs is further cut down by means of the *-ize* and *de-* formations, and banal statements are given an appearance of profundity by means of the *not un-* formation. Simple conjunctions and prepositions are replaced by such phrases as *with respect to, having regard to, the fact that, by dint of, in view of, in the interests of, on the hypothesis that;* and the ends of sentences are saved from anti-climax by such resounding commonplaces as *greatly to be desired, cannot be left out of account, a development to be expected in the near future, deserving of serious consideration, brought to a satisfactory conclusion,* and so on and so forth.

Pretentious diction. Words like *phenomenon, element, individual* (as noun), *objective, categorical, effective, virtual, basic, primary, promote, constitute, exhibit, exploit, utilize, eliminate, liquidate,* are used to dress up simple statement and give an air of scientific impartiality to biased judgements. Adjectives like *epoch-making, epic, historic, unforgettable, triumphant, age-old, inevitable, inexorable, veritable,* are used to dignify the sordid processes of international politics, while writing that aims at glorifying war usually takes on an archaic colour, its characteristic words being: *realm, throne, chariot, mailed fist, trident, sword, shield, buckler, banner, jackboot, clarion.* Foreign words and expressions such as *cul de sac, ancien régime, deus ex machina, mutatis mutandis, status quo, gleichschaltung, weltanschauung,* are used to give an air of culture and elegance. Except for the useful abbreviations *i.e., e.g.,* and *etc.,* there is no real need for any of the hundreds of foreign phrases now current in English. Bad writers, and especially scientific, political and sociological writers, are nearly always haunted by the notion that Latin or Greek words are grander than Saxon ones, and unnecessary words like *expedite, ameliorate, predict, extraneous, deracinated, clandestine, subaqueous* and hundreds of others constantly gain ground from their Anglo-Saxon opposite numbers.[1] The jargon peculiar to Marxist writing (*hyena, hangman, cannibal, petty bourgeois, these gentry, lacquey, flunkey, mad dog, White Guard,* etc.) consists largely of words and phrases translated from Russian, German or French; but the normal way of coining a new word is to use a Latin or Greek root with the appropriate affix and, where necessary, the -ize formation. It is often easier to make up words of this kind (*deregionalize, impermissible, extramarital, non-fragmentary,* and so forth) than to think up the English words that will cover one's meaning. The result, in general, is an increase in slovenliness and vagueness.

Meaningless words. In certain kinds of writing, particularly in art criticism and literary criticism, it is normal to come across long passages which are almost completely lacking in meaning.[2] Words like *romantic, plastic, values, human, dead, sentimental, natural, vitality,* as used in art criticism, are strictly meaningless, in the sense that they not only do not point to any discoverable object, but are hardly even expected to do so by the reader. When one critic writes, "The outstanding feature of Mr. X's work is its living quality," while another writes, "The immediately striking thing about Mr. X's work is its peculiar deadness," the reader accepts this as a simple difference of opinion. If words like *black* and *white* were involved, instead of the jargon words *dead* and *living,* he would see at once that language was being used in an improper way. Many

---

[1] An interesting illustration of this is the way in which the English flower names which were in use till very recently are being ousted by Greek ones, *snapdragon* becoming *antirrhinum, forget-me-not* becoming *myosotis,* etc. It is hard to see any practical reason for this change of fashion: it is probably due to an instinctive turning-away from the more homely word and a vague feeling that the Greek word is scientific.

[2] Example: "Comfort's catholicity of perception and image, strangely Whitmanesque in range, almost the exact opposite in aesthetic compulsion, continues to evoke that trembling atmospheric accumulative hinting at a cruel, an inexorably serene timelessness . . . Wrey Gardiner scores by aiming at simple bullseyes with precision. Only they are not so simple, and through this contented sadness runs more than the surface bitter-sweet of resignation." (*Poetry Quarterly.*)

political words are similarly abused. The word *Fascism* has now no meaning except in so far as it signifies "something not desirable." The words *democracy, socialism, freedom, patriotic, realistic, justice,* have each of them several different meanings which cannot be reconciled with one another. In the case of a word like *democracy,* not only is there no agreed definition, but the attempt to make one is resisted from all sides. It is almost universally felt that when we call a country democratic we are praising it: consequently the defenders of every kind of régime claim that it is a democracy, and fear that they might have to stop using the word if it were tied down to any one meaning. Words of this kind are often used in a consciously dishonest way. That is, the person who uses them has his own private definition, but allows his hearer to think he means something quite different. Statements like *Marshal Pétain was a true patriot, The Soviet Press is the freest in the world, The Catholic Church is opposed to persecution,* are almost always made with intent to deceive. Other words used in variable meanings, in most cases more or less dishonestly, are: *class, totalitarian, science, progressive, reactionary, bourgeois, equality.*

Now that I have made this catalogue of swindles and perversions, let me give another example of the kind of writing that they lead to. This time it must of its nature be an imaginary one. I am going to translate a passage of good English into modern English of the worst sort. Here is a well-known verse from *Ecclesiastes:*

I returned, and saw under the sun, that the race is not to the swift, nor the battle to the strong, neither yet bread to the wise, nor yet riches to men of understanding, nor yet favour to men of skill; but time and chance happeneth to them all.

Here it is in modern English:

Objective consideration of contemporary phenomena compels the conclusion that success or failure in competitive activities exhibits no tendency to be commensurate with innate capacity, but that a considerable element of the unpredictable must invariably be taken into account.

This is a parody, but not a very gross one. Exhibit (3), above, for instance, contains several patches of the same kind of English. It will be seen that I have not made a full translation. The beginning and ending of the sentence follow the original meaning fairly closely, but in the middle the concrete illustrations—race, battle, bread—dissolve into the vague phrase "success or failure in competitive activities." This had to be so, because no modern writer of the kind I am discussing—no one capable of using phrases like "objective consideration of contemporary phenomena"—would ever tabulate his thoughts in that precise and detailed way. The whole tendency of modern prose is away from concreteness. Now analyse these two sentences a little more closely. The first contains 49 words but only 60 syllables, and all its words are those of everyday life. The second contains 38 words of 90 syllables: 18 of its words are from Latin roots, and one from Greek. The first sentence contains six vivid images, and only one phrase ("time and chance") that could be called vague. The second contains not a single fresh, arresting phrase, and in spite of its 90 syllables it gives only a shortened version of the meaning contained in the first. Yet without a doubt it is the second kind of sentence that is gaining ground in modern English. I do not want to exaggerate. This kind of writing is not yet universal, and outcrops of simplicity will occur here and there in the worst-written page. Still, if you or I were told to write a few lines on the uncertainty of human fortunes, we should probably come much nearer to my imaginary sentence than to the one from *Ecclesiastes*.

As I have tried to show, modern writing at its worst does not consist in picking out words for the sake of their meaning and inventing images in order to make the meaning clearer. It consists in gumming together long strips of words which have already been set in order by someone else, and making the results presentable by sheer humbug. The attraction of this way of writing is that it is easy. It is easier—even quicker, once you have the habit—to say *In my opinion it is a not unjustifiable assumption that* than to say *I think*. If you use ready-made phrases, you not only don't have to hunt about for words; you also don't have to bother with the rhythms of your sentences, since these phrases are generally so arranged as to be more or less euphonious. When you are composing in a hurry—when you are dictating to a stenographer, for instance, or making a public speech—it is natural to fall into a pretentious, Latinized style. Tags like *a consideration which we should do well to bear in mind* or *a conclusion to which all of us would readily assent* will save many a sentence from coming down with a bump. By using stale metaphors, similes and idioms, you save much mental effort, at the cost of leaving your meaning vague, not only for your reader but for yourself. This is the significance of mixed metaphors. The sole aim of a metaphor is to call up a visual image. When these images clash—as in *The Fascist octopus has sung its swan song, the jackboot is thrown into the melting pot*—it can be taken as certain that the writer is not seeing a mental image of the objects he is naming; in other words he is not really thinking. Look again at the examples I gave at the beginning of this essay. Professor Laski (1) uses five negatives in 53 words. One of these is superfluous, making nonsense of the whole passage, and in addition there is the slip *alien* for akin, making further nonsense, and several avoidable pieces of clumsiness which increase the general vagueness. Professor Hogben (2) plays ducks and drakes with a battery which is able to write prescriptions, and, while disapproving of the everyday phrase *put up with,* is unwilling to look *egregious* up in the dictionary and see what it means. (3), If one takes an uncharitable attitude towards it, is simply meaningless: probably one could work out its intended meaning by reading the whole of the article in which it occurs. In (4), the writer knows more or less what he wants to say, but an accumulation of stale phrases chokes him like tea leaves blocking a sink. In (5), words and meaning have almost parted company. People who write in this manner usually have a general emotional meaning—they dislike one thing and want to express solidarity with another—but they are not interested in the detail of what they are saying. A scrupulous writer, in every sentence that he writes, will ask himself at least four questions, thus: What am I trying to say? What words will express it? What image or idiom will make it clearer? Is this image fresh enough to have an effect? And he will probably ask himself two more: Could I put it more shortly? Have I said anything that is avoidably ugly? But you are not obliged to go to all this trouble. You can shirk it by simply throwing your mind open and letting the ready-made phrases come crowding in. They will construct your sentences for you—even think your thoughts for you, to a certain extent—

and at need they will perform the important service of partially concealing your meaning even from yourself. It is at this point that the special connection between politics and the debasement of language becomes clear.

In our time it is broadly true that political writing is bad writing. Where it is not true, it will generally be found that the writer is some kind of rebel, expressing his private opinions and not a "party line." Orthodoxy, of whatever colour, seems to demand a lifeless, imitative style. The political dialects to be found in pamphlets, leading articles, manifestoes, White Papers and the speeches of undersecretaries do, of course, vary from party to party, but they are all alike in that one almost never finds in them a fresh, vivid, home-made turn of speech. When one watches some tired hack on the platform mechanically repeating the familiar phrases—*bestial atrocities, iron heel, bloodstained tyranny, free peoples of the world, stand shoulder to shoulder*—one often has a curious feeling that one is not watching a live human being but some kind of dummy: a feeling which suddenly becomes stronger at moments when the light catches the speaker's spectacles and turns them into blank discs which seem to have no eyes behind them. And this is not altogether fanciful. A speaker who uses that kind of phraseology has gone some distance towards turning himself into a machine. The appropriate noises are coming out of his larynx, but his brain is not involved as it would be if he were choosing his words for himself. If the speech he is making is one that he is accustomed to make over and over again, he may be almost unconscious of what he is saying, as one is when one utters the responses in church. And this reduced state of consciousness, if not indispensable, is at any rate favourable to political conformity.

In our time, political speech and writing are largely the defence of the indefensible. Things like the continuance of British rule in India, the Russian purges and deportations, the dropping of the atom bombs on Japan, can indeed be defended, but only by arguments which are too brutal for most people to face, and which do not square with the professed aims of political parties. Thus political language has to consist largely of euphemism, question-begging and sheer cloudy vagueness. Defenceless villages are bombarded from the air, the inhabitants driven out into the countryside, the cattle machine-gunned, the huts set on fire with incendiary bullets: this is called *pacification*. Millions of peasants are robbed of their farms and sent trudging along the roads with no more than they can carry: this is called *transfer of population* or *rectification of frontiers*. People are imprisoned for years without trial, or shot in the back of the neck or sent to die of scurvy in Arctic lumber camps: this is called *elimination of unreliable elements*. Such phraseology is needed if one wants to name things without calling up mental pictures of them. Consider for instance some comfortable English professor defending Russian totalitarianism. He cannot say outright, "I believe in killing off your opponents when you can get good results by doing so." Probably, therefore, he will say something like this:

While freely conceding that the Soviet régime exhibits certain features which the humanitarian may be inclined to deplore, we must, I think, agree that a certain curtailment of the right to political opposition is an unavoidable concomitant of transitional periods, and that the rigours which the Russian people have been called upon to undergo have been amply justified in the sphere of concrete achievement.

The inflated style is itself a kind of euphemism. A mass of Latin words falls upon the facts like soft snow, blurring the outlines and covering up all the details. The great enemy of clear language is insincerity. When there is a gap between one's real and one's declared aims, one turns as it were instinctively to long words and exhausted idioms, like a cuttlefish squirting out ink. In our age there is no such thing as "keeping out of politics." All issues are political issues, and politics itself is a mass of lies, evasions, folly, hatred and schizophrenia. When the general atmosphere is bad, language must suffer. I should expect to find—this is a guess which I have not sufficient knowledge to verify—that the German, Russian and Italian languages have all deteriorated in the last ten or fifteen years, as a result of dictatorship.

But if thought corrupts language, language can also corrupt thought. A bad usage can spread by tradition and imitation, even among people who should and do know better. The debased language that I have been discussing is in some ways very convenient. Phrases like *a not unjustifiable assumption, leaves much to be desired, would serve no good purpose, a consideration which we should do well to bear in mind,* are a continuous temptation, a packet of aspirins always at one's elbow. Look back through this essay, and for certain you will find that I have again and again committed the very faults I am protesting against. By this morning's post I have received a pamphlet dealing with conditions in Germany. The author tells me that he "felt impelled" to write it. I open it at random, and here is almost the first sentence that I see: "(The Allies) have an opportunity not only of achieving a radical transformation of Germany's social and political structure in such a way as to avoid a nationalistic reaction in Germany itself, but at the same time of laying the foundations of a co-operative and unified Europe." You see, he "feels impelled" to write—feels, presumably, that he has something new to say—and yet his words, like cavalry horses answering the bugle, group themselves automatically into the familiar dreary pattern. This invasion of one's mind by ready-made phrases (*lay the foundations, achieve a radical transformation*) can only be prevented if one is constantly on guard against them, and every such phrase anaesthetizes a portion of one's brain.

I said earlier that the decadence of our language is probably curable. Those who deny this would argue, if they produced an argument at all, that language merely reflects existing social conditions, and that we cannot influence its development by any direct tinkering with words and constructions. So far as the general tone or spirit of a language goes, this may be true, but it is not true in detail. Silly words and expressions have often disappeared, not through any evolutionary process but owing to the conscious action of a minority. Two recent examples were *explore every avenue* and *leave no stone unturned,* which were killed by the jeers of a few journalists. There is a long list of flyblown metaphors which could similarly be got rid of if enough people would interest themselves in the job; and it should also be possible to laugh the *not un-* formation out of existence,[3] to reduce the amount of Latin and Greek in the average sentence, to drive out foreign phrases and strayed scientific words, and, in general, to make preten-

---

[3] One can cure oneself of the *not un-* formation by memorizing this sentence: *A not unblack dog was chasing a not unsmall rabbit across a not ungreen field.*

tiousness unfashionable. But all these are minor points. The defence of the English language implies more than this, and perhaps it is best to start by saying what it does *not* imply.

To begin with, it has nothing to do with archaism, with the salvaging of obsolete words and turns of speech, or with the setting-up of a "standard English" which must never be departed from. On the contrary, it is especially concerned with the scrapping of every word or idiom which has outworn its usefulness. It has nothing to do with correct grammar and syntax, which are of no importance so long as one makes one's meaning clear, or with the avoidance of Americanisms, or with having what is called a "good prose style." On the other hand it is not concerned with fake simplicity and the attempt to make written English colloquial. Nor does it even imply in every case preferring the Saxon word to the Latin one, though it does imply using the fewest and shortest words that will cover one's meaning. What is above all needed is to let the meaning choose the word, and not the other way about. In prose, the worst thing one can do with words is to surrender to them. When you think of a concrete object, you think wordlessly, and then, if you want to describe the thing you have been visualizing, you probably hunt about till you find the exact words that seem to fit it. When you think of something abstract you are more inclined to use words from the start, and unless you make a conscious effort to prevent it, the existing dialect will come rushing in and do the job for you, at the expense of blurring or even changing your meaning. Probably it is better to put off using words as long as possible and get one's meaning as clear as one can through pictures or sensations. Afterwards one can choose—not simply *accept*—the phrases that will best cover the meaning, and then switch round and decide what impression one's words are likely to make on another person. This last effort of the mind cuts out all stale or mixed images, all prefabricated phrases, needless repetitions, and humbug and vagueness generally. But one can often be in doubt about the effect of a word or a phrase, and one needs rules that one can rely on when instinct fails. I think the following rules will cover most cases:

(i) Never use a metaphor, simile or other figure of speech which you are used to seeing in print.
(ii) Never use a long word where a short one will do.
(iii) If it is possible to cut a word out, always cut it out.
(iv) Never use the passive where you can use the active.
(v) Never use a foreign phrase, a scientific word or a jargon word if you can think of an everyday English equivalent.
(vi) Break any of these rules sooner than say anything outright barbarous.

These rules sound elementary, and so they are, but they demand a deep change of attitude in anyone who has grown used to writing in the style now fashionable. One could keep all of them and still write bad English, but one could not write the kind of stuff that I quoted in those five specimens at the beginning of this article.

I have not here been considering the literary use of language, but merely language as an instrument for expressing and not for concealing or preventing thought. Stuart Chase and others have come near to claiming that all abstract words are meaningless, and have used this as a pretext for advocating a kind of political quietism. Since you don't know what Fascism is, how can you struggle against Fascism? One need not swallow such absurdities as this, but one ought to recognize that the present political chaos is connected with the decay of language, and that one can probably bring about some improvement by starting at the verbal end. If you simplify your English, you are freed from the worst follies of orthodoxy. You cannot speak any of the necessary dialects, and when you make a stupid remark its stupidity will be obvious, even to yourself. Political language—and with variations this is true of all political parties, from Conservatives to Anarchists—is designed to make lies sound truthful and murder respectable, and to give an appearance of solidity to pure wind. One cannot change this all in a moment, but one can at least change one's own habits, and from time to time one can even, if one jeers loudly enough, send some worn-out and useless phrase—some *jackboot, Achilles' heel, hotbed, melting pot, acid test, veritable inferno* or other lump of verbal refuse—into the dustbin where it belongs.

from THE STORY OF A NOVEL
by Thomas Wolfe

I DON'T KNOW how I became a writer, but I think it was because of a certain force in me that had to write and that finally burst through and found a channel. My people were of the working class of people. My father, a stonecutter, was a man with a great respect and veneration for literature. He had a tremendous memory, and he loved poetry, and the poetry that he loved best was naturally of the rhetorical kind that such a man would like. Nevertheless it was good poetry, Hamlet's Soliloquy, "Macbeth," Mark Antony's Funeral Oration, Grey's "Elegy," and all the rest of it. I heard it all as a child; I memorized and learned it all.

He sent me to college to the state university. The desire to write, which had been strong during all my days in high school, grew stronger still. I was editor of the college paper, the college magazine, etc., and in my last year or two I was a member of a course in playwriting which had just been established there. I wrote several little one-act plays, still thinking I would become a lawyer or a newspaper man, never daring to believe I could seriously become a writer. Then I went to Harvard, wrote some more plays there, became obsessed with the idea that I had to be a playwright, left Harvard, had my plays rejected, and finally in the autumn of 1926, how, why, or in what manner I have never exactly been able to determine, but probably because the force in me that had to write at length sought out its channel, I began to write my first book in London. I was living all alone at that time. I had two rooms—a bedroom and a sitting room—in a little square in Chelsea in which all the houses had that familiar, smoked brick and cream-yellow-plaster look of London houses. They looked exactly alike.

As I say, I was living alone at that time and in a foreign country. I did not know why I was there or what the direction of my life should be, and that was the way I began to write my book. I think that is one of the hardest times a writer goes through. There is no standard, no outward judgment, by which he can measure

Reprinted from *The Story of a Novel* by Thomas Wolfe; copyright 1936 by Charles Scribner's Sons; used by permission of the publishers.

[144]

The Story of a Novel

what he has done. By day I would write for hours in big ledgers which I had bought for the purpose; then at night I would lie in bed and fold my hands behind my head and think of what I had done that day and hear the solid, leather footbeat of the London bobby as he came by my window, and remember that I was born in North Carolina and wonder why the hell I was now in London lying in the darkened bed, and thinking about words I had that day put down on paper. I would get a great, hollow, utterly futile feeling inside me, and then I would get up and switch on the light and read the words I had written that day, and then I would wonder: why am I here now? why have I come?

By day there would be the great, dull roar of London, the gold, yellow, foggy light you have there in October. The man-swarmed and old, weblike, smoky London! And I loved the place, and I loathed it and abhorred it. I knew no one there, and I had been a child in North Carolina long ago, and I was living there in two rooms in the huge octopal and illimitable web of that overwhelming city. I did not know why I had come, why I was there.

I worked there every day with such feelings as I have described, and came back to America in the winter and worked here. I would teach all day and write all night, and finally about two and a half years after I had begun the book in London, I finished it in New York.

My book was what is often referred to as an autobiographical novel. I protested against this term in a preface to the book upon the grounds that any serious work of creation is of necessity autobiographical and that few more autobiographical works than *Gulliver's Travels* have ever been written.

My conviction is that all serious creative work must be at bottom autobiographical, and that a man must use the material and experience of his own life if he is to create anything that has substantial value. But I also believe now that the young writer is often led through inexperience to a use of the materials of life which are, perhaps, somewhat too naked and direct for the purpose of a work of art. The thing a young writer is likely to do is to confuse the limits between actuality and reality. He tends unconciously to describe an event in such a way because it actually happened that way, and from an artistic point of view, I can now see that this is wrong. It is not, for example, important that one remembers a beautiful woman of easy virtue as having come from the state of Kentucky in the year 1907. She could perfectly well have come from Idaho or Texas or Nova Scotia. The important thing really is only to express as well as possible the character and quality of the beautiful woman of easy virtue. But the young writer, chained to fact and to his own inexperience, as yet unliberated by maturity, is likely to argue, "she must be described as coming from Kentucky because that is where she actually did come from."

In spite of this, it is impossible for a man who has the stuff of creation in him to make a literal transcription of his own experience. Everything in a work of art is changed and transfigured by the personality of the artist. And as far as my own first book is concerned, I can truthfully say that I do not believe that there is a single page of it that is true to fact. And from this circumstance, also, I learned another curious thing about writing. For although my book was not true to fact, it was true to the general experience of the town I came from and I hope, of course, to the general experience of all men living. The best way I

How Writing Is Written

can describe the situation is this: it was as if I were a sculptor who had found a certain kind of clay with which to model. Now a farmer who knew well the neighborhood from which this clay had come might pass by and find the sculptor at his work and say to him, "I know the farm from which you got that clay." But it would be unfair of him to say, "I know the figure, too." Now I think what happened in my native town is that having seen the clay, they became immediately convinced that they recognized the figure, too, and the results of this misconception were so painful and ludicrous that the telling of it is almost past belief.

It was my experience to be assured by people from my native town not only that they remembered incidents and characters in my first book, which may have had some basis in actuality, but also that they remembered incidents which so far as I know had no historical basis whatever. For example, there was one scene in the book in which a stonecutter is represented as selling to a notorious woman of the town a statue of a marble angel which he has treasured for many years. So far as I know, there was no basis in fact for this story, and yet I was informed by several people later that they not only remembered the incident perfectly, but had actually been witnesses to the transaction. Nor was this the end of the story. I heard that one of the newspapers sent a reporter and a photographer to the cemetery and a photograph was printed in the paper with a statement to the effect that the angel was the now famous angel which had stood upon the stonecutter's porch for so many years and had given the title to my book. The unfortunate part of this proceeding was that I had never seen or heard of this angel before, and that this angel was, in fact, erected over the grave of a well-known Methodist lady who had died a few years before and that her indignant family had immediately written the paper to demand a retraction of its story, saying that their mother had been in no way connected with the infamous book or the infamous angel which had given the infamous book its name. Such, then, were some of the unforeseen difficulties with which I was confronted after the publication of my first book.

Month was passing into month; I had had a success. The way was opened to me. There was only one thing for me to do and that was work, and I was spending my time consuming myself with anger, grief, and useless passion about the reception the book had had in my native town, or wasting myself again in exuberant elation because of the critics' and the readers' praise, or in anguish and bitterness because of their ridicule. For the first time, I realized the nature of one of the artist's greatest conflicts, and was faced with the need of meeting it. For the first time I saw not only that the artist must live and sweat and love and suffer and enjoy as other men, but that the artist must also work as other men and that furthermore, he must work even while these common events of life are going on. It seems a simple and banal assertion, but I learned it hardly, and in one of the worst moments of my life. There is no such thing as an artistic vacuum; there is no such thing as a time when the artist may work in a delightful atmosphere, free of agony that other men must know, or if the artist ever does find such a time, it is something not to be hoped for, something not to be sought for indefinitely.

At any rate, while my life and energy were absorbed in the emotional vortex which my first book had created, I was getting almost no work done on the sec-

The Story of a Novel

ond. And now I was faced with another fundamental problem which every young writer must meet squarely if he is to continue. How is a man to get his writing done? How long should he work at writing, and how often? What kind of method, if any, must he find in following his work? I suddenly found myself face to face with the grim necessity of constant, daily work. And as simple as this discovery may seem to everyone, I was not prepared for it. A young writer without a public does not feel the sense of necessity, the pressure of time, as does a writer who has been published and who must now begin to think of time schedules, publishing seasons, the completion of his next book. I realized suddenly with a sense of definite shock that I had let six months go by since the publication of my first book and that, save for a great many notes and fragments, I had done nothing. Meanwhile, the book continued to sell slowly but steadily, and in February 1930, about five months after its publication, I found it possible to resign from the faculty of New York University and devote my full time to the preparation of a second book. That spring I was also fortunate enough to be awarded the Guggenheim Fellowship which would enable me to live and work abroad for a year. And accordingly at the beginning of May, I went abroad again.

I was in Paris for a couple of months, until the middle of July, and although I now compelled myself to work for four or five hours a day, my effort at composition was still confused and broken, and there was nothing yet that had the structural form and unity of a book. The life of the great city fascinated me as it had always done, but also aroused all the old feelings of naked homelessness, rootlessness, and loneliness which I have always felt there. It was, and has always remained for me, at least, the most homesick city in the world; the place where I have felt mostly an alien and a stranger, and certainly for me as fascinating and seductive as the city is, it has never been a good place to work. But here I would like to say something about places to work because that is another problem which causes young writers a great deal of doubt, uncertainty, and confusion, and I think, uselessly.

I had gone through the whole experience and now I was almost done with it. I had come to Paris first six years before, a youth of twenty-four, filled with all the romantic faith and foolishness which many young men at that time felt when they saw Paris. I had come there that first time, so I told myself, to work, and so glamorous was the magic name of Paris at that time, that I really thought one could work far better there than anywhere on earth; that it was a place where the very air was impregnated with the energies of art; where the artist was bound to find a more fortunate and happy life than he could possibly find in America. Now I had come to see that this was wrong. I had come to understand very plainly that what many of us were doing in those years when we fled from our own country and sought refuge abroad was not really looking for a place to work, but looking for a place where we could escape from work; that what we were really fleeing from in those years was not the Philistinism, the materialism, and ugliness in American life which we said we were fleeing from, but from the necessity of grappling squarely with ourselves and the necessity of finding in ourselves, somehow, the stuff to live by, to get from our own lives and our own experience the substance of our art which every man who ever wrote a living thing has had to get

[147]

out of himself and without which he is lost.

The place to work! Yes, the place to work *was* Paris; it *was* Spain; it *was* Italy and Capri and Majorca, but great God, it was also Keokuk, and Portland, Maine, and Denver, Colorado, and Yancey County, North Carolina, and wherever we might be, if work was there within us at the time. If this was all that I had learned from these voyages to Europe, if the price of all this wandering had been just this simple lesson, it would have been worth the price, but that was not all. I had found out during these years that the way to discover one's own country was to leave it; that the way to find America was to find it in one's heart, one's memory, and one's spirit, and in a foreign land.

I think I may say that I discovered America during these years abroad out of my very need of her. The huge gain of this discovery seemed to come directly from my sense of loss. I had been to Europe five times now; each time I had come with delight, with maddening eagerness to return, and each time how, where, and in what way I did not know, I had felt the bitter ache of homelessness, a desperate longing for America, an overwhelming desire to return.

During that summer in Paris, I think I felt this great homesickness more than ever before, and I really believe that from this emotion, this constant and almost intolerable effort of memory and desire, the material and the structure of the books I now began to write were derived.

The quality of my memory is characterized, I believe, in a more than ordinary degree by the intensity of its sense impressions, its power to evoke and bring back the odors, sounds, colors, shapes, and feel of things with concrete vividness. Now my memory was at work night and day, in a way that I could at first neither check nor control and that swarmed unbidden in a stream of blazing pageantry across my mind, with the million forms and substances of the life that I had left, which was my own, America. I would be sitting, for example, on the terrace of a café watching the flash and play of life before me on the Avenue de l'Opéra and suddenly I would remember the iron railing that goes along the boardwalk at Atlantic City. I could see it instantly just the way it was, the heavy iron pipe; its raw, galvanized look; the way the joints were fitted together. It was all so vivid and concrete that I could feel my hand upon it and know the exact dimensions, its size and weight and shape. And suddenly I would realize that I had never seen any railing that looked like this in Europe. And this utterly familiar, common thing would suddenly be revealed to me with all the wonder with which we discover a thing which we have seen all our life and yet have never known before. Or again, it would be a bridge, the look of an old iron bridge across an American river, the sound the train makes as it goes across it; the spoke-and-hollow rumble of the ties below; the look of the muddy banks; the slow, thick, yellow wash of an American river; an old flat-bottomed boat half filled with water stogged in the muddy bank; or it would be, most lonely and haunting of all the sounds I know, the sound of a milk wagon as it entered an American street just at the first gray of the morning, the slow and lonely clopping of the hoof upon the street, the jink of bottles, the sudden rattle of a battered old milk can, the swift and hurried footsteps of the milkman, and again the jink of bottles, a low word spoken to his horse, and then the great, slow, clopping hoof receding into silence, and then quietness and a bird song rising in the street again. Or it would be a little wooden shed out in the country two miles from my home town where people waited for the street car, and I could see and feel again the dull and rusty color of the old green paint and see and feel all of the initials that had been carved out with jackknives on the planks and benches within the shed, and smell the warm and sultry smell so resinous and so thrilling, so filled with a strange and nameless excitement of an unknown joy, a coming prophecy, and hear the street car as it came to a stop, the moment of brooding, drowsing silence; a hot thrum and drowsy stitch at three o'clock; the smell of grass and hot sweet clover; and then the sudden sense of absence, loneliness and departure when the street car had gone and there was nothing but the hot and drowsy stitch at three o'clock again.

Or again, it would be an American street with all its jumble of a thousand ugly architectures. It would be Montague Street or Fulton Street in Brooklyn, or Eleventh Street in New York, or other streets where I had lived; and suddenly I would see the gaunt and savage webbing of the elevated structure along Fulton Street, and how the light swarmed through in dusty, broken bars, and I could remember the old, familiar rusty color, that incomparable rusty color that gets into so many things here in America. And this also would be like something I had seen a million times and lived with all my life.

I would sit there, looking out upon the Avenue de l'Opéra and my life would ache with the whole memory of it; the desire to see it again; somehow to find a word for it; a language that would tell its shape, its color, the way we have all known and felt and seen it. And when I understood this thing, I saw that I must find for myself the tongue to utter what I knew but could not say. And from the moment of that discovery, the line and purpose of my life was shaped. The end toward which every energy of my life and talent would be henceforth directed was in such a way as this defined. It was as if I had discovered a whole new universe of chemical elements and had begun to see certain relations between some of them but had by no means begun to organize the whole series into a harmonious and coherent union. From this time on, I think my efforts might be described as the effort to complete that organization, to discover that articulation for which I strove, to bring about that final coherent union. I know that I have failed thus far in doing so, but I believe I understand pretty thoroughly just where the nature of my failure lies, and of course my deepest and most earnest hope is that the time will come when I shall not fail.

At any rate, from this time on the general progress of the three books which I was to write in the next four and a half years could be fairly described in somewhat this way. It was a progress that began in a whirling vortex and a creative chaos and that proceeded slowly at the expense of infinite confusion, toil, and error toward clarification and the articulation of an ordered and formal structure. An extraordinary image remains to me from that year, the year I spent abroad when the material of these books first began to take on an articulate form. It seemed that I had inside me, swelling and gathering all the time, a huge black cloud, and that this cloud was loaded with electricity, pregnant, crested, with a kind of hurricane violence that could not be held in check much longer; that the moment was approaching fast when it must break.

Well, all I can say is that the storm did break. It broke that summer while I was in Switzerland. It came in torrents, and it is not over yet.

The life of the artist at any epoch of man's history has not been an easy one. And here in America, it has often seemed to me, it may well be the hardest life that man has ever known. I am not speaking of some frustration in our native life, some barrenness of spirit, some arid Philistinism which contends against the artist's life and which prevents his growth. I do not speak of these things because I do not put the same belief in them that I once did. I am speaking as I have tried to speak from first to last in the concrete terms of the artist's actual experience, of the nature of the physical task before him. It seems to me that the task is one whose physical proportions are vaster and more difficult here than in any other nation on the earth. It is not merely that in the cultures of Europe and of the Orient the American artist can find no antecedent scheme, no structural plan, no body of tradition that can give his own work the validity and truth that it must have. It is not merely that he must make somehow a new tradition for himself, derived from his own life and from the enormous space and energy of American life, the structure of his own design; it is not merely that he is confronted by these problems; it is even more than this, that the labor of a complete and whole articulation, the discovery of an entire universe and of a complete language, is the task that lies before him.

Such is the nature of the struggle to which henceforth our lives must be devoted. Out of the billion forms of America, out of the savage violence and the dense complexity of all its swarming life; from the unique and single substance of this land and life of ours, must we draw the power and energy of our own life, the articulation of our speech, the substance of our art.

For here it seems to me in hard and honest ways like these we may find the tongue, the language, and the conscience that as men and artists we have got to have. Here, too, perhaps, must we who have no more than what we have, who know no more than what we know, who are no more than what we are, find our America. Here, at this present hour and moment of my life, I seek for mine.

UNTRAGIC AMERICA

AFTER 12 YEARS of silence, a new drama by our No. 1 playwright, Eugene O'Neill, is an event. But this one, *The Iceman Cometh,* prompts the reflection that no first-rate American tragedy has ever been written, not even by O'Neill. This despite the fact that the world has been steeped in tragedy for many years and despite the fact that all the characters in *The Iceman* are miserable specimens indeed. Instead of the ennobling effect that tragedy is supposed to give, *The Iceman* is more like a cosmic bellyache. And O'Neill's best plays, as a writer in *Theatre Arts* magazine has pointed out, are not so much real tragedies as "dramatizations of the tragic fact that man has lost sight of his own greatness."

America's failure to create first-rate tragedies may not seem like a national disaster. Yet dramatic tragedy has been the chosen medium of history's greatest art-

From *Life*, December 2, 1946. Reprinted by permission of *Life*, New York. Copyright 1946.

ists, and our failure in it may betoken some deeper failure in the American character or scene. A people who cannot witness great reminders of the tragic aspect of their own existence are not getting the most out of life and perhaps cannot be ranked among the greatest civilizations. The people of Athens and of Shakespeare's England were able to suffer vicariously with their tragic heroes in an emotional workout that left them wiser and more serene. That, said Aristotle, is the purpose of tragedy—to purge the emotions through pity and fear. But Americans disapprove of fear and want to free the world of it. Are we an essentially untragic people?

What Is Tragedy?

First, a few definitions, necessarily dogmatic. According to Aristotle, the first authority on the subject, tragedy must be "serious, complete and of a certain magnitude," to which Webster's dictionary adds that the hero "is by some passion or limitation brought to a catastrophe," the action as a whole working out as "a manifestation of fate." Strictly speaking, first-rate tragedy has been written in only two eras, by only four men: by Aeschylus, Sophocles and Euripedes in the 5th Century B.C. and by Shakespeare. Grade B tragedy (still very fine stuff) has been achieved by Corneille, Racine, Goethe, Ibsen and others, including composers of 19th Century opera; and you can grade it on down from there. But high tragedy must not be confused with pathos, gloom or a mere unhappy ending.

A key word in Aristotle's definition is "magnitude." The Greek and Shakespearean heroes were princes, kings or generals at least, outsize characters whose fate involved the fate of whole cities or nations with their own. Compare King Oedipus or King Lear with what passes for a tragic hero on the American stage—the clerk-hero of Elmer Rice's *Adding Machine*, significantly named Mr. Zero, or the moronic Lennie in Steinbeck's *Of Mice and Men*. Our heroes appeal not to our awe but to our power of sympathetic identification. Aided by naturalistic settings and dialog, we are above all made to feel at home, among equals or inferiors. The characters on our stage and screen may be rich and admirable, but we are always reminded of their humble origin, their warts or some other comfortable and exceedingly nontragic flaw. *The Iceman* carries this democratic snobbism about as far as it can be carried: the characters all start out as a bunch of drunken bums and finish the same.

The requirement of "magnitude," which our drama fails to meet, suggests that great tragedy may be incompatible with American democracy. Except at the Sinatra-fan level, we don't really believe in heroes, and when they appear among us anyway we unfit them for tragedy by cutting them down to size. Just as we reacted to the phenomenon of Hitler by singing *Der Führer's Face*, so we debunk our own heroes, good or bad. American fiction has produced a few characters, such as Ahab in *Moby Dick*, who are of truly tragic magnitude. But the typical American reader tries to get around Ahab by dubbing him a fanatic.

One reason for the greatness of Ahab and for the high seriousness of much Victorian literature in comparison with our own was that our forebears shared a deep Christian sense of sin. This sense of sin was related to a sense of man's cosmic importance, which we seem to have lost. To a Greek, also, man was the center of the universe; his very gods had manlike attributes and were constantly involving themselves in man's affairs, whether guiding him in battle or making love to his wife. But modern man has moved from the center of the universe and reduced himself to a trivial biological specimen. He cannot esteem himself highly enough for high tragedy. He can appraise, analyze, respect and belittle himself, but he cannot regard himself with awe.

Without awe, tragedy cannot achieve its greatest impact. And it may be that our belief that all men are equal, our refusal to admit the very concept of aristocracy, debars us from ever feeling the awe that the Athenians felt toward Oedipus or the Elizabethan groundlings toward Lear. In that case our failure to produce great tragedy may be a virtue, or at least a fair price to pay for our democracy. Maybe we are more like the Romans, who also had great political gifts and never produced any great tragedy either.

Yet democracy does produce heroes, and our history is replete with tragic themes. These themes and heroes may make great American tragedy if we get over our belittling habit and admit to ourselves that the average man is not the measure of all things. But even that won't be enough. For while great tragedy is not necessarily incompatible with democracy, it is incompatible with another habit that lies deep in the American grain.

The Idea of Progress

This habit is an optimistic faith in progress. Professor J. B. Bury, who wrote a history of *The Idea of Progress,* defines it to mean "that civilization has moved, is moving and will move in a desirable direction." This idea is only about as old as modern science, stemming from Bacon and Descartes. But it has as firm a grip on the modern world as the expectation of Judgment Day had on the medieval world. And except among Russian Communists (for Marx swallowed it whole) the idea of progress has nowhere taken deeper root than in America.

Now why is this idea incompatible with high tragedy? Because we have let it replace the old convictions on which tragedy depends, that man is finite (or sinful) and that his destiny does not lie wholly in his own hands. The idea of progress grew from the observable fact of science's increasing conquest of material nature. But Darwin, Herbert Spencer and others stretched this observable fact into certain unprovable assumptions: namely, that "all environments [Darwin's words] will tend to progress toward perfection," that man himself is perfectible through scientific self-knowledge and that evil is not a permanent necessity in the world. Even devout men like Tennyson, whose *Locksley Hall* is the battle hymn of progress, could promote the new faith by assuming God was on its side.

As indeed He may be. But there is increasing evidence to the contrary. There is also evidence that the underpinnings of our faith in progress may be weakening, for the scientists themselves are no longer so sure. The leading physicists have long since regained an almost primitive awe of the universe, and H. G. Wells repudiated a lifelong worship of progress before he left a world for which his final epithet was "doomed formicary." Bury's book was written a generation before the atomic bomb, but the bomb gives these words of his a new point: "If there were good cause for believing that the earth would be uninhabitable in A.D. 2000 or 2100, the doctrine of Progress would lose its meaning and would automatically disappear."

Reversal of Values

To gain a sense of tragedy, Americans must therefore virtually reverse two of their dearest values: on the one hand, we must recover our awareness of evil, uncertainty and fear; on the other, we must gain a sense of man's occasional greatness (which is quite a different thing from "the dignity of the common man"). For tragedy, in essence, is the spectacle of a great man confronting his own finiteness and being punished for letting his reach exceed his grasp. The Greeks had two words for this—*hybris*, pride, and *moira*, fate—which told them that subtle dangers lurk in all human achievements and that the bigger they are the harder they fall. But if Americans believe that there are no insoluble questions, they can't ask tragic questions. And if they believe that punishment is only for ignorance or inadequate effort, they can't give tragic answers. They can't have the tragic sense.

That sense is to feel a due humility before the forces that are able to humble us, without wishing to avoid the contest where the humbling may take place. We will be a more civilized people when we get it.

THE ESSENCE OF TRAGEDY
by MAXWELL ANDERSON

ANYBODY WHO DARES to discuss the making of tragedy lays himself open to critical assault and general barrage, for the theorists have been hunting for the essence of tragedy since Aristotle without entire success. There is no doubt that playwrights have occasionally written tragedy successfully, from Aeschylus on, and there is no doubt that Aristotle came very close to a definition of what tragedy is in his famous passage on catharsis. But why the performance of tragedy should have a cleansing effect on the audience, why an audience is willing to listen to tragedy, why tragedy has a place in the education of men, has never, to my knowledge, been convincingly stated. I must begin by saying that I have not solved the Sphinx's riddle which fifty generations of skillful brains have left in shadow. But I have one suggestion which I think might lead to a solution if it were put to laboratory tests by those who know something about philosophical analysis and dialectic.

There seems no way to get at this suggestion except through a reference to my own adventures in playwriting, so I ask your tolerance while I use myself as an instance. A man who has written successful plays is usually supposed to know something about the theory of playwriting, and perhaps he usually does. In my own case, however, I must confess that I came into the theater unexpectedly, without preparation, and stayed in it because I had a certain amount of rather accidental success. It was not until after I had fumbled my way through a good many successes and an appalling number of failures that I began to doubt the sufficiency of dramatic instinct and to wonder whether or not there were general laws governing dramatic structure which so poor a head for theory as my own might

Reprinted with the permission of William Sloane Associates, Inc., from Maxwell Anderson's *Off Broadway*. Copyright, 1947, by Maxwell Anderson.

grasp and use. I had read the *Poetics* long before I tried playwriting, and I had looked doubtfully into a few well-known handbooks on dramatic structure, but the maxims and theories propounded always drifted by me in a luminous haze—brilliant, true, profound in context, yet quite without meaning for me when I considered the plan for a play or tried to clarify an emotion in dialogue. So far as I could make out every play was a new problem, and the old rules were inapplicable. There were so many rules, so many landmarks, so many pitfalls, so many essential reckonings, that it seemed impossible to find your way through the jungle except by plunging ahead, trusting to your sense of direction and keeping your wits about you as you went.

But as the seasons went by and my failures fell as regularly as the leaves in autumn I began to search again among the theorists of the past for a word of wisdom that might take some of the gamble out of playwriting. What I needed most of all, I felt, was a working definition of what a play is, or perhaps a formula which would include all the elements necessary to a play structure. A play is almost always, probably, an attempt to recapture a vision for the stage. But when you are working in the theater it's most unsatisfactory to follow the gleam without a compass, quite risky to trust "the light that never was on sea or land" without making sure beforehand that you are not being led straight into a slough of despond. In other words you must make a choice among visions, and you must check your chosen vision carefully before assuming that it will make a play. But by what rules, what maps, what fields of reference can you check so intangible a substance as a revelation, a dream, an inspiration, or any similar nudge from the subconscious mind?

I shan't trouble you with the details of my search for a criterion, partly because I can't remember it in detail. But I reread Aristotle's *Poetics* in the light of some bitter experience, and one of his observations led me to a comparison of ancient and modern playwriting methods. In discussing construction he made a point of *the recognition scene* as essential to tragedy. The recognition scene, as Aristotle isolated it in the tragedies of the Greeks, was generally an artificial device, a central scene in which the leading character saw through a disguise, recognized as a friend or as an enemy, perhaps as a lover or a member of his own family, some person whose identity had been hidden. Iphigeneia, for example, acting as priestess in an alien country, receives a victim for sacrifice and then recognizes her own brother in this victim. There is an instant and profound emotional reaction, instantly her direction in the play is altered. But occasionally, in the greatest of the plays, the recognition turned on a situation far more convincing, though no less contrived. Oedipus, hunting savagely for the criminal who has brought the plague upon Thebes, discovers that he is himself that criminal—and since this is a discovery that affects not only the physical well-being and happiness of the hero, but the whole structure of his life, the effect on him and on the direction of the story is incalculably greater than could result from the more superficial revelation made to Iphigeneia.

Now scenes of exactly this sort are rare in the modern drama except in detective stories adapted for the stage. But when I probed a little more deeply into the memorable pieces of Shakespeare's theater and our own I began to see that though modern recognition scenes are subtler and harder to find, they are none the less present in the plays we choose to remember. They seldom have to do with anything so naïve as disguise or the unveiling of a personal identity. But the element of discovery is just as important as ever. For the mainspring in the mechanism of a modern play is almost invariably a discovery by the hero of some element in his environment or in his own soul of which he has not been aware—or which he has not taken sufficiently into account. Moreover, nearly every teacher of playwriting has had some inkling of this, though it was not until after I had worked out my own theory that what they said on this point took on accurate meaning for me. I still think that the rule which I formulated for my own guidance is more concise than any other, and so I give it here: A play should lead up to and away from a central crisis, and this crisis should consist in a discovery by the leading character which has an indelible effect on his thought and emotion and completely alters his course of action. The leading character, let me say again, must make the discovery; it must affect him emotionally; and it must alter his direction in the play.

Try that formula on any play you think worthy of study, and you will find that, with few exceptions, it follows this pattern or some variation of this pattern. The turning point of *The Green Pastures,* for example, is the discovery by God, who is the leading character, that a God who is to endure must conform to the laws of change. The turning point of *Hamlet* is Hamlet's discovery, in the play scene, that his uncle was unquestionably the murderer of his father. In *Abe Lincoln in Illinois* Lincoln's discovery is that he has been a coward, that he has stayed out of the fight for the Union because he was afraid. In each case, you will note, the discovery has a profound emotional effect on the hero, and gives an entirely new direction to his action in the play.

I'm not writing a disquisition on playwriting and wouldn't be competent to write one, but I do want to make a point of the superlative usefulness of this one touchstone for play structure. When a man sets out to write a play his first problem is his subject and the possibilities of that subject as a story to be projected from the stage. His choice of subject matter is his personal problem, and one that takes its answer from his personal relation to his times. But if he wants to know a possible play subject when he finds it, if he wants to know how to mold the subject into play form after he has found it, I doubt that he'll ever discover another standard as satisfactory as the modern version of Aristotle which I have suggested. If the plot he has in mind does not contain a playable episode in which the hero or heroine makes an emotional discovery, a discovery that practically dictates the end of the story, then such an episode must be inserted—and if no place can be found for it the subject is almost certainly a poor one for the theater. If this emotional discovery is contained in the story, but is not central, then it must be made central, and the whole action must revolve around it. In a three-act play it should fall near the end of the second act, though it may be delayed till the last; in a five-act play it will usually be found near the end of the third, though here also it can be delayed. Everything else in the play should be subordinated to this one episode—should lead up to or away from it.

Now this prime rule has a corollary which is just as important as the rule itself. The hero who is to make the central discovery in a play must not be a perfect man. He must have some variation of what

Aristotle calls a tragic fault; and the reason he must have it is that when he makes his discovery he must change both in himself and in his action—and he must change for the better. The fault can be a very simple one—a mere unawareness, for example—but if he has no fault he cannot change for the better, but only for the worse, and for a reason which I shall discuss later, it is necessary that he must become more admirable, and not less so, at the end of the play. In other words, a hero must pass through an experience which opens his eyes to an error of his own. He must learn through suffering. In a tragedy he suffers death itself as a consequence of his fault or his attempt to correct it, but before he dies he has become a nobler person because of his recognition of his fault and the consequent alteration of his course of action. In a serious play which does not end in death he suffers a lesser punishment, but the pattern remains the same. In both forms he has a fault to begin with, he discovers that fault during the course of the action, and he does what he can to rectify it at the end. In *The Green Pastures* God's fault was that he believed himself perfect. He discovered that he was not perfect, that he had been in error and must make amends. Hamlet's fault was that he could not make up his mind to act. He offers many excuses for his indecision until he discovers that there is no real reason for hesitation and that he has delayed out of cowardice. Lincoln, in *Abe Lincoln in Illinois,* has exactly the same difficulty. In the climactic scene it is revealed to him that he had hesitated to take sides through fear of the consequences to himself, and he then chooses to go ahead without regard for what may be in store for him. From the point of view of the playwright, then, the essence of a tragedy, or even of a serious play, is the spiritual awakening, or regeneration, of his hero.

When a playwright attempts to reverse the formula, when his hero makes a discovery which has an evil effect, or one which the audience interprets as evil, on his character, the play is inevitably a failure on the stage. In *Troilus and Cressida* Troilus discovers that Cressida is a light woman. He draws from her defection the inference that all women are faithless—that faith in woman is the possession of fools. As a consequence he turns away from life and seeks death in a cause as empty as the love he has given up, the cause of the strumpet Helen. All the glory of Shakespeare's verse cannot rescue the play for an audience, and save in *Macbeth* Shakespeare nowhere wrote so richly, so wisely, or with such a flow of brilliant metaphor.

For the audience will always insist that the alteration in the hero be for the better —or for what it believes to be the better. As audiences change the standards of good and evil change, though slowly and unpredictably, and the meanings of plays change with the centuries. One thing only is certain: that an audience watching a play will go along with it only when the leading character responds in the end to what it considers a higher moral impulse than moved him at the beginning of the story, though the audience will of course define morality as it pleases and in the terms of its own day. It may be that there is no absolute up or down in this world, but the race believes that there is, and will not hear of any denial.

And now at last I come to the point toward which I've been struggling so laboriously. Why does the audience come to the theater to look on while an imaginary hero is put to an imaginary trial and comes out of it with credit to the race and to him-

[156]

The Essence of Tragedy

self? It was this question that prompted my essay, and unless I've been led astray by my own predilections there is a very possible answer in the rules for playwriting which I have just cited. The theater originated in two complementary religious ceremonies, one celebrating the animal in man and one celebrating the god. Old Greek Comedy was dedicated to the spirits of lust and riot and earth, spirits which are certainly necessary to the health and continuance of the race. Greek tragedy was dedicated to man's aspiration, to his kinship with the gods, to his unending, blind attempt to lift himself above his lusts and his pure animalism into a world where there are other values than pleasure and survival. However unaware of it we may be, our theater has followed the Greek patterns with no change in essence, from Aristophanes and Euripides to our own day. Our more ribald musical comedies are simply our approximation of the Bacchic rites of Old Comedy. In the rest of our theater we sometimes follow Sophocles, whose tragedy is always an exaltation of the human spirit, sometimes Euripides, whose tragicomedy follows the same pattern of an excellence achieved through suffering. The forms of both tragedy and comedy have changed a good deal in non-essentials, but in essentials—and especially in the core of meaning which they must have for audiences—they are in the main the same religious rites which grew up around the altars of Attica long ago.

It is for this reason that when you write for the theater you must choose between your version of a phallic revel and your vision of what mankind may or should become. Your vision may be faulty, or shallow, or sentimental, but it must conform to some aspiration in the audience, or the audience will reject it. Old Comedy, the celebration of the animal in us, still has a place in our theater, as it had in Athens, but here, as there, that part of the theater which celebrated man's virtue and his regeneration in hours of crisis is accepted as having the more important function. Our comedy is largely the Greek New Comedy, which grew out of Euripides' tragicomedy, and is separated from tragedy only in that it presents a happier scene and puts its protagonist through an ordeal which is less than lethal.

And since our plays, aside from those which are basically Old Comedy, are exaltations of the human spirit, since that is what an audience expects when it comes to the theater, the playwright gradually discovers, as he puts plays before audiences, that he must follow the ancient Aristotelian rule: he must build his plot around a scene wherein his hero discovers some mortal frailty or stupidity in himself and faces life armed with a new wisdom. He must so arrange his story that it will prove to the audience that men pass through suffering purified, that, animal though we are, despicable though we are in many ways, there is in us all some divine, incalculable fire that urges us to be better than we are.

It could be argued that what the audience demands of a hero is only conformity to race morality, to the code which seems to the spectators most likely to make for race survival. In many cases, especially in comedy, and obviously in the comedy of Molière, this is true. But in the majority of ancient and modern plays it seems to me that what the audience wants to believe is that men have a desire to break the molds of earth which encase them and claim a kinship with a higher morality than that which hems them in. The rebellion of Antigone, who breaks the laws of men through adherence to a higher law of affection, the rebellion of Prometheus, who

[157]

breaks the law of the gods to bring fire to men, the rebellion of God in *The Green Pastures* against the rigid doctrine of the Old Testament, the rebellion of Tony in *They Knew What They Wanted* against the convention that called on him to repudiate his cuckold child, the rebellion of Liliom against the heavenly law which asked him to betray his own integrity and make a hypocrisy of his affection, even the repudiation of the old forms and the affirmation of new by the heroes of Ibsen and Shaw, these are all instances to me of the groping of men toward an excellence dimly apprehended, seldom possible of definition. They are evidence to me that the theater at its best is a religious affirmation, an age-old rite restating and reassuring man's belief in his own destiny and his ultimate hope. The theater is much older than the doctrine of evolution, but its one faith, asseverated again and again for every age and every year, is a faith in evolution, in the reaching and the climb of men toward distant goals, glimpsed but never seen, perhaps never achieved, or achieved only to be passed impatiently on the way to a more distant horizon.

THE NEW WAY OF WRITING

by Bonamy Dobrée

Can we say that there is, definitely, "a new way of writing"? Is there such a thing as *modern* prose, with characteristics the older prose does not possess?[1] It may seem at first sight that the question cannot reasonably be put, for if we are agreed that style is the personal voice—which pierces through even the "impersonal" manner—and that the voice is the man; and if we assume, as we plausibly can, that man does not alter except over very long periods, can we talk of a modern as opposed to an old-fashioned style?

One can make two answers to this. The first is, that though time may not change man physically, nor perhaps mentally, leaving his vocal cords and what he wants to do with them still the same, two things do change: the social being, and with him the method of speech he must use to be effective with other social beings. Man as a social animal alters in tune with what we call, since a better term is lacking, "the spirit of the age," which we gauge by the different approaches men make to the external universe, and, more important perhaps, to their own emotions. Man may be fundamentally unchanged, but in the social process of his time, different facets are polished, unfamiliar aspects emerge. To take a simple example: How would a fourteenth-century man react if he were asked to think of "the wonders of the deep" compared with the way a twentieth-century man would react? To-day we should at once let our minds turn to what we might roughly call "scientific marvels," that is to various detailed manifestations of fish life, or of corals. The fourteenth-century man would shudder deliciously at a vision of leviathans, appallingly, even incredibly shaped, of mermaids, of ghostly

From Bonamy Dobrée, *Modern Prose Style*, Oxford, 1934. Reprinted by permission of The Clarendon Press, Oxford.

[1] I may suggest to begin with, that had I been writing thirty years ago, I would probably have felt constrained to write "with characteristics *which* the older . . ."

[158]

inhabitants. Not only, then, will men of various ages wish to *ex*press different things, but they will wish to *im*press men differently. What would be the good, for instance, of a member of the House of Lords rising up and saying:

> My Lords, this ruinous and ignominious situation, where we cannot act with success nor suffer with honour, calls upon us to remonstrate in the strongest and loudest language of truth, to rescue the ears of majesty from the delusions which surround it.

We can imagine a peer having similar feelings about, perhaps, the situation in India, but such language, used by Chatham in 1777, would have no result whatever now, though in its way it is splendid, and in its own age was no doubt very effective indeed. Our second answer arises out of the first: since the needs of the voice have changed, the instrument has been altered: we no longer use the same tool as our ancestors did to move other people. And there is still another consideration. If we use a different tool it is that our emotions have changed, or at any rate, if our emotions do not change, our attitude towards them differs with the age in which we live. These things, however, interact upon each other. We know, as once we did not know, that our emotions vary with the language we use in describing them: the spirit of an age may not only be reflected in its prose, it may be, indeed it is, to some extent conditioned by it. This, however, is an issue which would take us too far outside the bounds of our subject; nor am I qualified to pursue it.

Let us now take two passages, dealing with much the same range of ideas, written by men who were each in their day stylists. We have already done something of the sort in the Introduction, but we can use another example to reinforce the argument of the first. This time one writer is Sir Thomas Browne, the other William James, and I am taking Browne at his most straightforward.

> Let thy studies be free as thy thoughts and contemplations: but fly not only upon the wings of imagination; join sense unto reason, and experiment unto speculation, and so give life unto embryon truths, and verities yet in their chaos. There is nothing more acceptable unto the ingenious world, than this noble eluctation of truth; wherein, against the tenacity of prejudice and prescription, this century now prevaileth.

That is from *Christian Morals:* now let us take this from *The Will to Believe:*

> On the whole, then, we must conclude that no philosophy of ethics is possible in the old-fashioned absolute sense of the term. Everywhere the ethical philosopher must wait on facts. The thinkers who create the ideals come he knows not whence, their sensibilities are evolved he knows not how; and the question as to which of two conflicting ideals will give the best universe then and there, can be answered by him only through the aid of the experience of other men.

I take it that anybody, even neglecting Browne's obsolete forms, would at once recognize the first passage as belonging to the seventeenth century, and the second to our own time. Can we put our finger on where exactly the difference lies?

It is pretty obvious that the difference lies in the rhythm, but that is too easy a thing to say: and as a matter of fact, if we analyse these two passages into "prose rhythms" in the way that Saintsbury did in his fascinating book, they are not, prosodically speaking at least, so different after all. Are not such cadences as

embryŏn/trūths, ănd/vēritĭes/yĕt ĭn
their/chāos,

and

ōld-făshiŏned/ābsŏlūte/sēnse ŏf thĕ/tērm,

of much the same order? Both are, in a sense, dactylic. What is different is the way the metres are used. In modern writing there is far less insistence on the rhythms; the unit into which the rhythms are woven, that is to say the phrase, is far more flexible, on the whole longer. The antithetical balance has gone. But what is more significant is that the written language to-day is much nearer the spoken language, with implications we shall follow up in a moment. But first I must dispose of two possible objections. The first and lesser one is that for the seventeenth-century example we have a very conscious stylist. That is true, but Jeremy Taylor or Milton will give much the same result. Why do we remember, except for its insistence on rhythm, Milton's "rousing herself like a strong man after sleep, and shaking her invincible locks"? But how do I know, it will be asked in the second place, that the older people did not speak as they wrote? The suggestion is often made, most notably by Mr. Gordon Bottomley, that in the seventeenth century, especially in Shakespeare's time, the rhythms of everyday speech were more accentuated, approached even those of blank verse, or of obviously cadenced speech. Let us look at something from a contemporary of Sir Thomas Browne's:

Up, and by water, stopping at Michell's, and there saw Betty, but could have no discourse with her, but there drank. To White Hall, and there walked to St. James's, where I find the Court mighty full, it being the Duke of York's birthday; and he mighty fine, and all the musick, one after another, to my great content.

Pepys, you see at once, was not writing literary English: he was setting down his doings as he might have chatted about them to his wife—if, of course, he had been a brave enough man to do so.

It is fairly certain, I think, that the written language of the seventeenth century was farther from the spoken language than the written language of to-day is from our conversation, a division which probably began with Caxton. John Donne, one can be sure, never spoke at home in the way that he thundered from the pulpit. The proof is to be found in the correspondence of the time, much of which has been collected by Professor Wyld in his *History of Modern Colloquial English,* largely for this purpose; and what comes out is that the language of the Elizabethans was not essentially unlike our own. Here, for one example, is Sir Philip Sidney writing to Edward Molyneux:

Few words are best. My letters to my father have come to the eyes of some. Neither can I condemn any but you for it. If it be so you have played the very knave with me; and so I will make you know if I have good proof of it. But that for so much as is past. For that is to come, I assure you before God, that if ever I know you do so much as read any letter I write to my father, without his commandment, or my consent, I will thrust my dagger into you. And trust to it, for I speak it in earnest. In the mean time, farewell.

The sentiments of this prose (we trust) are not ours, and the forms are not quite so, but the ring of it is. If we were to say that sort of thing, we should say it in that kind of way. Sidney's prose here, we see, is altogether different from what he wrote for the press, his "Sidneyan showers of sweet discourse." Here is another example; and making allowance for stage speech, does it sound very quaint or old-fashioned, or very heavily rhythmed?

Thou are so fat-witted, with drinking of old sack, and unbuttoning thee after supper, and sleeping upon benches after noon, that thou hast forgotten to demand that truly which thou wouldst truly know. What a devil hast thou to do with the time of the day. . . .

Prince Hal probably spoke fairly current English; and the journalists of the time, Nashe, Greene, Dekker, wrote much in the way Prince Hal spoke, for they were not labouring after fine style, but trying to write as men talked. What appears to have happened is that in the seventeenth century a profound division developed between the spoken and the written language, a division bridged by the journalists and the comic writers. What seems to have occurred afterwards was, to cut a long story short, that the journalists, forgetting Dryden, deserted to the written side: one has only to think of Addison, and then of Dr. Johnson, who, far from trying to write as he naturally spoke, did his best to model his conversation on his writing. Everybody remembers how he let slip the remark about *The Rehearsal* not having wit enough to keep it sweet, and then, recoiling in horror from so natural an expression, hurriedly amended the phrase to "has not vitality enough to preserve it from corruption." The stylists of the eighteenth century seem to have taken their writing farther and farther away from their speech—Gibbon, Burke, Smollett. This process went on through the nineteenth century; we have only to think of Carlyle or Pater, though it is true that some people all the while kept up the spoken tradition, Defoe, Sterne, and even Lamb, for though Lamb's style is artificial as regards words, his rhythms are those of his talk, or at any rate of his possible talk. What I think is going on at the present day is a return to speech rhythms: the conscious stylists are, so to speak, ridding themselves of "style": not "style," but *a* style is what they are aiming at, a style that will faithfully reflect their mind as it utters itself naturally. What is curious is that now it is the leading authors who write naturally, style, so-called, being left to the journalists. I take the opening sentence of the first leading article of *The Times* of the day on which I happened to be taking notes for this chapter (19 August 1933): "As soon as it was announced, on the morrow of Parliament's rising. . . ." One need not go on. Who would dream of *saying* "on the morrow of Parliament's rising"? It is jargon. What we would probably say is, "the day after Parliament rose." Not that this *pompier* "style" is confined to the august heights of journalism: it runs all through, and not long ago *The Daily Worker* printed with regard to certain prisons: "No sound comes from out those walls." Does the man who wrote those words habitually say "from out"? Why does this happen? Why do people write forms which are dead, which they would never utter? In both the examples quoted one is tempted to diagnose insincerity of thought, or at least mental laziness.

Does it not seem, then, that the modern prosewriter, in returning to the rhythms of everyday speech, is trying to be more honest with himself than if he used, as is too wreckingly easy, the forms and terms already published as the expression of other people's minds? "Style . . . is not an ornament; it is not an exercise, not a caper, nor complication of any sort. It is the sense of one's self, the knowledge of what one wants to say, and the saying of it in the most fitting words."[2] And that is why it is extremely hard to achieve *a* style, for all these three things are very difficult to attain. Take only the last task, the saying of what one wants to say in the most fitting words. It seems almost impossible, for every time we speak we have virtually to re-create the instrument if we want to be faithful to our idea or feeling. Everywhere the words and phrasing of past generations interpose themselves between us and the reality. "It is . . . a true and lamentable fact that, in ultimate analysis, one cannot speak about anything without altering it to some extent."[3] It is the realization of this, a realization possibly new in our day, which impels authors to try to write as they speak in ordinary life on ordinary physical matters, for it is only in this way that one can achieve fidelity to one's self: otherwise the language and style of the literary tradition assert themselves. But the modern writer must not think of style: the man who thinks first of style is lost: the primary thing to do—this is an old observation—is to think clearly. As M. Jean Cocteau says, writing for modern authors: "Style cannot be a starting point: it happens. What is style? For a great many people it is a complicated way of saying very simple things. From our point of view it is a very simple way of saying complicated things."[4] How does a modern writer tackle this problem? Here, I think, is a good example:

I had great ambitions. I have none now—and have not even the fear of failing. What matters to me and to many of the survivors of my generation is only that which is common to us all, our fear for our children. If it were not for that, I should know how to act in what remains of my life—that would be to withdraw as far as possible from the little world of writing and talking about books which is a microcosm of the whole, its values no finer than those accepted by the rest of the world, and only valid on the assumption that to a writer success means precisely what it means to a stockbroker or a multiple grocer. That is, material wealth, and the respect paid to it. This seems to me a denial of all the writer, the "clerk," should stand for, but I can do nothing to alter it, and therefore I ought to run away for my life.

After all that turbulence of desire and ambitions it seems strange I should believe now that very little in me is real except the absolute need, intellectual and spiritual, for withdrawal, for resolving to satisfy in my life only the simple wants. It is as strange as that I am only just learning to write and don't care to.

There are days when I retract all this, and think how queer I shall grow if I live alone, and think too that what is needed is some effort to create cells inside the body social, groups of angry, last-minute saints. That would be no good. I should weary in a week of the company of persons who thought and felt no differently from myself.[5]

That, as prose, is simple, easy, fluent, and flexible; what is important, however, is that it is written, apparently, in the *tones*

---

[2] Introduction to *The London Book of English Prose,* by Herbert Read and Bonamy Dobrée, Eyre and Spottiswoode, 1931.
[3] *The Theory of Speech and Language,* by A. H. Gardiner, Oxford, 1932.
[4] *A Call to Order,* Allen and Unwin, trs. 1933.
[5] From *No Time Like the Present,* by Storm Jameson, Cassell, 1933.

of every day, though here and there we can detect traces of literary forms—"only that which" instead of "only what": "how to act" instead of "what to do": it is extraordinarily difficult to rid one's self of terms of that kind. But to show how new the tone is, here is a passage from another autobiography written, one always thought, in a natural, confidential manner:

There were perhaps twenty boys in the school at most, and often fewer. I made the excursion between home and school four times a day; if I walked fast, the transit might take five minutes, and, as there were several objects of interest on the way, it might be spread over an hour. In fine weather the going to and from school was very delightful, and small as the scope was, it could be varied almost indefinitely.[6]

There are, we see immediately, one or two obvious "literary" turns in that passage: "I made the excursion between home and school," instead of "I went to and from school": "If I walked fast, the transit might take five minutes," instead of "I could get there or back (or do the journey) in five minutes": "objects of interest," with others of the same sort. And the general run, which is the important thing, though simple and easy, and we might perhaps admit fluent, is not flexible. Each sentence contains an idea and completes it. The mind comes to a full stop at the end of each phrase. But our minds in life do not work in that way; they are always ready to frame the next sentence, carried on by the impetus of the last. Gosse, in common with the older writers, was concerned, not to follow the movements of his mind, but to present something concrete.

To say, then, that the hall-mark of good modern prose style is an essential fidelity does not imply that writers of previous generations were charlatans and liars, only that they owed fidelity to other things. And it is here that the spirit of our age imposes itself upon our style. All the previous ages whose writers have been quoted or referred to here had something they could take for granted, and it never occurred to the older writers that they could not take themselves for granted. We can be sure of nothing; our civilization is threatened, even the simplest things we live by: we are on the verge of amazing changes. In our present confusion our only hope is to be scrupulously honest with ourselves, so honest as to doubt our own minds and the conclusions they arrive at. Most of us have ceased to believe, except provisionally, in truths, and we feel that what is important is not so much truth as the way our minds move towards truths. Therefore, to quote M. Cocteau again, "Form must be the form of the mind. Not a way of saying things, but of thinking them." Perhaps that is why we nowadays instinctively mistrust any one who pontificates: and, as a matter of experience, if we examine the writings of the pontificators, people skilled in "a way of saying things," we invariably find that their style is bad, that falsity has crept in somewhere. The writer is not being faithful to the movement of his mind; he is taking things for granted, and he fills us of to-day with uneasiness.

We have, then, to judge of the integrity of a modern writer by this sense of himself that we feel he has. If we are to respond, he must (we suppose) be aware of himself as something a little uncertain in

[6] From *Father and Son,* by Edmund Gosse, Heinemann, 1907.

this shifting universe: he also is part of the material which he has to treat with respect: he must listen to himself, so to speak, to hear what he has to say. He must not prejudge, or force an issue: we must be able to imagine that he is talking to himself. In no other way can he achieve *a* style, which is the sound of his voice, which is the man himself.

It is not so simple as it sounds for a man to watch his own mind; it is as difficult as writing in the way you ordinarily talk: literary habits continually get in the way. Nor must a man write as he might lazily talk, and it is more important than ever for him to reject the dead metaphor which can never be more than an approximation, to choose the exact, the expressive word, to rid his style of fat, to make it athletic. What he must really do, as the first essential, is to keep his awareness athletic, especially his awareness of himself. And he must not watch his mind idly; he must watch it as he might a delicate piece of machinery doing its work, and he must watch it, not flickering about in every direction, as an active mind does, but only in the direction he wants it to go. Otherwise the result may be disastrous. Even the following extremely clever attempt seems to me an object-lesson:

The problem from this time on became more definite.

It was all so nearly alike it must be different and it is different, it is natural that if everything is used and there is a continuous present and a beginning again and again if it is all so alike it must be simply different and everything simply different was the natural way of creating it then.

In this natural way of creating it then that it was simply different everything being alike it was simply different, this kept on leading one to lists. Lists naturally for a while and by lists I mean a series. More and more in going back over what was done at this time I find that I naturally kept simply different as an intention. Whether there was or whether there was not a continuous present did not then any longer trouble me there was or there was, and using everything no longer troubled me if everything is alike using everything could no longer trouble me and beginning again and again could no longer trouble me because if lists were inevitable if series were inevitable and the whole of it was inevitable beginning again and again could not trouble me so then with nothing to trouble me I very completely began naturally since everything is alike making it as simply different naturally as simply different as possible. I began doing natural phenomena what I call natural phenomena and natural phenomena naturally everything being alike natural phenomena are making things be naturally simply different. This found its culmination later, in the beginning it began in a center confused with lists with series with geography with returning portraits and with particularly often four and three and often with five and four. It is easy to see that in the beginning such a conception as everything being naturally different would be very inarticulate and very slowly it began to emerge and take the form of anything, and then naturally if anything that is simply different is simply different what follows will follow.[7]

One cannot say whether Miss Stein's mind really moves like that: possibly it does, and possibly most of our minds move more like that than we are aware of, or at any rate are prepared to admit. What is clear is that the mere following of the mind, its echoes and repetitions, does not really give its shape; and this makes us realize that to write naturally as the mind would wish to utter, is just as much an

[7] From *Composition as Explanation*, by Gertrude Stein, Hogarth Press, 1926.

art—or an artifice—as to write in what we call an artificial style, say that of a Pater or Meredith. What has happened is that the modern writer is faced with new material, and what he has to do is to discover the new form that this material requires.

But because this new form can only be an adaptation of the old, it takes consummate art to prevent literature interposing itself between us and life. The problem, no doubt, has always existed, but if it has been realized the solution has rarely, if ever, been hit on. Yet there is Sterne, and what Mrs. Woolf has to say about him is illuminating:

... With the first words—They order, said I, this matter better in France—we are in the world of *Tristram Shandy*. It is a world in which anything may happen. We hardly know what jest, what jibe, what flash of poetry is not going to glance suddenly through the gap which this astonishingly agile pen has cut in the thick-set hedge of English prose. Is Sterne himself responsible? Does he know what he is going to say next for all his resolve to be on his best behaviour this time? The jerky disconnected sentences are as rapid and it would seem as little under control as the phrases that fall from the lips of a brilliant talker. The very punctuation is that of speech, not writing, and brings the sounds and associations of the speaking voice in with it. The order of the ideas, their suddenness and irrelevancy, is more true to life than to literature. ... Under the influence of this extraordinary style the book becomes semi-transparent. The usual ceremonies and conventions which keep reader and writer at arm's length disappear. We are as close to life as we can be.[8]

That passage is not quoted as being characteristic of Mrs. Woolf: to hear her real voice one must go to the novels: it is quoted as an aid to my argument. And it serves it in two ways, because of what it says, and because of the way it says it, for if the prose is not markedly Mrs. Woolf's, it is obviously modern: the voice that is speaking is a voice of to-day: I shall not be misunderstood, I hope, if I say that any one might have written it. Now let us compare this with the way Bagehot wrote about Sterne in the *National Review* in 1864:

But here the great excellence of Sterne ends as well as begins. In *Tristram Shandy* especially there are several defects which, while we are reading it, tease and disgust us so much that we are scarcely willing even to admire as we ought to admire the refined pictures of human emotion. The first of these, and perhaps the worst, is the fantastic disorder of the form. It is an imperative law of the writing art, that a book should go straight on. A great writer should be able to tell a great meaning as coherently as a small writer tells a small meaning. ...

and so it goes on. That is typical nineteenth-century prose: we get something very like it in Matthew Arnold, or Huxley, and in its way it is excellent. But the rhythms and inflexions are quite different from those of to-day: it consists, not of thoughts closely followed, not of ideas suggested, but of utterances, of pronouncements. Again, as with Gosse, we have the end-stopped phrase: there is a door banged at the end of each, and we feel as though we were on parade receiving orders.

What seems to us to be lacking in the older prose is the sense of the uninterrupted flow of the mind: Bagehot, for example, appears to cut off this continuum, shall we call it, into arbitrary lengths, as

---

[8] *The Common Reader*, ii, Hogarth Press, 1932.

we slice chunks off a cucumber. This is to force on our minds a logic that is not of their own making; and though it may be true that, as T. E. Hulme said, "All styles are only means of subduing the reader," we must not feel that our minds are being forced, and therefore distorted. Perhaps it was George Moore's principal achievement to give this sense of flow: there is hardly an instant's pause in his mental processes. His style is very distinctive; all the time one hears a voice, a personal utterance, though pursued to the lengths to which he took it, or allowed it to carry him, it becomes in the end monotonous. The mind runs on too much; it has no form but that of a stream: no solid shape emerges. But the sort of flow we are talking about can, and sometimes does, take form. Here is an extract from Henry James, whose whole being was directed to following the movement of his mind, and who gave form to this movement, not indeed in a language natural to us, but one which seems to have been natural to him, a way which he could not have escaped from even if he had wanted to:

Momentary side-winds—things of no real authority—break in every now and then to put their inferior little questions to me; but I come back, I come back, as I say, I all throbbingly and yearningly and passionately, oh mon bon come back to this way that is clearly the only one in which I can do anything now, and that will open out to me more and more, and that has overwhelming reasons pleading all beautifully in its breast. What really happens is that the closer I get to the problem of the application of it in any particular case, the more I get *into* that application, so that the more doubts and torments fall away from me, the more I know where I am, the more everything spreads and shines and draws me on and I'm justified in my logic and my passion. . . . Causons, causons, mon bon—oh celestial, soothing, sanctifying process, with all the high sane forces of the sacred time fighting, through it, on my side! Let me fumble it gently and patiently out—with fever and fidget laid to rest—as in all the old enchanted months! It only looms, it only shines and shimmers, *too* beautiful and too interesting, it only hangs there too rich and too full and with too much to give and to pay; it only presents itself too admirably and too vividly, too straight and square and vivid, as a little organic and effective Action.[9]

We may think that artificial, but we do not feel, complicated as it is, that this is a literary language. It is the language of Henry James's speech; it reflects his mind accurately, a mind with a very definite form. James, if you like, had a tortuous way of thinking, but he had broken down the barriers between his mind and the expression of it.

What we look for, however, is a style which shall be as free and individual as in that passage, but which smacks less of idiosyncrasy, for something we might all use, though, no doubt, not so well as our model, for something which does not give us, as some recent prose does, the uneasy effect of submitting us to a laboratory experiment. Perhaps this is what we want:

The trouble with her ship was that it would *not* sail. It rode water-logged in the rotting port of home. All very well to have wild, reckless moods of irony and independence, if you have to pay for them by withering dustily on the shelf.

Alvina fell again into humility and fear: she began to show symptoms of her mother's heart trouble. For day followed day, month followed month, season after season went

[9] *Letters*, Macmillan.

by, and she grubbed away like a housemaid in Manchester House, she hurried round doing the shopping, she sang in the choir on Sundays, she attended the various chapel events, she went out to visit friends, and laughed and talked and played games. But all the time, what was there actually in her life? Not much. She was withering towards old-maiddom. Already in her twenty-eighth year, she spent her days grubbing in the house, whilst her father became an elderly, frail man still too lively in mind and spirit. Miss Pinnegar began to grow grey and elderly too, money became scarcer and scarcer, there was a black day ahead when her father would die and the home be broken up, and she would have to tackle life as a worker.

There lay the only alternative: in work. She might slave her days away teaching the piano, as Miss Frost had done: she might find a subordinate post as nurse: she might sit in the cash-desk of some shop. Some work of some sort would be found for her. And she would sink into the routine of her job, as did so many women, and grow old and die, chattering and fluttering. She would have what is called her independence. But, seriously faced with that treasure, and without the option of refusing it, strange how hideous she found it.

Work!—a job! More even than she rebelled against the Withams did she rebel against a job. . . .[10]

It is clear, I imagine, that that could not have been written in the last century; it speaks with the authentic voice of this. It has the ring of what we hear around us every day: it has no air of "style," yet it is extremely expressive. Certain liberties are taken, such as leaving out "It is . . ." before "all very well . . ." in the first paragraph. Here and there we feel just a touch of literary formulas, and we wish they were not there: "as did so many women" instead of "as so many women did," but these things are very rare in Lawrence. We feel that he is nearly always completely free of "literature" and can be himself. We follow his mind working—and he speaks as it works. Or, at least, that is the impression we get. It is not true, of course: but at least he is using his material (part of which is his mind) with complete freedom, and finding a form which will make it tell.

Suppose that, before we go on to discuss experiments, we try to prophesy what direction our prose will take. We might perhaps say that it will be in that of greater flexibility and a more curious following of our mental processes, with, sometimes, violence offered to our old notions of syntax wherever we find them distorting or cumbrous. One would like to think that all of us will come to the stage of refusing to write what we would not, indeed could not, say, though that, of course, is not to limit our writing to what we actually do say. This is not to claim for a moment that by writing as we speak we shall achieve a style; before we do that we must go through at least three fundamental disciplines. First there is that of fidelity to thought, the extremely difficult task of complete honesty; we must not, as is so easy, allow language to condition our thought: then there is the labour of finding the exact words and the exact inflexion of phrase to carry the whole sense, the emotional colour, of the words; and thirdly, it is over and above these things that we have to model our prose to give it what seems to be the run and structure of our usual speaking. That is where the artifice comes in, and that is where we can achieve the art.

[10] From *The Lost Girl*, by D. H. Lawrence, Secker, 1920.

Speed photograph of a tennis player, 1939. Edgerton.

Used with the permission of H. E. Edgerton and publisher. From Siegfried Giedion, Space, Time and Architecture, *Harvard University Press.*

Guernica. 1937. Detail. Pablo Picasso.

Lent by the artist to the Museum of Modern Art, New York.

Many people today as in former days look at pictures for what they say rather than for what they are. Then, stories and sentiments were read; today, the reading is of formal relations. The authenticity in one case may be no greater than in the other.*

* From *Appreciation: Painting, Poetry and Prose* by Leo Stein, copyright 1947 by Leo Stein, used by permission of Crown Publishers, Inc.

HOW WRITING IS WRITTEN
by GERTRUDE STEIN

WHAT I WANT to talk about to you is just the general subject of how writing is written. The beginning of it is what everybody has to know: everybody is contemporary with his period. A very bad painter once said to a very great painter, 'Do what you like, you cannot get rid of the fact that we are contemporaries.' That is what goes on in writing. The whole crowd of you are contemporary to each other, and the whole business of writing is the question of living in the contemporariness. Each generation has to live in that. The thing that is important is that nobody knows what the contemporariness is. In other words, they don't know where they are going, but they are on their way.

Each generation has to do with what you would call the daily life: and a writer, painter, or any sort of creative artist, is not at all ahead of his time. He is contemporary. He can't live in the past, because it is gone. He can't live in the future, because no one knows what it is. He can live only in the present of his daily life. He is expressing the thing that is being expressed by everybody else in their daily lives. The thing you have to remember is that everybody lives a contemporary daily life. The writer lives it, too, and expresses it imperceptibly. The fact remains that in the act of living, everybody has to live contemporarily. But in the things concerning art and literature they don't have to live contemporarily, because it doesn't make any difference; and they live about forty years behind their time. And that is the real explanation of why the artist or painter is not recognized by his contemporaries. He is expressing the time-sense of his contemporaries, but nobody is really interested. After the new generation has come, after the grandchildren, so to speak, then the opposition dies out: because after all there is then a new contemporary expression to oppose.

That is really the fact about contemporariness. As I see the whole crowd of you, if there are any of you who are going to express yourselves contemporarily, you will do something which most people won't want to look at. Most of you will be so busy living the contemporary life that it will be like the tired business man: in the things of the mind you will want the things you know. And too, if you don't live contemporarily, you are a nuisance. That is why we live contemporarily. If a man goes along the street with horse and carriage in New York in the snow, that man is a nuisance; and he knows it, so now he doesn't do it. He would not be living, or acting, contemporarily: he would only be in the way, a drag.

The world can accept me now because there is coming out of *your* generation somebody they won't like, and therefore they accept me because I am sufficiently past in having been contemporary so they don't have to dislike me. So thirty years from now I shall be accepted. And the same thing will happen again: that is the reason why every generation has the same thing happen. It will always be the same story, because there is always the same situation presented. The contemporary thing in art and literature is the thing which doesn't make enough difference to the people of that generation so that they can accept it or reject it.

Reprinted by permission of Random House, Inc.

Most of you know that in a funny kind of way you are nearer your grandparents than your parents. Since this contemporariness is always there, nobody realizes that you cannot follow it up. That is the reason people discover—those interested in the activities of other people—that they cannot understand their contemporaries. If you kids started in to write, I wouldn't be a good judge of you, because I am of the third generation. What you are going to do I don't know any more than anyone else. But I created a movement of which you are the grandchildren. The contemporary thing is the thing you can't get away from. That is the fundamental thing in all writing.

Another thing you have to remember is that each period of time not only has its contemporary quality, but it has a time-sense. Things move more quickly, slowly, or differently, from one generation to another. Take the Nineteenth Century. The Nineteenth Century was roughly the Englishman's Century. And their method, as they themselves, in their worst moments, speak of it, is that of 'muddling through.' They begin at one end and hope to come out at the other: their grammar, parts of speech, methods of talk, go with this fashion. The United States began a different phase when, after the Civil War, they discovered and created out of their inner need a different way of life. They created the Twentieth Century. The United States, instead of having the feeling of beginning at one end and ending at another, had the conception of assembling the whole thing out of its parts, the whole thing which made the Twentieth Century productive. The Twentieth Century conceived an automobile as a whole, so to speak, and then created it, built it up out of its parts. It was an entirely different point of view from the Nineteenth Century's. The Nineteenth Century would have seen the parts, and worked towards the automobile through them.

Now in a funny sort of way this expresses, in different terms the difference between the literature of the Nineteenth Century and the literature of the Twentieth. Think of your reading. If you look at it from the days of Chaucer, you will see that what you might call the 'internal history' of a country always affects its use of writing. It makes a difference in the expression, in the vocabulary, even in the handling of grammar. In an amusing story in your *Literary Magazine,* when the author speaks of the fact that he is tired of using quotation marks and isn't going to use them any more, with him that is a joke; but when I began writing, the whole question of punctuation was a vital question. You see, I had this new conception: I had this conception of the whole paragraph, and in *The Making of Americans* I had this idea of a whole thing. But if you think of contemporary English writers, it doesn't work like that at all. They conceive of it as pieces put together to make a whole, and I conceived it as a whole made up of its parts. I didn't know what I was doing any more than you know, but in response to the need of my period I was doing this thing. That is why I came in contact with people who were unconsciously doing the same thing. They had the Twentieth Century conception of a whole. So the element of punctuation was very vital. The comma was just a nuisance. If you got the thing as a whole, the comma kept irritating you all along the line. If you think of a thing as a whole, and the comma keeps sticking out, it gets on your nerves; because, after all, it destroys the reality of the whole. So I got rid more and more of commas. Not because I had any prejudice against commas; but the comma was a stumbling-block. When you were conceiving a sentence, the comma stopped you. That is the illustration of the question of grammar and parts of speech, as part of the daily life as we live it.

The other thing which I accomplished was the getting rid of nouns. In the Twentieth Century you feel like movement. The Nineteenth Century didn't feel that way. The element of movement was not the predominating thing that they felt. You know that in your lives movement is the thing that occupies you most—you feel movement all the time. And the United States had the first instance of what I call Twentieth Century writing. You see it first in Walt Whitman. He was the beginning of movement. He didn't see it very clearly, but there was a sense of movement that the European was much influenced by, because the Twentieth Century has become the American Century. That is what I mean when I say that each generation has its own literature.

There is a third element. You see, everybody in this generation has his sense of time which belongs to his crowd. But then, you always have the memory of what you were brought up with. In most people that makes a double time, which makes confusion. When one is beginning to write he is always under the shadow of the thing that is just past. And that is the reason why the creative person always has the appearance of ugliness. There is this persistent drag of the habits that belong to you. And in struggling away from this thing there is always an ugliness. That is the other reason why the contemporary writer is always refused. It is the effort of escaping from the thing which is a drag upon you that is so strong that the result is an apparent ugliness; and the world always says of the new writer, 'It is so ugly!' And they are right, because it *is* ugly. If you disagree with your parents, there is an ugliness in the relation. There is a double resistance that makes the essence of this thing ugly.

You always have in your writing the resistance outside of you and inside of you, a shadow upon you, and the thing which you must express. In the beginning of your writing, this struggle is so tremendous that that result is ugly; and that is the reason why the followers are always accepted before the person who made the revolution. The person who has made the fight probably makes it seem ugly, although the struggle has the much greater beauty. But the followers die out; and the man who made the struggle and the quality of beauty remains in the intensity of the fight. Eventually it comes out all right, and so you have this very queer situation which always happens with the followers: the original person has to have in him a certain element of ugliness. You know that is what happens over and over again: the statement made that it is ugly—the statement made against me for the last twenty years. And they are quite right, because it *is* ugly. But the essence of that ugliness is the thing which will always make it beautiful. I myself think it is much more interesting when it seems ugly, because in it you see the element of the fight. The literature of one hundred years ago is perfectly easy to see, because the sediment of ugliness has settled down and you got the solemnity of its beauty. But to a person of my temperament, it is much more amusing when it has the vitality of the struggle.

In my own case, the Twentieth Century,

which America created after the Civil War, and which had certain elements, had a definite influence on me. And in *The Making of Americans,* which is a book I would like to talk about, I gradually and slowly found out that there were two things I had to think about; the fact that knowledge is acquired, so to speak, by memory; but that when you know anything, memory doesn't come in. At any moment that you are conscious of knowing anything, memory plays no part. When any of you feels anybody else, memory doesn't come into it. You have the sense of the immediate. Remember that my immediate forebears were people like Meredith, Thomas Hardy, and so forth, and you will see what a struggle it was to do this thing. This was one of my first efforts to give the appearance of one time-knowledge, and not to make it a narrative story. This is what I mean by immediacy of description: you will find it in *The Making of Americans:* 'It happens very often that a man has it in him, that a man does something, that he does very often that he does many things, when he is a young man when he is an old man, when he is an older man.' Do you see what I mean? And here is a description of a thing that is very interesting: 'One of such of these kind of them had a little boy and this one, the little son wanted to make a collection of butterflies and beetles and it was all exciting to him and it was all arranged then and then the father said to the son you are certain this is not a cruel thing that you are wanting to be doing, killing things to make collections of them, and the son was very disturbed then and they talked about it together the two of them and more and more they talked about it then and then at last the boy was convinced it was a cruel thing and he said he would not do it and the father said the little boy was a noble boy to give up pleasure when it was a cruel one. The boy went to bed then and then the father when he got up in the early morning saw a wonderfully beautiful moth in the room and he caught him and he killed him and he pinned him and he woke up his son then and showed it to him and he said to him "see what a good father I am to have caught and killed this one," the boy was all mixed up inside him and then he said he would go on with his collecting and that was all there was then of discussing and this is a little description of something that happened once and it is very interesting.'

I was trying to get this present immediacy without trying to drag in anything else. I had to use present participles, new constructions of grammar. The grammar-constructions are correct, but they are changed, in order to get this immediacy. In short, from that time I have been trying in every possible way to get the sense of immediacy, and practically all the work I have done has been in that direction.

In *The Making of Americans* I had an idea that I could get a sense of immediacy if I made a description of every kind of human being that existed, the rules for resemblances and all the other things, until really I had made a description of every human being—I found this out when I was at Harvard working under William James.

Did you ever see that article that came out in *The Atlantic Monthly* a year or two ago, about my experiments with automatic writing? It was very amusing. The experiment that I did was to take a lot of people in moments of fatigue and rest and activity of various kinds, and see if they could do anything with automatic writing

How Writing Is Written

I found they could not do anything with automatic writing, but I found out a great deal about how people act. I found there a certain kind of human being who acted in a certain way, and another kind who acted in another kind of way, and their resemblances and their differences. And then I wanted to find out if you could make a history of the whole world, if you could know the whole life history of everyone in the world, their slight resemblances and lack of resemblances. I made enormous charts, and I tried to carry these charts out. You start in and you take everyone that you know, and then when you see anybody who has a certain expression or turn of the face that reminds you of some one, you find out where he agrees or disagrees with the character, until you build up the whole scheme. I got to the place where I didn't know whether I knew people or not. I made so many charts that when I used to go down the streets of Paris I wondered whether they were people I knew or ones I didn't. That is what *The Making of Americans* was intended to be. I was to make a description of every kind of human being until I could know by these variations how everybody was to be known. Then I got very much interested in this thing, and I wrote about nine hundred pages, and I came to a logical conclusion that this thing could be done. Anybody who has patience enough could literally and entirely make of the whole world a history of human nature. When I found it could be done, I lost interest in it. As soon as I found definitely and clearly and completely that I could do it, I stopped writing the long book. It didn't interest me any longer. In doing the thing, I found out this question of resemblances, and I found in making these analyses that the resemblances were not of memory. I had to remember what person looked like the other person. Then I found this contradiction: that the resemblances were a matter of memory. There were two prime elements involved, the element of memory and the other of immediacy.

The element of memory was a perfectly feasible thing, so then I gave it up. I then started a book which I called *A Long Gay Book* to see if I could work the thing up to a faster tempo. I wanted to see if I could make that a more complete vision. I wanted to see if I could hold it in the frame. Ordinarily the novels of the Nineteenth Century live by association; they are wont to call up other pictures than the one they present to you. I didn't want, when I said 'water,' to have you think of running water. Therefore I began limiting my vocabulary, because I wanted to get rid of anything except the picture within the frame. While I was writing I didn't want, when I used one word, to make it carry with it too many associations. I wanted as far as possible to make it exact, as exact as mathematics; that is to say, for example, if one and one make two, I wanted to get words to have as much exactness as that. When I put them down they were to have this quality. The whole history of my work, from *The Making of Americans,* has been a history of that. I made a great many discoveries, but the thing that I was always trying to do was this thing.

One thing which came to me is that the Twentieth Century gives of itself a feeling of movement, and has in its way no feeling for events. To the Twentieth Century events are not important. You must know that. Events are not exciting. Events have lost their interest for people. You read them more like a soothing syrup, and if you listen over the radio you don't get very excited. The thing has got to this place, that events are so wonderful that they are not exciting. Now you have to remember that the business of an artist is to be exciting. If the thing has its proper vitality, the result must be exciting. I was struck with it during the War: the average dough-boy standing on a street corner doing nothing—(they say, at the end of their doing nothing, 'I guess I'll go home') —was much more exciting to people than when the soldiers went over the top. The populace were passionately interested in their standing on the street corners, more so than in the St. Mihiel drive. And it is a perfectly natural thing. Events had got so continuous that the fact that events were taking place no longer stimulated anybody. To see three men, strangers, standing, expressed their personality to the European man so much more than anything else they could do. That thing impressed me very much. But the novel which tells about what happens is of no interest to anybody. It is quite characteristic that in *The Making of Americans,* Proust, *Ulysses,* nothing much happens. People are interested in existence. Newspapers excite people very little. Sometimes a personality breaks through the newspapers—Lindbergh, Dillinger,—when the personality has vitality. It wasn't what Dillinger *did* that excited anybody. The feeling is perfectly simple. You can see it in my *Four Saints.* Saints shouldn't do anything. The fact that a saint is there is enough for anybody. The *Four Saints* was written about as static as I could make it. The saints conversed a little, and it all did something. It did something more than the theater which has tried to make events has done. For our purposes, for our contemporary purposes, events have no importance. I merely say that for the last thirty years events are of no importance. They may make a great many people unhappy, they may cause convulsions in history, but from the standpoint of excitement, the kind of excitement the Nineteenth Century got out of events doesn't exist.

And so what I am trying to make you understand is that every contemporary writer has to find out what is the inner time-sense of his contemporariness. The writer or painter, or what not, feels this thing more vibrantly, and he has a passionate need of putting it down; and that is what creativeness does. He spends his life in putting down this thing which he doesn't know is a contemporary thing. If he doesn't put down the contemporary thing, he isn't a great writer, for he has to live in the past. That is what I mean by 'everything is contemporary.' The minor poets of the period, or the precious poets of the period, are all people who are under the shadow of the past. A man who is making a revolution has to be contemporary. A minor person can live in the imagination. That tells the story pretty completely.

The question of repetition is very important. It is important because there is no such thing as repetition. Everybody tells every story in about the same way. You know perfectly well that when you and your roommates tell something, you are telling the same story in about the same way. But the point about it is this. Everybody is telling the story in the same way. But if you listen carefully, you will see that not all the story is the same. There is always a slight variation. Somebody comes in, and you tell the story over again. Every time you tell that story it is told slightly differently. All my early work was a careful listening to all the people telling their story, and I conceived the idea which is, funnily enough, the same as the idea of the cinema. The cinema goes on the same principle: each picture is just infinitesimally different from the one before. If you listen carefully, you say something, the other person says something; but each time it changes just a little, until finally you come to the point where you convince him or you don't convince him. I used to listen very carefully to people talking. I had a passion for knowing just what I call their 'insides.' And in *The Making of Americans* I did this thing; but of course to my mind there is no repetition. For instance, in these early 'Portraits,' and in a whole lot of them in this book (*Portraits and Prayers*) you will see that every time a statement is made about someone being somewhere, that statement is different. If I had repeated, nobody would listen. Nobody could be in the room with a person who said the same thing over and over. He would drive everybody mad. There has to be a very slight change. Really listen to the way you talk, and every time you change it a little bit. That change, to me, was a very important thing to find out. You will see that when I kept on saying something was something or somebody was somebody, I changed it just a little bit until I got a whole portrait. I conceived the idea of building this thing up. It was all based upon this thing of everybody's slightly building this thing up. What I was after was this immediacy. A single photograph doesn't give it. I was trying for this thing, and so to my mind there is no repetition. The only thing that is repetition is when somebody tells you what he has learned.

No matter how you say it, you say it differently. It was this that led me in all that early work.

You see, finally, after I got this thing as completely as I could, then, of course, it being my nature, I wanted to tear it down. I attacked the problem from another way. I listened to people. I condensed it in about three words. There again, if you read those later 'Portraits,' you will see that I used three or four words instead of making a cinema of it. I wanted to condense it as much as possible and change it around, until you could get the movement of a human being. If I wanted to make a picture of you as you sit there, I would wait until I got a picture of you as individuals and then I'd change them until I got a picture of you as a whole.

I did these 'Portraits,' and then I got the idea of doing plays. I had the 'Portraits' so much in my head that I would almost know how you differ one from the other. I got this idea of the play, and put it down in a few words. I wanted to put them down in that way, and I began writing plays and I wrote a great many of them. The Nineteenth Century wrote a great many plays, and none of them are now read, because the Nineteenth Century wanted to put their novels on the stage. The better the play the more static. The minute you try to make a play a novel, it doesn't work. That is the reason I got interested in doing these plays.

When you get to that point there is no essential difference between prose and poetry. This is essentially the problem with which your generation will have to wrestle. The thing has got to the point where poetry and prose have to concern themselves with the static thing. That is up to you.

Drawing by Steinberg, © 1957 The New Yorker Magazine, Inc.

PART III · STORIES

A PIECE OF FICTION is both a design of experience and somebody's truth about life. It must stand by itself as well as carry more than its own weight of meaning. This section opens with two examples of semi-fiction. In them the beginnings of the fictional method are easily discerned because we know, or can find out, more facts and details about the subjects than the author tells us. The section closes with stories where material and method have been merged, and we need to know little more than the overwhelming number of details the author has formed into his narrative.

In theme, Huxley and Forster explore, by projection into a future at least halfway recognized in the present, an aspect of modern life that is suggested by Dos Passos' subjects and his treatment of them. Thurber reminds us that the situation is a human one and that it may not be unenjoyable to the observer, while Mark Schorer and Eudora Welty return us to the fundamentally tragic view of a life rejected or lost without meaning. Four stories of learning and losing the values the world offers, of acceptance and rejection, follow, with glimpses here and there of some value that can be won, if men but knew how. These stories lead almost logically to the last two, where the need to assert life in death and to pronounce, however tentatively, some judgment upon it appear as the central problems of human existence.

The last few stories are a fair test of the art of reading fiction. If the reader has gone carefully through the other stories, leaving no relevant question unanswered and allowing no uncontrolled play of the fancy, he will come to know the persons, places and things out of which, in these last stories, the authors have created their special worlds for the truth's sake. He will then be learning that the imagination makes legitimate use of facts, that imagination and knowledge are mingled in the truth, and finally that fiction is truth.

THE CAMPERS AT KITTY HAWK

by JOHN DOS PASSOS

ON DECEMBER SEVENTEENTH, nineteen hundred and three, Bishop Wright of the United Brethren onetime editor of the *Religious Telescope* received in his frame house on Hawthorn Street in Dayton, Ohio, a telegram from his boys Wilbur and Orville who'd gotten it into their heads to spend their vacations in a little camp out on the dunes of the North Carolina coast tinkering with a homemade glider they'd knocked together themselves. The telegram read:

SUCCESS FOUR FLIGHTS THURSDAY MORNING ALL AGAINST TWENTYONE MILE WIND STARTED FROM LEVEL WITH ENGINEPOWER ALONE AVERAGE SPEED THROUGH AIR THIRTYONE MILES LONGEST FIFTYSEVEN SECONDS INFORM PRESS HOME CHRISTMAS

The figures were a little wrong because the telegraph operator misread Orville's hasty penciled scrawl
   but the fact remains
   that a couple of young bicycle mechanics from Dayton, Ohio
   had designed constructed and flown
   for the first time ever a practical airplane.

After running the motor a few minutes to heat it up I released the wire that held the machine to the track and the machine started forward into the wind. Wilbur ran at the side of the machine holding the wing to balance it on the track. Unlike the start on the 14th made in a calm the machine facing a 27 mile wind started very slowly. . . . Wilbur was able to stay with it until it lifted from the track after a forty-foot run. One of the lifesaving men snapped the camera for us taking a picture just as it reached the end of the track and the machine had risen to a height of about two feet. . . . The course of the flight up and down was extremely erratic, partly due to the irregularities of the air, partly to lack of experience in handling this machine. A sudden dart when a little over a hundred and twenty feet from the point at which it rose in the air ended the flight. . . . This flight lasted only 12 seconds but it was nevertheless the first in the history of the world in which a machine carrying a man had raised itself by its own power into the air in full flight, had sailed forward without reduction of speed and had finally landed at a point as high as that from which it started.

A little later in the day the machine was caught in a gust of wind and turned over and smashed, almost killing the coastguardsman who tried to hold it down;
   it was too bad
   but the Wright brothers were too happy to care
   they'd proved that the damn thing flew.

When these points had been definitely established we at once packed our goods and returned home knowing that the age of the flying machine had come at last.

From *U S A* by John Dos Passos, Houghton Mifflin Co. Copyright, 1933, 1934, 1935, 1936 by John Dos Passos. By permission of the author.

The Campers at Kitty Hawk

They were home for Christmas in Dayton, Ohio, where they'd been born in the seventies of a family who had been settled west of the Alleghenies since eighteen fourteen, in Dayton, Ohio, where they'd been to grammarschool and highschool and joined their father's church and played baseball and hockey and worked out on the parallel bars and the flying swing and sold newspapers and built themselves a printingpress out of odds and ends from the junkheap and flown kites and tinkered with mechanical contraptions and gone around town as boys doing odd jobs to turn an honest penny.

The folks claimed it was the bishop's bringing home a helicopter, a fiftycent mechanical toy made of two fans worked by elastic bands that was supposed to hover in the air, that had got his youngest boys hipped on the subject of flight

so that they stayed home instead of marrying the way the other boys did, and puttered all day about the house picking up a living with jobprinting,

bicyclerepair work

sitting up late nights reading books on aerodynamics.

Still they were sincere churchmembers, their bicycle business was prosperous, a man could rely on their word. They were popular in Dayton.

In those days flyingmachines were the big laugh of all the crackerbarrel philosophers. Langley's and Chanute's unsuccessful experiments had been jeered down with an I-told-you-so that rang from coast to coast. The Wrights' big problem was to find a place secluded enough to carry on their experiments without being the horselaugh of the countryside. Then they had no money to spend;

they were practical mechanics; when they needed anything they built it themselves.

They hit on Kitty Hawk,

on the great dunes and sandy banks that stretch south towards Hatteras seaward of Albemarle Sound,

a vast stretch of seabeach

empty except for a coastguard station, a few fishermen's shacks and the swarms of mosquitoes and the ticks and chiggers in the crabgrass behind the dunes

and overhead the gulls and swooping terns, in the evening fishhawks and cranes flapping across the saltmarshes, occasionally eagles

that the Wright brothers followed soaring with their eyes

as Leonardo watched them centuries before

straining his sharp eyes to apprehend the laws of flight.

Four miles across the loose sand from the scattering of shacks, the Wright brothers built themselves a camp and a shed for their gliders. It was a long way to pack their groceries, their tools, anything they happened to need; in summer it was hot as blazes, the mosquitoes were hell;

but they were alone there

and they figured out that the loose sand was as soft as anything they could find to fall in.

There with a glider made of two planes and a tail in which they lay flat on their bellies and controlled the warp of the planes by shimmying their hips, taking off again and again all day from a big dune named Kill Devil Hill,

they learned to fly.

Once they'd managed to hover for a few seconds

and soar ever so slightly on a rising aircurrent

they decided the time had come

to put a motor in their biplane

[181]

Back in the shop in Dayton, Ohio, they built an airtunnel, which is their first great contribution to the science of flying, and tried out model planes in it.

They couldn't interest any builders of gasoline engines so they had to build their own motor.

It worked; after that Christmas of nineteen three the Wright brothers weren't doing it for fun any more; they gave up their bicycle business, got the use of a big old cowpasture belonging to the local banker for practice flights, spent all the time when they weren't working on their machine in promotion, worrying about patents, infringements, spies, trying to interest government officials, to make sense out of the smooth involved heartbreaking remarks of lawyers.

In two years they had a plane that would cover twentyfour miles at a stretch round and round the cowpasture.

People on the interurban car used to crane their necks out of the windows when they passed along the edge of the field, startled by the clattering pop pop of the old Wright motor and the sight of the white biplane like a pair of ironing-boards one on top of the other chugging along a good fifty feet in the air. The cows soon got used to it.

As the flights got longer
The Wright brothers got backers,
engaged in lawsuits,
lay in their beds at night sleepless with the whine of phantom millions, worse than the mosquitoes at Kitty Hawk.

In nineteen seven they went to Paris,
allowed themselves to be togged out in dress suits and silk hats,
learned to tip waiters
talked with government experts, got used to gold braid and postponements and vandyke beards and the outspread palms of politicos. For amusement
they played diabolo in the Tuileries gardens.

They gave publicized flights at Fort Myers, where they had their first fatal crackup, St. Petersburg, Paris, Berlin; at Pau they were all the rage,
such an attraction that the hotelkeeper wouldn't charge them for their room.
Alfonso of Spain shook hands with them and was photographed sitting in the machine,
King Edward watched a flight,
the Crown Prince insisted on being taken up,
the rain of medals began.

They were congratulated by the Czar
and the King of Italy and the amateurs of sport, and the society climbers and the papal titles,
and decorated by a society for universal peace.

Aeronautics became the sport of the day.
The Wrights don't seem to have been very much impressed by the upholstery and the braid and the gold medals and the parades of plush horses,
they remained practical mechanics
and insisted on doing all their own work themselves,
even to filling the gasolinetank.

In nineteen eleven they were back on the dunes
at Kitty Hawk with a new glider.
Orville stayed up in the air for nine and a half minutes, which remained a long time the record for motorless flight.
The same year Wilbur died of typhoidfever in Dayton.

In the rush of new names: Farman, Blériot, Curtiss, Ferber, Esnault-Peltrie, Delagrange;

in the sporting impact of bombs and the whine and rattle of shrapnel and the sudden stutter of machineguns after the motor's been shut off overhead,

and we flatten into the mud

and make ourselves small cowering in the corners of ruined walls,

the Wright brothers passed out of the headlines

but not even headlines or the bitter smear of newsprint or the choke of smokescreen and gas or chatter of brokers on the stockmarket or barking of phantom millions or oratory of brasshats laying wreaths on new monuments

can blur the memory

of the chilly December day

two shivering bicycle mechanics from Dayton, Ohio,

first felt their homemade contraption whittled out of hickory sticks,

gummed together with Arnstein's bicycle cement,

stretched with muslin they'd sewn on their sister's sewingmachine in their own backyard on Hawthorn Street in Dayton, Ohio,

soar into the air

above the dunes and the wide beach

at Kitty Hawk.

PROTEUS

by John Dos Passos

Steinmetz was a hunchback, son of a hunchback lithographer.

He was born in Breslau in eighteen sixtyfive, graduated with highest honors at seventeen from the Breslau Gymnasium, went to the University of Breslau to study mathematics;

mathematics to Steinmetz was muscular strength and long walks over the hills and the kiss of a girl in love and big evenings spent swilling beer with your friends;

on his broken back he felt the topheavy weight of society the way workingmen felt it on their straight backs, the way poor students felt it, was a member of a socialist club, editor of a paper called *The People's Voice*.

Bismarck was sitting in Berlin like a big paperweight to keep the new Germany feudal, to hold down the empire for his bosses the Hohenzollerns.

Steinmetz had to run off to Zurich for fear of going to jail; at Zurich his mathematics woke up all the professors at the Polytechnic;

but Europe in the eighties was no place for a penniless German student with a broken back and a big head filled with symbolic calculus and wonder about electricity that is mathematics made power and a socialist at that.

With a Danish friend he sailed for America steerage on an old French line boat *La Champagne*,

lived in Brooklyn at first and commuted to Yonkers where he had a twelvedollar a week job with Rudolph Eichemeyer who was a German exile from fortyeight an

From *U S A* by John Dos Passos, Houghton Mifflin Co. Copyright, 1933, 1934, 1935, 1936 by John Dos Passos. By permission of the author.

inventor and electrician and owner of a factory where he made hatmaking machinery and electrical generators.

In Yonkers he worked out the theory of the Third Harmonics

and the law of hysteresis which states in a formula the hundredfold relations between the metallic heat, density, frequency when the poles change places in the core of a magnet under an alternating current.

It is Steinmetz's law of hysteresis that makes possible all the transformers that crouch in little boxes and gableroofed houses in all the hightension lines all over everywhere. The mathematical symbols of Steinmetz's law are the patterns of all transformers everywhere.

In eighteen ninetytwo when Eichemeyer sold out to the corporation that was to form General Electric, Steinmetz was entered in the contract along with other valuable apparatus. All his life Steinmetz was a piece of apparatus belonging to General Electric.

First his laboratory was at Lynn, then it was moved and the little hunchback with it to Schenectady, the electric city.

General Electric humored him, let him be a socialist, let him keep a greenhouseful of cactuses lit up by mercury lights, let him have alligators, talking crows and a gila monster for pets and the publicity department talked up the wizard, the medicine man who knew the symbols that opened up the doors of Ali Baba's cave.

Steinmetz jotted a formula on his cuff and next morning a thousand new powerplants had sprung up and the dynamos sang dollars and the silence of the transformers was all dollars,

and the publicity department poured oily stories into the ears of the American public every Sunday and Steinmetz became the little parlor magician,

who made a toy thunderstorm in his laboratory and made all the toy trains run on time and the meat stay cold in the icebox and the lamp in the parlor and the great lighthouses and the searchlights and the revolving beams of light that guide airplanes at night towards Chicago, New York, St. Louis, Los Angeles,

and they let him be a socialist and believe that human society could be improved the way you can improve a dynamo and they let him be pro-German and write a letter offering his services to Lenin because mathematicians are so impractical who make up formulas by which you can build powerplants, factories, subway systems, light, heat, air, sunshine but not human relations that affect the stockholders' money and the directors' salaries.

Steinmetz was a famous magician and he talked to Edison tapping with the Morse code on Edison's knee

because Edison was so very deaf

and he went out West

to make speeches that nobody understood

and he talked to Bryan about God on a railroad train

and all the reporters stood round while he and Einstein

met face to face,

but they couldn't catch what they said

and Steinmetz was the most valuable piece of apparatus General Electric had

until he wore out and died.

EDUCATION IN THE WORLD STATE
by Aldous Huxley

Mr. Foster was left in the decanting room. The D.H.C. and his students stepped into the nearest lift and were carried up to the fifth floor.

Infant Nurseries. Neo-Pavlovian Conditioning Rooms, announced the notice board.

The Director opened a door. They were in a large bare room, very bright and sunny; for the whole of the southern wall was a single window. Half a dozen nurses, trousered and jacketed in the regulation white viscose-linen uniform, their hair aseptically hidden under white caps, were engaged in setting out bowls of roses in a long row across the floor. Big bowls, packed tight with blossom. Thousands of petals, ripe-blown and silkily smooth, like the cheeks of innumerable little cherubs, but of cherubs, in that bright light, not exclusively pink and Aryan, but also luminously Chinese, also Mexican, also apoplectic with too much blowing of celestial trumpets, also pale as death, pale with the posthumous whiteness of marble.

The nurses stiffened to attention as the D.H.C. came in.

"Set out the books," he said curtly.

In silence the nurses obeyed his command. Between the rose bowls the books were duly set out—a row of nursery quartos opened invitingly each at some gaily colored image of beast or fish or bird.

"Now bring in the children."

They hurried out of the room and returned in a minute or two, each pushing a kind of tall dumbwaiter laden, on all its four wire-netted shelves, with eight-month-old babies, all exactly alike (a Bokanovsky Group, it was evident) and all (since their caste was Delta) dressed in khaki.

"Put them down on the floor."

The infants were unloaded.

"Now turn them so that they can see the flowers and books."

Turned, the babies at once fell silent, then began to crawl towards those clusters of sleek colors, those shapes so gay and brilliant on the white pages. As they approached, the sun came out of a momentary eclipse behind a cloud. The roses flamed up as though with a sudden passion from within; a new and profound significance seemed to suffuse the shining pages of the books. From the ranks of the crawling babies came little squeals of excitement, gurgles and twitterings of pleasure.

The Director rubbed his hands. "Excellent!" he said. "It might almost have been done on purpose."

The swiftest crawlers were already at their goal. Small hands reached out uncertainly, touched, grasped, unpetaling the transfigured roses, crumpling the illuminated pages of the books. The Director waited until all were happily busy. Then, "Watch carefully," he said. And, lifting his hand, he gave the signal.

The Head Nurse, who was standing by a switchboard at the other end of the room, pressed down a little lever.

There was a violent explosion. Shriller and even shriller, a siren shrieked. Alarm bells maddeningly sounded.

The children started, screamed: their faces were distorted with terror.

"And now," the Director shouted (for the noise was deafening), "now we pro-

---

From *Brave New World*, by Aldous Huxley. Harper & Brothers. Copyright, 1932, by Aldous Huxley.

ceed to rub in the lesson with a mild electric shock."

He waved his hand again, and the Head Nurse pressed a second lever. The screaming of the babies suddenly changed its tone. There was something desperate, almost insane, about the sharp spasmodic yelps to which they now gave utterance. Their little bodies twitched and stiffened; their limbs moved jerkily as if to the tug of unseen wires.

"We can electrify that whole strip of floor," bawled the Director in explanation. "But that's enough," he signaled to the nurse.

The explosions ceased, the bells stopped ringing, the shriek of the siren died down from tone to tone into silence. The stiffly twitching bodies relaxed, and what had become the sob and yelp of infant maniacs broadened out once more into a normal howl of ordinary terror.

"Offer them the flowers and the books again."

The nurses obeyed; but at the approach of the roses, at the mere sight of those gaily-colored images of pussy and cock-a-doodle-doo and baa-baa black sheep, the infants shrank away in horror; the volume of their howling suddenly increased.

"Observe," said the Director triumphantly, "observe."

Books and loud noises, flowers and electric shocks—already in the infant mind these couples were compromisingly linked; and after two hundred repetitions of the same or a similar lesson would be wedded indissolubly. What man has joined, nature is powerless to put asunder.

"They'll grow up with what the psychologists used to call an 'instinctive' hatred of books and flowers. Reflexes unalterably conditioned. They'll be safe from books and botany all their lives." The Director turned to his nurses. "Take them away again."

Still yelling, the khaki babies were loaded on to their dumbwaiters and wheeled out, leaving behind them the smell of sour milk and a most welcome silence.

One of the students held up his hand; and though he could see quite well why you couldn't have lower-caste people wasting the Community's time over books, and that there was always the risk of their reading something which might undesirably decondition one of their reflexes, yet . . . well, he couldn't understand about the flowers. Why go to the trouble of making it psychologically impossible for Deltas to like flowers?

Patiently the D.H.C. explained. If the children were made to scream at the sight of a rose, that was on grounds of high economic policy. Not so very long ago (a century or thereabouts), Gammas, Deltas, even Epsilons, had been conditioned to like flowers—flowers in particular and wild nature in general. The idea was to make them want to be going out into the country at every available opportunity, and so compel them to consume transport.

"And didn't they consume transport?" asked the student.

"Quite a lot," the D.H.C. replied. "But nothing else."

Primroses and landscapes, he pointed out, have one grave defect: they are gratuitous. A love of nature keeps no factories busy. It was decided to abolish the love of nature, at any rate among the lower classes: to abolish the love of nature, but *not* the tendency to consume transport. For of course it was essential that they should keep on going to the country, even though they hated it. The problem was to find an economically sounder reason for consuming transport

[186]

than a mere affection for primroses and landscapes. It was duly found.

"We condition the masses to hate the country," concluded the Director. "But simultaneously we condition them to love all country sports. At the same time, we see to it that all country sports shall entail the use of elaborate apparatus. So that they consume manufactured articles as well as transport. Hence those electric shocks."

"I see," said the student, and was silent, lost in admiration.

There was a silence; then, clearing his throat, "Once upon a time," the Director began, "while our Ford was still on earth, there was a little boy called Reuben Rabinovitch. Reuben was the child of Polish speaking parents." The Director interrupted himself. "You know what Polish is, I suppose?"

"A dead language."

"Like French and German," added another student, officiously showing off his learning.

"And 'parent'?" questioned the D.H.C.

There was an uneasy silence. Several of the boys blushed. They had not yet learned to draw the significant but often very fine distinction between smut and pure science. One, at least, had the courage to raise a hand.

"Human beings used to be . . ." he hesitated; the blood rushed to his cheeks. "Well, they used to be viviparous."

"Quite right." The Director nodded approvingly.

"And when the babies were decanted . . ."

" 'Born,' " came the correction.

"Well, then they were the parents—I mean, not the babies, of course; the other ones." The poor boy was overwhelmed with confusion.

"In brief," the Director summed up, "the parents were the father and the mother." The smut that was really science fell with a crash into the boys' eye-avoiding silence. "Mother," he repeated loudly, rubbing in the science; and, leaning back in his chair, "These," he said gravely, "are unpleasant facts; I know it. But then most historical facts *are* unpleasant."

He returned to Little Reuben—to Little Reuben, in whose room, one evening, by an oversight, his father and mother (crash, crash!) happened to leave the radio turned on.

("For you must remember that in those days of gross viviparous reproduction, children were always brought up by their parents and not in State Conditioning Centers.")

While the child was asleep, a broadcast program from London suddenly started to come through; and the next morning, to the astonishment of his crash and crash (the more daring of the boys ventured to grin at one another), Little Reuben woke up repeating word for word a long lecture by that curious old writer ("one of the very few whose works have been permitted to come down to us"), George Bernard Shaw, who was speaking, according to a well-authenticated tradition, about his own genius. To Little Reuben's wink and snigger, this lecture was, of course, perfectly incomprehensible and, imagining that their child had suddenly gone mad, they sent for a doctor. He, fortunately, understood English, recognized the discourse as that which Shaw had broadcasted the previous evening, realized the significance of what had happened, and sent a letter to the medical press about it.

"The principle of sleep-teaching, or hypnopaedia, had been discovered." The D.H.C. made an impressive pause.

The principle had been discovered; but

many, many years were to elapse before that principle was usefully applied.

"The case of Little Reuben occurred only twenty-three years after Our Ford's first T-Model was put on the market." (Here the Director made a sign of the T on his stomach and all the students reverently followed suit.) "And yet . . ."

Furiously the students scribbled. *"Hypnopaedia, first used officially in A.F. 214. Why not before? Two reasons. (a) . . ."*

"These early experimenters," the D.H.C. was saying, "were on the wrong track. They thought that hypnopaedia could be made an instrument of intellectual education . . ."

(A small boy asleep on his right side, the right arm stuck out, the right hand hanging limp over the edge of the bed. Through a round grating in the side of a box a voice speaks softly.

"The Nile is the longest river in Africa and the second in length of all the rivers of the globe. Although falling short of the length of the Mississippi-Missouri, the Nile is at the head of all rivers as regards the length of its basin, which extends through 35 degrees of latitude . . ."

At breakfast the next morning, "Tommy" someone says, "do you know which is the longest river in Africa?" A shaking of the head. "But don't you remember something that begins: The Nile is the . . ."

"The-Nile-is-the-longest-river-in-Africa-and-the-second-in-length-of-all-the-rivers-of-the-globe . . ." The words come rushing out. "Although-falling-short-of . . ."

"Well, now, which is the longest river in Africa?"

The eyes are blank. "I don't know."

"But the Nile, Tommy."

"The-Nile-is-the-longest-river-in-Africa-and-second . . ."

"Then which river is the longest, Tommy?"

Tommy bursts into tears. "I don't know," he howls.)

That howl, the Director made it plain, discouraged the earliest investigators. The experiments were abandoned. No further attempt was made to teach children the length of the Nile in their sleep. Quite rightly. You can't learn a science unless you know what it's all about.

"Whereas, if they'd only started on *moral* education," said the Director, leading the way towards the door. The students followed him, desperately scribbling as they walked and all the way up in the lift. "Moral education, which ought never, in any circumstance, to be rational."

"Silence, silence," whispered a loud speaker as they stepped out at the fourteenth floor, and "Silence, silence," the trumpet mouths indefatigably repeated at intervals down every corridor. The students and even the Director himself rose automatically to the tips of their toes. They were Alphas, of course; but even Alphas have been well conditioned. "Silence, silence." All the air of the fourteenth floor was sibilant with the categorical imperative.

Fifty yards of tiptoeing brought them to a door which the Director cautiously opened. They stepped over the threshold into the twilight of a shuttered dormitory. Eighty cots stood in a row against the wall. There was a sound of light regular breathing and a continuous murmur, as of very faint voices remotely whispering.

A nurse rose as they entered and came to attention before the Director.

"What's the lesson this afternoon?" he asked.

"We had Elementary Sex for the first forty minutes," she answered. "But now

Education in the World State

it's switched over to Elementary Class Consciousness."

The Director walked slowly down the long line of cots. Rosy and relaxed with sleep, eighty little boys and girls lay softly breathing. There was a whisper under every pillow. The D.H.C. halted and, bending over one of the little beds, listened attentively.

"Elementary Class Consciousness, did you say? Let's have it repeated a little louder by the trumpet."

At the end of the room a loud speaker projected from the wall. The Director walked up to it and pressed a switch.

". . . all wear green," said a soft but very distinct voice, beginning in the middle of a sentence, "and Delta children wear khaki. Oh, no, I don't want to play with Delta children. And Epsilons are still worse. They're too stupid to be able to read or write. Besides they wear black, which is such a beastly color. I'm *so* glad I'm a Beta."

There was a pause; then the voice began again.

"Alpha children wear gray. They work much harder than we do, because they're so frightfully clever. I'm really awfully glad I'm a Beta, because I don't work so hard. And then we are much better than the Gammas and Deltas. Gammas are stupid. They all wear green, and Delta children wear khaki. Oh, no, I *don't* want to play with Delta children. And Epsilons are still worse. They're too stupid to be able . . ."

The Director pushed back the switch. The voice was silent. Only its thin ghost continued to mutter from beneath the eighty pillows.

"They'll have that repeated forty or fifty times more before they wake; then again on Thursday, and again on Saturday. A hundred and twenty times three times a week for thirty months. After which they go on to a more advanced lesson."

Roses and electric shocks, the khaki of Deltas and a whiff of asafoetida—welded indissolubly before the child can speak. But wordless conditioning is crude and wholesale; cannot bring home the finer distinctions, cannot inculate the more complex courses of behavior. For that there must be words, but words without reason. In brief, hypnopaedia.

"The greatest moralizing and socializing force of all time."

The students took it down in their little books. Straight from the horse's mouth.

Once more the Director touched the switch.

". . . so frightfully clever," the soft, insinuating, indefatigable voice was saying. "I'm really awfully glad I'm a Beta, because . . ."

Not so much like drops of water, though water, it is true, can wear holes in the hardest granite; rather, drops of liquid sealing-wax, drops that adhere, incrust, incorporate themselves with what they fall on, till finally the rock is all one scarlet blob.

"Till at last the child's mind *is* these suggestions, and the sum of the suggestions *is* the child's mind. And not the child's mind only. The adult's mind too —all his life long. The mind that judges and desires and decides—made up of these suggestions. But all these suggestions are *our* suggestions!" The Director almost shouted in his triumph. "Suggestions from the State." He banged the nearest table. "It therefore follows . . ."

A noise made him turn round.

"Oh, Ford!" he said in another tone, "I've gone and woken the children."

The Subway   George Tooker
Collection of the Whitney Museum of American Art, New York

THE MACHINE STOPS
by E. M. Forster

Part I

The Air-ship

IMAGINE, if you can, a small room, hexagonal in shape, like the cell of a bee. It is lighted neither by window nor by lamp, yet it is filled with a soft radiance. There are no apertures for ventilation, yet the air is fresh. There are no musical instruments, and yet, at the moment that my meditation opens, this room is throbbing with melodious sounds. An arm-chair is in the center, by its side a reading-desk—that is all the furniture. And in the arm-chair there sits a swaddled lump of flesh—a woman, about five feet high, with a face as white as a fungus. It is to her that the little room belongs.

An electric bell rang.

The woman touched a switch and the music was silent.

"I suppose I must see who it is," she thought, and set her chair in motion. The chair, like the music, was worked by machinery, and it rolled her to the other side of the room, where the bell still rang importunately.

"Who is it?" she called. Her voice was irritable, for she had been interrupted often since the music began. She knew several thousand people; in certain directions human intercourse had advanced enormously.

But when she listened into the receiver, her white face wrinkled into smiles, and she said:

"Very well. Let us talk, I will isolate myself. I do not expect anything important will happen for the next five minutes—for I can give you fully five minutes, Kuno.

From *The Eternal Moment* by E. M. Forster. Copyright, 1928, by Harcourt, Brace and Company, Inc.

Then I must deliver my lecture on 'Music during the Australian Period.'"

She touched the isolation knob, so that no one else could speak to her. Then she touched the lighting apparatus, and the little room was plunged into darkness.

"Be quick!" she called, her irritation returning. "Be quick, Kuno; here I am in the dark wasting my time."

But it was fully fifteen seconds before the round plate that she held in her hands began to glow. A faint blue light shot across it, darkening to purple, and presently she could see the image of her son, who lived on the other side of the earth, and he could see her.

"Kuno, how slow you are."

He smiled gravely.

"I really believe you enjoy dawdling."

"I have called you before, mother, but you were always busy or isolated. I have something particular to say."

"What is it, dearest boy? Be quick. Why could you not send it by pneumatic post?"

"Because I prefer saying such a thing. I want—"

"Well?"

"I want you to come and see me."

Vashti watched his face in the blue plate.

"But I can see you!" she exclaimed. "What more do you want?"

"I want to see you not through the Machine," said Kuno. "I want to speak to you not through the wearisome Machine."

"Oh, hush!" said his mother, vaguely shocked. "You mustn't say anything against the Machine."

"Why not?"

"One mustn't."

"You talk as if a god had made the Machine," cried the other. "I believe that you pray to it when you are unhappy. Men made it, do not forget that. Great men, but men. The Machine is much, but it is not everything. I see something like you in this plate, but I do not see you. I hear something like you through this telephone, but I do not hear you. That is why I want you to come. Come and stop with me. Pay me a visit, so that we can meet face to face, and talk about the hopes that are in my mind."

She replied that she could scarcely spare the time for a visit.

"The air-ship barely takes two days to fly between me and you."

"I dislike air-ships."

"Why?"

"I dislike seeing the horrible brown earth, and the sea, and the stars when it is dark. I get no ideas in an air-ship."

"I do not get them anywhere else."

"What kind of ideas can the air give you?"

He paused for an instant.

"Do you not know four big stars that form an oblong, and three stars close together in the middle of the oblong, and hanging from these stars, three other stars?"

"No, I do not. I dislike the stars. But did they give you an idea? How interesting; tell me."

"I had an idea that they were like a man."

"I do not understand."

"The four big stars are the man's shoulders and his knees. The three stars in the middle are like the belts that men wore once, and the three stars hanging are like a sword."

"A sword?"

"Men carried swords about with them, to kill animals and other men."

"It does not strike me as a very good idea, but it is certainly original. When did it come to you first?"

"In the air-ship—" He broke off, and she fancied that he looked sad. She could not be sure, for the Machine did not transmit *nuances* of expression. It only gave a general idea of people—an idea that was good enough for all practical purposes, Vashti thought. The imponderable bloom, declared by a discredited philosophy to be the actual essence of intercourse, was rightly ignored by the Machine, just as the imponderable bloom of the grape was ignored by the manufacturers of artificial fruit. Something "good enough" had long since been accepted by our race.

"The truth is," he continued, "that I want to see these stars again. They are curious stars. I want to see them not from the air-ship, but from the surface of the earth, as our ancestors did, thousands of years ago. I want to visit the surface of the earth."

She was shocked again.

"Mother, you must come, if only to explain to me what is the harm of visiting the surface of the earth."

"No harm," she replied, controlling herself. "But no advantage. The surface of the earth is only dust and mud, no life remains on it, and you would need a respirator, or the cold of the outer air would kill you. One dies immediately in the outer air."

"I know; of course I shall take all precautions."

"And besides—"

"Well?"

She considered, and chose her words with care. Her son had a queer temper, and she wished to dissuade him from the expedition.

"It is contrary to the spirit of the age," she asserted.

"Do you mean by that, contrary to the Machine?"

"In a sense, but—"

His image in the blue plate faded.

"Kuno!"

He had isolated himself.

For a moment Vashti felt lonely.

Then she generated the light, and the sight of her room, flooded with radiance and studded with electric buttons, revived her. There were buttons and switches everywhere—buttons to call for food, for music, for clothing. There was the hot-bath button, by pressure of which a basin of (imitation) marble rose out of the floor, filled to the brim with a warm deodorized liquid. There was the cold-bath button. There was the button that produced literature. And there were of course the buttons by which she communicated with her friends. The room, though it contained nothing, was in touch with all that she cared for in the world.

Vashti's next move was to turn off the isolation-switch, and all the accumulations of the last three minutes burst upon her. The room was filled with the noise of bells, and speaking-tubes. What was the new food like? Could she recommend it? Had she had any ideas lately? Might one tell her one's own ideas? Would she make an engagement to visit the public nurseries at an early date?—say this day month.

To most of these questions she replied with irritation—a growing quality in that accelerated age. She said that the new food was horrible. That she could not visit the public nurseries through press of engagements. That she had no ideas of her own but had just been told one—that four stars and three in the middle were like a man: she doubted there was much in it. Then she switched off her correspondents, for it was time to deliver her lecture on Australian music.

The clumsy system of public gatherings

[192]

had been long since abandoned; neither Vashti nor her audience stirred from their rooms. Seated in her arm-chair she spoke, while they in their arm-chairs heard her, fairly well, and saw her, fairly well. She opened with a humorous account of music in the pre-Mongolian epoch, and went on to describe the great outburst of song that followed the Chinese conquest. Remote and primeval as were the methods of I-San-So and the Brisbane school, she yet felt (she said) that study of them might repay the musician of today: they had freshness; they had, above all, ideas.

Her lecture, which lasted ten minutes, was well received, and at its conclusion she and many of her audience listened to a lecture on the sea; there were ideas to be got from the sea; the speaker had donned a respirator and visited it lately. Then she fed, talked to many friends, had a bath, talked again, and summoned her bed.

The bed was not to her liking. It was too large, and she had a feeling for a small bed. Complaint was useless, for beds were of the same dimension all over the world, and to have had an alternative size would have involved vast alterations in the Machine. Vashti isolated herself—it was necessary, for neither day nor night existed under the ground—and reviewed all that had happened since she had summoned the bed last. Ideas? Scarcely any. Events— was Kuno's invitation an event?

By her side, on the little reading-desk, was a survival from the ages of litter—one book. This was the Book of the Machine. In it were instructions against every possible contingency. If she was hot or cold or dyspeptic or at loss for a word, she went to the Book, and it told her which button to press. The Central Committee published it. In accordance with a growing habit, it was richly bound.

Sitting up in the bed, she took it reverently in her hands. She glanced round the glowing room as if some one might be watching her. Then, half ashamed, half joyful, she murmured, "O Machine! O Machine!" and raised the volume to her lips. Thrice she kissed it, thrice inclined her head, thrice she felt the delirium of acquiescence. Her ritual performed, she turned to page 1367, which gave the times of the departure of the air-ships from the island in the southern hemisphere, under whose soil she lived, to the island in the northern hemisphere, whereunder lived her son.

She thought, "I have not the time."

She made the room dark and slept; she awoke and made the room light; she ate and exchanged ideas with her friends, and listened to music and attended lectures; she made the room dark and slept. Above her, beneath her, and around her, the Machine hummed eternally; she did not notice the noise, for she had been born with it in her ears. The earth, carrying her, hummed as it sped through silence, turning her now to the invisible sun, now to the invisible stars. She awoke and made the room light.

"Kuno!"

"I will not talk to you," he answered, "until you come."

"Have you been on the surface of the earth since we spoke last?"

His image faded.

Again she consulted the Book. She became very nervous and lay back in her chair palpitating. Think of her as without teeth or hair. Presently she directed the chair to the wall, and pressed an unfamiliar button. The wall swung apart slowly. Through the opening she saw a tunnel that curved slightly, so that its goal was not visible. Should she go to see her son, here was the beginning of the journey.

Of course she knew all about the communication-system. There was nothing mysterious in it. She would summon a car and it would fly with her down the tunnel until it reached the lift that communicated with the air-ship station: the system had been in use for many, many years, long before the universal establishment of the Machine. And of course she had studied the civilization that had immediately preceded her own—the civilization that had mistaken the functions of the system, and had used it for bringing people to things, instead of for bringing things to people. Those funny old days, when men went for change of air instead of changing the air in their rooms! And yet—she was frightened of the tunnel: she had not seen it since her last child was born. It curved—but not quite as she remembered; it was brilliant—but not quite as brilliant as a lecturer had suggested. Vashti was seized with the terrors of direct experience. She shrank back into the room, and the wall closed up again.

"Kuno," she said, "I cannot come to see you. I am not well."

Immediately an enormous apparatus fell on to her out of the ceiling, a thermometer was automatically inserted between her lips, a stethoscope was automatically laid upon her heart. She lay powerless. Cool pads soothed her forehead. Kuno had telegraphed to her doctor.

So the human passions still blundered up and down in the Machine. Vashti drank the medicine that the doctor projected into her mouth, and the machinery retired into the ceiling. The voice of Kuno was heard asking how she felt.

"Better." Then with irritation: "But why do you not come to me instead?"

"Because I cannot leave this place."

"Why?"

"Because, any moment, something tremendous may happen."

"Have you been on the surface of the earth yet?"

"Not yet."

"Then what is it?"

"I will not tell you through the Machine."

She resumed her life.

But she thought of Kuno as a baby, his birth, his removal to the public nurseries, her one visit to him there, his visits to her—visits which stopped when the Machine had assigned him a room on the other side of the earth. "Parents, duties of," said the Book of the Machine, "cease at the moment of birth. P. 422327483." True, but there was something special about Kuno—indeed there had been something special about all her children—and, after all, she must brave the journey if he desired it. And "something tremendous might happen." What did that mean? The nonsense of a youthful man, no doubt, but she must go. Again she pressed the unfamiliar button, again the wall swung back, and she saw the tunnel that curved out of sight. Clasping the Book, she rose, tottered onto the platform, and summoned the car. Her room closed behind her: the journey to the northern hemisphere had begun.

Of course it was perfectly easy. The car approached and in it she found arm-chairs exactly like her own. When she signaled, it stopped, and she tottered into the lift. One other passenger was in the lift, the first fellow creature she had seen face to face for months. Few traveled in these days, for, thanks to the advance of science, the earth was exactly alike all over. Rapid intercourse, from which the previous civilization had hoped so much, had ended by defeating itself. What was the good of going to Pekin when it was just like Shrewsbury? Why return to Shrewsbury when it would be just like Pekin? Men seldom moved their bodies; all unrest was concentrated in the soul.

The air-ship service was a relic from the former age. It was kept up, because it was easier to keep it up than to stop it or to diminish it, but it now far exceeded the wants of the population. Vessel after vessel would rise from the vomitories of Rye or of Christchurch (I use the antique names), would sail into the crowded sky, and would draw up at the wharves of the south—empty. So nicely adjusted was the system, so independent of meteorology, that the sky, whether calm or cloudy, resembled a vast kaleidoscope whereon the same patterns periodically recurred. The ship on which Vashti sailed started now at sunset, now at dawn. But always, as it passed above Rheims, it would neighbor the ship that served between Helsingfors and the Brazils, and, every third time it surmounted the Alps, the fleet of Palermo would cross its track behind. Night and day, wind and storm, tide and earthquake, impeded man no longer. He had harnessed Leviathan. All the old literature, with its praise of Nature, and its fear of Nature, rang false as the prattle of a child.

Yet as Vashti saw the vast flank of the ship, stained with exposure to the outer air, her horror of direct experience returned. It was not quite like the air-ship in the cinematophote. For one thing it smelt—not strongly or unpleasantly, but it did smell, and with her eyes shut she should have known that a new thing was close to her. Then she had to walk to it from the lift, had to submit to glances from the other passengers. The man in front dropped his Book—no great matter, but it disquieted them all. In the rooms, if the Book was dropped, the floor raised it mechanically, but the gangway to the air-ship was not so prepared, and the sacred volume lay motionless. They stopped —the thing was unforeseen—and the man, instead of picking up his property, felt the muscles of his arm to see how they had failed him. Then someone actually said with direct utterance: "We shall be late"— and they trooped on board, Vashti treading on the pages as she did so.

Inside, her anxiety increased. The arrangements were old-fashioned and rough. There was even a female attendant, to whom she would have to announce her wants during the voyage. Of course a revolving platform ran the length of the boat, but she was expected to walk from it to her cabin. Some cabins were better than others, and she did not get the best. She thought the attendant had been unfair, and spasms of rage shook her. The glass valves had closed, she could not go back. She saw, at the end of the vestibule, the lift in which she had ascended going quietly up and down, empty. Beneath those corridors of shining tiles were rooms, tier below tier, reaching far into the earth, and in each room there sat a human being, eating, or sleeping, or producing ideas. And buried deep in the hive was her own room. Vashti was afraid.

"O Machine! O Machine!" she murmured, and caressed her Book, and was comforted.

Then the sides of the vestibule seemed to melt together, as do the passages that we see in dreams, the lift vanished, the Book that had been dropped slid to the left and vanished, polished tiles rushed by like a stream of water, there was a slight jar, and the air-ship, issuing from its tunnel, soared above the waters of a tropical ocean.

It was night. For a moment she saw the coast of Sumatra edged by the phosphorescence of waves, and crowned by lighthouses, still sending forth their disregarded beams. They also vanished, and only the stars distracted her. They were not motionless, but swayed to and fro above her head, thronging out of one skylight into another, as if the universe and not the air-ship was careening. And, as often happens on clear nights, they seemed now to be in perspective, now on a plane; now piled tier beyond tier into the infinite heavens, now concealing infinity, a roof limiting for ever the visions of men. In either case they seemed intolerable. "Are we to travel in the dark?" called the passengers angrily, and the attendant, who had been careless, generated the light, and pulled down the blinds of pliable metal. When the air-ships had been built, the desire to look direct at things still lingered in the world. Hence the extraordinary number of skylights and windows, and the proportionate discomfort to those who were civilized and refined. Even in Vashti's cabin one star peeped through a flaw in the blind, and after a few hours' uneasy slumber, she was disturbed by an unfamiliar glow, which was the dawn.

Quick as the ship had sped westwards, the earth had rolled eastwards quicker still, and had dragged back Vashti and her companions towards the sun. Science could prolong the night, but only for a little, and those high hopes of neutralizing the earth's diurnal revolution had passed, together with hopes that were possibly higher. To "keep pace with the sun," or even to outstrip it, had been the aim of the civilization preceding this. Racing aeroplanes had been built for the purpose, capable of enormous speed, and steered by the greatest intellects of the epoch. Round the globe they went, round and round, westward, westward, round and round, amidst humanity's applause. In vain. The globe went eastward quicker still, horrible accidents occurred, and the Committee of the Machine, at the time rising into prominence, declared the pursuit illegal, unmechanical, and punishable by Homelessness.

Of Homelessness more will be said later.

Doubtless the Committee was right. Yet the attempt to "defeat the sun" aroused the last common interest that our race experienced about the heavenly bodies, or indeed about anything. It was the last time that men were compacted by thinking of a power outside the world. The sun had conquered, yet it was the end of his spiritual dominion. Dawn, midday, twilight, the zodiacal path, touched neither men's lives nor their hearts, and science retreated into the ground, to concentrate herself upon problems that she was certain of solving.

So when Vashti found her cabin invaded by a rosy finger of light, she was annoyed, and tried to adjust the blind. But the blind flew up altogether, and she saw through the skylight small pink clouds, swaying against a background of blue, and as the sun crept higher, its radiance entered direct, brimming down the wall, like a golden sea. It rose and fell with the air-ship's motion, just as waves rise and fall, but it advanced steadily, as a tide advances. Unless she was careful, it would strike her face. A spasm of horror shook her and she rang for the attendant. The attendant too was horrified, but she could do nothing; it was not her place to mend the blind. She could only suggest that the lady should change her cabin, which she accordingly prepared to do.

The Machine Stops

People were almost exactly alike all over the world, but the attendant of the airship, perhaps owing to her exceptional duties, had grown a little out of the common. She had often to address passengers with direct speech, and this had given her a certain roughness and originality of manner. When Vashti swerved away from the sunbeams with a cry, she behaved barbarically—she put out her hand to steady her.

"How dare you!" exclaimed the passenger. "You forget yourself!"

The woman was confused, and apologized for not having let her fall. People never touched one another. The custom had become obsolete, owing to the Machine.

"Where are we now?" asked Vashti haughtily.

"We are over Asia," said the attendant, anxious to be polite.

"Asia?"

"You must excuse my common way of speaking. I have got into the habit of calling places over which I pass by their unmechanical names."

"Oh, I remember Asia. The Mongols came from it."

"Beneath us, in the open air, stood a city that was once called Simla."

"Have you ever heard of the Mongols and of the Brisbane school?"

"No."

"Brisbane also stood in the open air."

"Those mountains to the right—let me show you them." She pushed back a metal blind. The main chain of the Himalayas was revealed. "They were once called the Roof of the World, those mountains."

"What a foolish name!"

"You must remember that, before the dawn of civilization, they seemed to be an impenetrable wall that touched the stars. It was supposed that no one but the gods could exist above their summits. How we have advanced, thanks to the Machine!"

"How we have advanced, thanks to the Machine!" said Vashti.

"How we have advanced, thanks to the Machine!" echoed the passenger who had dropped his Book the night before, and who was standing in the passage.

"And that white stuff in the cracks?—what is it?"

"I have forgotten its name."

"Cover the window, please. These mountains give me no ideas."

The northern aspect of the Himalayas was in deep shadow: on the Indian slope the sun had just prevailed. The forests had been destroyed during the literature epoch for the purpose of making newspaper-pulp, but the snows were awakening to their morning glory, and clouds still hung on the breasts of Kinchinjunga. In the plain were seen the ruins of cities, with diminished rivers creeping by their walls, and by the sides of these were sometimes the signs of vomitories, marking the cities of today. Over the whole prospect airships rushed, crossing and intercrossing with incredible aplomb, and rising nonchalantly when they desired to escape the perturbations of the lower atmosphere and to traverse the Roof of the World.

"We have indeed advanced, thanks to the Machine," repeated the attendant, and hid the Himalayas behind a metal blind.

The day dragged wearily forward. The passengers sat each in his cabin, avoiding one another with an almost physical repulsion and longing to be once more under the surface of the earth. There were eight or ten of them, mostly young males, sent out from the public nurseries to inhabit the rooms of those who had died in various parts of the earth. The man who had dropped his Book was on the homeward journey. He had been sent to Sumatra for the purpose of propagating the race. Vashti alone was traveling by her private will.

At midday she took a second glance at the earth. The air-ship was crossing another range of mountains, but she could see little, owing to clouds. Masses of black rock hovered below her, and merged indistinctly into gray. Their shapes were fantastic; one of them resembled a prostrate man.

"No ideas here," murmured Vashti, and hid the Caucasus behind a metal blind.

In the evening she looked again. They were crossing a golden sea, in which lay many small islands and one peninsula.

She repeated, "No ideas here," and hid Greece behind a metal blind.

Part II

The Mending Apparatus

By a vestibule, by a lift, by a tubular railway, by a platform, by a sliding door—by reversing all the steps of her departure did Vashti arrive at her son's room, which exactly resembled her own. She might well declare that the visit was superfluous. The buttons, the knobs, the reading-desk with the Book, the temperature, the atmosphere, the illumination—all were exactly the same. And if Kuno himself, flesh of her flesh, stood close beside her at last, what profit was there in that? She was too well-bred to shake him by the hand.

Averting her eyes, she spoke as follows:

"Here I am. I have had the most terrible journey and greatly retarded the development of my soul. It is not worth it, Kuno, it is not worth it. My time is too precious. The sunlight almost touched me, and I have met with the rudest people. I can only stop a few minutes. Say what you want to say, and then I must return."

"I have been threatened with Homelessness," said Kuno.

She looked at him now.

"I have been threatened with Homelessness, and I could not tell you such a thing through the Machine."

Homelessness means death. The victim is exposed to the air, which kills him.

"I have been outside since I spoke to you last. The tremendous thing has happened, and they have discovered me."

"But why shouldn't you go outside!" she exclaimed. "It is perfectly legal, perfectly mechanical, to visit the surface of the earth. I have lately been to a lecture on the sea; there is no objection to that; one simply summons a respirator and gets an Egression-permit. It is not the kind of thing that spiritually-minded people do, and I begged you not to do it, but there is no legal objection to it."

"I did not get an Egression-permit."

"Then how did you get out?"

"I found out a way of my own."

The phrase conveyed no meaning to her, and he had to repeat it.

"A way of your own?" she whispered. "But that would be wrong."

"Why?"

The question shocked her beyond measure.

"You are beginning to worship the Machine," he said coldly. "You think it irreligious of me to have found out a way of my own. It was just what the Committee thought, when they threatened me with Homelessness."

At this she grew angry. "I worship nothing!" she cried. "I am most advanced. I don't think you irreligious, for there is no such thing as religion left. All the fear and the superstition that existed once have been destroyed by the Machine. I only meant that to find out a way of your own was— Besides, there is no new way out."

"So it is always supposed."

"Except through the vomitories, for which one must have an Egression-permit, it is impossible to get out. The Book says so."

"Well, the Book's wrong, for I have been out on my feet."

For Kuno was possessed of a certain physical strength.

By these days it was a demerit to be muscular. Each infant was examined at birth, and all who promised undue strength were destroyed. Humanitarians may protest, but it would have been no true kindness to let an athlete live; he would never have been happy in that state of life to which the Machine had called him; he would have yearned for trees to climb, rivers to bathe in, meadows and hills against which he might measure his body. Man must be adapted to his surroundings, must he not? In the dawn of the world our weakly must be exposed on Mount Taygetus, in its twilight our strong will suffer Euthanasia, that the Machine may progress, that the Machine may progress, that the Machine may progress eternally.

"You know that we have lost the sense of space. We say 'space is annihilated,' but we have annihilated not space, but the sense thereof. We have lost a part of ourselves. I determined to recover it, and I began by walking up and down the platform of the railway outside my room. Up and down, until I was tired, and so did recapture the meaning of 'Near' and 'Far.' 'Near' is a place to which I can get quickly *on my feet,* not a place to which the train or the air-ship will take me quickly. 'Far' is a place to which I cannot get quickly on my feet; the vomitory is 'far,' though I could be there in thirty-eight seconds by summoning the train. Man is the measure. That was my first lesson. Man's feet are the measure for distance, his hands are the measure for ownership, his body is the measure for all that is lovable and desirable and strong. Then I went further: it was then that I called to you for the first time, and you would not come.

"This city, as you know, is built deep beneath the surface of the earth, with only the vomitories protruding. Having paced the platform outside my own room, I took the lift to the next platform and paced that also, and so with each in turn, until I came to the topmost, above which begins the earth. All the platforms were exactly alike, and all that I gained by visiting them was to develop my sense of space and my muscles. I think I should have been content with this—it is not a little thing—but as I walked and brooded, it occurred to me that our cities had been built in the days when men still breathed the outer air, and that there had been ventilation shafts for the workmen. I could think of nothing but these ventilation shafts. Had they been destroyed by all the food-tubes and medicine-tubes and music-tubes that the Machine has evolved lately? Or did traces of them remain? One thing was certain. If I came upon them anywhere, it would be in the railway-tunnels of the topmost story. Everywhere else, all space was accounted for.

"I am telling my story quickly, but don't think that I was not a coward or that your answers never depressed me. It is not the proper thing, it is not mechanical, it is not decent to walk along a railway-tunnel. I did not fear that I might tread upon a live rail and be killed. I feared something far more intangible—doing what was not contemplated by the Machine. Then I said to myself, 'Man is the measure,' and I went, and after many visits I found an opening.

"The tunnels, of course, were lighted. Everything is light, artificial light; darkness is the exception. So when I saw a black gap in the tiles, I knew that it was an exception, and rejoiced. I put in my arm—I could put in no more at first—and waved it round and round in ecstasy. I loosened another tile, and put in my head, and shouted into the darkness: 'I am coming, I shall do it yet,' and my voice reverberated down endless passages. I seemed to hear the spirits of those dead workmen who had returned each evening to the starlight and to their wives, and all the generations who had lived in the open air called back to me, 'You will do it yet, you are coming.'"

He paused, and, absurd as he was, his last words moved her. For Kuno had lately asked to be a father, and his request had been refused by the Committee. His was not a type that the Machine desired to hand on.

"Then a train passed. It brushed by me, but I thrust my head and arms into the hole. I had done enough for one day, so I crawled back to the platform, went down in the lift, and summoned my bed. Ah, what dreams! And again I called you, and again you refused."

She shook her head and said:

"Don't. Don't talk of these terrible things. You make me miserable. You are throwing civilization away."

"But I had got back the sense of space and a man cannot rest then. I determined to get in at the hole and climb the shaft. And so I exercised my arms. Day after day I went through ridiculous movements, until my flesh ached, and I could hang by my hands and hold the pillow of my bed outstretched for many minutes. Then I summoned a respirator, and started.

"It was easy at first. The mortar had somehow rotted, and I soon pushed some more tiles in, and clambered after them into the darkness, and the spirits of the dead comforted me. I don't know what I mean by that. I just say what I felt. I felt, for the first time, that a protest had been lodged against corruption, and that even as the dead were comforting me, so I was comforting the unborn. I felt that humanity existed, and that it existed without clothes. How can I possibly explain this? It was naked, humanity seemed naked, and all these tubes and buttons and machineries neither came into the world with us, nor will they follow us out, nor do they matter supremely while we are here. Had I been strong, I would have torn off every garment I had, and gone out into the outer air unswaddled. But this is not for me, nor perhaps for my generation. I climbed with my respirator and my hygienic clothes and my dietetic tabloids! Better thus than not at all.

"There was a ladder, made of some primeval metal. The light from the railway fell upon its lowest rungs, and I saw that it led straight upwards out of the rubble at the bottom of the shaft. Perhaps our ancestors ran up and down it a dozen times daily, in their building. As I climbed, the rough edges cut through my gloves so that my hands bled. The light

[200]

helped me for a little, and then came darkness and, worse still, silence which pierced my ears like a sword. The Machine hums! Did you know that? Its hum penetrates our blood, and may even guide our thoughts. Who knows! I was getting beyond its power. Then I thought: 'This silence means that I am doing wrong.' But I heard voices in the silence, and again they strengthened me." He laughed. "I had need of them. The next moment I cracked my head against something."

She sighed.

"I had reached one of those pneumatic stoppers that defend us from the outer air. You may have noticed them on the airship. Pitch dark, my feet on the rungs of an invisible ladder, my hands cut; I cannot explain how I lived through this part, but the voices still comforted me, and I felt for fastenings. The stopper, I suppose, was about eight feet across. I passed my hand over it as far as I could reach. It was perfectly smooth. I felt it almost to the center. Not quite to the center, for my arm was too short. Then the voice said: 'Jump. It is worth it. There may be a handle in the center, and you may catch hold of it and so come to us your own way. And if there is no handle, so that you may fall and are dashed to pieces—it is still worth it: you will still come to us your own way.' So I jumped. There was a handle, and—"

He paused. Tears gathered in his mother's eyes. She knew that he was fated. If he did not die today he would die tomorrow. There was not room for such a person in the world. And with her pity disgust mingled. She was ashamed at having borne such a son, she who had always been so respectable and so full of ideas. Was he really the little boy to whom she had taught the use of his stops and buttons, and to whom she had given his first lessons in the Book? The very hair that disfigured his lip showed that he was reverting to some savage type. On atavism the Machine can have no mercy.

"There was a handle, and I did catch it. I hung tranced over the darkness and heard the hum of these workings as the last whisper in a dying dream. All the things I had cared about and all the people I had spoken to through tubes appeared infinitely little. Meanwhile the handle revolved. My weight had set something in motion and I span slowly, and then—

"I cannot describe it. I was lying with my face to the sunshine. Blood poured from my nose and ears and I heard a tremendous roaring. The stopper, with me clinging to it, had simply been blown out of the earth, and the air that we make down here was escaping through the vent into the air above. It burst up like a fountain. I crawled back to it—for the upper air hurts—and, as it were, I took great sips from the edge. My respirator had flown goodness knows where, my clothes were torn. I just lay with my lips close to the hole, and I sipped until the bleeding stopped. You can imagine nothing so curious. This hollow in the grass—I will speak of it in a minute,—the sun shining into it, not brilliantly but through marbled clouds,—the peace, the nonchalance, the sense of space, and, brushing my cheek, the roaring fountain of our artificial air! Soon I spied my respirator, bobbing up and down in the current high above my head, and higher still were many air-ships. But no one ever looks out of air-ships, and in my case they could not have picked me up. There I was, stranded. The sun shone a little way down the shaft, and revealed the topmost rung of the ladder, but it was hopeless trying to reach it. I should either have been tossed up again by the escape, or else have fallen in, and died. I could only lie on the grass, sipping and sipping, and from time to time glancing around me.

"I knew that I was in Wessex, for I had taken care to go to a lecture on the subject before starting. Wessex lies above the room in which we are talking now. It was once an important state. Its kings held all the southern coast from the Andredswald to Cornwall, while the Wansdyke protected them on the north, running over the high ground. The lecturer was only concerned with the rise of Wessex, so I do not know how long it remained an international power, nor would the knowledge have assisted me. To tell the truth I could do nothing but laugh, during this part. There was I, with a pneumatic stopper by my side and a respirator bobbing over my head, imprisoned, all three of us, in a grass-grown hollow that was edged with fern."

Then he grew grave again.

"Lucky for me that it was a hollow. For the air began to fall back into it and to fill it as water fills a bowl. I could crawl about. Presently I stood. I breathed a mixture, in which the air that hurts predominated whenever I tried to climb the sides. This was not so bad. I had not lost my tabloids and remained ridiculously cheerful, and as for the Machine, I forgot about it altogether. My one aim now was to get to the top, where the ferns were, and to view whatever objects lay beyond.

"I rushed the slope. The new air was still too bitter for me and I came rolling back, after a momentary vision of something gray. The sun grew very feeble, and I remembered that he was in Scorpio—I had been to a lecture on that too. If the sun is in Scorpio and you are in Wessex, it means that you must be as quick as you can, or it will get too dark. (This is the first bit of useful information I have ever got from a lecture, and I expect it will be the last.) It made me try frantically to breathe the new air, and to advance as far as I dared out of my pond. The hollow filled so slowly. At times I thought that the fountain played with less vigor. My respirator seemed to dance nearer the earth; the roar was decreasing."

He broke off.

"I don't think this is interesting you. The rest will interest you even less. There are no ideas in it, and I wish that I had not troubled you to come. We are too different, mother."

She told him to continue.

"It was evening before I climbed the bank. The sun had very nearly slipped out of the sky by this time, and I could not get a good view. You, who have just crossed the Roof of the World, will not want to hear an account of the little hills that I saw—low colorless hills. But to me they were living and the turf that covered them was a skin, under which their muscles rippled, and I felt that those hills had called with incalculable force to men in the past, and that men had loved them. Now they sleep—perhaps forever. They commune with humanity in dreams. Happy the man, happy the woman, who awakes the hills of Wessex. For though they sleep, they will never die."

His voice rose passionately.

"Cannot you see, cannot all your lecturers see, that it is we who are dying, and that down here the only thing that really lives is the Machine? We created the

[202]

Machine, to do our will, but we cannot make it do our will now. It has robbed us of the sense of space and of the sense of touch, it has blurred every human relation and narrowed down love to a carnal act, it has paralyzed our bodies and our wills, and now it compels us to worship it. The Machine develops—but not on our lines. The Machine proceeds—but not to our goal. We only exist as the blood corpuscles that course through its arteries, and if it could work without us, it would let us die. Oh, I have no remedy—or, at least, only one—to tell men again and again that I have seen the hills of Wessex as Aelfrid saw them when he overthrew the Danes.

"So the sun set. I forgot to mention that a belt of mist lay between my hill and other hills, and that it was the color of pearl."

He broke off for the second time.

"Go on," said his mother wearily.

He shook his head.

"Go on. Nothing that you say can distress me now. I am hardened."

"I had meant to tell you the rest, but I cannot: I know that I cannot: good-by."

Vashti stood irresolute. All her nerves were tingling with his blasphemies. But she was also inquisitive.

"This is unfair," she complained. "You have called me across the world to hear your story, and hear it I will. Tell me—as briefly as possible, for this is a disastrous waste of time—tell me how you returned to civilization."

"Oh,—that!" he said, starting. "You would like to hear about civilization. Certainly. Had I got to where my respirator fell down?"

"No—but I understand everything now. You put on your respirator, and managed to walk along the surface of the earth to a vomitory, and there your conduct was reported to the Central Committee."

"By no means."

He passed his hand over his forehead, as if dispelling some strong impression. Then, resuming his narrative, he warmed to it again.

"My respirator fell about sunset. I had mentioned that the fountain seemed feebler, had I not?"

"Yes."

"About sunset, it let the respirator fall. As I said, I had entirely forgotten about the Machine, and I paid no great attention at the time, being occupied with other things. I had my pool of air, into which I could dip when the outer keenness became intolerable, and which would possibly remain for days, provided that no wind sprang up to disperse it. Not until it was too late, did I realize what the stoppage of the escape implied. You see—the gap in the tunnel had been mended; the Mending Apparatus, the Mending Apparatus, was after me.

"One other warning I had, but I neglected it. The sky at night was clearer than it had been in the day, and the moon, which was about half the sky behind the sun, shone into the dell at moments quite brightly. I was in my usual place—on the boundary between the two atmospheres—when I thought I saw something dark move across the bottom of the dell, and vanish into the shaft. In my folly, I ran down. I bent over and listened, and I thought I heard a faint scraping noise in the depths.

"At this—but it was too late—I took alarm. I determined to put on my respirator and to walk right out of the dell. But my respirator had gone. I knew exactly where it had fallen—between the stopper and the aperture—and I could even feel the mark that it had made in the turf. It had gone, and I realized that something evil was at work, and I had better escape to the other air, and, if I must die, die running towards the cloud that had been the color of a pearl. I never started. Out of the shaft—it is too horrible. A worm, a long white worm, had crawled out of the shaft and was gliding over the moonlit grass.

"I screamed. I did everything that I should not have done, I stamped upon the creature instead of flying from it, and it at once curled round the ankle. Then we fought. The worm let me run all over the dell, but edged up my leg as I ran. 'Help!' I cried. (That part is too awful. It belongs to the part that you will never know.) 'Help!' I cried. (Why cannot we suffer in silence?) 'Help!' I cried. Then my feet were wound together, I fell, I was dragged away from the dear ferns and the living hills, and past the great metal stopper (I can tell you this part), and I thought it might save me again if I caught hold of the handle. It also was enwrapped, it also. Oh, the whole dell was full of the things. They were searching it in all directions, they were denuding it, and the white snouts of others peeped out of the hole, ready if needed. Everything that could be moved they brought—brushwood, bundles of fern, everything, and down we all went intertwined into hell. The last things that I saw, ere the stopper closed after us, were certain stars, and I felt that a man of my sort lived in the sky. For I did fight, I fought till the very end, and it was only my head hitting against the ladder that quieted me. I woke up in this room. The worms had vanished. I was surrounded by artificial air, artificial light, artificial peace, and my friends were calling to me down speaking-tubes to know whether I had come across any new ideas lately."

Here his story ended. Discussion of it was impossible, and Vashti turned to go.

"It will end in Homelessness," she said quietly.

"I wish it would," retorted Kuno.

"The Machine has been most merciful."

"I prefer the mercy of God."

"By that superstitious phrase, do you mean that you could live in the outer air?"

"Yes."

"Have you ever seen, round the vomitories, the bones of those who were extruded after the Great Rebellion?"

"Yes."

"They were left where they perished for our edification. A few crawled away, but they perished, too—who can doubt it? And so with the Homeless of our own day. The surface of the earth supports life no longer."

"Indeed."

"Ferns and a little grass may survive, but all higher forms have perished. Has any air-ship detected them?"

"No."

"Has any lecturer dealt with them?"

"No."

"Then why this obstinacy?"

"Because I have seen them," he exploded.

"Seen *what?*"

"Because I have seen her in the twilight—because she came to my help when I called—because she, too, was entangled by the worms, and, luckier than I, was killed by one of them piercing her throat."

He was mad. Vashti departed, nor, in the troubles that followed, did she ever see his face again.

The Machine Stops

Part III

The Homeless

During the years that followed Kuno's escapade, two important developments took place in the Machine. On the surface they were revolutionary, but in either case men's minds had been prepared beforehand, and they did but express tendencies that were latent already.

The first of these was the abolition of respirators.

Advanced thinkers, like Vashti, had always held it foolish to visit the surface of the earth. Air-ships might be necessary, but what was the good of going out for mere curiosity and crawling along for a mile or two in a terrestrial motor? The habit was vulgar and perhaps faintly improper: it was unproductive of ideas, and had no connection with the habits that really mattered. So respirators were abolished, and with them, of course, the terrestrial motors, and except for a few lecturers, who complained that they were debarred access to their subject-matter, the development was accepted quietly. Those who still wanted to know what the earth was like had after all only to listen to some gramophone, or to look into some cinematophote. And even the lecturers acquiesced when they found that a lecture on the sea was none the less stimulating when compiled out of other lectures that had already been delivered on the same subject. "Beware of first-hand ideas!" exclaimed one of the most advanced of them. "First-hand ideas do not really exist. They are but the physical impressions produced by love and fear, and on this gross foundation who could erect a philosophy? Let your ideas be second-hand, and if possible tenth-hand, for then they will be far removed from that disturbing element— direct observation. Do not learn anything about this subject of mine—the French Revolution. Learn instead what I think that Enicharmon thought Urizen thought Gutch thought Ho-Yung thought Chi-Bo-Sing thought Lafcadio Hearn thought Carlyle thought Mirabeau said about the French Revolution. Through the medium of these eight great minds, the blood that was shed at Paris and the windows that were broken at Versailles will be clarified to an idea which you may employ most profitably in your daily lives. But be sure that the intermediates are many and varied, for in history one authority exists to counteract another. Urizen must counteract the skepticism of Ho-Yung and Enicharmon, I must myself counteract the impetuosity of Gutch. You who listen to me are in a better position to judge about the French Revolution than I am. Your descendants will be even in a better position than you, for they will learn what you think I think, and yet another intermediate will be added to the chain. And in time"—his voice rose—"there will come a generation that has got beyond facts, beyond impressions, a generation absolutely colorless, a generation

> seraphically free
> From taint of personality,

which will see the French Revolution not as it happened, nor as they would like it to have happened, but as it would have happened, had it taken place in the days of the Machine."

Tremendous applause greeted this lecture, which did but voice a feeling already latent in the minds of men—a feeling that terrestrial facts must be ignored, and that the abolition of respirators was a positive gain. It was even suggested that air-ships should be abolished too. This was not done, because air-ships had somehow worked themselves into the Machine's system. But year by year they were used less, and mentioned less by thoughtful men.

The second great development was the re-establishment of religion.

This, too, had been voiced in the celebrated lecture. No one could mistake the reverent tone in which the peroration had concluded, and it awakened a responsive echo in the heart of each. Those who had long worshiped silently, now began to talk. They described the strange feeling of peace that came over them when they handled the Book of the Machine, the pleasure that it was to repeat certain numerals out of it, however little meaning those numerals conveyed to the outward ear, the ecstasy of touching a button, however unimportant, or of ringing an electric bell, however superfluously.

"The Machine," they exclaimed, "feeds us and clothes us and houses us; through it we speak to one another, through it we see one another, in it we have our being. The Machine is the friend of ideas and the enemy of superstition: the Machine is omnipotent, eternal; blessed is the Machine." And before long this allocution was printed on the first page of the Book, and in subsequent editions the ritual swelled into a complicated system of praise and prayer. The word "religion" was sedulously avoided, and in theory the Machine was still the creation and the implement of man. But in practice all, save a few retrogrades, worshiped it as divine. Nor was it worshiped in unity. One believer would be chiefly impressed by the blue optic plates, through which he saw other believers; another by the Mending Apparatus, which sinful Kuno had compared to worms; another by the lifts, another by the Book. And each would pray to this or to that, and ask it to intercede for him with the Machine as a whole. Persecution—that also was present. It did not break out, for reasons that will be set forward shortly. But it was latent, and all who did not accept the minimum known as "undenominational Mechanism" lived in danger of Homelessness, which means death, as we know.

To attribute these two great developments to the Central Committee, is to take a very narrow view of civilization. The Central Committee announced the developments, it is true, but they were no more the cause of them than were the kings of the imperialistic period the cause of war. Rather did they yield to some invincible pressure, which came no one knew whither, and which, when gratified, was succeeded by some new pressure equally invincible. To such a state of affairs it is convenient to give the name of progress. No one confessed the Machine was out of hand. Year by year it was served with increased efficiency and decreased intelligence. The better a man knew his own duties upon it, the less he understood the duties of his neighbor, and in all the world there was not one who understood the monster as a whole. Those master brains had perished. They had left full directions, it is true, and their successors had each of them mastered a portion of those directions. But Humanity, in its desire for comfort, had over-reached itself. It had exploited the riches of nature too far. Quietly and complacently, it was sinking into decadence, and progress had come to mean the progress of the Machine.

As for Vashti, her life went peacefully forward until the final disaster. She made her room dark and slept; she awoke and made the room light. She lectured and attended lectures. She exchanged ideas with her innumerable friends and believed she was growing more spiritual. At times a friend was granted Euthanasia, and left his or her room for the homelessness that is beyond all human conception. Vashti did not much mind. After an unsuccessful lecture, she would sometimes ask for Euthanasia herself. But the death-rate was not permitted to exceed the birth-rate, and the Machine had hitherto refused it to her.

The troubles began quietly, long before she was conscious of them.

One day she was astonished at receiving a message from her son. They never communicated, having nothing in common, and she had only heard indirectly that he was still alive, and had been transferred from the northern hemisphere, where he had behaved so mischievously, to the southern—indeed, to a room not far from her own.

"Does he want me to visit him?" she thought. "Never again, never. And I have not the time."

No, it was madness of another kind.

He refused to visualize his face upon the blue plate, and speaking out of the darkness with solemnity said:

"The Machine stops."

"What do you say?"

"The Machine is stopping, I know it, I know the signs."

She burst into a peal of laughter. He heard her and was angry, and they spoke no more.

"Can you imagine anything more absurd?" she cried to a friend. "A man who was my son believes that the Machine is stopping. It would be impious if it was not mad."

"The Machine is stopping?" her friend replied. "What does that mean? The phrase conveys nothing to me."

"Nor to me."

"He does not refer, I suppose, to the trouble there has been lately with the music?"

"Oh, no, of course not. Let us talk about music."

"Have you complained to the authorities?"

"Yes, and they say it wants mending, and referred me to the Committee of the Mending Apparatus. I complained of those curious gasping sighs that disfigure the symphonies of the Brisbane school. They sound like someone in pain. The Committee of the Mending Apparatus say that it shall be remedied shortly."

Obscurely worried, she resumed her life. For one thing, the defect in the music irritated her. For another thing, she could not forget Kuno's speech. If he had known that the music was out of repair—he could not know it, for he detested music—if he had known that it was wrong, "the Machine stops" was exactly the venomous sort of remark he would have made. Of course he had made it at a venture, but the coincidence annoyed her, and she spoke with some petulance to the Committee of the Mending Apparatus.

They replied, as before, that the defect would be set right shortly.

"Shortly! At once!" she retorted. "Why should I be worried by imperfect music? Things are always put right at once. If you do not mend it at once, I shall complain to the Central Committee."

"No personal complaints are received by the Central Committee," the Committee of the Mending Apparatus replied.

"Through whom am I to make my complaint, then?"

"Through us."

"I complain then."

"Your complaint shall be forwarded in its turn."

"Have others complained?"

This question was unmechanical, and the Committee of the Mending Apparatus refused to answer it.

"It is too bad!" she exclaimed to another of her friends. "There never was such an unfortunate woman as myself. I can never be sure of my music now. It gets worse and worse each time I summon it."

"I too have my troubles," the friend replied. "Sometimes my ideas are interrupted by a slight jarring noise."

"What is it?"

"I do not know whether it is inside my head, or inside the wall."

"Complain, in either case."

"I have complained, and my complaint will be forwarded in its turn to the Central Committee."

Time passed, and they resented the defects no longer. The defects had not been remedied, but the human tissues in that latter day had become so subservient, that they readily adapted themselves to every caprice of the Machine. The sigh at the crisis of the Brisbane symphony no longer irritated Vashti; she accepted it as part of the melody. The jarring noise, whether in the head or in the wall, was no longer resented by her friend. And so with the moldy artificial fruit, so with the bath water that began to stink, so with the defective rhymes that the poetry machine had taken to emit. All were bitterly complained of at first, and then acquiesced in and forgotten. Things went from bad to worse unchallenged.

It was otherwise with the failure of the sleeping apparatus. That was a more serious stoppage. There came a day when over the whole world—in Sumatra, in Wessex, in the innumerable cities of Courland and Brazil—the beds, when summoned by their tired owners, failed to appear. It may seem a ludicrous matter, but from it we may date the collapse of humanity. The Committee responsible for the failure was assailed by complainants, whom it referred, as usual, to the Committee of the Mending Apparatus, who in its turn assured them that their complaints would be forwarded to the Central Committee. But the discontent grew, for mankind was not yet sufficiently adaptable to do without sleeping.

"Someone is meddling with the Machine—" they began.

"Someone is trying to make himself king, to reintroduce the personal element."

"Punish that man with Homelessness."

"To the rescue! Avenge the Machine! Avenge the Machine!"

"War! Kill the man!"

But the Committee of the Mending Apparatus now came forward, and allayed the panic with well-chosen words. It confessed that the Mending Apparatus was itself in need of repair.

The effect of this frank confession was admirable.

"Of course," said a famous lecturer—he of the French Revolution, who gilded each new decay with splendor—"of course we shall not press our complaints now. The Mending Apparatus has treated us so well in the past that we all sympathize with it, and will wait patiently for its recovery. In its own good time it will resume its duties. Meanwhile let us do without our beds, our tabloids, our other little wants. Such, I feel sure, would be the wish of the Machine."

Thousands of miles away his audience applauded. The Machine still linked them. Under the sea, beneath the roots of the mountains, ran the wires through which they saw and heard, the enormous eyes and ears that were their heritage, and the hum of many workings clothed their thoughts in one garment of subserviency. Only the old and the sick remained ungrateful, for it was rumored that Euthanasia, too, was out of order, and that pain had reappeared among men.

It became difficult to read. A blight entered the atmosphere and dulled its luminosity. At times Vashti could scarcely see across her room. The air, too, was foul. Loud were the complaints, impotent the remedies, heroic the tone of the lecturer as he cried: "Courage, courage! What matter so long as the Machine goes on? To it the darkness and the light are one." And though things improved again after a time, the old brilliancy was never recaptured, and humanity never recovered from its entrance into twilight. There was an hysterical talk of "measures," of "provisional dictatorship," and the inhabitants of Sumatra were asked to familiarize themselves with the workings of the central power station, the said power station being situated in France. But for the most part panic reigned, and men spent their strength praying to their Books, tangible proofs of the Machine's omnipotence. There were gradations of terror—at times came rumors of hope—the Mending Apparatus was almost mended—the enemies of the Machine had been got under—new "nerve-centers" were evolving which would do the work even more magnificently than before. But there came a day when, without the slightest warning, without any previous hint of feebleness, the entire communication-system broke down, all over the world, and the world, as they understood it, ended.

Vashti was lecturing at the time and her earlier remarks had been punctuated with applause. As she proceeded the audience became silent, and at the conclusion there was no sound. Somewhat displeased, she called to a friend who was a specialist in sympathy. No sound: doubtless the friend was sleeping. And so with the next friend whom she tried to summon, and so with the next, until she remembered Kuno's cryptic remark, "The Machine stops."

The phrase still conveyed nothing. If Eternity was stopping it would of course be set going shortly.

For example, there was still a little light and air—the atmosphere had improved a few hours previously. There was still the Book, and while there was the Book there was security.

Then she broke down, for with the cessation of activity came an unexpected terror—silence.

She had never known silence, and the coming of it nearly killed her—it did kill many thousands of people outright. Ever since her birth she had been surrounded by the steady hum. It was to the ear what artificial air was to the lungs, and agonizing pains shot across her head. And scarcely knowing what she did, she stumbled forward and pressed the unfamiliar button, the one that opened the door of her cell.

Now the door of the cell worked on a simple hinge of its own. It was not connected with the central power station, dying far away in France. It opened, rousing immoderate hopes in Vashti, for she thought that the Machine had been mended. It opened, and she saw the dim tunnel that curved far away towards freedom. One look, and then she shrank back. For the tunnel was full of people—she was almost the last in that city to have taken alarm.

People at any time repelled her, and these were nightmares from her worst dreams. People were crawling about, people were screaming, whimpering, gasping for breath, touching each other, vanishing in the dark, and ever and anon being pushed off the platform onto the live rail. Some were fighting round the electric bells, trying to summon trains which could not be summoned. Others were yelling for Euthanasia or for respirators, or blaspheming the Machine. Others stood at the doors of their cells fearing, like herself, either to stop in them or to leave them. And behind all the uproar was silence—the silence which is the voice of the earth and of the generations who have gone.

No—it was worse than solitude. She closed the door again and sat down to wait for the end. The disintegration went on, accompanied by horrible cracks and rumbling. The valves that restrained the Medical Apparatus must have been weakened, for it ruptured and hung hideously from the ceiling. The floor heaved and fell and flung her from her chair. A tube oozed towards her serpent fashion. And at last the final horror approached—light began to ebb, and she knew that civilization's long day was closing.

She whirled round, praying to be saved from this, at any rate, kissing the Book, pressing button after button. The uproar outside was increasing, and even penetrated the wall. Slowly the brilliancy of her cell was dimmed, the reflections faded from her metal switches. Now she could not see the reading-stand, now not the Book, though she held it in her hand. Light followed the flight of sound, air was following light, and the original void returned to the cavern from which it had been so long excluded. Vashti continued to whirl, like the devotees of an earlier religion, screaming, praying, striking at the buttons with bleeding hands.

It was thus that she opened her prison and escaped—escaped in the spirit: at least so it seems to me, ere my meditation closes. That she escapes in the body—I cannot perceive that. She struck, by chance, the switch that released the door, and the rush of foul air on her skin, the loud throbbing whispers in her ears, told her that she was facing the tunnel again, and that tremendous platform on which she had seen men fighting. They were not fighting now. Only the whispers remained, and the little whimpering groans. They were dying by hundreds out in the dark.

She burst into tears.

Tears answered her.

They wept for humanity, those two, not for themselves. They could not bear that this should be the end. Ere silence was completed their hearts were opened, and they knew what had been important on the earth. Man, the flower of all flesh, the noblest of all creatures visible, man who had once made god in his image, and had mirrored his strength on the constellations, beautiful naked man was dying, strangled in the garments that he had woven. Century after century had he toiled, and here was his reward. Truly the garment had seemed heavenly at first, shot with the colors of culture, sewn with the threads of self-denial. And heavenly it had been so long as it was a garment and no more, so long as man could shed it at will and live by the essence that is his soul, and the essence, equally divine, that is his body. The sin against the body—it was for that they wept in chief; the centuries of wrong against the muscles and the nerves, and those five portals by which we can alone apprehend—glozing it over with talk of evolution, until the body was white pap, the home of ideas as colorless, last sloshy stirrings of a spirit that had grasped the stars.

"Where are you?" she sobbed.

His voice in the darkness said, "Here."

"Is there any hope, Kuno?"

"None for us."

"Where are you?"

She crawled towards him over the bodies of the dead. His blood spurted over her hands.

"Quicker," he gasped, "I am dying—but we touch, we talk, not through the Machine."

He kissed her.

"We have come back to our own. We die, but we have recaptured life, as it was in Wessex, when Aelfrid overthrew the Danes. We know what they know outside, they who dwelt in the cloud that is the color of a pearl."

"But, Kuno, is it true? Are there still men on the surface of the earth? Is this—this tunnel, this poisoned darkness—really not the end?"

He replied:

"I have seen them, spoken to them, loved them. They are hiding in the mist and the ferns until our civilization stops. Today they are the Homeless—tomorrow—"

"Oh, tomorrow—some fool will start the Machine again, tomorrow."

"Never," said Kuno, "never. Humanity has learnt its lesson."

As he spoke, the whole city was broken like a honeycomb. An air-ship had sailed in through the vomitory into a ruined wharf. It crashed downwards, exploding as it went, rending gallery after gallery with its wings of steel. For a moment they saw the nations of the dead, and, before they joined them, scraps of the untainted sky.

THE DAY THE DAM BROKE

by JAMES THURBER

MY MEMORIES of what my family and I went through during the 1913 flood in Ohio I would gladly forget. And yet neither the hardships we endured nor the turmoil and confusion we experienced can alter my feeling toward my native state and city. I am having a fine time now and wish Columbus were here, but if anyone ever wished a city was in hell it was during that frightful and perilous afternoon in 1913 when the dam broke, or, to be more exact, when everybody in town thought that the dam broke. We were both ennobled and demoralized by the experience. Grandfather especially rose to magnificent heights which can never lose their splendor for me, even though his reactions to the flood were based upon a profound misconception, namely, that Nathan Bedford Forrest's cavalry was the menace we were called upon to face. The only possible means of escape for us was to flee the house, a step which grandfather sternly forbade, brandishing his old army saber in his hand. "Let the sons —— come!" he roared.

From *My Life and Hard Times,* by James Thurber. Harper & Brothers. Originally appeared in *The New Yorker.* Copyright, 1933, by James Thurber and reprinted with his permission.

Meanwhile hundreds of people were streaming by our house in wild panic, screaming "Go east! Go east!" We had to stun grandfather with the ironing board. Impeded as we were by the inert form of the old gentleman—he was taller than six feet and weighed almost a hundred and seventy pounds—we were passed, in the first half-mile, by practically everybody else in the city. Had grandfather not come to, at the corner of Parsons Avenue and Town Street, we would unquestionably have been overtaken and engulfed by the roaring waters—that is, if there had *been* any roaring waters. Later, when the panic had died down and people had gone rather sheepishly back to their homes and their offices, minimizing the distances they had run and offering various reasons for running, city engineers pointed out that even if the dam had broken, the water level would not have risen more than two additional inches in the West Side. The West Side was, at the time of the dam scare, under thirty feet of water—as, indeed, were all Ohio river towns during the great spring floods of twenty years ago. The East Side (where we lived and where all the running occurred) had never been in any danger at all. Only a rise of some ninety-five feet could have caused the flood waters to flow over High Street—the thoroughfare that divided the east side of town from the west—and engulf the East Side.

The fact that we were all as safe as kittens under a cookstove did not, however, assuage in the least the fine despair and the grotesque desperation which seized upon the residents of the East Side when the cry spread like a grass fire that the dam had given way. Some of the most dignified, staid, cynical, and clear-thinking men in town abandoned their wives, stenographers, homes, and offices and ran east. There are few alarms in the world more terrifying than "The dam has broken!" There are few persons capable of stopping to reason when that clarion cry strikes upon their ears, even persons who live in towns no nearer than five hundred miles to a dam.

The Columbus, Ohio, broken-dam rumor began, as I recall it, about noon of March 12, 1913. High Street, the main canyon of trade, was loud with the placid hum of business and the buzzing of placid businessmen arguing, computing, wheedling, offering, refusing, compromising. Darius Conningway, one of the foremost corporation lawyers in the Middle-West, was telling the Public Utilities Commission in the language of Julius Caesar that they might as well try to move the Northern star as to move him. Other men were making their little boasts and their little gestures. Suddenly somebody began to run. It may be that he had simply remembered, all of a moment, an engagement to meet his wife, for which he was now frightfully late. Whatever it was, he ran east on Broad Street (probably toward the Maramor Restaurant, a favorite place for a man to meet his wife). Somebody else began to run, perhaps a newsboy in high spirits. Another man, a portly gentleman of affairs, broke into a trot. Inside of ten minutes, everybody on High Street, from the Union Depot to the Courthouse was running. A loud mumble gradually crystallized into the dread word "dam." "The dam has broke!" The fear was put into words by a little old lady in an electric, or by a traffic cop, or by a small boy: nobody knows who, nor does it now really matter. Two thousand people were abruptly in full flight. "Go east!" was the cry that arose—east away from the river, east to safety. "Go east! Go east! Go east!"

Black streams of people flowed eastward down all the streets leading in that direction; these streams, whose headwaters were in the drygoods stores, office buildings, harness shops, movie theaters, were fed by trickles of housewives, children, cripples, servants, dogs, and cats, slipping out of the houses past which the main streams flowed, shouting and screaming. People ran out leaving fires burning and food cooking and doors wide open. I remember, however, that my mother turned out all the fires and that she took with her a dozen eggs and two loaves of bread. It was her plan to make Memorial Hall, just two blocks away, and take refuge somewhere in the top of it, in one of the dusty rooms where war veterans met and where old battle flags and stage scenery were stored. But the seething throngs, shouting "Go east!" drew her along and the rest of us with her. When grandfather regained full consciousness, at Parsons Avenue, he turned upon the retreating mob like a vengeful prophet and exhorted the men to form ranks and stand off the Rebel dogs, but at length he, too, got the idea that the dam had broken and, roaring "Go east!" in his powerful voice, he caught up in one arm a small child and in the other a slight clerkish man of perhaps forty-two and we slowly began to gain on those ahead of us.

A scattering of firemen, policemen, and army officers in dress uniforms—there had been a review at Fort Hayes, in the northern part of town—added color to the surging billows of people. "Go east!" cried a little child in a piping voice, as she ran past a porch on which drowsed a lieutenant-colonel of infantry. Used to quick decisions, trained to immediate obedience, the officer bounded off the porch and, running at full tilt, soon passed the child, bawling "Go east!" The two of them emptied rapidly the houses of the little street they were on. "What is it? What is it?" demanded a fat, waddling man who intercepted the colonel. The officer dropped behind and asked the little child what it was. "The dam has broke!" gasped the girl. "The dam has broke!" roared the colonel. "Go east! Go east!" He was soon leading, with the exhausted child in his arms, a fleeing company of three hundred persons who had gathered around him from living-rooms, shops, garages, backyards, and basements.

Nobody has ever been able to compute with any exactness how many people took part in the great rout of 1913, for the panic, which extended from the Winslow Bottling Works in the south end to Clintonville, six miles north, ended as abruptly as it began and the bobtail and ragtag and velvet-gowned groups of refugees melted away and slunk home, leaving the streets peaceful and deserted. The shouting, weeping, tangled evacuation of the city lasted not more than two hours in all. Some few people got as far east as Reynoldsburg, twelve miles away; fifty or more reached the Country Club, eight miles away; most of the others gave up, exhausted, or climbed trees in Franklin Park, four miles out. Order was restored and fear dispelled finally by means of militiamen riding about in motor lorries bawling through megaphones: "The dam has *not* broken!" At first this tended only to add to the confusion and increase the panic, for many stampeders thought the soldiers were bellowing "The dam has now broken!", thus setting an official seal of authentication on the calamity.

All the time, the sun shone quietly and

there was nowhere any sign of oncoming waters. A visitor in an airplane, looking down on the straggling, agitated masses of people below, would have been hard put to it to divine a reason for the phenomenon. It must have inspired, in such an observer, a peculiar kind of terror, like the sight of the *Marie Celeste,* abandoned at sea, its galley fires peacefully burning, its tranquil decks bright in the sunlight.

An aunt of mine, Aunt Edith Taylor, was in a movie theater on High Street when, over and above the sound of the piano in the pit (a W. S. Hart picture was being shown), there rose the steadily increasing tromp of running feet. Persistent shouts rose above the tromping. An elderly man, sitting near my aunt, mumbled something, got out of his seat, and went up the aisle at a dogtrot. This started everybody. In an instant the audience was jamming the aisles. "Fire!" shouted a woman who always expected to be burned up in a theater; but now the shouts outside were louder and coherent. "The dam has broke!" cried somebody. "Go east!" screamed a small woman in front of my aunt. And east they went, emerging finally into the street, torn and sprawling. Inside the theater, Bill Hart was calmly calling some desperado's bluff and the brave girl at the piano played "Row! Row! Row!" loudly and then "In My Harem." Outside, men were streaming across the Statehouse yard, others were climbing trees, a woman managed to get up onto the "These Are My Jewels" statue, whose bronze figures of Sherman, Stanton, Grant, and Sheridan watched with cold unconcern the going to pieces of the capital city.

"I ran south to State Street, east on State to Third, south on Third to Town, and out east on Town," my aunt Edith has written me. "A tall spare woman with grim eyes and a determined chin ran past me down the middle of the street. I was still uncertain as to what was the matter, in spite of all the shouting. I drew up alongside the woman with some effort, for although she was in her late fifties, she had a beautiful easy running form and seemed to be in excellent condition. 'What is it?' I puffed. She gave me a quick glance and then looked ahead again, stepping up her pace a trifle. 'Don't ask me, ask God!' she said.

"When I reached Grant Avenue, I was so spent that Dr. H. R. Mallory—you remember Dr. Mallory, the man with the white beard who looks like Robert Browning?—well, Dr. Mallory, whom I had drawn away from at the corner of Fifth and Town, passed me. 'It's got us!' he shouted, and I felt sure that whatever it was *did* have us, for you know what conviction Dr. Mallory's statements always carried. I didn't know at the time what he meant, but I found out later. There was a boy behind him on roller skates, and Dr. Mallory mistook the swishing of the skates for the sound of rushing water. He eventually reached the Columbus School for Girls, at the corner of Parsons Avenue and Town Street, where he collapsed, expecting the cold frothing waters of the Scioto to sweep him into oblivion. The boy on the skates swirled past him and Dr. Mallory realized for the first time what he had been running from. Looking back up the street, he could see no signs of water, but nevertheless, after resting a few minutes, he jogged east again. He caught up with me at Ohio Avenue, where we rested together. I should say that about seven hundred people passed us. A funny thing was that all of them were on foot. Nobody seemed to have had the courage to stop and start his car; but, as I remember it, all cars had to be cranked in those days, which is probably the reason."

The next day, the city went about its business as if nothing had happened, but there was no joking. It was two years or more before you dared treat the breaking of the dam lightly. And even now, twenty years after, there are a few persons, like Dr. Mallory, who will shut up like a clam if you mention the Afternoon of the Great Run.

Parade, 1930   Peter Blume
Collection of the Museum of Modern Art, New York. Gift of Mrs. John D. Rockefeller, Jr. Used with permission.

THE SECRET LIFE OF WALTER MITTY

by JAMES THURBER

"WE'RE GOING THROUGH!" The Commander's voice was like thin ice breaking. He wore his full-dress uniform, with the heavily braided white cap pulled down rakishly over one cold gray eye. "We can't make it, sir. It's spoiling for a hur-

From *My World—and Welcome to It*, copyright, 1942, by James Thurber. By permission of Harcourt, Brace and Company, Inc. Originally appeared in *The New Yorker*.

ricane, if you ask me." "I'm not asking you, Lieutenant Berg," said the Commander. "Throw on the power lights! Rev her up to 8,500! We're going through!" The pounding of the cylinders increased: ta-pocketa-pocketa-pocketa-*pocketa-pocketa*. The Commander stared at the ice forming on the pilot window. He walked over and twisted a row of complicated dials. "Switch on No. 8 auxiliary!" he shouted. "Switch on No. 8 auxiliary!" repeated Lieutenant Berg. "Full strength in No. 3 turret!" shouted the Commander. "Full strength in No. 3 turret!" The crew, bending to their various tasks in the huge, hurtling eight-engined Navy hydroplane, looked at each other and grinned. "The Old Man'll get us through," they said to one another. "The Old Man ain't afraid of Hell!" . . .

"Not so fast! You're driving too fast!" said Mrs. Mitty. "What are you driving so fast for?"

"Hmm?" said Walter Mitty. He looked at his wife, in the seat beside him, with shocked astonishment. She seemed grossly unfamiliar, like a strange woman who had yelled at him in a crowd. "You were up to fifty-five," she said. "You know I don't like to go more than forty. You were up to fifty-five." Walter Mitty drove on toward Waterbury in silence, the roaring of the SN202 through the worst storm in twenty years of Navy flying fading in the remote, intimate airways of his mind. "You're tensed up again," said Mrs. Mitty. "It's one of your days. I wish you'd let Dr. Renshaw look you over."

Walter Mitty stopped the car in front of the building where his wife went to have her hair done. "Remember to get those overshoes while I'm having my hair done," she said. "I don't need overshoes," said Mitty. She put her mirror back into her bag. "We've been all through that," she said, getting out of the car. "You're not a young man any longer." He raced the engine a little. "Why don't you wear your gloves? Have you lost your gloves?" Walter Mitty reached in a pocket and brought out the gloves. He put them on, but after she had turned and gone into the building and he had driven on to a red light, he took them off again. "Pick it up, brother!" snapped a cop as the light changed, and Mitty hastily pulled on his gloves and lurched ahead. He drove around the streets aimlessly for a time, and then he drove past the hospital on his way to the parking lot.

. . . "It's the millionaire banker, Wellington McMillan," said the pretty nurse. "Yes?" said Walter Mitty, removing his gloves slowly. "Who has the case?" "Dr. Renshaw and Dr. Benbow, but there are two specialists here, Dr. Remington from New York and Dr. Pritchard-Mitford from London. He flew over." A door opened down a long, cool corridor and Dr. Renshaw came out. He looked distraught and haggard. "Hello, Mitty," he said. "We're having the devil's own time with McMillan, the millionaire banker and close personal friend of Roosevelt. Obstreosis of the ductal tract. Tertiary. Wish you'd take a look at him." "Glad to," said Mitty.

In the operating room there were whispered introductions: "Dr. Remington, Dr. Mitty, Dr. Pritchard-Mitford, Dr. Mitty." "I've read your book on streptothricosis," said Pritchard-Mitford, shaking hands. "A brilliant performance, sir." "Thank you," said Walter Mitty. "Didn't know you were in the States, Mitty," grumbled Remington. "Coals to Newcastle, bringing Mitford and me up here for a tertiary." "You are very kind," said Mitty. A huge, complicated machine, connected to the operating table, with many tubes and wires, began at this moment to go pocketa-pocketa-pocketa. "The new anesthetizer is giving way!" shouted an interne. "There is no one in the East who knows how to fix it!" "Quiet, man!" said Mitty, in a low, cool voice. He sprang to the machine, which was now going pocketa-pocketa-queep-pocketa-queep. He began fingering delicately a row of glistening dials. "Give me a fountain pen!" he snapped. Someone handed him a fountain pen. He pulled a faulty piston out of the machine and inserted the pen in its place. "That will hold for ten minutes," he said. "Get on with the operation." A nurse hurried over and whispered to Renshaw, and Mitty saw the man turn pale. "Coreopsis has set in," said Renshaw nervously. "If you would take over, Mitty?" Mitty looked at him and at the craven figure of Benbow, who drank, and at the grave, uncertain faces of the two great specialists. "If you wish," he said. They slipped a white gown on him; he adjusted a mask and drew on thin gloves; nurses handed him shining . . .

"Back it up, Mac! Look out for that Buick!" Walter Mitty jammed on the brakes. "Wrong lane, Mac," said the parking-lot attendant, looking at Mitty closely. "Gee. Yeh," muttered Mitty. He began cautiously to back out of the lane marked "Exit Only." "Leave her sit there," said the attendant. "I'll put her away." Mitty got out of the car. "Hey, better leave the key." "Oh," said Mitty, handing the man the ignition key. The attendant vaulted into the car, backed it up with insolent skill, and put it where it belonged.

They're so damn cocky, thought Walter Mitty, walking along Main Street; they think they know everything. Once he had tried to take his chains off, outside New Milford, and he had got them wound around the axles. A man had had to come out in a wrecking car and unwind them, a young, grinning garageman. Since then Mrs. Mitty always made him drive to a garage to have the chains taken off. The next time, he thought, I'll wear my right arm in a sling; they won't grin at me then. I'll have my right arm in a sling and they'll see I couldn't possibly take the chains off myself. He kicked at the slush on the sidewalk. "Overshoes," he said to himself, and he began looking for a shoe store.

When he came out into the street again, with the overshoes in a box under his arm, Walter Mitty began to wonder what the other thing was his wife had told him to get. She had told him twice before they set out from their house for Waterbury. In a way he hated these weekly trips to town—he was always getting something wrong. Kleenex, he thought, Squibb's, razor blades? No. Toothpaste, toothbrush, bicarbonate, carborundum, initiative and referendum? He gave it up. But she would remember it. "Where's the what's-its-name?" she would ask. "Don't tell me you forgot the what's-its-name." A newsboy went by shouting something about the Waterbury trial.

. . . "Perhaps this will refresh your memory." The District Attorney suddenly thrust a heavy automatic at the quiet figure on the witness stand. "Have you ever seen this before?" Walter Mitty took the gun and examined it expertly. "This is my Webley-Vickers 50.80," he said calmly. An excited buzz ran around the courtroom. The Judge rapped for order. "You are a crack shot with any sort of firearms, I believe?" said the District Attorney, insinuatingly. "Objection!" shouted Mitty's attorney. "We have shown that the defendant could not have fired the shot. We have shown that he wore his right arm in a sling on the night of the fourteenth of July." Walter Mitty raised his hand briefly and the bickering attorneys were stilled. "With any known make of gun," he said evenly, "I could have killed Gregory Fitzhurst at three hundred feet *with my left hand.*" Pandemonium broke loose in the courtroom. A woman's scream rose above the bedlam and suddenly a lovely, dark-haired girl was in Walter Mitty's arms. The District Attorney struck at her savagely. Without rising from his chair, Mitty let the man have it on the point of the chin. "You miserable cur!" . . .

"Puppy biscuit," said Walter Mitty. He stopped walking and the buildings of Waterbury rose up out of the misty courtroom and surrounded him again. A woman who was passing laughed. "He said 'Puppy biscuit,'" she said to her companion. "That man said 'Puppy biscuit' to himself." Walter Mitty hurried on. He went into an A. & P., not the first one he came to but a smaller one farther up the street. "I want some biscuit for small, young dogs," he said to the clerk. "Any special brand, sir?" The greatest pistol shot in the world thought a moment. "It says 'Puppies Bark for It' on the box," said Walter Mitty.

His wife would be through at the hairdresser's in fifteen minutes, Mitty saw in looking at his watch, unless they had trouble drying it; sometimes they had trouble drying it. She didn't like to get to the hotel first; she would want him to be there waiting for her as usual. He found a big leather chair in the lobby, facing a window, and he put the overshoes and the puppy biscuit on the floor beside it. He picked up an old copy of *Liberty* and sank down into the chair. "Can Germany Conquer the World Through the Air?" Walter Mitty looked at the pictures of bombing planes and of ruined streets.

. . . "The cannonading has got the wind up in young Raleigh, sir," said the sergeant. Captain Mitty looked up at him through tousled hair. "Get him to bed," he said wearily, "with the others. I'll fly alone." "But you can't, sir," said the sergeant anxiously. "It takes two men to handle that bomber and the Archies are pounding hell out of the air. Von Richtman's circus is between here and Saulier." "Somebody's got to get that ammunition dump," said Mitty. "I'm going over. Spot of brandy?" He poured a drink for the sergeant and one for himself. War thundered and whined around the dugout and battered at the door. There was a rending of wood, and splinters flew through the room. "A bit of a near thing," said Captain Mitty carelessly. "The box barrage is closing in," said the sergeant. "We only live once, Sergeant," said Mitty, with his faint, fleeting smile. "Or do we?" He poured another brandy and tossed it off. "I never see a man could hold his brandy like you, sir," said the sergeant. "Begging your pardon, sir." Captain Mitty stood up and strapped on his huge Webley-Vickers automatic. "It's forty kilometers through hell, sir," said the sergeant. Mitty finished one last brandy. "After all," he said softly, "what isn't?" The pounding of the cannon increased; there was the rat-tat-tatting of machine guns, and from somewhere came the menacing pocketa-pocketa-pocketa of the new flame-throwers. Walter Mitty walked to the door of the dugout humming "Auprès de Ma Blonde." He turned and waved to the sergeant. "Cheerio!" he said. . . .

Something struck his shoulder. "I've been looking all over this hotel for you," said Mrs. Mitty. "Why do you have to hide in this old chair? How did you expect me to find you?" "Things close in," said Walter Mitty vaguely. "What?" Mrs. Mitty said. "Did you get the what's-its-

The Secret Life of Walter Mitty

name? The puppy biscuit? What's in that box?" "Overshoes," said Mitty. "Couldn't you have put them on in the store?" "I was thinking," said Walter Mitty. "Does it ever occur to you that I am sometimes thinking?" She looked at him. "I'm going to take your temperature when I get you home," she said.

They went out through the revolving doors that made a faintly derisive whistling sound when you pushed them. It was two blocks to the parking lot. At the drugstore on the corner she said, "Wait here for me. I forgot something. I won't be a minute." She was more than a minute. Walter Mitty lighted a cigarette. It began to rain, rain with sleet in it. He stood up against the wall of the drugstore, smoking. . . . He put his shoulders back and his heels together. "To hell with the handkerchief," said Walter Mitty scornfully. He took one last drag on his cigarette and snapped it away. Then, with that faint, fleeting smile playing about his lips, he faced the firing squad; erect and motionless, proud and disdainful, Walter Mitty the Undefeated, inscrutable to the last.

Home

From Men, Women and Dogs, copyright, 1943, by James Thurber. By permission of Harcourt, Brace and Company, Inc. Originally appeared in The New Yorker.

THE FACE WITHIN THE FACE

by Mark Schorer

"Don't!" Laura Newman said, too sharply for the occasion, and Robert, her husband, who had just begun to trace a light imaginary line along her smooth brown thigh, pulled his hand away and fell back on the sand. Laura did not move. In a white swimming suit, she lay stretched out on a white towel, as arranged and quiet as a statue, hair flowing back, eyes closed, lips a little parted, face and body gleaming, offering herself to the sun as supine marble figures on monuments coldly offer themselves to God.

On the sand beyond his father, staring out at the sea, sat David, their thirteen-year-old son, who looked over toward his mother speculatively now and asked, "Don't what?"

"She was talking to me," Robert said. He stretched out and, leaning on his elbow, looked gloomily down at his wife's ear—an object strange and perfect, as if wrought, like an artifact, by cautious, astonishing skill. He turned away, toward the boy. "Let's swim," he said.

Laura did not speak or move. *Burn, burn,* she was thinking, *burn, burn, burn,* in the rhythm of the small, lapping waves that endlessly, warmly buffeted the yellow shore. The perfect, paradoxical, immaculate pleasure as the hot sun burns and burns on the skin! The accumulated and clinging irritations and frustrations and dismal intensities of four wet and cold winter months seemed to dry upon her and fall away like scales, and she could almost feel herself emerging, with this hot balm, new and absolutely pure, and in her mind she likened the images, from a forgotten school poem, of fire and ice.

She could hear, high above her or far out over the blue cove, the distant, whimpering cry of gulls—shrill whispers—and behind her closed lids she pictured them wheeling in silvery arcs against the cool blue of the sky. Nearer, travelling along the sand to her ear, she heard the swishing sound of feet as Robert and David went down to the water. Then she heard them splashing. Then she thought, *Puberty,* and at once, with the thought, she shuddered, and her warm skin was chilled, as if the sun had gone under a cloud and a cold wind abruptly blew.

"You should take him South with you if you can manage," Mr. Lowell, the headmaster, had written. "He is well along toward puberty now, you know, growing a little too fast, and he needs some sun, needs to be built up. He's not a rugged boy by nature. Of course, we would be glad to keep him here at the school during the spring holiday—he's a most likable and tractable lad, and I'm confident that the arrangements could be made—but in his own interest we all feel that you should consider taking him with you." And so on, and, of course, there had been no question but that the headmaster was right, only there had been the somewhat irritating question of revising their plans, of cutting their three weeks to a little less than two. Yet here they were, their sixth gorgeous day, and she expressed her gratitude to the sun in a

"The Face within the Face." By Mark Schorer; reprinted by permission of the author; copyright 1949 The New Yorker Magazine, Inc.

luxurious arching of her back and stretching of her toes, until her body was taut with pleasure. Into this momentary intense delight, voices broke. She relaxed and slowly turned, and raised her head and shoulders with her elbows under her.

Robert and David were still in the water, Robert swimming briskly out, David standing still, water to his knees, a bony little figure in the forefront of the vast expanse of empty sea. Turning her head, she saw that other people had come and were settling themselves on the sand at a barely reasonable distance behind her—a man and woman and two girls and a boy.

Laura swore softly. On their first day, the Newmans had wandered away from the big stretch of beach in front of their hotel and had found this quiet cove, where the surf broke far out and where almost no one ever came. They had enjoyed the empty sea from the small empty beach fringed with barren dunes, where there was no intrusion of strident voices, no gross intimacy with other bodies. Then who were these people disposing themselves now on the sand just behind her, already shouting and calling and shrilling, the mother to her scattering children, the husband to the wife? Not, Laura thought, guests of the hotel.

She stared at them. The man wore droopy flowered trunks. He had a long, skinny white body, with a scrawny patch of black hair on his white chest, and black forearms and legs, and a narrow head with too much black hair above his ears, and the white scalp showing through the thin hair on top. The wife was short and round, with a round head and, again, too much black, untidy hair. The children were like their mother—short and round, with round heads and faces, the girls with fuzzy black pigtails, the boy with a black shock that stood up in ragged thrusts. The man was pulling towels from a basket and spreading them on the sand, and when the wife had seated herself on one, she reached into the basket and brought out a tube, and Laura watched her spread a thick layer of white salve over her nose, under her eyes, and on her cheekbones, so that she suddenly gave the fantastic impression of wearing a white domino that had been cut in half. Then Laura saw that something was wrong with her right arm; it seemed, somehow, crippled, the fingers that applied the ointment knotted in a queer way and the elbow not quite free. And when, suddenly, she shouted to her children, who had run down to the water, her face, too, or the right side of it, showed some similar defect—a partial paralysis, which made her seem to leer. When she stopped shouting, her face settled into what was apparently its perpetual expression—a horrid, rigid simper.

Laura shuddered with distaste, turned around and sat up, and determinedly faced the sea. Two things she passionately claimed as belonging to her life, and she wanted them in no less than large ways. They were privacy and self-possession. At this moment, in a small way, this family had snatched the second with the first. As she watched Robert helping David with his crawl in the quiet water of the cove, she wondered irritably how people such as these could disturb her composure, until, in a sudden misery of recollection, she knew that it was because of their disgusting domesticity; somehow they gave the impression of having brought their entire household onto the immaculate beach, spilled out on the sand the whole steamy clutter of their lives, so that Laura thought of a cantankerous parrot in a parlor cage, some potted ferns before stiff lace curtains, a kitchen sink full of greasy dishes, and soiled bed linen, gray.

Laura sat stiffly on the sand in the abrupt and heavy grip of a life long since dead—of a sordid beach town in New Jersey, of a cheap, flimsily built cottage, a girl lying at night with her head under her pillow to shut out the sounds that came through the walls from the bedroom next to hers, and the girl in the day, seeking out some lonely place on the beach where she could lie in the sun for hours, unmolested, to purge herself. The people behind her, by their presence alone, had destroyed her careful peace, and through closed teeth she swore in anger, because now the sun was helpless.

The woman was screaming at the boy, who had walked down to the water and was watching Robert and David. "Lou-ee! Lou-ee!" she shrilled, and then some word that came to Laura as "Ny-ah! Ny-ah!" —like an abstraction from all negatives. Laura glanced over her shoulder at the distorted mouth under the white mask, and the stiff arm gesticulating, and then, turning back, lowered her head into her cupped hands, so that she sat with her fingers pressed over her ears. Yet she could hear the father, calling more gently, "Lou-ee, come!" The boy stared at his parents and, at last, laggingly, came back to where they sat. Laura heard his grunt as he flung himself on the sand behind her, saying, "What's the fun? What'd we come for?" The mother said, "Just wait," and the father said, "We'll go in soon."

Dripping, gleaming in the sun, Robert and David came out of the water, up the sand. "We have company," Laura said quietly when they stood before her. With identical indifferences in their eyes, they looked at the group behind her. "What's wrong with the woman's face and arm, Robert?" she asked with whispered irritation.

"I don't know," Robert said. He dropped to the sand and sat cross-legged beside her towel, at her feet. David duplicated the position on her other side.

"Ny-ah, Ny-ah!" the woman called out to one of her little girls, who was digging in the sand and scattering it. Involuntarily, Laura glanced at her again.

"Some slight paralysis," Robert said, his face turned away, and Laura, watching the stiff arm stuck out with its twisted fingers, said "Ugh!" and turned away, too.

Briskly, Robert said, "Well, David's getting good," but even when he leaned over and slapped the boy lightly on the shoulder in congratulation, David continued to stare at the woman and then let his eyes move to the white-faced boy who sat near her, sifting sand through his fingers.

"Aren't you, David?" Robert said loudly.

"What?" the boy asked vaguely, blinking suddenly as he looked at his father.

"Your crawl. It's good."

"Oh."

The blank indifference in David's voice made Laura shift her gaze from the glinting sea to the boy's impassive face. Once more he was staring at the people behind her while his hands, too, idly sifted sand. Then, as she looked at him, she saw that some subtle difference had overtaken his features since she had last really studied them. He was on the way to becoming a different boy. Since his last holiday, she thought, his neck had visibly lengthened, and all the bones of his face had coarsened —the jaw longer, the cheekbones more prominent, the forehead higher. And yet he was still a little boy. It was almost as if, within the hairless, child's face, another face was pushing through. That was a man's face. It was—she glanced at her husband—it was, indeed, Robert's face. *Puberty,* she thought, staring at the boy with a kind of horror. She saw him lengthening out and broadening, the chest swelling, the arms swelling, nails thickening, hair—and her legs and arms were suddenly covered with goose flesh, shivering prickles sweeping her skin as, for the first time, she recognized in him the gross, inevitable thrust into manhood.

Then, behind her, the woman began noisily to scold, and Laura, who was clutching her arms to her sides, as if she were cold, lay back and tried to relax, closed her eyes once more, and sought to regain her private exchange with the sun, her perfect isolation in light. But she was too aware of everything around her to capture that pure sensation of complete and separate being. Even as her body warmed and her skin began to burn, she heard the people behind her moving about, preparing at last to go down to the water, and the sounds of running, sliding in the sand and their shifting cries told her when they went. Robert and David were talking together in low voices, and then she was aware of David's moving off a bit and beginning to dig in the sand. She heard the distant sound of splashing water, of voices laughing and shouting, of David's hands digging, slapping wet sand, scraping, and she felt Robert's eyes on her as he still sat at her feet.

Then he spoke. "What do you think of David?" he asked.

She lay completely quiet. "Think of him?"

"We haven't talked about him. How do you think he is?"

"I think he's fine. Don't you?"

"No. I think we should bring him home."

She sat up abruptly. "What did you say, Robert?" The sun seemed to blind her as she tried to see his face.

"The end of this term would be a good time to break. Bring him back to a school in the city."

"But why *break* from a good school to a less good one? There's no city school that—"

"The schooling isn't all that matters. He needs us. He needs a home."

"David? He's thirteen! He's been away for three years. What does he need with us now? I've just thought—he's—why, he's nearly a man. . . ."

"He's lonely."

"Lonely? David?"

"Lonely. Yes. It hurts me."

She looked at him with blind eyes, staring, and he said, "A man? He's nearly a *man?*"

With this question, the mad shimmering of the sun suddenly died, and she saw him clearly. He was *there,* thin and clear and brown and tractable. She said, "Yes. After all, only four or five more years . . . just now, I could see *you* in him, emerging. He's a big boy. He *needs* to be away from home. He shouldn't have to depend on us now. What can we do for him?"

"Everything we've never done," Robert said.

"I don't know what you're talking about."

"He doesn't seem to have any anchorage. Least of all in us. He's adrift—lost in himself some way."

She said curtly, "Nonsense."

He looked at her steadily before he spoke. "You're so beautiful," he said at last, almost as if he were meditating upon a theory, and then he went on quietly, "But something's wrong with our life. I don't know what it is, but . . ."

"But?" she asked.

"But. . . ."

"Yes?"

He began to run his hands through the sand aimlessly, letting the grains sift slowly between his fingers. She watched him, and at last she said, "Well, that's gratitude!" She looked away from him to the running figures on the shore—the man and his wife and the three children, in and out of the water at the shallow edge of beach, shouting and ridiculously running. "I thought that we lived the way you wanted. I thought we had a—"

"We have," he said for her. "It's a beautiful, smooth, perfectly organized life. But what's missing?"

"Is anything?"

"Well, for example, whatever it is that David ought to feel about you."

"I don't know what you're talking about."

"Do you think you know him?"

"Of course."

"Look," Robert said. "Does he ever *talk* to you? Do you know what he's thinking about? Do you know what he's *like?*"

Laura looked at him. "It's you—I don't know what *you're* like," she said.

"Ahh!" he said, a long, disparaging denial, and turned away from her.

She lay back and began to cry. With a certain luxury, she felt the tears push up through her locked lids and run down and over her cheeks. They must be dropping on her towel! She said, "At last. I knew it would come sometime—it had to —and now it has. You—always so reservedly kind and unclaiming. Now, at last, you're using your position that until now you've hardly ever admitted. Now you tell me that I've failed—from *my* position!"

"Position?" he cried. "Oh, my God!"

She felt her tears burning on her skin, and, eyes still closed, she said, "Don't exclaim. I know it's true. I've always waited. I knew it would come someday. *My* inadequacy. So now it's come." Then, roughly brushing her cheeks with her fingers, she sat up. She tossed her hair back and cried, "But why today? Why, on the day that . . ." She looked to the water's edge, where the other family, gathered in a group, was starting back up the beach. "Why today, with those people here?"

He glanced at them. "What of them? What have they got to do with anything?" And, looking back at her, he cried, "Oh, look, don't be a fool!" Then he came through the sand on his knees and seized her hands. He held them and rubbed them and looked at her blurred brown eyes. "Laura, don't be a fool," he said, and hearing the protestation of love in these unlikely words, she looked away from him and down at the sand. She detached her hands. She felt the sun blessedly burn away the dampness around her eyelids. She looked out to the sea—the miles of blue, endless blue, nothing but blue, and over it the interminable reaches of cool blue sky—and she looked back at Robert, anxious beside her, and said with slow ease, "I'm sorry."

"I am, too."

"But you agree, don't you, that David shouldn't be taken from his school?"

Robert looked past her face and said, "David's heard. Perhaps all of it," and when Laura turned, she saw that, yes, there he was, only twelve or fifteen feet away from them, his hands deep in the bowels of a sand castle, stopped there for Lord knew how long, and his face turned toward them, his eyes wide and watchful. She could think of nothing to say except "They're coming back."

The others were just passing David. They had walked in a group from the shore, the mother in the lead, her foolish round face, encumbered with its unintended grin and its ridiculous swath of white ointment, lifted as she led her throng, her tribe. Behind her was the skinny, hairy, fish-white husband, behind him the homely little girls and, lagging now at David's castle, the boy. He stopped there and watched while the others went on, until David made some gesture of invitation, and then he dropped to his knees and both began silently to dig. The rest of the family settled itself again in its place, and when the little girls began a tentative movement toward the boys, the mother said sharply, "Ny-ah! Esther! Mir!" Reluctantly, they turned back and sat on the sand beside her.

Laura looked away from her. "What mad possessiveness!" she said.

The two boys were standing over the castle now, facing the sea, and the strange boy asked David a question, which he answered by ducking his head, hunching his shoulders, and moving his arms in the motion of a crawl. The other boy imitated them. Then, talking, they moved down to the water, and both ran in. David swam and the other boy watched, but only for a moment. Then the boy's mother was on her feet and screaming again, "Ny-ah! Ny-ah! Lou-ee! Come!" Her right cheek was distorted in her excitement, and her injured arm flailed grotesquely at the air.

The boy turned slowly and looked at her. Now, at last, he was outraged. Over the bright distance, Laura could see the fury in his tense, white face. He did not look back at David but came walking with slow deliberation up the beach, past the Newmans, whose heads turned as he walked, to his mother, who was still shaking her hand at him. Then, standing perhaps six feet before her, his arms flailing too, but in a rage, he yelled at her, "Ny-ah! Ny-ah! Ny-ah!"

She looked at him in amazement for a moment and then seemed to wilt. All the perky animation left her round body as she turned slowly and settled saggingly on her towel and, at last, sinking prone, with her face pressed into its folds, wept. Her husband hurried to her, and Laura looked back to the sea. She saw David standing in the shallow water, watching intently, and then, glancing at his lifted hand, move his fingers experimentally. Then he started back to them.

The husband, kneeling beside his wife with his arm over her shoulders, murmured consolingly to her, and her sobs began to subside. The boy, quiet now, with a kind of shamed determination on his face, stood stiffly on the spot where he had faced her. Then the father summoned him with an uncompromising gesture, until the boy moved reluctantly to her. There were words that the Newmans could not hear, but the boy presently knelt beside his mother, where his father had been, and spoke softly to her. Then the mother swiftly twisted to a sitting position, her contorted face red, and, seizing the boy in her arms, she broke again into sobs as she embraced him in a convulsion of love.

"My God! Let's go," Laura said, and leaped up. Hastily, Robert helped her put their belongings in their beach basket and, without looking at the other family again, they walked away as rapidly as the loose sand allowed. Only David, lagging behind his parents, kept looking back, until the dunes cut off his view.

On the way to the hotel, the Newmans did not talk much, and they did not mention the other family, but a few hours later, when Laura was brushing her hair before a tall triple mirror in the dressing-room alcove off her bedroom, she suddenly exclaimed, "I can't get them out of my mind!"

Robert was sitting on the edge of her bed, leafing through a magazine, and he looked up and asked, "Who?"

"That awful family—that woman."

"Oh."

David, who was lying on his back on a chaise longue, his legs flung out in masculine abandon, was doing something with his hands, which he held close before his face. Apparently preoccupied with his fingers and oblivious of his parents, he nevertheless now said quietly, "They weren't bad."

"That man's—*drawers!* That's all you can call them."

Robert laughed, but David asked in an innocent tone, "Just ordinary trunks, weren't they?" He rolled over on his stomach, as if to study his hands more closely.

Laura said, "You could hardly blame the boy for screaming back at her."

David said, "The boy was O.K. I like him."

Laura watched him in the glass. "What are you doing, David?"

He stood up lazily. "Nothing," he said. He walked to a window and leaned against the frame, and then he was fooling with his fingers again.

Suddenly, Laura saw what he was doing. "Stop it, David!" she said sharply.

Robert looked up again. "What's the matter?"

She watched David closely. He was standing by the window in such a way that the late-afternoon sunlight made a nimbus of the down on one cheek and along his chin. She thought of that down as a precursor to coarse stubble, and she said, "David, get out of here, will you? You make me nervous. Go wash your face."

"It's clean," he said as he started toward the door. He watched her with empty eyes as he sidled away.

Robert moved, and presently he was standing behind her. She looked up in the central mirror and met his sad, inquiring, forgiving eyes. "What was he doing?" Robert asked.

"I think he was trying to make his fingers look paralyzed, like that grotesque woman's."

Robert laughed uneasily. "Curiosity, probably. You know boys—they're interested in oddity. Probably not at all grotesque to him. Perhaps the contrary. Rather fascinating."

Laura brushed her hair with renewed vigor, until she had counted ten, twenty, thirty strokes. "He practically said he liked them."

"Well," Robert allowed, "perhaps he did."

Her brush paused in her hair. "Is it time for a drink?"

"I'll get you one." But he did not go. He put his hands on her shoulders and stroked her upper arms. "You are beautiful," he said.

For a moment or two, she sat immobile, unprotesting, under his hand. Then she said, "What about that drink?" She watched his reflection move away, and when he was out of the room, she leaned

The Face Within the Face

toward the mirror, toward her reflection. Her face cleared, as if shadows were passing from it, as if shadows had vanished from the shadows of her mind, and she smiled.

She opened a drawer of the dressing table and took out two gold bracelets—one with square chunks of jewels held in heavy links, and one with coins the size of half dollars—and put one on each wrist. Late sunlight shone upon her and flashed off the chains and the jewels in darting angles on the glass surfaces around her. Then, in the triple mirror, she caught sight of a figure moving. It was David again—moving, stopping. She watched his reflection. He was looking not at her but at his right hand, as he held it before him and forced his fingers into an imitation of gnarled paralysis.

"David," she said quietly, "please don't do that. Why do you keep doing that?"

He looked up and met her eyes in the mirror. "I just want to know how it feels," he said. "That woman—how she feels."

"If her hand is paralyzed, she probably doesn't feel anything. And why should you want to know how *she* feels?"

"I kind of liked her." He looked at Laura blandly.

"She was so loud—screaming all the time."

"They just weren't used to a beach, that was all. She was worried."

Laura lifted her hands to fasten a gold barrette in her brushed hair so that one ear would show, but she still watched David manipulating his fingers.

Suddenly, his face brightened. At last, he had duplicated the crippled arm. "This is the way it feels!"

Her eyes searched the mirror until his glance met hers. Then she grimaced in disgust and said with sharp finality, "Don't be perverse! She was—ugly!"

David was standing rigid behind her. His arm rose until it pointed out at her with a stiff, accusing crook at the elbow and in the clumsy-knuckled fingers. His drawn face was stiff with revulsion, only his eyes alive, glimmering upon her. "Says who?" he asked in a dead voice, and as his wild, unhappy eyes held and held hers, her bracelets clanked down on the mirrored top of the dressing table with a metallic chorus, and the mirrors flashed.

Ruthlessness of modern man in a situation. The traveler who doesn't know what to do in an emergency. Kind of primitivism. He dies because he has no-one who is really interested in him.

DEATH OF A TRAVELLING SALESMAN
by Eudora Welty

R. J. Bowman, who for fourteen years had travelled for a shoe company through Mississippi, drove his Ford along a rutted dirt path. It was a long day! The time did not seem to clear the noon hurdle and settle into soft afternoon. The sun, keeping its strength here even in winter, stayed at the top of the sky, and every time Bowman stuck his head out of the dusty car to stare up the road, it seemed to reach a long arm down and push against the top of his head, right through his hat—like the practical joke of an old drummer, long on the road. It made him feel all the more angry and helpless. He was feverish, and he was not quite sure of the way.

This was his first day back on the road after a long siege of influenza. He had had very high fever, and dreams, and had become weakened and pale, enough to tell the difference in the mirror, and he could not think clearly. . . . All afternoon, in the midst of his anger, and for no reason, he had thought of his dead grandmother. She had been a comfortable soul. Once more Bowman wished he could fall into the big feather bed that had been in her room. . . . Then he forgot her again.

This desolate hill country! And he seemed to be going the wrong way—it was as if he were going back, far back. There was not a house in sight. . . . There was no use wishing he were back in bed, though. By paying the hotel doctor his bill he had proved his recovery. He had not even been sorry when the pretty trained nurse said good-bye. He did not like illness, he distrusted it, as he distrusted the road without signposts. It angered him. He had given the nurse a really expensive bracelet, just because she was packing up her bag and leaving.

But now—what if in fourteen years on the road he had never been ill before and never had an accident? His record was broken, and he had even begun almost to question it. . . . He had gradually put up at better hotels, in the bigger towns, but weren't they all, eternally, stuffy in summer and draughty in winter? Women? He could only remember little rooms within little rooms, like a nest of Chinese paper boxes, and if he thought of one woman he saw the worn loneliness that the furniture of that room seemed built of. And he himself—he was a man who always wore rather wide-brimmed black hats, and in the wavy hotel mirrors had looked something like a bull-fighter, as he paused for that inevitable instant on the landing, walking downstairs to supper. . . . He leaned out of the car again, and once more the sun pushed at his head.

Bowman had wanted to reach Beulah by dark, to go to bed and sleep off his fatigue. As he remembered, Beulah was fifty miles away from the last town, on a gravelled road. This was only a cow trail. How had he ever come to such a place? One hand wiped the sweat from his face, and he drove on.

He had made the Beulah trip before. But he had never seen this hill or this petering-out path before—or that cloud, he

From *A Curtain of Green and Other Stories*, copyright, 1936, 1937, 1938, 1939, 1941, by Eudora Welty. Reprinted by permission of Harcourt, Brace and Company, Inc., New York.

thought shyly, looking up and then down quickly—any more than he had seen this day before. Why did he not admit he was simply lost and had been for miles? . . . He was not in the habit of asking the way of strangers, and these people never knew where the very roads they lived on went to; but then he had not even been close enough to anyone to call out. People standing in the fields now and then, or on top of the haystacks, had been too far away, looking like leaning sticks or weeds, turning a little at the solitary rattle of his car across their countryside, watching the pale sobered winter dust where it chunked out behind like big squashes down the road. The stares of these distant people had followed him solidly like a wall, impenetrable, behind which they turned back after he had passed.

The cloud floated there to one side like the bolster on his grandmother's bed. It went over a cabin on the edge of a hill, where two bare chinaberry trees clutched at the sky. He drove through a heap of dead oak leaves, his wheels stirring their weightless sides to make a silvery melancholy whistle as the car passed through their bed. No car had been along this way ahead of him. Then he saw that he was on the edge of a ravine that fell away, a red erosion, and that this was indeed the road's end.

He pulled the brake. But it did not hold, though he put all his strength into it. The car, tipped toward the edge, rolled a little. Without doubt, it was going over the bank.

He got out quietly, as though some mischief had been done him and he had his dignity to remember. He lifted his bag and sample case out, set them down, and stood back and watched the car roll over the edge. He heard something—not the crash he was listening for, but a slow un-uproarious crackle. Rather distastefully he went to look over, and he saw that his car had fallen into a tangle of immense grape vines as thick as his arm, which caught it and held it, rocked it like a grotesque child in a dark cradle, and then, as he watched, concerned somehow that he was not still inside it, released it gently to the ground.

He sighed.

Where am I? he wondered with a shock. Why didn't I do something? All his anger seemed to have drifted away from him. There was the house, back on the hill. He took a bag in each hand and with almost childlike willingness went toward it. But his breathing came with difficulty, and he had to stop to rest.

It was a shotgun house, two rooms and an open passage between, perched on the hill. The whole cabin slanted a little under the heavy heaped-up vine that covered the roof, light and green, as though forgotten from summer. A woman stood in the passage.

He stopped still. Then all of a sudden his heart began to behave strangely. Like a rocket set off, it began to leap and expand into uneven patterns of beats which showered into his brain, and he could not think. But in scattering and falling it made no noise. It shot up with great power, almost elation, and fell gently, like acrobats into nets. It began to pound profoundly, then waited irresponsibly, hitting in some sort of inward mockery first at his ribs, then against his eyes, then under his shoulder blades, and against the roof of his mouth when he tried to say, "Good afternoon, madam." But he could not hear his heart—it was as quiet as ashes falling. This was rather comforting; still, it was shocking to Bowman to feel his heart beating at all.

Stockstill in his confusion, he dropped his bags, which seemed to drift in slow bulks gracefully through the air and to cushion themselves on the grey prostrate grass near the doorstep.

As for the woman standing there, he saw at once that she was old. Since she could not possibly hear his heart, he ignored the pounding and now looked at her carefully, and yet in his distraction dreamily, with his mouth open.

She had been cleaning the lamp, and held it, half blackened, half clear, in front of her. He saw her with the dark passage behind her. She was a big woman with a weather-beaten but unwrinkled face; her lips were held tightly together, and her eyes looked with a curious dulled brightness into his. He looked at her shoes, which were like bundles. If it were summer she would be barefoot. . . . Bowman, who automatically judged a woman's age on sight, set her age at fifty. She wore a formless garment of some grey coarse material, rough-dried from a washing, from which her arms appeared pink and unexpectedly round. When she never said a word, and sustained her quiet pose of holding the lamp, he was convinced of the strength in her body.

"Good afternoon, madam," he said.

She stared on, whether at him or at the air around him he could not tell, but after a moment she lowered her eyes to show that she would listen to whatever he had to say.

"I wonder if you would be interested—" He tried once more. "An accident—my car . . ."

Her voice emerged low and remote, like a sound across a lake. "Sonny he ain't here."

"Sonny?"

"Sonny ain't here now."

Her son—a fellow able to bring my car up, he decided in blurred relief. He pointed down the hill. "My car's in the bottom of the ditch. I'll need help."

"Sonny ain't here, but he'll be here."

She was becoming clearer to him and her voice stronger, and Bowman saw that she was stupid.

He was hardly surprised at the deepening postponement and tedium of his journey. He took a breath, and heard his voice speaking over the silent blows of his heart. "I was sick. I am not strong yet. . . . May I come in?"

He stooped and laid his big black hat over the handle on his bag. It was a humble motion, almost a bow, that instantly struck him as absurd and betraying of all his weakness. He looked up at the woman, the wind blowing his hair. He might have continued for a long time in this unfamiliar attitude; he had never been a patient man, but when he was sick he had learned to sink submissively into the pillows, to wait for his medicine. He waited on the woman.

Then she, looking at him with blue eyes, turned and held open the door, and after a moment Bowman, as if convinced in his action, stood erect and followed her in.

Inside, the darkness of the house touched him like a professional hand, the doctor's. The woman set the half-cleaned lamp on a table in the center of the room and pointed, also like a professional person, a guide, to a chair with a yellow cowhide seat. She herself crouched on the hearth, drawing her knees up under the shapeless dress.

At first he felt hopefully secure. His heart was quieter. The room was enclosed in the gloom of yellow pine boards. He could see the other room, with the foot of an iron bed showing, across the passage. The bed had been made up with a red-and-yellow pieced quilt that looked like a map or a picture, a little like his grandmother's girlhood painting of Rome burning.

He had ached for coolness, but in this room it was cold. He stared at the hearth with dead coals lying on it and iron pots in the corners. The hearth and smoked chimney were of the stone he had seen ribbing the hills, mostly slate. Why is there no fire? he wondered.

And it was so still. The silence of the fields seemed to enter and move familiarly through the house. The wind used the open hall. He felt that he was in a mysterious, quiet, cool danger. It was necessary to do what? . . . To talk.

"I have a nice line of women's low-priced shoes . . ." he said.

But the woman answered, "Sonny'll be here. He's strong. Sonny'll move your car."

"Where is he now?"

"Farms for Mr. Redmond."

Mr. Redmond. Mr. Redmond. That was someone he would never have to encounter, and he was glad. Somehow the name did not appeal to him. . . . In a flare of touchiness and anxiety, Bowman wished to avoid even mention of unknown men and their unknown farms.

"Do you two live here alone?" He was surprised to hear his old voice, chatty, confidential, inflected for selling shoes, asking a question like that—a thing he did not even want to know.

"Yes. We are alone."

He was surprised at the way she answered. She had taken a long time to say that. She had nodded her head in a deep way too. Had she wished to affect him with some sort of premonition? he wondered unhappily. Or was it only that she would not help him, after all, by talking with him? For he was not strong enough to receive the impact of unfamiliar things without a little talk to break their fall. He had lived a month in which nothing had happened except in his head and his body—an almost inaudible life of heartbeats and dreams that came back, a life of fever and privacy, a delicate life which had left him weak to the point of—what? Of begging. The pulse in his palm leapt like a trout in a brook.

He wondered over and over why the woman did not go ahead with cleaning the lamp. What prompted her to stay there across the room, silently bestowing her presence upon him? He saw that with her it was not a time for doing little tasks. Her face was grave; she was feeling how right she was. Perhaps it was only politeness. In docility he held his eyes stiffly wide; they fixed themselves on the woman's clasped hands as though she held the cord they were strung on.

Then, "Sonny's coming," she said.

He himself had not heard anything, but there came a man passing the window and then plunging in at the door, with two hounds beside him. Sonny was a big enough man, with his belt slung low about his hips. He looked at least thirty. He had a hot, red face that was yet full of silence. He wore muddy blue pants and an old military coat stained and patched. World War? Bowman wondered. Great God, it was a Confederate coat. On the back of his light hair he had a wide filthy black hat which seemed to insult Bowman's own. He pushed down the dogs from his chest.

[231]

He was strong with dignity and heaviness in his way of moving. . . . There was the resemblance to his mother.

They stood side by side. . . . He must account again for his presence here.

"Sonny, this man, he had his car to run off over the prec'pice an' wants to know if you will git it out for him," the woman said after a few minutes.

Bowman could not even state his case.

Sonny's eyes lay upon him.

He knew he should offer explanations and show money—at least appear either penitent or authoritative. But all he could do was to shrug slightly.

Sonny brushed by him going to the window, followed by the eager dogs, and looked out. There was effort even in the way he was looking, as if he could throw his sight out like a rope. Without turning Bowman felt that his own eyes could have seen nothing: it was too far.

"Got me a mule out there an' got me a block an' tackle," said Sonny meaningfully. "I *could* catch me my mule an' git me my ropes, an' before long I'd git your car out the ravine."

He looked completely round the room, as if in meditation, his eyes roving in their own distance. Then he pressed his lips firmly and yet shyly together, and with the dogs ahead of him this time, he lowered his head and strode out. The hard earth sounded, cupping to his powerful way of walking—almost a stagger.

Mischievously, at the suggestion of those sounds, Bowman's heart leapt again. It seemed to walk about inside him.

"Sonny's goin' to do it," the woman said. She said it again, singing it almost, like a song. She was sitting in her place by the hearth.

Without looking out, he heard some shouts and the dogs barking and the pounding of hoofs in short runs on the hill. In a few minutes Sonny passed under the window with a rope, and there was a brown mule with quivering, shining, purple-looking ears. The mule actually looked in the window. Under its eyelashes it turned target-like eyes into his. Bowman averted his head and saw the woman looking serenely back at the mule, with only satisfaction in her face.

She sang a little more, under her breath. It occurred to him, and it seemed quite marvellous, that she was not really talking to him, but rather following the thing that came about with words that were unconscious and part of her looking.

So he said nothing, and this time when he did not reply he felt a curious and strong emotion, not fear, rise up in him.

This time, when his heart leapt, something—his soul—seemed to leap too, like a little colt invited out of a pen. He stared at the woman while the frantic nimbleness of his feeling made his head sway. He could not move; there was nothing he could do, unless perhaps he might embrace this woman who sat there growing old and shapeless before him.

But he wanted to leap up, to say to her, I have been sick and I found out then, only then, how lonely I am. Is it too late? My heart puts up a struggle inside me, and you may have heard it, protesting against emptiness. . . . It should be full, he would rush on to tell her, thinking of his heart now as a deep lake, it should be holding love like other hearts. It should be flooded with love. There would be a warm spring day . . . Come and stand in my heart, whoever you are, and a whole river would cover your feet and rise higher and take your knees in whirlpools, and draw you down to itself, your whole body, your heart too.

But he moved a trembling hand across his eyes, and looked at the placid crouch-

Death of a Travelling Salesman

ing woman across the room. She was still as a statue. He felt ashamed and exhausted by the thought that he might, in one more moment, have tried by simple words and embraces to communicate some strange thing—something which seemed always to have just escaped him . . .

Sunlight touched the farthest pot on the hearth. It was late afternoon. This time tomorrow he would be somewhere on a good gravelled road, driving his car past things that happened to people, quicker than their happening. Seeing ahead to the next day, he was glad, and knew that this was no time to embrace an old woman. He could feel in his pounding temples the readying of his blood for motion and for hurrying away.

"Sonny's hitched up your car by now," said the woman. "He'll git it out the ravine right shortly."

"Fine!" he cried with his customary enthusiasm.

Yet it seemed a long time that they waited. It began to get dark. Bowman was cramped in his chair. Any man should know enough to get up and walk around while he waited. There was something like guilt in such stillness and silence.

But instead of getting up, he listened. . . . His breathing restrained, his eyes powerless in the growing dark, he listened uneasily for a warning sound, forgetting in wariness what it would be. Before long he heard something—soft, continuous, insinuating.

"What's the noise?" he asked, his voice jumping into the dark. Then wildly he was afraid it would be his heart beating so plainly in the quiet room, and she would tell him so.

"You might hear the stream," she said grudgingly.

Her voice was closer. She was standing by the table. He wondered why she did not light the lamp. She stood there in the dark and did not light it.

Bowman would never speak to her now, for the time was past. I'll sleep in the dark, he thought, in his bewilderment pitying himself.

Heavily she moved on to the window. Her arm, vaguely white, rose straight from her full side and she pointed out into the darkness.

"That white speck's Sonny," she said, talking to herself.

He turned unwillingly and peered over her shoulder; he hesitated to rise and stand beside her. His eyes searched the dusky air. The white speck floated smoothly toward her finger, like a leaf on a river, growing whiter in the dark. It was as if she had shown him something secret, part of her life, but had offered no explanation. He looked away. He was moved almost to tears, feeling for no reason that she had made a silent declaration equivalent to his own. His hand waited upon his chest.

Then a step shook the house, and Sonny was in the room. Bowman felt how the woman left him there and went to the other man's side.

"I done got your car out, mister," said Sonny's voice in the dark. "She's settin' a-waitin' in the road, turned to go back where she come from."

"Fine!" said Bowman, projecting his own voice to loudness. "I'm surely much obliged—I could never have done it myself—I was sick. . . ."

"I could do it easy," said Sonny.

Bowman could feel them both waiting in the dark, and he could hear the dogs panting out in the yard, waiting to bark when he should go. He felt strangely helpless and resentful. Now that he could go, he longed to stay. From what was he being deprived? His chest was rudely shaken by the violence of his heart. These people cherished something here that he could not see, they withheld some ancient promise of food and warmth and light. Between them they had a conspiracy. He thought of the way she had moved away from him and gone to Sonny, she had flowed toward him. He was shaking with cold, he was tired, and it was not fair. Humbly and yet angrily he stuck his hand into his pocket.

"Of course I'm going to pay you for everything—"

"We don't take money for such," said Sonny's voice belligerently.

"I want to pay. But do something more . . . Let me stay—to-night. . . ." He took another step toward them. If only they could see him, they would know his sincerity, his real need! His voice went on, "I'm not very strong yet, I'm not able to walk far, even back to my car, maybe, I don't know—I don't know exactly where I am—"

He stopped. He felt as if he might burst into tears. What would they think of him!

Sonny came over and put his hands on him. Bowman felt them pass (they were professional too) across his chest, over his hips. He could feel Sonny's eyes upon him in the dark.

"You ain't no revenuer come sneakin' here, mister, ain't got no gun?"

To this end of nowhere! And yet *he* had come. He made a grave answer. "No."

"You can stay."

"Sonny," said the woman, "you'll have to borry some fire."

"I'll go git it from Redmond's," said Sonny.

"What?" Bowman strained to hear their words to each other.

"Our fire, it's out, and Sonny's got to borry some, because it's dark an' cold," she said.

"But matches—I have matches—"

"We don't have no need for 'em," she said proudly. "Sonny's goin' after his own fire."

"I'm goin' to Redmond's," said Sonny with an air of importance, and he went out.

After they had waited a while, Bowman looked out the window and saw a light moving over the hill. It spread itself out like a little fan. It zigzagged along the field, darting and swift, not like Sonny at all. . . . Soon enough, Sonny staggered in, holding a burning stick behind him in tongs, fire flowing in his wake, blazing light into the corners of the room.

"We'll make a fire now," the woman said, taking the brand.

When that was done she lit the lamp. It showed its dark and light. The whole room turned golden-yellow like some sort of flower, and the walls smelled of it and seemed to tremble with the quiet rushing of the fire and the waving of the burning lampwick in its funnel of light.

The woman moved among the iron pots. With the tongs she dropped hot coals on top of the iron lids. They made a set of soft vibrations, like the sound of a bell far away.

She looked up and over at Bowman, but he could not answer. He was trembling. . . .

"Have a drink, mister?" Sonny asked. He had brought in a chair from the other room and sat astride it with his folded arms across the back. Now we are all visible to one another, Bowman thought, and cried, "Yes, sir, you bet, thanks!"

"Come after me and do just what I do," said Sonny.

It was another excursion into the dark. They went through the hall, out to the back of the house, past a shed and a

Death of a Travelling Salesman

hooded well. They came to a wilderness of thicket.

"Down on your knees," said Sonny.

"What?" Sweat broke out on his forehead.

He understood when Sonny began to crawl through a sort of tunnel that the bushes made over the ground. He followed, startled in spite of himself when a twig or a thorn touched him gently without making a sound, clinging to him and finally letting him go.

Sonny stopped crawling and, crouched on his knees, began to dig with both his hands into the dirt. Bowman shyly struck matches and made a light. In a few minutes Sonny pulled up a jug. He poured out some of the whisky into a bottle from his coat pocket, and buried the jug again. "You never know who's liable to knock at your door," he said, and laughed. "Start back," he said, almost formally. "Ain't no need for us to drink outdoors, like hogs."

At the table by the fire, sitting opposite each other in their chairs, Sonny and Bowman took drinks out of the bottle, passing it across. The dogs slept; one of them was having a dream.

"This is good," said Bowman. "That is what I needed." It was just as though he were drinking the fire off the hearth.

"He makes it," said the woman with quiet pride.

She was pushing the coals off the pots, and the smells of corn bread and coffee circled the room. She set everything on the table before the men, with a bone-handled knife stuck into one of the potatoes, splitting out its golden fibre. Then she stood for a minute looking at them, tall and full above them where they sat. She leaned a little toward them.

"You-all can eat now," she said, and suddenly smiled.

Bowman had just happened to be looking at her. He set his cup back on the table in unbelieving protest. A pain pressed at his eyes. He saw that she was not an old woman. She was young, still young. He could think of no number of years for her. She was the same age as Sonny, and she belonged to him. She stood with the deep dark corner of the room behind her, the shifting yellow light scattering over her head and her grey formless dress, trembling over her tall body when it bent over them in its sudden communication. She was young. Her teeth were shining and her eyes glowed. She turned and walked slowly and heavily out of the room, and he heard her sit down on the cot and then lie down. The pattern on the quilt moved.

"She goin' to have a baby," said Sonny, popping a bite into his mouth.

Bowman could not speak. He was shocked with knowing what was really in this house. A marriage, a fruitful marriage. That simple thing. Anyone could have had that.

Somehow he felt unable to be indignant or protest, although some sort of joke had certainly been played upon him. There was nothing remote or mysterious here—only something private. The only secret was the ancient communication between two people. But the memory of the woman's waiting silently by the cold hearth, of the man's stubborn journey a mile away to get fire, and how they finally brought out their food and drink and filled the room proudly with all they had to show, was suddenly too clear and too enormous within him for response. . . .

"You ain't as hungry as you look," said Sonny.

The woman came out of the bedroom as soon as the men had finished, and ate her supper while her husband stared peacefully into the fire.

Then they put the dogs out, with the food that was left.

"I think I'd better sleep here by the fire, on the floor," said Bowman.

He felt that he had been cheated, and that he could afford now to be generous. Ill though he was, he was not going to ask them for their bed. He was through with asking favours in this house, now that he understood what was there.

"Sure, mister."

But he had not known yet how slowly he understood. They had not meant to give him their bed. After a little interval they both rose and looking at him gravely went into the other room.

He lay stretched by the fire until it grew low and dying. He watched every tongue of blaze lick out and vanish. "There will be special reduced prices on all footwear during the month of January," he found himself repeating quietly, and then he lay with his lips tight shut.

How many noises the night had! He heard the stream running, the fire dying, and he was sure now that he heard his heart beating, too, the sound it made under his ribs. He heard breathing, round and deep, of the man and his wife in the room across the passage. And that was all. But emotion swelled patiently within him, and he wished that the child were his.

He must get back to where he had been before. He stood weakly before the red coals, and put on his overcoat. It felt too heavy on his shoulders. As he started out he looked and saw that the woman had never got through with cleaning the lamp. On some impulse he put all the money from his billfold under its fluted glass base, almost ostentatiously.

Ashamed, shrugging a little, and then shivering, he took his bags and went out. The cold of the air seemed to lift him bodily. The moon was in the sky.

On the slope he began to run, he could not help it. Just as he reached the road, where his car seemed to sit in the moonlight like a boat, his heart began to give off tremendous explosions like a rifle, bang bang bang.

He sank in fright on to the road, his bags falling about him. He felt as if all this had happened before. He covered his heart with both hands to keep anyone from hearing the noise it made.

But nobody heard it.

THE ROCKING-HORSE WINNER

by D. H. LAWRENCE

THERE WAS a woman who was beautiful, who started with all the advantages, yet she had no luck. She married for love, and the love turned to dust. She had bonny children, yet she felt they had been thrust upon her, and she could not love them. They looked at her coldly, as if they were finding fault with her. And hurriedly she felt she must cover up some fault in herself. Yet what it was that she must cover up she never knew. Nevertheless, when her children were present, she always felt the centre of her heart go hard. This troubled her, and in her manner she was all the more gentle and anxious for her children, as if she loved them very much. Only she

From *The Portable D. H. Lawrence*. Copyright, 1933, by the Estate of D. H. Lawrence. Reprinted by permission of The Viking Press, Inc., N. Y.

The Rocking-Horse Winner

herself knew that at the centre of her heart was a hard little place that could not feel love, no, not for anybody. Everybody else said of her: "She is such a good mother. She adores her children." Only she herself, and her children themselves, knew it was not so. They read it in each other's eyes.

There were a boy and two little girls. They lived in a pleasant house, with a garden, and they had discreet servants, and felt themselves superior to anyone in the neighbourhood.

Although they lived in style, they felt always an anxiety in the house. There was never enough money. The mother had a small income, and the father had a small income, but not nearly enough for the social position which they had to keep up. The father went into town to some office. But though he had good prospects, these prospects never materialized. There was always the grinding sense of the shortage of money, though the style was always kept up.

At last the mother said: "I will see if I can't make something." But she did not know where to begin. She racked her brains, and tried this thing and the other, but could not find anything successful. The failure made deep lines come into her face. Her children were growing up, they would have to go to school. There must be more money, there must be more money. The father, who was always very handsome and expensive in his tastes, seemed as if he never would be able to do anything worth doing. And the mother, who had a great belief in herself, did not succeed any better, and her tastes were just as expensive.

And so the house came to be haunted by the unspoken phrase: There must be more money! There must be more money! The children could hear it all the time, though nobody said it aloud. They heard it at Christmas, when the expensive and splendid toys filled the nursery. Behind the shining modern rocking-horse, behind the smart doll's-house, a voice would start whispering: "There must be more money! There must be more money!" And the children would stop playing, to listen for a moment. They would look into each other's eyes, to see if they had all heard. And each one saw in the eyes of the other two that they too had heard. "There must be more money! There must be more money!"

It came whispering from the springs of the still-swaying rocking-horse, and even the horse, bending his wooden, champing head, heard it. The big doll, sitting so pink and smirking in her new pram, could hear it quite plainly, and seemed to be smirking all the more self-consciously because of it. The foolish puppy, too, that took the place of the teddy-bear, he was looking so extraordinarily foolish for no other reason but that he heard the secret whisper all over the house: "There must be more money!"

Yet nobody ever said it aloud. The whisper was everywhere, and therefore no one spoke it. Just as no one ever says: "We are breathing!" in spite of the fact that breath is coming and going all the time.

"Mother," said the boy Paul one day, "why don't we keep a car of our own? Why do we always use uncle's, or else a taxi?"

"Because we're the poor members of the family," said the mother.

"But why are we, mother?"

"Well—I suppose," she said slowly and bitterly, "it's because your father has no luck."

The boy was silent for some time.

"Is luck money, mother?" he asked, rather timidly.

[237]

"No, Paul. Not quite. It's what causes you to have money."

"Oh!" said Paul vaguely. "I thought when Uncle Oscar said filthy lucker, it meant money."

"Filthy lucre does mean money," said the mother. "But it's lucre, not luck."

"Oh!" said the boy. "Then what is luck, mother?"

"It's what causes you to have money. If you're lucky you have money. That's why it's better to be born lucky than rich. If you're rich, you may lose your money. But if you're lucky, you will always get more money."

"Oh! Will you? And is father not lucky?"

"Very unlucky, I should say," she said bitterly.

The boy watched her with unsure eyes.

"Why?" he asked.

"I don't know. Nobody ever knows why one person is lucky and another unlucky."

"Don't they? Nobody at all? Does nobody know?"

"Perhaps God. But He never tells."

"He ought to, then. And aren't you lucky either, mother?"

"I can't be, if I married an unlucky husband."

"But by yourself, aren't you?"

"I used to think I was, before I married. Now I think I am very unlucky indeed."

"Why?"

"Well—never mind! Perhaps I'm not really," she said.

The child looked at her, to see if she meant it. But he saw, by the lines of her mouth, that she was only trying to hide something from him.

"Well, anyhow," he said stoutly, "I'm a lucky person."

"Why?" said his mother, with a sudden laugh.

He stared at her. He didn't even know why he had said it.

"God told me," he asserted, brazening it out.

"I hope He did, dear!" she said, again with a laugh, but rather bitter.

"He did, mother!"

"Excellent!" said the mother, using one of her husband's exclamations.

The boy saw she did not believe him; or, rather, that she paid no attention to his assertion. This angered him somewhat, and made him want to compel her attention.

He went off by himself, vaguely, in a childish way, seeking for the clue to "luck." Absorbed, taking no heed of other people, he went about with a sort of stealth, seeking inwardly for luck. He wanted luck, he wanted it, he wanted it. When the two girls were playing dolls in the nursery, he would sit on his big rocking-horse, charging madly into space, with a frenzy that made the little girls peer at him uneasily. Wildly the horse careered, the waving dark hair of the boy tossed, his eyes had a strange glare in them. The little girls dared not speak to him.

When he had ridden to the end of his mad little journey, he climbed down and stood in front of his rocking-horse, staring fixedly into its lowered face. Its red mouth was slightly open, its big eye was wide and glassy-bright.

"Now!" he would silently command the snorting steed. "Now, take me to where there is luck! Now take me!"

And he would slash the horse on the neck with the little whip he had asked Uncle Oscar for. He knew the horse could take him to where there was luck, if only he forced it. So he would mount again, and start on his furious ride, hoping at last to get there. He knew he could get there.

The Rocking-Horse Winner

"You'll break your horse, Paul!" said the nurse.

"He's always riding like that! I wish he'd leave off!" said his elder sister Joan.

But he only glared down on them in silence. Nurse gave him up. She could make nothing of him. Anyhow he was growing beyond her.

One day his mother and his Uncle Oscar came in when he was on one of his furious rides. He did not speak to them.

"Hallo, you young jockey! Riding a winner?" said his uncle.

"Aren't you growing too big for a rocking-horse? You're not a very little boy any longer, you know," said his mother.

But Paul only gave a blue glare from his big, rather close-set eyes. He would speak to nobody when he was in full tilt. His mother watched him with an anxious expression on her face.

At last he suddenly stopped forcing his horse into the mechanical gallop, and slid down.

"Well, I got there!" he announced fiercely, his blue eyes still flaring, and his sturdy long legs straddling apart.

"Where did you get to?" asked his mother.

"Where I wanted to go," he flared back at her.

"That's right, son!" said Uncle Oscar. "Don't you stop till you get there. What's the horse's name?"

"He doesn't have a name," said the boy.

"Gets on without all right?" asked the uncle.

"Well, he has different names. He was called Sansovino last week."

"Sansovino, eh? Won the Ascot. How did you know his name?"

"He always talks about horse-races with Bassett," said Joan.

The uncle was delighted to find that his small nephew was posted with all the racing news. Bassett, the young gardener, who had been wounded in the left foot in the war and had got his present job through Oscar Cresswell, whose batman he had been, was a perfect blade of the "turf." He lived in the racing events, and the small boy lived with him.

Oscar Cresswell got it all from Bassett.

"Master Paul comes and asks me, so I can't do more than tell him, sir," said Bassett, his face terribly serious, as if he were speaking of religious matters.

"And does he ever put anything on a horse he fancies?"

"Well—I don't want to give him away—he's a young sport, a fine sport, sir. Would you mind asking him yourself? He sort of takes a pleasure in it, and perhaps he'd feel I was giving him away, sir, if you don't mind."

Bassett was serious as a church.

The uncle went back to his nephew, and took him off for a ride in the car.

"Say, Paul, old man, do you ever put anything on a horse?" the uncle asked.

The boy watched the handsome man closely.

"Why, do you think I oughtn't to?" he parried.

"Not a bit of it! I thought perhaps you might give me a tip for the Lincoln."

The car sped on into the country, going down to Uncle Oscar's place in Hampshire.

"Honour bright?" said the nephew.

"Honour bright, son!" said the uncle.

"Well, then, Daffodil."

"Daffodil! I doubt it, sonny. What about Mirza?"

"I only know the winner," said the boy. "That's Daffodil."

"Daffodil, eh?"

There was a pause. Daffodil was an obscure horse comparatively.

"Uncle!"

[239]

"Yes, son?"

"You won't let it go any further, will you? I promised Bassett."

"Bassett be damned, old man! What's he got to do with it?"

"We're partners. We've been partners from the first. Uncle, he lent me my first five shillings, which I lost. I promised him, honour bright, it was only between me and him; only you gave me that ten-shilling note I started winning with, so I thought you were lucky. You won't let it go any further, will you?"

The boy gazed at his uncle from those big, hot, blue eyes, set rather close together. The uncle stirred and laughed uneasily.

"Right you are, son! I'll keep your tip private. Daffodil, eh? How much are you putting on him?"

"All except twenty pounds," said the boy. "I keep that in reserve."

The uncle thought it a good joke.

"You keep twenty pounds in reserve, do you, you young romancer? What are you betting, then?"

"I'm betting three hundred," said the boy gravely. "But it's between you and me, Uncle Oscar! Honour bright?"

The uncle burst into a roar of laughter.

"It's between you and me all right, you young Nat Gould," he said, laughing. "But where's your three hundred?"

"Bassett keeps it for me. We're partners."

"You are, are you? And what is Bassett putting on Daffodil?"

"He won't go quite as high as I do, I expect. Perhaps he'll go a hundred and fifty."

"What, pennies?" laughed the uncle.

"Pounds," said the child, with a surprised look at his uncle. "Bassett keeps a bigger reserve than I do."

Between wonder and amusement Uncle Oscar was silent. He pursued the matter no further, but he determined to take his nephew with him to the Lincoln races.

"Now, son," he said, "I'm putting twenty on Mirza, and I'll put five for you on any horse you fancy. What's your pick?"

"Daffodil, uncle."

"No, not the fiver on Daffodil!"

"I should if it was my own fiver," said the child.

"Good! Good! Right you are! A fiver for me and a fiver for you on Daffodil."

The child had never been to a race-meeting before, and his eyes were blue fire. He pursed his mouth tight, and watched. A Frenchman just in front had put his money on Lancelot. Wild with excitement, he flayed his arms up and down, yelling "Lancelot! Lancelot!" in his French accent.

Daffodil came in first, Lancelot second, Mirza third. The child, flushed and with eyes blazing, was curiously serene. His uncle brought him four five-pound notes, four to one.

"What am I to do with these?" he cried, waving them before the boy's eyes.

"I suppose we'll talk to Bassett," said the boy. "I expect I have fifteen hundred now; and twenty in reserve; and this twenty."

His uncle studied him for some moments.

"Look here, son!" he said. "You're not serious about Bassett and that fifteen hundred, are you?"

"Yes, I am. But it's between you and me, uncle. Honour bright!"

"Honour bright all right, son! But I must talk to Bassett."

"If you'd like to be a partner, uncle, with Bassett and me, we could all be partners. Only, you'd have to promise, honour bright, uncle, not to let it go beyond us three. Bassett and I are lucky, and you must be lucky, because it was your ten shillings I started winning with. . . ."

Uncle Oscar took both Bassett and Paul into Richmond Park for an afternoon, and there they talked.

"It's like this, you see, sir," Bassett said. "Master Paul would get me talking about racing events, spinning yarns, you know, sir. And he was always keen on knowing if I'd made or if I'd lost. It's about a year since, now, that I put five shillings on Blush of Dawn for him—and we lost. Then the luck turned, with that ten shillings he had from you, that we put on Singhalese. And since that time, it's been pretty steady, all things considering. What do you say, Master Paul?"

"We're all right when we're sure," said Paul. "It's when we're not quite sure that we go down."

"Oh, but we're careful then," said Bassett.

"But when are you sure?" smiled Uncle Oscar.

"It's Master Paul, sir," said Bassett, in a secret, religious voice. "It's as if he had it from heaven. Like Daffodil, now, for the Lincoln. That was as sure as eggs."

"Did you put anything on Daffodil?" asked Oscar Cresswell.

"Yes, sir. I made my bit."

"And my nephew?"

Bassett was obstinately silent, looking at Paul.

"I made twelve hundred, didn't I, Bassett? I told uncle I was putting three hundred on Daffodil."

"That's right," said Bassett, nodding.

"But where's the money?" asked the uncle.

"I keep it safe locked up, sir. Master Paul he can have it any minute he likes to ask for it."

"What, fifteen hundred pounds?"

"And twenty! And forty, that is, with the twenty he made on the course."

"It's amazing!" said the uncle.

"If Master Paul offers you to be partners, sir, I would, if I were you; if you'll excuse me," said Bassett.

Oscar Cresswell thought about it.

"I'll see the money," he said.

They drove home again, and sure enough, Bassett came round to the garden-house with fifteen hundred pounds in notes. The twenty pounds reserve was left with Joe Glee, in the Turf Commission deposit.

"You see, it's all right, uncle, when I'm sure! Then we go strong, for all we're worth. Don't we, Bassett?"

"We do that, Master Paul."

"And when are you sure?" said the uncle, laughing.

"Oh, well, sometimes I'm absolutely sure, like about Daffodil," said the boy; "and sometimes I have an idea; and sometimes I haven't even an idea, have I, Bassett? Then we're careful, because we mostly go down."

"You do, do you! And when you're sure, like about Daffodil, what makes you sure, sonny?"

"Oh, well, I don't know," said the boy uneasily. "I'm sure, you know, uncle; that's all."

"It's as if he had it from heaven, sir," Bassett reiterated.

"I should say so!" said the uncle.

But he became a partner. And when the Leger was coming on, Paul was "sure" about Lively Spark, which was a quite inconsiderable horse. The boy insisted on putting a thousand on the horse, Bassett went for five hundred, and Oscar Cresswell two hundred. Lively Spark came in first, and the betting had been ten to one against him. Paul had made ten thousand.

"You see," he said. "I was absolutely sure of him."

Even Oscar Cresswell had cleared two thousand.

"Look here, son," he said, "this sort of thing makes me nervous."

"It needn't, uncle! Perhaps I shan't be sure again for a long time."

"But what are you going to do with your money?" asked the uncle.

"Of course," said the boy, "I started it for mother. She said she had no luck, because father is unlucky, so I thought if I was lucky, it might stop whispering."

"What might stop whispering?"

"Our house. I hate our house for whispering."

"What does it whisper?"

"Why—why"—the boy fidgeted—"why, I don't know. But it's always short of money, you know, uncle."

"I know it, son, I know it."

"You know people send mother writs, don't you, uncle?"

"I'm afraid I do," said the uncle.

"And then the house whispers, like people laughing at you behind your back. It's awful, that is! I thought if I was lucky . . ."

"You might stop it," added the uncle.

The boy watched him with big blue eyes that had an uncanny cold fire in them, and he said never a word.

"Well, then!" said the uncle. "What are we doing?"

"I shouldn't like mother to know I was lucky," said the boy.

"Why not, son?"

"She'd stop me."

"I don't think she would."

"Oh!"—and the boy writhed in an odd way—"I don't want her to know, uncle."

"All right, son! We'll manage it without her knowing."

They managed it very easily. Paul, at the other's suggestion, handed over five thousand pounds to his uncle, who deposited it with the family lawyer, who was then to inform Paul's mother that a relative had put five thousand pounds into his hands, which sum was to be paid out a thousand pounds at a time, on the mother's birthday, for the next five years.

"So she'll have a birthday present of a thousand pounds for five successive years," said Uncle Oscar. "I hope it won't make it all the harder for her later."

Paul's mother had her birthday in November. The house had been "whispering" worse than ever lately, and, even in spite of his luck, Paul could not bear up against it. He was very anxious to see the effect of the birthday letter, telling his mother about the thousand pounds.

When there were no visitors, Paul now took his meals with his parents, as he was beyond the nursery control. His mother went into town nearly every day. She had discovered that she had an odd knack of sketching furs and dress materials, so she worked secretly in the studio of a friend who was the chief "artist" for the leading drapers. She drew the figures of ladies in furs and ladies in silk and sequins for the newspaper advertisements. This young woman artist earned several thousand pounds a year, but Paul's mother only made several hundreds, and she was again dissatisfied. She so wanted to be first in something, and she did not succeed, even in making sketches for drapery advertisements.

She was down to breakfast on the morning of her birthday. Paul watched her face as she read her letters. He knew the lawyer's letter. As his mother read it, her face hardened and became more expressionless. Then a cold, determined look came on her mouth. She hid the letter under the pile of others, and said not a word about it.

"Didn't you have anything nice in the post for your birthday, mother?" said Paul.

"Quite moderately nice," she said, her voice cold and absent.

She went away to town without saying more.

But in the afternoon Uncle Oscar appeared. He said Paul's mother had had a long interview with the lawyer, asking if the whole five thousand could be advanced at once, as she was in debt.

"What do you think, uncle?" said the boy.

"I leave it to you, son."

"Oh, let her have it, then! We can get some more with the other," said the boy.

"A bird in the hand is worth two in the bush, laddie!" said Uncle Oscar.

"But I'm sure to know for the Grand National; or the Lincolnshire; or else the Derby. I'm sure to know for one of them," said Paul.

So Uncle Oscar signed the agreement, and Paul's mother touched the whole five thousand. Then something very curious happened. The voices in the house suddenly went mad, like a chorus of frogs on a spring evening. There were certain new furnishings, and Paul had a tutor. He was really going to Eton, his father's school, in the following autumn. There were flowers in the winter, and a blossoming of the luxury Paul's mother had been used to. And yet the voices in the house, behind the sprays of mimosa and almond blossom, and from under the piles of iridescent cushions, simply trilled and screamed in a sort of ecstasy: "There must be more money! Oh-h-h, there must be more money. Oh, now, now-w! Now-w-w —there must be more money!—more than ever! More than ever!"

It frightened Paul terribly. He studied away at his Latin and Greek with his tutors. But his intense hours were spent with Bassett. The Grand National had gone by: he had not "known," and had lost a hundred pounds. Summer was at hand. He was in agony for the Lincoln. But even for the Lincoln he didn't "know" and he lost fifty pounds. He became wild-eyed and strange, as if something were going to explode in him.

"Let it alone, son! Don't you bother about it!" urged Uncle Oscar. But it was as if the boy couldn't really hear what his uncle was saying.

"I've got to know for the Derby! I've got to know for the Derby!" the child reiterated, his big blue eyes blazing with a sort of madness.

His mother noticed how overwrought he was.

"You'd better go to the seaside. Wouldn't you like to go now to the seaside, instead of waiting? I think you'd better," she said, looking down at him anxiously, her heart curiously heavy because of him.

But the child lifted his uncanny blue eyes.

"I couldn't possibly go before the Derby, mother!" he said. "I couldn't possibly!"

"Why not?" she said, her voice becoming heavy when she was opposed. "Why not? You can still go from the seaside to see the Derby with your Uncle Oscar, if that's what you wish. No need for you to wait here. Besides, I think you care too much about these races. It's a bad sign. My family has been a gambling family, and you won't know till you grow up how much damage it has done. But it has done damage. I shall have to send Bassett away, and ask Uncle Oscar not to talk racing to you, unless you promise to be reasonable about it; go away to the seaside and forget it. You're all nerves!"

"I'll do what you like, mother, so long as you don't send me away till after the Derby," the boy said.

"Send you away from where? Just from this house?"

"Yes," he said, gazing at her.

"Why, you curious child, what makes you care about this house so much, suddenly? I never knew you loved it."

He gazed at her without speaking. He had a secret within a secret, something he had not divulged, even to Bassett or to his Uncle Oscar.

But his mother, after standing undecided and a little bit sullen for some moments, said:

"Very well, then! Don't go to the seaside till after the Derby, if you don't wish it. But promise me you won't let your nerves go to pieces. Promise you won't think so much about horse-racing and events, as you call them!"

"Oh, no," said the boy casually. "I won't think much about them, mother. You needn't worry. I wouldn't worry, mother, if I were you."

"If you were me and I were you," said his mother, "I wonder what we should do!"

"But you know you needn't worry, mother, don't you?" the boy repeated.

"I should be awfully glad to know it," she said wearily.

"Oh, well, you can, you know. I mean, you ought to know you needn't worry," he insisted.

"Ought I? Then I'll see about it," she said.

Paul's secret of secrets was his wooden horse, that which had no name. Since he was emancipated from a nurse and a nursery-governess, he had had his rocking-horse removed to his own bedroom at the top of the house.

"Surely, you're too big for a rocking-horse!" his mother had remonstrated.

"Well, you see, mother, till I can have a real horse, I like to have some sort of animal about," had been his quaint answer.

"Do you feel he keeps you company?" she laughed.

"Oh, yes! He's very good, he always keeps me company, when I'm there," said Paul.

So the horse, rather shabby, stood in an arrested prance in the boy's bedroom.

The Derby was drawing near, and the boy grew more and more tense. He hardly heard what was spoken to him, he was very frail, and his eyes were really uncanny. His mother had sudden seizures of uneasiness about him. Sometimes, for half-an-hour, she would feel a sudden anxiety about him that was almost anguish. She wanted to rush to him at once, and know he was safe.

Two nights before the Derby, she was at a big party in town, when one of her rushes of anxiety about her boy, her firstborn, gripped her heart till she could hardly speak. She fought with the feeling, might and main, for she believed in common sense. But it was too strong. She had to leave the dance and go downstairs to telephone to the country. The children's nursery-governess was terribly surprised and startled at being rung up in the night.

"Are the children all right, Miss Wilmot?"

"Oh, yes, they are quite all right."

"Master Paul? Is he all right?"

"He went to bed as right as a trivet. Shall I run up and look at him?"

"No," said Paul's mother reluctantly. "No! Don't trouble. It's all right. Don't sit up. We shall be home fairly soon." She did not want her son's privacy intruded upon.

The Rocking-Horse Winner

"Very good," said the governess.

It was about one o'clock when Paul's mother and father drove up to their house. All was still. Paul's mother went to her room and slipped off her white fur cloak. She had told her maid not to wait up for her. She heard her husband downstairs, mixing a whisky-and-soda.

And then, because of the strange anxiety at her heart, she stole upstairs to her son's room. Noiselessly she went along the upper corridor. Was there a faint noise. What was it?

She stood, with arrested muscles, outside his door, listening. There was a strange, heavy, and yet not loud noise. Her heart stood still. It was a soundless noise, yet rushing and powerful. Something huge, in violent, hushed motion. What was it? What in God's name was it? She ought to know. She felt that she knew the noise. She knew what it was.

Yet she could not place it. She couldn't say what it was. And on and on it went, like a madness.

Softly, frozen with anxiety and fear, she turned the door-handle.

The room was dark. Yet in the space near the window, she heard and saw something plunging to and fro. She gazed in fear and amazement.

Then suddenly she switched on the light, and saw her son, in his green pyjamas, madly surging on the rocking-horse. The blaze of light suddenly lit him up, as he urged the wooden horse, and lit her up, as she stood, blonde, in her dress of pale green and crystal, in the doorway.

"Paul!" she cried. "Whatever are you doing?"

"It's Malabar!" he screamed, in a powerful, strange voice. "It's Malabar."

His eyes blazed at her for one strange and senseless second, as he ceased urging his wooden horse. Then he fell with a crash to the ground, and she, all her tormented motherhood flooding upon her, rushed to gather him up.

But he was unconscious, and unconscious he remained, with some brain-fever. He talked and tossed, and his mother sat stonily by his side.

"Malabar! It's Malabar! Bassett, Bassett, I know! It's Malabar!"

So the child tried, trying to get up and urge the rocking-horse that gave him his inspiration.

"What does he mean by Malabar?" asked the heart-frozen mother.

"I don't know," said the father stonily.

"What does he mean by Malabar?" she asked her brother Oscar.

"It's one of the horses running for the Derby," was the answer.

And, in spite of himself, Oscar Cresswell spoke to Bassett, and himself put a thousand on Malabar: at fourteen to one.

The third day of the illness was critical: they were waiting for a change. The boy, with his rather long, curly hair, was tossing ceaselessly on the pillow. He neither slept nor regained consciousness, and his eyes were like blue stones. His mother sat, feeling her heart had gone, turned actually into a stone.

In the evening, Oscar Cresswell did not come, but Bassett sent a message, saying could he come up for one moment, just one moment? Paul's mother was very angry at the intrusion, but on second thought she agreed. The boy was the same. Perhaps Bassett might bring him to consciousness.

The gardener, a shortish fellow with a little brown moustache, and sharp little brown eyes, tiptoed into the room, touched his imaginary cap to Paul's mother, and stole to the bedside, staring with glittering, smallish eyes, at the tossing, dying child.

Stories

"Master Paul!" he whispered. "Master Paul! Malabar come in first all right, a clean win. I did as you told me. You've made over seventy thousand pounds, you have; you've got over eighty thousand. Malabar came in all right, Master Paul!"

"Malabar! Malabar! Did I say Malabar, mother? Did I say Malabar? Do you think I'm lucky, mother? I knew Malabar, didn't I? Over eighty thousand pounds! I call that lucky, don't you, mother? Over eighty thousand pounds! I knew, didn't I know I knew? Malabar came in all right. If I ride my horse till I'm sure, then I tell you, Bassett, you can go as high as you like. Did you go for all you were worth, Bassett?"

"I went a thousand on it, Master Paul."

"I never told you, mother, that if I can ride my horse, and get there, then I'm absolutely sure—oh, absolutely! Mother, did I ever tell you? I am lucky."

"No, you never did," said the mother.

But the boy died in the night.

And even as he lay dead, his mother heard her brother's voice saying to her: "My God, Hester, you're eighty-odd thousand to the good and a poor devil of a son to the bad. But, poor devil, poor devil, he's best gone out of a life where he rides his rocking-horse to find a winner."

OF THIS TIME, OF THAT PLACE
by LIONEL TRILLING

IT WAS a fine September day. By noon it would be summer again, but now it was true autumn with a touch of chill in the air. As Joseph Howe stood on the porch of the house in which he lodged, ready to leave for his first class of the year, he thought with pleasure of the long indoor days that were coming. It was a moment when he could feel glad of his profession.

On the lawn the peach tree was still in fruit and young Hilda Aiken was taking a picture of it. She held the camera tight against her chest. She wanted the sun behind her, but she did not want her own long morning shadow in the foreground. She raised the camera, but that did not help, and she lowered it, but that made things worse. She twisted her body to the left, then to the right. In the end she had to step out of the direct line of the sun. At last she snapped the shutter and wound the film with intense care.

Howe, watching her from the porch, waited for her to finish and called good morning. She turned, startled, and almost sullenly lowered her glance. In the year Howe had lived at the Aikens', Hilda had accepted him as one of her family, but since his absence of the summer she had grown shy. Then suddenly she lifted her head and smiled at him, and the humorous smile confirmed his pleasure in the day. She picked up her bookbag and set off for school.

The handsome houses on the streets to the college were not yet fully awake, but they looked very friendly. Howe went by the Bradby house where he would be a guest this evening at the first dinner party of the year. When he had gone the length

Reprinted by permission of Lionel Trilling. Copyright 1944.

of the picket fence, the whitest in town, he turned back. Along the path there was a fine row of asters and he went through the gate and picked one for his buttonhole. The Bradbys would be pleased if they happened to see him invading their lawn and the knowledge of this made him even more comfortable.

He reached the campus as the hour was striking. The students were hurrying to their classes. He himself was in no hurry. He stopped at his dim cubicle of an office and lit a cigarette. The prospect of facing his class had suddenly presented itself to him and his hands were cold; the lawful seizure of power he was about to make seemed momentous. Waiting did not help. He put out his cigarette, picked up a pad of theme paper, and went to his classroom.

As he entered, the rattle of voices ceased, and the twenty-odd freshmen settled themselves and looked at him appraisingly. Their faces seemed gross, his heart sank at their massed impassivity, but he spoke briskly.

'My name is Howe,' he said, and turned and wrote it on the blackboard. The carelessness of the scrawl confirmed his authority. He went on, 'My office is 412 Slemp Hall, and my office-hours are Monday, Wednesday and Friday from eleven-thirty to twelve-thirty.'

He wrote, 'M., W., F., 11:30-12:30.' He said, 'I'll be very glad to see any of you at that time. Or if you can't come then, you can arrange with me for some other time.'

He turned again to the blackboard and spoke over his shoulder. 'The text for the course is Jarman's *Modern Plays*, revised edition. The Co-op has it in stock.' He wrote the name, underlined 'revised edition' and waited for it to be taken down in the new notebooks.

When the bent heads were raised again he began his speech of prospectus. 'It is hard to explain—' he said, and paused as they composed themselves. 'It is hard to explain what a course like this is intended to do. We are going to try to learn something about modern literature and something about prose composition.'

As he spoke, his hands warmed and he was able to look directly at the class. Last year on the first day the faces had seemed just as cloddish, but as the term wore on they became gradually alive and quite likable. It did not seem possible that the same thing could happen again.

'I shall not lecture in this course,' he continued. 'Our work will be carried on by discussion and we will try to learn by an exchange of opinion. But you will soon recognize that my opinion is worth more than anyone else's here.'

He remained grave as he said it, but two boys understood and laughed. The rest took permission from them and laughed too. All Howe's private ironies protested the vulgarity of the joke, but the laughter made him feel benign and powerful.

When the little speech was finished, Howe picked up the pad of paper he had brought. He announced that they would write an extemporaneous theme. Its subject was traditional, 'Who I am and why I came to Dwight College.' By now the class was more at ease and it gave a ritualistic groan of protest. Then there was a stir as fountain pens were brought out and the writing-arms of the chairs were cleared, and the paper was passed about. At last, all the heads bent to work, and the room became still.

Howe sat idly at his desk. The sun shone through the tall clumsy windows. The cool of the morning was already passing. There was a scent of autumn and of varnish and the stillness of the room was deep and oddly touching. Now and then a student's head was raised and scratched in the old, elaborate students' pantomime that calls the teacher to witness honest intellectual effort.

Suddenly a tall boy stood within the frame of the open door. 'Is this,' he said, and thrust a large nose into a college catalogue, 'is this the meeting place of English 1A? The section instructed by Dr. Joseph Howe?'

He stood on the very sill of the door, as if refusing to enter until he was perfectly sure of all his rights. The class looked up from work, found him absurd and gave a low mocking cheer.

The teacher and the new student, with equal pointedness, ignored the disturbance. Howe nodded to the boy, who pushed his head forward and then jerked it back in a wide elaborate arc to clear his brow of a heavy lock of hair. He advanced into the room and halted before Howe, almost at attention. In a loud, clear voice he announced, 'I am Tertan, Ferdinand R., reporting at the direction of Head of Department Vincent.'

The heraldic formality of this statement brought forth another cheer. Howe looked at the class with a sternness he could not really feel, for there was indeed something ridiculous about this boy. Under his displeased regard the rows of heads dropped to work again. Then he touched Tertan's elbow, led him up to the desk and stood so as to shield their conversation from the class.

'We are writing an extemporaneous theme,' he said. 'The subject is, "Who I am and why I came to Dwight College."'

He stripped a few sheets from the pad and offered them to the boy. Tertan hesitated and then took the paper, but he held it only tentatively. As if with the effort of making something clear, he gulped, and a slow smile fixed itself on his face. It was at once knowing and shy.

'Professor,' he said, 'to be perfectly fair to my classmates'—he made a large gesture over the room—'and to you'—he inclined his head to Howe—'this would not be for me an extemporaneous subject.'

Howe tried to understand. 'You mean you've already thought about it—you've heard we always give the same subject? That doesn't matter.'

Again the boy ducked his head and gulped. It was the gesture of one who wishes to make a difficult explanation with perfect candor. 'Sir,' he said, and made the distinction with great care, 'the topic I did not expect, but I have given much ratiocination to the subject.'

Howe smiled and said, 'I don't think that's an unfair advantage. Just go ahead and write.'

Tertan narrowed his eyes and glanced sidewise at Howe. His strange mouth smiled. Then in quizzical acceptance, he ducked his head, threw back the heavy, dank lock, dropped into a seat with a great loose noise and began to write rapidly.

The room fell silent again and Howe resumed his idleness. When the bell rang, the students who had groaned when the task had been set now groaned again because they had not finished. Howe took up the papers, and held the class while he made the first assignment. When he dismissed it, Tertan bore down on him, his slack mouth held ready for speech.

'Some professors,' he said, 'are pedants. They are Dryasdusts. However, some professors are free souls and creative spirits. Kant, Hegel and Nietzsche were all professors.' With this pronouncement he paused. 'It is my opinion,' he continued, 'that you occupy the second category.'

Of This Time, Of That Place

Howe looked at the boy in surprise and said with good-natured irony, 'With Kant, Hegel and Nietzsche?'

Not only Tertan's hand and head but his whole awkward body waved away the stupidity. 'It is the kind and not the quantity of the kind,' he said sternly.

Rebuked, Howe said as simply and seriously as he could, 'It would be nice to think so.' He added, 'Of course I am not a professor.'

This was clearly a disappointment but Tertan met it. 'In the French sense,' he said with composure. 'Generically, a teacher.'

Suddenly he bowed. It was such a bow, Howe fancied, as a stage-director might teach an actor playing a medieval student who takes leave of Abelard—stiff, solemn, with elbows close to the body and feet together. Then, quite as suddenly, he turned and left.

A queer fish, and as soon as Howe reached his office, he sifted through the batch of themes and drew out Tertan's. The boy had filled many sheets with his unformed headlong scrawl. 'Who am I?' he had begun. 'Here, in a mundane, not to say commercialized academe, is asked the question which from time long immemorably out of mind has accreted doubts and thoughts in the psyche of man to pester him as a nuisance. Whether in St. Augustine (or Austin as sometimes called) or Miss Bashkirtsieff or Frederic Amiel or Empedocles, or in less lights of the intellect than these, this posed question has been ineluctable.'

Howe took out his pencil. He circled 'academe' and wrote 'vocab.' in the margin. He underlined 'time long immemorably out of mind' and wrote 'Diction!' But this seemed inadequate for what was wrong. He put down his pencil and read ahead to discover the principle of error in the theme. 'Today as ever, in spite of gloomy prophets of the dismal science (economics) the question is uninvalidated. Out of the starry depths of heaven hurtles this spear of query demanding to be caught on the shield of the mind ere it pierces the skull and the limbs be unstrung.'

Baffled but quite caught, Howe read on. 'Materialism, by which is meant the philosophic concept and not the moral idea, provides no aegis against the question which lies beyond the tangible (metaphysics). Existence without alloy is the question presented. Environment and heredity relegated aside, the rags and old clothes of practical life discarded, the name and the instrumentality of livelihood do not, as the prophets of the dismal science insist on in this connection, give solution to the interrogation which not from the professor merely but veritably from the cosmos is given. I think, therefore I am (cogito etc.) but who am I? Tertan I am, but what is Tertan? Of this time, of that place, of some parentage, what does it matter?'

Existence without alloy: the phrase established itself. Howe put aside Tertan's paper and at random picked up another. 'I am Arthur J. Casebeer, Jr.,' he read. 'My father is Arthur J. Casebeer and my grandfather was Arthur J. Casebeer before him. My mother is Nina Wimble Casebeer. Both of them are college graduates and my father is in insurance. I was born in St. Louis eighteen years ago and we still make our residence there.'

Arthur J. Casebeer, who knew who he was, was less interesting than Tertan, but more coherent. Howe picked up Tertan's paper again. It was clear that none of the routine marginal comments, no 'sent. str.' or 'punct.' or 'vocab.' could cope with this torrential rhetoric. He read ahead, contenting himself with underscoring the errors against the time when he should have the necessary 'conference' with Tertan.

It was a busy and official day of cards and sheets, arrangements and small decisions, and it gave Howe pleasure. Even when it was time to attend the first of the weekly Convocations he felt the charm of the beginning of things when intention is still innocent and uncorrupted by effort. He sat among the young instructors on the platform, and joined in their humorous complaints at having to assist at the ceremony, but actually he got a clear satisfaction from the ritual of prayer and prosy speech, and even from wearing his academic gown. And when the Convocation was over the pleasure continued as he crossed the campus, exchanging greetings with men he had not seen since the spring. They were people who did not yet, and perhaps never would, mean much to him, but in a year they had grown amiably to be part of his life. They were his fellow-townsmen.

The day had cooled again at sunset, and there was a bright chill in the September twilight. Howe carried his voluminous gown over his arm, he swung his doctoral hood by its purple neckpiece, and on his head he wore his mortarboard with its heavy gold tassel bobbing just over his eye. These were the weighty and absurd symbols of his new profession and they pleased him. At twenty-six Joseph Howe had discovered that he was neither so well off nor so bohemian as he had once thought. A small income, adequate when supplemented by a sizable cash legacy, was genteel poverty when the cash was all spent. And the literary life—the room at the Lafayette, or the small apartment without a lease, the long summers on the Cape, the long afternoons and the social evenings—began to weary him. His writing filled his mornings and should perhaps have filled his life, yet it did not. To the amusement of his friends, and with a certain sense that he was betraying his own freedom, he had used the last of his legacy for a year at Harvard. The small but respectable reputation of his two volumes of verse had proved useful—he continued at Harvard on a fellowship and when he emerged as Doctor Howe he received an excellent appointment, with prospects, at Dwight.

He had his moments of fear when all that had ever been said of the dangers of the academic life had occurred to him. But after a year in which he had tested every possibility of corruption and seduction he was ready to rest easy. His third volume of verse, most of it written in his first years of teaching, was not only ampler but, he thought, better than its predecessors.

There was a clear hour before the Bradby dinner party, and Howe looked forward to it. But he was not to enjoy it, for lying with his mail on the hall table was a copy of this quarter's issue of *Life and Letters*, to which his landlord subscribed. Its severe cover announced that its editor, Frederic Woolley, had this month contributed an essay called 'Two Poets,' and Howe, picking it up, curious to see who the two poets might be, felt his own name start out at him with cabalistic power—Joseph Howe. As he continued to turn the pages his hand trembled.

Standing in the dark hall, holding the neat little magazine, Howe knew that his literary contempt for Frederic Woolley meant nothing, for he suddenly understood how he respected Woolley in the way of the world. He knew this by the trembling of his hand. And of the little world as well as the great, for although the literary groups of New York might dismiss Woolley, his name carried high authority in the academic world. At Dwight it was even a revered name, for it had been here at the college that Frederic Woolley had made the distinguished scholarly career from which he had gone on to literary journalism. In middle life he had been induced to take the editorship of *Life and Letters,* a literary monthly not widely read but heavily endowed, and in its pages he had carried on the defense of what he sometimes called the older values. He was not without wit, he had great knowledge and considerable taste, and even in the full movement of the 'new' literature he had won a certain respect for his refusal to accept it. In France, even in England, he would have been connected with a more robust tradition of conservatism, but America gave him an audience not much better than genteel. It was known in the college that to the subsidy of *Life and Letters* the Bradbys contributed a great part.

As Howe read, he saw that he was involved in nothing less than an event. When the Fifth Series of *Studies in Order and Value* came to be collected, this latest of Frederic Woolley's essays would not be merely another step in the old direction. Clearly and unmistakably, it was a turning point. All his literary life Woolley had been concerned with the relation of literature to morality, religion, and the private and delicate pieties, and he had been unalterably opposed to all that he had called 'inhuman humanitarianism.' But here, suddenly, dramatically late, he had made an about-face, turning to the public life and to the humanitarian politics he had so long despised. This was the kind of incident the histories of literature make much of. Frederic Woolley was opening for himself a new career and winning a kind of new youth. He contrasted the two poets, Thomas Wormser, who was admirable, Joseph Howe, who was almost dangerous. He spoke of the 'precious subjectivism' of Howe's verse. 'In times like ours,' he wrote, 'with millions facing penury and want, one feels that the qualities of the *tour d'ivoire* are well-nigh inhuman, nearly insulting. The *tour d'ivoire* becomes the *tour d'ivresse,* and it is not self-intoxicated poets that our people need.' The essay said more: 'The problem is one of meaning. I am not ignorant that the creed of the esoteric poets declares that a poem does not and should not *mean* anything, that it *is* something. But poetry is what the poet makes it, and if he is a true poet he makes what his society needs. And what is needed now is the tradition in which Mr. Wormser writes, the true tradition of poetry. The Howes do no harm, but they do no good when positive good is demanded of all responsible men. Or do the Howes indeed do no harm? Perhaps Plato would have said they do, that in some ways theirs is the Phrygian music that turns men's minds from the struggle. Certainly it is true that Thomas Wormser writes in the lucid Dorian mode which sends men into battle with evil.'

It was easy to understand why Woolley had chosen to praise Thomas Wormser. The long, lilting lines of *Corn Under Willows* hymned, as Woolley put it, the struggle for wheat in the Iowa fields, and expressed the real lives of real people. But why out of the dozen more notable examples he had chosen Howe's little volume as the example of 'precious subjectivism' was hard to guess. In a way it was funny, this multiplication of himself into 'the Howes.' And yet this becoming the multiform political symbol by whose creation Frederic Woolley gave the sign of a sudden new life, this use of him as a sacrifice whose blood was necessary for the rites of rejuvenation, made him feel oddly unclean.

Nor could Howe get rid of a certain practical resentment. As a poet he had a special and respectable place in the college life. But it might be another thing to be marked as the poet of a wilful and selfish obscurity.

As he walked to the Bradbys', Howe was a little tense and defensive. It seemed to him that all the world knew of the 'attack' and agreed with it. And, indeed, the Bradbys had read the essay but Professor Bradby, a kind and pretentious man, said, 'I see my old friend knocked you about a bit, my boy,' and his wife Eugenia looked at Howe with her childlike blue eyes and said, 'I shall *scold* Frederic for the untrue things he wrote about you. You aren't the least obscure.' They beamed at him. In their genial snobbery they seemed to feel that he had distinguished himself. He was the leader of Howeism. He enjoyed the dinner party as much as he had thought he would.

And in the following days, as he was more preoccupied with his duties, the incident was forgotten. His classes had ceased to be mere groups. Student after student detached himself from the mass and required or claimed a place in Howe's awareness. Of them all it was Tertan who first and most violently signaled his separate existence. A week after classes had begun Howe saw his silhouette on the frosted glass of his office door. It was motionless for a long time, perhaps stopped by the problem of whether or not to knock before entering. Howe called, 'Come in!' and Tertan entered with his shambling stride.

He stood beside the desk, silent and at attention. When Howe asked him to sit down, he responded with a gesture of head and hand, as if to say that such amenities were beside the point. Nevertheless, he did take the chair. He put his ragged, crammed briefcase between his legs. His face, which Howe now observed fully for the first time, was confusing, for it was made up of florid curves, the nose arched in the bone and voluted in the nostril, the mouth loose and soft and rather moist. Yet the face was so thin and narrow as to seem the very type of asceticism. Lashes of unusual length veiled the eyes and, indeed, it seemed as if there were a veil over the whole countenance. Before the words actually came, the face screwed itself into an attitude of preparation for them.

'You can confer with me now?' Tertan said.

'Yes, I'd be glad to. There are several things in your two themes I want to talk to you about.' Howe reached for the packet of themes on his desk and sought for Tertan's. But the boy was waving them away.

'These are done perforce,' he said. 'Under the pressure of your requirement. They are not significant; mere duties.' Again his great hand flapped vaguely to dismiss his themes. He leaned forward and gazed at his teacher.

'You are,' he said, 'a man of letters? You are a poet?' It was more declaration than question.

'I should like to think so,' Howe said.

At first Tertan accepted the answer with a show of appreciation, as though the understatement made a secret between himself and Howe. Then he chose to misunderstand. With his shrewd and disconcerting control of expression, he presented to Howe a puzzled grimace. 'What does that mean?' he said.

Howe retracted the irony. 'Yes. I am a poet.' It sounded strange to say.

'That,' Tertan said, 'is a wonder.' He corrected himself with his ducking head. 'I mean that is wonderful.'

Suddenly, he dived at the miserable briefcase between his legs, put it on his knees, and began to fumble with the catch, all intent on the difficulty it presented. Howe noted that his suit was worn thin, his shirt almost unclean. He became aware, even, of a vague and musty odor of garments worn too long in unaired rooms. Tertan conquered the lock and began to concentrate upon a search into the interior. At last he held in his hand what he was after, a torn and crumpled copy of *Life and Letters*.

'I learned it from here,' he said, holding it out.

Howe looked at him sharply, his hackles a little up. But the boy's face was not only perfectly innocent, it even shone with a conscious admiration. Apparently nothing of the import of the essay had touched him except the wonderful fact that his teacher was a 'man of letters.' Yet this seemed too stupid, and Howe, to test it, said, 'The man who wrote that doesn't think it's wonderful.'

Tertan made a moist hissing sound as he cleared his mouth of saliva. His head, oddly loose on his neck, wove a pattern of contempt in the air. 'A critic,' he said, 'who admits *prima facie* that he does not understand.' Then he said grandly, 'It is the inevitable fate.'

It was absurd, yet Howe was not only aware of the absurdity but of a tension suddenly and wonderfully relaxed. Now that the 'attack' was on the table between himself and this strange boy, and subject to the boy's funny and absolutely certain contempt, the hidden force of his feeling was revealed to him in the very moment that it vanished. All unsuspected, there had been a film over the world, a transparent but discoloring haze of danger. But he had no time to stop over the brightened aspect of things. Tertan was going on. 'I also am a man of letters. Putative.'

'You have written a good deal?' Howe meant to be no more than polite, and he was surprised at the tenderness he heard in his words.

Solemnly the boy nodded, threw back the dank lock, and sucked in a deep, anticipatory breath. 'First, a work of homiletics, which is a defense of the principles of religious optimism against the pessimism of Schopenhauer and the humanism of Nietzsche.'

'Humanism? Why do you call it humanism?'

'It is my nomenclature for making a deity of man,' Tertan replied negligently. 'Then three fictional works, novels. And numerous essays in science, combating materialism. Is it your duty to read these if I bring them to you?'

Howe answered simply, 'No, it isn't exactly my duty, but I shall be happy to read them.'

Tertan stood up and remained silent. He rested his bag on the chair. With a certain compunction—for it did not seem entirely proper that, of two men of letters, one should have the right to blue-pencil the other, to grade him or to question the quality of his 'sentence structure'—Howe reached for Tertan's papers. But before he could take them up, the boy suddenly made his bow-to-Abelard, the stiff inclination of the body with the hands seeming to emerge from the scholar's gown. Then he was gone.

But after his departure something was still left of him. The timbre of his curious sentences, the downright finality of so quaint a phrase as 'It is the inevitable fate' still rang in the air. Howe gave the warmth of his feeling to the new visitor who stood at the door announcing himself with a genteel clearing of the throat.

'Doctor Howe, I believe?' the student said. A large hand advanced into the room and grasped Howe's hand. 'Blackburn, sir, Theodore Blackburn, vice-president of the Student Council. A great pleasure, sir.'

Out of a pair of ruddy cheeks a pair of small eyes twinkled good-naturedly. The large face, the large body were not so much fat as beefy and suggested something 'typical'—monk, politician, or innkeeper.

Blackburn took the seat beside Howe's desk. 'I may have seemed to introduce myself in my public capacity, sir,' he said. 'But it is really as an individual that I came to see you. That is to say, as one of your students to be.'

He spoke with an English intonation and he went on, 'I was once an English major, sir.'

For a moment Howe was startled, for the roast-beef look of the boy and the manner of his speech gave a second's credibility to one sense of his statement. Then the collegiate meaning of the phrase asserted itself, but some perversity made Howe say what was not really in good taste even with so forward a student, 'Indeed? What regiment?'

Blackburn stared and then gave a little pouf-pouf of laughter. He waved the misapprehension away. '*Very* good, sir. It certainly is an ambiguous term.' He chuckled in appreciation of Howe's joke, then cleared his throat to put it aside. 'I look forward to taking your course in the romantic poets, sir,' he said earnestly. 'To me the romantic poets are the very crown of English literature.'

Howe made a dry sound, and the boy, catching some meaning in it, said, 'Little as I know them, of course. But even Shakespeare who is so dear to us of the Anglo-Saxon tradition is in a sense but the preparation for Shelley, Keats and Byron. And Wadsworth.'

Almost sorry for him, Howe dropped his eyes. With some embarrassment, for the boy was not actually his student, he said softly, 'Wordsworth.'

'Sir?'

'Wordsworth, not Wadsworth. You said Wadsworth.'

'Did I, sir?' Gravely he shook his head to rebuke himself for the error. 'Wordsworth, of course—slip of the tongue.' Then, quite in command again, he went on. 'I have a favor to ask of you, Doctor Howe. You see, I began my college course as an English major,'—he smiled—'as I said.'

'Yes?'

'But after my first year I shifted. I shifted to the social sciences. Sociology and government—I find them stimulating and very *real*.' He paused, out of respect for reality. 'But now I find that perhaps I have neglected the other side.'

'The other side?' Howe said.

'Imagination, fancy, culture. A well-rounded man.' He trailed off as if there were perfect understanding between them. 'And so, sir, I have decided to end my senior year with your course in the romantic poets.'

His voice was filled with an indulgence which Howe ignored as he said flatly and gravely, 'But that course isn't given until the spring term.'

'Yes, sir, and that is where the favor comes in. Would you let me take your romantic prose course? I can't take it for credit, sir, my program is full, but just for background it seems to me that I ought to take it. I do hope,' he concluded in a manly way, 'that you will consent.'

'Well, it's no great favor, Mr. Blackburn. You can come if you wish, though there's not much point in it if you don't do the reading.'

The bell rang for the hour and Howe got up.

'May I begin with this class, sir?' Blackburn's smile was candid and boyish.

Howe nodded carelessly and together, silently, they walked to the classroom down the hall. When they reached the door Howe stood back to let his student enter, but Blackburn moved adroitly behind him and grasped him by the arm to urge him over the threshold. They entered together with Blackburn's hand firmly on Howe's biceps, the student inducting the teacher into his own room. Howe felt a surge of temper rise in him and almost violently he disengaged his arm and walked to the desk, while Blackburn found a seat in the front row and smiled at him.

II

The question was, At whose door must the tragedy be laid?

All night the snow had fallen heavily and only now was abating in sparse little flurries. The windows were valanced high with white. It was very quiet; something of the quiet of the world had reached the class, and Howe found that everyone was glad to talk or listen. In the room there was a comfortable sense of pleasure in being human.

Casebeer believed that the blame for the tragedy rested with heredity. Picking up the book he read, 'The sins of the fathers are visited on their children.' This opinion was received with general favor. Nevertheless, Johnson ventured to say that the fault was all Pastor Manders' because the Pastor had made Mrs. Alving go back to her husband and was always hiding the truth. To this Hibbard objected with logic enough, 'Well then, it was really all her husband's fault. He *did* all the bad things.' De Witt, his face bright with an impatient idea, said that the fault was all society's. 'By society I don't mean upper-crust society,' he said. He looked around a little defiantly, taking in any members of the class who might be members of upper-crust society. 'Not in that sense. I mean the social unit.'

Howe nodded and said, 'Yes, of course.'

'If the society of the time had progressed far enough in science,' De Witt went on, 'then there would be no problem for Mr. Ibsen to write about. Captain Alving plays around a little, gives way to perfectly natural biological urges, and he gets a social disease, a venereal disease. If the disease is cured, no problem. Invent salvarsan and the disease is cured. The problem of heredity disappears and li'l Oswald just doesn't get paresis. No paresis, no problem—no problem, no play.'

This was carrying the ark into battle, and the class looked at De Witt with respectful curiosity. It was his usual way and on the whole they were sympathetic with his struggle to prove to Howe that science was better than literature. Still, there was something in his reckless manner that alienated them a little.

'Or take birth-control, for instance,' De Witt went on. 'If Mrs. Alving had some knowledge of contraception, she wouldn't have had to have li'l Oswald at all. No li'l Oswald, no play.'

The class was suddenly quieter. In the back row Stettenhover swung his great football shoulders in a righteous sulking gesture, first to the right, then to the left. He puckered his mouth ostentatiously. Intellect was always ending up by talking dirty.

Tertan's hand went up, and Howe said, 'Mr. Tertan.' The boy shambled to his feet and began his long characteristic gulp. Howe made a motion with his fingers, as small as possible, and Tertan ducked his head and smiled in apology. He sat down. The class laughed. With more than half the term gone, Tertan had not been able to remember that one did not rise to speak. He seemed unable to carry on the life of the intellect without this mark of respect for it. To Howe the boy's habit of rising seemed to accord with the formal shabbiness of his dress. He never wore the casual sweaters and jackets of his classmates. Into the free and comfortable air of the college classroom he brought the stuffy sordid strictness of some crowded, metropolitan high school.

'Speaking from one sense,' Tertan began slowly, 'there is no blame ascribable. From the sense of determinism, who can say where the blame lies? The preordained is the preordained and it cannot be said without rebellion against the universe, a palpable absurdity.'

In the back row Stettenhover slumped suddenly in his seat, his heels held out before him, making a loud, dry, disgusted sound. His body sank until his neck rested on the back of his chair. He folded his hands across his belly and looked significantly out of the window, exasperated not only with Tertan, but with Howe, with the class, with the whole system designed to encourage this kind of thing. There was a certain insolence in the movement and Howe flushed. As Tertan continued to speak, Howe stalked casually toward the window and placed himself in the line of Stettenhover's vision. He stared at the great fellow, who pretended not to see him. There was so much power in the big body, so much contempt in the Greek-athlete face under the crisp Greek-athlete curls, that Howe felt almost physical fear. But at last Stettenhover admitted him to focus and under his disapproving gaze sat up with slow indifference. His eyebrows raised high in resignation, he began to examine his hands. Howe relaxed and turned his attention back to Tertan.

'Flux of existence,' Tertan was saying, 'produces all things, so that judgment wavers. Beyond the phenomena, what? But phenomena are adumbrated and to them we are limited.'

Howe saw it for a moment as perhaps it existed in the boy's mind—the world of shadows which are cast by a great light upon a hidden reality as in the old myth of the Cave. But the little brush with Stettenhover had tired him, and he said irritably, 'But come to the point, Mr. Tertan.'

He said it so sharply that some of the class looked at him curiously. For three months he had gently carried Tertan through his verbosities, to the vaguely respectful surprise of the other students, who seemed to conceive that there existed between this strange classmate and their teacher some special understanding from which they were content to be excluded. Tertan looked at him mildly, and at once came brilliantly to the point. 'This is the summation of the play,' he said and took up his book and read, '"Your poor father never found any outlet for the overmastering joy of life that was in him. And I brought no holiday into his home, either. Everything seemed to turn upon duty and I am afraid I made your poor father's home unbearable to him, Oswald." Spoken by Mrs. Alving.'

Yes that was surely the 'summation' of the play and Tertan had hit it, as he hit, deviously and eventually, the literary point of almost everything. But now, as always, he was wrapping it away from sight. 'For

Of This Time, Of That Place

most mortals,' he said, 'there are only joys of biological urgings, gross and crass, such as the sensuous Captain Alving. For certain few there are the transmutations beyond these to a contemplation of the utter whole.'

Oh, the boy was mad. And suddenly the word, used in hyperbole, intended almost for the expression of exasperated admiration, became literal. Now that the word was used, it became simply apparent to Howe that Tertan was mad.

It was a monstrous word and stood like a bestial thing in the room. Yet it so completely comprehended everything that had puzzled Howe, it so arranged and explained what for three months had been perplexing him that almost at once its horror became domesticated. With this word Howe was able to understand why he had never been able to communicate to Tertan the value of a single criticism or correction of his wild, verbose themes. Their conferences had been frequent and long but had done nothing to reduce to order the splendid confusion of the boy's ideas. Yet, impossible though its expression was, Tertan's incandescent mind could always strike for a moment into some dark corner of thought.

And now it was suddenly apparent that it was not a faulty rhetoric that Howe had to contend with. With his new knowledge he looked at Tertan's face and wondered how he could have so long deceived himself. Tertan was still talking, and the class had lapsed into a kind of patient unconsciousness, a coma of respect for words which, for all that most of them knew, might be profound. Almost with a suffusion of shame, Howe believed that in some dim way the class had long ago had some intimation of Tertan's madness. He reached out as decisively as he could to seize the thread of Tertan's discourse before it should be entangled further.

'Mr. Tertan says that the blame must be put upon whoever kills the joy of living in another. We have been assuming that Captain Alving was a wholly bad man, but what if we assume that he became bad only because Mrs. Alving, when they were first married, acted toward him in the prudish way she says she did?'

It was a ticklish idea to advance to freshmen and perhaps not profitable. Not all of them were following.

'That would put the blame on Mrs. Alving herself, whom most of you admire. And she herself seems to think so.' He glanced at his watch. The hour was nearly over. 'What do you think, Mr. De Witt?'

De Witt rose to the idea; he wanted to know if society couldn't be blamed for educating Mrs. Alving's temperament in the wrong way. Casebeer was puzzled, Stettenhover continued to look at his hands until the bell rang.

Tertan, his brows louring in thought, was making as always for a private word. Howe gathered his books and papers to leave quickly. At this moment of his discovery and with the knowledge still raw, he could not engage himself with Tertan. Tertan sucked in his breath to prepare for speech and Howe made ready for the pain and confusion. But at that moment Casebeer detached himself from the group with which he had been conferring and which he seemed to represent. His constituency remained at a tactful distance. The mission involved the time of an assigned essay. Casebeer's presentation of the plea—it was based on the freshmen's heavy duties at the fraternities during Carnival Week—cut across Tertan's preparations for speech. 'And so some of us fellows thought,' Casebeer concluded with heavy solemnity, 'that we could do a better job, give our minds to it more, if we had more time.'

Tertan regarded Casebeer with mingled curiosity and revulsion. Howe not only said that he would postpone the assignment but went on to talk about the Carnival, and even drew the waiting constituency into the conversation. He was conscious of Tertan's stern and astonished stare, then of his sudden departure.

Now that the fact was clear, Howe knew that he must act on it. His course was simple enough. He must lay the case before the Dean. Yet he hesitated. His feeling for Tertan must now, certainly, be in some way invalidated. Yet could he, because of a word, hurry to assign to official and reasonable solicitude what had been, until this moment, so various and warm? He could at least delay and, by moving slowly, lend a poor grace to the necessary, ugly act of making his report.

It was with some notion of keeping the matter in his own hands that he went to the Dean's office to look up Tertan's records. In the outer office the Dean's secretary greeted him brightly, and at his request brought him the manila folder with the small identifying photograph pasted in the corner. She laughed. 'He was looking for the birdie in the wrong place,' she said.

Howe leaned over her shoulder to look at the picture. It was as bad as all the Dean's-office photographs were, but it differed from all that Howe had ever seen. Tertan, instead of looking into the camera, as no doubt he had been bidden, had, at the moment of exposure, turned his eyes upward. His mouth, as though conscious of the trick played on the photographer, had the sly superior look that Howe knew.

The secretary was fascinated by the picture. 'What a funny boy,' she said. 'He looks like Tartuffe!'

And so he did, with the absurd piety of the eyes and the conscious slyness of the mouth and the whole face bloated by the bad lens.

'Is he *like* that?' the secretary said.

'Like Tartuffe? No.'

From the photograph there was little enough comfort to be had. The records themselves gave no clue to madness, though they suggested sadness enough. Howe read of a father, Stanislaus Tertan, born in Budapest and trained in engineering in Berlin, once employed by the Hercules Chemical Corporation—this was one of the factories that dominated the sound end of the town—but now without employment. He read of a mother Erminie (Youngfellow) Tertan, born in Manchester, educated at a Normal School at Leeds, now housewife by profession. The family lived on Greenbriar Street which Howe knew as a row of once elegant homes near what was now the factory district. The old mansion had long ago been divided into small and primitive apartments. Of Ferdinand himself there was little to learn. He lived with his parents, had attended a Detroit high school and had transferred to the local school in his last year. His rating for intelligence, as expressed in numbers, was high, his scholastic record was remarkable, he held a college scholarship for his tuition.

Howe laid the folder on the secretary's desk. 'Did you find what you wanted to know?' she asked.

The phrases from Tertan's momentous first theme came back to him. 'Tertan I am, but what is Tertan? Of this time, of that place, of some parentage, what does it matter?'

'No, I didn't find it,' he said.

Now that he had consulted the sad, half-meaningless record he knew all the more firmly that he must not give the matter out of his own hands. He must not release Tertan to authority. Not that he anticipated from the Dean anything but the greatest kindness for Tertan. The Dean would have the experience and skill which he himself could not have. One way or another the Dean could answer the question, 'What is Tertan?' Yet this was precisely what he feared. He alone could keep alive—not forever but for a somehow important time—the question, 'What is Tertan?' He alone could keep it still a question. Some sure instinct told him that he must not surrender the question to a clean official desk in a clear official light to be dealt with, settled and closed.

He heard himself saying, 'Is the Dean busy at the moment? I'd like to see him.'

His request came thus unbidden, even forbidden, and it was one of the surprising and startling incidents of his life. Later when he reviewed the events, so disconnected in themselves, or so merely odd, of the story that unfolded for him that year, it was over this moment, on its face the least notable, that he paused longest. It was frequently to be with fear and never without a certainty of its meaning in his own knowledge of himself that he would recall this simple, routine request, and the feeling of shame and freedom it gave him as he sent everything down the official chute. In the end, of course, no matter what he did to 'protect' Tertan, he would have had to make the same request and lay the matter on the Dean's clean desk. But it would always be a landmark of his life that, at the very moment when he was rejecting the official way, he had been, without will or intention, so gladly drawn to it.

After the storm's last delicate flurry, the sun had come out. Reflected by the new snow, it filled the office with a golden light which was almost musical in the way it made all the commonplace objects of efficiency shine with a sudden sad and noble significance. And the light, now that he noticed it, made the utterance of his perverse and unwanted request even more momentous.

The secretary consulted the engagement pad. 'He'll be free any minute. Don't you want to wait in the parlor?'

She threw open the door of the large and pleasant room in which the Dean held his Committee meetings, and in which his visitors waited. It was designed with a homely elegance on the masculine side of the eighteenth-century manner. There was a small coal fire in the grate and the handsome mahogany table was strewn with books and magazines. The large windows gave on the snowy lawn, and there was such a fine width of window that the white casements and walls seemed at this moment but a continuation of the snow, the snow but an extension of casement and walls. The outdoors seemed taken in and made safe, the indoors seemed luxuriously freshened and expanded.

Howe sat down by the fire and lighted a cigarette. The room had its intended effect upon him. He felt comfortable and relaxed, yet nicely organized, some young diplomatic agent of the eighteenth century, the newly fledged Swift carrying out Sir William Temple's business. The rawness of Tertan's case quite vanished. He crossed his legs and reached for a magazine.

It was that famous issue of *Life and Letters* that his idle hand had found and his blood raced as he sifted through it, and the shape of his own name, Joseph Howe, sprang out at him, still cabalistic in its power. He tossed the magazine back on the table as the door of the Dean's office opened and the Dean ushered out Theodore Blackburn.

'Ah, Joseph!' the Dean said.

Blackburn said, 'Good morning, Doctor.' Howe winced at the title and caught the flicker of amusement over the Dean's face. The Dean stood with his hand high on the door-jamb and Blackburn, still in the doorway, remained standing almost under the long arm.

Howe nodded briefly to Blackburn, snubbing his eager deference. 'Can you give me a few minutes?' he said to the Dean.

'All the time you want. Come in.' Before the two men could enter the office, Blackburn claimed their attention with a long full 'er.' As they turned to him, Blackburn said, 'Can *you* give *me* a few minutes, Doctor Howe?' His eyes sparkled at the little audacity he had committed, the slightly impudent play with hierarchy. Of the three of them Blackburn kept himself the lowest, but he reminded Howe of his subaltern relation to the Dean.

'I mean, of course,' Blackburn went on easily, 'when you've finished with the Dean.'

'I'll be in my office shortly,' Howe said, turned his back on the ready 'Thank you, sir,' and followed the Dean into the inner room.

'Energetic boy,' said the Dean. 'A bit beyond himself but very energetic. Sit down.'

The Dean lighted a cigarette, leaned back in his chair, sat easy and silent for a moment, giving Howe no signal to go ahead with business. He was a young Dean, not much beyond forty, a tall handsome man with sad, ambitious eyes. He had been a Rhodes scholar. His friends looked for great things from him, and it was generally said that he had notions of education which he was not yet ready to try to put into practice.

His relaxed silence was meant as a compliment to Howe. He smiled and said, 'What's the business, Joseph?'

'Do you know Tertan—Ferdinand Tertan, a freshman?'

The Dean's cigarette was in his mouth and his hands were clasped behind his head. He did not seem to search his memory for the name. He said, 'What about him?'

Clearly the Dean knew something, and he was waiting for Howe to tell him more. Howe moved only tentatively. Now that he was doing what he had resolved not to do, he felt more guilty at having been so long deceived by Tertan and more need to be loyal to his error.

'He's a strange fellow,' he ventured. He said stubbornly, 'In a strange way he's very brilliant.' He concluded, 'But very strange.'

The springs of the Dean's swivel chair creaked as he came out of his sprawl and leaned forward to Howe. 'Do you mean he's so strange that it's something you could give a name to?'

Howe looked at him stupidly. 'What do you mean?' he said.

'What's his trouble?' the Dean said more neutrally.

'He's very brilliant, in a way. I looked him up and he has a top intelligence rating. But somehow, and it's hard to explain just how, what he says is always on the edge of sense and doesn't quite make it.'

The Dean looked at him and Howe flushed up. The Dean had surely read Woolley on the subject of 'the Howes' and the *tour d'ivresse*. Was that quick glance ironical?

The Dean picked up some papers from his desk, and Howe could see that they were in Tertan's impatient scrawl. Perhaps

[260]

the little gleam in the Dean's glance had come only from putting facts together.

'He sent me this yesterday,' the Dean said. 'After an interview I had with him. I haven't been able to do more than glance at it. When you said what you did, I realized there was something wrong.'

Twisting his mouth, the Dean looked over the letter. 'You seem to be involved,' he said without looking up. 'By the way, what did you give him at mid-term?'

Flushing, setting his shoulders, Howe said firmly, 'I gave him A-minus.'

The Dean chuckled. 'Might be a good idea if some of our nicer boys went crazy —just a little.' He said, 'Well,' to conclude the matter and handed the papers to Howe. 'See if this is the same thing you've been finding. Then we can go into the matter again.'

Before the fire in the parlor, in the chair that Howe had been occupying, sat Blackburn. He sprang to his feet as Howe entered.

'I said my office, Mr. Blackburn.' Howe's voice was sharp. Then he was almost sorry for the rebuke, so clearly and naively did Blackburn seem to relish his stay in the parlor, close to authority.

'I'm in a bit of a hurry, sir,' he said, 'and I did want to be sure to speak to you, sir.'

He was really absurd, yet fifteen years from now he would have grown up to himself, to the assurance and mature beefiness. In banks, in consular offices, in brokerage firms, on the bench, more seriously affable, a little sterner, he would make use of his ability to be administered by his job. It was almost reassuring. Now he was exercising his too-great skill on Howe. 'I owe you an apology, sir,' he said.

Howe knew that he did, but he showed surprise.

'I mean, Doctor, after your having been so kind about letting me attend your class, I stopped coming.' He smiled in deprecation. 'Extracurricular activities take up so much of my time. I'm afraid I undertook more than I could perform.'

Howe had noticed the absence and had been a little irritated by it after Blackburn's elaborate plea. It was an absence that might be interpreted as a comment on the teacher. But there was only one way for him to answer. 'You've no need to apologize,' he said. 'It's wholly your affair.'

Blackburn beamed. 'I'm so glad you feel that way about it, sir. I was worried you might think I had stayed away because I was influenced by—' he stopped and lowered his eyes.

Astonished, Howe said, 'Influenced by what?'

'Well, by—' Blackburn hesitated and for answer pointed to the table on which lay the copy of *Life and Letters*. Without looking at it, he knew where to direct his hand. 'By the unfavorable publicity, sir.' He hurried on. 'And that brings me to another point, sir. I am secretary of Quill and Scroll, sir, the student literary society, and I wonder if you would address us. You could read your own poetry, sir, and defend your own point of view. It would be very interesting.'

It was truly amazing. Howe looked long and cruelly into Blackburn's face, trying to catch the secret of the mind that could have conceived this way of manipulating him, this way so daring and inept— but not entirely inept—with its malice so without malignity. The face did not yield its secret. Howe smiled broadly and said, 'Of course I don't think you were influenced by the unfavorable publicity.'

'I'm still going to take—regularly, for credit—your romantic poets course next term,' Blackburn said.

'Don't worry, my dear fellow, don't worry about it.'

Howe started to leave and Blackburn stopped him with, 'But about Quill, sir?'

'Suppose we wait until next term? I'll be less busy then.'

And Blackburn said, 'Very good, sir, and thank you.'

In his office the little encounter seemed less funny to Howe, was even in some indeterminate way disturbing. He made an effort to put it from his mind by turning to what was sure to disturb him more, the Tertan letter read in the new interpretation. He found what he had always found, the same florid leaps beyond fact and meaning, the same headlong certainty. But as his eye passed over the familiar scrawl it caught his own name, and for the second time that hour he felt the race of his blood.

'The Paraclete,' Tertan had written to the Dean, 'from a Greek word meaning to stand in place of, but going beyond the primitive idea to mean traditionally the helper, the one who comforts and assists, cannot without fundamental loss be jettisoned. Even if taken no longer in the supernatural sense, the concept remains deeply in the human consciousness inevitably. Humanitarianism is no reply, for not every man stands in the place of every other man for this other comrade's comfort. But certain are chosen out of the human race to be the consoler of some other. Of these, for example, is Joseph Barker Howe, Ph.D. Of intellects not the first yet of true intellect and lambent instructions, given to that which is intuitive and irrational, not to what is logical in the strict word, what is judged by him is of the heart and not the head. Here is one chosen, in that he chooses himself to stand in the place of another for comfort and consolation. To him more than another I give my gratitude, with all respect to our Dean who reads this, a noble man, but merely dedicated, not consecrated. But not in the aspect of the Paraclete only is Dr. Joseph Barker Howe established, for he must be the Paraclete to another aspect of himself, that which is driven and persecuted by the lack of understanding in the world at large, so that he in himself embodies the full history of man's tribulations and, overflowing upon others, notably the present writer, is the ultimate end.'

This was love. There was no escape from it. Try as Howe might to remember that Tertan was mad and all his emotions invalidated, he could not destroy the effect upon him of his student's stern, affectionate regard. He had betrayed not only a power of mind but a power of love. And, however firmly he held before his attention the fact of Tertan's madness, he could do nothing to banish the physical sensation of gratitude he felt. He had never thought of himself as 'driven and persecuted' and he did not now. But still he could not make meaningless his sensation of gratitude. The pitiable Tertan sternly pitied him, and comfort came from Tertan's never-to-be-comforted mind.

III

In an academic community, even an efficient one, official matters move slowly. The term drew to a close with no action in the case of Tertan, and Joseph Howe had to confront a curious problem. How should he grade his strange student, Tertan?

Tertan's final examination had been no different from all his other writing, and what did one 'give' such a student? De Witt must have his A, that was clear. Johnson would get a B. With Casebeer it was a question of a B-minus or a C-plus, and Stettenhover, who had been crammed by the team tutor to fill half a blue-book with his thin feminine scrawl, would have his C-minus which he would accept with mingled indifference and resentment. But with Tertan it was not so easy.

The boy was still in the college process and his name could not be omitted from the grade sheet. Yet what should a mind under suspicion of madness be graded? Until the medical verdict was given, it was for Howe to continue as Tertan's teacher and to keep his judgment pedagogical. Impossible to give him an F: he had not failed. B was for Johnson's stolid mediocrity. He could not be put on the edge of passing with Stettenhover, for he exactly did not pass. In energy and richness of intellect he was perhaps even De Witte's superior, and Howe toyed grimly with the notion of giving him an A, but that would lower the value of the A De Witt had won with his beautiful and clear, if still arrogant, mind. There was a notation which the Registrar recognized—Inc., for Incomplete, and in the horrible comedy of the situation, Howe considered that. But really only a mark of M for Mad would serve.

In his perplexity, Howe sought the Dean, but the Dean was out of town. In the end, he decided to maintain the A-minus he had given Tertan at mid-term. After all, there had been no falling away from that quality. He entered it on the grade sheet with something like bravado.

Academic time moves quickly. A college year is not really a year, lacking as it does three months. And it is endlessly divided into units which, at their beginning, appear larger than they are—terms, half-terms, months, weeks. And the ultimate unit, the hour, is not really an hour, lacking as it does ten minutes. And so the new term advanced rapidly, and one day the fields about the town were all brown, cleared of even the few thin patches of snow which had lingered so long.

Howe, as he lectured on the romantic poets, became conscious of Blackburn emanating wrath. Blackburn did it well, did it with enormous dignity. He did not stir in his seat, he kept his eyes fixed on Howe in perfect attention, but he abstained from using his notebook, there was no mistaking what he proposed to himself as an attitude. His elbow on the writing-wing of the chair, his chin on the curled fingers of his hand, he was the embodiment of intellectual indignation. He was thinking his own thoughts, would give no public offense, yet would claim his due, was not to be intimidated. Howe knew that he would present himself at the end of the hour.

Blackburn entered the office without invitation. He did not smile; there was no cajolery about him. Without invitation he sat down beside Howe's desk. He did not speak until he had taken the blue-book from his pocket. He said, 'What does this mean, sir?'

It was a sound and conservative student tactic. Said in the usual way it meant, 'How could you have so misunderstood me?' or 'What does this mean for my future in the course?' But there were none of the humbler tones in Blackburn's way of saying it.

Howe made the established reply, 'I think that's for you to tell me.'

Blackburn continued icy. 'I'm sure I can't, sir.'

There was a silence between them. Both dropped their eyes to the blue-book on the desk. On its cover Howe had penciled: 'F. This is very poor work.'

Howe picked up the blue-book. There was always the possibility of injustice. The teacher may be bored by the mass of papers and not wholly attentive. A phrase, even the student's handwriting, may irritate him unreasonably. 'Well,' said Howe, 'Let's go through it.'

He opened the first page. 'Now here: you write, "In *The Ancient Mariner,* Coleridge lives in and transports us to a honey-sweet world where all is rich and strange, a world of charm to which we can escape from the humdrum existence of our daily lives, the world of romance. Here, in this warm and honey-sweet land of charming dreams we can relax and enjoy ourselves."'

Howe lowered the paper and waited with a neutral look for Blackburn to speak. Blackburn returned the look boldly, did not speak, sat stolid and lofty. At last Howe said, speaking gently, 'Did you mean that, or were you just at a loss for something to say?'

'You imply that I was just "bluffing"?' The quotation marks hung palpable in the air about the word.

'I'd like to know. I'd prefer believing that you were bluffing to believing that you really thought this.'

Blackburn's eyebrows went up. From the height of a great and firm-based idea he looked at his teacher. He clasped the crags for a moment and then pounced, craftily, suavely. 'Do you mean, Doctor Howe, that there aren't two opinions possible?'

It was superbly done in its air of putting all of Howe's intellectual life into the balance. Howe remained patient and simple. 'Yes, many opinions are possible, but not this one. Whatever anyone believes of *The Ancient Mariner,* no one can in reason believe that it represents a—a honey-sweet world in which we can relax.'

'But that is what I *feel,* sir.'

This was well-done, too. Howe said, 'Look, Mr. Blackburn. Do you really relax with hunger and thirst, the heat and the sea-serpents, the dead men with staring eyes, Life in Death and the skeletons? Come now, Mr. Blackburn.'

Blackburn made no answer, and Howe pressed forward. 'Now, you say of Wordsworth, "Of peasant stock himself, he turned from the effete life of the salons and found in the peasant the hope of a flaming revolution which would sweep away all the old ideas. This is the subject of his best poems."'

Beaming at his teacher with youthful eagerness, Blackburn said, 'Yes, sir, a rebel, a bringer of light to suffering mankind. I see him as a kind of Prothemeus.'

'A kind of what?'

'Prothemeus, sir.'

'Think, Mr. Blackburn. We were talking about him only today and I mentioned his name a dozen times. You don't mean Prothemeus. You mean—' Howe waited, but there was no response.

'You mean Prometheus.'

Blackburn gave no assent, and Howe took the reins. 'You've done a bad job here, Mr. Blackburn, about as bad as could be done.' He saw Blackburn stiffen and his genial face harden again. 'It shows either a lack of preparation or a complete lack of understanding.' He saw Blackburn's face begin to go to pieces and he stopped.

'Oh, sir,' Blackburn burst out, 'I've never had a mark like this before, never anything below a B, never. A thing like this has never happened to me before.'

It must be true, it was a statement too easily verified. Could it be that other instructors accepted such flaunting nonsense? Howe wanted to end the interview. 'I'll set it down to lack of preparation,' he said. 'I know you're busy. That's not an excuse, but it's an explanation. Now, suppose you really prepare, and then take another quiz in two weeks. We'll forget this one and count the other.'

Blackburn squirmed with pleasure and gratitude. 'Thank you, sir. You're really very kind, very kind.'

Howe rose to conclude the visit. 'All right, then—in two weeks.'

It was that day that the Dean imparted to Howe the conclusion of the case of Tertan. It was simple and a little anti-climactic. A physician had been called in, and had said the word, given the name.

'A classic case, he called it,' the Dean said. 'Not a doubt in the world,' he said. His eyes were full of miserable pity, and he clutched at a word. 'A classic case, a classic case.' To his aid and to Howe's there came the Parthenon and the form of the Greek drama, the Aristotelian logic, Racine and the Well-Tempered Clavichord, the blueness of the Aegean and its clear sky. Classic—that is to say, without a doubt, perfect in its way, a veritable model, and, as the Dean had been told, sure to take a perfectly predictable and inevitable course to a foreknown conclusion.

It was not only pity that stood in the Dean's eyes. For a moment there was fear too. 'Terrible,' he said, 'it is simply terrible.'

Then he went on briskly. 'Naturally, we've told the boy nothing. And, naturally, we won't. His tuition's paid by his scholarship, and we'll continue him on the rolls until the end of the year. That will be kindest. After that the matter will be out of our control. We'll see, of course, that he gets into the proper hands. I'm told there will be no change, he'll go on like this, be as good as this, for four to six months. And so we'll just go along as usual.'

So Tertan continued to sit in Section 5 of English 1A, to his classmates still a figure of curiously dignified fun, symbol to most of them of the respectable but absurd intellectual life. But to his teacher he was now very different. He had not changed—he was still the greyhound casting for the scent of ideas, and Howe could see that he was still the same Tertan, but he could not feel it. What he felt as he looked at the boy sitting in his accustomed place was the hard blank of a fact. The fact itself was formidable and depressing. But what Howe was chiefly aware of was that he had permitted the metamorphosis of Tertan from person to fact.

As much as possible he avoided seeing Tertan's upraised hand and eager eye. But the fact did not know of its mere factuality, it continued its existence as if it were Tertan, hand up and eye questioning, and one day it appeared in Howe's office with a document.

'Even the spirit who lives egregiously, above the herd, must have its relations with the fellowman,' Tertan declared. He laid the document on Howe's desk. It was headed 'Quill and Scroll Society of Dwight College. Application for Membership.'

'In most ways these are crass minds,' Tertan said, touching the paper. 'Yet as a whole, bound together in their common love of letters, they transcend their intellectual lacks since it is not a paradox that the whole is greater than the sum of its parts.'

'When are the elections?' Howe asked.

'They take place tomorrow.'

'I certainly hope you will be successful.'

'Thank you. Would you wish to implement that hope?' A rather dirty finger pointed to the bottom of the sheet. 'A faculty recommender is necessary,' Tertan said stiffly, and waited.

'And you wish me to recommend you?'

'It would be an honor.'

'You may use my name.'

Tertan's finger pointed again. 'It must be a written sponsorship, signed by the sponsor.' There was a large blank space on the form under the heading, 'Opinion of Faculty Sponsor.'

This was almost another thing and Howe hesitated. Yet there was nothing else to do and he took out his fountain pen. He wrote, 'Mr. Ferdinand Tertan is marked by his intense devotion to letters and by his exceptional love of all things of the mind.' To this he signed his name, which looked bold and assertive on the white page. It disturbed him, the strange affirming power of a name. With a businesslike air, Tertan whipped up the paper, folding it with decision, and put it into his pocket. He bowed and took his departure, leaving Howe with the sense of having done something oddly momentous.

And so much now seemed odd and momentous to Howe that should not have seemed so. It was odd and momentous, he felt, when he sat with Blackburn's second quiz before him, and wrote in an excessively firm hand the grade of C-minus. The paper was a clear, an indisputable failure. He was carefully and consciously committing a cowardice. Blackburn had told the truth when he had pleaded his past record. Howe had consulted it in the Dean's office. It showed no grade lower than a B-minus. A canvass of some of Blackburn's previous instructors had brought vague attestations to the adequate powers of a student imperfectly remembered, and sometimes surprise that his abilities could be questioned at all.

As he wrote the grade, Howe told himself that his cowardice sprang from an unwillingness to have more dealings with a student he disliked. He knew it was simpler than that. He knew he feared Blackburn: that was the absurd truth. And cowardice did not solve the matter after all. Blackburn, flushed with a first success, attacked at once. The minimal passing grade had not assuaged his feelings and he sat at Howe's desk and again the blue-book lay between them. Blackburn said nothing. With an enormous impudence, he was waiting for Howe to speak and explain himself.

At last Howe said sharply and rudely, 'Well?' His throat was tense and the blood was hammering in his head. His mouth was tight with anger at himself for his disturbance.

Blackburn's glance was almost baleful. 'This is impossible, sir.'

'But there it is,' Howe answered.

'Sir?' Blackburn had not caught the meaning but his tone was still haughty.

Impatiently Howe said, 'There it is, plain as day. Are you here to complain again?'

'Indeed I am, sir.' There was surprise in Blackburn's voice that Howe should ask the question.

'I shouldn't complain if I were you. You did a thoroughly bad job on your first quiz. This one is a little, only a very little, better.' This was not true. If anything, it was worse.

'That might be a matter of opinion, sir.'

'It is a matter of opinion. Of my opinion.'

'Another opinion might be different, sir.'

'You really believe that?' Howe said.

'Yes.' The omission of the 'sir' was monumental.

'Whose, for example?'

'The Dean's, for example.' Then the fleshy jaw came forward a little. 'Or a certain literary critic's, for example.'

It was colossal and almost too much for Blackburn himself to handle. The solidity of his face almost crumpled under it. But he withstood his own audacity and went

Of This Time, Of That Place

on. 'And the Dean's opinion might be guided by the knowledge that the person who gave me this mark is the man whom a famous critic, the most eminent judge of literature in this country, called a drunken man. The Dean might think twice about whether such a man is fit to teach Dwight students.'

Howe said in quiet admonition, 'Blackburn, you're mad,' meaning no more than to check the boy's extravagance.

But Blackburn paid no heed. He had another shot in the locker. 'And the Dean might be guided by the information, of which I have evidence, documentary evidence,'—he slapped his breast pocket twice—'that this same person personally recommended to the college literary society, the oldest in the country, that he personally recommended a student who is crazy, who threw the meeting into an uproar—a psychiatric case. The Dean might take that into account.'

Howe was never to learn the details of that 'uproar.' He had always to content himself with the dim but passionate picture which at that moment sprang into his mind, of Tertan standing on some abstract height and madly denouncing the multitude of Quill and Scroll who howled him down.

He sat quiet a moment and looked at Blackburn. The ferocity had entirely gone from the student's face. He sat regarding his teacher almost benevolently. He had played a good card and now, scarcely at all unfriendly, he was waiting to see the effect. Howe took up the blue-book and negligently sifted through it. He read a page, closed the book, struck out the C-minus and wrote an F.

'Now you may take the paper to the Dean,' he said. 'You may tell him that after reconsidering it, I lowered the grade.'

The gasp was audible. 'Oh, sir!' Blackburn cried. 'Please!' His face was agonized. 'It means my graduation, my livelihood, my future. Don't do this to me.'

'It's done already.'

Blackburn stood up. 'I spoke rashly, sir, hastily. I had no intention, no real intention, of seeing the Dean. it rests with you—entirely, entirely. I *hope* you will restore the first mark.'

'Take the matter to the Dean or not, just as you choose. The grade is what you deserve and it stands.'

Blackburn's head dropped. 'And will I be failed at mid-term, sir?'

'Of course.'

From deep out of Blackburn's great chest rose a cry of anguish. 'Oh, sir, if you want me to go down on my knees to you, I will, I will.'

Howe looked at him in amazement.

'I will, I will. On my knees, sir. This mustn't, mustn't happen.'

He spoke so literally, meaning so very truly that his knees and exactly his knees were involved and seeming to think that he was offering something of tangible value to his teacher, that Howe, whose head had become icy clear in the nonsensical drama, thought, 'The boy is mad,' and began to speculate fantastically whether something in himself attracted or developed aberration. He could see himself standing absurdly before the Dean and saying, 'I've found another. This time it's the vice-president of the Council, the manager of the debating team and secretary of Quill and Scroll.'

One more such discovery, he thought, and he himself would be discovered! And there, suddenly, Blackburn was on his knees with a thump, his huge thighs straining his trousers, his hand outstretched in a great gesture of supplication.

With a cry, Howe shoved back his swivel chair and it rolled away on its casters half across the little room. Blackburn knelt for a moment to nothing at all, then got to his feet.

Howe rose abruptly. He said, 'Blackburn, you will stop acting like an idiot. Dust your knees off, take your paper and get out. You've behaved like a fool and a malicious person. You have half a term to do a decent job. Keep your silly mouth shut and try to do it. Now get out.'

Blackburn's head was low. He raised it and there was a pious light in his eyes. 'Will you shake hands, sir?' he said. He thrust out his hand.

'I will not,' Howe said.

Head and hand sank together. Blackburn picked up his blue-book and walked to the door. He turned and said, 'Thank you, sir.' His back, as he departed, was heavy with tragedy and stateliness.

IV

After years of bad luck with the weather, the College had a perfect day for Commencement. It was wonderfully bright, the air so transparent, the wind so brisk that no one could resist talking about it.

As Howe set out for the campus he heard Hilda calling from the back yard. She called, 'Professor, professor,' and came running to him.

Howe said, 'What's this "professor" business?'

'Mother told me,' Hilda said. 'You've been promoted. And I want to take your picture.'

'Next year,' said Howe. 'I won't be a professor until next year. And you know better than to call anybody "professor."'

'It was just in fun,' Hilda said. She seemed disappointed.

'But you can take my picture if you want. I won't look much different next year.' Still, it was frightening. It might mean that he was to stay in this town all his life.

Hilda brightened. 'Can I take it in this?' she said, and touched the gown he carried over his arm.

Howe laughed. 'Yes, you can take it in this.'

'I'll get my things and meet you in front of Otis,' Hilda said. 'I have the background all picked out.'

On the campus the Commencement crowd was already large. It stood about in eager, nervous little family groups. As he crossed, Howe was greeted by a student, capped and gowned, glad of the chance to make an event for his parents by introducing one of his teachers. It was while Howe stood there chatting that he saw Tertan.

He had never seen anyone quite so alone, as though a circle had been woven about him to separate him from the gay crowd on the campus. Not that Tertan was not gay, he was the gayest of all. Three weeks had passed since Howe had last seen him, the weeks of examination, the lazy week before Commencement, and this was now a different Tertan. On his head he wore a panama hat, broad-brimmed and fine, of the shape associated with South American planters. He wore a suit of raw silk, luxurious, but yellowed with age and much too tight, and he sported a whangee cane. He walked sedately, the hat tilted at a devastating angle, the stick coming up and down in time to his measured tread. He had, Howe guessed, outfitted himself to greet the day in the clothes of that ruined father whose existence was on record in the Dean's office. Gravely and arrogantly he surveyed

[268]

Of This Time, Of That Place

the scene—in it, his whole bearing seemed to say, but not of it. With his haughty step, with his flashing eye, Tertan was coming nearer. Howe did not wish to be seen. He shifted his position slightly. When he looked again, Tertan was not in sight.

The chapel clock struck the quarter hour. Howe detached himself from his chat and hurried to Otis Hall at the far end of the campus. Hilda had not yet come. He went up into the high portico and, using the glass of the door for a mirror, put on his gown, adjusted the hood on his shoulders and set the mortarboard on his head. When he came down the steps, Hilda had arrived.

Nothing could have told him more forcibly that a year had passed than the development of Hilda's photographic possessions from the box camera of the previous fall. By a strap about her neck was hung a leather case, so thick and strong, so carefully stitched and so molded to its contents that it could only hold a costly camera. The appearance was deceptive, Howe knew, for he had been present at the Aikens' pre-Christmas conference about its purchase. It was only a fairly good domestic camera. Still, it looked very impressive. Hilda carried another leather case from which she drew a collapsible tripod. Decisively she extended each of its gleaming legs and set it up on the path. She removed the camera from its case and fixed it to the tripod. In its compact efficiency the camera almost had a life of its own, but Hilda treated it with easy familiarity, looked into its eye, glanced casually at its gauges. Then from a pocket she took still another leather case and drew from it a small instrument through which she looked first at Howe, who began to feel inanimate and lost, and then at the sky. She made some adjustment on the instrument, then some adjustment on the camera. She swept the scene with her eye, found a spot and pointed the camera in its direction. She walked to the spot, stood on it and beckoned to Howe. With each new leather case, with each new instrument, and with each new adjustment she had grown in ease and now she said, 'Joe, will you stand here?'

Obediently Howe stood where he was bidden. She had yet another instrument. She took out a tape-measure on a mechanical spool. Kneeling down before Howe, she put the little metal ring of the tape under the tip of his shoe. At her request, Howe pressed it with his toe. When she had measured her distance, she nodded to Howe who released the tape. At a touch, it sprang back into the spool. 'You have to be careful if you're going to get what you want,' Hilda said. 'I don't believe in all this snap-snap-snapping,' she remarked loftily. Howe nodded in agreement, although he was beginning to think Hilda's care excessive.

Now at last the moment had come. Hilda squinted into the camera, moved the tripod slightly. She stood to the side, holding the plunger of the shutter-cable. 'Ready,' she said. 'Will you relax, Joseph, please?' Howe realized that he was standing frozen. Hilda stood poised and precise as a setter, one hand holding the little cable, the other extended with curled dainty fingers like a dancer's, as if expressing to her subject the precarious delicacy of the moment. She pressed the plunger and there was the click. At once she stirred to action, got behind the camera, turned a new exposure. 'Thank you,' she said. 'Would you stand under that tree and let me do a character study with light and shade?'

The childish absurdity of the remark restored Howe's ease. He went to the little tree. The pattern the leaves made on his gown was what Hilda was after. He had just taken a satisfactory position when he heard in the unmistakable voice, 'Ah, Doctor! Having your picture taken?'

Howe gave up the pose and turned to Blackburn who stood on the walk, his hands behind his back, a little too large for his bachelor's gown. Annoyed that Blackburn should see him posing for a character study in light and shade, Howe said irritably, 'Yes, having my picture taken.'

Blackburn beamed at Hilda. 'And the little photographer?' he said. Hilda fixed her eyes on the ground and stood closer to her brilliant and aggressive camera. Blackburn, teetering on his heels, his hands behind his back, wholly prelatical and benignly patient, was not abashed at the silence. At last Howe said, 'If you'll excuse us, Mr. Blackburn, we'll go on with the picture.'

'Go right ahead, sir. I'm running along.' But he only came closer. 'Doctor Howe,' he said fervently, 'I want to tell you how glad I am that I was able to satisfy your standards at last.'

Howe was surprised at the hard, insulting brightness of his own voice, and even Hilda looked up curiously as he said, 'Nothing you have ever done has satisfied me, and nothing you could ever do would satisfy me, Blackburn.'

With a glance at Hilda, Blackburn made a gesture as if to hush Howe—as though all his former bold malice had taken for granted a kind of understanding between himself and his teacher, a secret which must not be betrayed to a third person. 'I only meant, sir,' he said, 'that I was able to pass your course after all.'

Howe said, 'You didn't pass my course. I passed you out of my course. I passed you without even reading your paper. I wanted to be sure the college would be rid of you. And when all the grades were in and I did read your paper, I saw I was right not to have read it first.'

Blackburn presented a stricken face. 'It was very bad, sir?'

But Howe had turned away. The paper had been fantastic. The paper had been, if he wished to see it so, mad. It was at this moment that the Dean came up behind Howe and caught his arm. 'Hello, Joseph,' he said. 'We'd better be getting along, it's almost late.'

He was not a familiar man, but when he saw Blackburn, who approached to greet him, he took Blackburn's arm, too. 'Hello, Theodore,' he said. Leaning forward on Howe's arm and on Blackburn's, he said, 'Hello, Hilda dear.' Hilda replied quietly, 'Hello, Uncle George.'

Still clinging to their arms, still linking Howe and Blackburn, the Dean said, 'Another year gone, Joe, and we've turned out another crop. After you've been here a few years, you'll find it reasonably upsetting—you wonder how there can be so many graduating classes while you stay the same. But of course you don't stay the same.' Then he said, 'Well,' sharply, to dismiss the thought. He pulled Blackburn's arm and swung him around to Howe. 'Have you heard about Teddy Blackburn?' he asked. 'He has a job already, before graduation—the first man of his class to be placed.' Expectant of congratulations, Blackburn beamed at Howe. Howe remained silent.

'Isn't that good?' the Dean said. Still Howe did not answer and the Dean, puzzled and put out, turned to Hilda. 'That's a very fine-looking camera, Hilda.' She touched it with affectionate pride.

'Instruments of precision,' said a voice. 'Instruments of precision.' Of the three with joined arms, Howe was the nearest to Tertan, whose gaze took in all the scene except the smile and the nod which Howe gave him. The boy leaned on his cane. The broad-brimmed hat, canting jauntily over his eye, confused the image of his face that Howe had established, suppressed the rigid lines of the ascetic and brought out the baroque curves. It made an effect of perverse majesty.

'Instruments of precision,' said Tertan for the last time, addressing no one, making a casual comment to the universe. And it occurred to Howe that Tertan might not be referring to Hilda's equipment. The sense of the thrice-woven circle of the boy's loneliness smote him fiercely. Tertan stood in majestic jauntiness, superior to all the scene, but his isolation made Howe ache with a pity of which Tertan was more the cause than the object, so general and indiscriminate was it.

Whether in his sorrow he made some unintended movement toward Tertan which the Dean checked, or whether the suddenly tightened grip on his arm was the Dean's own sorrow and fear, he did not know. Tertan watched them in the incurious way people watch a photograph being taken, and suddenly the thought that, to the boy, it must seem that the three were posing for a picture together made Howe detach himself almost rudely from the Dean's grasp.

'I promised Hilda another picture,' he announced—needlessly, for Tertan was no longer there, he had vanished in the last sudden flux of visitors who, now that the band had struck up, were rushing nervously to find seats.

'You'd better hurry,' the Dean said. 'I'll go along, it's getting late for me.' He departed and Blackburn walked stately by his side.

Howe again took his position under the little tree which cast its shadow over his face and gown. 'Just hurry, Hilda, won't you?' he said. Hilda held the cable at arm's length, her other arm crooked and her fingers crisped. She rose on her toes and said 'Ready,' and pressed the release. 'Thank you,' she said gravely and began to dismantle her camera as he hurried off to join the procession.

THE RICH BOY

by F. Scott Fitzgerald

BEGIN WITH AN INDIVIDUAL, and before you know it you find that you have created a type; begin with a type, and you find that you have created—nothing. That is because we are all queer fish, queerer behind our faces and voices than we want anyone to know or than we know ourselves. When I hear a man proclaiming himself an "average, honest, open fellow," I feel pretty sure that he has some definite and perhaps terrible abnormality which he has agreed to conceal—and his protestation of being average and honest and open is his way of reminding himself of his misprision.

There are no types, no plurals. There is

Reprinted from *All the Sad Young Men* by F. Scott Fitzgerald; copyright 1922, 1926 by Charles Scribner's Sons; used by permission of the publishers.

a rich boy, and this is his and not his brothers' story. All my life I have lived among his brothers but this one has been my friend. Besides, if I wrote about his brothers I should have to begin by attacking all the lies that the poor have told about the rich and the rich have told about themselves—such a wild structure they have erected that when we pick up a book about the rich, some instinct prepares us for unreality. Even the intelligent and impassioned reporters of life have made the country of the rich as unreal as fairyland.

Let me tell you about the very rich. They are different from you and me. They possess and enjoy early, and it does something to them, makes them soft where we are hard, and cynical where we are trustful, in a way that, unless you were born rich, it is difficult to understand. They think, deep in their hearts, that they are better than we are because we had to discover the compensations and refuges of life for ourselves. Even when they enter deep into our world or sink below us, they still think that they are better than we are. They are different. The only way I can describe young Anson Hunter is to approach him as if he were a foreigner and cling stubbornly to my point of view. If I accept his for a moment I am lost—I have nothing to show but a preposterous movie.

II

Anson was the eldest of six children who would some day divide a fortune of fifteen million dollars, and he reached the age of reason—is it seven?—at the beginning of the century when daring young women were already gliding along Fifth Avenue in electric "mobiles." In those days he and his brother had an English governess who spoke the language very clearly and crisply and well, so that the two boys grew to speak as she did—their words and sentences were all crisp and clear and not run together as ours are. They didn't talk exactly like English children but acquired an accent that is peculiar to fashionable people in the city of New York.

In the summer the six children were moved from the house on 71st Street to a big estate in northern Connecticut. It was not a fashionable locality—Anson's father wanted to delay as long as possible his children's knowledge of that side of life. He was a man somewhat superior to his class, which composed New York society, and to his period, which was the snobbish and formalized vulgarity of the Gilded Age, and he wanted his sons to learn habits of concentration and have sound constitutions and grow up into right-living and successful men. He and his wife kept an eye on them as well as they were able until the two older boys went away to school, but in huge establishments this is difficult—it was much simpler in the series of small and medium-sized houses in which my own youth was spent—I was never far out of the reach of my mother's voice, of the sense of her presence, her approval or disapproval.

Anson's first sense of his superiority came to him when he realized the half-grudging American deference that was paid to him in the Connecticut village. The parents of the boys he played with always inquired after his father and mother, and were vaguely excited when their own children were asked to the Hunters' house. He accepted this as the natural state of things, and a sort of impatience with all groups of which he was not the center—in money, in position, in authority—remained with him for the rest of his life. He disdained to struggle with other boys for precedence—he expected it to be given him freely, and when it wasn't he withdrew into his family. His family was sufficient, for in the East money is still a somewhat feudal thing, a clan-forming thing. In the snobbish West, money separates families to form "sets."

At eighteen, when he went to New Haven, Anson was tall and thick-set, with a clear complexion and a healthy color from the ordered life he had led in school. His hair was yellow and grew in a funny way on his head, his nose was beaked—these two things kept him from being handsome—but he had a confident charm and a certain brusque style, and the upper-class men who passed him on the street knew without being told that he was a rich boy and had gone to one of the best schools. Nevertheless, his very superiority kept him from being a success in college—the independence was mistaken for egotism, and the refusal to accept Yale standards with the proper awe seemed to belittle all those who had. So, long before he graduated, he began to shift the center of his life to New York.

He was at home in New York—there was his own house with "the kind of servants you can't get any more"—and his own family, of which, because of his good humor and a certain ability to make things go, he was rapidly becoming the center, and the débutante parties, and the correct manly world of the men's clubs, and the occasional wild spree with the gallant girls whom New Haven only knew from the fifth row. His aspirations were conventional enough—they included even the irreproachable shadow he would some day marry, but they differed from the aspirations of the majority of young men in that there was no mist over them, none of that quality which is variously known as "idealism" or "illusion." Anson accepted without reservation the world of high finance and high extravagance, of divorce and dissipation, of snobbery and of privilege. Most of our lives end as a compromise—it was as a compromise that his life began.

He and I first met in the late summer of 1917 when he was just out of Yale, and, like the rest of us, was swept up into the systematized hysteria of the war. In the blue-green uniform of the naval aviation he came down to Pensacola, where the hotel orchestras played *I'm Sorry, Dear,* and we young officers danced with the girls. Everyone liked him, and though he ran with the drinkers and wasn't an especially good pilot, even the instructors treated him with a certain respect. He was always having long talks with them in his confident, logical voice—talks which ended by his getting himself, or, more frequently, another officer, out of some impending trouble. He was convivial, bawdy, robustly avid for pleasure, and we were all surprised when he fell in love with a conservative and rather proper girl.

Her name was Paula Legendre, a dark, serious beauty from somewhere in California. Her family kept a winter residence just outside of town, and in spite of her primness she was enormously popular; there is a large class of men whose egotism can't endure humor in a woman. But Anson wasn't that sort, and I couldn't understand the attraction of her "sincerity"—that was the thing to say about her—for his keen and somewhat sardonic mind.

Nevertheless, they fell in love—and on her terms. He no longer joined the twilight gathering at the De Soto bar, and whenever they were seen together they were engaged in a long, serious dialogue, which must have gone on several weeks. Long afterward he told me that it was not about anything in particular but was composed on both sides of immature and even meaningless statements—the emotional content that gradually came to fill it grew up not out of the words but out of its enormous seriousness. It was a sort of hypnosis. Often it was interrupted, giving way to that emasculated humor we call fun; when they were alone it was resumed again, solemn, low-keyed, and pitched so as to give each other a sense of unity in feeling and thought. They came to resent any interruptions of it, to be unresponsible to facetiousness about life, even to the mild cynicism of their contemporaries. They were only happy when the dialogue was going on, and its seriousness bathed them like the amber glow of an open fire. Toward the end there came an interruption they did not resent—it began to be interrupted by passion.

Oddly enough, Anson was as engrossed in the dialogue as she was and as profoundly affected by it, yet at the same time aware that on his side much was insincere, and on hers much was merely simple. At first, too, he despised her emotional simplicity as well, but with his love her nature deepened and blossomed, and he could despise it no longer. He felt that if he could enter into Paula's warm safe life he would be happy. The long preparation of the dialogue removed any constraint—he taught her some of what he had learned from more adventurous women, and she responded with a rapt holy intensity. One evening after a dance they agreed to marry, and he wrote a long letter about her to his mother. The next day Paula told him that she was rich, that she had a personal fortune of nearly a million dollars.

III

It was exactly as if they could say "Neither of us has anything: we shall be poor together"—just as delightful that they should be rich instead. It gave them the same communion of adventure. Yet when Anson got leave in April, and Paula and her mother accompanied him North, she was impressed with the standing of his family in New York and with the scale on which they lived. Alone with Anson for the first time in the rooms where he had played as a boy, she was filled with a comfortable emotion, as though she was preeminently safe and taken care of. The pictures of Anson in a skull cap at his first school, of Anson on horseback with the sweetheart of a mysterious forgotten summer, of Anson in a gay group of ushers and bridesmaids at a wedding, made her jealous of his life apart from her in the past, and so completely did his authoritative person seem to sum up and typify these possessions of his that she was inspired with the idea of being married immediately and returning to Pensacola as his wife.

But an immediate marriage wasn't discussed—even the engagement was to be secret until after the war. When she realized that only two days of his leave remained, her dissatisfaction crystallized in the intention of making him as unwilling to wait as she was. They were driving to the country for dinner and she determined to force the issue that night.

Now a cousin of Paula's was staying with them at the Ritz, a severe, bitter girl who loved Paula but was somewhat jealous of her impressive engagement, and as Paula was late in dressing, the cousin, who wasn't going to the party, received Anson in the parlor of the suite.

Anson had met friends at five o'clock and drunk freely and indiscreetly with them for an hour. He left the Yale Club at a proper time, and his mother's chauffeur drove him to the Ritz, but his usual capacity was not in evidence, and the impact of the steam-heated sitting-room made him suddenly dizzy. He knew it, and he was both amused and sorry.

Paula's cousin was twenty-five, but she was exceptionally naïve, and at first failed to realize what was up. She had never met Anson before, and she was surprised when he mumbled strange information and nearly fell off his chair, but until Paula appeared it didn't occur to her that what she had taken for the odor of a dry-cleaned uniform was really whiskey. But Paula understood as soon as she appeared; her only thought was to get Anson away before her mother saw him, and at the look in her eyes the cousin understood too.

When Paula and Anson descended to the limousine they found two men inside, both asleep; they were the men with whom he had been drinking at the Yale Club, and they were also going to the party. He had entirely forgotten their presence in the car. On the way to Hempstead they awoke and sang. Some of the songs were rough, and though Paula tried to reconcile herself to the fact that Anson had few verbal inhibitions, her lips tightened with shame and distaste.

Back at the hotel the cousin, confused and agitated, considered the incident, and then walked into Mrs. Legendre's bedroom, saying: "Isn't he funny?"

"Who is funny?"

"Why—Mr. Hunter. He seemed so funny."

Mrs. Legendre looked at her sharply.

"How is he funny?"

"Why, he said he was French. I didn't know he was French."

"That's absurd. You must have misunderstood." She smiled: "It was a joke."

The cousin shook her head stubbornly.

"No. He said he was brought up in France. He said he couldn't speak any English, and that's why he couldn't talk to me. And he couldn't!"

Mrs. Legendre looked away with impatience just as the cousin added thoughtfully, "Perhaps it was because he was so drunk," and walked out of the room.

This curious report was true. Anson, finding his voice thick and uncontrollable, had taken the unusual refuge of announcing that he spoke no English. Years afterward he used to tell that part of the story, and he invariably communicated the uproarious laughter which the memory aroused in him.

Five times in the next hour Mrs. Legendre tried to get Hempstead on the phone. When she succeeded, there was a ten-minute delay before she heard Paula's voice on the wire.

"Cousin Jo told me Anson was intoxicated."

"Oh, no...."

"Oh, yes. Cousin Jo says he was intoxicated. He told her he was French, and fell off his chair and behaved as if he was very intoxicated. I don't want you to come home with him."

"Mother, he's all right! Please don't worry about—"

"But I do worry. I think it's dreadful. I want you to promise me not to come home with him."

"I'll take care of it, mother...."

"I don't want you to come home with him."

"All right, mother. Good-by."

"Be sure now, Paula. Ask some one to bring you."

Deliberately Paula took the receiver from her ear and hung it up. Her face was flushed with helpless annoyance. Anson was stretched out asleep in a bedroom upstairs, while the dinner-party below was proceeding lamely toward conclusion.

The hour's drive had sobered him somewhat—his arrival was merely hilarious—and Paula hoped that the evening was not

[275]

spoiled, after all, but two imprudent cocktails before dinner completed the disaster. He talked boisterously and somewhat offensively to the party at large for fifteen minutes, and then slid silently under the table; like a man in an old print—but, unlike an old print, it was rather horrible without being at all quaint. None of the young girls present remarked upon the incident—it seemed to merit only silence. His uncle and two other men carried him upstairs, and it was just after this that Paula was called to the phone.

An hour later Anson awoke in a fog of nervous agony, through which he perceived after a moment the figure of his Uncle Robert standing by the door.

". . . I said are you better?"

"What?"

"Do you feel better, old man?"

"Terrible," said Anson.

"I'm going to try you on another bromo-seltzer. If you can hold it down, it'll do you good to sleep."

With an effort Anson slid his legs from the bed and stood up.

"I'm all right," he said dully.

"Take it easy."

"I thin' if you gave me a glassbrandy I could go downstairs."

"Oh, no—"

"Yes, that's the only thin'. I'm all right now. . . . I suppose I'm in Dutch dow' there."

"They know you're a little under the weather," said his uncle deprecatingly. "But don't worry about it. Schuyler didn't even get here. He passed away in the locker-room over at the Links."

Indifferent to any opinion, except Paula's, Anson was nevertheless determined to save the débris of the evening, but when after a cold bath he made his appearance most of the party had already left. Paula got up immediately to go home.

In the limousine the old serious dialogue began. She had known that he drank, she admitted, but she had never expected anything like this—it seemed to her that perhaps they were not suited to each other, after all. Their ideas about life were too different, and so forth. When she finished speaking, Anson spoke in turn, very soberly. Then Paula said she'd have to think it over; she wouldn't decide tonight; she was not angry but she was terribly sorry. Nor would she let him come into the hotel with her, but just before she got out of the car she leaned and kissed him unhappily on the cheek.

The next afternoon Anson had a long talk with Mrs. Legendre while Paula sat listening in silence. It was agreed that Paula was to brood over the incident for a proper period and then, if mother and daughter thought it best, they would follow Anson to Pensacola. On his part he apologized with sincerity and dignity—that was all; with every card in her hand Mrs. Legendre was unable to establish any advantage over him. He made no promises, showed no humility, only delivered a few serious comments on life which brought him off with rather a moral superiority at the end. When they came South three weeks later, neither Anson in his satisfaction nor Paula in her relief at the reunion realized that the psychological moment had passed forever.

IV

He dominated and attracted her, and at the same time filled her with anxiety. Confused by his mixture of solidity and self-indulgence, of sentiment and cynicism—incongruities which her gentle mind was unable to resolve—Paula grew to think of him as two alternating personalities. When she saw him alone, or at a formal party, or with his casual inferiors, she felt a tremendous pride in his strong, attractive presence, the paternal, understanding stature of his mind. In other company she became uneasy when what had been a fine imperviousness to mere gentility showed its other face. The other face was gross, humorous, reckless of everything but pleasure. It startled her mind temporarily away from him, even led her into a short covert experiment with an old beau, but it was no use—after four months of Anson's enveloping vitality there was an anæmic pallor in all other men.

In July he was ordered abroad, and their tenderness and desire reached a crescendo. Paula considered a last-minute marriage—decided against it only because there were always cocktails on his breath now, but the parting itself made her physically ill with grief. After his departure she wrote him long letters of regret for the days of love they had missed by waiting. In August Anson's plane slipped down into the North Sea. He was pulled onto a destroyer after a night in the water and sent to hospital with pneumonia; the Armistice was signed before he was finally sent home.

Then, with every opportunity given back to them, with no material obstacle to overcome, the secret weavings of their temperaments came between them, drying up their kisses and their tears, making their voices less loud to one another, muffling the intimate chatter of their hearts until the old communication was only possible by letters, from far away. One afternoon a society reporter waited for two hours in the Hunters' home for a confirmation of their engagement. Anson denied it; nevertheless an early issue carried the report as a leading paragraph—they were "constantly seen together at Southampton, Hot Springs, and Tuxedo Park." But the serious dialogue had turned a corner into a long-sustained quarrel, and the affair was almost played out. Anson got drunk flagrantly and missed an engagement with her, whereupon Paula made certain behavioristic demands. His despair was helpless before his pride and his knowledge of himself: the engagement was definitely broken.

"Dearest," said their letters now, "Dearest, Dearest, when I wake up in the middle of the night and realize that after all it was not to be, I feel that I want to die. I can't go on living any more. Perhaps when we meet this summer we may talk things over and decide differently—we were so excited and sad that day, and I don't feel that I can live all my life without you. You speak of other people. Don't you know there are no other people for me, but only you. . . ."

But as Paula drifted here and there around the East she would sometimes mention her gaieties to make him wonder. Anson was too acute to wonder. When he saw a man's name in her letters he felt more sure of her and a little disdainful—he was always superior to such things. But he still hoped that they would some day marry.

Meanwhile he plunged vigorously into all the movements and glitter of postbellum New York, entering a brokerage house, joining half a dozen clubs, dancing late, and moving in three worlds—his own world, the world of young Yale graduates, and that section of the half-world which rests one end on Broadway. But there was always a thorough and infrangible eight hours devoted to his work in Wall Street, where the combination of his influential family connection, his sharp intelligence, and his abundance of sheer physical energy brought him almost immediately forward. He had one of those invaluable minds with partitions in it;

sometimes he appeared at his office refreshed by less than an hour's sleep, but such occurrences were rare. So early as 1920 his income in salary and commissions exceeded twelve thousand dollars.

As the Yale tradition slipped into the past he became more and more of a popular figure among his classmates in New York, more popular than he had ever been in college. He lived in a great house, and had the means of introducing young men into other great houses. Moreover, his life already seemed secure, while theirs, for the most part, had arrived again at precarious beginnings. They commenced to turn to him for amusement and escape, and Anson responded readily, taking pleasure in helping people and arranging their affairs.

There were no men in Paula's letters now, but a note of tenderness ran through them that had not been there before. From several sources he heard that she had "a heavy beau," Lowell Thayer, a Bostonian of wealth and position, and though he was sure she still loved him, it made him uneasy to think that he might lose her, after all. Save for one unsatisfactory day she had not been in New York for almost five months, and as the rumors multiplied he became increasingly anxious to see her. In February he took his vacation and went down to Florida.

Palm Beach sprawled plump and opulent between the sparkling sapphire of Lake Worth, flawed here and there by house-boats at anchor, and the great turquoise bar of the Atlantic Ocean. The huge bulks of the Breakers and the Royal Poinciana rose as twin paunches from the bright level of the sand, and around them clustered the Dancing Glade, Bradley's House of Chance, and a dozen modistes and milliners with goods at triple prices from New York. Upon the trellissed veranda of the Breakers two hundred women stepped right, stepped left, wheeled, and slid in that then celebrated calisthenic known as the double-shuffle, while in half-time to the music two thousand bracelets clicked up and down on two hundred arms.

At the Everglades Club after dark Paula and Lowell Thayer and Anson and a casual fourth played bridge with hot cards. It seemed to Anson that her kind, serious face was wan and tired—she had been around now for four, five, years. He had known her for three.

"Two spades."

"Cigarette? . . . Oh, I beg your pardon. By me."

"By."

"I'll double three spades."

There were a dozen tables of bridge in the room, which was filling up with smoke. Anson's eyes met Paula's, held them persistently even when Thayer's glance fell between them. . . .

"What was bid?" he asked abstractedly.

"*Rose of Washington Square*"

sang the young people in the corners:

"*I'm withering there
In basement air—*"

The smoke banked like fog, and the opening of a door filled the room with blown swirls of ectoplasm. Little Bright Eyes streaked past the tables seeking Mr. Conan Doyle among the Englishmen who were posing as Englishmen about the lobby.

"You could cut it with a knife."

". . . cut it with a knife."

". . . a knife."

At the end of the rubber Paula suddenly got up and spoke to Anson in a tense, low voice. With scarcely a glance at Lowell Thayer, they walked out the door and descended a long flight of stone steps—in a moment they were walking hand in hand along the moonlit beach.

"Darling, darling...." They embraced recklessly, passionately, in a shadow.... Then Paula drew back her face to let his lips say what she wanted to hear—she could feel the words forming as they kissed again.... Again she broke away, listening, but as he pulled her close once more she realized that he had said nothing —only *"Darling! Darling!"* in that deep, sad whisper that always made her cry. Humbly, obediently, her emotion yielded to him and the tears streamed down her face, but her heart kept on crying: "Ask me—oh, Anson, dearest, ask me!"

"Paula.... *Paula!*"

The words wrung her heart like hands, and Anson, feeling her tremble, knew that emotion was enough. He need say no more, commit their destinies to no practical enigma. Why should he, when he might hold her so, biding his own time, for another year—forever? He was considering them both, her more than himself. For a moment, when she said suddenly that she must go back to her hotel, he hesitated, thinking, first, "This is the moment, after all," and then: "No, let it wait—she is mine...."

He had forgotten that Paula too was worn away inside with the strain of three years. Her mood passed forever in the night.

He went back to New York next morning filled with a certain restless dissatisfaction. Late in April, without warning, he received a telegram from Bar Harbor in which Paula told him that she was engaged to Lowell Thayer, and that they would be married immediately in Boston. What he had never really believed could happen had happened at last.

Anson filled himself with whiskey that morning, and going to the office, carried on his work without a break—rather with a fear of what would happen if he stopped. In the evening he went out as usual, saying nothing of what had occurred; he was cordial, humorous, unabstracted. But one thing he could not help—for three days in any place, in any company, he would suddenly bend his head into his hands and cry like a child.

v

In 1922 when Anson went abroad with the junior partner to investigate some London loans, the journey intimated that he was to be taken into the firm. He was twenty-seven now, a little heavy without being definitely stout, and with a manner older than his years. Old people and young people liked him and trusted him, and mothers felt safe when their daughters were in his charge, for he had a way, when he came into a room, of putting himself on a footing with the oldest and most conservative people there. "You and I," he seemed to say, "we're solid. We understand."

He had an instinctive and rather charitable knowledge of the weaknesses of men and women, and, like a priest, it made him the more concerned for the maintenance of outward forms. It was typical of him that every Sunday morning he taught in a fashionable Episcopal Sunday-school—even though a cold shower and a quick change into a cutaway coat were all that separated him from the wild night before.

After his father's death he was the political head of his family, and, in effect, guided the destinies of the younger children. Through a complication his authority did not extend to his father's estate, which was administrated by his Uncle Robert, who was the horsey member of that set which centers about Wheatley Hills.

Uncle Robert and his wife, Edna, had been great friends of Anson's youth, and the former was disappointed when his nephew's superiority failed to take a horsey form. He backed him for a city club which was the most difficult in America to enter—one could only join if one's family had "helped to build up New York" (or, in other words, were rich before 1880)—and when Anson, after his election, neglected it for the Yale Club, Uncle Robert gave him a little talk on the subject. But when on top of that Anson declined to enter Robert Hunter's own conservative and somewhat neglected brokerage house, his manner grew cooler. Like a primary teacher who has taught all he knew, he slipped out of Anson's life.

There were so many friends in Anson's life—scarcely one for whom he had not done some unusual kindness and scarcely one whom he did not occasionally embarrass by his bursts of rough conversation or his habit of getting drunk whenever and however he liked. It annoyed him when anyone else blundered in that regard—about his own lapses he was always humorous. Odd things happened to him and he told them with infectious laughter.

I was working in New York that spring, and I used to lunch with him at the Yale Club, which my university was sharing until the completion of our own. I had read of Paula's marriage, and one afternoon, when I asked him about her, something moved him to tell me the story. After that he frequently invited me to family dinners at his house and behaved as though there was a special relation between us, as though with his confidence a little of that consuming memory had passed into me.

I found that despite the trusting mothers, his attitude toward girls was not indiscriminately protective. It was up to the girl—if she showed any inclination toward looseness, she must take care of herself, even with him.

"Life," he would explain sometimes, "has made a cynic of me."

By life he meant Paula. Sometimes, especially when he was drinking, it became a little twisted in his mind, and he thought that she had callously thrown him over.

This "cynicism," or rather his realization that naturally fast girls were not worth sparing, led to his affair with Dolly Karger. It wasn't his only affair in those years, but it came nearest to touching him deeply, and it had a profound effect upon his attitude toward life.

Dolly was the daughter of a notorious "publicist" who had married into society. She herself grew up into the Junior League, came out at the Plaza, and went to the Assembly; and only a few old families like the Hunters could question whether or not she "belonged," for her picture was often in the papers, and she had more enviable attention than many girls who undoubtedly did. She was dark-haired, with carmine lips and a high, lovely color, which she concealed under pinkish-gray powder all through the first year out, because high color was unfashionable—Victorian-pale was the thing to be. She wore black, severe suits and stood with her hands in her pockets leaning a little forward, with a humorous restraint on her face. She danced exquisitely—better than anything she liked to dance—better than anything except making love. Since she was ten she had always been in love, and, usually, with some boy who didn't respond to her. Those who did—and there were many—bored her after a brief encounter, but for her failures she reserved the warmest spot in her heart. When she met them she would always try once more—sometimes she succeeded, more often she failed.

It never occurred to this gypsy of the unattainable that there was a certain resemblance in those who refused to love her—they shared a hard intuition that saw through to her weakness, not a weakness of emotion but a weakness of rudder. Anson perceived this when he first met her, less than a month after Paula's marriage. He was drinking rather heavily, and he pretended for a week that he was falling in love with her. Then he dropped her abruptly and forgot—immediately he took up the commanding position in her heart.

Like so many girls of that day Dolly was slackly and indiscreetly wild. The unconventionality of a slightly older generation had been simply one facet of a post-war movement to discredit obsolete manners—Dolly's was both older and shabbier, and she saw in Anson the two extremes which the emotionally shiftless woman seeks, an abandon to indulgence alternating with a protective strength. In his character she felt both the sybarite and the solid rock, and these two satisfied every need of her nature.

She felt that it was going to be difficult, but she mistook the reason—she thought that Anson and his family expected a more spectacular marriage, but she guessed immediately that her advantage lay in his tendency to drink.

They met at the large débutante dances, but as her infatuation increased they managed to be more and more together. Like most mothers, Mrs. Karger believed that Anson was exceptionally reliable, so she allowed Dolly to go with him to distant country clubs and suburban houses without inquiring closely into their activities or questioning her explanations when they came in late. At first these explanations might have been accurate, but Dolly's worldly ideas of capturing Anson were soon engulfed in the rising sweep of her emotion. Kisses in the back of taxis and motorcars were no longer enough; they did a curious thing:

They dropped out of their world for a while and made another world just beneath it where Anson's tippling and Dolly's irregular hours would be less noticed and commented on. It was composed, this world, of varying elements—several of Anson's Yale friends and their wives, two or three young brokers and bond salesmen and a handful of unattached men, fresh from college, with money and a propensity to dissipation. What this world lacked in spaciousness and scale it made up for by allowing them a liberty that it scarcely permitted itself. Moreover, it centered around them and permitted Dolly the pleasure of a faint condescension—a pleasure which Anson, whose whole life was a condescension from the certitudes of his childhood, was unable to share.

He was not in love with her, and in the long feverish winter of their affair he frequently told her so. In the spring he was weary—he wanted to renew his life at some other source—moreover, he saw that either he must break with her now or accept the responsibility of a definite seduction. Her family's encouraging attitude precipitated his decision—one evening when Mr. Karger knocked discreetly at the library door to announce that he had left a bottle of old brandy in the dining-room, Anson felt that life was hemming him in. That night he wrote her a short letter in which he told her that he was going on his vacation, and that in view of all the circumstances they had better meet no more.

It was June. His family had closed up

the house and gone to the country, so he was living temporarily at the Yale Club. I had heard about his affair with Dolly as it developed—accounts salted with humor, for he despised unstable women, and granted them no place in the social edifice in which he believed—and when he told me that night that he was definitely breaking with her I was glad. I had seen Dolly here and there, and each time with a feeling of pity at the hopelessness of her struggle, and of shame at knowing so much about her that I had no right to know. She was what is known as "a pretty little thing," but there was a certain recklessness which rather fascinated me. Her dedication to the goddess of waste would have been less obvious had she been less spirited —she would most certainly throw herself away, but I was glad when I heard that the sacrifice would not be consummated in my sight.

Anson was going to leave the letter of farewell at her house next morning. It was one of the few houses left open in the Fifth Avenue district, and he knew that the Kargers, acting upon erroneous information from Dolly, had foregone a trip abroad to give their daughter her chance. As he stepped out the door of the Yale Club into Madison Avenue the postman passed him, and he followed back inside. The first letter that caught his eye was in Dolly's hand.

He knew what it would be—a lonely and tragic monologue, full of the reproaches he knew, the invoked memories, the "I wonder if's"—all the immemorial intimacies that he had communicated to Paula Legendre in what seemed another age. Thumbing over some bills, he brought it on top again and opened it. To his surprise it was a short, somewhat formal note, which said that Dolly would be unable to go to the country with him for the week-end, because Perry Hull from Chicago had unexpectedly come to town. It added that Anson had brought this on himself: "—if I felt that you loved me as I loved you I would go with you at any time, any place, but Perry is so nice, and he so much wants me to marry him—"

Anson smiled contemptuously—he had had experience with such decoy epistles. Moreover he knew how Dolly had labored over this plan, probably sent for the faithful Perry and calculated the time of his arrival—even labored over the note so that it would make him jealous without driving him away. Like most compromises, it had neither force nor vitality but only a timorous despair.

Suddenly he was angry. He sat down in the lobby and read it again. Then he went to the phone, called Dolly and told her in his clear, compelling voice that he had received her note and would call for her at five o'clock as they had previously planned. Scarcely waiting for the pretended uncertainty of her "Perhaps I can see you for an hour," he hung up the receiver and went down to his office. On the way he tore his own letter into bits and dropped it in the street.

He was not jealous—she meant nothing to him—but at her pathetic ruse everything stubborn and self-indulgent in him came to the surface. It was a presumption from a mental inferior and it could not be overlooked. If she wanted to know to whom she belonged she would see.

He was on the doorstep at quarter past five. Dolly was dressed for the street, and he listened in silence to the paragraph of "I can only see you for an hour," which she had begun on the phone.

"Put on your hat, Dolly," he said, "we'll take a walk."

They strolled up Madison Avenue and over to Fifth while Anson's shirt dampened upon his portly body in the deep heat. He talked little, scolding her, making no love to her, but before they had walked six blocks she was his again, apologizing for the note, offering not to see Perry at all as an atonement, offering anything. She thought that he had come because he was beginning to love her.

"I'm hot," he said when they reached 71st Street. "This is a winter suit. If I stop by the house and change, would you mind waiting for me downstairs? I'll only be a minute."

She was happy; the intimacy of his being hot, of any physical fact about him, thrilled her. When they came to the iron-grated door and Anson took out his key she experienced a sort of delight.

Downstairs it was dark, and after he ascended in the lift Dolly raised a curtain and looked out through opaque lace at the houses over the way. She heard the lift machinery stop, and with the notion of teasing him pressed the button that brought it down. Then on what was more than an impulse she got into it and sent it up to what she guessed was his floor.

"Anson," she called, laughing a little.

"Just a minute," he answered from his bedroom . . . then after a brief delay: "Now you can come in."

He had changed and was buttoning his vest. "This is my room," he said lightly. "How do you like it?"

She caught sight of Paula's picture on the wall and stared at it in fascination, just as Paula had stared at the pictures of Anson's childish sweethearts five years before. She knew something about Paula—sometimes she tortured herself with fragments of the story.

Suddenly she came close to Anson, raising her arms. They embraced. Outside the area window a soft artificial twilight already hovered, though the sun was still bright on a back roof across the way. In half an hour the room would be quite dark. The uncalculated opportunity overwhelmed them, made them both breathless, and they clung more closely. It was imminent, inevitable. Still holding one another, they raised their heads—their eyes fell together upon Paula's picture, staring down at them from the wall.

Suddenly Anson dropped his arms, and sitting down at his desk tried the drawer with a bunch of keys.

"Like a drink?" he asked in a gruff voice.

"No, Anson."

He poured himself half a tumbler of whiskey, swallowed it, and then opened the door into the hall.

"Come on," he said.

Dolly hesitated.

"Anson—I'm going to the country with you tonight, after all. You understand that, don't you?"

"Of course," he answered brusquely.

In Dolly's car they rode on to Long Island, closer in their emotions than they had ever been before. They knew what would happen—not with Paula's face to remind them that something was lacking, but when they were alone in the still, hot Long Island night they did not care.

The estate in Port Washington where they were to spend the week-end belonged to a cousin of Anson's who had married a Montana copper operator. An interminable drive began at the lodge and twisted under imported poplar saplings toward a huge, pink, Spanish house. Anson had often visited there before.

After dinner they danced at the Linx Club. About midnight Anson assured himself that his cousins would not leave before two—then he explained that Dolly was tired; he would take her home and return to the dance later. Trembling a little with excitement, they got into a borrowed car together and drove to Port Washington. As they reached the lodge he stopped and spoke to the night-watchman.

"When are you making a round, Carl?"

"Right away."

"Then you'll be here till everybody's in?"

"Yes, sir."

"All right. Listen: if any automobile, no matter whose it is, turns in at this gate, I want you to phone the house immediately." He put a five-dollar bill into Carl's hand. "Is that clear?"

"Yes, Mr. Anson." Being of the Old World, he neither winked nor smiled. Yet Dolly sat with her face turned slightly away.

Anson had a key. Once inside he poured a drink for both of them—Dolly left hers untouched—then he ascertained definitely the location of the phone, and found that it was within easy hearing distance of their rooms, both of which were on the first floor.

Five minutes later he knocked at the door of Dolly's room.

"Anson?" He went in, closing the door behind him. She was in bed, leaning up anxiously with elbows on the pillow; sitting beside her he took her in his arms.

"Anson, darling."

He didn't answer.

"Anson.... Anson! I love you.... Say you love me. Say it now—can't you say it now? Even if you don't mean it?"

He did not listen. Over her head he perceived that the picture of Paula was hanging here upon this wall.

He got up and went close to it. The frame gleamed faintly with thrice-reflected moonlight—within was a blurred shadow of a face that he saw he did not know. Almost sobbing, he turned around and stared with abomination at the little figure on the bed.

"This is all foolishness," he said thickly. "I don't know what I was thinking about. I don't love you and you'd better wait for somebody that loves you. I don't love you a bit, can't you understand?"

His voice broke, and he went hurriedly out. Back in the salon he was pouring himself a drink with uneasy fingers, when the front door opened suddenly, and his cousin came in.

"Why, Anson, I hear Dolly's sick," she began solicitously. "I hear she's sick...."

"It was nothing," he interrupted, raising his voice so that it would carry into Dolly's room. "She was a little tired. She went to bed."

For a long time afterward Anson believed that a protective God sometimes interfered in human affairs. But Dolly Karger, lying awake and staring at the ceiling, never again believed in anything at all.

VI

When Dolly married during the following autumn, Anson was in London on business. Like Paula's marriage, it was sudden, but it affected him in a different way. At first he felt that it was funny, and had an inclination to laugh when he thought of it. Later it depressed him—it made him feel old.

There was something repetitive about it —why, Paula and Dolly had belonged to different generations. He had a foretaste of the sensation of a man of forty who hears that the daughter of an old flame has married. He wired congratulations and, as was not the case with Paula, they were sincere—he had never really hoped that Paula would be happy.

When he returned to New York, he was made a partner in the firm, and, as his responsibilities increased, he had less time on his hands. The refusal of a life-insurance company to issue him a policy made such an impression on him that he stopped drinking for a year, and claimed that he felt better physically, though I think he missed the convivial recounting of those Celliniesque adventures which, in his early twenties, had played such a part in his life. But he never abandoned the Yale Club. He was a figure there, a personality, and the tendency of his class, who were now seven years out of college, to drift away to more sober haunts was checked by his presence.

His day was never too full nor his mind too weary to give any sort of aid to any one who asked it. What had been done at first through pride and superiority had become a habit and a passion. And there was always something—a younger brother in trouble at New Haven, a quarrel to be patched up between a friend and his wife, a position to be found for this man, an investment for that. But his specialty was the solving of problems for young married people. Young married people fascinated him and their apartments were almost sacred to him—he knew the story of their love-affair, advised them where to live and how, and remembered their babies' names. Toward young wives his attitude was circumspect: he never abused the trust which their husbands—strangely enough in view of his unconcealed irregularities—invariably reposed in him.

He came to take a vicarious pleasure in happy marriages, and to be inspired to an almost equally pleasant melancholy by those that went astray. Not a season passed that he did not witness the collapse of an affair that perhaps he himself had fathered. When Paula was divorced and almost immediately remarried to another Bostonian, he talked about her to me all one afternoon. He would never love any one as he had loved Paula, but he insisted that he no longer cared.

"I'll never marry," he came to say; "I've seen too much of it, and I know a happy marriage is a very rare thing. Besides, I'm too old."

But he did believe in marriage. Like all men who spring from a happy and successful marriage, he believed in it passionately—nothing he had seen would change his belief, his cynicism dissolved upon it like air. But he did really believe he was too old. At twenty-eight he began to accept with equanimity the prospect of marrying without romantic love; he resolutely chose a New York girl of his own class, pretty, intelligent, congenial, above reproach—and set about falling in love with her. The things he had said to Paula with sincerity, to other girls with grace, he could no longer say at all without smiling, or with the force necessary to convince.

"When I'm forty," he told his friends, "I'll be ripe. I'll fall for some chorus girl like the rest."

Nevertheless, he persisted in his attempt. His mother wanted to see him married, and he could now well afford it—he had a seat on the Stock Exchange, and his earned income came to twenty-five thousand a year. The idea was agreeable: when his friends—he spent most of his time with the set he and Dolly had evolved —closed themselves in behind domestic doors at night, he no longer rejoiced in his freedom. He even wondered if he should have married Dolly. Not even Paula had loved him more, and he was learning the rarity, in a single life, of encountering true emotion.

Just as this mood began to creep over him a disquieting story reached his ear.

His aunt Edna, a woman just this side of forty, was carrying on an open intrigue with a dissolute, hard-drinking young man named Cary Sloane. Every one knew of it except Anson's Uncle Robert, who for fifteen years had talked long in clubs and taken his wife for granted.

Anson heard the story again and again with increasing annoyance. Something of his old feeling for his uncle came back to him, a feeling that was more than personal, a reversion toward that family solidarity on which he had based his pride. His intuition singled out the essential point of the affair, which was that his uncle shouldn't be hurt. It was his first experiment in unsolicited meddling, but with his knowledge of Edna's character he felt that he could handle the matter better than a district judge or his uncle.

His uncle was in Hot Springs. Anson traced down the sources of the scandal so that there should be no possibility of mistake and then he called Edna and asked her to lunch with him at the Plaza next day. Something in his tone must have frightened her, for she was reluctant, but he insisted, putting off the date until she had no excuse for refusing.

She met him at the appointed time in the Plaza lobby, a lovely, faded, gray-eyed blond in a coat of Russian sable. Five great rings, cold with diamonds and emeralds, sparkled on her slender hands. It occurred to Anson that it was his father's intelligence and not his uncle's that had earned the fur and the stones, the rich brilliance that buoyed up her passing beauty.

Though Edna scented his hostility, she was unprepared for the directness of his approach.

"Edna, I'm astonished at the way you've been acting," he said in a strong, frank voice. "At first I couldn't believe it."

"Believe what?" she demanded sharply.

"You needn't pretend with me, Edna. I'm talking about Cary Sloane. Aside from any other consideration, I didn't think you could treat Uncle Robert—"

"Now look here, Anson—" she began angrily, but his peremptory voice broke through hers:

"—and your children in such a way. You've been married eighteen years, and you're old enough to know better."

"You can't talk to me like that! You—"

"Yes, I can. Uncle Robert has always been my best friend." He was tremendously moved. He felt a real distress about his uncle, about his three young cousins.

Edna stood up, leaving her crab-flake cocktail untasted.

"This is the silliest thing—"

"Very well, if you won't listen to me I'll go to Uncle Robert and tell him the whole story—he's bound to hear it sooner or later. And afterward I'll go to old Moses Sloane."

Edna faltered back into her chair.

"Don't talk so loud," she begged him. Her eyes blurred with tears. "You have no idea how your voice carries. You might have chosen a less public place to make all these crazy accusations."

He didn't answer.

"Oh, you never liked me, I know," she went on. "You're just taking advantage of some silly gossip to try and break up the only interesting friendship I've ever had. What did I ever do to make you hate me so?"

Still Anson waited. There would be the appeal to his chivalry, then to his pity, finally to his superior sophistication—when he had shouldered his way through all these there would be admissions, and he could come to grips with her. By being silent, by being impervious, by returning

The Rich Boy

constantly to his main weapon, which was his own true emotion, he bullied her into frantic despair as the luncheon hour slipped away. At two o'clock she took out a mirror and a handkerchief, shined away the marks of her tears and powdered the slight hollows where they had lain. She had agreed to meet him at her own house at five.

When he arrived she was stretched on a *chaise-longue* which was covered with cretonne for the summer, and the tears he had called up at luncheon seemed still to be standing in her eyes. Then he was aware of Cary Sloane's dark anxious presence upon the cold hearth.

"What's this idea of yours?" broke out Sloane immediately. "I understand you invited Edna to lunch and then threatened her on the basis of some cheap scandal."

Anson sat down.

"I have no reason to think it's only scandal."

"I hear you're going to take it to Robert Hunter, and to my father."

Anson nodded.

"Either you break it off—or I will," he said.

"What God damned business is it of yours, Hunter?"

"Don't lose your temper, Cary," said Edna nervously. "It's only a question of showing him how absurd—"

"For one thing, it's my name that's being handed around," interrupted Anson. "That's all that concerns you, Cary."

"Edna isn't a member of your family."

"She most certainly is!" His anger mounted. "Why—she owes this house and the rings on her fingers to my father's brains. When Uncle Robert married her she didn't have a penny."

They all looked at the rings as if they had a significant bearing on the situation. Edna made a gesture to take them from her hand.

"I guess they're not the only rings in the world," said Sloane.

"Oh, this is absurd," cried Edna. "Anson, will you listen to me? I've found out how the silly story started. It was a maid I discharged who went right to the Chilicheffs—all these Russians pump things out of their servants and then put a false meaning on them." She brought down her fist angrily on the table: "And after Tom lent them the limousine for a whole month when we were South last winter—"

"Do you see?" demanded Sloane eagerly. "This maid got hold of the wrong end of the thing. She knew that Edna and I were friends, and she carried it to the Chilicheffs. In Russia they assume that if a man and a woman—"

He enlarged the theme to a disquisition upon social relations in the Caucasus.

"If that's the case it better be explained to Uncle Robert," said Anson dryly, "so that when the rumors do reach him he'll know they're not true."

Adopting the method he had followed with Edna at luncheon he let them explain it all away. He knew that they were guilty and that presently they would cross the line from explanation into justification and convict themselves more definitely than he could ever do. By seven they had taken the desperate step of telling him the truth—Robert Hunter's neglect, Edna's empty life, the casual dalliance that had flamed up into passion—but like so many true stories it had the misfortune of being old, and its enfeebled body beat helplessly against the armor of Anson's will. The threat to go to Sloane's father sealed their helplessness, for the latter, a retired cotton broker out of Alabama, was a notorious fundamentalist who controlled his son by a rigid allowance and the promise that at his next vagary the allowance would stop forever.

They dined at a small French restaurant, and the discussion continued—at one time Sloane resorted to physical threats, a little later they were both imploring him to give them time. But Anson was obdurate. He saw that Edna was breaking up, and that her spirit must not be refreshed by any renewal of their passion.

At two o'clock in a small night-club on 53d Street, Edna's nerves suddenly collapsed, and she cried to go home. Sloane had been drinking heavily all evening, and he was faintly maudlin, leaning on the table and weeping a little with his face in his hands. Quickly Anson gave them his terms. Sloane was to leave town for six months, and he must be gone within forty-eight hours. When he returned there was to be no resumption of the affair, but at the end of a year Edna might, if she wished, tell Robert Hunter that she wanted a divorce and go about it in the usual way.

He paused, gaining confidence from their faces for his final word.

"Or there's another thing you can do," he said slowly, "if Edna wants to leave her children, there's nothing I can do to prevent your running off together."

"I want to go home!" cried Edna again. "Oh, haven't you done enough to us for one day?"

Outside it was dark, save for a blurred glow from Sixth Avenue down the street. In that light those two who had been lovers looked for the last time into each other's faces, realizing that between them there was not enough youth and strength to avert their eternal parting. Sloane walked suddenly off down the street and Anson tapped a dozing taxi-driver on the arm.

It was almost four; there was a patient flow of cleaning water along the ghostly pavement of Fifth Avenue, and the shadows of two night women flitted over the dark façade of St. Thomas's church. Then the desolate shrubbery of Central Park where Anson had often played as a child, and the mounting numbers, significant as names, of the marching streets. This was his city, he thought, where his name had flourished through five generations. No change could alter the permanence of its place here, for change itself was the essential substratum by which he and those of his name identified themselves with the spirit of New York. Resourcefulness and a powerful will—for his threats in weaker hands would have been less than nothing —had beaten the gathering dust from his uncle's name, from the name of his family, from even this shivering figure that sat beside him in the car.

Cary Sloane's body was found next morning on the lower shelf of a pillar of Queensboro Bridge. In the darkness and in his excitement he had thought that it was the water flowing black beneath him, but in less than a second it made no possible difference—unless he had planned to think one last thought of Edna, and call out her name as he struggled feebly in the water.

VII

Anson never blamed himself for his part in this affair—the situation which brought it about had not been of his making. But the just suffer with the unjust, and he found that his oldest and somehow his most precious friendship was over. He never knew what distorted story Edna told, but he was welcome in his uncle's house no longer.

Just before Christmas Mrs. Hunter retired to a select Episcopal heaven, and Anson became the responsible head of his family. An unmarried aunt who had lived with them for years ran the house, and attempted with helpless inefficiency to chaperone the younger girls. All the children were less self-reliant than Anson, more conventional both in their virtues and in their shortcomings. Mrs. Hunter's death had postponed the début of one daughter and the wedding of another. Also it had taken something deeply material from all of them, for with her passing the quiet, expensive superiority of the Hunters came to an end.

For one thing, the estate, considerably diminished by two inheritance taxes and soon to be divided among six children, was not a notable fortune any more. Anson saw a tendency in his youngest sisters to speak rather respectfully of families that hadn't "existed" twenty years ago. His own feeling of precedence was not echoed in them—sometimes they were conventionally snobbish, that was all. For another thing, this was the last summer they would spend on the Connecticut estate; the clamor against it was too loud: "Who wants to waste the best months of the year shut up in that dead old town?" Reluctantly he yielded—the house would go into the market in the fall, and next summer they would rent a smaller place in Westchester County. It was a step down from the expensive simplicity of his father's idea, and, while he symphathized with the revolt, it also annoyed him; during his mother's lifetime he had gone up there at least every other week-end—even in the gayest summers.

Yet he himself was part of this change, and his strong instinct for life had turned him in his twenties from the hollow obsequies of that abortive leisure class. He did not see this clearly—he still felt that there was a norm, a standard of society. But there was no norm, it was doubtful if there had ever been a true norm in New York. The few who still paid and fought to enter a particular set succeeded only to find that as a society it scarcely functioned—or, what was more alarming, that the Bohemia from which they fled sat above them at table.

At twenty-nine Anson's chief concern was his own growing loneliness. He was sure now that he would never marry. The number of weddings at which he had officiated as best man or usher was past all counting—there was a drawer at home that bulged with the official neckties of this or that wedding-party, neckties standing for romances that had not endured a year, for couples who had passed completely from his life. Scarfpins, gold pencils, cuff-buttons, presents from a generation of grooms had passed through his jewel-box and been lost—and with every ceremony he was less and less able to imagine himself in the groom's place. Under his hearty good-will toward all those marriages there was despair about his own.

And as he neared thirty he became not a little depressed at the inroads that marriage, especially lately, had made upon his friendships. Groups of people had a disconcerting tendency to dissolve and disappear. The men from his own college—and it was upon them he had expended the most time and affection—were the most elusive of all. Most of them were drawn deep into domesticity, two were dead, one lived abroad, one was in Hollywood writing continuities for pictures that Anson went faithfully to see.

Most of them, however, were permanent commuters with an intricate family life centering around some suburban country club, and it was from these that he felt his estrangement most keenly.

In the early days of their married life they had all needed him; he gave them advice about their slim finances, he exorcised their doubts about the advisability of bringing a baby into two rooms and a bath, especially he stood for the great world outside. But now their financial troubles were in the past and the fearfully expected child had evolved into an absorbing family. They were always glad to see old Anson, but they dressed up for him and tried to impress him with their present importance, and kept their troubles to themselves. They needed him no longer.

A few weeks before his thirtieth birthday the last of his early and intimate friends was married. Anson acted in his usual rôle of best man, gave his usual silver tea-service, and went down to the usual *Homeric* to say good-by. It was a hot Friday afternoon in May, and as he walked from the pier he realized that Saturday closing had begun and he was free until Monday morning.

"Go where?" he asked himself.

The Yale Club, of course; bridge until dinner, then four or five raw cocktails in somebody's room and a pleasant confused evening. He regretted that this afternoon's groom wouldn't be along—they had always been able to cram so much into such nights: they knew how to attach women and how to get rid of them, how much consideration any girl deserved from their intelligent hedonism. A party was an adjusted thing—you took certain girls to certain places and spent just so much on their amusement; you drank a little, not much, more than you ought to drink, and at a certain time in the morning you stood up and said you were going home. You avoided college boys, sponges, future engagements, fights, sentiment, and indiscretions. That was the way it was done. All the rest was dissipation.

In the morning you were never violently sorry—you made no resolutions, but if you had overdone it and your heart was slightly out of order, you went on the wagon for a few days without saying anything about it, and waited until an accumulation of nervous boredom projected you into another party.

The lobby of the Yale Club was unpopulated. In the bar three very young alumni looked up at him, momentarily and without curiosity.

"Hello there, Oscar," he said to the bartender. "Mr. Cahill been around this afternoon?"

"Mr. Cahill's gone to New Haven."

"Oh . . . that so?"

"Gone to the ball game. Lot of men gone up."

Anson looked once again into the lobby, considered for a moment, and then walked out and over to Fifth Avenue. From the broad window of one of his clubs—one that he had scarcely visited in five years—a gray man with watery eyes stared down at him. Anson looked quickly away—that figure sitting in vacant resignation, in supercilious solitude, depressed him. He stopped and, retracing his steps, started over 47th Street toward Teak Warden's apartment. Teak and his wife had once been his most familiar friends —it was a household where he and Dolly Karger had been used to go in the days of their affair. But Teak had taken to drink, and his wife had remarked publicly that Anson was a bad influence on him. The remark reached Anson in an exaggerated form—when it was finally cleared up, the delicate spell of intimacy was broken, never to be renewed.

"Is Mr. Warden at home?" he inquired.

"They've gone to the country."

The Rich Boy

The fact unexpectedly cut at him. They were gone to the country and he hadn't known. Two years before he would have known the date, the hour, come up at the last moment for a final drink, and planned his first visit to them. Now they had gone without a word.

Anson looked at his watch and considered a week-end with his family, but the only train was a local that would jolt through the aggressive heat for three hours. And tomorrow in the country, and Sunday—he was in no mood for porch-bridge with polite undergraduates, and dancing after dinner at a rural roadhouse, a diminutive of gaiety which his father had estimated too well.

"Oh, no," he said to himself. . . . "No."

He was a dignified, impressive young man, rather stout now, but otherwise unmarked by dissipation. He could have been cast for a pillar of something—at times you were sure it was not society, at others nothing else—for the law, for the church. He stood for a few minutes motionless on the sidewalk in front of a 47th Street apartment-house; for almost the first time in his life he had nothing whatever to do.

Then he began to walk briskly up Fifth Avenue, as if he had just been reminded of an important engagement there. The necessity of dissimulation is one of the few characteristics that we share with dogs, and I think of Anson on that day as some well-bred specimen who had been disappointed at a familiar back door. He was going to see Nick, once a fashionable bartender in demand at all private dances, and now employed in cooling non-alcoholic champagne among the labyrinthine cellars of the Plaza Hotel.

"Nick," he said, "what's happened to everything?"

"Dead," Nick said.

"Make me a whiskey sour." Anson handed a pint bottle over the counter. "Nick, the girls are different; I had a little girl in Brooklyn and she got married last week without letting me know."

"That a fact? Ha-ha-ha," responded Nick diplomatically. "Slipped it over on you."

"Absolutely," said Anson. "And I was not with her the night before."

"Ha-ha-ha," said Nick, "ha-ha-ha!"

"Do you remember the wedding, Nick, in Hot Springs where I had the waiters and the musicians singing 'God save the King'?"

"Now where was that, Mr. Hunter?" Nick concentrated doubtfully. "Seems to me that was—"

"Next time they were back for more, and I began to wonder how much I'd paid them," continued Anson.

"—seems to me that was at Mr. Trenholm's wedding."

"Don't know him," said Anson decisively. He was offended that a strange name should intrude upon his reminiscences; Nick perceived this.

"Naw—aw—" he admitted, "I ought to know that. It was one of your crowd—Brakins . . . Baker—"

"Bicker Baker," said Anson responsively. "They put me in a hearse after it was over and covered me up with flowers and drove me away."

"Ha-ha-ha," said Nick. "Ha-ha-ha."

Nick's simulation of the old family servant paled presently and Anson went upstairs to the lobby. He looked around—his eyes met the glance of an unfamiliar clerk at the desk, then fell upon a flower from the morning's marriage hesitating in the mouth of a brass cuspidor. He went out and walked slowly toward the blood-red sun over Columbus Circle. Suddenly he turned around and, retracing his steps to the Plaza, immured himself in a telephone-booth.

Later he said that he tried to get me three times that afternoon, that he tried everyone who might be in New York—men and girls he had not seen for years, an artist's model of his college days whose faded number was still in his address book—Central told him that even the exchange existed no longer. At length his quest roved into the country, and he held brief disappointing conversations with emphatic butlers and maids. So-and-so was out, riding, swimming, playing golf, sailed to Europe last week. Who shall I say phoned?

It was intolerable that he should pass the evening alone—the private reckonings which one plans for a moment of leisure lose every charm when the solitude is enforced. There were always women of a sort, but the ones he knew had temporarily vanished, and to pass a New York evening in the hired company of a stranger never occurred to him—he would have considered that that was something shameful and secret, the diversion of a travelling salesman in a strange town.

Anson paid the telephone bill—the girl tried unsuccessfully to joke with him about its size—and for the second time that afternoon started to leave the Plaza and go he knew not where. Near the revolving door the figure of a woman, obviously with child, stood sideways to the light—a sheer beige cape fluttered at her shoulders when the door turned and, each time, she looked impatiently toward it as if she were weary of waiting. At the first sight of her a strong nervous thrill of familiarity went over him, but not until he was within five feet of her did he realize that it was Paula.

"Why, Anson Hunter!"

His heart turned over.

"Why, Paula—"

"Why, this is wonderful. I can't believe it, *Anson!*"

She took both his hands, and he saw in the freedom of the gesture that the memory of him had lost poignancy to her. But not to him—he felt that old mood that she evoked in him stealing over his brain, that gentleness with which he had always met her optimism as if afraid to mar its surface.

"We're at Rye for the summer. Pete had to come East on business—you know of course I'm Mrs. Peter Hagerty now—so we brought the children and took a house. You've got to come out and see us."

"Can I?" he asked directly. "When?"

"When you like. Here's Pete." The revolving door functioned, giving up a fine tall man of thirty with a tanned face and a trim mustache. His immaculate fitness made a sharp contrast with Anson's increasing bulk, which was obvious under the faintly tight cutaway coat.

"You oughtn't to be standing," said Hagerty to his wife. "Let's sit down here." He indicated lobby chairs, but Paula hesitated.

"I've got to go right home," she said. "Anson, why don't you—why don't you come out and have dinner with us tonight? We're just getting settled, but if you can stand that—"

Hagerty confirmed the invitation cordially.

"Come out for the night."

Their car waited in front of the hotel, and Paula with a tired gesture sank back against silk cushions in the corner.

"There's so much I want to talk to you about," she said, "it seems hopeless."

"I want to hear about you."

"Well"—she smiled at Hagerty—"that would take a long time too. I have three children—by my first marriage. The oldest is five, then four, then three." She smiled again. "I didn't waste much time having them, did I?"

"Boys?"

"A boy and two girls. Then—oh, a lot of things happened, and I got a divorce in Paris a year ago and married Pete. That's all—except that I'm awfully happy."

In Rye they drove up to a large house near the Beach Club, from which there issued presently three dark, slim children who broke from an English governess and approached them with an esoteric cry. Abstractedly and with difficulty Paula took each one into her arms, a caress which they accepted stiffly, as they had evidently been told not to bump into Mummy. Even against their fresh faces Paula's skin showed scarcely any weariness—for all her physical languor she seemed younger than when he had last seen her at Palm Beach seven years ago.

At dinner she was preoccupied, and afterward, during the homage to the radio, she lay with closed eyes on the sofa, until Anson wondered if his presence at this time were not an intrusion. But at nine o'clock, when Hagerty rose and said pleasantly that he was going to leave them by themselves for a while, she began to talk slowly about herself and the past.

"My first baby," she said—"the one we call Darling, the biggest little girl—I wanted to die when I knew I was going to have her, because Lowell was like a stranger to me. It didn't seem as though she could be my own. I wrote you a letter and tore it up. Oh, you were so bad to me, Anson."

It was the dialogue again, rising and falling. Anson felt a sudden quickening of memory.

"Weren't you engaged once?" she asked —"a girl named Dolly something?"

"I wasn't ever engaged. I tried to be engaged, but I never loved anybody but you, Paula."

"Oh," she said. Then after a moment: "This baby is the first one I ever really wanted. You see, I'm in love now—at last."

He didn't answer, shocked at the treachery of her remembrance. She must have seen that the "at last" bruised him, for she continued:

"I was infatuated with you, Anson—you could make me do anything you liked. But we wouldn't have been happy. I'm not smart enough for you. I don't like things to be complicated like you do." She paused. "You'll never settle down," she said.

The phrase struck at him from behind —it was an accusation that of all accusations he had never merited.

"I could settle down if women were different," he said. "If I didn't understand so much about them, if women didn't spoil you for other women, if they had only a little pride. If I could go to sleep for a while and wake up into a home that was really mine—why, that's what I'm made for, Paula, that's what women have seen in me and liked in me. It's only that I can't get through the preliminaries any more."

Hagerty came in a little before eleven; after a whiskey Paula stood up and announced that she was going to bed. She went over and stood by her husband.

"Where did you go, dearest?" she demanded.

"I had a drink with Ed Saunders."

"I was worried. I thought maybe you'd run away."

She rested her head against his coat.

"He's sweet, isn't he, Anson?" she demanded.

"Absolutely," said Anson, laughing.

She raised her face to her husband.

"Well, I'm ready," she said. She turned

to Anson: "Do you want to see our family gymnastic stunt?"

"Yes," he said in an interested voice.

"All right. Here we go!"

Hagerty picked her up easily in his arms.

"This is called the family acrobatic stunt," said Paula. "He carries me upstairs. Isn't it sweet of him?"

"Yes," said Anson.

Hagerty bent his head slightly until his face touched Paula's.

"And I love him," she said. "I've just been telling you, haven't I, Anson?"

"Yes," he said.

"He's the dearest thing that ever lived in this world; aren't you, darling? . . . Well, good night. Here we go. Isn't he strong?"

"Yes," Anson said.

"You'll find a pair of Pete's pajamas laid out for you. Sweet dreams—see you at breakfast."

"Yes," Anson said.

VIII

The older members of the firm insisted that Anson should go abroad for the summer. He had scarcely had a vacation in seven years, they said. He was stale and needed a change. Anson resisted.

"If I go," he declared, "I won't come back any more."

"That's absurd, old man. You'll be back in three months with all this depression gone. Fit as ever."

"No." He shook his head stubbornly. "If I stop, I won't go back to work. If I stop, that means I've given up—I'm through."

"We'll take a chance on that. Stay six months if you like—we're not afraid you'll leave us. Why, you'd be miserable if you didn't work."

They arranged his passage for him. They liked Anson—every one liked Anson—and the change that had been coming over him cast a sort of pall over the office. The enthusiasm that had invariably signalled up business, the consideration toward his equals and his inferiors, the lift of his vital presence—within the past four months his intense nervousness had melted down these qualities into the fussy pessimism of a man of forty. On every transaction in which he was involved he acted as a drag and a strain.

"If I go I'll never come back," he said.

Three days before he sailed Paula Legendre Hagerty died in childbirth. I was with him a great deal then, for we were crossing together, but for the first time in our friendship he told me not a word of how he felt, nor did I see the slightest sign of emotion. His chief preoccupation was with the fact that he was thirty years old —he would turn the conversation to the point where he could remind you of it and then fall silent, as if he assumed that the statement would start a chain of thought sufficient to itself. Like his partners, I was amazed at the change in him, and I was glad when the *Paris* moved off into the wet space between the worlds, leaving his principality behind.

"How about a drink?" he suggested.

We walked into the bar with that defiant feeling that characterizes the day of departure and ordered four Martinis. After one cocktail a change came over him —he suddenly reached across and slapped my knee with the first joviality I had seen him exhibit for months.

"Did you see that girl in the red tam?" he demanded, "the one with the high color who had the two police dogs down to bid her good-by."

"She's pretty," I agreed.

"I looked her up in the purser's office and found out that she's alone. I'm going down to see the steward in a few minutes. We'll have dinner with her tonight."

After a while he left me, and within an hour he was walking up and down the deck with her, talking to her in his strong, clear voice. Her red tam was a bright spot of color against the steel-green sea, and from time to time she looked up with a flashing bob of her head, and smiled with amusement and interest, and anticipation. At dinner we had champagne, and were very joyous—afterward Anson ran the pool with infectious gusto, and several people who had seen me with him asked me his name. He and the girl were talking and laughing together on a lounge in the bar when I went to bed.

I saw less of him on the trip than I had hoped. He wanted to arrange a foursome, but there was no one available, so I saw him only at meals. Sometimes, though, he would have a cocktail in the bar, and he told me about the girl in the red tam, and his adventures with her, making them all bizarre and amusing, as he had a way of doing, and I was glad he was himself again, or at least the self that I knew, and with which I felt at home. I don't think he was ever happy unless someone was in love with him, responding to him like filings to a magnet, helping him to explain himself, promising him something. What it was I do not know. Perhaps they promised that there would always be women in the world who would spend their brightest, freshest, rarest hours to nurse and protect that superiority he cherished in his heart.

THE BEAR
by William Faulkner

He was ten. But it had already begun, long before that day when at last he wrote his age in two figures and he saw for the first time the camp where his father and Major de Spain and old General Compson and the others spent two weeks each November and two weeks again each June. He had already inherited then, without ever having seen it, the tremendous bear with one trap-ruined foot which, in an area almost a hundred miles deep, had earned for itself a name, a definite designation like a living man.

He had listened to it for years: the long legend of corncribs rifled, of shotes and grown pigs and even calves carried bodily into the woods and devoured, of traps and deadfalls overthrown and dogs mangled and slain, and shotgun and even rifle charges delivered at point-blank range and with no more effect than so many peas blown through a tube by a boy—a corridor of wreckage and destruction beginning back before he was born, through which sped, not fast but rather with the ruthless and irresistible deliberation of a locomotive, the shaggy tremendous shape.

It ran in his knowledge before he ever saw it. It looked and towered in his dreams before he even saw the unaxed woods where it left its crooked print, shaggy, huge, red-eyed, not malevolent but just big—too big for the dogs which tried to bay it, for the horses which tried to ride it down, for the men and the bullets they fired into it, too big for the very country which was its constricting scope. He seemed to see it entire with a

From William Faulkner, *Go Down, Moses*. Copyright, 1942, by William Faulkner. Reprinted by permission of Random House, Inc.

child's complete divination before he ever laid eyes on either—the doomed wilderness whose edges were being constantly and punily gnawed at by men with axes and plows who feared it because it was wilderness, men myriad and nameless even to one another in the land where the old bear had earned a name, through which ran not even a mortal animal but an anachronism, indomitable and invincible, out of an old dead time, a phantom, epitome and apotheosis of the old wild life at which the puny humans swarmed and hacked in a fury of abhorrence and fear, like pygmies about the ankles of a drowsing elephant; the old bear solitary, indomitable and alone, widowered, childless and absolved of mortality—old Priam reft of his old wife and having outlived all his sons.

Until he was ten, each November he would watch the wagon containing the dogs and the bedding and food and guns and his father and Tennie's Jim, the Negro, and Sam Fathers, the Indian, son of a slave woman and a Chickasaw chief, depart on the road to town, to Jefferson, where Major de Spain and the others would join them. To the boy, at seven and eight and nine, they were not going into the Big Bottom to hunt bear and deer, but to keep yearly rendezvous with the bear which they did not even intend to kill. Two weeks later they would return, with no trophy, no head and skin. He had not expected it. He had not even been afraid it would be in the wagon. He believed that even after he was ten and his father would let him go too, for those two November weeks, he would merely make another one, along with his father and Major de Spain and General Compson and the others, the dogs which feared to bay it and the rifles and shotguns which failed even to bleed it, in the yearly pageant of the old bear's furious immortality.

Then he heard the dogs. It was in the second week of his first time in the camp. He stood with Sam Fathers against a big oak beside the faint crossing where they had stood each dawn for nine days now, hearing the dogs. He had heard them once before, one morning last week—a murmur, sourceless, echoing through the wet woods, swelling presently into separate voices which he could recognize and call by name. He had raised and cocked the gun as Sam told him and stood motionless again while the uproar, the invisible course, swept up and past and faded; it seemed to him that he could actually see the deer, the buck, blond, smoke-colored, elongated with speed, fleeing, vanishing, the woods, the gray solitude, still ringing even when the cries of the dogs had died away.

"Now let the hammers down," Sam said.

"You knew they were not coming here too," he said.

"Yes," Sam said. "I want you to learn how to do when you didn't shoot. It's after the chance for the bear or the deer has done already come and gone that men and dogs get killed."

"Anyway," he said, "it was just a deer."

Then on the tenth morning he heard the dogs again. And he readied the too-long, too-heavy gun as Sam had taught him, before Sam even spoke. But this time it was no deer, no ringing chorus of dogs running strong on a free scent, but a moiling yapping an octave too high, with something more than indecision and even abjectness in it, not even moving very fast, taking a long time to pass completely out of hearing, leaving even then somewhere

[296]

The Bear

in the air that echo, thin, slightly hysterical, abject, almost grieving, with no sense of a fleeing, unseen, smoke-colored, grass-eating shape ahead of it, and Sam, who had taught him first of all to cock the gun and take position where he could see everywhere and then never move again, had himself moved up beside him; he could hear Sam breathing at his shoulder and he could see the arched curve of the old man's inhaling nostrils.

"Hah," Sam said. "Not even running. Walking."

"Old Ben!" the boy said. "But up here!" he cried. "Way up here!"

"He do it every year," Sam said. "Once. Maybe to see who in camp this time, if he can shoot or not. Whether we got the dog yet that can bay and hold him. He'll take them to the river, then he'll send them back home. We may as well go back, too; see how they look when they come back to camp."

When they reached the camp the hounds were already there, ten of them crouching back under the kitchen, the boy and Sam squatting to peer back into the obscurity where they huddled, quiet, the eyes luminous, glowing at them and vanishing, and no sound, only that effluvium of something more than dog, stronger than dog and not just animal, just beast, because still there had been nothing in front of that abject and almost painful yapping save the solitude, the wilderness, so that when the eleventh hound came in at noon and with all the others watching—even old Uncle Ash, who called himself first a cook—Sam daubed the tattered ear and the raked shoulder with turpentine and axle grease, to the boy it was still no living creature, but the wilderness which, leaning for the moment down, had patted lightly once the hound's temerity.

"Just like a man," Sam said. "Just like folks. Put off as long as she could having to be brave, knowing all the time that sooner or later she would have to be brave once to keep on living with herself, and knowing all the time beforehand what was going to happen to her when she done it."

That afternoon, himself on the one-eyed wagon mule which did not mind the smell of blood nor, as they told him, of bear, and with Sam on the other one, they rode for more than three hours through the rapid, shortening winter day. They followed no path, no trail even that he could see; almost at once they were in a country which he had never seen before. Then he knew why Sam had made him ride the mule which would not spook. The sound one stopped short and tried to whirl and bolt even as Sam got down, blowing its breath, jerking and wrenching at the rein while Sam held it, coaxing it forward with his voice, since he could not risk tying it, drawing it forward while the boy got down from the marred one.

Then, standing beside Sam in the gloom of the dying afternoon, he looked down at the rotted overturned log, gutted and scored with claw marks and, in the wet earth beside it, the print of the enormous warped two-toed foot. He knew now what he had smelled when he peered under the kitchen where the dogs huddled. He realized for the first time that the bear which had run in his listening and loomed in his dreams since before he could remember to the contrary, and which, therefore, must have existed in the listening and dreams of his father and Major de Spain and even old General Compson, too, before they began to remember in their turn, was a mortal animal, and that if they had departed for the camp each Novem-

[297]

ber without any actual hope of bringing its trophy back, it was not because it could not be slain, but because so far they had had no actual hope to.

"Tomorrow," he said.

"We'll try tomorrow," Sam said. "We ain't got the dog yet."

"We've got eleven. They ran him this morning."

"It won't need but one," Sam said. "He ain't here. Maybe he ain't nowhere. The only other way will be for him to run by accident over somebody that has a gun."

"That wouldn't be me," the boy said. "It will be Walter or Major or—"

"It might," Sam said. "You watch close in the morning. Because he's smart. That's how come he has lived this long. If he gets hemmed up and has to pick out somebody to run over, he will pick out you."

"How?" the boy said. "How will he know—" He ceased. "You mean he already knows me, that I ain't never been here before, ain't had time to find out yet whether I—" He ceased again, looking at Sam, the old man whose face revealed nothing until it smiled. He said humbly, not even amazed, "It was me he was watching. I don't reckon he did need to come but once."

The next morning they left the camp three hours before daylight. They rode this time because it was too far to walk, even the dogs in the wagon; again the first gray light found him in a place which he had never seen before, where Sam had placed him and told him to stay and then departed. With the gun which was too big for him, which did not even belong to him, but to Major de Spain, and which he had fired only once—at a stump on the first day, to learn the recoil and how to reload it—he stood against a gum tree beside a little bayou whose black still water crept without movement out of a canebrake and crossed a small clearing and into cane again, where, invisible, a bird—the big woodpecker called Lord-to-God by Negroes—clattered at a dead limb.

It was a stand like any other, dissimilar only in incidentals to the one where he had stood each morning for ten days; a territory new to him, yet no less familiar than that other one which, after almost two weeks, he had come to believe he knew a little—the same solitude, the same loneliness through which human beings had merely passed without altering it, leaving no mark, no scar, which looked exactly as it must have looked when the first ancestor of Sam Fathers' Chickasaw predecessors crept into it and looked about, club or stone ax or bone arrow drawn and poised; different only because, squatting at the edge of the kitchen, he smelled the hounds huddled and cringing beneath it and saw the raked ear and shoulder of the one who, Sam said, had had to be brave once in order to live with herself, and saw yesterday in the earth beside the gutted log the print of the living foot.

He heard no dogs at all. He never did hear them. He only heard the drumming of the woodpecker stop short off and knew that the bear was looking at him. He never saw it. He did not know whether it was in front of him or behind him. He did not move, holding the useless gun, which he had not even had warning to cock and which even now he did not cock, tasting in his saliva that taint as of brass which he knew now because he had smelled it when he peered under the kitchen at the huddled dogs.

Then it was gone. As abruptly as it had ceased, the woodpecker's dry, monotonous clatter set up again, and after a while he even believed he could hear the dogs—a

The Bear

murmur, scarce a sound even, which he had probably been hearing for some time before he even remarked it, drifting into hearing and then out again, dying away. They came nowhere near him. If it was a bear they ran, it was another bear. It was Sam himself who came out of the cane and crossed the bayou, followed by the injured bitch of yesterday. She was almost at heel, like a bird dog, making no sound. She came and crouched against his leg, trembling, staring off into the cane.

"I didn't see him," he said. "I didn't, Sam!"

"I know it," Sam said. "He done the looking. You didn't hear him neither, did you?"

"No," the boy said. "I—"

"He's smart," Sam said. "Too smart." He looked down at the hound, trembling faintly and steadily against the boy's knee. From the raked shoulder a few drops of fresh blood oozed and clung. "Too big. We ain't got the dog yet. But maybe someday. Maybe not next time. But someday."

So I must see him, he thought. *I must look at him.* Otherwise, it seemed to him that it would go on like this forever, as it had gone on with his father and Major de Spain, who was older than his father, and even with old General Compson, who had been old enough to be a brigade commander in 1865. Otherwise, it would go on so forever, next time and next time, after and after and after. It seemed to him that he could see the two of them, himself and the bear, shadowy in the limbo from which time emerged, becoming time; the old bear absolved of mortality and himself partaking, sharing a little of it, enough of it. And he knew now what he had smelled in the huddled dogs and tasted in his saliva. He recognized fear.

So I will have to see him, he thought, without dread or even hope. *I will have to look at him.*

It was in June of the next year. He was eleven. They were in camp again, celebrating Major de Spain's and General Compson's birthdays. Although the one had been born in September and the other in the depth of winter and in another decade, they had met for two weeks to fish and shoot squirrels and turkey and run coons and wildcats with the dogs at night. That is, he and Boon Hoggenbeck and the Negroes fished and shot squirrels and ran the coons and cats, because the proved hunters, not only Major de Spain and old General Compson, who spent those two weeks sitting in a rocking chair before a tremendous iron pot of Brunswick stew, stirring and tasting, with old Ash to quarrel with about how he was making it and Tennie's Jim to pour whisky from the demijohn into the tin dipper from which he drank it, but even the boy's father and Walter Ewell, who were still young enough, scorned such, other than shooting the wild gobblers with pistols for wagers on their marksmanship.

Or, that is, his father and the others believed he was hunting squirrels. Until the third day he thought that Sam Fathers believed that too. Each morning he would leave the camp right after breakfast. He had his own gun now, a Christmas present. He went back to the tree beside the little bayou where he had stood that morning. Using the compass which old General Compson had given him, he ranged from that point; he was teaching himself to be a better-than-fair woodsman without knowing he was doing it. On the second day he even found the gutted log where he had first seen the crooked print. It was almost completely crumbled now, healing with unbelievable speed, a passionate and almost visible relinquishment, back into the earth from which the tree had grown.

He ranged the summer woods now, green with gloom; if anything, actually dimmer than in November's gray dissolution, where, even at noon, the sun fell only in intermittent dappling upon the earth, which never completely dried out and which crawled with snakes—moccasins and water snakes and rattlers, themselves the color of the dappled gloom, so that he would not always see them until they moved, returning later and later, first day, second day, passing in the twilight of the third evening the little log pen enclosing the log stable where Sam was putting up the horses for the night.

"You ain't looked right yet," Sam said.

He stopped. For a moment he didn't answer. Then he said peacefully, in a peaceful rushing burst as when a boy's miniature dam in a little brook gives way, "All right. But how? I went to the bayou. I even found that log again. I—"

"I reckon that was all right. Likely he's been watching you. You never saw his foot?"

"I," the boy said—"I didn't—I never thought—"

"It's the gun," Sam said. He stood beside the fence, motionless—the old man, the Indian, in the battered faded overalls and the frayed five-cent straw hat which in the Negro's race had been the badge of his enslavement and was now the regalia of his freedom. The camp—the clearing, the house, the barn and its tiny lot with which Major de Spain in his turn had scratched punily and evanescently at the wilderness—faded in the dusk, back into the immemorial darkness of the woods. *The gun,* the boy thought. *The gun.*

"Be scared," Sam said. "You can't help that. But don't be afraid. Ain't nothing in the woods going to hurt you unless you corner it, or it smells that you are afraid. A bear or a deer, too, has got to be scared of a coward the same as a brave man has got to be."

The gun, the boy thought.

"You will have to choose," Sam said.

He left the camp before daylight, long before Uncle Ash would wake in his quilts on the kitchen floor and start the fire for breakfast. He had only the compass and a stick for snakes. He could go almost a mile before he would begin to need the compass. He sat on a log, the invisible compass in his invisible hand, while the secret night sounds, fallen still at his movements, scurried again and then ceased for good, and the owls ceased and gave over to the waking of day birds, and he could see the compass. Then he went fast yet still quietly; he was becoming better and better as a woodsman, still without having yet realized it.

He jumped a doe and a fawn at sunrise, walked them out of the bed, close enough to see them—the crash of undergrowth, the white scut, the fawn scudding behind her faster than he had believed it could run. He was hunting right, upwind, as Sam had taught him; not that it mattered now. He had left the gun; of his own will and relinquishment he had accepted not a gambit, not a choice, but a condition in which not only the bear's heretofore inviolable anonymity but all the old rules and balances of hunter and hunted had been abrogated. He would not even be afraid, not even in the moment when the fear would take him completely —blood, skin, bowels, bones, memory from the long time before it became his memory—all save that thin, clear, quench-

The Bear

less, immortal lucidity which alone differed him from this bear and from all the other bear and deer he would ever kill in the humility and pride of his skill and endurance, to which Sam had spoken when he leaned in the twilight on the lot fence yesterday.

By noon he was far beyond the little bayou, farther into the new and alien country than he had ever been. He was traveling now not only by the compass but by the old, heavy, biscuit-thick silver watch which had belonged to his grandfather. When he stopped at last, it was for the first time since he had risen from the log at dawn when he could see the compass. It was far enough. He had left the camp nine hours ago; nine hours from now, dark would have already been an hour old. But he didn't think that. He thought, *All right. Yes. But what?* and stood for a moment, alien and small in the green and topless solitude, answering his own question before it had formed and ceased. It was the watch, the compass, the stick—the three lifeless mechanicals with which for nine hours he had fended the wilderness off; he hung the watch and compass carefully on a bush and leaned the stick beside them and relinquished completely to it.

He had not been going very fast for the last two or three hours. He went no faster now, since distance would not matter even if he could have gone fast. And he was trying to keep a bearing on the tree where he had left the compass, trying to complete a circle which would bring him back to it or at least intersect itself, since direction would not matter now either. But the tree was not there, and he did as Sam had schooled him—made the next circle in the opposite direction, so that the two patterns would bisect somewhere, but crossing no print of his own feet, finding the tree at last, but in the wrong place—no bush, no compass, no watch—and the tree not even the tree, because there was a down log beside it and he did what Sam Fathers had told him was the next thing and the last.

As he sat down on the log he saw the crooked print—the warped, tremendous, two-toed indentation which, even as he watched it, filled with water. As he looked up, the wilderness coalesced, solidified—the glade, the tree he sought, the bush, the watch and the compass glinting where a ray of sunlight touched them. Then he saw the bear. It did not emerge, appear; it was just there, immobile, solid, fixed in the hot dappling of the green and windless noon, not as big as he had dreamed it, but as big as he had expected it, bigger, dimensionless against the dappled obscurity, looking at him where he sat quietly on the log and looked back at it.

Then it moved. It made no sound. It did not hurry. It crossed the glade, walking for an instant into the full glare of the sun; when it reached the other side it stopped again and looked back at him across one shoulder while his quiet breathing inhaled and exhaled three times.

Then it was gone. It didn't walk into the woods, the undergrowth. It faded sank back into the wilderness as he had watched a fish, a huge old bass, sink and vanish back into the dark depths of its pool without even any movement of its fins.

He thought, *It will be next fall*. But it was not next fall, nor the next nor the next. He was fourteen then. He had killed his buck, and Sam Fathers had marked his face with the hot blood, and in the next year he killed a bear. But even before that accolade he had become as competent in the woods as many grown men with the same experience; by his fourteenth year he was a better woodsman than most grown men with more. There was no territory within thirty miles of the camp that he did not know—bayou, ridge, brake, landmark tree and path. He could have led anyone to any point in it without deviation, and brought them out again. He knew game trails that even Sam Fathers did not know; in his thirteenth year he found a buck's bedding place, and unbeknown to his father he borrowed Walter Ewell's rifle and lay in wait at dawn and killed the buck when it walked back to the bed, as Sam had told him how the old Chickasaw fathers did.

But not the old bear, although by now he knew its footprint better than he did his own, and not only the crooked one. He could see any one of the three sound ones and distinguish it from any other, and not only by its size. There were other bears within those thirty miles which left tracks almost as large, but this was more than that. If Sam Fathers had been his mentor and the back-yard rabbits and squirrels at home his kindergarten, then the wilderness the old bear ran was his college, the old male bear itself, so long unwifed and childless as to have become its own ungendered progenitor, was his alma mater. But he never saw it.

He could find the crooked print now almost whenever he liked, fifteen or ten or five miles, or sometimes nearer the camp than that. Twice while on stand during the three years he heard the dogs strike its trail by accident; on the second time they jumped it seemingly, the voices high, abject, almost human in hysteria, as on that first morning two years ago.

But not the bear itself. He would remember that noon three years ago, the glade, himself and the bear fixed during that moment in the windless and dappled blaze, and it would seem to him that it had never happened, that he had dreamed that too. But it had happened. They had looked at each other, they had emerged from the wilderness old as earth, synchronized to that instant by something more than the blood that moved the flesh and bones which bore them, and touched, pledged something, affirmed something more lasting than the frail web of bones and flesh which any accident could obliterate.

Then he saw it again. Because of the very fact that he thought of nothing else, he had forgotten to look for it. He was still-hunting with Walter Ewell's rifle. He saw it cross the end of a long blowdown, a corridor where a tornado had swept, rushing through rather than over the tangle of trunks and branches as a locomotive would have, faster than he had ever believed it could move, almost as fast as a deer even, because a deer would have spent most of that time in the air, faster than he could bring the rifle sights up to it, so that he believed the reason he never let off the shot was that he was still behind it, had never caught up with it. And now he knew what had been wrong during all the three years. He sat on a log, shaking and trembling as if he had never seen the woods before nor anything that ran them, wondering with incredulous amazement how he could have forgotten the very thing which Sam Fathers had told him and which the bear itself had proved the next day and had now returned after three years to reaffirm.

And he now knew what Sam Fathers had meant about the right dog, a dog in

The Bear

which size would mean less than nothing. So when he returned alone in April—school was out then, so that the sons of farmers could help with the land's planting, and at last his father had granted him permission, on his promise to be back in four days—he had the dog. It was his own, a mongrel of the sort called by Negroes a fyce, a ratter, itself not much bigger than a rat and possessing that bravery which had long since stopped being courage and had become foolhardiness.

It did not take four days. Alone again, he found the trail on the first morning. It was not a stalk; it was an ambush. He timed the meeting almost as if it were an appointment with a human being. Himself holding the fyce muffled in a feed sack and Sam Fathers with two of the hounds on a piece of plowline rope, they lay down wind of the trail at dawn of the second morning. They were so close that the bear turned without even running, as if in surprised amazement at the shrill and frantic uproar of the released fyce, turning at bay against the trunk of a tree, on its hind feet; it seemed to the boy that it would never stop rising, taller and taller, and even the two hounds seemed to take a sort of desperate and despairing courage from the fyce, following it as it went in.

Then he realized that the fyce was actually not going to stop. He flung, threw the gun away, and ran; when he overtook and grasped the frantically pinwheeling little dog, it seemed to him that he was directly under the bear.

He could smell it, strong and hot and rank. Sprawling, he looked up to where it loomed and towered over him like a cloudburst and colored like a thunderclap, quite familiar, peacefully and even lucidly familiar, until he remembered:

This was the way he had used to dream about it. Then it was gone. He didn't see it go. He knelt, holding the frantic fyce with both hands, hearing the abased wailing of the hounds drawing farther and farther away, until Sam came up. He carried the gun. He laid it down quietly beside the boy and stood looking down at him.

"You've done seed him twice now with a gun in your hands," he said. "This time you couldn't have missed him."

The boy rose. He still held the fyce. Even in his arms and clear of the ground, it yapped frantically, straining and surging after the fading uproar of the two hounds like a tangle of wire springs. He was panting a little, but he was neither shaking nor trembling now.

"Neither could you!" he said. "You had the gun! Neither did you!"

"And you didn't shoot," his father said. "How close were you?"

"I don't know, sir," he said. "There was a big wood tick inside his right hind leg. I saw that. But I didn't have the gun then."

"But you didn't shoot when you had the gun," his father said. "Why?"

But he didn't answer, and his father didn't wait for him to, rising and crossing the room, across the pelt of the bear which the boy had killed two years ago and the larger one which his father had killed before he was born, to the bookcase beneath the mounted head of the boy's first buck. It was the room which his father called the office, from which all the plantation business was transacted; in it for the fourteen years of his life he had heard the best of all talking. Major de Spain would be there and sometimes old General Compson, and Walter Ewell and Boon Hoggenbeck and Sam Fathers and Tennie's Jim, too, because they, too, were hunters, knew the woods and what ran them.

He would hear it, not talking himself but listening—the wilderness, the big woods, bigger and older than any recorded document of white man fatuous enough to believe he had bought any fragment of it or Indian ruthless enough to pretend that any fragment of it had been his to convey. It was of the men, not white nor black nor red, but men, hunters with the will and hardihood to endure and the humility and skill to survive, and the dogs and the bear and deer juxtaposed and reliefed against it, ordered and compelled by and within the wilderness in the ancient and unremitting contest by the ancient and immitigable rules which voided all regrets and brooked no quarter, the voices quiet and weighty and deliberate for retrospection and recollection and exact remembering, while he squatted in the blazing firelight as Tennie's Jim squatted, who stirred only to put more wood on the fire and to pass the bottle from one glass to another. Because the bottle was always present, so that after a while it seemed to him that those fierce instants of heart and brain and courage and wiliness and speed were concentrated and distilled into that brown liquor which not women, not boys and children, but only hunters drank, drinking not of the blood they had spilled but some condensation of the wild immortal spirit, drinking it moderately, humbly even, not with the pagan's base hope of acquiring thereby the virtues of cunning and strength and speed, but in salute to them.

His father returned with the book and sat down again and opened it. "Listen," he said. He read the five stanzas aloud, his voice quiet and deliberate in the room where there was no fire now because it was already spring. Then he looked up. The boy watched him. "All right," his father said. "Listen." He read again, but only the second stanza this time, to the end of it, the last two lines, and closed the book and put it on the table beside him. "'She cannot fade, though thou hast not thy bliss, for ever wilt thou love, and she be fair,'" he said.

"He's talking about a girl," the boy said.

"He had to talk about something," his father said. Then he said, "He was talking about truth. Truth doesn't change. Truth is one thing. It covers all things which touch the heart—honor and pride and pity and justice and courage and love. Do you see now?"

He didn't know. Somehow it was simpler than that. There was an old bear, fierce and ruthless, not merely just to stay alive, but with the fierce pride of liberty and freedom, proud enough of that liberty and freedom to see it threatened without fear or even alarm; nay, who at times even seemed deliberately to put that freedom and liberty in jeopardy in order to savor them, to remind his old strong bones and flesh to keep supple and quick to defend and preserve them. There was an old man, son of a Negro slave and an Indian king, inheritor on the one side of the long chronicle of a people who had learned humility through suffering, and pride through the endurance which survived the suffering and injustice, and on the other side, the chronicle of a people even longer in the land than the first, yet who no longer existed in the land at all save in the solitary brotherhood of an old Negro's alien blood and the wild and invincible spirit of an old bear. There was a boy who wished to learn humility and pride in order to become skillful and

The Bear

worthy in the woods, who suddenly found himself becoming so skillful so rapidly that he feared he would never become worthy because he had not learned humility and pride, although he had tried to, until one day and as suddenly he discovered that an old man who could not have defined either had led him, as though by the hand, to that point where an old bear and a little mongrel dog showed him that, by possessing one thing other, he would possess them both.

And a little dog, nameless and mongrel and many-fathered, grown, yet weighing less than six pounds, saying as if to itself, "I can't be dangerous, because there's nothing much smaller than I am; I can't be fierce, because they would call it just noise; I can't be humble, because I'm already too close to the ground to genuflect; I can't be proud, because I wouldn't be near enough to it for anyone to know who was casting that shadow, and I don't even know that I'm not going to heaven, because they have already decided that I don't possess an immortal soul. So all I can be is brave. But it's all right. I can be that, even if they still call it just noise."

That was all. It was simple, much simpler than somebody talking in a book about a youth and a girl he would never need to grieve over, because he could never approach any nearer her and would never have to get any farther away. He had heard about a bear, and finally got big enough to trail it, and he trailed it four years and at last met it with a gun in his hands and he didn't shoot. Because a little dog— But he could have shot long before the little dog covered the twenty yards to where the bear waited, and Sam Fathers could have shot at any time during that interminable minute while Old Ben stood on his hind feet over them. He stopped. His father was watching him gravely across the spring-rife twilight of the room; when he spoke, his words were as quiet as the twilight, too, not loud, because they did not need to be, because they would last: "Courage, and honor, and pride," his father said, "and pity, and love of justice and of liberty. They all touch the heart, and what the heart holds to becomes truth, as far as we know truth. Do you see now?"

Sam, and Old Ben, and Nip, he thought. And himself too. He had been all right too. His father had said so. "Yes, sir," he said.

[305]

Mt. Kilimanjaro, in Tanganyika, called "House of God" by the Masai people

Photo from THREE LIONS

THE SNOWS OF KILIMANJARO

by Ernest Hemingway

Kilimanjaro is a snow-covered mountain 19,710 feet high, and is said to be the highest mountain in Africa. Its western summit is called the Masai "Ngàje Ngài," the House of God. Close to the western summit there is the dried and frozen carcass of a leopard. No one has explained what the leopard was seeking at that altitude.

"The marvellous thing is that it's painless," he said. "That's how you know when it starts."

"Is it really?"

"Absolutely. I'm awfully sorry about the odor, though. That must bother you."

"Don't! Please don't."

"Look at them," he said. "Now is it sight or is it scent that brings them like that?"

The cot the man lay on was in the wide shade of a mimosa tree and as he looked out past the shade onto the glare of the plain there were three of the big birds squatted obscenely, while in the sky a dozen more sailed, making quiet moving shadows as they passed.

"They've been there since the day the truck broke down," he said. "Today's the first time any have lit on the ground. I watched the way they sailed very carefully at first in case I ever wanted to use them in a story. That's funny now."

"I wish you wouldn't," she said.

"I'm only talking," he said. "It's much easier if I talk. But I don't want to bother you."

"You know it doesn't bother me," she said. "It's that I've gotten so very nervous not being able to do anything. I think we might make it as easy as we can until the plane comes."

"Or until the plane doesn't come."

"Please tell me what I can do. There must be something I can do."

"You can take the leg off and that might stop it, though I doubt it. Or you can shoot me. You're a good shot now. I taught you to shoot, didn't I?"

"Please don't talk that way. Couldn't I read to you?"

"Read what?"

"Anything in the book bag that we haven't read."

"I can't listen to it," he said. "Talking is the easiest. We quarrel and that makes the time pass."

"I don't quarrel. I never want to quarrel. Let's not quarrel any more. No matter how nervous we get. Maybe they will be back with another truck today. Maybe the plane will come."

"I don't want to move," the man said. "There is no sense in moving now except to make it easier for you."

"That's cowardly."

"Can't you let a man die as comfortably as he can without calling him names? What's the use of slanging me?"

"You're not going to die."

"Don't be silly. I'm dying now. Ask those bastards." He looked over to where the huge, filthy birds sat, their naked heads sunk in the hunched feathers. A fourth planed down, to run quick-legged and then waddle slowly toward the others.

Reprinted from *The Fifth Column and The First Forty-nine Stories* by Ernest Hemingway; copyright 1938 by Ernest Hemingway; used by permission of the publishers, Charles Scribner's Sons.

"They are around every camp. You never notice them. You can't die if you don't give up."

"Where did you read that? You're such a bloody fool."

"You might think about someone else."

"For Christ's sake," he said, "that's been my trade."

He lay then and was quiet for a while and looked across the heat shimmer of the plain to the edge of the bush. There were a few Tommies that showed minute and white against the yellow and, far off, he saw a herd of zebra, white against the green of the bush. This was a pleasant camp under big trees against a hill, with good water, and close by, a nearly dry waterhole where sand grouse flighted in the mornings.

"Wouldn't you like me to read?" she asked. She was sitting on a canvas chair beside his cot. "There's a breeze coming up."

"No, thanks."

"Maybe the truck will come."

"I don't give a damn about the truck."

"I do."

"You give a damn about so many things that I don't."

"Not so many, Harry."

"What about a drink?"

"It's supposed to be bad for you. It said in Black's to avoid all alcohol. You shouldn't drink."

"Molo!" he shouted.

"Yes, Bwana."

"Bring whiskey-soda."

"Yes, Bwana."

"You shouldn't," she said. "That's what I mean by giving up. It says it's bad for you. I know it's bad for you."

"No," he said. "It's good for me."

So now it was all over, he thought. So now he would never have a chance to finish it. So this was the way it ended in a bickering over a drink. Since the gangrene started in his right leg, he had no pain and with the pain the horror had gone, and all he felt now was a great tiredness and anger that this was the end of it. For this, that now was coming, he had very little curiosity. For years it had obsessed him; but now it meant nothing in itself. It was strange how easy being tired enough made it.

Now he would never write the things that he had saved to write until he knew enough to write them well. Well, he would not have to fail at trying to write them either. Maybe you could never write them, and that was why you put them off and delayed the starting. Well, he would never know, now.

"I wish we'd never come," the woman said. She was looking at him holding the glass and biting her lip. "You never would have gotten anything like this in Paris. You always said you loved Paris. We could have stayed in Paris or gone anywhere. I'd have gone anywhere. I said I'd go anywhere you wanted. If you wanted to shoot, we could have gone shooting in Hungary and been comfortable."

"Your bloody money," he said.

"That's not fair," she said. "It was always yours as much as mine. I left everything and I went wherever you wanted to go and I've done what you wanted to do. But I wish we'd never come here."

"You said you loved it."

"I did when you were all right. But now I hate it. I don't see why that had to happen to your leg. What have we done to have that happen to us?"

"I suppose what I did was to forget to put iodine on it when I first scratched it. Then I didn't pay any attention to it because I never infect. Then, later, when it got bad, it was probably using that weak carbolic solution when the other antiseptics

Character is dying on the plains, and keeps looking to the mountains. Character had ambitions, ideals and like the leopard he dies.

The Snows of Kilimanjaro

traditional techniques.

ran out that paralyzed the minute blood vessels and started the gangrene." He looked at her, "What else?"

"I don't mean that."

"If we would have hired a good mechanic instead of a half-baked kikuyu driver, he would have checked the oil and never burned out that bearing in the truck."

"I don't mean that."

"If you hadn't left your own people, your goddamned Old Westbury, Saratoga, Palm Beach people to take me on—"

"Why, I loved you. That's not fair. I love you now. I'll always love you. Don't you love me?"

"No," said the man. "I don't think so. I never have."

"Harry, what are you saying? You're out of your head."

"No. I haven't any head to go out of."

"Don't drink that," she said. "Darling, please don't drink that. We have to do everything we can."

"You do it," he said. "I'm tired."

Now in his mind he saw a railway station at Karagatch and he was standing with his pack and that was the headlight of the Simplon-Orient cutting the dark now and he was leaving Thrace then after the retreat. That was one of the things he had saved to write, with, in the morning at breakfast, looking out the window and seeing snow on the mountains in Bulgaria and Nansen's Secretary asking the old man if it were snow and the old man looking at it and saying, No, that's not snow. It's too early for snow. And the Secretary repeating to the other girls, No, you see. It's not snow and them all saying, It's not snow we were mistaken. But it was the snow all right and he sent them on into it when he evolved exchange of populations. And it was snow they tramped along in until they died that winter.

It was snow too that fell all Christmas week that year up in the Gauertal, that year they lived in the wood-cutter's house with the big square porcelain stove that filled half the room, and they slept on mattresses filled with beech leaves, the time the deserter came with his feet bloody in the snow. He said the police were right behind him and they gave him woolen socks and held the gendarmes talking until the tracks had drifted over.

In Schrunz, on Christmas day, the snow was so bright it hurt your eyes when you looked out from the Weinstube and saw every one coming home from church. That was where they walked up the sleigh-smoothed urine-yellowed road along the river with the steep pine hills, skis heavy on the shoulder, and where they ran that great run down the glacier above the Madlener-Haus, the snow as smooth to see as cake frosting and as light as powder and he remembered the noiseless rush the speed made as you dropped down like a bird.

They were snow-bound a week in the Madlener-Haus that time in the blizzard playing cards in the smoke by the lantern light and the stakes were higher all the time as Herr Lent lost more. Finally he lost it all. Everything, the skischule money and all the season's profit and then his capital. He could see him with his long nose, picking up the cards and then opening, "Sans Voir." There was always gambling then. When there was no snow you gambled and when there was too much you gambled. He thought of all the time in his life he had spent gambling.

But he had never written a line of that, nor of that cold, bright Christmas day with the mountains showing across the plain that Barker had flown across the lines to bomb the Austrian officers' leave train, machine-gunning them as they scattered and ran. He remembered Barker afterwards coming into the mess and starting to tell about it. And how quiet it got and then somebody saying, "You bloody murderous bastard."

Those were the same Austrians they killed then that he skied with later. No not the same. Hans, that he skied with all that year, had been in the Kaiser-Jägers and when they went hunting hares together up the little valley above the sawmill they had talked of the fighting on Pasubio and of the attack on Pertica and Asalone and he had never written a word of that. Nor of Monte Corno, nor the Siete Commum, nor of Arsiedo.

How many winters had he lived in the Voralberg and the Arlberg? It was four and then he remembered the man who had the fox to sell when they had walked into Bludenz, that time to buy presents, and the cherry-pit taste of good kirsch, the fast-slipping rush of running powder-snow on crust, singing "Hi! Ho! said Rolly!" as you ran down the last stretch to the steep drop, taking it straight, then running the orchard in three turns and out across the ditch and onto the icy road behind the inn. Knocking your bindings loose, kicking the skis free and leaning them up against the wooden wall of the inn, the lamplight coming from the window, where inside, in the smoky, new-wine smelling warmth, they were playing the accordion.

"Where did we stay in Paris?" he asked the woman who was sitting by him in a canvas chair, now, in Africa.

"At the Crillon. You know that."

"Why do I know that?"

"That's where we always stayed."

"No. Not always."

"There and at the Pavillon Henri-Quatre in St. Germain. You said you loved it there."

"Love is a dunghill," said Harry. "And I'm the cock that gets on it to crow."

"If you have to go away," she said, "is it absolutely necessary to kill off everything you leave behind? I mean do you have to take away everything? Do you have to kill your horse, and your wife, and burn your saddle and your armour?"

"Yes," he said. "Your damned money was my armour. My Swift and my Armour."

"Don't."

"All right. I'll stop that. I don't want to hurt you."

"It's a little bit late now."

"All right, then. I'll go on hurting you. It's more amusing. The only thing I ever really liked to do with you I can't do now."

"No, that's not true. You liked to do many things and everything you wanted to do I did."

"Oh, for Christ sake stop bragging, will you?"

He looked at her and saw her crying.

"Listen," he said. "Do you think that it is fun to do this? I don't know why I'm doing it. It's trying to kill to keep yourself alive, I imagine. I was all right when we started talking. I didn't mean to start this, and now I'm crazy as a coot and being as cruel to you as I can be. Don't pay any attention, darling, to what I say. I love you, really. You know I love you. I've never loved any one else the way I love you."

He slipped into the familiar lie he made his bread and butter by.

"You're sweet to me."

"You bitch," he said. "You rich bitch. That's poetry. I'm full of poetry now. Rot and poetry. Rotten poetry."

[310]

The Snows of Kilimanjaro

"Stop it. Harry, why do you have to turn into a devil now?"

"I don't like to leave anything," the man said. "I don't like to leave things behind."

It was evening now and he had been asleep. The sun was gone behind the hill and there was a shadow all across the plain and the small animals were feeding close to camp; quick-dropping heads and switching tails, he watched them keeping well out away from the bush now. The birds no longer waited on the ground. They were all perched heavily in a tree. There were many more of them. His personal boy was sitting by the bed.

"Memsahib's gone to shoot," the boy said. "Does Bwana want?"

"Nothing."

She had gone to kill a piece of meat and, knowing how he liked to watch the game, she had gone well away so she would not disturb this little pocket of the plain that he could see. She was always thoughtful, he thought. On anything she knew about, or had read, or that she had ever heard.

It was not her fault that when he went to her he was already over. How could a woman know that you meant nothing that you said; that you spoke only from habit and to be comfortable? After he no longer meant what he said, his lies were more successful with women than when he had told them the truth.

It was not so much that he lied as that there was no truth to tell. He had had his life and it was over and then he went on living it again with different people and more money, with the best of the same places, and some new ones.

You kept from thinking and it was all marvellous. You were equipped with good insides so that you did not go to pieces that way, the way most of them had, and you made an attitude that you cared nothing for the work you used to do, now that you could no longer do it. But, in yourself, you said that you would write about these people; about the very rich; that you were really not of them but a spy in their country; that you would leave it and write of it and for once it would be written by someone who knew what he was writing of. But he would never do it, because each day of not writing, of comfort, of being that which he despised, dulled his ability and softened his will to work so that, finally, he did no work at all. The people he knew now were all much more comfortable when he did not work. Africa was where he had been happiest in the good time of his life, so he had come out here to start again. They had made this safari with the minimum of comfort. There was no hardship; but there was no luxury and he had thought that he could get back into training that way. That in some way he could work the fat off his soul the way a fighter went into the mountains to work and train in order to burn it out of his body.

She had liked it. She said she loved it. She loved anything that was exciting, that involved a change of scene, where there were new people and where things were pleasant. And he had felt the illusion of returning strength of will to work. Now if this was how it ended, and he knew it was, he must not turn like some snake biting itself because its back was broken. It wasn't this woman's fault. If it had not been she, it would have been another. If he lived by a lie, he should try to die by it. He heard a shot beyond the hill.

She shot very well, this good, this rich bitch, this kindly caretaker and destroyer of his talent. Nonsense. He had destroyed his talent himself. Why should he blame this woman because she kept him well? He had destroyed his talent by not using it, by betrayals of himself and what he believed in, by drinking so much that he blunted the edge of his perceptions, by laziness, by sloth, and by snobbery, by pride and by prejudice, by hook and by crook. What was this? A catalogue of old books? What was his talent anyway? It was a talent all right, but instead of using it, he had traded on it. It was never what he had done, but always what he could do. And he had chosen to make his living with something else instead of a pen or a pencil. It was strange, too, wasn't it, that when he fell in love with another woman, that woman should always have more money than the last one? But when he no longer was in love, when he was only lying, as to this woman, now, who had the most money of all, who had all the money there was, who had had a husband and children, who had taken lovers and been dissatisfied with them, and who loved him dearly as a writer, as a man, as a companion, and as a proud possession; it was strange that, when he did not love her at all and was lying, he should be able to give her more for her money than when he had really loved.

We must all be cut out for what we do, he thought. However you make your living is where your talent lies. He had sold vitality, in one form or another, all his life, and when your affections are not too involved you give much better value for the money. He had found that out, but he would never write that, now, either. No, he would not write that, although it was well worth writing.

Now she came in sight, walking across the open toward the camp. She was wearing jodhpurs and carrying her rifle. The two boys had a Tommy slung and they were coming along behind her. She was still a good-looking woman, he thought, and she had a pleasant body. She had a great talent and appreciation for the bed, she was not pretty, but he liked her face, she read enormously, liked to ride and shoot and, certainly, she drank too much. Her husband had died when she was still a comparatively young woman and for a while she had devoted herself to her two just-grown children, who did not need her and were embarrassed at having her about, to her stable of horses, to books, and to bottles. She liked to read in the evening before dinner and she drank Scotch-and-soda while she read. By dinner she was fairly drunk and after a bottle of wine at dinner she was usually drunk enough to sleep.

That was before the lovers. After she had the lovers, she did not drink so much because she did not have to be drunk to sleep. But the lovers bored her. She had been married to a man who had never bored her and these people bored her very much.

Then one of her two children was killed in a plane crash and after that was over she did not want the lovers, and drink being no anaesthetic she had to make another life. Suddenly, she had been acutely frightened of being alone. But she wanted someone that she respected with her.

It had begun very simply. She liked what he wrote and she had always envied the life he led. She thought he did exactly what he wanted to. The steps by which she had acquired him and the way in which she had finally fallen in love with him were all part of a regular progression in which she had built herself a new life and he had traded away what remained of his old life.

He had traded it for security, for comfort, too, there was no denying that, and for what else? He did not know. She would have bought him anything he wanted. He knew that. She was a damned nice woman too. He would as soon be in bed with her as anyone; rather with her, because she was richer, because she was very pleasant and appreciative, and because she never made scenes. And now this life that she had built again was coming to a term because he had not used iodine two weeks ago when a thorn had scratched his knee as they moved forward trying to photograph a herd of waterbuck standing, their heads up, peering while their nostrils searched the air, their ears spread wide to hear the first noise that would send them rushing into the bush. They had bolted, too, before he got the picture.

Here she came now.

He turned his head on the cot to look toward her. "Hello," he said.

"I shot a Tommy ram," she told him. "He'll make you good broth and I'll have them mash some potatoes with the Klim. How do you feel?"

"Much better."

"Isn't that lovely? You know I thought perhaps you would. You were sleeping when I left."

"I had a good sleep. Did you walk far?"

"No. Just around behind the hill. I made quite a good shot on the Tommy."

"You shoot marvellously, you know."

"I love it. I've loved Africa. Really. If *you're* all right it's the most fun that I've ever had. You don't know the fun it's been to shoot with you. I've loved the country."

"I love it too."

"Darling, you don't know how marvelous it is to see you feeling better. I couldn't stand it when you felt that way. You won't talk to me like that again, will you? Promise me?"

"No," he said. "I don't remember what I said."

"You don't have to destroy me. Do you? I'm only a middle-aged woman who loves you and wants to do what you want to do. I've been destroyed two or three times already. You wouldn't want to destroy me again, would you?"

"I'd like to destroy you a few times in bed," he said.

"Yes. That's the good destruction. That's the way we're made to be destroyed. The plane will be here tomorrow."

"How do you know?"

"I'm sure. It's bound to come. The boys have the wood all ready and the grass to make the smudge. I went down and looked at it again today. There's plenty of room to land and we have the smudges ready at both ends."

"What makes you think it will come tomorrow?"

"I'm sure it will. It's overdue now. Then, in town, they will fix up your leg and then we will have some good destruction. Not that dreadful talking kind."

"Should we have a drink? The sun is down."

"Do you think you should?"

"I'm having one."

"We'll have one together. *Molo, letti dui whiskey-soda!*" she called.

"You'd better put on your mosquito boots," he told her.

"I'll wait till I bathe . . ."

While it grew dark they drank and just before it was dark and there was no longer enough light to shoot, a hyena crossed the open on his way around the hill.

"That bastard crosses there every night," the man said. "Every night for two weeks."

"He's the one makes the noise at night. I don't mind it. They're a filthy animal, though."

Drinking together, with no pain now except the discomfort of lying in the one position, the boys lighting a fire, its shadow jumping on the tents, he could feel the return of acquiescence in this life of pleasant surrender. She *was* very good to him. He had been cruel and unjust in the afternoon. She was a fine woman, marvelous really. And just then it occured to him that he was going to die.

It came with a rush; not as a rush of water nor of wind; but of a sudden evil-smelling emptiness and the odd thing was that the hyena slipped lightly along the edge of it.

"What is it, Harry?" she asked him.

"Nothing," he said. "You had better move over to the other side. To windward."

"Did Molo change the dressing?"

"Yes. I'm just using the boric now."

"How do you feel?"

"A little wobbly."

"I'm going in to bathe," she said. "I'll be right out. I'll eat with you and then we'll put the cot in."

So, he said to himself, we did well to stop the quarreling. He had never quarreled much with this woman, while with the women that he loved he had quarreled so much they had finally, always, with the corrosion of the quarreling, killed what they had together. He had loved too much, demanded too much, and he wore it all out.

He thought about alone in Constantinople that time, having quarreled in Paris before he had gone out. He had whored the whole time and then, when that was over, and he had failed to kill his loneliness, but only made it worse, he had written her, the first one, the one who left him, a letter telling her how he had never been able to kill it. . . . How when he thought he saw her outside the Régence one time it made him go all faint and sick inside, and that he would follow a woman who looked like her in some way, along the Boulevard, afraid to see it was not she, afraid to lose the feeling it gave him. How everyone he had slept with had only made him miss her more. How what she had done could never matter since he knew he could not cure himself of loving her. He wrote this letter at the Club, cold sober, and mailed it to New York asking her to write him at the office in Paris. That seemed safe. And that night, missing her so much it made him feel hollow sick inside, he wandered up past Taxim's, picked a girl up and took her out to supper. He had gone to a place to dance with her afterward, she danced badly, and left her for a hot Armenian slut, that swung her belly against him so it almost scalded. He took her away from a British gunner subaltern after a row. The gunner asked him outside and they fought in the street on the cobbles in the dark. He'd hit him twice, hard, on the side of the jaw and when he didn't go down he knew he was in for a fight. The gunner hit him in the body, then beside his eye. He swung with his left again and landed and the gunner fell on him and grabbed his coat and tore the sleeve off and he clubbed him twice behind the ear and then smashed him with his right as he pushed him away. When the gunner went down his head hit first and he ran with the girl because they heard the M.P.'s coming. They got into a taxi and drove out to Rimmily Hissa along the Bosphorus, and around, and back in the cool night and went to bed and she felt as overripe as she looked but smooth, rose-petal, syrupy, smooth-bellied, big-breasted, and needed no pillow under her buttocks, and he left her before she was awake looking blowzy enough in the first daylight and turned up at the Pera Palace with a black eye, carrying his coat because one sleeve was missing.

That same night he left for Anatolia and he remembered, later on that trip, riding all day through fields of the poppies that they raised for opium and how strange it made you feel, finally, and all the distances seemed wrong, to where they had made the attack with the newly arrived Constantine officers, that did not know a goddamned thing, and the artillery had fired into the troops and the British observer had cried like a child.

That was the day he'd first seen dead men wearing white ballet skirts and upturned shoes with pompons on them. The Turks had come steadily and lumpily and he had seen the skirted men running and the officers shooting into them and running then themselves, and he and the British observer had run, too, until his lungs ached and his mouth was full of the taste of pennies, and they stopped behind some rocks and there were the Turks coming as lumpily as ever. Later he had seen the things that he could never think of and later still he had seen much worse. So when he got back to Paris that time he could not talk about it or stand to have it mentioned. And there in the café as he passed was that American poet with a pile of saucers in front of him and a stupid look on his potato face talking about the Dada movement with a Roumanian who said his name was Tristan Tzara, who always wore a monocle and had a headache, and, back at the apartment with his wife that now he loved again, the quarrel all over, the madness all over, glad to be home, the office sent his mail up to the flat. So then the letter in answer to the one he'd written came in on a platter one morning and when he saw the handwriting he went cold all over and tried to slip the letter underneath another. But his wife said, "Who is that letter from, dear?" and that was the end of the beginning of that.

He remembered the good times with them all, and the quarrels. They always picked the finest places to have the quarrels. And why had they always quarreled when he was feeling best? He had never written any of that because, at first, he never wanted to hurt anyone and then it seemed as though there was enough to write without it. But he had always thought that he would write it finally. There was so much to write. He had seen the world change; not just the events; although he had seen many of them and had watched the people, but he had seen the subtler change and he could remember how the people were at different times. He had been in it and he had watched it and it was his duty to write of it; but now he never would.

"How do you feel?" she said. She had come out from the tent now after her bath.

"All right."

"Could you eat now?" He saw Molo behind her with the folding table and the other boy with the dishes.

"I want to write," he said.

"You ought to take some broth to keep your strength up."

"I'm going to die tonight," he said. "I don't need my strength up."

"Don't be melodramatic, Harry, please," she said.

"Why don't you use your nose? I'm rotted halfway up my thigh now. What the hell should I fool with broth for? Molo bring whiskey-soda."

"Please take the broth," she said gently.

"All right."

The broth was too hot. He had to hold it in the cup until it cooled enough to take it and then he just got it down without gagging.

"You're a fine woman," he said. "Don't pay any attention to me."

She looked at him with her well-known, well-loved face from *Spur* and *Town and Country,* only a little the worse for drink, only a little the worse for bed, but *Town and Country* never showed those good breasts and those useful thighs and those lightly small-of-back-caressing hands, and as he looked and saw her well-known pleasant smile, he felt death come again. This time there was no rush. It was a puff, as of a wind that makes a candle flicker and the flame go tall.

"They can bring my net out later and hang it from the tree and build the fire up. I'm not going in the tent tonight. It's not worth moving. It's a clear night. There won't be any rain."

So this was how you died, in whispers that you did not hear. Well, there would be no more quarreling. He could promise that. The one experience that he had never had he was not going to spoil now. He probably would. You spoiled everything. But perhaps he wouldn't.

"You can't take dictation, can you?"

"I never learned," she told him.

"That's all right."

There wasn't time, of course, although it seemed as though it telescoped so that you might put it all into one paragraph if you could get it right.

There was a log house, chinked white with mortar, on a hill above the lake. There was a bell on a pole by the door to call the people in to meals. Behind the house were fields and behind the fields was the timber. A line of Lombardy poplars ran from the house to the dock. Other poplars ran along the point. A road went up to the hills along the edge of the timber and along that road he picked blackberries. Then that log house was burned down and all the guns that had been on deer foot racks above the open fire place were burned and afterwards their barrels, with the lead melted in the magazines, and the stocks burned away, lay out on the heap of ashes that were used to make lye for the big iron soap kettles, and you asked Grandfather if you could have them to play with, and he said, no. You see they were his guns still and he never bought any others. Nor did he hunt any more. The house was rebuilt in the same place out of lumber now and painted white and from its porch you saw the poplars and the lake beyond; but there were never any more guns. The barrels of the guns that had hung on the deer feet on the wall of the log house lay out there on the heap of ashes and no one ever touched them.

In the Black Forest, after the war, we rented a trout stream and there were two ways to walk to it. One was down the valley from Triberg and around the valley road in the shade of the trees that bordered the white road, and then up a side road that went up through the hills past many small farms, with the big Schwarzwald houses, until that road crossed the stream. That was where our fishing began.

The other way was to climb steeply up to the edge of the woods and then go across the top of the hills through the pine woods, and then out to the edge of a meadow and down across this meadow to the bridge. There were birches along the stream and it was not big, but narrow, clear and fast, with pools where it had cut under the roots of the birches. At the hotel in Triberg the proprietor had a fine season. It was very pleasant and we were all great friends. The next year came the inflation and the money he had made the year before was not enough to buy sup-

plies to open the hotel and he hanged himself.

You could dictate that, but you could not dictate the Place Contrescarpe where the flower sellers dyed their flowers in the street and the dye ran over the paving where the autobus started and the old men and the women, always drunk on wine and bad marc; and the children with their noses running in the cold; the smell of dirty sweat and poverty and drunkenness at the Café des Amateurs and the whores at the Bal Musette they lived above. The Concierge who entertained the trooper of the Garde Républicaine in her loge, his horsehair plumed helmet on a chair. The locataire across the hall whose husband was a bicycle racer and her joy that morning at the Crémerie when she had opened L'Auto and seen where he placed third in Paris-Tours, his first big race. She had blushed and laughed and then gone upstairs crying with the yellow sporting paper in her hand. The husband of the woman who ran the Bal Musette drove a taxi, and when he, Harry, had to take an early plane the husband knocked upon the door to wake him and they each drank a glass of white wine at the zinc of the bar before they started. He knew his neighbors in that quarter then because they all were poor.

Around that Place there were two kinds; the drunkards and the sportifs. The drunkards killed their poverty that way; the sportifs took it out in exercise. They were the descendants of the Communards and it was no struggle for them to know their politics. They knew who had shot their fathers, their relatives, their brothers, and their friends when the Versailles troops came in and took the town after the Commune and executed anyone they could catch with calloused hands, or who wore a cap, or carried any other sign he was a workingman. And in that poverty, and in that quarter across the street from a Boucherie Chevaline and a wine co-operative, he had written the start of all he was to do. There never was another part of Paris that he loved like that, the sprawling trees, the old white plastered houses painted brown below, the long green of the autobus in that round square, the purple flower dye upon the paving, the sudden drop down the hill of the rue Cardinal Lemoine to the river, and the other way the narrow crowded world of the rue Mouffetard. The street that ran up toward the Pantheon and the other that he always took with the bicycle, the only asphalted street in all that quarter, smooth under the tires, with the high narrow houses and the cheap tall hotel where Paul Verlaine had died. There were only two rooms in the apartments where they lived and he had a room on the top floor of that hotel that cost him sixty francs a month where he did his writing, and from it he could see the roofs and chimney pots and all the hills of Paris.

From the apartment you could only see the wood and coal man's place. He sold wine too, bad wine. The golden horse's head outside the Boucherie Chevaline where the carcasses hung yellow gold and red in the open window, and the green painted co-operative where they bought their wine; good wine and cheap. The rest was plaster walls and the windows of the neighbors. The neighbors who, at night, when some one lay drunk in the street, moaning and groaning in that typical French *ivresse* that you were propaganded to believe did not exist, would open their windows and then the murmur of talk.

"Where is the policeman? When you don't want him the bugger is always there. He's sleeping with some concierge. Get *the* Agent." *Till some one threw a bucket of water from a window and the moaning stopped.* "*What's that? Water. Ah, that's intelligent.*" *And the windows shutting. Marie, his femme de ménage, protesting against the eight-hour day saying,* "*If a husband works until six he gets only a little drunk on the way home and does not waste too much. If he works only until five he is drunk every night and one has no money. It is the wife of the workingman who suffers from this shortening of hours.*"

"Wouldn't you like some more broth?" the woman asked him now.

"No, thank you very much. It is awfully good."

"Try just a little."

"I would like a whiskey-soda."

"It's not good for you."

"No. It's bad for me. Cole Porter wrote the words and the music. This knowledge that you're going mad for me."

"You know I like you to drink."

"Oh, yes. Only it's bad for me."

When she goes, he thought, I'll have all I want. Not all I want, but all there is. Ayee, he was tired. Too tired. He was going to sleep a little while. He lay still and death was not there. It must have gone around another street. It went in pairs, on bicycles, and moved absolutely silently on the pavements.

No, he had never written about Paris. Not the Paris that he cared about. But what about the rest that he had never written?

What about the ranch and the silvered gray of the sage brush, the quick, clear water in the irrigation ditches, and the heavy green of the alfalfa? The trail went up into the hills and the cattle in the summer were shy as deer. The bawling and the steady noise and slow moving mass raising a dust as you brought them down in the fall. And behind the mountains, the clear sharpness of the peak in the evening light and, riding down along the trail in the moonlight, bright across the valley. Now he remembered coming down through the timber in the dark holding the horse's tail when you could not see and all the stories that he meant to write.

About the half-wit chore boy who was left at the ranch that time and told not to let any one get any hay, and that old bastard from the Forks who had beaten the boy when he had worked for him stopping to get some feed. The boy refusing and the old man saying he would beat him again. The boy got the rifle from the kitchen and shot him when he tried to come into the barn and when they came back to the ranch he'd been dead a week, frozen in the corral, and the dogs had eaten part of him. But what was left you packed on a sled wrapped in a blanket and roped on and you got the boy to help you haul it, and the two of you took it out over the road on skis, and sixty miles down to town to turn the boy over. He having no idea that he would be arrested. Thinking he had done his duty and that you were his friend and he would be rewarded. He'd helped to haul the old man in so everybody could know how bad the old man had been and how he'd tried to steal some feed that didn't belong to him, and when the sheriff put the handcuffs on the boy he couldn't believe it. Then he'd started to cry. That was one story he had saved to write. He knew at least twenty good stories from out there and he had never written one. Why?

"You tell them why," he said.
"Why what, dear?"
"Why nothing."

She didn't drink so much, now, since she had him. But if he lived he would never write about her, he knew that now. Nor about any of them. The rich were dull and they drank too much, or they played too much backgammon. They were dull and they were repetitious. He remembered poor Julian and his romantic awe of them and how he had started a story once that began, "The very rich are different from you and me." And how someone had said to Julian, Yes, they have more money. But that was not humorous to Julian. He thought they were a special glamorous race and when he found they weren't it wrecked him just as much as any other thing that wrecked him.

He had been contemptuous of those who wrecked. You did not have to like it because you understood it. He could bear anything, he thought, because nothing could hurt him if he did not care.

All right. Now he would not care for death. One thing he had always dreaded was the pain. He could stand pain as well as any man, until it went on too long, and wore him out, but here he had something that had hurt frightfully and just when he had felt it breaking him, the pain had stopped.

He remembered long ago when Williamson, the bombing officer, had been hit by a stick bomb someone in a German patrol had thrown as he was coming in through the wire that night and, screaming, had begged everyone to kill him. He was a fat man, very brave, and a good officer, although addicted to fantastic shows. But that night he was caught in the wire, with a flare lighting him up and his bowels spilled out into the wire, so when they brought him in, alive, they had to cut him loose. Shoot me, Harry. For Christ sake, shoot me. They had had an argument one time about our Lord never sending you anything you could not bear and someone's theory had been that meant that at a certain time the pain passed you out automatically. But he had always remembered Williamson, that night. Nothing passed out Williamson until he gave him all his morphine tablets that he had always saved to use himself and then they did not work right away.

Still this now, that he had, was very easy; and if it was no worse as it went on there was nothing to worry about. Except that he would rather be in better company.

He thought a little about the company that he would like to have.

No, he thought, when everything you do, you do too long, and do too late, you can't expect to find the people still there. The people all are gone. The party's over and you are with your hostess now.

I'm getting as bored with dying as with everything else, he thought.

"It's a bore," he said out loud.

"What is, my dear?"

"Anything you do too bloody long."

He looked at her face between him and the fire. She was leaning back in the chair and the firelight shone on her pleasantly lined face and he could see that she was sleepy. He heard the hyena make a noise just outside the range of the fire.

"I've been writing," he said. "But I got tired."

"Do you think you will be able to sleep?"

"Pretty sure. Why don't you turn in?"

"I like to sit here with you."

"Do you feel anything strange?" he asked her.

"No. Just a little sleepy."

"I do," he said.

He had just felt death come by again.

"You know the only thing I've never lost is curiosity," he said to her.

"You've never lost anything. You're the most complete man I've ever known."

"Christ," he said. "How little a woman knows. What is that? Your intuition?"

Because, just then, death had come and rested its head on the foot of the cot and he could smell its breath.

"Never believe any of that about a scythe and a skull," he told her. "It can be two bicycle policemen as easily or be a bird. Or it can have a wide snout like a hyena."

It had moved up on him now, but it had no shape any more. It simply occupied space.

"Tell it to go away."

It did not go away, but moved a little closer.

"You've got a hell of a breath," he told it. "You stinking bastard."

It moved up closer to him still, and now he could not speak to it, and when it saw he could not speak, it came a little closer, and now he tried to send it away without speaking, but it moved in on him so its weight was all upon his chest, and while it crouched there and he could not move, or speak, he heard the woman say, "Bwana is asleep now. Take the cot up very gently and carry it into the tent."

He could not speak to tell her to make it go away and it crouched now, heavier, so he could not breathe. And then, while they lifted the cot, suddenly it was all right and the weight went from his chest.

It was morning and had been morning for some time and he heard the plane. It showed very tiny and then made a wide circle and the boys ran out and lit the fires, using kerosene, and piled on grass so there were two big smudges at each end of the level place and the morning breeze blew them toward the camp and the plane circled twice more, low this time, and then glided down and leveled off and landed smoothly and, coming walking toward him, was old Compton in slacks, a tweed jacket, and a brown felt hat.

"What's the matter, old cock?" Compton said.

"Bad leg," he told him. "Will you have some breakfast?"

"Thanks. I'll just have some tea. It's the Puss Moth, you know. I won't be able to take the Memsahib. There's only room for one. Your lorry is on the way."

Helen had taken Compton aside and was speaking to him. Compton came back more cheery than ever.

"We'll get you right in," he said. "I'll be back for the Mem. Now I'm afraid I'll have to stop at Arusha to refuel. We'd better get going."

"What about the tea?"

"I don't really care about it, you know."

The boys had picked up the cot and carried it around the green tents and down along the rock and out onto the plain and along past the smudges that were burning brightly now, the grass all consumed, and the wind fanning the fire, to the little plane. It was difficult getting him in, but once in he lay back in the leather seat, and the leg was stuck straight out to one side of the seat where Compton sat. Compton started the motor and got in. He waved to Helen and to the boys and, as the clatter moved into the old familiar roar, they swung around with Compie watching for wart-hog holes and roared, bumping, along the stretch between the fires and with the last bump rose and he saw them all standing below, waving, and the camp beside the hill, flattening now, and the plain spreading, clumps of trees, and the bush flattening, while the game trails ran

[320]

The Snows of Kilimanjaro

now smoothly to the dry waterholes, and there was a new water that he had never known of. The zebra, small rounded backs now, and the wildebeeste, big headed dots seeming to climb as they moved in long fingers across the plain, now scattering as the shadow came toward them, they were tiny now, and the movement had no gallop, and the plain as far as you could see, gray-yellow now and ahead old Compie's tweed back and the brown felt hat. Then they were over the first hills and the wildebeeste were trailing up them, and then they were over mountains with sudden depths of green-rising forest and the solid bamboo slopes, and then the heavy forest again, sculptured into peaks and hollows until they crossed, and hills sloped down and then another plain, hot now, and purple brown, bumpy with heat and Compie looking back to see how he was riding. Then there were other mountains dark ahead.

And then instead of going on to Arusha they turned left, he evidently figured that they had the gas, and looking down he saw a pink sifting cloud, moving over the ground, and in the air, like the first snow in a blizzard, that comes from nowhere, and he knew the locusts were coming up from the south. Then they began to climb and they were going to the east it seemed, and then it darkened and they were in a storm, the rain so thick it seemed like flying through a waterfall, and then they were out and Compie turned his head and grinned and pointed and there, ahead, all he could see, as wide as all the world, great, high, and unbelievably white in the sun, was the square top of Kilimanjaro. And then he knew that there was where he was going.

Just then the hyena stopped whimpering in the night and started to make a strange, human, almost crying sound. The woman heard it and stirred uneasily. She did not wake. In her dream she was at the house on Long Island and it was the night before her daughter's début. Somehow her father was there and he had been very rude. Then the noise the hyena made was so loud she woke and for a moment she did not know where she was and she was very afraid. Then she took the flashlight and shone it on the other cot that they had carried in after Harry had gone to sleep. She could see his bulk under the mosquito bar, but somehow he had gotten his leg out and it hung down alongside the cot. The dressings had all come down and she could not look at it.

"Molo," she called, "Molo! Molo!"

Then she said, "Harry, Harry!" Then her voice rising, "Harry! Please! Oh Harry!"

There was no answer and she could not hear him breathing.

Outside the tent the hyena made the same strange noise that had awakened her. But she did not hear him for the beating of her heart.

HEART OF DARKNESS
by Joseph Conrad

I

The *Nellie,* a cruising yawl, swung to her anchor without a flutter of the sails, and was at rest. The flood had made, the wind was nearly calm, and being bound down the river, the only thing for it was to come to and wait for the turn of the tide.

The sea-reach of the Thames stretched before us like the beginning of an interminable waterway. In the offing the sea and the sky were welded together without a joint, and in the luminous space the tanned sails of the barges drifting up with the tide seemed to stand still in red clusters of canvas sharply peaked, with gleams of varnished sprits. A haze rested on the low shores that ran out to sea in vanishing flatness. The air was dark above Gravesend, and farther back still seemed condensed into a mournful gloom, brooding motionless over the biggest, and the greatest, town on earth.

The Director of Companies was our captain and our host. We four affectionately watched his back as he stood in the bows looking to seaward. On the whole river there was nothing that looked half so nautical. He resembled a pilot, which to a seaman is trustworthiness personified. It was difficult to realize his work was not out there in the luminous estuary, but behind him, within the brooding gloom.

Between us there was, as I have already said somewhere, the bond of the sea. Besides holding our hearts together through long periods of separation, it had the effect of making us tolerant of each other's yarns—and even convictions. The Lawyer—the best of old fellows—had, because of his many years and many virtues, the only cushion on deck, and was lying on the only rug. The Accountant had brought out already a box of dominoes, and was toying architecturally with the bones. Marlow sat cross-legged right aft, leaning against the mizzen-mast. He had sunken cheeks, a yellow complexion, a straight back, an ascetic aspect, and, with his arms dropped, the palms of hands outwards, resembled an idol. The director, satisfied the anchor had good hold, made his way aft and sat down amongst us. We exchanged a few words lazily. Afterwards there was silence on board the yacht. For some reason or other we did not begin that game of dominoes. We felt meditative, and fit for nothing but placid staring. The day was ending in a serenity of still and exquisite brilliance. The water shone pacifically; the sky, without a speck, was a benign immensity of unstained light; the very mist on the Essex marshes was like a gauzy and radiant fabric, hung from the wooded rises inland, and draping the low shores in diaphanous folds. Only the gloom to the west, brooding over the upper reaches, became more somber every minute, as if angered by the approach of the sun.

And at last, in its curved and imperceptible fall, the sun sank low, and from glowing white changed to a dull red without rays and without heat, as if about to go out suddenly, stricken to death by the touch of that gloom brooding over a crowd of men.

Forthwith a change came over the waters, and the serenity became less brilliant but more profound. The old river in its broad reach rested unruffled at the decline

Copyright, Joseph Conrad. Reprinted by permission of J. M. Dent & Sons, Ltd.

of day, after ages of good service done to the race that peopled its banks, spread out in the tranquil dignity of a waterway leading to the uttermost ends of the earth. We looked at the venerable stream not in the vivid flush of a short day that comes and departs forever, but in the august light of abiding memories. And indeed nothing is easier for a man who has, as the phrase goes, "followed the sea" with reverence and affection, than to evoke the great spirit of the past upon the lower reaches of the Thames. The tidal current runs to and fro in its unceasing service, crowded with memories of men and ships it had borne to the rest of home or to the battles of the sea. It had known and served all the men of whom the nation is proud, from Sir Francis Drake to Sir John Franklin, knights all, titled and untitled—the knights-errant of the sea. It had borne all the ships whose names are like jewels flashing in the night of time, from the *Golden Hind* returning with her round flanks full of treasure, to be visited by the Queen's Highness and thus pass out of the gigantic tale, to the *Erebus* and *Terror,* bound on other conquests—and that never returned. It had known the ships and the men. They had sailed from Deptford, from Greenwich, from Erith—the adventurers and the settlers; kings' ships and the ships of men on 'Change; captains, admirals, the dark "interlopers" of the Eastern trade, and the commissioned "generals" of East India fleets. Hunters for gold or pursuers of fame, they all had gone out on that stream, bearing the sword, and often the torch, messengers of the might within the land, bearers of a spark from the sacred fire. What greatness had not floated on the ebb of that river into the mystery of an unknown earth! . . . The dreams of men, the seed of commonwealths, the germs of empires.

The sun set; the dusk fell on the stream, and lights began to appear along the shore. The Chapman lighthouse, a three-legged thing erect on a mudflat, shone strongly. Lights of ships moved in the fairway—a great stir of lights going up and going down. And farther west on the upper reaches the place of the monstrous town was still marked ominously on the sky, a brooding gloom in sunshine, a lurid glare under the stars.

"And this also," said Marlow suddenly, "has been one of the dark places on the earth."

He was the only man of us who still "followed the sea." The worst that could be said of him was that he did not represent his class. He was a seaman, but he was a wanderer, too, while most seamen lead, if one may so express it, a sedentary life. Their minds are of the stay-at-home order, and their home is always with them—the ship; and so is their country—the sea. One ship is very much like another, and the sea is always the same. In the immutability of their surroundings the foreign shores, the foreign faces, the changing immensity of life, glide past, veiled not by a sense of mystery but by a slightly disdainful ignorance; for there is nothing mysterious to a seaman unless it be the sea itself, which is the mistress of his existence and as inscrutable as Destiny. For the rest, after his hours of work, a casual stroll or a casual spree on shore suffices to unfold for him the secret of a whole continent, and generally he finds the secret not worth knowing. The yarns of seamen have a direct simplicity, the whole meaning of which lies within the shell of a cracked nut. But Marlow was not typical (if his propensity to spin yarns be excepted), and to him the meaning of an episode was not inside like a kernel but outside, enveloping the tale which brought it out only as a glow brings out a haze, in the likeness of one of these misty halos that sometimes are made visible by the spectral illumination of moonshine.

His remark did not seem at all surprising. It was just like Marlow. It was accepted in silence. No one took the trouble to grunt even; and presently he said, very slow—

"I was thinking of very old times, when the Romans first came here, nineteen hundred years ago—the other day. . . . Light came out of this river since—you say Knights? Yes; but it is like a running blaze on a plain, like a flash of lightning in the clouds. We live in the flicker—may it last as long as the old earth keeps rolling! But darkness was here yesterday. Imagine the feelings of a commander of a fine—what d'ye call 'em—trireme in the Mediterranean, ordered suddenly to the north; run overland across the Gauls in a hurry; put in charge of one of these craft the legionaries—a wonderful lot of handy men they must have been, too—used to build, apparently by the hundred, in a month or two, if we may believe what we read. Imagine him here—the very end of the world, a sea the color of lead, a sky the color of smoke, a kind of ship about as rigid as a concertina—and going up this river with stores, or orders, or what you like. Sand-banks, marshes, forests, savages,—precious little to eat fit for a civilized man, nothing but Thames water to drink. No Falernian wine here, no going ashore. Here and there a military camp lost in a wilderness, like a needle in a bundle of hay—cold, fog, tempests, disease, exile, and death,—death skulking in the air, in the water, in the bush. They must have been dying like flies here. Oh, yes—he did it. Did it very well, too, no doubt, and without thinking much about it either, except afterwards to brag of what he had gone through in his time, perhaps. They were men enough to face the darkness. And perhaps he was cheered by keeping his eye on a chance of promotion to the fleet at Ravenna by and by, if he had good friends in Rome and survived the awful climate. Or think of a decent young citizen in a toga—perhaps too much dice, you know—coming out here in the train of some prefect, or tax-gatherer, or trader even, to mend his fortunes. Land in a swamp, march through the woods, and in some inland post feel the savagery, the utter savagery, had closed round him,—all that mysterious life of the wilderness that stirs in the forest, in the jungles, in the hearts of wild men. There's no initiation either into such mysteries. He has to live in the midst of the incomprehensible, which is also detestable. And it has a fascination, too, that goes to work upon him. The fascination of the abomination—you know, imagine the growing regrets, the longing to escape, the powerless disgust, the surrender, the hate."

He paused.

"Mind," he began again, lifting one arm from the elbow, the palm of the hand outwards, so that, with his legs folded before him, he had the pose of a Buddha preaching in European clothes and without a lotus-flower—"Mind, none of us would feel exactly like this. What saves us is efficiency—the devotion to efficiency. But these chaps were not much account, really. They were no colonists; their administration was merely a squeeze, and nothing more, I suspect. They were conquerors, and for that you want only brute force—nothing to boast of, when you have it, since your strength is just an accident arising from the weakness of others. They grabbed what they could get for the sake of what was to be got. It was just robbery with violence, aggravated murder on a great scale, and men going at it blind—as is very proper for those who tackle a darkness. The conquest of the earth, which mostly means the taking it away from those who have a different complexion or slightly flatter noses than ourselves, is not a pretty thing when you look into it too much. What redeems it is the idea only. An idea at the back of it; not a sentimental pretense but an idea; and an unselfish belief in the idea—something you can set up, and bow down before, and offer a sacrifice to. . . ."

He broke off. Flames glided in the river, small green flames, red flames, white flames, pursuing, overtaking, joining, crossing each other—then separating slowly or hastily. The traffic of the great city went on in the deepening night upon the sleepless river. We looked on, waiting patiently—there was nothing else to do till the end of the flood; but it was only after a long silence, when he said, in a hesitating voice, "I suppose you fellows remember I did once turn fresh-water sailor for a bit," that we knew we were fated, before the ebb began to run, to hear one of Marlow's inconclusive experiences.

"I don't want to bother you much with what happened to me personally," he began, showing in this remark the weakness of many tellers of tales who seem so often unaware of what their audience would best like to hear; "yet to understand the effect of it on me you ought to know how I got out there, what I saw, how I went up that river to the place where I first met the poor chap. It was the farthest point of navigation and the culminating point of my experience. It seemed somehow to throw a kind of light on everything about me—and into my thoughts. It was somber enough, too—and pitiful—not extraordinary in any way—not very clear either. No, not very clear. And yet it seemed to throw a kind of light.

"I had then, as you remember, just returned to London after a lot of Indian Ocean, Pacific, China Seas—a regular dose of the East—six years or so, and I was loafing about, hindering you fellows in your work and invading your homes, just as though I had got a heavenly mission to civilize you. It was very fine for a time, but after a bit I did get tired of resting. Then I began to look for a ship—I should think the hardest work on earth. But the ships wouldn't even look at me. And I got tired of that game, too.

"Now when I was a little chap I had a passion for maps. I would look for hours at South America, or Africa, or Australia, and lose myself in all the glories of exploration. At that time there were many blank spaces on the earth, and when I saw one that looked particularly inviting on a map (but they all look that) I would put my finger on it and say, When I grow up I will go there. The North Pole was one of these places, I remember. Well, I haven't been there yet, and shall not try now. The glamour's off. Other places were scattered about the Equator, and in every sort of latitude all over the two hemispheres. I have been in some of them, and . . . well, we won't talk about that. But there was one yet—the biggest, the most blank, so to speak—that I had a hankering after.

"True, by this time it was not a blank space any more. It had got filled since my childhood with rivers and lakes and names. It had ceased to be a blank space of delightful mystery—a white patch for a boy to dream gloriously over. It had become a place of darkness. But there was in it one river especially, a mighty big river, that you could see on the map, resembling an immense snake uncoiled, with its head in the sea, its body at rest curving afar over a vast country, and its tail lost in the depths of the land. And as I looked at the map of it in a shop-window, it fascinated me as a snake would a bird—a silly little bird. Then I remembered there was a big concern, a Company for trade on that river. Dash it all! I thought to myself, they can't trade without using some kind of craft on that lot of fresh water—steamboats! Why shouldn't I try to get charge of one? I went on along Fleet Street, but could not shake off the idea. The snake had charmed me.

"You understand it was a Continental concern, that Trading society; but I have a lot of relations living on the Continent, because it's cheap and not so nasty as it looks, they say.

"I am sorry to own I began to worry them. This was already a fresh departure for me. I was not used to getting things that way, you know. I always went my own road and on my own legs where I had a mind to go. I wouldn't have believed it of myself; but, then—you see—I felt somehow I must get there by hook or by crook. So I worried them. The men said 'My dear fellow,' and did nothing. Then—would you believe it?—I tried the women. I, Charlie Marlow, set the women to work—to get a job. Heavens! Well, you see, the notion drove me. I had an aunt, a dear enthusiastic soul. She wrote: 'It will be delightful. I am ready to do anything, anything for you. It is a glorious idea. I know the wife of a very high personage in the Administration, and also a man who has lots of influence with,' etc., etc. She was determined to make no end of fuss to get me appointed skipper of a river steamboat, if such was my fancy.

"I got my appointment—of course; and I got it very quick. It appears the Company had received news that one of their captains had been killed in a scuffle with the natives. This was my chance, and it made me the more anxious to go. It was only months and months afterwards, when I made the attempt to recover what was left of the body, that I heard the original quarrel arose from a misunderstanding about some hens. Yes, two black hens. Fresleven—that was the fellow's name, a Dane—thought himself wronged somehow in the bargain, so he went ashore and started to hammer the chief of the village with a stick. Oh, it didn't surprise me in the least to hear this, and at the same time to be told that Fresleven was the gentlest, quietest creature that ever walked on two legs. No doubt he was; but he had been a couple of years already out there engaged in the noble cause, you know, and he probably felt the need at last of asserting his self-respect in some way. Therefore he whacked the old nigger mercilessly, while a big crowd of his people watched him, thunderstruck, till some man—I was told the chief's son—in desperation at hearing the old chap yell, made a tentative jab with a spear at the white man—and of course it went quite easy between the shoulder-blades. Then the whole population cleared into the forest, expecting all kinds of calamities to happen, while, on the other hand,

[326]

Heart of Darkness

the steamer Fresleven commanded left also in a bad panic, in charge of the engineer, I believe. Afterwards nobody seemed to trouble much about Fresleven's remains, till I got out and stepped into his shoes. I couldn't let it rest, though; but when an opportunity offered at last to meet my predecessor, the grass growing through his ribs was tall enough to hide his bones. They were all there. The supernatural being had not been touched after he fell. And the village was deserted, the huts gaped black, rotting, all askew within the fallen enclosures. A calamity had come to it, sure enough. The people had vanished. Mad terror had scattered them, men, women, and children, through the bush, and they had never returned. What became of the hens I don't know either. I should think the cause of progress got them, anyhow. However, through this glorious affair I got my appointment, before I had fairly begun to hope for it.

"I flew around like mad to get ready, and before forty-eight hours I was crossing the Channel to show myself to my employers, and sign the contract. In a very few hours I arrived in a city that always makes me think of a whited sepulcher. Prejudice no doubt. I had no difficulty in finding the Company's offices. It was the biggest thing in the town, and everybody I met was full of it. They were going to run an over-sea empire, and make no end of coin by trade.

"A narrow and deserted street in deep shadow, high houses, innumerable windows with venetian blinds, a dead silence, grass sprouting between the stones, imposing carriage archways right and left, immense double doors standing ponderously ajar. I slipped through one of these cracks, went up a swept and ungarnished staircase, as arid as a desert, and opened the first door I came to. Two women, one fat and the other slim, sat on straw-bottomed chairs, knitting black wool. The slim one got up and walked straight at me—still knitting with down-cast eyes—and only just as I began to think of getting out of her way, as you would for a somnambulist, stood still, and looked up. Her dress was as plain as an umbrella-cover, and she turned round without a word and preceded me into a waiting-room. I gave my name, and looked about. Deal table in the middle, plain chairs all around the walls, on one end a large shining map, marked with all the colors of a rainbow. There was a vast amount of red—good to see at any time, because one knows that some real work is done in there, a deuce of a lot of blue, a little green, smears of orange, and, on the East Coast, a purple patch, to show where the jolly pioneers of progress drink the jolly lager-beer. However, I wasn't going into any of these. I was going into the yellow. Dead in the center. And the river was there—fascinating—deadly—like a snake. Ough! A door opened, a white-haired secretarial head, but wearing a compassionate expression, appeared, and a skinny forefinger beckoned me into the sanctuary. Its light was dim, and a heavy writing-desk squatted in the middle. From behind that structure came out an impression of pale plumpness in a frock-coat. The great man himself. He was five feet six, I should judge, and had his grip on the handle-end of ever so many millions. He shook hands, I fancy, murmured vaguely, was satisfied with my French. *Bon voyage.*

"In about forty-five seconds I found myself again in the waiting-room with the compassionate secretary, who, full of desolation and sympathy, made me sign some document. I believe I undertook amongst other things not to disclose any trade secrets. Well, I am not going to.

"I began to feel slightly uneasy. You know I am not used to such ceremonies, and there was something ominous in the atmosphere. It was just as though I had been let into some conspiracy—I don't know—something not quite right; and I was glad to get out. In the outer room the two women knitted black wool feverishly. People were arriving, and the younger one was walking back and forth introducing them. The old one sat on her chair. Her flat cloth slippers were propped up on a foot-warmer, and a cat reposed on her lap. She wore a starched white affair on her head, had a wart on one cheek, and silver-rimmed spectacles hung on the tip of her nose. She glanced at me above the glasses. The swift and indifferent placidity of that look troubled me. Two youths with foolish and cheery countenances were being piloted over, and she threw at them the same quick glance of unconcerned wisdom. She seemed to know all about them and about me, too. An eerie feeling came over me. She seemed uncanny and fateful. Often far away there I thought of these two, guarding the door of Darkness, knitting black wool as for a warm pall, one introducing, introducing continuously to the unknown, the other scrutinizing the cheery and foolish faces with unconcerned old eyes. *Ave!* Old knitter of black wool. *Morituri te salutant.* Not many of those she looked at ever saw her again—not half, by a long way.

"There was yet a visit to the doctor. 'A simple formality,' assured me the secretary, with an air of taking an immense part in all my sorrows. Accordingly a young chap wearing his hat over the left eyebrow, some clerk I suppose,—there must have been clerks in the business, though the house was as still as a house in a city of the dead,—came from somewhere upstairs, and led me forth. He was shabby and careless, with inkstains on the sleeves of his jacket, and his cravat was large and billowy, under a chin shaped like the toe of an old boot. It was a little too early for the doctor, so I proposed a drink, and thereupon he developed a vein of joviality. As we sat over our vermouths he glorified the Company's business, and by and by I expressed casually my surprise at him not going out there. He became very cool and collected all at once. 'I am not such a fool as I look, quoth Plato to his disciples,' he said sententiously, emptied his glass with great resolution, and we rose.

"The old doctor felt my pulse, evidently thinking of something else the while. 'Good, good for there,' he mumbled, and then with a certain eagerness asked me whether I would let him measure my head. Rather surprised, I said Yes, when he produced a thing like calipers and got the dimensions back and front and every way, taking notes carefully. He was an unshaven little man in a threadbare coat like a gaberdine, with his feet in slippers, and I thought him a harmless fool. 'I always ask leave, in the interests of science, to measure the crania of those going out there,' he said. 'And when they come back, too?' I asked. 'Oh, I never see them,' he remarked; 'and, moreover, the changes take place inside, you know.' He smiled, as if at some quiet joke. 'So you are going out there. Famous. Interesting, too.' He gave me a searching glance, and made another note. 'Ever any madness in your family?' he asked, in a matter-of-fact tone. I felt very annoyed. 'Is that question in the interests of science, too?' 'It would be,' he said, without taking notice of my irritation, 'interesting for science to watch the mental changes of individuals, on the spot, but . . .' 'Are you an alienist?' I interrupted. 'Every doctor should be—a little,' answered that original, imperturbably. 'I have a little theory which you Messieurs who go out there must help me to prove. This is my share in the advantages my country shall reap from the possession of such a magnificent dependency. The mere wealth I leave to others. Pardon my questions, but you are the first Englishman coming under my observation . . .' I hastened to assure him I was not in the least typical. 'If I were,' said I, 'I wouldn't be talking like this with you.' 'What you say is rather profound, and probably erroneous,' he said, with a laugh. 'Avoid irritation more than exposure to the sun. Adieu. How do you English say, eh? Good-by. Ah! Good-by. Adieu. In the tropics one must before everything keep calm.' . . . He lifted a warning forefinger. . . . 'Du calme, du calme. Adieu.'

"One thing more remained to do—say good-by to my excellent aunt. I found her triumphant. I had a cup of tea—the last decent cup of tea for many days—and in a room that most soothingly looked just as you would expect a lady's drawing-room to look, we had a long quiet chat by the fireside. In the course of these confidences it became quite plain to me I had been represented to the wife of the high dignitary, and goodness knows to how many more people besides, as an exceptional and gifted creature—a piece of good fortune for the Company—a man you don't get hold of every day. Good heavens! and I was going to take charge of a two-penny-half-penny river-steamboat with a penny whistle attached! It appeared, however, I was also one of the Workers, with a capital—you know. Something like an emissary of light, something like a lower sort of apostle. There had been a lot of such rot let loose in print and talk just about that time, and the excellent woman, living right in the rush of all that humbug, got carried off her feet. She talked about 'weaning those ignorant millions from their horrid ways,' till, upon my word, she made me quite uncomfortable. I ventured to hint that the Company was run for profit.

"'You forget, dear Charlie, that the laborer is worthy of his hire,' she said, brightly. It's queer how out of touch with truth women are. They live in a world of their own, and there has never been anything like it, and never can be. It is too beautiful altogether, and if they were to set it up it would go to pieces before the first sunset. Some confounded fact we men have been living contentedly with ever since the day of creation would start up and knock the whole thing over.

"After this I got embraced, told to wear flannel, be sure to write often, and so on —and I left. In the street—I don't know why—a queer feeling came to me that I was an impostor. Odd thing that I, who used to clear out for any part of the world at twenty-four hours' notice, with less thought than most men give to the crossing of a street, had a moment—I won't say of hesitation, but of startled pause, before this commonplace affair. The best way I can explain it to you is by saying that, for a second or two, I felt as though, instead of going to the center of a continent, I were about to set off for the center of the earth.

"I left in a French steamer, and she

called in every blamed port they have out there, for, as far as I could see, the sole purpose of landing soldiers and custom-house officers. I watched the coast. Watching a coast as it slips by the ship is like thinking about an enigma. There it is before you—smiling, frowning, inviting, grand, mean, insipid, or savage, and always mute with an air of whispering, Come and find out. This one was almost featureless, as if still in the making, with an aspect of monotonous grimness. The edge of a colossal jungle, so dark-green as to be almost black, fringed with white surf, ran straight, like a ruled line, far, far away along a blue sea whose glitter was blurred by a creeping mist. The sun was fierce, the land seemed to glisten and drip with steam. Here and there grayish-whitish specks showed up clustered inside the white surf, with a flag flying above them perhaps. Settlements some centuries old, and still no bigger than pinheads on the untouched expanse of their background. We pounded along, stopped, landed soldiers; went on, landed custom-house clerks to levy toll in what looked like a God-forsaken wilderness, with a tin shed and a flag-pole lost in it; landed more soldiers—to take care of the custom-house clerks, presumably. Some, I heard, got drowned in the surf; but whether they did or not, nobody seemed particularly to care. They were just flung out there, and on we went. Every day the coast looked the same, as though we had not moved; but we passed various places —trading places—with names like Gran' Bassam, Little Popo; names that seemed to belong to some sordid farce acted in front of a sinister backcloth. The idleness of a passenger, my isolation amongst all these men with whom I had no point of contact, the oily and languid sea, the uniform somberness of the coast, seemed to keep me away from the truth of things, within the toil of a mournful and senseless delusion. The voice of the surf heard now and then was a positive pleasure, like the speech of a brother. It was something natural, that had its reason, that had a meaning. Now and then a boat from the shore gave one a momentary contact with reality. It was paddled by black fellows. You could see from afar the white of their eyeballs glistening. They shouted, sang; their bodies streamed with perspiration; they had faces like grotesque masks—these chaps; but they had bone, muscle, a wild vitality, an intense energy of movement, that was as natural and true as the surf along their coast. They wanted no excuse for being there. They were a great comfort to look at. For a time I would feel I belonged still to a world of straightforward facts; but the feeling would not last long. Something would turn up to scare it away. Once, I remember, we came upon a man-of-war anchored off the coast. There wasn't even a shed there, and she was shelling the bush. It appears the French had one of their wars going on thereabouts. Her ensign dropped limp like a rag; the muzzles of the long six-inch guns stuck out all over the low hull; the greasy, slimy swell swung her up lazily and let her down, swaying her thin masts. In the empty immensity of earth, sky, and water, there she was, incomprehensible, firing into a continent. Pop, would go one of the six-inch guns; a small flame would dart and vanish, a little white smoke would disappear, a tiny projectile would give a feeble screech—and nothing happened. Nothing could happen. There was a touch of insanity in the proceeding, a sense of lugubrious drollery in the sight;

and it was not dissipated by somebody on board assuring me earnestly there was a camp of natives—he called them enemies!—hidden out of sight somewhere.

"We gave her her letters (I heard the men in that lonely ship were dying of fever at the rate of three a day) and went on. We called at some more places with farcical names, where the merry dance of death and trade goes on in a still and earthy atmosphere as of an overheated catacomb; all along the formless coast bordered by dangerous surf, as if Nature herself had tried to ward off intruders; in and out of rivers, streams of death in life, whose banks were rotting into mud, whose waters, thickened into slime, invaded the contorted mangroves, that seemed to writhe at us in the extremity of an impotent despair. Nowhere did we stop long enough to get a particularized impression, but the general sense of vague and oppressive wonder grew upon me. It was like a weary pilgrimage amongst hints for nightmares.

"It was upward of thirty days before I saw the mouth of the big river. We anchored off the seat of the government. But my work would not begin till some two hundred miles farther on. So as soon as I could I made a start for a place thirty miles higher up.

"I had my passage on a little sea-going steamer. Her captain was a Swede, and knowing me for a seaman, invited me on the bridge. He was a young man, lean, fair, and morose, with lanky hair and a shuffling gait. As we left the miserable little wharf, he tossed his head contemptuously at the shore. 'Been living there?' he asked. I said, 'Yes.' 'Fine lot these government chaps—are they not?' he went on, speaking English with great precision and considerable bitterness. 'It is funny what some people will do for a few francs a month. I wonder what becomes of that kind when it goes up-country?' I said to him I expected to see that soon. 'So-o-o!' he exclaimed. He shuffled athwart, keeping one eye ahead vigilantly. 'Don't be too sure,' he continued. 'The other day I took up a man who hanged himself on the road. He was a Swede, too.' 'Hanged himself! Why, in God's name?' I cried. He kept on looking out watchfully. 'Who knows? The sun was too much for him, or the country perhaps.'

"At last we opened a reach. A rocky cliff appeared, mounds of turned-up earth by the shore, houses on a hill, others with iron roofs, amongst a waste of excavations, or hanging to the declivity. A continuous noise of the rapids above hovered over this scene of inhabited devastation. A lot of people, mostly black and naked, moved about like ants. A jetty projected into the river. A blinding sunlight drowned all this at times in a sudden recrudescence of glare. 'There's your Company's station,' said the Swede, pointing to three wooden barrack-like structures on the rocky slope. 'I will send your things up. Four boxes did you say? So. Farewell.'

"I came upon a boiler wallowing in the grass, then found a path leading up the hill. It turned aside for the bowlders, and also for an undersized railway-truck lying there on its back with its wheels in the air. One was off. The thing looked as dead as the carcass of some animal. I came upon more pieces of decaying machinery, a stack of rusty rails. To the left a clump of trees made a shady spot, where dark things seemed to stir feebly. I blinked, the path was steep. A horn tooted to the right, and I saw the black people run. A heavy and dull detonation shook the ground, a puff of smoke came out of the cliff, and that was all. No change appeared on the face of the rock. They were building a railway. The cliff was not in the way or anything; but this objectless blasting was all the work going on.

"A slight clinking behind me made me turn my head. Six black men advanced in a file, toiling up the path. They walked erect and slow, balancing small baskets full of earth on their heads, and the clink kept time with their footsteps. Black rags were wound round their loins, and the short ends behind waggled to and fro like tails. I could see every rib, the joints of their limbs were like knots in a rope; each had an iron collar on his neck, and all were connected together with a chain whose bights swung between them, rhythmically clinking. Another report from the cliff made me think suddenly of that ship of war I had seen firing into a continent. It was the same kind of ominous voice; but these men could by no stretch of imagination be called enemies. They were called criminals, and the outraged law, like the bursting shells, had come to them, an insoluble mystery from the sea. All their meager breasts panted together, the violently dilated nostrils quivered, the eyes stared stonily up-hill. They passed me within six inches, without a glance, with that complete, deathlike indifference of unhappy savages. Behind this raw matter one of the reclaimed, the product of the new forces at work, strolled despondently, carrying a rifle by its middle. He had a uniform jacket with one button off, and seeing a white man on the path, hoisted his weapon to his shoulder with alacrity. This was simple prudence, white men being so much alike at a distance that he could not tell who I might be. He was speedily reassured, and with a large, white rascally grin, and a glance at his charge, seemed to take me into partnership in his exalted trust. After all, I also was a part of the great cause of these high and just proceedings.

"Instead of going up, I turned and descended to the left. My idea was to let that chain-gang get out of sight before I climbed the hill. You know I am not particularly tender; I've had to strike and to fend off. I've had to resist and to attack sometimes—that's only one way of resisting—without counting the exact cost, according to the demands of such sort of life as I had blundered into. I've seen the devil of violence, and the devil of greed, and the devil of hot desire; but, by all the stars! these were strong, lusty, red-eyed devils, that swayed and drove men—men, I tell you. But as I stood on this hillside, I foresaw that in the blinding sunshine of that land I would become acquainted with a flabby, pretending, weak-eyed devil of a rapacious and pitiless folly. How insidious he could be, too, I was only to find out several months later and a thousand miles farther. For a moment I stood appalled, as though by a warning. Finally I descended the hill, obliquely, towards the trees I had seen.

"I avoided a vast artificial hole somebody had been digging on the slope, the purpose of which I found it impossible to divine. It wasn't a quarry or a sand-pit, anyhow. It was just a hole. It might have been connected with the philanthropic desire of giving the criminals something to do. I don't know. Then I nearly fell into a very narrow ravine, almost no more than a scar in the hillside. I discovered that a lot of imported drainage-pipes for the settlement had been tumbled in there. There wasn't one that was not broken. It was a wanton smash-up. At last I got under the trees. My purpose was to stroll into the shade for a moment; but no sooner within than it seemed to me I had stepped into the gloomy circle of some Inferno. The rapids were near, and an uninterrupted, uniform, headlong, rushing noise filled the mournful stillness of the grove, where not a breath stirred, not a leaf moved, with a mysterious sound—as though the tearing pace of the launched earth had suddenly become audible.

"Black shapes crouched, lay, sat between the trees leaning against the trunks, clinging to the earth, half coming out, half effaced within the dim light, in all the attitudes of pain, abandonment, and despair. Another mine on the cliff went off, followed by a slight shudder of the soil under my feet. The work was going on. The work! And this was the place where some of the helpers had withdrawn to die.

"They were dying slowly—it was very clear. They were not enemies, they were not criminals, they were nothing earthly now,—nothing but black shadows of disease and starvation, lying confusedly in the greenish gloom. Brought from all the recesses of the coast in all the legality of time contracts, lost in uncongenial surroundings, fed on unfamiliar food, they sickened, became inefficient, and were then allowed to crawl away and rest. These moribund shapes were free as air —and nearly as thin. I began to distinguish the gleam of the eyes under the trees. Then, glacing down, I saw a face near my hand. The black bones reclined at full length with one shoulder against the tree, and slowly the eyelids rose and the sunken eyes looked up at me, enormous and vacant, a kind of blind, white flicker in the depths of the orbs, which died out slowly. The man seemed young —almost a boy—but you know with them it's hard to tell. I found nothing else to do but to offer him one of my good Swede's ship's biscuits I had in my pocket. The fingers closed slowly on it and held —there was no other movement and no other glance. He had tied a bit of white worsted round his neck— Why? Where did he get it? Was it a badge—an ornament—a charm—a propitiatory act? Was there any idea at all connected with it? It looked startling round his black neck, this bit of white thread from beyond the seas.

"Near the same tree two more bundles of acute angles sat with their legs drawn up. One, with his chin propped on his knees, stared at nothing, in an intolerable and appalling manner: his brother phantom rested its forehead, as if overcome with a great weariness; and all about others were scattered in every pose of contorted collapse, as in some picture of a massacre or a pestilence. While I stood horror-struck, one of these creatures rose to his hands and knees, and went off on all-fours towards the river to drink. He lapped out of his hand, then sat up in the sunlight, crossing his shins in front of him, and after a time let his woolly head fall on his breastbone.

"I didn't want any more loitering in the shade, and I made haste towards the station. When near the buildings I met a white man, in such an unexpected elegance of get-up that in the first moment I took him for a sort of vision. I saw a high starched collar, white cuffs, a light alpaca jacket, snowy trousers, a clean necktie, and varnished boots. No hat. Hair parted, brushed, oiled, under a green-lined parasol held in a big white hand. He was amazing, and had a penholder behind his ear.

"I shook hands with this miracle, and I learned he was the Company's chief accountant, and that all the book-keeping was done at this station. He had come out for a moment, he said, 'to get a breath of fresh air.' The expression sounded wonderfully odd, with its suggestion of sedentary desk-life. I wouldn't have mentioned the fellow to you at all, only it was from his lips that I first heard the name of the man who is so indissolubly connected with the memories of that time. Moreover, I respected the fellow. Yes; I respected his collars, his vast cuffs, his brushed hair. His appearance was certainly that of a hairdresser's dummy; but in the great demoralization of the land he kept up his appearance. That's backbone. His starched collars and got-up shirt-fronts were achievements of character. He had been out nearly three years; and, later, I could not help asking him how he managed to sport such linen. He had just the faintest blush, and said modestly, 'I've been teaching one of the native women about the station. It was difficult. She had a distaste for the work.' Thus this man had verily accomplished something. And he was devoted to his books, which were in apple-pie order.

"Everything else in the station was in a muddle,—heads, things, buildings. Strings of dusty niggers with splay feet arrived and departed; a stream of manufactured goods, rubbishy cottons, beads, and brass-wire set into the depths of darkness, and in return came a precious trickle of ivory.

"I had to wait in the station for ten days—an eternity. I lived in a hut in the yard, but to be out of the chaos I would sometimes get into the accountant's office. It was built of horizontal planks, and so badly put together that, as he bent over his high desk, he was barred from neck to heels with narrow strips of sunlight. There was no need to open the big shutter to see. It was hot there, too; big flies buzzed fiendishly, and did not sting, but stabbed. I sat generally on the floor, while, of faultless appearance (and even slightly scented), perching on a high stool, he wrote, he wrote. Sometimes he stood up for exercise. When a trucklebed with a sick man (some invalid agent from up-country) was put in there, he exhibited a gentle annoyance. 'The groans of this sick person,' he said, 'distract my attention. And without that it is extremely difficult to guard against clerical errors in this climate.'

"One day he remarked, without lifting his head, 'In the interior you will no doubt meet Mr. Kurtz.' On my asking who Mr. Kurtz was, he said he was a first-class agent; and seeing my disappointment at this information, he added slowly, laying down his pen, 'He is a very remarkable person.' Further questions elicited from him that Mr. Kurtz was at present in charge of a trading post, a very important one, in the true ivory-country, at 'the very bottom of there. Sends in as much ivory as all the others put together. . . .' He began to write again. The sick man was too ill to groan. The flies buzzed in a great peace.

"Suddenly there was a growing murmur of voices and a great tramping of feet. A caravan had come in. A violent babble of uncouth sounds burst out on the other side of the planks. All the carriers were speaking together, and in the midst of the uproar the lamentable voice of the chief agent was heard 'giving it up' tearfully for the twentieth time that

Heart of Darkness

day.... He rose slowly. 'What a frightful row,' he said. He crossed the room gently to look at the sick man, and returning, said to me, 'He does not hear.' 'What! Dead?' I asked, startled. 'No, not yet,' he answered, with great composure. Then, alluding with a toss of the head to the tumult in the station yard, 'When one has got to make correct entries, one comes to hate those savages—hate them to the death.' He remained thoughtful for a moment. 'When you see Mr. Kurtz,' he went on, 'tell him for me that everything here'—he glanced at the desk—'is very satisfactory. I don't like to write to him—with those messengers of ours you never know who may get hold of your letter —at that Central Station.' He stared at me for a moment with his mild, bulging eyes. 'Oh, he will go far, very far,' he began again. 'He will be a somebody in the Administration before long. They, above—the Council in Europe, you know —mean him to be.'

"He turned to his work. The noise outside had ceased, and presently in going out I stopped at the door. In the steady buzz of flies the homeward-bound agent was lying flushed and insensible; the other, bent over his books, was making correct entries of perfectly correct transactions; and fifty feet below the doorstep I could see the still tree-tops of the grove of death.

"Next day I left that station at last, with a caravan of sixty men, for a two-hundred-mile tramp.

"No use telling you much about that. Paths, paths, everywhere; a stamped-in network of paths spreading over the empty land, through long grass, through burnt grass, through thickets, down and up chilly ravines, up and down stony hills ablaze with heat; and a solitude, a solitude, nobody, not a hut. The population had cleared out a long time ago. Well, if a lot of mysterious niggers armed with all kinds of fearful weapons suddenly took to traveling on the road between Deal and Gravesend, catching the yokels right and left to carry heavy loads for them, I fancy every farm and cottage thereabout would get empty very soon. Only here the dwellings were gone, too. Still I passed through several abandoned villages. There's something pathetically childish in the ruins of grass walls. Day after day, with the stamp and shuffle of sixty pair of bare feet behind me, each pair under a sixty-lb. load. Camp, cook, sleep, strike camp, march. Now and then a carrier dead in harness, at rest in the long grass near the path, with an empty water-gourd and his long staff lying by his side. A great silence around and above. Perhaps on some quiet night the tremor of far-off drums, sinking, swelling, a tremor vast, faint; a sound weird, appealing, suggestive, and wild—and perhaps with as profound a meaning as the sound of bells in a Christian country. Once a white man in an unbuttoned uniform, camping on the path with an armed escort of lank Zanzibars, very hospitable and festive— not to say drunk. Was looking after the upkeep of the road, he declared. Can't say I saw any road or any upkeep, unless the body of a middle-aged Negro, with a bullet-hole in the forehead, upon which I absolutely stumbled three miles farther on, may be considered as a permanent improvement. I had a white companion, too, not a bad chap, but rather too fleshy and with the exasperating habit of fainting on the hot hillsides, miles away from the least bit of shade and water. Annoying, you know, to hold your own coat like a parasol over a man's head while he is coming-to. I couldn't help asking him once what he meant by coming there at all. 'To make money, of course. What do you think?' he said, scornfully. Then he got fever, and had to be carried in a hammock slung under a pole. As he weighed sixteen stone I had no end of rows with the carriers. They jibbed, ran away, sneaked off with their loads in the night—quite a mutiny. So, one evening, I made a speech in English with gestures, not one of which was lost to the sixty pairs of eyes before me, and the next morning I started the hammock off in front all right. An hour afterwards I came upon the whole concern wrecked in a bush—man, hammock, groans, blankets, horrors. The heavy pole had skinned his poor nose. He was very anxious for me to kill somebody, but there wasn't the shadow of a carrier near. I remembered the old doctor—'It would be interesting for science to watch the mental changes of individuals, on the spot.' I felt I was becoming scientifically interesting. However, all that is to no purpose. On the fifteenth day I came in sight of the big river again, and hobbled into the Central Station. It was on a back water surrounded by scrub and forest, with a pretty border of smelly mud on one side, and on the three others enclosed by a crazy fence of rushes. A neglected gap was all the gate it had, and the first glance at the place was enough to let you see the flabby devil was running that show. White men with long staves in their hands appeared languidly from amongst the buildings, strolling up to take a look at me, and then retired out of sight somewhere. One of them, a stout, excitable chap with black mustaches, informed me with great volubility and many digressions, as soon as I told him who I was, that my steamer was at the bottom of the river. I was thunderstruck. What, how, why? Oh, it was 'all right.' The 'manager himself' was there. All quite correct. 'Everybody had behaved splendidly! splendidly!'—'you must,' he said in agitation, 'go and see the general manager at once. He is waiting!'

"I did not see the real significance of that wreck at once. I fancy I see it now, but I am not sure—not at all. Certainly the affair was too stupid—when I think of it—to be altogether natural. Still. . . . But at the moment it presented itself simply as a confounded nuisance. The steamer was sunk. They had started two days before in a sudden hurry up the river with the manager on board, in charge of some volunteer skipper, and before they had been out three hours they tore the bottom out of her on stones, and she sank near the south bank. I asked myself what I was to do there, now my boat was lost. As a matter of fact, I had plenty to do in fishing my command out of the river. I had to set about it the very next day. That, and the repairs when I brought the pieces to the station, took some months.

"My first interview with the manager was curious. He did not ask me to sit down after my twenty-mile walk that morning. He was commonplace in complexion, in feature, in manners, and in voice. He was of middle size and of ordinary build. His eyes, of the usual blue, were perhaps remarkably cold, and he certainly could make his glance fall on one as trenchant and heavy as an ax. But even at these times the rest of his person seemed to disclaim the intention. Otherwise there was only an indefinable, faint expression of his lips, something stealthy —a smile—not a smile—I remember it, but I can't explain. It was unconscious, this smile was, though just after he had said something it got intensified for an instant. It came at the end of his speeches like a seal applied on the words to make the meaning of the commonest phrase appear absolutely inscrutable. He was a common trader, from his youth up employed in these parts—nothing more. He was obeyed, yet he inspired neither love nor fear, nor even respect. He inspired uneasiness. That was it! Uneasiness. Not a definite mistrust—just uneasiness—nothing more. You have no idea how effective such a . . . a . . . faculty can be. He had no genius for organizing, for initiative, or for order even. That was evident in such things as the deplorable state of the station. He had no learning, and no intelligence. His position had come to him —why? Perhaps because he was never ill. . . . He had served three terms of three years out there. . . . Because triumphant health in the general rout of constitutions is a kind of power in itself. When he went home on leave he rioted on a large scale—pompously. Jack ashore—with a difference—in externals only. This one could gather from his casual talk. He originated nothing, he could keep the routine going—that's all. But he was great. He was great by this little thing that it was impossible to tell what could control such a man. He never gave that secret away. Perhaps there was nothing within him. Such a suspicion made one pause—for out there there were no external checks. Once when various tropical diseases had laid low almost every 'agent' in the station, he was heard to say, 'Men who come out here should have no entrails.' He sealed the utterance with that smile of his, as though it had been a door opening into a darkness he had in his keeping. You fancied you had seen things —but the seal was on. When annoyed at meal-times by the constant quarrels of the white men about precedence, he ordered an immense round table to be made, for which a special house had to be built. This was the station's mess-room. Where he sat was the first place—the rest were nowhere. One felt this to be his unalterable conviction. He was neither civil nor uncivil. He was quiet. He allowed his 'boy'—an overfed young Negro from the coast—to treat the white men, under his very eyes, with provoking insolence.

"He began to speak as soon as he saw me. I had been very long on the road. He could not wait. Had to start without me. The up-river stations had to be relieved. There had been so many delays already that he did not know who was dead and who was alive, and how they got on—and so on, and so on. He paid no attention to my explanations, and, playing with a stick of sealing-wax, repeated several times that the situation was 'very grave, very grave.' There were rumors that a very important station was in jeopardy, and its chief, Mr. Kurtz, was ill. Hoped it was not true. Mr. Kurtz was . . . I felt weary and irritable. Hang Kurtz, I thought. I interrupted him by saying I had heard of Mr. Kurtz on the coast. 'Ah! So they talk of him down there,' he murmured to himself. Then he began again, assuring me Mr. Kurtz was the best agent he had, an exceptional man, of the greatest importance to the Company; therefore I could understand his anxiety. He was, he said, 'very, very uneasy.' Certainly he fidgeted on his chair a good deal, exclaimed, 'Ah, Mr. Kurtz!' broke the stick of sealing-wax and seemed dumfounded by the accident. Next thing he wanted to know 'how long it would take to.' . . . I interrupted him again. Being hungry, you know, and kept on my feet too, I was getting savage. 'How can I tell?' I said. 'I haven't even seen the wreck yet—some months, no doubt.' All this talk seemed to me so futile. 'Some months,' he said. 'Well, let us say three months before we can make a start. Yes. That ought to do the affair.' I flung out of his hut (he lived all alone in a clay hut with a sort of veranda) muttering to myself my opinion of him. He was a chattering idiot. Afterwards I took it back when it was borne in upon me startlingly with what extreme nicety he had estimated the time requisite for the 'affair.'

"I went to work the next day, turning, so to speak, my back on that station. In that way only it seemed to me I could keep my hold on the redeeming facts of life. Still, one must look about sometimes; and then I saw this station, these men strolling aimlessly about in the sunshine of the yard. I asked myself sometimes what it all meant. They wandered here and there with their absurd long staves in their hands, like a lot of faithless pilgrims bewitched inside a rotten fence. The word 'ivory' rang in the air, was whispered, was sighed. You would think they were praying to it. A taint of imbecile rapacity blew through it all, like a whiff from some corpse. By Jove! I've never seen anything so unreal in my life. And outside, the silent wilderness surrounding this cleared speck on the earth struck me as something great and invincible, like evil or truth, waiting patiently for the passing away of this fantastic invasion.

"Oh, these months! Well, never mind. Various things happened. One evening a grass shed full of calico, cotton prints, beads, and I don't know what else, burst into a blaze so suddenly that you would have thought the earth had opened to let an avenging fire consume all that trash. I was smoking my pipe quietly by my dismantled steamer, and saw them all cutting capers in the light, with their arms lifted high, when the stout man with mustaches came tearing down to the river, a tin pail in his hand, assured me that everybody was 'behaving splendidly, splendidly,' dipped about a quart of water and tore back again. I noticed there was a hole in the bottom of his pail.

"I strolled up. There was no hurry. You see the thing had gone off like a box of matches. It had been hopeless from the very first. The flame had leaped high, driven everybody back, lighted up everything—and collapsed. The shed was already a heap of embers glowing fiercely. A nigger was being beaten near by. They said he had caused the fire in some way; be that as it may, he was screeching most horribly. I saw him, later, for several days, sitting in a bit of shade looking very sick and trying to recover himself: afterwards he arose and went out—and the wilderness without a sound took him into its bosom again. As I approached the glow from the dark I found myself at the back of two men, talking. I heard the name of Kurtz pronounced, then the words, 'take advantage of this unfortunate accident.' One of the men was the manager. I wished him a good evening. 'Did you ever see anything like it—eh? it is incredible,' he said, and walked off. The other man remained. He was a first-class agent, young, gentlemanly, a bit reserved, with a forked little beard and a hooked nose. He was stand-offish with the other agents, and they on their side said he was the manager's spy upon them. As to me, I had hardly ever spoken to him before. We got into talk, and by and by we strolled away from the hissing ruins. Then he asked me to his room, which was in the main building of the station. He struck a match, and I perceived that this young aristocrat had not only a silver-mounted dressing-case but also a whole candle all to himself. Just at that time the manager was the only man supposed to have any right to candles. Native mats covered the clay walls; a collection of spears, assegais, shields, knives was hung up in trophies. The business intrusted to this fellow was the making of bricks—so I had been informed; but there wasn't a fragment of a brick anywhere in the station, and he had been there more than a year—waiting. It seems he could not make bricks without something, I don't know what—straw, maybe. Anyway, it could not be found there, and as it was not likely to be sent from Europe, it did not appear clear to me what he was waiting for. An act of special creation perhaps. However, they were all waiting—all the sixteen or twenty pilgrims of them —for something; and upon my word it did not seem an uncongenial occupation, from the way they took it, though the only thing that ever came to them was disease—as far as I could see. They beguiled the time by backbiting and intriguing against each other in a foolish kind of way. There was an air of plotting about that station, but nothing came of it, of course. It was as unreal as everything else —as the philanthropic pretense of the whole concern, as their talk, as their government, as their show of work. The only real feeling was a desire to get appointed to a trading-post where ivory was to be had, so that they could earn percentages. They intrigued and slandered and hated each other only on that account,—but as to effectually lifting a little finger—oh, no. By heavens! there is something after all in the world allowing one man to steal a horse while another must not look at a halter. Steal a horse straight out. Very well. He has done it. Perhaps he can ride. But there is a way of looking at a halter that would provoke the most charitable of saints into a kick.

"I had no idea why he wanted to be sociable, but as we chatted in there it suddenly occurred to me the fellow was trying to get at something—in fact, pumping me. He alluded constantly to Europe, to the people I was supposed to know there —putting leading questions as to my acquaintances in the sepulchral city, and so on. His little eyes glittered like mica discs —with curiosity—though he tried to keep up a bit of superciliousness. At first I was astonished, but very soon I became awfully curious to see what he would find out from me. I couldn't possibly imagine what I had in me to make it worth his while. It was very pretty to see how he baffled himself, for in truth my body was full only of chills, and my head had nothing in it but that wretched steamboat business. It was evident he took me for a perfectly shameless prevaricator. At last he got angry, and, to conceal a movement of furious annoyance, he yawned. I rose. Then I noticed a small sketch in oils, on a panel, representing a woman, draped and blindfolded, carrying a lighted torch. The background was somber—almost black. The movement of the woman was stately, and the effect of the torchlight on the face was sinister.

"It arrested me, and he stood by civilly, holding an empty half-pint champagne bottle (medical comforts) with the candle stuck in it. To my question he said Mr. Kurtz had painted this—in this very station more than a year ago—while waiting for means to go to his trading-post. 'Tell me, pray,' said I, 'who is this Mr. Kurtz?'

"'The chief of the Inner Station,' he answered in a short tone, looking away. 'Much obliged,' I said, laughing. 'And you are the brickmaker of the Central Station. Every one knows that.' He was silent for a while. 'He is a prodigy,' he said at last. 'He is an emissary of pity, and science, and progress, and devil knows what else. We want,' he began to declaim suddenly, 'for the guidance of the cause intrusted to us by Europe, so to speak, higher intelligence, wide sympathies, a singleness of purpose.' 'Who says that?' I asked. 'Lots of them,' he replied. 'Some even write that; and so *he* comes here, a special being, as you ought to know.' 'Why ought I to know?' I interrupted, really surprised. He paid no attention. 'Yes. To-day he is chief of the best station, next year he will be assistant-manager, two years more and . . . but I daresay you know what he will be in two years' time. You are of the new gang—the gang of virtue. The same people who sent him specially also recommended you. Oh, don't say no. I've my own eyes to trust.' Light dawned upon me. My dear aunt's influential acquaintances were producing an unexpected effect upon that young man. I nearly burst into a laugh. 'Do you read the Company's confidential correspondence?' I asked. He hadn't a word to say. It was great fun. 'When Mr. Kurtz,' I continued, severely, 'is General Manager, you won't have the opportunity.'

"He blew the candle out suddenly, and we went outside. The moon had risen. Black figures strolled about listlessly, pouring water on the glow, whence proceeded a sound of hissing; steam ascended in the moonlight, the beaten nigger groaned somewhere. 'What a row the brute makes!' said the indefatigable man with the mustaches, appearing near us. 'Serves him right. Transgression—punishment—bang! Pitiless, pitiless. That's the only way. This will prevent all conflagrations for the future. I was just telling the manager . . .' He noticed my companion, and became crestfallen all at once. 'Not in bed yet,' he said, with a kind of servile heartiness; 'it's so natural. Ha! Danger—agitation.' He vanished. I went on to the river-side, and the other followed me. I heard a scathing murmur at my ear, 'Heap of muffs—go to.' The pilgrims could be seen in knots gesticulating, discussing. Several had still their staves in their hands. I verily believe they took these sticks to bed with them. Beyond the fence the forest stood up spectrally in the moonlight, and through the dim stir, through the faint sounds of that lamentable courtyard, the silence of the land went home to one's very heart—its mystery, its greatness, the amazing reality of its concealed life. The hurt nigger moaned feebly somewhere near by, and then fetched a deep sigh that made me mend my pace away from there. I felt a hand introducing itself under my arm. 'My dear sir,' said the fellow, 'I don't want to be misunderstood, and especially by you, who will see Mr. Kurtz long before I can have that pleasure. I wouldn't like him to get a false idea of my disposition. . . .'

"I let him run on, this papier-mâché Mephistopheles, and it seemed to me that if I tried I could poke my forefinger through him, and would find nothing inside but a little loose dirt, maybe. He, don't you see, had been planning to be assistant-manager by and by under the present man, and I could see that the coming of that Kurtz had upset them both not a little. He talked precipitately, and I did not try to stop him. I had my shoulders against the wreck of my steamer, hauled up on the slope like a carcass of some big river animal. The smell of mud, of primeval mud, by Jove! was in my nostrils, the high stillness of primeval forest was before my eyes; there were shiny patches on the black creek. The moon had spread over everything a thin layer of silver—over the rank grass, over the mud, upon the wall of matted vegetation standing higher than the wall of a temple, over the great river I could see through a somber gap glittering, glittering, as it flowed broadly by without a murmur. All this was great, expectant, mute, while the man jabbered about himself. I wondered whether the stillness on the face of the immensity looking at us two were meant as an appeal or as a menace. What were we who had strayed in here? Could we handle that dumb thing, or would it handle us? I felt how big, how confoundedly big, was that thing that couldn't talk, and perhaps was deaf as well. What was in there? I could see a little ivory coming out from there, and I had heard Mr. Kurtz was in there. I had heard enough about it, too—God knows! Yet somehow it didn't bring any image with it—no more than if I had been told an angel or a fiend was in there. I believed it in the same way one of you might believe there are inhabitants in the planet Mars. I knew once a Scotch sailmaker who was certain, dead sure, there were people in Mars. If you asked him for some idea how they looked and behaved, he would get shy and mutter something about 'walking on all-fours.' If you as much as smiled, he would—though a man of sixty-four—offer to fight you. I would not have gone so far as to fight for Kurtz, but I went for him near enough to a lie. You know I hate, detest, and can't bear a lie, not because I am straighter than the rest of us, but simply because it appalls me. There is a taint of death, a flavor of mortality in lies—which is exactly what I hate and detest in the world —what I want to forget. It makes me miserable and sick, like biting something rotten would do. Temperament, I suppose. Well, I went near enough to it by letting the young fool there believe anything he liked to imagine as to my influence in Europe. I became in an instant as much of a pretense as the rest of the bewitched pilgrims. This simply because I had a notion it somehow would be of help to that Kurtz whom at the time I did not see—you understand. He was just a word for me. I did not see the man in the name any more than you do. Do you see him? Do you see the story? Do you see anything? It seems to me I am trying to tell you a dream—making a vain attempt, because no relation of a dream can convey the dream-sensation, that commingling of absurdity, surprise, and bewilderment in a tremor of struggling revolt, that notion of being captured by the incredible which is of the very essence of dreams. . . ."

He was silent for a while.

". . . No, it is impossible; it is impossible to convey the life-sensation of any given epoch of one's existence—that which makes its truth, its meaning—its subtle and penetrating essence. It is impossible. We live, as we dream—alone. . . ."

He paused again as if reflecting, then added—

"Of course in this you fellows see more than I could then. You see me, whom you know. . . ."

It had become so pitch dark that we listeners could hardly see one another. For a long time already he, sitting apart, had been no more to us than a voice. There was not a word from anybody. The others might have been asleep, but I was awake. I listened, I listened on the watch for the sentence, for the word, that would give me the clew to the faint uneasiness inspired by this narrative that seemed to shape itself without human lips in the heavy night-air of the river.

". . . Yes—I let him run on," Marlow began again, "and think what he pleased about the powers that were behind me. I did! And there was nothing behind me! There was nothing but that wretched, old, mangled steamboat I was leaning against, while he talked fluently about 'the necessity for every man to get on.' 'And when one comes out here, you conceive, it is not to gaze at the moon.' Mr. Kurtz was a 'universal genius,' but even a genius would find it easier to work with 'adequate tools—intelligent men.' He did not make bricks—why, there was a physical impossibility in the way—as I was well aware; and if he did secretarial work for the manager, it was because 'no sensible man rejects wantonly the confidence of his superiors.' Did I see it? I saw it. What more did I want? What I really wanted was rivets, by heaven! Rivets. To get on with the work—to stop the hole. Rivets I wanted. There were cases of them down at the coast—cases—piled up—burst—split! You kicked a loose rivet at every second step in that station yard on the hillside. Rivets had rolled into the grove of death. You could fill your pockets with rivets for the trouble of stooping down—and there wasn't one rivet to be found where it was wanted. We had plates that would do, but nothing to fasten them with. And every week the messenger, a lone negro, letter-bag on shoulder and staff in hand, left our station for the coast. And several times a week a coast caravan came in with trade goods—ghastly glazed calico that made you shudder only to look at it, glass beads, valued about a penny a quart, confounded spotted cotton handkerchiefs. And no rivets. Three carriers could have brought all that was wanted to set that steamboat afloat.

"He was becoming confidential now, but I fancy my unresponsive attitude must have exasperated him at last, for he judged it necessary to inform me he feared neither God nor devil, let alone any mere man. I said I could see that very well, but what I wanted was a certain quantity of rivets—and rivets were what really Mr. Kurtz wanted, if he had only known it. Now letters went to the coast every week. . . . 'My dear sir,' he cried, 'I write from dictation.' I demanded rivets. There was a way—for an intelligent man. He changed his manner; became very cold, and suddenly began to talk about a hippopotamus; wondered whether sleeping on board the steamer (I stuck to my salvage night and day) I wasn't disturbed. There was an old hippo that had the bad habit of getting out on the bank and roaming at night over the station grounds. The pilgrims used to turn out in a body and empty every rifle they could lay hands on at him. Some even had sat up o' nights for him. All this energy was wasted, though. 'That animal has a charmed life,' he said; 'but you can say this only of brutes in this country. No man—you apprehend me?—no man here bears a charmed life.' He stood there for a moment in the moonlight with his delicate hooked nose set a little askew, and his mica eyes glittering without a wink, then, with a curt good night, he strode off. I could see he was disturbed and considerably puzzled, which made me feel more hopeful than I had been for days. It was a great comfort to turn from that chap to my influential friend, the battered, twisted, ruined, tin-pot steamboat. I clambered on board. She rang under my feet like an empty Huntley & Palmer biscuit-tin kicked along a gutter; she was nothing so solid in make, and rather less pretty in shape, but I had expended enough hard work on her to make me love her. No influential friend would have served me better. She had given me a chance to come out a bit —to find out what I could do. No, I don't like work. I had rather laze about and think of all the fine things that can be done. I don't like work—no man does— but I like what is in the work,—the chance to find yourself. Your own reality —for yourself, not for others—what no other man can ever know. They can only see the mere show, and never can tell what it really means.

"I was not surprised to see somebody sitting aft, on the deck, with his legs dangling over the mud. You see I rather chummed with the few mechanics there were in that station, whom the other pilgrims naturally despised—on account of their imperfect manners, I suppose. This was the foreman—a boiler-maker by trade —a good worker. He was a lank, bony, yellow-faced man, with big intense eyes. His aspect was worried, and his head was as bald as the palm of my hand; but his hair in falling seemed to have stuck to his chin, and had prospered in the new locality, for his beard hung down to his waist. He was a widower with six young children (he had left them in charge of a sister of his to come out there), and the passion of his life was pigeon-flying. He was an enthusiast and a connoisseur. He would rave about pigeons. After work hours he used sometimes to come over from his hut for a talk about his children and his pigeons; at work, when he had to crawl in the mud under the bottom of the steamboat, he would tie up that beard of his in a kind of white serviette he brought for the purpose. It had loops to go over his ears. In the evening he could be seen squatted on the bank rinsing that wrapper in the creek with great care, then spreading it solemnly on a bush to dry.

"I slapped him on the back and shouted, 'We shall have rivets!' He scrambled to his feet exclaiming, 'No! Rivets!' as though he couldn't believe his ears. Then in a low voice, 'You . . . eh?' I don't know why we behaved like lunatics. I put my finger to the side of my nose and nodded mysteriously. 'Good for you!' he cried, snapped his fingers above his head, lifting one foot. I tried a jig. We capered on the iron deck. A frightful clatter came out of that hulk, and the virgin forest on the other bank of the creek sent it back in a thundering roll upon the sleeping station. It must have made some of the pilgrims sit up in their hovels. A dark figure obscured the lighted doorway of the manager's hut, vanished, then, a second or so after, the doorway itself vanished, too. We stopped, and the silence driven away by the stamping of our feet flowed back again from the recesses of the land. The great wall of vegetation, an exuberant and entangled mass of trunks, branches, leaves, boughs, festoons, motionless in the moonlight, was like a rioting invasion of soundless life, a rolling wave of plants, piled up, crested, ready to topple over the creek, to sweep every little man of us out of his little existence. And it moved not. A deadened burst of mighty splashes and snorts reached us from afar, as though an ichthyosaurus had been taking a bath of glitter in the great river. 'After all,' said the boiler-maker in a reasonable tone, 'why shouldn't we get the rivets?' Why not, indeed? I did not know of any reason why we shouldn't. 'They'll come in three weeks,' I said, confidently.

"But they didn't. Instead of rivets there came an invasion, an infliction, a visitation. It came in sections during the next three weeks, each section headed by a donkey carrying a white man in new clothes and tan shoes, bowing from that elevation right and left to the impressed pilgrims. A quarrelsome band of footsore sulky niggers trod on the heels of the donkeys; a lot of tents, campstools, tin boxes, white cases, brown bales would be shot down in the courtyard, and the air of mystery would deepen a little over the muddle of the station. Five such installments came, with their absurd air of disorderly flight with the loot of innumerable outfit shops and provision stores, that, one would think, they were lugging, after a raid, into the wilderness for equitable division. It was an inextricable mess of things decent in themselves but that human folly made look like the spoils of thieving.

"This devoted band called itself the Eldorado Exploring Expedition, and I believe they were sworn to secrecy. Their talk, however, was the talk of sordid buccaneers: it was reckless without hardihood, greedy without audacity, and cruel without courage; there was not an atom of foresight or of serious intention in the whole batch of them, and they did not seem aware these things are wanted for the work of the world. To tear treasure out of the bowels of the land was their desire, with no more moral purpose at the back of it than there is in burglars breaking into a safe. Who paid the expenses of the noble enterprise I don't know; but the uncle of our manager was leader of that lot.

"In exterior he resembled a butcher in a poor neighborhood, and his eyes had a look of sleepy cunning. He carried his fat paunch with ostentation on his short legs, and during the time his gang infested the station spoke to no one but his nephew. You could see these two roaming about all day long with their heads close together in an everlasting confab.

"I had given up worrying myself about the rivets. One's capacity for that kind of folly is more limited than you would suppose. I said Hang!—and let things slide. I had plenty of time for meditation, and now and then I would give some thought to Kurtz. I wasn't very interested in him. No. Still, I was curious to see whether this man, who had come out equipped with moral ideas of some sort, would climb to the top after all and how he would set about his work when there."

II

"One evening as I was lying flat on the deck of my steamboat, I heard voices approaching—and there were the nephew and the uncle strolling along the bank. I laid my head on my arm again, and had nearly lost myself in a doze, when somebody said in my ear, as it were: 'I am as harmless as a little child, but I don't like to be dictated to. Am I the manager—or am I not? I was ordered to send him there. It's incredible.' . . . I became aware that the two were standing on the shore alongside the forepart of the steamboat, just below my head. I did not move; it did not occur to me to move: I was sleepy. 'It *is* unpleasant,' grunted the uncle. 'He has asked the Administration to be sent there,' said the other, 'with the idea of showing what he could do; and I was instructed accordingly. Look at the influence that man must have. Is it not frightful?' They both agreed it was frightful, then made several bizarre remarks: 'Make rain and fine weather—one man—the Council—by the nose'—bits of absurd sentences that got the better of my drowsiness, so that I had pretty near the whole of my wits about me when the uncle said, 'The climate may do away with this difficulty for you. Is he alone there?' 'Yes,' answered the manager; 'he sent his assistant down the river with a note to me in these terms: "Clear this poor devil out of the country, and don't bother sending more of that sort. I had rather be alone than have the kind of men you can dispose of with me." It was more than a year ago. Can you imagine such impudence!' 'Anything since then?' asked the other, hoarsely. 'Ivory,' jerked the nephew; 'lots of it—prime sort—lots —most annoying, from him.' 'And with that?' questioned the heavy rumble. 'Invoice,' was the reply fired out, so to speak. Then silence. They had been talking about Kurtz.

"I was broad awake by this time, but, lying perfectly at ease, remained still, having no inducement to change my position. 'How did that ivory come all this way?' growled the elder man, who seemed very vexed. The other explained that it had come with a fleet of canoes in charge of an English half-caste clerk Kurtz had with him; that Kurtz had apparently intended to return himself, the station being by that time bare of goods and stores, but after coming three hundred miles, had suddenly decided to go back, which he started to do alone in a small dugout with four paddlers, leaving the half-caste to continue down the river with the ivory. The two fellows there seemed astounded at anybody attempting such a thing. They were at a loss for an adequate motive. As to me, I seemed to see Kurtz for the first time. It was a distinct glimpse: the dugout, four paddling savages, and the lone white man turning his back suddenly on the headquarters, on relief, on thoughts of home—perhaps; setting his face towards the depths of the wilderness, towards his empty and desolate station. I did not know the motive. Perhaps he was just simply a fine fellow who stuck to his work for its own sake. His name, you understand, had not been pronounced once. He was 'that man.' The half-caste, who, as far as I could see, had conducted a difficult trip with great prudence and pluck, was invariably alluded to as 'that scoundrel.' The 'scoundrel' had reported that the 'man' had been very ill—had recovered imperfectly. . . . The two below me moved away then a few paces, and strolled back and forth at some little distance. I heard: 'Military post—doctor—two hundred miles—quite alone now —unavoidable delays—nine months—no news—strange rumors.' They approached again, just as the manager was saying, 'No one, as far as I know, unless a species of wandering trader—a pestilential fellow, snapping ivory from the natives.' Who was it they were talking about now? I gathered in snatches that this was some man supposed to be in Kurtz's district, and of whom the manager did not approve. 'We will not be free from unfair competition till one of these fellows is

[345]

hanged for an example,' he said. 'Certainly,' grunted the other; 'get him hanged! Why not? Anything—anything can be done in this country. That's what I say; nobody here, you understand, *here*, can endanger your position. And why? You stand the climate—you outlast them all. The danger is in Europe; but there before I left I took care to—' They moved off and whispered, then their voices rose again. 'The extraordinary series of delays is not my fault. I did my best.' The fat man sighed. 'Very sad.' 'And the pestiferous absurdity of his talk,' continued the other; 'he bothered me enough when he was here. "Each station should be like a beacon on the road towards better things, a center for trade, of course, but also for humanizing, improving, instructing." Conceive you—that ass! And he wants to be manager! No, it's—' Here he got choked by excessive indignation, and I lifted my head the least bit. I was surprised to see how near they were—right under me. I could have spat upon their hats. They were looking on the ground, absorbed in thought. The manager was switching his leg with a slender twig: his sagacious relative lifted his head. 'You have been well since you came out this time?' he asked. The other gave a start. 'Who? I? Oh! Like a charm—like a charm. But the rest—oh, my goodness! All sick. They die so quick, too, that I haven't the time to send them out of the country—it's incredible!' 'H'm. Just so,' grunted the uncle. 'Ah! my boy, trust to this—I say, trust to this.' I saw him extend his short flipper of an arm for a gesture that took in the forest, the creek, the mud, the river,—seemed to beckon with a dishonoring flourish before the sunlit face of the land a treacherous appeal to the lurking death, to the hidden evil, to the profound darkness of its heart. It was so startling that I leaped to my feet and looked back at the edge of the forest, as though I had expected an answer of some sort to that black display of confidence. You know the foolish notions that come to one sometimes. The high stillness confronted these two figures with its ominous patience, waiting for the passing away of a fantastic invasion.

"They swore aloud together—out of sheer fright, I believe—then pretending not to know anything of my existence, turned back to the station. The sun was low; and leaning forward side by side, they seemed to be tugging painfully uphill their two ridiculous shadows of unequal length, that trailed behind them slowly over the tall grass without bending a single blade.

"In a few days the Eldorado Expedition went into the patient wilderness, that closed upon it as the sea closes over a diver. Long afterwards the news came that all the donkeys were dead. I know nothing as to the fate of the less valuable animals. They, no doubt, like the rest of us, found what they deserved. I did not inquire. I was then rather excited at the prospect of meeting Kurtz very soon. When I say very soon I mean it comparatively. It was just two months from the day we left the creek when we came to the bank below Kurtz's station.

"Going up that river was like traveling back to the earliest beginnings of the world, when vegetation rioted on the earth and the big trees were kings. An empty stream, a great silence, an impenetrable forest. The air was warm, thick, heavy, sluggish. There was no joy in the brilliance of sunshine. The long stretches of the waterway ran on, deserted, into the gloom of overshadowed distances. On silvery sandbanks hippos and alligators sunned themselves side by side. The broadening waters flowed through a mob of wooded islands; you lost your way on that river as you would in a desert, and butted all day long against shoals, trying to find the channel, till you thought yourself bewitched and cut off forever from everything you had known once—somewhere—far away—in another existence perhaps. There were moments when one's past came back to one, as it will sometimes when you have not a moment to spare to yourself; but it came in the shape of an unrestful and noisy dream, remembered with wonder amongst the overwhelming realities of this strange world of plants, and water, and silence. And this stillness of life did not in the least resemble a peace. It was the stillness of an implacable force brooding over an inscrutable intention. It looked at you with a vengeful aspect. I got used to it afterwards; I did not see it any more; I had no time. I had to keep guessing at the channel; I had to discern, mostly by inspiration, the signs of hidden banks; I watched for sunken stones; I was learning to clap my teeth smartly before my heart flew out, when I shaved by a fluke some infernal sly old snag that would have ripped the life out of the tin-pot steamboat and drowned all the pilgrims; I had to keep a look-out for the signs of dead wood we could cut up in the night for next day's steaming. When you have to attend to things of that sort, to the mere incidents of the surface, the reality —the reality, I tell you—fades. The inner truth is hidden—luckily, luckily. But I felt it all the same; I felt often its mysterious stillness watching me at my monkey tricks, just as it watches you fellows performing on your respective tight-ropes for—what is it? half-a-crown a tumble—"

"'Try to be civil, Marlow,' growled a voice, and I knew there was at least one listener awake besides myself.

"I beg your pardon. I forgot the heartache which makes up the rest of the price. And indeed what does the price matter, if the trick be well done? You do your tricks very well. And I didn't do badly either, since I managed not to sink that steamboat on my first trip. It's a wonder to me yet. Imagine a blindfolded man set to drive a van over a bad road. I sweated and shivered over that business considerably, I can tell you. After all, for a seaman, to scrape the bottom of the thing that's supposed to float all the time under his care is the unpardonable sin. No one may know of it, but you never forget the thump—eh? A blow on the very heart. You remember it, you dream of it, you wake up at night and think of it—years after—and go hot and cold all over. I don't pretend to say that steamboat floated all the time. More than once she had to wade for a bit, with twenty cannibals splashing around and pushing. We had enlisted some of these chaps on the way for a crew. Fine fellows—cannibals—in their place. They were men one could work with, and I am grateful to them. And, after all, they did not eat each other before my face: they had brought along a provision of hippo-meat which went rotten, and made the mystery of the wilderness stink in my nostrils. Phoo! I can sniff it now. I had the manager on board and three or four pilgrims with their staves—all complete. Sometimes we came upon a station close by the bank, clinging to the skirts of the unknown, and the white men rushing out of a tumble-down hovel, with great gestures of joy and surprise and welcome, seemed very strange—had the appearance of being held there captive by a spell. The word ivory would ring in the air for a while—and on we went again into the silence, along empty reaches, round the still bends, between the high walls of our winding way, reverberating in hollow claps the ponderous beat of the stern-wheel. Trees, trees, millions of trees, massive, immense, running up high; and at their foot, hugging the bank against the stream, crept the little begrimed steamboat, like a sluggish beetle crawling on the floor of a lofty portico. It made you feel very small, very lost, and yet it was not altogether depressing, that feeling. After all, if you were small, the grimy beetle crawled on—which was just what you wanted it to do. Where the pilgrims imagined it crawled to I don't know. To some place where they expected to get something, I bet! For me it crawled towards Kurtz—exclusively; but when the steam-pipes started leaking we crawled very slow. The reaches opened before us and closed behind, as if the forest had stepped leisurely across the water to bar the way for our return. We penetrated deeper and deeper into the heart of darkness. It was very quiet there. At night sometimes the roll of drums behind the curtain of trees would run up the river and remain sustained faintly, as if hovering in the air high over our heads, till the first break of day. Whether it meant war, peace, or prayer we could not tell. The dawns were heralded by the descent of a chill stillness; the wood-cutters slept, their fires burned low; the snapping of a twig would make you start. We were wanderers on a prehistoric earth, on an earth that wore the aspect of an unknown planet. We could have fancied ourselves the first of men taking possession of an accursed inheritance, to be subdued at the cost of profound anguish and of excessive toil. But suddenly, as we struggled round a bend, there would be a glimpse of rush walls, of peaked grass-roofs, a burst of yells, a whirl of black limbs, a mass of hands clapping, of feet stamping, of bodies swaying, of eyes rolling, under the droop of heavy and motionless foliage. The steamer toiled along slowly on the edge of a black and incomprehensible frenzy. The prehistoric man was cursing us, praying to us, welcoming us—who could tell? We were cut off from the comprehension of our surroundings; we glided past like phantoms, wondering and secretly appalled, as sane men would be before an enthusiastic outbreak in a madhouse. We could not understand because we were too far and could not remember, because we were traveling in the night of first ages, of those ages that are gone, leaving hardly a sign—and no memories.

"The earth seemed unearthly. We are accustomed to look upon the shackled form of a conquered monster, but there—there you could look at a thing monstrous and free. It was unearthly, and the men were— No, they were not inhuman. Well, you know, that was the worst of it—this suspicion of their not being inhuman. It would come slowly to one. They howled and leaped, and spun, and made horrid faces; but what thrilled you was just the thought of their humanity—like yours—the thought of your remote kinship with this wild and passionate uproar. Ugly. Yes, it was ugly enough; but if you were man enough you would admit to yourself that there was in you just the faintest trace of a response to the terrible frankness of that noise, a dim suspicion of there being a meaning in it which you—you so remote from the night of first ages—could comprehend. And why not? The mind of man is capable of anything—because everything is in it, all the past as well as all the future. What was there after all? Joy, fear, sorrow, devotion, valor, rage—who can tell?—but truth—truth stripped of its cloak of time. Let the fool gape and shudder—the man knows, and can look on without a wink. But he must at least be as much of a man as these on the shore. He must meet that truth with his own true stuff—with his own inborn strength. Principles won't do. Acquisitions, clothes, pretty rags—rags that would fly off at the first good shake. No; you want a deliberate belief. An appeal to me in this fiendish row—is there? Very well; I hear; I admit, but I have a voice, too, and for good or evil mine is the speech that cannot be silenced. Of course, a fool, what with sheer fright and fine sentiments, is always safe. Who's that grunting? You wonder I didn't go ashore for a howl and a dance? Well, no—I didn't. Fine sentiments, you say? Fine sentiments, be hanged! I had no time. I had to mess about with whitelead and strips of woolen blanket helping to put bandages on those leaky steam-pipes—I tell you. I had to watch the steering, and circumvent those snags, and get the tin-pot along by hook or by crook. There was surface-truth enough in these things to save a wiser man. And between whiles I had to look after the savage who was fireman. He was an improved specimen; he could fire up a vertical boiler. He was there below me, and, upon my word, to look at him was as edifying as seeing a dog in a parody of breeches and a feather hat, walking on his hind-legs. A few months of training had done for that really fine chap. He squinted at the steam-gauge and at the water-gauge with an evident effort of intrepidity—and he had filed teeth, too, the poor devil, and the wool of his pate shaved into queer patterns, and three ornamental scars on each of his cheeks. He ought to have been clapping his hands and stamping his feet on the bank, instead of which he was hard at work, a thrall to strange witchcraft, full of improving knowledge. He was useful because he had been instructed; and what he knew was this—that should the water in that transparent thing disappear, the evil spirit inside the boiler would get angry through the greatness of his thirst, and take a terrible vengeance. So he sweated and fired up and watched the glass fearfully (with an impromptu charm, made of rags, tied to his arm, and a piece of polished bone, as big as a watch, stuck flatways through his lower lip), while the wooded banks slipped past us slowly, the short noise was left behind, the interminable miles of silence—and we crept on, towards Kurtz. But the snags were thick, the water was treacherous and shallow, the boiler seemed indeed to have a sulky devil in it, and thus neither that fireman nor I had any time to peer into our creepy thoughts.

"Some fifty miles below the Inner Station we came upon a hut of reeds, an inclined and melancholy pole, with the unrecognizable tatters of what had been a flag of some sort flying from it, and a neatly stacked wood-pile. This was unexpected. We came to the bank, and on the stack of firewood found a flat piece of board with some faded pencil-writing on it. When deciphered it said: 'Wood for you. Hurry up. Approach cautiously.' There was a signature, but it was illegible—not Kurtz—a much longer word. 'Hurry up.' Where? Up the river? 'Approach cautiously.' We had not done so.

But the warning could not have been meant for the place where it could be only found after approach. Something was wrong above. But what—and how much? That was the question. We commented adversely upon the imbecility of that telegraphic style. The bush around said nothing, and would not let us look very far, either. A torn curtain of red twill hung in the doorway of the hut, and flapped sadly in our faces. The dwelling was dismantled; but we could see a white man had lived there not very long ago. There remained a rude table—a plank on two posts; a heap of rubbish reposed in a dark corner, and by the door I picked up a book. It had lost its covers, and the pages had been thumbed into a state of extremely dirty softness; but the back had been lovingly stitched afresh with white cotton thread, which looked clean yet. It was an extraordinary find. Its title was, *An Inquiry into some Points of Seamanship,* by a man Towser, Towson—some such name—Master in his Majesty's Navy. The matter looked dreary reading enough, with illustrative diagrams and repulsive tables of figures, and the copy was sixty years old. I handled this amazing antiquity with the greatest possible tenderness, lest it should dissolve in my hands. Within, Towson or Towser was inquiring earnestly into the breaking strain of ships' chains and tackle, and other such matters. Not a very enthralling book; but at the first glance you could see there a singleness of intention, an honest concern for the right way of going to work, which made these humble pages, thought out so many years ago, luminous with another than a professional light. The simple old sailor, with his talk of chains and purchases, made me forget the jungle and the pilgrims in a delicious sensation of having come upon something unmistakably real. Such a book being there was wonderful enough; but still more astounding were the notes penciled in the margin, and plainly referring to the text. I couldn't believe my eyes! They were in cipher! Yes, it looked like cipher. Fancy a man lugging with him a book of that description into this nowhere and studying it—and making notes—in cipher at that! It was an extravagant mystery.

"I had been dimly aware for some time of a worrying noise, and when I lifted my eyes I saw the wood-pile was gone, and the manager, aided by all the pilgrims, was shouting at me from the riverside. I slipped the book into my pocket. I assure you to leave off reading was like tearing myself away from the shelter of an old and solid friendship.

"I started the lame engine ahead. 'It must be this miserable trader—this intruder,' exclaimed the manager, looking back malevolently at the place we had left. 'He must be English,' I said. 'It will not save him from getting into trouble if he is not careful,' muttered the manager darkly. I observed with assumed innocence that no man was safe from trouble in this world.

"The current was more rapid now, the steamer seemed at her last gasp, the stern-wheel flopped languidly, and I caught myself listening on tiptoe for the next beat of the boat, for in sober truth I expected the wretched thing to give up every moment. It was like watching the last flickers of a life. But still we crawled. Sometimes I would pick out a tree a little way ahead to measure our progress towards Kurtz by, but I lost it invariably before we got abreast. To keep the eyes so long on one thing was too much for human patience. The manager displayed a beautiful resignation. I fretted and fumed and took to arguing with myself whether or no I would talk openly with Kurtz; but before I could come to any conclusion it occurred to me that my speech or my silence, indeed any action of mine, would be a mere futility. What did it matter what any one knew or ignored? What did it matter who was manager? One gets sometimes such a flash of insight. The essentials of this affair lay deep under the surface, beyond my reach, and beyond my power of meddling.

"Towards the evening of the second day we judged ourselves about eight miles from Kurtz's station. I wanted to push on; but the manager looked grave, and told me the navigation up there was so dangerous that it would be advisable, the sun being very low already, to wait where we were till next morning. Moreover, he pointed out that if the warning to approach cautiously were to be followed, we must approach in daylight—not at dusk, or in the dark. This was sensible enough. Eight miles meant nearly three hours' steaming for us, and I could also see suspicious ripples at the upper end of the reach. Nevertheless, I was annoyed beyond expression at the delay, and most unreasonably, too, since one night more could not matter much after so many months. As we had plenty of wood, and caution was the word, I brought up in the middle of the stream. The reach was narrow, straight, with high sides like a railway cutting. The dusk came gliding into it long before the sun had set. The current ran smooth and swift, but a dumb immobility sat on the banks. The living trees, lashed together by the creepers and every living bush of the undergrowth, might have been changed into stone, even to the slenderest twig, to the lightest leaf.

It was not sleep—it seemed unnatural, like a state of trance. Not the faintest sound of any kind could be heard. You looked on amazed, and began to suspect yourself of being deaf—then the night came suddenly, and struck you blind as well. About three in the morning some large fish leaped, and the loud splash made me jump as though a gun had been fired. When the sun rose there was a white fog, very warm and clammy, and more blinding than the night. It did not shift or drive; it was just there, standing all round you like something solid. At eight or nine, perhaps, it lifted as a shutter lifts. We had a glimpse of the towering multitude of trees, of the immense matted jungle, with the blazing little ball of the sun hanging over it—all perfectly still—and then the white shutter came down again, smoothly, as if sliding in greased grooves. I ordered the chain, which we had begun to heave in, to be paid out again. Before it stopped running with a muffled rattle, a cry, a very loud cry, as of infinite desolation, soared slowly in the opaque air. It ceased. A complaining clamor, modulated in savage discords, filled our ears. The sheer unexpectedness of it made my hair stir under my cap. I don't know how it struck the others: to me it seemed as though the mist itself had screamed, so suddenly, and apparently from all sides at once, did this tumultuous and mournful uproar arise. It culminated in a hurried outbreak of almost intolerably excessive shrieking, which stopped short, leaving us stiffened in a variety of silly attitudes, and obstinately listening to the nearly as appalling and excessive silence. 'Good God! What is the meaning—' stammered at my elbow one of the pilgrims,—a little fat man, with sandy hair and red whiskers, who wore side-spring boots, and pink pajamas tucked into his socks. Two others remained open-mouthed a whole minute, then dashed into the little cabin, to rush out incontinently and stand darting scared glances, with Winchesters at 'ready' in their hands. What we could see was just the steamer we were on, her outlines blurred as though she had been on the point of dissolving, and a misty strip of water, perhaps two feet broad, around her —and that was all. The rest of the world was nowhere, as far as our eyes and ears were concerned. Just nowhere. Gone, disappeared; swept off without leaving a whisper or a shadow behind.

"I went forward, and ordered the chain to be hauled in short, so as to be ready to trip the anchor and move the steamboat at once if necessary. 'Will they attack?' whispered an awed voice. 'We will be all butchered in this fog,' murmured another. The faces twitched with the strain, the hands trembled slightly, the eyes forgot to wink. It was very curious to see the contrast of expressions of the white men and of the black fellows of our crew, who were as much strangers to that part of the river as we, though their homes were only eight hundred miles away. The whites, of course, greatly discomposed, had besides a curious look of being painfully shocked by such an outrageous row. The others had an alert, naturally interested expression; but their faces were essentially quiet, even those of the one or two who grinned as they hauled at the chain. Several exchanged short, grunting phrases, which seemed to settle the matter to their satisfaction. Their headman, a young, broad-chested black, severely draped in dark-blue fringed cloths, with fierce nostrils and his hair all done up artfully in oily ringlets, stood near me. 'Aha!' I said, just for good fellowship's sake. 'Catch 'im,' he snapped, with a bloodshot widening of his eyes and a flash of sharp teeth—'catch 'im. Give 'im to us.' 'To you, eh?' I asked; 'what would you do with them?' 'Eat 'im!' he said, curtly, and, leaning his elbow on the rail, looked out into the fog in a dignified and profoundly pensive attitude. I would no doubt have been properly horrified, had it not occurred to me that he and his chaps must be very hungry: that they must have been growing increasingly hungry for at least this month past. They had been engaged for six months (I don't think a single one of them had any clear idea of time, as we at the end of countless ages have. They still belonged to the beginnings of time—had no inherited experience to teach them as it were), and of course, as long as there was a piece of paper written over in accordance with some farcical law or other made down the river, it didn't enter anybody's head to trouble how they would live. Certainly they had brought with them some rotten hippo-meat, which couldn't have lasted very long, anyway, even if the pilgrims hadn't, in the midst of a shocking hullabaloo, thrown a considerable quantity of it overboard. It looked like a high-handed proceeding; but it was really a case of legitimate self-defense. You can't breathe dead hippo waking, sleeping, and eating, and at the same time keep your precarious grip on existence. Besides that, they had given them every week three pieces of brass wire, each about nine inches long; and the theory was they were to buy their provisions with that currency in river-side villages. You can see how *that* worked. There were either no villages, or the people were hostile, or the director, who like the rest of us fed out of tins, with an occasional old he-goat thrown in, didn't want to stop the steamer for some more or less recondite reason. So, unless they swallowed the wire itself, or made loops of it to snare the fishes with, I don't see what good their extravagant salary could be to them. I must say it was paid with a regularity worthy of a large and honorable trading company. For the rest, the only thing to eat—though it didn't look eatable in the least—I saw in their possession was a few lumps of some stuff like half-cooked dough, of a dirty lavender color, they kept wrapped in leaves, and now and then swallowed a piece of, but so small that it seemed done more for the looks of the thing than for any serious purpose of sustenance. Why in the name of all the gnawing devils of hunger they didn't go for us—they were thirty to five—and have a good tuck-in for once, amazes me now when I think of it. They were big powerful men, with not much capacity to weigh the consequences, with courage, with strength, even yet, though their skins were no longer glossy and their muscles no longer hard. And I saw that something restraining, one of those human secrets that baffle probability, had come into play there. I looked at them with a swift quickening of interest—not because it occurred to me I might be eaten by them before very long, though I own to you that just then I perceived—in a new light, as it were—how unwholesome the pilgrims looked, and I hoped, yes, I positively hoped, that my aspect was not so—what shall I say?—so—unappetizing: a touch of fantastic vanity which fitted well with the dream-sensation that pervaded all my days at that time. Perhaps I had a little fever, too. One can't live with one's finger everlastingly on one's pulse. I had often 'a little fever,' or a little touch of other things—the playful paw-strokes of the wilderness, the preliminary trifling before the more serious onslaught which came in due course. Yes; I looked at them as you would on any human being, with a curiosity of their impulses, motives, capacities, weaknesses, when brought to the test of an inexorable physical necessity. Restraint! What possible restraint? Was it superstition, disgust, patience, fear—or some kind of primitive honor? No fear can stand up to hunger, no patience can wear it out, disgust simply does not exist where hunger is; and as to superstition, beliefs, and what you may call principles, they are less than chaff in a breeze. Don't you know the devilry of lingering starvation, its exasperating torment, its black thoughts, its somber and brooding ferocity? Well, I do. It takes a man all his inborn strength to fight hunger properly. It's really easier to face bereavement, dishonor, and the perdition of one's soul—than this kind of prolonged hunger. Sad, but true. And these chaps, too, had no earthly reason for any kind of scruple. Restraint! I would just as soon have expected restraint from a hyena prowling amongst the corpses of a battlefield. But there was the fact facing me—the fact dazzling, to be seen, like the foam on the depths of the sea, like a ripple on an unfathomable enigma, a mystery greater—when I thought of it —than the curious, inexplicable note of desperate grief in this savage clamor that had swept by us on the river-bank, behind the blind whiteness of the fog.

"Two pilgrims were quarreling in hurried whispers as to which bank. 'Left.' 'No, no; how can you? Right, right, of course.' 'It is very serious,' said the manager's voice behind me; 'I would be desolated if anything should happen to Mr. Kurtz before we came up.' I looked at him, and had not the slightest doubt he was sincere. He was just the kind of man who would wish to preserve appearances. That was his restraint. But when he muttered something about going on at once, I did not even take the trouble to answer him. I knew, and he knew, that it was impossible. Were we to let go our hold of the bottom, we would be absolutely in the air—in space. We wouldn't be able to tell where we were going to—whether up or down stream, or across—till we fetched against one bank or the other,—and then we wouldn't know at first which it was. Of course I made no move. I had no mind for a smash-up. You couldn't imagine a more deadly place for a shipwreck. Whether drowned at once or not, we were sure to perish speedily in one way or another. 'I authorize you to take all the risks,' he said, after a short silence. 'I refuse to take any,' I said, shortly; which was just the answer he expected, though its tone might have surprised him. 'Well, I must defer to your judgment. You are captain,' he said, with marked civility. I turned my shoulder to him in sign of my appreciation, and looked into the fog. How long would it last? It was the most hopeless look-out. The approach to this Kurtz grubbing for ivory in the wretched bush was beset by as many dangers as though he had been an enchanted princess sleeping in a fabulous castle. 'Will they attack, do you think?' asked the manager, in a confidential tone.

"I did not think they would attack, for several obvious reasons. The thick fog was one. If they left the bank in their canoes they would get lost in it, as we would be if we attempted to move. Still, I had also judged the jungle of both banks quite impenetrable—and yet eyes were in it, eyes that had seen us. The river-side bushes were certainly very thick; but the undergrowth behind was evidently penetrable. However, during the short lift I had seen no canoes anywhere in the reach —certainly not abreast of the steamer. But what made the idea of attack inconceivable to me was the nature of the noise —of the cries we had heard. They had not the fierce character boding immediate hostile intention. Unexpected, wild, and violent as they had been, they had given me an irresistible impression of sorrow. The glimpse of the steamboat had for some reason filled those savages with unrestrained grief. The danger, if any, I expounded, was from our proximity to a great human passion let loose. Even extreme grief may ultimately vent itself in violence—but more generally takes the form of apathy. . . .

"You should have seen the pilgrims stare! They had no heart to grin, or even to revile me: but I believe they thought me gone mad—with fright, maybe. I delivered a regular lecture. My dear boys, it was no good bothering. Keep a lookout? Well, you may guess I watched the fog for the signs of lifting as a cat watches a mouse; but for anything else our eyes were of no more use to us than if we had been buried miles deep in a heap of cotton-wool. It felt like it, too—choking, warm, stifling. Besides, all I said, though it sounded extravagant, was absolutely true to fact. What we afterwards alluded to as an attack was really an attempt at repulse. The action was very far from being aggressive—it was not even defensive, in the usual sense: it was undertaken under the stress of desperation, and in its essence was purely protective.

"It developed itself, I should say, two

hours after the fog lifted, and its commencement was at a spot, roughly speaking, about a mile and a half below Kurtz's station. We had just floundered and flopped round a bend, when I saw an islet, a mere grassy hummock of bright green, in the middle of the stream. It was the only thing of the kind; but as we opened the reach more, I perceived it was the head of a long sandbank, or rather of a chain of shallow patches stretching down the middle of the river. They were discolored, just awash, and the whole lot was seen just under the water, exactly as a man's backbone is seen running down the middle of his back under the skin. Now, as far as I did see, I could go to the right or to the left of this. I didn't know either channel, of course. The banks looked pretty well alike, the depth appeared the same; but as I had been informed the station was on the west side, I naturally headed for the western passage.

"No sooner had we fairly entered it than I became aware it was much narrower than I had supposed. To the left of us there was the long uninterrupted shoal, and to the right a high, steep bank heavily overgrown with bushes. Above the bush the trees stood in serried ranks. The twigs overhung the current thickly, and from distance to distance a large limb of some tree projected rigidly over the stream. It was then well on in the afternoon, the face of the forest was gloomy, and a broad strip of shadow had already fallen on the water. In this shadow we steamed up—very slowly, as you may imagine. I sheered her well inshore—the water being deepest near the bank, as the sounding-pole informed me.

"One of my hungry and forbearing friends was sounding in the bows just below me. This steamboat was exactly like a decked scow. On the deck, there were two little teak-wood houses, with doors and windows. The boiler was in the fore-end, and the machinery right astern. Over the whole there was a light roof, supported on stanchions. The funnel projected through that roof, and in front of the funnel a small cabin built of light planks served for a pilot-house. It contained a couch, two camp-stools, a loaded Martini-Henry leaning in one corner, a tiny table, and the steering-wheel. It had a wide door in front and a broad shutter at each side. All these were always thrown open, of course. I spent my days perched up there on the extreme fore-end of that roof, before the door. At night I slept, or tried to, on the couch. An athletic black belonging to some coast tribe, and educated by my poor predecessor, was the helmsman. He sported a pair of brass earrings, wore a blue cloth wrapper from the waist to the ankles, and thought all the world of himself. He was the most unstable kind of fool I had ever seen. He steered with no end of a swagger while you were by; but if he lost sight of you, he became instantly the prey of an abject funk, and would let that cripple of a steamboat get the upper hand of him in a minute.

"I was looking down at the sounding-pole, and feeling much annoyed to see at each try a little more of it stick out of that river, when I saw my poleman give up the business suddenly, and stretch himself flat on the deck, without even taking the trouble to haul his pole in. He kept hold on it though, and it trailed in the water. At the same time the fireman, whom I could also see below me, sat down abruptly before his furnace and ducked his head. I was amazed. Then

I had to look at the river mighty quick, because there was a snag in the fairway. Sticks, little sticks, were flying about—thick: they were whizzing before my nose, dropping below me, striking behind me against my pilot-house. All this time the river, the shore, the woods, were very quiet—perfectly quiet. I could only hear the heavy splashing thump of the stern-wheel and the patter of these things. We cleared the snag clumsily. Arrows, by Jove! We were being shot at! I stepped in quickly to close the shutter on the land-side. That fool-helmsman, his hands on the spokes, was lifting his knees high, stamping his feet, champing his mouth, like a reined-in horse. Confound him! And we were staggering within ten feet of the bank. I had to lean right out to swing the heavy shutter, and I saw a face amongst the leaves on the level with my own, looking at me very fierce and steady; and then suddenly, as though a veil had been removed from my eyes, I made out, deep in the tangled gloom, naked breasts, arms, legs, glaring eyes,—the bush was swarming with human limbs in movement, glistening, of bronze color. The twigs shook, swayed, and rustled, the arrows flew out of them, and then the shutter came to. 'Steer her straight,' I said to the helmsman. He held his head rigid, face forward; but his eyes rolled, he kept on lifting and setting down his feet gently, his mouth foamed a little. 'Keep quiet!' I said in a fury. I might just as well have ordered a tree not to sway in the wind. I darted out. Below me there was a great scuffle of feet on the iron deck; confused exclamations; a voice screamed, 'Can you turn back?' I caught sight of a V-shaped ripple on the water ahead. What? Another snag! A fusillade burst out under my feet. The pilgrims had opened with their Winchesters, and were simply squirting lead into that bush. A deuce of a lot of smoke came up and drove slowly forward. I swore at it. Now I couldn't see the ripple or the snag either. I stood in the doorway, peering, and the arrows came in swarms. They might have been poisoned, but they looked as though they wouldn't kill a cat. The bush began to howl. Our wood-cutters raised a war-like whoop; the report of a rifle just at my back deafened me. I glanced over my shoulder, and the pilot-house was yet full of noise and smoke when I made a dash at the wheel. The fool-nigger had dropped everything, to throw the shutter open and let off that Martini-Henry. He stood before the wide opening, glaring, and I yelled at him to come back, while I straightened the sudden twist out of that steamboat. There was no room to turn even if I had wanted to, the snag was somewhere very near ahead in that confounded smoke, there was no time to lose, so I just crowded her into the bank—right into the bank, where I knew the water was deep.

"We tore slowly along the overhanging bushes in a whirl of broken twigs and flying leaves. The fusillade below stopped short, as I had foreseen it would when the squirts got empty. I threw my head back to a glinting whizz that traversed the pilot-house, in at one shutter-hole and out at the other. Looking past that mad helmsman, who was shaking the empty rifle and yelling at the shore, I saw vague forms of men running bent double, leaping, gliding, distinct, incomplete, evanescent. Something big appeared in the air before the shutter, the rifle went overboard, and the man stepped back swiftly, looked at me over his shoulder in an extraordinary, profound, familiar manner, and fell upon my feet. The side of his head hit the wheel twice, and the end of what appeared a long cane clattered round and knocked over a little camp-stool. It looked as though after wrenching that thing from somebody ashore he had lost his balance in the effort. The thin smoke had blown away, we were clear of the snag, and looking ahead I could see that in another hundred yards or so I would be free to sheer off, away from the bank; but my feet felt so very warm and wet that I had to look down. The man had rolled on his back and stared straight up at me; both his hands clutched that cane. It was the shaft of a spear that, either thrown or lunged through the opening, had caught him in the side just below the ribs; the blade had gone in out of sight, after making a frightful gash; my shoes were full; a pool of blood lay very still, gleaming dark-red under the wheel; his eyes shone with an amazing luster. The fusillade burst out again. He looked at me anxiously, gripping the spear like something precious, with an air of being afraid I would try to take it away from him. I had to make an effort to free my eyes from his gaze and attend to steering. With one hand I felt above my head for the line of the steam whistle, and jerked out screech after screech hurriedly. The tumult of angry and warlike yells was checked instantly, and then from the depths of the woods went out such a tremulous and prolonged wail of mournful fear and utter despair as may be imagined to follow the flight of the last hope from the earth. There was a great commotion in the bush; the shower of arrows stopped, a few dropping shots rang out sharply—then silence, in which the languid beat of the stern-wheel came plainly to my ears. I put the helm hard a-starboard at the moment when the pilgrim in pink pajamas, very hot and agitated, appeared in the doorway. 'The manager sends me—' he began in an official tone, and stopped short. 'Good God!' he said, glaring at the wounded man.

"We two whites stood over him, and his lustrous and inquiring glance enveloped us both. I declare it looked as though he would presently put to us some question in an understandable language; but he died without uttering a sound, without moving a limb, without twitching a muscle. Only in the very last moment, as though in response to some sign we could not see, to some whisper we could not hear, he frowned heavily, and that frown gave to his black death-mask an inconceivably somber, brooding, and menacing expression. The luster of inquiring glance faded swiftly into vacant glassiness. 'Can you steer?' I asked the agent eagerly. He looked very dubious; but I made a grab at his arm, and he understood at once I meant him to steer whether or no. To tell you the truth, I was morbidly anxious to change my shoes and socks. 'He is dead,' murmured the fellow, immensely impressed. 'No doubt about it,' said I, tugging like mad at the shoe-laces. 'And by the way, I suppose Mr. Kurtz is dead as well by this time.'

"For the moment that was the dominant thought. There was a sense of extreme disappointment, as though I had found out I had been striving after something altogether without a substance. I couldn't have been more disgusted if I had traveled all this way for the sole purpose of talking with Mr. Kurtz. Talking with . . . I flung one shoe overboard, and became aware that that was exactly what I had been looking forward to—a talk with Kurtz. I made the strange discovery that I had never imagined him as doing, you know, but as discoursing. I didn't say to myself, 'Now I will never see him,' or 'Now I will never shake him by the hand,' but, 'Now I will never hear him.' The man presented himself as a voice. Not of course that I did not connect him with some sort of action. Hadn't I been told in all the tones of jealousy and admiration that he had collected, bartered, swindled, or stolen more ivory than all the other agents together? That was not the point. The point was in his being a gifted creature, and that of all his gifts the one that stood out preëminently, that carried with it a sense of real presence, was his ability to talk, his words—the gift of expression, the bewildering, the illuminating, the most exalted and the most contemptible, the pulsating stream of light, or the deceitful flow from the heart of an impenetrable darkness.

"The other shoe went flying unto the devil-god of that river. I thought, by Jove! it's all over. We are too late; he has vanished—the gift has vanished, by means of some spear, arrow, or club. I will never hear that chap speak after all,—and my sorrow had a startling extravagance of emotion, even such as I had noticed in the howling sorrow of these savages in the bush. I couldn't have felt more lonely desolation somehow, had I been robbed of a belief or had missed my destiny in life. . . . Why do you sigh in this beastly way, somebody? Absurd? Well, absurd. Good Lord! mustn't a man ever— Here, give me some tobacco." . . .

There was a pause of profound stillness, then a match flared, and Marlow's lean face appeared, worn, hollow, with downward folds and drooped eyelids, with an aspect of concentrated attention; and as he took vigorous draws at his pipe, it seemed to retreat and advance out of the night in the regular flicker of the tiny flame. The match went out.

"Absurd!" he cried. "This is the worst of trying to tell. . . . Here you all are, each moored with two good addresses, like a hulk with two anchors, a butcher round one corner, a policeman round another, excellent appetites, and temperature normal—you hear—normal from year's end to year's end. And you say, Absurd! Absurd be—exploded! Absurd! My dear boys, what can you expect from a man who out of sheer nervousness had just flung overboard a pair of new shoes! Now I think of it, it is amazing I did not shed tears. I am, upon the whole, proud of my fortitude. I was cut to the quick at the idea of having lost the inestimable privilege of listening to the gifted Kurtz. Of course I was wrong. The privilege was waiting for me. Oh, yes, I heard more than enough. And I was right, too. A voice. He was very little more than a voice. And I heard—him—it—this voice —other voices—all of them were so little more than voices—and the memory of that time itself lingers around me, impalpable, like a dying vibration of one immense jabber, silly, atrocious, sordid, savage, or simply mean, without any kind of sense. Voices, voices—even the girl herself—now—"

He was silent for a long time.

"I laid the ghost of his gifts at last with a lie," he began, suddenly. "Girl! What? Did I mention a girl? Oh, she is out of it—completely. They—the women I mean —are out of it—should be out of it. We must help them to stay in that beautiful world of their own, lest ours gets worse. Oh, she had to be out of it. You should have heard the disinterred body of Mr. Kurtz saying, 'My Intended.' You would have perceived directly then how completely she was out of it. And the lofty frontal bone of Mr. Kurtz! They say the hair goes on growing sometimes, but this —ah—specimen, was impressively bald. The wilderness had patted him on the head, and, behold, it was like a ball—an ivory ball; it had caressed him, and—lo! —he had withered; it had taken him, loved him, embraced him, got into his veins, consumed his flesh, and sealed his soul to its own by the inconceivable ceremonies of some devilish initiation. He was its spoiled and pampered favorite. Ivory? I should think so. Heaps of it, stacks of it. The old mud shanty was bursting with it. You would think there was not a single tusk left either above or below the ground in the whole country. 'Mostly fossil,' the manager had remarked, disparagingly. It was no more fossil than I am; but they call it fossil when it is dug up. It appears these niggers do bury the tusks sometimes—but evidently they couldn't bury this parcel deep enough to save the gifted Mr. Kurtz from his fate. We filled the steamboat with it, and had to pile a lot on the deck. Thus he could see and enjoy as long as he could see, because the appreciation of this favor had remained with him to the last. You should have heard him say, 'My ivory.' Oh, yes, I heard him. 'My Intended, my ivory, my station, my river, my—' everything belonged to him. It made me hold my breath in expectation of hearing the wilderness burst into a prodigious peal of laughter that would shake the fixed stars in their places. Everything belonged to him—but that was a trifle. The thing was to know what he belonged to, how many powers of darkness claimed him for their own. That was the reflection that made you creepy all over. It was impossible—it was not good for one either—trying to imagine. He had taken a high seat amongst the devils of the land—I mean literally. You can't understand. How could you?—with solid pavement under your feet, surrounded by kind neighbors ready to cheer you or to fall on you, stepping delicately between the butcher and the policeman, in the holy terror of scandal and gallows and lunatic asylums—how can you imagine what particular region of the first ages a man's untrammeled feet may take him into by the way of solitude—utter solitude without a policeman—by the way of silence—utter silence, where no warning voice of a kind neighbor can be heard whispering of public opinion? These little things make all the great difference. When they are gone you must fall back upon your own innate strength, upon your own capacity for faithfulness. Of course you may be too much of a fool to go wrong—too dull even to know you are being assaulted by the powers of darkness. I take it, no fool ever made a bargain for his soul with the devil: the fool is too much of a fool, or the devil too much of a devil—I don't know which. Or you may be such a thunderingly exalted creature as to be altogether deaf and blind to anything but heavenly sights and sounds. Then the earth for you is only a standing place—and whether to be like this is your loss or your gain I won't pretend to say. But most of us are neither one nor the other. The earth for us is a place to live in, where we must put up with sights, with sounds, with smells, too, by Jove!—breathe dead hippo, so to speak, and not be contaminated. And there, don't you see? your strength comes in, the faith in your ability for the digging of unostentatious holes to bury the stuff in—your power of devotion, not to yourself, but to an obscure, back-breaking business. And that's difficult enough. Mind, I am not trying to excuse or even explain—I am trying to account to myself for—for—Mr. Kurtz—for the shade of Mr. Kurtz. This initiated wraith from the back of Nowhere honored me with its amazing confidence before it vanished altogether. This was because it could speak English to me. The original Kurtz had been educated partly in England, and—as he was good enough to say himself—his sympathies were in the right place. His mother was half-English, his father was half-French. All Europe contributed to the making of Kurtz; and by and by I learned that, most appropriately, the International Society for the Suppression of Savage Customs had intrusted him with the making of a report, for its future guidance. And he had written it, too. I've seen it. I've read it. It was eloquent, vibrating with eloquence, but too high-strung, I think. Seventeen pages of close writing he had found time for! But this must have been before his—let us say—nerves, went wrong, and caused him to preside at certain midnight dances ending with unspeakable rites, which—as far as I reluctantly gathered from what I heard at various times—were offered up to him—do you understand?—to Mr. Kurtz himself. But it was a beautiful piece of writing. The opening paragraph, however, in the light of later information, strikes me now as ominous. He began with the argument that we whites, from the point of development we had arrived at, 'must necessarily appear to them [savages] in the nature of supernatural beings—we approach them with the might as of a deity,' and so on, and so on. 'By the simple exercise of our will we can exert a power for good practically unbounded,' etc., etc. From that point he soared and took me with him. The peroration was magnificent, though difficult to remember, you know. It gave me the notion of an exotic Immensity ruled by an august Benevolence. It made me tingle with enthusiasm. This was the unbounded power of eloquence—of words—of burning noble words. There were no practical hints to interrupt the magic current of phrases, unless a kind of note at the foot of the last page, scrawled evidently much later, in an unsteady hand, may be regarded as the exposition of a method. It was very simple, and at the end of that moving appeal to every altruistic sentiment it blazed at you, luminous and terrifying, like a flash of lightning in a serene sky: 'Exterminate all the brutes!' The curious part was that he had apparently forgotten all about the valuable postscriptum, because, later on, when he in a sense came to himself, he repeatedly entreated me to take good care of 'my pamphlet' (he called it), as it was sure to have in the future a good influence upon his career. I had full information about all these things, and, besides, as it turned out, I was to have the care of his memory. I've done enough for it to give me the indisputable right to lay it, if I choose, for an everlasting rest in the dustbin of progress, amongst all the sweepings and, figuratively speaking, all the dead cats of civilization. But then, you see, I can't choose. He won't be forgotten. Whatever he was, he was not common. He had the power to charm or frighten rudimentary souls into an aggravated witch-dance in his honor; he could also fill the small souls of the pilgrims with bitter misgivings: he had one devoted friend at least, and he had conquered one soul in the world that was neither rudimentary nor tainted with self-seeking. No; I can't forget him, though I am not prepared to affirm the fellow was exactly worth the life we lost in getting to him. I missed my late helmsman awfully,—I missed him even while his body was still lying in the pilot-house. Perhaps you will think it passing strange this regret for a savage who was no more account than a grain of sand in a black Sahara. Well, don't you see, he had done something, he had steered; for months I had him at my back—a help—an instrument. It was a kind of partnership. He steered for me—I had to look after him, I worried about his deficiencies, and thus a subtle bond had been created, of which I only became aware when it was suddenly broken. And the intimate profundity of that look he gave me when he received his hurt remains to this day in my memory—like a claim of distant kinship affirmed in a supreme moment.

"Poor fool! If he had only left that shutter alone. He had no restraint, no restraint—just like Kurtz—a tree swayed by the wind. As soon as I had put on a dry pair of slippers, I dragged him out, after first jerking the spear out of his side, which operation I confess I performed with my eyes shut tight. His heels leaped together over the little door-step; his shoulders were pressed to my breast; I hugged him from behind desperately. Oh! he was heavy, heavy; heavier than any man on earth, I should imagine. Then without more ado I tipped him overboard. The current snatched him as though he had been a wisp of grass, and I saw the body roll over twice before I lost sight of it forever. All the pilgrims and the manager were then congregated on the awning-deck about the pilot-house, chattering at each other like a flock of excited magpies, and there was a scandalized murmur at my heartless promptitude. What they wanted to keep that body hanging about for I can't guess. Embalm it, maybe. But I had also heard another, and a very ominous, murmur on the deck below. My friends the wood-cutters were likewise scandalized, and with a better show of reason—though I admit that the reason itself was quite inadmissible. Oh, quite! I had made up my mind that if my late helmsman was to be eaten, the fishes alone should have him. He had been a very second-rate helmsman while alive, but now he was dead he might have become a first-class temptation, and possibly cause some startling trouble. Besides, I was anxious to take the wheel, the man in pink pajamas showing himself a hopeless duffer at the business.

"This I did directly the simple funeral was over. We were going half-speed, keeping right in the middle of the stream, and I listened to the talk about me. They had given up Kurtz, they had given up the station; Kurtz was dead, and the station had been burnt—and so on—and so on. The red-haired pilgrim was beside himself with the thought that at least this poor Kurtz had been properly avenged. 'Say! We must have made a glorious slaughter of them in the bush. Eh? What do you think? Say?' He positively danced, the bloodthirsty little gingery beggar. And he had nearly fainted when he saw the wounded man! I could not help saying, 'You made a glorious lot of smoke, anyhow.' I had seen, from the way the tops of the bushes rustled and flew, that almost all the shots had gone too high. You can't hit anything unless you take aim and fire from the shoulder; but these chaps fired from the hip with their eyes shut. The retreat, I maintained—and I was right—was caused by the screeching of the steam-whistle. Upon this they forgot Kurtz, and began to howl at me with indignant protests.

"The manager stood by the wheel murmuring confidentially about the necessity of getting well away down the river before dark at all events, when I saw in the distance a clearing on the river-side and the outlines of some sort of building. 'What's this?' I asked. He clapped his hands in wonder. 'The station!' he cried. I edged in at once, still going half-speed.

"Through my glasses I saw the slope of a hill interspersed with rare trees and perfectly free from undergrowth. A long decaying building on the summit was half buried in the high grass; the large holes in the peaked roof gaped black from afar; the jungle and the woods made a background. There was no enclosure or fence of any kind; but there had been one apparently, for near the house half-a-dozen slim posts remained in a row, roughly trimmed, and with their upper ends ornamented with round carved balls. The rails, or whatever there had been between, had disappeared. Of course the forest surrounded all that. The river-bank was clear, and on the water-side I saw a white man under a hat like a cartwheel beckoning persistently with his whole arm. Examining the edge of the forest above and below, I was almost certain I could see movements—human forms gliding here and there. I steamed past prudently, then stopped the engines and let her drift down. The man on the shore began to shout, urging us to land. 'We have been attacked,' screamed the manager. 'I know—I know. It's all right,' yelled back the other, as cheerful as you please. 'Come along. It's all right. I am glad.'

"His aspect reminded me of something I had seen—something funny I had seen somewhere. As I maneuvered to get alongside, I was asking myself, 'What does this fellow look like?' Suddenly I got it. He looked like a harlequin. His clothes had been made of some stuff that was brown holland probably, but it was covered with patches all over, with bright patches, blue, red and yellow,—patches on the back, patches on the front, patches on elbows, on knees; colored binding around his jacket, scarlet edging at the bottom of his trousers; and the sunshine made him look extremely gay and wonderfully neat withal, because you could see how beautifully all this patching had been done. A beardless, boyish face, very fair, no features to speak of, nose peeling, little blue eyes, smiles and frowns chasing each other over that open countenance like sunshine and shadow on a windswept plain. 'Look out, captain!' he cried; 'there's a snag lodged in her last night.' 'What! Another snag?' I confess I swore shamefully. I had nearly holed my cripple, to finish off that charming trip. The harlequin on the bank turned his little pug-nose up to me. 'You English?' he asked, all smiles. 'Are you?' I shouted from the wheel. The smiles vanished, and he shook his head as if sorry for my disappointment. Then he brightened up. 'Never mind!' he cried, encouragingly. 'Are we in time?' I asked. 'He is up there,' he replied, with a toss of the head up the hill, and becoming gloomy all of a sudden. His face was like the autumn sky, overcast one moment and bright the next.

"When the manager, escorted by the pilgrims, all of them armed to the teeth, had gone to the house this chap came on board. 'I say, I don't like this. These natives are in the bush,' I said. He assured me earnestly it was all right. 'They are simple people,' he added; 'well, I am glad you came. It took me all my time to keep them off.' 'But you said it was all right,' I cried. 'Oh, they meant no harm,' he said; and as I stared he corrected himself, 'Not exactly.' Then vivaciously, 'My faith, your pilot-house wants a clean-up!' In the next breath he advised me to keep enough steam on the boiler to blow the whistle in case of any trouble. 'One good screech will do more for you than all your rifles. They are simple people,' he repeated. He rattled away at such a rate he quite overwhelmed me. He seemed to be trying to make up for lots of silence, and actually hinted, laughing, that such was the case. 'Don't you talk with Mr. Kurtz?' I said. 'You don't talk with that man—you listen to him,' he exclaimed with severe exaltation. 'But now—' He waved his arm, and in the twinkling of an eye was in the uttermost depths of despondency. In a moment he came up again with a jump, possessed himself of both my hands, shook them continuously, while he gabbled: 'Brother sailor ... honor ... pleasure ... delight ... introduce myself ... Russian ... son of an arch-priest ... Government of Tambov. ... What? Tobacco! English tobacco; the excellent English tobacco! Now, that's brotherly. Smoke? Where's a sailor that does not smoke?'

"The pipe soothed him, and gradually I made out he had run away from school, had gone to sea in a Russian ship; ran away again; served some time in English ships; was now reconciled with the arch-priest. He made a point of that. 'But when one is young one must see things, gather experience, ideas; enlarge the mind.' 'Here!' I interrupted. 'You can never tell! Here I met Mr. Kurtz,' he said, youthfully solemn and reproachful. I held my tongue after that. It appears he had persuaded a Dutch trading house on the coast to fit him out with stores and goods, and had started for the interior with a light heart, and no more idea of what would happen to him than a baby. He had been wandering about that river for nearly two years alone, cut off from everybody and everything. 'I am not so young as I look. I am twenty-five,' he said. 'At first old Van Shuyten would tell me to go to the devil,' he narrated with keen enjoyment; 'but I stuck to him, and talked and talked, till at last he got afraid I would talk the hind-leg off his favorite dog, so he gave me some cheap things and a few guns, and told me he hoped he would never see my face again. Good old Dutchman, Van Shuyten. I've sent him one small lot of ivory a year ago, so that he can't call me a little thief when I get back. I hope he got it. And for the rest I don't care. I had some wood stacked for you. That was my old house. Did you see?'

"I gave him Towson's book. He made as though he would kiss me, but restrained himself. 'The only book I had left, and I thought I had lost it,' he said, looking at it ecstatically. 'So many accidents happen to a man going about alone, you know. Canoes get upset sometimes—and sometimes you've got to clear out so quick when the people get angry.' He thumbed the pages. 'You made notes in Russian?' I asked. He nodded. 'I thought they were written in cipher,' I said. He laughed, then became serious. 'I had lots of trouble to keep these people off,' he said. 'Did they want to kill you?' I asked. 'Oh, no!' he cried, and checked himself.

'Why did they attack us?' I pursued. He hesitated, then said shamefacedly, 'They don't want him to go.' 'Don't they?' I said curiously. He nodded a nod full of mystery and wisdom. 'I tell you,' he cried, 'this man has enlarged my mind.' He opened his arms wide, staring at me with his little blue eyes that were perfectly round."

III

"I looked at him, lost in astonishment. There he was before me, in motley, as though he had absconded from a troupe of mimes, enthusiastic, fabulous. His very existence was improbable, inexplicable, and altogether bewildering. He was an insoluble problem. It was inconceivable how he had existed, how he had succeeded in getting so far, how he had managed to remain—why he did not instantly disappear. 'I went a little farther,' he said, 'then still a little farther—till I had gone so far that I don't know how I'll ever get back. Never mind. Plenty time. I can manage. You take Kurtz away quick—quick—I tell you.' The glamour of youth enveloped his parti-colored rags, his destitution, his loneliness, the essential desolation of his futile wanderings. For months—for years—his life hadn't been worth a day's purchase; and there he was gallantly, thoughtlessly alive, to all appearance indestructible solely by the virtue of his few years and of his unreflecting audacity. I was seduced into something like admiration—like envy. Glamour urged him on, glamour kept him unscathed. He surely wanted nothing from the wilderness but space to breathe in and to push on through. His need was to exist, and to move onwards at the greatest possible risk, and with a maximum of privation. If the absolutely pure, uncalculating, unpractical spirit of adventure had ever ruled a human being, it ruled this be-patched youth. I almost envied him the possession of this modest and clear flame. It seemed to have consumed all thought of self so completely, that even while he was talking to you, you forgot that it was he—the man before your eyes—who had gone through these things. I did not envy him his devotion to Kurtz, though. He had not meditated over it. It came to him and he accepted it with a sort of eager fatalism. I must say that to me it appeared about the most dangerous thing in every way he had come upon so far.

"They had come together unavoidably, like two ships becalmed near each other, and lay rubbing sides at last. I suppose Kurtz wanted an audience, because on a certain occasion, when encamped in the forest, they had talked all night, or more probably Kurtz had talked. 'We talked of everything,' he said, quite transported at the recollection. 'I forgot there was such a thing as sleep. The night did not seem to last an hour. Everything! Everything! . . . Of love, too.' 'Ah, he talked to you of love!' I said, much amused. 'It isn't what you think,' he cried, almost passionately. 'It was in general. He made me see things—things.'

"He threw his arms up. We were on deck at the time, and the headman of my wood-cutters, lounging near by, turned upon him his heavy and glittering eyes. I looked around, and I don't know why, but I assure you that never, never before, did this land, this river, this jungle, the very arch of this blazing sky, appear to me so hopeless and so dark, so impenetrable to human thought, so pitiless to human weakness. 'And, ever since, you have been with him, of course?' I said.

"On the contrary. It appears their intercourse had been very much broken by various causes. He had, as he informed me proudly, managed to nurse Kurtz through two illnesses (he alluded to it as you would to some risky feat), but as a rule Kurtz wandered alone far in the depths of the forest. 'Very often coming to this station, I had to wait days and days before he would turn up,' he said. 'Ah, it was worth waiting for!—sometimes.' 'What was he doing? exploring or what?' I asked. 'Oh, yes, of course'; he had discovered lots of villages, a lake, too—he did not know exactly in what direction; it was dangerous to inquire too much—but mostly his expeditions had been for ivory. 'But he had no goods to trade with by that time,' I objected. 'There's a good lot of cartridges left even yet,' he answered, looking away. 'To speak plainly, he raided the country,' I said. He nodded. 'Not alone, surely!' He muttered something about the villages round that lake. 'Kurtz got the tribe to follow him, did he?' I suggested. He fidgeted a little. 'They adored him,' he said. The tone of these words was so extraordinary that I looked at him searchingly. It was curious to see his mingled eagerness and reluctance to speak of Kurtz. The man filled his life, occupied his thoughts, swayed his emotions. 'What can you expect?' he burst out; 'he came to them with thunder and lightning, you know—and they had never seen anything like it—and very terrible. He could be very terrible. You can't judge Mr. Kurtz as you would an ordinary man. No, no, no! Now—just to give you an idea—I don't mind telling you he wanted to shoot me, too, one day—but I don't judge him.' 'Shoot you!' I cried. 'What for?' 'Well, I had a small lot of ivory the chief of that village near my house gave me. You see I used to shoot game for them. Well, he wanted it, and wouldn't hear reason. He declared he would shoot me unless I gave him the ivory and then cleared out of the country, because he could do so, and had a fancy for it, and there was nothing on earth to prevent him killing whom he jolly well pleased. And it was true, too. I gave him the ivory. What did I care! But I didn't clear out. No, no, I couldn't leave him. I had to be careful, of course, till we got friendly again for a time. He had his second illness then. Afterwards I had to keep out of the way; but I didn't mind. He was living for the most part in those villages on the lake. When he came down to the river, sometimes he would take to me, and sometimes it was better for me to be careful. This man suffered too much. He hated all this, and somehow he couldn't get away. When I had a chance I begged him to try and leave while there was time; I offered to go back with him. And he would say yes, and then he would remain; go off on another ivory hunt; disappear for weeks; forget himself amongst these people—forget himself—you know.' 'Why! he's mad,' I said. He protested indignantly. Mr. Kurtz couldn't be mad. If I had heard him talk, only two days ago, I wouldn't dare hint at such a thing. . . . I had taken up my binoculars while we talked, and was looking at the shore, sweeping the limit of the forest at each side and at the back of the house. The consciousness of there being people in that bush, so silent, so quiet—as silent and quiet as the ruined house on the hill—made me uneasy. There was no sign on the face of nature of this amazing tale that was not so much told as suggested to me in desolate exclamations, completed by shrugs, in interrupted phrases, in hints ending in deep sighs. The woods were unmoved, like a mask—heavy, like the closed door of a prison—they looked with their air of hidden knowledge, of patient expectation, of unapproachable silence. The Russian was explaining to me that it was only lately that Mr. Kurtz had come down to the river, bringing along with him all the fighting men of that lake tribe. He had been absent for several months—getting himself adored, I suppose—and had come down unexpectedly, with the intention to all appearance of making a raid either across the river or down stream. Evidently the appetite for more ivory had got the better of the —what shall I say?—less material aspirations. However he had got much worse suddenly. 'I heard he was lying helpless, and so I came up—took my chance,' said the Russian. 'Oh, he is bad, very bad.' I directed my glass to the house. There were no signs of life, but there was the ruined roof, the long mud wall peeping above the grass, with three little square window-holes, no two of the same size; all this brought within reach of my hand, as it were. And then I made a brusque movement, and one of the remaining posts of that vanished fence leaped up in the field of my glass. You remember I told you I had been struck at the distance by certain attempts at ornamentation, rather remarkable in the ruinous aspect of the place. Now I had suddenly a nearer view, and its first result was to make me throw my head back as if before a blow. Then I went carefully from post to post with my glass, and I saw my mistake. These round knobs were not ornamental but symbolic; they were expressive and puzzling, striking and disturbing—food for thought and also for vultures if there had been any looking down from the sky; but at all events for such ants as were industrious enough to ascend the pole. They would have been even more impressive, those heads on the stakes, if their faces had not been turned to the house. Only one, the first I had made out, was facing my way. I was not so shocked as you may think. The start back I had given was really nothing but a movement of surprise. I had expected to see a knob of wood there, you know. I returned deliberately to the first I had seen—and there it was, black, dried, sunken, with closed eyelids,—a head that seemed to sleep at the top of that pole, and with the shrunken dry lips showing a narrow white line of the teeth, was smiling, too, smiling continuously at some endless and jocose dream of that eternal slumber.

"I am not disclosing any trade secrets. In fact, the manager said afterwards that Mr. Kurtz's methods had ruined the district. I have no opinion on that point, but I want you clearly to understand that there was nothing exactly profitable in these heads being there. They only showed that Mr. Kurtz lacked restraint in the gratification of his various lusts, that there was something wanting in him—some small matter which, when the pressing need arose, could not be found under his magnificent eloquence. Whether he knew of this deficiency himself I can't say. I think the knowledge came to him at last —only at the very last. But the wilderness had found him out early, and had taken on him a terrible vengeance for the fantastic invasion. I think it had whispered to him things about himself which he did not know, things of which he had no conception till he took counsel with this great solitude—and the whisper had proved irresistibly fascinating. It echoed loudly within him because he was hollow at the core. . . . I put down the glass, and the head that had appeared near enough to be spoken to seemed at once to have leaped away from me into inaccessible distance.

"The admirer of Mr. Kurtz was a bit crestfallen. In a hurried indistinct voice he began to assure me he had not dared to take these—say, symbols—down. He was not afraid of the natives; they would not stir till Mr. Kurtz gave the word. His ascendancy was extraordinary. The camps of these people surrounded the place, and the chiefs came every day to see him. They would crawl. . . . 'I don't want to know anything of the ceremonies used when approaching Mr. Kurtz,' I shouted. Curious, this feeling that came over me that such details would be more intolerable than those heads drying on the stakes under Mr. Kurtz's windows. After all, that was only a savage sight, while I seemed at one bound to have been transported into some lightless region of subtle horrors, where pure, uncomplicated savagery was a positive relief, being something that had a right to exist—obviously—in the sunshine. The young man looked at me with surprise. I suppose it did not occur to him that Mr. Kurtz was no idol of mine. He forgot I hadn't heard any of these splendid monologues on, what was it? on love, justice, conduct of life —or what not. If it had come to crawling before Mr. Kurtz, he crawled as much as the veriest savage of them all. I had no idea of the conditions, he said: these heads were the heads of rebels. I shocked him excessively by laughing. Rebels! What would be the next definition I was to hear? There had been enemies, criminals, workers—and these were rebels. Those rebellious heads looked very subdued to me on their sticks. 'You don't know how such a life tries a man like Kurtz,' cried Kurtz's last disciple. 'Well, and you?' I said. 'I! I! I am a simple man. I have no great thoughts. I want nothing from anybody. How can you compare me to . . . ?' His feelings were too much for speech, and suddenly he broke down. 'I don't understand,' he groaned, 'I've been doing my best to keep him alive and that's enough. I had no hand in all this. I have no abilities. There hasn't been a drop of medicine or a mouthful of invalid food for months here. He was shamefully abandoned. A man like this, with such ideas. Shamefully! Shamefully! I—I—haven't slept for the last ten nights. . . .'

"His voice lost itself in the calm of the evening. The long shadows of the forest had slipped downhill while we talked, had gone far beyond the ruined hovel, beyond the symbolic row of stakes. All this was in the gloom, while we down there were yet in the sunshine, and the stretch of the river abreast of the clearing glittered in a still and dazzling splendor, with a murky and overshadowed bend above and below. Not a living soul was seen on the shore. The bushes did not rustle.

"Suddenly round the corner of the house a group of men appeared, as though they had come up from the ground. They waded waist-deep in the grass, in a compact body, bearing an improvised stretcher in their midst. Instantly, in the emptiness of the landscape, a cry arose whose shrillness pierced the still air like a sharp arrow flying straight to the very heart of the land; and, as if by enchantment, streams of human beings— of naked human beings—with spears in their hands, with bows, with shields, with wild glances and savage movements, were poured into the clearing by the dark-faced and pensive forest. The bushes shook, the grass swayed for a time, and then everything stood still in attentive immobility.

"'Now, if he does not say the right thing to them we are all done for,' said the Russian at my elbow. The knot of men with the stretcher had stopped, too, halfway to the steamer, as if petrified. I saw the man on the stretcher sit up, lank and with an uplifted arm, above the shoulders of the bearers. 'Let us hope that the man who can talk so well of love in general will find some particular reason to spare us this time,' I said. I resented bitterly the absurd danger of our situation, as if to be at the mercy of that atrocious phantom had been a dishonoring necessity. I could not hear a sound, but through my glasses I saw the thin arm extended commandingly, the lower jaw moving, the eyes of that apparition shining darkly far in its bony head that nodded with grotesque jerks. Kurtz—Kurtz—that means short in German—don't it? Well, the name was as true as everything else in his life—and death. He looked at least seven feet long. His covering had fallen off, and his body emerged from it pitiful and appalling as from a winding-sheet. I could see the cage of his ribs all astir, the bones of his arm waving. It was as though an animated image of death carved out of old ivory had been shaking its hand with menaces at a motionless crowd of men made of dark and glittering bronze. I saw him open his mouth wide—it gave him a weirdly voracious aspect, as though he had wanted to swallow all the air, all the earth, all the men before him. A deep voice reached me faintly. He must have been shouting. He fell back suddenly. The stretcher shook as the bearers staggered forward again, and almost at the same time I noticed that the crowd of savages was vanishing without any perceptible movement of retreat, as if the forest that had ejected these beings so suddenly had drawn them in again as the breath is drawn in a long aspiration.

"Some of the pilgrims behind the stretcher carried his arms—two shotguns, a heavy rifle, and a light revolver-carbine—the thunderbolts of that pitiful Jupiter. The manager bent over him murmuring as he walked beside his head. They laid him down in one of the little cabins—just a room for a bedplace and a camp-stool or two, you know. We had brought his belated correspondence, and a lot of torn envelopes and open letters littered his bed. His hand roamed feebly amongst these papers. I was struck by the fire of his eyes and the composed languor of his expression. It was not so much the exhaustion of disease. He did not seem in pain. This shadow looked satiated and calm, as though for the moment it had had its fill of all the emotions.

"He rustled one of the letters, and looking straight in my face said, 'I am glad.' Somebody had been writing to him about me. These special recommendations were turning up again. The volume of tone he emitted without effort, almost without the trouble of moving his lips, amazed me. A voice! a voice! It was grave, profound, vibrating, while the man did not seem capable of a whisper. However, he had enough strength in him—factitious no doubt—to very nearly make an end of us, as you shall hear directly.

"The manager appeared silently in the doorway; I stepped out at once and he drew the curtain after me. The Russian, eyed curiously by the pilgrims, was staring at the shore. I followed the direction of his glance.

"Dark human shapes could be made out in the distance, flitting indistinctly against the gloomy border of the forest, and near the river two bronze figures, leaning on tall spears, stood in the sunlight under fantastic head-dresses of spotted skins, warlike and still in statuesque repose. And from right to left along the lighted shore moved a wild and gorgeous apparition of a woman.

"She walked with measured steps, draped in striped and fringed cloths, treading the earth proudly, with a slight jingle and flash of barbarous ornaments. She carried her head high; her hair was done in the shape of a helmet; she had brass leggings to the knee, brass wire gauntlets to the elbow, a crimson spot on her tawny cheek, innumerable necklaces of glass beads on her neck; bizarre things, charms, gifts of witch-men, that hung about her, glittered and trembled at every step. She must have had the value of several elephant tusks upon her. She was savage and superb, wild-eyed and magnificent; there was something ominous and stately in her deliberate progress. And in the hush that had fallen suddenly upon the whole sorrowful land, the immense wilderness, the colossal body of the fecund and mysterious life seemed to look at her, pensive, as though it had been looking at the image of its own tenebrous and passionate soul.

"She came abreast of the steamer, stood still, and faced us. Her long shadow fell to the water's edge. Her face had a tragic and fierce aspect of wild sorrow and of dumb pain mingled with the fear of some struggling, half-shaped resolve. She stood looking at us without a stir, and like the wilderness itself, with an air of brooding over an inscrutable purpose. A whole minute passed, and then she made a step forward. There was a low jingle, a glint of yellow metal, a sway of fringed draperies, and she stopped as if her heart had failed her. The young fellow by my side growled. The pilgrims murmured at my back. She looked at us all as if her life had depended upon the unswerving steadiness of her glance. Suddenly she opened her bared arms and threw them up rigid above her head, as though in an uncontrollable desire to touch the sky, and at the same time the swift shadows darted out on the earth, swept around on the river, gathering the steamer into a shadowy embrace. A formidable silence hung over the scene.

"She turned away slowly, walked on, following the bank, and passed into the bushes to the left. Once only her eyes gleamed back at us in the dusk of the thickets before she disappeared.

"'If she had offered to come aboard I really think I would have tried to shoot her,' said the man of patches, nervously. 'I have been risking my life every day for the last fortnight to keep her out of the house. She got in one day and kicked up a row about those miserable rags I picked up in the storeroom to mend my clothes with. I wasn't decent. At least it must have been that, for she talked like a fury to Kurtz for an hour, pointing at me now and then. I don't understand the dialect of this tribe. Luckily for me, I fancy Kurtz felt too ill that day to care, or there would have been mischief. I don't understand. . . . No—it's too much for me. Ah, well, it's all over now.'

"At this moment I heard Kurtz's deep voice behind the curtain: 'Save me!—save the ivory, you mean. Don't tell me. Save *me!* Why, I've had to save you. You are interrupting my plans now. Sick! Sick! Not so sick as you would like to believe. Never mind. I'll carry my ideas out yet —I will return. I'll show you what can be done. You with your little peddling notions—you are interfering with me. I will return. I . . .'

"The manager came out. He did me the honor to take me under the arm and lead me aside. 'He is very low, very low,' he said. He considered it necessary to sigh, but neglected to be consistently sorrowful. 'We have done all we could for him— haven't we? But there is no disguising the fact, Mr. Kurtz has done more harm than good to the Company. He did not see the time was not ripe for vigorous action. Cautiously, cautiously—that's my principle. We must be cautious yet. The district is closed to us for a time. Deplorable! Upon the whole, the trade will suffer. I don't deny there is a remarkable quantity of ivory—mostly fossil. We must save it, at all events—but look how precarious the position is—and why? Because the method is unsound.' 'Do you,' said I, looking at the shore, 'call it "unsound method"?' 'Without doubt,' he exclaimed hotly. 'Don't you?' . . . 'No method at all,' I murmured after a while. 'Exactly,' he exulted. 'I anticipated this. Shows a complete want of judgment. It is my duty to point it out in the proper quarter.' 'Oh,' said I, 'that fellow—what's his name?— the brickmaker, will make a readable report for you.' He appeared confounded for a moment. It seemed to me I had never breathed an atmosphere so vile, and I turned mentally to Kurtz for relief—positively for relief. 'Nevertheless I think Mr. Kurtz is a remarkable man,' I said with emphasis. He started, dropped on me a cold heavy glance, said very quietly, 'he *was*,' and turned his back on me. My hour of favor was over; I found myself lumped along with Kurtz as a partisan of methods for which the time was not ripe: I was unsound! Ah! but it was something to have at least a choice of nightmares.

"I had turned to the wilderness really, not to Mr. Kurtz, who, I was ready to admit, was as good as buried. And for a moment it seemed to me as if I also were buried in a vast grave full of unspeakable secrets. I felt an intolerable weight oppressing my breast, the smell of the damp earth, the unseen presence of victorious corruption, the darkness of an impenetrable night. . . . The Russian tapped me on the shoulder. I heard him mumbling and stammering something about 'brother seamen—couldn't conceal —knowledge of matters that would affect Mr. Kurtz's reputation.' I waited. For him evidently Mr. Kurtz was not in his grave; I suspect that for him Mr. Kurtz was one of the immortals. 'Well!' said I at last, 'speak out. As it happens, I am Mr. Kurtz's friend—in a way.'

"He stated with a good deal of formality that had we not been 'of the same profession,' he would have kept the matter to himself without regard to consequences. 'He suspected there was an active ill will towards him on the part of these white men that—' 'You are right,' I said, remembering a certain conversation I had overheard. 'The manager thinks you ought to be hanged.' He showed a concern at this intelligence which amused me at first. 'I had better get out of the way quietly,' he said, earnestly. 'I can do no more for Kurtz now, and they would soon find some excuse. What's to stop them? There's a military post three hundred miles from here.' 'Well, upon my

Heart of Darkness

word,' said I, 'perhaps you had better go if you have any friends amongst the savages near by.' 'Plenty,' he said. 'They are simple people—and I want nothing, you know.' He stood biting his lip, then: 'I don't want any harm to happen to these whites here, but of course I was thinking of Mr. Kurtz's reputation—but you are a brother seaman and—' 'All right,' said I, after a time. 'Mr. Kurtz's reputation is safe with me.' I did not know how truly I spoke.

"He informed me, lowering his voice, that it was Kurtz who had ordered the attack to be made on the steamer. 'He hated sometimes the idea of being taken away—and then again. . . . But I don't understand these matters. I am a simple man. He thought it would scare you away —that you would give it up, thinking him dead. I could not stop him. Oh, I had an awful time of it this last month.' 'Very well,' I said. 'He is all right now.' 'Ye-e-es,' he muttered, not very convinced apparently. 'Thanks,' said I; 'I shall keep my eyes open.' 'But quiet—eh?' he urged, anxiously. 'It would be awful for his reputation if anybody here—' I promised a complete discretion with great gravity. 'I have a canoe and three black fellows waiting not very far. I am off. Could you give me a few Martini-Henry cartridges?' I could, and did, with proper secrecy. He helped himself, with a wink at me, to a handful of my tobacco. 'Between sailors —you know—good English tobacco.' At the door of the pilot-house he turned round—'I say, haven't you a pair of shoes you could spare?' He raised one leg. 'Look.' The soles were tied with knotted strings sandal-wise under his bare feet. I rooted out an old pair, at which he looked with admiration before tucking them under his left arm. One of his pockets (bright red) was bulging with cartridges, from the other (dark blue) peeped 'Towson's Inquiry,' etc., etc. He seemed to think himself excellently well equipped for a renewed encounter with the wilderness. 'Ah! I'll never, never meet such a man again. You ought to have heard him recite poetry—his own, too, it was, he told me. Poetry!' He rolled his eyes at the recollection of these delights. 'Oh, he enlarged my mind!' 'Good-by,' said I. He shook hands and vanished in the night. Sometimes I ask myself whether I had ever really seen him—whether it was possible to meet such a phenomenon! . . .

"When I woke up shortly after midnight his warning came to my mind with its hint of danger that seemed, in the starred darkness, real enough to make me get up for the purpose of having a look round. On the hill a big fire burned, illuminating fitfully a crooked corner of the station-house. One of the agents with a picket of a few of our blacks, armed for the purpose, was keeping guard over the ivory; but deep within the forest, red gleams that wavered, that seemed to sink and rise from the ground amongst confused columnar shapes of intense blackness, showed the exact position of the camp where Mr. Kurtz's adorers were keeping their uneasy vigil. The monotonous beating of a big drum filled the air with muffled shocks and a lingering vibration. A steady droning sound of many men chanting each to himself some weird incantation came out from the black, flat wall of the woods as the humming of bees comes out of a hive, and had a strange narcotic effect upon my half-awake senses. I believe I dozed off leaning over the rail, till an abrupt burst of yells, an overwhelming outbreak of a pent-up and mysterious frenzy, woke me up in a bewildered wonder. It was cut short all at once, and the low droning went on with an effect of audible and soothing silence. I glanced casually into the little cabin. A light was burning within, but Mr. Kurtz was not there.

"I think I would have raised an outcry if I had believed my eyes. But I didn't believe them at first—the thing seemed so impossible. The fact is I was completely unnerved by a sheer blank fright, pure abstract terror, unconnected with any distinct shape of physical danger. What made this emotion so overpowering was—how shall I define it?—the moral shock I received, as if something altogether monstrous, intolerable to thought and odious to the soul, had been thrust upon me unexpectedly. This lasted of course the merest fraction of a second, and then the usual sense of commonplace, deadly danger, the possibility of a sudden onslaught and massacre, or something of the kind, which I saw impending, was positively welcome and composing. It pacified me, in fact, so much, that I did not raise an alarm.

"There was an agent buttoned up inside an ulster and sleeping on a chair on deck within three feet of me. The yells had not awakened him; he snored very slightly; I left him to his slumbers and leaped ashore. I did not betray Mr. Kurtz —it was ordered I should never betray him—it was written I should be loyal to the nightmare of my choice. I was anxious to deal with this shadow by myself alone,—and to this day I don't know why I was so jealous of sharing with any one the peculiar blackness of that experience.

"As soon as I got on the bank I saw a trail—a broad trail through the grass. I remember the exultation with which I said to myself, 'He can't walk—he is crawling on all-fours—I've got him.' The grass was wet with dew. I strode rapidly with clenched fists. I fancy I had some vague notion of falling upon him and giving him a drubbing. I don't know. I had some imbecile thoughts. The knitting old woman with the cat obtruded herself upon my memory as a most improper person to be sitting at the other end of such an affair. I saw a row of pilgrims squirting lead in the air out of Winchesters held to the hip. I thought I would never get back to the steamer, and imagined myself living alone and unarmed in the woods to an advanced age. Such silly things—you know. And I remember I confounded the beat of the drum with the beating of my heart, and was pleased at its calm regularity.

"I kept to the track though—then stopped to listen. The night was very clear; a dark blue space, sparkling with dew and starlight, in which black things stood very still. I thought I could see a kind of motion ahead of me. I was strangely cocksure of everything that night. I actually left the track and ran in a wide semicircle (I verily believe chuckling to myself) so as to get in front of that stir, of that motion I had seen —if indeed I had seen anything. I was circumventing Kurtz as though it had been a boyish game.

"I came upon him, and, if he had not heard me coming, I would have fallen over him, too, but he got up in time. He rose, unsteady, long, pale, indistinct, like a vapor exhaled by the earth, and swayed slightly, misty and silent before me; while at my back the fires loomed between the trees, and the murmur of many voices issued from the forest. I had cut him off cleverly; but when actually confronting him I seemed to come to my senses, I saw the danger in its right proportion. It was by no means over yet. Suppose he began to shout? Though he could hardly stand, there was still plenty of vigor in his voice. 'Go away—hide yourself,' he said, in that profound tone. It was very awful. I glanced back. We were within thirty yards from the nearest fire. A black figure stood up, strode on long black legs, waving long black arms, across the glow. It had horns—antelope horns, I think—on its head. Some sorcerer, some witch-man, no doubt: it looked fiend-like enough. 'Do you know what you are doing?' I whispered. 'Perfectly,' he answered, raising his voice for that single word: it sounded to me far off and yet loud, like a hail through a speaking-trumpet. If he makes a row we are lost, I thought to myself. This clearly was not a case for fisticuffs, even apart from the very natural aversion I had to beat that Shadow—this wandering and tormented thing. 'You will be lost,' I said —'utterly lost.' One gets sometimes such a flash of inspiration, you know. I did say the right thing, though indeed he could not have been more irretrievably lost than he was at this very moment, when the foundations of our intimacy were being laid—to endure—to endure— even to the end—even beyond.

" 'I had immense plans,' he muttered irresolutely. 'Yes,' said I; 'but if you try to shout I'll smash your head with—' There was not a stick or a stone near. 'I will throttle you for good,' I corrected myself. 'I was on the threshold of great things,' he pleaded, in a voice of longing, with a wistfulness of tone that made my blood run cold. 'And now for this stupid scoundrel—' 'Your success in Europe is assured in any case,' I affirmed, steadily. I did not want to have the throttling of him, you understand—and indeed it would have been very little use for any practical purpose. I tried to break the spell—the heavy, mute spell of the wilderness—that seemed to draw him to its pitiless breast by the awakening of forgotten and brutal instincts, by the memory of gratified and monstrous passions. This alone, I was convinced, had driven him out to the edge of the forest, to the bush, towards the gleam of fires, the throb of drums, the drone of weird incantations; this alone had beguiled his unlawful soul beyond the bounds of permitted aspirations. And, don't you see, the terror of the position was not in being knocked on the head—though I had a very lively sense of that danger, too—but in this, that I had to deal with a being to whom I could not appeal in the name of anything high or low. I had, even like the niggers, to invoke him—himself—his own exalted and incredible degradation. There was nothing either above or below him, and I knew it. He had kicked himself loose of the earth. Confound the man! he had kicked the very earth to pieces. He was alone, and I before him did not know whether I stood on the ground or floated in the air. I've been telling you what we said—repeating the phrases we pronounced—but what's the good? They were common everyday words—the familiar, vague sounds exchanged on every waking day of life. But what of that? They had behind them, to my mind, the terrific suggestiveness of words heard in dreams, of phrases spoken in nightmares. Soul! If anybody had ever struggled with a soul, I am the man. And I wasn't arguing with a lunatic either. Believe me or not, his intelligence was perfectly clear— concentrated, it is true, upon himself with horrible intensity, yet clear; and therein was my only chance—barring, of course, the killing him there and then, which wasn't so good, on account of unavoidable noise. But his soul was mad. Being alone in the wilderness, it had looked within itself, and, by heavens! I tell you, it had gone mad. I had—for my sins, I suppose—to go through the ordeal of looking into it myself. No eloquence could have been so withering to one's belief in mankind as his final burst of sincerity. He struggled with himself, too. I saw it, —I heard it. I saw the inconceivable mystery of a soul that knew no restraint, no faith, and no fear, yet struggling blindly with itself. I kept my head pretty well; but when I had him at last stretched on the couch, I wiped my forehead, while my legs shook under me as though I had carried half a ton on my back down that hill. And yet I had only supported him, his bony arm clasped round my neck—and he was not much heavier than a child.

"When next day we left at noon, the crowd, of whose presence behind the curtain of trees I had been acutely conscious all the time, flowed out of the woods again, filled the clearing, covered the slope with a mass of naked, breathing, quivering, bronze bodies. I steamed up a bit, then swung downstream, and two thousand eyes followed the evolutions of the splashing, thumping, fierce river-demon beating the water with its terrible tail and breathing black smoke into the air. In front of the first rank, along the river, three men, plastered with bright red earth from head to foot, strutted to and fro restlessly. When we came abreast again, they faced the river, stamped their feet, nodded their horned heads, swayed their scarlet bodies; they shook towards the fierce river-demon a bunch of black feathers, a mangy skin with a pendent tail—something that looked like a dried gourd; they shouted periodically together strings of amazing words that resembled no sounds of human language; and the deep murmurs of the crowd, interrupted suddenly, were like the responses of some satanic litany.

"We had carried Kurtz into the pilot-house; there was more air there. Lying on the couch, he stared through the open shutter. There was an eddy in the mass of human bodies, and the woman with helmeted head and tawny cheeks rushed out to the very brink of the stream. She put out her hands, shouted something, and all that wild mob took up the shout in a roaring chorus of articulated, rapid, breathless utterance.

"'Do you understand this?' I asked.

"He kept on looking out past me with fiery, longing eyes, with a mingled expression of wistfulness and hate. He made no answer, but I saw a smile, a smile of indefinable meaning, appear on his colorless lips that a moment after twitched convulsively. 'Do I not?' he said slowly, gasping, as if the words had been torn out of him by a supernatural power.

"I pulled the string of the whistle, and I did this because I saw the pilgrims on deck getting out their rifles with an air of anticipating a jolly lark. At the sudden screech there was a movement of abject terror through that wedged mass of bodies. 'Don't! don't you frighten them away,' cried some one on deck disconsolately. I pulled the string time after time. They broke and ran, they leaped, they crouched, they swerved, they dodged the flying terror of the sound. The three red chaps had fallen flat, face down on the shore, as though they had been shot dead. Only the barbarous and superb woman did not so much as flinch, and stretched tragically her bare arms after us over the somber and glittering river.

"And then that imbecile crowd down on the deck started their little fun, and I could see nothing more for smoke.

"The brown current ran swiftly out of the heart of darkness, bearing us down towards the sea with twice the speed of our upward progress; and Kurtz's life was running swiftly, too, ebbing, ebbing out of his heart into the sea of inexorable time. The manager was very placid, he had no vital anxieties now, he took us both in with a comprehensive and satisfied glance: the 'affair' had come off as well as could be wished. I saw the time approaching when I would be left alone of the party of 'unsound method.' The pilgrims looked upon me with disfavor. I was, so to speak, numbered with the dead. It is strange how I accepted this unforeseen partnership, this choice of nightmares forced upon me in the tenebrous land invaded by these mean and greedy phantoms.

"Kurtz discoursed. A voice! a voice! It rang deep to the very last. It survived his strength to hide in the magnificent folds of eloquence the barren darkness of his heart. Oh, he struggled! he struggled! The wastes of his weary brain were haunted by shadowy images now—images of wealth and fame revolving obsequiously round his unextinguishable gift of noble and lofty expression. My Intended, my station, my career, my ideas —these were the subjects for the occasional utterances of elevated sentiments. The shade of the original Kurtz frequented the bedside of the hollow sham, whose fate it was to be buried presently in the mold of primeval earth. But both the diabolic love and the unearthly hate of the mysteries it had penetrated fought for the possession of that soul satiated with primitive emotions, avid of lying fame, of sham distinction, of all the appearances of success and power.

"Sometimes he was contemptibly childish. He desired to have kings meet him at railway stations on his return from some ghastly Nowhere, where he intended to accomplish great things. 'You show them you have in you something that is really profitable, and then there will be no limits to the recognition of your ability,' he would say. 'Of course you must take care of the motives—right motives— always.' The long reaches that were like one and the same reach, monotonous bends that were exactly alike, slipped past the steamer, with their multitude of secular trees looking patiently after this grimy fragment of another world, the forerunner of change, of conquest, of trade, of massacres, of blessings. I looked ahead—piloting. 'Close the shutter,' said Kurtz suddenly one day; 'I can't bear to look at this.' I did so. There was a silence. 'Oh, but I will wring your heart yet!' he cried at the invisible wilderness.

"We broke down—as I had expected— and had to lie up for repairs at the head of an island. This delay was the first thing that shook Kurtz's confidence. One morning he gave me a packet of papers and a photograph—the lot tied together with a shoestring. 'Keep this for me,' he said. 'This noxious fool' (meaning the manager) 'is capable of prying into my boxes when I am not looking.' In the afternoon I saw him. He was lying on his back with closed eyes, and I withdrew quietly, but I heard him mutter, 'Live rightly, die, die. . . .' I listened. There was nothing more. Was he rehearsing some speech in his sleep, or was it a fragment of a phrase from some newspaper article? He had been writing for the papers and meant to do so again, 'for the furthering of my ideas. It's a duty.'

"His was an impenetrable darkness. I looked at him as you peer down at a man who is lying at the bottom of a precipice where the sun never shines. But I had not much time to give him, because I was helping the engine-driver to take to pieces the leaky cylinders, to straighten a bent connecting-rod, and in other such matters. I lived in an infernal mess of rust, filings, nuts, bolts, spanners, hammers, ratchet-drills—things I abominate, because I don't get on with them. I tended the little forge we fortunately had aboard; I toiled wearily in a wretched scrap-heap—unless I had the shakes too bad to stand.

"One evening coming in with a candle I was startled to hear him say a little tremulously, 'I am lying here in the dark waiting for death.' The light was within a foot of his eyes. I forced myself to murmur, 'Oh, nonsense!' and stood over him as if transfixed.

"Anything approaching the change that came over his features I have never seen before, and hope never to see again. Oh, I wasn't touched. I was fascinated. It was as though a veil had been rent. I saw on that ivory face the expression of somber pride, of ruthless power, of craven terror—of an intense and hopeless despair. Did he live his life again in every detail of desire, temptation, and surrender during that supreme moment of complete knowledge? He cried in a whisper at some image, at some vision—he cried out twice, a cry that was no more than a breath—

"'The horror! The horror!'

"I blew the candle out and left the cabin. The pilgrims were dining in the mess-room, and I took my place opposite the manager, who lifted his eyes to give me a questioning glance, which I successfully ignored. He leaned back, serene, with that peculiar smile of his sealing the unexpressed depths of his meanness. A continuous shower of small flies streamed upon the lamp, upon the cloth, upon our hands and faces. Suddenly the manager's boy put his insolent black head in the doorway, and said in a tone of scathing contempt—

"'Mistah Kurtz—he dead.'

"All the pilgrims rushed out to see. I remained, and went on with my dinner. I believe I was considered brutally callous. However, I did not eat much. There was a lamp in there—light, don't you know—and outside it was so beastly, beastly dark. I went no more near the remarkable man who had pronounced a judgment upon the adventures of his soul on this earth. The voice was gone. What else had been there? But I am of course aware that next day the pilgrims buried something in a muddy hole.

"And then they very nearly buried me.

"However, as you see I did not go to join Kurtz there and then. I did not. I remained to dream the nightmare out to the end, and to show my loyalty to Kurtz once more. Destiny. My destiny! Droll thing life is—that mysterious arrangement of merciless logic for a futile purpose. The most you can hope from it is some knowledge of yourself—that comes too late—a crop of unextinguishable regrets. I have wrestled with death. It is the most unexciting contest you can imagine. It takes place in an impalpable grayness, with nothing underfoot, with noth-

Heart of Darkness

ing around, without spectators, without clamor, without glory, without the great desire of victory, without the great fear of defeat, in a sickly atmosphere of tepid skepticism, without much belief in your own right, and still less in that of your adversary. If such is the form of ultimate wisdom, then life is a greater riddle than some of us think it to be. I was within a hair's breadth of the last opportunity for pronouncement, and I found with humiliation that probably I would have nothing to say. This is the reason why I affirm that Kurtz was a remarkable man. He had something to say. He said it. Since I had peeped over the edge myself, I understand better the meaning of his stare, that could not see the flame of the candle, but was wide enough to embrace the whole universe, piercing enough to penetrate all the hearts that beat in the darkness. He had summed up—he had judged. 'The horror!' He was a remarkable man. After all, this was the expression of some sort of belief; it had candor, it had conviction, it had a vibrating note of revolt in its whisper, it had the appalling face of a glimpsed truth—the strange commingling of desire and hate. And it is not my own extremity I remember best—a vision of grayness without form filled with physical pain, and a careless contempt for the evanescence of all things—even of this pain itself. No! It is his extremity that I seem to have lived through. True, he had made that last stride, he had stepped over the edge, while I had been permitted to draw back my hesitating foot. And perhaps in this is the whole difference; perhaps all the wisdom, and all truth, and all sincerity, are just compressed into the inappreciable moment of time in which we step over the threshold of the invisible.

Perhaps! I like to think my summing-up would not have been a word of careless contempt. Better his cry—much better. It was an affirmation, a moral victory paid for by innumerable defeats, by abominable terrors, by abominable satisfactions. But it was a victory! That is why I have remained loyal to Kurtz to the last, and even beyond, when a long time after I heard once more, not his own choice, but the echo of his magnificent eloquence thrown to me from a soul as translucently pure as a cliff of crystal.

"No, they did not bury me, though there is a period of time which I remember mistily, with a shuddering wonder, like a passage through some inconceivable world that had no hope in it and no desire. I found myself back in the sepulchral city resenting the sight of people hurrying through the streets to filch a little money from each other, to devour their infamous cookery, to gulp their unwholesome beer, to dream their insignificant and silly dreams. They trespassed upon my thoughts. They were intruders whose knowledge of life was to me an irritating pretense, because I felt so sure they could not possibly know the things I knew. Their bearing, which was simply the bearing of commonplace individuals going about their business in the assurance of perfect safety, was offensive to me like the outrageous flauntings of folly in the face of a danger it is unable to comprehend. I had no particular desire to enlighten them, but I had some difficulty in restraining myself from laughing in their faces, so full of stupid importance. I daresay I was not very well at that time. I tottered about the streets—there were various affairs to settle—grinning bitterly at perfectly respectable persons. I admit my behavior was inex-

[377]

[Handwritten margin notes at top: "self. Kurtz is an idealist and his ideas had become completely santed. He behaved in a manner like that of the blackest diamond. But all man-kind are this way. Kurtz has become ruled over by his passion rather his ideas."

Left margin: "Passion / 1. of power, / 2. of sway."]

cusable, but then my temperature was seldom normal in these days. My dear aunt's endeavors to 'nurse up my strength' seemed altogether beside the mark. It was not my strength that wanted nursing, it was my imagination that wanted soothing. I kept the bundle of papers given me by Kurtz, not knowing exactly what to do with it. His mother had died lately, watched over, as I was told, by his Intended. A clean-shaved man, with an official manner and wearing gold-rimmed spectacles, called on me one day and made inquiries, at first circuitous, afterwards suavely pressing, about what he was pleased to denominate certain 'documents.' I was not surprised, because I had had two rows with the manager on the subject out there. I had refused to give up the smallest scrap out of that package, and I took the same attitude with the spectacled man. He became darkly menacing at last, and with much heat argued that the Company had the right to every bit of information about its 'territories.' And said he, 'Mr. Kurtz's knowledge of unexplored regions must have been necessarily extensive and peculiar—owing to his great abilities and to the deplorable circumstances in which he had been placed: therefore—' I assured him Mr. Kurtz's knowledge, however extensive, did not bear upon the problems of commerce or administration. He invoked then the name of science. 'It would be an incalculable loss, if,' etc., etc. I offered him the report on the 'Suppression of Savage Customs,' with the postscriptum torn off. He took it up eagerly, but ended by sniffing at it with an air of contempt. 'This is not what we had a right to expect,' he remarked. 'Expect nothing else,' I said. 'There are only private letters.' He withdrew upon some threat of legal proceedings, and I saw him no more; but another fellow, calling himself Kurtz's cousin, appeared two days later, and was anxious to hear all the details about his dear relative's last moments. Incidentally he gave me to understand that Kurtz had been essentially a great musician. 'There was the making of an immense success,' said the man, who was an organist, I believe, with lank gray hair flowing over a greasy coat-collar. I had no reason to doubt his statement; and to this day I am unable to say what was Kurtz's profession, whether he ever had any—which was the greatest of his talents. I had taken him for a painter who wrote for the papers, or else for a journalist who could paint—but even the cousin (who took snuff during the interview) could not tell me what he had been—exactly. He was a universal genius—on that point I agreed with the old chap, who thereupon blew his nose noisily into a large cotton handkerchief and withdrew in senile agitation, bearing off some family letters and memoranda without importance. Ultimately a journalist anxious to know something of the fate of his 'dear colleague' turned up. This visitor informed me Kurtz's proper sphere ought to have been politics 'on the popular side.' He had furry straight eyebrows, bristly hair cropped short, an eye-glass on a broad ribbon, and, becoming expansive, confessed his opinion that Kurtz really couldn't write a bit—'but heavens! how that man could talk. He electrified large meetings. He had faith —don't you see?—he had the faith. He could get himself to believe anything— anything. He would have been a splendid leader of an extreme party.' 'What party?' I asked. 'Any party,' answered the other. 'He was an—an—extremist.' Did I not think so? I assented. Did I know, he asked, with a sudden flash of curiosity, 'what it was that had induced him to

Heart of Darkness

go out there?' 'Yes,' said I, and forthwith handed him the famous Report for publication, if he thought fit. He glanced through it hurriedly, mumbling all the time, judged 'it would do,' and took himself off with this plunder.

"Thus I was left at last with a slim packet of letters and the girl's portrait. She struck me as beautiful—I mean she had a beautiful expression. I know that the sunlight can be made to lie, too, yet one felt that no manipulation of light and pose could have conveyed the delicate shade of truthfulness upon those features. She seemed ready to listen without mental reservation, without suspicion, without a thought for herself. I concluded I would go and give her back her portrait and those letters myself. Curiosity? Yes; and also some other feeling perhaps. All that had been Kurtz's had passed out of my hands: his soul, his body, his station, his plans, his ivory, his career. There remained only his memory and his Intended—and I wanted to give that up, too, to the past, in a way—to surrender personally all that remained of him with me to that oblivion which is the last word of our common fate. I don't defend myself. I had no clear perception of what it was I really wanted. Perhaps it was an impulse of unconscious loyalty, or the fulfillment of one of those ironic necessities that lurk in the facts of human existence. I don't know. I can't tell. But I went.

"I thought his memory was like the other memories of the dead that accumulate in every man's life—a vague impress on the brain of shadows that had fallen on it in their swift and final passage; but before the high and ponderous door, between the tall houses of a street as still and decorous as a well-kept alley in a cemetery, I had a vision of him on the stretcher, opening his mouth voraciously, as if to devour all the earth with all its mankind. He lived then before me; he lived as much as he had ever lived—a shadow insatiable of splendid appearances, of frightful realities; a shadow darker than the shadow of the night, and draped nobly in the folds of a gorgeous eloquence. The vision seemed to enter the house with me—the stretcher, the phantom-bearers, the wild crowd of obedient worshipers, the gloom of the forest, the glitter of the reach between the murky bends, the beat of the drum, regular and muffled like the beating of a heart—the heart of a conquering darkness. It was a moment of triumph for the wilderness, an invading and vengeful rush which, it seemed to me, I would have to keep back alone for the salvation of another soul. And the memory of what I had heard him say afar there, with the horned shapes stirring at my back, in the glow of fires, within the patient woods, those broken phrases came back to me, were heard again in their ominous and terrifying simplicity. I remembered his abject pleading, his abject threats, the colossal scale of his vile desires, the meanness, the torment, the tempestuous anguish of his soul. And later on I seemed to see his collected languid manner, when he said one day, 'This lot of ivory now is really mine. The Company did not pay for it. I collected it myself at a very great personal risk. I am afraid they will try to claim it as theirs though. H'm. It is a difficult case. What do you think I ought to do—resist? Eh? I want no more than justice.' ... He wanted no more than justice—no more than justice. I rang the bell before a mahogany door on the first floor, and while I waited he seemed to stare at me out of the glassy panel—stare with that wide and immense stare embracing,

[379]

condemning, loathing all the universe. I seemed to hear the whispered cry, 'The horror! The horror!'

"The dusk was falling. I had to wait in a lofty drawing-room with three long windows from floor to ceiling that were like three luminous and bedraped columns. The bent gilt legs and backs of the furniture shone in indistinct curves. The tall marble fireplace had a cold and monumental whiteness. A grand piano stood massively in a corner; with dark gleams on the flat surfaces like a somber and polished sarcophagus. A high door opened—closed. I rose.

"She came forward, all in black, with a pale head, floating towards me in the dusk. She was in mourning. It was more than a year since his death, more than a year since the news came; she seemed as though she would remember and mourn forever. She took both my hands in hers and murmured, 'I had heard you were coming.' I noticed she was not very young—I mean not girlish. She had a mature capacity for fidelity, for belief, for suffering. The room seemed to have grown darker, as if all the sad light of the cloudy evening had taken refuge on her forehead. This fair hair, this pale visage, this pure brow, seemed surrounded by an ashy halo from which the dark eyes looked out at me. Their glance was guileless, profound, confident, and trustful. She carried her sorrowful head as though she were proud of that sorrow, as though she would say, I—I alone know how to mourn him as he deserves. But while we were still shaking hands, such a look of awful desolation came upon her face that I perceived she was one of those creatures that are not the playthings of Time. For her he had died only yesterday. And, by Jove! the impression was so powerful that for me, too, he seemed to have died only yesterday—nay, this very minute. I saw her and him in the same instant of time—his death and her sorrow—I saw her sorrow in the very moment of his death. Do you understand? I saw them together—I heard them together. She had said, with a deep catch of the breath, 'I have survived' while my strained ears seemed to hear distinctly, mingled with her tone of despairing regret, the summing up whisper of his eternal condemnation. I asked myself what I was doing there, with a sensation of panic in my heart as though I had blundered into a place of cruel and absurd mysteries not fit for a human being to behold. She motioned me to a chair. We sat down. I laid the packet gently on the little table, and she put her hand over it. . . . 'You knew him well,' she murmured, after a moment of mourning silence.

"'Intimacy grows quickly out there,' I said. 'I knew him as well as it is possible for one man to know another.'

"'And you admired him,' she said. 'It was impossible to know him and not to admire him. Was it?'

"'He was a remarkable man,' I said, unsteadily. Then before the appealing fixity of her gaze, that seemed to watch for more words on my lips, I went on, 'It was impossible not to—'

"'Love him,' she finished eagerly, silencing me into an appalled dumbness. 'How true! how true! But when you think that no one knew him so well as I! I had all his noble confidence. I knew him best.'

"'You knew him best,' I repeated. And perhaps she did. But with every word spoken the room was growing darker, and only her forehead, smooth and white, remained illumined by the unextinguishable light of belief and love.

Heart of Darkness

"'You were his friend,' she went on. 'His friend,' she repeated, a little louder. 'You must have been, if he had given you this, and sent you to me. I feel I can speak to you—and oh! I must speak. I want you—you have heard his last words—to know I have been worthy of him. . . . It is not pride. . . . Yes! I am proud to know I understood him better than any one on earth—he told me so himself. And since his mother died I have had no one —no one—to—to—'

"I listened. The darkness deepened. I was not even sure he had given me the right bundle. I rather suspect he wanted me to take care of another batch of his papers which, after his death, I saw the manager examining under the lamp. And the girl talked, easing her pain in the certitude of my sympathy; she talked as thirsty men drink. I had heard that her engagement with Kurtz had been disapproved by her people. He wasn't rich enough or something. And indeed I don't know whether he had not been a pauper all his life. He had given me some reason to infer that it was his impatience of comparative poverty that drove him out there.

"'. . . Who was not his friend who had heard him speak once?' she was saying. 'He drew men towards him by what was best in them.' She looked at me with intensity. 'It is the gift of the great,' she went on, and the sound of her low voice seemed to have the accompaniment of all the other sounds, full of mystery, desolation, and sorrow, I had ever heard—the ripple of the river, the soughing of the trees swayed by the wind, the murmurs of the crowds, the faint ring of incomprehensible words cried from afar, the whisper of a voice speaking from beyond the threshold of an eternal darkness. 'But you have heard him! You know!' she cried.

"'Yes, I know,' I said with something like despair in my heart, but bowing my head before the faith that was in her, before that great and saving illusion that shone with an unearthly glow in the darkness, in the triumphant darkness from which I could not have defended her—from which I could not even defend myself.

"'What a loss to me—to us!' she corrected herself with beautiful generosity; then added in a murmur, 'To the world.' By the last gleams of twilight I could see the glitter of her eyes, full of tears —of tears that would not fall.

"'I have been very happy—very fortunate—very proud,' she went on. 'Too fortunate. Too happy for a little while. And now I am unhappy for—for life.'

"She stood up; her fair hair seemed to catch all the remaining light in a glimmer of gold. I rose, too.

"'And of all this,' she went on, mournfully, 'of all his promise, and of all his greatness, of his generous mind, of his noble heart, nothing remains—nothing but a memory. You and I—'

"'We shall always remember him,' I said, hastily.

"'No!' she cried. 'It is impossible that all this should be lost—that such a life should be sacrificed to leave nothing—but sorrow. You know what vast plans he had. I knew of them, too—I could not perhaps understand—but others knew of them. Something must remain. His words, at least, have not died.'

"'His words will remain,' I said.

"'And his example,' she whispered to herself. 'Men looked up to him—his goodness shone in every act. His example—'

"'True,' I said; 'his example, too. Yes, his example. I forgot that.'

[381]

"'But I do not. I cannot—I cannot believe—not yet. I cannot believe that I shall never see him again, that nobody will see him again, never, never, never.'

"She put out her arms as if after a retreating figure, stretching them black and with clasped pale hands across the fading and narrow sheen of the window. Never see him! I saw him clearly enough then. I shall see this eloquent phantom as long as I live, and I shall see her, too, a tragic and familiar Shade, resembling in this gesture another one, tragic also, and bedecked with powerless charms, stretching bare brown arms over the glitter of the infernal stream, the stream of darkness. She said suddenly very low, 'He died as he lived.'

"'His end,' said I, with dull anger stirring in me, 'was in every way worthy of his life.'

"'And I was not with him,' she murmured. My anger subsided before a feeling of infinite pity.

"'Everything that could be done—' I mumbled.

"'Ah, but I believed in him more than any one on earth—more than his own mother, more than—himself. He needed me! Me! I would have treasured every sigh, every word, every sign, every glance.'

"I felt like a chill grip on my chest. 'Don't,' I said, in a muffled voice.

"'Forgive me. I—I—have mourned so long in silence—in silence. . . . You were with him—to the last? I think of his loneliness. Nobody near to understand him as I would have understood. Perhaps no one to hear. . . .'

"'To the very end,' I said, shakily. 'I heard his very last words. . . .' I stopped in a fright.

"'Repeat them,' she murmured in a heart-broken tone. 'I want—I want—something—something—to—live with.'

"I was on the point of crying at her, 'Don't you hear them?' The dusk was repeating them in a persistent whisper all around us, in a whisper that seemed to swell menacingly like the first whisper of a rising wind. 'The horror! The horror!'

"'His last word—to live with,' she insisted. 'Don't you understand I loved him —I loved him—I loved him!'

"I pulled myself together and spoke slowly.

"'The last word he pronounced was— your name.'

"I heard a light sigh and then my heart stood still, stopped dead short by an exulting and terrible cry, by the cry of inconceivable triumph and of unspeakable pain. 'I knew it—I was sure!' . . . She knew. She was sure. I heard her weeping; she had hidden her face in her hands. It seemed to me that the house would collapse before I could escape, that the heavens would fall upon my head. But nothing happened. The heavens do not fall for such a trifle. Would they have fallen, I wonder, if I had rendered Kurtz that justice which was his due? Hadn't he said he wanted only justice? But I couldn't. I could not tell her. It would have been too dark—too dark altogether. . . ."

Marlow ceased, and sat apart, indistinct and silent, in the pose of a meditating Buddha. Nobody moved for a time. "We have lost the first of the ebb," said the Director, suddenly. I raised my head. The offing was barred by a black bank of clouds, and the tranquil waterway leading to the uttermost ends of the earth flowed somber under an overcast sky— seemed to lead into the heart of an immense darkness.

PART IV · DRAMA

THE FOLLOWING PLAYS will suggest the range of dramatic forms in the twentieth-century theater, and provide material for discussion of numerous problems of our century.

In *Major Barbara* and in *The Philadelphia Story* will be found some of the wit, satire, and social criticism characteristic of the comedy of ideas and of the comedy of manners.

The Hairy Ape is an example of the dramatic expressionism introduced to the American theater by O'Neill in the early 1920s. At that time uninfluenced by German expressionist techniques, O'Neill found in August Strindberg, and in his own imagination, a dramatic form which broke sharply with contemporary realism and naturalism. As O'Neill said, "The old 'naturalism' —or 'realism,' if you prefer—. . . no longer applies. It represents our fathers' daring aspirations toward self-recognition by holding the family kodak up to ill-nature. . . . We have endured too much from the banality of surfaces."

The Glass Menagerie is a successful blend of several techniques. Basically a "memory play," as the author has said, it uses the expressionist device of "projecting the mind onto stage." The individual scenes are realistic, but the use of symbolism, thematic music, and projected slides moves the scenes beyond the "banality of surfaces."

When *Tiger at the Gates* was produced in New York, many people, intensely aware of our twentieth-century problems of war and peace, felt that there were tragic elements in a play billed as a comedy. This question might be considered by the reader in the light of the two articles on tragedy which will be found in Part II, and in the recalling of the meaning of "comedy" to Dante or Balzac or the Shakespeare of *Measure for Measure*.

The cry of Yank Smith in *The Hairy Ape,* "I ain't on 'oith and I ain't in heaven . . . I'm in de middle tryin' to separate 'em, takin' all de woist punches from bot' of 'em," has its bearing on the questions faced by Hector in *Tiger at the Gates* as well as by Barbara in *Major Barbara*. And it touches on the question of individualism in *The Philadelphia Story* and on the search for self-realization in *The Glass Menagerie*.

PREFACE TO MAJOR BARBARA
by GEORGE BERNARD SHAW

THE GOSPEL OF ST. ANDREW UNDERSHAFT

IN the millionaire Undershaft I have represented a man who has become intellectually and spiritually as well as practically conscious of the irresistible natural truth which we all abhor and repudiate: to wit, that the greatest of our evils, and the worst of our crimes is poverty, and that our first duty, to which every other consideration should be sacrificed, is not to be poor. "Holy poverty," "poor but honest," "the respectable poor," and such phrases are as intolerable and as immoral as "drunken but amiable," "fraudulent but a good after-dinner speaker," "splendidly criminal," or the like. Security, the chief pretence of civilization, cannot exist where the worst of dangers, the danger of poverty, hangs over everyone's head, and where the alleged protection of our persons from violence is only an accidental result of the existence of a police force whose real business is to force the poor man to see his children starve whilst the money that might feed and clothe them goes to overfeed pet dogs.

It is difficult to make people realize that an evil is an evil. For instance, we seize a man and deliberately do him a malicious injury: say, imprison him for years. One would not suppose that it needed any exceptional clearness of wit to recognize in this an act of diabolical cruelty. But in England such a recognition provokes a stare of surprise, followed by an explanation that the outrage is punishment or justice or something else that is all right, or perhaps by a heated attempt to argue that we should all be robbed and murdered in our beds if such stupid villainies as sentences of imprisonment were not committed daily. It is useless to argue that even if this were true, which it is not, the alternative to adding crimes of our own to the crimes from which we suffer is not helpless submission. Chickenpox is an evil; but if I were to declare that we must either submit to it or else repress it sternly by seizing everyone who suffers from it and punishing them by inoculation with smallpox, I should be laughed at; for though nobody could deny that the result would be to prevent chickenpox to some extent by making people avoid it much more carefully, and to effect a further apparent prevention by making them conceal it very anxiously, yet people would have sense enough to see that the deliberate propagation of smallpox was a creation of evil, and must therefore be ruled out in favor of purely humane and hygienic measures. Yet in the precisely parallel case of a man breaking into my house and stealing my wife's diamonds I am expected as a matter of course to steal ten years of his life, torturing him all the time. If he tries to defeat that monstrous retaliation by shooting me, my survivors hang him. The net result suggested by the police statistics is that we inflict atrocious injuries on the burglars we catch in order to make the rest take effectual precautions against detection; so that instead of saving our wives' diamonds from burglary we only greatly decrease our chances of ever getting them back,

Copyright © 1913, 1941 by George Bernard Shaw.

and increase our chances of being shot by the robber if we are unlucky enough to disturb him at his work.

But the thoughtless wickedness with which we scatter sentences of imprisonment, torture in the solitary cell and on the plank bed, privation of human intercourse and daily news, and flogging, on moral invalids and energetic rebels, is as nothing compared to the silly levity with which we tolerate poverty as if it were either a wholesome tonic for lazy people or else a virtue to be embraced as St. Francis embraced it. If a man is indolent, let him be poor. If he is drunken, let him be poor. If he is not a gentleman, let him be poor. If he is addicted to the fine arts or to pure science instead of to trade and finance, let him be poor. If he chooses to spend his wages on his beer and his family instead of saving it up for his old age, let him be poor. Let nothing be done for "the undeserving": let him be poor. Serve him right! Also—somewhat inconsistently —blessed are the poor!

Now what does this Let Him Be Poor mean? It means let him be weak. Let him be ignorant. Let him become a nucleus of disease. Let him be a standing exhibition and example of ugliness and dirt. Let him have rickety children. Let him be cheap, and drag his fellows down to his own price by selling himself to do their work. Let his habitations turn our cities into poisonous congeries of slums. Let his daughters infect our young men with the diseases of the streets, and his sons revenge him by turning the nation's manhood into scrofula, cowardice, cruelty, hypocrisy, political imbecility, and all the other fruits of oppression and malnutrition. Let the undeserving become still less deserving; and let the deserving lay up for himself, not treasures in heaven, but horrors in hell upon earth. This being so, is it really wise to let him be poor? Would he not do ten times less harm as a prosperous burglar, incendiary, ravisher or murderer, to the utmost limits of humanity's comparatively negligible impulses in' these directions? Suppose we were to abolish all penalties for such activities, and decide that poverty is the one thing we will not tolerate—that every adult with less than a thousand a year shall be painlessly but inexorably killed, and every hungry half naked child forcibly fattened and clothed, would not that be an enormous improvement on our existing system, which has already destroyed so many civilizations, and is visibly destroying ours? Surely the sensible course would be to give every man enough to live well on, so as to guarantee the community against the possibility of a case of the malignant disease of poverty, and then (necessarily) to see that he earned it.

Undershaft, the hero of Major Barbara, is a man who, having grasped the fact that poverty is a crime, knows that when society offered him the alternative of poverty or a lucrative trade in death and destruction, it offered him, not a choice between opulent villainy and humble virtue, but between energetic enterprise and cowardly infamy. His conduct stands the Kantian test, which Peter Shirley's does not. Peter Shirley is what we call the honest poor man. Undershaft is what we call the wicked rich one: Shirley is Lazarus, Undershaft Dives. Well, the misery of the world is due to the fact that the great mass of men act and believe as Peter Shirley acts and believes. If they acted and believed as Undershaft acts and believes, the immediate result would be a revolution of incalculable beneficence. To have money, says Undershaft, is with me a point of honor for which I am prepared to kill to make my own life worth living. This preparedness is, as he says, the final test of sincerity. Like Froissart's medieval hero, who saw that "to rob and pill was a good life" he is not the dupe of that public sentiment against killing which is propagated and endowed by people who but for it would be killed themselves, or of the mouth-honor paid to poverty and obedience by rich and insubordinate parasites who want to rob the poor without courage and command them without superiority. Froissart's knight, in placing the achievement of a good life before all the other duties —which indeed are not duties at all when they conflict with it, but plain wickednesses—behaved bravely, admirably, and, in the final analysis, public-spiritedly. Medieval society, on the other hand, behaved very badly indeed in organizing itself so stupidly that a good life could be achieved by robbing and pilling. If the knight's contemporaries had been all as resolute as he, robbing and pilling would have been the shortest way to the gallows, just as, if we were all as resolute and clearsighted as Undershaft, an attempt to live by means of what is called "an independent income" would be the shortest way to the lethal chamber. But as, thanks to our political ignorance and personal cowardice (fruits of poverty, both), the best imitation of a good life now procurable is life on an independent income, all sensible people aim at securing such an income, and are, of course, careful to legalize and moralize both it and all the actions and sentiments which lead to it and support it as an institution. What else can they do? They know, of course, that they are rich because others are poor. But they cannot help that: it is for the poor to repudiate poverty when they have had enough of it. The thing can be done easily enough: the demonstrations to the contrary made by the economists, jurists, moralists and sentimentalists hired by the rich to defend them, or even doing the work gratuitously out of sheer folly and abjectness, impose only on those who have leisure to read, and want to be imposed on.

The reason why the independent income-tax payers are not solid in defence of their position is that the poverty of those we rob prevents our having the good life for which we sacrifice them. Rich men or aristocrats with a developed sense of life—men like Ruskin and William Morris and Kropotkin—have enormous social appetites and very fastidious personal ones. They are not content with handsome houses: they want handsome cities. They are not content with bediamonded wives and blooming daughters: they complain because the charwoman is badly dressed, because the laundress smells of gin, because the sempstress is anemic, because every man they meet is not a friend and every woman not a romance. They turn up their noses at their neighbor's drains, and are made ill by the architecture of their neighbor's house. Trade patterns made to suit vulgar people do not please them; and they can get nothing else. The very air is not good enough for them: there is too much factory smoke in it. They even demand abstract conditions: justice, honor, a healthy moral atmosphere, an honest nexus to replace the cash nexus. Finally they declare that though to rob and pill with your own hand on horseback and in steel coat may have been a good life, to rob and pill by the hands of the policeman, the bailiff, and the soldier, and to underpay them meanly for doing it, is not a good life, but rather fatal to all possibility of even a tolerable one. They call on the poor to revolt, and, finding the poor shocked at their ungentlemanliness, despairingly revile them for their "damned wantlessness" (*verdammte Bedürfnislosigkeit*).

So far, however, their attack on society has lacked simplicity. The poor do not share their tastes, nor understand their art-criticisms, nor want the simple life, the aesthetic life, the literate life: on the contrary, they want very much to wallow in all the costly vulgarities from which the elect souls among the rich turn away with loathing. It is by surfeit and not by abstinence that they will be cured of their hankering after unwholesome sweets. What they do dislike and are ashamed of is their poverty. To ask them to fight for the difference between the Picture Post and the Kelmscott Chaucer is silly: they prefer the Post. "Cease to be slaves, in order that you may become cranks" is not a very inspiring call to arms; nor is it really improved by substituting saints for cranks. Both terms denote men of genius; and the common man does not want to live the life of a saint or a man of genius. But he does want more money. Whatever else he may be vague about, he is clear about that. He may or may not prefer Major Barbara to the Drury Lane pantomime; but he always prefers a pound to five shillings.

Now to deplore this preference as sordid, and teach children that it is sinful to desire money, is to strain towards the extreme limit of impudence in lying and corruption in hypocrisy. The universal regard for money is the one hopeful fact in our civilization, the one sound spot in our social conscience. Money is the most important thing in the world. It represents health, strength, honor, generosity and beauty as conspicuously and undeniably as the want of it represents illness, weakness, disgrace, meanness and ugliness. Not the least of its virtues is that it destroys base people as certainly as it fortifies and dignifies noble people. It is only when it is cheapened to worthlessness for some and made impossibly dear to others, that it becomes a curse. In short, it is a curse only in such foolish social conditions that life itself is a curse. For the two things are inseparable: money is the counter that enables life to be distributed socially: it *is* life as truly as gold coins and bank notes are money. The first duty of every citizen is to insist on having money on reasonable terms; and this demand is not complied with by giving four men a few shillings each for ten or twelve hours' drudgery and one man a thousand pounds for nothing. The crying need of the nation is not for better morals, cheaper bread, temperance, liberty, culture, redemption of fallen sisters and erring brothers, nor the grace, love and fellowship of the Trinity, but simply for enough money. And the evil to be attacked is not sin, suffering, greed, priestcraft, kingcraft, demogogy, monopoly, ignorance, drink, war, pestilence, nor any of the other consequences of poverty, but just poverty itself.

Once take your eyes from the ends of the earth and fix them on this truth just under your nose; and Andrew Undershaft's views will not perplex you in the least. Unless indeed his constant sense that he is only the instrument of a Will or Life Force which uses him for purposes wider than his own, may puzzle you. If so, that is because you are walking either in artificial Darwinian darkness, or in mere stupidity. All genuinely religious people have that consciousness. To them Undershaft the Mystic will be quite intelligible, and his perfect comprehension of his daughter the Salvationist and her lover the Euripidean Republican natural and inevitable. This, however, is not new, even on the stage. What is new, as far as I know, is that article in Undershaft's religion which recognizes in Money the first need, and in poverty the vilest sin of man and society.

This dramatic conception has not, of course, been reached in one step. Nor has it been borrowed from Nietzsche nor from any man born beyond the Channel. The late Samuel Butler, in his own department the greatest English writer of the latter half of the XIX century, steadily inculcated the necessity and morality of a conscientious Laodiceanism in religion and of an earnest and constant sense of the importance of money. It drives one almost to despair of English literature that when I produced plays in which Butler's extraordinarily fresh, free and future-piercing suggestions had an obvious share, I was reproached for echoing Schopenhauer, Ibsen, and Nietzsche. Really, the English do not deserve to have great men. They allowed Butler to die practically unknown whilst in Sicily there was already a Via Samuele Butler. When English tourists came upon it they asked either "Who the devil was Samuele Butler?" or wondered why the Sicilians should perpetuate the memory of the author of Hudibras.

The Salvation Army

When Major Barbara was produced in London, the second act was reported in an important northern newspaper as a withering attack on the Salvation Army, and the despairing ejaculation of Barbara deplored by a London daily as a tasteless blasphemy. And they were set right, not by the professed critics of the theatre, but by religious and philosophical publicists who not only understand the act as well as the Salvationists themselves, but also saw it in its relation to the religious life of the nation: a life which then lay not only outside the sympathy of many theatre critics, but outside their knowledge of society. Indeed nothing could be more ironically curious than the confrontation Major Barbara effected of the theatre enthusiasts with the religious enthusiasts. On the one hand was the playgoer, always seeking pleasure, paying exorbitantly for it, suffering unbearable discomforts for it, and not always getting it. On the other hand was the Salvationist, repudiating gaiety, courting effort and sacrifice, yet always in the wildest spirits, laughing, joking, singing, rejoicing, drumming, and tambourining: his life flying by in a flash of excitement, and his death arriving as a climax of triumph. And, if you please, the playgoer despising the Salvationist as a joyless person, shut out from the heaven of the theatre, self-condemned to a life of hideous gloom; and the Salvationist mourning over the playgoer as over a prodigal with vine leaves in his hair, careering outrageously to hell amid the popping of champagne corks and the ribald laughter of sirens! Could misunderstanding be more complete, or sympathy worse misplaced?

Fortunately, the Salvationists are more accessible to the religious character of the drama than the playgoers to the gay energy and artistic fertility of religion. They can see, when it is pointed out to them, that a theatre, as a place where two or three are gathered together, takes from that divine presence an inalienable sanctity of which the grossest and profanest farce can no more deprive it than a hypocritical sermon by a snobbish bishop can desecrate Westminster Abbey. But in our professional playgoers this indispensable preliminary conception of sanctity seems wanting. They talk of actors as mimes and mummers, and, I fear, think of playwrights as liars and pandars whose main business is the voluptuous soothing of the tired city speculator when what he calls the serious business of the day is over. Passion, the life of drama, means nothing to them but primitive sexual excitement: such phrases as "impassioned poetry" or "passionate love of truth" have fallen quite out of their vocabulary and been replaced by "passional crime" and the like. They assume, as far as I can gather, that people in whom passion has a larger scope are passionless and therefore uninteresting. Consequently they come to think of religious people either as figures of fun or as hypocrites, bores, and spoilsports. And so, when Barbara cracks Salvation Army jokes, and snatches a kiss from her lover across his drum, the devotees of the theatre think they ought to appear shocked, and conclude that the whole play is an elaborate mockery of the Army. And then either hypocritically rebuke me for mocking, or foolishly take part in the supposed mockery!

Even the handful of mentally competent critics got into difficulties over my demonstration of the economic deadlock in which the Salvation Army finds itself. Some of them thought that the Army would not have taken money from a distiller and a cannon founder: others thought it should not have taken it: all assumed more or less definitely that it reduced itself to absurdity or hypocrisy by taking it. On the first point the reply of the Army itself was prompt and conclusive. As one of its officers said, they would take money from the devil himself and be only too glad to get it out of his hands and into God's. They gratefully acknowledged that publicans not only give them money but allow them to collect it in the bar, sometimes even when there is a Salvation meeting outside preaching teetotalism. In fact, they questioned the verisimilitude of the play, not because Mrs. Baines took the money, but because Barbara refused it.

On the point that the Army ought not to take such money, its justification is obvious. It must take the money because it cannot exist without money, and there is no other money to be had. Practically all the spare money in the country consists of a mass of rent, interest, and profit, every penny of which is bound up with crime, drink, prostitution, disease, and all the evil fruits of poverty, as inextricably as with enterprise, wealth, commercial probity, and national prosperity. The notion that you can earmark certain coins as tainted is childish. None the less the fact that all our money is tainted gives a very severe shock to earnest young souls when some dramatic instance of the taint first makes them conscious of it. When an enthusiastic young clergyman of the Established Church first realizes that the Ecclesiastical Commissioners receive the rents of sporting public houses, brothels, and sweating dens; or that the most generous contributor at his last charity sermon was an employer trading in female labor cheapened by prostitution; or that the only patron who can afford to rebuild his church or his schools or give his boys' brigade a gymnasium or a library is the son-in-law of a Chicago meat King, that young clergyman has, like Barbara, a very bad quarter hour. But he cannot help himself by refusing to accept money from anybody except sweet old ladies with independent incomes and gentle and lovely ways of life. He has only to follow up the income of the sweet ladies to its industrial source, and there he will find Mrs. Warren's profession and all the rest of it. His own stipend has the same root. He must either share the world's guilt or go to another planet. He must save the world's honor if he is to save his own. This is what all the Churches find just as the Salvation Army and Barbara find it in the play. Her discovery is that she is her father's accomplice; that the Salvation Army is the accomplice of the distiller and the dynamite maker; that they can no more escape one another than they can escape the air they breathe; and that there is no salvation for them through personal righteousness, but only through the redemption of the whole nation from its vicious, lazy, competitive anarchy. Nevertheless we proceed without the least misgiving as to the elevation of our private characters, the purity of our private atmospheres, and our right to repudiate as foreign to ourselves the coarse depravity of the garret and the slum. Not that we mean any harm: we only desire to be, in our little private way, ladies and gen- ,tlemen. We do not understand Barbara's lesson because we have not, like her, learnt it by taking our part in the larger life of the nation.

Barbara's Return to the Colors

Barbara's return to the colors may yet provide a subject for the dramatic historian of the future. To go back to the Salvation Army with the knowledge that even the Salvationists themselves are not saved yet; that poverty is not blessed, but a most damnable sin; and that when General Booth chose Blood and Fire for the emblem of Salvation instead of the Cross, he was perhaps better inspired than he knew: such knowledge, for the daughter of Andrew Undershaft, will clearly lead to something hopefuller than distributing bread and treacle at the expense of Bodger.

It is a very significant thing, this instinctive choice of the military form of organization, this substitution of the drum for the organ, by the Salvation Army. Does it not suggest that the Salvationists divine that they must actually fight the devil instead of merely praying at him? At present, it is true, they have not quite ascertained his correct address. When they do, they may give a very rude shock to that sense of security which he has gained from his experience of the fact that hard words, even when uttered by eloquent essayists and lecturers, or carried unanimously at enthusiastic public meetings on the motion of eminent reformers, break no bones. It has been said that the French Revolution was the work of Voltaire, Rousseau and the Encyclopedists. It seems to me to have been the work of men who had observed that virtuous indignation, caustic criticism, conclusive argument, and instructive pamphleteering, even when done by the most earnest and witty literary geniuses, were as useless as praying, things going steadily from bad to worse whilst Rousseau's Social Contract and the pamphlets of Voltaire were at the height of their vogue. Eventually, as we know, perfectly respectable citizens and earnest philanthropists connived at the September massacres because hard experience had convinced them that if they contented themselves with appeals to humanity and patriotism, the aristocracy, though it would read their appeals with the greatest enjoyment and appreciation, flattering and admiring the writers, would none the less continue to conspire with foreign monarchists to undo the revolution and restore the old system with every circumstance of savage vengeance and ruthless repression of popular liberties.

The nineteenth century saw the same lesson repeated in England. It had its Utilitarians, its Christian Socialists, its Fabians (still extant): it had Bentham, Mill, Dickens, Ruskin, Carlyle, Butler, Henry George, and Morris. And the end of all their efforts is the Chicago described by Mr. Upton Sinclair, and the London in which the people who pay to be amused by my dramatic representation of Peter Shirley turned out to starve at forty because there are younger slaves to be had for his wages, do not take, and have not the slightest intention of taking, any effective step to organize society in such a way as to make that everyday infamy impossible. I, who have preached and pamphleteered like any Encyclopedist, have to confess that my methods are no use, and would be no use if I were Voltaire, Rousseau, Shelley, Bentham, Marx, Mill, Dickens, Carlyle, Ruskin, Butler, and Morris all rolled into one, with Euripides, Erasmus, More, Montaigne, Molière, Beaumarchais, Swift, Goethe, Wagner, Ibsen, Tolstoy, Jesus and the prophets all thrown in (as indeed in some sort I actually am, standing as I do on all their shoulders). The problem being to make heroes out of cowards, we paper apostles and artist-magicians have succeeded only in giving cowards all the sensations of heroes whilst they tolerate every abomination, accept every plunder, and submit to every oppression. Christianity, in making a merit of such submission, has marked only that depth in the abyss at which the very sense of shame is lost. The Christian has been like Dickens' doctor in the debtor's prison, who tells the newcomer of its ineffable peace and security: no duns, no tyrannical collectors of rates and taxes, no importunate hopes nor exacting duties, nothing but the rest and safety of having no farther to fall.

Yet in the poorest corner of this soul-destroying Christendom vitality suddenly begins to germinate again. Joyousness, a sacred gift long dethroned by the hellish laughter of derision and obscenity, rises like a flood miraculously out of the fetid dust and mud of the slums; rousing marches and impetuous dithyrambs rise to the heavens from people among whom the depressing noise called "sacred music" is a standing joke; a flag with Blood and Fire on it is unfurled, not in murderous rancor, but because fire is beautiful and blood a vital and splendid red; Fear, which we flatter by calling Self, vanishes; and transfigured men and women carry their gospel through a transfigured world, calling their leader General, themselves captains and brigadiers, and their whole body an Army: praying, but praying only for refreshment, for strength to fight, and for needful MONEY (a notable sign, that); preaching, but not preaching submission; daring ill-usage and abuse, but not putting up with more of it than is inevitable; and practising what the world will let them practise, including soap and water, color and music. There is danger in such activity; and where there is danger there is hope. Our present security is nothing, and can be nothing, but evil made irresistible.

Weaknesses of the Salvation Army

For the present, however, it is not my business to flatter the Salvation Army. Rather must I point out to it that it has almost as many weaknesses as the Church of England itself. It is building up a business organization which will compel it eventually to see that its original staffs of enthusiast-commanders shall be succeeded by a bureaucracy of men of business. That has always happened sooner or later to great orders founded by saints; and the order founded by Saint William Booth will not escape the same danger. It is even more dependent than the Church on rich people who would cut off supplies at once if it began to preach a revolt against poverty which must also be a revolt against riches. It is hampered by a heavy contingent of pious elders who are not really Salvationists at all, but Evangelicals of the old school. It still "sticks to Moses," which is flat nonsense at this time of day if it means, as I am afraid it does, that the Book of Genesis contains a trustworthy scientific account of the origin of species, and that the god to whom Jephthah sacrificed his daughter is any less obviously a tribal idol than Dagon or Chemosh.

Further, there is still too much otherworldliness about the Army. Like Frederick's grenadier, the Salvationist wants to live for ever (the most monstrous way of crying for the moon); and though it is evident to anyone who has ever heard General Booth and his best officers that they would work as hard for human salvation as they do at present if they believed that death would be the end of them individually, they and their followers have a bad habit of talking as if the Salvationists were heroically enduring a very bad time on earth as an investment which will bring them in dividends later on in the form, not of a better life to come for the whole world, but of an eternity spent by themselves personally in a sort of bliss which would bore any active person to a second death. Surely the truth is that the Salvationists are unusually happy people. And is it not the very diagnostic of true salvation that it shall overcome the fear of death? Now the man who has come to believe that there is no such thing as death, the change so called being merely the transition to an exquisitely happy and utterly careless life, has not overcome the fear of death at all: on the contrary, it has overcome him so completely that he refuses to die on any terms whatever. I do not call a Salvationist really saved until he is ready to lie down cheerfully on the scrap heap, having paid scot and lot and something over, and let his eternal life pass on to renew its youth in the battalions of the future.

Then there is the nasty lying habit called confession, which the Army encourages because it lends itself to dramatic oratory, with plenty of thrilling incident. For my part, when I hear a convert relating the violences and oaths and blasphemies he was guilty of before he was saved, making out that he was a very terrible fellow then and is the most contrite and chastened of Christians now, I believe him no more than I believe the millionaire who says he came up to London or Chicago as a boy with only three half-pence in his pocket. Salvationists have said to me that Barbara in my play would never have been taken in by so transparent a humbug as Snobby Price; and certainly I do not think Snobby could have taken in any experienced Salvationist on a point on which the Salvationist did not wish to be taken in. But on the point of conversion all Salvationists wish to be taken in; for the more obvious the sinner the more obvious the miracle of his conversion. When converted burglars and reclaimed drunkards are the attractions at an experience meeting, the burglars can hardly be too burglarious or the drunkards too drunken. As long as such attractions are relied on, you will have your Snobbies claiming to have beaten their mothers when they were as a matter of prosaic fact habitually beaten by them, and your Rummies of the tamest respectability pretending to a past of reckless and dazzling vice. Even when confessions are sincerely autobiographic we should beware of assuming that the impulse to make them was pious or that the interest of the hearers is wholesome. As well might we assume that the poor people who insist on shewing disgusting ulcers to district visitors are convinced hygienists, or that the curiosity which sometimes welcomes such exhibitions is a pleasant and creditable one. One is often tempted to suggest that those who pester our police superintendents with confessions of murder might very wisely be taken at their word and executed, except in the few cases in which a real murderer is seeking to be relieved of his guilt by confession and expiation. For though I am not, I hope, an unmerciful person, I do not think that the inexorability of the deed once done should be disguised by any ritual, whether in the confessional or on the scaffold.

And here my disagreement with the Salvation Army, and with all propagandists of the Cross (which I loathe as I loathe all gibbets) becomes deep indeed. Forgiveness, absolution, atonement, are figments: punishment is only a pretence of cancelling one crime by another; and we can no more have forgiveness without vindictiveness than a cure without a disease. We shall never get a high morality from people who conceive that their misdeeds are revocable and pardonable, nor in a society where absolution and expiation are officially provided for us all. The demand may be very real; but the supply is spurious.

Thus Bill Walker, in my play, having assaulted the Salvation Lass, presently finds himself overwhelmed with an intolerable conviction of sin under the skilled treatment of Barbara. Straightway he begins to try to unassault the lass and deruffianize his deed, first by getting punished for it in kind, and, when that relief is denied him, by fining himself a pound to compensate the girl. He is foiled both ways. He finds the Salvation Army as inexorable as the facts. It will not punish him: it will not take his money. It will not tolerate a redeemed ruffian: it leaves him no means of salvation except ceasing to be a ruffian. In doing this, the Salvation Army instinctively grasps the central truth of Christianity and discards its central superstition: that central truth being the vanity of revenge and punishment, and that central superstition the salvation of the world by the gibbet.

For, be it noted, Bill has assaulted an old and starving woman also; and for this worse offence he feels no remorse whatever, because she makes it clear that her malice is as great as his own. "Let her have the law of me, as she said she would," says Bill: "what I done to her is no more on what you might call my conscience than sticking a pig." This shews a perfectly natural and wholesome state of mind on his part. The old woman, like the law she threatens him with, is perfectly ready to play the game of retaliation with him: to rob him if he steals, to flog him if he strikes, to murder him if he kills. By example and precept the law and public opinion teach him to impose his will on others by anger, violence, and cruelty, and to wipe off the moral score by punishment. That is sound Crosstianity. But this Crosstianity has got entangled with something which Barbara calls Christianity, and which unexpectedly causes her to refuse to play the hangman's game of Satan casting out Satan. She refuses to prosecute a drunken ruffian; she converses on equal terms with a blackguard to whom no lady should be seen speaking in the public street: in short, she imitates Christ. Bill's conscience reacts to this just as naturally as it does to the old woman's threats. He is placed in a position of unbearable moral inferiority, and strives by every means in his power to escape from it, whilst he is still quite ready to meet the abuse of the old woman by attempting to smash a mug on her face. And that is the triumphant justification of Barbara's Christianity as against our system of judicial punishment and the vindictive villain-thrashings and "poetic justice" of the romantic stage.

For the credit of literature it must be pointed out that the situation is only partly novel. Victor Hugo long ago gave us the epic of the convict and the bishop's candlesticks, of the Crosstian policeman annihilated by his encounter with the Christian Valjean. But Bill Walker is not, like Valjean, romantically changed from a demon into an angel. There are millions of Bill Walkers in all classes of society today; and the point which I, as a professor of natural psychology, desire to demonstrate, is that Bill, without any change in his character or circumstances whatsoever, will react one way to one sort of treatment and another way to another.

In proof I might point to the sensational object lesson provided by our commercial millionaires today. They begin as brigands: merciless, unscrupulous, dealing out ruin and death and slavery to their competitors and employees, and facing desperately the worst that their competitors can do to them. The history of the English factories, the American Trusts, the exploitation of African gold, diamonds, ivory and rubber, outdoes in villainy the worst that has ever been imagined of the buccaneers of the Spanish Main. Captain Kidd would have marooned a modern Trust magnate for conduct unworthy of a gentleman of fortune. The law every day seizes on scoundrels who are not capitalists and punishes them with a cruelty worse than their own, with the result that they come out of the torture house more dangerous than they went in, and renew their evil doing (nobody will employ them at anything else) until they are again seized, again tormented, and again let loose, with the same result.

But the moneyed scoundrel is dealt with very differently, and very Christianly. He is not only forgiven: he is idolized, respected, made much of, all but worshipped. Society returns him good for evil in the most extravagant overmeasure. And with what result? He begins to idolize himself, to respect himself, to live up to the treatment he receives. He preaches sermons; he writes books of the most edifying advice to young men, actually persuading himself that he got on by taking his own advice; he endows educational institutions; he supports charities; he dies finally in the odor of sanctity, leaving a will which is a monument of public spirit and bounty. And all this without any change in his character. The spots of the leopard and the stripes of the tiger are as brilliant as ever; but the conduct of the world towards him has changed; and his conduct has changed accordingly. You have only to reverse your attitude towards him, to lay hands on his property, revile him, torture him, and he will be a brigand again in a moment, as ready to crush you as you are to crush him, and quite as full of pretentious moral reasons for doing it.

In short, when Major Barbara says that there are no scoundrels, she is right: there are no absolute scoundrels, though there are intolerable people of whom I shall treat presently. Every reasonable man (and woman) is a potential scoundrel and a potential good citizen. Whatever his character, what he does, and what we think of what he does, depend mostly on how we treat him. The characteristics that ruin a citizen in one class make him eminent in another. The characters that behave differently in different circumstances behave alike in similar circumstances. Take a common English character like that of Bill Walker. We meet Bill everywhere: on the judicial bench, on the episcopal bench, in the Privy Council, at the War Office and Admiralty, as well as in the Old Bailey dock or in the ranks of casual unskilled labor. And the morality of Bill's characteristics varies with these various circumstances. The faults of the burglar are the qualities of the financier: the manners and habits of a duke would cost a city clerk his situation. In short, though character is independent of circumstances, conduct is not; and our moral judgments of character are not: both are circumstantial. Take any condition of life in which the circumstances are for a mass of men practically alike: prison, the peerage, the army, the factory, the stables, the gipsy encampment or where you please! In spite of diversity of character and temperament, the conduct and morals of the individuals in each group are as predicable and as alike in the main as if they were a flock of sheep, morals being mostly only social habits and circumstantial necessities. Strong people know this and count upon it. In nothing have the master-minds of the world been distinguished from the ordinary suburban season-ticket holder more than in their straightforward perception of the fact that mankind in the lump is a single species, and not a menagerie of gentlemen and bounders, villains and heroes, cowards and daredevils, peers and peasants, shopkeepers and aristocrats, artisans and laborers, washerwomen and duchesses, in which all the grades of income and caste represent distinct animals who must not be introduced to one another or intermarry. Napoleon constructing a galaxy of generals and courtiers, and even of monarchs, out of his collection of social nobodies; Julius Cæsar appointing as governor of Egypt the son of a freedman who but a short time before would have been legally disqualified for the post even of a private soldier in the Roman army; Louis XI making his barber his privy councillor: all these had in their different ways a firm hold of the scientific fact of human equality, expressed by Barbara in the Christian formula that all men are children of one father. No use declaring that all men are born free if we deny that they are born good. Guarantee a man's goodness and his liberty will take care of itself. To guarantee his freedom on condition that we approve of his moral character is formally to abolish all freedom whatsoever, as every man's liberty is at the mercy of moral indictments which any bigot can trump up against everyone who violates custom, whether as a prophet or as a rascal. This is the lesson Democracy has to learn before it can become anything but the most oppressive of all the priesthoods.

Let us now return to Bill Walker and his case of conscience against the Salvation Army. Major Barbara, not being a modern Tetzel, or the treasurer of a hospital, refuses to sell absolution to Bill for a pound sterling. Unfortunately, what the Army can afford to refuse to Bill Walker, it cannot refuse to Bodger. Bodger is master of the situation because he holds the purse strings. "Strive as you will," says Bodger, in effect: "me you cannot do without. You cannot save Bill Walker without my money." And the Army answers, quite rightly under the circumstances, "We will take money from the devil himself sooner than abandon the work of Salvation." So Bodger pays his conscience-money and gets the absolution that is refused to Bill. In real life Bill would perhaps never know this. But I, the dramatist whose business it is to shew the connexion between things that seem apart and unrelated in the haphazard order of events in real life, have contrived to make it known to Bill, with the result that the Salvation Army loses its hold of him at once.

But Bill may not be lost, for all that. He is still in the grip of the facts and of his own conscience, and may find his taste for blackguardism permanently spoiled. Still, I cannot guarantee that happy ending. Walk through the poorer quarters of our cities on Sunday when the men are not working, but resting and chewing the cud of their reflections. You will find one expression common to every mature face: the expression of cynicism. The discovery made by Bill Walker about the Salvation Army has been made by everyone there. They have found that every man has his price; and they have been foolishly or corruptly taught to mistrust and despise him for that necessary and salutary condition of social existence. When they learn that General Booth, too, has his price, they do not admire him because it is a high one, and admit the need of organizing society so that he shall get it in an honorable way: they conclude that his character is unsound and that all religious men are hypocrites and allies of their sweaters and oppressors. They know that the large subscriptions which help to support the Army are endowments, not of religion, but of the wicked doctrine of docility in poverty and humility under oppression; and they are rent by the most agonizing of all the doubts of the soul, the doubt whether their true salvation must not come from their most abhorrent passions, from murder, envy, greed, stubbornness, rage, and terrorism, rather than from public spirit, reasonableness, humanity, generosity, tenderness, delicacy, pity and kindness. The confirmation of that doubt, at which our newspapers have been working so hard for years past, is the morality of militarism; and the justification of militarism is that circumstances may at any time make it the true morality of the moment. This, which I wrote before 1914, has been most bloodily confirmed by two world wars.

At such moments it becomes the duty of the Churches to rally their congregations against the existing order. But if they do this, the existing order must forcibly suppress them. Churches are suffered to exist only on condition that they preach submission to the State as at present capitalistically organized. The Church of England itself is compelled to add to the thirtysix articles in which it formulates its religious tenets, three more in which it apologetically protests that the moment any of these articles comes in conflict with the State it is to be entirely renounced, abjured, violated, abrogated and abhorred, the policeman being a much more important person than any of the Persons of the Trinity. And this is why no tolerated Church nor Salvation Army can ever win the entire confidence of the poor. It must be on the side of the police and the military, no matter what it believes or disbelieves; and as the police and the military are the instruments by which the rich rob and oppress the poor (on legal and moral principles made for the purpose), it is not possible to be on the side of the poor and of the police at the same time. Indeed the religious bodies, as the almoners of the rich, become a sort of auxiliary police, taking off the insurrectionary edge of poverty with coals and blankets, bread and treacle, soothing and cheering the victims with hopes of immense and inexpensive happiness in another world when the process of working them to premature death in the service of the rich is complete in this.

CHRISTIANITY AND ANARCHISM

Such is the false position from which neither the Salvation Army nor the Church of England nor any other religious organization whatever can escape except through a reconstitution of society. Nor can they merely endure the State passively, washing their hands of its sins. The State is constantly forcing the consciences of men by violence and cruelty. Not content with exacting money from us for the maintenance of its soldiers and policemen, its gaolers and executioners, it forces us to take an active personal part in its proceedings on pain of becoming ourselves the victims of its violence. As I wrote these lines forty years ago a sensational example was given to the world. A royal marriage had been celebrated, first by sacrament in a cathedral, and then by a bullfight having for its main amusement the spectacle of horses gored and disembowelled by the bull, after which, when the bull was so exhausted as to be no longer dangerous, he was killed by a cautious matador. But the ironic contrast between the bullfight and the sacrament of marriage does not move anyone. Another contrast—that between the splendor, the happiness, the atmosphere of kindly admiration surrounding the young couple, and the price paid for it under our abominable social arrangements in the misery, squalor and degradation of millions of other young couples—was drawn at the same moment by an American novelist, Mr. Upton Sinclair, who chipped a corner of the veneering from the huge meat packing industries of Chicago, and shewed it to us as a sample of what is going on all over the world underneath the top layer of prosperous plutocracy. One man was sufficiently moved by that contrast to pay his own life as the price of one terrible blow at the responsible parties. His poverty left him ignorant enough to be duped by the pretence that the innocent young bride and bridegroom, put forth and crowned by plutocracy as the heads of a State in which they had less personal power than any policeman, and less influence than any Chairman of a Trust, were responsible. At them accordingly he launched his sixpennorth of fulminate, missing his mark, but scattering the bowels of as many horses as any bull in the arena, and slaying twenty-three persons, besides wounding ninety-nine. And of all these, the horses alone were innocent of the guilt he was avenging: had he blown all Madrid to atoms with every adult person in it, not one could have escaped the charge of being an accessory, before, at, and after the facts, to poverty and prostitution, to such wholesale massacre of infants as Herod never dreamt of, to plague, pestilence and famine, battle, murder and lingering death: perhaps not one who had not helped, through example, precept, connivance, and even clamor, to teach the dynamiter his well-learnt gospel of hatred and vengeance, by approving every day of sentences of years of imprisonment so infernal in their unnatural stupidity and panic-stricken cruelty, that their advocates can disavow neither the dagger nor the bomb without stripping the mask of justice and humanity from themselves also.

At that very moment there appeared the biography of one of our dukes, who, being a Scot, could argue about politics, and therefore stood out as a great brain among our aristocrats. And what, if you please, was his Grace's favorite historical episode, which he declared he never read without intense satisfaction? Why, the young General Bonaparte's pounding of the Paris mob to pieces in 1795, called in playful approval by our respectable classes "the whiff of grapeshot," though Napoleon, to do him justice, took a deeper view of it, and would fain have had it forgotten. And since the Duke was not a demon, but a man of like passions with ourselves, by no means rancorous or cruel as men go, who can doubt that all over the world proletarians of the ducal kidney revelled in "the whiff of dynamite" (the flavor of the joke seems to evaporate a little, does it not?) because it was aimed at the class they hate even as our argute duke hated what he called the mob?

In such an atmosphere there could be only one sequel to the Madrid explosion. All Europe burned to emulate it. Vengeance! More blood! Tear "the Anarchist beast" to shreds. Drag him to the scaffold. Imprison him for life. Let all civilized States band together to drive his like off the face of the earth; and if any State refuses to join, make war on it. This time the leading London newspaper, then anti-Liberal and therefore anti-Tsarist in politics, did not say "Serve you right" to the victims, as it did, in effect, when Bobrikoff, and De Plehve, and Grand Duke Sergius, were in the same manner unofficially fulminated into fragments. No: fulminate our rivals in Asia by all means, ye brave Russian revolutionaries; but to aim at an English princess! monstrous! hideous! hound down the wretch to his doom; and observe, please, that we are a civilized and merciful people, and however much we may regret it, must not treat him as Ravaillac, Damiens, and our regicides of 1649 were treated.

Strangely enough, in the midst of this raging fire of malice, the one man who still had faith in the kindness and intelligence of human nature was the fulminator, a hunted wretch, with nothing, apparently, to secure his triumph over all the prisons and scaffolds of infuriate Europe except the revolver in his pocket and his readiness to discharge it at a moment's notice into his own head. Think of him setting out to find a gentleman and a Christian in the multitude of human wolves howling for his blood. Think also of this: that at the very first essay he found what he sought: a veritable grandee of Spain, a noble, high-thinking, unterrified, malice-void soul, in the guise—of all masquerades in the world!—of a modern editor. The Anarchist wolf, flying from the wolves of plutocracy, threw himself on the honor of the man. The man, not being a wolf (nor a London editor), and therefore not having enough sympathy with his exploit to be made bloodthirsty by it, did not throw him back to the pursuing wolves—gave him, instead, what help he could to escape, and sent him off acquainted at last with a force that goes deeper than dynamite, though you cannot buy so much of it for sixpence. That righteous and honorable high human deed was not wasted on Europe, let us hope, though it benefited the fugitive wolf for a moment only. The plutocratic wolves presently smelt him out. The fugitive shot the unlucky wolf whose nose was nearest; shot himself; and then convinced the world, by his photograph, that he was no monstrous freak of reversion to the tiger, but a good looking young man with nothing abnormal about him except his appalling courage and resolution (that is why the terrified shrieked Coward at him): one to whom murdering a happy young couple on their wedding morning would have been an unthinkably unnatural abomination under rational and kindly human circumstances.

Then comes the climax of irony and blind stupidity. The wolves, balked of their meal of fellow-wolf, turn on the Samaritan man, and proceed to torture him, after their manner, by imprisonment, for refusing to fasten his teeth in the throat of the dynamiter and hold him down until they came to finish him.

Thus, you see, a man may not be a gentleman nowadays even if he wishes to. As to being a Christian, he is allowed some latitude in that matter, because, I repeat, Christianity has two faces. Popular Christianity has for its emblem a gibbet; for its chief sensation a sanguinary execution after torture; for its central mystery an insane vengeance bought off by a trumpery expiation. But there is a nobler and profounder Christianity which affirms the sacred mystery of Equality, and forbids the glaring futility and folly of vengeance, often politely called punishment or justice. The gibbet part of Christianity is tolerated. The other is criminal felony. Connoisseurs in irony are well aware of the fact that the only editor in England who denounced punishment as radically wrong, also repudiated Christianity; called his paper The Freethinker; and was imprisoned for a year for "bad taste" under the law against blasphemy.

SANE CONCLUSIONS

And now I must ask the excited reader not to lose his head on one side or the other, but to draw a sane moral from these grim absurdities. It is not good sense to propose that laws against crime should apply to principals only and not to accessories whose consent, counsel, or silence may secure impunity to the principal. If you institute punishment as part of the law, you must punish people for refusing to punish. If you have a police, part of its duty must be to compel everybody to assist the police. No doubt if your laws are unjust, and your policemen agents of oppression, the result will be an unbearable violation of the private consciences of citizens. But that cannot be helped: the remedy is, not to license everybody to thwart the law if they please, but to make laws that will command the public assent, and not to deal cruelly and stupidly with lawbreakers. Everybody disapproves of burglars; but the modern burglar, when caught and overpowered by a householder, sometimes appeals, often, let us hope, with success, to his captor not to deliver him over to the useless horrors of penal servitude. In other cases the lawbreaker escapes because those who could give him up do not consider his breach of the law a guilty action. Private tribunals are formed in opposition to the official tribunals; and these private tribunals employ assassins as executioners, as was done, for example, by Mahomet before he had established his power officially, and by the Ribbon lodges of Ireland in their long struggle with the landlords. Under such circumstances, the assassin goes free although everybody in the district knows who he is and what he has done. They do not betray him, partly because they justify him exactly as the regular Government justifies its official executioner, and partly because they would themselves be assassinated if they betrayed him: another method learnt from the official government. Given a tribunal employing a slayer who has no personal quarrel with the slain, and there is clearly no moral difference between official and unofficial killing.

In short, all men are anarchists with regard to laws which are against their consciences, either in the preamble or in the penalty. In London our worst anarchists are the magistrates, because many of them are so old and ignorant that when they are called upon to administer any law that is based on ideas or knowledge less than half a century old, they disagree with it, and being mere ordinary homebred private Englishmen without any respect for law except in the abstract, naïvely set the example of violating it. In this instance the man lags behind the law; but when the law lags behind the man, he becomes equally an anarchist. When some huge change in social conditions, such as the industrial revolution of the eighteenth and nineteenth centuries, throws our legal and industrial institutions out of date, Anarchism becomes almost a religion. The whole force of the most energetic geniuses of the time in philosophy, economics, and art, concentrates itself on demonstrations and reminders that morality and law are only conventions, fallible and continually obsolescing. Tragedies in which the heroes are bandits, and comedies in which law-abiding and conventionally moral folk are compelled to satirize themselves by outraging the conscience of the spectators every time they do their duty, appear simultaneously with economic treatises entitled "What is Property? Theft!" and with histories of "The Conflict between Religion and Science."

Now this is not a healthy state of things. The advantages of living in society are proportionate, not to the freedom of the individual from a code, but to the complexity and subtlety of the code he is prepared not only to accept but to uphold as a matter of such vital importance that a lawbreaker at large is hardly to be tolerated on any plea. Such an attitude becomes impossible when the only men who can make themselves heard and remembered throughout the world spend all their energy in raising our gorge against current law, current morality, current respectability, and legal property. The ordinary man, uneducated in social theory even when he is schooled in Latin verse, cannot be set against all the laws of his country and yet persuaded to regard law in the abstract as vitally necessary to society. Once he is brought to repudiate the laws and institutions he knows, he will repudiate the very conception of law and the very groundwork of institutions, ridiculing human rights, extolling brainless methods as "historical," and tolerating nothing except opportunist empiricism in conduct, with dynamite as the basis of politics and vivisection as the basis of science. That is hideous; but what is to be done? Here am I, for instance, by class a respectable man, by common sense a hater of waste and disorder, by intellectual constitution legally minded to the verge of pedantry, and by temperament apprehensive and economically disposed to the limit of old-maidishness; yet I am, and have always been, and shall now always be, a revolutionary writer, because our laws make law impossible; our liberties destroy all freedom; our property is organized robbery; our morality is an impudent hypocrisy; our wisdom is administered by inexperienced or malexperienced dupes, our power wielded by cowards and weaklings, and our honor false in all its points. I am an enemy of the existing order for good reasons; but that does not make my attacks any less encouraging or helpful to people who are its enemies for bad reasons. I cannot help that, even if I could see what worse we could do than we are already doing. And society, with all its prisons and bayonets and whips and ostracisms and starvations, is powerless in the face of the Anarchist who is prepared to sacrifice his own life in the battle with it. Our natural safety from the cheap and devastating explosives which anybody can make, and every conscript learns to handle, lies in the fact that brave and resolute men, when they are rascals, will not risk their skins for the good of humanity, and, when they are not, are sympathetic enough to care for humanity, abhorring murder, and never committing it until their consciences are outraged beyond endurance. The remedy is, then, simply not to outrage their consciences.

Do not be afraid that they will not make allowances. All men make very large allowances indeed before they stake their own lives in a war to the death with society. Nobody demands or expects the millennium. But there are two things that must be set right, or we shall perish, like Rome, of soul atrophy disguised as empire.

The first is, that the daily ceremony of dividing the wealth of the country among its inhabitants shall be so conducted that no crumb shall, save as a criminal's ration, go to any able-bodied adults who are not producing by their personal exertions not only a full equivalent for what they take, but a surplus sufficient to provide for their superannuation and pay back the debt due for their nurture.

The second is that the deliberate infliction of malicious injuries which now goes on under the name of punishment be abandoned; so that the thief, the ruffian, the gambler, and the beggar, may without inhumanity be handed over to the law, and made to understand that a State which is too humane to punish will also be too thrifty to waste the life of honest men in watching or restraining dishonest ones. That is why we do not imprison dogs. We even take our chance of their first bite. But if a dog delights to bark and bite, it goes to the lethal chamber. That seems to me sensible. To allow the dog to expiate his bite by a period of torment, and then let him loose in a much more savage condition (for the chain makes a dog savage) to bite again and expiate again, having meanwhile spent a great deal of human life and happiness in the task of chaining and feeding and tormenting him, seems to me idiotic and superstitious. Yet that is what we do to men who bark and bite and steal. It would be far more sensible to put up with their vices, as we put up with their illnesses, until they give more trouble than they are worth, at which point we should, with many apologies and expressions of sympathy, and some generosity in complying with their last wishes, place them in the lethal chamber and get rid of them. Under no circumstances should they be allowed to expiate their misdeeds by a manufactured penalty, to subscribe to a charity, or to compensate the victims. If there is to be no punishment there can be no forgiveness. We shall never have real moral responsibility until everyone knows that his deeds are irrevocable, and that his life depends on his usefulness. Hitherto, alas! humanity has never dared face these hard facts. We frantically scatter conscience money and invent systems of conscience banking, with expiatory penalties, atonements, redemptions, salvations, hospital subscription lists and what not, to enable us to contract-out of the moral code. Not content with the old scapegoat and sacrificial lamb, we deify human saviors, and pray to miraculous virgin intercessors. We attribute mercy to the inexorable; soothe our consciences after committing murder by throwing ourselves on the bosom of divine love; and shrink even from our own gallows because we are forced to admit that it, at least, is irrevocable—as if one hour of imprisonment were not as irrevocable as any execution!

If a man cannot look evil in the face without illusion, he will never know what it really is, or combat it effectually. The few men who have been able (relatively) to do this have been called cynics, and have sometimes had an abnormal share of evil in themselves, corresponding to the abnormal strength of their minds; but they have never done mischief unless they intended to do it. That is why great scoundrels have been beneficent rulers whilst amiable and privately harmless monarchs have ruined their countries by trusting to the hocus-pocus of innocence and guilt, reward and punishment, virtuous indignation and pardon, instead of standing up to the facts without either malice or mercy. Major Barbara stands up to Bill Walker in that way, with the result that the ruffian who cannot get hated, has to hate himself. To relieve this agony he tries to get punished; but the Salvationist whom he tries to provoke is as merciless as Barbara, and only prays for him. Then he tries to pay, but can get nobody to take his money. His doom is the doom of Cain, who, failing to find either a savior, a policeman, or an almoner to help him to pretend that his brother's blood no longer cried from the ground, had to live and die a murderer. Cain took care not to commit another murder, unlike our railway shareholders (I am one) who kill and maim shunters by hundreds to save the cost of automatic couplings, and make atonement by annual subscriptions to deserving charities. Had Cain been allowed to pay off his score, he might possibly have killed Adam and Eve for the mere sake of a second luxurious reconciliation with God afterwards. Bodger, you may depend on it, will go on to the end of his life poisoning people with whisky, because he can always depend on the Salvation Army or the Church of England to negotiate a redemption for him in consideration of a trifling percentage of his profits.

There is a third condition too, which must be fulfilled before the great teachers of the world will cease to scoff at its religions. Creeds must become intellectually honest. At present there is not a single credible established religion in the world. That is perhaps the most stupendous fact in the whole world-situation. This play of mine, Major Barbara, is, I hope, both true and inspired; but whoever says that it all happened, and that faith in it and understanding of it consist in believing that it is a record of an actual occurrence, is, to speak according to Scripture, a fool and a liar, and is hereby solemnly denounced and cursed as such by me, the author, to all posterity.

London, June 1906
Revised, April 1944,
in Ayot Saint Lawrence

MAJOR BARBARA
by George Bernard Shaw

ACT I

[*It is after dinner in January 1906, in the library in* Lady Britomart Undershaft's *house in Wilton Crescent. A large and comfortable settee is in the middle of the room, upholstered in dark leather. A person sitting on it (it is vacant at present) would have, on his right,* Lady Britomart's *writing table, with the lady herself busy at it; a smaller writing table behind him on his left; the door behind him on* Lady Britomart's *side; and a window with a window seat directly on his left. Near the window is an armchair.*

Lady Britomart *is a woman of fifty or thereabouts, well dressed and yet careless of her dress, well bred and quite reckless of her breeding, well mannered and yet appallingly outspoken and indifferent to the opinion of her interlocutors, amiable and yet peremptory, arbitrary, and high-tempered to the last bearable degree, and withal a very typical managing matron of the upper class, treated as a naughty child until she grew into a scolding mother, and finally settling down with plenty of practical ability and worldly experience, limited in the oddest way with domestic and class limitations, conceiving the universe exactly as if it were a large house in Wilton Crescent, though handling her corner of it very effectively on that assumption, and being quite enlightened and liberal as to the books in the library, the pictures on the walls, the music in the portfolios, and the articles in the papers.*

Her son, Stephen, *comes in. He is a gravely correct young man under 25, taking himself very seriously, but still in some awe of his mother, from childish habit and bachelor shyness rather than from any weakness of character.*]

Stephen. What's the matter?

Lady Britomart. Presently, Stephen.

Stephen *submissively walks to the settee and sits down. He takes up a Liberal weekly called* The Speaker.

Lady Britomart. Don't begin to read, Stephen. I shall require all your attention.

STEPHEN. It was only while I was waiting—

LADY BRITOMART. Don't make excuses, Stephen. [*He puts down The Speaker.*] Now! [*She finishes her writing; rises; and comes to the settee.*] I have not kept you waiting very long, I think.

STEPHEN. Not at all, mother.

LADY BRITOMART. Bring me my cushion. [*He takes the cushion from the chair at the desk and arranges it for her as she sits down on the settee.*] Sit down. [*He sits down and fingers his tie nervously.*] Don't fiddle with your tie, Stephen: there is nothing the matter with it.

STEPHEN. I beg your pardon. [*He fiddles with his watch chain instead.*]

LADY BRITOMART. Now are you attending to me, Stephen?

STEPHEN. Of course, mother.

LADY BRITOMART. No: it's not of course. I want something much more than your everyday matter-of-course attention. I am going to speak to you very seriously, Stephen. I wish you would let that chain alone.

STEPHEN [*hastily relinquishing the chain*]. Have I done anything to annoy you, mother? If so, it was quite unintentional.

LADY BRITOMART [*astonished*]. Nonsense! [*With some remorse.*] My poor boy, did you think I was angry with you?

STEPHEN. What is it, then, mother? You are making me very uneasy.

LADY BRITOMART [*squaring herself at him rather aggressively*]. Stephen: may I ask how soon you intend to realize that you are a grown-up man, and that I am only a woman?

STEPHEN [*amazed*]. Only a—

LADY BRITOMART. Don't repeat my words, please: it is a most aggravating habit. You must learn to face life seriously, Stephen. I really cannot bear the whole burden of our family affairs any longer. You must advise me: you must assume the responsibility.

STEPHEN. I!

LADY BRITOMART. Yes, you, of course. You were 24 last June. You've been at Harrow and Cambridge. You've been to India and Japan. You must know a lot of things, now; unless you have wasted your time most scandalously. Well, advise me.

STEPHEN [*much perplexed*]. You know I have never interfered in the household—

LADY BRITOMART. No: I should think not. I don't want you to order the dinner.

STEPHEN. I mean in our family affairs.

LADY BRITOMART. Well, you must interfere now; for they are getting quite beyond me.

STEPHEN [*troubled*]. I have thought sometimes that perhaps I ought; but really, mother, I know so little about them; and what I do know is so painful! it is so impossible to mention some things to you— [*He stops, ashamed.*]

LADY BRITOMART. I suppose you mean your father.

STEPHEN [*almost inaudibly*]. Yes.

LADY BRITOMART. My dear: we can't go on all our lives not mentioning him. Of course you were quite right not to open the subject until I asked you to; but you are old enough now to be taken into my confidence, and to help me to deal with him about the girls.

STEPHEN. But the girls are all right. They are engaged.

LADY BRITOMART [*complacently*]. Yes: I have made a very good match for Sarah. Charles Lomax will be a millionaire at 35. But that is ten years ahead; and in the meantime his trustees cannot under the terms of his father's will allow him more than £800 a year.

STEPHEN. But the will says also that if he increases his income by his own exertions, they may double the increase.

LADY BRITOMART. Charles Lomax's exertions are much more likely to decrease his income than to increase it. Sarah will have to find at least another £800 a year for the next ten years; and even then they will be as poor as church mice. And what about Barbara? I thought Barbara was going to make the most brilliant career of all of you. And what does she do? Joins the Salvation Army; discharges her maid; lives on a pound a week; and walks in one evening with a professor of Greek whom she has picked up in the street, and who pretends to be a Salvationist, and actually plays the big drum for her in public because he has fallen head over ears in love with her.

STEPHEN. I was certainly rather taken aback when I heard they were engaged. Cusins is a very nice fellow, certainly: nobody would ever guess that he was born in Australia; but—

LADY BRITOMART. Oh, Adolphus Cusins will make a very good husband. After all, nobody can say a word against Greek: it stamps a man at once as an educated gentleman. And my family, thank Heaven, is not a pig-headed Tory one. We are Whigs, and believe in liberty. Let snobbish people say what they please: Barbara shall marry, not the man they like, but the man *I* like.

STEPHEN. Of course I was thinking only of his income. However, he is not likely to be extravagant.

LADY BRITOMART. Don't be too sure of that, Stephen. I know your quiet, simple, refined, poetic people like Adolphus: quite content with the best of everything! They cost more than your extravagant people, who are always as mean as they are second rate. No: Barbara will need at least £2000 a year. You see it means two additional households. Besides, my dear, you must marry soon. I don't approve of the present fashion of philandering bachelors and late marriages; and I am trying to arrange something for you.

STEPHEN. It's very good of you, mother; but perhaps I had better arrange that for myself.

LADY BRITOMART. Nonsense! you are much too young to begin matchmaking: you would be taken in by some pretty little nobody. Of course I don't mean that you are not to be consulted: you know that as well as I do. [*Stephen closes his lips and is silent.*] Now don't sulk, Stephen.

STEPHEN. I am not sulking, mother. What has all this got to do with—with —with my father?

LADY BRITOMART. My dear Stephen: where is the money to come from? It is easy enough for you and the other children to live on my income as long as we are in the same house; but I can't keep four families in four separate houses. You know how poor my father is: he has barely seven thousand a year now; and really, if he were not the Earl of Stevenage, he would have to give up society. He can do nothing for us. He says, naturally enough, that it is absurd that he should be asked to provide for the children of a man who is rolling in money. You see, Stephen, your father must be fabulously wealthy, because there is always a war going on somewhere.

STEPHEN. You need not remind me of that, mother. I have hardly ever opened a newspaper in my life without seeing our name in it. The Undershaft torpedo! The

Undershaft quick firers! The Undershaft ten inch! the Undershaft disappearing rampart gun! the Undershaft submarine! and now the Undershaft aerial battleship! At Harrow they called me the Woolwich Infant. At Cambridge it was the same. A little brute at King's who was always trying to get up revivals, spoilt my Bible—your first birthday present to me—by writing under my name, "Son and heir to Undershaft and Lazarus, Death and Destruction Dealers: address, Christendom and Judea." But that was not so bad as the way I was kowtowed to everywhere because my father was making millions by selling cannons.

Lady Britomart. It is not only the cannons, but the war loans that Lazarus arranges under cover of giving credit for the cannons. You know, Stephen, it's perfectly scandalous. Those two men, Andrew Undershaft and Lazarus, positively have Europe under their thumbs. That is why your father is able to behave as he does. He is above the law. Do you think Bismarck or Gladstone or Disraeli could have openly defied every social and moral obligation all their lives as your father has? They simply wouldn't have dared. I asked Gladstone to take it up. I asked The Times to take it up. I asked the Lord Chamberlain to take it up. But it was just like asking them to declare war on the Sultan. They wouldn't. They said they couldn't touch him. I believe they were afraid.

Stephen. What could they do? He does not actually break the law.

Lady Britomart. Not break the law! He is always breaking the law. He broke the law when he was born: his parents were not married.

Stephen. Mother! Is that true?

Lady Britomart. Of course it's true: that was why we separated.

Stephen. He married without letting you know this!

Lady Britomart [*rather taken aback by this inference*]. Oh no. To do Andrew justice, that was not the sort of thing he did. Besides, you know the Undershaft motto: Unashamed. Everybody knew.

Stephen. But you said that was why you separated.

Lady Britomart. Yes, because he was not content with being a foundling himself: he wanted to disinherit you for another foundling. That was what I couldn't stand.

Stephen [*ashamed*]. Do you mean for —for—for—

Lady Britomart. Don't stammer, Stephen. Speak distinctly.

Stephen. But this is so frightful to me, mother. To have to speak to you about such things!

Lady Britomart. It's not pleasant for me, either, especially if you are still so childish that you must make it worse by a display of embarrassment. It is only in the middle classes, Stephen, that people get into a state of dumb helpless horror when they find that there are wicked people in the world. In our class, we have to decide what is to be done with wicked people; and nothing should disturb our self-possession. Now ask your question properly.

Stephen. Mother: have you no consideration for me? For Heaven's sake either treat me as a child, as you always do, and tell me nothing at all; or tell me everything and let me take it as best I can.

Lady Britomart. Treat you as a child! What do you mean? It is most unkind and ungrateful of you to say such a thing. You know I have never treated any of you as children. I have always made you my companions and friends, and allowed you perfect freedom to do and say whatever you liked, so long as you liked what I could approve of.

STEPHEN [*desperately*]. I daresay we have been the very imperfect children of a very perfect mother; but I do beg you to let me alone for once, and tell me about this horrible business of my father wanting to set me aside for another son.

LADY BRITOMART [*amazed*]. Another son! I never said anything of the kind. I never dreamt of such a thing. This is what comes of interrupting me.

STEPHEN. But you said—

LADY BRITOMART [*cutting him short*]. Now be a good boy, Stephen, and listen to me patiently. The Undershafts are descended from a foundling in the parish of St. Andrew Undershaft in the city. That was long ago, in the reign of James the First. Well, this foundling was adopted by an armorer and gun-maker. In the course of time the foundling succeeded to the business; and from some notion of gratitude, or some vow or something, he adopted another foundling, and left the business to him. And that foundling did the same. Ever since that, the cannon business has always been left to an adopted foundling named Andrew Undershaft.

STEPHEN. But did they never marry? Were there no legitimate sons?

LADY BRITOMART. Oh yes: they married just as your father did; and they were rich enough to buy land for their own children and leave them well provided for. But they always adopted and trained some foundling to succeed them in the business; and of course they always quarrelled with their wives furiously over it. Your father was adopted in that way; and he pretends to consider himself bound to keep up the tradition and adopt somebody to leave the business to. Of course I was not going to stand that. There may have been some reason for it when the Undershafts could only marry women in their own class, whose sons were not fit to govern great estates. But there could be no excuse for passing over my son.

STEPHEN [*dubiously*]. I am afraid I should make a poor hand of managing a cannon foundry.

LADY BRITOMART. Nonsense! you could easily get a manager and pay him a salary.

STEPHEN. My father evidently had no great opinion of my capacity.

LADY BRITOMART. Stuff, child! you were only a baby: it had nothing to do with your capacity. Andrew did it on principle, just as he did every perverse and wicked thing on principle. When my father remonstrated, Andrew actually told him to his face that history tells us of only two successful institutions: one the Undershaft firm, and the other the Roman Empire under the Antonines. That was because the Antonine emperors all adopted their successors. Such rubbish! The Stevenages are as good as the Antonines, I hope; and you are a Stevenage. But that was Andrew all over. There you have the man! Always clever and unanswerable when he was defending nonsense and wickedness: always awkward and sullen when he had to behave sensibly and decently!

STEPHEN. Then it was on my account that your home life was broken up, mother. I am sorry.

LADY BRITOMART. Well, dear, there were other differences. I really cannot bear an immoral man. I am not a Pharisee, I hope; and I should not have minded his merely doing wrong things: we are none of us perfect. But your father didn't exactly do wrong things: he said them and thought them: that was what was so dreadful. He really had a sort of religion of wrongness. Just as one doesn't mind men practising immorality so long as they own that they are in the wrong by preaching morality; so I couldn't forgive Andrew for preaching immorality while he practised morality. You would all have grown up without principles, without any knowledge of right and wrong, if he had been in the house. You know, my dear, your father was a very attractive man in some ways. Children did not dislike him; and he took advantage of it to put the wickedest ideas into their heads, and make them quite unmanageable. I did not dislike him myself: very far from it; but nothing can bridge over moral disagreement.

STEPHEN. All this simply bewilders me, mother. People may differ about matters of opinion, or even about religion; but how can they differ about right and wrong? Right is right; and wrong is wrong; and if a man cannot distinguish them properly, he is either a fool or a rascal: that's all.

LADY BRITOMART [*touched*]. That's my own boy [*she pats his cheek*]! Your father never could answer that: he used to laugh and get out of it under cover of some affectionate nonsense. And now that you understand the situation, what do you advise me to do?

STEPHEN. Well, what can you do?

LADY BRITOMART. I must get the money somehow.

STEPHEN. We cannot take money from him. I had rather go and live in some cheap place like Bedford Square or even Hampstead than take a farthing of his money.

LADY BRITOMART. But after all, Stephen, our present income comes from Andrew.

STEPHEN [*shocked*]. I never knew that.

LADY BRITOMART. Well, you surely didn't suppose your grandfather had anything to give me. The Stevenages could not do everything for you. We gave you social position. Andrew had to contribute something. He had a very good bargain, I think.

STEPHEN [*bitterly*]. We are utterly dependent on him and his cannons, then?

LADY BRITOMART. Certainly not: the money is settled. But he provided it. So you see it is not a question of taking money from him or not: it is simply a question of how much. I don't want any more for myself.

STEPHEN. Nor do I.

LADY BRITOMART. But Sarah does; and Barbara does. That is, Charles Lomax and Adolphus Cusins will cost them more. So I must put my pride in my pocket and ask for it, I suppose. That is your advice, Stephen, is it not?

STEPHEN. No.

LADY BRITOMART [*sharply*]. Stephen!

STEPHEN. Of course if you are determined—

LADY BRITOMART. I am not determined: I ask your advice; and I am waiting for it. I will not have all the responsibility thrown on my shoulders.

STEPHEN [*obstinately*]. I would die sooner than ask him for another penny.

LADY BRITOMART [*resignedly*]. You mean that *I* must ask him. Very well, Stephen: it shall be as you wish. You will be glad to know that your grandfather concurs. But he thinks I ought to ask Andrew to come here and see the girls. After all, he must have some natural affection for them.

STEPHEN. Ask him here!!!

LADY BRITOMART. Do not repeat my words, Stephen. Where else can I ask him?

STEPHEN. I never expected you to ask him at all.

LADY BRITOMART. Now don't tease, Stephen. Come! you see that it is necessary that he should pay us a visit, don't you?

STEPHEN [*reluctantly*]. I suppose so, if the girls cannot do without his money.

LADY BRITOMART. Thank you, Stephen: I knew you would give me the right advice when it was properly explained to you. I have asked your father to come this evening. [*Stephen bounds from his seat.*] Don't jump, Stephen: it fidgets me.

STEPHEN [*in utter consternation*]. Do you mean to say that my father is coming here tonight—that he may be here at any moment?

LADY BRITOMART [*looking at her watch*]. I said nine. [*He gasps. She rises.*] Ring the bell, please. [STEPHEN *goes to the smaller writing table; presses a button on it; and sits at it with his elbows on the table and his head in his hands, outwitted and overwhelmed.*] It is ten minutes to nine yet; and I have to prepare the girls. I asked Charles Lomax and Adolphus to dinner on purpose that they might be here. Andrew had better see them in case he should cherish any delusions as to their being capable of supporting their wives. [*The butler enters:* LADY BRITOMART *goes behind the settee to speak to him.*] Morrison: go up to the drawing room and tell everybody to come down here at once. [MORRISON *withdraws.* LADY BRITOMART *turns to* STEPHEN.] Now remember, Stephen: I shall need all your countenance and authority. [*He rises and tries to recover some vestige of these attributes.*] Give me a chair, dear. [*He pushes a chair forward from the wall to where she stands, near the smaller writing table. She sits down; and he goes to the armchair, into which he throws himself.*] I don't know how Barbara will take it. Ever since they made her a major in the Salvation Army she has developed a propensity to have her own way and order people about which quite cows me sometimes. It's not ladylike: I'm sure I don't know where she picked it up. Anyhow, Barbara shan't bully me; but still it's just as well that your father should be here before she has time to refuse to meet him or make a fuss. Don't look nervous, Stephen: it will only encourage Barbara to make difficulties. *I* am nervous enough, goodness knows; but I don't shew it.

SARAH *and* BARBARA *come in with their respective young men,* CHARLES LOMAX *and* ADOLPHUS CUSINS. SARAH *is slender, bored, and mundane.* BARBARA *is robuster, jollier, much more energetic.* SARAH *is fashionably dressed:* BARBARA *is in Salvation Army uniform.* LOMAX, *a young man about town, is like many other young men about town. He is afflicted with a frivolous sense of humor which plunges him at the most inopportune moments into paroxysms of imperfectly suppressed laughter.* CUSINS *is a spectacled student, slight, thin haired, and sweet voiced, with a more complex form of* LOMAX'S *complaint. His sense of humor is intellectual and subtle, and is complicated by an appalling temper. The lifelong struggle of a benevolent temperament and a high conscience against impulses of inhuman ridicule and fierce impatience has set up a chronic strain which has visibly wrecked his constitution. He is a most implacable, determined, tenacious, intolerant person who by mere force of character presents himself as—and indeed actually is—considerate, gentle, explanatory, even mild and apologetic, capable possibly of murder, but not of cruelty or coarseness. By the operation of some instinct which is not merciful enough to blind him with the illusions of love, he is obstinately bent on marrying* BARBARA. LOMAX *likes* SARAH *and thinks it will be rather a lark to marry her. Consequently he has not attempted to resist* LADY BRITOMART's *arrangements to that end.*

All four look as if they had been having a good deal of fun in the drawing room. The girls enter first, leaving the swains outside. SARAH *comes to the settee.* BARBARA *comes in after her and stops at the door.*

BARBARA. Are Cholly and Dolly to come in?

LADY BRITOMART [*forcibly*]. Barbara: I will not have Charles called Cholly: the vulgarity of it positively makes me ill.

BARBARA. It's all right, mother: Cholly is quite correct nowadays. Are they to come in?

LADY BRITOMART. Yes, if they will behave themselves.

BARBARA [*through the door*]. Come in, Dolly; and behave yourself.

BARBARA *comes to her mother's writing table.* CUSINS *enters smiling, and wanders towards* LADY BRITOMART.

SARAH [*calling*]. Come in, Cholly. [LOMAX *enters, controlling his features very imperfectly, and places himself vaguely between* SARAH *and* BARBARA.]

LADY BRITOMART [*peremptorily*]. Sit down, all of you. [*They sit.* CUSINS *crosses to the window and seats himself there.* LOMAX *takes a chair.* BARBARA *sits at the writing table and* SARAH *on the settee.*] I don't in the least know what you are laughing at, Adolphus. I am surprised at you, though I expected nothing better from Charles Lomax.

CUSINS [*in a remarkably gentle voice*]. Barbara has been trying to teach me the West Ham Salvation March.

LADY BRITOMART. I see nothing to laugh at in that; nor should you if you are really converted.

CUSINS [*sweetly*]. You were not present. It was really funny, I believe.

LOMAX. Ripping.

LADY BRITOMART. Be quiet, Charles. Now listen to me, children. Your father is coming here this evening.

General stupefaction. LOMAX, SARAH, *and* BARBARA *rise:* SARAH *scared, and* BARBARA *amused and expectant.*

LOMAX [*remonstrating*]. Oh I say!

LADY BRITOMART. You are not called on to say anything, Charles.

SARAH. Are you serious, mother?

LADY BRITOMART. Of course I am serious. It is on your account, Sarah, and also on Charles's. [*Silence.* SARAH *sits, with a shrug.* CHARLES *looks painfully unworthy.*] I hope you are not going to object, Barbara.

BARBARA. I! why should I? My father has a soul to be saved like anybody else. He's quite welcome as far as I am concerned. [*She sits on the table, and softly whistles "Onward, Christian Soldiers."*]

LOMAX [*still remonstrant*]. But really, don't you know! Oh I say!

LADY BRITOMART [*frigidly*]. What do you wish to convey, Charles?

LOMAX. Well, you must admit that this is a bit thick.

LADY BRITOMART [*turning with ominous suavity to* CUSINS]. Adolphus: you are a professor of Greek. Can you translate Charles Lomax's remarks into reputable English for us?

CUSINS [*cautiously*]. If I may say so, Lady Brit, I think Charles has rather happily expressed what we all feel. Homer, speaking of Autolycus, uses the same phrase. πυκινὸν δόμον ἐλθεῖν means a bit thick.

LOMAX [*handsomely*]. Not that I mind, you know, if Sarah don't. [*He sits.*]

LADY BRITOMART [*crushingly*]. Thank you. Have I your permission, Adolphus, to invite my own husband to my own house?

CUSINS [*gallantly*]. You have my unhesitating support in everything you do.

LADY BRITOMART. Tush! Sarah: have you nothing to say?

SARAH. Do you mean that he is coming regularly to live here?

LADY BRITOMART. Certainly not. The spare room is ready for him if he likes to stay for a day or two and see a little more of you; but there are limits.

SARAH. Well, he can't eat us, I suppose. I don't mind.

LOMAX [*chuckling*]. I wonder how the old man will take it.

LADY BRITOMART. Much as the old woman will, no doubt, Charles.

LOMAX [*abashed*]. I didn't mean—at least—

LADY BRITOMART. You didn't think, Charles. You never do; and the result is, you never mean anything. And now please attend to me, children. Your father will be quite a stranger to us.

LOMAX. I suppose he hasn't seen Sarah since she was a little kid.

LADY BRITOMART. Not since she was a little kid, Charles, as you express it with that elegance of diction and refinement of thought that seem never to desert you. Accordingly—er— [*impatiently*]. Now I have forgotten what I was going to say. That comes of your provoking me to be sarcastic, Charles. Adolphus: will you kindly tell me where I was.

CUSINS [*sweetly*]. You were saying that as Mr. Undershaft has not seen his children since they were babies, he will form his opinion of the way you have brought them up from their behavior tonight, and that therefore you wish us all to be particularly careful to conduct ourselves well, especially Charles.

LADY BRITOMART [*with emphatic approval*]. Precisely.

LOMAX. Look here, Dolly: Lady Brit didn't say that.

LADY BRITOMART [*vehemently*]. I did, Charles. Adolphus's recollection is perfectly correct. It is most important that you should be good; and I do beg you for once not to pair off into opposite corners and giggle and whisper while I am speaking to your father.

BARBARA. All right, mother. We'll do you credit. [*She comes off the table, and sits in her chair with ladylike elegance.*]

LADY BRITOMART. Remember, Charles, that Sarah will want to feel proud of you instead of ashamed of you.

LOMAX. Oh I say! there's nothing to be exactly proud of, don't you know.

LADY BRITOMART. Well, try and look as if there was.

MORRISON, *pale and dismayed, breaks into the room in unconcealed disorder.*

MORRISON. Might I speak a word to you, my lady?

LADY BRITOMART. Nonsense! Shew him up.

MORRISON. Yes, my lady. [*He goes.*]

LOMAX. Does Morrison know who it is?

LADY BRITOMART. Of course. Morrison has always been with us.

LOMAX. It must be a regular corker for him, don't you know.

LADY BRITOMART. Is this a moment to get on my nerves, Charles, with your outrageous expressions?

LOMAX. But this is something out of the ordinary, really—

MORRISON [*at the door*]. The—er—Mr. Undershaft. [*He retreats in confusion.*]

ANDREW UNDERSHAFT *comes in. All rise.* LADY BRITOMART *meets him in the middle of the room behind the settee.*

ANDREW *is, on the surface, a stoutish, easygoing elderly man, with kindly patient manners, and an engaging simplicity of character. But he has a watchful, deliberate, waiting, listening face, and formidable reserves of power, both bodily and mental, in his capacious chest and long head. His gentleness is partly that of a strong man who has learnt by experience that his natural grip hurts ordinary people unless he handles them very carefully, and partly the mellowness of age and success. He is also a little shy in his present very delicate situation.*

LADY BRITOMART. Good evening, Andrew.

UNDERSHAFT. How d'ye do, my dear.

LADY BRITOMART. You look a good deal older.

UNDERSHAFT [*apologetically*]. I am somewhat older. [*Taking her hand with a touch of courtship.*] Time has stood still with you.

LADY BRITOMART [*throwing away his hand*]. Rubbish! This is your family.

UNDERSHAFT [*surprised*]. Is it so large? I am sorry to say my memory is failing very badly in some things. [*He offers his hand with paternal kindness to* LOMAX.]

LOMAX [*jerkily shaking his hand*]. Ahdedoo.

UNDERSHAFT. I can see you are my eldest. I am very glad to meet you again, my boy.

LOMAX [*remonstrating*]. No, but look here don't you know— [*Overcome.*] Oh I say!

LADY BRITOMART [*recovering from momentary speechlessness*]. Andrew: do you mean to say that you don't remember how many children you have?

UNDERSHAFT. Well, I am afraid I—. They have grown so much—er. Am I making any ridiculous mistake? I may as well confess: I recollect only one son. But so many things have happened since, of course—er—

LADY BRITOMART [*decisively*]. Andrew: you are talking nonsense. Of course you have only one son.

UNDERSHAFT. Perhaps you will be good enough to introduce me, my dear.

LADY BRITOMART. That is Charles Lomax, who is engaged to Sarah.

UNDERSHAFT. My dear sir, I beg your pardon.

LOMAX. Notatall. Delighted, I assure you.

LADY BRITOMART. This is Stephen.

UNDERSHAFT [*bowing*]. Happy to make your acquaintance, Mr. Stephen. Then [*going to* CUSINS] you must be my son. [*Taking* CUSINS' *hands in his.*] How are you, my young friend? [*To* LADY BRITOMART.] He is very like you, my love.

CUSINS. You flatter me, Mr. Undershaft. My name is Cusins: engaged to Barbara. [*Very explicitly.*] That is Major Barbara Undershaft, of the Salvation Army. That is Sarah, your second daughter. This is Stephen Undershaft, your son.

UNDERSHAFT. My dear Stephen, I beg your pardon.

STEPHEN. Not at all.

UNDERSHAFT. Mr. Cusins: I am much indebted to you for explaining so precisely. [*Turning to* SARAH.] Barbara, my dear—

SARAH [*prompting him*]. Sarah.

UNDERSHAFT. Sarah, of course. [*They*

shake hands. He goes over to BARBARA.] Barbara—I am right this time, I hope?

BARBARA. Quite right. [*They shake hands.*]

LADY BRITOMART [*resuming command*]. Sit down, all of you. Sit down, Andrew. [*She comes forward and sits on the settee.* CUSINS *also brings his chair forward on her left.* BARBARA *and* STEPHEN *resume their seats.* LOMAX *gives his chair to* SARAH *and goes for another.*]

UNDERSHAFT. Thank you, my love.

LOMAX [*conversationally, as he brings a chair forward between the writing table and the settee, and offers it to* UNDERSHAFT]. Takes you some time to find out exactly where you are, don't it?

UNDERSHAFT [*accepting the chair, but remaining standing*]. That is not what embarrasses me, Mr. Lomax. My difficulty is that if I play the part of a father, I shall produce the effect of an intrusive stranger; and if I play the part of a discreet stranger, I may appear a callous father.

LADY BRITOMART. There is no need for you to play any part at all, Andrew. You had much better be sincere and natural.

UNDERSHAFT [*submissively*]. Yes, my dear: I daresay that will be best. [*He sits down comfortably.*] Well, here I am. Now what can I do for you all?

LADY BRITOMART. You need not do anything, Andrew. You are one of the family. You can sit with us and enjoy yourself.

A painfully conscious pause. BARBARA *makes a face at* LOMAX, *whose too long suppressed mirth immediately explodes in agonized neighings.*

LADY BRITOMART [*outraged*]. Charles Lomax: if you can behave yourself, behave yourself. If not, leave the room.

LOMAX. I'm awfully sorry, Lady Brit; but really you know, upon my soul! [*He sits on the settee between* LADY BRITOMART *and* UNDERSHAFT, *quite overcome.*]

BARBARA. Why don't you laugh if you want to, Cholly? It's good for your inside.

LADY BRITOMART. Barbara: you have had the education of a lady. Please let your father see that; and don't talk like a street girl.

UNDERSHAFT. Never mind me, my dear. As you know, I am not a gentleman; and I was never educated.

LOMAX [*encouragingly*]. Nobody'd know it, I assure you. You look all right, you know.

CUSINS. Let me advise you to study Greek, Mr. Undershaft. Greek scholars are privileged men. Few of them know Greek; and none of them know anything else; but their position is unchallengeable. Other languages are the qualifications of waiters and commercial travellers: Greek is to a man of position what the hallmark is to silver.

BARBARA. Dolly: don't be insincere. Cholly: fetch your concertina and play something for us.

LOMAX [*jumps up eagerly, but checks himself to remark doubtfully to* UNDERSHAFT]. Perhaps that sort of thing isn't in your line, eh?

UNDERSHAFT. I am particularly fond of music.

LOMAX [*delighted*]. Are you? Then I'll get it. [*He goes upstairs for the instrument.*]

UNDERSHAFT. Do you play, Barbara?

BARBARA. Only the tambourine. But Cholly's teaching me the concertina.

UNDERSHAFT. Is Cholly also a member of the Salvation Army?

BARBARA. No: he says it's bad form to be a dissenter. But I don't despair of Cholly. I made him come yesterday to a meeting at the dock gates, and take the collection in his hat.

UNDERSHAFT [*looks whimsically at his wife*]!!

LADY BRITOMART. It is not my doing, Andrew. Barbara is old enough to take her own way. She has no father to advise her.

BARBARA. Oh yes she has. There are no orphans in the Salvation Army.

UNDERSHAFT. Your father there has a great many children and plenty of experience, eh?

BARBARA [*looking at him with quick interest and nodding*]. Just so. How did you come to understand that? [LOMAX *is heard at the door trying the concertina.*]

LADY BRITOMART. Come in, Charles. Play us something at once.

LOMAX. Righto! [*He sits down in his former place, and preludes.*]

UNDERSHAFT. One moment, Mr. Lomax. I am rather interested in the Salvation Army. Its motto might be my own: Blood and Fire.

LOMAX [*shocked*]. But not your sort of blood and fire, you know.

UNDERSHAFT. My sort of blood cleanses: my sort of fire purifies.

BARBARA. So do ours. Come down tomorrow to my shelter—the West Ham shelter—and see what we're doing. We're going to march to a great meeting in the Assembly Hall at Mile End. Come and see the shelter and then march with us: it will do you a lot of good. Can you play anything?

UNDERSHAFT. In my youth I earned pennies, and even shillings occasionally, in the streets and in public house parlors by my natural talent for stepdancing. Later on, I became a member of the Undershaft orchestral society, and performed passably on the tenor trombone.

LOMAX [*scandalized—putting down the concertina*]. Oh I say!

BARBARA. Many a sinner has played himself into heaven on the trombone, thanks to the Army.

LOMAX [*to* BARBARA, *still rather shocked*]. Yes; but what about the cannon business, don't you know? [*To* UNDERSHAFT.] Getting into heaven is not exactly in your line, is it?

LADY BRITOMART. Charles!!!

LOMAX. Well; but it stands to reason, don't it? The cannon business may be necessary and all that: we can't get on without cannons; but it isn't right, you know. On the other hand, there may be a certain amount of tosh about the Salvation Army—I belong to the Established Church myself—but still you can't deny that it's religion; and you can't go against religion, can you? At least unless you're downright immoral, don't you know.

UNDERSHAFT. You hardly appreciate my position, Mr. Lomax—

LOMAX [*hastily*]. I'm not saying anything against you personally—

UNDERSHAFT. Quite so, quite so. But consider for a moment. Here I am, a profiteer in mutilation and murder. I find myself in a specially amiable humor just now because, this morning, down at the foundry, we blew twenty-seven dummy soldiers into fragments with a gun which formerly destroyed only thirteen.

LOMAX [*leniently*]. Well, the more destructive war becomes, the sooner it will be abolished, eh?

UNDERSHAFT. Not at all. The more destructive war becomes the more fascinating we find it. No, Mr. Lomax: I am obliged to you for making the usual excuse for my trade; but I am not ashamed of it. I am not one of those men who keep their morals and their business in

Major Barbara

water-tight compartments. All the spare money my trade rivals spend on hospitals, cathedrals, and other receptacles for conscience money, I devote to experiments and researches in improved methods of destroying life and property. I have always done so; and I always shall. Therefore your Christmas card moralities of peace on earth and goodwill among men are of no use to me. Your Christianity, which enjoins you to resist not evil, and to turn the other cheek, would make me a bankrupt. My morality—my religion—must have a place for cannons and torpedoes in it.

STEPHEN [*coldly—almost sullenly*]. You speak as if there were half a dozen moralities and religions to choose from, instead of one true morality and one true religion.

UNDERSHAFT. For me there is only one true morality; but it might not fit you, as you do not manufacture aerial battleships. There is only one true morality for every man; but every man has not the same true morality.

LOMAX [*overtaxed*]. Would you mind saying that again? I didn't quite follow it.

CUSINS. It's quite simple. As Euripides says, one man's meat is another man's poison morally as well as physically.

UNDERSHAFT. Precisely.

LOMAX. Oh, that! Yes, yes, yes. True. True.

STEPHEN. In other words, some men are honest and some are scoundrels.

BARBARA. Bosh! There are no scoundrels.

UNDERSHAFT. Indeed? Are there any good men?

BARBARA. No. Not one. There are neither good men nor scoundrels: there are just children of one Father; and the sooner they stop calling one another names the better. You needn't talk to me: I know them. I've had scores of them through my hands: scoundrels, criminals, infidels, philanthropists, missionaries, county councillors, all sorts. They're all just the same sort of sinner; and there's the same salvation ready for them all.

UNDERSHAFT. May I ask have you ever saved a maker of cannons?

BARBARA. No. Will you let me try?

UNDERSHAFT. Well, I will make a bargain with you. If I go to see you tomorrow in your Salvation Shelter, will you come the day after to see me in my cannon works?

BARBARA. Take care. It may end in your giving up the cannons for the sake of the Salvation Army.

UNDERSHAFT. Are you sure it will not end in your giving up the Salvation Army for the sake of the cannons?

BARBARA. I will take my chance of that.

UNDERSHAFT. And I will take my chance of the other. [*They shake hands on it.*] Where is your shelter?

BARBARA. In West Ham. At the sign of the cross. Ask anybody in Canning Town. Where are your works?

UNDERSHAFT. In Perivale St. Andrews. At the sign of the sword. Ask anybody in Europe.

LOMAX. Hadn't I better play something?

BARBARA. Yes. Give us "Onward, Christian Soldiers."

LOMAX. Well, that's rather a strong order to begin with, don't you know. Suppose I sing Thou'rt passing hence, my brother. It's much the same tune.

BARBARA. It's too melancholy. You get saved, Cholly; and you'll pass hence, my brother, without making such a fuss about it.

LADY BRITOMART. Really, Barbara, you go on as if religion were a pleasant subject. Do have some sense of propriety.

UNDERSHAFT. I do not find it an unpleasant subject, my dear. It is the only one that capable people really care for.

LADY BRITOMART [*looking at her watch*]. Well, if you are determined to have it, I insist on having it in a proper and respectable way. Charles: ring for prayers.

General amazement. STEPHEN *rises in dismay.*

LOMAX [*rising*]. Oh I say!

UNDERSHAFT [*rising*]. I am afraid I must be going.

LADY BRITOMART. You cannot go now, Andrew: it would be most improper. Sit down. What will the servants think?

UNDERSHAFT. My dear: I have conscientious scruples. May I suggest a compromise? If Barbara will conduct a little service in the drawing room, with Mr. Lomax as organist, I will attend it willingly. I will even take part, if a trombone can be procured.

LADY BRITOMART. Don't mock, Andrew.

UNDERSHAFT [*shocked—to* BARBARA]. You don't think I am mocking, my love, I hope.

BARBARA. No, of course not; and it wouldn't matter if you were: half the Army came to their first meeting for a lark. [*Rising.*] Come along. [*She throws her arm round her father and sweeps him out, calling to the others from the threshold.*] Come, Dolly. Come, Cholly.

CUSINS *rises.*

LADY BRITOMART. I will not be disobeyed by everybody. Adolphus: sit down. [*He does not.*] Charles: you may go. You are not fit for prayers: you cannot keep your countenance.

LOMAX. Oh I say! [*He goes out.*]

LADY BRITOMART [*continuing*]. But you, Adolphus, can behave yourself if you choose to. I insist on your staying.

CUSINS. My dear Lady Brit: there are things in the family prayer book that I couldn't bear to hear you say.

LADY BRITOMART. What things, pray?

CUSINS. Well, you would have to say before all the servants that we have done things we ought not to have done, and left undone things we ought to have done, and that there is no health in us. I cannot bear to hear you doing yourself such an injustice, and Barbara such an injustice. As for myself, I flatly deny it: I have done my best. I shouldn't dare to marry Barbara—I couldn't look you in the face —if it were true. So I must go to the drawing room.

LADY BRITOMART [*offended*]. Well, go. [*He starts for the door.*] And remember this, Adolphus [*he turns to listen*]: I have a very strong suspicion that you went to the Salvation Army to worship Barbara and nothing else. And I quite appreciate the very clever way in which you systematically humbug me. I have found you out. Take care Barbara doesn't. That's all.

CUSINS [*with unruffled sweetness*]. Don't tell on me. [*He steals out.*]

LADY BRITOMART. Sarah: if you want to go, go. Anything's better than to sit there as if you wished you were a thousand miles away.

SARAH [*languidly*]. Very well, mamma. [*She goes.*]

LADY BRITOMART, *with a sudden flounce, gives way to a little gust of tears.*

STEPHEN [*going to her*]. Mother: what's the matter?

LADY BRITOMART [*swishing away her tears with her handkerchief*]. Nothing. Foolishness. You can go with him, too, if you like, and leave me with the servants.

STEPHEN. Oh, you mustn't think that, mother. I—I don't like him.

LADY BRITOMART. The others do. That is the injustice of a woman's lot. A woman has to bring up her children; and that means to restrain them, to deny them things they want, to set them tasks, to punish them when they do wrong, to do all the unpleasant things. And then the father, who has nothing to do but pet them and spoil them, comes in when all her work is done and steals their affection from her.

STEPHEN. He has not stolen our affection from you. It is only curiosity.

LADY BRITOMART [*violently*]. I won't be consoled, Stephen. There is nothing the matter with me. [*She rises and goes towards the door.*]

STEPHEN. Where are you going, mother?

LADY BRITOMART. To the drawing room, of course. [*She goes out. "Onward, Christian Soldiers," on the concertina, with tambourine accompaniment, is heard when the door opens.*] Are you coming, Stephen?

STEPHEN. No. Certainly not. [*She goes. He sits down on the settee, with compressed lips and an expression of strong dislike.*]

ACT II

[*The yard of the West Ham shelter of the Salvation Army is a cold place on a January morning. The building itself, an old warehouse, is newly whitewashed. Its gabled end projects into the yard in the middle, with a door on the ground floor, and another in the loft above it without any balcony or ladder, but with a pulley rigged over it for hoisting sacks. Those who come from this central gable end into the yard have the gateway leading to the street on their left, with a stone horse-trough just beyond it, and, on the right, a penthouse shielding a table from the weather. There are forms at the table; and on them are seated a man and a woman, both much down on their luck, finishing a meal of bread (one thick slice each, with margarine and golden syrup) and diluted milk.*

THE MAN, a workman out of employment, is young, agile, a talker, a poser, sharp enough to be capable of anything in reason except honesty or altruistic considerations of any kind. THE WOMAN is a commonplace old bundle of poverty and hard-worn humanity. She looks sixty and probably is forty-five. If they were rich people, gloved and muffed and well wrapped up in furs and overcoats, they would be numbed and miserable; for it is a grindingly cold raw January day; and a glance at the background of grimy warehouses and leaden sky visible over the whitewashed walls of the yard would drive any idle rich person straight to the Mediterranean. But these two, being no more troubled with visions of the Mediterranean than of the moon, and being compelled to keep more of their clothes in the pawnshop, and less on their persons, in winter than in summer, are not depressed by the cold: rather are they stung into vivacity, to which their meal has just now given an almost jolly turn. THE MAN *takes a pull at his mug, and then gets up and moves about the yard with his hands deep in his pockets, occasionally breaking into a stepdance.*]

THE WOMAN. Feel better arter your meal, sir?

THE MAN. No. Call that a meal! Good enough for you, praps; but wot is it to me, an intelligent workin man.

THE WOMAN. Workin man! Wot are you?

THE MAN. Painter.

THE WOMAN [*sceptically*]. Yus, I dessay.

THE MAN. Yus, you dessay! I know. Every loafer that can't do nothink calls isself a painter. Well, I'm a real painter: grainer, finisher, thirty-eight bob a week when I can get it.

THE WOMAN. Then why don't you go and get it?

THE MAN. I'll tell you why. Fust: I'm intelligent—fffff! it's rotten cold here [*he dances a step or two*]—yes: intelligent beyond the station o life into which it has pleased the capitalists to call me; and they don't like a man that sees through em. Second, an intelligent bein needs a doo share of appiness; so I drink somethink cruel when I get the chawnce. Third, I stand by my class and do as little as I can so's to leave arf the job for me fellow workers. Fourth, I'm fly enough to know wot's inside the law and wot's outside it; and inside it I do as the capitalists do: pinch wot I can lay me ands on. In a proper state of society I am sober, industrious and honest: in Rome, so to speak, I do as the Romans do. Wot's the consequence? When trade is bad—and it's rotten bad just now—and the employers az to sack arf their men, they generally start on me.

THE WOMAN. What's your name?

THE MAN. Price. Bronterre O'Brien Price. Usually called Snobby Price, for short.

THE WOMAN. Snobby's a carpenter, ain't it? You said you was a painter.

PRICE. Not that kind of snob, but the genteel sort. I'm too uppish, owing to my intelligence, and my father being a Chartist and a reading, thinking man: a stationer, too. I'm none of your common hewers of wood and drawers of water; and don't you forget it. [*He returns to his seat at the table, and takes up his mug.*] Wot's your name?

THE WOMAN. Rummy Mitchens, sir.

PRICE [*quaffing the remains of his milk to her*]. Your elth, Miss Mitchens.

RUMMY [*correcting him*]. Missis Mitchens.

PRICE. Wot! Oh Rummy, Rummy! Respectable married woman, Rummy, gittin rescued by the Salvation Army by pretendin to be a bad un. Same old game!

RUMMY. What am I to do? I can't starve. Them Salvation lasses is dear good girls; but the better you are, the worse they likes to think you were before they rescued you. Why shouldn't they av a bit o credit, poor loves? they're worn to rags by their work. And where would they get the money to rescue us if we was to let on we're no worse than other people? You know what ladies and gentlemen are.

PRICE. Thievin swine! Wish I ad their job, Rummy, all the same. Wot does Rummy stand for? Pet name praps?

RUMMY. Short for Romola.

PRICE. For wot!?

RUMMY. Romola. It was out of a new book. Somebody me mother wanted me to grow up like.

PRICE. We're companions in misfortune,

[418]

Rummy. Both on us got names that nobody cawnt pronounce. Consequently I'm Snobby and you're Rummy because Bill and Sally wasn't good enough for our parents. Such is life!

RUMMY. Who saved you, Mr. Price? Was it Major Barbara?

PRICE. No: I come here on my own. I'm going to be Bronterre O'Brien Price, the converted painter. I know wot they like. I'll tell em how I blasphemed and gambled and wopped my poor old mother—

RUMMY [shocked]. Used you to beat your mother?

PRICE. Not likely. She used to beat me. No matter: you come and listen to the converted painter, and you'll hear how she was a pious woman that taught me me prayers at er knee, an how I used to come home drunk and drag her out o bed be er snow white airs, an lam into er with the poker.

RUMMY. That's what's so unfair to us women. Your confessions is just as big lies as ours: you don't tell what you really done no more than us; but you men can tell your lies right out at the meetins and be made much of for it; while the sort o confessions we az to make az to be wispered to one lady at a time. It ain't right, spite of all their piety.

PRICE. Right! Do you spose the Army'd be allowed if it went and did right? Not much. It combs our air and makes us good little blokes to be robbed and put upon. But I'll play the game as good as any of em. I'll see somebody struck by lightnin, or hear a voice sayin "Snobby Price: where will you spend eternity?" I'll av a time of it, I tell you.

RUMMY. You won't be let drink, though.

PRICE. I'll take it out in gorspellin, then. I don't want to drink if I can get fun enough any other way.

JENNY HILL, *a pale, overwrought, pretty Salvation lass of 18, comes in through the yard gate, leading* PETER SHIRLEY, *a half hardened, half worn-out elderly man, weak with hunger.*

JENNY [supporting him]. Come! pluck up. I'll get you something to eat. You'll be all right then.

PRICE [rising and hurrying officiously to take the old man off JENNY's hands]. Poor old man! Cheer up, brother: you'll find rest and peace and appiness ere. Hurry up with the food, miss: e's fair done. [JENNY hurries into the shelter.] Ere, buck up, daddy! she's fetchin y'a thick slice o breadn treacle, an a mug o skyblue. [He seats him at the corner of the table.]

RUMMY [gaily]. Keep up your old art! Never say die!

SHIRLEY. I'm not an old man. I'm ony 46. I'm as good as ever I was. The grey patch come in my hair before I was thirty. All it wants is three pennorth o hair dye: am I to be turned on the streets to starve for it? Holy God! I've worked ten to twelve hours a day since I was thirteen, and paid my way all through; and now am I to be thrown into the gutter and my job given to a young man that can do it no better than me because I've black hair that goes white at the first change?

PRICE [cheerfully]. No good jawrin about it. You're ony a jumped-up, jerked-off, orspittle-turned-out incurable of an ole workin man: who cares about you? Eh? Make the thievin swine give you a meal: they've stole many a one from you. Get a bit o your own back. [JENNY returns with the usual meal.] There you are, brother. Awsk a blessin an tuck that into you.

[419]

SHIRLEY [*looking at it ravenously but not touching it, and crying like a child*]. I never took anything before.

JENNY [*petting him*]. Come, come! the Lord sends it to you: he wasn't above taking bread from his friends; and why should you be? Besides, when we find you a job you can pay us for it if you like.

SHIRLEY [*eagerly*]. Yes, yes: that's true. I can pay you back: it's only a loan. [*Shivering.*] Oh Lord! oh Lord! [*He turns to the table and attacks the meal ravenously.*]

JENNY. Well, Rummy, are you more comfortable now?

RUMMY. God bless you, lovey! you've fed my body and saved my soul, havn't you? [JENNY, *touched, kisses her.*] Sit down and rest a bit: you must be ready to drop.

JENNY. I've been going hard since morning. But there's more work than we can do. I mustn't stop.

RUMMY. Try a prayer for just two minutes. You'll work all the better after.

JENNY [*her eyes lighting up*]. Oh isn't it wonderful how a few minutes' prayer revives you! I was quite lightheaded at twelve o'clock, I was so tired; but Major Barbara just sent me to pray for five minutes; and I was able to go on as if I had only just begun. [*To* PRICE.] Did you have a piece of bread?

PRICE [*with unction*]. Yes, miss; but I've got the piece that I value more; and that's the peace that passeth hall hannerstennin.

RUMMY [*fervently*]. Glory Hallelujah!

BILL WALKER, *a rough customer of about 25, appears at the yard gate and looks malevolently at* JENNY.

JENNY. That makes me so happy. When you say that, I feel wicked for loitering here. I must get to work again.

She is hurrying to the shelter, when the new-comer moves quickly up to the door and intercepts her. His manner is so threatening that she retreats as he comes at her truculently, driving her down the yard.

BILL. Aw knaow you. You're the one that took awy maw girl. You're the one that set er agen me. Well, Aw'm gowin to ev er aht. Not that Aw care a carse for er or you: see? Bat Aw'll let er knaow; and Aw'll let you knaow. Aw'm gowing to give her a doin that'll teach er to cat awy from me. Nah in wiv you and tell er to cam aht afore Aw cam in and kick er aht. Tell er Bill Walker wants er. She'll knaow wot thet means; and if she keeps me witin it'll be worse. You stop to jawr beck at me; and Aw'll stawt on you: d'ye eah? There's your wy. In you gow. [*He takes her by the arm and slings her towards the door of the shelter. She falls on her hand and knee.* RUMMY *helps her up again.*]

PRICE [*rising, and venturing irresolutely towards* BILL]. Easy there, mate. She ain't doin you no arm.

BILL. Oo are you callin mite? [*Standing over him threateningly.*] You're gowin to stend ap for er, aw yer? Put ap your ends.

RUMMY [*running indignantly to him to scold him*]. Oh, you great brute— [*He instantly swings his left hand back against her face. She screams and reels back to the trough, where she sits down, covering her bruised face with her hands and rocking herself and moaning with pain.*]

JENNY [*going to her*]. Oh, God forgive you! How could you strike an old woman like that?

BILL [*seizing her by the hair so vio-*

lently that she also screams, and tearing her away from the old woman]. You Gawd forgimme again an Aw'll Gawd forgive you one on the jawr thet'll stop you pryin for a week. [*Holding her and turning fiercely on* PRICE.] Ev you ennything to sy agen it?

PRICE [*intimidated*]. No, matey: she ain't anything to do with me.

BILL. Good job for you! Aw'd pat two meals into you and fawt you with one finger arter, you stawved cur. [*To* JENNY.] Nah are you gowin to fetch aht Mog Ebijem; or em Aw to knock your fice off you and fetch her meself?

JENNY [*writhing in his grasp*]. Oh please someone go in and tell Major Barbara— [*She screams again as he wrenches her head down; and* PRICE *and* RUMMY *flee into the shelter.*]

BILL. You want to gow in and tell your Mijor of me, do you?

JENNY. Oh please don't drag my hair. Let me go.

BILL. Do you or down't you? [*She stifles a scream.*] Yus or nao?

JENNY. God give me strength—

BILL [*striking her with his fist in the face*]. Gow an shaow her thet, and tell her if she wants one lawk it to cam and interfere with me. [JENNY, *crying with pain, goes into the shed. He goes to the form and addresses the old man.*] Eah: finish your mess; an git aht o maw wy.

SHIRLEY [*springing up and facing him fiercely, with the mug in his hand*]. You take a liberty with me, and I'll smash you over the face with the mug and cut your eye out. Ain't you satisfied—young whelps like you—with takin the bread out o the mouths of your elders that have brought you up and slaved for you, but you must come shovin and cheekin and bullyin in here, where the bread o charity is sickenin in our stummicks?

BILL [*contemptuously, but backing a little*]. Wot good are you, you aold palsy mag? Wot good are you?

SHIRLEY. As good as you and better. I'll do a day's work agen you or any fat young soaker of your age. Go and take my job at Horrockses, where I worked for ten year. They want young men there: they can't afford to keep men over forty-five. They're very sorry—give you a character and happy to help you to get anything suited to your years—sure a steady man won't be long out of a job. Well, let em try you. They'll find the differ. What do you know? Not as much as how to beeyave yourself—layin your dirty fist across the mouth of a respectable woman!

BILL. Downt provowk me to ly it acrost yours: d'ye eah?

SHIRLEY [*with blighting contempt*]. Yes: you like an old man to hit, don't you, when you've finished with the women. I ain't seen you hit a young one yet.

BILL [*stung*]. You loy, you aold soup-kitchener, you. There was a yang menn eah. Did Aw offer to itt him or did Aw not?

SHIRLEY. Was he starvin or was he not? Was he a man or only a crosseyed thief an a loafer? Would you hit my son-in-law's brother?

BILL. Oo's ee?

SHIRLEY. Todger Fairmile o Balls Pond. Him that won £20 off the Japanese wrastler at the music hall by standin out 17 minutes 4 seconds agen him.

BILL [*sullenly*]. Aw'm nao music awl wrastler. Ken he box?

SHIRLEY. Yes: an you can't.

[421]

BILL. Wot! Aw cawn't, cawn't Aw? Wot's thet you sy [*threatening him*]?

SHIRLEY [*not budging an inch*]. Will you box Todger Fairmile if I put him on to you? Say the word.

BILL [*subsiding with a slouch*]. Aw'll stend ap to enny menn alawy, if he was ten Todger Fairmawls. But Aw don't set ap to be a perfeshnal.

SHIRLEY [*looking down on him with unfathomable disdain*]. You box! Slap an old woman with the back o your hand! You hadn't even the sense to hit her where a magistrate couldn't see the mark of it, you silly young lump of conceit and ignorance. Hit a girl in the jaw and ony make her cry! If Todger Fairmile'd done it, she wouldn't a got up inside o ten minutes, no more than you would if he got on to you. Yah! I'd set about you myself if I had a week's feedin in me instead o two months' starvation. [*He turns his back on him and sits down moodily at the table.*]

BILL [*following him and stooping over him to drive the taunt in*]. You loy! you've the bread and treacle in you that you cam eah to beg.

SHIRLEY [*bursting into tears*]. Oh God! it's true: I'm only an old pauper on the scrap heap. [*Furiously.*] But you'll come to it yourself; and then you'll know. You'll come to it sooner than a teetotaller like me, fillin yourself with gin at this hour o the mornin!

BILL. Aw'm nao gin drinker, you oald lawr; bat wen Aw want to give my girl a bloomin good awdin Aw lawk to ev a bit o devil in me: see? An eah Aw emm, talkin to a rotten aold blawter like you sted o givin her wot for. [*Working himself into a rage.*] Aw'm gowin in there to fetch her aht. [*He makes vengefully for the shelter door.*]

SHIRLEY. You're goin to the station on a stretcher, more likely; and they'll take the gin and the devil out of you there when they get you inside. You mind what you're about: the major here is the Earl o Stevenage's granddaughter.

BILL [*checked*]. Garn!

SHIRLEY. You'll see.

BILL [*his resolution oozing*]. Well, Aw ain't dan nathin to er.

SHIRLEY. Spose she said you did! who'd believe you?

BILL [*very uneasy, skulking back to the corner of the penthouse*]. Gawd! there's no jastice in this cantry. To think wot them people can do! Aw'm as good as er.

SHIRLEY. Tell her so. It's just what a fool like you would do.

BARBARA, *brisk and businesslike, comes from the shelter with a note book, and addresses herself to* SHIRLEY. BILL, *cowed, sits down in the corner on a form, and turns his back on them.*

BARBARA. Good morning.

SHIRLEY [*standing up and taking off his hat*]. Good morning, miss.

BARBARA. Sit down: make yourself at home. [*He hesitates; but she puts a friendly hand on his shoulder and makes him obey.*] Now then! since you've made friends with us, we want to know all about you. Names and addresses and trades.

SHIRLEY. Peter Shirley. Fitter. Chucked out two months ago because I was too old.

BARBARA [*not at all surprised*]. You'd pass still. Why didn't you dye your hair?

SHIRLEY. I did. Me age come out at a coroner's inquest on me daughter.

BARBARA. Steady?

SHIRLEY. Teetotaller. Never out of a job

[422]

before. Good worker. And sent to the knackers like an old horse!

BARBARA. No matter: if you did your part God will do his.

SHIRLEY [*suddenly stubborn*]. My religion's no concern of anybody but myself.

BARBARA [*guessing*]. I know. Secularist?

SHIRLEY [*hotly*]. Did I offer to deny it?

BARBARA. Why should you? My own father's a Secularist, I think. Our Father—yours and mine—fulfils himself in many ways; and I daresay he knew what he was about when he made a Secularist of you. So buck up, Peter! we can always find a job for a steady man like you. [SHIRLEY, *disarmed and a little bewildered, touches his hat. She turns from him to* BILL.] What's your name?

BILL [*insolently*]. Wot's thet to you?

BARBARA [*calmly making a note*]. Afraid to give his name. Any trade?

BILL. Oo's afride to give is nime? [*Doggedly, with a sense of heroically defying the House of Lords in the person of Lord Stevenage.*] If you want to bring a chawge agen me, bring it. [*She waits, unruffled.*] Moy nime's Bill Walker.

BARBARA [*as if the name were familiar: trying to remember how*]. Bill Walker? [*Recollecting.*] Oh, I know: you're the man that Jenny Hill was praying for inside just now. [*She enters his name in her note book.*]

BILL. Oo's Jenny Ill? And wot call as she to pry for me?

BARBARA. I don't know. Perhaps it was you that cut her lip.

BILL [*defiantly*]. Yus, it was me that cat her lip. Aw ain't afride o you.

BARBARA. How could you be, since you're not afraid of God? You're a brave man, Mr. Walker. It takes some pluck to do our work here; but none of us dare lift our hand against a girl like that, for fear of her father in heaven.

BILL [*sullenly*]. I want nan o your kentin jawr. I spowse you think Aw cam eah to beg from you, like this demmiged lot eah. Not me. Aw down't want your bread and scripe and ketlep. Aw don't blieve in your Gawd, no more than you do yourself.

BARBARA [*sunnily apologetic and ladylike, as on a new footing with him*]. Oh, I beg your pardon for putting your name down, Mr. Walker. I didn't understand. I'll strike it out.

BILL [*taking this as a slight, and deeply wounded by it*]. Eah! you let maw nime alown. Ain't it good enaff to be in your book?

BARBARA [*considering*]. Well, you see, there's no use putting down your name unless I can do something for you, is there? What's your trade?

BILL [*still smarting*]. Thets nao concern o yours.

BARBARA. Just so. [*Very businesslike.*] I'll put you down as [*writing*] the man who—struck—poor little Jenny Hill—in the mouth.

BILL [*rising threateningly*]. See eah. Awve ed enaff o this.

BARBARA [*quite sunny and fearless*]. What did you come to us for?

BILL. Aw cam for maw gel, see? Aw cam to tike her aht o this and to brike er jawr for er.

BARBARA [*complacently*]. You see I was right about your trade. [BILL, *on the point of retorting furiously, finds himself, to his great shame and terror, in danger of crying instead. He sits down again suddenly.*] What's her name?

BILL [*dogged*]. Er nime's Mog Ebbijem: thets whot her nime is.

BARBARA. Mog Habbijam! Oh, she's

[423]

gone to Canning Town, to our barracks there.

BILL [*fortified by his resentment of* MOG's *perfidy*]. Is she? [*Vindictively.*] Then Aw'm gowin to Kennintahn arter er. [*He crosses to the gate; hesitates; finally comes back at* BARBARA.] Are you loyin to me to git shat o me?

BARBARA. I don't want to get shut of you. I want to keep you here and save your soul. You'd better stay: you're going to have a bad time today, Bill.

BILL. Oo's gowin to give it to me? You, preps?

BARBARA. Someone you don't believe in. But you'll be glad afterwards.

BILL [*slinking off*]. Aw'll gow to Kennintahn to be aht o reach o your tangue. [*Suddenly turning on her with intense malice.*] And if Aw down't fawnd Mog there, Aw'll cam beck and do two years for you, selp me Gawd if Aw down't!

BARBARA [*a shade kindlier, if possible*]. It's no use, Bill. She's got another bloke.

BILL. Wot!

BARBARA. One of her own converts. He fell in love with her when he saw her with her soul saved, and her face clean, and her hair washed.

BILL [*surprised*]. Wottud she wash it for, the carroty slat? It's red.

BARBARA. It's quite lovely now, because she wears a new look in her eyes with it. It's a pity you're too late. The new bloke has put your nose out of joint, Bill.

BILL. Aw'll put his nowse aht o joint for him. Not that Aw care a carse for er, mawnd thet. But Aw'll teach er to drop me as if Aw was dirt. And Aw'll teach him to meddle with maw judy. Wots iz bleedin nime?

BARBARA. Sergeant Todger Fairmile.

SHIRLEY [*rising with grim joy*]. I'll go with him, miss. I want to see them two meet. I'll take him to the infirmary when it's over.

BILL [*to* SHIRLEY, *with undissembled misgiving*]. Is thet im you was speakin on?

SHIRLEY. That's him.

BILL. Im that wrastled in the music awl?

SHIRLEY. The competitions at the National Sportin Club was worth nigh a hundred a year to him. He's gev em up now for religion; so he's a bit fresh for want of the exercise he was accustomed to. He'll be glad to see you. Come along.

BILL. Wots is wight?

SHIRLEY. Thirteen four. [BILL's *last hope expires.*]

BARBARA. Go and talk to him, Bill. He'll convert you.

SHIRLEY. He'll convert your head into a mashed potato.

BILL [*sullenly*]. Aw ain't afride of im. Aw ain't afride of ennybody. Bat e can lick me. She's dan me. [*He sits down moodily on the edge of the horse trough.*]

SHIRLEY. You ain't goin. I thought not. [*He resumes his seat.*]

BARBARA [*calling*]. Jenny!

JENNY [*appearing at the shelter door with a plaster on the corner of her mouth*]. Yes, Major.

BARBARA. Send Rummy Mitchens out to clear away here.

JENNY. I think she's afraid.

BARBARA [*her resemblance to her mother flashing out for a moment*]. Nonsense! she must do as she's told.

JENNY [*calling into the shelter*]. Rummy: the Major says you must come.

JENNY *comes to* BARBARA, *purposely keeping on the side next* BILL, *lest he should suppose that she shrank from him or bore malice.*

BARBARA. Poor little Jenny! Are you

[424]

tired? [*Looking at the wounded cheek.*] Does it hurt?

JENNY. No: it's all right now. It was nothing.

BARBARA [*critically*]. It was as hard as he could hit, I expect. Poor Bill! You don't feel angry with him, do you?

JENNY. Oh no, no, no: indeed I don't, Major, bless his poor heart! [BARBARA *kisses her; and she runs away merrily into the shelter.* BILL *writhes with an agonizing return of his new and alarming symptoms, but says nothing.* RUMMY MITCHENS *comes from the shelter.*]

BARBARA [*going to meet* RUMMY]. Now, Rummy, bustle. Take in those mugs and plates to be washed; and throw the crumbs about for the birds.

RUMMY *takes the three plates and mugs; but* SHIRLEY *takes back his mug from her, as there is still some milk left in it.*

RUMMY. There ain't any crumbs. This ain't a time to waste good bread on birds.

PRICE [*appearing at the shelter door*]. Gentleman come to see the shelter, Major. Says he's your father.

BARBARA. All right. Coming. [SNOBBY *goes back into the shelter, followed by* BARBARA.]

RUMMY [*stealing across to* BILL *and addressing him in a subdued voice, but with intense conviction*]. I'd av the lor of you, you flat eared pignosed potwalloper, if she'd let me. You're no gentleman, to hit a lady in the face. [BILL, *with greater things moving in him, takes no notice.*]

SHIRLEY [*following her*]. Here! in with you and don't get yourself into more trouble by talking.

RUMMY [*with hauteur*]. I ain't ad the pleasure o being hintroduced to you, as I can remember. [*She goes into the shelter with the plates.*]

SHIRLEY. That's the—

BILL [*savagely*]. Down't you talk to me, d'ye eah? You lea me alown, or Aw'll do you a mischief. Aw'm not dirt under your feet, ennywy.

SHIRLEY [*calmly*]. Don't you be afeerd. You ain't such prime company that you need expect to be sought after. [*He is about to go into the shelter when* BARBARA *comes out, with* UNDERSHAFT *on her right.*]

BARBARA. Oh, there you are, Mr. Shirley! [*Between them.*] This is my father: I told you he was a Secularist, didn't I? Perhaps you'll be able to comfort one another.

UNDERSHAFT [*startled*]. A Secularist! Not the least in the world: on the contrary, a confirmed mystic.

BARBARA. Sorry, I'm sure. By the way, papa, what is your religion? in case I have to introduce you again.

UNDERSHAFT. My religion? Well, my dear, I am a Millionaire. That is my religion.

BARBARA. Then I'm afraid you and Mr. Shirley won't be able to comfort one another after all. You're not a Millionaire, are you, Peter?

SHIRLEY. No; and proud of it.

UNDERSHAFT [*gravely*]. Poverty, my friend, is not a thing to be proud of.

SHIRLEY [*angrily*]. Who made your millions for you? Me and my like. What's kep us poor? Keepin you rich. I wouldn't have your conscience, not for all your income.

UNDERSHAFT. I wouldn't have your income, not for all your conscience, Mr. Shirley. [*He goes to the penthouse and sits down on a form.*]

BARBARA [*stopping* SHIRLEY *adroitly as he is about to retort*]. You wouldn't think he was my father, would you, Peter? Will you go into the shelter and lend the lasses a hand for a while: we're worked off our feet.

SHIRLEY [*bitterly*]. Yes: I'm in their debt for a meal, ain't I?

BARBARA. Oh, not because you're in their debt, but for love of them, Peter, for love of them. [*He cannot understand, and is rather scandalized.*] There! don't stare at me. In with you; and give that conscience of yours a holiday [*bustling him into the shelter*].

SHIRLEY [*as he goes in*]. Ah! it's a pity you never was trained to use your reason, miss. You'd have been a very taking lecturer on Secularism.

BARBARA *turns to her father.*

UNDERSHAFT. Never mind me, my dear. Go about your work; and let me watch it for a while.

BARBARA. All right.

UNDERSHAFT. For instance, what's the matter with that outpatient over there?

BARBARA [*looking at* BILL, *whose attitude has never changed, and whose expression of brooding wrath has deepened*]. Oh, we shall cure him in no time. Just watch. [*She goes over to* BILL *and waits. He glances up at her and casts his eyes down again, uneasy, but grimmer than ever.*] It would be nice to just stamp on Mog Habbijam's face, wouldn't it, Bill?

BILL [*starting up from the trough in consternation*]. It's a loy: Aw never said so. [*She shakes her head.*] Oo taold you wot was in moy mawnd?

BARBARA. Only your new friend.

BILL. Wot new friend?

BARBARA. The devil, Bill. When he gets round people they get miserable, just like you.

BILL [*with a heartbreaking attempt at devil-may-care cheerfulness*]. Aw ain't miserable. [*He sits down again, and stretches his legs in an attempt to seem indifferent.*]

BARBARA. Well, if you're happy, why don't you look happy, as we do?

BILL [*his legs curling back in spite of him*]. Aw'm eppy enaff, Aw tell you. Woy cawn't you lea me alown? Wot ev I dan to you? Aw ain't smashed your fice, ev Aw?

BARBARA [*softly: wooing his soul*]. It's not me that's getting at you, Bill.

BILL. Oo else is it?

BARBARA. Somebody that doesn't intend you to smash women's faces, I suppose. Somebody or something that wants to make a man of you.

BILL [*blustering*]. Mike a menn o me! Ain't Aw a menn? eh? Oo sez Aw'm not a menn?

BARBARA. There's a man in you somewhere, I suppose. But why did he let you hit poor little Jenny Hill? That wasn't very manly of him, was it?

BILL [*tormented*]. Ev dan wiv it, Aw tell you. Chack it. Aw'm sick o your Jenny Ill and er silly little fice.

BARBARA. Then why do you keep thinking about it? Why does it keep coming up against you in your mind? You're not getting converted, are you?

BILL [*with conviction*]. Not ME. Not lawkly.

BARBARA. That's right, Bill. Hold out against it. Put out your strength. Don't let's get you cheap. Todger Fairmile said he wrestled for three nights against his salvation harder than he ever wrestled with the Jap at the music hall. He gave in to the Jap when his arm was going to break. But he didn't give in to his salvation until his heart was going to break. Perhaps you'll escape that. You haven't any heart, have you?

Major Barbara

BILL. Wot d'ye mean? Woy ain't Aw got a awt the sime as ennybody else?

BARBARA. A man with a heart wouldn't have bashed poor little Jenny's face, would he?

BILL [*almost crying*]. Ow, will you lea me alown? Ev Aw ever offered to meddle with you, that you cam neggin and provowkin me lawk this? [*He writhes convulsively from his eyes to his toes.*]

BARBARA [*with a steady soothing hand on his arm and a gentle voice that never lets him go*]. It's your soul that's hurting you, Bill, and not me. We've been through it all ourselves. Come with us, Bill. [*He looks wildly round.*] To brave manhood on earth and eternal glory in heaven. [*He is on the point of breaking down.*] Come. [*A drum is heard in the shelter; and* BILL, *with a gasp, escapes from the spell as* BARBARA *turns quickly.* ADOLPHUS *enters from the shelter with a big drum.*] Oh! there you are, Dolly. Let me introduce a new friend of mine, Mr. Bill Walker. This is my bloke, Bill: Mr. Cusins. [CUSINS *salutes with his drumstick.*]

BILL. Gowin to merry im?

BARBARA. Yes.

BILL [*fervently*]. Gawd elp im! Gawaw-aw-awd elp im!

BARBARA. Why? Do you think he won't be happy with me?

BILL. Awve aony ed to stend it for a mawnin: e'll ev to stend it for a lawf-tawm.

CUSINS. That is a frightful reflection, Mr. Walker. But I can't tear myself away from her.

BILL. Well, Aw ken. [*To* BARBARA.] Eah! do you knaow where Aw'm gowin to, and wot Aw'm gowin to do?

BARBARA. Yes: you're going to heaven; and you're coming back here before the week's out to tell me so.

BILL. You loy. Aw'm gowin to Kennintahn, to spit in Todger Fairmawl's eye. Aw beshed Jenny Ill's fice; an nar Aw'll git me aown fice beshed and cam beck and shaow it to er. Ee'll itt me ardern Aw itt er. That'll mike us square. [*To* ADOLPHUS.] Is thet fair or is it not? You're a genlmn: you oughter knaow.

BARBARA. Two black eyes won't make one white one, Bill.

BILL. Aw didn't awst you. Cawn't you never keep your mahth shat? Oy awst the genlmn.

CUSINS [*reflectively*]. Yes: I think you're right, Mr. Walker. Yes: I should do it. It's curious: it's exactly what an ancient Greek would have done.

BARBARA. But what good will it do?

CUSINS. Well, it will give Mr. Fairmile some exercise; and it will satisfy Mr. Walker's soul.

BILL. Rot! there ain't nao sach a thing as a saoul. Ah kin you tell wevver Awve a saoul or not? You never seen it.

BARBARA. I've seen it hurting you when you went against it.

BILL [*with compressed aggravation*]. If you was maw gel and took the word aht o me mahth lawk thet, Aw'd give you sathink you'd feel urtin, Aw would. [*To* ADOLPHUS.] You tike maw tip, mite. Stop er jawr; or you'll doy afoah your tawm. [*With intense expression.*] Wore aht: thets wot you'll be: wore aht. [*He goes away through the gate.*]

CUSINS [*looking after him*]. I wonder!

BARBARA. Dolly! [*indignant, in her mother's manner*].

CUSINS. Yes, my dear, it's very wearing to be in love with you. If it lasts, I quite think I shall die young.

BARBARA. Should you mind?

CUSINS. Not at all. [*He is suddenly softened, and kisses her over the drum, evidently not for the first time, as people cannot kiss over a big drum without practice.* UNDERSHAFT *coughs.*]

BARBARA. It's all right, papa, we've not forgotten you. Dolly: explain the place to papa: I haven't time. [*She goes busily into the shelter.*]

UNDERSHAFT *and* ADOLPHUS *now have the yard to themselves.* UNDERSHAFT, *seated on a form, and still keenly attentive, looks hard at* ADOLPHUS. ADOLPHUS *looks hard at him.*

UNDERSHAFT. I fancy you guess something of what is in my mind, Mr. Cusins. [CUSINS *flourishes his drumsticks as if in the act of beating a lively rataplan, but makes no sound.*] Exactly so. But suppose Barbara finds you out!

CUSINS. You know, I do not admit that I am imposing on Barbara. I am quite genuinely interested in the views of the Salvation Army. The fact is, I am a sort of collector of religions; and the curious thing is that I find I can believe them all. By the way, have you any religion?

UNDERSHAFT. Yes.

CUSINS. Anything out of the common?

UNDERSHAFT. Only that there are two things necessary to Salvation.

CUSINS [*disappointed, but polite*]. Ah, the Church Catechism. Charles Lomax also belongs to the Established Church.

UNDERSHAFT. The two things are—

CUSINS. Baptism and—

UNDERSHAFT. No. Money and gunpowder.

CUSINS [*surprised, but interested*]. That is the general opinion of our governing classes. The novelty is in hearing any man confess it.

UNDERSHAFT. Just so.

CUSINS. Excuse me: is there any place in your religion for honor, justice, truth, love, mercy and so forth?

UNDERSHAFT. Yes: they are the graces and luxuries of a rich, strong, and safe life.

CUSINS. Suppose one is forced to choose between them and money or gunpowder?

UNDERSHAFT. Choose money and gunpowder; for without enough of both you cannot afford the others.

CUSINS. That is your religion?

UNDERSHAFT. Yes.

The cadence of this reply makes a full close in the conversation. CUSINS *twists his face dubiously and contemplates* UNDERSHAFT. UNDERSHAFT *contemplates him.*

CUSINS. Barbara won't stand that. You will have to choose between your religion and Barbara.

UNDERSHAFT. So will you, my friend. She will find out that that drum of yours is hollow.

CUSINS. Father Undershaft: you are mistaken: I am a sincere Salvationist. You do not understand the Salvation Army. It is the army of joy, of love, of courage: it has banished the fear and remorse and despair of the old hell-ridden evangelical sects: it marches to fight the devil with trumpet and drum, with music and dancing, with banner and palm, as becomes a sally from heaven by its happy garrison. It picks the waster out of the public house and makes a man of him: it finds a worm wriggling in a back kitchen, and lo! a woman! Men and women of rank too, sons and daughters of the Highest. It takes the poor professor of Greek, the most artificial and self-suppressed of human creatures, from his meal of roots, and lets loose the rhapsodist in him; reveals the true worship of Dionysos to him; sends him down the public street drumming dithyrambs [*he plays a thundering flourish on the drum*].

UNDERSHAFT. You will alarm the shelter.

CUSINS. Oh, they are accustomed to these sudden ecstasies. However, if the drum worries you—[*he pockets the drumsticks; unhooks the drum; and stands it on the ground opposite the gateway*].

UNDERSHAFT. Thank you.

CUSINS. You remember what Euripides says about your money and gunpowder?

UNDERSHAFT. No.

CUSINS [*declaiming*].

> One and another
> In money and guns may outpass his
>   brother;
> And men in their millions float and
>   flow
> And seethe with a million hopes as
>   leaven;
> And they win their will; or they miss
>   their will;
> And their hopes are dead or are pined
>   for still;
>   But who'er can know
>   As the long days go
> That to live is happy, has found his
>   heaven.

My translation: what do you think of it?

UNDERSHAFT. I think, my friend, that if you wish to know, as the long days go, that to live is happy, you must first acquire money enough for a decent life, and power enough to be your own master.

CUSINS. You are damnably discouraging. [*He resumes his declamation.*]

> Is it so hard a thing to see
> That the spirit of God—whate'er it
>   be—
> The law that abides and changes not,
>   ages long,
> The Eternal and Nature-born: these
>   things be strong?
> What else is Wisdom? What of Man's
>   endeavor,
> Or God's high grace so lovely and so
>   great?
> To stand from fear set free? to breathe
>   and wait?
> To hold a hand uplifted over Fate?
> And shall not Barbara be loved for
>   ever?

UNDERSHAFT. Euripides mentions Barbara, does he?

CUSINS. It is a fair translation. The word means Loveliness.

UNDERSHAFT. May I ask—as Barbara's father—how much a year she is to be loved for ever on?

CUSINS. As Barbara's father, that is more your affair than mine. I can feed her by teaching Greek: that is about all.

UNDERSHAFT. Do you consider it a good match for her?

CUSINS [*with polite obstinacy*]. Mr. Undershaft: I am in many ways a weak, timid, ineffectual person; and my health is far from satisfactory. But whenever I feel that I must have anything, I get it, sooner or later. I feel that way about Barbara. I don't like marriage: I feel intensely afraid of it; and I don't know what I shall do with Barbara or what she will do with me. But I feel that I and nobody else must marry her. Please regard that as settled.—Not that I wish to be arbitrary; but why should I waste your time in discussing what is inevitable?

UNDERSHAFT. You mean that you will stick at nothing: not even the conversion of the Salvation Army to the worship of Dionysos.

CUSINS. The business of the Salvation Army is to save, not to wrangle about the name of the pathfinder. Dionysos or another: what does it matter?

UNDERSHAFT [*rising and approaching him*]. Professor Cusins: you are a young man after my own heart.

CUSINS. Mr. Undershaft: you are, as far as I am able to gather, a most infernal old rascal; but you appeal very strongly to my sense of ironic humor.

UNDERSHAFT *mutely offers his hand. They shake.*

UNDERSHAFT [*suddenly concentrating himself*]. And now to business.

CUSINS. Pardon me. We are discussing religion. Why go back to such an uninteresting and unimportant subject as business?

UNDERSHAFT. Religion is our business at present, because it is through religion alone that we can win Barbara.

CUSINS. Have you, too, fallen in love with Barbara?

UNDERSHAFT. Yes, with a father's love.

CUSINS. A father's love for a grown-up daughter is the most dangerous of all infatuations. I apologize for mentioning my own pale, coy, mistrustful fancy in the same breath with it.

UNDERSHAFT. Keep to the point. We have to win her; and we are neither of us Methodists.

CUSINS. That doesn't matter. The power Barbara wields here—the power that wields Barbara herself—is not Calvinism, not Presbyterianism, not Methodism—

UNDERSHAFT. Not Greek Paganism either, eh?

CUSINS. I admit that. Barbara is quite original in her religion.

UNDERSHAFT [*triumphantly*]. Aha! Barbara Undershaft would be. Her inspiration comes from within herself.

CUSINS. How do you suppose it got there?

UNDERSHAFT [*in towering excitement*]. It is the Undershaft inheritance. I shall hand on my torch to my daughter. She shall make my converts and preach my gospel—

CUSINS. What! Money and gunpowder!

UNDERSHAFT. Yes, money and gunpowder. Freedom and power. Command of life and command of death.

CUSINS [*urbanely: trying to bring him down to earth*]. This is extremely interesting, Mr. Undershaft. Of course you know that you are mad.

UNDERSHAFT [*with redoubled force*]. And you?

CUSINS. Oh, mad as a hatter. You are welcome to my secret since I have discovered yours. But I am astonished. Can a madman make cannons?

UNDERSHAFT. Would anyone else than a madman make them? And now [*with surging energy*] question for question. Can a sane man translate Euripides?

CUSINS. No.

UNDERSHAFT [*seizing him by the shoulder*]. Can a sane woman make a man of a waster or a woman of a worm?

CUSINS [*reeling before the storm*]. Father Colossus—Mammoth Millionaire—

UNDERSHAFT [*pressing him*]. Are there two mad people or three in this Salvation shelter today?

CUSINS. You mean Barbara is as mad as we are?

UNDERSHAFT [*pushing him lightly off and resuming his equanimity suddenly and completely*]. Pooh, Professor! let us call things by their proper names. I am a millionaire; you are a poet; Barbara is a savior of souls. What have we three to do with the common mob of slaves and idolaters? [*He sits down again with a shrug of contempt for the mob.*]

CUSINS. Take care! Barbara is in love with the common people. So am I. Have you never felt the romance of that love?

UNDERSHAFT [*cold and sardonic*]. Have you ever been in love with Poverty, like St. Francis? Have you ever been in love with Dirt, like St. Simeon! Have you ever been in love with disease and suffering, like our nurses and philanthropists? Such passions are not virtues, but the most unnatural of all the vices. This love of the common people may please an earl's granddaughter and a university professor; but I have been a common man and a poor man; and it has no romance for me. Leave it to the poor to pretend that poverty is a blessing: leave it to the coward to make a religion of his cowardice by preaching humility: we know better than that. We three must stand together above the common people: how else can we help their children to climb up beside us? Barbara must belong to us, not to the Salvation Army.

CUSINS. Well, I can only say that if you think you will get her away from the Salvation Army by talking to her as you have been talking to me, you don't know Barbara.

UNDERSHAFT. My friend: I never ask for what I can buy.

CUSINS [*in a white fury*]. Do I understand you to imply that you can buy Barbara?

UNDERSHAFT. No; but I can buy the Salvation Army.

CUSINS. Quite impossible.

UNDERSHAFT. You shall see. All religious organizations exist by selling themselves to the rich.

CUSINS. Not the Army. That is the Church of the poor.

UNDERSHAFT. All the more reason for buying it.

CUSINS. I don't think you quite know what the Army does for the poor.

UNDERSHAFT. Oh yes I do. It draws their teeth: that is enough for me as a man of business.

CUSINS. Nonsense! It makes them sober—

UNDERSHAFT. I prefer sober workmen. The profits are larger.

CUSINS. —honest—

UNDERSHAFT. Honest workmen are the most economical.

CUSINS. —attached to their homes—

UNDERSHAFT. So much the better: they will put up with anything sooner than change their shop.

CUSINS. —happy—

UNDERSHAFT. An invaluable safeguard against revolution.

CUSINS. —unselfish—

UNDERSHAFT. Indifferent to their own interests, which suits me exactly.

CUSINS. —with their thoughts on heavenly things—

UNDERSHAFT [*rising*]. And not on Trade Unionism nor Socialism. Excellent.

CUSINS [*revolted*]. You really are an infernal old rascal.

UNDERSHAFT [*indicating* PETER SHIRLEY, *who has just come from the shelter and strolled dejectedly down the yard between them*]. And this is an honest man!

SHIRLEY. Yes; and what av I got by it? [*He passes on bitterly and sits on the form, in the corner of the penthouse.*]

SNOBBY PRICE, *beaming sanctimoniously, and* JENNY HILL, *with a tambourine full of coppers, come from the shelter and go to the drum, on which* JENNY *begins to count the money.*

UNDERSHAFT [*replying to* SHIRLEY]. Oh, your employers must have got a good deal by it from first to last. [*He sits on the table, with one foot on the side form,* CUSINS, *overwhelmed, sits down on the same form nearer the shelter.* BARBARA *comes from the shelter to the middle of the yard. She is excited and a little overwrought.*]

BARBARA. We've just had a splendid experience meeting at the other gate in Cripps's Lane. I've hardly ever seen them so much moved as they were by your confession, Mr. Price.

PRICE. I could almost be glad of my past wickedness if I could believe that it would elp to keep hathers stright.

BARBARA. So it will, Snobby. How much, Jenny?

JENNY. Four and tenpence, Major.

BARBARA. Oh Snobby, if you had given your poor mother just one more kick, we should have got the whole five shillings!

PRICE. If she heard you say that, miss, she'd be sorry I didn't. But I'm glad. Oh what a joy it will be to her when she hears I'm saved!

UNDERSHAFT. Shall I contribute the odd twopence, Barbara? The millionaire's mite, eh? [*He takes a couple of pennies from his pocket.*]

BARBARA. How did you make that twopence?

UNDERSHAFT. As usual. By selling cannons, torpedoes, submarines, and my new patent Grand Duke hand grenade.

BARBARA. Put it back in your pocket. You can't buy your salvation here for twopence: you must work it out.

UNDERSHAFT. Is twopence not enough? I can afford a little more, if you press me.

BARBARA. Two million millions would not be enough. There is bad blood on your hands; and nothing but good blood can cleanse them. Money is no use. Take it away. [*She turns to* CUSINS]. Dolly: you must write another letter for me to the papers. [*He makes a wry face.*] Yes: I know you don't like it; but it must be done. The starvation this winter is beating us: everybody is unemployed. The General says we must close this shelter if we can't get more money. I force the collections at the meetings until I am ashamed: don't I, Snobby?

PRICE. It's a fair treat to see you work it, miss. The way you got them up from three-and-six to four-and-ten with that hymn, penny by penny and verse by verse, was a caution. Not a Cheap Jack on Mile End Waste could touch you at it.

BARBARA. Yes; but I wish we could do without it. I am getting at last to think more of the collection than of the people's souls. And what are those hatfuls of pence and halfpence? We want thousands! tens of thousands! hundreds of thousands! I want to convert people, not to be always begging for the Army in a way I'd die sooner than beg for myself.

UNDERSHAFT [*in profound irony*]. Genuine unselfishness is capable of anything, my dear.

BARBARA [*unsuspectingly, as she turns away to take the money from the drum and put it in a cash bag she carries*]. Yes, isn't it? [UNDERSHAFT *looks sardonically at* CUSINS.]

CUSINS [*aside to* UNDERSHAFT]. Mephistopheles! Machiavelli!

BARBARA [*tears coming into her eyes as she ties the bag and pockets it*]. How are we to feed them? I can't talk religion to a man with bodily hunger in his eyes. [*Almost breaking down.*] It's frightful.

JENNY [*running to her*]. Major, dear—

BARBARA [*rebounding*]. No: don't comfort me. It will be all right. We shall get the money.

UNDERSHAFT. How?

JENNY. By praying for it, of course. Mrs. Baines says she prayed for it last night; and she has never prayed for it in vain; never once. [*She goes to the gate and looks out into the street.*]

BARBARA [*who has dried her eyes and regained her composure*]. By the way, dad, Mrs. Baines has come to march with us to our big meeting this afternoon; and she is very anxious to meet you, for some reason or other. Perhaps she'll convert you.

UNDERSHAFT. I shall be delighted, my dear.

JENNY [*at the gate: excitedly*]. Major! Major! here's that man back again.

JENNY. The man that hit me. Oh, I hope he's coming back to join us.

BILL WALKER, *with frost on his jacket, comes through the gate, his hands deep in his pockets and his chin sunk between his shoulders, like a cleaned-out gambler. He halts between* BARBARA *and the drum*.

BARBARA. Hullo, Bill! Back already!

BILL [*nagging at her*]. Bin talkin ever sence, ev you?

BARBARA. Pretty nearly. Well, has Todger paid you out for poor Jenny's jaw?

BILL. Nao e ain't.

BARBARA. I thought your jacket looked a bit snowy.

BILL. Sao it is snaowy. You want to knaow where the snaow cam from, down't you?

BARBARA. Yes.

BILL. Well, it cam from orf the grahnd in Pawkinses Corner in Kennintahn. It got grabbed orf be maw shaoulders: see?

BARBARA. Pity you didn't rub some off with your knees, Bill! That would have done you a lot of good.

BILL [*with sour mirthless humor*]. Aw was sivin anather menn's knees at the tawm. E was kneelin on moy ed, e was.

JENNY. Who was kneeling on your head?

BILL. Todger was. E was pryin for me: pryin comfartable wiv me as a cawpet. Sow was Mog. Sao was the aol bloomin meetin. Mog she sez, "Ow Lawd brike is stabborn sperrit; bat down't urt is dear art." Thet was wot she said. "Down't urt is dear art"! An er blowk—thirteen stun four!—kneelin wiv all is wight on me. Fanny, ain't it?

JENNY. Oh no. We're so sorry, Mr. Walker.

BARBARA [*enjoying it frankly*]. Nonsense! of course it's funny. Served you right, Bill! You must have done something to him first.

BILL [*doggedly*]. Aw did wot Aw said Aw'd do. Aw spit in is eye. E looks ap at the skoy and sez, "Ow that Aw should be fahnd worthy to be spit upon for the gospel's sike!" e sez; an Mog sez, "Glaory Allelloolier!"; an then e called me Braddher, and dahned me as if Aw was a kid and e was me mather worshin me a Setterda nawt. Aw ednt jast nao shaow wiv im at all. Arf the street pryed; an the tather arf larfed fit to split theirselves. [*To* BARBARA.] There! are you settisfawd nah?

BARBARA [*her eyes dancing*]. Wish I'd been there, Bill.

BILL. Yus: you'd a got in a hextra bit o talk on me, wouldn't you?

JENNY. I'm so sorry, Mr. Walker.

BILL [*fiercely*]. Down't you gow bein sorry for me: you've no call. Listen eah. Aw browk your jawr.

JENNY. No, it didn't hurt me: indeed it didn't, except for a moment. It was only that I was frightened.

[433]

BILL. Aw down't want to be forgive be you, or be ennybody. Wot Aw did Aw'll py for. Aw trawd to gat me aown jawr browk to settisfaw you—

JENNY [*distressed*]. Oh no—

BILL [*impatiently*]. Tell y' Aw did: cawn't you listen to wots bein taold you? All Aw got be it was bein mide a sawt of in the pablic street for me pines. Well, if Aw cawn't settisfaw you one wy, Aw ken anather. Listen eah! Aw ed two quid sived agen the frost; an Awve a pahnd of it left. A mite o mawn last week ed words with the judy e's gowin to merry. E give er wot-for; an e's bin fawnd fifteen bob. E ed a rawt to itt er cause they was gowin to be merrid; but Aw ednt nao rawt to itt you; sao put another fawv bob on an call it a pahnd's worth. [*He produces a sovereign.*] Eahs the manney. Tike it; and lets ev no more o your forgivin an pryin and your Mijor jawrin me. Let wot Aw dan be dan an pide for; and let there be a end of it.

JENNY. Oh, I couldn't take it, Mr. Walker. But if you would give a shilling or two to poor Rummy Mitchens! you really did hurt her; and she's old.

BILL [*contemptuously*]. Not lawkly. Aw'd give her anather as soon as look at er. Let her ev the lawr o me as she threatened! She ain't forgiven me: not mach. Wot Aw dan to er is not on me mawnd—wot she [*indicating* BARBARA] mawt call on me conscience—no more than stickin a pig. It's this Christian gime o yours that Aw wownt ev plyed agen me: this bloomin forgivin an neggin an jawrin that mikes a menn thet sore that iz lawf's a burdn to im. Aw wownt ev it, Aw tell you; sao tike your manney and stop thrawin your silly beshed fice hap agen me.

JENNY. Major: may I take a little of it for the Army?

BARBARA. No: the Army is not to be bought. We want your soul, Bill; and we'll take nothing less.

BILL [*bitterly*]. Aw knaow. Me an maw few shillins is not good enaff for you. You're a earl's grendorter, you are. Nathink less than a anderd pahnd for you.

UNDERSHAFT. Come, Barbara! you could do a great deal of good with a hundred pounds. If you will set this gentleman's mind at ease by taking his pound, I will give the other ninety-nine.

BILL, *dazed by such opulence, instinctively touches his cap.*

BARBARA. Oh, you're too extravagant, papa. Bill offers twenty pieces of silver. All you need offer is the other ten. That will make the standard price to buy anybody who's for sale. I'm not; and the Army's not. [*To* BILL.] You'll never have another quiet moment, Bill, until you come round to us. You can't stand out against your salvation.

BILL [*sullenly*]. Aw cawn't stend aht agen music awl wrastlers and awtful tangued women. Awve offered to py. Aw can do no more. Tike it or leave it. There it is. [*He throws the sovereign on the drum, and sits down on the horse-trough. The coin fascinates* SNOBBY PRICE, *who takes an early opportunity of dropping his cap on it.*]

MRS. BAINES *comes from the shelter. She is dressed as a Salvation Army Commissioner. She is an earnest looking woman of about 40, with a caressing, urgent voice, and an appealing manner.*

BARBARA. This is my father, Mrs. Baines. [UNDERSHAFT *comes from the table, taking his hat off with marked civility.*] Try what you can do with him. He won't listen to me, because he remembers what a fool I was when I was a baby. [*She leaves them together and chats with* JENNY.]

MRS. BAINES. Have you been shewn over the shelter, Mr. Undershaft? You know the work we're doing, of course.

UNDERSHAFT [*very civilly*]. The whole nation knows it, Mrs. Baines.

MRS. BAINES. No, sir: the whole nation does not know it, or we should not be crippled as we are for want of money to carry our work through the length and breadth of the land. Let me tell you that there would have been rioting this winter in London but for us.

UNDERSHAFT. You really think so?

MRS. BAINES. I know it. I remember 1886, when you rich gentlemen hardened your hearts against the cry of the poor. They broke the windows of your clubs in Pall Mall.

UNDERSHAFT [*gleaming with approval of their method*]. And the Mansion House Fund went up next day from thirty thousand pounds to seventy-nine thousand! I remember quite well.

MRS. BAINES. Well, won't you help me to get at the people? They won't break windows then. Come here, Price. Let me shew you to this gentleman. [PRICE *comes to be inspected.*] Do you remember the window breaking?

PRICE. My ole father thought it was the revolution, maam.

MRS. BAINES. Would you break windows now?

PRICE. Oh no, maam. The windows of eaven av bin opened to me. I know now that the rich man is a sinner like myself.

RUMMY [*appearing above at the loft door*]. Snobby Price!

SNOBBY. Wot is it?

RUMMY. Your mother's askin for you at the other gate in Cripps's Lane. She's heard about your confession. [PRICE *turns pale.*]

MRS. BAINES. Go, Mr. Price; and pray with her.

JENNY. You can go through the shelter, Snobby.

PRICE [*to* MRS. BAINES]. I couldnt face her now, maam, with all the weight of my sins fresh on me. Tell her she'll find her son at ome, waitin for her in prayer. [*He skulks off through the gate, incidentally stealing the sovereign on his way out by picking up his cap from the drum.*]

MRS. BAINES [*with swimming eyes*]. You see how we take the anger and the bitterness against you out of their hearts, Mr. Undershaft.

UNDERSHAFT. It is certainly most convenient and gratifying to all large employers of labor, Mrs. Baines.

MRS. BAINES. Barbara: Jenny: I have good news: most wonderful news. [JENNY *runs to her.*] My prayers have been answered. I told you they would, Jenny, didn't I?

JENNY. Yes, yes.

BARBARA [*moving nearer to the drum*]. Have we got money enough to keep the shelter open?

MRS. BAINES. I hope we shall have enough to keep all the shelters open. Lord Saxmundham has promised us five thousand pounds—

BARBARA. Hooray!

JENNY. Glory!

MRS. BAINES. —if—

BARBARA. "If!" If what?

MRS. BAINES. —if five other gentlemen will give a thousand each to make it up to ten thousand.

BARBARA. Who is Lord Saxmundham? I never heard of him.

UNDERSHAFT [*who has pricked up his ears at the peer's name, and is now watch-*

ing BARBARA *curiously*]. A new creation, my dear. You have heard of Sir Horace Bodger?

BARBARA. Bodger! Do you mean the distiller? Bodger's whisky!

UNDERSHAFT. That is the man. He is one of the greatest of our public benefactors. He restored the cathedral at Hakington. They made him a baronet for that. He gave half a million to the funds of his party: they made him a baron for that.

SHIRLEY. What will they give him for the five thousand?

UNDERSHAFT. There is nothing left to give him. So the five thousand, I should think, is to save his soul.

MRS. BAINES. Heaven grant it may! Oh Mr. Undershaft, you have some very rich friends. Can't you help us towards the other five thousand? We are going to hold a great meeting this afternoon at the Assembly Hall in the Mile End Road. If I could only announce that one gentleman had come forward to support Lord Saxmundham, others would follow. Don't you know somebody? couldn't you? wouldn't you? [*her eyes fill with tears*] oh, think of those poor people, Mr. Undershaft: think of how much it means to them, and how little to a great man like you.

UNDERSHAFT [*sardonically gallant*]. Mrs. Baines: you are irresistible. I can't disappoint you; and I can't deny myself the satisfaction of making Bodger pay up. You shall have your five thousand pounds.

MRS. BAINES. Thank God!

UNDERSHAFT. You don't thank me?

MRS. BAINES. Oh sir, don't try to be cynical: don't be ashamed of being a good man. The Lord will bless you abundantly; and our prayers will be like a strong fortification round you all the days of your life. [*With a touch of caution.*] You will let me have the cheque to shew at the meeting, won't you? Jenny: go in and fetch a pen and ink. [JENNY *runs to the shelter door.*]

UNDERSHAFT. Do not disturb Miss Hill: I have a fountain pen. [JENNY *halts. He sits at the table and writes the cheque.* CUSINS *rises to make room for him. They all watch him silently.*]

BILL [*cynically, aside to* BARBARA, *his voice and accent horribly debased.*] Wot prawce selvytion nah?

BARBARA. Stop. [UNDERSHAFT *stops writing: they all turn to her in surprise.*] Mrs. Baines: are you really going to take this money?

MRS. BAINES [*astonished*]. Why not, dear?

BARBARA. Why not! Do you know what my father is? Have you forgotten that Lord Saxmundham is Bodger the whisky man? Do you remember how we implored the County Council to stop him from writing Bodger's Whisky in letters of fire against the sky; so that the poor drink-ruined creatures on the Embankment could not wake up from their snatches of sleep without being reminded of their deadly thirst by that wicked sky sign? Do you know that the worst thing I have had to fight here is not the devil, but Bodger, Bodger, Bodger, with his whisky, his distilleries, and his tied houses? Are you going to make our shelter another tied house for him, and ask me to keep it?

BILL. Rotten dranken whisky it is too.

MRS. BAINES. Dear Barbara: Lord Saxmundham has a soul to be saved like any of us. If heaven has found the way to make a good use of his money, are we to set ourselves up against the answer to our prayers?

BARBARA. I know he has a soul to be saved. Let him come down here; and I'll do my best to help him to his salvation. But he wants to send his cheque down to buy us, and go on being as wicked as ever.

UNDERSHAFT [*with a reasonableness which* CUSINS *alone perceives to be ironical*]. My dear Barbara: alcohol is a very necessary article. It heals the sick—

BARBARA. It does nothing of the sort.

UNDERSHAFT. Well, it assists the doctor: that is perhaps a less questionable way of putting it. It makes life bearable to millions of people who could not endure their existence if they were quite sober. It enables Parliament to do things at eleven at night that no sane person would do at eleven in the morning. Is it Bodger's fault that this inestimable gift is deplorably abused by less than one per cent of the poor? [*He turns again to the table; signs the cheque; and crosses it.*]

MRS. BAINES. Barbara: will there be less drinking or more if all those poor souls we are saving come tomorrow and find the doors of our shelters shut in their faces? Lord Saxmundham gives us the money to stop drinking—to take his own business from him.

CUSINS [*impishly*]. Pure self-sacrifice on Bodger's part, clearly! Bless dear Bodger! [BARBARA *almost breaks down as* ADOLPHUS, *too, fails her.*]

UNDERSHAFT [*tearing out the cheque and pocketing the book as he rises and goes past* CUSINS *to* MRS. BAINES]. I also, Mrs. Baines, may claim a little disinterestedness. Think of my business! think of the widows and orphans! the men and lads torn to pieces with shrapnel and poisoned with lyddite! [MRS. BAINES *shrinks; but he goes on remorselessly*] the oceans of blood, not one drop of which is shed in a really just cause! the ravaged crops! the peaceful peasants forced, women and men, to till their fields under the fire of opposing armies on pain of starvation! the bad blood of the fierce little cowards at home who egg on others to fight for the gratification of their national vanity! All this makes money for me: I am never richer, never busier than when the papers are full of it. Well, it is your work to preach peace on earth and goodwill to men. [MRS. BAINES'S *face lights up again.*] Every convert you make is a vote against war. [*Her lips move in prayer.*] Yet I give you this money to help you to hasten my own commercial ruin. [*He gives her the cheque.*]

CUSINS [*mounting the form in an ecstasy of mischief*]. The millennium will be inaugurated by the unselfishness of Undershaft and Bodger. Oh be joyful! [*He takes the drumsticks from his pocket and flourishes them.*]

MRS. BAINES [*taking the cheque*]. The longer I live the more proof I see that there is an Infinite Goodness that turns everything to the work of salvation sooner or later. Who would have thought that any good could have come out of war and drink? And yet their profits are brought today to the feet of salvation to do its blessed work. [*She is affected to tears.*]

JENNY [*running to* MRS. BAINES *and throwing her arms round her*]. Oh dear! how blessed, how glorious it all is!

CUSINS [*in a convulsion of irony*]. Let us seize this unspeakable moment. Let us march to the great meeting at once. Excuse me just an instant. [*He rushes into the shelter.* JENNY *takes her tambourine from the drum head.*]

MRS. BAINES. Mr. Undershaft: have you

ever seen a thousand people fall on their knees with one impulse and pray? Come with us to the meeting. Barbara shall tell them that the Army is saved, and saved through you.

CUSINS [*returning impetuously from the shelter with a flag and a trombone, and coming between* MRS. BAINES *and* UNDERSHAFT]. You shall carry the flag down the first street, Mrs. Baines. [*He gives her the flag.*] Mr. Undershaft is a gifted trombonist: he shall intone an Olympian diapason to the West Ham Salvation March. [*Aside to* UNDERSHAFT, *as he forces the trombone on him.*] Blow, Machiavelli, blow.

UNDERSHAFT [*aside to him, as he takes the trombone*]. The trumpet in Zion! [CUSINS *rushes to the drum, which he takes up and puts on.* UNDERSHAFT *continues, aloud.*] I will do my best. I could vamp a bass if I knew the tune.

CUSINS. It is a wedding chorus from one of Donizetti's operas; but we have converted it. We convert everything to good here, including Bodger. You remember the chorus. "For thee immense rejoicing—immenso giubilo—immenso giubilo." [*With drum obbligato.*] Rum tum ti tum tum, tum tum ti ta—

BARBARA. Dolly: you are breaking my heart.

CUSINS. What is a broken heart more or less here? Dionysos Undershaft has descended. I am possessed.

MRS. BAINES. Come, Barbara: I must have my dear Major to carry the flag with me.

JENNY. Yes, yes, Major darling.

CUSINS *snatches the tambourine out of* JENNY's *hand and mutely offers it to* BARBARA.

BARBARA [*coming forward a little as she puts the offer behind her with a shudder, whilst* CUSINS *recklessly tosses the tambourine back to* JENNY *and goes to the gate*]. I can't come.

JENNY. Not come!

MRS. BAINES [*with tears in her eyes*]. Barbara: do you think I am wrong to take the money?

BARBARA [*impulsively going to her and kissing her*]. No, no: God help you, dear, you must: you are saving the Army. Go; and may you have a great meeting!

JENNY. But aren't you coming?

BARBARA. No. [*She begins taking off the silver S brooch from her collar.*]

MRS. BAINES. Barbara: what are you doing?

JENNY. Why are you taking your badge off? You can't be going to leave us, Major.

BARBARA [*quietly*]. Father: come here.

UNDERSHAFT [*coming to her*]. My dear! [*Seeing that she is going to pin the badge on his collar, he retreats to the penthouse in some alarm.*]

BARBARA [*following him*]. Don't be frightened. [*She pins the badge on and steps back towards the table, shewing him to the others.*] There! It's not much for £5000, is it?

MRS. BAINES. Barbara: if you won't come and pray with us, promise me you will pray for us.

BARBARA. I can't pray now. Perhaps I shall never pray again.

MRS. BAINES. Barbara!

JENNY. Major!

BARBARA [*almost delirious*]. I can't bear any more. Quick march!

CUSINS [*calling to the procession in the street outside*]. Off we go. Play up, there! Immenso giubilo. [*He gives the time with his drum; and the band strikes up the march, which rapidly becomes more dis-*

tant as the procession moves briskly away.]

MRS. BAINES. I must go, dear. You're overworked: you will be all right tomorrow. We'll never lose you. Now Jenny: step out with the old flag. Blood and Fire! [*She marches out through the gate with her flag.*]

JENNY. Glory Hallelujah! [*flourishing her tambourine and marching*].

UNDERSHAFT [*to* CUSINS, *as he marches out past him easing the slide of his trombone*]. "My ducats and my daughter"!

CUSINS [*following him out*]. Money and gunpowder!

BARBARA. Drunkenness and Murder! My God: why hast thou forsaken me?

She sinks on the form with her face buried in her hands. The march passes away into silence. BILL WALKER *steals across to her.*

BILL [*taunting*]. Wot prawce selvytion nah?

SHIRLEY. Don't you hit her when she's down.

BILL. She itt me wen Aw wiz dahn. Waw shouldn't Aw git a bit o me aown beck?

BARBARA [*raising her head*]. I didn't take your money, Bill. [*She crosses the yard to the gate and turns her back on the two men to hide her face from them.*]

BILL [*sneering after her*]. Naow, it warn't enaff for you. [*Turning to the drum, he misses the money.*] Ellow! If you ain't took it sammun else ez. Were's it gorn? Bly me if Jenny Ill didn't tike it arter all!

RUMMY [*screaming at him from the loft*]. You lie, you dirty blackguard! Snobby Price pinched it off the drum when he took up his cap. I was up here all the time an see im do it.

BILL. Wot! Stowl maw manney! Waw didn't you call thief on him, you silly aold macker you?

RUMMY. To serve you aht for ittin me acrost the fice. It's cost y'pahnd, that az. [*Raising a paean of squalid triumph.*] I done you. I'm even with you. I've ad it aht o y— [BILL *snatches up* SHIRLEY'S *mug and hurls it at her. She slams the loft door and vanishes. The mug smashes against the door and falls in fragments.*]

BILL [*beginning to chuckle*]. Tell us, aol menn, wot o'clock this mawnin was it wen im as they call Snobby Prawce was sived?

BARBARA [*turning to him more composedly, and with unspoiled sweetness*]. About half past twelve, Bill. And he pinched your pound at a quarter to two. I know. Well, you can't afford to lose it. I'll send it to you.

BILL [*his voice and accent suddenly improving*]. Not if Aw wiz to stawve for it. Aw ain't to be bought.

SHIRLEY. Ain't you? You'd sell yourself to the devil for a pint o beer; ony there ain't no devil to make the offer.

BILL [*unshamed*]. Sao Aw would, mite, and often ev, cheerful. But she cawn't baw me. [*Approaching* BARBARA.] You wanted maw saoul, did you? Well, you ain't got it.

BARBARA. I nearly got it, Bill. But we've sold it back to you for ten thousand pounds.

SHIRLEY. And dear at the money!

BARBARA. No, Peter: it was worth more than money.

BILL [*salvationproof*]. It's nao good: you cawn't get rahnd me nah. Aw down't blieve in it; and Awve seen tody that Aw was rawt. [*Going.*] Sao long, aol soupkitchener! Ta, ta, Mijor Earl's Grendorter! [*Turning at the gate.*] Wot prawce selvytion nah? Snobby Prawce! Ha! ha!

BARBARA [*offering her hand*]. Goodbye, Bill.

BILL [*taken aback, half plucks his cap off; then shoves it on again defiantly*]. Git aht. [BARBARA *drops her hand, discouraged. He has a twinge of remorse.*] But thets aw rawt, you knaow. Nathink pasnl. Naow mellice. Sao long, Judy. [*He goes.*]

BARBARA. No malice. So long, Bill.

SHIRLEY [*shaking his head*]. You make too much of him, miss, in your innocence.

BARBARA [*going to him*]. Peter: I'm like you now. Cleaned out, and lost my job.

SHIRLEY. You've youth an hope. That's two better than me.

BARBARA. I'll get you a job, Peter. That's hope for you: the youth will have to be enough for me. [*She counts her money.*] I have just enough left for two teas at Lockharts, a Rowton doss for you, and my tram and bus home. [*He frowns and rises with offended pride. She takes his arm.*] Don't be proud, Peter: it's sharing between friends. And promise me you'll talk to me and not let me cry. [*She draws him towards the gate.*]

SHIRLEY. Well, I'm not accustomed to talk to the like of you—

BARBARA [*urgently*]. Yes, yes: you must talk to me. Tell me about Tom Paine's books and Bradlaugh's lectures. Come along.

SHIRLEY. Ah, if you would only read Tom Paine in the proper spirit, miss! [*They go out through the gate together.*]

ACT III

[*Next day after lunch* LADY BRITOMART *is writing in the library in Wilton Crescent.* SARAH *is reading in the armchair near the window.* BARBARA, *in ordinary fashionable dress, pale and brooding, is on the settee.* CHARLES LOMAX *enters. He starts on seeing* BARBARA *fashionably attired and in low spirits.*]

LOMAX. You've left off your uniform!

BARBARA *says nothing; but an expression of pain passes over her face.*

LADY BRITOMART [*warning him in low tones to be careful*]. Charles!

LOMAX [*much concerned, coming behind the settee and bending sympathetically over* BARBARA]. I'm awfully sorry, Barbara. You know I helped you all I could with the concertina and so forth. [*Momentously.*] Still, I have never shut my eyes to the fact that there is a certain amount of tosh about the Salvation Army. Now the claims of the Church of England—

LADY BRITOMART. That's enough, Charles. Speak of something suited to your mental capacity.

LOMAX. But surely the Church of England is suited to all our capacities.

BARBARA [*pressing his hand*]. Thank you for your sympathy, Cholly. Now go and spoon with Sarah.

LOMAX [*dragging a chair from the writing table and seating himself affectionately by* SARAH'S *side*]. How is my ownest today?

SARAH. I wish you wouldn't tell Cholly to do things, Barbara. He always comes straight and does them. Cholly: we're going to the works this afternoon.

LOMAX. What works?

SARAH. The cannon works.

LOMAX. What? your governor's shop!

[440]

SARAH. Yes.

LOMAX. Oh I say!

CUSINS *enters in poor condition. He also starts visibly when he sees* BARBARA *without her uniform.*

BARBARA. I expected you this morning, Dolly. Didn't you guess that?

CUSINS [*sitting down beside her*]. I'm sorry. I have only just breakfasted.

SARAH. But we've just finished lunch.

BARBARA. Have you had one of your bad nights?

CUSINS. No: I had rather a good night: in fact, one of the most remarkable nights I have ever passed.

BARBARA. The meeting?

CUSINS. No: after the meeting.

LADY BRITOMART. You should have gone to bed after the meeting. What were you doing?

CUSINS. Drinking.

LADY BRITOMART. Adolphus!
SARAH. Dolly!
BARBARA. Dolly!
LOMAX. Oh I say!

LADY BRITOMART. What were you drinking, may I ask?

CUSINS. A most devilish kind of Spanish burgundy, warranted free from added alcohol: a Temperance burgundy in fact. Its richness in natural alcohol made any addition superfluous.

BARBARA. Are you joking, Dolly?

CUSINS [*patiently*]. No. I have been making a night of it with the nominal head of this household: that is all.

LADY BRITOMART. Andrew made you drunk!

CUSINS. No: he only provided the wine. I think it was Dionysos who made me drunk. [*To* BARBARA.] I told you I was possessed.

LADY BRITOMART. You're not sober yet. Go home to bed at once.

CUSINS. I have never before ventured to reproach you, Lady Brit; but how could you marry the Prince of Darkness?

LADY BRITOMART. It was much more excusable to marry him than to get drunk with him. That is a new accomplishment of Andrew's, by the way. He usen't to drink.

CUSINS. He doesn't now. He only sat there and completed the wreck of my moral basis, the rout of my convictions, the purchase of my soul. He cares for you, Barbara. That is what makes him so dangerous to me.

BARBARA. That has nothing to do with it, Dolly. There are larger loves and diviner dreams than the fireside ones. You know that, don't you?

CUSINS. Yes: that is our understanding. I know it. I hold to it. Unless he can win me on that holier ground he may amuse me for a while; but he can get no deeper hold, strong as he is.

BARBARA. Keep to that; and the end will be right. Now tell me what happened at the meeting?

CUSINS. It was an amazing meeting. Mrs. Baines almost died of emotion. Jenny Hill simply gibbered with hysteria. The Prince of Darkness played his trombone like a madman: its brazen roarings were like the laughter of the damned. 117 conversions took place then and there. They prayed with the most touching sincerity and gratitude for Bodger, and for the anonymous donor of the £5000. Your father would not let his name be given.

LOMAX. That was rather fine of the old man, you know. Most chaps would have wanted the advertisement.

CUSINS. He said all the charitable institutions would be down on him like kites on a battle-field if he gave his name.

LADY BRITOMART. That's Andrew all

over. He never does a proper thing without giving an improper reason for it.

Cusins. He convinced me that I have all my life been doing improper things for proper reasons.

Lady Britomart. Adolphus: now that Barbara has left the Salvation Army, you had better leave it too. I will not have you playing that drum in the streets.

Cusins. Your orders are already obeyed, Lady Brit.

Barbara. Dolly: were you ever really in earnest about it? Would you have joined if you had never seen me?

Cusins [*disingenuously*]. Well—er—well, possibly, as a collector of religions—

Lomax [*cunningly*]. Not as a drummer, though, you know. You are a very clearheaded brainy chap, Dolly; and it must have been apparent to you that there is a certain amount of tosh about—

Lady Britomart. Charles: if you must drivel, drivel like a grown-up man and not like a schoolboy.

Lomax [*out of countenance*]. Well, drivel is drivel, don't you know, whatever a man's age.

Lady Britomart. In good society in England, Charles, men drivel at all ages by repeating silly formulas with an air of wisdom. Schoolboys make their own formulas out of slang, like you. When they reach your age, and get political private secretaryships and things of that sort, they drop slang and get their formulas out of The Spectator or The Times. You had better confine yourself to The Times. You will find that there is a certain amount of tosh about The Times; but at least its language is reputable.

Lomax [*overwhelmed*]. You are so awfully strong-minded, Lady Brit—

Lady Britomart. Rubbish! [Morrison *comes in.*] What is it?

Morrison. If you please, my lady, Mr. Undershaft has just drove up to the door.

Lady Britomart. Well, let him in. [Morrison *hesitates.*] What's the matter with you?

Morrison. Shall I announce him, my lady; or is he at home here, so to speak, my lady?

Lady Britomart. Announce him.

Morrison. Thank you, my lady. You won't mind my asking, I hope. The occasion is in a manner of speaking new to me.

Lady Britomart. Quite right. Go and let him in.

Morrison. Thank you, my lady. [*He withdraws.*]

Lady Britomart. Children: go and get ready. [Sarah *and* Barbara *go upstairs for their out-of-door wraps.*] Charles: go and tell Stephen to come down here in five minutes: you will find him in the drawing room. [Charles *goes.*] Adolphus: tell them to send round the carriage in about fifteen minutes. [Adolphus *goes.*]

Morrison [*at the door*]. Mr. Undershaft.

Undershaft *comes in.* Morrison *goes out.*

Undershaft. Alone! How fortunate!

Lady Britomart [*rising*]. Don't be sentimental, Andrew. Sit down. [*She sits on the settee: he sits beside her, on her left. She comes to the point before he has time to breathe.*] Sarah must have £800 a year until Charles Lomax comes into his property. Barbara will need more, and need it permanently, because Adolphus hasn't any property.

Undershaft [*resignedly*]. Yes, my dear: I will see to it. Anything else? for yourself, for instance?

LADY BRITOMART. I want to talk to you about Stephen.

UNDERSHAFT [*rather wearily*]. Don't, my dear. Stephen doesn't interest me.

LADY BRITOMART. He does interest me. He is our son.

UNDERSHAFT. Do you really think so? He has induced us to bring him into the world; but he chose his parents very incongruously, I think. I see nothing of myself in him, and less of you.

LADY BRITOMART. Andrew: Stephen is an excellent son, and a most steady, capable, highminded young man. You are simply trying to find an excuse for disinheriting him.

UNDERSHAFT. My dear Biddy: the Undershaft tradition disinherits him. It would be dishonest of me to leave the cannon foundry to my son.

LADY BRITOMART. It would be most unnatural and improper of you to leave it to anyone else, Andrew. Do you suppose this wicked and immoral tradition can be kept up for ever? Do you pretend that Stephen could not carry on the foundry just as well as all the other sons of the big business houses?

UNDERSHAFT. Yes: he could learn the office routine without understanding the business, like all the other sons; and the firm would go on by its own momentum until the real Undershaft—probably an Italian or a German—would invent a new method and cut him out.

LADY BRITOMART. There is nothing that any Italian or German could do that Stephen could not do. And Stephen at least has breeding.

UNDERSHAFT. The son of a foundling! Nonsense!

LADY BRITOMART. My son, Andrew! And even you may have good blood in your veins for all you know.

UNDERSHAFT. True. Probably I have. That is another argument in favor of a foundling.

LADY BRITOMART. Andrew: don't be aggravating. And don't be wicked. At present you are both.

UNDERSHAFT. This conversation is part of the Undershaft tradition, Biddy. Every Undershaft's wife has treated him to it ever since the house was founded. It is mere waste of breath. If the tradition be ever broken it will be for an abler man than Stephen.

LADY BRITOMART [*pouting*]. Then go away.

UNDERSHAFT [*deprecatory*]. Go away!

LADY BRITOMART. Yes: go away. If you will do nothing for Stephen, you are not wanted here. Go to your foundling, whoever he is; and look after him.

UNDERSHAFT. The fact is, Biddy—

LADY BRITOMART. Don't call me Biddy. I don't call you Andy.

UNDERSHAFT. I will not call my wife Britomart: it is not good sense. Seriously, my love, the Undershaft tradition has landed me in a difficulty. I am getting on in years; and my partner Lazarus has at last made a stand and insisted that the succession must be settled one way or the other; and of course he is quite right. You see, I haven't found a fit successor yet.

LADY BRITOMART [*obstinately*]. There is Stephen.

UNDERSHAFT. That's just it: all the foundlings I can find are exactly like Stephen.

LADY BRITOMART. Andrew!!

UNDERSHAFT. I want a man with no relations and no schooling: that is, a man who would be out of the running altogether if he were not a strong man. And I can't find him. Every blessed foundling nowadays is snapped up in his infancy by Barnardo homes, or School Board officers, or Boards of Guardians; and if he shews the least ability he is fastened on by schoolmasters; trained to win scholarships like a racehorse; crammed with secondhand ideas; drilled and disciplined in docility and what they call good taste; and lamed for life so that he is fit for nothing but teaching. If you want to keep the foundry in the family, you had better find an eligible foundling and marry him to Barbara.

LADY BRITOMART. Ah! Barbara! Your pet! You would sacrifice Stephen to Barbara.

UNDERSHAFT. Cheerfully. And you, my dear, would boil Barbara to make soup for Stephen.

LADY BRITOMART. Andrew: this is not a question of our likings and dislikings: it is a question of duty. It is your duty to make Stephen your successor.

UNDERSHAFT. Just as much as it is your duty to submit to your husband. Come, Biddy! these tricks of the governing class are of no use with me. I am one of the governing class myself; and it is waste of time giving tracts to a missionary. I have the power in this matter; and I am not to be humbugged into using it for your purposes.

LADY BRITOMART. Andrew: you can talk my head off; but you can't change wrong into right. And your tie is all on one side. Put it straight.

UNDERSHAFT [*disconcerted*]. It won't stay unless it's pinned [*he fumbles at it with childish grimaces*]—

STEPHEN *comes in.*

STEPHEN [*at the door*]. I beg your pardon [*about to retire*].

LADY BRITOMART. No: come in, Stephen. [STEPHEN *comes forward to his mother's writing table.*]

UNDERSHAFT [*not very cordially*]. Good afternoon.

STEPHEN [*coldly*]. Good afternoon.

UNDERSHAFT [*to* LADY BRITOMART]. He knows all about the tradition, I suppose?

LADY BRITOMART. Yes. [*To* STEPHEN.] It is what I told you last night, Stephen.

UNDERSHAFT [*sulkily*]. I understand you want to come into the cannon business.

STEPHEN. *I* go into trade! Certainly not.

UNDERSHAFT [*opening his eyes, greatly eased in mind and manner*]. Oh! in that case—

LADY BRITOMART. Cannons are not trade, Stephen. They are enterprise.

STEPHEN. I have no intention of becoming a man of business in any sense. I have no capacity for business and no taste for it. I intend to devote myself to politics.

UNDERSHAFT [*rising*]. My dear boy: this is an immense relief to me. And I trust it may prove an equally good thing for the country. I was afraid you would consider yourself disparaged and slighted. [*He moves towards* STEPHEN *as if to shake hands with him.*]

LADY BRITOMART [*rising and interposing*]. Stephen: I cannot allow you to throw away an enormous property like this.

STEPHEN [*stiffly*]. Mother: there must be an end of treating me as a child, if you please. [LADY BRITOMART *recoils, deeply wounded by his tone.*] Until last night I did not take your attitude seriously, because I did not think you meant it seriously. But I find now that you left me in the dark as to matters which you should have explained to me years ago. I am extremely hurt and offended. Any further discussion of my intentions had better take place with my father, as between one man and another.

[444]

Major Barbara

Lady Britomart. Stephen! [*She sits down again, her eyes filling with tears.*]

Undershaft [*with grave compassion*]. You see, my dear, it is only the big men who can be treated as children.

Stephen. I am sorry, mother, that you have forced me—

Undershaft [*stopping him*]. Yes, yes, yes, yes: that's all right, Stephen. She won't interfere with you any more: your independence is achieved: you have won your latchkey. Don't rub it in; and above all, don't apologize. [*He resumes his seat.*] Now what about your future, as between one man and another—I beg your pardon, Biddy: as between two men and a woman.

Lady Britomart [*who has pulled herself together strongly*]. I quite understand, Stephen. By all means go your own way if you feel strong enough. [Stephen *sits down magisterially in the chair at the writing table with an air of affirming his majority.*]

Undershaft. It is settled that you do not ask for the succession to the cannon business.

Stephen. I hope it is settled that I repudiate the cannon business.

Undershaft. Come, come! don't be so devilishly sulky: it's boyish. Freedom should be generous. Besides, I owe you a fair start in life in exchange for disinheriting you. You can't become prime minister all at once. Haven't you a turn for something? What about literature, art, and so forth?

Stephen. I have nothing of the artist about me, either in faculty or character, thank Heaven!

Undershaft. A philosopher, perhaps? Eh?

Stephen. I make no such ridiculous pretension.

Undershaft. Just so. Well, there is the army, the navy, the Church, the Bar. The Bar requires some ability. What about the Bar?

Stephen. I have not studied law. And I am afraid I have not the necessary push —I believe that is the name barristers give to their vulgarity—for success in pleading.

Undershaft. Rather a difficult case, Stephen. Hardly anything left but the stage, is there? [Stephen *makes an impatient movement.*] Well, come! is there anything you know or care for?

Stephen [*rising and looking at him steadily*]. I know the difference between right and wrong.

Undershaft [*hugely tickled*]. You don't say so! What! no capacity for business, no knowledge of law, no sympathy with art, no pretension to philosophy; only a simple knowledge of the secret that has puzzled all the philosophers, baffled all the lawyers, muddled all the men of business, and ruined most of the artists: the secret of right and wrong. Why, man, you're a genius, a master of masters, a god! At twentyfour, too!

Stephen [*keeping his temper with difficulty*]. You are pleased to be facetious. I pretend to nothing more than any honorable English gentleman claims as his birthright [*he sits down angrily*].

Undershaft. Oh, that's everybody's birthright. Look at poor little Jenny Hill, the Salvation lassie! she would think you were laughing at her if you asked her to stand up in the street and teach grammar or geography or mathematics or even drawing room dancing; but it never occurs to her to doubt that she can teach morals and religion. You are all alike, you respectable people. You can't tell me the bursting strain of a ten-inch gun, which is a very simple matter; but you all think you can tell me the bursting strain of a man under temptation. You daren't handle high explosives; but you're all ready to handle honesty and truth and justice and the whole duty of man, and kill one another at that game. What a country! What a world!

Lady Britomart [*uneasily*]. What do you think he had better do, Andrew?

Undershaft. Oh, just what he wants to do. He knows nothing and he thinks he knows everything. That points clearly to a political career. Get him a private secretaryship to someone who can get him an Under Secretaryship; and then leave him alone. He will find his natural and proper place in the end on the Treasury Bench.

Stephen [*springing up again*]. I am sorry, sir, that you force me to forget the respect due to you as my father. I am an Englishman and I will not hear the Government of my country insulted. [*He thrusts his hands in his pockets, and walks angrily across to the window.*]

Undershaft [*with a touch of brutality*]. The government of your country! *I* am the government of your country: I, and Lazarus. Do you suppose that you and half a dozen amateurs like you, sitting in a row in that foolish gabble shop, can govern Undershaft and Lazarus? No, my friend: you will do what pays us. You will make war when it suits us, and keep peace when it doesn't. You will find out that trade requires certain measures when we have decided on those measures. When I want anything to keep my dividends up, you will discover that my want is a national need. When other people want something to keep my dividends down, you will call out the police and military. And in return you shall have the support and applause of my newspapers, and the delight of imagining that you are a great statesman. Government of your country! Be off with you, my boy, and play with your caucuses and leading articles and historic parties and great leaders and burning questions and the rest of your toys. *I* am going back to my counting-house to pay the piper and call the tune.

Stephen [*actually smiling, and putting his hand on his father's shoulder with indulgent patronage*]. Really, my dear father, it is impossible to be angry with you. You don't know how absurd all this sounds to me. You are very properly proud of having been industrious enough to make money; and it is greatly to your credit that you have made so much of it. But it has kept you in circles where you are valued for your money and deferred to for it, instead of in the doubtless very old-fashioned and behind-the-times public school and university where I formed my habits of mind. It is natural for you to think that money governs England; but you must allow me to think I know better.

Undershaft. And what does govern England, pray?

Stephen. Character, father, character.

Undershaft. Whose character? Yours or mine?

Stephen. Neither yours nor mine, father, but the best elements in the English national character.

Undershaft. Stephen: I've found your profession for you. You're a born journalist. I'll start you with a high-toned weekly review. There!

Before Stephen *can reply* Sarah, Barbara, Lomax, *and* Cusins *come in ready for walking.* Barbara *crosses the room to the window and looks out.* Cusins *drifts amiably to the armchair.* Lomax *remains near the door, whilst* SARAH *comes to her mother.*

STEPHEN *goes to the smaller writing table and busies himself with his letters.*

SARAH. Go and get ready, mamma: the carriage is waiting. [LADY BRITOMART *leaves the room.*]

UNDERSHAFT [*to* SARAH]. Good day, my dear. Good afternoon, Mr. Lomax.

LOMAX [*vaguely*]. Ahdedoo.

UNDERSHAFT [*to* CUSINS]. Quite well after last night, Euripides, eh?

CUSINS. As well as can be expected.

UNDERSHAFT. That's right. [*To* BARBARA.] So you are coming to see my death and devastation factory, Barbara?

BARBARA [*at the window*]. You came yesterday to see my salvation factory. I promised you a return visit.

LOMAX [*coming forward between* SARAH *and* UNDERSHAFT]. You'll find it awfully interesting. I've been through the Woolwich Arsenal; and it gives you a ripping feeling of security, you know, to think of the lot of beggars we could kill if it came to fighting. [*To* UNDERSHAFT, *with sudden solemnity.*] Still, it must be rather an awful reflection for you, from the religious point of view as it were. You're getting on, you know, and all that.

SARAH. You don't mind Cholly's imbecility, papa, do you?

LOMAX [*much taken aback*]. Oh I say!

UNDERSHAFT. Mr. Lomax looks at the matter in a very proper spirit, my dear.

LOMAX. Just so. That's all I meant, I assure you.

SARAH. Are you coming, Stephen?

STEPHEN. Well, I am rather busy—er— [*Magnanimously.*] Oh well, yes: I'll come. That is, if there is room for me.

UNDERSHAFT. I can take two with me in a little motor I am experimenting with for field use. You won't mind its being rather unfashionable. It's not painted yet; but it's bullet proof.

LOMAX [*appalled at the prospect of confronting Wilton Crescent in an unpainted motor*]. Oh I say!

SARAH. The carriage for me, thank you. Barbara doesn't mind what she's seen in.

LOMAX. I say, Dolly, old chap: do you really mind the car being a guy? Because of course if you do I'll go in it. Still—

CUSINS. I prefer it.

LOMAX. Thanks awfully, old man. Come, my ownest. [*He hurries out to secure his seat in the carriage.* SARAH *follows him.*]

CUSINS [*moodily walking across to* LADY BRITOMART'S *writing table*]. Why are we two coming to this Works Department of Hell? that is what I ask myself.

BARBARA. I have always thought of it as a sort of pit where lost creatures with blackened faces stirred up smoky fires and were driven and tormented by my father? Is it like that, dad?

UNDERSHAFT [*scandalized*]. My dear! It is a spotlessly clean and beautiful hillside town.

CUSINS. With a Methodist chapel? Oh do say there's a Methodist chapel.

UNDERSHAFT. There are two: a Primitive one and a sophisticated one. There is even an Ethical Society; but it is not much patronized, as my men are all strongly religious. In the High Explosives Sheds they object to the presence of Agnostics as unsafe.

CUSINS. And yet they don't object to you!

BARBARA. Do they obey all your orders?

UNDERSHAFT. I never give them any orders. When I speak to one of them it is, "Well, Jones, is the baby doing well? and has Mrs. Jones made a good recovery?"

"Nicely, thank you, sir." And that's all.

CUSINS. But Jones has to be kept in order. How do you maintain discipline among your men?

UNDERSHAFT. I don't. They do. You see, the one thing Jones won't stand is any rebellion from the man under him, or any assertion of social equality between the wife of the man with 4 shillings a week less than himself, and Mrs. Jones! Of course they all rebel against me, theoretically. Practically, every man of them keeps the man just below him in his place. I never meddle with them. I never bully them. I don't even bully Lazarus. I say that certain things are to be done; but I don't order anybody to do them. I don't say, mind you, that there is no ordering about and snubbing and even bullying. The men snub the boys and order them about; the carmen snub the sweepers; the artisans snub the unskilled laborers; the foremen drive and bully both the laborers and artisans; the assistant engineers find fault with the foremen; the chief engineers drop on the assistants; the departmental managers worry the chiefs; and the clerks have tall hats and hymnbooks and keep up the social tone by refusing to associate on equal terms with anybody. The result is a colossal profit, which comes to me.

CUSINS [revolted]. You really are a—well, what I was saying yesterday.

BARBARA. What was he saying yesterday?

UNDERSHAFT. Never mind, my dear. He thinks I have made you unhappy. Have I?

BARBARA. Do you think I can be happy in this vulgar silly dress? I! who have worn the uniform. Do you understand what you have done to me? Yesterday I had a man's soul in my hand. I set him in the way of life with his face to salvation. But when we took your money he turned back to drunkenness and derision. [With intense conviction.] I will never forgive you that. If I had a child, and you destroyed its body with your explosives—if you murdered Dolly with your horrible guns—I could forgive you if my forgiveness would open the gates of heaven to you. But to take a human soul from me, and turn it into the soul of a wolf! that is worse than any murder.

UNDERSHAFT. Does my daughter despair so easily? Can you strike a man to the heart and leave no mark on him?

BARBARA [her face lighting up]. Oh, you are right: he can never be lost now: where was my faith?

CUSINS. Oh, clever, clever devil!

BARBARA. You may be a devil; but God speaks through you sometimes. [She takes her father's hands and kisses them.] You have given me back my happiness: I feel it deep down now, though my spirit is troubled.

UNDERSHAFT. You have learnt something. That always feels at first as if you had lost something.

BARBARA. Well, take me to the factory of death; and let me learn something more. There must be some truth or other behind all this frightful irony. Come, Dolly. [She goes out.]

CUSINS. My guardian angel! [To UNDERSHAFT.] Avaunt! [He follows BARBARA.]

STEPHEN [quietly, at the writing table]. You must not mind Cusins, father. He is a very amiable good fellow; but he is a Greek scholar and naturally a little eccentric.

UNDERSHAFT. Ah, quite so. Thank you, Stephen. Thank you. [He goes out.]

STEPHEN *smiles patronizingly; buttons his coat responsibly; and crosses the room to the door.* LADY BRITOMART, *dressed for out-of-doors, opens it before he reaches it. She looks round for the others; looks at* STEPHEN; *and turns to go without a word.*

STEPHEN [*embarrassed*]. Mother—

LADY BRITOMART. Don't be apologetic, Stephen. And don't forget that you have outgrown your mother. [*She goes out.*]

Perivale St. Andrews lies between two Middlesex hills, half climbing the northern one. It is an almost smokeless town of white walls, roofs of narrow green slates or red tiles, tall trees, domes, campaniles, and slender chimney shafts, beautifully situated and beautiful in itself. The best view of it is obtained from the crest of a slope about half a mile to the east, where the high explosives are dealt with. The foundry lies hidden in the depths between, the tops of its chimneys sprouting like huge skittles into the middle distance. Across the crest runs an emplacement of concrete, with a firestep, and a parapet which suggests a fortification, because there is a huge cannon of the obsolete Woolwich Infant pattern peering across it at the town. The cannon is mounted on an experimental gun carriage: possibly the original model of the Undershaft disappearing rampart gun alluded to by STEPHEN. *The firestep, being a convenient place to sit, is furnished here and there with straw disc cushions; and at one place there is the additional luxury of a fur rug.*

BARBARA *is standing on the firestep, looking over the parapet towards the town. On her right is the cannon; on her left the end of a shed raised on piles, with a ladder of three or four steps up to the door, which opens outwards and has a little wooden landing at the threshold, with a fire bucket in the corner of the landing. Several dummy soldiers more or less mutilated, with straw protruding from their gashes, have been shoved out of the way under the landing. A few others are nearly upright against the shed; and one has fallen forward and lies, like a grotesque corpse, on the emplacement. The parapet stops short of the shed, leaving a gap which is the beginning of the path down the hill through the foundry to the town. The rug is on the firestep near this gap. Down on the emplacement behind the cannon is a trolley carrying a huge conical bombshell with a red band painted on it. Further to the right is the door of an office, which, like the sheds, is of the lightest possible construction.*

CUSINS *arrives by the path from the town.*

BARBARA. Well?

CUSINS. Not a ray of hope. Everything perfect! wonderful! real! It only needs a cathedral to be a heavenly city instead of a hellish one.

BARBARA. Have you found out whether they have done anything for old Peter Shirley?

CUSINS. They have found him a job as gatekeeper and timekeeper. He's frightfully miserable. He calls the time-keeping brainwork, and says he isn't used to it; and his gate lodge is so splendid that he's ashamed to use the rooms, and skulks in the scullery.

BARBARA. Poor Peter!

STEPHEN *arrives from the town. He carries a fieldglass.*

STEPHEN [*enthusiastically*]. Have you two seen the place? Why did you leave us?

CUSINS. I wanted to see everything I was not intended to see; and Barbara wanted to make the men talk.

STEPHEN. Have you found anything discreditable?

CUSINS. No. They call him Dandy Andy and are proud of his being a cunning old rascal; but it's all horribly, frightfully, immorally, unanswerably perfect.

SARAH *arrives.*

SARAH. Heavens! what a place! [*She crosses to the trolley.*] Did you see the nursing home!? [*She sits down on the shell.*]

STEPHEN. Did you see the libraries and schools!?

SARAH. Did you see the ball room and the banqueting chamber in the Town Hall!?

STEPHEN. Have you gone into the insurance fund, the pension fund, the building society, the various applications of cooperation!?

UNDERSHAFT *comes from the office, with a sheaf of telegrams in his hand.*

UNDERSHAFT. Well, have you seen everything? I'm sorry I was called away. [*Indicating the telegrams.*] Good news from Manchuria.

STEPHEN. Another Japanese victory?

UNDERSHAFT. Oh, I don't know. Which side wins does not concern us here. No: the good news is that the aerial battleship is a tremendous success. At the first trial it has wiped out a fort with three hundred soldiers in it.

CUSINS [*from the platform*]. Dummy soldiers?

UNDERSHAFT [*striding across to* STEPHEN *and kicking the prostrate dummy brutally out of his way*]. No: the real thing.

CUSINS *and* BARBARA *exchange glances. Then* CUSINS *sits on the step and buries his face in his hands.* BARBARA *gravely lays her hand on his shoulder. He looks up at her in whimsical desperation.*

UNDERSHAFT. Well, Stephen, what do you think of the place?

STEPHEN. Oh, magnificent. A perfect triumph of modern industry. Frankly, my dear father, I have been a fool: I had no idea of what it all meant: of the wonderful forethought, the power of organization, the administrative capacity, the financial genius, the colossal capital it represents. I have been repeating to myself as I came through your streets "Peace hath her victories no less renowned than War." I have only one misgiving about it all.

UNDERSHAFT. Out with it.

STEPHEN. Well, I cannot help thinking that all this provision for every want of your workmen may sap their independence and weaken their sense of responsibility. And greatly as we enjoyed our tea at that splendid restaurant—how they gave us all that luxury and cake and jam and cream for threepence I really cannot imagine!—still you must remember that restaurants break up home life. Look at the continent, for instance! Are you sure so much pampering is really good for the men's characters?

UNDERSHAFT. Well, you see, my dear boy, when you are organizing civilization you have to make up your mind whether trouble and anxiety are good things or not. If you decide that they are, then, I take it, you simply don't organize civilization; and there you are, with trouble and anxiety enough to make us all angels! But if you decide the other way, you may as well go through with it. However, Stephen, our characters are safe here. A sufficient dose of anxiety is always provided by the fact that we may be blown to smithereens at any moment.

SARAH. By the way, papa, where do you make the explosives?

UNDERSHAFT. In separate little sheds, like that one. When one of them blows up, it costs very little; and only the people quite close to it are killed.

STEPHEN, *who is quite close to it, looks at it rather scaredly, and moves away quickly to the cannon. At the same moment the door of the shed is thrown abruptly open; and a foreman in overalls and list slippers comes out on the little landing and holds the door for* LOMAX, *who appears in the doorway.*

LOMAX [*with studied coolness*]. My good fellow: you needn't get into a state of nerves. Nothing's going to happen to you; and I suppose it wouldn't be the end of the world if anything did. A little bit of British pluck is what you want, old chap. [*He descends and strolls across to* SARAH.]

UNDERSHAFT [*to the foreman*]. Anything wrong, Bilton?

BILTON [*with ironic calm*]. Gentleman walked into the high explosives shed and lit a cigaret, sir: that's all.

UNDERSHAFT. Ah, quite so. [*Going over to* LOMAX.] Do you happen to remember what you did with the match?

LOMAX. Oh come! I'm not a fool. I took jolly good care to blow it out before I chucked it away.

BILTON. The top of it was red hot inside, sir.

LOMAX. Well, suppose it was! I didn't chuck it into any of your messes.

UNDERSHAFT. Think no more of it, Mr. Lomax. By the way, would you mind lending me your matches.

LOMAX [*offering his box*]. Certainly.

UNDERSHAFT. Thanks. [*He pockets the matches.*]

LOMAX [*lecturing to the company generally*]. You know, these high explosives don't go off like gunpowder, except when they're in a gun. When they're spread loose, you can put a match to them without the least risk: they just burn quietly like a bit of paper. [*Warming to the scientific interest of the subject.*] Did you know that, Undershaft? Have you ever tried?

UNDERSHAFT. Not on a large scale, Mr. Lomax. Bilton will give you a sample of guncotton when you are leaving if you ask him. You can experiment with it at home. [BILTON *looks puzzled.*]

SARAH. Bilton will do nothing of the sort, papa. I suppose it's your business to blow up the Russians and Japs; but you might really stop short of blowing up poor Cholly. [BILTON *gives it up and retires into the shed.*]

LOMAX. My ownest, there is no danger. [*He sits beside her on the shell.*]

LADY BRITOMART *arrives from the town with a bouquet.*

LADY BRITOMART [*impetuously*]. Andrew: you shouldn't have let me see this place.

UNDERSHAFT. Why, my dear?

LADY BRITOMART. Never mind why: you shouldn't have: that's all. To think of all that [*indicating the town*] being yours! and that you have kept it to yourself all these years!

UNDERSHAFT. It does not belong to me. I belong to it. It is the Undershaft inheritance.

LADY BRITOMART. It is not. Your ridiculous cannons and that noisy banging foundry may be the Undershaft inheritance; but all that plate and linen, all that furniture and those houses and orchards and gardens belong to us. They belong to me: they are not a man's business. I won't give them up. You must be out of your senses to throw them all away; and if you persist in such folly, I will call in a doctor.

UNDERSHAFT [*stooping to smell the bouquet*]. Where did you get the flowers, my dear?

LADY BRITOMART. Your men presented them to me in your William Morris Labor Church.

CUSINS. Oh! It needed only that. A Labor Church! [*He mounts the firestep distractedly, and leans with his elbows on the parapet, turning his back to them.*]

LADY BRITOMART. Yes, with Morris's words in mosaic letters ten feet high round the dome. NO MAN IS GOOD ENOUGH TO BE ANOTHER MAN'S MASTER. The cynicism of it!

UNDERSHAFT. It shocked the men at first, I am afraid. But now they take no more notice of it than of the ten commandments in church.

LADY BRITOMART. Andrew: you are trying to put me off the subject of the inheritance by profane jokes. Well, you shan't. I don't ask it any longer for Stephen: he has inherited far too much of your perversity to be fit for it. But Barbara has rights as well as Stephen. Why should not Adolphus succeed to the inheritance? I could manage the town for him; and he can look after the cannons, if they are really necessary.

UNDERSHAFT. I should ask nothing better if Adolphus were a foundling. He is exactly the sort of new blood that is wanted in English business. But he's not a foundling; and there's an end of it. [*He makes for the office door.*]

CUSINS [*turning to them*]. Not quite. [*They all turn and stare at him.*] I think —Mind! I am not committing myself in any way as to my future course—but I think the foundling difficulty can be got over. [*He jumps down to the emplacement.*]

UNDERSHAFT [*coming back to him*]. What do you mean?

CUSINS. Well, I have something to say which is in the nature of a confession.

SARAH.
LADY BRITOMART. } Confession!
BARBARA.
STEPHEN.

LOMAX. Oh I say!

CUSINS. Yes, a confession. Listen, all. Until I met Barbara I thought myself in the main an honorable, truthful man, because I wanted the approval of my conscience more than I wanted anything else. But the moment I saw Barbara, I wanted her far more than the approval of my conscience.

LADY BRITOMART. Adolphus!

CUSINS. It is true. You accused me yourself, Lady Brit, of joining the Army to worship Barbara; and so I did. She bought my soul like a flower at a street corner; but she bought it for herself.

UNDERSHAFT. What! Not for Dionysos or another?

CUSINS. Dionysos and all the others are in herself. I adored what was divine in her, and was therefore a true worshipper. But I was romantic about her too. I thought she was a woman of the people, and that a marriage with a professor of Greek would be far beyond the wildest social ambitions of her rank.

LADY BRITOMART. Adolphus!!

LOMAX. Oh I say!!!

CUSINS. When I learnt the horrible truth—

LADY BRITOMART. What do you mean by the horrible truth, pray?

CUSINS. That she was enormously rich; that her grandfather was an earl; that her father was the Prince of Darkness—

[452]

UNDERSHAFT. Chut!

CUSINS. —and that I was only an adventurer trying to catch a rich wife, then I stooped to deceive her about my birth.

BARBARA [*rising*]. Dolly!

LADY BRITOMART. Your birth! Now, Adolphus, don't dare to make up a wicked story for the sake of these wretched cannons. Remember: I have seen photographs of your parents; and the Agent General for South Western Australia knows them personally and has assured me that they are most respectable married people.

CUSINS. So they are in Australia; but here they are outcasts. Their marriage is legal in Australia, but not in England. My mother is my father's deceased wife's sister; and in this island I am consequently a foundling. [*Sensation.*]

BARBARA. Silly! [*She climbs to the cannon, and leans, listening, in the angle it makes with the parapet.*]

CUSINS. Is the subterfuge good enough, Machiavelli?

UNDERSHAFT [*thoughtfully*]. Biddy: this may be a way out of the difficulty.

LADY BRITOMART. Stuff! A man can't make cannons any the better for being his own cousin instead of his proper self. [*She sits down on the rug with a bounce that expresses her downright contempt for their casuistry.*]

UNDERSHAFT [*to* CUSINS]. You are an educated man. That is against the tradition.

CUSINS. Once in ten thousand times it happens that the schoolboy is a born master of what they try to teach him. Greek has not destroyed my mind: it has nourished it. Besides, I did not learn it at an English public school.

UNDERSHAFT. Hm! Well, I cannot afford to be too particular: you have cornered the foundling market. Let it pass. You are eligible, Euripides: you are eligible.

BARBARA. Dolly: yesterday morning, when Stephen told us all about the tradition, you became very silent; and you have been strange and excited ever since. Were you thinking of your birth then?

CUSINS. When the finger of Destiny suddenly points at a man in the middle of his breakfast, it makes him thoughtful.

UNDERSHAFT. Aha! You have had your eye on the business, my young friend, have you?

CUSINS. Take care! There is an abyss of moral horror between me and your accursed aerial battleships.

UNDERSHAFT. Never mind the abyss for the present. Let us settle the practical details and leave your final decision open. You know that you will have to change your name. Do you object to that?

CUSINS. Would any man named Adolphus—any man called Dolly!—object to be called something else?

UNDERSHAFT. Good. Now, as to money! I propose to treat you handsomely from the beginning. You shall start at a thousand a year.

CUSINS [*with sudden heat, his spectacles twinkling with mischief*]. A thousand! You dare offer a miserable thousand to the son-in-law of a millionaire! No, by Heavens, Machiavelli! you shall not cheat me. You cannot do without me; and I can do without you. I must have two thousand five hundred a year for two years. At the end of that time, if I am a failure, I go. But if I am a success, and stay on, you must give me the other five thousand.

UNDERSHAFT. What other five thousand?

CUSINS. To make the two years up to five thousand a year. The two thousand five hundred is only half pay in case I should turn out a failure. The third year I must have ten per cent on the profits.

UNDERSHAFT [*taken aback*]. Ten per cent! Why, man, do you know what my profits are?

CUSINS. Enormous, I hope: otherwise I shall require twenty-five per cent.

UNDERSHAFT. But, Mr. Cusins, this is a serious matter of business. You are not bringing any capital into the concern.

CUSINS. What! no capital! Is my mastery of Greek no capital? Is my access to the subtlest thought, the loftiest poetry yet attained by humanity, no capital? My character! my intellect! my life! my career! what Barbara calls my soul! are these no capital? Say another word, and I double my salary.

UNDERSHAFT. Be reasonable—

CUSINS [*peremptorily*]. Mr. Undershaft: you have my terms. Take them or leave them.

UNDERSHAFT [*recovering himself*]. Very well. I note your terms; and I offer you half.

CUSINS [*disgusted*]. Half!

UNDERSHAFT [*firmly*]. Half.

CUSINS. You call yourself a gentleman; and you offer me half!!

UNDERSHAFT. I do not call myself a gentleman; but I offer you half.

CUSINS. This to your future partner! your successor! your son-in-law!

BARBARA. You are selling your own soul, Dolly, not mine. Leave me out of the bargain, please.

UNDERSHAFT. Come! I will go a step further for Barbara's sake. I will give you three fifths; but that is my last word.

CUSINS. Done!

LOMAX. Done in the eye! Why, *I* get only eight hundred, you know.

CUSINS. By the way, Mac, I am a classical scholar, not an arithmetical one. Is three fifths more than half or less?

UNDERSHAFT. More, of course.

CUSINS. I would have taken two hundred and fifty. How you can succeed in business when you are willing to pay all that money to a University don who is obviously not worth a junior clerk's wages!—well! What will Lazarus say?

UNDERSHAFT. Lazarus is a gentle romantic Jew who cares for nothing but string quartets and stalls at fashionable theatres. He will be blamed for your rapacity in money matters, poor fellow! as he has hitherto been blamed for mine. You are a shark of the first order, Euripides. So much the better for the firm!

BARBARA. Is the bargain closed, Dolly? Does your soul belong to him now?

CUSINS. No: the price is settled: that is all. The real tug of war is still to come. What about the moral question?

LADY BRITOMART. There is no moral question in the matter at all, Adolphus. You must simply sell cannons and weapons to people whose cause is right and just, and refuse them to foreigners and criminals.

UNDERSHAFT [*determinedly*]. No: none of that. You must keep the true faith of an Armorer, or you don't come in here.

CUSINS. What on earth is the true faith of an Armorer?

UNDERSHAFT. To give arms to all men who offer an honest price for them, without respect of persons or principles: to aristocrat and republican, to Nihilist and Tsar, to Capitalist and Socialist, to Protestant and Catholic, to burglar and policeman, to black man, white man and yellow man, to all sorts and conditions, all nationalities, all faiths, all follies, all causes and all crimes. The first Undershaft wrote up in his shop IF GOD GAVE THE HAND, let not Man withhold the sword. The second wrote up all have the right to fight: none have the right to judge. The third wrote up to Man the weapon: to Heaven the victory. The fourth had no literary turn; so he did not write up anything; but he sold cannons to Napoleon under the nose of George the Third. The fifth wrote up peace shall not prevail save with a sword in her hand. The sixth, my master, was the best of all. He wrote up nothing is ever done in this world until men are prepared to kill one another if it is not done. After that, there was nothing left for the seventh to say. So he wrote up, simply, unashamed.

Cusins. My good Machiavelli, I shall certainly write something up on the wall; only, as I shall write it in Greek, you won't be able to read it. But as to your Armorer's faith, if I take my neck out of the noose of my own morality I am not going to put it into the noose of yours. I shall sell cannons to whom I please and refuse them to whom I please. So there!

Undershaft. From the moment when you become Andrew Undershaft, you will never do as you please again. Don't come here lusting for power, young man.

Cusins. If power were my aim I should not come here for it. You have no power.

Undershaft. None of my own, certainly.

Cusins. I have more power than you, more will. You do not drive this place: it drives you. And what drives the place?

Undershaft [*enigmatically*]. A will of which I am a part.

Barbara [*startled*]. Father! Do you know what you are saying; or are you laying a snare for my soul?

Cusins. Don't listen to his metaphysics, Barbara. The place is driven by the most rascally part of society, the money hunters, the pleasure hunters, the military promotion hunters; and he is their slave.

Undershaft. Not necessarily. Remember the Armorer's Faith. I will take an order from a good man as cheerfully as from a bad one. If you good people prefer preaching and shirking to buying my weapons and fighting the rascals, don't blame me. I can make cannons: I cannot make courage and conviction. Bah! you tire me, Euripides, with your morality mongering. Ask Barbara: she understands. [*He suddenly reaches up and takes* Barbara's *hands, looking powerfully into her eyes.*] Tell him, my love, what power really means.

Barbara [*hypnotized*]. Before I joined the Salvation Army, I was in my own power; and the consequence was that I never knew what to do with myself. When I joined it, I had not time enough for all the things I had to do.

Undershaft [*approvingly*]. Just so. And why was that, do you suppose?

Barbara. Yesterday I should have said, because I was in the power of God. [*She resumes her self-possession, withdrawing her hands from his with a power equal to his own.*] But you came and shewed me that I was in the power of Bodger and Undershaft. Today I feel—oh! how can I put it into words? Sarah: do you remember the earthquake at Cannes, when we were little children?—how little the surprise of the first shock mattered compared to the dread and horror of waiting for the second? That is how I feel in this place today. I stood on the rock I thought eternal; and without a word of warning it reeled and crumbled under me. I was safe with an infinite wisdom watching me, an army marching to Salvation with me; and in a moment, at a stroke of your pen in a cheque book, I stood alone; and the heavens were empty. That was the first shock of the earthquake: I am waiting for the second.

UNDERSHAFT. Come, come, my daughter! don't make too much of your little tinpot tragedy. What do we do here when we spend years of work and thought and thousands of pounds of solid cash on a new gun or an aerial battleship that turns out just a hairsbreadth wrong after all? Scrap it. Scrap it without wasting another hour or another pound on it. Well, you have made for yourself something that you call a morality or a religion or what not. It doesn't fit the facts. Well, scrap it. Scrap it and get one that does fit. That is what is wrong with the world at present. It scraps its obsolete steam engines and dynamos; but it won't scrap its old prejudices and its old moralities and its old religions and its old political constitutions. What's the result? In machinery it does very well; but in morals and religion and politics it is working at a loss that brings it nearer bankruptcy every year. Don't persist in that folly. If your old religion broke down yesterday, get a newer and a better one for tomorrow.

BARBARA. Oh how gladly I would take a better one to my soul! But you offer me a worse one. [*Turning on him with sudden vehemence.*] Justify yourself: shew me some light through the darkness of this dreadful place, with its beautifully clean workshops, and respectable workmen, and model homes.

UNDERSHAFT. Cleanliness and respectability do not need justification, Barbara: they justify themselves. I see no darkness here, no dreadfulness. In your Salvation shelter I saw poverty, misery, cold and hunger. You gave them bread and treacle and dreams of heaven. I give from thirty shillings a week to twelve thousand a year. They find their own dreams; but I look after the drainage.

BARBARA. And their souls?

UNDERSHAFT. I save their souls just as I saved yours.

BARBARA [*revolted*]. You saved my soul! What do you mean?

UNDERSHAFT. I fed you and clothed you and housed you. I took care that you should have money enough to live handsomely—more than enough; so that you could be wasteful, careless, generous. That saved your soul from the seven deadly sins.

BARBARA [*bewildered*]. The seven deadly sins!

UNDERSHAFT. Yes, the deadly seven. [*Counting on his fingers.*] Food, clothing, firing, rent, taxes, respectability and children. Nothing can lift those seven millstones from Man's neck but money; and the spirit cannot soar until the millstones are lifted. I lifted them from your spirit. I enabled Barbara to become Major Barbara; and I saved her from the crime of poverty.

CUSINS. Do you call poverty a crime?

UNDERSHAFT. The worst of crimes. All the other crimes are virtues beside it: all the other dishonors are chivalry itself by comparison. Poverty blights whole cities; spreads horrible pestilences; strikes dead the very souls of all who come within sight, sound, or smell of it. What you call crime is nothing: a murder here and a theft there, a blow now and a curse then: what do they matter? they are only the accidents and illnesses of life: there are not fifty genuine professional criminals in London. But there are millions of poor people, abject people, dirty people, ill fed, ill clothed people. They poison us morally and physically: they kill the happiness of society: they force us to do away with our own liberties and to organize unnatural cruelties for fear they should rise against us and drag us down into their abyss. Only fools fear crime: we all fear poverty. Pah! [*turning on Barbara*] you talk of your half-saved ruffian in West Ham: you accuse me of dragging his soul back to perdition. Well, bring him to me here; and I will drag his soul back again to salvation for you. Not by words and dreams; but by thirtyeight shillings a week, a sound house in a handsome street, and a permanent job. In three weeks he will have a fancy waistcoat; in three months a tall hat and a chapel sitting; before the end of the year he will shake hands with a duchess at a Primrose League meeting, and join the Conservative Party.

BARBARA. And will he be the better for that?

UNDERSHAFT. You know he will. Don't be a hypocrite, Barbara. He will be better fed, better housed, better clothed, better behaved; and his children will be pounds heavier and bigger. That will be better than an American cloth mattress in a shelter, chopping firewood, eating bread and treacle, and being forced to kneel down from time to time to thank heaven for it: knee drill, I think you call it. It is cheap work converting starving men with a Bible in one hand and a slice of bread in the other. I will undertake to convert West Ham to Mahometanism on the same terms. Try your hand on my men: their souls are hungry because their bodies are full.

BARBARA. And leave the east end to starve?

UNDERSHAFT [*his energetic tone dropping into one of bitter and brooding remembrance*]. *I* was an east ender. I moralized and starved until one day I swore that I would be a full-fed free man at all costs; that nothing should stop me except a bullet, neither reason nor morals nor the lives of other men. I said, "Thou shalt starve ere I starve"; and with that word I became free and great. I was a dangerous man until I had my will: now I am a useful, beneficent, kindly person. That is the history of most self-made millionaires, I fancy. When it is the history of every Englishman we shall have an England worth living in.

LADY BRITOMART. Stop making speeches, Andrew. This is not the place for them.

UNDERSHAFT [*punctured*]. My dear: I have no other means of conveying my ideas.

LADY BRITOMART. Your ideas are nonsense. You got on because you were selfish and unscrupulous.

UNDERSHAFT. Not at all. I had the strongest scruples about poverty and starvation. Your moralists are quite unscrupulous about both: they make virtues of them. I had rather be a thief than a pauper. I had rather be a murderer than a slave. I don't want to be either; but if you force the alternative on me, then, by Heaven, I'll choose the braver and more moral one. I hate poverty and slavery worse than any other crimes whatsoever. And let me tell you this. Poverty and slavery have stood up for centuries to your sermons and leading articles: they will not stand up to my machine guns. Don't preach at them: don't reason with them. Kill them.

BARBARA. Killing. Is that your remedy for everything?

UNDERSHAFT. It is the final test of conviction, the only lever strong enough to overturn a social system, the only way of saying Must. Let six hundred and seventy fools loose in the streets; and three policemen can scatter them. But huddle them together in a certain house in Westminster; and let them go through certain ceremonies and call themselves certain names until at last they get the courage to kill; and your six hundred and seventy fools become a government. Your pious mob fills up ballot papers and imagines it is governing its masters; but the ballot paper that really governs is the paper that has a bullet wrapped up in it.

Cusins. That is perhaps why, like most intelligent people, I never vote.

Undershaft. Vote! Bah! When you vote, you only change the names of the cabinet. When you shoot, you pull down governments, inaugurate new epochs, abolish old orders and set up new. Is that historically true, Mr. Learned Man, or is it not?

Cusins. It is historically true. I loathe having to admit it. I repudiate your sentiments. I abhor your nature. I defy you in every possible way. Still, it is true. But it ought not to be true.

Undershaft. Ought! ought! ought! ought! ought! Are you going to spend your life saying ought, like the rest of our moralists? Turn your oughts into shalls, man. Come and make explosives with me. Whatever can blow men up can blow society up. The history of the world is the history of those who had courage enough to embrace this truth. Have you the courage to embrace it, Barbara?

Lady Britomart. Barbara: I positively forbid you to listen to your father's abominable wickedness. And you, Adolphus, ought to know better than to go about saying that wrong things are true. What does it matter whether they are true if they are wrong?

Undershaft. What does it matter whether they are wrong if they are true?

Lady Britomart [*rising*]. Children: come home instantly. Andrew: I am exceedingly sorry I allowed you to call on us. You are wickeder than ever. Come at once.

Barbara [*shaking her head*]. It's no use running away from wicked people, mamma.

Lady Britomart. It is every use. It shews your disapprobation of them.

Barbara. It does not save them.

Lady Britomart. I can see that you are going to disobey me. Sarah: are you coming home or are you not?

Sarah. I daresay it's very wicked of papa to make cannons; but I don't think I shall cut him on that account.

Lomax [*pouring oil on the troubled waters*]. The fact is, you know, there is a certain amount of tosh about this notion of wickedness. It doesn't work. You must look at facts. Not that I would say a word in favor of anything wrong; but then, you see, all sorts of chaps are always doing all sorts of things; and we have to fit them in somehow, don't you know. What I mean is that you can't go cutting everybody; and that's about what it comes to. [*Their rapt attention to his eloquence makes him nervous.*] Perhaps I don't make myself clear.

Lady Britomart. You are lucidity itself, Charles. Because Andrew is successful and has plenty of money to give to Sarah, you will flatter him and encourage him in his wickedness.

Lomax [*unruffled*]. Well, where the carcase is, there will the eagles be gathered, don't you know. [*To* Undershaft.] Eh? What?

Undershaft. Precisely. By the way, may I call you Charles?

LOMAX. Delighted. Cholly is the usual ticket.

UNDERSHAFT [*to* LADY BRITOMART]. Biddy—

LADY BRITOMART [*violently*]. Don't dare call me Biddy. Charles Lomax: you are a fool. Adolphus Cusins: you are a Jesuit. Stephen: you are a prig. Barbara: you are a lunatic. Andrew: you are a vulgar tradesman. Now you all know my opinion; and my conscience is clear, at all events. [*She sits down with a vehemence that the rug fortunately softens.*]

UNDERSHAFT. My dear: you are the incarnation of morality. [*She snorts.*] Your conscience is clear and your duty done when you have called everybody names. Come, Euripides! it is getting late; and we all want to go home. Make up your mind.

CUSINS. Understand this, you old demon—

LADY BRITOMART. Adolphus!

UNDERSHAFT. Let him alone, Biddy. Proceed, Euripides.

CUSINS. You have me in a horrible dilemma. I want Barbara.

UNDERSHAFT. Like all young men, you greatly exaggerate the difference between one young woman and another.

BARBARA. Quite true, Dolly.

CUSINS. I also want to avoid being a rascal.

UNDERSHAFT [*with biting contempt*]. You lust for personal righteousness, for self-approval, for what you call a good conscience, for what Barbara calls salvation, for what I call patronizing people who are not so lucky as yourself.

CUSINS. I do not: all the poet in me recoils from being a good man. But there are things in me that I must reckon with. Pity—

UNDERSHAFT. Pity! The scavenger of misery.

CUSINS. Well, love.

UNDERSHAFT. I know. You love the needy and the outcast: you love the oppressed races, the Negro, the Indian ryot, the underdog everywhere. Do you love the Japanese? Do you love the French? Do you love the English?

CUSINS. No. Every true Englishman detests the English. We are the wickedest nation on earth; and our success is a moral horror.

UNDERSHAFT. That is what comes of your gospel of love, is it?

CUSINS. May I not love even my father-in-law?

UNDERSHAFT. Who wants your love, man? By what right do you take the liberty of offering it to me? I will have your due heed and respect, or I will kill you. But your love! Damn your impertinence!

CUSINS [*grinning*]. I may not be able to control my affections, Mac.

UNDERSHAFT. You are fencing, Euripides. You are weakening: your grip is slipping. Come! try your last weapon. Pity and love have broken in your hand: forgiveness is still left.

CUSINS. No: forgiveness is a beggar's refuge. I am with you there: we must pay our debts.

UNDERSHAFT. Well said. Come! you will suit me. Remember the words of Plato.

CUSINS [*starting*]. Plato! You dare quote Plato to me!

UNDERSHAFT. Plato says, my friend, that society cannot be saved until either the Professors of Greek take to making gunpowder, or else the makers of gunpowder become Professors of Greek.

CUSINS. Oh, tempter, cunning tempter!

UNDERSHAFT. Come! choose, man, choose.

CUSINS. But perhaps Barbara will not marry me if I make the wrong choice.

BARBARA. Perhaps not.

CUSINS [*desperately perplexed*]. You hear!

BARBARA. Father: do you love nobody?

UNDERSHAFT. I love my best friend.

LADY BRITOMART. And who is that, pray?

UNDERSHAFT. My bravest enemy. That is the man who keeps me up to the mark.

CUSINS. You know, the creature is really a sort of poet in his way. Suppose he is a great man, after all!

UNDERSHAFT. Suppose you stop talking and make up your mind, my young friend.

CUSINS. But you are driving me against my nature. I hate war.

UNDERSHAFT. Hatred is the coward's revenge for being intimidated. Dare you make war on war? Here are the means: my friend Mr. Lomax is sitting on them.

LOMAX [*springing up*]. Oh I say! You don't mean that this thing is loaded, do you? My ownest: come off it.

SARAH [*sitting placidly on the shell*]. If I am to be blown up, the more thoroughly it is done the better. Don't fuss, Cholly.

LOMAX [*to* UNDERSHAFT, *strongly remonstrant*]. Your own daughter, you know!

UNDERSHAFT. So I see. [*To* CUSINS.] Well, my friend, may we expect you here at six tomorrow morning?

CUSINS [*firmly*]. Not on any account. I will see the whole establishment blown up with its own dynamite before I will get up at five. My hours are healthy, rational hours: eleven to five.

UNDERSHAFT. Come when you please: before a week you will come at six and stay until I turn you out for the sake of your health. [*Calling.*] Bilton! [*He turns to* LADY BRITOMART, *who rises.*] My dear: let us leave these two young people to themselves for a moment. [BILTON *comes from the shed.*] I am going to take you through the guncotton shed.

BILTON [*barring the way*]. You can't take anything explosive in here, sir.

LADY BRITOMART. What do you mean? Are you alluding to me?

BILTON [*unmoved*]. No, ma'am. Mr. Undershaft has the other gentleman's matches in his pocket.

LADY BRITOMART [*abruptly*]. Oh! I beg your pardon. [*She goes into the shed.*]

UNDERSHAFT. Quite right, Bilton, quite right: here you are. [*He gives* BILTON *the box of matches.*] Come, Stephen. Come, Charles. Bring Sarah. [*He passes into the shed.*]

BILTON *opens the box and deliberately drops the matches into the fire-bucket.*

LOMAX. Oh! I say. [BILTON *stolidly hands him the empty box.*] Infernal nonsense! Pure scientific ignorance! [*He goes in.*]

SARAH. Am I all right, Bilton?

BILTON. You'll have to put on list slippers, miss: that's all. We've got 'em inside. [*She goes in.*]

STEPHEN [*very seriously to* CUSINS]. Dolly, old fellow, think. Think before you decide. Do you feel that you are a sufficiently practical man? It is a huge undertaking, an enormous responsibility. All this mass of business will be Greek to you.

CUSINS. Oh, I think it will be much less difficult than Greek.

STEPHEN. Well, I just want to say this before I leave you to yourselves. Don't let anything I have said about right and wrong prejudice you against this great

Major Barbara

chance in life. I have satisfied myself that the business is one of the highest character and a credit to our country. [*Emotionally.*] I am very proud of my father. I— [*Unable to proceed, he presses* CUSINS' *hand and goes hastily into the shed, followed by* BILTON.]

BARBARA *and* CUSINS, *left alone together, look at one another silently.*

CUSINS. Barbara: I am going to accept this offer.

BARBARA. I thought you would.

CUSINS. You understand, don't you, that I had to decide without consulting you. If I had thrown the burden of the choice on you, you would sooner or later have despised me for it.

BARBARA. Yes: I did not want you to sell your soul for me any more than for this inheritance.

CUSINS. It is not the sale of my soul that troubles me: I have sold it too often to care about that. I have sold it for a professorship. I have sold it for an income. I have sold it to escape being imprisoned for refusing to pay taxes for hangmen's ropes and unjust wars and things that I abhor. What is all human conduct but the daily and hourly sale of our souls for trifles? What I am now selling it for is neither money nor position nor comfort, but for reality and for power.

BARBARA. You know that you will have no power, and that he has none.

CUSINS. I know. It is not for myself alone. I want to make power for the world.

BARBARA. I want to make power for the world too; but it must be spiritual power.

CUSINS. I think all power is spiritual: these cannons will not go off by themselves. I have tried to make spiritual power by teaching Greek. But the world can never be really touched by a dead language and a dead civilization. The people must have power; and the people cannot have Greek. Now the power that is made here can be wielded by all men.

BARBARA. Power to burn women's houses down and kill their sons and tear their husbands to pieces.

CUSINS. You cannot have power for good without having power for evil too. Even mother's milk nourishes murderers as well as heroes. This power which only tears men's bodies to pieces has never been so horribly abused as the intellectual power, the imaginative power, the poetic, religious power that can enslave men's souls. As a teacher of Greek I gave the intellectual man weapons against the common man. I now want to give the common man weapons against the intellectual man. I love the common people. I want to arm them against the lawyers, the doctors, the priests, the literary men, the professors, the artists, and the politicians, who, once in authority, are more disastrous and tyrannical than all the fools, rascals, and impostors. I want a power simple enough for common men to use, yet strong enough to force the intellectual oligarchy to use its genius for the general good.

BARBARA. Is there no higher power than that [*pointing to the shell*]?

CUSINS. Yes; but that power can destroy the higher powers just as a tiger can destroy a man: therefore Man must master that power first. I admitted this when the Turks and Greeks were last at war. My best pupil went out to fight for Hellas. My parting gift to him was not a copy of Plato's Republic, but a revolver and a hundred Undershaft cartridges. The blood of every Turk he shot—if he shot any—is on my head as well as on Undershaft's. That act committed me to this place for ever. Your father's challenge has beaten me. Dare I make war on war? I dare. I must. I will. And now, is it all over between us?

BARBARA [*touched by his evident dread of her answer*]. Silly baby Dolly! How could it be!

CUSINS [*overjoyed*]. Then you—you—you— Oh for my drum! [*He flourishes imaginary drumsticks.*]

BARBARA [*angered by his levity*]. Take care, Dolly, take care. Oh, if only I could get away from you and from father and from it all! if I could have the wings of a dove and fly away to heaven!

CUSINS. And leave me!

BARBARA. Yes, you, and all the other naughty mischievous children of men. But I can't. I was happy in the Salvation Army for a moment. I escaped from the world into a paradise of enthusiasm and prayer and soul saving; but the moment our money ran short, it all came back to Bodger: it was he who saved our people: he, and the Prince of Darkness, my papa. Undershaft and Bodger: their hands stretch everywhere: when we feed a starving fellow creature, it is with their bread, because there is no other bread; when we tend the sick, it is in the hospitals they endow; if we turn from the churches they build, we must kneel on the stones of the streets they pave. As long as that lasts, there is no getting away from them. Turning our backs on Bodger and Undershaft is turning our backs on life.

CUSINS. I thought you were determined to turn your back on the wicked side of life.

BARBARA. There is no wicked side: life is all one. And I never wanted to shirk my share in whatever evil must be endured, whether it be sin or suffering. I wish I could cure you of middle-class ideas, Dolly.

CUSINS [*gasping*]. Middle cl—! A snub! A social snub to me! from the daughter of a foundling!

BARBARA. That is why I have no class, Dolly: I come straight out of the heart of the whole people. If I were middle-class I should turn my back on my father's business; and we should both live in an artistic drawing room, with you reading the reviews in one corner, and I in the other at the piano, playing Schumann: both very superior persons, and neither of us a bit of use. Sooner than that, I would sweep out the guncotton shed, or be one of Bodger's barmaids. Do you know what would have happened if you had refused papa's offer?

CUSINS. I wonder!

BARBARA. I should have given you up and married the man who accepted it. After all, my dear old mother has more sense than any of you. I felt like her when I saw this place—felt that I must have it —that never, never, never could I let it go; only she thought it was the houses and the kitchen ranges and the linen and china, when it was really all the human souls to be saved: not weak souls in starved bodies, sobbing with gratitude for a scrap of bread and treacle, but full-fed, quarrelsome, snobbish, uppish creatures, all standing on their little rights and dignities, and thinking that my father ought to be greatly obliged to them for making so much money for him—and so he ought. That is where salvation is really wanted. My father shall never throw it in my teeth again that my converts were bribed with bread. [*She is transfigured.*] I have got rid of the bribe of bread. I have got rid of the bribe of heaven. Let God's work be done for its own sake: the work he had to create us to do because it cannot be done except by living men and women. When I die, let him be in my debt, not I in his; and let me forgive him as becomes a woman of my rank.

CUSINS. Then the way of life lies through the factory of death?

BARBARA. Yes, through the raising of hell to heaven and of man to God, through the unveiling of an eternal light in the Valley of The Shadow. [*Seizing him with both hands.*] Oh, did you think my courage would never come back? did you believe that I was a deserter? that I, who have stood in the streets, and taken my people to my heart, and talked of the holiest and greatest things with them, could ever turn back and chatter foolishly to fashionable people about nothing in a drawing room? Never, never, never, never: Major Barbara will die with the colors. Oh! and I have my dear little Dolly boy still; and he has found me my place and my work. Glory Hallelujah! [*She kisses him.*]

CUSINS. My dearest: consider my delicate health. I cannot stand as much happiness as you can.

BARBARA. Yes: it is not easy work being in love with me, is it? But it's good for you. [*She runs to the shed, and calls, childlike.*] Mamma! Mamma! [BILTON *comes out of the shed, followed by* UNDERSHAFT.] I want Mamma.

UNDERSHAFT. She is taking off her list slippers, dear. [*He passes on to* CUSINS.] Well? What does she say?

CUSINS. She has gone right up into the skies.

LADY BRITOMART [*coming from the shed and stopping on the steps, obstructing* SARAH, *who follows with* LOMAX. BARBARA *clutches like a baby at her mother's skirt*]. Barbara: when will you learn to be independent and to act and think for yourself? I know as well as possible what that cry of "Mamma, Mamma," means. Always running to me!

SARAH [*touching* LADY BRITOMART'S *ribs with her finger tips and imitating a bicycle horn*]. Pip! pip!

LADY BRITOMART [*highly indignant*]. How dare you say Pip! pip! to me, Sarah? You are both very naughty children. What do you want, Barbara?

BARBARA. I want a house in the village to live in with Dolly. [*Dragging at the skirt.*] Come and tell me which one to take.

UNDERSHAFT [*to* CUSINS]. Six o'clock tomorrow morning, Euripides.

THE END

THE PHILADELPHIA STORY
by PHILIP BARRY

CHARACTERS

SETH LORD
MARGARET LORD
ALEXANDER LORD
TRACY LORD
DINAH LORD
WILLIAM TRACY
C. K. DEXTER HAVEN
ELIZABETH IMBRIE

MACAULAY CONNOR
GEORGE KITTREDGE
DR. PARSONS
THOMAS
EDWARD
ELSIE
MAY
MAC

ACTION AND SCENE: *The play takes place in the course of twenty-four hours at the Seth Lords' house in the country near Philadelphia. The Time is the present, late June, and the Scenes are as follows:*

ACT I. The Sitting Room. Late morning, Friday
ACT II. Scene 1: The Porch. Late evening, Friday
Scene 2: The Porch. Early morning, Saturday
ACT III. The Sitting Room. Late morning, Saturday

ACT I

[*The Sitting Room of the Lords' house in the country near Philadelphia is a large, comfortably furnished room of a somewhat faded elegance containing a number of very good Victorian pieces. The entrance from the Hall is at Right, upstage, down two broad, shallow steps. The entrance into what the family still call "the Parlor" is through double doors downstage Right. At Left are two glass doors leading to the Porch. A writing desk stands between them. There is a large marble fireplace in the back wall and a grand piano in the corner at Left. Chairs and a table are at downstage Right and at downstage Left another table, an easy chair and a sofa. There is a large and fine portrait over the fireplace and other paintings here and there. A wall cabinet contains a quantity of bric-a-brac and there is more of it, together with a number of signed photographs in silver frames, upon the tables and piano. There are also several cardboard boxes strewn about. It is late on a Friday morning, in June, an overcast day.* DINAH, *who is all of thirteen years old, is stretched out on the sofa reading a set of printers' galley proofs.* TRACY, *a strikingly lovely girl of 24, sits in the chair at Left, a leather writing set upon her knees, scribbling notes. She wears slacks and a blouse.* MARGARET LORD, *their mother, a young and smart 47, comes in from the Hall with three more boxes in*

Copyright 1939 by Philip Barry and Ellen S. Barry.

[464]

The Philadelphia Story

her arms. *She places them upon the table near* TRACY.]

MARGARET. I'm terribly afraid that some of the cards for these last-minute presents have got themselves mixed. Look at them, Tracy—perhaps you can tell.

TRACY. In a minute, Mother. I'm up to my neck in these blank thank-you notes. [DINAH *folds one of the proof sheets she is reading under another.*]

DINAH. This stinks.

MARGARET. Not "stinks," darling. If absolutely necessary, "smells"—but only if absolutely necessary. What is it?

DINAH. I found it in Sandy's room. It's something that's going to be in a magazine. It certainly stinks, all right.

MARGARET. Keep out of your brother's things, dear—and his house. [*She studies a list of names.*] Ninety-four for the ceremony, five hundred and six for the reception—I don't know where we'll put them all, if it should rain.

DINAH. It won't rain.

MARGARET. Uncle Willie wanted to insure against it with Lloyd's but I wouldn't let him. If I was God and someone bet I wouldn't let it rain, I'd show him fast enough. This second page is solid Cadwalader. Twenty-six.

DINAH. That's a lot of Cadwalader.

MARGARET. One, my child, is a lot of Cadwalader.

TRACY. How do you spell omelet?

MARGARET. O-m-m-e-l-e-t.

TRACY. I thought there was another "l."

MARGARET. The omelet dish from the—?

TRACY. You said it was an omelet dish.

MARGARET. It might be for fish.

TRACY. "Fish dish"? Sounds idiotic.

MARGARET. I should simply say "Thank you so much for your lovely silver dish."

TRACY. Here's the tag. "Old Dutch Muffin Ear, Circa 1810." What the—? [*She drops the card.*] I am simply enchanted with your old Dutch Muffin Ear—with which my husband and I will certainly hear any muffin coming a mile away.

DINAH. Lookit, Tracy: don't you think you've done enough notes for one day?

TRACY. Don't disturb me. [*She examines another card.*] From Cousin Horace Macomber, one pair of game shears, looking like hell. [*Picks up shears.*]

DINAH. He's so awful. What did he send the other time?

TRACY. No one to speak of sent anything the other time.

MARGARET. It's such a pity your brother Junius can't be here for your wedding. London's so far away.

DINAH. I miss old Junius: you did a good job when you had him, Mother.

MARGARET. The first is always the best. They deteriorate as you go on.

TRACY. There was no occasion to send anything the other time.

DINAH [*Reading the proof sheets.*] This is certainly pretty rooty-tooty all right.

TRACY. It could scarcely be considered a wedding at all, the other time. When you run off to Maryland, on a sudden impulse, the way Dexter and I did—

DINAH. Ten months is quite long to be married, though. You can have a baby in nine, can't you?

TRACY. I guess—if you put your mind to it.

DINAH. Why didn't you?

TRACY. Mother, don't you think it's time for her nap?

DINAH. I imagine you and George'll have slews of 'em.

TRACY. I hope so—all like you, dear, with the same wild grace. [*She rises from*

[465]

[handwritten at top: Is not either a comedy or a tragic, but rather a melodrama. Has the qualities of being tragic, but turns out quite happy at the end.]

Drama

[handwritten in margin: Going to happy thing?]

her chair with a box of envelopes, which she places upon the desk.]

DINAH. Lookit: "the other time"—he's back from wherever he's been.

MARGARET. What do you mean?

DINAH. Dexter, of course. I saw his car in front of his house: the roadster. It must be him.

MARGARET. When? When did you?

DINAH. This morning, early, when I was out exercising The Hoofer.

MARGARET. Why didn't you tell us? [TRACY *moves to her unconcernedly.*]

TRACY. I'm not worried, Mother. The only trouble Mr. C. K. Dexter Haven ever gave me was when he married me.—You might say the same for one Seth Lord. If you'd just face it squarely as I did—

MARGARET. That will do! I will allow none of you to criticize your father.

TRACY. What are we expected to do when he treats you—

MARGARET. Did you hear me, Tracy?

TRACY. All right, I give up.

MARGARET.—And in view of this second attempt of yours, it might pay you to remind yourself that neither of us has proved to be a very great success as a wife.

TRACY. We just picked the wrong first husbands, that's all.

MARGARET. That is an extremely vulgar remark.

TRACY. Oh, who cares about either of them any more— [*She leans over the back of* MARGARET's *chair and hugs her.*] Golly Moses, I'm going to be happy now!

MARGARET. Darling.

TRACY. Isn't George an angel?

MARGARET. George is an angel.

TRACY. Is he handsome, or is he not?

MARGARET. George is handsome.

TRACY. Suds. I'm a lucky girl. [*She gathers up her boxes and writing case.*]

DINAH. *I* like Dexter. [TRACY *moves toward the Hall doorway.*]

TRACY. Really? Why don't you ask him to lunch, or something? [*And goes out.*]

DINAH [*looking after her*]. She's awfully mean about him, isn't she?

MARGARET. He was rather mean to her, my dear.

DINAH. Did he really sock her?

MARGARET. Don't say "sock," darling. "Strike" is quite an ugly enough word.

DINAH. But did he really?

MARGARET. I'm afraid I don't know the details.

DINAH. Cruelty and drunkenness, it said.

MARGARET. Dinah!

DINAH. It was right in the papers.

MARGARET. You read too much. You'll spoil your eyes.

DINAH. I think it's an awful thing to say about a man. I don't think they like things like that said about them.

MARGARET. I'm sure they don't. [DINAH *picks up the proof sheets again.*]

DINAH. Father's going to be hopping when he reads all this about himself in that magazine, *Destiny,* when it comes out.

MARGARET. All what? *About whom?*

DINAH. Father—that they're going to publish.

MARGARET. Dinah, what *are* you talking about?

DINAH. It's what they call proof sheets for some article they're going to call "Broadway and Finance," and Father's in it, and so they just sent it on to Sandy—sort of you know, on approval. It was just there on the table in his room, and so I—

MARGARET. But the article! What does the article say? [*She takes the proof sheets and examines them.*]

[466]

DINAH. Oh, it's partly about Father backing three shows for that dancer—what's her name—Tina Mara—and his early history—and about the stables—and why he's living in New York, instead of with us any more, and—

MARGARET. Great heaven—what on earth can we do?

DINAH. Couldn't Father sue them for—for liable?

MARGARET. But it's true—it's all— [*She glances at* DINAH.] That is, I mean to say—

DINAH. I don't think the part about Tina Mara is, the way they put it. It's simply full of innundo.

MARGARET. Of what?

DINAH. Of innundo. [*She rests her chin on her hand and stares into space.*] Oh, I do wish something would happen here. Nothing ever possibly in the least ever happens. [*Then suddenly hops up and goes to her mother.*] Next year can I go to the Conservatory in New York? They teach you to sing and dance and act and everything at once. *Can* I, Mother?

MARGARET. Save your dramatics, Dinah. [*She folds the proof sheets and puts them down.*] Oh, why didn't Sandy tell me!

DINAH. Mother, why won't Tracy at least *ask* her own *father* to her *wedding?*

MARGARET. Your sister has very definite opinions about certain things. [*She moves toward the desk at Left.*]

DINAH. [*following her*]. She's sort of— you know—hard, isn't she?

MARGARET. Not hard—none of my children is that, I hope. Tracy sets exceptionally high standards for herself, that's all— and although she lives up to them, other people aren't always quite able to. If your Uncle Willie Tracy comes in, tell him to wait. I want to see him. [*Having put the desk in order, she moves toward the Porch door.*]

DINAH. Tell me one thing: don't you think it's stinking not at least to *want* Father? [MARGARET *stops in the doorway and turns to her.*]

MARGARET. Yes, darling, between ourselves I think it's good and stinking. [*And goes out.*]

DINAH.—And I bet if Dexter knew what she— [*She waits a moment, then goes to the telephone and dials four numbers.*] Hello, may I please speak to Mr. Dexter Haven—what?—Dexter! It's you! [*Then affectionately.*] A very great pleasure to have you back.—Dinah, you goat, Dinah Lord. What?—You bet!—Lookit, Dexter, Tracy says why don't you come right over for lunch? What? But she told me to ask you.—Listen, though, maybe it would be better if you'd—Hello!—Hello! [*She replaces the telephone as* TRACY *comes in from the Hall with a large roll of paper.*]

TRACY. Who was that?

DINAH. Wrong number. [TRACY *spreads the roll of paper out on the table.*]

TRACY. Listen, darling, give me a hand with this cockeyed seating arrangement, will you? At least hold it down.—George doesn't want the Grants at the bridal table. [ALEXANDER (SANDY) LORD, 26, *comes in from the Hall.*] He says they're fast. He—

SANDY. Hello, kids.

TRACY. Sandy! [*She reaches up to him, hugs him.*]

SANDY. Where's Mother?

TRACY. She's around. How's New York? How's Sue?—How's the baby?

SANDY. Blooming. They sent their love, sorry they can't make the wedding. Is there a party tonight, of course?

TRACY. Aunt Geneva's throwing a monster.

SANDY. Boy, am I going to get plastered. [*To* DINAH.] Hello, little fellah.

DINAH. Hello, yourself. [*He gives her a small, flat box.*]

SANDY. This is for you, Mug. Get the three race horses into the paddock. It's tough. Work it out.

DINAH. Oh, thanks! [*She begins to work at the puzzle.*]

SANDY [*to* TRACY]. Sue's and my wedding present comes by registered mail, Tracy—and a pretty penny it set me back.

TRACY. You're a bonny boy, Sandy. I love you.

SANDY. Mutual. [MARGARET *re-enters from the Porch.*]

MARGARET. I was wondering about you. [SANDY *goes to her and embraces her.*]

SANDY. Give us a kiss.—You look fine.—Imagine this, a *grand*mother! How's everything?

MARGARET. Absolute chaos.

SANDY. Just how you like it, eh? Just when you function best!

MARGARET. How's my precious grandchild?

SANDY. Couldn't be better, Sue too. Ten more days in the hospital, and back home they'll be.

MARGARET. I broke into your house and did up the nursery.

SANDY. Good girl. Where's George, Tracy?

TRACY. He's staying in the Gatehouse. He still had business things to clear up and I thought he'd be quieter there.

SANDY. Did he see his picture in *Dime*? Was he sore at the "Former Coal Miner" caption? [MARGARET *picks up the proof sheets once more.*]

MARGARET. What about this absurd article about your father and—er—Tina Mara in *Destiny,* Sandy? Can't it be stopped?

TRACY. About Father and—? Let me see! [*She takes the proof sheets.*]

SANDY. Where'd you get hold of that? [*He tries unsuccessfully to recover them.*]

MARGARET. Get ready for lunch, Dinah.

DINAH. In a minute. I'm busy. [*She flops down on the Hall step and continues to work at her puzzle.*]

TRACY [*reading*]. Oh, the absolute devils!—Who publishes *Destiny*?

SANDY. Sidney Kidd.—Also *Dime*, also *Spy*, the picture sheet. I worked on *Dime* for two summers. You know that.

TRACY. Stopped? It's got to be! I'll go to him myself.

SANDY. A fat lot of good that would do. You're too much alike. God save us from the strong. [*He seats himself.*] I saw Kidd the day before yesterday. It took about three hours, but I finally got through to him.

TRACY. What happened?

SANDY. I think I fixed things.

TRACY. How?

SANDY. That would be telling.

MARGARET. Just so long as your father never hears of it.

SANDY. I had a copy of the piece made and sent it around to his flat, with a little note saying, "How do you like it?" [TRACY *laughs shortly.*]

TRACY. You are a fellah.

MARGARET. Sandy!

SANDY. Why not? Let him worry a little.

TRACY. Let him worry a lot! [THOMAS *enters from Hall.*]

SANDY. Yes, Thomas?

THOMAS. Mr. Connor and the lady say they will be down directly, sir.

SANDY. Thanks, that's fine. Tell May or Elsie to look after Miss Imbrie, will you?

THOMAS. Very good, sir. [*He goes out.*]

MARGARET. What's all this?

TRACY. "Mr. Connor and—?"

The Philadelphia Story

SANDY. Mike Connor—Macaulay Connor, his name is.—And—er—Elizabeth Imbrie. I'm putting them up for over the wedding. They're quite nice, you'll like them.

TRACY. You asked people to stay in this house without even asking us?

MARGARET. I think it's very queer indeed.

TRACY. I think it's queerer than that—*I* think it's paranoiac.

SANDY. Keep your shirt on.—I just sort of drifted into them and we sort of got to talking about what riots weddings are as a rule, and they'd never been to a Philadelphia one, and—

TRACY. You're lying, Sandy.—I can always tell.

SANDY. Now look here, Tracy—

TRACY. Look where? "Elizabeth Imbrie"—I know that name! She's a—wait—damn your eyes, Sandy, she's a photographer!

SANDY. For a fact?

TRACY. For a couple of facts—and a famous one!

SANDY. Well, it might be nice to have some good shots of the wedding.

TRACY. What are they doing here?

SANDY. Just now I suppose they're brushing up and going to the bathroom. They're very interesting people. [*He moves uneasily about the room.*] She's practically an artist, and he's written a couple of books—and—and I thought you liked interesting people. [DINAH *rises from her step.*]

DINAH. *I* do!

TRACY [*suddenly*]. I know—now I know! They're from *Destiny*.—*Destiny* sent them!

MARGARET. *Destiny?*

SANDY. You're just a mass of intuition, Tray.

TRACY. Well, they can go right back again.

SANDY. No, they can't. Not till they get their story.

TRACY. Story? What story?

SANDY. The Philadelphia story.

MARGARET. And what on earth's that?

SANDY. Well, it seems Kidd has had Connor and Imbrie and a couple of others down here for two months doing the town: I mean writing it up. It's to come out in three parts in the Autumn. "Industrial Philadelphia," "Historical Philadelphia"—and then the third—

TRACY. I'm going to be sick.

SANDY. Yes, dear: "Fashionable Philadelphia."

TRACY. I *am* sick.

MARGARET. But why us? Surely there are other families who—

TRACY. Yes—why not the Drexels or the Biddles or the *qu'est-ce-que-c'est* Cassatts? [SANDY *seats himself again.*]

SANDY. We go even further back: it's those Quakers.—And of course there's your former marriage and your looks and your general prowess in golf and fox-hunting, with a little big game on the side, and your impending second marriage into the coal fields—

TRACY. Never mind that!

SANDY. I don't, but they do. It's news, darling, news.

MARGARET. Is there no such thing as privacy any more?

TRACY. Only in bed, Mother, and not always there.

SANDY. Anyhow, I thought I was licked—and what else could I do?

TRACY. A trade, eh? So we're to let them publish the inside story of my wedding in order to keep Father's wretched little affair quiet!

MARGARET. It's utterly and completely disgusting.

SANDY. It was my suggestion, not Kidd's. I may have been put in the way of making it, I don't know. It's hard to tell, with a future President of the United States.

TRACY. What's the writer's name again?

SANDY. Connor, Macaulay Connor. I don't think he likes the assignment any more than we do—the gal either. They were handling the Industrial end. [TRACY *goes to the telephone, and dials.*]

TRACY. My heart's breaking for them.

MARGARET. I don't know what the world is coming to. It's an absolute invasion: two strange people tramping through the house, prying and investigating—

TRACY. Maybe we're going through a revolution without knowing it. [*To the telephone.*] Hello, is Mr. Briggs there?— This is Tracy Lord, Mr. Briggs.—Look, I wonder if you happen to have on hand any books by Macaulay Connor? [SANDY *rises.*]—You have? Could you surely send them out this afternoon?—Thanks, Mr. Briggs, you're sweet. [*She replaces the telephone, raging.*]—If they've got to have a story, I'll give them a story—I'll give them one they can't get through the mails!

SANDY. Oh—oh—I was afraid of this.

TRACY. Who the hell do they think they are, barging in on peaceful people—watching every little mannerism—jotting down notes on how we sit, and stand, and eat and move—

DINAH [*eagerly*]. Will they do that?

TRACY.—And all in the horrible, snide corkscrew English! Well, if we have to submit to it to save Father's face—which incidentally doesn't deserve it—I'm for giving them a picture of home life that will stand their hair on end.

MARGARET. You will do nothing of the sort, Tracy.

SANDY. She thinks she'll be the outrageous Miss Lord. The fact is, she'll probably be Sweetness and Light to the neck.

TRACY. Oh, will I!

SANDY. You don't know yet what being under the microscope does to people. I felt it a little coming out in the car. It's a funny feeling.

MARGARET. It's odd how self-conscious we've all become over the worldly possessions that once made us so confident.

SANDY. I know: you catch yourself explaining away your dough, the way you would a black eye: you've just run into it in the dark or something.

MARGARET. We shall be ourselves with them, very much ourselves.

DINAH. But, Mother, you want us to create a good impression, don't you?

MARGARET [*to* SANDY]. They don't know that *we* know what they're here for, I hope?

SANDY. No: that was understood.

DINAH. I should think it would look awfully funny to them, Father's not being here for his own daughter's wedding.

TRACY. Would you, now?

SANDY. That's all right; I fixed that, too.

TRACY. How do you mean you did?

SANDY. I told Sue to send a telegram before dinner. "Confined to bed with a cold, unable to attend nuptials, oceans of love, Father."

MARGARET. Not just in those words!

SANDY. Not exactly.—It'll come on the telephone and Thomas will take it and you won't have your glasses and he'll read it aloud to you.

MARGARET. Tracy, will you promise to behave like a lady, if only for my sake?

TRACY. I'll do my best, Mrs. Lord. I don't know how good that is.

MARGARET. Go put a dress on.

TRACY. Yes, Mother.

MARGARET. There are too many legs around here.

TRACY. Suds! I'll be pure Victorian, all frills and ruffles, conversationally chaste as an egg. [WILLIAM (UNCLE WILLIE) TRACY, 62, *enters from the Parlor.*] Hello, Uncle Willie. Where did you come from?

UNCLE WILLIE. Your Great-aunt Geneva has requested my absence from the house until dinner time. Can you give me lunch, Margaret?

MARGARET. But of course! With pleasure.

DINAH. Hello, Uncle Willie.

SANDY. How are you, Uncle Willie?

UNCLE WILLIE. Alexander and Dinah, good morning. [*To* TRACY.]—My esteemed wife, the old war horse, is certainly spreading herself for your party. I seriously question the propriety of any such display in such times, but she—why aren't you being married in church, Tracy?

TRACY. I like the parlor here so much better. Didn't you think it looked pretty as you came through?

UNCLE WILLIE. That is not the point. The point is that I've sunk thousands in that church, and I'd like to get some use of it.—Give me a glass of sherry, Margaret.

MARGARET. Not until lunch time, my dear.

UNCLE WILLIE. These women.

DINAH. You're really a wicked old man, aren't you? [*He points beyond her, to the Porch.*]

UNCLE WILLIE. What's that out there? [DINAH *turns to look. He vigorously pinches her behind.*]

DINAH. Ouch!

UNCLE WILLIE. Never play with fire, child. [*He looks at the others.*] What's a-lack here? What's a-stirrin'? What's amiss?

SANDY. Uncle Willie, do you know anything about the laws of libel? [UNCLE WILLIE *seats himself.*]

UNCLE WILLIE. Certainly, I know about the laws of libel. Why shouldn't I? I know all about them. In 1916, I, Willie Q. Tracy, successfully defended the *Post*, and George Lorimer personally, against one of the cleverest, one of the subtlest—why? What do you want to say?

SANDY. It isn't what *I* want to say—

TRACY. Is it enough if they can simply prove that it is true?

UNCLE WILLIE. Certainly not! Take me: if I was totally bald and wore a toupee, if I had flat feet, with these damnable metal arches, false teeth, and a case of double—

DINAH. Poor Uncle Willie.

UNCLE WILLIE. I said *"If* I had"—And if such facts were presented in the public prints in such a manner as to hold me up to public ridicule, I could collect substantial damages—and would, if it took me all winter.

TRACY. Suppose the other way around. Suppose they printed things that weren't true.

UNCLE WILLIE. Suppose they did? Suppose it was erroneously stated, that during my travels as a young man I was married in a native ceremony to a dusky maiden in British Guinea, I doubt if I could collect a cent. [*He looks past her, toward the Hall door.*] Who are these two strange people coming down the hall? [*The entire family rises.*]

MARGARET. Oh, good gracious! [TRACY *takes* UNCLE WILLIE *by the arm.*]

TRACY. Come on—out! [*She leads him toward the Parlor at Right.*] What was she like, Uncle Willie?

UNCLE WILLIE. Who?

TRACY. British Guinea?

UNCLE WILLIE. So very unlike your Aunt Geneva, my dear. [*They go out.*]

MARGARET. Dinah—

DINAH. But, Mother, oughtn't we—?

MARGARET. Come! Sandy can entertain them until we—until we collect ourselves. [*She directs* DINAH *into the Parlor.*]

SANDY. What'll I say?

MARGARET. I wish I could tell you—in a few very well-chosen words. [*She goes out.* SANDY *is alone for a moment. He hunches his shoulders uncomfortably and clears his throat.* MACAULAY (MIKE), *30, and* ELIZABETH (LIZ) IMBRIE, *28, come in from the Hall.* LIZ *has a small and important camera hanging from a leather strap around her neck.*]

LIZ.—In here?

MIKE. He said the sitting room. I suppose that's contrasted to the living room, the ballroom, the drawing room, the morning room, the—[*He sees* SANDY.] Oh, hello again. Here you are.

SANDY. Here I am.

MIKE. It's quite a place.

SANDY. It is, isn't it?—I couldn't help overhearing you as you came in. Do you mind if I say something?

MIKE. Not at all. What?

SANDY. Your approach to your job seems definitely antagonistic. I don't think it's fair. I think you ought to give us a break.

MIKE. It's not a job I asked for.

SANDY. I know it's not. But in spite of it, and in spite of certain of our regrettable inherited characteristics, we just might be fairly decent. Why not wait and see? [MIKE *and* LIZ *seat themselves.*]

MIKE. You have quite a style yourself.— You're on the *Saturday Evening Post*, did you say? [SANDY *seats himself, facing* MIKE *and* LIZ.]

SANDY. I work for it.

MIKE. Which end?

SANDY. Editorial.

MIKE. I have to tell you, in all honesty, that I'm opposed to everything you represent.

SANDY. *Destiny* is hardly a radical sheet: what is it you're doing—boring from within?

MIKE.—And I'm not a communist, not by a long shot.

LIZ. Just a small pin-feather in the Left Wing. [MIKE *looks at her.*]—Sorry.

SANDY. Jeffersonian Democrat?

MIKE. That's more like it.

SANDY. Have you ever seen his house at Monticello? *It's* quite a place too.

LIZ. Home Team One; Visitors Nothing. [*She rises and looks about her.*] Is this house very old, Mr. Lord?

SANDY. No, there are a very few old ones on the Main Line.—The Gatehouse is, of course. Father's grandfather built that for a summer place when they all lived on Rittenhouse Square. Father and Mother did this about 1910—the spring before my brother Junius was born. He's the eldest. You won't meet him, he's in the diplomatic service in London.

MIKE [*to* LIZ]. Wouldn't you know?

SANDY. *I* worked for Sidney Kidd once. What do you make of him?

MIKE [*after a moment*]. A brilliant editor, and a very wonderful man.

LIZ. Also, our bread and butter.

SANDY. Sorry to have been rude. [MIKE *takes a sheaf of typewritten cards from his pocket and begins to glance through them.*]

MIKE. I suppose you're all opposed to the Administration?

SANDY. The present one? No—as a matter of fact we're Loyalists.

MIKE. Surprise, surprise.—The Research Department didn't give us much data.— Your sister's fiancé—George Kittredge—

aged 32.—Since last year General Manager Quaker State Coal, in charge of operation.—Is that right?

SANDY. That's right.—And brilliant at it.

MIKE. So I've heard tell. I seem to have read about him first back in '35 or '36.—Up from the bottom, wasn't he?

SANDY. Just exactly—and of the mines.

MIKE. Reorganized the entire works?

SANDY. He did.

MIKE. National hero, new model: makes drooping family incomes to revive again. Anthracite, sweet anthracite.—How did your sister happen to meet him?

SANDY. She and I went up a month ago to look things over.

MIKE. I see. And was it instant?

SANDY. Immediate.

MIKE. Good for her. He must be quite a guy.—Which side of this—er—fine aboriginal family does she resemble most, would you say? [SANDY *looks at him, rises.*]

SANDY. The histories of both are in the library: I'll get them out for you. I'll also see if I can round up some of the Living Members.

LIZ. They don't know about us, do they? [SANDY, *in the doorway, stops and turns.*]

SANDY.—Pleasanter not, don't you think?

LIZ. Much.

SANDY. That's what *I* thought—also what Kidd thought. [*Suddenly* MIKE *rises.*]

MIKE. Look here, Lord—

SANDY. Yes—?

MIKE. Why don't you throw us out? [SANDY *laughs shortly, then goes out.*]

SANDY. I hope you'll never know!

LIZ. Meaning what?

MIKE. Search me.

LIZ. Maybe Der Kidder has been up to his little tricks.

MIKE. If only I could get away from his damned paper—

LIZ. It's Sidney himself you can't get away from, dear. [*She begins to tour the room with her camera.*]

MIKE. I tried to resign again on the phone this morning.

LIZ.—Knickknacks—gimcracks—signed photographs! Wouldn't you know you'd have to be as rich as the Lords to live in a dump like this? [*Sees the portrait over the mantel.*] Save me—it's a Gilbert Stuart!

MIKE. A what?

LIZ. Catch me, Mike!

MIKE. Faint to the left, will you? [*He returns to the typewritten cards.*] "First husband, C. K.—"—Can you imagine what a guy named "C. K. Dexter Haven" must be like?

LIZ. "Macaulay Connor" is not such a homespun tag, my pet.

MIKE. I've been called Mike ever since I can remember.

LIZ. Well, maybe Dexter is "Ducky" to his friends.

MIKE. I wouldn't doubt it.—But I wonder what the "C. K." is for—

LIZ. Maybe it's Pennsylvania Dutch for "William Penn."

MIKE. "C. K. Dexter Haven"—God!

LIZ. I knew a plain Joe Smith once. He was only a clerk in a hardware store, but he was an absolute louse.

MIKE.—Also he plays polo. Also designs and races sailboats. "Class" boats, I think they call them. Very upper class, of course.

LIZ. Don't despair. He's out, and Kittredge, man of the people, is in.

MIKE. From all reports, quite a comer too. Political timber.—Poor fellow, I wonder how he fell for it.

Liz. I imagine she's a young lady who knows what she wants when she wants it.

Mike. The young, rich, rapacious American female—there's no other country where she exists.

Liz. I'll admit the idea of *her* scares even me.—Would I change places with her, for all her wealth and beauty? Boy! Just ask me!

Mike. I know how I'm going to begin. [*He leans back on the sofa, closes his eyes, and declaims.*] "—So much for Historical Philadelphia, so much for Industrial. Now, Gentle Reader, consider an entire section of American Society which, closely following the English tradition, lives on the land, but in a new sense. It is not the land that provides the living, it is—"

Liz. You're ahead of yourself. Wait till you do your documentation.

Mike. I'm tired. Kidd is a slave driver. I wish I was home in bed. Also I'm hungry. Tell four footmen to call me in time for lunch. [Dinah *re-enters from the Porch, her manner now very much that of a woman of the world. She rises upon her toes like a ballet dancer and advances toward them.*]

Dinah. Oh—how do you do?—Friends of Alexander's, are you not? [Mike *rises.*]

Mike. How do you do.—Why yes, we—

Dinah. I am Dinah Lord. My real name is Diana, but my sister changed it.

Liz. I'm Elizabeth Imbrie and this is Macaulay Connor. It's awfully nice of— [Dinah *extends an arched hand to each.*]

Dinah. Enchantée de vous voir. Enchantée de faire votre connaisance.—I spoke French before I spoke English. My early childhood was spent in Paris, where my father worked in a bank—the House of Morgan.

Liz. Really?

Dinah. C'est vrai—absolument! [*She runs up to the piano, leaping a low stool as she goes.*] Can you play the piano? I can. And sing at the same time. Listen— [*She plays and sings.*] "Pepper Sauce Woman, Pepper Sauce Woman—" [Liz *speaks lowly to* Mike.]

Liz. What is this?

Mike. An idiot, probably. They happen in the best of families, especially in the best.

Dinah.
"—Oh, what a shame; she has lost her name
Don't know who to blame, walkin' along in Shango Batchelor."
[*She stops singing and continues in a dreamy voice:*] The Bahamas—how well I remember them.—Those perfumed nights—the flowers—the native wines. I was there, once, on a little trip with Leopold Stokowski. [Tracy *comes in from the Porch. She has changed into a rather demure dress, high in neck and ample in skirt.*]

Tracy. You were there with your governess, after the whooping cough. [Dinah *gestures airily.*]

Dinah.—My sister Tracy. Greetings, Sister.

Tracy. Mother wants to see you at once. At once! [Dinah *rises from the piano.*]

Dinah. You've got on my hair ribbon.

Tracy. Your face is still dirty. [*As* Dinah *passes her,* Tracy *gives her one, deft, smart spank, then, as* Dinah *goes out into the Hall, comes up to* Mike *and* Liz, *cool, collected and charming, all Sweetness and Light.*] It's awfully nice having you here. [*She shakes hands with them.*] I do hope you'll stay for my wedding.

Liz. We'd like to very much.

Mike. In fact, that was our idea.

TRACY. I'm so pleased that it occurred to you. [*She indicates the sofa. They seat themselves there and* TRACY *takes a chair facing them.*] The house is in rather a mess, of course. We all have to huddle here, and overflow onto the porch.—I hope your rooms are comfortable. [MIKE *takes out a pack of cigarettes.*]

LIZ. Oh, very, thanks.

TRACY. Anything you want, ask Mary or Elsie. They're magic. [*She holds a cigarette box out to them. Each takes one.* LIZ's *camera catches her eye.*] What a cunning little camera. [MIKE *has struck a match. He sees that* TRACY *is holding an automatic lighter toward him as she talks to* LIZ.—*He slowly bends forward to accept a light for his cigarette, then blows his match out.* TRACY *graciously smiles at him.*]

LIZ. It's a Contax. I'm afraid I'm rather a nuisance with it. [*She accepts a light from the lighter.*]

TRACY. But, you couldn't be: I hope you'll take loads. Dear Papá and Mamá aren't allowing any reporters in—that is, except for little Mr. Grace, who does the social news. [*To* MIKE.] Can you imagine a grown-up man, having to sink so low?

MIKE. It does seem pretty bad.

TRACY. People have always been so kind about letting us live our simple and uneventful little life here unmolested. Of course, after my divorce last year—but I expect that always happens, and is more or less deserved. Dear Papá was quite angry, though, and swore he'd never let another reporter inside the gate. He thought some of their methods were a trifle underhanded.—You're a writer, aren't you, Mr. Connor?

MIKE. In a manner of speaking.

TRACY. Sandy told me. I've sent for your books. "Macaulay Connor"—What's the "Macaulay" for?

MIKE. My father taught English history. I'm "Mike" to my friends.

TRACY.—Of whom you have many, I'm sure. English history has always fascinated me. Cromwell—Bloody Mary, John the Bastard.—Where did he teach? I mean your father—

MIKE. In the high school in South Bend, Indiana.

TRACY. "South Bend"! It sounds like dancing, doesn't it? You must have had a most happy childhood there.

MIKE. It was terrific.

TRACY. I'm so glad.

MIKE. I don't mean it that way.

TRACY. I'm so sorry. Why?

MIKE. Largely due to the lack of the wherewithal, I guess.

TRACY. But that doesn't always cause unhappiness, does it?—not if you're the right kind of man. George Kittredge, my fiancé, never had anything either, but he—. Are either of you married?

MIKE. No.

LIZ. I—er—that is, no.

TRACY. You mean *you* were, but now you're divorced?

LIZ. Well, the fact is—

TRACY. Suds—you can't mean you're ashamed of it!

LIZ. Of course I'm not ashamed of it. [MIKE *is staring at her.*]

MIKE. Wha-at?

LIZ. It was ages ago, when I was a mere kid, in Duluth.

MIKE. Good Lord, Liz—you never told me you were—

LIZ. You never asked.

MIKE. I know, but—

LIZ. Joe Smith. Hardware.

MIKE. Liz, you're the damnedest girl.

LIZ. *I* think I'm sweet. [MIKE *rises,*

turns once around the sofa and seats himself again.]

TRACY. Duluth—that must be a lovely spot. It's west of here, isn't it?

LIZ. Sort of.—But occasionally we get the breezes.

TRACY. Is this your first visit in Philadelphia?

LIZ. Just about.

TRACY. It's a quaint old place, don't you think? I suppose it's affected somewhat by being the only really big city that's near New York.

LIZ. I think that's a very good point to make about it.

TRACY.—Though I suppose you consider us somewhat provincial.

LIZ. Not at all, I assure you.

TRACY. Odd customs, and such. Where the scrapples eat Biddle on Sunday. Of course it *is* very old—Philadelphia, I mean; the scrapple is fresh weekly. How old are *you*, Mr. Connor?

MIKE. I was thirty last month.

TRACY. Two books isn't much for a man of thirty. I don't mean to criticize. You probably have other interests outside your work.

MIKE. None.—Unless— [*He looks at* LIZ *and smiles.*]

TRACY. How sweet! Are you living together?

MIKE. Why, er—that is—

LIZ. That's an odd question, I must say!

TRACY. Why?

LIZ. Well—it just is.

TRACY. I don't see why. I think it's very interesting. [*She leans forward seriously, elbow on knee, chin on hand.*] Miss Imbrie—don't you agree that all this marrying and giving in marriage is the damnedest gyp that's ever been put over on an unsuspecting public?

MIKE [*to* LIZ]. Can she be human?

TRACY. Please, Mr. Connor!—I asked Miss Imbrie a question.

LIZ. No. The fact is, I don't.

TRACY. Good. Nor do I. That's why I'm putting my chin out for the second time tomorrow. [GEORGE, *off stage, Left, calls "Tracy." She rises and moves toward the Porch.*] Here's the lucky man now. I'll bring him right in and put him on view—a one-man exhibition.—In here, George! In here, my dear! [*She goes out,* LIZ *rises and turns to* MIKE.]

LIZ. My God—who's doing the interviewing here?

MIKE. She's a lot more than I counted on.

LIZ. Do you suppose she's caught on somehow?

MIKE. No. She's just a hellion.

LIZ. I'm beginning to feel the size of a pinhead.

MIKE. Don't let her throw you.

LIZ. Do you want to take over?

MIKE. I want to go home. [TRACY *re-enters with* GEORGE KITTREDGE, *aged 32, and brings him up to them.*]

TRACY. Miss Imbrie—Mr. Connor—Mr. Kittredge, my beau.—Friends of Sandy's, George.

GEORGE. Any friend of Sandy's— [*He shakes hands with them.*]

LIZ. How do you do?

MIKE. How are you?

GEORGE. Fine as silk, thanks.

LIZ. You certainly look it.

GEORGE. Thanks! I've shaken quite a lot of coal dust from my feet in the last day or two.

TRACY. Isn't he beautiful? Isn't it wonderful what a little soap and water will do?

MIKE. Didn't I read a piece about you in the *Nation* a while ago?

GEORGE. Quite a while ago: I've been

resting on my laurels since that—and a couple of others.

MIKE. Quite a neat piece of work—anticipating the Guffey Coal Act the way you did.—Or do I remember straight?

GEORGE. Anyone should have foreseen that. I was just lucky.

LIZ. A becoming modesty.

GEORGE. That's nothing to what's yet to be done with Labor relations.

TRACY. You ought to see him with the men—they simply adore him.

GEORGE. Oh—come on, Tracy!

TRACY. Oh, but they do! Never in my life will I forget that first night I saw you: all those wonderful faces, and the torch lights, and the way his voice boomed—

GEORGE. You see, I'm really a spellbinder. That's the way I got her.

TRACY. Except it was me who got you! —I'm going to put these two at the bridal table, in place of the Grants.

GEORGE. That's a good idea.

TRACY. George, it won't rain, will it?— Promise me it won't rain.

GEORGE. Tracy, I'll see to that personally.

TRACY. I almost believe you could.

MIKE. I guess this must be love.

GEORGE. Your guess is correct, Mr. Connor.

TRACY. I'm just his faithful Old Dog Tray.

GEORGE. Give me your paw. [*She presents her hand.*]

TRACY. You've got it. [*He takes it and kisses it.* MARGARET *enters from the Parlor, followed by* DINAH. DINAH *remains in the doorway.* MARGARET *goes directly to* LIZ *and* MIKE.]

MARGARET. How do you do? We're so happy to have you. Forgive me for not coming in sooner, but things are in such a state. I'd no idea that a simple country wedding could involve so much. [*She crosses to* TRACY *and* TRACY *to her. They beam fatuously upon one another.*] My little girl—[*She pats her face, then turns back to* LIZ.]—I do hope you'll be comfortable. Those rooms are inclined to be hot in this weather.—Aren't you pretty, my dear! [SANDY *comes in from the Hall.*] Look at the way she wears her hair, Tracy. Isn't it pretty?

TRACY. Mighty fine.

MARGARET. I do wish my husband might be here to greet you, but we expect him presently. He's been detained in New York on business for that lovely Tina Mara. You know her work?

LIZ. Only vaguely!

MARGARET. So talented—and such a lovely person! But like so many artists— no business head, none whatever. [*She gives* TRACY *a knowing smile.* TRACY *and* SANDY *smile.* SANDY *then smirks for* TRACY's *sole benefit.* EDWARD *comes in from the Hall, carrying a tray with a carafe of sherry and several glasses.* THOMAS *follows him.* EDWARD *pours,* THOMAS *serves.* MARGARET *beams upon* GEORGE.] Good morning, George!

GEORGE. Good morning, Mrs. Lord.

MARGARET. And this is my youngest daughter, Diana— [DINAH *curtseys.*]

MIKE. I think we've met. [THOMAS *gives* MARGARET *a glass of sherry.*]

MARGARET. Thank you, Thomas. [SANDY *stretches himself out in an easy chair.*]

SANDY. Now let's all relax, and throw ourselves into things. Hi, George!

GEORGE. Hello, Sandy—Welcome home! [*All take sherry, with the exception of* TRACY *and* DINAH.]

MARGARET. After lunch Sandy must show you some of the sights—the model dairy, and the stables, and the chicken farm—and perhaps there'll be time to run

[477]

you out to some other places on the Main Line—Devon, St. Davids, Bryn Mawr, where my daughter Tracy went to college—

DINAH. Till she got bounced out on her—

MARGARET.—Dinah! [UNCLE WILLIE re-enters from the Parlor.]

UNCLE WILLIE. It's a pretty kettle of fish when a man has to wait two mortal hours— [Suddenly TRACY runs to him with her arms out.]

TRACY. Papá!—Dear Papá— [She embraces him warmly.] Didn't the car meet you? [UNCLE WILLIE is completely bewildered.]

WILLIE. The car?

TRACY. You angel—to drop everything and get here in time for lunch!—Isn't he, Mamá?

MARGARET. In—indeed he is. [UNCLE WILLIE stares at them.]

UNCLE WILLIE. I'm not one to jump at conclusions, but—

TRACY. These are our friends, Mr. Connor and Miss Imbrie, Father.—They're here for the wedding.

MIKE and LIZ. How do you do, Mr. Lord?

UNCLE WILLIE. Dashed fine. How are you?

SANDY. Hi, Pops!

UNCLE WILLIE.—Alexander.

DINAH. Welcome back, Daddy!

UNCLE WILLIE. Dinah—Kittredge— [He turns to MARGARET and bows.] Margaret, my sweet. [THOMAS comes down to his Left with a glass of sherry. UNCLE WILLIE tosses it off and returns the glass.]

TRACY. Mother, don't you think you ought to explain the new arrangement to Father before lunch?

MARGARET. Why—yes—I think I'd best. [She slips her arm through UNCLE WILLIE'S and leads him to the desk which stands between the Porch doors.] See here—here is the list now—Seth. [In from the Porch comes DEXTER HAVEN, 28. SANDY sees him and exclaims.]

SANDY. Holy Cats! [MARGARET turns quickly.]

MARGARET. Dexter Haven!

DEXTER. Hello, friends and enemies. I came the short way, across the fields.

MARGARET. Well, this is a surprise.

GEORGE. I should think it is. [DEXTER kisses MARGARET lightly upon the cheek.]

DEXTER. Hello, you sweet thing.

MARGARET. Now you go right home at once!

UNCLE WILLIE. Remove yourself, young man!

DEXTER. But I've been invited. [He shakes UNCLE WILLIE'S hand.] How are you, sir?

UNCLE WILLIE. No better, no worse. Get along.

DEXTER. Hello, Sandy. [They shake hands.]

SANDY. How are you, boy?

DEXTER. Never better. In fact, it's immoral how good I feel.

DINAH. What—what brings you here, Mr. Haven?

DEXTER. Dinah, my angel! [He kisses her cheek.] Why, she's turned into a raving beauty! [He turns to TRACY.]—Awfully sweet and thoughtful of you to ask me to lunch, Tray.

TRACY. Not at all.—Extra place, Thomas.

THOMAS. Yes, Miss Tracy. [He and EDWARD go out, into the Hall. UNCLE WILLIE and MARGARET talk inaudibly at the desk. TRACY gestures toward MIKE and LIZ.]

TRACY. Miss Imbrie—Mr. Connor—my former husband, whose name for the moment escapes me.

DEXTER. How do you do?
LIZ. How do you do?
MIKE. How do you do?
DEXTER.—Of course I intended to come anyway, but it did make it pleasanter.—Hello, Kittredge.
GEORGE. How are you, Haven? [DEXTER *peers at him.*]
DEXTER. What's the matter? You don't look as well as when I last saw you. [*He pats his arm sympathetically.*] Poor fellow—I know just how you feel. [*He turns to* TRACY, *gazes at her fondly.*] Redhead—isn't *she* in the pink, though!—*You* don't look old enough to marry anyone, even for the first time—you never did! She needs trouble to mature her, Kittredge. Give her lots of it.
GEORGE. I'm afraid she can't count on me for that.
DEXTER. No? Too bad.—Sometimes, for your own sake, I think you should have stuck to me longer, Red. [TRACY *goes to* GEORGE *and takes his arm.*]
TRACY. I thought it was for life, but the nice Judge gave me a full pardon.
DEXTER. That's the kind of talk I like to hear: no bitterness, no recrimination—just a good quick left to the jaw.
GEORGE. Very funny. [THOMAS *reappears in the Hall doorway.*]
THOMAS. Luncheon is served, Madam.
MARGARET. Thank you, Thomas. [*He goes out.* UNCLE WILLIE *advances from the desk.*]
UNCLE WILLIE. I don't suppose a man ever had a better or finer family. [*He turns and takes* MARGARET's *arm.*] I wake in the night and say to myself—"Seth, you lucky dog. What have you done to deserve it?"

MARGARET. And what *have* you? [*Arm in arm they go out into the Hall.*]
TRACY. Do you mind if I go in with Mr. Connor, Miss Imbrie?
LIZ. Why, not in the least. [SANDY *offers* LIZ *his arm.*]
SANDY. Sandy's your boy.
TRACY [*takes* MIKE's *arm*]—Because I think he's such an interesting man.
GEORGE. Come on, Dinah, I draw you, I guess.
DINAH. Dexter—
DEXTER [*to* GEORGE]. Isn't snatching one of my girls enough, you cad?
GEORGE. You're a very bright fellow, Haven. I'll hire you.
MIKE [*to* TRACY]. No wonder you want to get away from all this.
TRACY. That's very insulting—but consistently interesting. We must talk more. [*They are all approaching the Hall when* SETH LORD, 50, *appears in the Porch doorway, hat in hand, a light topcoat over his arm.*]
SETH. I don't know how welcome I am, but after Sandy's note, I thought the least I could do was to— [DINAH *starts down the Hall steps to him but is stopped by* TRACY, *who suddenly cries out to* SETH.]
TRACY. Uncle Willie! [*She turns to others.*] Please go on in to lunch, everyone, I want a word with Uncle Willie. [*They go out.* TRACY *crosses the room and faces her father.*]
SETH. Well, daughter?
TRACY. Well?
SETH. Still Justice, with her shining sword—eh? Who's on the spot?
TRACY. We are; thanks to you—Uncle Willie.

CURTAIN

ACT II

SCENE I

[*The Porch, which is more like a room than a porch. Entrance from the Sitting Room is through the glass doors at back and to the Library, through glass doors at Stage Left; to the Garden, down broad stone steps from the Porch and along a gravel path past shrubbery to Left and Right. The open side of the Porch is shielded with latticework, and there are pots of geraniums on the steps. Early evening, Friday. The sky has cleared.* MIKE *is in a chair on the Porch, making additional notes.* LIZ *is seated on the steps, reloading her camera.*]

LIZ. I may need more film.

MIKE. I may need more paper.

LIZ. There's a cousin Joanna who's definitely crazy.

MIKE. Who told you?

LIZ. Dinah.

MIKE. Dinah should know.

LIZ. Where is she now? I want some more shots of her, while it's still light.

MIKE. She's out schooling a horse somewhere. It's the horses that get the schooling hereabouts. Did you shoot the old Tycoon milking his cows?

LIZ. Several times. He shot one at me, but he missed.

MIKE. Caption: "Seventy Times Seven Fat Kine Has He." [*He consults his notes.*] "George Kittredge, Important Official, Important Company. Controlling interest owned by Seth Lord."

LIZ. What a coincidence and will wonders never cease?

MIKE. I'm inclined to like Kittredge—I can see how she fell for him. I think he's in a tough spot, with Haven prowling around, though.

LIZ. Is a sinister fellow, Dexter.

MIKE. Is very.—But George is interesting. Get him on coal some time.

LIZ. I'd rather have him on toast.

MIKE. Answer me honestly, Liz: What right has a girl like Tracy Lord to exist?

LIZ. Politically, socially, or economically?

MIKE. But what place has she got in the world today? Come the Revolution and she'd be the first to go.

LIZ. Sure: right out under the Red General's arm.

MIKE. She's a new one on me. Maybe Philadelphia produces a different brand of monkey. [LIZ *looks at him keenly.*]

LIZ. You're a funny one, Mike.

MIKE. Why?

LIZ. Use the name "Wanamaker" in a sentence.

MIKE. I bite.

LIZ. I met a girl this morning. I hate her, but I—

MIKE. I get you, but you're wrong. You couldn't be wronger. Women like that bore the pants off me.

LIZ. For a writer, you use your figures of speech most ineptly. You know, I wish they knew why we were here. They're all such sweet innocents, it makes me feel like— [UNCLE WILLIE *and* SETH *enter from the Garden down Right.*]

UNCLE WILLIE. Would you accept this perfect rose, Miss Imbrie?

LIZ. Why, thank you, Mr. Lord. It's a beauty.

SETH. Miss Imbrie is amused at something.

LIZ. I'm sorry, Mr. Tracy, but it's so funny, you being uncle and nephew. Could I have a picture of you together?

UNCLE WILLIE. Certainly! [*He slips his arm through* SETH's.] Now then, stand up

[480]

straight, Uncle Willie. He *is* younger than I. It was a matter of half-sisters marrying stepbrothers.

Liz. I see. That is, I think I do. [*She snaps a picture.*]

Uncle Willie. No incest, however.

Liz. Of course not. [*And snaps another.*]

Uncle Willie. There have been other things, however. [*He looks at* Seth.] Uncle Willie—I'm thinking of asking that little dancer, Tina Mara, to come down and dance for the wedding guests tomorrow. Do you think it's a good idea?

Seth. Excellent. It might put an end to the ridiculous gossip about you and her.

Uncle Willie. Is there gossip?

Seth. There seems to be.

Uncle Willie. Is it ridiculous?

Seth. All gossip is ridiculous. [Sandy *comes from the Library at Left and crosses the Porch to the Sitting-Room door.*]

Sandy. Look alive, men! Time to dress!

Seth. Right you are. Thanks, Sandy— [*He goes up the steps and over the Porch into the Sitting Room.* Sandy *follows him.*]

Uncle Willie. Miss Imbrie, as a camera-fiend, I think I have another interesting subject for you.

Liz. Will I have time?

Uncle Willie. Time is an illusion. Come with me, please. [*He offers his arm, which she takes gingerly.*] It's part of the old house, a little removed from it.

Liz. But what?

Uncle Willie. An ancient granite privy, of superb design—a dream of loveliness.

Liz.—At sunset—idyllic! [Liz *and* Uncle Willie *go out into the Garden.* Mike *pockets his notebook and moves toward the Sitting Room. Suddenly* Tracy *appears in the Library doorway. She wears a bright-colored dressing gown over the foundation for a white evening dress and has a book in her hand, her finger marking a place toward the end of it.*]

Tracy. Please wait a minute.

Mike. With pleasure. [*He stops where he is. She goes to him, turns him about and looks at him wonderingly.*] What's the matter?

Tracy. I've been reading these stories. They're so damned beautiful.

Mike. You like? Thanks—

Tracy. Why, Connor, they're almost poetry. [*He laughs shortly.*]

Mike. Don't fool yourself: they *are!*

Tracy. I can't make you out at all, now.

Mike. Really? I thought I was easy.

Tracy. So did I, but you're not. You talk so big and tough—and then you write like this. Which is which?

Mike. I guess I'm both.

Tracy. No—I believe you put the toughness on, to save your skin.

Mike. You think?

Tracy. Yes. *I* know a little about that—

Mike. Do you?

Tracy. Quite a lot. [*They look at each other for a moment. Then* Tracy *laughs a little embarrassedly and glances away.*] It—the book—it was just such a complete —hell of a surprise, that's all.

Mike. Yes—it seems you do.

Tracy. What?

Mike. Know about it.

Tracy. The one called "With The Rich and Mighty"—I think I liked *it* best.

Mike. I got it from a Spanish peasant's proverb—"With The Rich and Mighty, always a little patience." [Tracy *laughs.*]

Tracy. Good! [*She seats herself, gazes again at the book.*] Tell me something, will you? When you can do a thing like this, how can you possibly do anything else?

Mike. Such as what?

[481]

TRACY. You said after lunch—what was it you said? "Cheap stuff for expensive magazines."

MIKE. Did I?

TRACY. Yes. You did. You said you spent most of your time that way. [MIKE *seats himself, facing her.*]

MIKE. Practically all. Why? What about it?

TRACY. I can't understand it. And I like to understand things.

MIKE. You'll never believe it, but there are people in this world who have to earn their living.

TRACY. Of course! But people buy books, don't they?

MIKE. Sure they do: they even read them.

TRACY. Well, then!

MIKE. That one represents two solid years' work. It netted Connor something under six hundred dollars.

TRACY. But that shouldn't *be!*

MIKE.—Only unhappily it is. [*There is a pause.*]

TRACY. And what about your Miss Imbrie?

MIKE. Miss Imbrie is in somewhat the same fix. She's a born painter, and might be an important one. But Miss Imbrie must eat. Also, she prefers a roof over her head to being constantly out in the rain and snow. [TRACY *ponders this.*]

TRACY. Food and a roof—food and a roof—

MIKE. Those charming essentials.

TRACY [*suddenly*]. Listen: I've got an idea! [*She rises, goes to him, stands over him.*] Listen: I've got the most marvelous little house in Unionville. It's up on a hill, with a view that would knock you silly. I'm never there except in the hunting season, and not much then, and I'd be so happy to know it was of some use to someone. [*She moves swiftly across the Porch and back again.*] There's a brook and a small lake, no size really, and a patch of woods, and in any kind of weather, it's the— [*She is down the steps now, looking up at the sky.*] —And look at that sky now, will you! Suddenly it's clear as clear! It's going to be fine tomorrow! It's going to be fair! Good for you, God! [*She glances down the path.*] Hell! [*And quickly returns to the Porch.*] Someone's coming—someone I don't want to be alone with. Stand by for a couple of minutes, will you?

MIKE. Certainly—if you like.

TRACY.—You *will* think about the house, won't you?

MIKE. Why, it's terribly nice of you, but—

TRACY. Don't think I'd come trooping in every minute, because I wouldn't. I'd never come, except when expressly asked to.

MIKE. It isn't that.

TRACY. What is it?

MIKE. Well, you see—er—you see the idea of artists having a patron has more or less gone out, and— [*She looks at him steadily.*]

TRACY. I see. [*Then waits a moment.*] That wasn't especially kind of you, Mr. Connor. There's no need to rub our general uselessness in.

MIKE. I'm afraid I don't get you.

TRACY. Don't bother. I'm sorry to have seemed—patronizing.

MIKE. I didn't quite mean—

TRACY. Please don't bother, really. [DEXTER *comes in down the Garden path. He carries a small picture, wrapped in tissue paper.*]

DEXTER. Hello.

TRACY. Hello. Fancy seeing you here.

The Philadelphia Story

[*He mounts the Porch and goes to the table.*]

DEXTER. Orange juice? Certainly!—

TRACY. You're sure you don't want something stronger? I'll ring if you like. [*He pours himself a glass of orange juice from a pitcher.*]

DEXTER. Not now, thanks. This is fine.

TRACY. Don't tell me you've forsaken your beloved whisky-and-whiskies—

DEXTER. No, indeed. I've just changed their color, that's all. I go in for the pale pastel shades now. I find they're more becoming. [*He looks at* MIKE *over his glass.*] We met at lunch, didn't we?

MIKE. Yes, I seem to remember. Connor's my name.

DEXTER.—The writer—of course! Do you drink, Mr. Connor?

MIKE. A little. Why?

DEXTER. Not to excess?

MIKE. Not often.

DEXTER.—And a writer! It's extraordinary. I thought all writers drank to excess, and beat their wives. I expect that at one time *I* secretly wanted to be a writer.

TRACY. Dexter, would you mind doing something for me? [*He replaces the glass upon the table and puts the picture beside it.*]

DEXTER. Anything. What?

TRACY. Get the hell out of here.

DEXTER. Oh, no, I couldn't do that. That wouldn't be fair to you. You need me too much.

TRACY. Would you mind telling me just what it is you're hanging around for? [MIKE *moves toward the Library door.*] No—please don't go! I'd honestly much prefer it if you wouldn't. [*Reluctantly* MIKE *seats himself near the door.*]

DEXTER. So should I. Do stay, Mr. Connor. As a writer this ought to be right up your street.

TRACY [*to* MIKE]. Miss not a word! [DEXTER *gazes at her.*]

DEXTER. Honestly, you never looked better in your life. You're getting a fine tawny look.

TRACY. Oh, we're going to talk about me, are we? Goody.

DEXTER.—It's astonishing what money can do for people, don't you agree, Mr. Connor? Not too much, you know—just more than enough. Particularly for girls. Look at Tracy: there's never been a blow that hasn't been softened for her. There'll never be one that won't be softened. Why, it even changed her shape—she was a dumpy little thing originally.

TRACY.—Only as it happens, I'm not interested in myself, for the moment. What interests me now, is what, if any, your real point is, in—

DEXTER. Not interested in yourself? My dear, you're fascinated! You're far and away your favorite person in the world.

TRACY. Dexter, in case you don't know it, I—!

DEXTER. Shall I go on—?

TRACY. Oh, yes, please do, by all means— [*She seats herself.*]

DEXTER. Of course, she is kindness itself, Mr. Connor—

TRACY.—Itself, Mr. Connor.

DEXTER. She is generous to a fault—that is, except to other people's faults. For instance, she never had the slightest sympathy toward nor understanding of what used to be known as my deep and gorgeous thirst.

TRACY. That was your problem!

DEXTER. It was the problem of a young man of exceptionally high spirit, who drank to slow down that damned engine he'd found nothing yet to do with.—I refer to my mind. You took on that problem with me, when you took me.—You

[483]

were no helpmate there, Tracy—you were a scold.

TRACY. It was disgusting. It made you so unattractive.

DEXTER. A weakness—sure. And strength is her religion, Mr. Connor. She is a goddess, without patience for any kind of human imperfection. And when I gradually discovered that my relation to her was expected to be not that of a loving husband and a good companion, but— [*He turns away from her.*] Oh—never mind—

TRACY. Say it!

DEXTER.—But that of a kind of high priest to a virgin goddess, then my drinks grew more frequent and deeper in hue, that's all.

TRACY. I never considered you as that, nor myself!

DEXTER. You did without knowing it. And the night that *you* got drunk on champagne, and climbed out on the roof and stood there naked, with your arms out to the moon, wailing like a banshee— [MIKE, *with a startled expression, moves sideways out into the Library.*]

TRACY. I told you I never had the slightest recollection of doing any such thing!

DEXTER. I know; you drew a blank. You wanted to.—Mr. Connor, what would you say in the case of— [*He turns and sees that* MIKE *has gone.*]

TRACY. He's a reporter, incidentally. He's doing us for *Destiny*.

DEXTER. Sandy told me. A pity we can't supply photographs of you on the roof.

TRACY. Honestly, the fuss you made over that silly, childish—!

DEXTER. It was enormously important, and most revealing. The moon is also a goddess, chaste and virginal.

TRACY. Stop using those foul words! We were married nearly a year, weren't we?

DEXTER. Marriage doesn't change a true case like yours, my dear. It's an affair of the spirit—not of the flesh.

TRACY. Dexter, what are you trying to make me out as?

DEXTER. Tracy, what do you fancy yourself as?

TRACY. I don't know that I fancy myself as anything.

DEXTER. When I read you were going to marry Kittredge, I couldn't believe it. How in the world can you even think of it? [*She turns on him.*]

TRACY. I love him, that's why! As I never even began to love you!

DEXTER. It may be true, but I doubt it. *I* think it's just a swing from me, and what I represent—but I think it's too violent a swing. That's why I came on. Kittredge is no great tower of strength, you know, Tracy. He's just a tower.

TRACY. You've known him how long? —half a day.

DEXTER. I knew him for two days two years ago, the time I went up to the fields with your father, but half a day would have done, I think.

TRACY. It's just personal, then—

DEXTER. Purely and completely.

TRACY. You couldn't possibly understand him or his qualities. I shouldn't expect you to.

DEXTER. I suppose when you come right down to it, Tray, it just offends my vanity to have anyone who was even remotely my wife, marry so obviously beneath her.

TRACY. "Beneath" me! How dare you —any of you—in this day and age, use such a—?

DEXTER. I'm talking about differences in mind and imagination. You could marry Mac, the night watchman, and I'd cheer for you.

TRACY. And what's wrong with George?

[484]

The Philadelphia Story

DEXTER. Nothing—utterly nothing. He's a wizard at his job, and I'm sure he is honest, sober, and industrious. He's just not for you.

TRACY. He *is* for me—he's a great man and a good man: already he's of national importance.

DEXTER. Good Lord—you sound like *Destiny* talking.—Well, whatever he is, you'll have to stick, Tray. He'll give you no out as I did.

TRACY. I won't require one.

DEXTER. I suppose you'd still be attractive to any man of spirit, though. There's something engaging about it, this virgin goddess business, something more challenging to the male than the more obvious charms.

TRACY. Really?

DEXTER. Oh, yes! We're very vain, you know—"This citadel can and shall be taken—and I'm just the boy to do it."

TRACY. You seem quite contemptuous of me, all of a sudden.

DEXTER. Not of you, Red, never of you. You could be the damnedest, finest woman on this earth. If I'm contemptuous of anything, it's of something in you you either can't help, or make no attempt to: your so-called "strength"—your prejudice against weakness—your blank intolerance—

TRACY. Is that all?

DEXTER. That's the gist of it; because you'll never be a first-class woman or a first-class human being, till you have learned to have some small regard for human frailty. It's a pity your own foot can't slip a little some time—but no, your sense of inner divinity won't allow it. The goddess must and shall remain intact.— You know, I think there are more of you around than people realize. You're a special class of American Female now—the Married Maidens.—And of Type Philadelphiaensis, you're the absolute tops, my dear.

TRACY. Damn your soul, Dext, if you say another—! [*He sees* GEORGE *coming in from the Library at Left.*]

DEXTER. I'm through, Tracy—for the moment I've said my say. [GEORGE *smiles at them with a great attempt at good humor.*]

GEORGE. I suppose I ought to object to this twosome.

DEXTER. That would be most objectionable. Well, any time either of you wants more advice from me— [*He moves toward the steps.*]

GEORGE. When we do, we'll give you a ring, Haven.

DEXTER. Do that, will you? You'll find that I have a most sympathetic and understanding ear— [*He turns to* TRACY.] I left you a little wedding present there on the table, Red—I'm sorry I hadn't any ribbon to tie it up with. [*Then goes out down the path.*]

GEORGE. You see—it's no use even attempting to be friendly.

TRACY. Certainly not. You were a dear to try. Please don't mind him. [DINAH *comes in from the Garden, down the opposite path. She mounts the Porch and crosses to the Sitting-Room door.*]

DINAH [*to* TRACY]. You got taken when you bought that roan. She's parrot-jawed.

TRACY. Get into a tub. You're revolting.

DINAH. What's more, she swallows wind by the bucket.

TRACY. Where's Miss Imbrie? Wasn't she with you?

DINAH. No. She's gone to the privy with Uncle Willie. [*She goes out, into the Sitting Room.* TRACY *picks up the package left by* DEXTER, *scrutinizes it, shakes it.*]

TRACY. It's anyone's guess what this

might be. [*She unwraps it.*] It's—why it's a photograph of the "True Love."

GEORGE.—The?—What's that?

TRACY. A boat he designed—and built, practically. We sailed her down the coast of Maine and back, the summer we were married. My, she was yare.

GEORGE. "Yare?" What does that mean?

TRACY. It means—oh, what does it mean?—Easy to handle—quick to the helm—fast—bright—everything a boat should be. [*She gazes at the photograph for a moment without speaking, then drops it upon the table.*] —And the hell with it.

GEORGE. Rather bad taste, I'd say, giving you that.

TRACY. Dexter never concerns himself much with taste.

GEORGE. How'd you ever happen to marry a fellow like that, Tracy?

TRACY. Oh, I don't know—I expect it was kind of a hangover from childhood days. We grew up together, you know.

GEORGE. I see—propinquity.

TRACY. Oh, George—to get away—to get away—! Somehow to feel useful in the world—

GEORGE. Useful?—I'm going to build you an ivory tower with my own two hands.

TRACY. Like fun you are.

GEORGE. You mean you've been in one too long?

TRACY. I mean that, and a lot of things.

GEORGE. I'm going to make a grand life for us, dear—and you can help, all right.

TRACY. I hope I can.

GEORGE. From now on we'll both stop wasting time on unimportant people.

TRACY. That's all right with me.

GEORGE. Our little house on the river up there—I'd like people to consider it an honor to be asked there.

TRACY. Why an honor, especially?

GEORGE. We're going to represent something, Tracy—something straight and sound and fine.—And then perhaps young Mr. Haven may be somewhat less condescending. [*She looks at him.*]

TRACY. George—you don't really mind him, do you? I mean the fact of him—

GEORGE. The—? I don't see what you mean, Tracy.

TRACY. I mean that—you know—that he ever was—was my lord and master— That we ever were—

GEORGE. I don't believe he ever was—not really. I don't believe anyone ever was, or ever will be. That's the wonderful thing about you, Tracy. [*She looks at him startled.*]

TRACY. What? How—?

GEORGE. You're like some marvelous, distant—oh, queen, I guess. You're so cool and fine and—and always so much your own. That's the wonderful *you* in you—that no one can ever really possess—that no one can touch, hardly. It's—it's a kind of beautiful purity, Tracy, that's the only word for it. [*She is now really frightened.*]

TRACY. George—

GEORGE. Oh, it's grand, Tracy—it's just grand! Everyone feels it about you. It's what I first worshiped you for, Tracy, from afar.

TRACY. George, listen—

GEORGE. First, now, and always! [*He leans toward her.*] Only from a little nearer, now—eh, darling?

TRACY. I don't want to be worshiped! I want to be loved!

GEORGE. You're that, too. You're that, all right.

TRACY. I mean really loved.

GEORGE. But that goes without saying, Tracy.

The Philadelphia Story

TRACY. And now it's you—who doesn't see what *I* mean. [EDWARD, *carrying a tray with cocktail things and a bottle of champagne enters from the Sitting Room, followed by* ELSIE. ELSIE *picks up the orange-juice tray from the table.*] You can just leave them, Edward. [EDWARD *places the tray.* ELSIE *looks down at* DEXTER'S *present.*]

ELSIE. Shall I put this picture with the other presents, Miss Tracy?

TRACY. No—just leave it there, please.

ELSIE. Yes, Miss. [*They go out, into the Sitting Room.*]

GEORGE [*to* TRACY]. Don't let Miss Imbrie get hold of it.

TRACY. I should say not. [*She rewraps the picture.*]

GEORGE. I hope they'll soft pedal the first-marriage angle.

TRACY. I wish they'd pedal themselves right out of here.

GEORGE [*after a moment*]. They've got a job to do. And it's an honor, you know, Tracy.

TRACY. What is?

GEORGE. Why—to be done by *Destiny*. [TRACY *frowns at him.*]

TRACY. Are you joking?

GEORGE. Joking—?

TRACY. But you can't seriously mean that you think—!

GEORGE. I think *Destiny* fills a very definite place, Tracy. [TRACY *stares at him uncomprehendingly.* MARGARET *comes in from the Library, followed by* SETH. *Both are in evening clothes.*]

MARGARET. George, you aren't dressed! —And Tracy, you're guests of honor—you mustn't be late. [GEORGE *moves swiftly to the steps.*]

GEORGE. Right on my way, Ma'am! [*He stops and turns to* TRACY.] Wait for me, Tracy! I make the Gatehouse in nothing flat, now! [*He is away, down the path, practically at a run.*]

SETH. Does he by any chance ever walk anywhere?

TRACY. When he likes, I expect.

SETH. I have a feeling he's going to take the ring tomorrow and go through center with it. [MARGARET *laughs and seats herself.*]

MARGARET. Seth, you idiot.

TRACY. That's very amusing, I'm sure.

SETH. Oh, don't take things to heart so, Tracy. You'll wear yourself out. [LIZ *hurries in from the Garden.*]

LIZ. I won't be a minute!

MARGARET. There's no hurry, Miss Imbrie. [LIZ *smiles, and goes out, into the Sitting Room.* SETH *is preparing cocktails.*]

SETH. What bothers me at the moment, is the spectacle we're all making of ourselves for the benefit of the young man and woman from *Destiny*.

TRACY. Whose fault is it?

SETH. That's beside the point.

MARGARET. Never in my life have I felt so self-conscious. It's all simply dreadful.

SETH. It's worse: it's stupid and childish and completely undignified.

TRACY. So are other things.

SETH. They can publish what they like about me, but—

TRACY.—My idea is, they'll publish nothing about any of us.

SETH. How do you propose to stop them?

TRACY. I don't quite know yet.

SETH. Well, at present the least we can do is to inform Connor and the camera-lady that we are all quite aware of their purpose here. I insist on that.

TRACY. All right! I'll tell them myself.

SETH. I think it will come better from me, don't you—as, at least, titular head of the family? [*He gives* MARGARET *a cocktail. A moment, then* TRACY *speaks deliberately harshly.*]

TRACY. Of course—inasmuch as you let us in for it in the first place.

SETH. Do keep that note out of your voice, Tracy. It's most unattractive.

TRACY. Oh? How does Miss Mara talk? Or does she purr?

MARGARET. Tracy!

SETH. It's all right, Margaret.

TRACY. Sweet and low, I suppose. Dulcet. Very ladylike.—You've got a fine right, you have—after the way you've treated Mother—after the way you've treated us all—a magnificent right you've got to come back here in your best county manner and strike attitudes and make stands and criticize my fiancé and give orders and mess things up generally, just as if you'd done—

MARGARET. Stop it instantly, Tracy! [TRACY *rises abruptly.*]

TRACY. I can't help it. It's sickening.— As if he'd done nothing at all!

MARGARET. It is no concern of yours. If it concerns anyone, it concerns—well, actually, I don't know whom it concerns, except your father.

SETH. That's very wise of you, Margaret. What most wives won't seem to realize, is that their husband's philandering—particularly the middle-aged kind—has nothing whatever to do with them.

TRACY. Oh? Then what has it to do with? [SETH *reseats himself.*]

SETH. A reluctance to grow old, I think. I suppose the best mainstay a man can have as he gets along in years is a daughter—the right kind of daughter.

TRACY. That's interesting, to say the least.

SETH.—One who loves him blindly—as no good wife ever should, of course.— One for whom he can do no wrong—

TRACY. How sweet.

SETH. I'm talking seriously about something I've thought out thoroughly. I've had to. I think a devoted young daughter gives a man the illusion that youth is still his.

TRACY. Very important, I suppose.

SETH. Very—and without her, he's inclined to go in search of it again, because it's as precious to him as it is to any woman.—But with a girl of his own full of warmth for him, full of foolish, unquestioning, uncritical affection—

TRACY.—None of which I've got.

SETH. None. You have a good mind, a pretty face and a disciplined body that does what you tell it. You have more wealth than any of us, thanks to one grandfather's name and another's red hair, and a shameless play for both of them since about age three. In fact—

TRACY. I never! I loved them!

SETH.—In fact, you have everything it takes to make a lovely woman except the one essential—an understanding heart. Without it, you might just as well be made of bronze.

TRACY [*after a moment*]. That's an awful thing to say to anyone.

SETH. Indeed it is.

TRACY. So I'm to blame for Tina Mara, am I?

SETH. If any blame attaches, to some extent I expect you are.

TRACY. You coward.

SETH. No.—But better to be one than a prig—and a perennial spinster, however many marriages.

MARGARET. Seth! That's too much.

SETH. I'm afraid it's not enough [TRACY *is staring at him.*]

TRACY. Wha-what did you say I was?

[488]

SETH. Do you want me to repeat it?

MARGARET. Seth—now I understand a great deal that I didn't. [*He goes to her.*]

SETH. It's all past now, Margaret. It has been for some time. Forgive me. You won't have to again. *I* understand a lot more than I did, as well. [MARGARET *touches his hand understandingly. Still* TRACY *stares.*]

TRACY. "A prig and a—?" You mean—you mean you think *I* think I'm some kind of a virgin goddess or something?

SETH. If your ego wishes to call it that, yes.—Also, you've been talking like a jealous woman.

TRACY. A—? [*She turns away, her face a study.*] What's the matter with everyone all at once, anyhow? [UNCLE WILLIE *comes in from the Garden.*]

UNCLE WILLIE. Miss Imbrie preferred dressing, to my company. [*To* SETH.] What do you make of that, Uncle Willie?

SETH. We're going to drop all this. From now on you're yourself again—and so am I. I shall tell Connor and Miss Imbrie we know what their tender mission is, and at the first opportunity. [SANDY *and* DINAH, *in evening clothes, come in from the house.*]

UNCLE WILLIE. It's a pity. It was jolly good fun. Let's have a drink—

SANDY. Damme, let's do that. [*He pours cocktails.*]

DINAH. We're all so completely commonplace. *I* don't see how we interest anyone. [MARGARET *frowns over* DINAH'S *costume.*]

MARGARET. I think that dress hikes up a little behind. [DINAH *sighs.*]

DINAH. No—it's me that does. [TRACY *speaks briefly, out of her preoccupation.*]

TRACY. You look adorable, Dinah.

DINAH. Oh, thanks, Tracy! Thanks ever so much!

SANDY. A wedding without ushers and bridesmaids. Peace! It's wonderful—

DINAH. *I'm* the bridesmaid!—So can I have a cocktail at last? Can I?

MARGARET. Certainly not.

DINAH. It's a dirty gyp. [*She throws herself down in a chair.* SANDY *offers* TRACY *a cocktail.*]

SANDY. Tracy? [*She shakes her head.*] Champagne, instead?

TRACY. No, thanks.

SANDY. Excuse, please. I forgot, you never.

UNCLE WILLIE. Never? The girl's demented.

TRACY.—But prigs don't.

UNCLE WILLIE. What's that?

TRACY. Nor spinsters.

SANDY. We don't get you.

TRACY. Nor goddesses, virgin or otherwise.

SANDY [*to* UNCLE WILLIE].—Not completely: just a borderline case. [MIKE *and* LIZ, *dressed for dinner, enter from the house.* MIKE *wears a soft shirt.* SANDY *greets them.*] Hello! You were quick. [TRACY *is now standing away from them, leaning against a column of the Porch, noticing nothing.*]

UNCLE WILLIE. Miss Imbrie, you are a dream of loveliness. A cocktail or champagne?

LIZ. Thanks, champagne. I've never had enough.

SANDY. You will tonight. [UNCLE WILLIE *gives* LIZ *and* MIKE *a glass.*]

MIKE. Champagne flew. [*He clears his throat, straightens his tie and begins, to* UNCLE WILLIE.] Mr. Lord—er—that is to say— [SETH *speaks simultaneously.*]

SETH. Mr. Connor—oh—excuse me.

MIKE [*again to* UNCLE WILLIE]. Mr. Lord, Miss Imbrie and I have something on our minds—

UNCLE WILLIE. That's splendid; just the place for it. What?

MIKE. Well—er—it's sort of hard to explain—it's—er—about the reason we're here and so forth.

SETH. I think perhaps there's something I ought to explain too—

MIKE.—But did you ever hear of a man named Sidney Kidd? [THOMAS *enters with a tray and note.*]

SETH.—And did you ever hear of a man named Seth—er—? What is it, Thomas?

THOMAS. They've just phoned a telegram, Mr. Lord—

UNCLE WILLIE. Give it here.

THOMAS [*turns to him*]. It's for Mrs. Lord, Mr. Tracy. [LIZ *and* MIKE *exchange glances.*]

UNCLE WILLIE. Then why didn't you say so?

THOMAS.—Mrs. Lord and Miss Lord, that is. [MARGARET, *with a half-smile, glances at* SANDY.]

MARGARET. Read it, Thomas. I haven't my glasses.

SANDY. Hey! Wait a minute!

MARGARET. Read it, Thomas.

THOMAS. "Most frightfully sorry will not be able to get down for the wedding as am confined to my bed with everything wrong. Baby better. It was only gas. Love, Father." Is there any answer, Madam?

MARGARET. No, Thomas—none in this world. [*He goes out.*]

LIZ [*to* UNCLE WILLIE]. He got you a little mixed up, didn't he?

UNCLE WILLIE. A common mistake.

SETH. Now do you understand, Mr. Connor?

MIKE. I think we do.

LIZ. It's wonderful! Lord only knows where we go from here.

SANDY. To Aunt Geneva's!—Come on, everybody.

DINAH. My first party, and about time. [UNCLE WILLIE *moves to* LIZ, *speaks invitingly.*]

UNCLE WILLIE. Who'll come in my little car with me? [MARGARET *moves between them, separating them.*]

MARGARET. Seth and Dinah and I.—Sandy, will you bring Miss Imbrie and Mr. Connor?

SANDY. Like a shot.

DINAH. The evening is pregnant with possibilities. [MARGARET *takes her gently by the shoulders and ushers her out the Library door.*]

MARGARET. "Full of" is better, dear. [UNCLE WILLIE *passes behind* LIZ, *on his way out. She exclaims suddenly.*]

LIZ. Ouch! [SETH *moves to her solicitously.*]

SETH. What was it?

LIZ. N-nothing. [SETH *goes out. She turns to* SANDY.] You know, I felt exactly as if I'd been pinched.

SANDY. Don't think you weren't! [*He and* LIZ *go out.* MIKE *turns to follow them, then stops as he sees* TRACY *still standing motionless against the column.*]

MIKE. Aren't you coming?

TRACY. I'll follow along with George.

MIKE [*after a moment*]. What's the matter with you, Tracy?

TRACY. You tell *me*, will you? [*He looks at her intently.*]

MIKE. Damn if I know. I'd like to. [*She smiles uncertainly.*]

TRACY. Well, if you ever happen to find out—

MIKE.—I'll tell you. Sure. [*After another moment, she speaks again.*]

TRACY.—And remember, Mike—"With the Rich and Mighty—"

MIKE. "—Always a Little Patience"— Yes, Highness, I will.

TRACY. Do that. Please do. [*He looks*

[490]

The Philadelphia Story

at her for an instant longer, then turns abruptly and goes out. She is alone. She brushes her hair back from her brow. She sees the champagne upon the table before her. She takes up a glass, lifts it to her lips, drinks it deliberately, then thoughtfully reaches for another.]

CURTAIN

SCENE 2

[The Porch. About half-past five on Saturday morning. It is going to be a clear day, and throughout the scene the light increases. MAC, *the night watchman, about 30, crosses the path from Left to Right smoking a pipe and swinging a lighted lantern. He goes out, Right.* SANDY *enters from the house. He is carrying a tray with two bottles of champagne, one already opened, a pitcher of milk and glasses. He is followed by* TRACY. *Both are in evening dress.]*

SANDY. The question is, can we get away with it?

TRACY. You've got to get away with it! You must, Sandy!

SANDY. It's your idea, not mine.

TRACY. What difference does that make? *[She pours herself a glass of champagne.]*

SANDY. You get the ideas and I do all the work.

TRACY. Sandy!

SANDY. Okay.

TRACY. What you don't already know about the great Sidney Kidd, you can certainly fill in from Mike's ravings tonight.

SANDY. I used to have that *Dime* lingo down pretty pat.

TRACY. It's a chance to write a beauty: you know it is.

SANDY. Then I swap it with Kidd for Connor's piece on us—and where am I?

TRACY. You'll have the satisfaction of knowing you saved the lot of us single-handed.

SANDY. And if he won't swap?

TRACY. I'm not worried about that.

SANDY. I suppose there's a fair chance the *Post* would go for it.

TRACY. Of course! You can't possibly lose. Quick—they'll be here! How long will it take you?

SANDY. Three thousand words—all night —what there's left of it. *[He looks at his watch.]* Holy cats! You get to bed.

TRACY. Have you got a typewriter?

SANDY. My old Corona is upstairs, I think.

TRACY. Make it smoke.

SANDY. You bet.

TRACY. Suds. I can't stand it. You won't fall asleep?

SANDY. I've drunk nothing but black coffee since Connor began his lecture.

TRACY. "Sidney Kidd—his habits—his habitat—and how to hunt him."

SANDY. Poor Connor! It must have been bottled up in him for years.

TRACY. Waiter, another bottle.

SANDY. No. I've got enough for three articles now: profile, full-face—

TRACY.—Also rear elevation.—Mike and Liz—they mustn't suspect, Sandy.

SANDY. Oh, no—oh, my, no!

TRACY. They have simply stepped in their own chewing gum.—I suppose Kidd has one of those private numbers the rich and the mighty hide behind in New York.

SANDY. I'll dig it out of Liz and give him a buzz.

TRACY. What will you say?

SANDY. I'll be brief, bluff, belligerent. *[*TRACY *laughs and pours herself another glass of champagne.]* Here—lay off that!

[491]

TRACY. Why?

SANDY. You are already in wine, sister.

TRACY. Me? You lie. It never affects me, not in the slightest.

SANDY. That's because you never take it.

TRACY. Even if I did, it wouldn't.

SANDY. Don't say that: it's unlucky. [*She drains the glass.* SANDY *shakes his head over her.*] I have seen people fly in the face of Pommery before.

TRACY. I've just got a good head, I guess.

SANDY. Don't say it, don't say it! [TRACY *seats herself upon the steps.*]

TRACY. Sandy, you fool.

SANDY. George will spank.

TRACY. I could spank George for the way he behaved. [SANDY *seats himself beside her.*]

SANDY. He had a right to be sore. You and Mike disappeared for two hours, at least.

TRACY. You were along.

SANDY. All the same, tongues were wagging like tails. George said—

TRACY. George wanted to leave sharp at twelve—how could we?

SANDY. They need a lot of sleep, those big fellows.

TRACY. They must.—Then at one, with Father and Mother and Dinah.—Then at two, then at three—every hour on the hour. We fought like wolves in the car coming home.

SANDY. I hope you explained.

TRACY. Certainly not. He should have known. He was extremely rude. You'd have thought I had been out with Dexter, or something.—[*She thinks for a moment.*] I wonder where Dext was? I half expected him to— I don't like the look behind Dexter's eyes, Sandy. It makes me sad.

SANDY. Don't be sad, Tracy. [*He puts an arm about her and for an instant she rests her head against his shoulder.*]

TRACY. Oh, Sandy, if you knew how I envy you and Sue that darling fat little creature you've just produced—

SANDY. You'll probably have four or five of your own any day now.

TRACY. Six! Oh, I hope—I do hope!—I hope I'm good for something besides knocking out golf balls and putting horses over fences.

SANDY. You're good for my money any day.

TRACY. Thanks! [*She gets up from the step and moves again to the table.*] Was I really mean to George I wonder? I don't want to be.

SANDY. You're in an odd mood, little fellah. What's amiss—what's afoot?

TRACY. I guess it's just that—a lot of things I always thought were terribly important, I find now are—and the other way around—and—oh, what the hell. [*She refills her glass, looks at it and puts it down upon the table.*]

SANDY. I don't think I'd spend much more time with Connor tonight, if I were you.

TRACY. Why not?

SANDY. Writers with wine sauce intoxicate little girls. [*She laughs uncertainly.*]

TRACY. They sort of do, don't they?— He fascinates me. He's so violent, Sandy.

SANDY. He's fallen, Tray. I could hear him bump.

TRACY. Mind your own beeswax, old Nosey Parker.

SANDY. Get thee to bed. [*She reaches for her glass—he stops her hand.*]

TRACY. No!

SANDY.—Before you have to be carried.

TRACY. No! No! No! [*She throws up her arms, her head back.*] I feel too delicious!—Sandy, I feel just elegant. [*Then cocks her head, listening.*] Is that my bedroom telephone?

SANDY. Now you're hearing things.

TRACY. It couldn't be anyone but George. I *was* sort of swinish to him. Perhaps I'd better— [*She starts toward the Sitting Room.*] As for you—get to work, you dog. Stop leaning on your shovel. [*She stops, as* MIKE *comes out upon the Porch from the Library. He is in fine fettle, coatless, his soft shirt open at the neck. He goes directly to the table.*]

MIKE. Listen! Now I'm really under way. Miss not an inflection.

TRACY. Is it Connor the poet, or Connor the conspirator?

MIKE. Both! [*He pours himself a glass of wine and begins to declaim.*] "No lightweight is balding, beetlebrowed Sidney Kidd, no mean displacement, his: for windy bias, bicarbonate." [*He drinks the wine, looks at the glass.*] This is funny stuff. I'm used to whisky. Whisky is a clap on the back. Champagne, entwining arms.

TRACY. That's pretty. Is it poetry?

MIKE. *Dime* will tell.

SANDY. "None before him but Writer Wolfgang Goethe has known all about all. Gigantic was Goethe's output, bigger already is Kidd's. Sample from his own pen: 'Pittsburgh is a gentle city.'"

TRACY. Sidney is a gentle man. [MIKE *points a finger at* SANDY.)

MIKE. Potent, able, beady-eyed scion of great wealth in Quakertown, why don't you do a piece on our great and good friend?

SANDY. On Kidd?

MIKE. On none other.

SANDY. Nimble scrivener, it's an idea.

TRACY. Brilliant. I wish *I'd* thought of it. [MIKE *turns and points a finger at her.*]

MIKE. Baby Giant Tycooness.

TRACY. But would it not be a low, dirty deed?

MIKE. *He'd* print a scandal about his best friend: he's said he would.

SANDY. Who is his best friend?

MIKE. I guess Santa Claus. [*He passes his hand vaguely over his face.*] What is this mist before my eyes? [TRACY *rises suddenly and goes to the table.*]

TRACY. *I* tell you what! Let's all have a quick swim to brighten us up. Go get Liz, Sandy. [*She strips off her bracelets and rings and leaves them on table.*]

SANDY. Not me: It's too cold this early.

TRACY. It's the best hour of the day! Dexter and I always swam after parties.

MIKE. I haven't got any bathing suit.

TRACY. But we won't need any! It's just ourselves. [*He looks at her uncertainly for an instant, then quickly fills two glasses, moves one gingerly toward her, and raises the other.*]

MIKE. Let's dip into this instead.

TRACY. [*after a brief pause, to* SANDY]. No takers.—Get Liz anyway, Sandy.

SANDY. If she's not in bed. [*He goes out into the Sitting Room.*]—Or even if she is.

TRACY [*to* MIKE, *after a moment*]. That was an odd thing you just did—

MIKE. Me?

TRACY [*turning away*]. You. For a moment you made me—self-conscious.

MIKE. How? About what?

TRACY. Never mind. [*She raises her glass.*] Hello, you. [*He raises his.*]

MIKE. Hello.

TRACY. You look fine.

MIKE. I *feel* fine.

TRACY. Quite a fellah.

MIKE. They say. [*They drink.*]

TRACY. Did you enjoy the party?

MIKE. Sure. The prettiest sight in this fine pretty world is the Privileged Class enjoying its privileges.

TRACY.—Also somewhat of a snob.

MIKE. How do you mean?

TRACY. I'm wondering.

MIKE. Consider, Gentle Reader: they toil not, neither do they spin.

TRACY. Oh, yes, they do! They spin in circles. [*She spins once and seats herself upon the step at Left.* MIKE *goes to her.*]

MIKE. Nicely put. "Awash with champagne was Mrs. Willie Q. Tracy (born Geneva Biddle)'s stately pleasure dome on a hilltop in smart Radnor, Pa., on a Saturday night late in June, the eve of her great-niece's—" [*He sits beside her.*] Tracy, you can't marry that guy.

TRACY. George?—I'm going to. Why not?

MIKE. I don't know. I'd have thought I'd be for it. But somehow you just don't seem to match up.

TRACY. Then the fault's with me.

MIKE. Maybe so: all the same, you can't do it. [TRACY *rises and moves a little way along the path.*]

TRACY. No? Come around about noon tomorrow—I mean today. [*After a moment he rises and faces her.*]

MIKE. Tracy—

TRACY. Yes, Mr. Connor?

MIKE. How do you mean, I'm "a snob"?

TRACY. You're the worst kind there is: an intellectual snob. You've made up your mind awfully young, it seems to me. [MIKE *goes to her.*]

MIKE. Thirty's about time to make up your mind.—And I'm nothing of the sort, not Mr. Connor.

TRACY. The time to make up your mind about people is never. Yes, you are—and a complete one.

MIKE. You're quite a girl.

TRACY. You think?

MIKE. I know.

TRACY. Thank you, Professor. I don't think I'm exceptional.

MIKE. You are, though.

TRACY. I know any number like me. You ought to get around more.

MIKE. In the Upper Clahss? No, thanks.

TRACY. You're just a mass of prejudices, aren't you? You're so much thought and so little feeling, Professor. [*She moves Right, further away from him.*]

MIKE. Oh, I am, am I? [*She wheels about on him.*]

TRACY. Yes, you am, are you!—Your damned intolerance furiates me. I mean *in*furiates me! I should think, of all people, a writer would need tolerance. The fact is, you'll never—you can't be a first-rate writer or a first-rate human being until you learn to have some small regard for— [*Suddenly she stops. Her eyes widen, remembering. She turns from him.*] Aren't the geraniums pretty, Professor? Is it not a handsome day that begins? [MIKE *mounts the Porch, looks down upon her.*]

MIKE. Lay off that "Professor."

TRACY. Yes, Professor. [*She mounts the Porch, faces him.*]

MIKE. You've got all the arrogance of your class all right, haven't you?

TRACY. Holy suds, what have "classes" to do with it!

MIKE. Quite a lot.

TRACY. Why? What do they matter—except for the people in them? George comes from the so-called "lower" class, Dexter comes from the upper. Well?

MIKE. Well?

TRACY.—Though there's a great deal to be said for Dexter—and don't you forget it!

MIKE. I'll try not to. [TRACY *moves to the table.*]

TRACY. Mac, the night watchman, is a prince among men and Joey, the stable boy, is a rat. Uncle Hugh is a saint. Uncle Willie's a pincher. [*She fills her glass again.*]

MIKE. So what?

TRACY. There aren't any rules about human beings, that's all!—You're teaching me things, Professor: this is new to me. Thanks, I am beholden to you. [*She raises her glass to him.*]

MIKE. Not at all.

TRACY. "Upper" and "lower" my eye! I'll take the lower, thanks. [*She brings the glass to her lips.*]

MIKE.—If you can't get a drawing-room. [*She puts the glass down, untasted, and turns on him.*]

TRACY. What do you mean by that?

MIKE. My mistake.

TRACY. Decidedly.

MIKE. Okay.

TRACY. You're insulting.

MIKE. I'm sorry.

TRACY. Oh, don't apologize!

MIKE. Who the hell's apologizing?

TRACY. I never knew such a man.

MIKE. You wouldn't be likely to, dear—not from where *you* sit.

TRACY. Talk about arrogance!

MIKE [*after a moment*]. Tracy—

TRACY. What do you want?

MIKE. You're wonderful. [*She laughs.*]

TRACY. Professor—may I go out?

MIKE. Class is dismissed. [*She moves Left.*] Miss Lord will please wait. [*She stops, turns and meets his gaze steadily.*]

TRACY. Miss Lord is privileged. [MIKE *speaks in a lower voice.*]

MIKE. There's magnificence in you, Tracy. I'm telling you.

TRACY. I'm—! [*A moment.*] Now I'm getting self-conscious again. I—it's funny— [*Another moment. Then she moves toward him, impulsively.*] Mike, let's— [*She stops herself.*]

MIKE. What?

TRACY. I—I don't know—go up, I guess. It's late.

MIKE.—A magnificence that comes out of your eyes, that's in your voice, in the way you stand there, in the way you walk. You're lit from within, bright, bright, bright. There are fires banked down in you, hearth-fires and holocausts— [*She moves another step toward him, stands before him.*]

TRACY. You—I don't seem to you—made of bronze, then—

MIKE. You're made of flesh and blood—that's the blank, unholy surprise of it. You're the golden girl, Tracy, full of love and warmth and delight— What the hell's this? You've got tears in your eyes.

TRACY. Shut up, shut up!—Oh, Mike—keep talking—keep talking! *Talk*, will you?

MIKE. I've stopped. [*For a long moment they look at each other. Then* TRACY *speaks, deliberately, harshly.*]

TRACY. Why? Has your mind taken hold again, dear Professor?

MIKE. You think so? [*She moves Right, away from him.*]

TRACY. Yes, Professor.

MIKE. A good thing, don't you agree? [*She leans against the column of the Porch, facing him.*]

TRACY. No, Professor.

MIKE. Drop that Professor—you hear me?

TRACY. Yes, Professor. [*He moves to her slowly, stands almost against her.*]

MIKE. That's really all I am to you, is it?

TRACY. Of course, Professor.

MIKE. Are you sure? [*She looks up at him.*]

TRACY. Why, why yes—yes, of course, Profess— [*His kiss stops the word. The*

[495]

kiss is taken and returned. After it she exclaims softly.] Golly. [She gazes at him wonderingly, then raises her face to receive another. Then she stands in his arms, her cheek against his breast, amazement in her eyes.] Golly Moses.

MIKE. Tracy dear—

TRACY. Mr. Connor—Mr. Connor—

MIKE. Let me tell you something—

TRACY. No, don't— All of a sudden I've got the shakes.

MIKE. I have, too.

TRACY. What *is* it?

MIKE. It must be something like love.

TRACY. No, no! It mustn't be. It can't—

MIKE. Why? Would it be inconvenient?

TRACY. Terribly. Anyway, it isn't. I know it's not. Oh, Mike, I'm a bad girl—

MIKE. Not you.

TRACY. We're out of our minds.

MIKE. —Right into our hearts.

TRACY. That ought to have music.

MIKE. It has, hasn't it?—Tracy, you lovely— [*She hears something, looks quickly toward the door, whispers.*]

TRACY. They're coming.

MIKE. The hell. [*She holds a hand out to him.*]

TRACY. It's—it's not far to the pool. It's only over the lawn, in the birch-grove— it'll be lovely now.

MIKE. Come on—

TRACY. Oh, it's as—it's as if my insteps —were melting away.—What is it? Have I—have I got feet of clay, or something?

MIKE. —Quick! Here they are— [*He takes her hand and hurries her down the steps.*]

TRACY. I—I feel so small all at once.

MIKE. You're immense—you're tremendous.

TRACY. Not me—oh, not me! Put me in your pocket, Mike— [*They are gone. A moment, then* SANDY *comes quickly in from the house, a sheaf of photographs in his hand. He is followed by* LIZ, *in pajamas and wrapper.*]

LIZ. You give those back!

SANDY. Look, Tracy— [*He sees that the Porch is empty.*]

LIZ. May I have them, please?

SANDY. Did Kidd *know* you took these shots of him?

LIZ. Some of them.

SANDY. Sit down. Have a drink.

LIZ. I should say not. A drink would be redundant, tautological, and a mistake. [*Wearily she drops into a chair and eyes the pitcher on the table.*] Is that milk?

SANDY. That is milk.

LIZ. Gimme. Milk, I will accept. [*He pours and gives her a glass.*] I met this cow this afternoon. Nice Bossy.

SANDY. Let me keep just these three shots.

LIZ. What for?

SANDY. A low purpose.

LIZ. Sufficiently low?

SANDY. Nefarious.

LIZ. You won't reproduce them?

SANDY. Nope.

LIZ. Nor cause them to be reproduced?

SANDY. Honest.

LIZ. —In any way, shape, or manner, without permission?

SANDY. So help me, Sidney Kidd.

LIZ. Amen.

SANDY. What's his private number?

LIZ. You mean his private number or his sacred private number?

SANDY. The one by the bed and the bathtub.

LIZ. Regent 4-1416— [*She settles lower in the chair.* SANDY *goes to the telephone just inside the near Sitting-Room door.*] I won't tell you. [*She listens a moment, as he dials. Then.*] Is Mr. Kittredge pure gold, Lord? [SANDY *comes into the doorway, the telephone in hand.*]

SANDY. We must never doubt that, Missy. [*He stands behind her chair, looking down upon her.*]

LIZ [*sleepily*]. Lèse majesté—excuse it, please.

SANDY [*to the telephone*]. Regent 4-1416 New York.—Wayne 22-23. [*To Liz.*]—And Mr. Connor—what of him?

LIZ. Percentage of base metal. Alloy.

SANDY. So.

LIZ.—Which imparts a certain shape and firmness.

SANDY [*to the telephone*]. Hello?—Mr. Kidd? This is Alexander Lord. [LIZ *listens intently.*]

LIZ. I know nothing about this.

SANDY. No, I'm in Philadelphia.—Yes, I know it is. It's early here, too. Look, Mr. Kidd, I think you'd better get over here as fast as you can. What?—I'm sorry to have to tell you, sir, but Connor has had an accident—yes, pretty bad—he had a pretty bad fall.—No, it's his heart we're worried about now.—Yes, I'm afraid so: He keeps talking about you, calling you names—I mean calling your name.—How's that?—No, the eleven o'clock's time enough. We don't expect him to regain consciousness much before then.

LIZ. His only hope is to get fired—I know it is.

SANDY. Sorry, Miss Imbrie's sleeping. Shock.—The newspapers? No, they don't know a thing about it. I understand. What? I said I understood, didn't I?—Twelve-twenty North Philadelphia—I'll have you met. [*He disappears briefly into the Sitting Room and returns without the telephone.*] He wants no publicity. [LIZ *has suppressed her broadening grin. She stirs lazily in her chair and inquires.*]

LIZ. Who was that?

SANDY. God. [*She looks toward the Garden path.*]

LIZ. Do I hear someone?

SANDY. It's Mac, the night watchman.—Liz—you're in love with Connor, aren't you?

LIZ. People ask the oddest questions.

SANDY. Why don't you marry him?

LIZ. I can't hear you.

SANDY. I say, why don't you—? [DEXTER *comes along the path and stops at the steps. He wears flannels and an old jacket.*] Hello, here's an early one!

DEXTER. Hello. I saw quite a full day ahead, and got myself up. [*He seats himself on the steps.*]—A good party?

SANDY. Fine.

DEXTER. Good. [*He lights a cigarette.* LIZ *rises from her chair.*]

LIZ.—And sufficient. Hell or high water, I'm going to bed. [*She moves toward the far Sitting-Room door.*]

SANDY [*following her*]. Why don't you, Liz—*you* know—what I asked?

LIZ. He's still got a lot to learn, and I don't want to get in his way yet a while. Okay?

SANDY. Okay.—Risky, though. Suppose another girl came along in the meantime?

LIZ. Oh, I'd just scratch her eyes out, I guess.—That is, unless she was going to marry someone else the next day.

SANDY. You're a good number, Liz.

LIZ. No, I just photograph well. [*She goes out.*]

DEXTER. Complications? [SANDY *re-examines the photographs.*]

SANDY. There might be.

DEXTER. Where are they?

SANDY. Who?

DEXTER. The complications.

SANDY. They went up—at least I hope and pray that they did.

[497]

DEXTER. Well, well. [SANDY *waves the photographs at him and moves toward the Library door.*]

SANDY. Make yourself comfortable, Dext. I've got a little blackmailing to do. [SANDY *goes out.* DEXTER *smokes quietly for a moment, then rises and stamps out his cigarette as he hears someone coming along the path.* GEORGE *enters, still in evening clothes. He stops in surprise at the sight of* DEXTER.]

GEORGE. What are you doing here?

DEXTER. Oh, I'm a friend of the family's—just dropped in for a chat.

GEORGE. Don't try to be funny. I asked you a question.

DEXTER. I might ask you the same one.

GEORGE. I telephoned Tracy and her phone didn't answer.

DEXTER. I didn't telephone. I just came right over.

GEORGE. I was worried, so I—

DEXTER. Yes, I was worried, too.

GEORGE. About what?

DEXTER. What do you think of this Connor—or do you?

GEORGE. What about him?

DEXTER. I just wondered. [*He moves away from him, toward the table.*]

GEORGE. Listen: If you're trying to insinuate some—

DEXTER. My dear fellow, I wouldn't dream of it! I was only— [*He stops suddenly as* TRACY'S *rings and bracelets upon the table catch his eye.* GEORGE *looks down the Garden path.*]

GEORGE. Who's that I hear? [DEXTER *glances quickly down the path in the direction of the swimming pool, then pockets the rings and bracelets. He turns to* GEORGE.]

DEXTER. Look, Kittredge: I advise you to go to bed.

GEORGE. Oh, you do, do you?

DEXTER. Yes. I strongly urge you to do so at once.

GEORGE. I'm staying right here. [DEXTER *looks at him.*]

DEXTER. You're making a mistake. Somehow I don't think you'll understand.

GEORGE. You'd better leave that to—! I hear someone walking—

DEXTER. Yes?—Must be Mac. [*He calls out down the path, making every word clear.*] It's all right, Mac—it's only us! [*He turns to* GEORGE—*comes down to him.*] Come on—I'll walk along with you.

GEORGE. I'm staying right here—so are you.

DEXTER. All right, then: take the works, and may God be with you. [*He retires into a corner of the Porch. Heavy steps on the gravel path draw nearer. Finally,* MIKE *appears, carrying* TRACY *in his arms. Both are in bathrobes and slippers and there is a jumble of clothes, his and hers, slung over* MIKE'S *shoulder. He stops with her for a moment at the top of the steps. She stirs in his arms, speaks lowly, as if from a long way away.*]

TRACY. Take me upstairs, Mike—

MIKE. Yes, dear. Here we go. [GEORGE *looms up.*]

GEORGE. What the—! [DEXTER *comes swiftly in between him and* MIKE.]

DEXTER. Easy, old boy! [*To* MIKE.] She's not hurt?

MIKE. No. She's just— [TRACY *murmurs dreamily.*]

TRACY. Not wounded, sire—but dead.

GEORGE. She—she hasn't any clothes on!

TRACY [*into* MIKE'S *shoulder*]. Not a stitch—it's delicious. [MIKE *speaks lowly.*]

MIKE. It seems the minute she hit the water, the wine— [DEXTER *glances at* GEORGE, *who can only stare.*]

[498]

DEXTER. A likely story, Connor.
MIKE. What did you say?
DEXTER. I said, a likely story!
MIKE. Listen: if—!
DEXTER. You'll come down again directly?
MIKE. Yes, if you want.
DEXTER. I want. [TRACY *lifts her head limply and looks at them.*]
TRACY. Hello, Dexter. Hello, George. [*She crooks her head around and looks vaguely up at* MIKE.] Hello, Mike. [DEXTER *goes and opens the screen door for them.*]
DEXTER. The second door on the right at the top of the stairs. Mind you don't wake Dinah. [MIKE *moves toward the door with* TRACY.]
TRACY. My feet are of clay—made of clay—did you know it? [*She drops her head again and tightens her arms around* MIKE'S *neck.*] Goo' nigh'—sleep well, little man. [MIKE *carries her out, past* DEXTER.]
DEXTER [*calling after them*]. Look out for Dinah! [*He comes forward.*] How are the mighty fallen!—But if I know Tracy—and I know her very well—she'll remember very little of this. For the second time in her life, she may draw quite a tidy blank.—Of course she may worry, though—
GEORGE. Good God! [DEXTER *turns on him swiftly.*]
DEXTER. You believe it, then?
GEORGE. Believe what?
DEXTER. The—er—the implications of what you've seen, let's say.
GEORGE. What else is there to believe?
DEXTER. Why, I suppose that's entirely up to you.
GEORGE. I've got eyes, and I've got imagination, haven't I?

DEXTER. I don't know. Have you?
GEORGE. So you pretend not to believe it—
DEXTER. Yes, I pretend not to.
GEORGE. Then you don't know women.
DEXTER. Possibly not.
GEORGE. You're a blind fool!
DEXTER. Oh, quite possibly!
GEORGE.—God! [DEXTER *studies him.*]
DEXTER. You won't be too hard on her, will you?
GEORGE. I'll make up my own mind what I'll be!
DEXTER. But we're all only human, you know.
GEORGE. You—all of you—with your damned sophisticated ideas!
DEXTER. Isn't it hell? [MIKE *comes swiftly through the door and up to* DEXTER.]
MIKE. Well? [GEORGE *advances.*]
GEORGE. Why, you lowdown—!
DEXTER [*quickly*]. The lady is my wife, Mr. Connor. [*His uppercut to* MIKE'S *jaw sends him across the Porch and to the floor.*]
GEORGE. You!—What right have—?
DEXTER.—A husband's, till tomorrow, Kittredge.
GEORGE. I'll make up my mind, all right! [*He turns, and storms out down the Garden path.* DEXTER *bends over* MIKE.]
DEXTER. Okay, old man? [MIKE *sits up, nursing his chin.*]
MIKE. Listen: if you think—!
DEXTER. I know—I'm sorry. But I thought I'd better hit you before he did. [MAC, *the night watchman, comes along the Garden path from the opposite direction taken by* GEORGE. *He is putting his lantern out.* DEXTER *straightens up.*] Hello, Mac. How are you?
MAC. Hello, Dexter! Anything wrong?

DEXTER. Not a thing, Mac.—Just as quiet as a church.

MAC. Who is it? [MIKE *turns his face to him.*] Hell!—I thought it might be Kittredge.

DEXTER. We can't have everything, Mac. [MAC *laughs, shakes his head, and continues along the path.*]

CURTAIN

ACT III

[*The Sitting Room. Late morning, Saturday. The room is full of bright noonday sun and there are flowers everywhere.* UNCLE WILLIE, *in a morning coat, fancy waistcoat, and Ascot, stands in the center of the room facing* THOMAS.]

THOMAS. I am trying to think, Mr. Tracy. [*A moment, then* UNCLE WILLIE *demands impatiently.*]

UNCLE WILLIE. Well? Well?

THOMAS. She wakened late, sir, and had a tray in her room. I believe May and Elsie are just now dressing her.

UNCLE WILLIE. It's not the bride I'm asking about—it's her sister.

THOMAS. I haven't seen Miss Dinah since breakfast, sir. She came down rather early.

UNCLE WILLIE. Is there anything wrong with her?

THOMAS. I did notice that she seemed a trifle silent, took only one egg and neglected to finish her cereal. The hot cakes and bacon, however, went much as usual.

UNCLE WILLIE. She was telephoning me like a mad woman before I was out of my tub. [DINAH, *in blue-jeans, tiptoes in from the Porch and up behind him.*] I expected at least two bodies, hacked beyond recognition, the house stiff with police, and— [DINAH *tugs at his coattail. He starts and turns.*] Good God, child—don't do that! I drank champagne last night.

DINAH. Hello, Uncle Willie.

UNCLE WILLIE. *Why* must I come on ahead of your Aunt Geneva? Why must I waste not one minute? What's amiss? What's about? Speak up! Don't stand there with your big eyes like a stuffed owl. [DINAH *glances significantly at* THOMAS.]

THOMAS. Is there anything else, sir? If not—

UNCLE WILLIE. Thanks, Thomas, nothing. [THOMAS *goes out. Again* DINAH *tugs at* UNCLE WILLIE'S *coattail, drawing him to an armchair.*]

DINAH. Come over here—and speak very low. Nobody's allowed to come in here this morning but Tracy—and speak terribly low.

UNCLE WILLIE. What the Sam Hill for? What's alack? What's afoot?

DINAH. I had no one to turn to but you, Uncle Willie.

UNCLE WILLIE. People are always turning to me. I wish they'd stop. [*She kneels on another chair, leaning over the table to him.*]

DINAH. It's desperate. It's about Tracy.

UNCLE WILLIE. Tracy? What's she up to now? Tracy this, and Tracy that. Upstairs and downstairs and in my lady's chamber.

DINAH. How did you know?

UNCLE WILLIE. Know what?

DINAH. It seems to me you know just about everything.

UNCLE WILLIE. I have a fund of information accumulated through the years. I am old, seasoned, and full of instruction.

The Philadelphia Story

But there are gaps in my knowledge. Ask me about falconry, say, or ballistics, and you will get nowhere.

DINAH. I meant more about people and—and sin.

UNCLE WILLIE. I know only that they are inseparable. I also know that the one consolation for being old is the realization that, however you live, you will never die young.—Get to the point, child. What do you want of me?

DINAH. Advice.

UNCLE WILLIE. On what subject or subjects?

DINAH [*after a moment*]. Well, lookit: you don't like George, do you?

UNCLE WILLIE. Kittredge? I deplore him.

DINAH. And you'd like it if Tracy didn't go ahead and have married him after all—or would you?

UNCLE WILLIE. Where do you go to school?

DINAH. I don't, yet. I'm going some place next fall.

UNCLE WILLIE. And high time.—Like it? I would cheer. I would raise my voice in song.

DINAH. Well, I think I know a way to stop her from, but I need advice on how.

UNCLE WILLIE. Proceed, child—proceed cautiously.

DINAH. Well, suppose she all of a sudden developed an illikit passion for someone—

UNCLE WILLIE. Can you arrange it?

DINAH. It doesn't need to be. It is already.

UNCLE WILLIE. Ah? Since when?

DINAH. Last night—and well into the morning.

UNCLE WILLIE. You surprise me, Dinah.

DINAH. Imagine what *I* was—and just imagine what *George* would be.

UNCLE WILLIE. And—er—the object of this—er—illikit passion—

DINAH. Let him be nameless.—Only tell me, should I tell George?—It's getting late. [*Unnoticed by them* DEXTER *has come in from the Porch.*]

UNCLE WILLIE. Maybe he'll want to marry her anyway.

DINAH. But she can't! If she marries anyone, it's got to be Mr. Connor!

UNCLE WILLIE. Connor? Why Connor?

DINAH. She's just got to, that's all! [DEXTER *comes forward.*]

DEXTER. Why, Dinah? What makes you think she should? [DINAH *looks at him, appalled.*]

DINAH. Dexter!

DEXTER. Isn't that a pretty big order to swing at this late date?

DINAH. I—I didn't say anything. What did *I* say?

DEXTER. Of course, you might talk it over with her.—But maybe you have.

DINAH. Certainly not, I haven't!

UNCLE WILLIE. Apparently the little cherub has seen or heard something.

DEXTER. That's Dexter's own Dinah.

UNCLE WILLIE. I must say *you* show a certain amount of cheek, walking in here on this, of all mornings.

DEXTER. Tracy just did a very sweet thing: she telephoned and asked me what to do for a feeling of fright accompanied by headache.

DINAH. I should think it would be bad luck for a first husband to see the bride before the wedding.

DEXTER. That's what I figured.—Why all this about Connor, Dinah? Did the party give you bad dreams?

DINAH. It wasn't any dream.

DEXTER. I wouldn't be too sure. Once you've gone to bed it's pretty hard to tell, isn't it? [DINAH *ponders this.*]

DINAH. Is it?

DEXTER. You bet your hat it is. It's practically impossible.

DINAH. I thought it was Sandy's typewriter woke me up. [TRACY *comes in from the Hall, in the dress in which she is to be married. A leather-strapped wrist watch dangles from her hand. She moves to the sofa.*]

TRACY. Hello! Isn't it a fine day, though! Is everyone fine? That's fine! [*She seats herself uncertainly.*] My, I'm hearty.

DEXTER. How are you otherwise?

TRACY. I don't know what's the matter with me. I must have had too much sun yesterday.

DEXTER. It's awfully easy to get too much. [*She picks up a silver cigarette box and looks at herself in it.*]

TRACY. My eyes don't open properly. [*She blinks up at* DEXTER.] Please go home, Dext.

DEXTER. Not till we get those eyes open. [*He seats himself beside her upon the sofa. She notices* UNCLE WILLIE.]

TRACY. Uncle Willie, good morning.

UNCLE WILLIE. That remains to be seen.

TRACY. Aren't you here early?

UNCLE WILLIE. Weddings get me out like nothing else.

DINAH. It's nearly half-past twelve.

TRACY. It can't be!

DINAH. Maybe it can't, but it is.

TRACY. Where—where's Mother? [DINAH *springs up.*]

DINAH. Do you want her?

TRACY. No, I just wondered. [DINAH *reseats herself.*]

DINAH. She's talking with the orchestra, and Father with the minister, and—

TRACY. Dr. Parsons—already?

DINAH.—And Miss Imbrie's gone with her camera to shoot the horses, and Sandy's in his room and—and Mr. Connor, he hasn't come down yet.

DEXTER. And it's Saturday.

TRACY. Thanks loads. It's nice to have things accounted for. [*She passes the hand with the wrist watch across her brow, then looks at the watch.*]—Only I wonder what this might be?

DEXTER. It looks terribly like a wrist watch.

TRACY. But whose? I found it in my room. I nearly stepped on it.

DINAH. Getting out of bed?

TRACY. Yes. Why?

DINAH. I just wondered. [TRACY *puts the watch on the table before her.*]

TRACY. There's another mystery, Uncle Willie.

UNCLE WILLIE. Mysteries irritate me.

TRACY. I was robbed at your house last night.

UNCLE WILLIE. You don't say.

TRACY. Yes—my bracelets and my engagement ring are missing everywhere.

UNCLE WILLIE. Probably someone's house guest from New York. [DEXTER *brings them out of his pocket.*]

DEXTER. Here you are. [*She takes them, stares at them, then at him.*]

TRACY.—But you weren't at the party!

DEXTER. Wasn't I?

TRACY. Were you?

DEXTER. Don't tell me you don't remember!

TRACY. I—I do now, sort of—but there were such a lot of people. [DEXTER *rises.*]

DEXTER. You should have taken a quick swim to shake them off. There's nothing like a swim after a late night.

TRACY.—A swim. [*And her eyes grow rounder.* DEXTER *laughs.*]

DEXTER. There! Now they're open!

DINAH. That was just the beginning—

and it was no dream. [DEXTER *glances at her, then moves to* UNCLE WILLIE.]

DEXTER. Don't you think, sir, that if you and I went to the pantry at this point—you know: speaking of eye-openers? [UNCLE WILLIE *rises and precedes him toward the Porch.*]

UNCLE WILLIE. The only sane remark I've heard this morning. I know a formula that is said to pop the pennies off the eyelids of dead Irishmen. [*He goes out.* DEXTER *stops beside* DINAH.]

DEXTER. Oh, Dinah—if conversation drags, you might tell Tracy your dream. [*He goes out.* DINAH *turns and gazes reflectively at* TRACY.]

TRACY. What did he say?

DINAH. Oh, nothing. [*She goes to* TRACY *and puts an arm around her shoulder.*] Tray—I hate you to get married and go away.

TRACY. I'll miss you, darling. I'll miss all of you.

DINAH. We'll miss you, too.—It—it isn't like when you married Dexter, and just moved down the road a ways.

TRACY. I'll come back often. It's only Wilkes-Barre.

DINAH. It gripes me.

TRACY [*fondly*]. Baby— [*There is another silence.* DINAH *gazes at her intently, then gathers her forces and speaks.*]

DINAH. You know, I did have the funniest dream about you last night.

TRACY [*without interest*]. Did you? What was it?

DINAH. It was terribly interesting, and —and awfully scary, sort of— [TRACY *rises from the sofa.*]

TRACY. Do you like my dress, Dinah?

DINAH. Yes, ever so much. [TRACY *has risen too quickly. She wavers a moment, steadies herself, then moves to the Porch door.*]

TRACY. It feels awfully heavy.—You'd better rush and get ready yourself.

DINAH. You know me: I don't take a minute. [MARGARET, *dressed for the wedding, comes in from the Parlor, from whence violins are now heard, tuning up.*]

MARGARET. Turn around, Tracy. [TRACY *turns.*] Yes, it looks lovely.

TRACY. What's that—that scratching sound I hear?

MARGARET. The orchestra tuning. Yes— I'm glad we decided against the blue one. [*She moves to the Hall door.*] Where's your father? You know, I feel completely impersonal about all this. I can't quite grasp it. Get dressed, Dinah. [*She goes out into the Hall.* TRACY *turns and blinks into the sunlight, blazing in from the Porch.*]

TRACY. That sun is certainly bright all right, isn't it?

DINAH. It was up awfully early.

TRACY. Was it?

DINAH. Unless I dreamed that, too.—It's supposed to be the longest day of the year or something, isn't it?

TRACY. I wouldn't doubt it for a minute.

DINAH. It was all certainly pretty rooty-tooty.

TRACY. What was?

DINAH. My dream. [TRACY *moves back from the Porch door.*]

TRACY. Dinah, you'll have to learn sooner or later that no one is interested in anyone else's dreams.

DINAH.—I thought I got up and went over to the window and looked out across the lawn. And guess what I thought I saw coming over out of the woods?

TRACY. I haven't the faintest idea. A skunk?

DINAH. Well, sort of.—It was Mr. Connor.

TRACY. Mr. Connor?

DINAH. Yes—with his both arms full of something. And guess what it turned out to be?

TRACY. What?

DINAH. You—and some clothes. [TRACY *turns slowly and looks at her.*] Wasn't it funny? It was sort of like as if you were coming from the pool— [TRACY *closes her eyes.*]

TRACY. The pool.—I'm going crazy. I'm standing here solidly on my own two hands going crazy.—And then what?

DINAH. Then I thought I heard something outside in the hall, and I went and opened my door a crack and there he was, still coming along with you, puffing like a steam engine. His wind can't be very good.

TRACY. And then what?—

DINAH. And you were sort of crooning—

TRACY. I never crooned in my life!

DINAH. I guess it just sort of sounded like you were. Then he—guess what?

TRACY. I—couldn't possibly.

DINAH. Then he just sailed right into your room with you and—and that scared me so, that I just flew back to bed—or thought I did—and pulled the covers up over my head and laid there shaking and thinking: if *that's* the way it is, why doesn't she marry him, instead of old George? And then I must have fallen even faster asleep, because the next thing I knew it was eight o'clock, and the typewriter still going.

TRACY. Sandy—the typewriter—

DINAH. So in a minute I got up and went to your door and peeked in, to make sure you were all right—and guess what?

TRACY [*agonized*]. What?

DINAH. You were. He was gone by then. [TRACY *assumes a high indignation.*]

TRACY. Gone? Of course he was gone—he was never there!

DINAH. I know, Tracy.

TRACY. Well! I should hope you did! [*She seats herself firmly in an armchair.*]

DINAH. I'm certainly glad I do, because if I didn't and if in a little while I heard Dr. Parsons saying, "If anyone knows any just cause or reason why these two should not be united in holy matrimony"—I just wouldn't know what to do. [*She sighs profoundly.*]—And it was all only a dream.

TRACY. Naturally!

DINAH. I know. Dexter said so, straight off.—But isn't it funny, how—

TRACY. Dexter!

DINAH. Yes.—He said— [TRACY *rises and seizes her by the arm.*]

TRACY. You told Dexter all that?

DINAH. Not a word. Not a single word. —But you know how quick he is.

TRACY. Dinah Lord—you little fiend, how can you stand here and—! [SETH *comes in from the Hall, in morning coat and striped trousers.*]

SETH. Tracy, the next time you marry, choose a different Man of God, will you? This one wears me out. [*He goes to the Parlor doors, opens them, glances in, and closes them again.*] Good heavens!—Dinah! Get into your clothes! You look like a tramp.

DINAH. I'm going. [SETH *is about to go out again into the Hall, when* TRACY'S *voice stops him.*]

TRACY. Father. [*He turns to her.*]

SETH. Yes, Tracy?

TRACY. I'm glad you came back. I'm glad you're here. [*He comes to her.*]

SETH. Thank you, child.

TRACY. I'm sorry—I'm truly sorry I'm a disappointment to you.

SETH. I never said that, daughter—and I never will. [*He looks at her fondly for a moment, touches her arm, then turns abruptly and goes out into the Hall.*]

Where's your mother? Where's George? [MIKE, *in a blue suit, comes in from the Porch. He goes to the table and puts a cigarette out there.*]

MIKE. Good morning.

TRACY. Oh, hello!

MIKE. I was taking the air. I like it, but it doesn't like me.—Hello, Dinah.

DINAH [*replies with great dignity*]. How do you do?

TRACY. Did—did you have a good sleep?

MIKE. Wonderful. How about you?

TRACY. Marvelous. Have you ever seen a handsomer day?

MIKE. Never. What did it set you back?

TRACY. I got it for nothing, for being a good girl.

MIKE. Good. [*There is a brief silence. They look at* DINAH, *who is regarding them fixedly.*]

DINAH. I'm going, don't worry. [*She moves toward the Parlor doors.*]

TRACY. Why should you?

DINAH. I guess you must have things you wish to discuss.

TRACY. "Things to"—? What are you talking about!

DINAH. Only remember, it's getting late. [*Gingerly she opens the Parlor doors a crack, and peers in.*] Some of them are in already. My, they look solemn. [*She moves toward the Hall.*] I'll be ready when you are! [*And goes out.*]

TRACY. She's always trying to make situations.—How's your work coming—are you doing us up brown?

MIKE. I've—somehow I've lost my angle.

TRACY. How do you mean, Mike?

MIKE. I've just got so damn tolerant all at once, I doubt if I'll ever be able to write another line. [TRACY *laughs uncertainly.*]

TRACY. You are a fellah, Mike.

MIKE. Or the mug of this world: I don't know.

TRACY. When you're at the work you ought to be doing, you'll soon see that tolerance— What's the matter with your chin?

MIKE. Does it show?

TRACY. A little. What happened?

MIKE. I guess I just stuck it out too far.

TRACY.—Into a door, in the dark?

MIKE. That's it. [*His voice lowers solicitously.*] Are you—are *you* all right, Tracy? [*The startled look comes back into her eyes. She laughs, to cover it.*]

TRACY. Me? Of course! Why shouldn't I be?

MIKE. That was a flock of wine we put away.

TRACY. I never felt better in my life. [*She moves away from him.*]

MIKE. That's fine. That's just daisy.

TRACY. I—I guess we're lucky both to have such good heads.

MIKE. Yes, I guess. [*He moves toward her.*]

TRACY. It must be awful for people who —you know—get up and make speeches or—or try to start a fight—or, you know, misbehave in general.

MIKE. It certainly must.

TRACY. It must be—some sort of hidden weakness coming out.

MIKE. Weakness? I'm not so sure of that. [*Again she moves away from him.*]

TRACY. Anyhow, I had a simply wonderful evening. I hope you enjoyed it too.

MIKE. I enjoyed the last part of it. [*She turns to him uncertainly.*]

TRACY. Really? Why—why especially the last?

MIKE. Are you asking me, Tracy?

TRACY. Oh, you mean the swim!—We did swim, and so forth, didn't we?

MIKE. We swam, and so forth. [*She advances to him suddenly.*]

TRACY. Mike—

[505]

MIKE [*gazing*]. You darling, darling girl—

TRACY. Mike!

MIKE. What can I say to you? Tell me, darling— [*She recovers herself and again moves away.*]

TRACY. Not anything—don't say anything. And especially not "Darling."

MIKE. Never in this world will I ever forget you.

TRACY.—Not anything, I said.

MIKE. You're going to go through with it, then—

TRACY. Through with what?

MIKE. The wedding.

TRACY. Why—why shouldn't I?

MIKE. Well, you see, I've made a funny discovery: that in spite of the fact that someone's up from the bottom, he may be quite a heel. And that even though someone else is born to the purple, he still may be quite a guy.—Hell, I'm only saying what you said last night!

TRACY. I said a lot of things last night, it seems.

MIKE [*after a moment*]. All right, no dice. But understand: also no regrets about last night.

TRACY. Why should I have?

MIKE. That's it! That's the stuff; you're wonderful. You're aces, Tracy. [*Now she is in full retreat.*]

TRACY. You don't know what I mean! I'm asking you—tell me straight out—tell me the reason why I should have any— [*But she cannot finish. Her head drops.*] No—don't.—Just tell me—what time is it?

MIKE [*glancing at his wrist*]. It's— what's happened to my wrist watch? [TRACY *stops, frozen, speaks without turning.*]

TRACY. Why? Is it broken?

MIKE. It's gone. I've lost it somewhere.

TRACY [*after a moment*]. I can't tell you how extremely sorry I am to hear that.

MIKE. Oh, well—I'd always just as soon not know the time.

TRACY [*her back to him*]. There on the table—

MIKE.—What is? [*He goes to the table, finds the watch.*] Well, for the love of—! Who found it? I'll give a reward, or something. [*He straps the watch on his wrist.*]

TRACY. I don't think any reward will be expected. [*She drops miserably down into an armchair.* DEXTER *comes in from the Porch, a small glass in hand.*]

DEXTER. Now then! This medicine indicated in cases of— [*He stops at the sight of* MIKE.] Hello, Connor. How are you?

MIKE. About as you'd think.—Is that for me?

DEXTER. For Tracy.—Why? Would you like one?

MIKE. I would sell my grandmother for a drink—and you know how I love my grandmother.

DEXTER. Uncle Willie's around in the pantry, doing weird and wonderful things. Just say I said, One of the same. [MIKE *moves toward the Porch.*]

MIKE. Is it all right if I say Two?

DEXTER. That's between you and your grandmother. [MIKE *goes out.* DEXTER *calls after him.*]—And find Liz! [DEXTER *goes to* TRACY *with the drink.*] Doctor's orders, Tray.

TRACY. What is it?

DEXTER. Just the juice of a few flowers. [TRACY *takes the glass and looks at it, and tastes it.*]

TRACY. Peppermint— [DEXTER *smiles.*]

DEXTER.—White.—And one other simple ingredient. It's called a stinger. It removes the sting. [TRACY *sets the glass down and looks away.*]

TRACY. Oh, Dext—don't say that!

DEXTER. Why not, Tray?
TRACY.—Nothing will—nothing ever can! [*She rises from the chair.*] Oh, Dexter—I've done the most terrible thing to you!
DEXTER [*after a moment*]. To *me*, did you say? [*She nods vigorously.*] I doubt that, Red. I doubt it very much.
TRACY. You don't know, you don't know!
DEXTER. Well, maybe I shouldn't.
TRACY. You've got to—you must! I couldn't stand it, if you didn't! Oh, Dext —what am I going to do?
DEXTER.—But why to *me*, Darling? [*She looks at him.*] Where do I come into it any more? [*Still she looks.*] Aren't you confusing me with someone else?—A fellow named Kittredge, or something?
TRACY [*a sudden, awful thought*]. George—
DEXTER. That's right; George Kittredge. A splendid chap—very high morals—very broad shoulders.— [TRACY *goes to the telephone.*]
TRACY. I've got to tell him. [DEXTER *follows her.*]
DEXTER. Tell him what?
TRACY. I've got to tell him! [*She dials a number.*]
DEXTER. But if he's got any brain at all, he'll have realized by this time what a fool he made of himself, when he—
TRACY.—When he what? [*To the telephone.*] Hello? Hello, George—this is Tracy. Look—I don't care whether it's bad luck or not, but I've got to see you for a minute before the wedding.—What? *What* note? I didn't get any note.—When? Well, why didn't someone tell me?— Right! Come on the run. [*She replaces the telephone, goes up to the fireplace, finds the wall bell and rings it.*] He sent a note over at ten o'clock.

DEXTER. I told you he'd come to his senses. [TRACY *turns slowly.*]
TRACY. Was—was he here, too?
DEXTER. Sure.
TRACY. My God—why didn't you sell tickets? [DEXTER *brings her her drink.*]
DEXTER. Finish your drink.
TRACY. Will it help?
DEXTER. There's always the hope. [EDWARD *comes into the Hall doorway.*]
EDWARD. You rang, Miss?
TRACY. Isn't there a note for me from Mr. Kittredge somewhere?
EDWARD. I believe it was put on the hall table upstairs. Mrs. Lord said not to disturb you.
TRACY. I'd like to have it, if I may.
EDWARD. Very well, Miss. [*He goes out,* TRACY *finishes her drink and gives* DEXTER *the empty glass.*]
TRACY. Say something, Dext—anything.
DEXTER. No—you do.
TRACY. Oh, Dext—I'm wicked! [*She moves away from him.*] I'm such an unholy mess of a girl.
DEXTER. That's no good. That's not even conversation.
TRACY. But never in all my life—not if I live to be a hundred—will I ever forget the way you tried to—to stand me on my feet again this morning.
DEXTER. You—you're in grand shape. Tell me: what did you think of my wedding present? I like my presents at least to be acknowledged.
TRACY. It was beautiful and sweet, Dext.
DEXTER. She was quite a boat, the "True Love."
TRACY. Was, and is.
DEXTER. She had the same initials as yours—did you ever realize that? [TRACY *seats herself in the armchair at* Left *of the table.*]
TRACY. No, I never did.

[507]

DEXTER. Nor did I, till I last saw her.—Funny we missed it. My, she was yare.

TRACY. She was yare, all right. [*A moment.*] *I* wasn't, was I?

DEXTER. Wasn't what?

TRACY. Yare. [DEXTER *laughs shortly and seats himself in the chair across the table from her.*]

DEXTER. Not very!—You were good at the bright-work, though. I'll never forget you down on your knees on the deck every morning, with your little can of polish. [*They speak without looking at each other, straight out in front of them.*]

TRACY. I wouldn't let even you help, would I?

DEXTER. Not even me.

TRACY. I made her shine.—Where is she now?

DEXTER. In the yard at Seven Hundred Acre, getting gone over. I'm going to sell her to Rufe Watriss at Oyster Bay. [*There is a silence. Then she speaks, incredulously.*]

TRACY. You're going to sell the "True Love"?

DEXTER. Why not?

TRACY. For money?

DEXTER. He wired an offer yesterday.

TRACY.—To *that* fat old rum pot?

DEXTER. What the hell does it matter?

TRACY. She's too clean, she's too yare!

DEXTER. I know—but when you're through with a boat, you're— [*He looks at her.*] That is, of course, unless *you* want her. [*She turns away, without replying.*] Of course she's good for nothing but racing—and only really comfortable for two people—and not so damned so, for them. So I naturally thought— But of course, if *you* should want her—

TRACY. No—I don't want her.

DEXTER. I'm going to design another for myself, along a little more practical lines.

TRACY. Are you?

DEXTER. I started on the drawings a couple of weeks ago.

TRACY. What will you call her?

DEXTER. I thought the "True Love II."—What do you think? [TRACY *rises abruptly.*]

TRACY. Dexter, if you call any boat that, I promise you I'll blow you and it right out of the water!

DEXTER. I know it's not very imaginative, but—

TRACY. Just try it, that's all! [*She moves away from him.*] *I'll* tell you what you can call it, if you like—

DEXTER. What?

TRACY. In fond remembrance of me—

DEXTER. What?

TRACY. The "Easy Virtue." [DEXTER *goes to her.*]

DEXTER. Tray, I'll be damned if I'll have you thinking such things of yourself!

TRACY. What would you like me to think?

DEXTER. I don't know. But I do know that virtue, so-called, is no matter of a single misstep or two.

TRACY. You don't think so?

DEXTER. I know so. It's something inherent, it's something regardless of anything.

TRACY. Like fun it is.

DEXTER. You're wrong. The occasional misdeeds are often as good for a person as—as the more persistent virtues.—That is, if the person is there. Maybe you haven't committed enough, Tray. Maybe this is your coming-of-age.

TRACY. I don't know.—Oh, I don't know anything any more!

DEXTER. That sounds very hopeful. That's just fine, Tray.

TRACY. Oh, be still, you! [EDWARD *comes in with a note on a tray.*] Thanks, Edward.

EDWARD. They are practically all in, Miss—and quite a number standing in the back. [MIKE *and* LIZ *comes in from the Porch.*] All our best wishes, Miss.

TRACY. Thanks, Edward. Thanks, very much.

LIZ. —And all ours, Tracy.

TRACY. Thank you, thank everybody. [EDWARD *goes out, into the Hall, passing* SANDY, *who rushes in and up to* TRACY. *He wears a short morning coat.*]

SANDY. Tray—he's here! He's arrived!

TRACY [*opening the note*]. Who has?

SANDY. Kidd—Sidney Kidd.

TRACY. What for? What does *he* want?

LIZ. May I scream?

MIKE. What the—!

TRACY. Oh, now I remember!

SANDY. Well, I should hope you did. I haven't been to bed at all. I gave him the Profile. He's reading it now. I couldn't stand the suspense, so I—

MIKE. Profile, did you say? What profile?

SANDY. The Kidd himself, complete with photographs. Do you want to see a copy?

MIKE. Holy St. Rose of South Bend!

SANDY. —Offered in exchange for yours of us. I told him what a help you've both been to me.

LIZ. I don't think you'll find it so hard to resign now, Mike. Me neither.

MIKE. That's all right with me.

LIZ. Belts will be worn tighter this winter.

SANDY. I'll see how he's bearing up. [*He moves toward the Hall, meeting* DR. PARSONS, *a middle-aged clergyman, in surplice and stole, as he comes in.*] Good morning, Dr. Parsons. How's everything?

DR. PARSONS. Where is your sister? [SANDY *points to her and goes out.* TRACY *is now reading the note.* DR. PARSONS *calls to her.*] Tracy? Tracy! [*She looks up startled.*]

TRACY. Yes? [*He smiles, and beckons engagingly.*]

DEXTER. One minute, Dr. Parsons, Mr. Kittredge is on his way. [DR. PARSONS *smiles again, and goes out into the Parlor, carefully closing the door behind him.* DEXTER *turns to* TRACY.] I'm afraid it's the deadline, Tracy.

TRACY. So is this. Listen—"My dear Tracy: Your conduct last night was so shocking to my ideals of womanhood, that my attitude toward you and the prospects of a happy and useful life together, has changed materially. Your, to me, totally unexpected breach of common decency, not to mention the moral aspect—" [GEORGE *comes in from the Porch.*]

GEORGE. Tracy!

TRACY. Hello, George.

GEORGE. Tracy—all these people!

TRACY. It's only a letter from a friend. They're my friends, too. "—not to mention the moral aspect, certainly entitles me to a full explanation, before going through with our proposed marriage. In the light of day, I am sure that you will agree with me. Otherwise, with profound regrets and all best wishes, yours very sincerely—" [*She folds the note and returns it to its envelope.*] Yes, George, I quite agree with you—in the light of day or the dark of night, for richer, for poorer, for better, for worse, in sickness and in health—and thank you so very much for your good wishes at this time.

GEORGE. That's all you've got to say?

TRACY. What else? I wish for your sake, as well as mine, I had an explanation. But unfortunately, I've none. You'd better just say "good riddance," George.

GEORGE. It isn't easy, you know.

TRACY. I don't see why.

Liz [*to* Mike]. Say something, Stupid.

Mike. Wait a minute. [*Preparatory music—Debussy—is now faintly heard from the Parlor.*]

George. You'll grant I had a right to be angry, and very angry.

Tracy. You certainly had, you certainly have.

George. "For your sake, as well," you said—

Tracy. Yes—it would be nice to know.

Liz [*to* Mike]. Will you say something?

Mike. Wait!

Liz. What for?

Mike. Enough rope.

George.—On the very eve of your wedding, an affair with another man—

Tracy. I told you I agreed, George—and I tell you again: good riddance to me.

George. That's for me to decide.

Tracy. Well, I wish you would a—a—little more quickly.

Mike. Look, Kittredge—

Tracy. If there was some way to make you see that—that regardless of it—or even because of it—I'm—somehow I feel more of a person, George.

George. That's a little difficult to understand. [Tracy *lets herself down into an armchair.*]

Tracy. Yes, I can see that it would be.

Dexter. Not necessarily.

George. You keep out of it!

Dexter. You forget: I am out of it. [*He seats himself upon the sofa, away from them all.*]

Mike [*advancing*]. Kittredge, it just might interest you to know that the so-called "affair" consisted of exactly two kisses and one rather late swim.

Tracy [*unwilling to accept the gallant gesture*]. Thanks, Mike, but there's no need to— [Mike *turns to her.*]

Mike. All of which I thoroughly enjoyed, and the memory of which I wouldn't part with for anything.

Tracy. It's no use, Mike.

Mike [*again to* George].—After which, I accompanied her to her room, deposited her on her bed, and promptly returned to you two on the porch—as you will doubtless remember.

Dexter. Doubtless without a doubt.

George. You mean to say that was all there was to it?

Mike. I do. [George *ponders.* Tracy *is looking at* Mike *in astonishment. Suddenly she rises and demands indignantly of him.*]

Tracy. Why? Was I so damned unattractive—so distant, so forbidding, or something, that—?

George. This is fine talk, too!

Tracy. I'm asking a question! [*The music has stopped now.*]

Mike. You were extremely attractive—and as for "distant and forbidding," on the contrary. But you were also somewhat the worse—or the better—for wine, and there are rules about that, damn it.

Tracy [*after a moment*]. Thank you, Mike. I think men are wonderful.

Liz. The little dears.

George. Well, that's a relief, I'll admit. Still—

Tracy. Why? Where's the difference? If my wonderful, marvelous, beautiful virtue is still intact, it's no thanks to me, I assure you.

George. I don't think you—

Tracy.—It's purely by courtesy of the gentleman from South Bend.

Liz. Local papers, please copy.

George. I fail to see the humor in this situation, Miss Imbrie.

Liz. I appreciate that. It was a little hard for me too, at first—

[510]

The Philadelphia Story

Tracy. Oh, Liz— [*She goes to her, gropes for her hand.*]

Liz. It's all right, Tracy. We all go a little haywire at times—and if we don't, maybe we ought to.

Tracy. Liz.

Liz. You see, it really wasn't Tracy at all, Mr. Kittredge. It was another girl: a Miss Pommery, '28.

George. You'd had too much to drink—

Tracy. That seems to be the consensus of opinion.

George. Will you promise me never to touch the stuff again? [*She looks at him, speaking slowly.*]

Tracy. No, George, I don't believe I will. There are certain things about that other girl I rather like.

George. But a man expects his wife to—

Tracy.—To behave herself. Naturally.

Dexter. To behave herself naturally. [George *glances angrily at him.*] Sorry.

George [*to* Tracy]. But if it hadn't been for the drink last night, all this might not have happened.

Tracy. But apparently nothing did. What made you think it had?

George. It didn't take much imagination, I can tell you that.

Tracy. Not much, perhaps—but just of a certain kind.

George. It seems *you* didn't think any too well of yourself.

Tracy. That's the odd thing, George: somehow I'd have hoped you'd think better of me than I did.

George. I'm not going to quibble, Tracy: all the evidence was there.

Tracy. And I was guilty straight off— that is, until I was proved innocent.

George. Well?

Dexter. Downright un-American, if you ask me.

George. No one is asking you! [Sandy *comes into the Hall doorway, consternation on his face.*]

Sandy. Listen—he's read it—and holy cats, guess what?

Liz. What?

Sandy. He loves it! He says it's brilliant— He wants it for *Destiny!*

Mike. I give up.

George. Who wants what?

Liz. Sidney Kidd—Sidney Kidd.

George [*hardly believing the good news.*] Sidney Kidd is here himself?!

Sandy. Big as life, and twice as handsome. Boy, is this wedding a National Affair now! [*He goes out.*]

George [*after a moment*]. It's extremely kind and thoughtful of him. [*Another moment. Then.*] Come on, Tracy—it must be late. Let's let bygones be bygones—what do you say?

Tracy. Yes—and good-by, George.

George. I don't understand you.

Tracy. Please—good-by.

George. But what on earth—?

Liz. I imagine she means that your explanation is inadequate.

George. Look here, Tracy—

Tracy. You're too good for me, George. You're a hundred times too good.

George. I never said I—

Tracy. And I'd make you most unhappy, most.—That is, I'd do my best to. [George *looks at her.*]

George. Well, if that's the way you want it—

Tracy. That is the way it is.

George. All right. Possibly it's just as well. [*He starts toward the Hall.*]

Dexter. I thought you'd eventually think so. [George *turns and confronts him.*]

George. I've got a feeling you've had more to do with this than anyone.

[511]

DEXTER. A novel and interesting idea, I'm sure.

GEORGE. You and your whole rotten class.

DEXTER. Oh, class my—! [*But he stops himself.*]

MIKE. Funny—I heard a truck driver say that yesterday—only with a short "a."

GEORGE. Listen: you're all on your way out—the lot of you—and don't think you aren't.—Yes, and good riddance! [*He goes out.*]

MIKE. Well, there goes George. [*Again the orchestra is heard. This time it is "Oh Promise Me."* TRACY *moves swiftly to the Parlor doors, opens them slightly, peers in, and exclaims.*]

TRACY. Oh, my sainted aunt—that welter of faces! [*She closes the doors and returns.*] What in the name of all that's holy am I to do? [MAY, *the housemaid, comes in with* TRACY'S *hat and gloves.*]

MAY. You forgot your hat, Miss Tracy. [TRACY *takes the broad-brimmed hat, the immaculate gloves, and gazes at them helplessly.*]

TRACY. Oh, God— Oh, dear God—have mercy on Tracy! [MIKE *rises and goes to her.*]

MIKE. Tracy—

TRACY. Yes, Mike?

MIKE. Forget the license!

TRACY. License? [DEXTER *fumbles in his pocket.*]

DEXTER. I've got an old one here that we never used, Maryland being quicker—

MIKE. Forget it! [*To* TRACY.] Old Parson Parsons—he's never seen Kittredge, has he? Nor have most of the others. I got you into this, I'll get you out.—Will you marry me, Tracy? [*She looks at him for a long, grateful moment before speaking. Then.*]

TRACY. No, Mike.—Thanks, but no.

MIKE. But listen: I've never asked a girl to marry me before in my life!—I've avoided it!—You've got me all confused—why not—?

TRACY.—Because I don't think Liz would like it—and I'm not sure that you would—and I'm even a little doubtful about myself.—But I'm beholden to you, Mike, I'm most beholden. [MIKE *gestures impatiently.*]

MIKE. They're in there! They're waiting!

LIZ. Don't get too conventional all at once, will you?—There'll be a reaction.

MIKE [*an appeal*]. Liz—

LIZ. I count on your sustaining the mood. [*She beckons to him and he joins her.* DEXTER *rises.*]

DEXTER. It'll be all right, Tracy: you've been got out of jams before.

TRACY.—Been *got out* of them, did you say?

DEXTER. That's what I said, Tracy. Don't worry, you always are. [MARGARET *and* SETH *come in from the Hall.*]

MARGARET. Tracy, we met George in the hall—it's all right, dear: your father will make a very simple announcement.

SETH. Is there anything special you want me to say?

TRACY. No! I'll say it, whatever it is.— I won't be got out of anything more, thanks. [*She moves to the Parlor door.* UNCLE WILLIE *and* DINAH *enter from the Hall.*]

UNCLE WILLIE. What's alack? What's amiss?

MARGARET. Oh, this just can't be happening—it can't! [TRACY *throws open the Parlor doors and stands in the doorway gazing into the Parlor. She addresses her wedding guests.*]

TRACY. I'm—I'm—hello! Good morning. —I'm—that is to say—I'm terribly sorry to have kept you waiting, but—but there's been a little hitch in the proceedings. I've made a terrible fool of myself—which isn't unusual—and my fiancé—my fiancé— [*She stops and swallows.*]

MARGARET. Seth!

SETH. Wait, my dear.

TRACY. —my fiancé, that was, that is— he thinks we'd better call it a day and I quite agree with him. [*She half turns and whispers.*] Dexter—Dexter—what the hell next?

DEXTER. "Two years ago you were invited to a wedding in this house and I did you out of it by eloping to Maryland—" [*He moves swiftly to* MARGARET.]

TRACY. "Two years ago you were invited to a wedding in this house and I did you out of it by eloping to Maryland—" [*Then, desperately.*] Dexter, Dexter, where are you?

DEXTER [*simultaneously, to* MARGARET.] May I? Just as a loan? [*He takes a ring from her finger and goes to* MIKE *with it.*] Here, put this in your vest pocket.

MIKE. But I haven't got a vest.

DEXTER. Then hold it in your hand! [*He goes quickly to* TRACY.]

DEXTER. "Which was very bad manners—"

TRACY [*into the Parlor*]. "—Which was very bad manners—"

DEXTER. "But I hope to make it up to you by going through with it now, as originally planned."

TRACY. "But I hope to make it up to you by—by going—" [*Suddenly she realizes what she is saying and turns to* DEXTER *with blank wonder in her eyes. He gestures, and she turns again and continues.*] —by going beautifully through with it now—as originally and—most beautifully—planned. [DEXTER *moves to* MIKE.]

DEXTER. I'd like you to be my best man, if you will, because I think you're one hell of a guy, Mike.

MIKE. I'd be honored, C. K.

UNCLE WILLIE. Ladies, follow me! No rushing please! [LIZ *and* MARGARET *go out with him into the Hall.*]

TRACY [*simultaneously, into the Parlor*]. —Because there's something awfully nice about a wedding—I don't know—they're so gay and attractive—and I've always wanted one, and—

DEXTER. "So if you'll just keep your seats a minute—"

TRACY. "So if you'll just keep your seats a minute—"

DEXTER. That's all.

TRACY. "That's all!" [*She closes the doors and turns breathlessly to* DEXTER.] Dexter—are you sure?

DEXTER. Not in the least.—But I'll risk it—will you?

TRACY. You bet!—And you didn't do it just to soften the blow?

DEXTER. No, Tray.

TRACY. Nor to save my face?

DEXTER. It's a nice little face.

TRACY. Oh—I'll be yare now—I'll promise to be yare!

DEXTER. Be whatever you like, you're my Redhead.—All set?

TRACY. All set! [*She runs and snatches her hat from a chair, puts it on before a mirror.*]—Oh, how did this ever happen?

SETH. Don't inquire.—Go on, Dinah: tell Mr. Dutton to start the music. [DINAH *goes out into the Hall, exclaiming triumphantly.*]

DINAH. I did it—I did it all! [DEXTER *and* MIKE *go to the Hall doorway, wait there for the signal;* SETH *turns to* TRACY.]

SETH. Daughter— [*She moves to him.*]

[513]

TRACY. I love you, Father.

SETH. And I love you, daughter.

TRACY. Never in my life have I been so full of love before.—[*The Wedding March begins to be heard from the Parlor.*]

DEXTER. See you soon, Red!

TRACY. See you soon, Dext! [DEXTER *and* MIKE *go out.* TRACY *stands before* SETH.] How do I look?

SETH. Like a queen—like a goddess.

TRACY. Do you know how I feel?

SETH. How?

TRACY. Like a human—like a human being! [SETH *smiles.*]

SETH.—And is that all right? [*She tightens her arm in his. They start to move slowly across the room in the direction of the Parlor.*]

TRACY. All right? Oh, Father, it's Heaven!

CURTAIN

"THE HAIRY APE"

A Comedy of Ancient and Modern Life in Eight Scenes

by Eugene O'Neill

CHARACTERS

Robert Smith, "Yank"
Paddy
Long
Mildred Douglas
Her Aunt
Second Engineer
A Guard
A Secretary of an Organization
Stokers, Ladies, Gentlemen, etc.

SCENES

Scene I: *The firemen's forecastle of an ocean liner —an hour after sailing from New York.*
Scene II: *Section of promenade deck, two days out—morning*
Scene III: *The stokehole. A few minutes later.*
Scene IV: *Same as Scene I. Half an hour later.*
Scene V: *Fifth Avenue, New York. Three weeks later.*
Scene VI: *An island near the city. The next night.*
Scene VII: *In the city. About a month later.*
Scene VIII: *In the city. Twilight of the next day.*

SCENE I

[*The firemen's forecastle of a transatlantic liner an hour after sailing from New York for the voyage across. Tiers of narrow, steel bunks, three deep, on all sides. An entrance in rear. Benches on the floor before the bunks. The room is crowded with men, shouting, cursing, laughing, singing—a confused, inchoate uproar swelling into a sort of unity, a meaning—the bewildered, furious, baffled defiance of a beast in a cage. Nearly all the men are drunk. Many bottles are passed from hand to hand. All are dressed in dungaree pants, heavy ugly shoes. Some wear singlets, but the majority are stripped to the waist.*

The treatment of this scene, or of any other scene in the play, should by no means be naturalistic. The effect sought after is a cramped space in the bowels of a ship, imprisoned by white steel. The lines of bunks, the uprights supporting them, cross each other like the steel framework of a cage. The ceiling crushes down upon the men's heads. They cannot stand upright. This accentuates the natural stooping posture which shoveling coal and the resultant over-development of back and shoulder muscles have given them. The men themselves should resemble those pictures in which the appearance of Neanderthal Man is guessed at. All are

---

Eugene O'Neill, *The Hairy Ape*, *1922*. Copyright, 1925, by Eugene O'Neill. Reprinted by permission of Random House, Inc.

hairy-chested, with long arms of tremendous power, and low, receding brows above their small, fierce, resentful eyes. All the civilized white races are represented, but except for the slight differentiation in color of hair, skin, eyes, all these men are alike.

The curtain rises on a tumult of sound. YANK *is seated in the foreground. He seems broader, fiercer, more truculent, more powerful, more sure of himself than the rest. They respect his superior strength—the grudging respect of fear. Then, too, he represents to them a self-expression, the very last word in what they are, their most highly developed individual.*]

VOICES. Gif me trink dere, you!
'Ave a wet!
Salute!
Gesundheit!
Skoal!
Drunk as a lord, God stiffen you!
Here's how!
Luck!
Pass back that bottle, damn you!
Pourin' it down his neck!
Ho, Froggy! Where the devil have you been?
La Touraine.
I hit him smash in yaw, py Gott!
Jenkins—the First—he's a rotten swine—
And the coppers nabbed him—and I run—
I like peer better. It don't pig head gif you.
A slut, I'm sayin'! She robbed me aslape—
To hell with 'em all!
You're a bloody liar!
Say dot again! [*Commotion. Two men about to fight are pulled apart.*]
No scrappin' now!
Tonight—
See who's the best man!
Bloody Dutchman!
Tonight on the for'ard square.
I'll bet on Dutchy.
He packa da wallop, I tella you!
Shut up, Wop!
No fightin', maties. We're all chums, ain't we?
[*A voice starts bawling a song.*]

"Beer, beer, glorious beer!
Fill yourselves right up to here."

YANK [*for the first time seeming to take notice of the uproar about him, turns around threateningly—in a tone of contemptuous authority*]. Choke off dat noise! Where d'yuh get dat beer stuff? Beer, hell! Beer's for goils—and Dutchmen. Me for somep'n wit a kick to it! Gimme a drink, one of youse guys. [*Several bottles are eagerly offered. He takes a tremendous gulp at one of them; then, keeping the bottle in his hand, glares belligerently at the owner, who hastens to acquiesce in this robbery by saying*] All righto, Yank. Keep it and have another. [YANK *contemptuously turns his back on the crowd again. For a second there is an embarrassed silence. Then—*]

VOICES. We must be passing the Hook.
She's beginning to roll to it.
Six days in hell—and then Southampton.
Py Yesus, I vish somepody take my first vatch for me!
Gittin' seasick, Square-head?
Drink up and forget it!
What's in your bottle?
Gin.
Dot's nigger trink.
Absinthe? It's doped. You'll go off your chump, Froggy!
Cochon!
Whisky, that's the ticket!
Where's Paddy?
Going asleep.

"The Hairy Ape"

Sing us that whisky song, Paddy. [*They all turn to an old, wizened Irishman who is dozing, very drunk, on the benches forward. His face is extremely monkey-like with all the sad, patient pathos of that animal in his small eyes.*]

Singa da song, Caruso Pat!
He's gettin' old. The drink is too much for him.
He's too drunk.

PADDY [*blinking about him, starts to his feet resentfully, swaying, holding on to the edge of a bunk*]. I'm never too drunk to sing. 'Tis only when I'm dead to the world I'd be wishful to sing at all. [*With a sort of sad contempt.*] "Whisky Johnny," ye want? A chanty, ye want? Now that's a queer wish from the ugly like of you, God help you. But no matther. [*He starts to sing in a thin, nasal, doleful tone.*]

Oh, whisky is the life of man!
    Whisky! O Johnny! [*They all join in on this.*]
Oh, whisky is the life of man!
    Whisky for my Johnny! [*Again chorus.*]

Oh, whisky drove my old man mad!
    Whisky! O Johnny!
Oh, whisky drove my old man mad!
    Whisky for my Johnny!

YANK [*again turning around scornfully*]. Aw hell! Nix on dat old sailing ship stuff! All dat bull's dead, see? And you're dead, too, yuh damned old Harp, on'y yuh don't know it. Take it easy, see. Give us a rest. Nix on de loud noise. [*With a cynical grin*] Can't youse see I'm tryin' to t'ink?

ALL [*repeating the word after him as one with the same cynical amused mockery*]. Think! [*The chorused word has a brazen metallic quality as if their throats were phonograph horns. It is followed by a general uproar of hard, barking laughter*].

VOICES. Don't be cracking your head wit ut, Yank.
You gat headache, py yingo!
One thing about it—it rhymes with drink!
Ha, ha, ha!
Drink, don't think!
Drink, don't think!
Drink, don't think!
[*A whole chorus of voices has taken up this refrain, stamping on the floor, pounding on the benches with fists.*]

YANK [*taking a gulp from his bottle—good-naturedly*]. Aw right. Can de noise. I got yuh de foist time. [*The uproar subsides. A very drunken sentimental tenor begins to sing.*]

"Far away in Canada,
    Far across the sea,
There's a lass who fondly waits
    Making a home for me—"

YANK [*fiercely contemptuous*]. Shut up, yuh lousy boob! Where d'yuh get dat tripe? Home? Home, hell! I'll make a home for yuh! I'll knock yuh dead. Home! T'hell wit home! Where d'yuh get dat tripe? Dis is home, see? What d'yuh want wit home? [*Proudly.*] I runned away from mine when I was a kid. On'y too glad to beat it, dat was me. Home was lickings for me, dat's all. But yuh can bet your shoit no one ain't never licked me since! Wanter try it, any of youse? Huh! I guess not. [*In a more placated but still contemptuous tone.*] Goils waitin' for yuh, huh? Aw, hell! Dat's all tripe. Dey don't wait for no one. Dey'd double-

[517]

cross yuh for a nickel. Dey're all tarts, get me? Treat 'em rough, dat's me. To hell wit 'em. Tarts, dat's what, de whole bunch of 'em.

LONG [*very drunk, jumps on a bench excitedly, gesticulating with a bottle in his hand*]. Listen 'ere, Comrades! Yank 'ere is right. 'E says this 'ere stinkin' ship is our 'ome. And 'e says as 'ome is 'ell. And 'e's right! This is 'ell. We lives in 'ell, Comrades—and right enough we'll die in it. [*Raging.*] And who's ter blame, I arsks yer? We ain't. We wasn't born this rotten way. All men is born free and ekal. That's in the bleedin' Bible, maties. But what d'they care for the Bible—them lazy, bloated swine what travels first cabin? Them's the ones. They dragged us down 'til we're on'y wage slaves in the bowels of a bloody ship, sweatin', burnin' up, eatin' coal dust! Hit's them's ter blame—the damned Capitalist clarss! [*There had been a gradual murmur of contemptuous resentment rising among the men until now he is interrupted by a storm of catcalls, hisses, boos, hard laughter.*]

VOICES. Turn it off!
Shut up!
Sit down!
Closa da face!
Tamn fool! [*Etc.*]

YANK [*standing up and glaring at* LONG]. Sit down before I knock yuh down! [LONG *makes haste to efface himself.* YANK *goes on contemptuously.*] De Bible, huh? De Cap'tlist class, huh? Aw nix on dat Salvation Army-Socialist bull. Git a soapbox! Hire a hall! Come and be saved, huh? Jerk us to Jesus, huh? Aw g'wan! I've listened to lots of guys like you, see. Yuh're all wrong. Wanter know what I t'ink? Yuh ain't no good for no one. Yuh're de bunk. Yuh ain't got no noive, get me? Yuh're yellow, dat's what.

Yellow, dat's you. Say! What's dem slobs in de foist cabin got to do wit us? We're better men dan dey are, ain't we? Sure! One of us guys could clean up de whole mob wit one mit. Put one of 'em down here for one watch in de stokehole, what'd happen? Dey'd carry him off on a stretcher. Dem boids don't amount to nothin'. Dey're just baggage. Who makes dis old tub run? Ain't it us guys? Well den, we belong, don't we? We belong and dey don't. Dat's all. [*A loud chorus of approval.* YANK *goes on.*] As for dis bein' hell—aw, nuts! Yuh lost your noive, dat's what. Dis is a man's job, get me? It belongs. It runs dis tub. No stiffs need apply. But yuh're a stiff, see? Yuh're yellow, dat's you.

VOICES [*with a great hard pride in them*].
Righto!
A man's job!
Talk is cheap, Long.
He never could hold up his end.
Divil take him!
Yank's right. We make it go.
Py Gott, Yank say right ting!
We don't need no one cryin' over us.
Makin' speeches.
Throw him out!
Yellow!
Chuck him overboard!
I'll break his jaw for him!
[*They crowd around* LONG *threateningly.*]

YANK [*half good-natured again—contemptuously*]. Aw, take it easy. Leave him alone. He ain't woith a punch. Drink up. Here's how, whoever owns dis. [*He takes a long swallow from his bottle. All drink with him. In a flash all is hilarious amiability again, backslapping, loud talk, etc.*]

PADDY [*who has been sitting in a blinking, melancholy daze—suddenly cries out in a voice full of old sorrow*]. We belong to this, you're saying? We make the ship to go, you're saying? Yerra then, that Almighty God have pity on us! [*His voice runs into the wail of a keen, he rocks back and forth on his bench. The men stare at him, startled and impressed in spite of themselves.*] Oh, to be back in the fine days of my youth, ochone! Oh, there was fine beautiful ships them days—clippers wid tall masts touching the sky—fine strong men in them—men that was sons of the sea as if 'twas the mother that bore them. Oh, the clean skins of them, and the clear eyes, the straight backs and full chests of them! Brave men they was, and bold men surely! We'd be sailing out, bound down round the Horn maybe. We'd be making sail in the dawn, with a fair breeze, singing a chanty song wid no care to it. And astern the land would be sinking low and dying out, but we'd give it no heed but a laugh, and never a look behind. For the day that was, was enough, for we was free men—and I'm thinking 'tis only slaves do be giving heed to the day that's gone or the day to come—until they're old like me. [*With a sort of religious exaltation.*] Oh, to be scudding south again wid the power of the Trade Wind driving her on steady through the nights and the days! Full sail on her! Nights and days! Nights when the foam of the wake would be flaming wid fire, when the sky'd be blazing and winking wid stars. Or the full of the moon maybe. Then you'd see her driving through the gray night, her sails stretching aloft all silver and white, not a sound on the deck, the lot of us dreaming dreams, till you'd believe 'twas no real ship at all you was on but a ghost ship like the *Flying Dutchman* they say does be roaming the seas forevermore widout touching a port. And there was the days, too. A warm sun on the clean decks. Sun warming the blood of you, and wind over the miles of shiny green ocean like strong drink to your lungs. Work—aye, hard work—but who'd mind that at all? Sure, you worked under the sky and 'twas work wid skill and daring to it. And wid the day done, in the dog watch, smoking me pipe at ease, the lookout would be raising land maybe, and we'd see the mountains of South Americy wid the red fire of the setting sun painting their white tops and the clouds floating by them! [*His tone of exaltation ceases. He goes on mournfully.*] Yerra, what's the use of talking? 'Tis a dead man's whisper. [*To* YANK *resentfully.*] 'Twas them days men belonged to ships, not now. 'Twas them days a ship was part of the sea, and a man was part of a ship, and the sea joined all together and made it one. [*Scornfully.*] Is it one wid this you'd be, Yank—black smoke from the funnels smudging the sea, smudging the decks—the bloody engines pounding and throbbing and shaking—wid divil a sight of sun or a breath of clean air—choking our lungs wid coal dust—breaking our backs and hearts in the hell of the stokehole—feeding the bloody furnace—feeding our lives along wid the coal, I'm thinking—caged in by steel from a sight of the sky like bloody apes in the Zoo! [*With a harsh laugh.*] Ho-ho, divil mend you! Is it to belong to that you're wishing? Is it a flesh and blood wheel of the engines you'd be?

YANK [*who has been listening with a contemptuous sneer, barks out the answer*]. Sure ting! Dat's me. What about it?

PADDY [*as if to himself—with great sorrow*]. Me time is past due. That a great wave wid sun in the heart of it may sweep me over the side sometime I'd be dreaming of the days that's gone!

YANK. Aw, yuh crazy Mick! [*He springs to his feet and advances on* PADDY *threateningly—then stops, fighting some queer struggle within himself—lets his hands fall to his sides—contemptuously.*] Aw, take it easy. Yuh're aw right, at dat. Yuh're bugs, dat's all—nutty as a cuckoo. All dat tripe yuh been pullin'— Aw, dat's all right. On'y it's dead, get me? Yuh don't belong no more, see. Yuh don't get de stuff. Yuh're too old. [*Disgustedly.*] But aw say, come up for air onct in a while, can't yuh? See what's happened since yuh croaked. [*He suddenly bursts forth vehemently, growing more and more excited.*] Say! Sure! Sure I meant it! What de hell— Say, lemme talk! Hey! Hey, you old Harp! Hey, youse guys! Say, listen to me—wait a moment—I gotter talk, see. I belong and he don't. He's dead but I'm livin'. Listen to me! Sure I'm part of de engines! Why de hell not! Dey move, don't dey? Dey're speed, ain't dey? Dey smash trou, don't dey? Twenty-five knots a hour! Dat's goin' some! Dat's new stuff! Dat belongs! But him, he's too old. He gets dizzy. Say, listen. All dat crazy tripe about nights and days; all dat crazy tripe about stars and moons; all dat crazy tripe about suns and winds, fresh air and de rest of it— Aw hell, dat's all a dope dream! Hittin' de pipe of de past, dat's what he's doin'. He's old and don't belong no more. But me, I'm young! I'm in de pink! I move wit it! It, get me! I mean de ting dat's de guts of all dis. It ploughs trou all de tripe he's been sayin'. It blows dat up! It knocks dat dead! It slams dat offen de face of de oith! It, get me! De engines and de coal and de smoke and all de rest of it! He can't breathe and swallow coal dust, but I kin, see? Dat's fresh air for me! Dat's food for me! I'm new, get me? Hell in de stokehole? Sure! It takes a man to work in hell. Hell, sure, dat's my fav'rite climate. I eat it up! I git fat on it! It's me makes it hot! It's me makes it roar! It's me makes it move! Sure, on'y for me everyting stops. It all goes dead, get me? De noise and smoke and all de engines movin' de woild, dey stop. Dere ain't nothin' no more! Dat's what I'm sayin'. Everyting else dat makes de woild move, somep'n makes it move. It can't move witout somep'n else, see? Den yuh get down to me. I'm at de bottom, get me! Dere ain't nothin' foither. I'm de end! I'm de start! I start somep'n and de woild moves! It—dat's me!—de new dat's moiderin' de old! I'm de ting in coal dat makes it boin; I'm steam and oil for de engines; I'm de ting in noise dat makes yuh hear it; I'm smoke and express trains and steamers and factory whistles; I'm de ting in gold dat makes it money! And I'm what makes iron into steel! Steel, dat stands for de whole ting! And I'm steel—steel—steel! I'm de muscles in steel, de punch behind it! [*As he says this he pounds with his fist against the steel bunks. All the men, roused to a pitch of frenzied self-glorification by his speech, do likewise. There is a deafening metallic roar, through which* YANK'S *voice can be heard bellowing.*] Slaves, hell! We run de whole woiks. All de rich guys dat tink dey're somep'n, dey ain't nothin'! Dey don't belong. But us guys, we're in de move, we're at de bottom, de whole ting is us! [PADDY *from the start of* YANK'S *speech has been taking one gulp after another from his bottle, at first frightenedly, as if he were afraid to listen, then desperately, as if to drown his senses, but finally has achieved complete indifferent, even amused, drunkenness.* YANK *sees his lips moving. He quells the uproar with a shout.*] Hey, youse guys, take it easy!

[520]

"The Hairy Ape"

Wait a moment! De nutty Harp is sayin' somep'n.

PADDY [*is heard now—throws his head back with a mocking burst of laughter*]. Ho-ho-ho-ho-ho—

YANK [*drawing back his fist, with a snarl*]. Aw! Look out who yuh're givin' the bark!

PADDY [*begins to sing the "Miller of Dee" with enormous good nature*].

"I care for nobody, no, not I,
And nobody cares for me."

YANK [*good-natured himself in a flash, interrupts* PADDY *with a slap on the bare back like a report*]. Dat's de stuff! Now yuh're gettin' wise to somep'n. Care for nobody, dat's de dope! To hell wit 'em all! And nix on nobody else carin'. I kin care for myself, get me! [*Eight bells sound, muffled, vibrating through the steel walls as if some enormous brazen gong were imbedded in the heart of the ship. All the men jump up mechanically, file through the door silently close upon each other's heels in what is very like a prisoners' lockstep.* YANK *slaps* PADDY *on the back.*] Our watch, yuh old Harp! [*Mockingly.*] Come on down in hell. Eat up de coal dust. Drink in de heat. It's it, see! Act like yuh liked it, yuh better—or croak yuhself.

PADDY [*with jovial defiance*]. To the divil wid it! I'll not report this watch. Let them log me and be damned. I'm no slave the like of you. I'll be sittin' here at me ease, and drinkin', and thinkin', and dreaming dreams.

YANK [*contemptuously*]. Tinkin' and dreamin', what'll that get yuh? What's tinkin' got to do with it? We move, don't we? Speed, ain't it? Fog, dat's all you stand for. But we drive trou dat, don't we? We split dat up and smash trou—twenty-five knots a hour! [*Turns his back on* PADDY *scornfully.*] Aw, yuh make me sick! Yuh don't belong! [*He strides out the door in rear.* PADDY *hums to himself, blinking drowsily.*]

CURTAIN

SCENE II

[*Two days out. A section of the promenade deck.* MILDRED DOUGLAS *and her aunt are discovered reclining in deck chairs. The former is a girl of twenty, slender, delicate, with a pale, pretty face marred by a self-conscious expression of disdainful superiority. She looks fretful, nervous and discontented, bored by her own anemia. Her aunt is a pompous and proud—and fat—old lady. She is a type even to the point of a double chin and lorgnettes. She is dressed pretentiously, as if afraid her face alone would never indicate her position in life.* MILDRED *is dressed all in white.*

The impression to be conveyed by this scene is one of the beautiful, vivid life of the sea all about—sunshine on the deck in a great flood, the fresh sea wind blowing across it. In the midst of this, these two incongruous, artificial figures, inert and disharmonious, the elder like a gray lump of dough touched up with rouge, the younger looking as if the vitality of her stock had been sapped before she was conceived, so that she is the expression not of its life energy but merely of the artificialities that energy had won for itself in the spending.]

MILDRED [*looking up with affected dreaminess*]. How the black smoke swirls back against the sky! Is it not beautiful?

AUNT [*without looking up*]. I dislike smoke of any kind.

MILDRED. My great-grandmother smoked a pipe—a clay pipe.

AUNT [*ruffling*]. Vulgar!

MILDRED. She was too distant a relative to be vulgar. Time mellows pipes.

AUNT [*pretending boredom but irritated*]. Did the sociology you took up at college teach you that—to play the ghoul on every possible occasion, excavating old bones? Why not let your great-grandmother rest in her grave?

MILDRED [*dreamily*]. With her pipe beside her—puffing in Paradise.

AUNT [*with spite*]. Yes, you are a natural born ghoul. You are even getting to look like one, my dear.

MILDRED [*in a passionless tone*]. I detest you, Aunt. [*Looking at her critically.*] Do you know what you remind me of? Of a cold pork pudding against a background of linoleum tablecloth in the kitchen of a—but the possibilities are wearisome. [*She closes her eyes.*]

AUNT [*with a bitter laugh*]. Merci for your candor. But since I am and must be your chaperon—in appearance, at least—let us patch up some sort of armed truce. For my part you are quite free to indulge any pose of eccentricity that beguiles you —as long as you observe the amenities—

MILDRED [*drawling*]. The inanities?

AUNT [*going on as if she hadn't heard*]. After exhausting the morbid thrills of social service work on New York's East Side—how they must have hated you, by the way, the poor that you made so much poorer in their own eyes!—you are now bent on making your slumming international. Well, I hope Whitechapel will provide the needed nerve tonic. Do not ask me to chaperon you there, however. I told your father I would not. I loathe deformity. We will hire an army of detectives and you may investigate everything—they allow you to see.

MILDRED [*protesting with a trace of genuine earnestness*]. Please do not mock at my attempts to discover how the other half lives. Give me credit for some sort of groping sincerity in that at least. I would like to help them. I would like to be some use in the world. Is it my fault I don't know how? I would like to be sincere, to touch life somewhere. [*With weary bitterness.*] But I'm afraid I have neither the vitality nor integrity. All that was burnt out in our stock before I was born. Grandfather's blast furnaces, flaming to the sky, melting steel, making millions—then father keeping those home fires burning, making more millions—and little me at the tail-end of it all. I'm a waste product in the Bessemer process—like the millions. Or rather, I inherit the acquired trait of the by-product, wealth, but none of the energy, none of the strength of the steel that made it. I am sired by gold and damned by it, as they say at the race track—damned in more ways than one. [*She laughs mirthlessly.*]

AUNT [*unimpressed—superciliously*]. You seem to be going in for sincerity today. It isn't becoming to you, really—except as an obvious pose. Be as artificial as you are, I advise. There's a sort of sincerity in that, you know. And, after all, you must confess you like that better.

MILDRED [*again affected and bored*]. Yes, I suppose I do. Pardon me for my outburst. When a leopard complains of its spots, it must sound rather grotesque. [*In a mocking tone.*] Purr, little leopard. Purr, scratch, tear, kill, gorge yourself and be happy—only stay in the jungle where your spots are camouflage. In a cage they make you conspicuous.

AUNT. I don't know what you are talking about.

MILDRED. It would be rude to talk about anything to you. Let's just talk. [*She looks at her wrist watch.*] Well, thank goodness, it's about time for them to come for me. That ought to give me a new thrill, Aunt.

AUNT [*affectedly troubled*]. You don't mean to say you're really going? The dirt—the heat must be frightful—

MILDRED. Grandfather started as a puddler. I should have inherited an immunity to heat that would make a salamander shiver. It will be fun to put it to the test.

AUNT. But don't you have to have the captain's—or someone's—permission to visit the stokehole?

MILDRED [*with a triumphant smile*]. I have it—both his and the chief engineer's. Oh, they didn't want to at first, in spite of my social service credentials. They didn't seem a bit anxious that I should investigate how the other half lives and works on a ship. So I had to tell them that my father, the president of Nazareth Steel, chairman of the board of directors of this line, had told me it would be all right.

AUNT. He didn't.

MILDRED. How naïve age makes one! But I said he did, Aunt. I even said he had given me a letter to them—which I had lost. And they were afraid to take the chance that I might be lying. [*Excitedly.*] So it's ho! for the stokehole. The second engineer is to escort me. [*Looking at her watch again.*] It's time. And here he comes, I think. [*The* SECOND ENGINEER *enters. He is a husky, fine-looking man of thirty-five or so. He stops before the two and tips his cap, visibly embarrassed and ill-at-ease.*]

SECOND ENGINEER. Miss Douglas?

MILDRED. Yes. [*Throwing off her rugs and getting to her feet.*] Are we all ready to start?

SECOND ENGINEER. In just a second, ma'am. I'm waiting for the Fourth. He's coming along.

MILDRED [*with a scornful smile*]. You don't care to shoulder this responsibility alone, is that it?

SECOND ENGINEER [*forcing a smile*]. Two are better than one. [*Disturbed by her eyes, glances out to sea—blurts out.*] A fine day we're having.

MILDRED. Is it?

SECOND ENGINEER. A nice warm breeze—

MILDRED. It feels cold to me.

SECOND ENGINEER. But it's hot enough in the sun—

MILDRED. Not hot enough for me. I don't like Nature. I was never athletic.

SECOND ENGINEER [*forcing a smile*]. Well, you'll find it hot enough where you're going.

MILDRED. Do you mean hell?

SECOND ENGINEER [*flabbergasted, decides to laugh*]. Ho-ho! No, I mean the stokehole.

MILDRED. My grandfather was a puddler. He played with boiling steel.

SECOND ENGINEER [*all at sea—uneasily*]. Is that so? Hum, you'll excuse me, ma'am, but are you intending to wear that dress?

MILDRED. Why not?

SECOND ENGINEER. You'll likely rub against oil and dirt. It can't be helped.

MILDRED. It doesn't matter. I have lots of white dresses.

SECOND ENGINEER. I have an old coat you might throw over—

MILDRED. I have fifty dresses like this. I will throw this one into the sea when I come back. That ought to wash it clean, don't you think?

SECOND ENGINEER [*doggedly*]. There's ladders to climb down that are none too clean—and dark alleyways—

MILDRED. I will wear this very dress and none other.

SECOND ENGINEER. No offense meant. It's none of my business. I was only warning you—

MILDRED. Warning? That sounds thrilling.

SECOND ENGINEER [*looking down the deck—with a sigh of relief*]. There's the Fourth now. He's waiting for us. If you'll come—

MILDRED. Go on. I'll follow you. [*He goes.* MILDRED *turns a mocking smile on her aunt.*] An oaf—but a handsome, virile oaf.

AUNT [*scornfully*]. Poser!

MILDRED. Take care. He said there were dark alleyways—

AUNT [*in the same tone*]. Poser!

MILDRED [*biting her lips angrily*]. You are right. But would that my millions were not so anemically chaste!

AUNT. Yes, for a fresh pose I have no doubt you would drag the name of Douglas in the gutter!

MILDRED. From which it sprang. Good-by, Aunt. Don't pray too hard that I may fall into the fiery furnace.

AUNT. Poser!

MILDRED [*viciously*]. Old hag. [*She slaps her aunt insultingly across the face and walks off, laughingly gaily.*]

AUNT [*screams after her*]. I said poser!

CURTAIN

SCENE III

[*The stokehole. In the rear, the dimly-outlined bulks of the furnaces and boilers. High overhead one hanging electric bulb sheds just enough light through the murky air laden with coal dust to pile up masses of shadows everywhere. A line of men, stripped to the waist, is before the furnace doors. They bend over, looking neither to right nor left, handling their shovels as if they were part of their bodies, with a strange, awkward, swinging rhythm. They use the shovels to throw open the furnace doors. Then from these fiery round holes in the black a flood of terrific light and heat pours full upon the men who are outlined in silhouette in the crouching, inhuman attitudes of chained gorillas. The men shovel with a rhythmic motion, swinging as on a pivot from the coal which lies in heaps on the floor behind to hurl it into the flaming mouths before them. There is a tumult of noise—the brazen clang of the furnace doors as they are flung open or slammed shut, the grating, teeth-gritting grind of steel against steel, of crunching coal. This clash of sounds stuns one's ears with its rending dissonance. But there is order in it, rhythm, a mechanical regulated recurrence, a tempo. And rising above all, making the air hum with the quiver of liberated energy, the roar of leaping flames in the furnaces, the monotonous throbbing beat of the engines.*

As the curtain rises, the furnace doors are shut. The men are taking a breathing spell. One or two are arranging the coal behind them, pulling it into more accessible heaps. The others can be dimly made out leaning on their shovels in relaxed attitudes of exhaustion.]

PADDY [*from somewhere in the line—plaintively*]. Yerra, will this divil's own watch nivir end? Me back is broke. I'm destroyed entirely.

YANK [*from the center of the line—with exuberant scorn*]. Aw, yuh make me sick! Lie down and croak, why don't yuh? Always beefin', dat's you! Say, dis is a cinch! Dis was made for me! It's my meat, get me! [*A whistle is blown—a thin, shrill note from somewhere overhead in the darkness.* YANK *curses without resentment.*] Dere's de damn engineer crackin' de whip. He tinks we're loafin'.

PADDY [*vindictively*]. God stiffen him!

YANK [*in an exultant tone of command*]. Come on, youse guys! Git into de game! She's gittin' hungry! Pile some grub in her. Trow it into her belly! Come on now, all of youse! Open her up! [*At this last all the men, who have followed his movements of getting into position, throw open their furnace doors with a deafening clang. The fiery light floods over their shoulders as they bend round for the coal. Rivulets of sooty sweat have traced maps on their backs. The enlarged muscles form bunches of high light and shadow.*]

YANK [*chanting a count as he shovels without seeming effort*]. One—two—tree— [*His voice rising exultantly in the joy of battle.*] Dat's de stuff! Let her have it! All togedder now! Sling it into her! Let her ride! Shoot de piece now! Call de toin on her! Drive her into it! Feel her move! Watch her smoke! Speed, dat's her middle name! Give her coal, youse guys! Coal, dat's her booze! Drink it up, baby! Let's see yuh sprint! Dig in and gain a lap! Dere she go-o-es. [*This last in the chanting formula of the gallery gods at the six-day bike race. He slams his furnace door shut. The others do likewise with as much unison as their wearied bodies will permit. The effect is of one fiery eye after another being blotted out with a series of accompanying bangs.*]

PADDY [*groaning*]. Me back is broke. I'm bate out—bate— [*There is a pause. Then the inexorable whistle sounds again from the dim regions above the electric light. There is a growl of cursing rage from all sides.*]

YANK [*shaking his fist upward—contemptuously*]. Take it easy dere, you! Who d'yuh tink's runnin' dis game, me or you? When I git ready, we move. Not before! When I git ready, get me!

VOICES [*approvingly*].
That's the stuff!
Yank tal him, py golly!
Yank ain't affeerd.
Goot poy, Yank!
Give him hell!
Tell 'im 'e's a bloody swine!
Bloody slave-driver!

YANK [*contemptuously*]. He ain't got no noive. He's yellow, get me? All de engineers is yellow. Dey got streaks a mile wide. Aw, to hell wit him! Let's move, youse guys. We had a rest. Come on, she needs it! Give her pep! It ain't for him. Him and his whistle, dey don't belong. But we belong, see! We gotter feed de baby! Come on! [*He turns and flings his furnace door open. They all follow his lead. At this instant the* SECOND *and* FOURTH ENGINEERS *enter from the darkness on the left with* MILDRED *between them. She starts, turns paler, her pose is crumbling, she shivers with fright in spite of the blazing heat, but forces herself to leave the* ENGINEERS *and take a few steps nearer the men. She is right behind* YANK. *All this happens quickly while the men have their backs turned.*]

YANK. Come on, youse guys! [*He is turning to get coal when the whistle sounds again in a peremptory, irritating note. This drives* YANK *into a sudden fury. While the other men have turned full* around and stopped dumfounded by the spectacle of MILDRED standing there in her white dress, YANK does not turn far enough to see her. Besides, his head is thrown back, he blinks upward through the murk trying to find the owner of the whistle, he brandishes his shovel murderously over his head in one hand, pounding on his chest, gorilla-like, with the other, shouting.] Toin off dat whistle! Come down outa dere, yuh yellow, brass-buttoned, Belfast bum, yuh! Come down and I'll knock yer brains out! Yuh lousy, stinkin', yellow mut of a Catholic-moiderin' bastard! Come down and I'll moider yuh! Pullin' dat whistle on me, huh? I'll show yuh! I'll crash yer skull in! I'll drive yer teet' down yer troat! I'll slam yer nose trou de back of yer head! I'll cut yer guts out for a nickel, yuh lousy boob, yuh dirty, crummy, muck-eatin' son of a— [Suddenly he becomes conscious of all the other men staring at something directly behind his back. He whirls defensively with a snarling, murderous growl, crouching to spring, his lips drawn back over his teeth, his small eyes gleaming ferociously. He sees MILDRED, like a white apparition in the full light from the open furnace doors. He glares into her eyes, turned to stone. As for her, during his speech she has listened, paralyzed with horror, terror, her whole personality crushed, beaten in, collapsed, by the terrific impact of this unknown, abysmal brutality, naked and shameless. As she looks at his gorilla face, as his eyes bore into hers, she utters a low, choking cry and shrinks away from him, putting both hands up before her eyes to shut out the sight of his face, to protect her own. This startles YANK to a reaction. His mouth falls open, his eyes grow bewildered.]

MILDRED [about to faint—to the ENGINEERS, who now have her one by each arm—whimperingly]. Take me away! Oh, the filthy beast! [She faints. They carry her quickly back, disappearing in the darkness at the left, rear. An iron door clangs shut. Rage and bewildered fury rush back on YANK. He feels himself insulted in some unknown fashion in the very heart of his pride. He roars]: God damn yuh! [And hurls his shovel after them at the door which has just closed. It hits the steel bulkhead with a clang and falls clattering on the steel floor. From overhead the whistle sounds again in a long, angry, insistent command.]

CURTAIN

SCENE IV

[The firemen's forecastle. YANK'S watch has just come off duty and had dinner. Their faces and bodies shine from a soap and water scrubbing but around their eyes, where a hasty dousing does not touch, the coal dust sticks like black make-up, giving them a queer, sinister expression. YANK has not washed either face or body. He stands out in contrast to them, a blackened, brooding figure. He is seated forward on a bench in the exact attitude of Rodin's "The Thinker." The others, most of them smoking pipes, are staring at YANK half-apprehensively, as if fearing an outburst; half-amusedly, as if they saw a joke somewhere that tickled them.]

VOICES. He ain't ate nothin'.
Py golly, a fallar gat to gat grub in him.
Divil a lie.

Yank feeda da fire, no feeda da face.
Ha-ha.
He ain't even washed hisself.
He's forgot.
Hey, Yank, you forgot to wash.

YANK [*sullenly*]. Forgot nothin'! To hell wit washin'.

VOICES. It'll stick to you.
It'll get under your skin.
Give yer the bleedin' itch, that's wot.
It makes spots on you—like a leopard.
Like a piebald nigger, you mean.
Better wash up, Yank.
You sleep better.
Wash up, Yank.
Wash up! Wash up!

YANK [*resentfully*]. Aw say, youse guys. Lemme alone. Can't youse see I'm tryin' to tink?

ALL [*repeating the word after him as one with cynical mockery*]. Think! [*The word has a brazen, metallic quality as if their throats were phonograph horns. It is followed by a chorus of hard, barking laughter.*]

YANK [*springing to his feet and glaring at them belligerently*]. Yes, tink! Tink, dat's what I said! What about it? [*They are silent, puzzled by his sudden resentment at what used to be one of his jokes.* YANK *sits down again in the same attitude of "The Thinker".*]

VOICES. Leave him alone.
      He's got a grouch on.
      Why wouldn't he?

PADDY [*with a wink at the others*]. Sure I know what's the matther. 'Tis aisy to see. He's fallen in love, I'm telling you.

ALL [*repeating the word after him as one with cynical mockery*]. Love! [*The word has a brazen, metallic quality as if their throats were phonograph horns. It is followed by a chorus of hard, barking laughter.*]

YANK [*with a contemptuous snort*]. Love, hell! Hate, dat's what. I've fallen in hate, get me?

PADDY [*philosophically*]. 'Twould take a wise man to tell one from the other. [*With a bitter, ironical scorn, increasing as he goes on.*] But I'm telling you it's love that's in it. Sure what else but love for us poor bastes in the stokehole would be bringing a fine lady, dressed like a white quane, down a mile of ladders and steps to be havin' a look at us? [*A growl of anger goes up from all sides.*]

LONG [*jumping on a bench—hecticly*]. Hinsultin' us! Hinsultin' us, the bloody cow! And them bloody engineers! What right 'as they got to be exhibitin' us 's if we was bleedin' monkeys in a menagerie? Did we sign for hinsults to our dignity as 'onest workers? Is that in the ship's articles? You kin bloody well bet it ain't! But I knows why they done it. I arsked a deck steward 'o she was and 'e told me. 'Er old man's a bleedin' millionaire, a bloody Capitalist! 'E's got enuf bloody gold to sink this bleedin' ship! 'E makes arf the bloody steel in the world! 'E owns this bloody boat! And you and me, Comrades, we're 'is slaves! And the skipper and mates and engineers, they're 'is slaves! And she's 'is bloody daughter and we're all 'er slaves, too! And she gives 'er orders as 'ow she wants to see the bloody animals below decks and down they takes 'er! [*There is a roar of rage from all sides.*]

YANK [*blinking at him bewilderedly*]. Say! Wait a moment! Is all dat straight goods?

LONG. Straight as string! The bleedin' steward as waits on 'em, 'e told me about 'er. And what're we goin' ter do, I arsks yer? 'Ave we got ter swaller 'er hinsults like dogs? It ain't in the ship's articles. I tell yer we got a case. We kin go to law—

YANK [*with abysmal contempt*]. Hell! Law!

ALL [*repeating the word after him as one with cynical mockery*]. Law! [*The word has a brazen metallic quality as if their throats were phonograph horns. It is followed by a chorus of hard, barking laughter.*]

LONG [*feeling the ground slipping from under his feet—desperately*]. As voters and citizens we kin force the bloody governments—

YANK [*with abysmal contempt*]. Hell! Governments!

ALL [*repeating the word after him as one with cynical mockery*]. Governments! [*The word has a brazen metallic quality as if their throats were phonograph horns. It is followed by a chorus of hard, barking laughter.*]

LONG [*hysterically*]. We're free and equal in the sight of God—

YANK [*with abysmal contempt*]. Hell! God!

ALL [*repeating the word after him as one with cynical mockery*]. God! [*The word has a brazen metallic quality as if their throats were phonograph horns. It is followed by a chorus of hard, barking laughter.*]

YANK [*witheringly*]. Aw, join de Salvation Army!

ALL. Sit down! Shut up! Damn fool! Sea-lawyer! [LONG *slinks back out of sight.*]

PADDY [*continuing the trend of his thoughts as if he had never been interrupted—bitterly*]. And there she was standing behind us, and the Second pointing at us like a man you'd hear in a circus would be saying: In this cage is a queerer kind of baboon than ever you'd find in darkest Africy. We roast them in their own sweat—and be damned if you won't hear some of them saying they like it! [*He glances scornfully at* YANK.]

YANK [*with a bewildered uncertain growl*]. Aw!

PADDY. And there was Yank roarin' curses and turning round wid his shovel to brain her—and she looked at him, and him at her—

YANK [*slowly*]. She was all white. I tought she was a ghost. Sure.

PADDY [*with heavy, biting sarcasm*]. 'Twas love at first sight, divil a doubt of it! If you'd seen the endearin' look on her pale mug when she shriveled away with her hands over her eyes to shut out the sight of him! Sure, 'twas as if she'd seen a great hairy ape escaped from the Zoo!

YANK [*stung—with a growl of rage*]. Aw!

PADDY. And the loving way Yank heaved his shovel at the skull of her, only she was out the door! [*A grin breaking over his face.*] 'Twas touching, I'm telling you! It put the touch of home, swate home in the stokehole. [*There is a roar of laughter from all.*]

YANK [*glaring at* PADDY *menacingly*]. Aw, choke dat off, see!

PADDY [*not heeding him—to the others*]. And her grabbin' at the Second's arm for protection. [*With a grotesque imitation of a woman's voice.*] Kiss me, Engineer dear, for it's dark down here and me old man's in Wall Street making money! Hug me tight, darlin', for I'm afeerd in the dark and me mother's on deck makin' eyes at the skipper! [*Another roar of laughter.*]

YANK [*threateningly*]. Say! What yuh tryin' to do, kid me, yuh old Harp?

PADDY. Divil a bit! Ain't I wishin' myself you'd brained her?

YANK [*fiercely*]. I'll brain her! I'll brain her yet, wait 'n' see! [*Coming over to*

"The Hairy Ape"

PADDY—*slowly.*] Say, is dat what she called me—a hairy ape?

PADDY. She looked it at you if she didn't say the word itself.

YANK [*grinning horribly*]. Hairy ape, huh? Sure! Dat's de way she looked at me, aw right. Hairy ape! So dat's me, huh? [*Bursting into rage—as if she were still in front of him.*] Yuh skinny tart! Yuh white-faced bum, yuh! I'll show yuh who's a ape! [*Turning to the others, bewilderment seizing him again.*] Say, youse guys. I was bawlin' him out for pullin' de whistle on us. You heard me. And den I seen youse lookin' at somep'n and I tought he'd sneaked down to come up in back of me, and I hopped round to knock him dead wit de shovel. And dere she was wit de light on her! Christ, yuh coulda pushed me over with a finger! I was scared, get me? Sure! I tought she was a ghost, see? She was all in white like dey wrap around stiffs. You seen her. Kin yuh blame me? She didn't belong, dat's what. And den when I come to and seen it was a real skoit and seen de way she was lookin' at me—like Paddy said—Christ, I was sore, get me? I don't stand for dat stuff from nobody. And I flung de shovel —on'y she'd beat it. [*Furiously.*] I wished it'd banged her! I wished it'd knocked her block off!

LONG. And be 'anged for murder or 'lectrocuted? She ain't bleedin' well worth it.

YANK. I don't give a damn what! I'd be square wit her, wouldn't I? Tink I wanter let her put somep'n over on me? Tink I'm goin' to let her git away wit dat stuff? Yuh don't know me! No one ain't never put nothin' over on me and got away wit it, see!—not dat kind of stuff—no guy and no skoit neither! I'll fix her! Maybe she'll come down again—

VOICE. No chance, Yank. You scared her out of a year's growth.

YANK. I scared her? Why de hell should I scare her? Who de hell is she? Ain't she de same as me? Hairy ape, huh? [*With his old confident bravado.*] I'll show her I'm better'n her, if she on'y knew it. I belong and she don't, see! I move and she's dead! Twenty-five knots a hour, dat's me! Dat carries her but I make dat. She's on'y baggage. Sure! [*Again bewilderedly.*] But, Christ, she was funny lookin'! Did yuh pipe her hands? White and skinny. Yuh could see de bones through 'em. And her mush, dat was dead white, too. And her eyes, dey was like dey'd seen a ghost. Me, dat was! Sure! Hairy ape! Ghost, huh? Look at dat arm! [*He extends his right arm, swelling out the great muscles.*] I coulda took her wit dat, wit just my little finger even, and broke her in two. [*Again bewilderedly.*] Say, who is dat skoit, huh? What is she? What's she come from? Who made her? Who give her de noive to look at me like dat? Dis ting's got my goat right. I don't get her. She's new to me. What does a skoit like her mean, huh? She don't belong, get me! I can't see her. [*With growing anger.*] But one ting I'm wise to, aw right, aw right! Youse all kin bet your shoits I'll git even wit her. I'll show her if she tinks she— She grinds de organ and I'm on de string, huh? I'll fix her! Let her come down again and I'll fling her in de furnace! She'll move den! She won't shiver at nothin', den! Speed, dat'll be her! She'll belong den! [*He grins horribly.*]

PADDY. She'll never come. She's had her belly-full, I'm telling you. She'll be in bed now, I'm thinking, wid ten doctors and nurses feedin' her salts to clean the fear out of her.

YANK [*enraged*]. Yuh tink I made her sick, too, do yuh? Just lookin' at me, huh? Hairy ape, huh? [*In a frenzy of rage.*] I'll

Drama

fix her! I'll tell her where to git off! She'll git down on her knees and take it back or I'll bust de face offen her! [*Shaking one fist upward and beating on his chest with the other.*] I'll find yuh! I'm comin', d'yuh hear? I'll fix yuh, God damn yuh! [*He makes a rush for the door.*]

Voices. Stop him!
    He'll get shot!
    He'll murder her!
    Trip him up!
    Hold him!
    He's gone crazy!
    Gott, he's strong!
    Hold him down!
    Look out for a kick!
    Pin his arms!

[*They have all piled on him and, after a fierce struggle, by sheer weight of numbers have borne him to the floor just inside the door.*]

Paddy [*who has remained detached*]. Kape him down till he's cooled off. [*Scornfully.*] Yerra, Yank, you're a great fool. Is it payin' attention at all you are to the like of that skinny sow widout one drop of rale blood in her?

Yank [*frenziedly, from the bottom of the heap*]. She done me doit! She done me doit, didn't she? I'll git square wit her! I'll get her some way! Git offen me, youse guys! Lemme up! I'll show her who's a ape!

CURTAIN

SCENE V

[*Three weeks later. A corner of Fifth Avenue in the Fifties on a fine Sunday morning. A general atmosphere of clean, well-tidied, wide street; a flood of mellow, tempered sunshine; gentle, genteel breezes. In the rear, the show windows of two shops, a jewelry establishment on the corner, a furrier's next to it. Here the adornments of extreme wealth are tantalizingly displayed. The jeweler's window is gaudy with glittering diamonds, emeralds, rubies, pearls, etc., fashioned in ornate tiaras, crowns, necklaces, collars, etc. From each piece hangs an enormous tag from which a dollar sign and numerals in intermittent electric lights wink out the incredible prices. The same in the furrier's. Rich furs of all varieties hang there bathed in a downpour of artificial light. The general effect is of a background of magnificence cheapened and made grotesque by commercialism, a background in tawdry disharmony with the clear light and sunshine on the street itself.*]

Up the side street Yank and Long come swaggering. Long *is dressed in shore clothes, wears a black Windsor tie, cloth cap.* Yank *is in his dirty dungarees. A fireman's cap with black peak is cocked defiantly on the side of his head. He has not shaved for days and around his fierce, resentful eyes—as around those of* Long *to a lesser degree—the black smudge of coal dust still sticks like make-up. They hesitate and stand together at the corner, swaggering, looking about them with a forced, defiant contempt.*]

Long [*indicating it all with an oratorical gesture*]. Well, 'ere we are. Fif' Avenoo. This 'ere's their bleedin' private lane, as yer might say. [*Bitterly.*] We're trespassers 'ere. Proletarians keep orf the grass!

Yank [*dully*]. I don't see no grass, yuh boob. [*Staring at the sidewalk.*] Clean, ain't it? Yuh could eat a fried egg offen it. The white wings got some job sweepin'

"The Hairy Ape"

dis up. [*Looking up and down the avenue—surlily.*] Where's all de white-collar stiffs yuh said was here—and de skoits—*her* kind?

LONG. In church, blarst 'em! Arskin' Jesus to give 'em more money.

YANK. Choich, huh? I useter go to choich onct—sure—when I was a kid. Me old man and woman, dey made me. Dey never went demselves, dough. Always got too big a head on Sunday mornin', dat was dem. [*With a grin.*] Dey was scrappers for fair, bot' of dem. On Satiday nights when dey bot' got a skinful dey could put up a bout oughter been staged at de Garden. When dey got trough dere wasn't a chair or table wit a leg under it. Or else dey bot' jumped on me for somep'n. Dat was where I loined to take punishment. [*With a grin and a swagger.*] I'm a chip offen de old block, get me?

LONG. Did yer old man follow the sea?

YANK. Naw. Worked along shore. I runned away when me old lady croaked wit de tremens. I helped at truckin' and in de market. Den I shipped in de stokehole. Sure. Dat belongs. De rest was nothin'. [*Looking around him.*] I ain't never seen dis before. De Brooklyn waterfront, dat was where I was dragged up. [*Taking a deep breath.*] Dis ain't so bad at dat, huh?

LONG. Not bad? Well, we pays for it wiv our bloody sweat, if yer wants to know!

YANK [*with sudden angry disgust*]. Aw, hell! I don't see no one, see—like her. All dis gives me a pain. It don't belong. Say, ain't dere a back room around dis dump? Let's go shoot a ball. All dis is too clean and quiet and dolled up, get me! It gives me a pain.

LONG. Wait and yer'll bloody well see—

YANK. I don't wait for no one. I keep on de move. Say, what yuh drag me up here for, anyway? Tryin' to kid me, yuh simp, yuh?

LONG. Yer wants to get back at 'er, don't yer? That's what yer been sayin' every bloomin' hour since she hinsulted yer.

YANK [*vehemently*]. Sure ting I do! Didn't I try to get even wit her in Southampton? Didn't I sneak on de dock and wait for her by de gangplank? I was goin' to spit in her pale mug, see! Sure, right in her pop-eyes! Dat woulda made me even, see? But no chanct. Dere was a whole army of plainclothes bulls around. Dey spotted me and gimme de bum's rush. I never seen her. But I'll git square wit her yet, you watch! [*Furiously.*] De lousy tart! She tinks she kin get away wit moider—but not wit me! I'll fix her! I'll tink of a way!

LONG [*as disgusted as he dares to be*]. Ain't that why I brought yer up 'ere—to show yer? Yer been lookin' at this 'ere 'ole affair wrong. Yer been actin' an' talkin' 's if it was all a bleedin' personal matter between yer and that bloody cow. I wants to convince yer she was on'y a representative of 'er clarss. I wants to awaken yer bloody clarss consciousness. Then yer'll see it's 'er clarss yer've got to fight, not 'er alone. There's a 'ole mob of 'em like 'er, Gawd blind 'em!

YANK [*spitting on his hands—belligerently*]. De more de merrier when I gits started. Bring on de gang!

LONG. Yer'll see 'em in arf a mo', when that church lets out. [*He turns and sees the window display in the two stores for the first time.*] Blimey! Look at that, will yer? [*They both walk back and stand looking in the jeweler's.* LONG *flies into a fury.*] Just look at this 'ere bloomin' mess! Just look at it! Look at the bleedin' prices on 'em—more'n our 'ole bloody stokehole makes in ten voyages sweatin'

[531]

in 'ell! And they—'er and 'er bloody clarss—buys 'em for toys to dangle on 'em! One of these 'ere would buy scoff for a starvin' family for a year!

YANK. Aw, cut de sob stuff! T' hell wit de starvin' family! Yuh'll be passin' de hat to me next. [*With naïve admiration.*] Say, dem tings is pretty, huh? Bet yuh dey'd hock for a piece of change aw right. [*Then turning away, bored.*] But, aw hell, what good are dey? Let her have 'em. Dey don't belong no more'n she does. [*With a gesture of sweeping the jewelers into oblivion.*] All dat don't count, get me?

LONG [*who has moved to the furrier's—indignantly*]. And I s'pose this 'ere don't count neither—skins of poor, 'armless animals slaughtered so as 'er and 'ers can keep their bleedin' noses warm!

YANK [*who has been staring at something inside—with queer excitement*]. Take a slant at dat! Give it de once-over! Monkey fur—two t'ousand bucks! [*Bewilderedly.*] Is dat straight goods—monkey fur? What de hell—?

LONG [*bitterly*]. It's straight enuf. [*With grim humor.*] They wouldn't bloody well pay that for a 'airy ape's skin—no, nor for the 'ole livin' ape with all 'is 'ead, and body, and soul thrown in!

YANK [*clenching his fists, his face growing pale with rage as if the skin in the window were a personal insult*]. Trowin' it up in my face! Christ! I'll fix her!

LONG [*excitedly*]. Church is out. 'Ere they come, the bleedin' swine. [*After a glance at* YANK's *lowering face—uneasily.*] Easy goes, Comrade. Keep yer bloomin' temper. Remember force defeats itself. It ain't our weapon. We must impress our demands through peaceful means—the votes of the on-marching proletarians of the bloody world!

YANK [*with abysmal contempt*]. Votes, hell! Votes is a joke, see. Votes for women! Let dem do it!

LONG [*still more uneasily*]. Calm, now. Treat 'em wiv the proper contempt. Observe the bleedin' parasites but 'old yer 'orses.

YANK [*angrily*]. Git away from me! Yuh're yellow, dat's what. Force, dat's me! De punch, dat's me every time, see! [*The crowd from church enter from the right, sauntering slowly and affectedly, their heads held stiffly up, looking neither to right nor left, talking in toneless, simpering voices. The women are rouged, calcimined, dyed, overdressed to the nth degree. The men are in Prince Alberts, high hats, spats, canes, etc. A procession of gaudy marionettes, yet with something of the relentless horror of Frankensteins in their detached, mechanical unawareness.*]

VOICES. Dear Doctor Caiaphas! He is so sincere!

What was the sermon? I dozed off.

About the radicals, my dear—and the false doctrines that are being preached.

We must organize a hundred per cent American bazaar.

And let everyone contribute one one-hundredth per cent of their income tax.

What an original idea!

We can devote the proceeds to rehabilitating the veil of the temple.

But that has been done so many times.

YANK [*glaring from one to the other of them—with an insulting snort of scorn*]. Huh! Huh! [*Without seeming to see him, they make wide detours to avoid the spot where he stands in the middle of the sidewalk.*]

LONG [*frightenedly*]. Keep yer bloomin' mouth shut, I tells yer.

YANK [*viciously*]. G'wan! Tell it to Sweeney! [*He swaggers away and delib-*

erately *lurches into a top-hatted gentleman, then glares at him pugnaciously.*] Say, who d'yuh tink yuh're bumpin'? Tink yuh own de oith?

GENTLEMAN [*coldly and affectedly*]. I beg your pardon. [*He has not looked at* YANK *and passes on without a glance, leaving him bewildered.*]

LONG [*rushing up and grabbing* YANK's *arm*]. 'Ere! Come away! This wasn't what I meant. Yer'll 'ave the bloody coppers down on us.

YANK [*savagely—giving him a push that sends him sprawling*]. G'wan!

LONG [*picks himself up—hysterically*]. I'll pop orf then. This ain't what I meant. And whatever 'appens, yer can't blame me. [*He slinks off left.*]

YANK. T' hell wit youse! [*He approaches a lady—with a vicious grin and a smirking wink.*] Hello, Kiddo. How's every little ting? Got anyting on for tonight? I know an old boiler down to de docks we kin crawl into. [*The lady stalks by without a look, without a change of pace.* YANK *turns to others—insultingly.*] Holy smokes, what a mug! Go hide yuhself before de horses shy at yuh. Gee, pipe de heine on dat one! Say, youse, yuh look like de stoin of a ferryboat. Paint and powder! All dolled up to kill! Yuh look like stiffs laid out for de boneyard! Aw, g'wan, de lot of youse! Yuh give me de eye-ache. Yuh don't belong, get me! Look at me, why don't youse dare? I belong, dat's me! [*Pointing to a skyscraper across the street which is in process of construction—with bravado.*] See dat building goin' up dere? See de steel work? Steel, dat's me! Youse guys live on it and tink yuh're somep'n. But I'm *in* it, see! I'm de hoistin' engine dat makes it go up! I'm it—de inside and bottom of it! Sure! I'm steel and steam and smoke and de rest of it! It moves—speed—twenty-five stories up—and me at de top and bottom—movin'! Youse simps don't move. Yuh're on'y dolls I winds up to see 'm spin. Yuh're de garbage, get me—de leavins—de ashes we dump over de side! Now, what 'a' yuh gotta say? [*But as they seem neither to see nor hear him, he flies into a fury.*] Bums! Pigs! Tarts! Bitches! [*He turns in a rage on the men, bumping viciously into them but not jarring them the least bit. Rather it is he who recoils after each collision. He keeps growling.*] Git off de oith! G'wan, yuh bum! Look where yuh're goin', can't yuh? Git outa here! Fight, why don't yuh? Put up yer mits! Don't be a dog! Fight or I'll knock yuh dead! [*But, without seeming to see him, they all answer with mechanical affected politeness*]: I beg your pardon. [*Then at a cry from one of the women, they all scurry to the furrier's window.*]

THE WOMAN [*ecstatically, with a gasp of delight*]. Monkey fur! [*The whole crowd of men and women chorus after her in the same tone of affected delight*]: Monkey fur!

YANK [*with a jerk of his head back on his shoulders, as if he had received a punch full in the face—raging*]. I see yuh, all in white! I see yuh, yuh white-faced tart, yuh! Hairy ape, huh? I'll hairy ape yuh! [*He bends down and grips at the street curbing as if to pluck it out and hurl it. Foiled in this, snarling with passion, he leaps to the lamp-post on the corner and tries to pull it up for a club. Just at that moment a bus is heard rumbling up. A fat, high-hatted, spatted gentleman runs out from the side street. He calls out plaintively*]: Bus! Bus! Stop there! [*and runs full tilt into the bending, straining* YANK, *who is bowled off his balance.*]

YANK [*seeing a fight—with a roar of joy as he springs to his feet*]. At last! Bus, huh? I'll bust yuh! [*He lets drive a ter-

rific swing, his fist landing full on the fat gentleman's face. But the gentleman stands unmoved as if nothing had happened.]

GENTLEMAN. I beg your pardon. [*Then irritably.*] You have made me lose my bus. [*He claps his hands and begins to scream.*] Officer! Officer! [*Many police whistles shrill out on the instant and a whole platoon of policemen rush in on* YANK *from all sides. He tries to fight but is clubbed to the pavement and fallen upon. The crowd at the window have not moved or noticed this disturbance. The clanging gong of the patrol wagon approaches with a clamoring din.*]

CURTAIN

SCENE VI

[*Night of the following day. A row of cells in the prison on Blackwells Island. The cells extend back diagonally from right front to left rear. They do not stop, but disappear in the dark background as if they ran on, numberless, into infinity. One electric bulb from the low ceiling of the narrow corridor sheds its light through the heavy steel bars of the cell at the extreme front and reveals part of the interior.* YANK *can be seen within, crouched on the edge of his cot in the attitude of Rodin's "The Thinker." His face is spotted with black and blue bruises. A bloodstained bandage is wrapped around his head.*]

YANK [*suddenly starting as if awakening from a dream, reaches out and shakes the bars—aloud to himself, wonderingly*]. Steel. Dis is de Zoo, huh? [*A burst of hard, barking laughter comes from the unseen occupants of the cells, runs back down the tier, and abruptly ceases.*]

VOICES [*mockingly*]. The Zoo? That's a new name for this coop—a damn good name!
Steel, eh? You said a mouthful. This is the old iron house.
Who is that boob talkin'?
He's the bloke they brung in out of his head. The bulls had beat him up fierce.

YANK [*dully*]. I musta been dreamin'. I tought I was in a cage at de Zoo—but de apes don't talk, do dey?

VOICES [*with mocking laughter*]. You're in a cage aw right.
A coop!
A pen!
A sty!
A kennel! [*Hard laughter—a pause.*]
Say, guy! Who are you? No, never mind lying. What are you?
Yes, tell us your sad story. What's your game?
What did they jug yuh for?

YANK [*dully*]. I was a fireman—stokin' on de liners. [*Then with sudden rage, rattling his cell bars.*] I'm a hairy ape, get me? And I'll bust youse all in de jaw if yuh don't lay off kiddin' me.

VOICES. Huh! You're a hard boiled duck, ain't you!
When you spit, it bounces! [*Laughter.*]
Aw, can it. He's a regular guy. Ain't you?
What did he say he was—a ape?

YANK [*defiantly*]. Sure ting! Ain't dat what youse all are—apes? [*A silence. Then a furious rattling of bars from down the corridor.*]

A VOICE [*thick with rage*]. I'll show yuh who's a ape, yuh bum!
VOICES. Ssshh! Nix!
Can de noise!
Piano!

[534]

You'll have the guard down on us!

YANK [*scornfully*]. De guard? Yuh mean de keeper, don't yuh? [*Angry exclamations from all the cells.*]

VOICE [*placatingly*]. Aw, don't pay no attention to him. He's off his nut from the beatin'-up he got. Say, you guy! We're waitin' to hear what they landed you for—or ain't yuh tellin'?

YANK. Sure, I'll tell youse. Sure! Why de hell not? On'y—youse won't get me. Nobody gets me but me, see? I started to tell de Judge and all he says was: "Toity days to tink it over." Tink it over! Christ, dat's all I been doin' for weeks! [*After a pause.*] I was tryin' to git even wit someone, see?—someone dat done me doit.

VOICES [*cynically*]. De old stuff, I bet. Your goil, huh?
Give yuh the double-cross, huh?
That's them every time!
Did yuh beat up de odder guy?

YANK [*disgustedly*]. Aw, yuh're all wrong! Sure dere was a skoit in it—but not what youse mean, not dat old tripe. Dis was a new kind of skoit. She was dolled up all in white—in de stokehole. I tought she was a ghost. Sure. [*A pause.*]

VOICES [*whispering*]. Gee, he's still nutty.
Let him rave. It's fun listenin'.

YANK [*unheeding—groping in his thoughts*]. Her hands—dey was skinny and white like dey wasn't real but painted on somep'n. Dere was a million miles from me to her—twenty-five knots a hour. She was like some dead ting de cat brung in. Sure, dat's what. She didn't belong. She belonged in de window of a toy store, or on de top of a garbage can, see! Sure! [*He breaks out angrily.*] But would yuh believe it, she had de noive to do me doit. She lamped me like she was seein' somep'n broke loose from de menagerie. Christ, yuh'd oughter seen her eyes! [*He rattles the bars of his cell furiously.*] But I'll get back at her yet, you watch! And if I can't find her I'll take it out on de gang she runs wit. I'm wise to where dey hangs out now. I'll show her who belongs! I'll show her who's in de move and who ain't. You watch my smoke!

VOICES [*serious and joking*]. Dat's de talkin'!
Take her for all she's got!
What was this dame, anyway? Who was she, eh?

YANK. I dunno. First cabin stiff. Her old man's a millionaire, dey says—name of Douglas.

VOICES. Douglas? That's the president of the Steel Trust, I bet.
Sure. I seen his mug in de papers.
He's filthy with dough.

VOICE. Hey, feller, take a tip from me. If you want to get back at that dame, you better join the Wobblies. You'll get some action then.

YANK. Wobblies? What de hell's dat?

VOICE. Ain't you ever heard of the I. W. W.?

YANK. Naw. What is it?

VOICE. A gang of blokes—a tough gang. I been readin' about 'em today in the paper. The guard give me the *Sunday Times*. There's a long spiel about 'em. It's from a speech made in the Senate by a guy named Senator Queen. [*He is in the cell next to* YANK's. *There is a rustling of paper.*] Wait'll I see if I got light enough and I'll read you. Listen. [*He reads.*] "There is a menace existing in this country today which threatens the vitals of our fair Republic—as foul a menace against the very life-blood of the American Eagle as was the foul conspiracy of Cataline against the eagles of ancient Rome!"

VOICE [*disgustedly*]. Aw, hell! Tell him to salt de tail of dat eagle!

[535]

VOICE [*reading*]. "I refer to that devil's brew of rascals, jailbirds, murderers and cutthroats who libel all honest working men by calling themselves the Industrial Workers of the World; but in the light of their nefarious plots, I call them the Industrious *Wreckers* of the World!"

YANK [*with vengeful satisfaction*]. Wreckers, dat's de right dope! Dat belongs! Me for dem!

VOICE. Ssshh! [*Reading.*] "This fiendish organization is a foul ulcer on the fair body of our Democracy—"

VOICE. Democracy, hell! Give him the boid, fellers— the raspberry! [*They do.*]

VOICE. Ssshh! [*Reading.*] "Like Cato I say to this Senate, the I. W. W. must be destroyed! For they represent an ever-present dagger pointed at the heart of the greatest nation the world has ever known, where all men are born free and equal, with equal opportunities to all, where the Founding Fathers have guaranteed to each one happiness, where Truth, Honor, Liberty, Justice, and the Brotherhood of Man are a religion absorbed with one's mother's milk, taught at our father's knee, sealed, signed, and stamped upon in the glorious Constitution of these United States!" [*A perfect storm of hisses, catcalls, boos, and hard laughter.*]

VOICES [*scornfully*]. Hurrah for de Fort' of July!
Pass de hat!
Liberty!
Justice!
Honor!
Opportunity!
Brotherhood!

ALL [*with abysmal scorn*]. Aw, hell!

VOICE. Give that Queen Senator guy the bark. All togedder now—one—two—tree— [*A terrific chorus of barking and yapping.*]

GUARD [*from a distance*]. Quiet there, youse—or I'll git the hose. [*The noise subsides.*]

YANK [*with growling rage*]. I'd like to catch dat senator guy alone for a second. I'd loin him some trute!

VOICE. Ssshh! Here's where he gits down to cases on the Wobblies. [*Reads.*] "They plot with fire in one hand and dynamite in the other. They stop not before murder to gain their ends, nor at the outraging of defenseless womanhood. They would tear down society, put the lowest scum in the seats of the mighty, turn Almighty God's revealed plan for the world topsy-turvy, and make of our sweet and lovely civilization a shambles, a desolation where man, God's masterpiece, would soon degenerate back to the ape!"

VOICE [*to* YANK]. Hey, you guy. There's your ape stuff again.

YANK [*with a growl of fury*]. I got him. So dey blow up tings, do dey? Dey turn tings round, do dey? Hey, lend me dat paper, will yuh?

VOICE. Sure. Give it to him. On'y keep it to yourself, see. We don't wanter listen to no more of that slop.

VOICE. Here you are. Hide it under your mattress.

YANK [*reaching out*]. Tanks. I can't read much but I kin manage. [*He sits, the paper in the hand at his side, in the attitude of Rodin's "The Thinker." A pause. Several snores from down the corridor. Suddenly* YANK *jumps to his feet with a furious groan as if some appalling thought had crashed on him—bewilderedly.*] Sure—her old man—president of de Steel Trust—makes half de steel in de world—steel—where I tought I belonged —drivin' trou—movin'—in dat—to make her—and cage me in for her to spit on!

Christ! [*He shakes the bars of his cell door till the whole tier trembles. Irritated, protesting exclamations from those awakened or trying to get to sleep.*] He made dis—dis cage! Steel! *It* don't belong, dat's what! Cages, cells, locks, bolts, bars—dat's what it means!—holdin' me down with him at de top! But I'll drive trou! Fire, dat melts it! I'll be fire—under de heap—fire dat never goes out—hot as hell—breakin' out in de night—[*While he has been saying this last he has shaken his cell door to a clanging accompaniment. As he comes to the "breakin' out" he seizes one bar with both hands and, putting his two feet up against the others so that his position is parallel to the floor like a monkey's, he gives a great wrench backwards. The bar bends like a licorice stick under his tremendous strength. Just at this moment the* PRISON GUARD *rushes in, dragging a hose behind him.*]

GUARD [*angrily*]. I'll loin youse bums to wake me up! [*Sees* YANK.] Hello, it's you, huh? Got the D. Ts., hey? Well, I'll cure 'em. I'll drown your snakes for yuh! [*Noticing the bar.*] Hell, look at dat bar bended! On'y a bug is strong enough for dat!

YANK [*glaring at him*]. Or a hairy ape, yuh big yellow bum! Look out! Here I come! [*He grabs another bar.*]

GUARD [*scared now—yelling off left*]. Toin de hose on, Ben!—full pressure! And call de others—and a straitjacket! [*The curtain is falling. As it hides* YANK *from view, there is a splattering smash as the stream of water hits the steel of* YANK'S *cell.*]

CURTAIN

SCENE VII

[*Nearly a month later. An I. W. W. local near the waterfront, showing the interior of a front room on the ground floor, and the street outside. Moonlight on the narrow street, buildings massed in black shadow. The interior of the room, which is general assembly room, office, and reading room, resembles some dingy settlement boys' club. A desk and high stool are in one corner. A table with papers, stacks of pamphlets, chairs about it, is at center. The whole is decidedly cheap, banal, commonplace and unmysterious as a room could well be. The secretary is perched on the stool making entries in a large ledger. An eye shade casts his face into shadows. Eight or ten men, longshoremen, iron workers, and the like, are grouped about the table. Two are playing checkers. One is writing a letter. Most of them are smoking pipes. A big signboard is on the wall at the rear, "Industrial Workers of the World—Local No. 57."*]

YANK [*comes down the street outside. He is dressed as in Scene Five. He moves cautiously, mysteriously. He comes to a point opposite the door; tiptoes softly up to it, listens, is impressed by the silence within, knocks carefully, as if he were guessing at the password to some secret rite. Listens. No answer. Knocks again a bit louder. No answer. Knocks impatiently, much louder.*]

SECRETARY [*turning around on his stool*]. What the hell is that—someone knocking? [*Shouts.*] Come in, why don't you? [*All the men in the room look up.* YANK *opens the door slowly, gingerly, as if afraid of an ambush. He looks around for secret doors, mystery, is taken aback by the commonplaceness of the room and the men in it, thinks he may have gotten in the wrong place, then sees the signboard on the wall and is reassured.*]

YANK [*blurts out*]. Hello.

MEN [*reservedly*]. Hello.

YANK [*more easily*]. I tought I'd bumped into de wrong dump.

SECRETARY [*scrutinizing him carefully*]. Maybe you have. Are you a member?

YANK. Naw, not yet. Dat's what I come for—to join.

SECRETARY. That's easy. What's your job—longshore?

YANK. Naw. Fireman—stoker on de liners.

SECRETARY [*with satisfaction*]. Welcome to our city. Glad to know you people are waking up at last. We haven't got many members in your line.

YANK. Naw. Dey're all dead to de woild.

SECRETARY. Well, you can help to wake 'em. What's your name? I'll make out your card.

YANK [*confused*]. Name? Lemme tink.

SECRETARY [*sharply*]. Don't you know your own name?

YANK. Sure; but I been just Yank for so long—Bob, dat's it—Bob Smith.

SECRETARY [*writing*]. Robert Smith. [*Fills out the rest of card.*] Here you are. Cost you half a dollar.

YANK. Is dat all—four bits? Dat's easy. [*Gives the Secretary the money.*]

SECRETARY [*throwing it in drawer*]. Thanks. Well, make yourself at home. No introductions needed. There's literature on the table. Take some of those pamphlets with you to distribute aboard ship. They may bring results. Sow the seed, only go about it right. Don't get caught and fired. We got plenty out of work. What we need is men who can hold their jobs—and work for us at the same time.

YANK. Sure. [*But he still stands, embarrassed and uneasy.*]

SECRETARY [*looking at him—curiously*]. What did you knock for? Think we had a coon in uniform to open doors?

YANK. Naw. I tought it was locked—and dat yuh'd wanter give me the once-over trou a peep-hole or somep'n to see if I was right.

SECRETARY [*alert and suspicious but with an easy laugh*]. Think we were running a crap game? That door is never locked. What put that in your nut?

YANK [*with a knowing grin, convinced that this is all camouflage, a part of the secrecy*]. Dis burg is full of bulls, ain't it?

SECRETARY [*sharply*]. What have the cops got to do with us? We're breaking no laws.

YANK [*with a knowing wink*]. Sure. Youse wouldn't for woilds. Sure. I'm wise to dat.

SECRETARY. You seem to be wise to a lot of stuff none of us knows about.

YANK [*with another wink*]. Aw, dat's aw right, see. [*Then made a bit resentful by the suspicious glances from all sides.*] Aw, can it! Youse needn't put me trou de toid degree. Can't youse see I belong? Sure! I'm reg'lar. I'll stick, get me? I'll shoot de woiks for youse. Dat's why I wanted to join in.

SECRETARY [*breezily, feeling him out*]. That's the right spirit. Only are you sure you understand what you've joined? It's all plain and above board; still, some guys get a wrong slant on us. [*Sharply.*] What's your notion of the purpose of the I. W. W.?

YANK. Aw, I know all about it.

SECRETARY [*sarcastically*]. Well, give us some of your valuable information.

YANK [*cunningly*]. I know enough not to speak outa my toin. [*Then resentfully*

"The Hairy Ape"

again.] Aw, say! I'm reg'lar. I'm wise to de game. I know yuh got to watch your step wit a stranger. For all youse know, I might be a plain-clothes dick, or somep'n, dat's what yuh're tinkin', huh? Aw, forget it! I belong, see? Ask any guy down to de docks if I don't.

SECRETARY. Who said you didn't?

YANK. After I'm 'nitiated, I'll show yuh.

SECRETARY [*astounded*]. Initiated? There's no initiation.

YANK [*disappointed*]. Ain't there no password—no grip nor nothin'?

SECRETARY. What'd you think this is—the Elks—or the Black Hand?

YANK. De Elks, hell! De Black Hand, dey're a lot of yellow back-stickin' Ginees. Naw. Dis is a man's gang, ain't it?

SECRETARY. You said it! That's why we stand on our two feet in the open. We got no secrets.

YANK [*surprised but admiringly*]. Yuh mean to say yuh always run wide open—like dis?

SECRETARY. Exactly.

YANK. Den yuh sure got your noive wit youse!

SECRETARY [*sharply*]. Just what was it made you want to join us? Come out with that straight.

YANK. Yuh call me? Well, I got noive, too! Here's my hand. Yuh wanter blow tings up, don't yuh? Well, dat's me! I belong!

SECRETARY [*with pretended carelessness*]. You mean change the unequal conditions of society by legitimate direct action—or with dynamite?

YANK. Dynamite! Blow it offen de oith—steel—all de cages—all de factories, steamers, buildings, jails—de Steel Trust and all dat makes it go.

SECRETARY. So—that's your idea, eh? And did you have any special job in that line you wanted to propose to us? [*He makes a sign to the men, who get up cautiously one by one and group behind* YANK.]

YANK [*boldly*]. Sure, I'll come out wit it. I'll show youse I'm one of de gang. Dere's dat millionaire guy, Douglas—

SECRETARY. President of the Steel Trust, you mean? Do you want to assassinate him?

YANK. Naw, dat don't get yuh nothin'. I mean blow up de factory, de woiks, where he makes de steel. Dat's what I'm after—to blow up de steel, knock all de steel in de woild up to de moon. Dat'll fix tings! [*Eagerly, with a touch of bravado.*] I'll do it by me lonesome! I'll show yuh! Tell me where his woiks is, how to git there, all de dope. Gimme de stuff, de old butter—and watch me do de rest! Watch de smoke and see it move! I don't give a damn if dey nab me—long as it's done! I'll soive life for it—and give 'em de laugh! [*Half to himself.*] And I'll write her a letter and tell her de hairy ape done it. Dat'll square tings.

SECRETARY [*stepping away from* YANK]. Very interesting. [*He gives a signal. The men, huskies all, throw themselves on* YANK *and before he knows it they have his legs and arms pinioned. But he is too flabbergasted to make a struggle, anyway. They feel him over for weapons.*]

MAN. No gat, no knife. Shall we give him what's what and put the boots to him?

SECRETARY. No. He isn't worth the trouble we'd get into. He's too stupid. [*He comes closer and laughs mockingly in* YANK'S *face.*] Ho-ho! By God, this is the biggest joke they've put up on us yet. Hey, you Joke! Who sent you—Burns or Pinkerton? No, by God, you're such a bonehead I'll bet you're in the Secret Ser-

[539]

vice! Well, you dirty spy, you rotten agent provocator, you can go back and tell whatever skunk is paying you bloodmoney for betraying your brothers that he's wasting his coin. You couldn't catch a cold. And tell him that all he'll ever get on us, or ever has got, is just his own sneaking plots that he's framed up to put us in jail. We are what our manifesto says we are, neither more nor less—and we'll give him a copy of that any time he calls. And as for you— [*He glares scornfully at* YANK, *who is sunk in an oblivious stupor.*] Oh, hell, what's the use of talking? You're a brainless ape.

YANK [*aroused by the word to fierce but futile struggles*]. What's dat, yuh Sheeny bum, yuh!

SECRETARY. Throw him out, boys. [*In spite of his struggles, this is done with gusto and éclat. Propelled by several parting kicks,* YANK *lands sprawling in the middle of the narrow cobbled street. With a growl he starts to get up and storm the closed door, but stops bewildered by the confusion in his brain, pathetically impotent. He sits there, brooding, in as near to the attitude of Rodin's "Thinker" as he can get in his position.*]

YANK [*bitterly*]. So dem boids don't tink I belong, neider. Aw, to hell wit 'em! Dey're in de wrong pew—de same old bull—soapboxes and Salvation Army—no guts! Cut out an hour offen de job a day and make me happy! Gimme a dollar more a day and make me happy! Tree square a day, and cauliflowers in de front yard—ekal rights—a woman and kids—a lousy vote—and I'm all fixed for Jesus, huh? Aw, hell! What does dat get yuh? Dis ting's in your inside, but it ain't your belly. Feedin' your face—sinkers and coffee—dat don't touch it. It's way down—at de bottom. Yuh can't grab it, and yuh can't stop it. It moves, and everything moves. It stops and de whole woild stops. Dat's me now—I don't tick, see?—I'm a busted Ingersoll, dat's what. Steel was me, and I owned de woild. Now I ain't steel, and de woild owns me. Aw, hell! I can't see—it's all dark, get me? It's all wrong! [*He turns a bitter mocking face up like an ape gibbering at the moon.*] Say, youse up dere, Man in de Moon, yuh look so wise, gimme de answer, huh? Slip me de inside dope, de information right from de stable—where do I get off at, huh?

A POLICEMAN [*who has come up the street in time to hear this last—with grim humor*]. You'll get off at the station, you boob, if you don't get up out of that and keep movin'.

YANK [*looking up at him—with a hard, bitter laugh*]. Sure! Lock me up! Put me in a cage! Dat's de on'y answer yuh know. G'wan, lock me up!

POLICEMAN. What you been doin'?

YANK. Enuf to gimme life for! I was born, see? Sure, dat's de charge. Write it in de blotter. I was born, get me!

POLICEMAN [*jocosely*]. God pity your old woman! [*Then matter-of-fact.*] But I've no time for kidding. You're soused. I'd run you in but it's too long a walk to the station. Come on now, get up, or I'll fan your ears with this club. Beat it now! [*He hauls* YANK *to his feet.*]

YANK [*in a vague mocking tone*]. Say, where do I go from here?

POLICEMAN [*giving him a push—with a grin, indifferently*]. Go to hell.

CURTAIN

"The Hairy Ape"

SCENE VIII

[*Twilight of the next day. The monkey house at the Zoo. One spot of clear gray light falls on the front of one cage so that the interior can be seen. The other cages are vague, shrouded in shadow from which chatterings pitched in a conversational tone can be heard. On the one cage a sign from which the word "gorilla" stands out. The gigantic animal himself is seen squatting on his haunches on a bench in much the same attitude as Rodin's "Thinker." YANK enters from the left. Immediately a chorus of angry chattering and screeching breaks out. The gorilla turns his eyes but makes no sound or move.*]

YANK [*with a hard, bitter laugh*]. Welcome to your city, huh? Hail, hail, de gang's all here! [*At the sound of his voice the chattering dies away into an attentive silence.* YANK *walks up to the gorilla's cage and, leaning over the railing, stares in at its occupant, who stares back at him, silent and motionless. There is a pause of dead stillness. Then* YANK *begins to talk in a friendly confidential tone, half-mockingly, but with a deep undercurrent of sympathy.*] Say, yuh're some hard-lookin' guy, ain't yuh? I seen lots of tough nuts dat de gang called gorillas, but yuh're de foist real one I ever seen. Some chest yuh got, and shoulders, and dem arms and mits! I bet yuh got a punch in eider fist dat'd knock 'em all silly! [*This with genuine admiration. The gorilla, as if he understood, stands upright, swelling out his chest and pounding on it with his fist.* YANK *grins sympathetically.*] Sure, I get yuh. Yuh challenge de whole woild, huh? Yuh got what I was sayin' even if yuh muffed de woids. [*Then bitterness creeping in.*] And why wouldn't yuh get me? Ain't we both members of de same club—de Hairy Apes? [*They stare at each other—a pause—then* YANK *goes on slowly and bitterly.*] So yuh're what she seen when she looked at me, de white-faced tart! I was you to her, get me? On'y outa de cage—broke out—free to moider her, see? Sure! Dat's what she tought. She wasn't wise dat I was in a cage, too—worser'n yours—sure—a damn sight—'cause you got some chanct to bust loose —but me— [*He grows confused.*] Aw, hell! It's all wrong, ain't it? [*A pause.*] I s'pose yuh wanter know what I'm doin' here, huh? I been warmin' a bench down to de Battery—ever since last night. Sure. I seen de sun come up. Dat was pretty, too—all red and pink and green. I was lookin' at de skyscrapers—steel—and all de ships comin' in, sailin' out, all over de oith—and dey was steel, too. De sun was warm, dey wasn't no clouds, and dere was a breeze blowin'. Sure, it was great stuff. I got it aw right—what Paddy said about dat bein' de right dope—on'y I couldn't get *in* it, see? I couldn't belong in dat. It was over my head. And I kept tinkin'—and den I beat it up here to see what youse was like. And I waited till dey was all gone to git yuh alone. Say, how d'yuh feel sittin' in dat pen all de time, havin' to stand for 'em comin' and starin' at yuh—de white-faced, skinny tarts and de boobs what marry 'em—makin' fun of yuh, laughin' at yuh, gittin' scared of yuh—damn 'em! [*He pounds on the rail with his fist. The gorilla rattles the bars of his cage and snarls. All the other monkeys set up an angry chattering in the darkness.* YANK *goes on excitedly.*] Sure! Dat's de way it hits me, too. On'y yuh're lucky, see? Yuh don't belong wit

[541]

Drama

'em and yuh know it. But me, I belong wit 'em—but I don't, see? Dey don't belong wit me, dat's what. Get me? Tinkin' is hard— [*He passes one hand across his forehead with a painful gesture. The gorilla growls impatiently.* YANK *goes on groping.*] It's dis way, what I'm drivin' at. Youse can sit and dope dream in de past, green woods, de jungle and de rest of it. Den yuh belong and dey don't. Den yuh kin laugh at 'em, see? Yuh're de champ of de woild. But me—I ain't got no past to tink in, nor nothin' dat's comin', on'y what's now—and dat don't belong. Sure, yuh're de best off! Yuh can't tink, can yuh? Yuh can't talk neider. But I kin make a bluff at talkin' and tinkin'—a'most git away wit it—a'most!—and dat's where de joker comes in. [*He laughs.*] I ain't on oith and I ain't in heaven, get me? I'm in de middle tryin' to separate 'em, takin' all de woist punches from bot' of 'em. Maybe dat's what dey call hell, huh? But you, yuh're at de bottom. You belong! Sure! Yuh're de on'y one in de woild dat does, yuh lucky stiff! [*The gorilla growls proudly.*] And dat's why dey gotter put yuh in a cage, see? [*The gorilla roars angrily.*] Sure! Yuh get me. It beats it when you try to tink it or talk it—it's way down—deep—behind—you 'n' me we feel it. Sure! Bot' members of dis club! [*He laughs—then in a savage tone.*] What de hell! T' hell wit it! A little action, dat's our meat! Dat belongs! Knock 'em down and keep bustin' 'em till dey croaks yuh wit a gat—wit steel; Sure! Are yuh game? Dey've looked at youse, ain't dey—in a cage? Wanter git even? Wanter wind up like a sport 'stead of croakin' slow in dere? [*The gorilla roars an emphatic affirmative.* YANK *goes on with a sort of furious exaltation.*] Sure! Yuh're reg'lar! Yuh'll stick to de finish! Me 'n' you, huh?—bot' members of dis club! We'll put up one last star bout dat'll knock 'em offen deir seats! Dey'll have to make de cages stronger after we're trou! [*The gorilla is straining at his bars, growling, hopping from one foot to the other.* YANK *takes a jimmy from under his coat and forces the lock on the cage door. He throws this open.*] Pardon from de governor! Step out and shake hands. I'll take yuh for a walk down Fif' Avenoo. We'll knock 'em offen de oith and croak wit de band playin'. Come on, Brother. [*The gorilla scrambles gingerly out of his cage. Goes to* YANK *and stands looking at him.* YANK *keeps his mocking tone—holds out his hand.*] Shake—de secret grip of our order. [*Something, the tone of mockery, perhaps, suddenly enrages the animal. With a spring he wraps his huge arms around* YANK *in a murderous hug. There is a crackling snap of crushed ribs—a gasping cry, still mocking, from* YANK.] Hey, I didn't say kiss me! [*The gorilla lets the crushed body slip to the floor; stands over it uncertainly, considering; then picks it up, throws it in the cage, shuts the door, and shuffles off menacingly into the darkness at left. A great uproar of frightened chattering and whimpering comes from the other cages. Then* YANK *moves, groaning, opening his eyes, and there is silence. He mutters painfully.*] Say—dey oughter match him—wit Zybszko. He got me, aw right. I'm trou. Even him didn't tink I belonged. [*Then, with sudden passionate despair.*] Christ, where do I get off at? Where do I fit in? [*Checking himself as suddenly.*] Aw, what de hell! No squawkin', see! No quittin', get me! Croak wit your boots on! [*He grabs hold of the bars of the cage and hauls himself painfully to his feet—*

[542]

The Glass Menagerie

looks around him bewilderedly—forces a mocking laugh.] In de cage, huh? [*In the strident tones of a circus barker.*] Ladies and gents, step forward and take a slant at de one and only— [*His voice weakening.*]—one and original—Hairy Ape from de wilds of— [*He slips in a heap on the floor and dies. The monkeys set up a chattering, whimpering wail. And, perhaps, the Hairy Ape at last belongs.*]

CURTAIN

THE GLASS MENAGERIE
A Play
by TENNESSEE WILLIAMS

THE GLASS MENAGERIE *was first produced by Eddie Dowling and Louis J. Singer at the Civic Theatre, Chicago, Ill., on December 26, 1944, and at the Playhouse Theatre, New York City, on March 31, 1945, with the following cast:*

THE MOTHER	Laurette Taylor
HER SON	Eddie Dowling
HER DAUGHTER	Julie Haydon
THE GENTLEMAN CALLER	Anthony Ross

SETTING DESIGNED AND LIGHTED by Jo Mielziner
ORIGINAL MUSIC COMPOSED by Paul Bowles
STAGED by Eddie Dowling and Margo Jones

THE CHARACTERS

AMANDA WINGFIELD (*the mother*) .... Laurette Taylor
   A little woman of great but confused vitality clinging frantically to another time and place. Her characterization must be carefully created, not copied from type. She is not paranoiac, but her life is paranoia. There is much to admire in Amanda, and as much to love and pity as there is to laugh at. Certainly she has endurance and a kind of heroism, and though her foolishness makes her unwittingly cruel at times, there is tenderness in her slight person.

LAURA WINGFIELD (*her daughter*) .... Julie Haydon
   Amanda, having failed to establish contact with reality, continues to live vitally in her illusions, but Laura's situation is even graver. A childhood illness has left her

Reprinted by permission of Random House, Inc. Copyright 1945 by Tennessee Williams and Edwina D. Williams.

crippled, one leg slightly shorter than the other, and held in a brace. This defect need not be more than suggested on the stage. Stemming from this, Laura's separation increases till she is like a piece of her own glass collection, too exquisitely fragile to move from the shelf.

TOM WINGFIELD (*her son*)..Eddie Dowling
And the narrator of the play. A poet with a job in a warehouse. His nature is not remorseless, but to escape from a trap he has to act without pity.

JIM O'CONNOR (*the gentleman caller*)..........................Anthony Ross
A nice, ordinary, young man.

SCENE

An Alley in St. Louis

PART I. *Preparation for a Gentleman Caller.*
PART II. *The Gentleman calls.*
Time: Now and the Past.

PRODUCTION NOTES

Being a "memory play," *The Glass Menagerie* can be presented with unusual freedom of convention. Because of its considerably delicate or tenuous material, atmospheric touches and subtleties of direction play a particularly important part. Expressionism and all other unconventional techniques in drama have only one valid aim, and that is a closer approach to truth. When a play employs unconventional techniques, it is not, or certainly shouldn't be, trying to escape its responsibility of dealing with reality, or interpreting experience, but is actually or should be attempting to find a closer approach, a more penetrating and vivid expression of things as they are. The straight realistic play with its genuine frigidaire and authentic ice-cubes, its characters that speak exactly as its audience speaks, corresponds to the academic landscape and has the same virtue of a photographic likeness. Everyone should know nowadays the unimportance of the photographic in art: that truth, life, or reality is an organic thing which the poetic imagination can represent or suggest, in essence, only through transformation, through changing into other forms than those which were merely present in appearance.

These remarks are not meant as a preface only to this particular play. They have to do with a conception of a new, plastic theatre which must take the place of the exhausted theatre of realistic conventions if the theatre is to resume vitality as a part of our culture.

THE SCREEN DEVICE. There is *only one important difference between the original and acting version of the play* and that is the *omission* in the latter of the device which I tentatively included in my *original* script. This device was the use of a screen

The Glass Menagerie

on which were projected magic-lantern slides bearing images or titles. I do not regret the omission of this device from the present Broadway production. The extraordinary power of Miss Taylor's performance made it suitable to have the utmost simplicity in the physical production. But I think it may be interesting to some readers to see how this device was conceived. So I am putting it into the published manuscript. These images and legends, projected from behind, were cast on a section of wall between the front-room and dining-room areas, which should be indistinguishable from the rest when not in use.

The purpose of this will probably be apparent. It is to give accent to certain values in each scene. Each scene contains a particular point (or several) which is structurally the most important. In an episodic play, such as this, the basic structure or narrative line may be obscured from the audience; the effect may seem fragmentary rather than architectural. This may not be the fault of the play so much as a lack of attention in the audience. The legend or image upon the screen will strengthen the effect of what is merely allusion in the writing and allow the primary point to be made more simply and lightly than if the entire responsibility were on the spoken lines. Aside from this structural value, I think the screen will have a definite emotional appeal, less definable but just as important. An imaginative producer or director may invent many other uses for this device than those indicated in the present script. In fact the possibilities of the device seem much larger to me than the instance of this play can possibly utilize.

THE MUSIC. Another extra-literary accent in this play is provided by the use of music. A single recurring tune, "The Glass Menagerie," is used to give emotional emphasis to suitable passages. This tune is like circus music, not when you are on the grounds or in the immediate vicinity of the parade, but when you are at some distance and very likely thinking of something else. It seems under those circumstances to continue almost interminably and it weaves in and out of your preoccupied consciousness; then it is the lightest, most delicate music in the world and perhaps the saddest. It expresses the surface vivacity of life with the underlying strain of immutable and inexpressible sorrow. When you look at a piece of delicately spun glass you think of two things: how beautiful it is and how easily it can be broken. Both of those ideas should be woven into the recurring tune, which dips in and out of the play as if it were carried on a wind that changes. It serves as a thread of connection and allusion between the narrator with his separate point in time and space and the subject of his story. Between each episode it returns as reference to the emotion, nostalgia, which is the first condition of the play. It is primarily Laura's music and therefore comes out most clearly when the play focuses upon her and the lovely fragility of glass which is her image.

THE LIGHTING. The lighting in the play is not realistic. In keeping with the atmosphere of memory, the stage is dim. Shafts of light are focused on selected areas or actors, sometimes in contradistinction to what is the apparent center. For instance, in the quarrel scene between Tom and Amanda, in which Laura has no active part, the clearest pool of light is on her figure. This is also true of the supper scene, when her silent figure on the sofa should remain the visual center. The light upon Laura should be distinct from the others, having a peculiar pristine clarity such as

[545]

light used in early religious portraits of female saints or madonnas. A certain correspondence to light in religious paintings, such as El Greco's, where the figures are radiant in atmosphere that is relatively dusky, could be effectively used throughout the play. (It will also permit a more effective use of the screen.) A free, imaginative use of light can be of enormous value in giving a mobile, plastic quality to plays of a more or less static nature.

T. W.

SCENE I

[*The Wingfield apartment is in the rear of the building, one of those vast hive-like conglomerations of cellular living-units that flower as warty growths in overcrowded urban centers of lower middle-class population and are symptomatic of the impulse of this largest and fundamentally enslaved section of American society to avoid fluidity and differentiation and to exist and function as one interfused mass of automatism.*

The apartment faces an alley and is entered by a fire-escape, a structure whose name is a touch of accidental poetic truth, for all of these huge buildings are always burning with the slow and implacable fires of human desperation. The fire-escape is included in the set—that is, the landing of it and steps descending from it.

The scene is memory and is therefore nonrealistic. Memory takes a lot of poetic license. It omits some details; others are exaggerated, according to the emotional value of the articles it touches, for memory is seated predominantly in the heart. The interior is therefore rather dim and poetic.

At the rise of the curtain, the audience is faced with the dark, grim rear wall of the Wingfield tenement. This building, which runs parallel to the footlights, is flanked on both sides by dark, narrow alleys which run into murky canyons of tangled clotheslines, garbage cans and the sinister latticework of neighboring fire-escapes. It is up and down these side alleys that exterior entrances and exits are made, during the play. At the end of TOM'S *opening commentary, the dark tenement wall slowly reveals (by means of a transparency) the interior of the ground floor Wingfield apartment.*

Downstage is the living room, which also serves as a sleeping room for LAURA, *the sofa unfolding to make her bed. Upstage, center, and divided by a wide arch or second proscenium with transparent faded portieres (or second curtain), is the dining room. In an old-fashioned what-not in the living room are seen scores of transparent glass animals. A blown-up photograph of the father hangs on the wall of the living room, facing the audience, to the left of the archway. It is the face of a very handsome young man in a doughboy's First World War cap. He is gallantly smiling, ineluctably smiling, as if to say, "I will be smiling forever."*

The audience hears and sees the opening scene in the dining room through both the transparent fourth wall of the building and the transparent gauze portieres of the dining-room arch. It is during this revealing scene that the fourth wall slowly ascends, out of sight. This transparent exterior wall is not brought down again until the very end of the play, during TOM'S *final speech.*

The narrator is an undisguised convention of the play. He takes whatever license

The Glass Menagerie

with dramatic convention as is convenient to his purposes.

TOM *enters dressed as a merchant sailor from alley, stage left, and strolls across the front of the stage to the fire-escape. There he stops and lights a cigarette. He addresses the audience.*]

TOM. Yes, I have tricks in my pocket, I have things up my sleeve. But I am the opposite of a stage magician. He gives you illusion that has the appearance of truth. I give you truth in the pleasant disguise of illusion.

To begin with, I turn back time. I reverse it to that quaint period, the thirties, when the huge middle class of America was matriculating in a school for the blind. Their eyes had failed them, or they had failed their eyes, and so they were having their fingers pressed forcibly down on the fiery Braille alphabet of a dissolving economy.

In Spain there was revolution. Here there was only shouting and confusion.

In Spain there was Guernica. Here there were disturbances of labor, sometimes pretty violent, in otherwise peaceful cities such as Chicago, Cleveland, Saint Louis . . .

This is the social background of the play. [MUSIC.]

The play is memory.

Being a memory play, it is dimly lighted, it is sentimental, it is not realistic.

In memory everything seems to happen to music. That explains the fiddle in the wings.

I am the narrator of the play, and also a character in it.

The other characters are my mother, Amanda, my sister, Laura, and a gentleman caller who appears in the final scenes.

He is the most realistic character in the play, being an emissary from a world of reality that we were somehow set apart from.

But since I have a poet's weakness for symbols, I am using this character also as a symbol; he is the long delayed but always expected something that we live for.

There is a fifth character in the play who doesn't appear except in this larger-than-life-size photograph over the mantel.

This is our father who left us a long time ago.

He was a telephone man who fell in love with long distances; he gave up his job with the telephone company and skipped the light fantastic out of town . . .

The last we heard of him was a picture post-card from Mazátlan, on the Pacific coast of Mexico, containing a message of two words—

"Hello— Good-bye!" and no address.

I think the rest of the play will explain itself. . . . [AMANDA'S *voice becomes audible through the portieres.* LEGEND ON SCREEN: "OÙ SONT LES NEIGES." *He divides the portieres and enters the upstage area.* AMANDA *and* LAURA *are seated at a drop-leaf table. Eating is indicated by gestures without food or utensils.* AMANDA *faces the audience.* TOM *and* LAURA *are seated in profile. The interior has lit up softly and through the scrim we see* AMANDA *and* LAURA *seated at the table in the upstage area.*]

AMANDA [*calling*]. Tom?

TOM. Yes, Mother.

AMANDA. We can't say grace until you come to the table!

TOM. Coming, Mother. [*He bows slightly and withdraws, reappearing a few moments later in his place at the table.*]

AMANDA [*to her son*]. Honey, don't *push* with your *fingers*. If you have to push with something, the thing to push with is a crust of bread. And chew—chew! Animals have sections in their stomachs

Amanda never forgets that she was born of gentleman.

Drama

which enable them to digest food without mastication, but human beings are supposed to chew their food before they swallow it down. Eat food leisurely, son, and really enjoy it. A well-cooked meal has lots of delicate flavors that have to be held in the mouth for appreciation. So chew your food and give your salivary glands a chance to function! [TOM *deliberately lays his imaginary fork down and pushes his chair back from the table.*]

TOM. I haven't enjoyed one bite of this dinner because of your constant directions on how to eat it. It's you that make me rush through meals with your hawk-like attention to every bite I take. Sickening—spoils my appetite—all this discussion of—animals' secretion—salivary glands—mastication!

AMANDA [*lightly*]. Temperament like a Metropolitan star! [*He rises and crosses downstage.*] You're not excused from the table.

TOM. I'm getting a cigarette.

AMANDA. You smoke too much. [LAURA *rises.*]

LAURA. I'll bring in the blanc mange. [*He remains standing with his cigarette by the portieres during the following.*]

AMANDA [*rising*]. No, sister, no, sister—you be the lady this time and I'll be the darky.

LAURA. I'm already up.

AMANDA. Resume your seat, little sister—I want you to stay fresh and pretty—for gentlemen callers!

LAURA. I'm not expecting any gentlemen callers.

AMANDA [*crossing out to kitchenette. Airily*]. Sometimes they come when they are least expected! Why, I remember one Sunday afternoon in Blue Mountain—[*Enters kitchenette.*]

TOM. I know what's coming!

LAURA. Yes. But let her tell it.

TOM. Again?

LAURA. She loves to tell it. [AMANDA *returns with bowl of dessert.*]

AMANDA. One Sunday afternoon in Blue Mountain—your mother received—*seventeen!*—gentlemen callers! Why, sometimes there weren't chairs enough to accommodate them all. We had to send the nigger over to bring in folding chairs from the parish house.

TOM [*remaining at portieres*]. How did you entertain those gentlemen callers?

AMANDA. I understood the art of conversation!

TOM. I bet you could talk.

AMANDA. Girls in those days *knew* how to talk, I can tell you.

TOM. Yes? [IMAGE: AMANDA AS A GIRL ON A PORCH, GREETING CALLERS.]

AMANDA. They knew how to entertain their gentlemen callers. It wasn't enough for a girl to be possessed of a pretty face and a graceful figure—although I wasn't slighted in either respect. She also needed to have a nimble wit and a tongue to meet all occasions.

TOM. What did you talk about?

AMANDA. Things of importance going on in the world! Never anything coarse or common or vulgar. [*She addresses* TOM *as though he were seated in the vacant chair at the table though he remains by portieres. He plays this scene as though he held the book.*] My callers were gentlemen—all! Among my callers were some of the most prominent young planters of the Mississippi Delta—planters and sons of planters! [TOM *motions for music and a spot of light on* AMANDA. *Her eyes lift, her face glows, her voice becomes rich and elegiac.* SCREEN LEGEND: "OÙ SONT LES NEIGES."]

There was young Champ Laughlin who later became vice-president of the Delta Planters Bank.

[548]

Hadley Stevenson who was drowned in Moon Lake and left his widow one hundred and fifty thousand in Government bonds.

There were the Cutrere brothers, Wesley and Bates. Bates was one of my bright particular beaux! He got in a quarrel with that wild Wainwright boy. They shot it out on the floor of Moon Lake Casino. Bates was shot through the stomach. Died in the ambulance on his way to Memphis. His widow was also well-provided for, came into eight or ten thousand acres, that's all. She married him on the rebound —never loved her—carried my picture on him the night he died!

And there was that boy that every girl in the Delta had set her cap for! That beautiful, brilliant young Fitzhugh boy from Greene County!

TOM. What did he leave his widow?

AMANDA. He never married! Gracious, you talk as though all of my old admirers had turned up their toes to the daisies!

TOM. Isn't this the first you've mentioned that still survives?

AMANDA. That Fitzhugh boy went North and made a fortune—came to be known as the Wolf of Wall Street! He had the Midas touch, whatever he touched turned to gold!

And I could have been Mrs. Duncan J. Fitzhugh, mind you! But—I picked your father!

LAURA [*rising*]. Mother, let me clear the table.

AMANDA. No, dear, you go in front and study your typewriter chart. Or practice your shorthand a little. Stay fresh and pretty!—It's almost time for our gentlemen callers to start arriving. [*She flounces girlishly toward the kitchenette.*] How many do you suppose we're going to entertain this afternoon? [TOM *throws down the paper and jumps up with a groan.*]

LAURA [*alone in the dining room*]. I don't believe we're going to receive any, Mother.

AMANDA [*reappearing, airily*]. What? No one—not one? You must be joking! [LAURA *nervously echoes her laugh. She slips in a fugitive manner through the half-open portieres and draws them gently behind her. A shaft of very clear light is thrown on her face against the faded tapestry of the curtains.* MUSIC: "THE GLASS MENAGERIE" UNDER FAINTLY. *Lightly.*] Not one gentleman caller? It can't be true! There must be a flood, there must have been a tornado!

LAURA. It isn't a flood, it's not a tornado, Mother. I'm just not popular like you were in Blue Mountain. . . . [TOM *utters another groan.* LAURA *glances at him with a faint, apologetic smile. Her voice catching a little.*] Mother's afraid I'm going to be an old maid.

[THE SCENE DIMS OUT WITH "GLASS MENAGERIE" MUSIC.]

SCENE II

["*Laura, Haven't You Ever Liked Some Boy?*"

On the dark stage the screen is lighted with the image of blue roses.

Gradually LAURA's figure becomes apparent and the screen goes out.

The music subsides.

LAURA *is seated in the delicate ivory chair at the small claw-foot table.*

She wears a dress of soft violet material for a kimono—her hair tied back from her forehead with a ribbon.

She is washing and polishing her collection of glass.

[549]

AMANDA *appears on the fire-escape steps. At the sound of her ascent,* LAURA *catches her breath, thrusts the bowl of ornaments away and seats herself stiffly before the diagram of the typewriter keyboard as though it held her spellbound.*

Something has happened to AMANDA. *It is written in her face as she climbs to the landing: a look that is grim and hopeless and a little absurd.*

She has on one of those cheap or imitation velvety-looking cloth coats with imitation fur collar. Her hat is five or six years old, one of those dreadful cloche hats that were worn in the late twenties and she is clasping an enormous black patent-leather pocketbook with nickel clasps and initials. This is her full-dress outfit, the one she usually wears to the D.A.R.

Before entering she looks through the door.

She purses her lips, opens her eyes very wide, rolls them upward and shakes her head.

Then she slowly lets herself in the door. Seeing her mother's expression LAURA *touches her lips with a nervous gesture.*]

LAURA. Hello, Mother, I was— [*She makes a nervous gesture toward the chart on the wall.* AMANDA *leans against the shut door and stares at* LAURA *with a martyred look.*]

AMANDA. Deception? Deception? [*She slowly removes her hat and gloves, continuing the sweet suffering stare. She lets the hat and gloves fall on the floor—a bit of acting.*]

LAURA [*shakily*]. How was the D.A.R. meeting? [AMANDA *slowly opens her purse and removes a dainty white handkerchief which she shakes out delicately and delicately touches to her lips and nostrils.*]

Didn't you go to the D.A.R. meeting, Mother?

AMANDA [*faintly, almost inaudibly*]. —No.—No. [*Then more forcibly.*] I did not have the strength—to go to the D.A.R. In fact, I did not have the courage! I wanted to find a hole in the ground and hide myself in it forever! [*She crosses slowly to the wall and removes the diagram of the typewriter keyboard. She holds it in front of her for a second, staring at it sweetly and sorrowfully—then bites her lips and tears it in two pieces.*]

LAURA [*faintly*]. Why did you do that, Mother? [AMANDA *repeats the same procedure with the chart of the Gregg Alphabet.*] Why are you—

AMANDA. Why? Why? How old are you, Laura?

LAURA. Mother, you know my age.

AMANDA. I thought that you were an adult; it seems that I was mistaken. [*She crosses slowly to the sofa and sinks down and stares at* LAURA.]

LAURA. Please don't stare at me, Mother. [AMANDA *closes her eyes and lowers her head. Count ten.*]

AMANDA. What are we going to do, what is going to become of us, what is the future? [*Count ten.*]

LAURA. Has something happened, Mother? [AMANDA *draws a long breath and takes out the handkerchief again. Dabbing process.*] Mother, has—something happened?

AMANDA. I'll be all right in a minute, I'm just bewildered—[*Count five.*]—by life. . . .

LAURA. Mother, I wish that you would tell me what's happened!

AMANDA. As you know, I was supposed to be inducted into my office at the D.A.R. this afternoon. [IMAGE: A SWARM OF TYPEWRITERS.] But I stopped off at Rubicam's business college to speak to your teachers about your having a cold and ask them what progress they thought you were making down there.

LAURA. Oh. . . .

AMANDA. I went to the typing instructor and introduced myself as your mother. She didn't know who you were. Wingfield, she said. We don't have any such student enrolled at the school!

I assured her she did, that you had been going to classes since early in January.

"I wonder," she said, "if you could be talking about that terribly shy little girl who dropped out of school after only a few days' attendance?"

"No," I said, "Laura, my daughter, has been going to school every day for the past six weeks!"

"Excuse me," she said. She took the attendance book out and there was your name, unmistakably printed, and all the dates you were absent until they decided that you had dropped out of school.

I still said, "No, there must have been some mistake! There must have been some mix-up in the records!"

And she said, "No—I remember her perfectly now. Her hands shook so that she couldn't hit the right keys! The first time we gave a speed-test, she broke down completely—was sick at the stomach and almost had to be carried into the washroom! After that morning she never showed up any more. We phoned the house but never got any answer—while I was working at Famous and Barr, I suppose, demonstrating those— Oh!"

I felt so weak I could barely keep on my feet!

I had to sit down while they got me a glass of water!

Fifty dollars' tuition, all of our plans— my hopes and ambitions for you—just gone up the spout, just gone up the spout like that. [LAURA *draws a long breath and gets awkwardly to her feet. She crosses to the victrola and winds it up.*]

What are you doing?

LAURA. Oh! [*She releases the handle and returns to her seat.*]

AMANDA. Laura, where have you been going when you've gone out pretending that you were going to business college?

LAURA. I've just been going out walking.

AMANDA. That's not true.

LAURA. It is. I just went walking.

AMANDA. Walking? Walking? In winter? Deliberately courting pneumonia in that light coat? Where did you walk to, Laura?

LAURA. All sorts of places—mostly in the park.

AMANDA. Even after you'd started catching that cold?

LAURA. It was the lesser of two evils, Mother. [IMAGE: WINTER SCENE IN PARK.] I couldn't go back up. I—threw up—on the floor!

AMANDA. From half past seven till after five every day you mean to tell me you walked around in the park, because you wanted to make me think that you were still going to Rubicam's Business College?

LAURA. It wasn't as bad as it sounds. I went inside places to get warmed up.

AMANDA. Inside where?

LAURA. I went in the art museum and the bird-houses at the Zoo. I visited the penguins every day! Sometimes I did without lunch and went to the movies. Lately I've been spending most of my afternoons in the Jewel-box, that big glass house where they raise the tropical flowers.

AMANDA. You did all this to deceive me, just for deception? [LAURA *looks down.*] Why?

Drama

LAURA. Mother, when you're disappointed, you get that awful suffering look on your face, like the picture of Jesus' mother in the museum!

AMANDA. Hush!

LAURA. I couldn't face it. [*Pause. A whisper of strings.* LEGEND: "THE CRUST OF HUMILITY."]

AMANDA [*hopelessly fingering the huge pocketbook*]. So what are we going to do the rest of our lives? Stay home and watch the parades go by? Amuse ourselves with the glass menagerie, darling? Eternally play those worn-out phonograph records your father left as a painful reminder of him?

We won't have a business career—we've given that up because it gave us nervous indigestion! [*Laughs wearily.*] What is there left but dependency all our lives? I know so well what becomes of unmarried women who aren't prepared to occupy a position. I've seen such pitiful cases in the South—barely tolerated spinsters living upon the grudging patronage of sister's husband or brother's wife!—stuck away in some little mouse-trap of a room—encouraged by one in-law to visit another—little birdlike women without any nest—eating the crust of humility all their life!

Is that the future that we've mapped out for ourselves?

I swear it's the only alternative I can think of!

It isn't a very pleasant alternative, is it?

Of course—some girls *do marry.* [LAURA *twists her hands nervously.*]

Haven't you ever liked some boy?

LAURA. Yes. I liked one once. [*Rises.*] I came across his picture a while ago.

AMANDA [*with some interest*]. He gave you his picture?

LAURA. No, it's in the year-book.

AMANDA [*disappointed*]. Oh—a high-school boy. [SCREEN IMAGE: JIM AS HIGH-SCHOOL HERO BEARING A SILVER CUP.]

LAURA. Yes. His name was Jim. [LAURA *lifts the heavy annual from the claw-foot table.*] Here he is in *The Pirates of Penzance.*

AMANDA [*absently*]. The what?

LAURA. The operetta the senior class put on. He had a wonderful voice and we sat across the aisle from each other Mondays, Wednesdays and Fridays in the Aud. Here he is with the silver cup for debating! See his grin?

AMANDA [*absently*]. He must have had a jolly disposition.

LAURA. He used to call me—Blue Roses. [IMAGE: BLUE ROSES.]

AMANDA. Why did he call you such a name as that?

LAURA. When I had that attack of pleurosis—he asked me what was the matter when I came back. I said pleurosis—he thought that I said Blue Roses! So that's what he always called me after that. Whenever he saw me, he'd holler, "Hello, Blue Roses!" I didn't care for the girl that he went out with. Emily Meisenbach. Emily was the best-dressed girl at Soldan. She never struck me, though, as being sincere . . . It says in the Personal Section—they're engaged. That's—six years ago! They must be married by now.

AMANDA. Girls that aren't cut out for business careers usually wind up married to some nice man. [*Gets up with a spark of revival.*] Sister, that's what you'll do! [LAURA *utters a startled, doubtful laugh. She reaches quickly for a piece of glass.*]

LAURA. But, Mother—

AMANDA. Yes? [*Crossing to photograph.*]

LAURA [*in a tone of frightened apology*]. I'm—crippled! [IMAGE: SCREEN.]

[552]

The Glass Menagerie

AMANDA. Nonsense! Laura, I've told you never, never to use that word. Why, you're not crippled, you just have a little defect—hardly noticeable, even! When people have some slight disadvantage like that, they cultivate other things to make up for it—develop charm—and vivacity— and—*charm!* That's all you have to do! [*She turns again to the photograph.*] One thing your father had *plenty of*—was charm! [TOM *motions to the fiddle in the wings.*]

[THE SCENE FADES OUT WITH MUSIC.]

SCENE III

[LEGEND ON SCREEN: "AFTER THE FIASCO—" TOM *speaks from the fire-escape landing.*]

TOM. After the fiasco at Rubicam's Business College, the idea of getting a gentleman caller for Laura began to play a more and more important part in Mother's calculations.

It became an obsession. Like some archetype of the universal unconscious, the image of the gentleman caller haunted our small apartment. . . . [IMAGE: YOUNG MAN AT DOOR WITH FLOWERS.]

An evening at home rarely passed without some allusion to this image, this specter, this hope. . . .

Even when he wasn't mentioned, his presence hung in Mother's preoccupied look and in my sister's frightened, apologetic manner—hung like a sentence passed upon the Wingfields!

Mother was a woman of action as well as words.

She began to take logical steps in the planned direction.

Late that winter and in the early spring —realizing that extra money would be needed to properly feather the nest and plume the bird—she conducted a vigorous campaign on the telephone, roping in subscribers to one of those magazines for matrons called *The Home-maker's Companion,* the type of journal that features the serialized sublimations of ladies of letters who think in terms of delicate cup- like breasts, slim, tapering waists, rich, creamy thighs, eyes like wood-smoke in autumn, fingers that soothe and caress like strains of music, bodies as powerful as Etruscan sculpture.

[SCREEN IMAGE: GLAMOR MAGAZINE COVER. AMANDA *enters with phone on long extension cord. She is spotted in the dim stage.*]

AMANDA. Ida Scott? This is Amanda Wingfield!

We *missed* you at the D.A.R. last Monday!

I said to myself: She's probably suffering with that sinus condition! How is that sinus condition?

Horrors! Heaven have mercy!—You're a Christian martyr, yes, that's what you are, a Christian martyr!

Well, I just now happened to notice that your subscription to the *Companion's* about to expire! Yes, it expires with the next issue, honey!—just when that wonderful new serial by Bessie Mae Hopper is getting off to such an exciting start. Oh, honey, it's something that you can't miss! You remember how *Gone With the Wind* took everybody by storm? You simply couldn't go out if you hadn't read it. All everybody *talked* was Scarlett O'Hara. Well, this is a book that critics already compare to *Gone With the Wind.* It's the *Gone With the Wind* of the post-World War generation!—What?—Burning?—Oh, honey, don't let them burn,

[553]

Drama

go take a look in the oven and I'll hold the wire! Heavens—I think she's hung up!

[DIM OUT]

[LEGEND ON SCREEN: "YOU THINK I'M IN LOVE WITH CONTINENTAL SHOEMAKERS?" Before the stage is lighted, the violent voices of TOM and AMANDA are heard. They are quarreling behind the portieres. In front of them stands LAURA with clenched hands and panicky expression. A clear pool of light on her figure throughout this scene.]

TOM. What in Christ's name am I—
AMANDA [shrilly]. Don't you use that—
TOM. Supposed to do!
AMANDA. Expression! Not in my—
TOM. Ohhh!
AMANDA. Presence! Have you gone out of your senses?
TOM. I have, that's true, *driven* out!
AMANDA. What is the matter with you, you—big—big—IDIOT!
TOM. Look!—I've got *no thing,* no single thing—
AMANDA. Lower your voice!
TOM. In my life here that I can call my own! Everything is—
AMANDA. Stop that shouting!
TOM. Yesterday you confiscated my books! You had the nerve to—
AMANDA. I took that horrible novel back to the library—yes! That hideous book by that insane Mr. Lawrence. [TOM *laughs wildly.*] I cannot control the output of diseased minds or people who cater to them— [TOM *laughs still more wildly.*] BUT I WON'T ALLOW SUCH FILTH BROUGHT INTO MY HOUSE! No, no, no, no, no!
TOM. House, house! Who pays rent on it, who makes a slave of himself to—
AMANDA [*fairly screeching*]. Don't you DARE to—

TOM. No, no, *I* mustn't say things! *I've* got to just—
AMANDA. Let me tell you—
TOM. I don't want to hear any more! [*He tears the portieres open. The upstage area is lit with a turgid smoky red glow.* AMANDA's *hair is in metal curlers and she wears a very old bathrobe, much too large for her slight figure, a relic of the faithless Mr. Wingfield. An upright typewriter and a wild disarray of manuscripts is on the drop-leaf table. The quarrel was probably precipitated by* AMANDA's *interruption of his creative labor. A chair lying overthrown on the floor. Their gesticulating shadows are cast on the ceiling by the fiery glow.*]
AMANDA. You *will* hear more, you—
TOM. No, I won't hear more, I'm going out!
AMANDA. You come right back in—
TOM. Out, out, out! Because I'm—
AMANDA. Come back here, Tom Wingfield! I'm not through talking to you!
TOM. Oh, go—
LAURA [*desperately*]. —Tom!
AMANDA. You're going to listen, and no more insolence from you! I'm at the end of my patience! [*He comes back toward her.*]
TOM. What do you think I'm at? Aren't I supposed to have any patience to reach the end of, Mother? I know, I know. It seems unimportant to you, what I'm *doing*—what I *want* to do—having a little *difference* between them! You don't think that—
AMANDA. I think you've been doing things that you're ashamed of. That's why you act like this. I don't believe that you go every night to the movies. Nobody goes to the movies night after night. Nobody in their right minds goes to the

[554]

movies as often as you pretend to. People don't go to the movies at nearly midnight, and movies don't let out at two A.M. Come in stumbling. Muttering to yourself like a maniac! You get three hours' sleep and then go to work. Oh, I can picture the way you're doing down there. Moping, doping, because you're in no condition.

TOM [*wildly*]. No, I'm in no condition!

AMANDA. What right have you got to jeopardize your job? Jeopardize the security of us all? How do you think we'd manage if you were—

TOM. Listen! You think I'm crazy *about* the *warehouse?* [*He bends fiercely toward her slight figure.*] You think I'm in love with the Continental Shoemakers? You think I want to spend fifty-five *years* down there in that—*celotex interior!* with—*fluorescent—tubes!* Look! I'd rather somebody picked up a crowbar and battered out my brains—than go back mornings! I *go!* Every time you come in yelling that God damn *"Rise and Shine!" "Rise and Shine!"* I say to myself, "How *lucky dead* people are!" But I get up. I *go!* For sixty-five dollars a month I give up all that I dream of doing and being *ever!* And you say self—*self's* all I ever think of. Why, listen, if self is what I thought of, Mother, I'd be where he is—GONE! [*Pointing to father's picture.*] As far as the system of transportation reaches! [*He starts past her. She grabs his arm.*] Don't grab at me, Mother!

AMANDA. Where are you going?

TOM. I'm going to the *movies!*

AMANDA. I don't believe that lie!

TOM [*crouching toward her, overtowering her tiny figure. She backs away, gasping.*] I'm going to opium dens! Yes, opium dens, dens of vice and criminals' hangouts, Mother. I've joined the Hogan gang, I'm a hired assassin, I carry a tommy gun in a violin case! I run a string of cathouses in the Valley! They call me Killer, Killer Wingfield, I'm leading a double-life, a simple, honest warehouse worker by day, by night a dynamic *czar* of the *underworld, Mother.* I go to gambling casinos, I spin away fortunes on the roulette table! I wear a patch over one eye and a false mustache, sometimes I put on green whiskers. On those occasions they call me—*El Diablo!* Oh, I could tell you things to make you sleepless! My enemies plan to dynamite this place. They're going to blow us all sky-high some night! I'll be glad, very happy, and so will you! You'll go up, up on a broomstick, over Blue Mountain with seventeen gentlemen callers! You ugly—babbling old—*witch.* . . . [*He goes through a series of violent, clumsy movements, seizing his overcoat, lunging to the door, pulling it fiercely open. The women watch him, aghast. His arm catches in the sleeve of the coat as he struggles to pull it on. For a moment he is pinioned by the bulky garment. With an outraged groan he tears the coat off again, splitting the shoulder of it, and hurls it across the room. It strikes against the shelf of* LAURA's *glass collection, there is a tinkle of shattering glass.* LAURA *cries out as if wounded.* MUSIC. LEGEND: "THE GLASS MENAGERIE."]

LAURA [*shrilly*]. My glass!—menagerie. . . . [*She covers her face and turns away. But* AMANDA *is still stunned and stupefied by the "ugly witch" so that she barely notices this occurrence. Now she recovers her speech.*]

AMANDA [*in an awful voice*]. I won't speak to you—until you apologize! [*She crosses through portieres and draws them together behind her.* TOM *is left with*

[555]

LAURA. LAURA *clings weakly to the mantel with her face averted.* TOM *stares at her stupidly for a moment. Then he crosses to shelf. Drops awkwardly on his knees to collect the fallen glass, glancing at* LAURA *as if he would speak but couldn't.*]

["*The Glass Menagerie*" *steals in as* THE SCENE DIMS OUT.]

SCENE IV

[*The interior is dark. Faint light in the alley.*

A deep-voiced bell in a church is tolling the hour of five as the scene commences.

TOM *appears at the top of the alley. After each solemn boom of the bell in the tower, he shakes a little noise-maker or rattle as if to express the tiny spasm of man in contrast to the sustained power and dignity of the Almighty. This and the unsteadiness of his advance make it evident that he has been drinking.*

As he climbs the few steps to the fire-escape landing light steals up inside. LAURA *appears in night-dress, observing* TOM's *empty bed in the front room.*

TOM *fishes in his pockets for door-key, removing a motley assortment of articles in the search, including a perfect shower of movie-ticket stubs and an empty bottle. At last he finds the key, but just as he is about to insert it, it slips from his fingers. He strikes a match and crouches below the door.*]

TOM [*bitterly*]. One crack—and it falls through! [LAURA *opens the door.*]

LAURA. Tom! Tom, what are you doing?

TOM. Looking for a door-key.

LAURA. Where have you been all this time?

TOM. I have been to the movies.

LAURA. All this time at the movies?

TOM. There was a very long program. There was a Garbo picture and a Mickey Mouse and a travelogue and a newsreel and a preview of coming attractions. And there was an organ solo and a collection for the milk-fund—simultaneously—which ended up in a terrible fight between a fat lady and an usher!

LAURA [*innocently.*] Did you have to stay through everything?

TOM. Of course! And, oh, I forgot! There was a big stage show! The headliner on this stage show was Malvolio the Magician. He performed wonderful tricks, many of them, such as pouring water back and forth between pitchers. First it turned to wine and then it turned to beer and then it turned to whiskey. I know it was whiskey it finally turned into because he needed somebody to come up out of the audience to help him, and I came up—both shows! It was Kentucky Straight Bourbon. A very generous fellow, he gave souvenirs. [*He pulls from his back pocket a shimmering rainbow-colored scarf.*] He gave me this. This is his magic scarf. You can have it, Laura. You wave it over a canary cage and you get a bowl of gold-fish. You wave it over the gold-fish bowl and they fly away canaries. . . . But the wonderfullest trick of all was the coffin trick. We nailed him into a coffin and he got out of the coffin without removing one nail. [*He has come inside.*] There is a trick that would come in handy for me—get me out of this 2 by 4 situation! [*Flops onto bed and starts removing shoes.*]

LAURA. Tom—Shhh!

TOM. What're you shushing me for?

LAURA. You'll wake up Mother.

TOM. Goody, goody! Pay 'er back for all those "Rise an' Shines." [*Lies down,*

[556]

groaning.] You know it don't take much intelligence to get yourself into a nailed-up coffin, Laura. But who in hell ever got himself out of one without removing one nail? [*As if in answer, the father's grinning photograph lights up.*]

[SCENE DIMS OUT]

[*Immediately following: The church bell is heard striking six. At the sixth stroke the alarm clock goes off in* AMANDA'S *room, and after a few moments we hear her calling:* "Rise and Shine! Rise and Shine! Laura, go tell your brother to rise and shine!"]

TOM [*sitting up slowly*]. I'll rise—but I won't shine. [*The light increases.*]

AMANDA. Laura, tell your brother his coffee is ready. [LAURA *slips into front room.*]

LAURA. Tom!—It's nearly seven. Don't make Mother nervous. [*He stares at her stupidly. Beseechingly.*] Tom, speak to Mother this morning. Make up with her, apologize, speak to her!

TOM. She won't to me. It's her that started not speaking.

LAURA. If you just say you're sorry she'll start speaking.

TOM. Her not speaking—is that such a tragedy?

LAURA. Please—please!

AMANDA [*calling from kitchenette*]. Laura, are you going to do what I asked you to do, or do I have to get dressed and go out myself?

LAURA. Going, going—soon as I get on my coat! [*She pulls on a shapeless felt hat with nervous, jerky movement, pleadingly glancing at* TOM. *Rushes awkwardly for coat. The coat is one of* AMANDA'S, *inaccurately made-over, the sleeves too short for* LAURA.] Butter and what else?

AMANDA [*entering upstage*]. Just butter. Tell them to charge it.

LAURA. Mother, they make such faces when I do that.

AMANDA. Sticks and stones can break our bones, but the expression on Mr. Garfinkel's face won't harm us! Tell your brother his coffee is getting cold.

LAURA [*at door*]. Do what I asked you, will you, will you, Tom? [*He looks sullenly away.*]

AMANDA. Laura, go now or just don't go at all!

LAURA [*rushing out*]. Going—going! [*A second later she cries out.* TOM *springs up and crosses to door.* AMANDA *rushes anxiously in.* TOM *opens the door.*]

TOM. Laura?

LAURA. I'm all right. I slipped, but I'm all right.

AMANDA [*peering anxiously after her*]. If anyone breaks a leg on those fire-escape steps, the landlord ought to be sued for every cent he possesses! [*She shuts door. Remembers she isn't speaking and returns to other room. As* TOM *enters listlessly for his coffee, she turns her back to him and stands rigidly facing the window on the gloomy gray vault of the areaway. Its light on her face with its aged but childish features is cruelly sharp, satirical as a Daumier print.* MUSIC UNDER: "AVE MARIA." TOM *glances sheepishly but sullenly at her averted figure and slumps at the table. The coffee is scalding hot; he sips it and gasps and spits it back in the cup. At his gasp,* AMANDA *catches her breath and half turns. Then catches herself and turns back to window.* TOM *blows on his coffee, glancing sidewise at his mother. She clears her throat.* TOM *clears his. He starts to rise. Sinks back down again, scratches his head, clears his throat again.* AMANDA *coughs.* TOM *raises his cup in both hands to blow on it, his eyes staring over the rim of it at his mother for several moments. Then he slowly sets the cup down*

[557]

and awkwardly and hesitantly rises from the chair.]

Tom [hoarsely]. Mother. I—I apologize, Mother. [Amanda draws a quick, shuddering breath. Her face works grotesquely. She breaks into childlike tears.] I'm sorry for what I said, for everything that I said, I didn't mean it.

Amanda [sobbingly]. My devotion has made me a witch and so I make myself hateful to my children!

Tom. No, you don't.

Amanda. I worry so much, don't sleep, it makes me nervous!

Tom [gently]. I understand that.

Amanda. I've had to put up a solitary battle all these years. But you're my right-hand bower! Don't fall down, don't fail!

Tom [gently]. I try, Mother.

Amanda [with great enthusiasm]. Try and you will succeed! [The notion makes her breathless.] Why, you—you're just full of natural endowments! Both of my children—they're unusual children! Don't you think I know it? I'm so—proud! Happy and—feel I've—so much to be thankful for but— Promise me one thing, Son!

Tom. What, Mother?

Amanda. Promise, son, you'll—never be a drunkard!

Tom [turns to her grinning]. I will never be a drunkard, Mother.

Amanda. That's what frightened me so, that you'd be drinking! Eat a bowl of Purina!

Tom. Just coffee, Mother.

Amanda. Shredded wheat biscuit?

Tom. No. No, Mother, just coffee.

Amanda. You can't put in a day's work on an empty stomach. You've got ten minutes—don't gulp! Drinking too-hot liquids makes cancer of the stomach. . . . Put cream in.

Tom. No, thank you.

Amanda. To cool it.

Tom. No! No, thank you, I want it black.

Amanda. I know, but it's not good for you. We have to do all that we can to build ourselves up. In these trying times we live in, all that we have to cling to is—each other. . . . That's why it's so important to— Tom, I— I sent out your sister so I could discuss something with you. If you hadn't spoken I would have spoken to you. [Sits down.]

Tom [gently]. What is it, Mother, that you want to discuss?

Amanda. Laura! [Tom puts his cup down slowly. Legend on screen: "laura." Music: "the glass menagerie."]

Tom.—Oh.—Laura . . .

Amanda [touching his sleeve]. You know how Laura is. So quiet but—still water runs deep! She notices things and I think she—broods about them. [Tom looks up.] A few days ago I came in and she was crying.

Tom. What about?

Amanda. You.

Tom. Me?

Amanda. She has an idea that you're not happy here.

Tom. What gave her that idea?

Amanda. What gives her any idea? However, you do act strangely. I—I'm not criticizing, understand *that!* I know your ambitions do not lie in the warehouse, that like everybody in the whole wide world—you've had to—make sacrifices, but —Tom—Tom—life's not easy, it calls for —Spartan endurance! There's so many things in my heart that I cannot describe to you! I've never told you but I—*loved* your father. . . .

Tom [gently]. I know that, Mother.

Amanda. And you—when I see you tak-

[558]

ing after his ways! Staying out late—and —well, you *had* been drinking the night you were in that—terrifying condition! Laura says that you hate the apartment and that you go out nights to get away from it! Is that true, Tom?

Tom. No. You say there's so much in your heart that you can't describe to me. That's true of me, too. There's so much in my heart that I can't describe to *you!* So let's respect each other's—

Amanda. But, why—*why,* Tom—are you always so *restless?* Where do you *go* to, nights?

Tom. I—go to the movies.

Amanda. Why do you go to the movies so much, Tom?

Tom. I go to the movies because—I like adventure. Adventure is something I don't have much of at work, so I go to the movies.

Amanda. But, Tom, you go to the movies *entirely* too *much!*

Tom. I like a lot of adventure. [Amanda *looks baffled, then hurt. As the familiar inquisition resumes he becomes hard and impatient again.* Amanda *slips back into her querulous attitude toward him.* Image on screen: sailing vessel with jolly roger.]

Amanda. Most young men find adventure in their careers.

Tom. Then most young men are not employed in a warehouse.

Amanda. The world is full of young men employed in warehouses and offices and factories.

Tom. Do all of them find adventure in their careers?

Amanda. They do or they do without it! Not everybody has a craze for adventure.

Tom. Man is by instinct a lover, a hunter, a fighter, and none of those instincts are given much play at the warehouse!

Amanda. Man is by instinct! Don't quote instinct to me! Instinct is something that people have got away from! It belongs to animals! Christian adults don't want it!

Tom. What do Christian adults want, then, Mother?

Amanda. Superior things! Things of the mind and the spirit! Only animals have to satisfy instincts! Surely your aims are somewhat higher than theirs! Than monkeys—pigs—

Tom. I reckon they're not.

Amanda. You're joking. However, that isn't what I wanted to discuss.

Tom [*rising*]. I haven't much time.

Amanda [*pushing his shoulders*]. Sit down.

Tom. You want me to punch in red at the warehouse, Mother?

Amanda. You have five minutes. I want to talk about Laura. [Legend: "plans and provisions."]

Tom. All right! What about Laura?

Amanda. We have to be making some plans and provisions for her. She's older than you, two years, and nothing has happened. She just drifts along doing nothing. It frightens me terribly how she just drifts along.

Tom. I guess she's the type that people call home girls.

Amanda. There's no such type, and if there is, it's a pity! That is unless the home is hers, with a husband!

Tom. What?

Amanda. Oh, I can see the handwriting on the wall as plain as I see the nose in front of my face! It's terrifying! More and more you remind me of your

[559]

father! He was out all hours without explanation!—Then *left!* Good-bye!

And me with the bag to hold. I saw that letter you got from the Merchant Marine. I know what you're dreaming of. I'm not standing here blindfolded.

Very well, then. Then *do* it!

But not till there's somebody to take your place.

TOM. What do you mean?

AMANDA. I mean that as soon as Laura has got somebody to take care of her, married, a home of her own, independent—why, then you'll be free to go wherever you please, on land, on sea, whichever way the wind blows you!

But until that time you've got to look out for your sister. I don't say me because I'm old and don't matter! I say for your sister because she's young and dependent.

I put her in business college—a dismal failure! Frightened her so it made her sick at the stomach.

I took her over to the Young People's League at the church. Another fiasco. She spoke to nobody, nobody spoke to her. Now all she does is fool with those pieces of glass and play those worn-out records. What kind of a life is that for a girl to lead?

TOM. What can I do about it?

AMANDA. Overcome selfishness! Self, self, self is all that you ever think of! [TOM *springs up and crosses to get his coat. It is ugly and bulky. He pulls on a cap with earmuffs.*] Where is your muffler? Put your wool muffler on! [*He snatches it angrily from the closet and tosses it around his neck and pulls both ends tight.*] Tom! I haven't said what I had in mind to ask you.

TOM. I'm too late to—

AMANDA [*catching his arm—very importunately. Then shyly*]. Down at the warehouse, aren't there some—nice young men?

TOM. No!

AMANDA. There *must* be—*some* . . .

TOM. Mother— [*Gesture.*]

AMANDA. Find out one that's clean-living—doesn't drink and—ask him out for sister!

TOM. What?

AMANDA. For *sister!* To *meet!* Get acquainted!

TOM [*stamping to door*]. Oh, my gosh!

AMANDA. Will you? [*He opens door. Imploringly.*] Will you? [*He starts down.*] Will you? *Will* you, dear?

TOM [*calling back*]. YES! [AMANDA *closes the door hesitantly and with a troubled but faintly hopeful expression.* SCREEN IMAGE: GLAMOR MAGAZINE COVER. *Spot* AMANDA *at phone.*]

AMANDA. Ella Cartwright? This is Amanda Wingfield!

How are you, honey?

How is that kidney condition? [*Count five.*] Horrors! [*Count five.*]

You're a Christian martyr, yes, honey, that's what you are, a Christian martyr!

Well, I just now happened to notice in my little red book that your subscription to the *Companion* has just run out! I knew that you wouldn't want to miss out on the wonderful serial starting in this new issue. It's by Bessie Mae Hopper, the first thing she's written since *Honeymoon for Three.*

Wasn't that a strange and interesting story? Well, this one is even lovelier, I believe. It has a sophisticated, society background. It's all about the horsey set on Long Island!

[FADE OUT]

The Glass Menagerie

SCENE V

[LEGEND ON SCREEN: "ANNUNCIATION." *Fade with music. It is early dusk of a spring evening. Supper has just been finished in the Wingfield apartment.* AMANDA *and* LAURA *in light-colored dresses are removing dishes from the table, in the upstage area, which is shadowy, their movements formalized almost as a dance or ritual, their moving forms as pale and silent as moths.* TOM, *in white shirt and trousers, rises from the table and crosses toward the fire-escape.*]

AMANDA [*as he passes her*]. Son, will you do me a favor?

TOM. What?

AMANDA. Comb your hair! You look so pretty when your hair is combed! [TOM *slouches on sofa with evening paper. Enormous caption "Franco Triumphs."*] There is only one respect in which I would like you to emulate your father.

TOM. What respect is that?

AMANDA. The care he always took of his appearance. He never allowed himself to look untidy. [*He throws down the paper and crosses to fire-escape.*] Where are you going?

TOM. I'm going out to smoke.

AMANDA. You smoke too much. A pack a day at fifteen cents a pack. How much would that amount to in a month? Thirty times fifteen is how much, Tom? Figure it out and you will be astounded at what you could save. Enough to give you a night-school course in accounting at Washington U! Just think what a wonderful thing that would be for you, Son! [TOM *is unmoved by the thought.*]

TOM. I'd rather smoke. [*He steps out on landing, letting the screen door slam.*]

AMANDA [*sharply*]. I know! That's the tragedy of it. . . . [*Alone, she turns to look at her husband's picture.* DANCE MUSIC: "ALL THE WORLD IS WAITING FOR THE SUNRISE!"]

TOM [*to the audience*]. Across the alley from us was the Paradise Dance Hall. On evenings in spring the windows and doors were open and the music came outdoors. Sometimes the lights were turned out except for a large glass sphere that hung from the ceiling. It would turn slowly about and filter the dusk with delicate rainbow colors. Then the orchestra played a waltz or a tango, something that had a slow and sensuous rhythm. Couples would come outside, to the relative privacy of the alley. You could see them kissing behind ash-pits and telephone poles.

This was the compensation for lives that passed like mine, without any change or adventure.

Adventure and change were imminent in this year. They were waiting around the corner for all these kids.

Suspended in the mist over Berchtesgaden, caught in the folds of Chamberlain's umbrella—

In Spain there was Guernica!

But here there was only hot swing music and liquor, dance halls, bars, and movies, and sex that hung in the gloom like a chandelier and flooded the world with brief, deceptive rainbows. . . .

All the world was waiting for bombardments! [AMANDA *turns from the picture and comes outside.*]

AMANDA [*sighing*]. A fire-escape landing's a poor excuse for a porch. [*She spreads a newspaper on a step and sits down, gracefully and demurely as if she were settling into a swing on a Mississippi veranda.*] What are you looking at?

TOM. The moon.

AMANDA. Is there a moon this evening?

TOM. It's rising over Garfinkel's Delicatessen.

AMANDA. So it is! A little silver slipper of a moon. Have you made a wish on it yet?

TOM. Um-hum.

AMANDA. What did you wish for?

TOM. That's a secret.

AMANDA. A secret, huh? Well, I won't tell mine either. I will be just as mysterious as you.

TOM. I bet I can guess what yours is.

AMANDA. Is my head so transparent?

TOM. You're not a sphinx.

AMANDA. No, I don't have secrets. I'll tell you what I wished for on the moon. Success and happiness for my precious children! I wish for that whenever there's a moon, and when there isn't a moon, I wish for it, too.

TOM. I thought perhaps you wished for a gentleman caller.

AMANDA. Why do you say that?

TOM. Don't you remember asking me to fetch one?

AMANDA. I remember suggesting that it would be nice for your sister if you brought home some nice young man from the warehouse. I think that I've made that suggestion more than once.

TOM. Yes, you have made it repeatedly.

AMANDA. Well?

TOM. We are going to have one.

AMANDA. *What?*

TOM. A gentleman caller! [THE ANNUNCIATION IS CELEBRATED WITH MUSIC. AMANDA *rises.* IMAGE ON SCREEN: CALLER WITH BOUQUET.]

AMANDA. You mean you have asked some nice young man to come over?

TOM. Yep. I've asked him to dinner.

AMANDA. You really did?

TOM. I did!

AMANDA. You did, and did he—*accept?*

TOM. He did!

AMANDA. Well, well—well, well! That's —lovely!

TOM. I thought that you would be pleased.

AMANDA. It's definite, then?

TOM. Very definite.

AMANDA. Soon?

TOM. Very soon.

AMANDA. For heaven's sake, stop putting on and tell me some things, will you?

TOM. What things do you want me to tell you?

AMANDA. *Naturally* I would like to know when he's *coming!*

TOM. He's coming tomorrow.

AMANDA. *Tomorrow?*

TOM. Yep. Tomorrow.

AMANDA. But, Tom!

TOM. Yes, Mother?

AMANDA. Tomorrow gives me no time!

TOM. Time for what?

AMANDA. Preparations! Why didn't you phone me at once, as soon as you asked him, the minute that he accepted? Then, don't you see, I could have been getting ready!

TOM. You don't have to make any fuss.

AMANDA. Oh, Tom, Tom, Tom, of course I have to make a fuss! I want things nice, not sloppy! Not thrown together. I'll certainly have to do some fast thinking, won't I?

TOM. I don't see why you have to think at all.

AMANDA. You just don't know. We can't have a gentleman caller in a pig-sty! All my wedding silver has to be polished, the monogrammed table linen ought to be laundered! The windows have to be washed and fresh curtains put up. And how about clothes? We have to *wear* something, don't we?

TOM. Mother, this boy is no one to make a fuss over!

AMANDA. Do you realize he's the first young man we've introduced to your sister?

It's terrible, dreadful, disgraceful that poor little sister has never received a single gentleman caller! Tom, come inside! [*She opens the screen door.*]

TOM. What for?

AMANDA. I want to ask you some things.

TOM. If you're going to make such a fuss, I'll call it off, I'll tell him not to come!

AMANDA. You certainly won't do anything of the kind. Nothing offends people worse than broken engagements. It simply means I'll have to work like a Turk! We won't be brilliant, but we will pass inspection. Come on inside. [TOM *follows, groaning.*] Sit down.

TOM. Any particular place you would like me to sit?

AMANDA. Thank heavens I've got that new sofa! I'm also making payments on a floor lamp I'll have sent out! And put the chintz covers on, they'll brighten things up! Of course I'd hoped to have these walls re-papered.... What is the young man's name?

TOM. His name is O'Connor.

AMANDA. That, of course, means fish—tomorrow is Friday! I'll have that salmon loaf—with Durkee's dressing! What does he do? He works at the warehouse?

TOM. Of course! How else would I—

AMANDA. Tom, he—doesn't drink?

TOM. Why do you ask me that?

AMANDA. Your father *did*!

TOM. Don't get started on that!

AMANDA. He *does* drink, then?

TOM. Not that I know of!

AMANDA. Make sure, be certain! The last thing I want for my daughter's a boy who drinks!

TOM. Aren't you being a little bit premature? Mr. O'Connor has not yet appeared on the scene!

AMANDA. But will tomorrow. To meet your sister, and what do I know about his character? Nothing! Old maids are better off than wives of drunkards!

TOM. Oh, my God!

AMANDA. Be still!

TOM [*leaning forward to whisper*]. Lots of fellows meet girls whom they don't marry!

AMANDA. Oh, talk sensibly, Tom—and don't be sarcastic! [*She has gotten a hairbrush.*]

TOM. What are you doing?

AMANDA. I'm brushing that cow-lick down!

What is this young man's position at the warehouse?

TOM [*submitting grimly to the brush and the interrogation*]. This young man's position is that of a shipping clerk, Mother.

AMANDA. Sounds to me like a fairly responsible job, the sort of a job *you* would be in if you just had more *get-up*.

What is his salary? Have you any idea?

TOM. I would judge it to be approximately eighty-five dollars a month.

AMANDA. Well—not princely, but—

TOM. Twenty more than I make.

AMANDA. Yes, how well I know! But for a family man, eighty-five dollars a month is not much more than you can just get by on....

TOM. Yes, but Mr. O'Connor is not a family man.

AMANDA. He might be, mightn't he? Some time in the future?

TOM. I see. Plans and provisions.

AMANDA. You are the only young man that I know of who ignores the fact that the future becomes the present, the present the past, and the past turns into everlasting regret if you don't plan for it!

TOM. I will think that over and see what I can make of it.

AMANDA. Don't be supercilious with your mother! Tell me some more about this—what do you call him?

TOM. James D. O'Connor. The D. is for Delaney.

AMANDA. Irish on *both* sides! *Gracious!* And doesn't drink?

TOM. Shall I call him up and ask him right this minute?

AMANDA. The only way to find out about those things is to make discreet inquiries at the proper moment. When I was a girl in Blue Mountain and it was suspected that a young man drank, the girl whose attentions he had been receiving, if any girl *was,* would sometimes speak to the minister of his church, or rather her father would if her father was living, and sort of feel him out on the young man's character. That is the way such things are discreetly handled to keep a young woman from making a tragic mistake!

TOM. Then how did you happen to make a tragic mistake?

AMANDA. That innocent look of your father's had everyone fooled!

He *smiled*—the world was *enchanted!*

No girl can do worse than put herself at the mercy of a handsome appearance!

I hope that Mr. O'Connor is not too good-looking.

TOM. No, he's not too good-looking. He's covered with freckles and hasn't too much of a nose.

AMANDA. He's not right-down homely, though?

TOM. Not right-down homely. Just medium homely, I'd say.

AMANDA. Character's what to look for in a man.

TOM. That's what I've always said, Mother.

AMANDA. You've never said anything of the kind and I suspect you would never give it a thought.

TOM. Don't be so suspicious of me.

AMANDA. At least I hope he's the type that's up and coming.

TOM. I think he really goes in for self-improvement.

AMANDA. What reason have you to think so?

TOM. He goes to night school.

AMANDA [*beaming*]. Splendid! What does he do, I mean study?

TOM. Radio engineering and public speaking!

AMANDA. Then he has visions of being advanced in the world!

Any young man who studies public speaking is aiming to have an executive job some day!

And radio engineering? A thing for the future!

Both of these facts are very illuminating. Those are the sort of things that a mother should know concerning any young man who comes to call on her daughter. Seriously or—not.

TOM. One little warning. He doesn't know about Laura. I didn't let on that we had dark ulterior motives. I just said, why don't you come and have dinner with us? He said okay and that was the whole conversation.

AMANDA. I bet it was! You're eloquent as an oyster.

However, he'll know about Laura when he gets here. When he sees how lovely and sweet and pretty she is, he'll thank his lucky stars he was asked to dinner.

TOM. Mother, you mustn't expect too much of Laura.

AMANDA. What do you mean?

TOM. Laura seems all those things to you and me because she's ours and we love her. We don't even notice she's crippled any more.

AMANDA. Don't say crippled! You know that I never allow that word to be used!

TOM. But face facts, Mother. She is and —that's not all—

AMANDA. What do you mean "not all"?

TOM. Laura is very different from other girls.

AMANDA. I think the difference is all to her advantage.

TOM. Not quite all—in the eyes of others—strangers—she's terribly shy and lives in a world of her own and those things make her seem a little peculiar to people outside the house.

AMANDA. Don't say peculiar.

TOM. Face the facts. She is. [THE DANCE-HALL MUSIC CHANGES TO A TANGO THAT HAS A MINOR AND SOMEWHAT OMINOUS TONE.]

AMANDA. In what way is she peculiar—may I ask?

TOM [gently]. She lives in a world of her own—a world of—little glass ornaments, Mother.... [Gets up. AMANDA remains holding brush, looking at him, troubled.] She plays old phonograph records and—that's about all— [He glances at himself in the mirror and crosses to door.]

AMANDA [sharply]. Where are you going?

TOM. I'm going to the movies. [Out screen door.]

AMANDA. Not to the movies, every night to the movies! [Follows quickly to screen door.] I don't believe you always go to the movies! [He is gone. AMANDA looks worriedly after him for a moment. Then vitality and optimism return and she turns from the door. Crossing to portieres.] Laura! Laura! [LAURA answers from kitchenette.]

LAURA. Yes, Mother.

AMANDA. Let those dishes go and come in front! [LAURA appears with dish towel. Gaily.] Laura, come here and make a wish on the moon! [SCREEN IMAGE: MOON.]

LAURA [entering]. Moon—moon?

AMANDA. A little silver slipper of a moon. Look over your left shoulder, Laura, and make a wish! [LAURA looks faintly puzzled as if called out of sleep. AMANDA seizes her shoulders and turns her at an angle by the door.] Now! Now, darling, wish!

LAURA. What shall I wish for, Mother?

AMANDA [her voice trembling and her eyes suddenly filling with tears.] Happiness! Good fortune! [The violin rises and the stage dims out.]

[CURTAIN]

SCENE VI

[IMAGE: HIGH SCHOOL HERO.]

And so the following evening I brought Jim home to dinner. I had known Jim slightly in high school. In high school Jim was a hero. He had tremendous Irish good nature and vitality with the scrubbed and polished look of white chinaware. He seemed to move in a continual spotlight. He was a star in basketball, captain of the debating club, president of the senior class and the glee club and he sang the male lead in the annual light operas. He was always running or bounding, never just walking. He seemed always at the point of defeating the law of gravity. He was shooting with such velocity through his adolescence that you would logically expect him to arrive at nothing short of the

White House by the time he was thirty. But Jim apparently ran into more interference after his graduation from Soldan. His speed had definitely slowed. Six years after he left high school he was holding a job that wasn't much better than mine. [IMAGE: CLERK.]

He was the only one at the warehouse with whom I was on friendly terms. I was valuable to him as someone who could remember his former glory, who had seen him win basketball games and the silver cup in debating. He knew of my secret practice of retiring to a cabinet of the wash-room to work on poems when business was slack in the warehouse. He called me Shakespeare. And while the other boys in the warehouse regarded me with suspicious hostility, Jim took a humorous attitude toward me. Gradually his attitude affected the others, their hostility wore off and they also began to smile at me as people smile at an oddly fashioned dog who trots across their path at some distance.

I knew that Jim and Laura had known each other at Soldan, and I had heard Laura speak admiringly of his voice. I didn't know if Jim remembered her or not. In high school Laura had been as unobtrusive as Jim had been astonishing. If he did remember Laura, it was not as my sister, for when I asked him to dinner, he grinned and said, "You know, Shakespeare, I never thought of you as having folks!"

He was about to discover that I did. . . .

[LIGHT UPSTAGE. LEGEND ON SCREEN: "THE ACCENT OF A COMING FOOT." *Friday evening. It is about five o'clock of a late spring evening which comes "scattering poems in the sky." A delicate lemony light is in the Wingfield apartment.* AMANDA *has worked like a Turk in preparation for the gentleman caller. The results are astonishing. The new floor lamp with its rose-silk shade is in place, a colored paper lantern conceals the broken light fixture in the ceiling, new billowing white curtains are at the windows, chintz covers are on chairs and sofa, a pair of new sofa pillows make their initial appearance. Open boxes and tissue paper are scattered on the floor.* LAURA *stands in the middle with lifted arms while* AMANDA *crouches before her, adjusting the hem of the new dress, devout and ritualistic. The dress is colored and designed by memory. The arrangement of* LAURA's *hair is changed; it is softer and more becoming. A fragile, unearthly prettiness has come out in* LAURA: *she is like a piece of translucent glass touched by light, given a momentary radiance, not actual, not lasting.*]

AMANDA [*impatiently*]. Why are you trembling?

LAURA. Mother, you've made me so nervous!

AMANDA. How have I made you nervous?

LAURA. By all this fuss! You make it seem so important!

AMANDA. I don't understand you, Laura. You couldn't be satisfied with just sitting home, and yet whenever I try to arrange something for you, you seem to resist it. [*She gets up.*] Now take a look at yourself. No, wait! Wait just a moment—I have an idea!

LAURA. What is it now? [AMANDA *produces two powder puffs which she wraps in handkerchiefs and stuffs in* LAURA's *bosom.*] Mother, what are you doing?

AMANDA. They call them "Gay Deceivers"!

LAURA. I won't wear them!

AMANDA. You will!

LAURA. Why should I?

The Glass Menagerie

AMANDA. Because, to be painfully honest, your chest is flat.

LAURA. You make it seem like we were setting a trap.

AMANDA. All pretty girls are a trap, a pretty trap, and men expect them to be. [LEGEND: "A PRETTY TRAP."] Now look at yourself, young lady. This is the prettiest you will ever be!

I've got to fix myself now! You're going to be surprised by your mother's appearance! [*She crosses through portieres, humming gaily.* LAURA *moves slowly to the long mirror and stares solemnly at herself. A wind blows the white curtains inward in a slow, graceful motion and with a faint, sorrowful sighing.*]

AMANDA [*off stage*]. It isn't dark enough yet. [*She turns slowly before the mirror with a troubled look.*]

[LEGEND ON SCREEN: "THIS IS MY SISTER: CELEBRATE HER WITH STRINGS!" MUSIC.]

AMANDA [*laughing, off*]. I'm going to show you something. I'm going to make a spectacular appearance!

LAURA. What is it, Mother?

AMANDA. Possess your soul in patience—you will see!

Something I've resurrected from that old trunk! Styles haven't changed so terribly much after all.... [*She parts the portieres.*] Now just look at your mother! [*She wears a girlish frock of yellowed voile with a blue silk sash. She carries a bunch of jonquils—the legend of her youth is nearly revived. Feverishly.*] This is the dress in which I led the cotillion. Won the cakewalk twice at Sunset Hill, wore one spring to the Governor's ball in Jackson!

See how I sashayed around the ballroom, Laura? [*She raises her skirt and does a mincing step around the room.*] I wore it on Sundays for my gentlemen callers! I had it on the day I met your father—I had malaria fever all that spring. The change of climate from East Tennessee to the Delta—weakened resistance—I had a little temperature all the time—not enough to be serious—just enough to make me restless and giddy!—Invitations poured in—parties all over the Delta!—"Stay in bed," said Mother, "you have fever!"—but I just wouldn't.—I took quinine but kept on going, going!—Evenings, dances!—Afternoons, long, long rides! Picnics—lovely!—So lovely, that country in May.—All lacy with dogwood, literally flooded with jonquils!—That was the spring I had the craze for jonquils. Jonquils became an absolute obsession. Mother said, "Honey, there's no more room for jonquils." And still I kept on bringing in more jonquils. Whenever, wherever I saw them, I'd say, "Stop! Stop! I see jonquils!" I made the young men help me gather the jonquils! It was a joke, Amanda and her jonquils! Finally there were no more vases to hold them, every available space was filled with jonquils. No vases to hold them? All right, I'll hold them myself! And then I— [*She stops in front of the picture.* MUSIC.] met your father!

Malaria fever and jonquils and then—this—boy.... [*She switches on the rose-colored lamp.*] I hope they get here before it starts to rain. [*She crosses upstage and places the jonquils in bowl on table.*] I gave your brother a little extra change so he and Mr. O'Connor could take the service car home.

LAURA [*with altered look*]. What did you say his name was?

AMANDA. O'Connor.

LAURA. What is his first name?

AMANDA. I don't remember. Oh, yes, I do. It was—Jim! [LAURA *sways slightly and catches hold of a chair.* LEGEND ON SCREEN: "NOT JIM!"]

LAURA [*faintly*]. Not—Jim!

AMANDA. Yes, that was it, it was Jim! I've never known a Jim that wasn't nice! [MUSIC: OMINOUS.]

LAURA. Are you sure his name is Jim O'Connor?

AMANDA. Yes. Why?

LAURA. Is he the one that Tom used to know in high school?

AMANDA. He didn't say so. I think he just got to know him at the warehouse.

LAURA. There was a Jim O'Connor we both knew in high school— [*Then, with effort.*] If that is the one that Tom is bringing to dinner—you'll have to excuse me, I won't come to the table.

AMANDA. What sort of nonsense is this?

LAURA. You asked me once if I'd ever liked a boy. Don't you remember I showed you this boy's picture?

AMANDA. You mean the boy you showed me in the year book?

LAURA. Yes, that boy.

AMANDA. Laura, Laura, were you in love with that boy?

LAURA. I don't know, Mother. All I know is I couldn't sit at the table if it was him!

AMANDA. It won't be him! It isn't the least bit likely. But whether it is or not, you will come to the table. You will not be excused.

LAURA. I'll have to be, Mother.

AMANDA. I don't intend to humor your silliness, Laura. I've had too much from you and your brother, both! So just sit down and compose yourself till they come. Tom has forgotten his key so you'll have to let them in, when they arrive.

LAURA [*panicky*]. Oh, Mother—*you* answer the door!

AMANDA [*lightly*]. I'll be in the kitchen—busy!

LAURA. Oh, Mother, please answer the door, don't make me do it!

AMANDA [*crossing into kitchenette*]. I've got to fix the dressing for the salmon. Fuss, fuss—silliness!—over a gentleman caller!

[*Door swings shut.* LAURA *is left alone.* LEGEND: "TERROR!" *She utters a low moan and turns off the lamp—sits stiffly on the edge of the sofa, knotting her fingers together.* LEGEND ON SCREEN: "THE OPENING OF A DOOR!" TOM *and* JIM *appear on the fire-escape steps and climb to landing. Hearing their approach,* LAURA *rises with a panicky gesture. She retreats to the portieres. The doorbell.* LAURA *catches her breath and touches her throat. Low drums.*]

AMANDA [*calling*]. Laura, sweetheart! The door! [LAURA *stares at it without moving.*]

JIM. I think we just beat the rain.

TOM. Uh-huh. [*He rings again, nervously.* JIM *whistles and fishes for a cigarette.*]

AMANDA [*very, very gaily*]. Laura, that is your brother and Mr. O'Connor! Will you let them in, darling? [LAURA *crosses toward kitchenette door.*]

LAURA [*breathlessly*]. Mother—you go to the door! [AMANDA *steps out of kitchenette and stares furiously at* LAURA. *She points imperiously at the door.*]

LAURA. Please, please!

AMANDA [*in a fierce whisper*]. What is the matter with you, you silly thing?

LAURA [*desperately*]. Please, you answer it, *please!*

AMANDA. I told you I wasn't going to humor you, Laura. Why have you chosen this moment to lose your mind?

LAURA. Please, please, please, you go!

AMANDA. You'll have to go to the door because I can't!

LAURA [*despairingly*]. I can't either!

AMANDA. *Why?*

LAURA. I'm *sick!*

AMANDA. I'm sick, too—of your nonsense! Why can't you and your brother be normal people? Fantastic whims and behavior! [TOM *gives a long ring.*] Preposterous goings on! Can you give me one reason— [*Calls out lyrically.*] COMING! JUST ONE SECOND!—why you should be afraid to open a door? Now you answer it, Laura!

LAURA. Oh, oh, oh . . . [*She returns through the portieres. Darts to the victrola and winds it frantically and turns it on.*]

AMANDA. Laura Wingfield, you march right to that door!

LAURA. Yes—yes, Mother! [*A faraway, scratchy rendition of "Dardanella" softens the air and gives her strength to move through it. She slips to the door and draws it cautiously open.* TOM *enters with the caller,* JIM O'CONNOR.]

TOM. Laura, this is Jim. Jim, this is my sister, Laura.

JIM [*stepping inside*]. I didn't know that Shakespeare had a sister!

LAURA [*retreating stiff and trembling from the door*]. How—how do you do?

JIM [*heartily extending his hand*]. Okay! [LAURA *touches it hesitantly with hers.*]

JIM. Your hand's *cold*, Laura!

LAURA. Yes, well—I've been playing the victrola. . . .

JIM. Must have been playing classical music on it! You ought to play a little hot swing music to warm you up!

LAURA. Excuse me—I haven't finished playing the victrola. . . . [*She turns awkwardly and hurries into the front room. She pauses a second by the victrola. Then catches her breath and darts through the portieres like a frightened deer.*]

JIM [*grinning*]. What was the matter?

TOM. Oh—with Laura? Laura is—terribly shy.

JIM. Shy, huh? It's unusual to meet a shy girl nowadays. I don't believe you ever mentioned you had a sister.

TOM. Well, now you know. I have one. Here is the *Post Dispatch.* You want a piece of it?

JIM. Uh-huh.

TOM. What piece? The comics?

JIM. Sports! [*Glances at it.*] Ole Dizzy Dean is on his bad behavior.

TOM [*disinterest*]. Yeah? [*Lights cigarette and crosses back to fire-escape door.*]

JIM. Where are *you* going?

TOM. I'm going out on the terrace.

JIM [*goes after him*]. You know, Shakespeare—I'm going to sell you a bill of goods!

TOM. What goods?

JIM. A course I'm taking.

TOM. Huh?

JIM. In public speaking! You and me, we're not the warehouse type.

TOM. Thanks—that's good news. But what has public speaking got to do with it?

JIM. It fits you for—executive positions!

TOM. Awww.

JIM. I tell you it's done a helluva lot for me. [IMAGE: EXECUTIVE AT DESK.]

TOM. In what respect?

JIM. In every! Ask yourself what is the difference between you an' me and men in the office down front? Brains?—No!— Ability?—No! Then what? Just one little thing—

TOM. What is that one little thing?

JIM. Primarily it amounts to—social poise! Being able to square up to people and hold your own on any social level!

AMANDA [*off stage*]. Tom?

TOM. Yes, Mother?

AMANDA. Is that you and Mr. O'Connor?

TOM. Yes, Mother.

AMANDA. Well, you just make yourselves comfortable in there.

TOM. Yes, Mother.

AMANDA. Ask Mr. O'Connor if he would like to wash his hands.

JIM. Aw, no—no—thank you—I took care of that at the warehouse. Tom—

TOM. Yes?

JIM. Mr. Mendoza was speaking to me about you.

TOM. Favorably?

JIM. What do you think?

TOM. Well—

JIM. You're going to be out of a job if you don't wake up.

TOM. I am waking up—

JIM. You show no signs.

TOM. The signs are interior. [IMAGE ON SCREEN: THE SAILING VESSEL WITH JOLLY ROGER AGAIN.] I'm planning to change. [*He leans over the rail speaking with quiet exhilaration. The incandescent marquees and signs of the first-run movie houses light his face from across the alley. He looks like a voyager.*] I'm right at the point of committing myself to a future that doesn't include the warehouse and Mr. Mendoza or even a night-school course in public speaking.

JIM. What are you gassing about?

TOM. I'm tired of the movies.

JIM. Movies!

TOM. Yes, movies! Look at them— [*A wave toward the marvels of Grand Avenue.*] All of those glamorous people—having adventures—hogging it all, gobbling the whole thing up! You know what happens? People go to the *movies* instead of *moving!* Hollywood characters are supposed to have all the adventures for everybody in America, while everybody in America sits in a dark room and watches them have them! Yes, until there's a war. That's when adventure becomes available to the masses! *Everyone's* dish, not only Gable's! Then the people in the dark room come out of the dark room to have some adventures themselves— Goody, goody!— It's our turn now, to go to the South Sea Island—to make a safari—to be exotic, far-off!—But I'm not patient. I don't want to wait till then. I'm tired of the *movies* and I am *about* to *move!*

JIM [*incredulously*]. Move?

TOM. Yes.

JIM. When?

TOM. Soon!

JIM. Where? Where? [THEME THREE MUSIC SEEMS TO ANSWER THE QUESTION, WHILE TOM THINKS IT OVER. HE SEARCHES AMONG HIS POCKETS.]

TOM. I'm starting to boil inside. I know I seem dreamy, but inside—well, I'm boiling!—Whenever I pick up a shoe, I shudder a little thinking how short life is and what I am doing!—Whatever that means, I know it doesn't mean shoes—except as something to wear on a traveler's feet! [*Finds paper.*] Look—

JIM. What?

TOM. I'm a member.

JIM [*reading*]. The Union of Merchant Seamen.

TOM. I paid my dues this month, instead of the light bill.

JIM. You will regret it when they turn the lights off.

TOM. I won't be here.

JIM. How about your mother?

TOM. I'm like my father. The bastard son of a bastard! See how he grins? And he's been absent going on sixteen years!

JIM. You're just talking, you drip. How does your mother feel about it?

The Glass Menagerie

Tom. Shhh!—Here comes Mother! Mother is not acquainted with my plans!

Amanda [*enters portieres*]. Where are you all?

Tom. On the terrace, Mother. [*They start inside. She advances to them. Tom is distinctly shocked at her appearance. Even Jim blinks a little. He is making his first contact with girlish Southern vivacity and in spite of the night-school course in public speaking is somewhat thrown off the beam by the unexpected outlay of social charm. Certain responses are attempted by Jim but are swept aside by Amanda's gay laughter and chatter. Tom is embarrassed but after the first shock Jim reacts very warmly. Grins and chuckles, is altogether won over.* IMAGE: AMANDA AS A GIRL.]

Amanda [*coyly smiling, shaking her girlish ringlets*]. Well, well, well, so this is Mr. O'Connor. Introductions entirely unnecessary. I've heard so much about you from my boy. I finally said to him, Tom—good gracious!—why don't you bring this paragon to supper? I'd like to meet this nice young man at the warehouse!—Instead of just hearing him sing your praises so much!

I don't know why my son is so stand-offish—that's not Southern behavior!

Let's sit down and—I think we could stand a little more air in here! Tom, leave the door open. I felt a nice fresh breeze a moment ago. Where has it gone to?

Mmm, so warm already! And not quite summer, even. We're going to burn up when summer really gets started.

However, we're having—we're having a very light supper. I think light things are better fo' this time of year. The same as light clothes are. Light clothes an' light food are what warm weather calls fo'. You know our blood gets so thick during th' winter—it takes a while fo' us to *adjust* ou'selves!—when the season changes . . .

It's come so quick this year. I wasn't prepared. All of a sudden—heavens! Already summer!—I ran to the trunk an' pulled out this light dress— Terribly old! Historical almost! But feels so good—so good an' co-ol, y' know. . . .

Tom. Mother—

Amanda. Yes, honey?

Tom. How about—supper?

Amanda. Honey, you go ask Sister if supper is ready! You know that Sister is in full charge of supper!

Tell her you hungry boys are waiting for it. [*To* Jim.] Have you met Laura?

Jim. She—

Amanda. Let you in? Oh, good, you've met already! It's rare for a girl as sweet an' pretty as Laura to be domestic! But Laura is, thank heavens, not only pretty but also very domestic. I'm not at all. I never was a bit. I never could make a thing but angel-food cake. Well, in the South we had so many servants. Gone, gone, gone. All vestige of gracious living! Gone completely! I wasn't prepared for what the future brought me. All of my gentlemen callers were sons of planters and so of course I assumed that I would be married to one and raise my family on a large piece of land with plenty of servants. But man proposes—and woman accepts the proposal!—To vary that old, old saying a little bit—I married no planter! I married a man who worked for the telephone company!—That gallantly smiling gentleman over there! [*Points to the picture.*] A telephone man who—fell in love with long-distance!—Now he travels and I don't even know where!—But what am I going on for about my—tribulations?

[571]

Tell me yours—I hope you don't have any! Tom?

TOM [*returning*]. Yes, Mother?

AMANDA. Is supper nearly ready?

TOM. It looks to me like supper is on the table.

AMANDA. Let me look— [*She rises prettily and looks through portieres.*] Oh, lovely!—But where is Sister?

TOM. Laura is not feeling well and she says that she thinks she'd better not come to the table.

AMANDA. What?—Nonsense!—Laura? Oh, Laura!

LAURA [*off stage, faintly*]. Yes, Mother.

AMANDA. You really must come to the table. We won't be seated until you come to the table!

Come in, Mr. O'Connor. You sit over there, and I'll—

Laura? Laura Wingfield!

You're keeping us waiting, honey! We can't say grace until you come to the table! [*The back door is pushed weakly open and* LAURA *comes in. She is obviously quite faint, her lips trembling, her eyes wide and staring. She moves unsteadily toward the table.* LEGEND: "TERROR!" *Outside a summer storm is coming abruptly. The white curtains billow inward at the windows and there is a sorrowful murmur and deep blue dusk.* LAURA *suddenly stumbles—she catches at a chair with a faint moan.*]

TOM. Laura!

AMANDA. Laura! [*There is a clap of thunder.* LEGEND: "AH!" *Despairingly.*]

Why, Laura, you *are* sick, darling! Tom, help your sister into the living room, dear!

Sit in the living room, Laura—rest on the sofa.

Well! [*To the gentleman caller.*] Standing over the hot stove made her ill!—I told her that it was just too warm this evening, but— [TOM *comes back in.* LAURA *is on the sofa.*] Is Laura all right now?

TOM. Yes.

AMANDA. What *is* that? Rain? A nice cool rain has come up! [*She gives the gentleman caller a frightened look.*] I think we may—have grace—now . . . [TOM *looks at her stupidly.*] Tom, honey—you say grace!

TOM. Oh . . . "For these and all thy mercies—" [*They bow their heads,* AMANDA *stealing a nervous glance at* JIM. *In the living room* LAURA, *stretched on the sofa, clenches her hand to her lips, to hold back a shuddering sob.*] God's Holy Name be praised—

[THE SCENE DIMS OUT]

SCENE VII

[A Souvenir.

Half an hour later. Dinner is just being finished in the upstage area which is concealed by the drawn portieres.

As the curtain rises LAURA *is still huddled upon the sofa, her feet drawn under her, her head resting on a pale blue pillow, her eyes wide and mysteriously watchful. The new floor lamp with its shade of rose-colored silk gives a soft, becoming light to her face, bringing out the fragile, unearthly prettiness which usually escapes attention. There is a steady murmur of rain, but it is slackening and stops soon after the scene begins; the air outside becomes pale and luminous as the moon breaks out.*

A moment after the curtain rises, the lights in both rooms flicker and go out.]

JIM. Hey, there, Mr. Light Bulb! [AMANDA *laughs nervously.* LEGEND: "SUSPENSION OF A PUBLIC SERVICE."]
AMANDA. Where was Moses when the lights went out? Ha-ha. Do you know the answer to that one, Mr. O'Connor?
JIM. No, Ma'am, what's the answer?
AMANDA. In the dark! [JIM *laughs appreciatively.*] Everybody sit still. I'll light the candles. Isn't it lucky we have them on the table? Where's a match? Which of you gentlemen can provide a match?
JIM. Here.
AMANDA. Thank you, sir.
JIM. Not at all, Ma'am!
AMANDA. I guess the fuse has burnt out. Mr. O'Connor, can you tell a burnt-out fuse? I know I can't and Tom is a total loss when it comes to mechanics. [SOUND: GETTING UP: VOICES RECEDE A LITTLE TO KITCHENETTE.] Oh, be careful you don't bump into something. We don't want our gentleman caller to break his neck. Now wouldn't that be a fine howdy-do?
JIM. Ha-ha! Where is the fuse-box?
AMANDA. Right here next to the stove. Can you see anything?
JIM. Just a minute.
AMANDA. Isn't electricity a mysterious thing? Wasn't it Benjamin Franklin who tied a key to a kite? We live in such a mysterious universe, don't we? Some people say that science clears up all the mysteries for us. In my opinion it only creates more!
Have you found it yet?
JIM. No, Ma'am. All these fuses look okay to me.
AMANDA. Tom!
TOM. Yes, Mother?
AMANDA. That light bill I gave you several days ago. The one I told you we got the notices about? [LEGEND: "HA!"]
TOM. Oh.—Yeah.

AMANDA. You didn't neglect to pay it by any chance?
TOM. Why, I—
AMANDA. Didn't! I might have known it!
JIM. Shakespeare probably wrote a poem on that light bill, Mrs. Wingfield.
AMANDA. I might have known better than to trust him with it! There's such a high price for negligence in this world!
JIM. Maybe the poem will win a ten-dollar prize.
AMANDA. We'll just have to spend the remainder of the evening in the nineteenth century, before Mr. Edison made the Mazda lamp!
JIM. Candlelight is my favorite kind of light.
AMANDA. That shows you're romantic! But that's no excuse for Tom.
Well, we got through dinner. Very considerate of them to let us get through dinner before they plunged us into everlasting darkness, wasn't it, Mr. O'Connor?
JIM. Ha-ha!
AMANDA. Tom, as a penalty for your carelessness you can help me with the dishes.
JIM. Let me give you a hand.
AMANDA. Indeed you will not!
JIM. I ought to be good for something.
AMANDA. Good for something? [*Her tone is rhapsodic.*] You? Why, Mr. O'Connor, nobody, *nobody's* given me this much entertainment in years—as you have!
JIM. Aw, now, Mrs. Wingfield!
AMANDA. I'm not exaggerating, not one bit! But Sister is all by her lonesome. You go keep her company in the parlor!
I'll give you this lovely old candelabrum that used to be on the altar at the church of the Heavenly Rest. It was melted a little out of shape when the church burnt down. Lightning struck it one spring. Gypsy

Jones was holding a revival at the time and he intimated that the church was destroyed because the Episcopalians gave card parties.

Jim. Ha-ha.

Amanda. And how about you coaxing Sister to drink a little wine? I think it would be good for her! Can you carry both at once?

Jim. Sure. I'm Superman!

Amanda. Now, Thomas, get into this apron! [*The door of kitchenette swings closed on* Amanda's *gay laughter; the flickering light approaches the portieres.* Laura *sits up nervously as he enters. Her speech at first is low and breathless from the almost intolerable strain of being alone with a stranger.* The legend: "i don't suppose you remember me at all!" *In her first speeches in this scene, before* Jim's *warmth overcomes her paralyzing shyness,* Laura's *voice is thin and breathless as though she has just run up a steep flight of stairs.* Jim's *attitude is gently humorous. In playing this scene it should be stressed that while the incident is apparently unimportant, it is to* Laura *the climax of her secret life.*]

Jim. Hello, there, Laura.

Laura [*faintly*]. Hello. [*She clears her throat.*]

Jim. How are you feeling now? Better?

Laura. Yes. Yes, thank you.

Jim. This is for you. A little dandelion wine. [*He extends it toward her with extravagant gallantry.*]

Laura. Thank you.

Jim. Drink it—but don't get drunk! [*He laughs heartily.* Laura *takes the glass uncertainly; laughs shyly.*] Where shall I set the candles?

Laura. Oh—oh, anywhere . . .

Jim. How about here on the floor? Any objections?

Laura. No.

Jim. I'll spread a newspaper under to catch the drippings. I like to sit on the floor. Mind if I do?

Laura. Oh, no.

Jim. Give me a pillow?

Laura. What?

Jim. A pillow!

Laura. Oh . . . [*Hands him one quickly.*]

Jim. How about you? Don't you like to sit on the floor?

Laura. Oh—yes.

Jim. Why don't you, then?

Laura. I—will.

Jim. Take a pillow! [Laura *does. Sits on the other side of the candelabrum.* Jim *crosses his legs and smiles engagingly at her.*] I can't hardly see you sitting way over there.

Laura. I can—see you.

Jim. I know, but that's not fair, I'm in the limelight. [Laura *moves her pillow closer.*] Good! Now I can see you! Comfortable?

Laura. Yes.

Jim. So am I. Comfortable as a cow! Will you have some gum?

Laura. No, thank you.

Jim. I think that I will indulge, with your permission. [*Musingly unwraps it and holds it up.*] Think of the fortune made by the guy that invented the first piece of chewing gum. Amazing, huh? The Wrigley Building is one of the sights of Chicago.—I saw it summer before last when I went up to the Century of Progress. Did you take in the Century of Progress?

Laura. No, I didn't.

Jim. Well, it was quite a wonderful exposition. What impressed me most was the Hall of Science. Gives you an idea of what the future will be in America, even more wonderful than the present time is!

The Glass Menagerie

[*Pause. Smiling at her.*] Your brother tells me you're shy. Is that right, Laura?

LAURA. I—don't know.

JIM. I judge you to be an old-fashioned type of girl. Well, I think that's a pretty good type to be. Hope you don't think I'm being too personal—do you?

LAURA [*hastily, out of embarrassment*]. I believe I *will* take a piece of gum, if you —don't mind. [*Clearing her throat.*] Mr. O'Connor, have you—kept up with your singing?

JIM. Singing? Me?

LAURA. Yes. I remember what a beautiful voice you had.

JIM. When did you hear me sing?

[VOICE OFF STAGE IN THE PAUSE.]

VOICE [*off stage*].

O blow, ye winds, heigh-ho,
A-roving I will go!
　I'm off to my love
　With a boxing glove—
Ten thousand miles away!

JIM. You say you've heard me sing?

LAURA. Oh, yes! Yes, very often . . . I —don't suppose—you remember me—at all?

JIM [*smiling doubtfully*]. You know I have an idea I've seen you before. I had that idea soon as you opened the door. It seemed almost like I was about to remember your name. But the name that I started to call you—wasn't a name! And so I stopped myself before I said it.

LAURA. Wasn't it—Blue Roses?

JIM [*springs up. Grinning*]. Blue Roses! —My gosh, yes—Blue Roses! That's what I had on my tongue when you opened the door! Isn't it funny what tricks your memory plays? I didn't connect you with high school somehow or other. But that's where it was; it was high school. I didn't even know you were Shakespeare's sister! Gosh, I'm sorry.

LAURA. I didn't expect you to. You— barely knew me!

JIM. But we did have a speaking acquaintance, huh?

LAURA. Yes, we—spoke to each other.

JIM. When did you recognize me?

LAURA. Oh, right away!

JIM. Soon as I came in the door?

LAURA. When I heard your name I thought it was probably you. I knew that Tom used to know you a little in high school. So when you came in the door— Well, then I was—sure.

JIM. Why didn't you *say* something, then?

LAURA [*breathlessly*]. I didn't know what to say, I was—too surprised!

JIM. For goodness' sakes! You know, this sure is funny!

LAURA. Yes! Yes, isn't it, though . . .

JIM. Didn't we have a class in something together?

LAURA. Yes, we did.

JIM. What class was that?

LAURA. It was—singing—Chorus!

JIM. Aw!

LAURA. I sat across the aisle from you in the Aud.

JIM. Aw.

LAURA. Mondays, Wednesdays and Fridays.

JIM. Now I remember—you always came in late.

LAURA. Yes, it was so hard for me, getting upstairs. I had that brace on my leg— it clumped so loud!

JIM. I never heard any clumping.

LAURA [*wincing at the recollection*]. To me it sounded like—thunder!

JIM. Well, well, well, I never even noticed.

LAURA. And everybody was seated before I came in. I had to walk in front of all those people. My seat was in the back row. I had to go clumping all the way up the aisle with everyone watching!

JIM. You shouldn't have been self-conscious.

LAURA. I know, but I was. It was always such a relief when the singing started.

JIM. Aw, yes, I've placed you now! I used to call you Blue Roses. How was it that I got started calling you that?

LAURA. I was out of school a little while with pleurosis. When I came back you asked me what was the matter. I said I had pleurosis—you thought I said Blue Roses. That's what you always called me after that!

JIM. I hope you didn't mind.

LAURA. Oh, no—I liked it. You see, I wasn't acquainted with many—people. . . .

JIM. As I remember you sort of stuck by yourself.

LAURA. I—I—never have had much luck at—making friends.

JIM. I don't see why you wouldn't.

LAURA. Well, I—started out badly.

JIM. You mean being—

LAURA. Yes, it sort of—stood between me—

JIM. You shouldn't have let it!

LAURA. I know, but it did, and—

JIM. You were shy with people!

LAURA. I tried not to be but never could—

JIM. Overcome it?

LAURA. No, I—I never could!

JIM. I guess being shy is something you have to work out of kind of gradually.

LAURA [*sorrowfully*]. Yes—I guess it—

JIM. Takes time!

LAURA. Yes—

JIM. People are not so dreadful when you know them. That's what you have to remember! And everybody has problems, not just you, but practically everybody has got some problem. You think of yourself as having the only problems, as being the only one who is disappointed. But just look around you and you will see lots of people as disappointed as you are. For instance, I hoped when I was going to high school that I would be further along at this time, six years later, than I am now— You remember that wonderful write-up I had in *The Torch?*

LAURA. Yes! [*She rises and crosses to table.*]

JIM. It said I was bound to succeed in anything I went into! [LAURA *returns with the annual.*] Holy Jeez! *The Torch!* [*He accepts it reverently. They smile across it with mutual wonder.* LAURA *crouches beside him and they begin to turn through it.* LAURA'S *shyness is dissolving in his warmth.*]

LAURA. Here you are in *The Pirates of Penzance!*

JIM [*wistfully*]. I sang the baritone lead in that operetta.

LAURA [*raptly*]. So—*beautifully!*

JIM [*protesting*]. Aw—

LAURA. Yes, yes—beautifully—beautifully!

JIM. You heard me?

LAURA. All three times!

JIM. No!

LAURA. Yes!

JIM. All three performances?

LAURA [*looking down*]. Yes.

JIM. Why?

LAURA. I—wanted to ask you to—autograph my program.

JIM. Why didn't you ask me to?

LAURA. You were always surrounded by your own friends so much that I never had a chance to.

JIM. You should have just—

LAURA. Well, I—thought you might think I was—

JIM. Thought I might think you was— what?

[576]

The Glass Menagerie

LAURA. Oh—

JIM [*with reflective relish*]. I was beleaguered by females in those days.

LAURA. You were terribly popular!

JIM. Yeah—

LAURA. You had such a—friendly way—

JIM. I was spoiled in high school.

LAURA. Everybody—liked you!

JIM. Including you?

LAURA. I—yes, I—I did, too— [*She gently closes the book in her lap.*]

JIM. Well, well, well!—Give me that program, Laura. [*She hands it to him. He signs it with a flourish.*] There you are—better late than never!

LAURA. Oh, I—what a—surprise!

JIM. My signature isn't worth very much right now. But some day—maybe—it will increase in value! Being disappointed is one thing and being discouraged is something else. I am disappointed but I am not discouraged. I'm twenty-three years old. How old are you?

LAURA. I'll be twenty-four in June.

JIM. That's not old age!

LAURA. No, but—

JIM. You finished high school?

LAURA [*with difficulty*]. I didn't go back.

JIM. You mean you dropped out?

LAURA. I made bad grades in my final examinations. [*She rises and replaces the book and the program. Her voice strained.*] How is—Emily Meisenbach getting along?

JIM. Oh, that kraut-head!

LAURA. Why do you call her that?

JIM. That's what she was.

LAURA. You're not still—going with her?

JIM. I never see her.

LAURA. It said in the Personal Section that you were—engaged!

JIM. I know, but I wasn't impressed by that—propaganda!

LAURA. It wasn't—the truth?

JIM. Only in Emily's optimistic opinion!

LAURA. Oh— [LEGEND: "WHAT HAVE YOU DONE SINCE HIGH SCHOOL?"] JIM *lights a cigarette and leans indolently back on his elbows smiling at* LAURA *with a warmth and charm which lights her inwardly with altar candles. She remains by the table and turns in her hands a piece of glass to cover her tumult.*]

JIM [*after several reflective puffs on a cigarette*]. What have you done since high school? [*She seems not to hear him.*] Huh? [LAURA *looks up.*] I said what have you done since high school, Laura?

LAURA. Nothing much.

JIM. You must have been doing something these six long years.

LAURA. Yes.

JIM. Well, then, such as what?

LAURA. I took a business course at business college—

JIM. How did that work out?

LAURA. Well, not very—well—I had to drop out, it gave me—indigestion— [JIM *laughs gently.*]

JIM. What are you doing now?

LAURA. I don't do anything—much. Oh, please don't think I sit around doing nothing! My glass collection takes up a good deal of time. Glass is something you have to take good care of.

JIM. What did you say—about glass?

LAURA. Collection I said—I have one— [*She clears her throat and turns away again, acutely shy.*]

JIM [*abruptly*]. You know what I judge to be the trouble with you?

Inferiority complex! Know what that is? That's what they call it when someone low-rates himself!

I understand it because I had it, too. Although my case was not so aggravated as yours seems to be. I had it until I took up public speaking, developed my voice, and learned that I had an aptitude for science. Before that time I never thought of

[577]

myself as being outstanding in any way whatsoever!

Now I've never made a regular study of it, but I have a friend who says I can analyze people better than doctors that make a profession of it. I don't claim that to be necessarily true, but I can sure guess a person's psychology, Laura! [*Takes out his gum.*] Excuse me, Laura. I always take it out when the flavor is gone. I'll use this scrap of paper to wrap it in. I know how it is to get it stuck on a shoe.

Yep—that's what I judge to be your principal trouble. A lack of confidence in yourself as a person. You don't have the proper amount of faith in yourself. I'm basing that fact on a number of your remarks and also on certain observations I've made. For instance that clumping you thought was so awful in high school. You say that you even dreaded to walk into class. You see what you did? You dropped out of school, you gave up an education because of a clump, which as far as I know was practically non-existent! A little physical defect is what you have. Hardly noticeable even! Magnified thousands of times by imagination!

You know what my strong advice to you is? Think of yourself as *superior* in some way!

LAURA. In what way would I think?

JIM. Why, man alive, Laura! Just look about you a little. What do you see? A world full of common people! All of 'em born and all of 'em going to die!

Which of them has one-tenth of your good points! Or mine! Or anyone else's, as far as that goes— Gosh!

Everybody excels in some one thing. Some in many! [*Unconsciously glances at himself in the mirror.*] All you've got to do is discover in *what!*

Take me, for instance. [*He adjusts his tie at the mirror.*]

My interest happens to lie in electro-dynamics. I'm taking a course in radio engineering at night school, Laura, on top of a fairly responsible job at the warehouse. I'm taking that course and studying public speaking.

LAURA. Ohhhh.

JIM. Because I believe in the future of television! [*Turning back to her.*] I wish to be ready to go up right along with it. Therefore I'm planning to get in on the ground floor. In fact I've already made the right connections and all that remains is for the industry itself to get under way! Full steam— [*His eyes are starry.*] Knowledge—Zzzzzp! Money—Zzzzzzp!—Power! That's the cycle democracy is built on! [*His attitude is convincingly dynamic.* LAURA *stares at him, even her shyness eclipsed in her absolute wonder. He suddenly grins.*] I guess you think I think a lot of myself!

LAURA. No—o-o-o, I—

JIM. Now how about you? Isn't there something you take more interest in than anything else?

LAURA. Well, I do—as I said—have my—glass collection— [*A peal of girlish laughter from the kitchen.*]

JIM. I'm not right sure I know what you're talking about. What kind of glass is it?

LAURA. Little articles of it, they're ornaments mostly!

Most of them are little animals made out of glass, the tiniest little animals in the world. Mother calls them a glass menagerie!

Here's an example of one, if you'd like to see it!

This one is one of the oldest. It's nearly thirteen. [MUSIC: "THE GLASS MENAGERIE." *He stretches out his hand.*] Oh, be careful—if you breathe, it breaks!

The Glass Menagerie

JIM. I'd better not take it. I'm pretty clumsy with things.

LAURA. Go on, I trust you with him! [*Places it in his palm.*] There now—you're holding him gently! Hold him over the light, he loves the light! You see how the light shines through him?

JIM. It sure does shine!

LAURA. I shouldn't be partial, but he is my favorite one.

JIM. What kind of a thing is this one supposed to be?

LAURA. Haven't you noticed the single horn on his forehead?

JIM. A unicorn, huh?

LAURA. Mmm-hmmm!

JIM. Unicorns, aren't they extinct in the modern world?

LAURA. I know!

JIM. Poor little fellow, he must feel sort of lonesome.

LAURA [*smiling*]. Well, if he does he doesn't complain about it. He stays on a shelf with some horses that don't have horns and all of them seem to get along nicely together.

JIM. How do you know?

LAURA [*lightly*]. I haven't heard any arguments among them!

JIM [*grinning*]. No arguments, huh? Well, that's a pretty good sign! Where shall I set him?

LAURA. Put him on the table. They all like a change of scenery once in a while!

JIM [*stretching*]. Well, well, well, well—Look how big my shadow is when I stretch!

LAURA. Oh, oh, yes—it stretches across the ceiling!

JIM [*crossing to door*]. I think it's stopped raining. [*Opens fire-escape door.*] Where does the music come from?

LAURA. From the Paradise Dance Hall across the alley.

JIM. How about cutting the rug a little, Miss Wingfield?

LAURA. Oh, I—

JIM. Or is your program filled up? Let me have a look at it. [*Grasps imaginary card.*] Why, every dance is taken! I'll just have to scratch some out. [WALTZ MUSIC: "LA GOLONDRINA."] Ahhh, a waltz! [*He executes some sweeping turns by himself then holds his arms toward* LAURA.]

LAURA [*breathlessly*]. I—can't dance!

JIM. There you go, that inferiority stuff!

LAURA. I've never danced in my life!

JIM. Come on, try!

LAURA. Oh, but I'd step on you!

JIM. I'm not made out of glass.

LAURA. How—how—how do we start?

JIM. Just leave it to me. You hold your arms out a little.

LAURA. Like this?

JIM. A little bit higher. Right. Now don't tighten up, that's the main thing about it—relax.

LAURA [*laughing breathlessly*]. It's hard not to.

JIM. Okay.

LAURA. I'm afraid you can't budge me.

JIM. What do you bet I can't? [*He swings her into motion.*]

LAURA. Goodness, yes, you can!

JIM. Let yourself go, now, Laura, just let yourself go.

LAURA. I'm—

JIM. Come on!

LAURA. Trying!

JIM. Not so stiff— Easy does it!

LAURA. I know but I'm—

JIM. Loosen th' backbone! There now, that's a lot better.

LAURA. Am I?

JIM. Lots, lots better! [*He moves her about the room in a clumsy waltz.*]

LAURA. Oh, my!

JIM. Ha-ha!

LAURA. Oh, my goodness!

JIM. Ha-ha-ha! [*They suddenly bump into the table.* JIM *stops.*] What did we hit on?

LAURA. Table.

JIM. Did something fall off it? I think—

LAURA. Yes.

JIM. I hope that it wasn't the little glass horse with the horn!

LAURA. Yes.

JIM. Aw, aw, aw. Is it broken?

LAURA. Now it is just like all the other horses.

JIM. It's lost its—

LAURA. Horn! It doesn't matter. Maybe it's a blessing in disguise.

JIM. You'll never forgive me. I bet that that was your favorite piece of glass.

LAURA. I don't have favorites much. It's no tragedy, Freckles. Glass breaks so easily. No matter how careful you are. The traffic jars the shelves and things fall off them.

JIM. Still I'm awfully sorry that I was the cause.

LAURA [*smiling*]. I'll just imagine he had an operation. The horn was removed to make him feel less—freakish! [*They both laugh.*] Now he will feel more at home with the other horses, the ones that don't have horns...

JIM. Ha-ha, that's very funny! [*Suddenly serious.*] I'm glad to see that you have a sense of humor. You know—you're—well —very different!

Surprisingly different from anyone else I know! [*His voice becomes soft and hesitant with a genuine feeling.*] Do you mind me telling you that? [LAURA *is abashed beyond speech.*] I mean it in a nice way... [LAURA *nods shyly, looking away.*] You make me feel sort of—I don't know how to put it! I'm usually pretty good at expressing things, but— This is something that I don't know how to say! [LAURA *touches her throat and clears it—turns the broken unicorn in her hands. Even softer.*]

Has anyone ever told you that you were pretty? [PAUSE: MUSIC. LAURA *looks up slowly, with wonder, and shakes her head.*] Well, you are! In a very different way from anyone else. And all the nicer because of the difference, too. [*His voice becomes low and husky.* LAURA *turns away, nearly faint with the novelty of her emotions.*]

I wish that you were my sister. I'd teach you to have some confidence in yourself. The different people are not like other people, but being different is nothing to be ashamed of. Because other people are not such wonderful people. They're one hundred times one thousand. You're one times one! They walk all over the earth. You just stay here. They're common as —weeds, but—you—well, you're—Blue Roses! [IMAGE ON SCREEN: BLUE ROSES. MUSIC CHANGES.]

LAURA. But blue is wrong for—roses...

JIM. It's right for you!—You're—pretty!

LAURA. In what respect am I pretty?

JIM. In all respects—believe me! Your eyes—your hair—are pretty! Your hands are pretty! [*He catches hold of her hand.*] You think I'm making this up because I'm invited to dinner and have to be nice. Oh, I could do that! I could put on an act for you, Laura, and say lots of things without being very sincere. But this time I am. I'm talking to you sincerely. I happened to notice you had this inferiority complex that keeps you from feeling comfortable with people. Somebody needs to build your confidence up and make you proud instead of shy and turning away and—blushing—

Somebody—ought to—

Ought to—*kiss* you, Laura! [*His hand slips slowly up her arm to her shoulder.* MUSIC SWELLS TUMULTUOUSLY. *He suddenly turns her about and kisses her on the lips. When he releases her,* LAURA *sinks* on the sofa with a bright, dazed look. JIM backs away and fishes in his pocket for a cigarette. LEGEND ON SCREEN: "SOUVENIR."] Stumble-john! [*He lights the cigarette, avoiding her look. There is a peal of girlish laughter from* AMANDA *in the kitchen.* LAURA *slowly raises and opens her hand. It still contains the little broken glass animal. She looks at it with a tender, bewildered expression.*] Stumble-john! I shouldn't have done that— That was way off the beam. You don't smoke, do you? [*She looks up, smiling, not hearing the question. He sits beside her a little gingerly. She looks at him speechlessly—waiting. He coughs decorously and moves a little further aside as he considers the situation and senses her feelings, dimly, with perturbation. Gently.*] Would you—care for a—mint? [*She doesn't seem to hear him but her look grows brighter even.*] Peppermint—Life-Saver? My pocket's a regular drug store—wherever I go . . . [*He pops a mint in his mouth. Then gulps and decides to make a clean breast of it. He speaks slowly and gingerly.*] Laura, you know, if I had a sister like you, I'd do the same thing as Tom. I'd bring out fellows and—introduce her to them. The right type of boys of a type to—appreciate her.

Only—well—he made a mistake about me.

Maybe I've got no call to be saying this. That may not have been the idea in having me over. But what if it was?

There's nothing wrong about that. The only trouble is that in my case—I'm not in a situation to—do the right thing.

I can't take down your number and say I'll phone.

I can't call up next week and—ask for a date.

I thought I had better explain the situation in case you—misunderstood it and—

hurt your feelings. . . . [*Pause. Slowly, very slowly,* LAURA'S *look changes, her eyes returning slowly from his to the ornament in her palm.* AMANDA *utters another gay laugh in the kitchen.*]

LAURA [*faintly*]. You — won't — call again?

JIM. No, Laura, I can't. [*He rises from the sofa.*] As I was just explaining, I've—got strings on me. Laura, I've—been going steady! I go out all of the time with a girl named Betty. She's a home-girl like you, and Catholic, and Irish, and in a great many ways we—get along fine. I met her last summer on a moonlight boat trip up the river to Alton, on the *Majestic*. Well—right away from the start it was—love! [LEGEND: LOVE! LAURA *sways slightly forward and grips the arm of the sofa. He fails to notice, now enrapt in his own comfortable being.*] Being in love has made a new man of me! [*Leaning stiffly forward, clutching the arm of the sofa,* LAURA *struggles visibly with her storm. But* JIM *is oblivious, she is a long way off.*] The power of love is really pretty tremendous!

Love is something that—changes the whole world, Laura! [*The storm abates a little and* LAURA *leans back. He notices her again.*]

It happened that Betty's aunt took sick, she got a wire and had to go to Centralia. So Tom—when he asked me to dinner—I naturally just accepted the invitation, not knowing that you—that he—that I— [*He stops awkwardly.*] Huh—I'm a stumble-john! [*He flops back on the sofa. The holy candles in the altar of* LAURA'S *face have been snuffed out. There is a look of almost infinite desolation.* JIM *glances at her uneasily.*]

I wish that you would—say something. [*She bites her lip which was trembling and then bravely smiles. She opens her* hand again on the broken glass ornament. Then she gently takes his hand and raises it level with her own. She carefully places the unicorn in the palm of his hand, then pushes his fingers closed upon it.] What are you—doing that for? You want me to have him?—Laura? [She nods.] What for?

LAURA. A—souvenir... [She rises unsteadily and crouches beside the victrola to wind it up. LEGEND ON SCREEN: "THINGS HAVE A WAY OF TURNING OUT SO BADLY!" OR IMAGE: "GENTLEMAN CALLER WAVING GOODBYE!—GAILY." At this moment AMANDA rushes brightly back in the front room. She bears a pitcher of fruit punch in an old-fashioned cut-glass pitcher and a plate of macaroons. The plate has a gold border and poppies painted on it.]

AMANDA. Well, well, well! Isn't the air delightful after the shower? I've made you children a little liquid refreshment. [Turns gaily to the gentleman caller.] Jim, do you know that song about lemonade?

"Lemonade, lemonade
Made in the shade and stirred with a spade—
Good enough for any old maid!"

JIM [uneasily]. Ha-ha! No—I never heard it.

AMANDA. Why, Laura! You look so serious!

JIM. We were having a serious conversation.

AMANDA. Good! Now you're better acquainted!

JIM [uncertainly]. Ha-ha! Yes.

AMANDA. You modern young people are much more serious-minded than my generation. I was so gay as a girl!

JIM. You haven't changed, Mrs. Wingfield.

AMANDA. Tonight I'm rejuvenated! The gaiety of the occasion, Mr. O'Connor! [She tosses her head with a peal of laughter. Spills lemonade.] Oooo! I'm baptizing myself!

JIM. Here—let me—

AMANDA [setting the pitcher down]. There now. I discovered we had some maraschino cherries. I dumped them in, juice and all!

JIM. You shouldn't have gone to that trouble, Mrs. Wingfield.

AMANDA. Trouble, trouble? Why, it was loads of fun!

Didn't you hear me cutting up in the kitchen? I bet your ears were burning! I told Tom how outdone with him I was for keeping you to himself so long a time! He should have brought you over much, much sooner! Well, now that you've found your way, I want you to be a very frequent caller! Not just occasional but all the time. Oh, we're going to have a lot of gay times together! I see them coming!

Mmm, just breathe that air! So fresh, and the moon's so pretty!

I'll skip back out—I know where my place is when young folks are having a—serious conversation!

JIM. Oh, don't go out, Mrs. Wingfield. The fact of the matter is I've got to be going.

AMANDA. Going, now? You're joking! Why, it's only the shank of the evening, Mr. O'Connor!

JIM. Well, you know how it is.

AMANDA. You mean you're a young workingman and have to keep workingmen's hours. We'll let you off early tonight. But only on the condition that next time you stay later.

What's the best night for you? Isn't Saturday night the best night for you workingmen?

JIM. I have a couple of time-clocks to punch, Mrs. Wingfield. One at morning, another one at night!

The Glass Menagerie

AMANDA. My, but you *are* ambitious! You work at night, too?

JIM. No, Ma'am, not work but—Betty! [*He crosses deliberately to pick up his hat. The band at the Paradise Dance Hall goes into a tender waltz.*]

AMANDA. Betty? Betty? Who's—Betty! [*There is an ominous cracking sound in the sky.*]

JIM. Oh, just a girl. The girl I go steady with! [*He smiles charmingly. The sky falls.* LEGEND: "THE SKY FALLS."]

AMANDA [*a long-drawn exhalation*]. Ohhhh . . . Is it a serious romance, Mr. O'Connor?

JIM. We're going to be married the second Sunday in June.

AMANDA. Ohhhh—how nice! Tom didn't mention that you were engaged to be married.

JIM. The cat's not out of the bag at the warehouse yet. You know how they are. They call you Romeo and stuff like that. [*He stops at the oval mirror to put on his hat. He carefully shapes the brim and the crown to give a discreetly dashing effect.*] It's been a wonderful evening, Mrs. Wingfield. I guess this is what they mean by Southern hospitality.

AMANDA. It really wasn't anything at all.

JIM. I hope it don't seem like I'm rushing off. But I promised Betty I'd pick her up at the Wabash depot, an' by the time I get my jalopy down there her train'll be in. Some women are pretty upset if you keep 'em waiting.

AMANDA. Yes, I know— The tyranny of women! [*Extends her hand.*] Good-bye, Mr. O'Connor. I wish you luck—and happiness—and success! All three of them, and so does Laura!—Don't you, Laura?

LAURA. Yes!

JIM [*taking her hand*]. Good-bye, Laura. I'm certainly going to treasure that souvenir. And don't you forget the good advice I gave you. [*Raises his voice to a cheery shout.*] So long, Shakespeare! Thanks again, ladies— Good night! [*He grins and ducks jauntily out. Still bravely grimacing,* AMANDA *closes the door on the gentleman caller. Then she turns back to the room with a puzzled expression. She and* LAURA *don't dare to face each other.* LAURA *crouches beside the victrola to wind it.*]

AMANDA [*faintly*]. Things have a way of turning out so badly. I don't believe that I would play the victrola. Well, well —well— Our gentleman caller was engaged to be married! Tom!

TOM [*from back*]. Yes, Mother?

AMANDA. Come in here a minute. I want to tell you something awfully funny.

TOM [*enters with macaroon and a glass of the lemonade*]. Has the gentleman caller gotten away already?

AMANDA. The gentleman caller has made an early departure. What a wonderful joke you played on us!

TOM. How do you mean?

AMANDA. You didn't mention that he was engaged to be married.

TOM. Jim? Engaged?

AMANDA. That's what he just informed us.

TOM. I'll be jiggered! I didn't know about that.

AMANDA. That seems very peculiar.

TOM. What's peculiar about it?

AMANDA. Didn't you call him your best friend down at the warehouse?

TOM. He is, but how did I know?

AMANDA. It seems extremely peculiar that you wouldn't know your best friend was going to be married!

TOM. The warehouse is where I work, not where I know things about people!

AMANDA. You don't know things anywhere! You live in a dream; you manu-

[583]

facture illusions! [*He crosses to door.*] Where are you going?

TOM. I'm going to the movies.

AMANDA. That's right, now that you've had us make such fools of ourselves. The effort, the preparations, all the expense! The new floor lamp, the rug, the clothes for Laura! All for what? To entertain some other girl's fiancé!

Go to the movies, go! Don't think about us, a mother deserted, an unmarried sister who's crippled and has no job! Don't let anything interfere with your selfish pleasure!

Just go, go, go—to the movies!

TOM. All right, I will! The more you shout about my selfishness to me the quicker I'll go, and I won't go to the movies!

AMANDA. Go, then! Then go to the moon—you selfish dreamer!

[TOM *smashes his glass on the floor. He plunges out on the fire-escape, slamming the door.* LAURA *screams—cut by door. Dance-hall music up.* TOM *goes to the rail and grips it desperately, lifting his face in the chill white moonlight penetrating the narrow abyss of the alley.* LEGEND ON SCREEN: "AND SO GOOD-BYE . . ." TOM'S *closing speech is timed with the interior pantomime. The interior scene is played as though viewed through soundproof glass.* AMANDA *appears to be making a comforting speech to* LAURA *who is huddled upon the sofa. Now that we cannot hear the mother's speech, her silliness is gone and she has dignity and tragic beauty.* LAURA'S *dark hair hides her face until at the end of the speech she lifts it to smile at her mother.* AMANDA'S *gestures are slow and graceful, almost dance-like, as she comforts the daughter. At the end of her speech she glances a moment at the father's picture—then withdraws through the portieres. At close of* TOM'S *speech,* LAURA *blows out the candles, ending the play.*]

TOM. I didn't go to the moon, I went much further—for time is the longest distance between two places—

Not long after that I was fired for writing a poem on the lid of a shoe-box.

I left Saint Louis. I descended the steps of this fire-escape for a last time and followed, from then on, in my father's footsteps, attempting to find in motion what was lost in space—

I traveled around a great deal. The cities swept about me like dead leaves, leaves that were brightly colored but torn away from the branches.

I would have stopped, but I was pursued by something.

It always came upon me unawares, taking me altogether by surprise. Perhaps it was a familiar bit of music. Perhaps it was only a piece of transparent glass—

Perhaps I am walking along a street at night, in some strange city, before I have found companions. I pass the lighted window of a shop where perfume is sold. The window is filled with pieces of colored glass, tiny transparent bottles in delicate colors, like bits of a shattered rainbow.

Then all at once my sister touches my shoulder. I turn around and look into her eyes . . .

Oh, Laura, Laura, I tried to leave you behind me, but I am more faithful than I intended to be!

I reach for a cigarette, I cross the street, I run into the movies or a bar, I buy a drink, I speak to the nearest stranger—anything that can blow your candles out! [LAURA *bends over the candles.*] —for nowadays the world is lit by lightning! Blow out your candles, Laura—and so good-bye. . . . [*She blows the candles out.*]

[THE SCENE DISSOLVES]

Christina's World   Andrew Wyeth
Collection, The Museum of Modern Art, New York

"My aim is to escape from the medium with which I work. To leave no residue of technical mannerisms to stand between my expression and the observer. To seek freedom through significant form and design rather than through the diversion of so-called free and accidental brush handling . . . Not to exhibit craft, but rather to submerge it, and make it rightfully the handmaiden of beauty, power and emotional content."—Andrew Wyeth

TIGER AT THE GATES

(LA GUERRE DE TROIE N'AURA PAS LIEU)

by JEAN GIRAUDOUX

Translated by
CHRISTOPHER FRY

CHARACTERS

ANDROMACHE
CASSANDRA
LAUNDRESS
HECTOR
PARIS
PRIAM
DEMOKOS
HECUBA
MATHEMATICIAN
SERVANT
POLYXENE
HELEN

MESSENGER
TROILUS
ABNEOS
BUSIRIS
AJAX
ULYSSES
A TOPMAN
OLPIDES
SERVANT
SENATOR
SAILOR

PEACE, IRIS, FIRST OLD MAN, SECOND OLD MAN, MESSENGERS, GUARDS, CROWD

THE PLAYWRIGHTS' COMPANY (in association with Henry M. Margolis) presented TIGER AT THE GATES in the Robert L. Joseph production on October 3, 1955, at the Plymouth Theatre, New York City, with the following cast:

HECTOR	MICHAEL REDGRAVE
Andromache, *wife to Hector*	Barbara Jefford
Cassandra, *sister to Hector*	Leueen MacGrath
Laundress	Judith Braun
Paris, *brother to Hector*	Leo Ciceri
First Old Man	Howard Caine
Second Old Man	Jack Bittner
Priam, *King of Troy, father to Hector*	Morris Carnovsky
Demekos, *a Poet, Leader of the Senate*	John Laurie
Hecuba, *mother to Hector*	Catherine Lacey
Mathematician	Milton Selzer
Lady in Waiting	Jacqueline Brookes
Polyxene, *young sister to Hector*	Ellen Christopher

Tiger at the Gates, by Jean Giraudoux, translated by Christopher Fry. Copyright 1955 by Christopher Fry. Reprinted by permission of Oxford University Press, Inc.

Tiger at the Gates

Helen	Diane Cilento
Messenger	Ernest Graves
Troilus, *young brother to Hector*	Peter Kerr
Abneos, *a Senator*	Howard Caine
Busiris, *a Lawyer*	Wyndham Goldie
Ajax, *a Greek Captain*	Felix Munso
Ulysses	Walter Fitzgerald
A Topman, *Officer on Paris' Ship*	Nehemiah Persoff
Olpides, *Sailor on Paris' Ship*	Jack Bittner
Senator	Tom McDermott
Sailor	Louis Criss

Directed by Harold Clurman
Designed by Loudon Sainthill
Incidental Music by Lennox Berkeley

ACT I

ANDROMACHE. There's not going to be a Trojan War, Cassandra!

CASSANDRA. I shall take that bet, Andromache.

ANDROMACHE. The Greeks are quite right to protest. We are going to receive their ambassador very civilly. We shall wrap up his little Helen and give her back to him.

CASSANDRA. We shall receive him atrociously. We shall refuse to give Helen back. And there *will* be a Trojan War.

ANDROMACHE. Yes, if Hector were not here. But he is here, Cassandra, he is home again. You can hear the trumpets. At this moment he is marching into the city, victorious. And Hector is certainly going to have something to say. When he left, three months ago, he promised me this war would be the last.

CASSANDRA. It is the last. The next is still ahead of him.

ANDROMACHE. Doesn't it ever tire you to see and prophesy only disasters?

CASSANDRA. I see nothing. I prophesy nothing. All I ever do is to take account of two great stupidities: the stupidity of men, and the wild stupidity of the elements.

ANDROMACHE. Why should there be a war? Paris and Helen don't care for each other any longer.

CASSANDRA. Do you think it will matter if Paris and Helen don't care for each other any longer? Has destiny ever been interested in whether things were still true or not?

ANDROMACHE. I don't know what destiny is.

CASSANDRA. I'll tell you. It is simply the relentless logic of each day we live.

ANDROMACHE. I don't understand abstractions.

CASSANDRA. Never mind. We can try a metaphor. Imagine a tiger. You can understand that? It's a nice, easy metaphor. A sleeping tiger.

ANDROMACHE. Let it sleep.

CASSANDRA. There's nothing I should like better. But certain cocksure statements have been prodding him out of his sleep. For some considerable time Troy has been full of them.

ANDROMACHE. Full of what?

CASSANDRA. Of cocksure statements, a confident belief that the world, and the supervision of the world, is the province of mankind in general, and Trojan men and women in particular.

ANDROMACHE. I don't follow you.

CASSANDRA. Hector at this very moment is marching into Troy?

ANDROMACHE. Yes. Hector at this very moment has come home to his wife.

CASSANDRA. And Hector's wife is going to have a child?

ANDROMACHE. Yes; I am going to have a child.

CASSANDRA. Don't you call these statements a little overconfident?

ANDROMACHE. Don't frighten me, Cassandra.

[*A* YOUNG LAUNDRESS *goes past with an armful of linen*]

LAUNDRESS. What a beautiful day, miss!

CASSANDRA. Does it seem so, indeed?

LAUNDRESS. It's the most beautiful Spring day Troy has seen this year.

[*Exit*]

CASSANDRA. Even the laundrymaid is confident!

ANDROMACHE. And so she should be, Cassandra. How can you talk of a war on a day like this? Happiness is falling on us out of the sky.

CASSANDRA. Like a blanket of snow.

ANDROMACHE. And beauty, as well. Look at the sunshine. It is finding more mother-of-pearl on the rooftops of Troy than was ever dragged up from the bed of the sea. And do you hear the sound coming up from the fishermen's houses, and the movement of the trees, like the murmuring of sea shells? If ever there were a chance to see men finding a way to live in peace, it is today. To live in peace, in humility. And to be immortal.

CASSANDRA. Yes, I am sure those cripples who have been carried out to lie in their doorways feel how immortal they are.

ANDROMACHE. And to be good. Do you see that horseman, in the advance-guard, leaning from his saddle to stroke a cat on the battlements? Perhaps this is also going to be the first day of true fellowship between men and the animals.

CASSANDRA. You talk too much. Destiny, the tiger, is getting restive, Andromache!

ANDROMACHE. Restive, maybe, in young girls looking for husbands; but not otherwise.

CASSANDRA. You are wrong. Hector has come home in triumph to the wife he adores. The tiger begins to rouse, and opens one eye. The incurables lie out on their benches in the sun and feel immortal. The tiger stretches himself. Today is the chance for peace to enthrone herself over all the world. The tiger licks his lips. And Andromache is going to have a son! And the horsemen have started leaning from their saddles to stroke tom-cats on the battlements! The tiger starts to prowl.

ANDROMACHE. Be quiet!

CASSANDRA. He climbs noiselessly up the palace steps. He pushes open the doors with his snout. And here he is, here he is!

[HECTOR'S *voice:* Andromache!]

ANDROMACHE. You are lying! It is Hector!

CASSANDRA. Whoever said it was not?

[*Enter* HECTOR]

ANDROMACHE. Hector!

HECTOR. Andromache!

[*They embrace*]

And good morning to you, too, Cas-

sandra. Ask Paris to come to me, if you will. As soon as he can.
[CASSANDRA *lingers*]
Have you something to tell me?
ANDROMACHE. Don't listen to her! Some catastrophe or other!
HECTOR. Tell me.
CASSANDRA. Your wife is going to have a child.
[*Exit* CASSANDRA]
[HECTOR *takes* ANDROMACHE *in his arms, leads her to a stone bench, and sits beside her. A short pause*]
HECTOR. Will it be a son or a daughter?
ANDROMACHE. Which did you want to create when you called it into life?
HECTOR. A thousand boys. A thousand girls.
ANDROMACHE. Why? Because it would give you a thousand women to hold in your arms? You are going to be disappointed. It will be a son, one single son.
HECTOR. That may very well be. Usually more boys are born than girls at the end of a war.
ANDROMACHE. And before a war? Which, before a war?
HECTOR. Forget wars, Andromache, even this war. It's over. It lost you a father and a brother, but it gave you back a husband.
ANDROMACHE. It has been too kind. It may think better of it presently.
HECTOR. Don't worry. We won't give it the chance. Directly I leave you I shall go into the square, and formally close the Gates of War. They will never open again.
ANDROMACHE. Close them, then. But they will open again.
HECTOR. You can even tell me the day, perhaps?
ANDROMACHE. I can even tell you the day: the day when the cornfields are heavy and golden, when the vines are stooping, ready for harvest, and every house is sheltering a contented couple.
HECTOR. And peace, no doubt, at its very height?
ANDROMACHE. Yes. And my son is strong and glowing with life.
[HECTOR *embraces her*]
HECTOR. Perhaps your son will be a coward. That's one possible safeguard.
ANDROMACHE. He won't be a coward. But perhaps I shall have cut off the index finger of his right hand.
HECTOR. If every mother cut off her son's right-hand index finger, the armies of the world would fight without index fingers. And if they cut off their sons' right legs, the armies would be one-legged. And if they put out their eyes, the armies would be blind, but there would still be armies: blind armies groping to find the fatal place in the enemy's groin, or to get at his throat.
ANDROMACHE. I would rather kill him.
HECTOR. There's a truly maternal solution to war!
ANDROMACHE. Don't laugh. I can still kill him before he is born.
HECTOR. Don't you want to see him at all, not even for a moment? After that, you would think again. Do you mean never to see your son?
ANDROMACHE. It is your son that interests me. Hector, it's because he is yours, because he is you, that I'm so afraid. You don't know how like you he is. Even in this no-man's-land where he is waiting, he already has everything, all those qualities you brought to this life we live together. He has your tenderness, your silences. If you love war, he will love it. Do you love war?
HECTOR. Why ask such a question?

ANDROMACHE. Admit, sometimes you love it.

HECTOR. If a man can love what takes away hope, and happiness, and all those nearest to his heart.

ANDROMACHE. And you know it can be so. Men do love it.

HECTOR. If they let themselves be fooled by that little burst of divinity the gods give them at the moment of attack.

ANDROMACHE. Ah, there, you see! At the moment of attack you feel like a god.

HECTOR. More often not as much as a man. But sometimes, on certain mornings, you get up from the ground feeling lighter, astonished, altered. Your whole body, and the armour on your back, have a different weight, they seem to be made of a different metal. You are invulnerable. A tenderness comes over you, submerging you, a kind of tenderness of battle: you are tender because you are pitiless; what, in fact, the tenderness of the gods must be. You advance towards the enemy slowly, almost absent-mindedly, but lovingly. And you try not to crush a beetle crossing your path. You brush off the mosquito without hurting it. You never at any time had more respect for the life you meet on your way.

ANDROMACHE. And then the enemy comes?

HECTOR. Then the enemy comes, frothing at the mouth. You pity him; you can see him there, behind the swollen veins and the whites of his eyes, the helpless, willing little man of business, the well-meaning husband and son-in-law who likes to grow his own vegetables. You feel a sort of love for him. You love the wart on his cheek and the cast in his eye. You love him. But he comes on; he is insistent. Then you kill him.

ANDROMACHE. And you bend over the wretched corpse as though you are a god; but you are not a god; you can't give back his life again.

HECTOR. You don't wait to bend over him. There are too many more waiting for you, frothing at the mouth and howling hate. Too many more unassuming, law-abiding family men.

ANDROMACHE. Then you kill them.

HECTOR. You kill them. Such is war.

ANDROMACHE. All of them: you kill them all?

HECTOR. This time we killed them all. Quite deliberately. They belonged to an incorrigibly warlike race, the reason why wars go on and multiply in Asia. Only one of them escaped.

ANDROMACHE. In a thousand years' time, there the warlike race will be again, descended from that one man. His escape made all that slaughter futile after all. My son is going to love war, just as you do.

HECTOR. I think, now that I've lost my love for it, I hate it.

ANDROMACHE. How do you come to hate what you once worshipped?

HECTOR. You know what it's like when you find out a friend is a liar? Whatever he says, after that, sounds false, however true it may be. And strangely enough, war used to promise me many kinds of virtue: goodness, generosity, and a contempt for anything base and mean. I felt I owed it all my strength and zest for life, even my private happiness, you, Andromache. And until this last campaign there was no enemy I haven't loved.

ANDROMACHE. Very soon you will say you only kill what you love.

HECTOR. It's hard to explain how all the sounds of war combined to make me think it was something noble. The galloping of horse in the night, the clatter of bowls and dishes where the cooks were moving in and out of the firelight, the brush of silk and metal against your tent as the night-patrol went past, and the cry of the falcon wheeling high above the sleeping army and their unsleeping captain: it all seemed then so right, marvellously right.

Andromache. But not this time: this time war had no music for you?

Hector. Why was that? Because I am older? Or was it just the kind of weariness with your job which, for instance, a carpenter will be suddenly seized by, with a table half finished, as I was seized one morning, standing over an adversary of my own age, about to put an end to him? Up to that time, a man I was going to kill had always seemed my direct opposite. This time I was kneeling on a mirror, the death I was going to give was a kind of suicide. I don't know what the carpenter does at such a time, whether he throws away his hammer and plane, or goes on with it. I went on with it. But after that nothing remained of the perfect trumpet note of war. The spear as it slid against my shield rang suddenly false; so did the shock of the killed against the ground, and, some hours later, the palace crumbling into ruin. And, moreover, war knew that I understood, and gave up any pretence of shame. The cries of the dying sounded false. I had come to that.

Andromache. But it all still sounded right for the rest of them.

Hector. The rest of them heard it as I did. The army I brought back hates war.

Andromache. An army with poor hearing.

Hector. No. When we first came in sight of Troy, an hour ago, you can't imagine how everything in that moment sounded true for them. There wasn't a regiment which didn't halt, racked to the heart by this sense of returning music. So much so, we were afraid to march boldly in through the gates: we broke up into groups outside the walls. It feels like the only job worthy of a good army, laying peaceful siege to the open cities of your own country.

Andromache. You haven't understood, this is where things are falser than anywhere. War is here, in Troy, Hector. That is what welcomed you at the gates.

Hector. What do you mean?

Andromache. You haven't heard that Paris has carried off Helen?

Hector. They told me so. What else?

Andromache. Did you know that the Greeks are demanding her back? And their ambassador arrives today? And if we don't give her up, it means war.

Hector. Why shouldn't we give her up? I shall give her back to them myself.

Andromache. Paris will never agree to it.

Hector. Paris will agree, and very soon. Cassandra is bringing him to me.

Andromache. But Paris can't agree. His honour, as you all call it, won't let him. Nor his love either, he may tell you.

Hector. Well, we shall see. Run and ask Priam if he will let me speak to him at once. And set your heart at rest. All the Trojans who have been fighting, or who can fight, are against a war.

Andromache. There are still the others, remember.

[*As* Andromache *goes* . . .
Cassandra *enters with* Paris]

Cassandra. Here is Paris.

Hector. Congratulations, Paris. I hear you have been very well occupied while we were away.

Paris. Not badly. Thank you.

HECTOR. What is this story they tell me about Helen?

PARIS. Helen is a very charming person. Isn't she, Cassandra?

CASSANDRA. Fairly charming.

PARIS. Why these reservations today? It was only yesterday you said you thought she was extremely pretty.

CASSANDRA. She is extremely pretty, and fairly charming.

PARIS. Hasn't she the ways of a young, gentle gazelle?

CASSANDRA. No.

PARIS. But you were the one who first said she was like a gazelle.

CASSANDRA. I made a mistake. Since then I have seen a gazelle again.

HECTOR. To hell with gazelles! Doesn't she look any more like a woman than that?

PARIS. She isn't the type of woman we know here, obviously.

CASSANDRA. What is the type of woman we know here?

PARIS. Your type, my dear sister. The fearfully unremote sort of woman.

CASSANDRA. When your Greek makes love she is a long way off, I suppose?

PARIS. You know perfectly well what I'm trying to say. I have had enough of Asiatic women. They hold you in their arms as though they were glued there, their kisses are like battering-rams, their words chew right into you. The more they undress the more elaborate they seem, until when they're naked they are more overdressed than ever. And they paint their faces to look as though they mean to imprint themselves on you. And they do imprint themselves on you. In short, you are definitely *with* them. But Helen is far away from me, even held in my arms.

HECTOR. Very interesting! But, one wonders, is it really worth a war, to allow Paris to make love at a distance?

CASSANDRA. With distance. He loves women to be distant but right under his nose.

PARIS. To have Helen with you not with you is worth anything in the world.

HECTOR. How did you fetch her away? Willingly, or did you compel her?

PARIS. Listen, Hector! You know women as well as I do. They are only willing when you compel them, but after that they're as enthusiastic as you are.

HECTOR. On horseback, in the usual style of seducers, leaving a heap of horse manure under the windows.

PARIS. Is this a court of enquiry?

HECTOR. Yes, it is. Try for once to answer precisely and accurately. Have you insulted her husband's house, or the Greek earth?

PARIS. The Greek water, a little. She was bathing.

CASSANDRA. She is born of the foam, is she? This cold one is born of the foam, like Venus.

HECTOR. You haven't disfigured the walls of the palace with offensive drawings, as you usually do? You didn't shout to the echoes any word which they would at once repeat to the betrayed husband?

PARIS. No. Menelaus was naked on the river bank, busy removing a crab from his big toe. He watched my boat sail past as if the wind were carrying his clothes away.

HECTOR. Looking furious?

PARIS. The face of a king being nipped by a crab isn't likely to look beatific.

HECTOR. No onlookers?

PARIS. My crew.

HECTOR. Perfect!

PARIS. Why perfect? What are you getting at?

HECTOR. I say perfect, because you have done nothing irrevocable. In other words: she was undressed, so neither her clothes nor her belongings have been insulted. Nothing except her body, which is negligible. I've enough acquaintance with the Greeks to know they will concoct a divine adventure out of it, to their own glory, the story of this little Greek queen who goes down into the sea, and quietly comes up again a few months later, with a look on her face of perfect innocence.

CASSANDRA. We can be quite sure of the look on her face.

PARIS. You think that I'm going to take Helen back to Menelaus?

HECTOR. We don't ask so much of you, or of her. The Greek ambassador will take care of it. He will put her back in the sea himself, like a gardener planting waterlilies, at a particular chosen spot. You will give her into his hands this evening.

PARIS. I don't know whether you are allowing yourself to notice how monstrous you are being, to suppose that a man who has the prospect of a night with Helen will agree to giving it up.

CASSANDRA. You still have an afternoon with Helen. Surely that's more Greek?

HECTOR. Don't be obstinate. We know you of old. This isn't the first separation you've accepted.

PARIS. My dear Hector, that's true enough. Up to now I have always accepted separations fairly cheerfully. Parting from a woman, however well you love her, induces a most pleasant state of mind, which I know how to value as well as anybody. You come out of her arms and take your first lonely walk through the town, and, the first little dressmaker you meet, you notice with a shock of surprise how fresh and unconcerned she looks, after that last sight you have had of the dear face you parted from, her nose red with weeping. Because you have come away from such broken, despairing farewells, the laundrygirls and the fruitsellers laughing their heads off, more than make up for whatever you've lost in the parting. By losing one person your life has become entirely re-peopled. All the women in the world have been created for you afresh; they are all your own, in the liberty, honour, and peace of your conscience. Yes, you're quite right: when a love-affair is broken off it reaches its highest point of exaltation. Which is why I shall never be parted from Helen, because with Helen I feel as though I had broken with every other woman in the world, and that gives me the sensation of being free a thousand times over instead of once.

HECTOR. Because she doesn't love you. Everything you say proves it.

PARIS. If you like. But, if I had to choose one out of all the possible ways of passion, I would choose the way Helen doesn't love me.

HECTOR. I'm extremely sorry. But you will give her up.

PARIS. You are not the master here.

HECTOR. I am your elder brother, and the future master.

PARIS. Then order me about in the future. For the present, I obey my father.

HECTOR. That's all I want! You're willing that we should put this to Priam and accept his judgment?

PARIS. Perfectly willing.

HECTOR. On your solemn word? We both swear to accept that?

CASSANDRA. Mind what you're doing, Hector! Priam is mad for Helen. He would rather give up his daughters.

HECTOR. What nonsense is this?

PARIS. For once she is telling the truth about the present instead of the future.

CASSANDRA. And all our brothers, and all our uncles, and all our great-great uncles! Helen has a guard-of-honour which includes every old man in the city. Look there. It is time for her walk. Do you see, there's a fringe of white beards draped all along the battlements?

HECTOR. A beautiful sight. The beards are white, and the faces red.

CASSANDRA. Yes; it's the blood pressure. They should be waiting at the Scamander Gate, to welcome the victorious troops. But no; they are all at the Sceean Gate, waiting for Helen.

HECTOR. Look at them, all leaning forward as one man, like storks when they see a rat going by.

CASSANDRA. The rat is Helen.

PARIS. Is it?

CASSANDRA. There she is: on the second terrace, standing to adjust her sandal, and giving careful thought to the crossing of her legs.

HECTOR. Incredible. All the old men of Troy are there looking down at her.

CASSANDRA. Not all. There are certain crafty ones looking up at her.

[*Cries offstage:* Long live Beauty!]

HECTOR. What are they shouting?

PARIS. They're shouting "Long live Beauty!"

CASSANDRA. I quite agree with them, if they mean that they themselves should die as quickly as possible.

[*Cries offstage:* Long live Venus!]

HECTOR. And what now?

CASSANDRA. "Long live Venus." They are shouting only words without R's in them because of their lack of teeth. Long live Beauty, long live Venus, long live Helen. At least they imagine they're shouting, though, as you can hear, all they are doing is simply increasing a mumble to its highest power.

HECTOR. What has Venus to do with it?

CASSANDRA. They imagine it was Venus who gave us Helen. To show her gratitude to Paris for awarding her the apple on first sight.

HECTOR. That was another brilliant stroke of yours.

PARIS. Stop playing the elder brother!

[*Enter* TWO OLD MEN]

1ST OLD MAN. Down there we see her better.

2ND OLD MAN. We had a very good view.

1ST OLD MAN. But she can hear us better from up here. Come on. One, two, three!

BOTH. Long live Helen!

2ND OLD MAN. It's a little tiring, at our age, to have to climb up and down these impossible steps all the time, according to whether we want to look at her or to cheer her.

1ST OLD MAN. Would you like us to alternate? One day we will cheer her? Another day we will look at her?

2ND OLD MAN. You are mad! One day without looking at Helen, indeed! Goodness me, think what we've seen of her today! One, two, three!

BOTH. Long live Helen!

1ST OLD MAN. And now down we go again!

[*They run off*]

CASSANDRA. You see what they're like, Hector. I don't know how their poor lungs are going to stand it.

HECTOR. But our father can't be like this.

PARIS. Hector, before we have this out in front of my father, I suppose you wouldn't like to take just one look at Helen.

HECTOR. I don't care a fig about Helen. Ah: greetings to you, father!

[PRIAM *enters, with* HECUBA, ANDROMACHE, *the poet* DEMOKOS *and another old man.* HECUBA *leads by the hand little* POLYXENE]

PRIAM. What was it you said?

HECTOR. I said that we should make haste to shut the Gates of War, father, see them bolted and padlocked, so that not even a gnat can get between them.

PRIAM. I thought what you said was somewhat shorter.

DEMOKOS. He said he didn't care a fig about Helen.

PRIAM. Look over here.

[HECTOR *obeys*]

Do you see her?

HECUBA. Indeed he sees her. Who, I ask myself, doesn't see her, or hasn't seen her? She takes the road which goes the whole way round the city.

DEMOKOS. It is Beauty's perfect circle.

PRIAM. Do you see her?

HECTOR. Yes, I see her. What of it?

DEMOKOS. Priam is asking you what you see.

HECTOR. I see a young woman adjusting her sandal.

CASSANDRA. She takes some time to adjust her sandal.

PARIS. I carried her off naked; she left her clothes in Greece. Those are your sandals, Cassandra. They're a bit big for her.

CASSANDRA. Anything's too big for these little women.

HECTOR. I see two charming buttocks.

HECUBA. He sees what all of you see.

PRIAM. I'm sorry for you!

HECTOR. Why?

PRIAM. I had no idea that the young men of Troy had come to this.

HECTOR. What have they come to?

PRIAM. To being impervious to beauty.

DEMOKOS. And, consequently, ignorant of love. And, consequently, unrealistic. To us who are poets reality is love or nothing.

HECTOR. But the old men, you think, can appreciate love and beauty?

HECUBA. But of course. If you make love, or if you are beautiful, you don't need to understand these things.

HECTOR. You come across beauty, father, at every street corner. I'm not alluding to Helen, though at the moment she condescends to walk our streets.

PRIAM. You are being unfair, Hector. Surely there have been occasions in your life when a woman has seemed to be more than merely herself, as though a radiance of thoughts and feelings glowed from her flesh, taking a special brilliance from it.

DEMOKOS. As a ruby represents blood.

HECTOR. Not to those who have seen blood. I have just come back from a close acquaintance with it.

DEMOKOS. A symbol, you understand. Soldier though you are, you have surely heard of symbolism! Surely you have come across women who as soon as you saw them seemed to you to personify intelligence, harmony, gentleness, whatever it might be?

HECTOR. It has happened.

DEMOKOS. And what did you do?

HECTOR. I went closer, and that was the end of it. And what does this we see here personify?

DEMOKOS. We have told you before: Beauty.

HECUBA. Then send her quickly back to the Greeks if you want her to personify that for long. Blonde beauty doesn't usually last for ever.

DEMOKOS. It's impossible to talk to these women!

HECUBA. Then don't talk *about* women. You're not showing much gallantry, I might say; nor patriotism either. All other races choose one of their own women as their symbol, even if they have flat noses and lips like two fishes on a plate. It's only you who have to go outside your own country to find it.

HECTOR. Listen, father: we are just back from a war, and we have come home exhausted. We have made quite certain of peace on our continent for ever. From now on we mean to live in happiness, and we mean our wives to be able to love us without anxiety, and to bear our children.

DEMOKOS. Wise principles, but war has never prevented wives from having children.

HECTOR. So explain to me why we have come back to find the city transformed, all because of Helen? Explain to me what you think she has given to us, worth a quarrel with the Greeks?

MATHEMATICIAN. Anybody will tell you! I can tell you myself!

HECUBA. Listen to the mathematician!

MATHEMATICIAN. Yes, listen to the mathematician! And don't think that mathematicians have no concern with women! We're the land-surveyors of your personal landscape. I can't tell you how we mathematicians suffer to see any slight disproportion of the flesh, on the chin or the thigh, any infringement of your geometrical desirability. Well now, until this day mathematicians have never been satisfied with the countryside surrounding Troy. The line linking the plain with the hills seemed to us too slack: the line from the hills to the mountains too taut. Now, since Helen came, the country has taken on meaning and vigour. And, what is particularly evident to true mathematicians, space and volume have now found in Helen a common denominator. We can abolish all the instruments we have invented to reduce the universe to a manageable equation. There are no more feet and inches, ounces, pounds, milligrams or leagues. There is only the weight of Helen's footfall, the length of Helen's arm, the range of Helen's look or voice; and the movement of the air as she goes past is the measure of the winds. That is what the mathematicians will tell you.

HECUBA. The old fool is crying.

PRIAM. My dear son, you have only to look at this crowd, and you will understand what Helen is. She is a kind of absolution. To each one of these old men, whom you can see now like a frieze of grotesque heads all round the city walls: to the old swindler, the old thief, the old pandar, to all the old failures, she has shown they always had a secret longing to rediscover the beauty they had lost. If throughout their lives beauty had always been as close at hand as Helen is today, they would never have tricked their friends, or sold their daughters, or drunk away their inheritance. Helen is like a pardon to them: a new beginning for them, their whole future.

HECTOR. These old men's ancient futures are no concern of mine.

DEMOKOS. Hector, as a poet I approach things by the way of poetry. Imagine if beauty, never, at any time, touched our language. Imagine there being no such word as "delight."

HECTOR. We should get on well enough without it. I get on without it already. "Delight" is a word I use only when I'm absolutely driven to it.

DEMOKOS. Well, then the word "desirable": you could get on without that as well, I suppose?

HECTOR. If it could be bought only at the cost of war, yes, I could get on without the word "desirable."

DEMOKOS. One of the most beautiful words there are was found only at the cost of war: the word "courage."

HECTOR. It has been well paid for.

HECUBA. And the word "cowardice" was inevitably found at the same time.

PRIAM. My son, why do you so deliberately not understand us?

HECTOR. I understand you very well. With the help of a quibble, by pretending to persuade us to fight for beauty you want to get us to fight for a woman.

PRIAM. Would you never go to war for any woman?

HECTOR. Certainly not!

HECUBA. And he would be unchivalrously right.

CASSANDRA. If there were only one woman, then perhaps he would go to war for her. But we have exceeded that number, quite extravagantly.

DEMOKOS. Wouldn't you go to war to rescue Andromache?

HECTOR. Andromache and I have already made our secret plans for escaping from any prison in the world, and finding our way back to each other again.

DEMOKOS. Even if there's no hope of it on earth?

HECTOR. Even then.

HECUBA. You have done well to unmask them, Hector. They want you to make war for the sake of a woman; it's the kind of lovemaking men believe in who are past making love in any other way.

DEMOKOS. And doesn't that make you all the more valuable?

HECUBA. Ah yes! You may say so!

DEMOKOS. Excuse me, but I can't agree with you. The sex which gave me my mother will always have my respect, even its least worthy representatives.

HECUBA. We know that. You have, as we know, shown your respect for instance to—

[*The* SERVANTS *who have stood by to hear the argument burst out laughing*]

PRIAM. Hecuba! Daughters! What can this mean? Why on earth are you all so up in arms? The Council are considering giving the city a public holiday in honour of one of your sex.

ANDROMACHE. I know of only one humiliation for a woman: injustice.

DEMOKOS. It's painful to say so, but there's no one knows less what a woman is than a woman.

[*The* YOUNG SERVANT, *passing:* Oh, dear! dear!]

HECUBA. We know perfectly well. I will tell you myself what a woman is.

DEMOKOS. Don't let them talk, Priam. You never know what they might say.

HECUBA. They might tell the truth.

PRIAM. I have only to think of one of you, my dears, to know what a woman is.

DEMOKOS. In the first place, she is the source of our energy. You know that, Hector. The soldiers who haven't a portrait of a woman in their kit aren't worth anything.

CASSANDRA. The source of your pride, yes, I agree.

HECUBA. Of your vices.

ANDROMACHE. She is a poor bundle of uncertainty, a poor mass of fears, who detests whatever is difficult, and adores whatever is vulgar and easy.

HECTOR. Dear Andromache!

HECUBA. It's very simple. I have been a woman for fifty years, and I've never yet been able to discover precisely what it is I am.

DEMOKOS. Secondly, whether she likes it or not, she's the only reward for courage. Ask any soldier. To kill a man is to merit a woman.

ANDROMACHE. She loves cowards and libertines. If Hector were a coward or a libertine I shouldn't love him less; I might even love him more.

PRIAM. Don't go too far, Andromache. You will prove the very opposite of what you want to prove.

POLYXENE. She is greedy. She tells lies.

DEMOKOS. So we're to say nothing of her fidelity, her purity: we are not to mention them?

THE SERVANT. Oh, dear! dear!

DEMOKOS. What did you say?

THE SERVANT. I said "Oh, dear! dear!" I say what I think.

POLYXENE. She breaks her toys. She puts them headfirst into boiling water.

HECUBA. The older we women grow, the more clearly we see what men really are: hypocrites, boasters, he-goats. The older men grow, the more they doll us up with every perfection. There isn't a slut you've hugged behind a wall who isn't transformed in your memories into a loved and lovely creature.

PRIAM. Have you ever deceived me, Hecuba?

HECUBA. Only with yourself; scores of times with yourself.

DEMOKOS. Has Andromache ever deceived Hector?

HECUBA. You can leave Andromache out of this. There is nothing she could recognize in the sad histories of erring women.

ANDROMACHE. But I know if Hector were not my husband, if he were a club-footed, bandy-legged fisherman I should run after him and find him in his hovel, and lie down on the pile of oyster-shells and seaweed, and give him a son in adultery.

POLYXENE. She pretends to go to sleep at night, but she's really playing games in her head with her eyes shut.

HECUBA [to POLYXENE]. You may well say so! It's dreadful! You know how I scold you for it!

THE SERVANT. The only thing worse than a woman is a man; there are no words to describe him.

DEMOKOS. Then more's the pity if a woman deceives us! More's the pity if she scorns her own value and dignity! If she can't be true to a pattern of perfection which would save her from the ravages of conscience, we have to do it for her.

THE SERVANT. Oh, the kind guardian angel!

PARIS. One thing they've forgotten to say of themselves: they are never jealous.

PRIAM. My dear daughters, the fact that you're so furious is a proof in itself that we are right. I can't conceive of any greater unselfishness than the way you now fight for peace, when peace will give you idle, feeble, chicken-hearted husbands, and war would turn them into men.

DEMOKOS. Into heroes.

HECUBA. Yes, we know the jargon. In war-time a man is called a hero. It doesn't make him any braver, and he runs for his life. But at least it's a hero who is running away.

ANDROMACHE. Father, I must beg you to listen. If you have such a fondness for women, listen to what they have to say to you, for I can promise I speak for all the women in the world. Let us keep our husbands as they are. The gods took care to see they were surrounded with enough obstacles and dangers to keep them brave and vigorous. Quite enough if they had nothing to cope with except floods and storms! Or only wild animals! The small game, foxes and hares and pheasants, which a woman can scarcely distinguish from the heather they hide in, prove a man's quickness of eye far better than this target you propose: the enemy's heart hiding in flesh and metal. Whenever I have seen a man kill a stag or an eagle, I have offered up thanks to them. I know they died for Hector. Why should you want me to owe Hector to the deaths of other men?

Priam. I don't want it, my dear child. But why do you think you are here now, all looking so beautiful, and valiantly demanding peace? Why: because your husbands and your fathers, and their fathers, and theirs, were fighting men. If they had been too lazy and self-indulgent to spring to arms, if they hadn't known how this dull and stupid business we call life suddenly leaps into flame and justifies itself through the scorn men have for it, you would find *you* were the cowards now, and you would be clamouring for war. A man has only one way of being immortal on this earth: he has to forget he is mortal.

Andromache. Why, exactly so, father: you're only too right. The brave men die in war. It takes great luck or judgment not to be killed. Once at least the head has to bow and the knee has to bend to danger. The soldiers who march back under the triumphal arches are death's deserters. How can a country increase in strength and honour by sending them both to their graves?

Priam. Daughter, the first sign of cowardice in a people is their first moment of decay.

Andromache. But which is the worse cowardice? To appear cowardly to others, and make sure of peace? Or to be cowardly in your own eyes, and let loose a war?

Demokos. Cowardice is not to prefer death on every hand rather than the death of one's native land.

Hecuba. I was expecting poetry at this point. It never lets us down.

Andromache. Everyone always dies for his country. If you have lived in it, well and wisely and actively, you die for it too.

Hecuba. It would be better if only the old men fought the wars. Every country is the country of youth. When its youth dies it dies with them.

Demokos. All this nonsense about youth! In thirty years' time youth is nothing but these old men you talk about.

Cassandra. Wrong.

Hecuba. Wrong! When a grown man reaches forty we change him for an old one. He has completely disappeared. There's only the most superficial resemblance between the two of them. Nothing is handed on from one to the other.

Demokos. I still take a serious concern in my fame as a poet.

Hecuba. Yes, that's quite true. And your rheumatism.

[*Another outburst of laughter from the* Servants]

Hector. And you can listen to all this without saying a word, Paris? Can you still not decide to give up an adventure to save us from years of unhappiness and massacre?

Paris. What do you want me to say? My case is an international problem.

Hector. Are you really in love with Helen, Paris?

Cassandra. They've become now a kind of symbol of love's devotion. They don't still have to love each other.

Paris. I worship Helen.

CASSANDRA [*at the rampart*]. Here she is.

HECTOR. If I persuade her to set sail, will you agree?

PARIS. Yes, I'll agree.

HECTOR. Father, if Helen is willing to go back to Greece, will you hold her here by force?

PRIAM. Why discuss the impossible?

HECTOR. Do you call it impossible? If women are a tenth of what you say they are, Helen will go of her own free will.

PARIS. Father, now *I'm* going to ask you to let him do what he wants. You have seen what it's like. As soon as the question of Helen cropped up, this whole tribe royal turned itself into a family conclave of all the poor girl's sisters-in-law, mother- and father-in-law, brother-in-law, worthy of the best middle-class tradition. I doubt if there's anything more humiliating than to be cast for the part of the seducer son in a large family. I've had quite enough of their insinuations. I accept Hector's challenge.

DEMOKOS. Helen's not only yours, Paris. She belongs to the city. She belongs to our country.

MATHEMATICIAN. She belongs to the landscape.

HECUBA. You be quiet, mathematician.

CASSANDRA. Here's Helen; here she is.

HECTOR. Father, I must ask you to let me handle this. Listen; they are calling us to go to the ceremony, to close the Gates of War. Leave this to me. I'll join you soon.

PRIAM. Do you really agree to this, Paris?

PARIS. I'm eager for it.

PRIAM. Very well, then; let it be so. Come along, the rest of you; we will see that the Gates of War are made ready.

CASSANDRA. Those poor gates. They need more oil to shut them than to open them.

[PARIS *and the rest withdraw.* DEMOKOS *stays*]

HECTOR. What are you waiting for?

DEMOKOS. The visitation of my genius.

HECTOR. Say that again?

DEMOKOS. Every time Helen walks my way I am thrown into a transport of inspiration. I shake all over, break into sweat, and improvise. Good heavens, here it is! [*He declaims:*]

Beautiful Helen, Helen of Sparta,
  Singular as the evening star,
The gods forbid that we should part a
  Pair as fair as you and Paris are.

HECTOR. Your line-endings give me a headache.

DEMOKOS. It's an invention of mine. I can obtain effects even more surprising. Listen: [*declaims*]

Face the great Hector with no qualm,
  Troy's glory though he be, and the world's terror:
He is the storm, and you the after-calm,
  Yours is the right, and his the boist'rous error.

HECTOR. Get out!

DEMOKOS. What are you glaring at? You look as though you have as little liking for poetry as you have for war.

HECTOR. They make a pretty couple! Now vanish.

[*Exit* DEMOKOS]
[*Enter* CASSANDRA]

CASSANDRA. Helen!

[*Enter* HELEN *and* PARIS]

PARIS. Here he is, Helen darling; this is Hector. He has a proposition to make to you, a perfectly simple proposition. He wants to hand you over to the Greeks, and prove to you that you don't love me.

Tell me you do love me, before I leave you with him. Tell me in your own words.

HELEN. I adore you, my sweet.

PARIS. Tell me how beautiful the wave was which swept you away from Greece.

HELEN. Magnificent! A magnificent wave! Where did you see a wave? The sea was so calm.

PARIS. Tell me you hate Menelaus.

HELEN. Menelaus? I hate him.

PARIS. You haven't finished yet. I shall never again return to Greece. Say that.

HELEN. You will never again return to Greece.

PARIS. No, no, this is about you, my darling.

HELEN. Oh, of course! How silly I am! I shall never again return to Greece.

PARIS. I didn't make her say it.—Now it's up to you.

[*He goes off*]

HECTOR. Is Greece a beautiful country?

HELEN. Paris found it ravishing.

HECTOR. I meant is Greece itself beautiful, apart from Helen?

HELEN. How very charming of you.

HECTOR. I was simply wondering what it is really like.

HELEN. Well, there are quite a great many kings, and a great many goats, dotted about on marble.

HECTOR. If the kings are in gold, and the goats angora, that would look pretty well when the sun was rising.

HELEN. I don't get up very early.

HECTOR. And a great many gods as well, I believe? Paris tells me the sky is crawling with them; he tells me you can see the legs of goddesses hanging down from the clouds.

HELEN. Paris always goes about with his nose in the air. He may have seen them.

HECTOR. But you haven't?

HELEN. I am not gifted that way. I will look out for them when I go back there again.

HECTOR. You were telling Paris you would never be going back there.

HELEN. He asked me to tell him so. I adore doing what Paris wants me to do.

HECTOR. I see. Is that also true of what you said about Menelaus? Do you not, after all, hate him?

HELEN. Why should I hate him?

HECTOR. For the one reason which might certainly make for hate. You have seen too much of him.

HELEN. Menelaus? Oh, no! I have never seen Menelaus. On the contrary.

HECTOR. You have never seen your husband?

HELEN. There are some things, and certain people, that stand out in bright colours for me. They are the ones I can see. I believe in them. I have never been able to see Menelaus.

HECTOR. Though I suppose he must have come very close to you sometimes.

HELEN. I have been able to touch him. But I can't honestly tell you I saw him.

HECTOR. They say he never left your side.

HELEN. Apparently. I must have walked across him a great many times without knowing it.

HECTOR. Whereas you have seen Paris.

HELEN. Vividly; in the clearest outline against the sky and the sun.

HECTOR. Does he still stand out as vividly as he did? Look down there: leaning against the rampart.

HELEN. Are you sure that's Paris, down there?

HECTOR. He is waiting for you.

HELEN. Good gracious! He's not nearly as clear as usual!

HECTOR. And yet the wall is freshly

whitewashed. Look again: there he is in profile.

HELEN. It's odd how people waiting for you stand out far less clearly than people you are waiting for.

HECTOR. Are you sure that Paris loves you?

HELEN. I don't like knowing about other people's feelings. There is nothing more embarrassing. Just as when you play cards and you see your opponent's hand. You are sure to lose.

HECTOR. What about yourself? Do you love him?

HELEN. I don't much like knowing my own feelings either.

HECTOR. But, listen: when you make love with Paris, when he sleeps in your arms, when you are circled round with Paris, overwhelmed with Paris, haven't you any thoughts about it?

HELEN. My part is over. I leave any thinking to the universe. It does it much better than I do.

HECTOR. Have there been many others, before Paris?

HELEN. Some.

HECTOR. And there will be others after him, wouldn't you say, as long as they stand out in clear relief against the sky, or the wall, or the white sheets on the bed? It is just as I thought it was. You don't love Paris particularly, Helen; you love men.

HELEN. I don't dislike them. They're as pleasant as soap and a sponge and warm water; you feel cleansed and refreshed by them.

HECTOR. Cassandra! Cassandra!

CASSANDRA [*entering*]. What do you want?

HECTOR. Cassandra, Helen is going back this evening with the Greek ambassador.

HELEN. I? What makes you think so?

HECTOR. Weren't you telling me that you didn't love Paris particularly?

HELEN. That was your interpretation. Still, if you like.

HECTOR. I quote my authority. You have the same liking for men as you have for a cake of soap.

HELEN. Yes; or pumice stone perhaps is better. What about it?

HECTOR. Well, then, you're not going to hesitate in your choice between going back to Greece, which you don't mind, and a catastrophe as terrible as war?

HELEN. You don't understand me at all, Hector. Of course I'm not hesitating. It would be very easy to say "I will do this or that, so that this can happen or that can happen." You've discovered my weakness and you are overjoyed. The man who discovers a woman's weakness is like the huntsman in the heat of the day who finds a cool spring. He wallows in it. But you mustn't think, because you have convinced me, you've convinced the future, too. Merely by making children behave as you want them to, you don't alter the course of destiny.

HECTOR. I don't follow your Greek shades and subtleties.

HELEN. It's not a question of shades and subtleties. It's no less than a question of monsters and pyramids.

HECTOR. Do you choose to leave here, yes or no?

HELEN. Don't bully me. I choose what happens in the way I choose men, or anything else. I choose whatever is not indefinite and vague. I choose what I see.

HECTOR. I know, you said that: what you see in the brightest colours. And you don't see yourself returning to Menelaus in a few days' time?

HELEN. No. It's very difficult.

HECTOR. We could no doubt persuade

your husband to dress with great brilliance for your return.

HELEN. All the purple dye from all the murex shells in the sea wouldn't make him visible to me.

HECTOR. Here you have a rival, Cassandra. Helen can read the future, too.

HELEN. No, I can't read the future. But when I imagine the future some of the pictures I see are coloured, and some are dull and drab. And up to now it has always been the coloured scenes which have happened in the end.

HECTOR. We are going to give you back to the Greeks at high noon, on the blinding sand, between the violet sea and the ochre-coloured wall. We shall all be in golden armour with red skirts; and my sisters, dressed in green and standing between my white stallion and Priam's black mare, will return you to the Greek ambassador, over whose silver helmet I can imagine tall purple plumes. You see that, I think?

HELEN. No, none of it. It is all quite sombre.

HECTOR. You are mocking me, aren't you?

HELEN. Why should I mock you? Very well, then. Let us go, if you like! Let us go and get ready to return me to the Greeks. We shall see what happens.

HECTOR. Do you realize how you insult humanity, or is it unconscious?

HELEN. I don't know what you mean.

HECTOR. You realize that your coloured picture-book is holding the world up to ridicule? While we are all battling and making sacrifices to bring about a time we can call our own, there are you, looking at your pictures which nothing in all eternity can alter. What's wrong? Which one has made you stop and stare at it with those blind eyes? I don't doubt it's the one where you are standing here on the ramparts, watching the battle going on below. Is it the battle you see?

HELEN. Yes.

HECTOR. And the city is in ruins or burning, isn't that so?

HELEN. Yes. It's a vivid red.

HECTOR. And what about Paris? You are seeing his body dragged behind a chariot?

HELEN. Oh, do you think that is Paris? I see what looks like a flash of sunlight rolling in the dust. A diamond sparkling on his hand. Yes, it is! Often I don't recognize faces, but I always recognize the jewellery. It's his ring, I'm quite certain.

HECTOR. Exactly. Do I dare to ask you about Andromache, and myself, the scene of Andromache and Hector? You are looking at us. Don't deny it. How do you see us? Happy, grown old, bathed in light?

HELEN. I am not trying to see it.

HECTOR. The scene of Andromache weeping over the body of Hector, does that shine clearer?

HELEN. You seem to know. But sometimes I see things shining, brilliantly shining, and they never happen. No one is infallible.

HECTOR. You needn't go on. I understand. There is a son between the weeping mother and the father stretched on the ground?

HELEN. Yes. He is playing with his father's tangled hair. He is a sweet boy.

HECTOR. And these scenes are there in your eyes, down in the depths of them. Could I see them there?

HELEN. I don't know. Look.

HECTOR. Nothing. Nothing except the ashes of all those fires, the gold and the emerald in dust. How innocent it is, this crystal where the future is waiting. But there should be tears bathing it, and where are they? Would you cry, Helen, if you were going to be killed?

HELEN. I don't know. But I should scream. And I feel I shall scream if you go on at me like this, Hector. I am going to scream.

HECTOR. You will leave for Greece this evening, Helen, otherwise I shall kill you.

HELEN. But I want to leave! I'm prepared to leave. All that I'm trying to tell is that I simply can't manage to distinguish the ship that is going to carry me there. Nothing is shining in the least, neither the metal on the mast, nor the ring in the captain's nose, nor the cabin-boy's eyes, nor anything.

HECTOR. You will go back on a grey sea under a grey sun. But we must have peace.

HELEN. I cannot see peace.

HECTOR. Ask Cassandra to make her appear for you. Cassandra is a sorceress. She can summon up shapes and spirits.

A MESSENGER [*entering*]. Hector, Priam is asking for you. The priests are opposed to our shutting the Gates of War. They say the gods will consider it an insult.

HECTOR. It is curious how the gods can never speak for themselves in these difficult matters.

MESSENGER. They have spoken for themselves. A thunderbolt has fallen on the temple, several men have been killed, the entrails of the victims have been consulted, and they are unanimously against Helen's return to Greece.

HECTOR. I would give a good deal to be able to consult the entrails of the priests . . . I'll follow you.

[*The* MESSENGER *goes*]

Well, now, Helen, do we agree about this?

HELEN. Yes.

HECTOR. From now on you will say what I tell you to say? You will do what I tell you to do?

HELEN. Yes.

HECTOR. When we come in front of Ulysses you won't contradict me, you will bear out everything I say?

HELEN. Yes.

HECTOR. Do you hear this, Cassandra? Listen to this solid wall of negation which says Yes! They have all given in to me. Paris has given in to me, Priam has given in to me, Helen has given in to me. And yet I can't help feeling that in each of these apparent victories I have been defeated. You set out, thinking you are going to have to wrestle with giants; you brace yourself to conquer them, and you find yourself wrestling with something inflexible reflected in a woman's eye. You have said yes beautifully, Helen, and you're brimful of a stubborn determination to defy me!

HELEN. That's possible. But how can I help it? It isn't my own determination.

HECTOR. By what peculiar vagary did the world choose to place its mirror in this obtuse head?

HELEN. It's most regrettable, obviously. But can you see any way of defeating the obstinacy of a mirror?

HECTOR. Yes. I've been considering that for the past several minutes.

ANOTHER MESSENGER [*entering*]. Hector, make haste. They are in a turmoil of revolt down on the beach. The Greek ships have been sighted, and they have hoisted their flag not masthead but hatchway. The honour of our navy is at stake. Priam is afraid the ambassador may be murdered as soon as he lands.

HECTOR. I leave you in charge of Helen, Cassandra. I must go and give my orders.

HELEN. If you break the mirror, will what is reflected in it cease to exist?

HECTOR. That is the whole question.

[*Exit* HECTOR]

CASSANDRA. I never see anything at all, you know, either coloured or not. But I can feel the weight on me of every person who comes towards me. I know what is in store for them by the sensation of suffering which flows into my veins.

HELEN. Is it true that you are a sorceress? Could you really make Peace take shape and appear for us?

CASSANDRA. Peace? Very easily. She is always standing in her beggarly way on every threshold. Wait ... you will see her now.

[PEACE *appears*]

HELEN. Oh, how pretty she is!

PEACE. Come to my rescue, Helen: help me!

HELEN. But how pale and wan she is.

PEACE. Pale and wan? What do you mean? Don't you see the gold shining in my hair?

HELEN. Gold? Well, perhaps a golden grey. It's very original.

PEACE. Golden grey? Is my gold now grey?

[*She disappears*]

CASSANDRA. I think she means to make herself clearer.

[PEACE *re-appears, outrageously painted*]

PEACE. Is that better now?

HELEN. I don't see her as well as I did before.

PEACE. Is that better?

CASSANDRA. Helen doesn't see you as well as she did.

PEACE. But you can see me: you are speaking to me.

CASSANDRA. It's my speciality to speak to the invisible.

PEACE. What is going on, then? Why are all the men in the city and along the beach making such a pandemonium?

CASSANDRA. Apparently their gods are insulted, and their honour is at stake.

PEACE. Their gods! Their honour!

CASSANDRA. Yes ... You are ill!

THE CURTAIN FALLS

ACT II

[*A palace enclosure. At each corner a view of the sea. In the middle a monument, the Gates of War. They are wide open.*]

[HELEN. *The young* TROILUS]

HELEN. You, you, hey! You down there! Yes, it's you I'm calling. Come here.

TROILUS. No.

HELEN. What is your name?

TROILUS. Troilus.

HELEN. Come here.

TROILUS. No.

HELEN. Come here, Troilus!

[TROILUS *draws near*]

That's the way. You obey when you're called by your name: you are still very like a puppy. It's rather beguiling. Do you know you have made me call out to a man for the first time in my life. They keep so close to my side I have only usually to move my lips. I have called out to sea-gulls, to dogs, to the echoes, but never before to a man. You will pay for that. What's the matter? Are you trembling?

TROILUS. No, I'm not.

HELEN. You tremble, Troilus.

TROILUS. Yes, I do.

HELEN. Why are you always just behind me? If I walk with my back to the sun and suddenly stop, the head of your shadow stubs itself against my feet. That doesn't matter, as long as it doesn't overshoot them. Tell me what you want.

TROILUS. I don't want anything.

HELEN. Tell me what you want, Troilus!

TROILUS. Everything! I want everything!

HELEN. You want everything. The moon?

TROILUS. Everything! Everything and more!

HELEN. You're beginning to talk like a real man already; you want to kiss me!

TROILUS. No!

HELEN. You want to kiss me, isn't that it, Troilus?

TROILUS. I would kill myself directly afterwards!

HELEN. Come nearer. How old are you?

TROILUS. Fifteen. Alas!

HELEN. Bravo that alas. Have you kissed girls of your own age?

TROILUS. I hate them.

HELEN. But you have kissed them?

TROILUS. Well, yes, you're bound to kiss them, you kiss them all. I would give my life not to have kissed any of them.

HELEN. You seem prepared to get rid of quite a number of lives. Why haven't you said to me frankly: Helen, I want to kiss you! I don't see anything wrong in your kissing me. Kiss me.

TROILUS. Never.

HELEN. And then, when the day came to an end, you would have come quietly to where I was sitting on the battlements watching the sun go down over the islands, and you would have turned my head towards you with your hands—from golden it would have become dark, only shadow now, you would hardly have been able to see me—and you would have kissed me, and I should have been very happy. Why this is Troilus, I should have said to myself: young Troilus is kissing me! Kiss me.

TROILUS. Never.

HELEN. I see. You think, once you have kissed me, you would hate me?

TROILUS. Oh! Older men have all the luck, knowing how to say what they want to!

HELEN. You say it well enough.

[Enter PARIS]

PARIS. Take care, Helen, Troilus is a dangerous fellow.

HELEN. On the contrary. He wants to kiss me.

PARIS. Troilus, you know that if you kiss Helen, I shall kill you?

HELEN. Dying means nothing to him; no matter how often.

PARIS. What's the matter with him? Is he crouching to spring? Is he going to take a leap at you? He's too nice a boy. Kiss Helen, Troilus. I'll let you.

HELEN. If you can make up his mind to it you're cleverer than I am.

[TROILUS who was about to hurl himself on HELEN immediately draws back]

PARIS. Listen, Troilus! Here's a committee of our revered elders coming to shut the Gates of War. Kiss Helen in front of them; it will make you famous. You want to be famous, don't you, later on in life?

TROILUS. No. I want nobody to have heard of me.

PARIS. You don't want to be famous? You don't want to be rich and powerful?

TROILUS. No. Poor. Ugly.

PARIS. Let me finish! So that you can have all the women you want.

TROILUS. I don't want any, none at all, none.

PARIS. Here come the senators! Now you can choose: either you kiss Helen in front of them, or I shall kiss her in front of you. Would you rather I did it? All right! Look! ... Why, this was a new version of kiss you gave me, Helen. What was it?

HELEN. The kiss I had ready for Troilus.

PARIS. You don't know what you're missing, my boy! Are you leaving us? Goodbye, then.

HELEN. We shall kiss one another, Troilus. I'll answer for that.

[TROILUS *goes*]

Troilus!

PARIS [*slightly unnerved*]. You called very loudly, Helen.

[*Enter* DEMOKOS]

DEMOKOS. Helen, one moment! Look me full in the face. I've got here in my hand a magnificent bird which I'm going to set free. Are you looking? Here it is. Smooth back your hair, and smile a beautiful smile.

PARIS. I don't see how the bird will fly any better if Helen smooths her hair and gives a beautiful smile.

HELEN. It can't do me any harm, anyway.

DEMOKOS. Don't move. One! Two! Three! There! It's all over, you can go now.

HELEN. Where was the bird?

DEMOKOS. It's a bird who knows how to make himself invisible.

HELEN. Ask him next time to tell you how he does it.

[*She goes*]

PARIS. What is this nonsense?

DEMOKOS. I am writing a song on the subject of Helen's face. I needed to look at it closely, to engrave it, smiling, on my memory.

[*Enter* HECUBA, POLYXENE, ABNEOS, *the* MATHEMATICIAN, *and some* OLD MEN]

HECUBA. Well, are you going to shut these Gates for us?

DEMOKOS. Certainly not. We might well have to open them again this very evening.

HECUBA. It is Hector's wish. And Hector will persuade Priam.

DEMOKOS. That is as we shall see. And what's more I have a surprise in store for Hector.

POLYXENE. Where do the Gates lead to, mama?

ABNEOS. To war, my child. When they are open it means there is war.

DEMOKOS. My friends ...

HECUBA. War or not, it's an absurd symbolism, your Gateway, and those two great doors always left open look very unsightly. All the dogs stop there.

MATHEMATICIAN. This is no domestic matter. It concerns war and the gods.

HECUBA. Which is just as I said: the gods never remember to shut their doors.

POLYXENE. I remember to shut them very well, don't I, mama?

PARIS. And you even include your fingers in them, don't you, my pretty one?

DEMOKOS. May I ask for a moment of silence, Paris? Abneos, and you, Mathematician, and you, my friends: I asked you to meet here earlier than the time fixed for the ceremony so that we could hold our first council. And it promises well that this first council of war should be, not a council of generals, but a council of intellectuals. For it isn't enough in war-time to have our soldiers drilled, well-armed, and spectacular. It is absolutely necessary to bring their enthusiasm up to fever pitch. The physical intoxication which their officers will get from them by a generous allowance of cheap wine supplied at the right moment, will still be ineffective against the Greeks, unless it is reinforced by the spiritual and moral intoxication which the poets can pour into them. If we are too old to fight we can at least make sure that the fighting is savage. I see you have something to say on the subject, Abneos.

ABNEOS. Yes. We must make a war-song.

DEMOKOS. Very proper. A war requires a war-song.

PARIS. We have done without one up to now.

HECUBA. War itself sings quite loud enough.

ABNEOS. We have done without one because up to now we were fighting only barbarians. It was nothing more than a hunt, and the hunting horn was all we needed. But now with the Greeks we're entering a different region of war altogether.

DEMOKOS. Exactly so, Abneos. The Greeks don't fight with everybody.

PARIS. We already have a national anthem.

ABNEOS. Yes. But it's a song of peace.

PARIS. If you sing a song of peace with enough gestures and grimaces it becomes a war-song. What are the words we have already?

ABNEOS. You know them perfectly well. There's no spirit in them:

"We cut and bind the harvest,
We tread the vineyard's blood."

DEMOKOS. At the very most it's a war-song against farm produce. You won't frighten the Spartans by threatening a wheatfield.

PARIS. Sing it with a spear in your hand, and a dead body at your feet, you will be surprised.

HECUBA. It includes the word "blood," there's always that.

PARIS. The word "harvest" as well. War rather approves of the word "harvest."

ABNEOS. Why discuss it, when Demokos can invent an entirely new one in a couple of hours.

DEMOKOS. A couple of hours is rather short.

HECUBA. Don't be afraid; it's more than you need for it. And after the song will come the hymn, and after the hymn the cantata. As soon as war is declared it will be impossible to hold the poets back. Rhyme is still the most effective drum.

DEMOKOS. And the most useful, Hecuba: you don't know how wisely you speak. I know war. As long as war isn't with us, and the Gates are shut, each of us is free to insult it and execrate it as we will. But once war comes, its pride and autocracy is huge. You can gain its goodwill only by flattery and adoration. So the mission of those who understand how to speak and write is to compliment and praise war ceaselessly and indiscriminately, otherwise we shut ourselves out from his favour.

PARIS. Have you got an idea for your song already?

DEMOKOS. A marvellous idea, which no one will understand better than you. War must be tired of the mask we always give it, of Medusa's venomous hair and a Gorgon's lips. I have had the notion to compare War's face with Helen's. It will be enchanted by the comparison.

POLYXENE. What does War look like, mama?

HECUBA. Like your Aunt Helen.

POLYXENE. She is very pretty.

DEMOKOS. Then the discussion is closed. You can expect the war-song. Why are you looking worried, Mathematician?

MATHEMATICIAN. Because there are other things far more urgent than this war-song, far more urgent!

DEMOKOS. You think we should discuss the question of medals, false information, atrocity stories, and so on?

MATHEMATICIAN. I think we should discuss the insulting epithets.

HECUBA. The insulting epithets?

MATHEMATICIAN. Before they hurl their spears the Greek fighting-men hurl insults. You third cousin of a toad, they yell! You son of a sow!—They insult each other, like that! And they have a good reason for it. They know that the body is more vulnerable when self-respect has fled. Soldiers famous for their composure lose it immediately when they're treated as warts or maggots. We Trojans suffer from a grave shortage of insults.

DEMOKOS. The Mathematician is quite right. We are the only race in the world which doesn't insult its enemies before it kills them.

PARIS. You don't think it's enough that the civilians insult the enemy civilians?

MATHEMATICIAN. The armies have to show the same hatred the civilians do. You know what dissemblers armies can be in this way. Leave them to themselves and they spend their time admiring each other. Their front lines very soon become the only ranks of real brotherhood in the world. So naturally, when the theatre of war is so full of mutual consideration, hatred is driven back on to the schools, the salons, the trades-people. If our soldiers aren't at least equal to the Greeks in the fury of their epithets, they will lose all taste for insults and calumny, and as a natural consequence all taste for war.

DEMOKOS. Suggestion adopted! We will organize a cursing parade this evening.

PARIS. I should have thought they're big enough to find their own curses.

DEMOKOS. What a mistake! Could you, adroit as you are, find your own effective curses?

PARIS. I believe so.

DEMOKOS. You fool yourself. Come and stand face to face with Abneos and begin.

PARIS. Why Abneos?

DEMOKOS. Because he lends himself to this sort of thing, with his corpulence and one thing and another.

ABNEOS. Come on, then, speak up, you piece of pie-crust!

PARIS. No. Abneos doesn't inspire me. I'll start with you, if you don't mind.

DEMOKOS. With me? Certainly. You can let fly at ten paces. There we are. Begin.

HECUBA. Take a good look at him. You will be inspired.

PARIS. You old parasite! You filthy-footed iambic pentameter!

DEMOKOS. Just one second. To avoid any mistake you had better say who it is you're addressing.

PARIS. You're quite right! Demokos! Bloodshot bullock's eye! You fungus-ridden plum tree!

DEMOKOS. Grammatically reasonable, but very naive. What is there in a fungus-ridden plum-tree to make me rise up foaming at the lips?

HECUBA. He also called you a bloodshot bullock's eye.

DEMOKOS. Bloodshot bullock's eye is better. But you see how you flounder, Paris? Search for something that can strike home to me. What are my faults, in your opinion?

PARIS. You are cowardly: your breath smells, and you have no talent.

DEMOKOS. You're asking for trouble!
PARIS. I was trying to please you.
POLYXENE. Why are we scolding Uncle Demokos, mama?
HECUBA. Because he is a cuckoo, dearest!
DEMOKOS. What did you say, Hecuba?
HECUBA. I was saying that you're a cuckoo, Demokos. If cuckoos had the absurdity, the affectation, the ugliness and the stench of vultures, you would be a cuckoo.
DEMOKOS. Wait a bit, Paris! Your mother is better at this than you are. Model yourselves on her. One hour's exercise each day for each soldier, and Hecuba has given us the superiority in insults which we badly need. As for the war-song, I'm not sure it wouldn't be wiser to entrust that to her as well.
HECUBA. If you like. But if so, I shouldn't say that war looks like Helen.
DEMOKOS. What would you say it looks like, in your opinion?
HECUBA. I will tell you when the Gates have been shut.

[*Enter* PRIAM, HECTOR, ANDROMACHE, *and presently* HELEN. *During the closing of the Gates,* ANDROMACHE *takes little* POLYXENE *aside and whispers a secret or an errand to her*]

HECTOR. As they nearly are.
DEMOKOS. One moment, Hector!
HECTOR. Aren't we ready to begin the ceremony?
HECUBA. Surely? The hinges are swimming in oil.
HECTOR. Well, then.
PRIAM. What our friends want you to understand, Hector, is that war is ready, too. Consider carefully. They're not mistaken. If you shut these Gates, in a minute we may have to open them again.

HECUBA. Even one minute of peace is worth taking.
HECTOR. Father, you should know what peace means to men who have been fighting for months. It's like solid ground to someone who was drowning or sinking in the quicksands. Do let us get our feet on to a few inches of peace, touch it, if only with the tips of our toes.
PRIAM. Hector: consider: inflicting the word peace on to the city today is as ruthless as though you gave it poison. You will take her off her guard, undermine her iron determination, debase, with the word peace, the accepted values of memory, affection, and hope. The soldiers will rush to buy the bread of peace, to drink the wine of peace, to hold in their arms the woman of peace, and in an hour you will put them back to face a war.
HECTOR. The war will never take place!
[*The sound of clamour near the Gates*]
DEMOKOS. No? Listen!
HECTOR. Shut the Gates. This is where we shall meet the Greeks. Conversation will be bitter enough as it is. We must receive them in peace.
PRIAM. My son, are we even sure we should let the Greeks disembark?
HECTOR. Disembark they shall. This meeting with Ulysses is our last chance of peace.
DEMOKOS. Disembark they shall not. Our honour is at stake. We shall be the laughing-stock of the whole world.
HECTOR. And you're taking it upon yourself to recommend to the Senate an action which would certainly mean war?
DEMOKOS. Upon myself? No, not at all. Will you come forward now, Busiris. This is where your mission begins.
HECTOR. Who is this stranger?
DEMOKOS. He is the greatest living ex-

[610]

pert on the rights of nations. It's a lucky chance he should be passing through Troy today. You can't say that he's a biased witness. He is neutral. Our Senate is willing to abide by his decision, a decision which all other nations will agree with tomorrow.

HECTOR. And what is your opinion?

BUSIRIS. My opinion, Princes, based on my own observation and further enquiry, is that the Greeks, in relation to Troy, are guilty of three breaches of international law. If you give them permission to disembark you will have sacrificed your position as the aggrieved party, and so lost the universal sympathy which would certainly have been yours in the conflict to follow.

HECTOR. Explain yourself.

BUSIRIS. Firstly, they have hoisted their flag hatchway and not masthead. A ship of war, my dear Princes and colleagues, hoists its flag hatchway only when replying to a salute from a boat carrying cattle. Clearly, then, so to salute a city and a city's population is an insult. As it happens, we have a precedent. Last year the Greeks hoisted their flag hatchway when they were entering the port of Orphea. The reply was incisive. Orphea declared war.

HECTOR. And what happened?

BUSIRIS. Orphea was beaten. Orphea no longer exists, nor the Orpheans either.

HECUBA. Perfect.

BUSIRIS. But the annihilation of a people doesn't alter in the least their superior moral position.

HECTOR. Go on.

BUSIRIS. Secondly, on entering your territorial waters the Greeks adopted the formation known as frontal. At the last congress there was some talk of including this formation in the paragraph of measures called defensive-aggressive. I was very happy to be able to get it restored under its proper heading of aggressive-defensive: so without doubt it is now one of the subtle forms of naval manœuvre which is a disguised form of blockade: that is to say, it constitutes a fault of the first degree! We have a precedent for this, as well. Five years ago the Greek navy adopted the frontal formation when they anchored outside Magnesia. Magnesia at once declared war.

HECTOR. Did they win it?

BUSIRIS. They lost it. There's not one stone of Magnesia still standing on another. But my redraft of the paragraph is still standing.

HECUBA. I congratulate you. We were beginning to be anxious.

HECTOR. Go on.

BUSIRIS. The third fault is not so serious. One of the Greek triremes has crept close in to shore without permission. Its captain, Ajax, the most unruly and impossible man among the Greeks, is climbing up towards the city, shouting scandal and provocation, and swearing he would like to kill Paris. But this is a very minor matter, from the international point of view; because it isn't, in any way, a formal breach of the law.

DEMOKOS. You have your information. The situation can only be resolved in one of two ways. To swallow an outrage, or return it. Choose.

HECTOR. Oneah, go and find Ajax. Head him off in this direction.

PARIS. I'm waiting here for him.

HECTOR. You will be good enough to stay in the Palace until I call for you. As for you, Busiris, you must understand that our city has no intention of being insulted by the Greeks.

BUSIRIS. I am not surprised. Troy's incorruptible pride is a legend all the world over.

HECTOR. You are going to provide me, here and now, with an argument which will allow our Senate to say that there has been no fault whatever on the part of our visitors, and with our pride untouched we welcome them here as our guests.

DEMOKOS. What nonsense is this?

BUSIRIS. It isn't in keeping with the facts, Hector.

HECTOR. My dear Busiris, all of us here know there's no better way of exercising the imagination than the study of law. No poet ever interpreted nature as freely as a lawyer interprets truth.

BUSIRIS. The Senate asked me for an opinion: I gave it.

HECTOR. And I ask you for an interpretation. An even subtler point of law.

BUSIRIS. It goes against my conscience.

HECTOR. Your conscience has seen Orphea destroyed, Magnesia destroyed: is it now contemplating, just as lightheartedly, the destruction of Troy?

HECUBA. Yes. He comes from Syracuse.

HECTOR. I do beg of you, Busiris. The lives of two countries depend on this. Help us.

BUSIRIS. Truth is the only help I can give you.

HECTOR. Precisely. Discover a truth which saves us. What is the use of justice if it doesn't hammer out a shield for innocent people? Forge us a truth. If you can't, there is one thing I can tell you, quite simply: we shall hold you here for as long as the war goes on.

BUSIRIS. What are you saying?

DEMOKOS. You're abusing your position, Hector!

HECUBA. During war we imprison the rights of man. There seems no reason why we shouldn't imprison a lawyer.

HECTOR. I mean what I say, Busiris. I've never failed yet to keep my promises, or my threats. And now either these guards are going to take you off to prison for a year or two, or else you leave here, this evening, heaped with gold. With this in mind, you can dispassionately examine the evidence once again.

BUSIRIS. Actually there are certain mitigating arguments.

HECTOR. I was sure there were.

BUSIRIS. In the case of the first fault, for instance, when the cattle-boat salute is given in certain seas where the shores are fertile, it could be interpreted as a salute from the sailors to the farmers.

HECTOR. That would be, in fact, the logical interpretation. The salute of the sea to the earth.

BUSIRIS. Not to mention that the cargo of cattle might easily be a cargo of bulls. In that case the homage would verge on flattery.

HECTOR. There you are. You've understood what I meant. We've arrived at our point of view.

BUSIRIS. And as to the frontal formation, that could as easily mean a promise as a provocation. Women wanting children give themselves not from the side but face to face.

HECTOR. Decisive argument.

BUSIRIS. Then, again, the Greek ships have huge carved nymphs for figureheads. A woman who comes towards you naked and open-armed is not a threat but an offer. An offer to talk, at any rate.

HECTOR. So there we have our honour safe and sound, Demokos. The next step is to make this consultation with Busiris public. Meanwhile, Minos, tell the port authorities to let Ulysses disembark without any loss of time.

DEMOKOS. It's no use even trying to

discuss honour with these fighting men. They trade on the fact that you can't treat them as cowards.

MATHEMATICIAN. At any rate, Hector, deliver the Oration for the Dead. That will make you think again.

HECTOR. There's not going to be an Oration for the Dead.

PRIAM. But it's a part of the ceremony. The victorious general must always speak in honour of the dead when the Gates are closed.

HECTOR. An Oration for the Dead of a war is a hypocritical speech in defence of the living, a plea for acquittal. I am not so sure of my innocence.

DEMOKOS. The High Command is not responsible.

HECTOR. Alas, no one is: nor the gods either. Besides, I have given my oration for the dead already. I gave it to them in their last minute of life, when they were lying on the battlefield, on a little slope of olive-trees, while they could still attend me with what was left of their sight and hearing. I can tell you what I said to them. There was one, disembowelled, already turning up the whites of his eyes, and I said to him: "It's not so bad, you know, it's not so bad; you will do all right, old man." And one with his skull split in two; I said: "You look pretty comical with that broken nose." And my little equerry, with his left arm hanging useless and his last blood flowing out of him; and I said, "It's a good thing for you it's the left arm you've splintered." I am happy I gave them one final swig of life; it was all they asked for; they died drinking it. And there's nothing else to be said. Shut the Gates.

POLYXENE. Did the little equerry die, as well?

HECTOR. Yes, puss-cat. He died. He stretched out his right arm. Someone I couldn't see took him by his perfect hand. And then he died.

DEMOKOS. Our general seems to confuse remarks made to the dying with the Oration for the Dead.

PRIAM. Why must you be so stubborn, Hector?

HECTOR. Very well: you shall have the Oration. [*He takes a position below the gates*]—You who cannot hear us, who cannot see us, listen to these words, look at those who come to honour you. We have won the war. I know that's of no moment to you. You are the victors, too. But we are victorious, and still live. That's where the difference is between us and why I'm ashamed. I don't know whether, among the crowd of the dead, any privilege is given to men who died victorious. But the living, whether victorious or not, have privilege enough. We have our eyes. We see the sun. We do what all men do under the sun. We eat. We drink. By the moon, we sleep with our wives. And with yours, now you have gone.

DEMOKOS. You insult the dead!

HECTOR. Do you think so?

DEMOKOS. Either the dead or the living.

HECTOR. There is a distinction.

PRIAM. Come to the peroration, Hector. The Greeks are coming ashore.

HECTOR. I will come to it now... Breathe in this incense, touch these offerings, you who can neither smell nor touch. And understand, since I speak to you sincerely, I haven't an equal tenderness and respect for all of you. Though all of you are the dead, with you as with us who survive there are men of courage and men of fear, and you can't make me confuse, for the sake of a ceremony, the dead I admire with those I can't admire. But what I have to say to you today is that war seems to me the most sordid, hypocritical way of making all men equal: and I accept death neither as a punishment or expiation for the coward, nor as a reward to the living. So, whatever you may be, absent, forgotten, purposeless, unresting, without existence, one thing is certain when we close these Gates: we must ask you to forgive us, we, the deserters who survive you, who feel we have stolen two great privileges, I hope the sound of their names will never reach you: the warmth of the living body, and the sky.

POLYXENE. The gates are shutting, mama!

HECUBA. Yes, darling.

POLYXENE. The dead men are pushing them shut.

HECUBA. They help, a little.

POLYXENE. They're helping quite a lot, especially over on the right.

HECTOR. Is it done? Are they shut?

GUARD. Tight as a clam.

HECTOR. We're at peace, father, we're at peace.

HECUBA. We're at peace!

POLYXENE. It feels much better, doesn't it, mama?

HECTOR. Indeed it does.

POLYXENE. I feel much better, anyway.

[*The sound of the* GREEKS' *music*]

A MESSENGER. The Greeks have landed, Priam!

DEMOKOS. What music! What frightful music! It's the most anti-Trojan music there could possibly be! Let's go and give them a welcome to match it.

HECTOR. Receive them royally, bring them here safely. You are responsible.

MATHEMATICIAN. At any rate we ought to counter with some Trojan music. Hector, if we can't be indignant any other way, you can authorize a battle of music.

CROWD. The Greeks! The Greeks!

MESSENGER. Ulysses is on the landing-stage, Priam. Where are we to take him?

PRIAM. Conduct him here. Send word to us in the palace when he comes. Keep with us, Paris. We don't want you too much in evidence just yet.

HECTOR. Let's go and prepare what we shall say to the Greeks, father.

DEMOKOS. You'd better prepare it somewhat better than your speech for the dead; you're likely to meet more contradiction.

[*Exeunt* PRIAM *and his* SONS]

If you are going with them, tell us before you go, Hecuba, what it is you think war looks like.

HECUBA. You insist on knowing?

DEMOKOS. If you've seen what it looks like, tell us.

HECUBA. Like the bottom of a baboon. When the baboon is up in a tree, with its hind end facing us, there is the face of war exactly: scarlet, scaley, glazed, framed in a clotted, filthy wig.

DEMOKOS. So he has two faces: this you describe, and Helen's.

[*Exit*]

ANDROMACHE. Here is Helen now. Polyxene, you remember what you have to say to her?

POLYXENE. Yes.

ANDROMACHE. Go to her, then.

[*Enter* HELEN]

HELEN. Do you want to talk to me, darling?

POLYXENE. Yes, Aunt Helen.

HELEN. It must be important, you're so very tense.

POLYXENE. Yes, Aunt Helen.

HELEN. Is it something you can't tell me without standing so stiffly?

POLYXENE. No, Aunt Helen.

HELEN. Do tell me, then; you make me feel terrible when you stand there like a little stick.

[614]

POLYXENE. Aunt Helen, if you love anyone, please go away.

HELEN. Why should I go away, darling?

POLYXENE. Because of the war.

HELEN. Do you know about war already, then?

POLYXENE. I don't exactly know about it. I think it means we have to die.

HELEN. And do you know what dying is?

POLYXENE. I don't exactly. I think it means we don't feel anything any more.

HELEN. What exactly was it that Andromache told you to ask me?

POLYXENE. If you love us at all, please to go away.

HELEN. That doesn't seem to me very logical. If you loved someone you wouldn't leave them?

POLYXENE. Oh, no! Never!

HELEN. Which would you rather do: go right away from Hecuba, or never feel anything any more?

POLYXENE. Oh, never feel anything! I would rather stay, and never feel anything any more.

HELEN. You see how badly you put things to me. If I'm to leave you, I mustn't love you. Would you rather I didn't love you?

POLYXENE. Oh, no! I want you to love me.

HELEN. In other words, you didn't know what you were saying, did you?

POLYXENE. No.

HECUBA [*offstage*]. Polyxene!

[*Enter* HECUBA]

Are you deaf, Polyxene? Why did you shut your eyes when you saw me? Are you playing at being a statue? Come with me.

HELEN. She is teaching herself not to feel anything. But she has no gift for it.

HECUBA. Can you hear me, Polyxene? And see me?

POLYXENE. Yes, I can hear you. I can see you, too.

HECUBA. Why are you crying? Don't you like to see and hear me?

POLYXENE. If I do, you will go away.

HECUBA. I think it would be better, Helen, if you left Polyxene alone. She is too sensitive to touch the insensitive, even through your beautiful dress and your beautiful voice.

HELEN. I quite agree with you. I advise Andromache to carry her own messages. Kiss me, Polyxene. I shall go away this evening, since that is what you would like.

POLYXENE. Don't go! Don't go!

HELEN. Bravo! You are quite loosened up again!

HECUBA. Are you coming with us, Andromache?

ANDROMACHE. No: I shall wait here.

[*Exeunt* HECUBA *and* POLYXENE]

HELEN. You want an explanation?

ANDROMACHE. I believe it's necessary.

HELEN. Listen to the way they're shouting and arguing down below. Isn't that enough? Do you and I have to have explanations, too? And what explanations, since I'm leaving here anyway?

ANDROMACHE. Whether you go or stay isn't any longer the problem.

HELEN. Tell Hector that. You will make his day easier.

ANDROMACHE. Yes, Hector is obsessed by the thought of getting you away. All men are the same. They take no notice of the stag in the thicket because they're already chasing the hare. Perhaps men can hunt like that. But not the gods.

HELEN. If you have discovered what the gods are after in this affair, I congratulate you.

ANDROMACHE. I don't know that the gods are after anything. But there is something the universe is after. Ever since this morning, it seems to me, everything has begged and cried out for it, men, animals, even the leaves on the trees and my own child, not yet born.

HELEN. Cried out for what?

ANDROMACHE. That you should love Paris.

HELEN. If they know so certainly that I don't love Paris, they are better informed than I am.

ANDROMACHE. But you don't love him! You could love him, perhaps. But, at present, you are both living in a misunderstanding.

HELEN. I live with him happily, amicably, in complete agreement. We understand each other so well, I don't really see how this can be called a misunderstanding.

ANDROMACHE. Agreement is never reached in love. The life of a wife and husband who love each other is never at rest. Whether the marriage is true or false, the marriage portion is the same: elemental discord. Hector is my absolute opposite. He shares none of my tastes. We pass our days either getting the better of one another, or sacrificing ourselves. There is no tranquillity for lovers.

HELEN. And if I went pale whenever I saw Paris: and my eyes filled with tears, and the palms of my hands were moist, you think Menelaus would be delighted, and the Greeks pleased and quite satisfied?

ANDROMACHE. It wouldn't much matter then what the Greeks thought.

HELEN. And the war would never happen?

ANDROMACHE. Perhaps, indeed, it would never happen. Perhaps if you loved him, love would call to the rescue one of its own equals: generosity or intelligence. No one, not even destiny itself, attacks devotion lightheartedly. And even if the war did happen, why, I think even then—

HELEN. Then it wouldn't be the same war, I suppose.

ANDROMACHE. Oh, no, Helen! You know what this struggle is going to be. Fate would never take so many precautions for an ordinary quarrel. It means to build the future on this war, the future of our countries and our peoples, and our ways of thinking. It won't be so bad if our thoughts and our future are built on the story of a man and a woman who truly love each other. But fate hasn't noticed yet that you are lovers only on paper, officially. To think that we're going to suffer and die only for a pair of theoretical lovers: and the splendour and calamity of the age to come will be founded on a trivial adventure between two people who don't love each other—that's what is so horrible.

HELEN. If everybody thinks that we love each other, it comes to the same thing.

ANDROMACHE. They don't think so. But no one will admit that he doesn't. Everyone, when there's war in the air, learns to live in a new element: falsehood. Everybody lies. Our old men don't worship beauty: they worship themselves, they worship ugliness. And this indignation the Greeks are showing us is a lie. God knows, they're amused enough at what you can do with Paris! Their boats, in the bay, with their patriotic anthems and their streamers flying, are a falsehood of the sea. And Hector's life and my son's life, too, are going to be played out in hypocrisy and pretence.

HELEN. So?

ANDROMACHE. I beg of you, Helen. You

see how I'm pressed against you as though I were begging you to love me. Love Paris! Or tell me that I'm mistaken! Tell me that you would kill yourself if Paris were to die! Tell me that you would even let yourself be disfigured if it would keep him alive. Then the war will only be a scourge, not an injustice.

HELEN. You are being very difficult. I don't think my way of loving is as bad as all that. Certainly I don't get upset and ill when Paris leaves me to play bowls or go fishing for eels. But I do feel commanded by him, magnetically attracted. Magnetism is a kind of love, as much as devotion. And it's an old and fruitful passion in its own way, as desperate devotion and passionate weeping are in theirs. I'm as content in this love as a star in a constellation. It's my own centre of gravity; I shine there; it's the way I breathe, and the way I take life in my arms. And it's easy to see what sons this love can produce: tall, clear-cut boys, of great distinction, with fine fingers and short noses. What will it all become if I fill it with jealousy, with emotion, and anxiety? The world is nervous enough already: look at yourself!

ANDROMACHE. Fill it with pity, Helen. That's the only help the world needs.

HELEN. There we are; I knew it would come; the word has been said.

ANDROMACHE. What word?

HELEN. The word "pity." You must talk to someone else. I'm afraid I'm not very good at pity.

ANDROMACHE. Because you don't know unhappiness.

HELEN. Maybe. It could also be that I think of unhappy people as my equals, I accept them, and I don't think of my health and my position and beauty as any better than their misery. It's a sense of brotherhood I have.

ANDROMACHE. You're blaspheming, Helen.

HELEN. I am sure people pity others to the same extent that they would pity themselves. Unhappiness and ugliness are mirrors they can't bear to look into. I haven't any pity for myself. You will see, if war breaks out. I'll put up with hunger and pain better than you will. And insults, too. Do you think I don't hear what the Trojan women say when I'm going past them? They treat me like a slut. They say that the morning light shows me up for what they think me. It may be true, or it may not be. It doesn't matter to me, one way or the other.

ANDROMACHE. Stop, Helen!

HELEN. And of course I can see, in what your husband called the coloured picture-book in my head, pictures of Helen grown old, flabby, toothless, sitting hunched-up in the kitchen, sucking sweets. I can see the white enamel I've plastered over my wrinkles, and the bright colours the sweets are, very clearly. But it leaves me completely indifferent.

ANDROMACHE. I am lost.

HELEN. Why? If you're content with one perfect couple to make the war acceptable, there is always you and Hector, Andromache.

[*Enter* AJAX, *then* HECTOR]

AJAX. Where is he? Where's he hiding himself? A coward! A typical Trojan!

HECTOR. Who are you looking for?

AJAX. I'm looking for Paris.

HECTOR. I am his brother.

AJAX. Beautiful family! I am Ajax! What's your name?

HECTOR. My name's Hector.

AJAX. It ought to be pimp!

HECTOR. I see that Greece has sent over her diplomats. What do you want?

AJAX. War.

HECTOR. Not a hope. Why do you want it?

AJAX. Your brother carried off Helen.

HECTOR. I am told she was willing.

AJAX. A Greek woman can do what she likes. She doesn't have to ask permission from you. He carried her off. It's a reason for war.

HECTOR. We can offer our apologies.

AJAX. What's a Trojan apology? We're not leaving here without your declaration of war.

HECTOR. Declare it yourselves.

AJAX. All right, we will. As from this evening.

HECTOR. That's a lie. You won't declare war. There isn't an island in the Archipelago that will back you if we aren't in any way responsible. And we don't intend to be.

AJAX. Will you declare it yourself, personally, if I call you a coward?

HECTOR. That is a name I accept.

AJAX. I've never known such unmilitary reaction! Suppose I tell you what the people of Greece thinks of Troy, that Troy is a cess-pit of vice and stupidity?

HECTOR. Troy is obstinate. You won't get your war.

AJAX. Suppose I spit on her?

HECTOR. Spit.

AJAX. Suppose I strike you, you, one of her princes?

HECTOR. Try it.

AJAX. Suppose I slap your face, you disgusting example of Troy's conceit and her spurious honour?

HECTOR. Strike.

AJAX [*striking him*]. There. If this lady's your wife she must be proud of you.

HECTOR. I know her. She is proud.
[*Enter* DEMOKOS]

DEMOKOS. What's all the noise about? What does this drunkard want, Hector?

HECTOR. He has got what he wants.

DEMOKOS. What is going on, Andromache?

ANDROMACHE. Nothing.

AJAX. Two times nothing. A Greek hits Hector, and Hector puts up with it.

DEMOKOS. Is this true, Hector?

HECTOR. Completely false, isn't it, Helen?

HELEN. The Greeks are great liars. Greek men, I mean.

AJAX. Is it natural for him to have one cheek redder than the other?

HECTOR. Yes. I am healthier on that side.

DEMOKOS. Tell the truth, Hector. Has he dared to raise his hand against you?

HECTOR. That is my concern.

DEMOKOS. It's the concern of war. You are the figurehead of Troy.

HECTOR. Exactly. No one is going to slap a figurehead.

DEMOKOS. Who are you, you brute? I am Demokos, second son of Achichaos!

AJAX. The second son of Achichaos? How do you do? Tell me: is it as serious to slap a second son of Achichaos as to strike Hector?

DEMOKOS. Quite as serious, you drunk. I am the head of the senate. If you want war, war to the death, you have only to try.

AJAX. All right. I'll try. [*He slaps* DEMOKOS]

DEMOKOS. Trojans! Soldiers! To the rescue!

HECTOR. Be quiet, Demokos!

DEMOKOS. To arms! Troy's been insulted! Vengeance!

HECTOR. Be quiet, I tell you.

[618]

DEMOKOS. I *will* shout! I'll rouse the city!

HECTOR. Be quiet! If you won't, I shall hit you, too!

DEMOKOS. Priam! Anchises! Come and see the shame of Troy burning on Hector's face!

[HECTOR *strikes* DEMOKOS. AJAX *laughs. During the scene,* PRIAM *and his lords group themselves ready to receive* ULYSSES]

PRIAM. What are you shouting for, Demokos?

DEMOKOS. I have been struck.

AJAX. Go and complain to Achichaos!

PRIAM. Who struck you?

DEMOKOS. Hector! Ajax! Ajax! Hector!

PARIS. What is he talking about? He's mad!

HECTOR. Nobody struck him, did they, Helen?

HELEN. I was watching most carefully, and I didn't notice anything.

AJAX. Both his cheeks are the same colour.

PARIS. Poets often get upset for no reason. It's what they call their inspiration. We shall get a new national anthem out of it.

DEMOKOS. You will pay for this, Hector.

VOICES. Ulysses! Here is Ulysses!

[AJAX *goes amicably to* HECTOR]

AJAX. Well done. Plenty of pluck. Noble adversary. A beautiful hit.

HECTOR. I did my best.

AJAX. Excellent method, too. Straight elbow. The wrist on an angle. Safe position for the carpus and metacarpus. Your slap must be stronger than mine is.

HECTOR. I doubt it.

AJAX. You must be able to throw a javelin magnificently with this iron forearm and this shoulder-bone for a pivot.

HECTOR. Eighty yards.

AJAX. My deepest respect! My dear Hector, forgive me. I withdraw my threats, I take back my slap. We have enemies in common, in the sons of Achichaos. I won't fight with anybody who shares with me an enmity for the sons of Achichaos. Not another mention of war. I don't know what Ulysses has got in mind, but count on me to arrange the whole thing.

[*He goes towards* ULYSSES *and comes back with him*]

ANDROMACHE. I love you, Hector.

HECTOR. [*Showing his cheek.*] Yes; but don't kiss me just yet.

ANDROMACHE. You have won this round, as well. Be confident.

HECTOR. I win every round. But still with each victory the prize escapes me.

ULYSSES. Priam and Hector?

PRIAM. Yes. And behind us, Troy, and the suburbs of Troy, and the land of Troy, and the Hellespont.

ULYSSES. I am Ulysses.

PRIAM. This is Anchises.

ULYSSES. There are many people here for a diplomatic conversation.

PRIAM. And here is Helen.

ULYSSES. Good morning, my queen.

HELEN. I've grown younger here, Ulysses. I've become a princess again.

PRIAM. We are ready to listen to you.

AJAX. Ulysses, you speak to Priam. I will speak to Hector.

ULYSSES. Priam, we have come to take Helen home again.

AJAX. You do understand, don't you, Hector? We can't have things happening like this.

ULYSSES. Greece and Menelaus cry out for vengeance.

AJAX. If deceived husbands can't cry out for vengeance, what can they do?

ULYSSES. Deliver Helen over to us within an hour. Otherwise it means war.

HECTOR. But if we give Helen back to you give us your assurance there will be peace.

AJAX. Utter tranquillity.

HECTOR. If she goes on board within an hour, the matter is closed.

AJAX. And all is forgotten.

HECTOR. *I* think there's no doubt we can come to an understanding, can we not, Helen?

HELEN. Yes, no doubt.

ULYSSES. You don't mean to say that Helen is being given back to us?

HECTOR. Exactly that. She is ready.

AJAX. What about her baggage? She is sure to have more to take back than when she came.

HECTOR. We return her to you, bag and baggage, and you guarantee peace. No reprisals, no vengeance!

AJAX. A woman is lost, a woman is found, and we're back where we were. Perfect! Isn't it, Ulysses?

ULYSSES. Just wait a moment. I guarantee nothing. Before we say there are going to be no reprisals we have to be sure there has been no cause for reprisals. We have to make sure that Menelaus will find Helen exactly as she was when she was taken from him.

HECTOR. How is he going to discover any difference?

ULYSSES. A husband is very perceptive when a world-wide scandal has put him on his guard. Paris will have had to have respected Helen. And if that isn't so . . .

CROWD. Oh, no! It isn't so!

ONE VOICE. Not exactly!

HECTOR. And if it is so?

ULYSSES. Where is this leading us, Hector?

HECTOR. Paris has not touched Helen. They have both taken me into their confidence.

ULYSSES. What is this absurd story?

HECTOR. The true story, isn't it, Helen?

HELEN. Why does it seem to you so extraordinary?

A VOICE. It's terrible! It puts us to shame!

HECTOR. Why do you have to smile, Ulysses? Do you see the slightest indication in Helen that she has failed in her duty?

ULYSSES. I'm not looking for one. Water leaves more mark on a duck's back than dishonour does on a woman.

PARIS. You're speaking to a queen.

ULYSSES. Present queens excepted, naturally. So, Paris, you have carried off this queen, carried her off naked; and I imagine that you didn't go into the water wearing all your armour; and yet you weren't seized by any taste or desire for her?

PARIS. A naked queen is dressed in her dignity.

HELEN. She has only to remember to keep it on.

ULYSSES. How long did the voyage last? I took three days with my ships, which are faster than yours.

VOICES. What are these intolerable insults to the Trojan navy?

A VOICE. Your winds are faster! Not your ships!

ULYSSES. Let us say three days, if you like. Where was the queen during those three days?

PARIS. Lying down on the deck.

ULYSSES. And Paris was where? In the crow's nest?

HELEN. Lying beside me.

ULYSSES. Was he reading as he lay beside you? Or fishing for goldfish?

HELEN. Sometimes he fanned me.

ULYSSES. Without ever touching you?

HELEN. One day, the second day, I think it was, he kissed my hand.

ULYSSES. Your hand! I see. An outbreak of the animal in him.

HELEN. I thought it was more dignified to take no notice.

ULYSSES. The rolling of the ship didn't throw you towards each other? I don't think it's an insult to the Trojan navy to suggest that its ships roll?

A VOICE. They roll much less than the Greek ships pitch!

AJAX. Pitch? Our Greek ships? If they seem to be pitching it's because of their high prows and their scooped-out sterns!

A VOICE. Oh, yes! The arrogant face and the flat behind, that's Greek all right.

ULYSSES. And what about the three nights you were sailing? The stars appeared and vanished again three times over the pair of you. Do you remember nothing of those three nights?

HELEN. I don't know. Oh, yes! I'd forgotten. I learnt a lot more about the stars.

ULYSSES. While you were asleep, perhaps, he might have taken you . . .

HELEN. A mosquito can wake me.

HECTOR. They will both swear to you, if you like, by our goddess Aphrodite.

ULYSSES. We can do without that. I know what Aphrodite is. Her favourite oath is a perjury.—It's a curious story you're telling me: and it will certainly destroy the idea that the rest of the Archipelago has always had of the Trojans.

PARIS. Why, what do they think of us in the Archipelago?

ULYSSES. You're thought of as less accomplished at trading than we are, but handsome and irresistible. Go on with your story, Paris. It's an interesting contribution to the study of human behaviour. What good reason could you have possibly had for respecting Helen when you had her at your mercy?

PARIS. I . . . I loved her.

HELEN. If you don't know what love is, Ulysses, I shouldn't venture on the subject.

ULYSSES. You must admit, Helen, you would never have followed him if you had known the Trojans were impotent.

VOICES. Shame! Muzzle him! Bring your women here, and you'll soon see! And your grandmother!

ULYSSES. I expressed myself badly. I meant that Paris, the handsome Paris, is impotent.

A VOICE. Why don't you say something, Paris? Are you going to make us the laughing-stock of the world?

PARIS. Hector, you can see, this is a most unpleasant situation for me!

HECTOR. You have to put up with it only a few minutes longer. Goodbye, Helen. And I hope your virtue will become as proverbial as your frailty might have done.

HELEN. That doesn't worry me. The centuries always give us the recognition we deserve.

ULYSSES. Paris the impotent, that's a very good surname! If you care to, Helen, you can kiss him for once.

PARIS. Hector!

FIRST TOPMAN. Are you going to tolerate this farce, commander?

HECTOR. Be quiet! I am in charge here!

TOPMAN. And a rotten job you make of it! We've stood quite enough. We'll tell you, we, Paris's own seamen, we'll tell you what he did with your queen!

VOICES. Bravo! Tell him!

TOPMAN. He's sacrificing himself on his brother's orders. I was an officer on board his ship. I saw everything.

HECTOR. You were quite wrong.

TOPMAN. Do you think a Trojan sailor doesn't know what he sees? I can tell the sex of a seagull thirty yards off. Come over here, Olpides. Olpides was up in the crow's nest. He saw everything from on top. I was standing on the stairs in the hatchway. My head was exactly on a level with them, like a cat on the end of a bed. Shall I tell him, Trojans?

HECTOR. Silence!

VOICES. Tell him! Go on and tell him!

TOPMAN. And they hadn't been on board more than two minutes, wasn't that true, Olpides?

OLPIDES. Only time enough for the queen to dry herself, being just come up out of the water, and to comb the parting into her hair again. I could see her parting, from her forehead over to the nape of her neck, from where I was.

TOPMAN. And he sent us all down into the hold, except the two of us who he couldn't see.

OLPIDES. And without a pilot, the ship drifted due north. There was no wind, and yet the sails were bellied out full.

TOPMAN. And when I looked out from where I was hiding, what I should have seen was the outline of one body, but what I did see was in the shape of two, like a wheaten loaf and rye bread, baking in the oven together.

OLPIDES. But from up where I was, I more often saw one body than two, but sometimes it was white, and sometimes it was golden brown.

TOPMAN. So much for impotence! And as for respectful, inexpressive love, and unspoken affection, you tell him, Olpides, what you heard from your ledge up there! Women's voices carry upwards, men's voices stay on the ground. I shall tell you what Paris said.

OLPIDES. She called him her ladybird, her little ewe-lamb.

TOPMAN. And he called her his lion, his panther. They reversed the sexes. Because they were being so affectionate. It's not unusual.

OLPIDES. And then she said: "You are my darling oak-tree, I put my arms round you as if you were an oak-tree." When you're at sea you think about trees, I suppose.

TOPMAN. And he called her his birch-tree: "My trembling silver birch-tree!" I remember the word birch-tree very well. It's a Russian tree.

OLPIDES. And I had to stay up in the crow's nest all night. You don't half get thirsty up there, and hungry, and everything else.

TOPMAN. And when at last they got up from the deck to go to bed they swayed on their feet. And that's how your wife Penelope would have got on with Trojan impotence.

VOICES. Bravo! Bravo!

A WOMAN'S VOICE. All praise to Paris.

A JOVIAL MAN. Render to Paris what belongs to Paris!

HECTOR. This is a pack of lies, isn't it, Helen?

ULYSSES. Helen is listening enraptured.

HELEN. I forgot they were talking about me. They sound so wonderfully convincing.

ULYSSES. Do you dare to say they are lying, Paris?

PARIS. In some of the particulars, yes, I think they are.

TOPMAN. We're not lying, either in the general or the particular. Are we, Olpides? Do you deny the expressions of love you used? Do you deny the word panther?

PARIS. Not especially the word panther.

TOPMAN. Well, birch-tree, then? I see. It's the phrase "trembling silver birch-tree" that embarrasses you. Well, like it or not, you used it. I swear you used it, and anyway what is there to blush about in the word "birch-tree"? I have seen these silver birch-trees trembling against the snow in wintertime, by the shores of the Caspian, with their rings of black bark apparently separated by rings of space, so that you wondered what was carrying the branches. And I've seen them at the height of summer, beside the canal at Astrakhan, with their white rings like fresh mushrooms. And the leaves talked and made signs to me. To see them quivering, gold above and silver underneath, it makes your heart melt! I could have wept like a woman, isn't that true, Olpides? That's how I feel about the birch-tree.

CROWD. Bravo! Bravo!

ANOTHER SAILOR. And it wasn't only the topman and Olpides who saw them, Priam. The entire crew came wriggling up through the hatches and peering under the handrails. The whole ship was one great spy-glass.

THIRD SAILOR. Spying out love.

ULYSSES. There you have it, Hector!

HECTOR. Be quiet, the lot of you.

TOPMAN. Well, keep this quiet, if you can!

[IRIS *appears in the sky*]

PEOPLE. Iris! Iris!

PARIS. Has Aphrodite sent you?

IRIS. Yes, Aphrodite sent me, and told me that I should say to you that love is the world's chief law. Whatever strengthens love becomes in itself sacred, even falsehood, avarice, or luxury. She takes all lovers under her protection, from the king to the goat-herd. And she forbids both of you, Hector and Ulysses, to separate Paris from Helen. Or else there will be war.

PARIS AND THE OLD MEN. Thank you, Iris.

HECTOR. Is there any message from Pallas Athene?

IRIS. Yes; Pallas Athene told me that I should say to you that reason is the chief law of the world. All who are lovers, she wishes me to say, are out of their minds. She would like you to tell her quite frankly what is more ridiculous than the mating of cocks with hens or flies with flies. And she orders both of you, Hector and Ulysses, to separate Helen from this Paris of the curly hair. Or else there will be war.

HECTOR AND THE WOMEN. Thank you, Iris!

PRIAM. Oh, my son, it isn't Aphrodite nor Pallas Athene who rules the world. What is it Zeus commands us to do in this time of uncertainty?

IRIS. Zeus, the master of the Gods, told me that I should say to you that those who see in the world nothing but love are as foolish as those who cannot see it at all. It is wise, Zeus, master of the Gods, informs you, it is wise sometimes to make love, and at other times not to make love. The decision he gives to Hector and Ulysses, is to separate Helen and Paris without separating them. He orders all the rest of you to go away and leave the negotiators to face each other. And let them so arrange matters that there will be no war. Or else—he swears to you: he swears there will be war.

[*Exit* IRIS]

HECTOR. At your service, Ulysses!

ULYSSES. At your service.

[ALL *withdraw*]

[*A great rainbow is seen in the sky*]

HELEN. How very like Iris to leave her scarf behind.

HECTOR. Now we come to the real tussle, Ulysses.

ULYSSES. Yes: out of which either war or peace is going to come.

HECTOR. Will war come of it?

ULYSSES. We shall know in five minutes' time.

HECTOR. If it's to be a battle of words, my chances are small.

ULYSSES. I believe it will be more a battle of weight. It's as though we were one on each side of a pair of scales. How we weigh in the balance will be what counts in the end.

HECTOR. How we weigh in the balance? And what is my weight, Ulysses? My weight is a young man, a young woman, an unborn child. Joy of life, belief in life, a response to whatever's natural and good.

ULYSSES. And my weight is the mature man, the wife thirty-five years old, the son whose height I measure each month with notches against the doorpost of the palace. My weight is the pleasures of living, and a mistrust of life.

HECTOR. Hunting, courage, loyalty, love.

ULYSSES. Circumspection in the presence of the gods, of men, and everything else.

HECTOR. The Phrygian oak-tree, all the leafy, thick-set oak-trees that grow on our hills with our curly-coated oxen.

ULYSSES. The power and wisdom of the olive-tree.

HECTOR. I weigh the hawk, I look straight into the sun.

ULYSSES. I weigh the owl.

HECTOR. I weigh the whole race of humble peasants, hard-working craftsmen, thousands of ploughs and looms, forges and anvils . . . Why is it, when I put all these in the scale in front of you, all at once they seem to me to weigh so light?

ULYSSES. I am the weight of this incorruptible, unpitying air of these coasts and islands.

HECTOR. Why go on? The scales have tipped.

ULYSSES. To my side? Yes, I think so.

HECTOR. And you want war?

ULYSSES. I don't want it. But I'm less sure whether war may not want us.

HECTOR. Our peoples have brought us together to prevent it. Our meeting itself shows that there is still some hope.

ULYSSES. You are young, Hector! It's usual on the eve of every war, for the two leaders of the peoples concerned to meet privately at some innocent village, on a terrace in a garden overlooking a lake. And they decide together that war is the world's worst scourge, and as they watch the rippling reflections in the water, with magnolia petals dropping on to their shoulders, they are both of them peace-loving, modest and friendly. They study one another. They look into each other's eyes. And, warmed by the sun and mellowed by the claret, they can't find anything in the other man's face to justify hatred, nothing, indeed, which doesn't inspire human affection, nothing incompatible in their languages any more, or in their particular way of scratching the nose or drinking wine. They really are exuding peace, and the world's desire for peace. And when their meeting is over, they shake hands in a most sincere brotherly fashion, and turn to smile and wave as they drive away. And the next day war breaks out. And so it is with us both at this moment. Our peoples, who have drawn aside, saying nothing while we have this interview, are not expecting us to win a victory over the inevitable. They have merely given us full powers, isolated here together, to stand above the catastrophe and taste the essential brotherhood of enemies. Taste it. It's a rare dish. Savour it. But that is all. One of the privileges of the great is to witness catastrophes from a terrace.

HECTOR. Do you think this is a conversation between enemies we are having?

ULYSSES. I should say a duet before the full orchestra. Because we have been created sensible and courteous, we can talk to each other, an hour or so before the war, in the way we shall talk to each other long after it's over, like old antagonists. We are merely having our reconciliation before the struggle instead of after it. That may be unwise. If one day one of us should have to kill the other, it might be as well if it wasn't a friend's face we recognized as the body dropped to the ground. But, as the universe well knows, we are going to fight each other.

HECTOR. The universe might be mistaken. One way to recognize error is the fact that it's universal.

ULYSSES. Let's hope so. But when destiny has brought up two nations, as for years it has brought up yours and mine, to a future of similar invention and authority, and given to each a different scale of values (as you and I saw just now, when we weighed pleasure against pleasure, conscience against conscience, even nature itself against nature): when the nation's architects and poets and painters have created for them opposing kingdoms of sound, and form, and subtlety, when we have a Trojan tile roof, a Theban arch, Phrygian red, Greek blue: the universe knows that destiny wasn't preparing alternative ways for civilization to flower. It was contriving the dance of death, letting loose the brutality and human folly which is all that the gods are really contented by. It's a mean way to contrive things, I agree. But we are Heads of State, you and I; we can say this between ourselves: it is Destiny's way of contriving things, inevitably.

HECTOR. And this time it has chosen to match Greece with Troy?

ULYSSES. This morning I was still in doubt. As soon as I stepped on to your landing stage I was certain of it.

HECTOR. You mean you felt yourself on enemy soil?

ULYSSES. Why will you always harp on the word enemy? Born enemies don't fight. Nations you would say were designed to go to war against each other—by their skins, their language, their smell: always jealous of each other, always hating each other—they're not the ones who fight. You will find the real antagonists in nations fate has groomed and made ready for the same war.

HECTOR. And you think we have been made ready for the Greek war?

ULYSSES. To an astonishing extent. Just as nature, when she foresees a struggle between two kinds of insects, equips them with weaknesses and weapons which correspond, so we, living well apart, unknown to ourselves, not even suspecting it, have both been gradually raised up to the level where war begins. All our weapons and habits correspond with each other and balance against each other like the beams of a gable. No other women in the world excite less brutality in us, or less desire, than your wives and daughters do; they give us a joy and an anguish of heart which is a sure sign of impending war between us. Doom has transfigured everything here with the colour of storm: your grave buildings shaking with shadow and fire, the neighing horses, figures disappearing into the dark of a colonnade: the future has never impressed me before with such startling clarity. There is nothing to be done. You're already living in the light of the Greek war.

HECTOR. And do the rest of the Greeks think this?

ULYSSES. What they think is no more reassuring. The rest of the Greeks think Troy is wealthy, her warehouses bulging, her soil prolific. They think that they, on the other hand, are living cramped on a rock. And your golden temples and golden wheatfields flashed from your promontories a signal our ships will never forget. It isn't very wise to have such golden gods and vegetables.

HECTOR. This is more like the truth, at last. Greece has chosen Troy for her prey. Then why a declaration of war? It would have been simpler to have taken Troy by surprise when I was away with the army. You would have had her without striking a blow.

ULYSSES. There's a kind of permission for war which can be given only by the world's mood and atmosphere, the feel of its pulse. It would have been madness to undertake a war without that permission. We didn't have it.

HECTOR. But you have it now.

ULYSSES. I think we do.

HECTOR. But why against us? Troy is famous for her arts, her justice, her humanity.

ULYSSES. A nation doesn't put itself at odds with its destiny by its crimes, but by its faults. Its army may be strong, its treasury well filled, its poets at the height of inspiration. But one day, why it is no one knows, because of some simple event, such as the citizens wantonly cutting down the trees, or their prince wickedly making off with a woman, or the children getting out of hand, the nation is suddenly lost. Nations, like men, die by imperceptible disorders. We recognize a doomed people by the way they sneeze or pare their nails. There's no doubt you carried off Helen badly.

HECTOR. What fairness of proportion can you see between the rape of one woman, and the possible destruction of a whole people, yours or mine, in war?

ULYSSES. We are speaking of Helen. You and Paris have made a great mistake about Helen. I've known her fifteen years, and watched her carefully. There's no doubt about it: she is one of the rare creatures destiny puts on the earth for its own personal use. They're apparently quite unimportant. It might be not even a person, but a small town, or a village: a little queen, or a child; but if you lay hands on them, watch out! It's very hard to know how to recognize one of these hostages of fate among all the other people and places. You haven't recognized it. You could have laid hands with impunity on our great admirals or one of our kings. Paris could have let himself go with perfect safety in a Spartan bed, or a Theban bed, with generous returns twenty times over; but he chose the shallowest brain, the hardest heart, the narrowest understanding of sex. And so you are lost.

HECTOR. We are giving Helen back to you.

ULYSSES. The insult to destiny can't be taken back.

HECTOR. What are we discussing, then? I'm beginning to see what is really behind your words. Admit it. You want our wealth! You had Helen carried off to give you an honourable pretext for war! I blush for Greece. She will be responsible and ashamed for the rest of time.

ULYSSES. Responsible and ashamed? Do you think so? The two words hardly agree. Even if we believed we were responsible for the war, all our generation would have to do would be to deny it, and lie, to appease the conscience of future generations. And we shall lie. We'll make that sacrifice.

HECTOR. Ah, well, the die is cast, Ulysses. On with the war! The more I hate it, the more I find growing in me an irresistible need to kill. If you won't help me, it were better you should leave here.

ULYSSES. Understand me, Hector; you have my help. Don't ask me to interpret fate. All I have tried to do is to read the world's hand, in the great lines of desert caravans, the wake of ships, and the track of migrant birds and wandering peoples. Give me your hand. There are lines there, too. We won't search to see if their lesson tells the same story. We'll suppose that these three little lines at the base of Hector's hand contradict the waves, the wings, and the furrows. I am inquisitive by nature, and not easily frightened. I'm quite willing to join issue with fate. I accept your offer of Helen. I will take her back to Menelaus. I've more than enough eloquence to convince a husband of his wife's virtue. I will even persuade Helen to believe it herself. And I'll leave at once, to avoid any chance of disturbance. Once back on my ship perhaps we can take the risk of running war on to the rocks.

HECTOR. Is this part of Ulysses' cunning, or his greatness?

ULYSSES. In this particular instance, I'm using my cunning against destiny, not against you. It's my first attempt, so I deserve some credit for it. I am sincere, Hector. If I wanted war, I should have asked for a ransom more precious to you than Helen. I am going now. But I can't shake off the feeling that the road from here to my ship is a long way.

HECTOR. My guard will escort you.

ULYSSES. As long as the road of a visiting king, when he knows there has been a threat against his life. Where are the assassins hiding? We're lucky if it's not in the heavens themselves. And the distance from here to the corner of the palace is a long way. A long way, taking this first step. Where is it going to carry me among all these perils? Am I going to slip and kill myself? Will part of the cornice fall down on me? It's all new stonework here; at any moment a stone may be dislodged. But courage. Let us go. [*He takes a first step*]

HECTOR. Thank you, Ulysses.

ULYSSES. The first step is safely over. How many more?

HECTOR. Four hundred and sixty.

ULYSSES. Now the second! You know what made me decide to go, Hector?

HECTOR. Yes. Your noble nature.

ULYSSES. Not precisely. Andromache's eyelashes dance as my wife Penelope's do.

[*Enter* ANDROMACHE *and* CASSANDRA]

HECTOR. Were you there all the time, Andromache?

ANDROMACHE. Let me take your arm. I've no more strength.

HECTOR. Did you hear what we said?

ANDROMACHE. Yes. I am broken.

HECTOR. You see, we needn't despair.

ANDROMACHE. We needn't despair for ourselves, perhaps. But for the world, yes. That man is terrible. All the unhappiness of the world is in me.

HECTOR. A moment or two more, and Ulysses will be on board. You see how fast he is travelling. You can follow his progress from here. There he is, on a level with the fountains. What are you doing?

ANDROMACHE. I haven't the strength any longer to hear any more. I am covering up my ears. I won't take my hands away until we know what our fate is to be.

HECTOR. Find Helen, Cassandra!
[AJAX *enters, more drunk than ever. He sees* ANDROMACHE. *Her back is towards him*]

CASSANDRA. Ulysses is waiting for you down at the harbour, Ajax. Helen will be brought to you there.

AJAX. Helen! To hell with Helen! This is the one I want to get my arms around.

CASSANDRA. Go away, Ajax. That is Hector's wife.

AJAX. Hector's wife! Bravo! I've always liked my friends' wives, my best friends' wives!

CASSANDRA. Ulysses is already half-way there. Hurry.

AJAX. Don't worry, my dear. She's got her hands over her ears. I can say what I like, she can't hear me. If I touched her, now, if I kissed her, certainly! But words she can't hear, what's the matter with that?

CASSANDRA. Everything is the matter with that. Go away, Ajax!

[AJAX, *while* CASSANDRA *tries to force him away from* ANDROMACHE *and* HECTOR, *slowly raises his javelin*]

AJAX. Do you think so? Then I might as well touch her. Might as well kiss her. But chastely, always chastely, with your best friends' wives! What's the most chaste part of your wife, Hector, her neck? So much for her neck. Her ear has a pretty little look of chastity to me. So much for her ear. I'll tell you what I've always found the chastest thing about a woman . . . Let me alone, now; let me alone! She can't even hear when I kiss her . . . You're so cursed strong! All right, I'm going, I said I was going. Goodbye.
[*He goes*]
[HECTOR *imperceptibly lowers his javelin. At this moment* DEMOKOS *bursts in*]

DEMOKOS. What's this cowardice? You're giving Helen back? Trojans, to arms! They've betrayed us. Fall in! And your war-song is ready! Listen to your war-song!

HECTOR [*striking him*]. Have that for your war-song!

DEMOKOS [*falling*]. He has killed me!

HECTOR. The war isn't going to happen, Andromache!

[*He tries to take* ANDROMACHE's *hands from her ears: she resists, her eyes fixed on* DEMOKOS. *The curtain which had begun to fall is lifted little by little*]

ABNEOS. They have killed Demokos! Who killed Demokos?

DEMOKOS. Who killed me? Ajax! Ajax! Kill him!

ABNEOS. Kill Ajax!

HECTOR. He's lying. I am the man who struck him.

DEMOKOS. No. It was Ajax.

ABNEOS. Ajax has killed Demokos. Catch him! Punish him!

HECTOR. I struck you, Demokos, admit it! Admit it, or I'll put an end to you!

DEMOKOS. No, my dear Hector, my good dear Hector. It was Ajax. Kill Ajax!

CASSANDRA. He is dying, just as he lived, croaking like a frog.

ABNEOS. There. They have taken Ajax. There. They have killed him!

HECTOR [*drawing* ANDROMACHE's *hands away from her ears*]. The war will happen.

[*The Gates of War slowly open, to show* HELEN *kissing* TROILUS]

CASSANDRA. The Trojan poet is dead. And now the Grecian poet will have his word.

THE CURTAIN FINALLY FALLS

PART V · POETRY

THE CONTEMPORARY POET writes against, and draws from, a large background of American, British, and Continental literature. Because that British background is usually studied in a Survey course, and because the Continental (particularly the French) could not be adequately represented in this volume, we have chosen to introduce this section with selections from the work of three nineteenth-century American poets. The different patterns of thought and technique found in Emerson, Dickinson, and Whitman have done their share in shaping the contemporary poet and his poem.

Thomas Hardy and A. E. Housman are frequently considered the first of the "modern" poets. Certainly the ruggedness of Hardy's poems and the precision of Housman's did much to rescue poetry from the sentimentality and false rhetoric so frequently found in the early part of this century.

The twelve poets who continue this part of the anthology range in technique from the "traditional" structures of Robinson and Frost through the symbolist patterns of Eliot to the typographical tricks of Cummings. They deal with a large and diverse subject matter: such precise things as an express train, a peach tree, a shooting gallery, and such general problems as the meaning of history, the individual's role in a world society, and the search for truth. The attitudes of the poets are also diverse: Whitman's determined optimism, Frost's search for a "Vantage Point," Eliot's early despair, Jeffers' rejection of man and society, Auden's insistence that "we must love one another or die," and Thomas' "true joy" that "sang burning in the sun."

We conclude this part of the book with a selection, necessarily limited, of the poets who have been publishing their work since 1950. These seven "new" poets deal with the old and with the new in old and new techniques. They are skillful, imaginative, moving. They are "influenced," and they are original. We have chosen these particular poems not only because they speak so poetically of our present world but also because they augur so well the future of poetry in our time.

The work of nine of the poets is preceded by excerpts from their own prose statements on the nature of poetry, the poetic process, or their attitudes toward the world. These comments can be most helpful to the reader in fully

Poetry

understanding the intentions of the individual poets. In the Appendix will be found a list of poems recorded by the poets. As we hear the poet read his own work, our understanding of the poem and our pleasure in it are almost always increased.

We have included only one commentary on a poem. The Kimon Friar analysis of Yeats' "Byzantium" is a clear explication of a difficult poem. The interested student will find many similar analyses of poems in the critical literature of recent years. We have provided no other commentaries or questions on the poems, believing that they should be left to the individual reader. We like to think of Robert Frost's reply to the question, "I understand the poem all right, but won't you tell me what it *means?*" He said, "If I had wanted you to know, I would have told you in the poem."

Lake Through the Locusts — Luigi Lucioni
Used with the permission of J. Watson Webb, Jr.

Ode

THE RHODORA:

ON BEING ASKED, WHENCE IS THE FLOWER?

by RALPH WALDO EMERSON

In May, when sea-winds pierced our solitudes,
I found the fresh Rhodora in the woods,
Spreading its leafless blooms in a damp nook,
To please the desert and the sluggish brook.
The purple petals, fallen in the pool,
Made the black water with their beauty gay;
Here might the red-bird come his plumes to cool,
And court the flower that cheapens his array.
Rhodora! if the sages ask thee why
This charm is wasted on the earth and sky,
Tell them, dear, that if eyes were made for seeing,
Then Beauty is its own excuse for being:
Why thou wert there, O rival of the rose!
I never thought to ask, I never knew:
But, in my simple ignorance, suppose
The self-same Power that brought me there brought you.

ODE

INSCRIBED TO W. H. CHANNING

by RALPH WALDO EMERSON

Though loath to grieve
The evil time's sole patriot,
I cannot leave
My honied thought
For the priest's cant,
Or statesman's rant.

If I refuse
My study for their politique,
Which at the best is trick,
The angry Muse
Puts confusion in my brain.

But who is he that prates
Of the culture of mankind,
Of better arts and life?
Go, blindworm, go,
Behold the famous States

Harrying Mexico
With rifle and with knife!

Or who, with accent bolder,
Dare praise the freedom-loving mountaineer?
I found by thee, O rushing Contoocook!
And in thy valleys, Agiochook!
The jackals of the negro-holder.

The God who made New Hampshire
Taunted the lofty land
With little men;—
Small bat and wren
House in the oak:—
If earth-fire cleave
The upheaved land, and bury the folk,
The southern crocodile would grieve.

Virtue palters; Right is hence;
Freedom praised, but hid;
Funeral eloquence
Rattles the coffin-lid.

What boots thy zeal,
O glowing friend,
That would indignant rend
The northland from the south?
Wherefore? To what good end?
Boston Bay and Bunker Hill
Would serve things still;—
Things are of the snake.
The horseman serves the horse,
The neatherd serves the neat,
The merchant serves the purse,
The eater serves his meat;
'Tis the day of the chattel,
Web to weave, and corn to grind;
Things are in the saddle,
And ride mankind.

There are two laws discrete,
Not reconciled,—
Law for man, and law for thing;
The last builds town and fleet,
But it runs wild,
And doth the man unking.
'Tis fit the forest fall,
The steep be graded,
The mountain tunnelled,
The sand shaded,
The orchard planted,
The glebe tilled,
The prairie granted,
The steamer built.

Let man serve law for man;
Live for friendship, live for love,
For truth's and harmony's behoof;
The state may follow how it can,
As Olympus follows Jove.

    Yet do not I implore
The wrinkled shopman to my sounding
    woods,
Nor bid the unwilling senator
Ask votes of thrushes in the solitudes.
Every one to his chosen work;—
Foolish hands may mix and mar;
Wise and sure the issues are.
Round they roll till dark is light,
Sex to sex, and even to odd;—
The over-god
Who marries Right to Might,
Who peoples, unpeoples,—
He who exterminates
Races by stronger races,
Black by white faces,—
Knows to bring honey
Out of the lion;
Grafts gentlest scion
On pirate and Turk.

The Cossack eats Poland,
Like stolen fruit;
Her last noble is ruined,
Her last poet mute:
Straight, into double band
The victors divide;
Half for freedom strike and stand;—
The astonished Muse finds thousands at
    her side.

Days

GIVE ALL TO LOVE
by Ralph Waldo Emerson

Give all to love;
Obey thy heart;
Friends, kindred, days,
Estate, good-fame,
Plans, credit and the Muse,—
Nothing refuse.

'T is a brave master;
Let it have scope:
Follow it utterly,
Hope beyond hope:
High and more high
It dives into noon,
With wing unspent,
Untold intent;
But it is a god,
Knows its own path
And the outlets of the sky.

It was never for the mean;
It requireth courage stout.
Souls above doubt,
Valor unbending,
It will reward,—
They shall return
More than they were,
And ever ascending.

Leave all for love;
Yet, hear me, yet,
One word more thy heart behoved,
One pulse more of firm endeavor,—
Keep thee to-day,
To-morrow, forever,
Free as an Arab
Of thy beloved.

Cling with life to the maid;
But when the surprise,
First vague shadow of surmise
Flits across her bosom young,
Of a joy apart from thee,
Free be she, fancy-free;
Nor thou detain her vesture's hem,
Nor the palest rose she flung
From her summer diadem.

Though thou loved her as thyself,
As a self of purer clay,
Though her parting dims the day,
Stealing grace from all alive;
Heartily know,
When half-gods go,
The gods arrive.

DAYS[1]
by Ralph Waldo Emerson

Daughters of Time, the hypocritic Days,
Muffled and dumb like barefoot dervishes,
And marching single in an endless file,
Bring diadems and fagots in their hands.
To each they offer gifts after his will,
Bread, kingdoms, stars, and sky that holds them all.
I, in my pleached garden, watched the pomp,
Forgot my morning wishes, hastily
Took a few herbs and apples, and the Day
Turned and departed silent. I, too late,
Under her solemn fillet saw the scorn.

[1] "The days are ever divine, as to the first Aryans. They come and go like muffled and veiled figures, sent from a distant friendly party; but they say nothing, and if we so not use the gifts they bring, they carry them as silently away."
—Emerson, "Works and Days."

Poetry

BRAHMA[1]

by Ralph Waldo Emerson

If the red slayer think he slays,
  Or if the slain think he is slain,
They know not well the subtle ways
  I keep, and pass, and turn again.

Far or forgot to me is near;
  Shadow and sunlight are the same;
The vanished gods to me appear;
  And one to me are shame and fame.

They reckon ill who leave me out;
  When me they fly, I am the wings;
I am the doubter and the doubt,
  And I the hymn the Brahmin sings.

The strong gods pine for my abode,
  And pine in vain the sacred Seven;
But thou, meek lover of the good!
  Find me, and turn thy back on heaven

[1] "In all nations there are minds which incline to dwell in the conception of the fundamental Unity . . . This tendency finds its highest expression in the religious writings of the East, and chiefly in the Indian Scriptures."
—Emerson, essay on Plato.

Brahma is the soul or essence of all creation. The strong gods are Indra, Agni, and Yama. Emerson, aware of the difficulty of the poem, suggested, "Say Jehovah instead of Brahma," and approved the interpretation by a girl of Concord: "It simply means God everywhere."

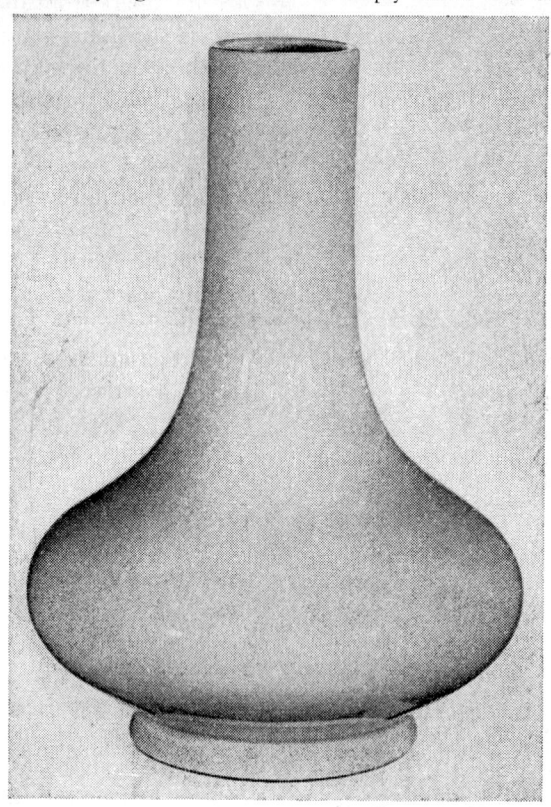

Courtesy, Museum of Fine Arts, Boston

Chinese vase, Ch'ien-lung period.

THIS IS MY LETTER

by Emily Dickinson

This is my letter to the world,
   That never wrote to me,—
The simple news that Nature told,
   With tender majesty.

Her message is committed
   To hands I cannot see;
For love of her, sweet countrymen,
   Judge tenderly of me!

I NEVER SAW

by Emily Dickinson

I never saw a moor,
I never saw the sea;
Yet know I how the heather looks,
And what a wave must be.

I never spoke with God,
Nor visited in heaven;
Yet certain am I of the spot
As if the chart were given.

ELYSIUM IS AS FAR

by Emily Dickinson

Elysium is as far as to
The very nearest room,
If in that room a friend await
Felicity or doom.

What fortitude the soul contains,
That it can so endure
The accent of a coming foot,
The opening of a door!

MUCH MADNESS

by Emily Dickinson

Much madness is divinest sense
To a discerning eye;
Much sense the starkest madness.
'T is the majority

In this, as all, prevails.
Assent, and you are sane;
Demur,—you're straightway dangerous,
And handled with a chain.

All poems except "Although I put away" from *Poems by Emily Dickinson*, edited by Martha Dickinson Bianchi and Alfred Leete Hampson, Little, Brown and Company.

THERE'S A CERTAIN SLANT
by Emily Dickinson

There's a certain slant of light,
On winter afternoons,
That oppresses, like the weight
Of cathedral tunes.

Heavenly hurt it gives us;
We can find no scar,
But internal difference
Where the meanings are.

None may teach it anything,
'T is the seal, despair,—
An imperial affliction
Sent us of the air.

When it comes, the landscape listens,
Shadows hold their breath;
When it goes, 't is like the distance
On the look of death.

SUCCESS IS COUNTED
by Emily Dickinson

Success is counted sweetest
By those who ne'er succeed.
To comprehend a nectar
Requires sorest need.

Not one of all the purple host
Who took the flag to-day
Can tell the definition,
So clear, of victory,

As he, defeated, dying,
On whose forbidden ear
The distant strains of triumph
Break, agonized and clear.

THE SOUL SELECTS
by Emily Dickinson

The soul selects her own society,
Then shuts the door;
On her divine majority
Obtrude no more.

Unmoved, she notes the chariot's pausing
At her low gate;

Unmoved, an emperor is kneeling
Upon her mat.

I've known her from an ample nation
Choose one;
Then close the valves of her attention
Like stone.

TO FIGHT ALOUD
by Emily Dickinson

To fight aloud is very brave,
But gallanter, I know,
Who charge within the bosom,
The cavalry of woe.

Who win, and nations do not see,
Who fall, and none observe,
Whose dying eyes no country
Regards with patriot love.

We trust, in plumed procession,
For such the angels go,
Rank after rank, with even feet
And uniforms of snow.

ALTHOUGH I PUT AWAY*
by Emily Dickinson

Although I put away his life,
An ornament too grand
For forehead low as mine to wear,
This might have been the hand

That sowed the flowers he preferred,
Or smoothed a homely pain,
Or pushed a pebble from his path,
Or played his chosen tune

On lute the least, the latest,
But just his ear could know
That whatsoe'er delighted it
I never would let go.

The foot to bear his errand
A little boot I know
Would leap abroad like antelope
With just the grant to do.

His weariest commandment
A sweeter to obey
Than "Hide and Seek," or skip to flutes,
Or all day chase the bee.

Your servant, Sir, will weary,
The surgeon will not come,
The world will have its own to do,
The dust will vex your fame.

The cold will force your tightest door
Some February day,
But say my apron bring the sticks
To make your cottage gay,

That I may take that promise
To Paradise with me—
To teach the angels avarice
Your kiss first taught to me!

*Copyright 1929 by Martha Dickinson Bianchi.

MY LIFE CLOSED TWICE
by Emily Dickinson

My life closed twice before its close;
It yet remains to see
If Immortality unveil
A third event to me,

So huge, so hopeless to conceive,
As these that twice befell.
Parting is all we know of heaven,
And all we need of hell.

JUST LOST
by Emily Dickinson

Just lost when I was saved!
Just felt the world go by!
Just girt me for the onset with eternity,
When breath blew back,
And on the other side
I heard recede the disappointed tide!

Therefore, as one returned, I feel,
Odd secrets of the line to tell!
Some sailor, skirting foreign shores,
Some pale reporter from the awful doors
Before the seal!

Next time, to stay!
Next time, the things to see
By ear unheard,
Unscrutinized by eye.

Next time, to tarry,
While the ages steal,—
Slow tramp the centuries,
And the cycles wheel.

Song of Myself

ONE'S-SELF I SING

by WALT WHITMAN

One's-self I sing, a simple separate person,
Yet utter the word Democratic, the word En-Masse.

Of physiology from top to toe I sing,
Not physiognomy alone nor brain alone is worthy for the Muse,
    I say the Form complete is worthier far,
The Female equally with the Male I sing.

Of Life immense in passion, pulse, and power,
Cheerful, for freest action form'd under the laws divine,
The Modern Man I sing.

from SONG OF MYSELF

by WALT WHITMAN

I

I celebrate myself, and sing myself,
And what I assume you shall assume,
For every atom belonging to me as good belongs to you.

I loafe and invite my soul,
I lean and loafe at my ease observing a spear of summer grass.

My tongue, every atom of my blood, form'd from this soil, this air,
Born here of parents born here from parents the same, and their parents the same,
I, now thirty-seven years old in perfect health begin,
Hoping to cease not till death.

Creeds and schools in abeyance,
Retiring back a while sufficed at what they are, but never forgotten,
I harbor for good or bad, I permit to speak at every hazard,
Nature without check with original energy.

  .   .   .   .   .   .

3

I have heard what the talkers were talking, the talk of the beginning and the end,
But I do not talk of the beginning or the end.

Poetry

There was never any more inception than there is now,
Nor any more youth or age than there is now,
And will never be any more perfection than there is now,
Nor any more heaven or hell than there is now.

Urge and urge and urge,
Always the procreant urge of the world.
Out of the dimness opposite equals advance, always substance and increase, always sex,
Always a knit of identity, always distinction, always a breed of life.

To elaborate is no avail, learn'd and unlearn'd feel that it is so.

Sure as the most certain sure, plumb in the uprights, well entretied, braced in the beams,
Stout as a horse, affectionate, haughty, electrical,
I and this mystery here we stand.

Clear and sweet is my soul, and clear and sweet is all that is not my soul.

Lack one lacks both, and the unseen is proved by the seen,
Till that becomes unseen and receives proof in its turn.

Showing the best and dividing it from the worst age vexes age,
Knowing the perfect fitness and equanimity of things, while they discuss I am silent, and go bathe and admire myself.
Welcome is every organ and attribute of me, and of any man hearty and clean,
Not an inch nor a particle of an inch is vile, and none shall be less familiar than the rest.

I am satisfied—I see, dance, laugh, sing;
As the hugging and loving bed-fellow sleeps at my side through the night, and withdraws at the peep of the day with stealthy tread,
Leaving me baskets cover'd with white towels swelling the house with their plenty,
Shall I postpone my acceptation and realization and scream at my eyes,
That they turn from gazing after and down the road,
And forthwith cipher and show me to a cent,
Exactly the value of one and exactly the value of two, and which is ahead? . . .

30

All truths wait in all things,
They neither hasten their own delivery nor resist it,

[640]

Song of Myself

They do not need the obstetric forceps of the surgeon,
The insignificant is as big to me as any,
(What is less or more than a touch?)

Logic and sermons never convince,
The damp of the night drives deeper into my soul.

(Only what proves itself to every man and woman is so,
Only what nobody denies is so.)

A minute and a drop of me settle my brain,
I believe the soggy clods shall become lovers and lamps,
And a compend of compends is the meat of a man or woman,
And a summit and flower there is the feeling they have for each other,
And they are to branch boundlessly out of that lesson until it becomes omnific,
And until one and all shall delight us, and we them.

. . . .

52

The spotted hawk swoops by and accuses me, he complains of my gab and my
    loitering.

I too am not a bit tamed, I too am untranslatable,
I sound my barbaric yawp over the roofs of the world.

The last scud of day holds back for me,
It flings my likeness after the rest and true as any on the shadow'd wilds,
It coaxes me to the vapor and the dusk.

I depart as air, I shake my white locks at the runaway sun,
I effuse my flesh in eddies, and drift it in lacy jags.

I bequeath myself to the dirt to grow from the grass I love,
If you want me again look for me under your boot-soles.

You will hardly know who I am or what I mean,
But I shall be good health to you nevertheless,
And filter and fibre your blood.

Failing to fetch me at first keep encouraged,
Missing me one place search another,
I stop somewhere waiting for you.

WHEN LILACS LAST IN THE DOORYARD BLOOM'D
by Walt Whitman

1

When lilacs last in the dooryard bloom'd,
And the great star early droop'd in the western sky in the night,
I mourn'd, and yet shall mourn with ever-returning spring.

Ever-returning spring, trinity sure to me you bring,
Lilac blooming perennial and drooping star in the west,
And thought of him I love.

2

O powerful western fallen star!
O shades of night—O moody, tearful night!
O great star disappear'd—O the black murk that hides the star!
O cruel hands that hold me powerless—O helpless soul of me!
O harsh surrrounding cloud that will not free my soul.

3

In the dooryard fronting an old farm-house near the white-wash'd palings,
Stands the lilac-bush tall-growing with heart-shaped leaves of rich green,
With many a pointed blossom rising delicate, with the perfume strong I love,
With every leaf a miracle—and from this bush in the dooryard,
With delicate-color'd blossoms and heart-shaped leaves of rich green,
A sprig with its flower I break.

4

In the swamp in secluded recesses,
A shy and hidden bird is warbling a song.
Solitary the thrush,
The hermit withdrawn to himself, avoiding the settlements,
Sings by himself a song.

Song of the bleeding throat,
Death's outlet song of life, (for well dear brother I know,
If thou wast not granted to sing thou would'st surely die.)

When Lilacs Last in the Dooryard Bloom'd

5

Over the breast of the spring, the land, amid cities,
Amid lanes and through old woods, where lately the violets peep'd from the ground,
    spotting the gray debris,
Amid the grass in the fields each side of the lanes, passing the endless grass,
Passing the yellow-spear'd wheat, every grain from its shroud in the dark-brown
    fields uprisen,
Passing the apple-tree blows of white and pink in the orchards,
Carrying a corpse to where it shall rest in the grave,
Night and day journeys a coffin.

6

Coffin that passes through lanes and streets,
Through day and night with the great cloud darkening the land,
With the pomp of the inloop'd flags with the cities draped in black,
With the show of the States themselves as of crape-veil'd women standing,
With processions long and winding and the flambeaus of the night,
With the countless torches lit, with the silent sea of faces and the unbared heads,
With the waiting depot, the arriving coffin, and the sombre faces,
With dirges through the night, with the thousand voices rising strong and solemn,
With all the mournful voices of the dirges pour'd around the coffin,
The dim-lit churches and the shuddering organs—where amid these you journey,
With the tolling tolling bells' perpetual clang,
Here, coffin that slowly passes,
I give you my sprig of lilac.

7

(Nor for you, for one alone,
Blossoms and branches green to coffins all I bring,
For fresh as the morning, thus would I chant a song for you O sane and sacred death.

All over bouquets of roses,
O death, I cover you over with roses and early lilies,
But mostly and now the lilac that blooms the first,
Copious I break, I break the sprigs from the bushes,
With loaded arms I come, pouring for you,
For you and the coffins all of you O death.)

8

O western orb sailing the heaven,
Now I know what you must have meant as a month since I walk'd,

As I walk'd in silence the transparent shadowy night,
As I saw you had something to tell as you bent to me night after night,
As you droop'd from the sky low down as if to my side, (while the other stars all look'd on,)
As we wander'd together the solemn night, (for something I know not what kept me from sleep,)
As the night advanced, and I saw on the rim of the west how full you were of woe,
As I stood on the rising ground in the breeze in the cool transparent night,
As I watch'd where you pass'd and was lost in the netherward black of the night,
As my soul in its trouble dissatisfied sank, as where you sad orb,
Concluded, dropt in the night, and was gone.

9

Sing on there in the swamp,
O singer bashful and tender, I hear your notes, I hear your call,
I hear, I come presently, I understand you,
But a moment I linger, for the lustrous star has detain'd me,
The star my departing comrade holds and detains me.

10

O how shall I warble myself for the dead one there I loved?
And how shall I deck my song for the large sweet soul that has gone?
And what shall my perfume be for the grave of him I love?

Sea-winds blown from east and west,
Blown from the Eastern sea and blown from the Western sea, till there on the prairies meeting,
These and with these and the breath of my chant,
I'll perfume the grave of him I love.

11

O what shall I hang on the chamber walls?
And what shall the pictures be that I hang on the walls,
To adorn the burial-house of him I love?

Pictures of growing spring and farms and homes,
With the Fourth-month eve at sundown, and the gray smoke lucid and bright,
With floods of the yellow gold of the gorgeous, indolent, sinking sun, burning, expanding the air,
With the fresh sweet herbage under foot, and the pale green leaves of the trees prolific,

When Lilacs Last in the Dooryard Bloom'd

In the distance the flowing glaze, the breast of the river, with a wind-dapple here and there,
With ranging hills on the banks, with many a line against the sky, and shadows,
And the city at hand with dwellings so dense, and stacks of chimneys,
And all the scenes of life and the workshops, and the workmen homeward returning.

12

Lo, body and soul—this land,
My own Manhattan with spires, and the sparkling and hurrying tides, and the ships,
The varied and ample land, the South and the North in the light, Ohio's shores and flashing Missouri,
And ever the far-spreading prairies cover'd with grass and corn.

Lo, the most excellent sun so calm and haughty,
The violet and purple morn with just-felt breezes,
The gentle soft-born measureless light,
The miracle spreading bathing all, the fulfill'd noon,
The coming eve delicious, the welcome night and the stars,
Over my cities shining all, enveloping man and land.

13

Sing on, sing on you gray-brown bird,
Sing from the swamps, the recesses, pour your chant from the bushes,
Limitless out of the dusk, out of the cedars and pines.

Sing on dearest brother, warble your reedy song,
Loud human song, with voice of uttermost woe.

O liquid and free and tender!
O wild and loose to my soul—O wondrous singer!
You only I hear—yet the star holds me, (but will soon depart,)
Yet the lilac with mastering odor holds me.

14

Now while I sat in the day and look'd forth,
In the close of the day with its light and the fields of spring, and the farmers preparing their crops,
In the large unconscious scenery of my land with its lakes and forests,
In the heavenly aerial beauty, (after the perturb'd winds and the storms,)
Under the arching heavens of the afternoon swift passing, and the voices of children and women,

The many-moving sea-tides, and I saw the ships how they sail'd,
And the summer approaching with richness, and the fields all busy with labor,
And the infinite separate houses, how they all went on, each with its meals and minutia of daily usages,
And the streets how their throbbings throbb'd, and the cities pent—lo, then and there,
Falling upon them all and among them all, enveloping me with the rest,
Appear'd the cloud, appear'd the long black trail,
And I knew death, its thought, and the sacred knowledge of death.

Then with the knowledge of death as walking one side of me,
And the thought of death close-walking the other side of me,
And I in the middle as with companions, and as holding the hands of companions,
I fled forth to the hiding receiving night that talks not,
Down to the shores of the water, the path by the swamp in the dimness,
To the solemn shadowy cedars and ghostly pines so still.

And the singer so shy to the rest receiv'd me,
The gray-brown bird I know receiv'd us comrades three,
And he sang the carol of death, and a verse for him I love.

From deep secluded recesses,
From the fragrant cedars and the ghostly pines so still,
Came the carol of the bird.

And the charm of the carol rapt me,
As I held as if by their hands my comrades in the night,
And the voice of my spirit tallied the song of the bird.

Come lovely and soothing death,
Undulate round the world, serenely arriving, arriving,
In the day, in the night, to all, to each,
Sooner or later delicate death.

Prais'd be the fathomless universe,
For life and joy, and for objects and knowledge curious,
And for love, sweet love—but praise! praise! praise!
For the sure-enwinding arms of cool-enfolding death.

Dark mother always gliding near with soft feet,
Have none chanted for thee a chant of fullest welcome?

When Lilacs Last in the Dooryard Bloom'd

Then I chant it for thee, I glorify thee above all,
I bring thee a song that when thou must indeed come, come unfalteringly.

Approach strong deliveress,
When it is so, when thou hast taken them I joyously sing the dead,
Lost in the loving floating ocean of thee,
Laved in the flood of thy bliss O death.

From me to thee glad serenades,
Dances for thee I propose saluting thee, adornments and feastings for thee,
And the sights of the open landscape and the high-spread sky are fitting,
And life and the fields, and the huge and thoughtful night.

The night in silence under many a star,
The ocean shore and the husky whispering wave whose voice I know,
And the soul turning to thee O vast and well-veil'd death,
And the body gratefully nestling close to thee.

Over the tree-tops I float thee a song,
Over the rising and sinking waves, over the myriad fields and the prairies wide,
Over the dense-pack'd cities all and the teeming wharves and ways,
I float this carol with joy, with joy to thee O death.

15

To the tally of my soul,
Loud and strong kept up the gray-brown bird,
With pure deliberate notes spreading filling the night.

Loud in the pines and cedars dim,
Clear in the freshness moist and the swamp-perfume,
And I with my comrades there in the night.

While my sight that was bound in my eyes unclosed,
As to long panoramas of visions.

And I saw askant the armies,
I saw as in noiseless dreams hundreds of battle-flags,
Borne through the smoke of the battles and pierc'd with missiles I saw them,
And carried hither and yon through the smoke, and torn and bloody,
And at last but a few shreds left in the staffs, (and all in silence,)
And the staffs all splinter'd and broken.

I saw battle-corpses, myriads of them,
And the white skeletons of young men, I saw them,
I saw the debris and debris of all the slain soldiers of the war,
But I saw they were not as was thought,
They themselves were fully at rest, they suffer'd not,
The living remain'd and suffer'd, the mother suffer'd,
And the wife and the child and the musing comrade suffer'd,
And the armies that remain'd suffer'd.

16

Passing the visions, passing the night,
Passing, unloosing the hold of my comrades' hands,
Passing the song of the hermit bird and the tallying song of my soul,
Victorious song, death's outlet song, yet varying ever-altering song,
As low and wailing, yet clear the notes, rising and falling, flooding the night,
Sadly sinking and fainting, as warning and warning, and yet again bursting with joy,
Covering the earth and filling the spread of the heaven,
As that powerful psalm in the night I heard from recesses,
Passing, I leave thee lilac with heart-shaped leaves,
I leave thee there in the door-yard, blooming, returning with spring.

I cease from my song for thee,
From my gaze on thee in the west, fronting the west, communing with thee,
O comrade lustrous with silver face in the night.

Yet each to keep and all, retrievements out of the night,
The song, the wondrous chant of the gray-brown bird,
And the tallying chant, the echo arous'd in my soul,
With the lustrous and drooping star with the countenance full of woe,
With the holders holding my hand nearing the call of the bird,
Comrades mine and I in the midst, and their memory ever to keep, for the dead I
    loved so well,
For the sweetest, wisest soul of all my days and lands—and this for his dear sake,
Lilac and star and bird twined with the chant of my soul,
There in the fragrant pines and the cedars dusk and dim.

WHEN I HEARD THE LEARN'D ASTRONOMER
by Walt Whitman

When I heard the learn'd astronomer,
When the proofs, the figures, were ranged in columns before me,
When I was shown the charts and diagrams, to add, divide, and measure them,
When I sitting heard the astronomer where he lectured with much applause in the lecture-room,
How soon unaccountable I became tired and sick,
Till rising and gliding out I wander'd off by myself,
In the mystical moist night-air, and from time to time,
Look'd up in perfect silence at the stars.

"Preface" to LATE LYRICS AND EARLIER
by Thomas Hardy

I believe that a good deal of the robustious, swaggering optimism of recent literature is at bottom cowardly and insincere . . . but my pessimism, if pessimism it be, does not involve the assumption that the world is going to the dogs. On the contrary, my practical philosophy is distinctly meliorist. What are my books but one plea against man's inhumanity to man—to woman—and to the lower animals. . . .

. . . while I am quite aware that a thinker is not expected, and, indeed, is scarcely allowed, now more than heretofore, to state all that crosses his mind concerning existence in this universe, in his attempts to explain or excuse the presence of evil and the incongruity of penalizing the irresponsible—it must be obvious to open intelligences that, without denying the beauty and faithful service of certain venerable cults, such disallowance of "obstinate questionings" and "blank misgivings" tends to a paralysed intellectual stalemate. Heine observed nearly a hundred years ago that the soul has her eternal rights; that she will not be darkened by statutes, nor lullabied by the music of bells. And what is to-day, in allusions to the present author's pages, alleged to be "pessimism" is, in truth, only such "questionings" in the exploration of reality and is the first step towards the soul's betterment, and the body's also.

If I may be forgiven for quoting my own old words, let me repeat what I printed in this relation more than twenty years ago, and wrote much earlier, in a poem entitled "In Tenebris":

"If way to the Better there be, it exacts a full look at the Worst": that is to say, by the exploration of reality, and its frank recognition stage by stage along the survey, with an eye to the best consummation possible: briefly, evolutionary meliorism. But it is called pessimism nevertheless; under which word, expressed with condemnatory emphasis, it is regarded by many as some pernicious new thing (though so old as to underlie the Gospel scheme, and even to permeate the Greek

The selections from Thomas Hardy, *Collected Poems*, copyright 1925, by The Macmillan Company and used with their permission.

drama); and the subject is charitably left to decent silence, as if further comment were needless.

Happily there are some who feel such Levitical passing-by to be, alas, by no means a permanent dismissal of the matter; that comment on where the world stands is very much the reverse of needless in these disordered years of our prematurely afflicted century: that amendment and not madness lies that way. And looking down the future these few hold fast to the same: that whether the human and kindred animal races survive till the exhaustion or destruction of the globe, or whether these races perish and are succeeded by others before that conclusion comes, pain to all upon it, tongued or dumb, shall be kept down to a minimum by loving-kindness, operating through scientific knowledge, and actuated by the modicum of free will conjecturally possessed by organic life when the mighty necessitating forces—unconscious or other —that have the "balancings of the clouds" happen to be in equilibrium, which may or may not be often.

. . . .

Whether owing to the barbarizing of taste in the younger minds by the dark madness of the late war, the unabashed cultivation of selfishness in all classes, the plethoric growth of knowledge simultaneously with the stunting of wisdom, "a degrading search after outrageous stimulation" (to quote Wordsworth again), or from any other cause we seem threatened with a new Dark Age. . . . In any event poetry, pure literature in general, religion —I include religion, in its essential and undogmatic sense, because poetry and religion touch each other, or rather modulate into each other; are, indeed, often but different names for the same thing—these, I say, the visible signs of mental and emotional life, must like all other things keep moving, becoming; even though at present . . . men's minds appear as above noted, to be moving backwards rather than on.

. . . .

It may indeed be a forlorn hope, a mere dream, that of an alliance between religion which must be retained unless the world is to perish, and complete rationality, which must come, unless also the world is to perish, by means of the interfusing effect of poetry—"the breath and finer spirit of all knowledge; the impassioned expression of science," as it was defined by an English poet who was quite orthodox in his ideas. But if it be true, as Comte argued, that advance is never in a straight line, but in a looped orbit, we may, in the aforesaid ominous moving backward, be doing it *pour mieux sauter,* drawing back for a spring. I repeat that I forlornly hope so. . . . But one dares not prophesy.

HAP

by THOMAS HARDY

If but some vengeful god would call to me
From up the sky, and laugh: "Thou suffering thing,
Know that thy sorrow is my ecstasy,
That thy love's loss is my hate's profiting!"

The Impercipient

Then would I bear it, clench myself, and die,
  Steeled by the sense of ire unmerited;
Half-eased in that a Powerfuller than I
  Had willed and meted me the tears I shed.

But not so. How arrives it joy lies slain,
  And why unblooms the best hope ever sown?
—Crass Casualty obstructs the sun and rain,
  And dicing Time for gladness casts a moan....
These purblind Doomsters had as readily strown
  Blisses about my pilgrimage as pain.

THE IMPERCIPIENT
(AT A CATHEDRAL SERVICE)
by Thomas Hardy

That with this bright believing band
  I have no claim to be,
That faiths by which my comrades stand
  Seem fantasies to me,
And mirage-mists their Shining Land,
  Is a strange destiny.

Why thus my soul should be consigned
  To infelicity,
Why always I must feel as blind
  To sights my brethren see,
Why joys they've found I cannot find,
  Abides a mystery.

Since heart of mine knows not that ease
  Which they know; since it be
That He who breathes All's-Well to these
  Breathes no All's-Well to me,
My lack might move their sympathies
  And Christian charity!

I am like a gazer who should mark
  An inland company
Standing upfingered with, "Hark! hark!
  The glorious distant sea!"
And feel, "Alas, 'tis but yon dark
  And wind-swept pine to me!"

Yet I would bear my shortcomings
  With meet tranquillity,
But for the charge that blessed things
  I'd liefer not have be.
O, doth a bird deprived of wings
  Go earth-bound wilfully!

Enough. As yet disquiet clings
  About us. Rest shall we.

[651]

"AH, ARE YOU DIGGING ON MY GRAVE?"
by Thomas Hardy

"Ah, are you digging on my grave,
  My loved one?—planting rue?"
—"No: yesterday he went to wed
One of the brightest wealth has bred.
'It cannot hurt her now,' he said,
  'That I should not be true.'"

"Then who is digging on my grave?
  My nearest dearest kin?"
—"Ah, no: they sit and think, 'What use!
What good will planting flowers produce?
No tendance of her mound can loose
  Her spirits from Death's gin.'"

"But some one digs upon my grave?
  My enemy?—prodding sly?"
—"Nay: when she heard you had passed
  the Gate
That shuts on all flesh soon or late,
She thought you no more worth her hate,
  And cares not where you lie."

"Then who is digging on my grave?
  Say—since I have not guessed!"
—"O it is I, my mistress dear,
Your little dog, who still lives near,
And much I hope my movements here
  Have not disturbed your rest?"

"Ah, yes! *You* dig upon my grave . . .
  Why flashed it not on me
That one true heart was left behind!
What feeling do we ever find
To equal among human kind
  A dog's fidelity!"

"Mistress, I dug upon your grave
  To bury a bone, in case
I should be hungry near this spot
When passing on my daily trot.
I am sorry, but I quite forgot
  It was your resting-place."

IN TENEBRIS
by Thomas Hardy

"Considerabam ad dexteram, et videbam; et non erat qui cognosceret me . . . Non est qui requirat animam meam."—*Ps. cxlii.*

When the cloud's swoln bosoms echo back the shouts of the many and strong
That things are all as they best may be, save a few to be right ere long,
And my eyes have not the vision in them to discern what to these is so clear
The blot seems straightway in me alone; one better he were not here.

The stout upstanders say, All's well with us; ruers have nought to rue!
And what the potent say so oft, can it fail to be somewhat true?
Breezily go they, breezily come; their dust smokes around their career,
Till I think I am one born out of due time, who has no calling here.

[652]

To an Unborn Pauper Child

Their dawns bring lusty joys it seems; their evenings all that is sweet;
Our times are blessed times, they cry: Life shapes it as is most meet,
And nothing is much the matter; there are many smiles to a tear;
Then what is the matter is I, I say. Why should such an one be here? . . .

Let him in whose ears the low-voiced Best is killed by the clash of the First,
Who holds that if way to the Better there be, it exacts a full look at the Worst,
Who feels that delight is a delicate growth cramped by crookedness, custom, and fear,
Get him up and be gone as one shaped awry; he disturbs the order here.

TO AN UNBORN PAUPER CHILD

by Thomas Hardy

I

Breathe not, hid Heart: cease silently,
And though thy birth-hour beckons thee,
   Sleep the long sleep:
   The Doomsters heap
Travails and teens around us here,
And Time-wraiths turn our songsingings to fear.

II

Hark, how the peoples surge and sigh,
And laughters fail, and greetings die:
   Hopes dwindle; yea,
   Faiths waste away,
Affections and enthusiasms numb;
Thou canst not mend these things if thou dost come.

III

Had I the ear of wombèd souls
Ere their terrestrial chart unrolls,
   And thou wert free
   To cease, or be,
Then would I tell thee all I know,
And put it to thee: wilt thou take Life so?

IV

Vain vow! No hint of mine may hence
To theeward fly; to thy locked sense

Explain none can
Life's pending plan:
Thou will thy ignorant entry make
Though skies spout fire and blood and nations quake.

v

Fain would I, dear, find some shut plot
Of earth's wide wold for thee, where not
One tear, one qualm,
Should break the calm.
But I am weak as thou and bare;
No man can change the common lot to rare.

vi

Must come and bide. And such are we—
Unreasoning, sanguine, visionary—
That I can hope
Health, love, friends, scope
In full for thee; can dream thou wilt find
Joys seldom yet attained by humankind!

THE OXEN

by Thomas Hardy

Christmas Eve, and twelve of the clock.
"Now they are all on their knees,"
An elder said as we sat in a flock
By the embers in hearthside ease.

We pictured the meek mild creatures where
They dwelt in their strawy pen,
Nor did it occur to one of us there
To doubt they were kneeling then.

So fair a fancy few would weave
In these years! Yet, I feel,
If someone said on Christmas Eve,
"Come; see the oxen kneel,

Afterwards

"In the lonely barton by yonder coomb
  Our childhood used to know,"
I should go with him in the gloom,
  Hoping it might be so.

AFTERWARDS

by THOMAS HARDY

When the Present has latched its postern behind my tremulous stay,
  And the May month flaps its glad green leaves like wings,
Delicate-filmed as new-spun silk, will the neighbors say,
  "He was a man who used to notice such things"?

If it be in the dusk when, like an eyelid's soundless blink,
  The dewfall-hawk comes crossing the shades to alight
Upon the wind-warped upland thorn, a gazer may think,
  "To him this must have been a familiar sight."

If I pass during some nocturnal blackness, mothy and warm,
  When the hedgehog travels furtively over the lawn,
One may say, "He strove that such innocent creatures should come to no harm,
  But he could do little for them; and now he is gone."

If, when hearing that I have been stilled at last, they stand at the door,
  Watching the full-starred heavens that winter sees,
Will this thought rise on those who will meet my face no more,
  "He was one who had an eye for such mysteries"?

And will any say when my bell of quittance is heard in the gloom,
  And a crossing breeze cuts a pause in its outrollings,
Till they rise again, as they were a new bell's boom,
  "He hears it not now, but used to notice such things"?

from THE NAME AND NATURE OF POETRY
by A. E. HOUSMAN

POETRY indeed seems to me more physical than intellectual. A year or two ago, in common with others, I received from America a request that I would define poetry. I replied that I could no more define poetry than a terrier can define a rat, but that I thought we both recognized the object by the symptoms it provokes in us. One of these symptoms was described in connection with another object by Eliphaz the Temanite: "A spirit passed before my face: the hair of my flesh stood up." Experience has taught me, while I am shaving of a morning, to keep watch over my thoughts, because, if a line of poetry strays into my memory, my skin bristles so that the razor ceases to act. This particular symptom is accompanied by a shiver down the spine; there is another which consists in a constriction of the throat and a precipitation of water to the eyes; and there is a third which I can only describe by borrowing a phrase from one of Keats's last letters, where he says, speaking of Fanny Brawne, "everything that reminds me of her goes through me like a spear." The seat of this sensation is the pit of the stomach.

My opinions on poetry are necessarily tinged, perhaps I should say tainted, by the circumstance that I have come into contact with it on two sides. We were saying a while ago that poetry is a very wide term, and inconveniently comprehensive: so comprehensive is it that it embraces two books, fortunately not large ones, of my own. I know how this stuff came into existence; and though I have no right to assume that any other poetry came into existence in the same way, yet I find reason to believe that some poetry, and quite good poetry, did. Wordsworth for instance says that poetry is the spontaneous overflow of powerful feelings, and Burns has left us this confession, "I have two or three times in my life composed from the wish rather than the impulse, but I never succeeded to any purpose." In short I think that the production of poetry, in its first stage, is less an active than a passive and involuntary process; and if I were obliged, not to define poetry, but to name the class of things to which it belongs, I should call it a secretion; whether a natural secretion, like turpentine in the fir, or a morbid secretion, like the pearl in the oyster, I think that my own case, though I may not deal with the material so cleverly as the oyster does, is the latter; because I have seldom written poetry unless I was rather out of health, and the experience, though pleasurable, was generally agitating and exhausting. If only that you may know what to avoid, I will give some account of the process.

Having drunk a pint of beer at luncheon—beer is a sedative to the brain, and my afternoons are the least intellectual portion of my life—I would go out for a walk of two or three hours. As I went along, thinking of nothing in particular, only looking at things around me and following the progress of the seasons, there would flow into my mind, with sudden and unaccountable emotion, sometimes a line or two of verse, sometimes a whole stanza at once, accompanied, not preceded, by a vague notion of the poem which they

From A. E. Housman, *The Name and Nature of Poetry*. By permission of The Macmillan Company, publishers.

were destined to form part of. Then there would usually be a lull of an hour or so, then perhaps the spring would bubble up again. I say bubble up because, so far as I could make out, the source of the suggestions thus proffered to the brain was an abyss which I have already had occasion to mention, the pit of the stomach. When I got home I wrote them down, leaving gaps, and hoping that further inspiration might be forthcoming another day. Sometimes it was, if I took my walks in a receptive and expectant frame of mind; but sometimes the poem had to be taken in hand and completed by the brain, which was apt to be a matter of trouble and anxiety, involving trial and disappointment, and sometimes ending in failure. I happen to remember distinctly the genesis of the piece which stands last in my first volume. Two of the stanzas, I do not say which, came into my head, just as they are printed, while I was crossing the corner of Hampstead Heath between the Spaniard's Inn and the footpath to Temple Fortune. A third stanza came with a little coaxing after tea. One more was needed, but it did not come: I had to turn to and compose it myself, and that was a laborious business. I wrote it thirteen times, and it was more than a twelvemonth before I got it right.

SOLDIER FROM THE WARS RETURNING
by A. E. HOUSMAN

Soldier from the wars returning,
    Spoiler of the taken town,
Here is ease that asks not earning;
    Turn you in and sit you down.

Peace is come and wars are over,
    Welcome you and welcome all,
While the charger crops the clover
    And his bridle hangs in stall.

Now no more of winters biting,
    Filth in trench from fall to spring,
Summers full of sweat and fighting
    For the Kesar or the King.

Rest you, charger, rust you, bridle;
    Kings and kesars, keep your pay;
Soldier, sit you down and idle
    At the inn of night for aye.

THE HALF-MOON WESTERS LOW, MY LOVE
by A. E. HOUSMAN

The half-moon westers low, my love,
    And the wind brings up the rain;
And wide apart lie we, my love,
    And seas between the twain.

I know not if it rains, my love,
    In the land where you do lie;
And oh, so sound you sleep, my love,
    You know no more than I.

Poems on pages 621-625 from A. E. Housman, *Collected Poems*, Henry Holt and Company, Inc.

THINK NO MORE, LAD
by A. E. Housman

Think no more, lad; laugh, be jolly:
  Why should men make haste to die?
Empty heads and tongues a-talking
Make the rough road easy walking,
And the feather pate of folly
  Bears the falling sky.

Oh, 'tis jesting, dancing, drinking
  Spins the heavy world around.
If young hearts were not so clever,
Oh, they would be young for ever:
Think no more; 'tis only thinking
  Lays lads underground.

THE LAWS OF GOD, THE LAWS OF MAN
by A. E. Housman

The laws of God, the laws of man,
He may keep that will and can;
Not I: let God and man decree
Laws for themselves and not for me;
And if my ways are not as theirs
Let them mind their own affairs.
Their deeds I judge and much condemn,
Yet when did I make laws for them?
Please yourselves, say I, and they
Need only look the other way.
But no, they will not; they must still
Wrest their neighbour to their will,
And make me dance as they desire
With jail and gallows and hell-fire.
And how am I to face the odds
Of man's bedevilment and God's?
I, a stranger and afraid
In a world I never made.
They will be master, right or wrong;
Though both are foolish, both are strong
And since, my soul, we cannot fly
To Saturn nor to Mercury,
Keep we must, if keep we can,
These foreign laws of God and man.

THE CHESTNUT CASTS HIS FLAMBEAUX
by A. E. Housman

The chestnut casts his flambeaux, and the flowers
  Stream from the hawthorn on the wind away,
The doors clap to, the pane is blind with showers.
  Pass me the can, lad; there's an end of May.

These poems from A. E. Housman, *Last Poems*, Henry Holt and Company, Inc.

"Terence, This Is Stupid Stuff"

There's one spoilt spring to scant our mortal lot,
  One season ruined of our little store.
May will be fine next year as like as not:
  Oh ay, but then we shall be twenty-four.

We for a certainty are not the first
  Have sat in taverns while the tempest hurled
Their hopeful plans to emptiness, and cursed
  Whatever brute and blackguard made the world.

It is in truth iniquity on high
  To cheat our sentenced souls of aught they crave,
And mar the merriment as you and I
  Fare on our long fool's-errand to the grave.

Iniquity it is; but pass the can.
  My lad, no pair of kings our mothers bore;
Our only portion is the estate of man:
  We want the moon, but we shall get no more.

If here to-day the cloud of thunder lours
  To-morrow it will hie on far behests;
The flesh will grieve on other bones than ours
  Soon, and the soul will mourn in other breasts.

The troubles of our proud and angry dust
  Are from eternity, and shall not fail.
Bear them we can, and if we can we must.
  Shoulder the sky, my lad, and drink your ale.

"TERENCE, THIS IS STUPID STUFF"
by A. E. Housman

"Terence, this is stupid stuff:
You eat your victuals fast enough;
There can't be much amiss, 'tis clear,
To see the rate you drink your beer.
But oh, good Lord, the verse you make,
It gives a chap the belly-ache.
The cow, the old cow, she is dead;
It sleeps well, the hornèd head:
We poor lads, 'tis our turn now
To hear such tunes as killed the cow.
Pretty friendship 'tis to rhyme
Your friends to death before their time
Moping melancholy mad:
Come, pipe a tune to dance to, lad."

Why, if 'tis dancing you would be,
There's brisker pipes than poetry.
Say, for what were hop-yards meant,
Or why was Burton built on Trent?
Oh many a peer of England brews
Livelier liquor than the Muse,

From A. E. Housman, *A Shropshire Lad*, Henry Holt and Company, Inc.

Poetry

And malt does more than Milton can
To justify God's ways to man.
Ale, man, ale's the stuff to drink
For fellows whom it hurts to think:
Look into the pewter pot
To see the world as the world's not.
And faith, 'tis pleasant till 'tis past:
The mischief is that 'twill not last.
Oh I have been to Ludlow fair
And left my necktie God knows where,
And carried half-way home, or near,
Pints and quarts of Ludlow beer:
Then the world seemed none so bad,
And I myself a sterling lad;
And down in lovely muck I've lain,
Happy till I woke again.
Then I saw the morning sky:
Heigho, the tale was all a lie;
The world, it was the old world yet,
I was I, my things were wet,
And nothing now remained to do
But begin the game anew.

 Therefore, since the world has still
Much good, but much less good than ill,
And while the sun and moon endure
Luck's a chance, but trouble's sure,
I'd face it as a wise man would,
And train for ill and not for good.

'Tis true, the stuff I bring for sale
Is not so brisk a brew as ale:
Out of a stem that scored the hand
I wrung it in a weary land.
But take it: if the smack is sour,
The better for the embittered hour;
It should do good to heart and head
When your soul is in my soul's stead;
And I will friend you, if I may,
In the dark and cloudy day.

 There was a king reigned in the East:
There, when kings will sit to feast,
They get their fill before they think
With poisoned meat and poisoned drink.
He gathered all that springs to birth
From the many-venomed earth;
First a little, thence to more,
He sampled all her killing store;
And easy, smiling, seasoned sound,
Sate the king when healths went round.
They put arsenic in his meat
And stared aghast to watch him eat;
They poured strychnine in his cup
And shook to see him drink it up:
They shook, they stared as white's their
 shirt:
Them it was their poison hurt.
—I tell the tale that I heard told.
Mithridates, he died old.

[660]

WHEN I WAS ONE-AND-TWENTY
by A. E. Housman

When I was one-and-twenty
  I heard a wise man say,
"Give crowns and pounds and guineas
  But not your heart away;
Give pearls away and rubies
  But keep your fancy free."
But I was one-and-twenty,
  No use to talk to me.

When I was one-and-twenty
  I heard him say again,
"The heart out of the bosom
  Was never given in vain;
'Tis paid with sighs aplenty
  And sold for endless rue."
And I am two-and-twenty,
  And oh, 'tis true, 'tis true.

REVEILLE
by A. E. Housman

Wake: the silver dusk returning
  Up the beach of darkness brims,
And the ship of sunrise burning
  Strands upon the eastern rims.

Wake: the vaulted shadow shatters,
  Trampled to the floor it spanned,
And the tent of night in tatters
  Straws the sky-pavilioned land.

Up, lad, up, 'tis late for lying:
  Hear the drums of morning play;
Hark, the empty highways crying
  "Who'll beyond the hills away?"

Towns and countries woo together,
  Forelands beacon, belfries call;
Never lad that trod on leather
  Lived to feast his heart with all.

Up, lad: thews that lie and cumber
  Sunlit pallets never thrive;
Morns abed and daylight slumber
  Were not meant for man alive.

Clay lies still, but blood's a rover;
  Breath's a ware that will not keep.
Up, lad: when the journey's over
  There'll be time enough to sleep.

LOVELIEST OF TREES, THE CHERRY NOW
by A. E. Housman

Loveliest of trees, the cherry now
Is hung with bloom along the bough,
And stands about the woodland ride
Wearing white for Eastertide.

Now, of my threescore years and ten,
Twenty will not come again,
And take from seventy springs a score,
It only leaves me fifty more.

And since to look at things in bloom
Fifty springs are little room,
About the woodlands I will go
To see the cherry hung with snow.

These poems from A. E. Housman, *A Shropshire Lad*, Henry Holt and Company, Inc.

Poetry

from SELECTED LETTERS
by EDWIN ARLINGTON ROBINSON

Not long ago I attempted . . . to define poetry as "a language that tells us, through a more or less emotional reaction, something that cannot be said." This might be an equally good, or bad, definition of music, but for the fact that the reader would balk instinctively at the qualifying "more or less" before "emotional"—the emotional reaction in the case of music that endures being unquestionably "more." And this, no doubt, is equally true of much of the best poetry . . . poetry is language and music at the same time.*

There is no "philosophy" in my poetry beyond an implication of an ordered universe and a sort of deterministic negation of the general futility that appears to be the basis of "rational" thought. So I suppose you will have to put me down as a mystic, if that means a man who cannot prove all his convictions to be true.*

The world is not a "prison house" but a kind of spiritual kindergarten, where millions of bewildered infants are trying to spell God with the wrong blocks.

—*from The Bookman*

CREDO
by EDWIN ARLINGTON ROBINSON

I cannot find my way: there is no star
In all the shrouded heavens anywhere;
And there is not a whisper in the air
Of any living voice but one so far
That I can hear it only as a bar
Of lost, imperial music, played when fair
And angel fingers wove, and unaware,
Dead leaves to garlands where no roses are.

No, there is not a glimmer, nor a call,
For one that welcomes, welcomes when he fears,
The black and awful chaos of the night;
For through it all—above, beyond it all—
I know the far-sent message of the years,
I feel the coming glory of the Light.

* These selections from E. A. Robinson, *Selected Letters*, edited by Ridgely Torrence, copyright 1940 by The Macmillan Company and used with their permission.

MR. FLOOD'S PARTY

by Edwin Arlington Robinson

Old Eben Flood, climbing alone one night
Over the hill between the town below
And the forsaken upland hermitage
That held as much as he should ever know
On earth again of home, paused warily.
The road was his with not a native near;
And Eben, having leisure, said aloud,
For no man else in Tilbury Town to hear:

"Well, Mr. Flood, we have the harvest moon
Again, and we may not have many more;
The bird is on the wing, the poet says,
And you and I have said it here before.
Drink to the bird." He raised up to the light
The jug that he had gone so far to fill,
And answered huskily: "Well, Mr. Flood,
Since you propose it, I believe I will."

Alone, as if enduring to the end
A valiant armor of scarred hopes outworn,
He stood there in the middle of the road
Like Roland's ghost winding a silent horn.
Below him, in the town among the trees,
Where friends of other days had honored him,
A phantom salutation of the dead
Rang thinly till old Eben's eyes were dim.

Then, as a mother lays her sleeping child
Down tenderly, fearing it may awake,
He set the jug down slowly at his feet
With trembling care, knowing that most things break;
And only when assured that on firm earth
It stood, as the uncertain lives of men
Assuredly did not, he paced away,
And with his hand extended paused again:

"Well, Mr. Flood, we have not met like this
In a long time; and many a change has come
To both of us, I fear, since last it was
We had a drop together. Welcome home!"
Convivially returning with himself,
Again he raised the jug up to the light;
And with an acquiescent quaver said:
"Well, Mr. Flood, if you insist, I might.

"Only a very little, Mr. Flood—
For auld lang syne. No more, sir; that will do."
So, for the time, apparently it did,
And Eben evidently thought so too;
For soon amid the silver loneliness
Of night he lifted up his voice and sang,
Secure, with only two moons listening,
Until the whole harmonious landscape rang—

"For auld lang syne." The weary throat gave out,
The last word wavered, and the song was done.
He raised again the jug regretfully
And shook his head, and was again alone.
There was not much that was ahead of him,
And there was nothing in the town below—
Where strangers would have shut the many doors
That many friends had opened long ago.

From E. A. Robinson, *Collected Poems*. By permission of The Macmillan Company, publishers.

SONNET

by Edwin Arlington Robinson

Never until our souls are strong enough
To plunge into the crater of the Scheme—
Triumphant in the flash there to redeem
Love's handsel and forevermore to slough,
Like cerements at a played-out masque, the rough
And reptile skins of us whereon we set
The stigma of scared years—are we to get
Where atoms and the ages are one stuff.

Nor ever shall we know the cursed waste
Of life in the beneficence divine
Of starlight and of sunlight and soul-shine
That we have squandered in sin's frail distress,
Till we have drunk, and trembled at the taste,
The mead of Thought's prophetic endlessness.

THE MILL

by Edwin Arlington Robinson

The miller's wife had waited long,
  The tea was cold, the fire was dead;
And there might yet be nothing wrong
  In how he went and what he said:
"There are no millers any more,"
  Was all that she had heard him say;
And he had lingered at the door
  So long that it seemed yesterday.

Sick with a fear that had no form
  She knew that she was there at last;
And in the mill there was a warm
  And mealy fragrance of the past.

What else there was would only seem
  To say again what he had meant;
And what was hanging from a beam
  Would not have heeded where she went

And if she thought it followed her,
  She may have reasoned in the dark
That one way of the few there were
  Would hide her and would leave no mark:
Black water, smooth above the weir
  Like starry velvet in the night,
Though ruffled once, would soon appear
  The same as ever to the sight.

From E. A. Robinson, *Collected Poems*. By permission of The Macmillan Company, publishers.

RICHARD CORY
by Edwin Arlington Robinson

Whenever Richard Cory went down town,
  We people on the pavement looked at him:
He was a gentleman from sole to crown,
  Clean favored, and imperially slim.

And he was always quietly arrayed,
  And he was always human when he talked;
But still he fluttered pulses when he said,
  "Good-morning," and he glittered when he walked.

And he was rich—yes, richer than a king,
  And admirably schooled in every grace:
In fine, we thought that he was everything
  To make us wish that we were in his place.

So on we worked, and waited for the light,
  And went without the meat, and cursed the bread;
And Richard Cory, one calm summer night,
  Went home and put a bullet through his head.

From Edwin Arlington Robinson, *The Children of the Night;* used by permission of the publishers, Charles Scribner's Sons.

FLAMMONDE
by Edwin Arlington Robinson

The man Flammonde, from God knows where,
With firm address and foreign air,
With news of nations in his talk
And something royal in his walk,
With glint of iron in his eyes,
But never doubt, nor yet surprise,
Appeared, and stayed, and held his head
As one by kings accredited.

Erect, with his alert repose
About him, and about his clothes,
He pictured all tradition hears
Of what we owe to fifty years.
His cleansing heritage of taste
Paraded neither want nor waste;
And what he needed for his fee
To live, he borrowed graciously.

From E. A. Robinson, *Collected Poems.* By permission of The Macmillan Company, publishers.

He never told us what he was,
Or what mischance, or other cause,
Had banished him from better days
To play the Prince of Castaways.
Meanwhile he played surpassing well
A part, for most, unplayable;
In fine, one pauses, half afraid
To say for certain that he played.

For that, one may as well forego
Conviction as to yes or no;
Nor can I say just how intense
Would then have been the difference
To several, who, having striven
In vain to get what he was given,
Would see the stranger taken on
By friends not easy to be won.

Moreover, many a malcontent
He soothed and found munificent;
His courtesy beguiled and foiled
Suspicion that his years were soiled;
His mien distinguished any crowd,
His credit strengthened when he bowed;
And women, young and old, were fond
Of looking at the man Flammonde.

There was a woman in our town
On whom the fashion was to frown;
But while our talk renewed the tinge
Of a long-faded scarlet fringe,
The man Flammonde saw none of that,
And what he saw we wondered at—
That none of us, in her distress,
Could hide or find our littleness.

There was a boy that all agreed
Had shut within him the rare seed
Of learning. We could understand,
But none of us could lift a hand.
The man Flammonde appraised the youth,
And told a few of us the truth;
And thereby, for a little gold,
A flowered future was unrolled.

There were two citizens who fought
For years and years, and over nought;
They made life awkward for their friends,
And shortened their own dividends.
The man Flammonde said what was wrong
Should be made right; nor was it long
Before they were again in line,
And had each other in to dine.

And these I mention are but four
Of many out of many more.
So much for them. But what of him—
So firm in every look and limb?
What small satanic sort of kink
Was in his brain? What broken link
Withheld him from the destinies
That came so near to being his?

What was he, when we came to sift
His meaning, and to note the drift
Of incommunicable ways
That make us ponder while we praise?
Why was it that his charm revealed
Somehow the surface of a shield?
What was it that we never caught?
What was he, and what was he not?

How much it was of him we met
We cannot ever know; nor yet
Shall all he gave us quite atone
For what was his, and his alone;
Nor need we now, since he knew best,
Nourish an ethical unrest:
Rarely at once will nature give
The power to be Flammonde and live.

We cannot know how much we learn
From those who never will return,
Until a flash of unforeseen
Remembrance falls on what has been.
We've each a darkening hill to climb;
And this is why, from time to time
In Tilbury Town, we look beyond
Horizons for the man Flammonde.

THE MASTER
(Lincoln)
by Edwin Arlington Robinson

A flying word from here and there
Had sown the name at which we sneered,
But soon the name was everywhere,
To be reviled and then revered—
A presence to be loved and feared,
We cannot hide it, or deny
That we, the gentlemen who jeered,
May be forgotten by and by.

He came when days were perilous
And hearts of men were sore beguiled;
And having made his note of us,
He pondered and was reconciled.
Was ever master yet so mild
As he, and so untamable?
We doubted, even when he smiled,
Not knowing what he knew so well.

He knew that undeceiving fate
Would shame us whom he served unsought;
He knew that he must wince and wait—
The jest of those for whom he fought;
He knew devoutly what he thought
Of us and of our ridicule;
He knew that we must all be taught
Like little children in a school.

We gave a glamour to the task
That he encountered and saw through;
But little of us did he ask,
And little did we ever do.
And what appears if we review
The season when we railed and chaffed?—
It is the face of one who knew
That we were learning while we laughed.

The face that in our vision feels
Again the venom that we flung,
Transfigured to the world reveals
The vigilance to which we clung.
Shrewd, hallowed, harassed, and among
The mysteries that are untold—
The face we see was never young,
Nor could it wholly have been old.

For he, to whom we had applied
Our shopman's test of age and worth,
Was elemental when he died,
As he was ancient at his birth:
The saddest among kings of earth,
Bowed with a galling crown, this man
Met rancor with a cryptic mirth,
Laconic—and Olympian.

The love, the grandeur, and the fame
Are bounded by the world alone;
The calm, the smoldering, and the flame
Of awful patience were his own:
With him they are forever flown
Past all our fond self-shadowings,
Wherewith we cumber the Unknown
As with inept, Icarian wings.

For we were not as other men:
'Twas ours to soar and his to see;
But we are coming down again,
And we shall come down pleasantly;
Nor shall we longer disagree
On what it is to be sublime,
But flourish in our perigee
And have one Titan at a time.

Reprinted from *The Town Down the River* by Edwin Arlington Robinson; copyright 1910 by Charles Scribner's Sons, 1938 by Ruth Nivison; used by permission of the publishers.

Weary of the Truth Marsden Hartley
Courtesy Whitney Museum
of American Art

from "THE FIGURE A POEM MAKES"
by Robert Frost

The figure a poem makes. It begins in delight and ends in wisdom. The figure is the same as for love. No one can really hold that the ecstasy should be static and stand still in one place. It begins in delight, it inclines to the impulse, it assumes direction with the first line laid down, it runs a course of lucky events, and ends in a clarification of life—not necessarily a great clarification, such as sects and cults are founded on, but in a momentary stay against confusion. It has denouement. It has an outcome that though unforeseen was predestined from the first image of the original mood—and indeed from the very mood. It is but a trick poem and no poem at all if the best of it was thought of first and saved for the last. It finds its own name as it goes and discovers the best waiting for it in some final phrase at once wise and sad—the happy-sad blend of the drinking song.

No tears in the writer, no tears in the reader. No surprise for the writer, no surprise for the reader. For me the initial delight is in the surprise of remembering something I didn't know I knew. I am in a place, a situation, as if I had materialized from cloud or risen out of the ground. There is a glad recognition of the long lost and the rest follows. Step by step the wonder of unexpected supply keeps growing. The impressions most useful to my purpose seem always those I was unaware of and so made no note of at the time when taken, and the conclusion is come to that like giants we are always hurling experience ahead of us to pave the future with against the day when we may want to strike a line of purpose across it for somewhere. The line will have the more charm for not being mechanically straight. We enjoy the straight crookedness of a good walking stick....

More than once I should have lost my soul to radicalism if it had been the originality it was mistaken for by its young converts. Originality and initiative are what I ask for my country. For myself, the originality need be no more than the freshness of a poem run in the way I have described: from delight to wisdom. The figure is the same as for love. Like a piece of ice on a hot stove the poem must ride on its own melting. A poem may be worked over once it is in being, but may not be worried into being. Its most precious quality will remain its having run itself and carried away the poet with it.

TWO TRAMPS IN MUD TIME
by Robert Frost

Out of the mud two strangers came
And caught me splitting wood in the yard.
And one of them put me off my aim
By hailing cheerily 'Hit them hard!'

I knew pretty well why he dropped behind
And let the other go on a way.
I knew pretty well what he had in mind:
He wanted to take my job for pay.

From Robert Frost, *Collected Poems*, copyright Henry Holt and Company, Inc., 1939.

Poetry

Good blocks of beech it was I split,
As large around as the chopping block;
And every piece I squarely hit
Fell splinterless as a cloven rock.
The blows that a life of self-control
Spares to strike for the common good
That day, giving a loose to my soul,
I spent on the unimportant wood.

The sun was warm but the wind was chill.
You know how it is with an April day
When the sun is out and the wind is still,
You're one month on in the middle of May.
But if you so much as dare to speak,
A cloud comes over the sunlit arch,
A wind comes off a frozen peak,
And you're two months back in the middle of March.

A bluebird comes tenderly up to alight
And fronts the wind to unruffle a plume,
His song so pitched as not to excite
A single flower as yet to bloom.
It is snowing a flake: and he half knew
Winter was only playing possum.
Except in color he isn't blue,
But he wouldn't advise a thing to blossom.

The water for which we may have to look
In summertime with a witching-wand,
In every wheelrut's now a brook,
In every print of a hoof a pond.
Be glad of water, but don't forget
The lurking frost in the earth beneath
That will steal forth after the sun is set
And show on the water its crystal teeth.

The time when most I loved my task
These two must make me love it more
By coming with what they came to ask.
You'd think I never had felt before
The weight of an ax-head poised aloft,
The grip on earth of outspread feet,
The life of muscles rocking soft
And smooth and moist in vernal heat.

Out of the woods two hulking tramps
(From sleeping God knows where last night,
But not long since in the lumber camps).
They thought all chopping was theirs of right.
Men of the woods and lumberjacks,
They judged me by their appropriate tool.
Except as a fellow handled an ax,
They had no way of knowing a fool.

Nothing on either side was said.
They knew they had but to stay their stay
And all their logic would fill my head:
As that I had no right to play
With what was another man's work for gain.
My right might be love but theirs was need.
And where the two exist in twain
Theirs was the better right—agreed.

But yield who will to their separation,
My object in living is to unite
My avocation and my vocation
As my two eyes make one in sight.
Only where love and need are one,
And the work is play for mortal stakes,
Is the deed ever really done
For Heaven and the future's sakes.

[670]

THE LOCKLESS DOOR

by Robert Frost

It went many years,
But at last came a knock,
And I thought of the door
With no lock to lock.

I blew out the light,
I tip-toed the floor,
And raised both hands
In prayer to the door.

But the knock came again.
My window was wide;

I climbed on the sill
And descended outside.

Back over the sill
I bade a 'Come in'
To whatever the knock
At the door may have been.

So at a knock
I emptied my cage
To hide in the world
And alter with age.

From *New Hampshire* by Robert Frost. Copyright, 1923, by Henry Holt and Company, Inc. Copyright, 1951, by Robert Frost.

THE STAR-SPLITTER

by Robert Frost

"You know Orion always comes up sideways.
Throwing a leg up over our fence of mountains,
And rising on his hands, he looks in on me
Busy outdoors by lantern-light with something
I should have done by daylight, and indeed,
After the ground is frozen, I should have done
Before it froze, and a gust flings a handful
Of waste leaves at my smoky lantern chimney
To make fun of my way of doing things,
Or else fun of Orion's having caught me.
Has a man, I should like to ask, no rights
These forces are obliged to pay respect to?"
So Brad McLaughlin mingled reckless talk
Of heavenly stars with hugger-mugger farming,
Till having failed at hugger-mugger farming,
He burned his house down for the fire insurance
And spent the proceeds on a telescope
To satisfy a life-long curiosity
About our place among the infinities.

From Robert Frost, *Collected Poems*, Henry Holt and Company, Inc.

[671]

Poetry

"What do you want with one of those blame things?"
I asked him well beforehand. "Don't you get one!"
"Don't call it blamed; there isn't anything
More blameless in the sense of being less
A weapon in our human fight," he said.
"I'll have one if I sell my farm to buy it."
There where he moved the rocks to plow the ground
And plowed between the rocks he couldn't move,
Few farms changed hands; so rather than spend years
Trying to sell his farm and then not selling,
He burned his house down for the fire insurance
And bought the telescope with what it came to.
He had been heard to say by several:
"The best thing that we're put here for's to see;
The strongest thing that's given us to see with's
A telescope. Someone in every town
Seems to me owes it to the town to keep one.
In Littleton it may as well be me."
After such loose talk it was no surprise
When he did what he did and burned his house down.

Mean laughter went about the town that day
To let him know we weren't the least imposed on,
And he could wait—we'd see to him to-morrow.
But the first thing next morning we reflected
If one by one we counted people out
For the least sin, it wouldn't take us long
To get so we had no one left to live with.
For to be social is to be forgiving.
Our thief, the one who does our stealing from us,
We don't cut off from coming to church suppers,
But what we miss we go to him and ask for.
He promptly gives it back, that is if still
Uneaten, unworn out, or undisposed of.
It wouldn't do to be too hard on Brad
About his telescope. Beyond the age
Of being given one's gift for Christmas,
He had to take the best way he knew how
To find himself in one. Well, all we said was
He took a strange thing to be roguish over.
Some sympathy was wasted on the house,
A good old-timer dating back along;
But a house isn't sentient; the house
Didn't feel anything. And if it did,

[672]

The Star-Splitter

Why not regard it as a sacrifice,
And an old-fashioned sacrifice by fire,
Instead of a new-fashioned one at auction?

Out of a house and so out of a farm
At one stroke (of a match), Brad had to turn
To earn a living on the Concord railroad,
As under-ticket-agent at a station
Where his job, when he wasn't selling tickets,
Was setting out up track and down, not plants
As on a farm, but planets, evening stars
That varied in their hue from red to green.

He got a good glass for six hundred dollars.
His new job gave him leisure for star-gazing.
Often he bid me come and have a look
Up the brass barrel, velvet black inside,
At a star quaking in the other end.
I recollect a night of broken clouds
And underfoot snow melted down to ice,
And melting further in the wind to mud.
Bradford and I had out the telescope.
We spread our two legs as we spread its three,
Pointed our thoughts the way we pointed it,
And standing at our leisure till the day broke,
Said some of the best things we ever said.
That telescope was christened the Star-splitter,
Because it didn't do a thing but split
A star in two or three the way you split
A globule of quicksilver in your hand
With one stroke of your finger in the middle.
It's a star-splitter if there ever was one
And ought to do some good if splitting stars
'Sa thing to be compared with splitting wood.

We've looked and looked, but after all where are we?
Do we know any better where we are,
And how it stands between the night to-night
And a man with a smoky lantern chimney?
How different from the way it ever stood?

[673]

DEPARTMENTAL

by ROBERT FROST

An ant on the table cloth
Ran into a dormant moth
Of many times his size.
He showed not the least surprise.
His business wasn't with such.
He gave it scarcely a touch,
And was off on his duty run.
Yet if he encountered one
Of the hive's enquiry squad
Whose work is to find out God
And the nature of time and space,
He would put him onto the case.
Ants are a curious race;
One crossing with hurried tread
The body of one of their dead
Isn't given a moment's arrest—
Seems not even impressed.
But he no doubt reports to any
With whom he crosses antennae,
And they no doubt report
To the higher up at court.

Then word goes forth in Formic:
"Death's come to Jerry McCormic,
Our selfless forager Jerry.
Will the special Janizary
Whose office it is to bury
The dead of the commissary
Go bring him home to his people.
Lay him in state on a sepal.
Wrap him for shroud in a petal.
Embalm him with ichor of nettle.
This is the word of your Queen."
And presently on the scene
Appears a solemn mortician;
And taking formal position
With feelers calmly atwiddle,
Seizes the dead by the middle,
And heaving him high in the air,
Carries him out of there.
No one stands round to stare.
It is nobody else's affair.

It couldn't be called ungentle.
But how thoroughly departmental.

From Robert Frost, *Collected Poems,* Henry Holt and Company, Inc.

TO A THINKER

by ROBERT FROST

The last step taken found your heft
Decidedly upon the left.
One more would throw you on the right.
Another still—you see your plight.

You call this thinking, but it's walking.
Not even that, it's only rocking,
Or weaving like a stabled horse:
From force to matter and back to force,

The Vantage Point

From form to content and back to form,
From norm to crazy and back to norm,
From bound to free and back to bound,
From sound to sense, and back to sound.
So back and forth. It almost scares
A man the way things come in pairs.
Just now you're off democracy
(With a polite regret to be),
And leaning on dictatorship;
But if you will accept the tip,
In less than no time, tongue and pen,
You'll be a democrat again.
A reasoner and good as such,
Don't let it bother you too much

If it makes you look helpless please
And a temptation to the tease.
Suppose you've no direction in you,
I don't see but you must continue
To use the gift you do possess,
And sway with reason more or less.
I own I never really warmed
To the reformer or reformed,
And yet conversion has its place
Not half way down the scale of grace.
So if you find you must repent
From side to side in argument,
At least don't use your mind too hard,
But trust my instinct—I'm a bard.

THE VANTAGE POINT
by Robert Frost

If tired of trees I seek again mankind,
    Well I know where to hie me—in the dawn,
    To a slope where the cattle keep the lawn.
There amid lolling juniper reclined,
Myself unseen, I see in white defined
    Far off the homes of men, and farther still,
    The graves of men on an opposing hill,
Living or dead, whichever are to mind.

And if by noon I have too much of these,
    I have but to turn on my arm, and lo,
    The sun-burned hillside sets my face aglow,
My breathing shakes the bluet like a breeze,
    I smell the earth, I smell the bruisèd plant,
    I look into the crater of the ant.

A DRUMLIN WOODCHUCK

by ROBERT FROST

One thing has a shelving bank,
Another a rotting plank,
To give it cozier skies
And make up for its lack of size.

My own strategic retreat
Is where two rocks almost meet,
And still more secure and snug,
A two-door burrow I dug.

With those in mind at my back
I can sit forth exposed to attack
As one who shrewdly pretends
That he and the world are friends.

All we who prefer to live
Have a little whistle we give,
And flash, at the least alarm
We dive down under the farm.

We allow some time for guile
And don't come out for a while
Either to eat or drink.
We take occasion to think.

And if after the hunt goes past
And the double-barrelled blast
(Like war and pestilence
And the loss of common sense),

If I can with confidence say
That still for another day,
Or even another year,
I will be there for you, my dear,

It will be because, though small
As measured against the All,
I have been so instinctively thorough
About my crevice and burrow.

STOPPING BY WOODS ON A SNOWY EVENING

by ROBERT FROST

Whose woods these are I think I know.
His house is in the village though;
He will not see me stopping here
To watch his woods fill up with snow.

My little horse must think it queer
To stop without a farmhouse near
Between the woods and frozen lake
The darkest evening of the year.

He gives his harness bells a shake
To ask if there is some mistake.
The only other sound's the sweep
Of easy wind and downy flake.

The woods are lovely, dark and deep.
But I have promises to keep,
And miles to go before I sleep,
And miles to go before I sleep.

NEITHER OUT FAR NOR IN DEEP

by Robert Frost

The people along the sand
All turn and look one way.
They turn their back on the land.
They look at the sea all day.

As long as it takes to pass
A ship keeps raising its hull;
The wetter ground like glass
Reflects a standing gull.

The land may vary more;
But wherever the truth may be—
The water comes ashore,
And the people look at the sea.

They cannot look out far.
They cannot look in deep.
But when was that ever a bar
To any watch they keep?

WEST-RUNNING BROOK

by Robert Frost

"Fred, where is north?"

"North? North is there, my love.
The brook runs west."

"West-running Brook then call it."
(West-running Brook men call it to this day.)
"What does it think it's doing running west
When all the other country brooks flow east
To reach the ocean? It must be the brook
Can trust itself to go by contraries
The way I can with you—and you with me—
Because we're—we're—I don't know what we are.
What are we?"

"Young or new?"

"We must be something.
We've said we two. Let's change that to we three.
As you and I are married to each other,
We'll both be married to the brook. We'll build

From *Complete Poems of Robert Frost.* Copyright, 1930, 1949, by Henry Holt & Company, Inc. Copyright 1936, 1948, by Robert Frost. By permission of the publishers.

[677]

Our bridge across it, and the bridge shall be
Our arm thrown over it asleep beside it.
Look, look, it's waving to us with a wave
To let us know it hears me."
                              "Why, my dear,
That wave's been standing off this jut of shore—"
(The black stream, catching on a sunken rock,
Flung backward on itself in one white wave,
And the white water rode the black forever,
Not gaining but not losing, like a bird
White feathers from the struggle of whose breast
Flecked the dark stream and flecked the darker pool
Below the point, and were at last driven wrinkled
In a white scarf against the far shore alders.)
"That wave's been standing off this jut of shore
Ever since rivers, I was going to say,
Were made in heaven. It wasn't waved to us."

"It wasn't, yet it was. If not to you
It was to me—in an annunciation."

"Oh, if you take it off to lady-land,
As't were the country of the Amazons
We men must see you to the confines of
And leave you there, ourselves forbid to enter,—
It is your brook! I have no more to say."

"Yes, you have, too. Go on. You thought of something."

"Speaking of contraries, see how the brook
In that white wave runs counter to itself.
It is from that in water we were from
Long, long before we were from any creature.
Here we, in our impatience of the steps,
Get back to the beginning of beginnings,
The stream of everything that runs away.
Some say existence like a Pirouot
And Pirouette, forever in one place,
Stands still and dances, but it runs away,
It seriously, sadly, runs away
To fill the abyss' void with emptiness.
It flows beside us in this water brook,
But it flows over us. It flows between us
To separate us for a panic moment.

Fire and Ice

It flows between us, over us, and *with* us.
And it is time, strength, tone, light, life and love—
And even substance lapsing unsubstantial;
The universal cataract of death
That spends to nothingness—and unresisted,
Save by some strange resistance in itself,
Not just a swerving, but a throwing back,
As if regret were in it and were sacred.
It has this throwing backward on itself
So that the fall of most of it is always
Raising a little, sending up a little.
Our life runs down in sending up the clock.
The brook runs down in sending up our life.
The sun runs down in sending up the brook.
And there is something sending up the sun.
It is this backward motion toward the source,
Against the stream, that most we see ourselves in,
The tribute of the current to the source.
It is from this in nature we are from.
It is most us."

"Today will be the day
You said so."

"No, today will be the day
You said the brook was called West-running Brook."

"Today will be the day of what we both said."

FIRE AND ICE

by Robert Frost

Some say the world will end in fire,
Some say in ice.
From what I've tasted of desire
I hold with those who favor fire.
But if it had to perish twice,
I think I know enough of hate
To know that for destruction ice
Is also great
And would suffice.

From *Complete Poems of Robert Frost.* Copyright, 1930, 1949, by Henry Holt & Company, Inc. Copyright, 1936, 1948, by Robert Frost. By permission of the publishers.

MENDING WALL
by Robert Frost

Something there is that doesn't love a wall,
That sends the frozen-ground-swell under it,
And spills the upper boulders in the sun;
And makes gaps even two can pass abreast.
The work of hunters is another thing:
I have come after them and made repair
Where they have left not one stone on a stone,
But they would have the rabbit out of hiding,
To please the yelping dogs. The gaps I mean,
No one has seen them made or heard them made,
But at spring mending-time we find them there.
I let my neighbour know beyond the hill;
And on a day we meet to walk the line
And set the wall between us once again.
We keep the wall between us as we go.
To each the boulders that have fallen to each.
And some are loaves and some so nearly balls
We have to use a spell to make them balance:
"Stay where you are until our backs are turned!"
We wear our fingers rough with handling them.
Oh, just another kind of out-door game,
One on a side. It comes to little more:
There where it is we do not need the wall:
He is all pine and I am apple orchard.
My apple trees will never get across
And eat the cones under his pines, I tell him.
He only says, "Good fences make good neighbours."
Spring is the mischief in me, and I wonder
If I could put a notion in his head:
"*Why* do they make good neighbours? Isn't it
Where there are cows? But here there are no cows.

There Are Roughly Zones

Before I built a wall I'd ask to know
What I was walling in or walling out,
And to whom I was like to give offence.
Something there is that doesn't love a wall,
That wants it down." I could say "Elves" to him,
But it's not elves exactly, and I'd rather
He said it for himself. I see him there,
Bringing a stone grasped firmly by the top
In each hand, like an old-stone savage armed.
He moves in darkness as it seems to me,
Not of woods only and the shade of trees.
He will not go behind his father's saying,
And he likes having thought of it so well
He says again, "Good fences make good neighbours."

THERE ARE ROUGHLY ZONES
by Robert Frost

We sit indoors and talk of the cold outside.
And every gust that gathers strength and heaves
Is a threat to the house. But the house has long been tried.
We think of the tree. If it never again has leaves,
We'll know, we say, that this was the night it died.
It is very far north, we admit, to have brought the peach.
What comes over a man, is it soul or mind—
That to no limits and bounds he can stay confined?
You would say his ambition was to extend the reach
Clear to the Arctic of every living kind.
Why is his nature forever so hard to teach
That though there is no fixed line between wrong and right,
There are roughly zones whose laws must be obeyed.
There is nothing much we can do for the tree tonight,
But we can't help feeling more than a little betrayed
That the northwest wind should rise to such a height
Just when the cold went down so many below.

Poetry

The tree has no leaves and may never have them again.
We must wait till some months hence in the spring to know.
But if it is destined never again to grow,
It can blame this limitless trait in the hearts of men.

ACQUAINTED WITH THE NIGHT
by Robert Frost

I have been one acquainted with the night.
I have walked out in rain—and back in rain.
I have outwalked the furthest city light.

I have looked down the saddest city lane.
I have passed by the watchman on his beat.
And dropped my eyes, unwilling to explain.

I have stood still and stopped the sound of feet
When far away an interrupted cry
Came over houses from another street,

But not to call me back or say good-bye;
And further still at an unearthly height,
One luminary clock against the sky

Proclaimed the time was neither wrong nor right.
I have been one acquainted with the night.

Nighthawks. Edward Hopper.   *Courtesy Art Institute of Chicago*

from THE PEOPLE, YES
by Carl Sandburg

57

Lincoln?
He was a mystery in smoke and flags
saying yes to the smoke, yes to the flags,
yes to the paradoxes of democracy,
yes to the hopes of government
of the people by the people for the people,
no to debauchery of the public mind,
no to personal malice nursed and fed,
yes to the Constitution when a help,
no to the Constitution when a hindrance,
yes to man as a struggler amid illusions,
each man fated to answer for himself:
Which of the faiths and illusions of mankind
must I choose for my own sustaining light
to bring me beyond the present wilderness?

Lincoln? was he a poet?
and did he write verses?
"I have not willingly planted a thorn
in any man's bosom."
"I shall do nothing through malice; what
I deal with is too vast for malice."

Death was in the air.
So was birth.
What was dying few could say.
What was being born none could know.

He took the wheel in a lashing roaring
   hurricane.
And by what compass did he steer the course
   of the ship?
"My policy is to have no policy," he said in
   the early months,
And three years later, "I have been controlled
   by events."

From *The People, Yes* by Carl Sandburg. Copyright, 1936, by Harcourt, Brace and Company, Inc.

Poetry

He could play with the wayward human mind, saying at Charleston, Illinois, September 18, 1858, it was no answer to an argument to call a man a liar.

"I assert that you [pointing a finger in the face of a man in the crowd] are here today, and you undertake to prove me a liar by showing that you were in Mattoon yesterday.

"I say that you took your hat off your head and you prove me a liar by putting it on your head."

He saw personal liberty across wide horizons.

"Our progress in degeneracy appears to me to be pretty rapid," he wrote Joshua F. Speed, August 24, 1855. "As a nation we began by declaring that 'all men are created equal, except Negroes.' When the Know-Nothings get control, it will read 'all men are created equal except Negroes and foreigners and Catholics.' When it comes to this, I shall prefer emigrating to some country where they make no pretense of loving liberty."

Did he look deep into a crazy pool
and see the strife and wrangling
with a clear eye, writing the military
head of a stormswept area:
"If both factions, or neither, shall abuse
you, you will probably be about right. Beware of being assailed by one and praised
by the other"?

Lincoln? was he a historian?
did he know mass chaos?
did he have an answer for those
who asked him to organize chaos?

"Actual war coming, blood grows hot, and blood is spilled. Thought is forced from old channels into confusion. Deception breeds and thrives. Confidence dies and universal suspicion reigns.

"Each man feels an impulse to kill his neighbor, lest he be first killed by him. Revenge and retaliation follow. And all this, as before said, may be among honest men only; but this is not all.

"Every foul bird comes abroad and every dirty reptile rises up. These add crime to confusion.

"Strong measures, deemed indispensable, but harsh at best, such men make worse by maladministration. Murders for old grudges, and murders for pelf, proceed under any cloak that will best cover for the occasion. These causes amply account for what has happened in Missouri."

Early in '64 the Committee of the New York Workingman's Democratic Republican Association called on him with assurances and he meditated aloud for them, recalling race and draft riots:

[684]

The People, Yes

"The most notable feature of a disturbance in your city last summer was the hanging of some working people by other working people. It should never be so.

"The strongest bond of human sympathy, outside of the family relation, should be one uniting all working people, of all nations and tongues and kindreds.

"Let not him who is houseless pull down the house of another, but let him labor diligently and build one for himself, thus by example assuring that his own shall be safe from violence when built."

>Lincoln? did he gather
>the feel of the American dream
>and see its kindred over the earth?

"As labor is the common burden of our race,
so the effort of some to shift
their share of the burden
onto the shoulders of others
is the great durable curse of the race."

>"I hold,
if the Almighty had ever made a set of men
that should do all of the eating
and none of the work,
he would have made them
with mouths only, and no hands;
and if he had ever made another class,
that he had intended should do all the work
and none of the eating,
he would have made them
without mouths and all hands."

"—the same spirit that says, 'You toil and work and earn bread, and I'll eat it.' No matter in what shape it comes, whether from the mouth of a king who seeks to bestride the people of his own nation and live by the fruit of their labor, or from one race of men as an apology for enslaving another race, it is the same tyrannical principle."

"As I would not be a *slave,* so I would not be a *master.* This expresses my idea of democracy. Whatever differs from this, to the extent of the difference, is no democracy."

[685]

"I never knew a man who wished to be himself a slave. Consider if you know any *good* thing that no man desires for himself."

"The sheep and the wolf
 are not agreed upon a definition
 of the word liberty."

"The whole people of this nation
 will ever do well
 if well done by."

"The plainest print cannot be read
through a gold eagle."

"How does it feel to be President?" an Illinois friend asked.
"Well, I'm like the man they rode out of town on a rail. He said if it wasn't for the honor of it he would just as soon walk."

>   Lincoln? he was a dreamer.
>   He saw ships at sea,
>   he saw himself living and dead
>   in dreams that came.

Into a secretary's diary December 23, 1863, went an entry: "The President tonight had a dream. He was in a party of plain people, and, as it became known who he was, they began to comment on his appearance. One of them said: 'He is a very common-looking man.' The President replied: 'The Lord prefers common-looking people. That is the reason he makes so many of them.'"

He spoke one verse for then and now:
 "If we could first know where we are,
 and whither we are tending,
 we could better judge
 what to do, and how to do it."

THE ROSE OF THE WORLD

by WILLIAM BUTLER YEATS

Who dreamed that beauty passes like a dream?
For these red lips with all their mournful pride,
Mournful that no new wonder may betide,
Troy passed away in one high funeral gleam,
And Usna's children died.

We and the laboring world are passing by:
Amid men's souls, that waver and give place,
Like the pale waters in their wintry race,
Under the passing stars, frame of the sky,
Lives on this lonely face.

Bow down, archangels, in your dim abode:
Before you were, or any hearts to beat,
Weary and kind, one lingered by His seat;
He made the world to be a grassy road
Before her wandering feet.

THE SECOND COMING

by WILLIAM BUTLER YEATS

Turning and turning in the widening gyre
The falcon cannot hear the falconer;
Things fall apart; the centre cannot hold;
Mere anarchy is loosed upon the world,
The blood-dimmed tide is loosed, and everywhere
The ceremony of innocence is drowned;
The best lack all conviction, while the worst
Are full of passionate intensity.

Surely some revelation is at hand;
Surely the Second Coming is at hand.
The Second Coming! Hardly are those words out
When a vast image out of *Spiritus Mundi*
Troubles my sight: somewhere in sands of the desert
A shape with lion body and the head of a man,
A gaze blank and pitiless as the sun,
Is moving its slow thighs, while all about it
Reel shadows of the indignant desert birds.
The darkness drops again; but now I know
That twenty centuries of stony sleep
Were vexed to nightmare by a rocking cradle,
And what rough beast, its hour come round at last,
Slouches towards Bethlehem to be born?

From W. B. Yeats, *Collected Poems*. Copyright, 1925, by The Macmillan Company and used with their permission.

[687]

LEDA AND THE SWAN

by William Butler Yeats

A sudden blow: the great wings beating still
Above the staggering girl, her thighs caressed
By the dark webs, her nape caught in his bill,
He holds her helpless breast upon his breast.

How can those terrified vague fingers push
The feathered glory from her loosening thighs?
And how can body, laid in that white rush,
But feel the strange heart beating where it lies?

A shudder in the loins engenders there
The broken wall, the burning roof and tower
And Agamemnon dead.
　　　　　　　　Being so caught up,
So mastered by the brute blood of the air,
Did she put on his knowledge with his power
Before the indifferent beak could let her drop?

I think if I could be given a month of Antiquity and leave to spend it where I chose, I would spend it in Byzantium a little before Justinian opened St. Sophia and closed the Academy of Plato. I think I could find in some little wine-shop some philosophical worker in mosaic who could answer all my questions, the supernatural descending nearer to him than to Plotinus even. . . . I think that in early Byzantium, maybe never before or since in recorded history, religious, aesthetic and practical life were one . . .

—*A Vision*

SAILING TO BYZANTIUM

by William Butler Yeats

That is no country for old men. The young
In one another's arm, birds in the trees,
—Those dying generations—at their song,
The salmon-falls, the mackerel-crowded seas,
Fish, flesh, or fowl, commend all summer long
Whatever is begotten, born, and dies.
Caught in that sensual music all neglect
Monuments of unageing intellect.

Byzantium

II

An aged man is but a paltry thing,
A tattered coat upon a stick, unless
Soul clap its hands and sing, and louder sing
For every tatter in its mortal dress,
Nor is there singing school but studying
Monuments of its own magnificence;
And therefore I have sailed the seas and come
To the holy city of Byzantium.

III

O sages standing in God's holy fire
As in the gold mosaic of a wall,
Come from the holy fire, perne in a gyre,
And be the singing-masters of my soul.
Consume my heart away; sick with desire
And fastened to a dying animal
It knows not what it is; and gather me
Into the artifice of eternity.

IV

Once out of nature I shall never take
My bodily form from any natural thing,
But such a form as Grecian goldsmiths make
Of hammered gold and gold enamelling
To keep a drowsy Emperor awake;
Or set upon a golden bough to sing
To lords and ladies of Byzantium
Of what is past, or passing, or to come.

BYZANTIUM

by WILLIAM BUTLER YEATS

The unpurged images of day recede;
The Emperor's drunken soldiery are abed;
Night resonance recedes, night-walkers' song
After great cathedral gong;
A starlit or a moonlit dome disdains

[689]

Poetry

All that man is,
All mere complexities,
The fury and the mire of human veins.

Before me floats an image, man or shade,
Shade more than man, more image than a shade;
For Hades' bobbin bound in mummy-cloth
May unwind the winding path;
A mouth that has no moisture and no breath
Breathless mouths may summon;
I hail the superhuman;
I call it death-in-life and life-in-death.

Miracle, bird or golden handiwork,
More miracle than bird or handiwork,
Planted on the starlit golden bough,
Can like the cocks of Hades crow,
Or, by the moon embittered, scorn aloud
In glory of changeless metal
Common bird or petal
And all complexities of mire or blood.

At midnight on the Emperor's pavement flit
Flames that no faggot feeds, nor steel has lit,
Nor storm disturbs, flames begotten of flame,
Where blood-begotten spirits come
And all complexities of fury leave,
Dying into a dance,
An agony of trance,
An agony of flame that cannot singe a sleeve.

Astraddle on the dolphin's mire and blood,
Spirit after spirit! The smithies break the flood,
The golden smithies of the Emperor!
Marbles of the dancing floor
Break bitter furies of complexity,
Those images that yet
Fresh images beget,
That dolphin-torn, that gong-tormented sea.

[690]

A NOTE ON BYZANTIUM

In his Diary for April 30, 1930, Yeats wrote: "Subject for a poem . . . Describe Byzantium as it is in the system towards the end of the first Christian millennium. A walking mummy. Flames at the street corners where the soul is purified, birds of hammered gold singing in the golden trees, in the harbour [sic], offering their backs to the wailing dead that they may carry them to paradise." Yeats depicts the spirits of the dead purifying themselves from the impurities of the living. It is night in Byzantium. The impure and unpurged living have withdrawn. The sounds of night have receded, the songs of night-walkers and the sound of the cathedral gong, which is not only a symbol of religious ritual tolling out the living and tolling in the dead, but also of the sensual music of impurities which later torments the sea. A cathedral dome, as of Santa Sophia, is lit by the stars or the moon; that is, during Phase 1 at the dark of the moon, or during Phase 15 when the stars recede in the glare of the full moon. Both are supernatural phases where no human incarnation is possible, for Phase 1 "is a supernatural incarnation, like Phase 15, because there is complete objectivity, and human life cannot be completely objective. At Phase 15 mind was completely absorbed by being, but now body is completely absorbed in its supernatural environment . . . mind and body take whatever shape, accept whatever image is imprinted upon them . . . are indeed the instruments of supernatural manifestation, the final link between the living and more powerful beings."—*A Vision*, p. 183. In this great silence, the starlit or moonlit dome disdains the fury and mire of human duality. The spirits now begin to float in from the realm of the dead.

Yeats describes various forms which the spirit may take during the second state: "In the *Meditation* it wears the form it had immediately before death; in the *Dreaming Back* and the *Phantasmagoria*, should it appear to the living, it has the form of the dream, in the *Return* the form worn during the event explored, in the *Shiftings* whatever form was most familiar to others during its life; in the *Purification* whatever form it fancies."—*A Vision*, p. 235. The spirits live in Hades; the bobbin, or spindle of Hades, symbolizes the revolving and gyrating motions of the dead undergoing their purifications, and the mummy-cloth is a symbol of their lives revolving on that spindle. Reliving their previous lives in memory, by *Dreaming Back* and in *Return*, they thus unwind a similar natural spindle or gyre of their lives upon earth called the "winding path" so that they may become freed of all natural attributes or memories. Caught in a limbo of air between the Condition of Fire and the terrestrial condition, they receive an inflowing from both directions and must continually shuttle between them. "The inflowing from their mirrored life, who themselves receive it from the Condition of Fire, falls upon the Winding Path called the Path of the Serpent, and that inflowing coming alike to men and to animals is called natural. . . . In so far as a man is like all other men, the inflow finds him upon the winding path, and in so far as he is a saint or sage, upon the straight path." The spirit's "descending power," however, "is neither the winding

By Kimon Friar. From Friar and Brinnin, *Modern Poetry*, copyright, 1951, by Appleton-Century-Crofts, Inc. Reprinted by permission of Appleton-Century-Crofts, Inc.

nor the straight line but zigzag . . . it is the sudden lightning, for all his acts of power are instantaneous. We perceive in the pulsation of the artery, and after slowly decline."—*Essays* (New York, Macmillan, 1924), pp. 528-529. Spirit now calls to spirit, and the poet, himself a spirit having neither the moisture nor the breath of the living, calls upon the superhuman in whom the dualities of life and death are being simultaneously resolved. The poet then turns to images of hammered golden birds wrought by human hands to such artifice that they seem inhuman and miraculous, identical in symbol to the spirits. In starlight these birds can crow like the cocks of Hades, a suggestion that if the spirits of the dead must recede before the crowing of a terrestrial cock, as legend has it, then the unpurged images of the living must recede before the cocks of Hades or the singing artificial birds of Byzantium. They sing of their singleness and changelessness, and scorn the passing, decaying birds and flowers of nature, the evil and passion of human complexity. The poet then turns again to the spirits of flame who in an agony of fire and trance are trying to die out of the complexities of human fury in a flaming dance which symbolizes the underlining rhythmic, gyrating pulse of creation. Since these spirits are composed of spiritual and not physical fire, no faggot can feed them, no flint can ignite them, no storm can disturb them, and they in turn cannot singe anything. They were once begotten out of the complexities of human blood which they must now purge away; also, like the bird who came out of the fire, spirit can beget spirit, flame beget flame "as one candle takes light from another."

In discussing that aspect of the second stage called *Phantasmagoria*, Yeats writes of those spirits that appear under the impulse of moral and emotional suffering, and recounts the story of a Japanese girl whose ghost tells a priest of a slight sin, which seems great to her because of her exaggerated conscience: "She is surrounded by flames, and though the priest explains that if she but ceased to believe in those flames they would cease to exist, believe she must, and the play ends in an elaborate dance, the dance of her agony." —*A Vision*, p. 231. Yeats reports the following conversation between himself and a spirit from the fifth state, that of *Purification:* " 'We have no power,' said an inhabitant of the state, 'except to purify our intention,' and when I asked of what, replied: 'Of complexity.' "—*A Vision*, p. 233. The poet finally turns to a vision of the spirits astraddle on the backs of dolphins plunging in an element of water and who carry them back and forth between the terrestrial condition of the living and the spiritual condition of fire and air. (According to Mrs. Arthur Strong's *Apotheosis and After-Life,* dolphins, in the art of the ancient world, were symbols of the soul and its transit.) The miraculous handiwork of the Byzantium goldsmiths, which are themselves now symbols of spirit, break in upon this spiritual flood, and also, in another sense of "break," transcend, overcome, or defeat the flood. The marble mosaics on the dancing floor of the Emperor's pavement (the Forum of Constantine known as "The Pavement" because of its marble floor), also break in upon and are involved in the dance. Thus the poem ends with a whirling dance broken into fragmented images, images begetting images of both symbol and spirit, and all tossed upon a dolphin-torn and gong-tormented sea of complexity, fury, and blood.

from SELECTED ESSAYS
by T. S. Eliot

Dante

In my experience of the appreciation of poetry I have always found that the less I knew about the poet and his work, before I began to read it, the better.

Tradition and the Individual Talent

I am alive to a usual objection to what is clearly part of my programme for the *metier* of poetry. The objection is that the doctrine requires a ridiculous amount of erudition (pedantry), a claim which can be rejected by appeal to the lives of poets in any pantheon. It will even be affirmed that much learning deadens or perverts poetic sensibility.

The Metaphysical Poets

It is not a permanent necessity that poets should be interested in philosophy, or in any other subject. We can only say that it appears likely that poets in our civilization, as it exists at present, must be *difficult*. Our civilization comprehends great variety and complexity, and this variety and complexity, playing upon a refined sensibility, must produce various and complex results. The poet must become more and more comprehensive, more allusive, more indirect, in order to force, to dislocate if necessary, language into his meaning.

William Blake

Blake was endowed with a capacity for considerable understanding of human nature with a remarkable and original sense of language, and a gift of hallucinated vision. Had these been controlled by a respect for impersonal reason, for common sense, for the objectivity of science, it would have been better for him.

From *Selected Essays 1917-1932* by T. S. Eliot, copyright, 1932, by Harcourt, Brace and Company, Inc.

Poetry

ANIMULA

by T. S. Eliot

"Issues from the hand of God, the simple soul"
To a flat world of changing lights and noise,
To light, dark, dry or damp, chilly or warm;
Moving between the legs of tables and of chairs,
Rising or falling, grasping at kisses and toys,
Advancing boldly, sudden to take alarm,
Retreating to the corner of arm and knee,
Eager to be reassured, taking pleasure
In the fragrant brilliance of the Christmas tree,
Pleasure in the wind, the sunlight and the sea;
Studies the sunlit pattern on the floor
And running stags around a silver tray;
Confounds the actual and the fanciful,
Content with playing-cards and kings and queens,
What the fairies do and what the servants say.
The heavy burden of the growing soul
Perplexes and offends more, day by day;
Week by week, offends and perplexes more
With the imperatives of "is and seems"
And may and may not, desire and control
The pain of living and the drug of dreams
Curl up the small soul in the window seat
Behind the *Encylopædia Britannica.*
Issues from the hand of time the simple soul
Irresolute and selfish, misshapen, lame,
Unable to fare forward or retreat,
Fearing the warm reality, the offered good,
Denying the importunity of the blood,
Shadow of its own shadows, specter in its own gloom,
Leaving disordered papers in a dusty room;
Living first in the silence after the viaticum.

Pray for Guiterriez, avid of speed and power,
For Boudin, blown to pieces,
For this one who made a great fortune,
And that one who went his own way.
Pray for Floret, by the boarhound slain between the yew trees,
Pray for us now and at the hour of our birth.

From *Collected Poems of T. S. Eliot.* Copyright, 1936, by Harcourt, Brace and Company, Inc.

THE LOVE SONG OF J. ALFRED PRUFROCK

by T. S. Eliot

*S'io credesse che mia risposta fosse
A persona che mai tornasse al mondo,
Questa fiamma staria senza piu scosse.
Ma perciocche giammai di questo fondo
Non torno vivo alcun, s'i'odo il vero,
Senza tema d'infamia ti rispondo.**

Let us go then, you and I,
When the evening is spread out against the sky
Like a patient etherized upon a table;
Let us go, through certain half-deserted streets,
The muttering retreats
Of restless nights in one-night cheap hotels
And sawdust restaurants with oyster-shells:
Streets that follow like a tedious argument
Of insidious intent
To lead you to an overwhelming question . . .
Oh, do not ask, "What is it?"
Let us go and make our visit.

In the room the women come and go
Talking of Michelangelo.

The yellow fog that rubs its back upon the window-panes,
The yellow smoke that rubs its muzzle on the window-panes
Licked its tongue into the corners of the evening,
Lingered upon the pools that stand in drains,

---

* If I thought my answer were to one who ever could return to the world, this flame should shake no more. But since none ever did return alive from this depth, if what I hear be true, without fear of infamy I answer thee.

From *Collected Poems of T. S. Eliot*. Copyright, 1936, by Harcourt, Brace and Company, Inc.

Let fall upon its back the soot that falls from chimneys,
Slipped by the terrace, made a sudden leap,
And seeing that it was a soft October night,
Curled once about the house, and fell asleep.

And indeed there will be time
For the yellow smoke that slides along the street,
Rubbing its back upon the window-panes;
There will be time, there will be time
To prepare a face to meet the faces that you meet;
There will be time to murder and create,
And time for all the works and days of hands
That lift and drop a question on your plate;
Time for you and time for me,
And time yet for a hundred indecisions,
And for a hundred visions and revisions,
Before the taking of a toast and tea.

In the room the women come and go
Talking of Michelangelo.

And indeed there will be time
To wonder, "Do I dare?" and, "Do I dare?"
Time to turn back and descend the stair,
With a bald spot in the middle of my hair—
(They will say: "How his hair is growing thin!")
My morning coat, my collar mounting firmly to the chin,
My necktie rich and modest, but asserted by a simple pin—
(They will say: "But how his arms and legs are thin!")
Do I dare
Disturb the universe?
In a minute there is time
For decisions and revisions which a minute will reverse.

For I have known them all already, known them all:—
Have known the evenings, mornings, afternoons,
I have measured out my life with coffee spoons;
I know the voices dying with a dying fall
Beneath the music from a farther room.
  So how should I presume?

And I have known the eyes already, known them all—
The eyes that fix you in a formulated phrase,
And when I am formulated, sprawling on a pin,

The Love Song of J. Alfred Prufrock

When I am pinned and wriggling on the wall,
Then how should I begin
To spit out all the butt-ends of my days and ways?
    And how should I presume?

And I have known the arms already, known them all—
Arms that are braceleted and white and bare
(But in the lamplight, downed with light brown hair!)
Is it perfume from a dress
That makes me so digress?
Arms that lie along a table, or wrap about a shawl.
    And should I then presume?
    And how should I begin?

.   .   .   .   .

Shall I say, I have gone at dusk through narrow streets
And watched the smoke that rises from the pipes
Of lonely men in shirt-sleeves, leaning out of windows? . . .

I should have been a pair of ragged claws
Scuttling across the floors of silent seas.

.   .   .   .   .

And the afternoon, the evening, sleeps so peacefully!
Smoothed by long fingers,
Asleep . . . tired . . . or it malingers,
Stretched on the floor, here beside you and me.
Should I, after tea and cakes and ices,
Have the strength to force the moment to its crisis?
But though I have wept and fasted, wept and prayed,
Though I have seen my head (grown slightly bald) brought in upon a platter
I am no prophet—and here's no great matter;
I have seen the moment of my greatness flicker,
And I have seen the eternal Footman hold my coat, and snicker,
And in short, I was afraid.

And would it have been worth it, after all,
After the cups, the marmalade, the tea,
Among the porcelain, among some talk of you and me,
Would it have been worth while,
To have bitten off the matter with a smile,
To have squeezed the universe into a ball
To roll it toward some overwhelming question,
To say: "I am Lazarus, come from the dead,

Come back to tell you all, I shall tell you all"—
If one, settling a pillow by her head,
    Should say: "That is not what I meant at all.
    That is not it, at all."

And would it have been worth it, after all,
Would it have been worth while,
After the sunsets and the dooryards and the sprinkled streets,
After the novels, after the teacups, after the skirts that trail along the floor—
And this, and so much more?—
It is impossible to say just what I mean!
But as if a magic lantern threw the nerves in patterns on a screen:
Would it have been worth while
If one, settling a pillow or throwing off a shawl,
And turning toward the window, should say:
    "That is not it at all,
    That is not what I meant, at all."

  .   .   .   .   .   .

No! I am not Prince Hamlet, nor was meant to be;
Am an attendant lord, one that will do
To swell a progress, start a scene or two,
Advise the prince; no doubt, an easy tool,
Deferential, glad to be of use,
Politic, cautious, and meticulous;
Full of high sentence, but a bit obtuse;
At times, indeed, almost ridiculous—
Almost, at times, the Fool.

I grow old . . . I grow old . . .
I shall wear the bottoms of my trousers rolled.

Shall I part my hair behind? Do I dare to eat a peach?
I shall wear white flannel trousers, and walk upon the beach.
I have heard the mermaids singing, each to each.

I do not think that they will sing to me.

I have seen them riding seaward on the waves
Combing the white hair of the waves blown back
When the wind blows the water white and black.

We have lingered in the chambers of the sea
By sea-girls wreathed with seaweed red and brown
Till human voices wake us, and we drown.

"Promise you'll wait for me. I want something real to come back to."

Permission The New Yorker. Copyright The F-R. Publishing Corporation.

PORTRAIT OF A LADY
by T. S. Eliot

Thou hast committed—
Fornication: but that was in another country,
And besides, the wench is dead.
—*The Jew of Malta.*

I

Among the smoke and fog of a December afternoon
You have the scene arrange itself—as it will seem to do—
With "I have saved this afternoon for you";
And four wax candles in the darkened room,
Four rings of light upon the ceiling overhead,
An atmosphere of Juliet's tomb
Prepared for all the things to be said, or left unsaid.
We have been, let us say, to hear the latest Pole
Transmit the Preludes, through his hair and finger-tips.
"So intimate, this Chopin, that I think his soul
Should be resurrected only among friends
Some two or three, who will not touch the bloom
That is rubbed and questioned in the concert room."
—And so the conversation slips
Among velleities and carefully caught regrets
Through attenuated tones of violins
Mingled with remote cornets
And begins.
"You do not know how much they mean to me, my friends,
And how, how rare and strange it is, to find
In a life composed so much, so much of odds and ends,
(For indeed I do not love it . . . you knew? you are not blind!
How keen you are!)
To find a friend who has these qualities,
Who has, and gives
Those qualities upon which friendship lives.
How much it means that I say this to you—
Without these friendships—life, what *cauchemar!*"

Among the windings of the violins
And the ariettes
Of cracked cornets
Inside my brain a dull tom-tom begins
Absurdly hammering a prelude of its own,
Capricious monotone
That is at least one definite "false note."
—Let us take the air, in a tobacco trance,
Admire the monuments,
Discuss the late events,
Correct our watches by the public clocks.
Then sit for half an hour and drink our bocks.

II

Now that lilacs are in bloom
She has a bowl of lilacs in her room
And twists one in her fingers while she talks.
"Ah, my friend, you do not know, you do not know
What life is, you who hold it in your hands";

From *Collected Poems of T. S. Eliot.* Copyright, 1936, by Harcourt, Brace and Company, Inc.

Portrait of a Lady

(Slowly twisting the lilac stalks)
"You let it flow from you, you let it flow,
And youth is cruel, and has no remorse
And smiles at situations which it cannot see."
I smile, of course,
And go on drinking tea.
"Yet with these April sunsets, that somehow recall
My buried life, and Paris in the Spring,
I feel immeasurably at peace, and find the world
To be wonderful and youthful, after all."

The voice returns like the insistent out-of-tune
Of a broken violin on an August afternoon:
"I am always sure that you understand
My feelings, always sure that you feel,
Sure that across the gulf you reach your hand.

You are invulnerable, you have no Achilles' heel.
You will go on, and when you have prevailed.
You can say: at this point many a one has failed.
But what have I, but what have I, my friend,
To give you, what can you receive from me?
Only the friendship and the sympathy
Of one about to reach her journey's end.

I shall sit here, serving tea to friends. . . ."

I take my hat: how can I make a cowardly amends
For what she has said to me?
You will see me any morning in the park
Reading the comics and the sporting page.
Particularly I remark
An English countess goes upon the stage.
A Greek was murdered at a Polish dance,
Another bank defaulter has confessed.
I keep my countenance,
I remain self-possessed
Except when a street piano, mechanical and tired
Reiterates some worn-out common song
With the smell of hyacinths across the garden
Recalling things that other people have desired.
Are these ideas right or wrong?

III

The October night comes down; returning as before
Except for a slight sensation of being ill at ease
I mount the stairs and turn the handle of the door
And feel as if I had mounted on my hands and knees.

"And so you are going abroad; and when do you return?
But that's a useless question.
You hardly know when you are coming back,
You will find so much to learn."
My smile falls heavily among the bric-à-brac.

"Perhaps you can write to me."
My self-possession flares up for a second;
This is as I had reckoned.
"I have been wondering frequently of late
(But our beginnings never know our ends!)
Why we have not developed into friends."
I feel like one who smiles, and turning shall remark
Suddenly, his expression in a glass.

My self-possession gutters; we are really
    in the dark.

"For everybody said so, all our friends,
They all were sure our feelings would re-
    late
So closely! I myself can hardly under-
    stand.
We must leave it now to fate.
You will write, at any rate.
Perhaps it is not too late.
I shall sit here, serving tea to friends."

And I must borrow every changing shape
To find expression . . . dance, dance
Like a dancing bear,
Cry like a parrot, chatter like an ape.
Let us take the air, in a tobacco trance—

Well! and what if she should die some
    afternoon,
Afternoon gray and smoky, evening yel-
    low and rose;
Should die and leave me sitting pen in
    hand
With the smoke coming down above the
    housetops;
Doubtful, for a while
Not knowing what to feel or if I under-
    stand
Or whether wise or foolish, tardy or too
    soon . . .
Would she not have the advantage, after
    all?
This music is successful with a "dying
    fall"
Now that we talk of dying—
And should I have the right to smile?

THE HOLLOW MEN

by T. S. Eliot

A penny for the Old Guy.

MISTAH KURTZ—HE DEAD.

I

We are the hollow men
We are the stuffed men
Leaning together
Headpiece filled with straw. Alas!
Our dried voices, when
We whisper together
Are quiet and meaningless
As wind in dry grass
Or rats' feet over broken glass
In our dry cellar

Shape without form, shade without colour,
Paralysed force, gesture without motion;

Those who have crossed
With direct eyes, to death's other King-
    dom
Remember us—if at all—not as lost
Violent souls, but only
As the hollow men
The stuffed men.

II

Eyes I dare not meet in dreams
In death's dream kingdom
These do not appear:
There, the eyes are
Sunlight on a broken column
There, is a tree swinging
And voices are
In the wind's singing

From *Collected Poems of T. S. Eliot.* Copyright, 1936, by Harcourt, Brace and Company, Inc.

The Hollow Men

More distant and more solemn
Than a fading star.

Let me be no nearer
In death's dream kingdom
Let me also wear
Such deliberate disguises
Rat's skin, crowskin, crossed staves
In a field
Behaving as the wind behaves
No nearer—

Not that final meeting
In the twilight kingdom

III

This is the dead land
This is cactus land
Here the stone images
Are raised, here they receive
The supplication of a dead man's hand
Under the twinkle of a fading star.

Is it like this
In death's other kingdom
Waking alone
At the hour when we are
Trembling with tenderness
Lips that would kiss
Form prayers to broken stone.

IV

The eyes are not here
There are no eyes here
In this valley of dying stars
In this hollow valley
This broken jaw of our lost kingdoms

In this last of meeting places
We grope together
And avoid speech
Gathered on this beach of the tumid river

Sightless, unless
The eyes reappear
As the perpetual star
Multifoliate rose
Of death's twilight kingdom
The hope only
Of empty men.

V

Here we go round the prickly pear
Prickly pear prickly pear
Here we go round the prickly pear
At five o'clock in the morning.

Between the idea
And the reality
Between the motion
And the act
Falls the Shadow
    For Thine is the Kingdom

Between the conception
And the creation
Between the emotion
And the response
Falls the Shadow
    Life is very long

Between the desire
And the spasm
Between the potency
And the existence
Between the essence
And the descent
Falls the Shadow
    For Thine is the Kingdom

For Thine is
Life is
For Thine is the

This is the way the world ends
This is the way the world ends
This is the way the world ends
Not with a bang but a whimper.

Poetry

JOURNEY OF THE MAGI—
by T. S. Eliot

'A cold coming we had of it,
Just the worst time of the year
For a journey, and such a long journey:
The ways deep and the weather sharp,
The very dead of winter.'
And the camels galled, sore-footed, refractory,
Lying down in the melting snow.
There were times we regretted
The summer palaces on slopes, the terraces,
And the silken girls bringing sherbet.
Then the camel men cursing and grumbling
And running away, and wanting their liquor and women,
And the night-fires going out, and the lack of shelters,
And the cities hostile and the towns unfriendly
And the villages dirty and charging high prices:
A hard time we had of it.
At the end we preferred to travel all night,
Sleeping in snatches,
With the voices singing in our ears, saying
That this was all folly.

Then at dawn we came down to a temperate valley,
Wet, below the snow line, smelling of vegetation;
With a running stream and a water-mill beating the darkness,
And three trees on the low sky,
And an old white horse galloped away in the meadow.
Then we came to a tavern with vine-leaves over the lintel,
Six hands at an open door dicing for pieces of silver,
And feet kicking the empty wine-skins.
But there was no information, and so we continued
And arrived at evening, not a moment too soon
Finding the place; it was (you may say) satisfactory.

All this was a long time ago, I remember,
And I would do it again, but set down
This set down
This: were we led all that way for
Birth or Death? There was a Birth, certainly,
We had evidence and no doubt. I had seen birth and death,

Triumphal March

But had thought they were different; this Birth was
Hard and bitter agony for us, like Death, our death.
We returned to our places, these Kingdoms,
But no longer at ease here, in the old dispensation,
With an alien people clutching their gods.
I should be glad of another death.

TRIUMPHAL MARCH
by T. S. Eliot

Stone, bronze, stone, steel, stone, oakleaves horses' heels
Over the paving.
And the flags. And the trumpets. And so many eagles.
How many? Count them. And such a press of people.
We hardly knew ourselves that day, or knew the City.
This is the way to the temple, and we so many crowding the way.
So many waiting, how many waiting? what did it matter, on such a day?
Are they coming? No, not yet. You can see some eagles. And hear the trumpets.
Here they come. Is he coming?
The natural wakeful life of our Ego is a perceiving.
We can wait with our stools and our sausages.
What comes first? Can you see? Tell us. It is

	5,800,000	rifles and carbines,
	102,000	machine guns,
	28,000	trench mortars,
	53,000	field and heavy guns,
I cannot tell how many projectiles, mines and fuses,
	13,000	aeroplanes,
	24,000	aeroplane engines,
	50,000	ammunition waggons,
now	55,000	army waggons,
	11,000	field kitchens,
	1,150	field bakeries.

What a time that took. Will it be he now? No,
Those are the golf club Captains, these the Scouts,
And now the *société gymnastique de Poissy*
And now come the Mayor and the Liverymen. Look
There he is now, look:
There is no interrogation in his eyes
Or in the hands, quiet over the horse's neck,
And the eyes watchful, waiting, perceiving, indifferent.

[705]

Poetry

O hidden under the dove's wing, hidden in the turtle's breast,
Under the palmtree at noon, under the running water
At the still point of the turning world. O hidden.

Now they go up to the temple. Then the sacrifice.
Now come the virgins bearing urns, urns containing
Dust
Dust
Dust of dust, and now
Stone, bronze, stone, steel, stone, oakleaves, horses' heels
Over the paving.

That is all we could see. But how many eagles! and how many trumpets!
(And Easter Day, we didn't get to the country,
So we took young Cyril to church. And they rang a bell
And he said right out loud, *crumpets*.)
           Don't throw away that sausage,
It'll come in handy. He's artful. Please, will you
Give us a light?
Light
Light
Et les soldats faisaient la haie? ILS LA FAISAIENT.

EAST COKER
by T. S. Eliot

I

In my beginning is my end. In succession
Houses rise and fall, crumble, are extended,
Are removed, destroyed, restored, or in their place
Is an open field, or a factory, or a by-pass.
Old stone to new building, old timber to new fires,
Old fires to ashes, and ashes to the earth,
Which is already flesh, fur and faeces,
Bone of man and beast, cornstalk and leaf.
Houses live and die: there is a time for building
And a time for living and for generation
And a time for the wind to break the loosened pane.
And to shake the wainscot where the field-mouse trots
And to shake the tattered arras woven with a silent motto.

  From *Four Quartets*, copyright, 1943, by T. S. Eliot. Reprinted by permission of Harcourt, Brace and Company, Inc.

East Coker

In my beginning is my end. Now the light falls
Across the open field, leaving the deep lane
Shuttered with branches, dark in the afternoon,
Where you lean against a bank while a van passes,
And the deep lane insists on the direction
Into the village, in the electric heat
Hypnotised. In a warm haze the sultry light
Is absorbed, not refracted, by grey stone.
The dahlias sleep in the empty silence.
Wait for the early owl.
                    In that open field
If you do not come too close, if you do not come too close,
On a Summer midnight, you can hear the music
Of the weak pipe and the little drum
And see them dancing around the bonfire
The association of man and woman
In daunsinge, signifying matrimonie—
A dignified and commodious sacrament.
Two and two, necessarye coniunction,
Holding eche other by the hand or the arm
Whiche betokeneth concorde. Round and round the fire
Leaping through the flames, or joined in circles,
Rustically solemn or in rustic laughter
Lifting heavy feet in clumsy shoes,
Earth feet, loam feet, lifted in country mirth
Mirth of those long since under earth
Nourishing the corn. Keeping time,
Keeping the rhythm in their dancing
As in their living in the living seasons
The time of the seasons and the constellations
The time of milking and the time of harvest
The time of the coupling of man and woman
And that of beasts. Feet rising and falling.
Eating and drinking. Dung and death.

Dawn points, and another day
Prepares for heat and silence. Out at sea the dawn wind
Wrinkles and slides. I am here
Or there, or elsewhere. In my beginning.

II

What is the late November doing
With the disturbance of the spring
And creatures of the summer heat,
And snowdrops writhing under feet
And hollyhocks that aim too high
Red into grey and tumble down
Late roses filled with early snow?
Thunder rolled by the rolling stars
Simulates triumphal cars
Deployed in constellated wars
Scorpion fights against the Sun
Until the Sun and Moon go down
Comets weep and Leonids fly
Hunt the heavens and the plains
Whirled in a vortex that shall bring
The world to that destructive fire
Which burns before the ice-cap reigns.

That was a way of putting it—not very satisfactory:
A periphrastic study in a worn-out poetical fashion,
Leaving one still with the intolerable wrestle
With words and meanings. The poetry does not matter.
It was not (to start again) what one had expected.
What was to be the value of the long looked forward to,
Long hoped for calm, the autumnal serenity
And the wisdom of age? Had they deceived us
Or deceived themselves, the quiet-voiced elders,
Bequeathing us merely a receipt for deceit?
The serenity only a deliberate hebetude,
The wisdom only the knowledge of dead secrets
Useless in the darkness into which they peered
Or from which they turned their eyes. There is, it seems to us,
At best, only a limited value
In the knowledge derived from experience.
The knowledge imposes a pattern, and falsifies,
For the pattern is new in every moment
And every moment is a new and shocking
Valuation of all we have been. We are only undeceived
Of that which, deceiving, could no longer harm.
In the middle, not only in the middle of the way
But all the way, in a dark wood, in a bramble,

[708]

East Coker

On the edge of a grimpen, where is no secure foothold,
And menaced by monsters, fancy lights,
Risking enchantment. Do not let me hear
Of the wisdom of old men, but rather of their folly,
Their fear of fear and frenzy, their fear of possession,
Of belonging to another, or to others, or to God.
The only wisdom we can hope to acquire
Is the wisdom of humility: humility is endless.

The houses are all gone under the sea.

The dancers are all gone under the hill.

III

O dark dark dark. They all go into the dark,
The vacant interstellar spaces, the vacant into the vacant,
The captains, merchant bankers, eminent men of letters,
The generous patrons of art, the statesmen and the rulers,
Distinguished civil servants, chairmen of many committees,
Industrial lords and petty contractors, all go into the dark,
And dark the Sun and Moon, and the Almanach de Gotha
And the Stock Exchange Gazette, the Directory of Directors,
And cold the sense and lost the motive of action.
And we all go with them, into the silent funeral,
Nobody's funeral, for there is no one to bury.
I said to my soul, be still, and let the dark come upon you
Which shall be the darkness of God. As, in a theatre,
The lights are extinguished, for the scene to be changed
With a hollow rumble of wings, with a movement of darkness on darkness,
And we know that the hills and the trees, the distant panorama
And the bold imposing façade are all being rolled away—
Or as, when an underground train, in the tube, stops too long between stations
And the conversation rises and slowly fades into silence
And you see behind every face the mental emptiness deepen
Leaving only the growing terror of nothing to think about;
Or when, under ether, the mind is conscious but conscious of nothing—
I said to my soul, be still, and wait without hope
For hope would be hope for the wrong thing; wait without love
For love would be love of the wrong thing; there is yet faith
But the faith and the love and the hope are all in the waiting.
Wait without thought, for you are not ready for thought:
So the darkness shall be the light, and the stillness the dancing.

Poetry

Whisper of running streams, and winter lightning.
The wild thyme unseen and the wild strawberry,
The laughter in the garden, echoed ecstasy
Not lost, but requiring, pointing to the agony
Of death and birth.
                  You say I am repeating
Something I have said before. I shall say it again.
Shall I say it again? In order to arrive there,
To arrive where you are, to get from where you are not,
   You must go by a way wherein there is no ecstasy.
In order to arrive at what you do not know
   You must go by a way which is the way of ignorance.
In order to possess what you do not possess
   You must go by the way of dispossession.
In order to arrive at what you are not
   You must go through the way in which you are not.
And what you do not know is the only thing you know
And what you own is what you do not own
And where you are is where you are not.

IV

The wounded surgeon plies the steel
That questions the distempered part;
Beneath the bleeding hands we feel
The sharp compassion of the healer's art
Resolving the enigma of the fever chart.

Our only health is the disease
If we obey the dying nurse
Whose constant care is not to please
But to remind of our, and Adam's curse,
And that, to be restored, our sickness must grow worse.

The whole earth is our hospital
Endowed by the ruined millionaire,
Wherein, if we do well, we shall
Die of the absolute paternal care
That will not leave us, but prevents us everywhere.

The chill ascends from feet to knees,
The fever sings in mental wires.
If to be warmed, then I must freeze

[710]

East Coker

And quake in frigid purgatorial fires
Of which the flame is roses, and the smoke is briars.

The dripping blood our only drink,
The bloody flesh our only food:
In spite of which we like to think
That we are sound, substantial flesh and blood—
Again, in spite of that, we call this Friday good.

V

So here I am, in the middle way, having had twenty years—
Twenty years largely wasted, the years of *l'entre deux guerres*—
Trying to learn to use words, and every attempt
Is a wholly new start, and a different kind of failure
Because one has only learnt to get the better of words
For the thing one no longer has to say, or the way in which
One is no longer disposed to say it. And so each venture
Is a new beginning, a raid on the inarticulate
With shabby equipment always deteriorating
In the general mess of imprecision of feeling,
Undisciplined squads of emotion. And what there is to conquer
By strength and submission, has already been discovered
Once or twice, or several times, by men whom one cannot hope
To emulate—but there is no competition—
There is only the fight to recover what has been lost
And found and lost again and again: but now, under conditions
That seem unpropitious. But perhaps neither gain nor loss.
For us, there is only the trying. The rest is not our business.

Home is where one starts from. As we grow older
The world becomes stranger, the pattern more complicated
Of dead and living. Not the intense moment
Isolated, with no before and after,
But a lifetime burning in every moment
And not the lifetime of one man only
But of old stones that cannot be deciphered.
There is a time for the evening under starlight,
A time for the evening under lamplight
(The evening with the photograph album).
Love is most nearly itself
When here and now cease to matter.
Old men ought to be explorers

[711]

Poetry

Here and there does not matter
We must be still and still moving
Into another intensity
For a further union, a deeper communion
Through the dark cold and the empty desolation,
The wave cry, the wind cry, the vast waters
Of the petrel and the porpoise. In my end is my beginning.

MACAVITY: THE MYSTERY CAT
by T. S. Eliot

Macavity's a Mystery Cat: he's called the Hidden Paw—
For he's the master criminal who can defy the Law.
He's the bafflement of Scotland Yard, the Flying Squad's despair:
For when they reach the scene of crime—*Macavity's not there!*

Macavity, Macavity, there's no one like Macavity,
He's broken every human law, he breaks the law of gravity.
His powers of levitation would make a fakir stare,
And when you reach the scene of crime—*Macavity's not there!*
You may seek him in the basement, you may look up in the air—
But I tell you once and once again, *Macavity's not there!*

Macavity's a ginger cat, he's very tall and thin;
You would know him if you saw him, for his eyes are sunken in.
His brow is deeply lined with thought, his head is highly domed;
His coat is dusty from neglect, his whiskers are uncombed.
He sways his head from side to side, with movements like a snake;
And when you think he's half asleep, he's always wide awake.

Macavity, Macavity, there's no one like Macavity,
For he's a fiend in feline shape, a monster of depravity.
You may meet him in a by-street, you may see him in the square—
But when a crime's discovered, then *Macavity's not there!*

He's outwardly respectable. (They say he cheats at cards.)
And his footprints are not found in any file of Scotland Yard's.
And when the larder's looted, or the jewel-case is rifled,
Or when the milk is missing, or another Peke's been stifled,
Or the greenhouse glass is broken, and the trellis past repair—
Ay, there's the wonder of the thing! *Macavity's not there!*

From *Old Possum's Book of Practical Cats*, copyright 1939, by T. S. Eliot. Reprinted by permission of Harcourt, Brace and Company, Inc.

Macavity: The Mystery Cat

And when the Foreign Office find a Treaty's gone astray,
Or the Admiralty lose some plans and drawings by the way,
There may be a scrap of paper in the hall or on the stair—
But it's useless to investigate—*Macavity's not there!*
And when the loss has been disclosed, the Secret Service say:
"It *must* have been Macavity!"—but he's a mile away.
You'll be sure to find him resting, or a-licking of his thumbs,
Or engaged in doing complicated long division sums.

Macavity, Macavity, there's no one like Macavity,
There never was a Cat of such deceitfulness and suavity.
He always has an alibi, and one or two to spare:
At whatever time the deed took place—MACAVITY WASN'T THERE!
And they say that all the Cats whose wicked deeds are widely known
(I might mention Mungojerrie, I might mention Griddlebone)
Are nothing more than agents for the Cat who all the time
Just controls their operations: the Napoleon of Crime!

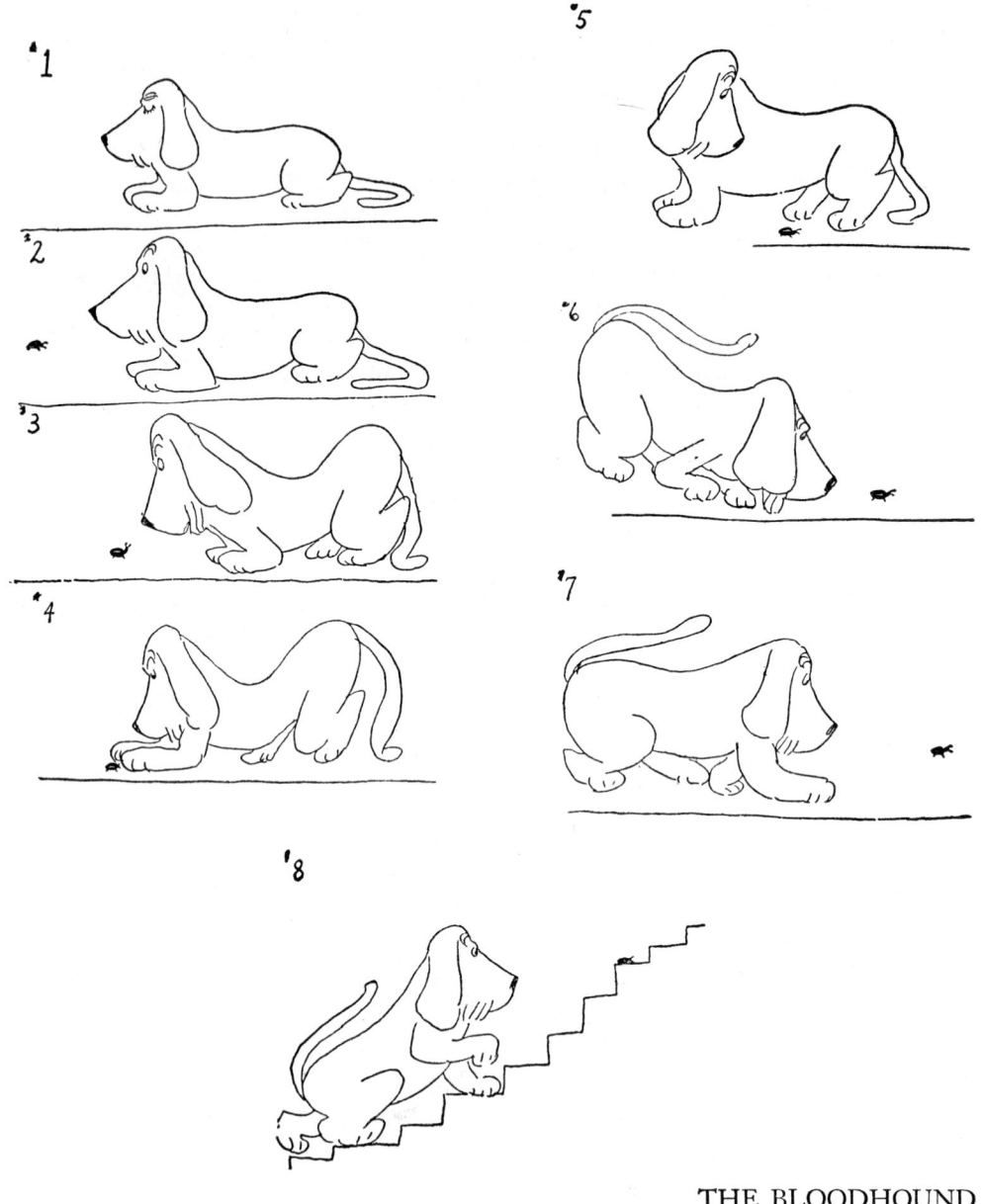

THE BLOODHOUND

[714]

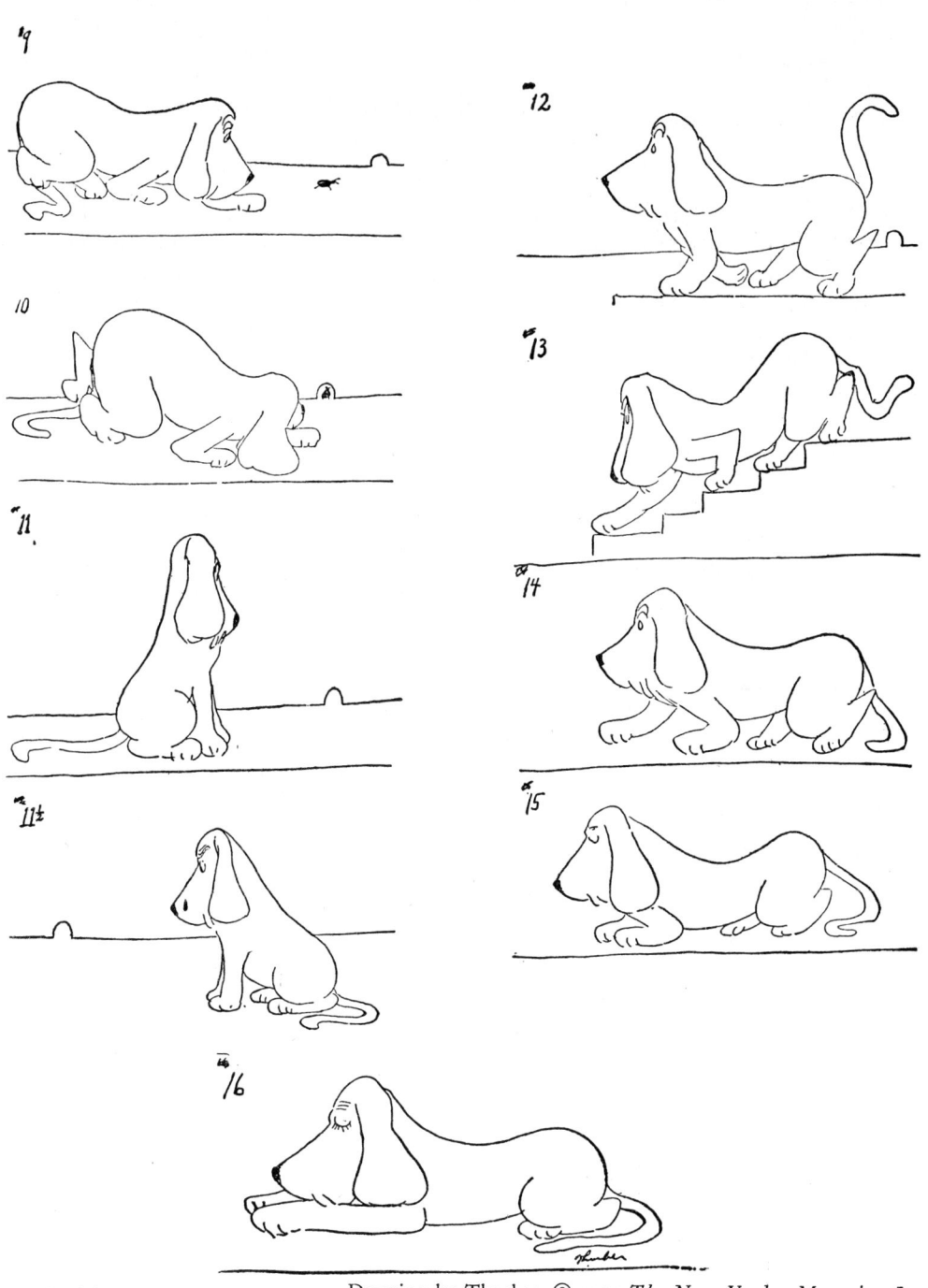

AND THE BUG   Drawing by Thurber, © 1932 *The New Yorker Magazine*, Inc.

from Foreword to THE SELECTED POETRY OF ROBINSON JEFFERS

by Robinson Jeffers

Long ago, ... it became evident to me that poetry—if it was to survive at all—must reclaim some of the power and reality that it was so hastily surrendering to prose. The modern French poetry of that time, and the most "modern" of the English poetry, seemed to me thoroughly defeatist, as if poetry were in terror of prose, and desperately trying to save its soul from the victor by giving up its body. It was becoming slight and fantastic, abstract, unreal, eccentric; and was not even saving its soul, for these are generally antipoetic qualities. It must reclaim substance and sense, and physical and psychological reality. This feeling has been basic in my mind since then. It led me to write narrative poetry, and to draw subjects from contemporary life; to present aspects of life that modern poetry had generally avoided; and to attempt the expression of philosophic and scientific ideas in verse. It was not in my mind to open new fields for poetry, but only to reclaim old freedom.

Still it was obvious that poetry and prose are different things; their provinces overlap, but must not be confused. Prose, of course, is free of all fields; it seemed to me, reading poetry and trying to write it, that poetry is bound to concern itself chiefly with permanent things and the permanent aspects of life. That was perhaps the great distinction between them, as regards subject and material. Prose can discuss matters of the moment; poetry must deal with things that a reader two thousand years away could understand and be moved by. This excludes much of the circumstance of modern life, especially in the cities. Fashions, forms of machinery, the more complex social, financial, political adjustments, and so forth, are all ephemeral, exceptional; they exist but will never exist again. Poetry must concern itself with (relatively) permanent things. These have poetic value; the ephemeral has only news value.

Another formative principle came to me from a phrase of Nietzsche's: "The poets? The poets lie too much." I was nineteen when the phrase stuck in my mind; a dozen years passed before it worked effectively, and I decided not to tell lies in verse. Not to feign any emotion that I did not feel; not to pretend to believe in optimism or pessimism, or unreversible progress; not to say anything because it was popular, or generally accepted, or fashionable in intellectual circles, unless I myself believed it; and not to believe easily. These negatives limit the field; I am not recommending them but for my own occasions.

Here are the principles that conditioned the verse in this book before it was written; but it would not have been written at all except for certain accidents that changed and directed my life. (Some kind of verse I should have written, of course, but not this kind.) The first of these accidents was my meeting with the woman

This and the following poems from *The Selected Poetry of Robinson Jeffers*. Copyright, 1937, by Robinson Jeffers. Reprinted by permission of Random House, Inc.

to whom this book is dedicated, and her influence, constant since that time. My nature is cold and undiscriminating; she excited and focused it, gave it eyes and nerves and sympathies. She never saw any of my poems until they were finished and typed, yet by her presence and conversation she has co-authored every one of them. Sometimes I think there must be some value in them, if only for that reason. She is more like a woman in a Scotch ballad, passionate, untamed and rather heroic—or like a falcon—than like any ordinary person.

A second piece of pure accident brought us to the Monterey coast mountains, where for the first time in my life I could see people living—amid magnificent unspoiled scenery—essentially as they did in the Idyls or the Sagas, or in Homer's Ithaca. Here was life purged of its ephemeral accretions. Men were riding after cattle, or plowing the headland, hovered by white sea-gulls, as they have done for thousands of years, and will for thousands of years to come. Here was contemporary life that was also permanent life; and not shut from the modern world but conscious of it and related to it; capable of expressing its spirit, but unencumbered by the mass of poetically irrelevant details and complexities that make a civilization.

By this time I was nearing thirty, and still a whole series of accidents was required to stir my lazy energies to the point of writing verse that seemed to be —whether good or bad—at least my own voice.

HURT HAWKS

by ROBINSON JEFFERS

I

The broken pillar of the wing jags from the clotted shoulder,
The wing trails like a banner in defeat,
No more to use the sky forever but live with famine
And pain a few days: cat nor coyote
Will shorten the week of waiting for death, there is game without talons.
He stands under the oak-bush and waits
The lame feet of salvation; at night he remembers freedom
And flies in a dream, the dawns ruin it.
He is strong and pain is worse to the strong, incapacity is worse.
The curs of the day come and torment him
At distance, no one but death the redeemer will humble that head,
The intrepid readiness, the terrible eyes.
The wild God of the world is sometimes merciful to those
That ask mercy, not often to the arrogant.
You do not know him, you communal people, or you have forgotten him;
Intemperate and savage, the hawk remembers him;
Beautiful and wild, the hawks, and men that are dying, remember him.

Poetry

II

I'd sooner, except the penalties, kill a man than a hawk; but the great redtail
Had nothing left but unable misery
From the bone too shattered for mending, the wing that trailed under his talons when he moved.
We had fed him six weeks, I gave him freedom,
He wandered over the foreland hill and returned in the evening, asking for death,
Not like a beggar, still eyed with the old
Implacable arrogance. I gave him the lead gift in the twilight. What fell was relaxed,
Owl-downy, soft feminine feathers; but what
Soared: the fierce rush: the night-herons by the flooded river cried fear at its rising
Before it was quite unsheathed from reality.

TO THE STONE-CUTTERS
by ROBINSON JEFFERS

Stone-cutters fighting time with marble, you foredefeated
Challengers of oblivion,
Eat cynical earnings, knowing rock splits, records fall down,
The square-limbed Roman letters
Scale in the thaws, wear in the rain. The poet as well
Builds his monument mockingly;
For man will be blotted out, the blithe earth die, the brave sun
Die blind and blacken to the heart:
Yet stones have stood for a thousand years, and pained thoughts found
The honey of peace in old poems.

SHINE, PERISHING REPUBLIC
by ROBINSON JEFFERS

While this America settles in the mould of its vulgarity, heavily thickening to empire,
And protest, only a bubble in the molten mass, pops and sighs out, and the mass hardens,

I sadly smiling remember that the flower fades to make fruit, the fruit rots to make earth.
Out of the mother; and through the spring exultances, ripeness and decadence; and home to the mother.

You making haste haste on decay: not blameworthy; life is good, be it stubbornly long or suddenly
A mortal splendor: meteors are not needed less than mountains: shine, perishing republic.

But for my children, I would have them keep their distance from the thickening center; corruption
Never has been compulsory, when the cities lie at the monster's feet there are left the mountains.

And boys, be in nothing so moderate as in love of man, a clever servant, insufferable master.
There is the trap that catches noblest spirits, that caught—they say—God, when he walked on earth.

THE PURSE-SEINE

by Robinson Jeffers

Our sardine fishermen work at night in the dark of the moon; daylight or moonlight
They could not tell where to spread the net, unable to see the phosphorescence of the shoals of fish.
They work northward from Monterey, coasting Santa Cruz; off New Year's Point or off Pigeon Point
The look-out man will see some lakes of milk-color light on the sea's night-purple; he points, and the helmsman
Turns the dark prow, the motorboat circles the gleaming shoal and drifts out her seine-net. They close the circle
And purse the bottom of the net, then with great labor haul it in.

I cannot tell you
How beautiful the scene is, and a little terrible, then, when the crowded fish
Know they are caught, and wildly beat from one wall to the other of their closing destiny the phosphorescent
Water to a pool of flame, each beautiful slender body sheeted with flame, like a live rocket
A comet's tail wake of clear yellow flame; while outside the narrowing
Floats and cordage of the net great sea-lions come up to watch, sighing in the dark; the vast walls of night
Stand erect to the stars.

Lately I was looking from a night mountain-top
On a wide city, the colored splendor, galaxies of light: how could I help but recall the seine-net
Gathering the luminous fish? I cannot tell you how beautiful the city appeared, and a little terrible.
I thought, We have geared the machines and locked all together into interdependence; we have built the great cities; now
There is no escape. We have gathered vast populations incapable of free survival, insulated
From the strong earth, each person in himself helpless, on all dependent. The circle is closed, and the net
Is being hauled in. They hardly feel the cords drawing, yet they shine already. The inevitable mass-disasters
Will not come in our time nor in our children's, but we and our children
Must watch the net draw narrower, government take all powers—or revolution, and the new government
Take more than all, add to kept bodies kept souls—or anarchy, the mass-disasters.

These things are Progress;
Do you marvel our verse is troubled or frowning, while it keeps its reason? Or it lets go, lets the mood flow
In the manner of the recent young men into mere hysteria, splintered gleams, crackled laughter. But they are quite wrong.
There is no reason for amazement: surely one always knew that cultures decay, and life's end is death.

THE ANSWER
by ROBINSON JEFFERS

Then what is the answer?—Not to be deluded by dreams.
To know that great civilizations have broken down into violence, and their tyrants come, many times before.
When open violence appears, to avoid it with honor or choose the least ugly faction; these evils are essential.
To keep one's own integrity, be merciful and uncorrupted and not wish for evil; and not be duped
By dreams of universal justice or happiness. These dreams will not be fulfilled.
To know this, and know that however ugly the parts appear the whole remains beautiful. A severed hand
Is an ugly thing, and man dissevered from the earth and stars and his history . . . for contemplation or in fact . . .

The Inquisitors

Often appears atrociously ugly. Integrity is wholeness, the greatest beauty is
Organic wholeness, the wholeness of life and things, the divine beauty of the universe. Love that, not man
Apart from that, or else you will share man's pitiful confusions, or drown in despair when his days darken.

THE INQUISITORS

by ROBINSON JEFFERS

Coming around a corner of the dark trail . . . what was wrong with the valley?
Azevedo checked his horse and sat staring: it was all changed. It was occupied. There were three hills
Where none had been: and firelight flickered red on their knees between them: if they were hills:
They were more like Red Indians around a camp-fire, grave and dark, mountain-high, hams on heels
Squatting around a little fire of hundred-foot logs. Azevedo remembers he felt an ice-brook
Glide on his spine; he slipped down from the saddle and hid
In the brush by the trail, above the black redwood forest. This was the Little Sur South Fork,
Its forest valley; the man had come in at nightfall over Bowcher's Gap, and a high moon hunted
Through running clouds. He heard the rumble of a voice, heavy not loud, saying, "I gathered some,
You can inspect them." One of the hills moved a huge hand
And poured its contents on a table-topped rock that stood in the firelight; men and women fell out;
Some crawled and some lay quiet; the hills leaned to eye them. One said: "It seems hardly possible
Such fragile creatures could be so noxious." Another answered,
"True, but we've seen. But it is only recently they have the power." The third answered, "That bomb?"
"Oh," he said, "—and the rest." He reached across and picked up one of the mites from the rock, and held it
Close to his eyes, and very carefully with finger and thumbnail peeled it: by chance a young female

"The Inquisitors," from *The Double Axe*. Copyright, 1948, by Robinson Jeffers. Reprinted by permission of Random House, Inc.

With long black hair: it was too helpless even to scream. He held it by one white
   leg and stared at it:
"I can see nothing strange: only so fragile." The third hill answered, "We suppose
   it is something
Inside the head." Then the other split the skull with his thumbnail, squinting his
   eyes and peering, and said,
"A drop of marrow. How could that spoil the earth?" "Nevertheless," he answered,
"They have that bomb. The blasts and the fires are nothing: freckles on the earth:
   the emanations
Might set the whole planet into a tricky fever
And destroy much." "Themselves," he answered. "Let them. Why not?" "No," he
   answered, "life."

                        Azevedo
Still watched in horror, and all three of the hills
Picked little animals from the rock, peeled them and cracked them, or toasted them
On the red coals, or split their bodies from the crotch upward
To stare inside. They said, "It remains a mystery. However," they said,
"It is not likely they can destroy all life: the planet is capacious. Life would surely
   grow up again
From grubs in the soil, or the newt and toad level, and be beautiful again. And
   again perhaps break its legs
On its own cleverness: who can forecast the future?" The speaker yawned, and with
   his flat hand
Brushed the rock clean; the three slowly stood up,
Taller than Pico Blanco into the sky, their Indian-beaked heads in the moon-cloud,
And trampled their watchfire out and went away southward, stepping across the
   Ventana mountains.

YOU, ANDREW MARVELL
by Archibald MacLeish

And here face down beneath the sun
And here upon earth's noonward height
To feel the always coming on
The always rising of the night

To feel creep up the curving east
The earthy chill of dusk and slow
Upon those under lands the vast
And ever climbing shadow grow

And strange at Ecbatan the trees
Take leaf by leaf the evening strange
The flooding dark about their knees
The mountains over Persia change

And now at Kermanshah the gate
Dark empty and the withered grass
And through the twilight now the late
Few travelers in the westward pass

And Baghdad darken and the bridge
Across the silent river gone

And through Arabia the edge
Of evening widen and steal on

And deepen on Palmyra's street
The wheel rut in the ruined stone
And Lebanon fade out and Crete
High through the clouds and overblown

And over Sicily the air
Still flashing with the landward gulls
And loom and slowly disappear
The sails above the shadowy hulls

And Spain go under and the shore
Of Africa the gilded sand
And evening vanish and no more
The low pale light across that land

Nor now the long light on the sea

And here face downward in the sun
To feel how swift how secretly
The shadow of the night comes on . . .

from THE HAMLET OF A. MACLEISH
by Archibald MacLeish

Night after night I lie like this listening.
Night after night I cannot sleep. I wake
Knowing something, thinking something has happened.
I have this feeling a great deal. I have
Sadness often. At night I have this feeling.
Waking I feel this pain as though I knew
Something not to be thought of, something unbearable.
I feel this pain at night as though some
Terrible thing had happened. At night the sky
Opens, the near things vanish, the bright walls
Fall, and the stars were always there, and the dark

The selections from Archibald MacLeish's *Poems 1924-1933* are used by permission of the publishers, Houghton Mifflin Company.

There and the cold and the stillness. I wake and stand
A long time by the window. I always think
The trees know the way they are silent. I always
Think some one has spoken, some one has told me.
Reading the books I always think so, reading
Words overheard in the books, reading the words
Like words in a strange language. I always hear
Music like that. I almost remember with music . . .
This is not what you think. It is not that. I swim
Every day at the beach under the fig tree.
I swim very well and far out. The smell
Of pine comes over the water. The wind blurs
Seaward. And afternoons I walk to the phare.
Much of the time I do not think anything;
Much of the time I do not even notice.
And then, speaking, closing a door, I see
Strangely as though I almost saw now, some
Shape of things I have always seen, the sun
White on a house and the windows open and swallows
In and out of the wallpaper, the moon's face
Faint by day in a mirror; I see some
Changed thing that is telling, something that almost
Tells—and this pain then, then this pain. And no
Words, only these shapes of things that seem
Ways of knowing what it is I am knowing.
I write these things in books, on pieces of paper.
I have written 'The wind rises . . .' I have written 'Bells
Plunged in the wind . . .' I have written 'Like
Doors . . .' 'Like evening . . .'
It is always the same: I cannot read what the words say.
It is always the same: there are signs and I cannot read them.
There are empty streets and the blinds drawn and the sky
Sliding in windows. There are lights before
Dawn in the yellow transoms over the doors.
There are steps that pass and pass all night that are always
One, always the same step passing . . .
I have traveled a great deal. I have seen at Homs
The cranes over the river and Isfahan
The fallen tiles in the empty garden, and Shiraz
Far off, the cypresses under the hill.
It is always the same. I have seen on the Kazvin road
On the moon grey desert the leafless wind,
The wind raging in moon-dusk. Or the light that comes
Seaward with slow oars from the mouth of the Euphrates.

American Letter

I have heard the nightingales in the thickets of Gilan,
And at dawn, at Teheran, I have heard from the ancient
Westward greying face of the wandering planet
The voices calling the small new name of god,
The voices answered with cockcrow, answered at dusk
With the cry of jackals far away in the gardens.
I have heard the name of the moon beyond those mountains.
It is always the same. It is always as though some
Smell of leaves had made me not quite remember;
As though I had turned to look and there were no one.
It has always been secret like that with me.
Always something has not been said. Always
The stones were there, the trees were there, the motionless
Hills have appeared in the dusk to me, the moon
Has stood a long time white and still in the window.
Always the earth has been turned away from me hiding
The veiled eyes and the wind in the leaves has not spoken . . .

As now the night is still. As the night now
Stands at the farthest off of touch and like
A raised hand held upon the empty air
Means and is silent.
                Look! It waves me still . . .
   I say Go on! Go on!

                As the whole night now
Made visible behind this darkness seems
To beckon to me . . .

AMERICAN LETTER

for Gerald Murphy

by Archibald MacLeish

The wind is east but the hot weather continues,
Blue and no clouds, the sound of the leaves thin,
Dry like the rustling of paper, scored across
With the slate-shrill screech of the locusts.
                              The tossing of
Pines is the low sound. In the wind's running
The wild carrots smell of the burning sun.
Why should I think of the dolphins at Capo di Mele?

Why should I see in my mind the taut sail
And the hill over St.-Tropez and your hand on the tiller?
Why should my heart be troubled with palms still?
I am neither a sold boy nor a Chinese official
Sent to sicken in Pa for some Lo-Yang dish.
This is my own land, my sky, my mountain:
This—not the humming pines and the surf and the sound
At the Ferme Blanche, nor Port Cros in the dusk and the harbor
Floating the motionless ship and the sea-drowned star.
I am neither Po Chü-i nor another after
Far from home, in a strange land, daft
For the talk of his own sort and the taste of his lettuces.
This land is my native land. And yet
I am sick for home for the red roofs and the olives,
And the foreign words and the smell of the sea fall.
How can a wise man have two countries?
How can a man have the earth and the wind and want
A land far off, alien, smelling of palm-trees
And the yellow gorse at noon in the long calms?

It is a strange thing—to be an American.
Neither an old house it is with the air
Tasting of hung herbs and the sun returning
Year after year to the same door and the churn
Making the same sound in the cool of the kitchen
Mother to son's wife, and the place to sit
Marked in the dusk by the worn stone at the wellhead—
That—nor the eyes like each other's eyes and the skull
Shaped to the same fault and the hands' sameness.
Neither a place it is nor a blood name.
America is West and the wind blowing.
America is a great word and the snow,
A way, a white bird, the rain falling,
A shining thing in the mind and the gulls' call.
America is neither a land nor a people,
A word's shape it is, a wind's sweep—
America is alone: many together,
Many of one mouth, of one breath,
Dressed as one—and none brothers among them:
Only the taught speech and the aped tongue.
America is alone and the gulls calling.

It is a strange thing to be an American.
It is strange to live on the high world in the stare
Of the naked sun and the stars as our bones live.
Men in the old lands housed by their rivers.

American Letter

They built their towns in the vales in the earth's shelter.
We first inhabit the world. We dwell
On the half earth, on the open curve of a continent.
Sea is divided from sea by the day-fall. The dawn
Rides the low east with us many hours;
First are the capes, then are the shorelands, now
The blue Appalachians faint at the day rise;
The willows shudder with light on the long Ohio:
The Lakes scatter the low sun: the prairies
Slide out of dark: in the eddy of clean air
The smoke goes up from the high plains of Wyoming:
The steep Sierras arise: the struck foam
Flames at the wind's heel on the far Pacific.
Already the noon leans to the eastern cliff:
The elms darken the door and the dust-heavy lilacs.

It is strange to sleep in the bare stars and to die
On an open land where few bury before us:
(From the new earth the dead return no more.)
It is strange to be born of no race and no people.
In the old lands they are many together. They keep
The wise past and the words spoken in common.
They remember the dead with their hands, their mouths dumb.
They answer each other with two words in their meeting.
They live together in small things. They eat
The same dish, their drink is the same and their proverbs.
Their youth is like. They are like in their ways of love.
They are many men. There are always others beside them.
Here it is one man and another and wide
On the darkening hills the faint smoke of the houses.
Here it is one man and the wind in the boughs.

Therefore our hearts are sick for the south water.
The smell of the gorse comes back to our night thought.
We are sick at heart for the red roofs and the olives;
We are sick at heart for the voice and the footfall...

Therefore we will not go though the sea call us.

This, this is our land, this is our people,
This that is neither a land nor a race. We must reap
The wind here in the grass for our soul's harvest:
Here we must eat our salt or our bones starve.
Here we must live or live only as shadows.
This is our race, we that have none, that have had
Neither the old walls nor the voices around us,

This is our land, this is our ancient ground—
The raw earth, the mixed bloods and the strangers,
The different eyes, the wind, and the heart's change.
These we will not leave though the old call us.
This is our country-earth, our blood, our kind.
Here we will live our years till the earth blind us—
The wind blows from the east. The leaves fall.
Far off in the pines a jay rises.
The wind smells of haze and the wild ripe apples.

I think of the masts at Cette and the sweet rain.

MEN

(*On a phrase of Apollinaire*)

by Archibald MacLeish

Our history is grave noble and tragic
We trusted the look of the sun on the green leaves
We built our towns of stone with enduring ornaments
We worked the hard flint for basins of water

We believed in the feel of the earth under us
We planted corn grapes apple-trees rhubarb
Nevertheless we knew others had died
Everything we have done has been faithful and dangerous

We believed in the promises made by the brows of women
We begot children at night in the warm wool
We comforted those who wept in fear on our shoulders
Those who comforted us had themselves vanished

We fought at the dikes in the bright sun for the pride of it
We beat drums and marched with music and laughter
We were drunk and lay with our fine dreams in the straw
We saw the stars through the hair of lewd women

Our history is grave noble and tragic
Many of us have died and are not remembered
Many cities are gone and their channels broken
We have lived a long time in this land and with honor

The selection from Archibald MacLeish's *Poems 1924-1933* is used by permission of the publishers, Houghton Mifflin Company.

SPEECH TO THOSE WHO SAY COMRADE
by Archibald MacLeish

The brotherhood is not by the blood certainly:
But neither are men brothers by speech—by saying so:
Men are brothers by life lived and are hurt for it:

Hunger and hurt are the great begetters of brotherhood:
Humiliation has gotten much love:
Danger I say is the nobler father and mother:

Those are as brothers whose bodies have shared fear
Or shared harm or shared hurt or indignity.
Why are the old soldiers brothers and nearest?

For this: with their minds they go over the sea a little
And find themselves in their youth again as they were in
Soissons and Meaux and at Ypres and those cities:

A French loaf and the girls with their eyelids painted
Bring back to aging and lonely men
Their twentieth year and the metal odor of danger:

It is this in life which of all things is tenderest—
To remember together with the unknown men the days
Common also to them and perils ended:

It is this which makes of many a generation—
A wave of men who having the same years
Have in common the same dead and the changes.

The solitary and unshared experience
Dies of itself like the violations of love
Or lives on as the dead live eerily.

The unshared and single man must cover his
Loneliness as a girl her shame for the way of
Life is neither by one man nor by suffering.

Who are the born brothers in truth? The puddlers
Scorched by the same flame in the same foundries:
Those who have spit on the same boards with the blood in it:

From *Public Speech*, copyright, 1936, by Archibald MacLeish, and reprinted by permission of Rinehart & Company, Inc., publishers.

Ridden the same rivers with green logs:
Fought the police in the parks of the same cities:
Grinned for the same blows: the same flogging:

Veterans out of the same ships—factories—
Expeditions for fame: the founders of continents:
Those that hid in Geneva a time back:

Those that have hidden and hunted and all such—
Fought together: labored together: they carry the
Common look like a card and they pass touching.

Brotherhood! No word said can make you brothers!
Brotherhood only the brave earn and by danger or
Harm or by bearing hurt and by no other

Brotherhood here in the strange world is the rich and
Rarest giving of life and the most valued:
Not to be had for a word or a week's wishing.

AMERICA WAS PROMISES

by Archibald MacLeish

Who is the voyager in these leaves?
Who is the traveler in this journey
Deciphers the revolving night: receives
The signal from the light returning?

America was promises to whom?

            East were the
Dead kings and the remembered sepulchres:
West was the grass.
                The groves of the oaks were at evening.

Eastward are the nights where we have slept.

And we move on: we move down:
With the first light we push forward:
We descend from the past as a wandering people from mountains.
We cross into the day to be discovered.
The dead are left where they fall—at dark
At night late under the coverlets.

Archibald MacLeish, *America Was Promises*. Reprinted by permission of the publishers, Duell, Sloan & Pearce, Inc.

America Was Promises

We mark the place with the shape of our teeth on our fingers.
The room is left as it was: the love

Who is the traveler in these leaves these
Annual waters and beside the doors
Jonquils: then the rose: the eaves
Heaping the thunder up: the mornings
Opening on like great valleys
Never till now approached: the familiar trees
Far off: distant with the future:
The hollyhocks beyond the afternoons:
The butterflies over the ripening fruit on the balconies:
And all beautiful
All before us

America was always promises.
From the first voyage and the first ship there were promises—
'the tropic bird which does not sleep at sea'
'the great mass of dark heavy clouds which is a sign'
'the drizzle of rain without wind which is a sure sign'
'the whale which is an indication'
'the stick appearing to be carved with iron'
'the stalk loaded with roseberries'
'and all these signs were from the west'
'and all night heard birds passing.'

Who is the voyager on these coasts?
Who is the traveler in these waters
Expects the future as a shore: foresees
Like Indies to the west the ending—he
The rumor of the surf intends?

America was promises—to whom?

Jefferson knew:
Declared it before God and before history:
Declares it still in the remembering tomb.
The promises were Man's: the land was his—
Man endowed by his Creator:
Earnest in love: perfectible by reason:
Just and perceiving justice: his natural nature
Clear and sweet at the source as springs in trees are.
It was Man the promise contemplated.
The times had chosen Man: no other:

Bloom on his face of every future:
Brother of stars and of all travelers:
Brother of time and of all mysteries:
Brother of grass also: of fruit trees.
It was Man who had been promised: who should have.
Man was to ride from the Tidewater: over the Gap:
West and South with the water: taking the book with him:
Taking the wheat seed: corn seed: pip of apple:
Building liberty a farmyard wide
Breeding for useful labor: for good looks:
For husbandry: humanity: for pride—
Practising self-respect and common decency.

And Man turned into men in Philadelphia
Practising prudence on a long-term lease:
Building liberty to fit the parlor:
Bred for crystal on the frontroom shelves:
Just and perceiving justice by the dollar:
Patriotic with the bonds at par
(And their children's children brag of their deeds for the Colonies).
Man rode up from the Tidewater: over the Gap:
Turned into men: turned into two-day settlers:
Lawyers with the land-grants in their caps:
Coon-skin voters wanting theirs and getting it.

Turned the promises to capital: invested it.

America was always promises:
'the wheel like a sun as big as a cart wheel
    with many sorts of pictures on it
    the whole of fine gold'

'twenty golden ducks
    beautifully worked and very natural looking
    and some like dogs of the kind they keep'

And they waved us west from the dunes: they cried out
Colua! Colua!
Mexico! Mexico! . . . Colua!

America was promises to whom?

Old Man Adams knew. He told us—
An aristocracy of compound interest
Hereditary through the common stock!
We'd have one sure before the mare was older.
"The first want of every man was his dinner:

America Was Promises

The second his girl." Kings were by the pocket.
Wealth made blood made wealth made blood made wealthy.
Enlightened selfishness gave lasting light.
Winners bred grandsons: losers only bred!

And the Aristocracy of politic selfishness
Bought the land up: bought the towns: the sites:
The goods: the government: the people. Bled them.
Sold them. Kept the profit. Lost itself.

The Aristocracy of Wealth and Talents
Turned its talents into wealth and lost them.
Turned enlightened selfishness to wealth.
Turned self-interest into bankbooks: balanced them.
Bred out: bred to fools: to hostlers:
Card sharps: well dressed women: dancefloor doublers.
The Aristocracy of Wealth and Talents
Sold its talents: bought the public notice:
Drank in public: went to bed in public:
Patronized the arts in public: pall'd with
Public authors public beauties: posed in
Public postures for the public page.
The Aristocracy of Wealth and Talents
Withered of talent and ashamed of wealth
Bred to sonsinlaw: insane relations:
Girls with open secrets: sailors' Galahads:
Prurient virgins with the tales to tell:
Women with dead wombs and living wishes.

The Aristocracy of Wealth and Talents
Moved out: settled on the Continent:
Sat beside the water at Rapallo:
Died in a rented house: unwept: unhonored.

And the child says I see the lightning on you.

The weed between the railroad tracks
Tasting of sweat: tasting of poverty:
The bitter and pure taste where the hawk hovers:
Native as the deer bone in the sand

O my America for whom?

For whom the promises? For whom the river
"It flows west! Look at the ripple of it!"

The grass "So that it was wonderful to see
And endless without end with wind wonderful!"
The Great Lakes: landless as oceans: their beaches
Coarse sand: clean gravel: pebbles:
Their bluffs smelling of sunflowers: smelling of surf:
Of fresh water: of wild sunflowers . . . wilderness.
For whom the evening mountains on the sky:
The night wind from the west: the moon descending?

Tom Paine knew.
Tom Paine knew the People.
The promises were spoken to the People.
History was voyages toward the People.
Americas were landfalls of the People.
Stars and expectations were the signals of the People.

Whatever was truly built the People had built it.
Whatever was taken down they had taken down.
Whatever was worn they had worn—ax-handles: fiddle-bows:
Sills of doorways: names for children: for mountains.
Whatever was long forgotten they had forgotten—
Fame of the great: names of the rich and their mottos.
The People had the promises: they'd keep them.
They waited their time in the world: they had wise sayings.
They counted out their time by day to day.
They counted it out day after day into history.
They had time and to spare in the spill of their big fists.
They had all the time there was like a handful of wheat seed.
When the time came they would speak and the rest would listen.

And the time came and the People did not speak.

The time came: the time comes: the speakers
Come and these who speak are not the People.

These who speak with gunstocks at the doors:
These the coarse ambitious priest
Leads by the bloody fingers forward:
These who reach with stiffened arm to touch
What none who took dared touch before:
These who touch the truth are not the People.

These the savage fables of the time
Lick at the fingers as a bitch will waked at morning:
These who teach the lie are not the People.

The time came: the time comes

America Was Promises

Comes and to whom? To these? Was it for these
The surf was secret on the new-found shore?
Was it for these the branch was on the water?—
These whom all the years were toward
The golden images the clouds the mountains?

Never before: never in any summer:
Never were days so generous: stars so mild:
Even in old men's talk or in books or remembering
Far back in a gone childhood
Or farther still to the light where Homer wanders—
The air all lucid with the solemn blue
That hills take at the distance beyond change. . . .
That time takes also at the distances.

Never were there promises as now:
Never was green deeper: earth warmer:
Light more beautiful to see: the sound of
Water lovelier: the many forms of
Leaves: stones: clouds: beasts: shadows
Clearer more admirable or the faces
More like answering faces or the hands
Quicker: more brotherly:
                  the aching taste of
Time more salt upon the tongue: more human
Never in any summer: and to whom?

At dusk: by street lights: in the rooms we ask this.

We do not ask for Truth now from John Adams.
We do not ask for Tongues from Thomas Jefferson.
We do not ask for Justice from Tom Paine.
We ask for answers.

And there is an answer.

There is Spain Austria Poland China Bohemia.
There are dead men in the pits in all those countries.
Their mouths are silent but they speak. They say
"The promises are theirs who take them."

Listen! Brothers! Generation!
Listen! You have heard these words. Believe it!
Believe the promises are theirs who take them!

Poetry

Believe unless we take them for ourselves
Others will take them for the use of others!

Believe unless we take them for ourselves
All of us: one here: another there:
Men not Man: people not the People:
Hands: mouths: arms: eyes: not syllables—
Believe unless we take them for ourselves
Others will take them: not for us: for others!

Believe unless we take them for ourselves
Now: soon: by the clock: before tomorrow:
Others will take them: not for now: for longer!

Listen! Brothers! Generation!
Companions of leaves: of the sun: of the slow evenings:
Companions of the many days: of all of them:
Listen! Believe the speaking dead! Believe
The journey is our journey. O believe
The signals were to us: the signs: the birds by
Night: the breaking surf.

        Believe
America is promises to
Take!

America is promises to
Us
To take them
Brutally
With love but
Take them.

O believe this!

MEMORIAL RAIN

by Archibald MacLeish

Ambassador Puser the ambassador
Reminds himself in French, felicitous tongue,
What these (young men no longer) lie here for
In rows that once, and somewhere else, were young—

The selections from Archibald MacLeish *Poems 1924-1933* are used by permission of the publishers, Houghton Mifflin Company.

Memorial Rain

All night in Brussels the wind had tugged at my door:
I had heard the wind at my door and the trees strung
Taut, and to me who had never been before
In that country it was a strange wind blowing
Steadily, stiffening the walls, the floor,
The roof of my room. I had not slept for knowing
He too, dead, was a stranger in that land
And felt beneath the earth in the wind's flowing
A tightening of roots and would not understand,
Remembering lake winds in Illinois,
That strange wind. I had felt his bones in the sand
Listening.

   —Reflects that these enjoy
Their country's gratitude, that deep repose,
That peace no pain can break, no hurt destroy,
That rest, that sleep—

    At Ghent the wind rose.
There was a smell of rain and a heavy drag
Of wind in the hedges but not as the wind blows
Over fresh water when the waves lag
Foaming and the willows huddle and it will rain:
I felt him waiting.

    —Indicates the flag
Which (may he say) enisles in Flanders' plain
This little field these happy, happy dead
Have made America—

    In the ripe grain
The wind coiled glistening, darted, fled,
Dragging its heavy body: at Waereghem
The wind coiled in the grass above his head:
Waiting—listening—

    —Dedicates to them
This earth their bones have hallowed, this last gift
A grateful country—

    Under the dry grass stem
The words are blurred, are thickened, the words sift
Confused by the rasp of the wind, by the thin grating

Poetry

Of ants under the grass, the minute shift
And tumble of dusty sand separating
From dusty sand. The roots of the grass strain,
Tighten, the earth is rigid, waits—he is waiting—

And suddenly, and all at once, the rain!
The living scatter, they run into houses, the wind
Is trampled under the rain, shakes free, is again
Trampled. The rain gathers, running in thinned
Spurts of water that ravel in the dry sand
Seeping in the sand under the grass roots, seeping
Between cracked boards to the bones of a clenched hand:
The earth relaxes, loosens; he is sleeping,
He rests, he is quiet, he sleeps in a strange land.

EPISTLE TO BE LEFT IN THE EARTH
by Archibald MacLeish

   . . . It is colder now
                      there are many stars
                                          we are drifting
North by the Great Bear
                        the leaves are falling
The water is stone in the scooped rocks
                                  to southward
Red sun grey air
                the crows are
Slow on their crooked wings
                                the jays have left us
Long since we passed the flares of Orion
Each man believes in his heart he will die
Many have written last thoughts and last letters
None know if our deaths are now or forever
None know if this wandering earth will be found

We lie down and the snow covers our garments
I pray you
           you (if any open this writing)
Make in your mouths the words that were our names

[738]

Geography of This Time

    I will tell you all we have learned
                    I will tell you everything
    The earth is round
               there are springs under the orchards

    The loam cuts with a blunt knife
                    beware of
Elms in thunder
            the lights in the sky are stars
We think they do not see
              we think also
The trees do not know nor the leaves of the grasses
                              hear us
The birds too are ignorant
              Do not listen
Do not stand at dark in the open windows
We before you have heard this
                they are voices
They are not words at all but the wind rising
Also none among us has seen God
(. . . We have thought often
The flaws of sun in the late and driving weather
Pointed to one tree but it was not so)
As for the nights I warn you the nights are dangerous
The wind changes at night and the dreams come

It is very cold
              there are strange stars near Arcturus

Voices are crying an unknown name in the sky

GEOGRAPHY OF THIS TIME
by Archibald MacLeish

What is required of us is the recognition of the frontiers between the centuries. And to take heart: to cross over.

Those who are killed in the place between out of ignorance, those who wander like cattle and are shot, those who are shot

From *The New Republic,* Oct. 28, 1942. Reprinted by permission of Mr. Archibald MacLeish and the editors.

and are left in the stone fields between the histories—these men may be pitied as the victims of accidents are pitied but their deaths do not signify. They are neither buried nor otherwise remembered but lie in the dead grass in the dry thorn in the worn light. Their years have no monuments.

There are many such in the sand here—many who did not perceive, who thought the time went on, the years went forward, the history was continuous—who thought tomorrow was of the same nation as today. There are many who came to the frontiers between the times and did not know them —who looked for the sentry-box at the stone bridge, for the barricade in the pines and the declaration in two languages—the warning and the opportunity to turn. They are dead there in the down light, in the sheep's barren.

What is required of us is the recognition

with no sign, with no word, with the roads raveled out into ruts and the ruts into dust and the dust stirred by the wind —the roads from behind us ending in the dust.

What is required of us is the recognition of the frontiers where the roads end.

We are very far. We are past the place where the light lifts from us and farther on than the relinquishment of leaves—farther even than the persistence in the east of the green color. Beyond are the confused tracks, the guns, the watchers.

What is required of us, Companions, is the recognition of the frontiers across this history, and to take heart: to cross over

—to persist and to cross over and survive

But to survive

To cross over

SPACE BEING CURVED

by E. E. CUMMINGS

Space being(don't forget to remember)Curved
(and that reminds me who said o yes Frost
Something there is which isn't fond of walls)

Copyright, 1931, by E. E. Cummings. From *Collected Poems,* published by Harcourt, Brace and Company, Inc.

O Sweet Spontaneous

an electromagnetic (now I've lost
the)Einstein expanded Newton's law preserved
conTinuum(but we read that beFore)

of Course life being just a Reflex you
know since Everything is Relative or

to sum it All Up god being Dead(not to

mention inTerred)
                    LONG LIVE that Upwardlooking
Serene Illustrious and Beatific
Lord of Creation,MAN:
                    at a least crooking
of Whose compassionate digit,earth's most terrific

quadruped swoons into billiardBalls!

O SWEET SPONTANEOUS
by E. E. Cummings

O sweet spontaneous
earth how often have
the
doting
        fingers of
prurient philosophers pinched
and
poked
thee
, has the naughty thumb
of science prodded
thy
    beauty   . how
often have religions taken
thee upon their scraggy knees

squeezing and
buffeting thee that thou mightest
            conceive
gods
        (but
true

to the incomparable
couch of death thy
rhythmic
lover
            thou answerest
them only with

                spring)

Copyright, 1923, by E. E. Cummings. From *Collected Poems,* published by Harcourt, Brace and Company, Inc.

[741]

"Well, it looks like a buttercup to me."

Permission The New Yorker. *Copyright* The F-R. Publishing Corporation.

NOBODY LOSES ALL THE TIME
by E. E. Cummings

nobody loses all the time

i had an uncle named
Sol who was a born failure and
nearly everybody said he should have gone
into vaudeville perhaps because my Uncle
  Sol could
sing McCann He Was A Diver on Xmas
  Eve like Hell Itself which
may or may not account for the fact that
  my Uncle

Sol indulged in that possibly most inex-
  cusable
of all to use a highfalootin phrase
luxuries that is or to
wit farming and be
it needlessly
added

my Uncle Sol's farm
failed because the chickens
ate the vegetables so
my Uncle Sol had a
chicken farm till the
skunks ate the chickens when

my Uncle Sol
had a skunk farm but
the skunks caught cold and
died so
my Uncle Sol imitated the
skunks in a subtle manner

or by drowning himself in the watertank
but somebody who'd given my Uncle Sol
  a Victor
Victrola and records while he lived presented to
him upon the auspicious occasion of his
  decease a
scrumptious not to mention splendiferous
  funeral with
tall boys in black gloves and flowers and
  everything and

i remember we all cried like the Missouri
when my Uncle Sol's coffin lurched because
somebody pressed a button
(and down went
my Uncle
Sol

and started a worm farm)

Copyright, 1926, by Horace Liveright. From: *Collected Poems,* published by Harcourt, Brace and Company, Inc.

IF YOU CAN'T EAT YOU GOT TO
by E. E. Cummings

If you can't eat you got to

smoke and we aint got
nothing to smoke:come on kid

let's go to sleep
if you can't smoke you got to

Sing and we aint got

nothing to sing;come on kid
let's go to sleep

if you can't sing you got to
die and we aint got

Nothing to die,come on kid

let's go to sleep
if you can't die you got to

dream and we aint got
nothing to dream(come on kid

Let's go to sleep)

Reprinted by permission of the publishers, Duell, Sloan & Pearce, Inc.

SINCE FEELING IS FIRST
by E. E. Cummings

since feeling is first
who pays any attention
to the syntax of things
will never wholly kiss you;

wholly to be a fool
while Spring is in the world

my blood approves,
and kisses are a better fate

than wisdom
lady i swear by all flowers. Don't cry
—the best gesture of my brain is less than
your eyelids' flutter which says

we are for each other: then
laugh, leaning back in my arms
for life's not a paragraph

And death i think is no parenthesis

Copyright, 1926, by Horace Liveright. From: *Collected Poems,* published by Harcourt, Brace and Company, Inc.

ANYONE LIVED IN A PRETTY HOW TOWN
by E. E. Cummings

anyone lived in a pretty how town
(with up so floating many bells down)

spring summer autumn winter
he sang his didn't he danced his did.

Reprinted by permission of the publishers, Duell, Sloan & Pearce, Inc.

These Children Singing

Women and men(both little and small)
cared for anyone not at all
they sowed their isn't they reaped their
 same
sun moon stars rain

children guessed(but only a few
and down they forgot as up they grew
autumn winter spring summer)
that noone loved him more by more

when by now and tree by leaf
she laughed his joy she cried his grief
bird by snow and stir by still
anyone's any was all to her

someones married their everyones
laughed their cryings and did their dance
(sleep wake hope and then)they
said their nevers they slept their dream

stars rain sun moon
(and only the snow can begin to explain
how children are apt to forget to remember
with up so floating many bells down)

one day anyone died i guess
(and noone stooped to kiss his face)
busy folk buried them side by side
little by little and was by was

all by all and deep by deep
and more by more they dream their sleep
noone and anyone earth by april
wish by spirit and if by yes.

Women and men(both dong and ding)
summer autumn winter spring
reaped their sowing and went their came
sun moon stars rain

THESE CHILDREN SINGING
by E. E. CUMMINGS

these children singing in stone a
silence of stone these
little children wound with stone
flowers opening for

ever these silently lit
tle children are petals
their song is a flower of
always their flowers

of stone are
silently singing
a song more silent
than silence these always

children forever
singing wreathed with singing
blossoms children of
stone with blossoming

eyes
know if a
lit tle
tree listens

forever to always children singing forever
a song made
of silent as stone silence of
song

Reprinted by permission of the publishers, Duell, Sloan & Pearce, Inc.

LOVE IS MORE THICKER
by E. E. Cummings

love is more thicker than forget
more thinner than recall
more seldom than a wave is wet
more frequent than to fail

it is most mad and moonly
and less it shall unbe
than all the sea which only
is deeper than the sea

love is less always than to win
less never than alive
less bigger than the least begin
less littler than forgive

it is most sane and sunly
and more it cannot die
than all the sky which only
is higher than the sky

Reprinted by permission of the publishers, Duell, Sloan & Pearce, Inc.

WHEN SERPENTS BARGAIN
by E. E. Cummings

when serpents bargain for the right to squirm
and the sun strikes to gain a living wage—
when thorns regard their roses with alarm
and rainbows are insured against old age

when every thrush may sing no new moon in
if all screech-owls have not okayed his voice
—and any wave signs on the dotted line
or else an ocean is compelled to close

when the oak begs permission of the birch
to make an acorn—valleys accuse their
mountains of having altitude—and march
denounces april as a saboteur

then we'll believe in that incredible
unanimal mankind(and not until)

From *Poems 1923-1954*, Harcourt, Brace and Company. Copyright © 1950 by E. E. Cummings.

[746]

TRAVELOGUE IN A SHOOTING-GALLERY
by Kenneth Fearing

There is a jungle, there is a jungle, there is a vast, vivid, wild, wild, marvelous, marvelous, marvelous jungle,
Open to the public during business hours,
A jungle not very far from an Automat, between a hat store there, and a radio shop.

There, there, whether it rains, or it snows, or it shines,
Under the hot, blazing, cloudless, tropical neon skies that the management always arranges there,
Rows and rows of marching ducks, dozens and dozens and dozens of ducks, move steadily along on smoothly-oiled ballbearing feet,
Ducks as big as telephone books, slow and fearless and out of this world,
While lines and lines of lions, lions, rabbits, panthers, elephants, crocodiles, zebras, apes,
Filled with jungle hunger and jungle rage and jungle love,
Stalk their prey on endless, endless rotary belts through never-ending forests, and burning deserts, and limitless veldts,
To the sound of tom-toms, equipped with silencers, beaten by thousands of savages hidden there.

And there it is that all the big game hunters go, there the traders and the explorers come,
Leanfaced men with windswept eyes who arrive by streetcar, auto or subway, taxi or on foot, streetcar or bus,
And they nod, and they say, and they need no more:
"There . . . there . . .
There they come and there they go."

And weighing machines, in this civilized jungle, will read your soul like an open book, for a penny at a time, and tell you all,
There, there, where smoking is permitted,
In a jungle that lies, like a rainbow's end, at the very end of every trail,
There, in the only jungle in the whole wide world where ducks are waiting for streetcars,
And hunters can be psychoanalyzed, while they smoke and wait for ducks.

From *Afternoon of a Pawnbroker and Other Poems*, copyright, 1943, by Kenneth Fearing. By permission of Harcourt, Brace and Company, Inc. Originally appeared in *The New Yorker*.

Return to Normal

From It's a long way to Heaven, *copyright, 1945, by Abner Dean, and reproduced by permission of Rinehart & Company, Inc., Publishers.*

RECEPTION GOOD

by Kenneth Fearing

Now, at a particular spot on the radio dial, "—in this corner, wearing purple trunks,"
Mingles, somehow, with the news that "—powerful enemy units have been surrounded in the drive—"
And both of these with the information that "—there is a way to avoid having chapped and roughened hands."

Such are the new and complex harmonies, it seems, of a strange and still more complex age;
It is not that the reception is confused or poor, but rather it is altogether too clear and good,

And no worse, in any case, than that other receiving set, the mind,
Forever faithfully transmitting the great and little impulses that arrive, however wavering or loud, from near and far:
"It is an ill wind—" it is apt to report, underscoring this with "—the bigger they are the harder they fall," and simultaneously reminding, darkly, that "Things are seldom as they seem,"

Reconciling, with ease, the irreconcilable,
Piecing together fragments of a flashing past with clouded snapshots of the present and the future,
("Something old, something new," its irrelevant announcer states. "Something borrowed, something blue.")

Fashioning a raw, wild symphony of a wedding march, a drinking song, and a dirge,
Multiplying enormous figures with precision, then raising the question: But after all, what is a man?
Somehow creating hope and fresh courage out of ancient doubt.

"Both boys are on their feet, they're going to it," the radio reports,
"—the sinking was attended by a heavy loss of life—"
"—this amazing cream for quick, miraculous results."

How many pieces are there, in a simple jigsaw puzzle?
How many phases of a man's life can crowd their way into a single moment?
How many angels, actually, can dance on the point of a pin?

From *Afternoon of a Pawnbroker and Other Poems,* copyright, 1943, by Kenneth Fearing. By permission of Harcourt, Brace and Company, Inc.

NO CREDIT

by Kenneth Fearing

Whether dinner was pleasant, with the windows lit by gunfire, and no one disagreed; or whether, later, we argued in the park, and there was a touch of vomit-gas in the evening air;
Whether we found a greater, deeper, more perfect love, by courtesy of Camels, over NBC; whether the comics amused us, or the newspapers carried a hunger death and a White House prayer for mother's day;
Whether the bills were paid or not, whether or not we had our doubts, whether we spoke our minds at Joe's, and the receipt said "Not Returnable," and the cash-register rang up "No Sale,"
Whether the truth was then, or later, or whether the best had already gone—

Nevertheless, we know; as every turn is measured; as every unavoidable risk is known;
As nevertheless, the flesh grows old, dies, dies in its only life, is gone;
The reflection goes from the mirror; as the shadow, of even a rebel, is gone from the wall;
As nevertheless, the current is thrown and the wheels revolve; and nevertheless, as the word is spoken and the wheat grows tall and the ships sail on—

None but the fool is paid in full; none but the broker, none but the scab is certain of profit;
The sheriff alone may attend a third degree in formal attire; alone, the academy artists multiply in dignity as trooper's bayonet guards the door;
Only Steve, the side-show robot, knows content; only Steve, the mechanical man in love with a photo-electric beam, remains aloof; only Steve, who sits and smokes or stands in salute, is secure;
Steve, whose shoebutton eyes are blind to terror, whose painted ears are deaf to appeal, whose welded breast will never be slashed by bullets, whose armature soul can hold no fear.

PORTRAIT (2)

by Kenneth Fearing

The clear brown eyes, kindly and alert, with 12-20 vision, give confident regard to the passing world through R. K. Lampert & Company lenses framed in gold;
His soul, however, is all his own;

From Kenneth Fearing, *Collected Poems*. Copyright, 1940, by Random House, Inc. Reprinted by permission of Random House, Inc. "Portrait (2)" originally appeared in *The New Yorker*.

American Rhapsody

Arndt Brothers necktie and hat (with feather) supply a touch of youth.
With his soul his own, he drives, drives, chats and drives,
The first and second bicuspids, lower right, replaced by bridgework, while two incisors have porcelain crowns;

(Render unto Federal, state and city Caesar, but not unto time;
Render nothing unto time until Amalgamated Death serves final notice, in proper form;

  The vault is ready;
  The will has been drawn by Clagget, Clagget, Clagget & Brown;
  The policies are adequate, Confidential's best, reimbursing for disability, partial or complete, with double indemnity should the end be a pure and simple accident)

Nothing unto time,
Nothing unto change, nothing unto fate,
Nothing unto you, and nothing unto me, or to any other known or unknown party or parties, living or deceased;

But Mercury shoes, with special arch supports, take much of the wear and tear;
On the course, a custombuilt driver corrects a tendency to slice;
Love's ravages have been repaired (it was a textbook case) by Drs. Schultz, Lightner, Mannheim, and Goode,
While all of it is enclosed in excellent tweed, with Mr. Baumer's personal attention to the shoulders and the waist;

And all of it now roving, chatting amiably through space in a Plymouth 6.
With his soul (his own) at peace, soothed by Walter Lippmann, and sustained by Haig & Haig.

AMERICAN RHAPSODY (4)

by Kenneth Fearing

First you bite your fingernails. And then you comb your hair again. And then you wait. And wait.
(They say, you know, that first you lie. And then you steal, they say. And then, they say, you kill.)

Then the doorbell rings. Then Peg drops in. And Bill. And Jane. And Doc.
And first you talk, and smoke, and hear the news and have a drink. Then you walk down the stairs.

From Kenneth Fearing, *Collected Poems*. Copyright, 1940, by Random House, Inc. Reprinted by permission of Random House, Inc. Originally appeared in *The New Yorker*.

And you dine, then, and go to a show after that, perhaps, and after that a night
    spot, and after that come home again, and climb the stairs again, and again go
    to bed.

But first Peg argues, and Doc replies. First you dance the same dance and you
    drink the same drink you always drank before.
And the piano builds a roof of notes above the world.
And the trumpet weaves a dome of music through space. And the drum makes a
    ceiling over space and time and night.
And then the table-wit. And then the check. Then home again to bed.
But first, the stairs

And do you now, baby, as you climb the stairs, do you still feel as you felt back
    there?
Do you feel again as you felt this morning? And the night before? And then the
    night before that?

(They say, you know, that first you hear voices. And then you have visions, they
    say. Then, they say, you kick and scream and rave.)
Or do you feel: What is one more night in a lifetime of nights?
What is one more death, or friendship, or divorce out of two, or three? Or four?
    Or five?
One more face among so many, many faces, one more life among so many million
    lives?

But first, baby, as you climb and count the stairs (and they total the same) did you,
    sometime or somewhere, have a different idea?
Is this, baby, what you were born to feel, and do, and be?

READINGS, FORECASTS, PERSONAL GUIDANCE
by KENNETH FEARING

It is not—I swear by every fiery omen to be seen these nights in every quarter of
    the heavens, I affirm it by all the monstrous portents of the earth and of the
    sea—
It is not that my belief in the true and mystic science is shaken, nor that I have
    lost faith in the magic of the cards, or in the augury of dreams, or in the great
    and good divinity of the stars.
No, I know still whose science fits the promise to the inquirer's need, invariably, for
    a change: Mine. My science foretells the wished-for journey, the business ad-
    justment, the handsome stranger. (Each of these is considered a decided change.)

From Kenneth Fearing, *Collected Poems*. Copyright, 1940, by Random House, Inc. Reprinted by permission of Random House, Inc. Originally appeared in *The New Yorker*.

Readings, Forecasts, Personal Guidance

And I know whose skill weighs matrimony, risks a flyer in steel or wheat against the vagaries of the moon.
(Planet of dreams, of mothers and of children, goddess of sailors and of all adventurers, forgive the liberty. But a man must eat.) My skill,
Mine, and the cunning and the patience. (Two dollars for the horoscope in brief and five for a twelve months' forecast in detail.)

No, it is this: The wonders that I have seen with my own eyes.

It is this: That still these people know, as I do not, that what has never been on earth before may still well come to pass,
That always, always there are new and brighter things beneath the sun,
That surely, in bargain basements or in walk-up flats, it must be so that still from time to time they hear wild angel voices speak.
It is this: That I have known them for what they are,
Seen thievery written plainly in their planets, found greed and murder and worse in their birth dates and their numbers, guilt etched in every line of every palm,
But still a light burns through the eyes they turn to me, a need more moving than the damned and dirty dollars (which I must take) that form the pattern of their larger hopes and deeper fears.

And it comes to this: That always I feel another hand, not mine, has drawn and turned the card to find some incredible ace,
Always another word I did not write appears in the spirit parchment prepared by me,
Always another face I do not know shows in the dream, the crystal globe, or the flame.

And finally, this: Corrupt, in a world bankrupt and corrupt, what have I got to do with these miracles?
If they want miracles, let them consult some one else.
Would they, in extremity, ask them of a physician? Or expect them, in desperation, of an attorney? Or of a priest? Or of a poet?

Nevertheless, a man must eat.
Mrs. Raeburn is expected at five. She will communicate with a number of friends and relatives long deceased.

DEVIL'S DREAM
by Kenneth Fearing

But it could never be true;
How could it ever happen, if it never did before, and it's not so now?

But suppose that the face behind those steel prison bars—
Why do you dream about a face lying cold in the trenches streaked with rain and dirt and blood?
Is it the very same face seen so often in the mirror?
Just as though it could be true—

But what if it is, what if it is, what if it is, what if the thing that cannot happen really happens just the same,
Suppose the fever goes a hundred, then a hundred and one,
What if Holy Savings Trust goes from 98 to 88 to 78 to 68, then drops down to 28 and 8 and out of sight,
And the fever shoots a hundred two, a hundred three, a hundred four, then a hundred five and out?

But now there's only the wind and the sky and sunlight and the clouds,
With everyday people walking and talking as they always have before along the everyday street,
Doing ordinary things with ordinary faces and ordinary voices in the ordinary way,
Just as they always will—

Then why does it feel like a bomb, why does it feel like a target,
Like standing on the gallows with the trap about to drop,
Why does it feel like a thunderbolt the second before it strikes, why does it feel like a tight-rope walk high over hell?

Because it is not, will not, never could be true
That the whole wide, bright, green, warm, calm world goes:
CRASH.

From Kenneth Fearing, *Collected Poems*. Copyright, 1940, by Random House, Inc. Reprinted by permission of Random House, Inc.

The Express

from Foreword to THE STILL CENTRE
by STEPHEN SPENDER

POETRY does not state truth, it states the conditions within which something felt is true. Even while he is writing about the little portion of reality which is part of his experience, the poet may be conscious of a different reality outside. His problem is to relate the small truth to the sense of a wider, perhaps theoretically known, truth outside his experience. Poems exist within their own limits, they do not exclude the possibility of other things, which might also be subjects of poetry, being different. They remain true to experience and they establish the proportions of that experience. One day a poet will write truthfully about the heroism as well as the fears and anxiety of today; but such a poetry will be very different from the utilitarian heroics of the moment.

I think that there is a certain pressure of external events on poets today, making them tend to write about what is outside their own limited experience. The violence of the times we are living in, the necessity of sweeping and general and immediate action, tend to dwarf the experience of the individual, and to make his immediate environment and occupations perhaps something that he is even ashamed of. For this reason, in my most recent poems, I have deliberately turned back to a kind of writing which is more personal, and I have included within my subjects weakness and fantasy and illusion.

From Stephen Spender, *The Still Centre*. Copyright, 1942, by Stephen Spender. Reprinted by permission of Random House, Inc.

THE EXPRESS
by STEPHEN SPENDER

After the first powerful plain manifesto
The black statement of pistons, without more fuss
But gliding like a queen, she leaves the station.
Without bowing and with restrained unconcern
She passes the houses which humbly crowd outside,
The gasworks and at last the heavy page
Of death, printed by gravestones in the cemetery.
Beyond the town there lies the open country
Where, gathering speed, she acquires mystery,
The luminous self-possession of ships on ocean.
It is now she begins to sing—at first quite low
Then loud, and at last with a jazzy madness—

From Stephen Spender, *Poems*. Copyright, 1934, by the Modern Library, Inc. Reprinted by permission of Random House, Inc.

The song of her whistle screaming at curves,
Of deafening tunnels, brakes, innumerable bolts.
And always light, aerial, underneath
Goes the elate meter of her wheels.
Steaming through metal landscape on her lines
She plunges new eras of wild happiness
Where speed throws up strange shapes, broad curves
And parallels clean like the steel of guns.
At last, further than Edinburgh or Rome,
Beyond the crest of the world, she reaches night
Where only a low streamline brightness
Of phosphorus on the tossing hills is white.
Ah, like a comet through flames she moves entranced
Wrapt in her music no bird song, no, nor bough
Breaking with honey buds, shall ever equal.

NOT PALACES, AN ERA'S CROWN
by Stephen Spender

Not palaces, an era's crown
Where the mind dwells, intrigues, rests;
The architectural gold-leaved flower
From people ordered like a single mind,
I build. This only what I tell:
It is too late for rare accumulation
For family pride, for beauty's filtered dusts;
I say, stamping the words with emphasis,
Drink from here energy and only energy,
As from the electric charge of a battery,
To will this Time's change.
Eye, gazelle, delicate wanderer,
Drinker of horizon's fluid line;
Ear that suspends on a chord
The spirit drinking timelessness;
Touch, love, all senses;
Leave your gardens, your singing feasts,
Your dreams of suns circling before our sun,
Of heaven after our world.
Instead, watch images of flashing brass
That strike the outward sense, the polished will
Flag of our purpose which the wind engraves.
No spirit seek here rest. But this: No man
Shall hunger: Man shall spend equally.
Our goal which we compel: Man shall be man.

—That programme of the antique Satan
Bristling with guns on the indented page
With battleship towering from hilly waves:
For what? Drive of a ruining purpose
Destroying all but its age-long exploiters.
Our programme like this, yet opposite,
Death to the killers, bringing light to life.

THE LANDSCAPE NEAR AN AERODROME
by Stephen Spender

More beautiful and soft than any moth
With burring furred antennae feeling its huge path
Through dusk, the air-liner with shut-off engines
Glides over suburbs and the sleeves set trailing tall
To point the wind. Gently, broadly, she falls
Scarcely disturbing charted currents of air.

Lulled by descent, the travellers across sea
And across feminine land indulging its easy limbs
In miles of softness, now let their eyes trained by watching
Penetrate through dusk the outskirts of this town
Here where industry shows a fraying edge.
Here they may see what is being done.

Beyond the winking masthead light
And the landing-ground, they observe the outposts
Of work: chimneys like lank black fingers
Or figures frightening and mad: and squat buildings
With their strange air behind trees, like women's faces
Shattered by grief. Here where few houses
Moan with faint light behind their blinds
They remark the unhomely sense of complaint, like a dog
Shut out and shivering at the foreign moon.

In the last sweep of love, they pass over fields
Behind the aerodrome, where boys play all day
Hacking dead grass: whose cries, like wild birds,
Settle upon the nearest roofs
But soon are hid under the loud city.

Then, as they land, they hear the tolling bell
Reaching across the landscape of hysteria
To where, larger than all the charcoaled batteries
And imaged towers against that dying sky,
Religion stands, the church blocking the sun.

Poetry

ULTIMA RATIO REGUM
by Stephen Spender

The guns spell money's ultimate reason
In letters of lead on the spring hillside.
But the boy lying dead under the olive trees
Was too young and too silly
To have been notable to their important eye.
He was a better target for a kiss.

When he lived, tall factory hooters never summoned him.
Nor did restaurant plate-glass doors revolve to wave him in.
His name never appeared in the papers.
The world maintained its traditional wall
Round the dead with their gold sunk deep as a well,
Whilst his life, intangible as a Stock Exchange rumour, drifted outside.

O too lightly he threw down his cap
One day when the breeze threw petals from the trees.
The unflowering wall sprouted with guns,
Machine-gun anger quickly scythed the grasses;
Flags and leaves fell from hands and branches;
The tweed cap rotted in the nettles.

Consider his life which was valueless
In terms of employment, hotel ledgers, news files.
Consider. One bullet in ten thousand kills a man.
Ask. Was so much expenditure justified
On the death of one so young and so silly
Lying under the olive trees, O world, O death?

from SPIRITUAL EXPLORATIONS
by Stephen Spender

VI

I am that witness through whom the whole
Knows it exists. Within the coils of blood,
Whispering under sleep, there moves the flood

From *Poems of Dedication*. Copyright, 1947, by Stephen Spender. Reprinted by permission of Random House, Inc.

I Think Continually of Those Who Were Truly Great

      Of stars, battles, dark and frozen pole.
      All that I am I am not. The cold stone
      Unfolds its angel for me. On my dreams ride
      The racial legends. The stars outside
      Glitter under my ribs. Being all, I am alone.
         I who say I call that eye I
      Which is the mirror in which things see
      Nothing except themselves. I die.
      The things, the vision, still will be.
      Upon this eye reflections of stars lie
      And that which passes, passes away, is I.

I THINK CONTINUALLY OF THOSE WHO WERE TRULY GREAT

by STEPHEN SPENDER

I think continually of those who were truly great.
Who, from the womb, remembered the soul's history
Through corridors of light where the hours are suns
Endless and singing. Whose lovely ambition
Was that their lips, still touched with fire,
Should tell of the Spirit clothed from head to foot in song.
And who hoarded from the Spring branches
The desires falling across their bodies like blossoms.

What is precious is never to forget
The essential delight of the blood drawn from ageless springs
Breaking through rocks in worlds before our earth.
Never to deny its pleasure in the morning simple light
Nor its grave evening demand for love.
Never to allow gradually the traffic to smother
With noise and fog the flowering of the spirit.

Near the snow, near the sun, in the highest fields
See how these names are fêted by the waving grass
And by the streamers of white cloud
And whispers of wind in the listening sky.
The names of those who in their lives fought for life
Who wore at their hearts the fire's centre.
Born of the sun they travelled a short while towards the sun,
And left the vivid air signed with their honour.

from "SQUARES AND OBLONGS" in POETS AT WORK
by W. H. AUDEN

A poet is, before anything else, a person who is passionately in love with language. Whether this love is a sign of his poetic gift or the gift itself—for falling in love is given not chosen—I don't know, but it is certainly the sign by which one recognizes whether a young man is potentially a poet or not.

Two theories of poetry. Poetry as a magical means for inducing desirable emotions and repelling undesirable emotions in oneself and others, or Poetry as a game of knowledge, a bringing to consciousness, by naming them, of emotions and their hidden relationships.

The first view was held by the Greeks, and is now held by MGM, Agit-Prop, and the collective public of the world. They are wrong.

The girl whose boy-friend starts writing her love poems should be on her guard. Perhaps he really does love her, but one thing is certain: while he was writing his poems he was not thinking of her but of his own feeling about her, and that is suspicious. Let her remember St. Augustine's confession of his feelings after the death of someone he loved very much: "I would rather have been deprived of my friend than of my grief."

How can I know what I think till I see what I say? A poet writes "The chestnut's comfortable root" and then changes this to "The chestnut's customary root." In this alteration there is no question of replacing one emotion by another, or of strengthening an emotion, but of discovering what the emotion is. The emotion is unchanged, but waiting to be identified like a telephone number one cannot remember. "8357. No, that's not it. 8557, 8457, no, it's on the tip of my tongue, wait a moment, I've got it, 8657. That's it."

The low-brow says: "I don't like poetry. It requires too much effort to understand and I'm afraid that if I learnt exactly what I feel, it would make me most uncomfortable." He is in the wrong, of course, but not so much in the wrong as the high-brow whose gifts make the effort to understand very little and who, having learned what he feels, is not at all uncomfortable, only interested.

From *Poets at Work*, by W. H. Auden, Karl Shapiro, Rudolf Arnheim, and Donald A. Stauffer, copyright, 1948, by Harcourt, Brace and Company, Inc.

Letter to Lord Byron

NOW THROUGH NIGHT'S CARESSING GRIP

by W. H. AUDEN

Now through night's caressing grip
Earth and all her oceans slip,
Capes of China slide away
From her fingers into day,
And the Americas incline
Coasts toward her shadow line.
Now the ragged vagrants creep
Into crooked holes to sleep;
Just and unjust, worst and best,
Change their places as they rest;
Awkward lovers lie in fields
Where disdainful beauty yields;
While the splendid and the proud
Naked stand before the crowd,
And the losing gambler gains,
And the begger entertains.
May sleep's healing power extend
Through these hours to each friend;
Unpursued by hostile force
Traction engine bull or horse
Or revolting succubus;
Calmly till the morning break
Let them lie, then gently wake.

From *The Collected Poetry of W. H. Auden*. Copyright, 1945, by W. H. Auden. Reprinted by permission of Random House, Inc.

from LETTER TO LORD BYRON, Part IV

by W. H. AUDEN

The Great War had begun: but masters' scrutiny
  And fists of big boys were the war to us;
It was as harmless as the Indian Mutiny,
  A beating from the Head was dangerous.
  But once when half the form put down *Bellus*.
We were accused of that most deadly sin,
Wanting the Kaiser and the Huns to win.

From W. H. Auden and Louis MacNeice, *Letters from Iceland*. Copyright, 1937, by W. H Auden and Louis MacNeice. Reprinted by permission of Random House, Inc.

[761]

Poetry

The way in which we really were affected
  Was having such a varied lot to teach us.
The best were fighting, as the King expected,
  The remnant either elderly grey creatures,
  Or characters with most peculiar features.
Many were raggable, a few were waxy,
One had to leave abruptly in a taxi.

Surnames I must not write—O Reginald,
  You at least taught us that which fadeth not,
Our earliest visions of the great wide world;
  The beer and biscuits that your favourites got,
  Your tales revealing you a first-class shot,
Your riding breeks, your drama called *The Waves*,
A few of us will carry to our graves.

'Half a lunatic, half a knave.' No doubt
  A holy terror to the staff at tea;
A good headmaster must have soon found out
  Your moral character was all at sea;
  I question if you'd got a pass degree:
But little children bless your kind that knocks
Away the edifying stumbling blocks.

How can I thank you? For it only shows
  (Let me ride just this once my hobby-horse),
There're things a good headmaster never knows.
  There must be sober schoolmasters, of course,
  But what a prep school really puts across
Is knowledge of the world we'll soon be lost in:
To-day it's more like Dickens than Jane Austen.

I hate the modern trick, to tell the truth,
  Of straightening out the kinks in the young mind,
Our passion for the tender plant of youth,
  Our hatred for all weeds of any kind.
  Slogans are bad: the best that I can find
Is this: 'Let each child have that's in our care
As much neurosis as the child can bear.'

In this respect, at least, my bad old Adam is
  Pigheadedly against the general trend;
And has no use for all these new academies
  Where readers of the better weeklies send
  The child they probably did not intend,

Letter to Lord Byron

To paint a lampshade, marry, or keep pigeons,
Or make a study of the world religions.

Goddess of bossy underlings, Normality!
    What murders are committed in thy name!
Totalitarian is thy state Reality,
    Reeking of antiseptics and the shame
    Of faces that all look and feel the same.
Thy Muse is one unknown to classic histories,
The topping figure of the hockey mistress.

From thy dread Empire not a soul's exempted:
    More than the nursemaids pushing prams in parks,
By thee the intellectuals are tempted,
    O, to commit the treason of the clerks,
    Bewitched by thee to literary sharks.
But I must leave thee to thy office stool,
I must get on now to my public school.

Men had stopped throwing stones at one another,
    Butter and Father had come back again;
Gone were the holidays we spent with Mother
    In furnished rooms on mountain, moor, and fen;
    And gone those summer Sunday evenings, when
Along the seafronts fled a curious noise,
'Eternal Father,' sung by three young boys.

Nation spoke Peace, or said she did, with nation;
    The sexes tried their best to look the same;
Morals lost value during the inflation,
    The great Victorians kindly took the blame:
    Visions of Dada to the Post-War came,
Sitting in cafés, nostrils stuffed with bread,
Above the recent and the straight-laced dead.

I've said my say on public schools elsewhere:
    Romantic friendship, prefects, bullying,
I shall not deal with, c'est une autre affaire.
    Those who expect them, will get no such thing,
    It is the strictly relevant I sing.
Why should they grumble? They've the Greek Anthology,
And all the spicier bits of Anthropology.

Poetry

We all grow up the same way, more or less;
   Life is not known to give away her presents;
She only swops. The unself-consciousness
    That children share with animals and peasants
    Sinks in the 'stürm und drang' of Adolescence.
Like other boys I lost my taste for sweets,
Discovered sunsets, passion, God, and Keats.

I shall recall a single incident
   No more. I spoke of mining engineering
As the career on which my mind was bent,
    But for some time my fancies had been veering;
    Mirages of the future kept appearing;
Crazes had come and gone in short, sharp gales,
For motor-bikes, photography, and whales.

But indecision broke off with a clean-cut end
   One afternoon in March at half-past three
When walking in a ploughed field with a friend;
    Kicking a little stone, he turned to me
    And said, 'Tell me, do you write poetry?'
I never had, and said so, but I knew
That very moment what I wished to do.

Without a bridge passage this leads me straight
   Into the theme marked 'Oxford' on my score
From pages twenty-five to twenty-eight.
    Aesthetic trills I'd never heard before
    Rose from the strings, shrill poses from the cor;
The woodwind chattered like a pre-war Russian,
'Art' boomed the brass, and 'Life' thumped the percussion.

A raw provincial, my good taste was tardy,
   And Edward Thomas I as yet preferred;
I was still listening to Thomas Hardy
    Putting divinity about a bird;
    But Eliot spoke the still unspoken word;
For gasworks and dried tubers I forsook
The clock at Granchester, the English rook.

All youth's intolerant certainty was mine as
   I faced life in a double-breasted suit;
I bought and praised but did not read Aquinas,

Letter to Lord Byron

At the *Criterion's* verdict I was mute,
   Though Arnold's I was ready to refute;
And through the quads dogmatic words rang clear,
   'Good poetry is classic and austere.'

So much for Art. Of course Life had its passions too;
   The student's flesh like his imagination
Makes facts fit theories and has fashions too.
   We were the tail, a sort of poor relation
   To that debauched, eccentric generation
That grew up with their fathers at the War,
And made new glosses on the noun Amor.

Three years passed quickly while the Isis went
   Down to the sea for better or for worse;
Then to Berlin, not Carthage, I was sent
   With money from my parents in my purse,
   And ceased to see the world in terms of verse.
I met a chap called Layard and he fed
New doctrines into my receptive head.

Part came from Lane, and part from D. H. Lawrence;
   Gide, though I didn't know it then, gave part.
They taught me to express my deep abhorrence
   If I caught anyone preferring Art
   To Life and Love and being Pure-in-Heart.
I lived with crooks but seldom was molested;
The Pure-in-Heart can never be arrested.

He's gay; no bludgeonings of chance can spoil it,
   The Pure-in-Heart loves all men on a par,
And has no trouble with his private toilet;
   The Pure-in-Heart is never ill; catarrh
   Would be the yellow streak, the brush of tar;
Determined to be loving and forgiving,
I came back home to try and earn my living.

The only thing you never turned your hand to
   Was teaching English in a boarding school.
To-day it's a profession that seems grand to
   Those whose alternative's an office stool;
   For budding authors it's become the rule.
To many an unknown genius postmen bring
Typed notices from Rabbitarse and String.

The Head's M.A., a bishop is a patron,
  The assistant staff is highly qualified;
Health is the care of an experienced matron,
  The arts are taught by ladies from outside;
  The food is wholesome and the grounds are wide;
Their aim is training character and poise,
With special coaching for the backward boys.

I found the pay good and had time to spend it,
  Though others may not have the good luck I did:
For You I'd hesitate to recommend it;
  Several have told me that they can't abide it.
  Still, if one tends to get a bit one-sided,
It's pleasant as it's easy to secure
The hero worship of the immature.

More, it's a job, and jobs to-day are rare:
  All the ideals in the world won't feed us
Although they give our crimes a certain air.
  So barons of the press who know their readers
  Employ to write their more appalling leaders,
Instead of Satan's horned and hideous minions,
Clever young men of liberal opinions.

Which brings me up to nineteen-thirty-five;
  Six months of film work is another story
I can't tell now. But, here I am, alive
  Knowing the true source of that sense of glory
  That still surrounds the England of the Tory,
Come only to the rather tame conclusion
That no man by himself has life's solution.

MUSÉE DES BEAUX ARTS
by W. H. AUDEN

ABOUT suffering they were never wrong,
The Old Masters: how well they understood
Its human position; how it takes place
While someone else is eating or opening a window or just walking dully along;

From *The Collected Poetry of W. H. Auden.* Copyright, 1945, by W. H. Auden. Reprinted by permission of Random House, Inc.

Auden believed that if we can't learn to love in the Christian sense we can't survive at all.

Law Like Love

How, when the aged are reverently, passionately waiting
For the miraculous birth, there always must be
Children who did not specially want it to happen, skating
On a pond at the edge of the wood:
They never forgot
That even the dreadful martyrdom must run its course
Anyhow in a corner, some untidy spot
Where the dogs go on with their doggy life and the torturer's horse
Scratches its innocent behind on a tree.

In Brueghel's *Icarus,* for instance: how everything turns away
Quite leisurely from the disaster; the ploughman may
Have heard the splash, the forsaken cry,
But for him it was not an important failure; the sun shone
As it had to on the white legs disappearing into the green
Water; and the expensive delicate ship that must have seen
Something amazing, a boy falling out of the sky,
Had somewhere to get to and sailed calmly on.

LAW LIKE LOVE
by W. H. AUDEN

Law, say the gardeners, is the sun,
Law is the one
All gardeners obey
Tomorrow, yesterday, today.

Law is the wisdom of the old
The impotent grandfathers shrilly scold;
The grandchildren put out a treble tongue,
Law is the senses of the young.

Law, says the priest with a priestly look,
Expounding to an unpriestly people,
Law is the words in my priestly book,
Law is my pulpit and my steeple.

Law, says the judge as he looks down his
  nose,
Speaking clearly and most severely,
Law is as I've told you before,
Law is as you know I suppose,
Law is but let me explain it once more,
Law is the Law.

Yet law-abiding scholars write;
Law is neither wrong nor right,
Law is only crimes
Punished by places and by times,
Law is the clothes men wear
Anytime, anywhere,
Law is Good-morning and Good-night.

Others say, Law is our Fate;
Others say, Law is our State;
Others say, others say
Law is no more
Law has gone away.

And always the loud angry crowd
Very angry and very loud
Law is We,
And always the soft idiot softly Me.

If we, dear, know we know no more
Than they about the law,
If I no more than you

[767]

Know what we should and should not do
Except that all agree
Gladly or miserably
That the law is
And that all know this,
If therefore thinking it absurd
To identify Law with some other word.
Unlike so many men
I cannot say Law is again,
No more than they can we suppress
The universal wish to guess
Or slip out of our own position
Into an unconcerned condition.
Although I can at least confine
Your vanity and mine
To stating timidly
A timid similarity
We shall boast anyway:
Like love I say.

Like love we don't know where or why
Like love we can't compel or fly
Like love we often weep
Like love we seldom keep.

CASINO
by W. H. AUDEN

Only the hands are living; to the wheel attracted,
Are moved as deer trek desperately towards a creek
  Through the dust and scrub of the desert, or gently
  As sunflowers turn to the light.

And, as the night takes up the cries of feverish children,
The cravings of lions in dens, the loves of dons,
  Gathers them all and remains the night, the
  Great room is full of their prayers

To the last feast of isolation self-invited
They flock, and in the rite of disbelief are joined;
  From numbers all their stars are recreated,
  The enchanted, the world, the sad.

Without, the rivers flow among the wholly living,
Quite near their trysts; and the mountains part them; and the bird
  Deep in the greens and moistures of summer
  Sings towards their work.

But here no nymph comes naked to the youngest shepherd;
The fountain is deserted; the laurel will not grow;
  The labyrinth is safe but endless, and broken
  Is Ariadne's thread.

As deeper in these hands is grooved their fortune: "Lucky
Were few, and it is possible that none was loved;
  And what was godlike in this generation
  Was never to be born."

PRIME

by W. H. AUDEN

Simultaneously, as soundlessly,
  Spontaneously, suddenly
As, at the vaunt of the dawn, the kind
  Gates of the body fly open
To its world beyond, the gates of the mind,
  The horn gate and the ivory gate
Swing to, swing shut, instantaneously
  Quell the nocturnal rummage
Of its rebellious fronde, ill-favored,
  Ill-natured and second-rate,
Disenfranchised, widowed and orphaned
  By an historical mistake:
Recalled from the shades to be a seeing being,
  From absence to be on display,
Without a name or history I wake
  Between my body and the day.

Holy this moment, wholly in the right,
  As, in complete obedience
To the light's laconic outcry, next
  As a sheet, near as a wall,
Out there as a mountain's poise of stone,
  The world is present, about,
And I know that I am, here, not alone
  But with a world, and rejoice
Unvexed, for the will has still to claim
  This adjacent arm as my own.
The memory to name me, resume
  Its routine of praise and blame,
And smiling to me is this instant while
  Still the day is intact and I
The Adam sinless in our beginning,
  Adam still previous to any act.

I draw breath; that is of course to wish
  No matter what to be wise
To be different to die and the cost
  No matter how is Paradise

From *Nones* by W. H. Auden. Copyright, 1951, by W. H. Auden. Reprinted by permission of Random House, Inc.

Lost of course and myself owing a death:
  The eager ridge, the steady sea,
The flat roofs of the fishing village
  Still asleep in its bunny,
Though as fresh and sunny still are not friends
  But things to hand, this ready flesh
No honest equal but my accomplice now
  My assassin to be and my name
Stands for my historical share of care
  For a lying self-made city,
Afraid of our living task, the dying
  Which the coming day will ask.

NONES

by W. H. AUDEN

What we know to be not possible,
  Though time after time foretold
By wild hermits, by shaman and sybil
  Gibbering in their trances,
Or revealed to a child in some chance rhyme
  Like *will* and *kill,* comes to pass
Before we realize it: we are surprised
  At the ease and speed of our deed
And uneasy: It is barely three,
  Mid-afternoon, yet the blood
Of our sacrifice is already
  Dry on the grass; we are not prepared
For silence so sudden and so soon;
  The day is too hot, too bright, too still,
Too ever, the dead remains too nothing.
  What shall we do till nightfall?

The wind has dropped and we have lost
  our public.
  The faceless many who always
Collect when any world is to be wrecked,
  Blown up, burnt down, cracked open,
Felled, sawn in two, hacked through, torn apart,
  Have all melted away: not one
Of these who in the shade of walls and trees
  Lie sprawled now, calmly sleeping,
Harmless as sheep, can remember why
  He shouted or what about
So loudly in the sunshine this morning;
  All if challenged would reply
—"It was a monster with one red eye,
  A crowd that saw him die, not I."—

From *Nones,* by W. H. Auden. Copyright, 1951, by W. H. Auden. Reprinted by permission of Random House, Inc.

[770]

Nones

The hangman has gone to wash, the sol-
    diers to eat:
  We are left alone with our feat.

The Madonna with the green woodpecker,
  The Madonna of the fig-tree,
The Madonna beside the yellow dam,
  Turn their kind faces from us
And our projects under construction,
  Look only in one direction,
Fix their gaze on our completed work:
  Pile-driver, concrete-mixer,
Crane and pickaxe wait to be used again,
  But how can we repeat this?
Outliving our act, we stand where we are,
  As disregarded as some
Discarded artifact of our own,
  Like torn gloves, rusted kettles,
Abandoned branch-lines, worn lop-sided
  Grindstones buried in nettles.

This mutilated flesh, our victim,
  Explains too nakedly, too well,
The spell of the asparagus-garden,
  The aim of our chalk-pit game; stamps,
Birds' eggs are not the same, behind the
  wonder
  Of tow-paths and sunken lanes,
Behind the rapture on the spiral stair,
  We shall always now be aware
Of the deed into which they lead, under
  The mock chase and mock capture,
The racing and tussling and splashing,
  The panting and the laughter,
Be listening for the cry and stillness
  To follow after: wherever
The sun shines, brooks run, books are
  written,
  There will also be this death.

Soon cool tramontana will stir the leaves,
  The shops will re-open at four,
The empty blue bus in the empty pink
  square
  Fill up and depart: we have time

To misrepresent, excuse, deny,
  Mythify, use this event
While, under a hotel bed, in prison,
  Down wrong turnings, its meaning
Waits for our lives: sooner than we would
  choose,
  Bread will melt, water will burn,
And the great quell begin, Abaddon
  Set up his triple gallows
At our seven gates, fat Belial make
  Our wives waltz naked; meanwhile
It would be best to go home, if we have
  a home,
  In any case good to rest.

That our dreaming wills may seem to es-
  cape
  This dead calm, wander instead
On knife edges, on black and white
  squares,
  Across moss, baize, velvet, boards,
Over cracks and hillocks, in mazes
  Of string and penitent cones,
Down granite ramps and damp passages,
  Through gates that will not relatch
And doors marked *Private,* pursued by
  Moors
  And watched by latent robbers,
To hostile villages at the heads of fjords,
  To dark châteaux where wind sobs
In the pine-trees and telephones ring,
  Inviting trouble, to a room,
Lit by one weak bulb, where our Double
  sits
  Writing and does not look up.

That, while we are thus away, our own
  wronged flesh
  May work undisturbed, restoring
The order we try to destroy, the rhythm
  We spoil out of spite: valves close
And open exactly, glands secrete,
  Vessels contract and expand
At the right moment, essential fluids
  Flow to renew exhausted cells,

Not knowing quite what has happened,
    but awed
By death like all the creatures
Now watching this spot, like the hawk
    looking down

Without blinking, the smug hens
    Passing close by in their pecking order,
The bug whose view is balked by grass,
Or the deer who shyly from afar
    Peer through chinks in the forest.

UNDER WHICH LYRE

A Reactionary Tract for the Times
(Phi Beta Kappa Poem. Harvard. 1946)

by W. H. AUDEN

Ares at last has quit the field,
The bloodstains on the bushes yield
    To seeping showers,
And in their convalescent state
The fractured towns associate
    With summer flowers.

Encamped upon the college plain
Raw veterans already train
    As freshman forces;
Instructors with sarcastic tongue
Shepherd the battle-weary young
    Through basic courses.

Among bewildering appliances
For mastering the arts and sciences
    They stroll or run,
And nerves that never flinched at slaughter
Are shot to pieces by the shorter
    Poems of Donne.

From *Nones* by W. H. Auden. Copyright, 1951, by W. H. Auden. Reprinted by permission of Random House, Inc.

Under Which Lyre

Professors back from secret missions
Resume their proper eruditions,
    Though some regret it;
They liked their dictaphones a lot,
They met some big wheels, and do **not**
    Let you forget it.

But Zeus' inscrutable decree
Permits the will-to-disagree
    To be pandemic,
Ordains that vaudeville shall preach
And every commencement speech
    Be a polemic.

Let Ares doze, that other war
Is instantly declared once more
    'Twixt those who follow
Precocious Hermes all the way
And those who without qualms obey
    Pompous Apollo.

Brutal like all Olympic games,
Though fought with smiles and Christian **names**
    And less dramatic,
This dialectic strife between
The civil gods is just as mean,
    And more fanatic.

What high immortals do in mirth
Is life and death on Middle Earth;
    Their a-historic
Antipathy forever gripes
All ages and somatic types,
    The sophomoric

Who face the future's darkest hints
With giggles or with prairie squints
    As stout as Cortez,
And those who like myself turn pale
As we approach with ragged sail
    The fattening forties.

The sons of Hermes love to play,
And only do their best when they
    Are told they oughtn't;

Poetry

Apollo's children never shrink
From boring jobs but have to think
    Their work important.

Related by antithesis,
A compromise between us is
    Impossible;
Respect perhaps but friendship never:
Falstaff the fool confronts forever
    The prig Prince Hal.

If he would leave the self alone,
Apollo's welcome to the throne,
    Fasces and falcons;
He loves to rule, has always done it;
The earth would soon, did Hermes run it,
    Be like the Balkans.

But jealous of our god of dreams,
His common-sense in secret schemes
    To rule the heart;
Unable to invent the lyre,
Creates with simulated fire
    Official art.

And when he occupies a college,
Truth is replaced by Useful Knowledge;
    He pays particular
Attention to Commercial Thought,
Public Relations, Hygiene, Sport,
    In his curricula

Athletic, extrovert and crude,
For him, to work in solitude
    Is the offence,
The goal a populous Nirvana:
His shield bears this device: *Mens sana*
    Qui mal y pense.

Today his arms, we must confess,
From Right to Left have met success,
    His banners wave
From Yale to Princeton, and the news
From Broadway to the Book Reviews
    Is very grave.

Under Which Lyre

His radio Homers all day long
In over-Whitmanated song
    That does not scan,
With adjectives laid end to end,
Extol the doughnut and commend
    The Common Man.

His, too, each homely lyric thing
On sport or spousal love or spring
    Or dogs or dusters,
Invented by some court-house bard
For recitation by the yard
    In filibusters.

To him ascend the prize orations
And sets of fugal variations
    On some folk-ballad,
While dietitians sacrifice
A glass of prune-juice or a nice
    Marsh-mallow salad.

Charged with his compound of sensational
Sex plus some undenominational
    Religious matter,
Enormous novels by co-eds
Rain down on our defenceless heads
    Till our teeth chatter.

In fake Hermetic uniforms
Behind our battle-line, in swarms
    That keep alighting,
His existentialists declare
That they are in complete despair,
    Yet go on writing.

No matter; He shall be defied;
White Aphrodite is on our side:
    What though his threat
To organize us grow more critical?
Zeus willing, we, the unpolitical,
    Shall beat him yet.

Lone scholars, sniping from the walls
Of learned periodicals,
    Our facts defend,

Our intellectual marines,
Landing in little magazines
    Capture a trend.

By night our student Underground
At cocktail parties whisper round
    From ear to ear;
Fat figures in the public eye
Collapse next morning, ambushed by
    Some witty sneer.

In our morale must lie our strength:
So, that we may behold at length
    Routed Apollo's
Battalions melt away like fog,
Keep well the Hermetic Decalogue,
    Which runs as follows:—

Thou shalt not do as the dean pleases,
Thou shalt not write thy doctor's thesis
    On education,
Thou shalt not worship projects nor
Shalt thou or thine bow down before
    Administration.

Thou shalt not answer questionnaires
Or quizzes upon World-Affairs,
    Nor with compliance
Take any test. Thou shalt not sit
With statisticians nor commit
    A social science.

Thou shalt not be on friendly terms
With guys in advertising firms,
    Nor speak with such
As read the Bible for its prose,
Nor, above all, make love to those
    Who wash too much.

Thou shalt not live within thy means
Nor on plain water and raw greens.
    If thou must choose
Between the chances, choose the odd;
Read *The New Yorker,* trust in God;
    And take short views.

"The Hand that Signed the Paper Felled a City"

from SELECTED WRITINGS
by Dylan Thomas

Poetry is the rhythmic, inevitably narrative, movement from an over-clothed blindness to a naked vision ... the physical and mental task of constructing a formally watertight compartment of words. ... Poetry must drag further into the clear nakedness of light more even of the hidden causes than Freud could realize.

IN MY CRAFT OR SULLEN ART
by Dylan Thomas

In my craft or sullen art
Exercised in the still night
When only the moon rages
And the lovers lie abed
With all their griefs in their arms,
I labour by singing light
Not for ambition or bread
Or the strut and trade of charms
On the ivory stages
But for the common wages

Of their most secret heart.
Not for the proud man apart
From the raging moon I write
On these spindrift pages
Not for the towering dead
With their nightingales and psalms
But for the lovers, their arms
Round the griefs of the ages,
Who pay no praise or wages
Nor heed my craft or art.

"THE HAND THAT SIGNED THE PAPER FELLED A CITY"
by Dylan Thomas

The hand that signed the paper felled a city;
Five sovereign fingers taxed the breath,
Doubled the globe of dead and halved a country;
These five kings did a king to death.

The mighty hand leads to a sloping shoulder,
The finger joints are cramped with chalk;
A goose's quill has put an end to murder
That put an end to talk.

The hand that signed the treaty bred a fever,
And famine grew, and locusts came;
Great is the hand that holds dominion over
Man by a scribbled name.

The five kings count the dead but do not soften
The crusted wound nor pat the brow;
A hand rules pity as a hand rules heaven;
Hands have no tears to flow.

From *The Selected Writings of Dylan Thomas*, Dylan Thomas, copyright, 1946, by New Directions. Reprinted by permission of New Directions, 333 Sixth Avenue, New York, N. Y.

POEM IN OCTOBER
by Dylan Thomas

It was my thirtieth year to heaven
Woke to my hearing from harbour and neighbour wood
   And the mussel pooled and the heron
      Priested shore
      The morning beckon
With water praying and call of seagull and rook
And the knock of sailing boats on the net webbed wall
      Myself to set foot
         That second
In the still sleeping town and set forth.

My birthday began with the water-
Birds and the birds of the winged trees flying my name
   Above the farms and the white horses
      And I rose
      In rainy autumn
And walked abroad in a shower of all my days.
High tide and the heron dived when I took the road
     Over the border
        And the gates
Of the town closed as the town awoke.

A springful of larks in a rolling
Cloud and the roadside bushes brimming with whistling
   Blackbirds and the sun of October
      Summery
      On the hill's shoulder,
Here were fond climates and sweet singers suddenly
Come in the morning where I wandered and listened
     To the rain wringing
       Wind blow cold
In the wood faraway under me.

Pale rain over the dwindling harbour
And over the sea wet church the size of a snail
   With its horns through mist, and the castle
      Brown as owls,
      But all the gardens
Of spring and summer were blooming in the tall tales

Poem in October

Beyond the border and under the lark full cloud.
    There could I marvel
        My birthday
Away but the weather turned around.

    It turned away from the blithe country
And down the other air and the blue altered sky
    Streamed again a wonder of summer
        With apples
      Pears and red currants
And I saw in the turning so clearly a child's
Forgotten mornings when he walked with his mother
    Through the parables
      Of sun light
    And the legends of the green chapels

    And the twice told fields of infancy
That his tears burned my cheeks and his heart moved in mine.
    These were the woods the river and sea
        Where a boy
      In the listening
Summertime of the dead whispered the truth of his joy
To the trees and the stones and the fish in the tide.
    And the mystery
      Sang alive
Still in the water and singing birds.

    And there could I marvel my birthday
Away but the weather turned around. And the true
    Joy of the long dead child sang burning
        In the sun.
      It was my thirtieth
Year to heaven stood there then in the summer noon
Though the town below lay leaved with October blood.
    O may my heart's truth
      Still be sung
On this high hill in a year's turning.

Poetry

IN THE WHITE GIANT'S THIGH
by Dylan Thomas

Through throats where many rivers meet, the curlews cry,
Under the conceiving moon, on the high chalk hill,
And there this night I walk in the white giant's thigh
Where barren as boulders women lie longing still

To labour and love though they lay down long ago.

Through throats where many rivers meet, the women pray,
Pleading in the waded bay for the seed to flow
Though the names on their weed grown stones are rained away,

And alone in the night's eternal, curving act
They yearn with tongues of curlews for the unconceived
And immemorial sons of the cudgelling, hacked

Hill. Who once in gooseskin winter loved all ice leaved
In the courters' lanes, or twined in the ox roasting sun
In the wains tonned so high that the wisps of the hay
Clung to the pitching clouds, or gay with any one
Young as they in the after milking moonlight lay

Under the lighted shapes of faith and their moonshade
Petticoats galed high, or shy with the rough riding boys,
Now clasp me to their grains in the gigantic glade,

Who once, green countries since, were a hedgerow of joys.
Time by, their dust was flesh the swineherd rooted sly,
Flared in the reek of the wiving sty with the rush
Light of his thighs, spreadeagle to the dunghill sky,
Or with their orchard man in the core of the sun's bush
Rough as cows' tongues and thrashed with brambles their buttermilk
Manes, under his quenchless summer barbed gold to the bone,

Or rippling soft in the spinney moon as the silk
And ducked and draked white lake that harps to a hail stone.

Who once were a bloom of wayside brides in the hawed house
And heard the lewd, wooed field flow to the coming frost,

Copyright 1953 by Dylan Thomas, reprinted by permission of New Directions, 333 Sixth Avenue, New York 14.

In the White Giant's Thigh

The scurrying, furred small friars squeal, in the dowse
Of day, in the thistle aisles, till the white owl crossed

Their breast, the vaulting does roister, the horned bucks climb
Quick in the wood at love, where a torch of foxes foams,
All birds and beasts of the linked night uproar and chime

And the mole snout blunt under his pilgrimage of domes,
Or, butter fat goosegirls, bounced in a gambo bed,
Their breasts full of honey, under their gander king
Trounced by his wings in the hissing shippen, long dead
And gone that barley dark where their clogs danced in the spring,
And their firefly hairpins flew, and the ricks ran round—

(But nothing bore, no mouthing babe to the veined hives
Hugged, and barren and bare on Mother Goose's ground
They with the simple Jacks were a boulder of wives)—

Now curlew cry me down to kiss the mouths of their dust.

The dust of their kettles and clocks swings to and fro
Where the hay rides now or the bracken kitchens rust
As the arc of the billhooks that flashed the hedges low
And cut the birds' boughs that the minstrel sap ran red.
They from houses where the harvest kneels, hold me hard,
Who heard the tall bell sail down the Sundays of the dead
And the rain wring out its tongues on the faded yard,
Teach me the love that is evergreen after the fall leaved
Grave, after Belovèd on the grass gulfed cross is scrubbed
Off by the sun and Daughters no longer grieved
Save by their long desirers in the fox cubbed
Streets or hungering in the crumbled wood: to these
Hale dead and deathless do the women of the hill
Love for ever meridian through the courters' trees

And the daughters of darkness flame like Fawkes fires still.

ON NO WORK OF WORDS
by Dylan Thomas

On no work of words now for three lean months in the bloody
Belly of the rich year and the big purse of my body
I bitterly take to task my poverty and craft:

To take to give is all, return what is hungrily given
Puffing the pounds of manna up through the dew to heaven,
The lovely gift of the gab bangs back on a blind shaft.

To lift to leave from the treasures of man is pleasing death
That will rake at last all currencies of the marked breath
And count the taken, forsaken mysteries in a bad dark.

To surrender now is to pay the expensive ogre twice.
Ancient woods of my blood, dash down to the nut of the seas
If I take to burn or return this world which is each man's work.

POEM ON HIS BIRTHDAY
by Dylan Thomas

In the mustardseed sun,
By full tilt river and switchback sea
  Where the cormorants scud,
In his house on stilts high among beaks
  And palavers of birds
This sandgrain day in the bent bay's grave
  He celebrates and spurns
His driftwood thirty-fifth wind turned
    age;
  Herons spire and spear.

Under and round him go
Flounders, gulls, on their cold, dying
    trails,
  Doing what they are told,

Curlews aloud in the congered waves
  Work at their ways to death,
And the rhymer in the long tongued
    room,
  Who tolls his birthday bell,
Toils towards the ambush of his wounds;
  Herons, steeple stemmed, bless.

In the thistledown fall,
He sings towards anguish; finches fly
  In the claw tracks of hawks
On a seizing sky; small fishes glide
  Through wynds and shells of drowned
Ship towns to pastures of otters. He
  In his slant, racking house

Poem on His Birthday

And the hewn coils of his trade perceives
   Herons walk in their shroud,

The livelong river's robe
   Of minnows wreathing around their
     prayer;
And far at sea he knows,
Who slaves to his crouched, eternal end
   Under a serpent cloud,
Dolphins dive in their turnturtle dust,
   The rippled seals streak down
To kill and their own tide daubing blood
   Slides good in the sleek mouth.

In a cavernous, swung
Wave's silence, wept white angelus knells.
   Thirty-five bells sing struck
On skull and scar where his loves lie
     wrecked,
   Steered by the falling stars.
And to-morrow weeps in a blind cage
   Terror will rage apart
Before chains break to a hammer flame
   And love unbolts the dark

And freely he goes lost
In the unknown, famous light of great
   And fabulous, dear God.
Dark is a way and light is a place,
   Heaven that never was
Nor will be ever is always true,
   And, in that brambled void,
Plenty as blackberries in the woods
   The dead grow for His joy.

There he might wander bare
With the spirits of the horseshoe bay
   Or the stars' seashore dead,
Marrow of eagles, the roots of whales
   And wishbones of wild geese,
With blessed, unborn God and His Ghost,
   And every soul His priest,

Gulled and chanter in young Heaven's
     fold
   Be at cloud quaking peace,

But dark is a long way.
He, on the earth of the night, alone
   With all the living, prays,
Who knows the rocketing wind will blow
   The bones out of the hills,
And the scythed boulders bleed, and the
     last
   Rage shattered waters kick
Masts and fishes to the still quick stars,
   Faithlessly unto Him

Who is the light of old
And air shaped Heaven where souls grow
     wild
   As horses in the foam:
Oh, let me midlife mourn by the shrined
   And druid herons' vows
The voyage to ruin I must run,
   Dawn ships clouted aground,
Yet, though I cry with tumbledown
     tongue,
   Count my blessings aloud:

Four elements and five
Senses, and man a spirit in love
   Tangling through this spun slime
To his nimbus bell cool kingdom come
   And the lost, moonshine domes,
And the sea that hides his secret selves
   Deep in its black, base bones,
Lulling of spheres in the seashell flesh,
   And this last blessing most,

That the closer I move
To death, one man through his sundered
     hulks,
   The louder the sun blooms
And the tusked, ramshackling sea exults;
   And every wave of the way
And gale I tackle, the whole world then,
   With more triumphant faith

Than ever was since the world was said,
  Spins its morning of praise,

I hear the bouncing hills
Grow larked and greener at berry brown
  Fall and the dew larks sing

Taller this thunderclap spring, and how
  More spanned with angels ride
The mansouled fiery islands! Oh,
  Holier then their eyes,
And my shining men no more alone
  As I sail out to die.

A WINTER'S TALE
by Dylan Thomas

  It is a winter's tale
That the snow blind twilight ferries over the lakes
And floating fields from the farm in the cup of the vales,
Gliding windless through the hand folded flakes,
The pale breath of cattle at the stealthy sail,

  And the stars falling cold,
And the smell of hay in the snow, and the far owl
Warning among the folds, and the frozen hold
Flocked with the sheep white smoke of the farm house cowl
In the river wended vales where the tale was told.

  Once when the world turned old
On a star of faith pure as the drifting bread,
As the food and flames of the snow, a man unrolled
The scrolls of fire that burned in his heart and head,
Torn and alone in a farm house in a fold

  Of fields. And burning then
In his firelit island ringed by the winged snow
And the dung hills white as wool and the hen
Roosts sleeping chill till the flame of the cock crow
Combs through the mantled yards and the morning men

  Stumble out with their spades,
The cattle stirring, the mousing cat stepping shy,
The puffed birds hopping and hunting, the milk maids
Gentle in their clogs over the fallen sky,
And all the woken farm at its white trades,

A Winter's Tale

   He knelt, he wept, he prayed,
By the spit and the black pot in the log bright light
And the cup and the cut bread in the dancing shade,
In the muffled house, in the quick of night,
At the point of love, forsaken and afraid.

   He knelt on the cold stones,
He wept from the crest of grief, he prayed to the veiled sky
May his hunger go howling on bare white bones
Past the statues of the stables and the sky roofed sties
And the duck pond glass and the blinding byres alone

   Into the home of prayers
And fires where he should prowl down the cloud
Of his snow blind love and rush in the white lairs.
His naked need struck him howling and bowed
Though no sound flowed down the hand folded air

   But only the wind strung
Hunger of birds in the fields of the bread of water, tossed
In high corn and the harvest melting on their tongues.
And his nameless need bound him burning and lost
When cold as snow he should run the wended vales among

   The rivers mouthed in night,
And drown in the drifts of his need, and lie curled caught
In the always desiring center of the white
Inhuman cradle and the bride bed forever sought
By the believer lost and the hurled outcast of light.

   Deliver him, he cried,
By losing him all in love, and cast his need
Alone and naked in the engulfing bride,
Never to flourish in the fields of the white seed
Or flower under the time dying flesh astride.

   Listen. The minstrels sing
In the departed villages. The nightingale,
Dust in the buried wood, flies on the grains of her wings
And spells on the winds of the dead his winter's tale.
The voice of the dust of water from the withered spring

   Is telling. The wizened
Stream with bells and baying water bounds. The dew rings

On the gristed leaves and the long gone glistening
Parish of snow. The carved mouths in the rock are wind swept strings.
Time sings through the intricately dead snow drop. Listen.

  It was a hand or sound
In the long ago land that glided the dark door wide
And there outside on the bread of the ground
A she bird rose and rayed like a burning bride.
A she bird dawned, and her breast with snow and scarlet downed.

  Look. And the dancers move
On the departed, snow bushed green, wanton in moon light
As a dust of pigeons. Exulting, the grave hooved
Horses, centaur dead, turn and tread the drenched white
Paddocks in the farms of birds. The dead oak walks for love.

  The carved limbs in the rock
Leap, as to trumpets. Calligraphy of the old
Leaves is dancing. Lines of age on the stones weave in a flock.
And the harp shaped voice of the water's dust plucks in a fold
Of fields. For love, the long ago she bird rises. Look.

  And the wild wings were raised
Above her folded head, and the soft feathered voice
Was flying through the house as though the she bird praised
And all the elements of the slow fall rejoiced
That a man knelt alone in the cup of the vales,

  In the mantle and calm,
By the spit and the black pot in the log bright light.
And the sky of birds in the plumed voice charmed
Him up and he ran like a wind after the kindling flight
Past the blind barns and byres of the windless farm.

  In the poles of the year
When black birds died like priests in the cloaked hedge row
And over the cloth of counties the far hills rode near,
Under the one leaved trees ran a scarecrow of snow
And fast through the drifts of the thickets antlered like deer,

  Rags and prayers down the knee-
Deep hillocks and loud on the numbed lakes,
All night lost and long wading in the wake of the she-
Bird through the times and lands and tribes of the slow flakes.
Listen and look where she sails the goose plucked sea,

A Winter's Tale

   The sky, the bird, the bride,
The cloud, the need, the planted stars, the joy beyond
The fields of seed and the time dying flesh astride,
The heavens, the heaven, the grave, the burning font.
In the far ago land the door of his death glided wide,

   And the bird descended.
On a bread white hill over the cupped farm
And the lakes and floating fields and the river wended
Vales where he prayed to come to the last harm
And the home of prayers and fires, the tale ended.

   The dancing perishes
On the white, no longer growing green, and, minstrel dead,
The singing breaks in the snow shoed villages of wishes
That once cut the figures of birds on the deep bread
And over the glazed lakes skated the shapes of fishes

   Flying. The rite is shorn
Of nightingale and centaur dead horse. The springs wither
Back. Lines of age sleep on the stones till trumpeting dawn.
Exultation lies down. Time buries the spring weather
That belled and bounded with the fossil and the dew reborn.

   For the bird lay bedded
In a choir of wings, as though she slept or died,
And the wings glided wide and he was hymned and wedded,
And through the thighs of the engulfing bride,
The woman breasted and the heaven headed

   Bird, he was brought low
Burning in the bride bed of love, in the whirl-
Pool at the wanting center, in the folds
Of paradise, in the spun bud of the world.
And she rose with him flowering in her melting snow.

Poetry

DO NOT GO GENTLE INTO THAT GOOD NIGHT
by Dylan Thomas

Do not go gentle into that good night,
Old age should burn and rave at close of day;
Rage, rage against the dying of the light.

Though wise men at their end know dark is right,
Because their words had forked no lightning they
Do not go gentle into that good night.

Good men, the last wave by, crying how bright
Their frail deeds might have danced in a green bay
Rage, rage against the dying of the light.

Wild men who caught and sang the sun in flight,
And learn, too late, they grieved it on its way,
Do not go gentle into that good night.

Grave men, near death, who see with blinding sight
Blind eyes could blaze like meteors and be gay,
Rage, rage against the dying of the light.

And you, my father, there on the sad height,
Curse, bless, me now with your fierce tears, I pray.
Do not go gentle into that good night.
Rage, rage against the dying of the light.

GUIDED MISSILES EXPERIMENTAL RANGE
by Robert Conquest

Soft sounds and odours brim up through the night
A wealth below the level of the eye;
Out of a black, an almost violet sky
Abundance flowers into points of light.

Till from the south-west, as their low scream mars
And halts this warm hypnosis of the dark,
Three black automata cut swift and stark,
Shaped clearly by the backward flow of stars.

Stronger than lives, by empty purpose blinded,
The only thought their circuits can endure is
The target-hunting rigour of their flight;

And by that loveless haste I am reminded
Of Aeschylus' description of the Furies:
"O barren daughters of the fruitful night."

A GIRL IN THE SNOW (For T.)
by Robert Conquest

Autumn's attrition. Then this world laid waste
Under a low white sky, diffusing glare
On blurs of snow as motionless and bare
As the dead epoch where our luck is placed.

Till from the imprecise close distance flies,
Winged on your skis and stillness-breaking nerve
Colour, towards me down this vital curve,
Blue suit, bronze hair and honey-coloured eyes.

Under this hollow cloud, a sky of rime,
The eyes' one focus in an empty mirror
You come towards my arms until I hold

Close to my heart, beyond all fear and error,
A clear-cut warmth in this vague waste of cold:
A road of meaning through the shapeless time.

From *Poems*, by Robert Conquest; reprinted by permission of Macmillan & Company Ltd., and St. Martin's Press.

Poetry

A LEVEL OF ABSTRACTION
by Robert Conquest

Summer, stream and stillness:
A solstice of the heart
Where she calls to its fullness
That endless search, that art.

The clear sweet known stream
Could not abstract to absolute
Crystal: he broke from that dream
A heart made desolate
In preparation for
Extremes of fruitfulness.

Briefly a kingfisher
Slashes the motionless
Vision of soft grey water
Where grey-green willows bend
With violent speed and colour.

And yet is congruent
To blue deep clarities
Of a delighting mind
As he looks deep into eyes
Through which strong virtues bind
Into the body's grace
The reciprocal beauties
Of her heart and face.

The apparatus of paradise
Is here, is made their own.
Roses and dragonflies
Glow on water or lawn;
The gold leaf does not move;
The soft air has not stirred;
She stands, the form of love.

Love is a general word.

EPISTEMOLOGY OF POETRY
by Robert Conquest

Across the long-curved bight or bay
The waves move clear beneath the day
And, rolling in obliquely, each
Unwinds its white torque up the beach.

Beneath the full semantic sun
The twisting currents race and run.
Words and evaluations start.
And yet the verse should play its part.

Below a certain threshold light
Is insufficient to excite
Those mechanisms which the eye
Constructs its daytime objects by:

A different system wakes behind
The dark, wide pupils till the mind
Accepts an image of this sea
As clear, but in an altered key.

Now darkness falls. And poems attempt
Light reconciling done and dreamt.
I do not find it in the rash
Disruption of the lightning flash.

Those vivid rigours stun the verse
And neural structure still prefers
The moon beneath whose moderate light
The great seas glitter in the bight.

HUMANITIES
by Robert Conquest

Hypnotized and told they're seeing red
When really looking at a yellow wall
The children speak of orange seen instead:
Split to such rainbow through that verbal lens
It takes a whole heart's effort to see all
The human plenum as a single ens.

The word on the objective breath must be
A wind to winnow the emotive out;
Music can generalize the inner sea
In dark harmonics of the blinded heart;
But, hot with certainty and keen with doubt,
Verse sweats out heartfelt knowledge, clear-eyed art.

Is it, when paper roses make us sneeze,
A mental or a physical event?
The word can freeze us to such categories,
Yet verse can warm the mirrors of the word
And through their loose distortions represent
The scene, the heart, the life, as they occurred.

—In a dream's blueness or a sunset's bronze
Poets seek the images of love and wonder,
But absolutes of music, gold or swans
Are only froth unless they go to swell
That harmony of science pealing under
The poem's waters like a sunken bell.

CHILD WAKING
by E. J. Scovell

The child sleeps in the daytime,
With his abandoned, with his jetsam look,
On the bare mattress, across the cot's corner;
Covers and toys thrown out, a routine labour.

Relaxed in sleep and light,
Face upwards, never so clear a prey to eyes;
Like a walled town surprised out of the air
All life called in, yet all laid bare

To the enemy above—
He has taken cover in daylight, gone to ground
In his own short length, his body strong in bleached
Blue cotton and his arms outstretched.

From *The River Steamer*, 1956. Reprinted by permission of The Cresset Press.

Now he opens eyes but not
To see at first; they reflect the light like snow,
And I wait in doubt if he sleeps or wakes, till I see
Slight pain of effort at the boundary,

And hear how the trifling wound
Of bewilderment fetches a caverned cry
As he crosses out of sleep—at once to recover
His place and poise, and smile as I lift him over.

But I recall the blue-
White snowfield of his eyes empty of sight
High between dream and day, and think how there
The soul might rise visible as a flower.

The Piper   Eugene Harris
Courtesy of POPULAR PHOTOGRAPHY

GENESIS

by Geoffrey Hill

I

Against the burly air I strode,
Where the tight ocean heaves its load,
Crying the miracles of God.

And first I brought the sea to bear
Upon the dead weight of the land;
And the waves flourished at my prayer,
The rivers spawned their sand.

And where the streams were salt and full
The tough pig-headed salmon strove,
Curbing the ebb and the tide's pull,
To reach the steady hills above.

II

The second day I stood and saw
The osprey plunge with triggered claw,
Feathering blood along the shore,
To lay the living sinew bare.

And the third day I cried: "Beware
The soft-voiced owl, the ferret's smile,
The hawk's deliberate stoop in air,
Cold eyes, and bodies hooped in steel,
Forever bent upon the kill."

III

And I renounced, on the fourth day,
This fierce and unregenerate clay,

Building as a huge myth for man
The watery Leviathan,

And made the glove-winged albatross
Scour the ashes of the sea
Where Capricorn and Zero cross,
A brooding immortality—
Such as the charmed phoenix has
In the unwithering tree.

IV

The phoenix burns as cold as frost;
And, like a legendary ghost,
The phantom-bird goes wild and lost,
Upon a pointless ocean tossed.

So, the fifth day, I turned again
To flesh and blood and the blood's pain.

V

On the sixth day, as I rode
In haste about the works of God,
With spurs I plucked the horse's blood.

By blood we live, the hot, the cold,
To ravage and redeem the world:
There is no bloodless myth will hold.

And by Christ's blood are men made free
Though in close shrouds their bodies lie
Under the rough pelt of the sea;

Though Earth has rolled beneath her weight
The bones that cannot bear the light.

Reprinted by permission of Geoffrey Hill and Andre Deutsch Ltd.

TIME AND MOTION STUDY
by Iain Fletcher

What are they? Why, only qualities of light
That once or twice were fractured into form:
Short wisps or rags that sting the touch or sight,
Dancing in famine through a night of storm:
   Cold images of Heat corrupt within,
   Whose mercies rattle in a bowl of tin.

But being not worshipped, being forgotten, brood
In eyes that fire the night with mysteries
And drag the heart to manufacture good
Where no good thing was ever held to rise:
   What I would do, I do not, doing
   All that I hate; pursued, myself pursuing.

Hunting myself in others, hunting what
Was never life to be quarry, only sired—
Member of darkness—by a swirling phantom, not
That warmth and tenseness have desired,
   Gifts never nourished by my cruel arts:
   A blinding Grace can only crack dry hearts.

But these all breathe out "illusion," are
Heavily unreal, a drugged metaphysician,
Plotting a marriage of retina and star
At some rare locus that is not position.
   Somewhere to find that sweet duality
   Of mind and flesh the heart would magnify.

My life is after Fall and Flood and Passion,
When Prophets wither into irony;
When the dead cosmos in a formal fashion
Translates all grievings into vanity,
   My life is after Unity, and wanders still
   In penitential valleys of the will.

A cradle swayed under a barren roof,
Or on the waves where Orpheus sowed his faith;
The horned God raging on a bull's black hoof.
My life lies in the diocese of wraith,
   My life lies after wrath, being so unreal
   There are no darker flashes to conceal.

Nor the severities of beauty, nor
The haunting disk of one occulted face;
The moral charm that all too many wore,
Too pertinently confident of Grace,
   My life is after Space and Time and Will,
   My life is always moved, but always still,

None moves me but my weakness, weak
Beyond all judgment, as beyond all law;
How should I ask for witnesses to speak,
Tethered in graves, watchmen who never saw,
   But in their majesty of distance gave
   Me mandate to believe these sighs might save.

Reprinted by permission of Iain Fletcher.

MASTERS
by Kingsley Amis

That horse whose rider fears to jump will fall,
Riflemen miss if orders sound unsure;
They only are secure who seem secure;
   Who lose their voice, lose all.

Those whom heredity or guns have made
Masters, must show it by a common speech;
Expected words in the same tone from each
   Will always be obeyed.

Likewise with stance, with gestures, and with face;
No more than mouth need move when words are said,
No more than hand to strike, or point ahead;
   Like slaves, limbs learn their place.

In triumph as in mutiny unmoved,
These make their public act their private good,
Their words in lounge or courtroom understood,
   But themselves never loved.

The eyes that will not look, the twitching cheek,
The hands that sketch what mouth would fear to own,
These only make us known, and we are known
   Only as we are weak:

By yielding mastery the will is freed,
For it is by surrender that we live,
And we are taken if we wish to give,
   Are needed if we need.

From *A Case of Samples* by Kingsley Amis. Harcourt, Brace and Company. Copyright 1956 by Kingsley Amis.

THE SOURCES OF THE PAST

by KINGSLEY AMIS

A broken flower-stem, a broken vase,
   A match-box torn in two and thrown
Among the lumps of glass:
   At the last meeting, these alone
Record its ruptures, point its violence,
   And, it seems, are ready to maintain
This charted look of permanence
   In the first moment's pain.

But now the door slams, the steps retreat;
   Into one softness night will blur
The diverse, the hard street;
   And memory will soon prefer
That polished set of symbols, glass and
   rose
(By slight revision), to the real mess
   Of stumbling, arguing, yells, blows
Or tears: to real distress.

All fragments of the past, near and far,
   Come down to us framed in a calm
No contemplations jar;
   But they grub it up from lapse of time,
And, could we strip that firm order away,
   What crude agitation would be shown:
What aimless hauntings behind clay,
   What fevers behind stone?

A DREAM OF FAIR WOMEN

by KINGSLEY AMIS

The door still swinging to, and girls revive,
Aeronauts in the utmost altitudes
   Of boredom fainting, dive
Into the bright oxygen of my nod;
Angels as well, a squadron of draped nudes,
   They roar towards their god.

Militant all, they fight to take my hat,
No more as yet; the other men retire
   Insulted, gestured at;
Each girl presses on me her share of what
Makes up the barn-door target of desire;
   And I am a crack shot.

Speech fails them, amorous, but each one's look,
Endorsed in other ways, begs me to sign
   Her body's autograph-book;
"Me first, Kingsley; I'm cleverest," each declares,
But no gourmet races downstairs to dine,
   Nor will I race upstairs.

Feigning aplomb, perhaps for half an hour,
I hover, and am shown by each princess
   The entrance to her tower,
Open, in that its tenant throws the key
At once to anyone, but not unless
   That anyone is me.

Now from the corridor their fathers cheer,
Their brothers, their young men; the cheers increase
   As soon as I appear;

The World, the Times

From each I win a handshake and sincere
Congratulations; from the chief of police
   A nod, a wink, a leer.

This over, all delay is over too;
The first eight girls (the roster now agreed)
   Leap on me and undo . . .
But honesty impels me to confess
That this is "all a dream," which was, indeed,
   Not difficult to guess.

But wait: not "just a dream," because, though good
And beautiful, it is also true, and hence
   Is rarely understood;

Who would choose any feasible ideal
In here and now's giant circumference
   If that small room were real?

Only the best; the others find, have found
Love's ordinary distances too great,
   And eager, stand their ground;
Map-drunk explorers, dry-land sailors, they
See no arrival that can compensate
   For boredom on the way.

And, seeming doctrinaire, but really weak,
Limelighted dolls guttering in their brain,
   They come with me, to seek
The halls of theoretical delight,
The women of that ever-fresh terrain,
   The night after tonight.

THE WORLD, THE TIMES
by Donald Hall

The habit of these years is constant choice.
Each act, each moment, is political.
Enormous power responds to one man's voice.
The President and Cabinet are on call.
Great freedom walks in us, and we command
The universe forever to expand.

The world, the times, the country, and the age
Maneuver toward eventuality.
We wait the coming; maybe in a rage
Great conquerors will come, our leaders be,
To take the generations into war
Until we men and women are no more;

Or maybe at some Easter we will find
A martyr who by absence wins the earth,
Who walked in life before us who were blind,
And whom we will await in second birth;
So live in holy darkness, and be sure
Our souls if not our bodies are secure.

However may the future be disguised,
I praise the moment, when no world is made.
Anarchy works to kill the civilized
And nothing will prevent a mortal raid
Except defense with violence again
Within the minds of many single men.

Now men are Persian in their ease, and fling

From *Exiles and Marriages* by Donald Hall. Copyright 1955 by Donald Hall. Reprinted by permission of The Viking Press, Inc., New York.

All difficulties out, for the freed man
Believes no good or ill in anything,
But loves his minute's pleasure, or what can
So glorify his days that they will be
Productive of his own security.

There's no security except the grave;
There's much belief in what does not exist.
All that is excellent is hard to save,
Since every man is partly anarchist.

We live by choice, and choose with every act
That form or chaos move from mind to fact.

I name an age of choice and discontent
Whose emblem is "the difficult to choose."
Each man is free to act, but his intent
Must circumscribe what he may not refuse.
Each moment is political, and we
Are clothed in nothing but mortality.

LOVE CALLS US TO THE THINGS OF THIS WORLD
by Richard Wilbur

    The eyes open to a cry of pulleys,
And spirited from sleep, the astounded soul
Hangs for a moment bodiless and simple
As false dawn.
               Outside the open window
The morning air is all awash with angels.

    Some are in bed-sheets, some are in blouses,
Some are in smocks: but truly there they are.
Now they are rising together in calm swells
Of halcyon feeling, filling whatever they wear
With the deep joy of their impersonal breathing;

    Now they are flying in place, conveying
The terrible speed of their omnipresence, moving
And staying like white water; and now of a sudden
They swoon down into so rapt a quiet
That nobody seems to be there.
               The soul shrinks

    From all that it is about to remember
From the punctual rape of every blessèd day,
And cries,
      "Oh, let there be nothing on earth but laundry,

Copyright, 1956 by Richard Wilbur. Reprinted from his volume, *Things of This World*, by permission of Harcourt, Brace and Company, Inc.

Looking into History

Nothing but rosy hands in the rising steam
And clear dances done in the sight of heaven."

Yet, as the sun acknowledges
With a warm look the world's hunks and colors,
The soul descends once more in bitter love
To accept the waking body, saying now
In a changed voice as the man yawns and rises,

"Bring them down from their ruddy gallows;
Let there be clean linen for the backs of thieves;
Let lovers go fresh and sweet to be undone,
And the heaviest nuns walk in a pure floating
Of dark habits,
         keeping their difficult balance."

LOOKING INTO HISTORY

by Richard Wilbur

I. Five soldiers fixed by Mathew Brady's eye
   Stand in a land subdued beyond belief.
   Belief might lend them life again. I try
   Like orphaned Hamlet working up his grief

   To see my spellbound fathers in these men
   Who, breathless in their amber atmosphere,
   Show but the postures men affected then
   And the hermit faces of a finished year.

   The guns and gear and all are strange until
   Beyond the tents I glimpse a file of trees
   Verging a road that struggles up a hill.
   They're sycamores.
                The long-abated breeze

   Flares in those boughs I know, and hauls the sound
   Of guns and a great forest in distress.
   Fathers, I know my cause, and we are bound
   Beyond that hill to fight at Wilderness.

II. But trick your eyes with Birnam Wood, or think
   How fire-cast shadows of the bankside trees

Poetry

    Rode on the back of Simois to sink
    In the wide waters. Reflect how history's

    Changes are like the sea's, which mauls and mulls
    Its salvage of the world in shifty waves,
    Shrouding in evergreen the oldest hulls
    And yielding views of its confounded graves

    To the new moon, the sun, or any eye
    That in its shallow shoreward version sees
    The pebbles charging with a deathless cry
    And caragreen memorials of trees.

III. Now, old man of the sea,
    I start to understand:
    The will will find no stillness
    Back in a stilled land.

    The dead give no command
    And shall not find their voice
    Till they be mustered by
    Some present fatal choice.

    Let me now rejoice
    In all impostures, take
    The shape of lion or leopard,
    Boar, or watery snake,

    Or like the comber break,
    Yet in the end stand fast
    And by some fervent fraud
    Father the waiting past,

    Resembling at the last
    The self-established tree
    That draws all waters toward
    Its live formality.

PART VI · PROSE

During the last half-century mankind has suffered a first great war, a futile peace, a world-wide depression, mass unemployment, the fearful rise of political nationalisms, a second even greater war, and a second even more doubtful peace. These were gigantic events, in a troubled century. Before them the individual has often seemed to dwindle into insignificance, or at least to feel helpless, as if historically lost, and full of self-distrust. The essays in this section are intended to present the human problems that arise in such a time, to explore causes and effects, and to suggest ways out, even if only paths and not highways.

William Faulkner's recent remarks on "the old verities and truths of the heart" would have sounded strange and irrelevant thirty years ago, but today his words may well set us looking for a sense of the individual and society, as earlier expressed by such men as Jefferson and Macaulay, a sense of the sort we have lost and may wish again to possess. Whitman and Turner recall us to the origins of a still powerful optimism in America, while Hayes reminds us of an even older responsibility, that we must identify our place in a world society with traditions of its own. It is only within this society that we, with the help of discussions like those by Kouwenhoven and Adams, can begin to name and evaluate our own characteristics.

Though, as White suggests, we are all fond of the old, Beard and Drucker indicate some of the issues, both general and specific, that will face us during our time and demand new solutions. Beard also raises the question whether anything has really changed and offers some hope for believing that the old human forces are still strong, working under new conditions.

World War II accentuated the existing problems for individual and society while bringing men and nations together as never before to assert their desire for freedom and to work for common goals. It solved few of the old problems for long: *The Races of Mankind* indicates one of the oldest even as it persuades us that we ought to be able to solve it. But there was still war, and the war had become unlike any other men had seen, for it brought the atomic bomb. The methods of modern science, described by Barnett, had led, when pressed into military service, to the test over New Mexico and the bomber over Nagasaki. In Frisch's narrative, we are made aware of the hu-

Prose

man element in the scientific discoveries that led to this event. The following essays warn us of the limitations of science and persuade us that its activities must be directed to human ends, the "old verities" of Faulkner's phrase.

The concluding selections suggest that human belief is central to all the concerns of the writers in this section. Arnold's poem is the most famous of nineteenth-century statements of doubt, the terms of which Lippmann makes clear for our time. Forster, as a thinking wise man, represents the honesty and self-trust men must regain if they are to deserve any freedom within their society or earn the right to solve their own problems and live by their chosen values.

REMARKS UPON RECEIVING THE NOBEL PRIZE
by WILLIAM FAULKNER

I FEEL that this award was not made to me as a man but to my work—a life's work in the agony and sweat of the human spirit, not for glory and least of all for profit, but to create out of the materials of the human spirit something which did not exist before. So this award is only mine in trust. It will not be difficult to find a dedication for the money part of it commensurate with the purpose and significance of its origin. But I would like to do the same with the acclaim too, by using this moment as a pinnacle from which I might be listened to by the young men and women already dedicated to the same anguish and travail, among whom is already that one who will some day stand here where I am standing.

Our tragedy today is a general and universal physical fear so long sustained by now that we can even bear it. There are no longer problems of the spirit. There is only the question: when will I be blown up? Because of this, the young man or woman writing today has forgotten the problems of the human heart in conflict with itself which alone can make good writing because only that is worth writing about, worth the agony and the sweat.

He must learn them again. He must teach himself that the basest of all things is to be afraid; and, teaching himself that, forget it forever, leaving no room in his workshop for anything but the old verities and truths of the heart, the old universal truths lacking which any story is ephemeral and doomed—love and honor and pity and pride and compassion and sacrifice. Until he does so he labors under a curse. He writes not of love but of lust, of defeats in which nobody loses anything of value, of victories without hope and worst of all without pity or compassion. His griefs grieve on no universal bones, leaving no scars. He writes not of the heart but of the glands.

Until he relearns these things he will write as though he stood among and watched the end of man. I decline to accept the end of man. It is easy enough to say that man is immortal simply because he will endure; that when the last ding-dong of doom has clanged and faded from the last worthless rock hanging tideless in the last red and dying evening, that even then there will still be one more sound: that of his puny inexhaustible voice, still talking. I refuse to accept this. I believe that man will not merely endure: he will prevail. He is immortal, not because he alone among creatures has an inexhaustible voice, but because he has a soul, a spirit capable of compassion and sacrifice and endurance. The poet's, the writer's, duty is to write about these things. It is his privilege to help man endure by lifting his heart, by reminding him of the courage and honor and hope and pride and compassion and pity and sacrifice which have been the glory of his past. The poet's voice need not merely be the record of man, it can be one of the props, the pillars to help him endure and prevail.

William Faulkner, Nobel Prize Speech. Used with the permission of Random House, Inc.

ON NATURAL ARISTOCRACY

by Thomas Jefferson

Monticello, *October 28, 1813.*

[To John Adams]

... I agree with you that there is a natural aristocracy among men. The grounds of this are virtue and talents. Formerly, bodily powers gave place among the aristoi. But since the invention of gunpowder has armed the weak as well as the strong with missile death, bodily strength, like beauty, good humor, politeness and other accomplishments, has become but an auxiliary ground for distinction. There is also an artificial aristocracy, founded on wealth and birth, without either virtue or talents; for with these it would belong to the first class. The natural aristocracy I consider as the most precious gift of nature, for the instruction, the trusts, and government of society. And indeed, it would have been inconsistent in creation to have formed man for the social state, and not to have provided virtue and wisdom enough to manage the concerns of the society. May we not even say, that that form of government is the best, which provides the most effectually for a pure selection of these natural aristoi into the offices of government? The artificial aristocracy is a mischievous ingredient in government, and provision should be made to prevent its ascendancy. On the question, what is the best provision, you and I differ; but we differ as rational friends, using the free exercise of our own reason, and mutually indulging its errors. You think it best to put the pseudo-aristoi into a separate chamber of legislation, where they may be hindered from doing mischief by their co-ordinate branches, and where, also, they may be a protection to wealth against the Agrarian and plundering enterprises of the majority of the people. I think that to give them power in order to prevent them from doing mischief, is arming them for it, and increasing instead of remedying the evil. For if the co-ordinate branches can arrest their action, so may they that of the co-ordinates. Mischief may be done negatively as well as positively. Of this, a cabal in the Senate of the United States has furnished many proofs. Nor do I believe them necessary to protect the wealthy; because enough of these will find their way into every branch of the legislation, to protect themselves. From fifteen to twenty legislatures of our own, in action for thirty years past, have proved that no fears of an equalization of property are to be apprehended from them. I think the best remedy is exactly that provided by all our constitutions, to leave to the citizens the free election and separation of the aristoi from the pseudo-aristoi, of the wheat from the chaff. In general they will elect the really good and wise. In some instances, wealth may corrupt, and birth blind them; but not in sufficient degree to endanger the society.

It is probable that our difference of opinion may, in some measure, be produced by a difference of character in those among whom we live. From what I have seen of Massachusetts and Connecticut myself, and still more from what I have heard, and the character given of the former by yourself, who know them so much better, there seems to be in those two States a traditionary reverence for certain families, which has rendered the offices of the government nearly hereditary in those families. I presume that from an early period of your history, members of those families happening to possess virtue and talents, have honestly exercised them for the good of the people, and by their services have endeared their names to them. In coupling Connecticut with you, I mean it politically only, not morally. For having made the Bible the common law of their land, they seemed to have modeled their morality on the story of Jacob and Laban. But although this hereditary succession to office with you, may, in some degree, be founded in real family merit, yet in a much higher degree, it has proceeded from your strict alliance of Church and State. These families are canonized in the eyes of the people on common principles, "you tickle me, and I will tickle you." In Virginia we have nothing of this. Our clergy, before the revolution, having been secured against rivalship by fixed salaries, did not give themselves the trouble of acquiring influence over the people. Of wealth, there were great accumulations in particular families, handed down from generation to generation, under the English law of entails. But the only object of ambition for the wealthy was a seat in the King's Council. All their court then was paid to the crown and its creatures; and they Philipised in all collisions between the King and the people. Hence they were unpopular; and that unpopularity continues attached to their names. A Randolph, a Carter, or a Burwell must have great personal superiority over a common competitor to be elected by the people even at this day. At the first session of our legislature after the Declaration of Independence, we passed a law abolishing entails. And this was followed by one abolishing the privilege of primogeniture, and dividing the lands of intestates equally among all their children, or other representatives. These laws, drawn by myself, laid the ax to the foot of pseudo-aristocracy. And had another which I prepared been adopted by the legislature, our work would have been complete. It was a bill for the more general diffusion of learning. This proposed to divide every county into wards of five or six miles square, like your townships; to establish in each ward a free school for reading, writing and common arithmetic; to provide for the annual selection of the best subjects from these schools, who might receive, at the public expense, a higher degree of education at a district school; and from these district schools to select a certain number of the most promising subjects, to be completed at an University, where all the useful sciences should be taught. Worth and genius would thus have been sought out from every condition of life, and completely prepared by education for defeating the competition of wealth and birth for public trusts. My proposition had, for a further object, to impart to these wards those portions of self-government for which they are best qualified, by confiding to them the care of their poor, their roads, police, elections, the nomination of jurors, administration of justice in small cases, elementary exercises of militia; in short, to have made them little republics, with a warden at the head of each, for all those concerns which, being under their eye, they would better manage than the larger republics of the county or State. A general call of ward meetings by their wardens on the same day through the State, would at any time produce the genuine sense of the people on any required point, and would enable the State to act in mass, as your people have so often done, and with so much effect by their town meetings. The law for religious freedom, which made a part of this system, having put down the aristocracy of the clergy, and restored to the citizen the freedom of the mind, and those of entails and descents nurturing an equality of condition among them, this on education would have raised the mass of the people to the high ground of moral respectability necessary to their own safety, and to orderly government; and would have completed the great object of qualifying them to select the veritable aristoi, for the trusts of government, to the exclusion of the pseudalists; and the same Theognis who has furnished the epigraphs of your two letters, assures us that "Ουδεμιαν πω, Κυρν', αγαθοι πολιν ωλεσαν ανδρες." [Not any state, Curnus, have good men yet destroyed.] Although this law has not yet been acted on but in a small and inefficient degree, it is still considered as before the legislature, with other bills of the revised code, not yet taken up, and I have great hope that some patriotic spirit will, at a favorable moment, call it up, and make it the key-stone of the arch of our government.

With respect to aristocracy, we should further consider, that before the establishment of the American States, nothing was known to history but the man of the old world, crowded within limits either small or overcharged, and steeped in the vices which that situation generates. A government adapted to such men would be one thing; but a very different one, that for the man of these States. Here everyone may have land to labor for himself, if he chooses; or, preferring the exercise of any other industry, may exact for it such compensation as not only to afford a comfortable subsistence, but wherewith to provide for a cessation from labor in old age. Everyone, by his property, or by his satisfactory situation, is interested in the support of law and order. And such men may safely and advantageously reserve to themselves a wholesome control over their public affairs, and a degree of freedom, which, in the hands of the *canaille* of the cities of Europe, would be instantly perverted to the demolition and destruction of everything public and private. The history of the last twenty-five years of France, and of the last forty years in America, nay of its last two hundred years, proves the truth of both parts of this observation.

But even in Europe a change has sensibly taken place in the mind of man. Science had liberated the ideas of those who read and reflect, and the American example had kindled feelings of right in the people. An insurrection has consequently begun, of science, talents, and courage, against rank and birth, which have fallen into contempt. It has failed in its first effort, because the mobs of the cities, the instrument used for its accomplishment, debased by ignorance, poverty and vice, could not be restrained to rational action. But the world will recover from the panic of this first catastrophe. Science is progressive, and talents and enterprise on the alert. Resort may be had to the people of the country, a more governable power from their principles and subordination; and rank, and birth, and tinsel-aristocracy will finally shrink into insignificance, even there. This, however, we have no right to meddle with. It suffices for us, if the moral and physical condition of our own citizens qualifies them to select the able and good for the direction of their government, with a recurrence of elections at such short periods as will enable them to displace an unfaithful servant, before the mischief he meditates may be irremediable.

I have thus stated my opinion on a point on which we differ, not with a view to controversy, for we are both too old to change opinions which are the result of a long life of inquiry and reflection; but on the suggestions of a former letter of yours, that we ought not to die before we have explained ourselves to each other. We acted in perfect harmony, through a long and perilous contest for our liberty and independence. A constitution has been acquired, which, though neither of us thinks perfect, yet both consider as competent to render our fellow citizens the happiest and the securest on whom the sun has ever shone. If we do not think exactly alike as to its imperfections, it matters little to our country, which, after devoting to it long lives of disinterested labor, we have delivered over to our successors in life, who will be able to take care of it and of themselves.

Of the pamphlet on aristocracy which has been sent to you, or who may be its author, I have heard nothing but through your letter. If the person you suspect, it may be known from the quaint, mystical, and hyperbolical ideas, involved in affected, new-fangled and pedantic terms which stamp his writings. Whatever it be, I hope your quiet is not to be affected at this day by the rudeness or intemperance of scribblers; but that you may continue in tranquillity to live and to rejoice in the prosperity of our country, until it shall be your own wish to take your seat among the aristoi who have gone before you. Ever and affectionately yours.

LETTER TO A CORRESPONDENT IN AMERICA
by Thomas Babington Macaulay

Sir: The four volumes of the *Colonial History of New York* reached me safely. I assure you that I shall value them highly. They contain much to interest an English as well as an American reader. Pray, accept my thanks, and convey them to the Regents of the University.

You are surprised to learn that I have not a high opinion of Mr. Jefferson, and I am surprised at your surprise. I am certain that I never wrote a line, and that I never in Parliament, in conversation or even on the hustings—a place where it is the fashion to court the populace—uttered a word indicating an opinion that the supreme authority in a State ought to be entrusted to the majority of citizens, in other words, to the poorest and most ignorant part of society. I have long been convinced that institutions purely democratic must, sooner or later, destroy liberty or civilization, or both.

In Europe, where the population is dense, the effect of such institutions would be almost instantaneous. What happened lately in France is an example. In 1848 a pure democracy was established there. During a short time there was reason to expect a general spoliation, a national bankruptcy, a new partition of the soil, a maximum of prices, a ruinous load of taxation laid on the rich for the purpose of supporting the poor in idleness. Such a system would, in twenty years, have made France as poor and barbarous as the France of the Carlovingians. Happily, the danger was averted; and now there is a despotism, a silent tribune, an enslaved press. Liberty is gone, but civilization has been saved.

I have not the smallest doubt that, if we had a purely democratic government here, the effect would be the same. Either the poor would plunder the rich and civilization would perish, or order and property would be saved by a strong military government, and liberty would perish. You may think that your country enjoys an exemption from these evils. I will frankly own to you that I am of a very different opinion. Your fate I believe to be certain, though it is deferred by a physical cause. As long as you have a boundless extent of fertile and unoccupied land, your laboring population will be far more at ease than the laboring population of the old world, and, while that is the case, the Jeffersonian polity may continue to exist without causing any fatal calamity. But the time will come when New England will be as thickly populated as Old England. Wages will be as low, and will fluctuate as much with you as with us. You will have your Manchesters and Birminghams, and in those Manchesters and Birminghams hundreds of thousands of artisans will assuredly be sometimes out of work. Then your institutions will be fairly brought to the test. Distress everywhere makes the laborer mutinous and discontented, and inclines him to listen with eagerness to agitators who tell him that it is a monstrous iniquity that one man should have a million while another cannot get a full meal.

In bad years there is plenty of grumbling here, and sometimes a little rioting. But it matters little, for here the sufferers are not the rulers. The supreme power is in the hands of a class, numerous indeed, but select; of an educated class; of a class which is, and knows itself to be, deeply interested in the security of property and maintenance of order. Accordingly, the malcontents are firmly yet gently restrained. The bad time is got over without robbing the wealthy to relieve the indigent. The springs of national prosperity soon begin to flow again; work is plentiful, wages rise, and all is tranquillity and cheerfulness. I have seen England pass three or four times through such critical seasons as I have described.

Through such seasons, the United States will have to pass in the course of the next century, if not of this. How will you pass through them? I heartily wish you a good deliverance. But my reason and my wishes are at war, and I cannot help foreboding the worst. It is quite plain that your government will never be able to restrain a distressed and discontented majority. For with you the majority is the government, and has the rich, who are always a minority, absolutely at its mercy.

The day will come when, in the State of New York, a multitude of people, none of whom has had more than half a breakfast, or expects to have more than half a dinner, will choose a Legislature. Is it possible to doubt what sort of Legislature will be chosen? On one side is a statesman preaching patience, respect for vested rights, strict observance of public faith. On the other is a demagogue ranting about the tyranny of capitalists and usurers, and asking why anybody should be permitted to drink champagne and to ride in a carriage, while thousands of honest folks are in want of necessaries. Which of the two candidates is likely to be preferred by a workingman who hears his children cry for more bread? I seriously apprehend that you will in some such season of adversity as I have described, do things which will prevent prosperity from returning; that you will act like people who should in a year of scarcity devour all the seed corn, and thus make the next year a year not of scarcity, but of absolute famine. There will be, I fear, spoliation. There is nothing to stop you. Your Constitution is all sail and no anchor.

As I said before, when a society has entered on this downward progress, either civilization or liberty must perish. Either some Caesar or Napoleon will seize the reins of government with a strong hand, or your Republic will be as fearfully plundered and laid waste by barbarians in the 20th Century as the Roman Empire was in the fifth—with this difference, that the Huns and Vandals who ravaged the Roman Empire came from without, and that your Huns and Vandals will have been engendered within your own country by your own institutions.

Thinking thus, of course, I cannot reckon Jefferson among the benefactors of mankind. I readily admit that his intentions were good and his abilities considerable. Odious stories have been circulated about his private life; but I do not know on what evidence those stories rest, and I think it probable that they are false or monstrously exaggerated. I have no doubt that I shall derive both pleasure and information from your account of him.

T. B. MACAULAY

Holly Lodge
May 23, 1857

---

from Preface to 1855 Edition of "LEAVES OF GRASS"
by WALT WHITMAN

AMERICA DOES NOT REPEL the past or what it has produced under its forms or amid other politics or the idea of castes or the old religions . . . accepts the lesson with calmness . . . is not so impatient as has been supposed that the slough still sticks to opinions and manners and literature while the life which served its requirements has passed into the new life of the new forms . . . perceives that the corpse

Used with the permission of Doubleday & Company, Inc.

is slowly borne from the eating and sleeping rooms of the house . . . perceives that it waits a little while in the door . . . that it was fittest for its days . . . that its action has descended to the stalwart and well-shaped heir who approaches . . . and that he shall be fittest for his days.

The Americans of all nations at any time upon the earth have probably the fullest poetical nature. The United States themselves are essentially the greatest poem. . . . Other states indicate themselves in their deputies . . . but the genius of the United States is not best or most in its executives or legislatures, nor in its ambassadors or authors or colleges or churches or parlors, nor even in its newspapers or inventors . . . but always most in the common people. Their manners, speech, dress, friendships—the freshness and candor of their physiognomy—the picturesque looseness of their carriage . . . their deathless attachment to freedom—their aversion to anything indecorous or soft or mean—the practical acknowledgment of the citizens of one state by the citizens of all other states—the fierceness of their roused resentment—their curiosity and welcome of novelty—their self-esteem and wonderful sympathy—their susceptibility to a slight—the air they have of persons who never knew how it felt to stand in the presence of superiors—the fluency of their speech—their delight in music, the sure symptom of manly tenderness and native elegance of soul . . . their good temper and openhandedness—the terrible significance of their elections—the President's taking off his hat to them not they to him—these too are unrhymed poetry. It awaits the gigantic and generous treatment worthy of it. . . .

The American poets are to enclose old and new, for America is the race of races. Of them a bard is to be commensurate with a people. To him the other continents arrive as contributions . . . he gives them reception for their sake and his own sake. His spirit responds to his country's spirit . . . he incarnates its geography and natural life and rivers and lakes. Mississippi with annual freshets and changing chutes, Missouri and Columbia and Ohio and Saint Lawrence with the falls and beautiful masculine Hudson, do not embouchure where they spend themselves more than they embouchure into him. The blue breadth over the inland sea of Virginia and Maryland and the sea off Massachusetts and Maine and over Manhattan bay and over Champlain and Erie and over Ontario and Huron and Michigan and Superior, and over the Texan and Mexican and Floridian and Cuban seas and over the seas off California and Oregon, is not tallied by the blue breadth of the waters below more than the breadth of above and below is tallied by him. When the long Atlantic coast stretches longer and the Pacific coast stretches longer he easily stretches with them north or south. He spans between them also from east to west and reflects what is between them. On him rise solid growths that offset the growths of pine and cedar and hemlock and liveoak and locust and chestnut and cypress and hickory and limetree and cottonwood and tuliptree and cactus and wildvine and tamarind and persimmon . . . and tangles as tangled as any canebreak or swamp . . . and forests coated with transparent ice and icicles hanging from the boughs and crackling in the wind . . . and sides and peaks of mountains . . . and pasturage sweet and free as savannah or upland or prairie . . . with flights and songs and screams that answer those of the wildpigeon and highhold and orchard-oriole and coot and surf-duck and redshouldered-hawk and fish-hawk and white-ibis and indian-hen and cat-owl and water-pheasant and qua-bird and pied-sheldrake and blackbird and mockingbird and buzzard and condor and night-heron and eagle. . . .

Of all nations the United States with veins full of poetical stuff most need poets and will doubtless have the greatest and use them the greatest. Their Presidents shall not be their common referee so much as their poets shall. Of all mankind the great poet is the equable man. Not in him but off from him things are grotesque or eccentric or fail of their sanity. Nothing out of its place is good and nothing in its place is bad. He bestows on every object or quality its fit proportions neither more nor less. He is the arbiter of the diverse and he is the key. He is the equalizer of his age and land . . . he supplies what wants supplying and checks what wants checking. . . .

The greatest poet hardly knows pettiness or triviality. If he breathes into any thing that was before thought small it dilates with the grandeur and life of the universe. He is a seer . . . he is individual . . . he is complete in himself . . . the others are as good as he, only he sees it and they do not. He is not one of the chorus . . . he does not stop for any regulations . . . he is the president of regulation. . . .

The land and sea, the animals, fishes and birds, the sky of heaven and the orbs, the forests mountains and rivers, are not small themes . . . but folks expect of the poet to indicate more than the beauty and dignity which always attach to dumb real objects . . . they expect him to indicate the path between reality and their souls. Men and women perceive the beauty well enough . . . probably as well as he. The passionate tenacity of hunters, woodmen, early risers, cultivators of gardens and orchards and fields, the love of healthy women for the manly form, seafaring persons, drivers of horses, the passion for light and the open air, all is an old varied sign of the unfailing perception of beauty and of a residence of the poetic in outdoor people. They can never be assisted by poets to perceive . . . some may but they never can. The poetic quality is not marshalled in rhyme or uniformity or abstract addresses to things nor in melancholy complaints or good precepts, but is the life of these and much else and is in the soul. . . . All beauty comes from beautiful blood and a beautiful brain. If the greatnesses are in conjunction in a man or woman it is enough . . . the fact will prevail through the universe . . . but the gaggery and gilt of a million years will not prevail. Who troubles himself about his ornaments or fluency is lost. This is what you shall do: Love the earth and sun and the animals, despise riches, give alms to every one that asks, stand up for the stupid and crazy, devote your income and labor to others, hate tyrants, argue not concerning God, have patience and indulgence toward the people, take off your hat to nothing known or unknown or to any man or number of men, go freely with powerful uneducated persons and with the young and with the mothers of families, read these leaves in the open air every season of every year of your life, re-examine all you have been told at school or church or in any book, dismiss whatever insults your own soul, and your very flesh shall be a great poem and have the richest fluency not only in its words but in the silent lines of its lips and face and between the lashes of your eyes and in every motion and joint of your body. . . . The poet shall not spend his time in unneeded work. He shall know that the ground is always ready plowed and manured . . . others may not know it but he shall. He shall go directly to the creation. His trust shall master the trust of everything he touches . . . and shall master all attachment. . . .

The art of art, the glory of expression and the sunshine of the light of letters is simplicity. Nothing is better than simplicity . . . nothing can make up for excess or for the lack of definiteness. To carry on the heave of impulse and pierce intellectual depths and give all subjects their articulations are powers neither common nor very uncommon. But to speak in literature with the perfect rectitude and insouciance of the movements of animals and the unimpeachableness of the sentiment of trees in the woods and grass by the roadside is the flawless triumph of art. If you have looked on him who has achieved it you have looked on one of the masters of the artists of all nations and times. . . . The greatest poet has less a marked style and is more the channel of thoughts and things without increase or diminution, and is the free channel of himself. He swears to his art, I will not be meddlesome, I will not have in my writing any elegance or effect or originality to hang in the way between me and the rest like curtains. I will have nothing hang in the way, not the richest curtains. What I tell I tell for precisely what it is. Let who may exalt or startle or fascinate or sooth I will have purposes as health or heat or snow has and be as regardless of observation. What I experience or portray shall go from my composition without a shred of my composition. You shall stand by my side and look in the mirror with me. . . .

The messages of great poets to each man and woman are, Come to us on equal terms, Only then can you understand us, We are no better than you, What we enclose you enclose, What we enjoy you may enjoy. Did you suppose there could be only one Supreme? We affirm there can be unnumbered Supremes, and that one does not countervail another any more than one eyesight countervails another . . . and that men can be good or grand only of the consciousness of their supremacy within them. What do you think is the grandeur of storms and dismemberments and the deadliest battles and wrecks and the wildest fury of the elements and the power of the sea and the motion of nature and of the throes of human desires and dignity and hate and love? It is that something in the soul which says, Rage on, Whirl on, I tread master here and everywhere, Master of the spasms of the sky and of the shatter of the sea, Master of nature and passion and death, And of all terror and all pain. . . .

Exact science and its practical movements are no checks on the greatest poet but always his encouragement and support. The outset and remembrance are there . . . there are the arms that lifted him first and brace him best . . . there he returns after all his goings and comings. The sailor and traveler . . . the anatomist chemist astronomer geologist phrenologist spiritualist mathematician historian and lexicographer are not poets, but they are the lawgivers of poets and their construction underlies the structure of every perfect poem. No matter what rises or is uttered they sent the seed of the conception of it . . . of them and by them stand the visible proofs of souls . . . always of their fatherstuff must be begotten the sinewy races of bards. If there shall be love and content between the father and the son and if the greatness of the son is the exuding of the greatness of the father there shall be love between the poet and the man of demonstrable science. In the beauty of poems are the tuft and final applause of science....

In the make of the great masters the idea of political liberty is indispensable. Liberty takes the adherence of heroes wherever men and women exist . . . but never takes any adherence or welcome from the rest more than from poets. They are the voice and exposition of liberty. They out of ages are worthy the grand idea . . . to them it is confided and they must sustain it. Nothing has precedence of it and nothing can warp or degrade it. The attitude of great poets is to cheer up slaves and horrify despots. The turn of their necks, the sound of their feet, the motions of their wrists, are full of hazard to the one and hope to the other. Come nigh them awhile and though they neither speak nor advise you shall learn the faithful American lesson. Liberty is poorly served by men whose good intent is quelled from one failure or two failures or any number of failures, or from the casual indifference or ingratitude of the people, or from the sharp show of the tushes of power, or the bringing to bear soldiers and cannon or any penal statutes. Liberty relies upon itself, invites no one, promises nothing, sits in calmness and light, is positive and composed, and knows no discouragement. The battle rages with many a loud alarm and frequent advance and retreat . . . the enemy triumphs . . . the prison, the handcuffs, the iron necklace and anklet, the scaffold, garrote and leadballs do their work . . . the cause is asleep . . . the strong throats are choked with their own blood . . . the young men drop their eyelashes toward the ground when they pass each other . . . and is liberty gone out of that place? No never. When liberty goes it is not the first to go nor the second or third to go . . . it waits for all the rest to go . . . it is the last.

. . . When the memories of the old martyrs are faded utterly away . . . when the large names of patriots are laughed at in the public halls from the lips of the orators . . . when the boys are no more christened after the same but christened after tyrants and traitors instead . . . when the laws of the free are grudgingly permitted and laws for informers and bloodmoney are sweet to the taste of the people . . . when I and you walk abroad upon the earth stung with compassion at the sight of numberless brothers answering our equal friendship and calling no man master—and when we are elated with noble joy at the sight of slaves . . . when the soul retires in the cool communion of the night and surveys its experience and has much extasy over the word and deed that put back a helpless innocent person into the gripe of the gripers or into any cruel inferiority . . . when those in all parts of these states who could easier realize the true American character but do not yet—when the swarms of cringers, suckers, doughfaces, lice of politics, planners of sly involutions for their own preferment to city offices or state legislatures or the judiciary or congress or the presidency, obtain a response of love and natural deference from the people whether they get the offices or no . . . when it is better to be a bound booby and rogue in office at a high salary than the poorest free mechanic or farmer with his hat unmoved from his head and firm eyes and a candid and generous heart . . . and when servility by town or state or the federal government or any oppression on a large scale or small scale can be tried on without its own punishment following duly after in exact proportion against the smallest chance of escape . . . or rather when all life and all the souls of men and women are discharged from any part of the earth—then only shall the instinct of liberty be discharged from that part of the earth. . . .

. . . It has been thought that the prudent citizen was the citizen who applied himself to solid gains and did well for himself and his family and completed a lawful life without debt or crime. The greatest poet sees and admits these economies as he sees the economies of food and sleep, but has higher notions of prudence than to think he gives much when he gives a few slight attentions at the latch of the gate. The premises of the prudence of life are not the hospitality of it or the ripeness and harvest of it.

The direct trial of him who would be the greatest poet is today. If he does not flood himself with the immediate age as with vast oceanic tides . . . and if he does not attract his own land body and soul to himself and hang on its neck with incomparable love and plunge his semitic muscle into its merits and demerits . . . and if he be not himself the age transfigured . . . and if to him is not opened the eternity which gives similitude to all periods and locations and processes and animate and inanimate forms, and which is the bond of time, and rises up from its inconceivable vagueness and infiniteness in the swimming shape of today, and is held by the ductile anchors of life, and makes the present spot the passage from what was to what shall be, and commits itself to the representation of this wave of an hour and this one of the sixty beautiful children of the wave—let him merge in the general run and wait his development. . . . Still the final test of poems or any character or work remains. The prescient poet projects himself centuries ahead and judges performer or performance after the changes of time. . . .

A great poem is for ages and ages in common and for all degrees and complexions and all departments and sects and for a woman as much as a man and a man as much as a woman. A great poem is no finish to a man or woman but rather a beginning. Has any one fancied he could sit at last under some due authority and rest satisfied with explanations and realize and be content and full? To no such terminus does the greatest poet bring . . . he brings neither cessation nor sheltered fatness and ease. The touch of him tells in action. Whom he takes he takes with firm sure grasp into live regions previously unattained . . . thenceforward is no rest . . . they see the space and ineffable sheen that turn the old spots and lights into dead vacuums. The companion of him beholds the birth and progress of stars and learns one of the meanings. Now there shall be a man cohered out of tumult and chaos . . . the elder encourages the younger and shows him how . . . they two shall launch off fearlessly together till the new world fits an orbit for itself and looks unabashed on the lesser orbits of the stars and sweeps through the ceaseless rings and shall never be quiet again. . . .

The poems distilled from other poems will probably pass away. The coward will surely pass away. The expectation of the vital and great can only be satisfied by the demeanor of the vital and great. The swarms of the polished deprecating and reflectors and the polite float off and leave no remembrance. America prepares with composure and goodwill for the visitors that have sent word. It is not intellect that is to be their warrant and welcome. The talented, the artist, the ingenious, the editor, the statesman, the erudite . . . they are not unappreciated . . . they fall in their place and do their work. The soul of the nation also does its work. No disguise can pass on it . . . no disguise can conceal from it. It rejects none, it permits all. Only toward as good as itself and toward the like of itself will it advance half-way. An individual is as superb as a nation when he has the qualities which make a superb nation. The soul of the largest and wealthiest and proudest nation may well go half-way to meet that of its poets. The signs are effectual. There is no fear of mistake. If the one is true the other is true. The proof of a poet is that his country absorbs him as affectionately as he has absorbed it.

Prose

THE SIGNIFICANCE OF THE FRONTIER IN AMERICAN HISTORY

by Frederick Jackson Turner

IN A RECENT BULLETIN of the Superintendent of the Census for 1890 appear these significant words: "Up to and including 1880 the country had a frontier of settlement, but at present the unsettled area has been so broken into by isolated bodies of settlement that there can hardly be said to be a frontier line. In the discussion of its extent, its westward movement, etc., it can not, therefore, any longer have a place in the census reports." This brief official statement marks the closing of a great historic movement. Up to our own day American history has been in a large degree the history of the colonization of the Great West. The existence of an area of free land, its continuous recession, and the advance of American settlement westward, explain American development.

Behind institutions, behind constitutional forms and modifications, lie the vital forces that call these organs into life and shape them to meet changing conditions. The peculiarity of American institutions is the fact that they have been compelled to adapt themselves to the changes of an expanding people—to the changes involved in crossing a continent, in winning a wilderness, and in developing at each area of this progress out of the primitive economic and political conditions of the frontier into the complexity of city life. Said Calhoun in 1817, "We are great, and rapidly—I was about to say fearfully—growing!" So saying, he touched the distinguishing feature of American life. All peoples show development; the germ theory of politics has been sufficiently emphasized. In the case of most nations, however, the development has occurred in a limited area; and if the nation has expanded, it has met other growing peoples whom it has conquered. But in the case of the United States we have a different phenomenon. Limiting our attention to the Atlantic coast, we have the familiar phenomenon of the evolution of institutions in a limited area, such as the rise of representative government; the differentiation of simple colonial governments into complex organs; the progress from primitive industrial society, without division of labor, up to manufacturing civilization. But we have in addition to this a recurrence of the process of evolution in each western area reached in the process of expansion. Thus American development has exhibited not merely advance along a single line, but a return to primitive conditions on a continually advancing fron-

From *The Frontier in American History* by Frederick J. Turner. Copyright, 1920, by Frederick J. Turner. Copyright, 1948, by Caroline M. S. Turner. Used by permission of Henry Holt and Company, Inc.

tier line, and a new development for that area. American social development has been continually beginning over again on the frontier. This perennial rebirth, this fluidity of American life, this expansion westward with its new opportunities, its continuous touch with the simplicity of primitive society, furnish the forces dominating American character. The true point of view in the history of this nation is not the Atlantic coast, it is the Great West. Even the slavery struggle, which is made so exclusive an object of attention by writers like Professor von Holst, occupies its important place in American history because of its relation to westward expansion.

In this advance, the frontier is the outer edge of the wave—the meeting point between savagery and civilization. Much has been written about the frontier from the point of view of border warfare and the chase, but as a field for the serious study of the economist and the historian it has been neglected.

The American frontier is sharply distinguished from the European frontier—a fortified boundary line running through dense populations. The most significant thing about the American frontier is, that it lies at the hither edge of free land. In the census reports it is treated as the margin of that settlement which has a density of two or more to the square mile. The term is an elastic one, and for our purposes does not need sharp definition. We shall consider the whole frontier belt, including the Indian country and the outer margin of the "settled area" of the census reports. This paper will make no attempt to treat the subject exhaustively; its aim is simply to call attention to the frontier as a fertile field for investigation, and to suggest some of the problems which arise in connection with it.

In the settlement of America we have to observe how European life entered the continent, and how America modified and developed that life and reacted on Europe. Our early history is the study of European germs developing in an American environment. Too exclusive attention has been paid by institutional students to the Germanic origins, too little to the American factors. The frontier is the line of most rapid and effective Americanization. The wilderness masters the colonist. It finds him a European in dress, industries, tools, modes of travel, and thought. It takes him from the railroad car and puts him in the birch canoe. It strips off the garments of civilization and arrays him in the hunting shirt and the moccasin. It puts him in the log cabin of the Cherokee and Iroquois and runs an Indian palisade around him. Before long he has gone to planting Indian corn and plowing with a sharp stick; he shouts the war cry and takes the scalp in orthodox Indian fashion. In short, at the frontier the environment is at first too strong for the man. He must accept the conditions which it furnishes, or perish, and so he fits himself into the Indian clearings and follows the Indian trails. Little by little he transforms the wilderness, but the outcome is not the old Europe, not simply the development of Germanic germs, any more than the first phenomenon was a case of reversion to the Germanic mark. The fact is, that here is a new product that is American. At first, the frontier was the Atlantic coast. It was the frontier of Europe in a very real sense. Moving westward, the frontier became more and more American. As successive terminal moraines result from successive glaciations, so each frontier leaves its traces behind it, and when it becomes a settled area the region still partakes of the frontier characteristics. Thus the advance of the frontier has meant a steady movement away from the influence of Europe, a steady growth of independence on American lines. And to study this advance, the men who grew up under these conditions, and the political, economic, and social results of it, is to study the really American part of our history.

In the course of the seventeenth century the frontier was advanced up the Atlantic river courses, just beyond the "fall line," and the tidewater region became the settled area. In the first half of the eighteenth century another advance occurred. Traders followed the Delaware and Shawnese Indians to the Ohio as early as the end of the first quarter of the century. Gov. Spotswood, of Virginia, made an expedition in 1714 across the Blue Ridge. The end of the first quarter of the century saw the advance of the Scotch-Irish and the Palatine Germans up the Shenandoah Valley into the western part of Virginia, and along the Piedmont region of the Carolinas. The Germans in New York pushed the frontier of settlement up the Mohawk to German Flats. In Pennsylvania the town of Bedford indicates the line of settlement. Settlements had begun on New River, a branch of the Kanawha, and on the sources of the Yadkin and French Broad. The King attempted to arrest the advance by his proclamation of 1763, forbidding settlements beyond the sources of the rivers flowing into the Atlantic; but in vain. In the period of the Revolution the frontier crossed the Alleghenies into Kentucky and Tennessee, and the upper waters of the Ohio were settled. When the first census was taken in 1790, the continuous settled area was bounded by a line which ran near the coast of Maine, and included New England except a portion of Vermont and New Hampshire, New York along the Hudson and up the Mohawk about Schenectady, eastern and southern Pennsylvania, Virginia well across the Shenandoah Valley, and the Carolinas and eastern Georgia. Beyond this region of continuous settlement were the small settled areas of Kentucky and Tennessee, and the Ohio, with the mountains intervening between them and the Atlantic area, thus giving a new and important character to the frontier. The isolation of the region increased its peculiarly American tendencies, and the need of transportation facilities to connect it with the East called out important schemes of internal improvement, which will be noted farther on. The "West," as a self-conscious section, began to evolve.

From decade to decade distinct advances of the frontier occurred. By the census of 1820 the settled area included Ohio, southern Indiana and Illinois, southeastern Missouri, and about one-half of Louisiana. This settled area had surrounded Indian areas, and the management of these tribes became an object of political concern. The frontier region of the time lay along the Great Lakes, where Astor's American Fur Company operated in the Indian trade, and beyond the Mississippi, where Indian traders extended their activity even to the Rocky Mountains; Florida also furnished frontier conditions. The Mississippi River region was the scene of typical frontier settlements.

The rising steam navigation on western waters, the opening of the Erie Canal, and the westward extension of cotton culture added five frontier states to the Union in this period. Grund, writing in 1836, declares: "It appears then that the universal disposition of Americans to emigrate to the western wilderness, in order to enlarge their dominion over inanimate nature, is the actual result of an expansive power which is inherent in them, and which by continually agitating all classes of society is constantly throwing a large portion of the whole population on the extreme confines of the State, in order to gain space for its development. Hardly is a new State or Territory formed before the same principle manifests itself again and gives rise to a further emigration; and so is it destined to go on until a physical barrier must finally obstruct its progress."

In the middle of this century the line indicated by the present eastern boundary of Indian Territory, Nebraska, and Kansas marked the frontier of the Indian country. Minnesota and Wisconsin still exhibited frontier conditions, but the distinctive frontier of the period is found in California, where the gold discoveries had sent a sudden tide of adventurous miners, and in Oregon, and the settlements in Utah. As the frontier had leaped over the Alleghenies, so now it skipped the Great Plains and the Rocky Mountains; and in the same way that the advance of the frontiersmen beyond the Alleghenies had caused the rise of important questions of transportation and internal improvement, so now the settlers beyond the Rocky Mountains needed means of communication with the East, and in the furnishing of these arose the settlement of the Great Plains and the development of still another kind of frontier life. Railroads, fostered by land grants, sent an increasing tide of immigrants into the Far West. The United States Army fought a series of Indian wars in Minnesota, Dakota, and the Indian Territory.

By 1880 the settled area had been pushed into northern Michigan, Wisconsin, and Minnesota, along Dakota rivers, and in the Black Hills region, and was ascending the rivers of Kansas and Nebraska. The development of mines in Colorado had drawn isolated frontier settlements into that region, and Montana and Idaho were receiving settlers. The frontier was found in these mining camps and the ranches of the Great Plains. The superintendent of the census for 1890 reports, as previously stated, that the settlements of the West lie so scattered over the region that there can no longer be said to be a frontier line.

In these successive frontiers we find natural boundary lines which have served to mark and to affect the characteristics of the frontiers, namely: the "fall line"; the Allegheny Mountains; the Mississippi; the Missouri where its direction approximates north and south; the line of the arid lands, approximately the ninety-ninth meridian; and the Rocky Mountains. The fall line marked the frontier of the seventeenth century; the Alleghenies that of the eighteenth; the Mississippi that of the first quarter of the nineteenth; the Missouri that of the middle of this century (omitting the California movement); and the belt of the Rocky Mountains and the arid tract, the present frontier. Each was won by a series of Indian wars.

At the Atlantic frontier one can study the germs of processes repeated at each successive frontier. We have the complex European life sharply precipitated by the wilderness into the simplicity of primitive conditions. The first frontier had to meet its Indian question, its question of the disposition of the public domain, of the means of intercourse with older settlements, of the extension of political organization, of religious and educational activity. And the settlement of these and similar questions for one frontier served as a guide for the next. The American student needs not to go to the "prim little townships of Sleswick" for illustrations of the law of continuity and development. For example, he may study the origin of our land policies in the colonial land policy; he may see how the system grew by adapting the statutes to the customs of the successive frontiers. He may see how the mining experience in the lead regions of Wisconsin, Illinois, and Iowa was applied to the mining laws of the Sierras, and how our Indian policy has been a series of experimentations on successive frontiers. Each tier of new States has found in the older ones material for its constitutions. Each frontier has made similar contributions to American characters, as will be discussed farther on.

But with all these similarities there are essential differences, due to the place element and the time element. It is evident that the farming frontier of the Mississippi Valley presents different conditions from the mining frontier of the Rocky Mountains. The frontier reached by the Pacific Railroad, surveyed into rectangles, guarded by the United States Army, and recruited by the daily immigrant ship, moves forward at a swifter pace and in a different way than the frontier reached by the birch canoe or the pack horse. The geologist traces patiently the shores of ancient seas, maps their areas, and compares the older and the newer. It would be a work worth the historian's labors to mark these various frontiers and in detail compare one with another. Not only would there result a more adequate conception of American development and characteristics, but invaluable additions would be made to the history of society.

Loria, the Italian economist, has urged the study of colonial life as an aid in understanding the stages of European development, affirming that colonial settlement is for economic science what the mountain is for geology, bringing to light primitive stratifications. "America," he says, "has the key to the historical enigma which Europe has sought for centuries in vain, and the land which has no history reveals luminously the course of universal history." There is much truth in this. The United States lies like a huge page in the history of society. Line by line as we read this continental page from West to East we find the record of social evolution. It begins with the Indian and the hunter; it goes on to tell of the disintegration of savagery by the entrance of the trader, the pathfinder of civilization; we read the annals of the pastoral stage in ranch life; the exploitation of the soil by the raising of unrotated crops of corn and wheat in sparsely settled farming communities; the intensive culture of the denser farm settlement; and finally the manufacturing organization with city and factory system. This page is familiar to the student of census statistics, but how little of it has been used by our historians. Particularly in eastern States this page is a palimpsest. What is now a manufacturing State was in an earlier decade an area of intensive farming. Earlier yet it had been a wheat area, and still earlier the "range" had attracted the cattle-herder. Thus Wisconsin, now developing manufacture, is a State with varied agricultural interests. But earlier it was given over to almost exclusive grain-raising, like North Dakota at the present time.

Each of these areas has had an influence in our economic and political history; the evolution of each into a higher stage has worked political transformations. But what constitutional historian has made any adequate attempt to interpret political facts by the light of these social areas and changes?

The Atlantic frontier was compounded of fisherman, fur-trader, miner, cattle-raiser, and farmer. Excepting the fisherman, each type of industry was on the march toward the West, impelled by an

Significance of Frontier in American History

irresistible attraction. Each passed in successive waves across the continent. Stand at Cumberland Gap and watch the procession of civilization, marching single file—the buffalo following the trail to the salt springs, the Indian, the fur-trader and hunter, the cattle-raiser, the pioneer farmer—and the frontier has passed by. Stand at South Pass in the Rockies a century later and see the same procession with wider intervals between. The unequal rate of advance compels us to distinguish the frontier into the trader's frontier, the rancher's frontier, or the miner's frontier, and the farmer's frontier. When the mines and the cowpens were still near the fall line the traders' pack trains were tinkling across the Alleghenies, and the French on the Great Lakes were fortifying their posts, alarmed by the British trader's birch canoe. When the trappers scaled the Rockies, the farmer was still near the mouth of the Missouri.

Why was it that the Indian trader passed so rapidly across the continent? What effects followed from the trader's frontier? The trade was coeval with American discovery. The Norsemen, Vespuccius, Verrazani, Hudson, John Smith, all trafficked for furs. The Plymouth pilgrims settled in Indian cornfields, and their first return cargo was of beaver and lumber. The records of the various New England colonies show how steadily exploration was carried into the wilderness by this trade. What is true for New England is, as would be expected, even plainer for the rest of the colonies. All along the coast from Maine to Georgia the Indian trade opened up the river courses. Steadily the trader passed westward, utilizing the older lines of French trade. The Ohio, the Great Lakes, the Mississippi, the Missouri, and the Platte, the lines of western advance, were ascended by traders. They found the passes in the Rocky Mountains and guided Lewis and Clark, Frémont, and Bidwell. The explanation of the rapidity of this advance is connected with the effects of the trader on the Indian. The trading post left the unarmed tribes at the mercy of those that had purchased firearms—a truth which the Iroquois Indians wrote in blood, and so the remote and unvisited tribes gave eager welcome to the trader. "The savages," wrote La Salle, "take better care of us French than of their own children; from us only can they get guns and goods." This accounts for the trader's power and the rapidity of his advance. Thus the disintegrating forces of civilization entered the wilderness. Every river valley and Indian trail became a fissure in Indian society, and so that society became honeycombed. Long before the pioneer farmer appeared on the scene, primitive Indian life had passed away. The farmers met Indians armed with guns. The trading frontier, while steadily undermining Indian power by making the tribes ultimately dependent on the whites, yet, through its sale of guns, gave to the Indian increased power of resistance to the farming frontier. French colonization was dominated by its trading frontier; English colonization by its farming frontier. There was an antagonism between the two frontiers as between the two nations. Said Duquesne to the Iroquois, "Are you ignorant of the difference between the king of England and the king of France? Go see the forts that our king has established and you will see that you can still hunt under their very walls. They have been placed for your advantage in places which you frequent. The English, on the contrary, are no sooner in possession of a place than the game is driven away. The forest falls before them as they advance, and the soil is laid bare so that you can scarce find the wherewithal to erect a shelter for the night."

And yet, in spite of this opposition of the interests of the trader and the farmer, the Indian trade pioneered the way for civilization. The buffalo trail became the Indian trail, and this became the trader's "trace"; the trails widened into roads, and the roads into turnpikes, and these in turn were transformed into railroads. The same origin can be shown for the railroads of the South, the Far West, and the Dominion of Canada. The trading posts reached by these trails were on the sites of Indian villages which had been placed in positions suggested by nature; and these trading posts, situated so as to command the water systems of the country, have grown into such cities as Albany, Pittsburgh, Detroit, Chicago, St. Louis, Council Bluffs, and Kansas City. Thus civilization in America has followed the arteries made by geology, pouring an ever richer tide through them, until at last the slender paths of aboriginal intercourse have been broadened and interwoven into the complex mazes of modern commercial lines; the wilderness has been interpenetrated by lines of civilization growing ever more numerous. It is like the steady growth of a complex nervous system for the originally simple, inert continent. If one would understand why we are to-day one nation, rather than a collection of isolated states, he must study this economic and social consolidation of the country. In this progress from savage conditions lie topics for the evolutionist.

The effect of the Indian frontier as a consolidating agent in our history is important. From the close of the seventeenth century various intercolonial congresses have been called to treat with Indians and establish common measures of defense. Particularism was strongest in colonies with no Indian frontier. This frontier stretched along the western border like a cord of union. The Indian was a common danger, demanding united action. Most celebrated of these conferences was the Albany congress of 1754, called to treat with the Six Nations, and to consider plans of union. Even a cursory reading of the plan proposed by the congress reveals the importance of the frontier. The powers of the general council and the officers were, chiefly, the determination of peace and war with the Indians, the regulation of Indian trade, the purchase of Indian lands, and the creation and government of new settlements as a security against the Indians. It is evident that the unifying tendencies of the Revolutionary period were facilitated by the previous cooperation in the regulation of the frontier. In this connection may be mentioned the importance of the frontier, from that day to this, as a military training school, keeping alive the power of resistance to aggression, and developing the stalwart and rugged qualities of the frontiersman.

It would not be possible in the limits of this paper to trace the other frontiers across the continent. Travelers of the eighteenth century found the "cowpens" among the canebrakes and peavine pastures of the South, and the "cow drivers" took their droves to Charleston, Philadelphia, and New York. Travelers at the close of the War of 1812 met droves of more than a thousand cattle and swine from the interior of Ohio going to Pennsylvania to fatten for the Philadelphia market. The ranges of the Great Plains, with ranch and cowboy and nomadic life, are things of yesterday and of to-day. The experience of the Carolina cowpens guided the ranchers of Texas. One element favoring the rapid extension of the rancher's frontier is the fact that in a remote country lacking transportation facilities the product must be in small bulk, or must be able to transport itself, and the cattle-raiser could easily drive his product to market. The effect of these great ranches on the subsequent agrarian history of the localities in which they existed should be studied.

The maps of the census reports show an uneven advance of the farmer's frontier, with tongues of settlement pushed forward and with indentations of wilderness. In part this is due to Indian resistance, in part to the location of river valleys and passes, in part to the unequal force of the centers of frontier attraction. Among the important centers of attraction may be mentioned the following: fertile and favorably situated soils, salt springs, mines, and army posts.

The frontier army post, serving to protect the settlers from the Indians, has also acted as a wedge to open the Indian country, and has been a nucleus for settlement. In this connection mention should also be made of the government military and exploring expeditions in determining the lines of settlement. But all the more important expeditions were greatly indebted to the earliest pathmakers, the Indian guides, the traders and trappers, and the French voyageurs, who were inevitable parts of governmental expeditions from the days of Lewis and Clark. Each expedition was an epitome of the previous factors in western advance.

In an interesting monograph, Victor Hehn has traced the effect of salt upon early European development, and has pointed out how it affected the lines of settlement and the form of administration. A similar study might be made for the salt springs of the United States. The early settlers were tied to the coast by the need of salt, without which they could not preserve their meats or live in comfort. Writing in 1752, Bishop Spangenburg says of a colony for which he was seeking lands in North Carolina, "They will require salt & other necessaries which they can neither manufacture nor raise. Either they must go to Charleston, which is 300 miles distant . . . Or else they must go to Boling's Point in V^a on a branch of the James & is also 300 miles from here . . . Or else they must go down the Roanoke—I know not how many miles—where salt is brought up from the Cape Fear." This may serve as a typical illustration. An annual pilgrimage to the coast for salt thus became essential. Taking flocks or furs and ginseng root, the early settlers sent their pack trains after seeding time each year to the coast. This proved to be an important educational influence, since it was almost the only way in which the pioneer learned what was going on in the East. But when discovery was made of the salt springs of the Kanawha, and the Holston, and Kentucky, and central New York, the West began to be freed from dependence on the coast. It was in part the effect of finding these salt springs that enabled settlement to cross the mountains.

From the time the mountains rose between the pioneer and the seaboard, a new order of Americanism arose. The West and the East began to get out of touch of each other. The settlements from the sea to the mountains kept connection with the rear and had a certain solidarity. But the over-mountain men grew more and more independent. The East took a narrow view of American advance, and nearly lost these men. Kentucky and Tennessee history bears abundant witness to the truth of this statement. The East began to try to hedge and limit westward expansion. Though Webster could declare that there were no Alleghenies in his politics, yet in politics in general they were a very solid factor.

The exploitation of the beasts took hunter and trader to the west, the exploitation of the grasses took the rancher west, and the exploitation of the virgin soil of the river valleys and prairies attracted the farmer. Good soils have been the most continuous attraction to the farmer's frontier. The land hunger of the Virginians drew them down the rivers into Carolina, in early colonial days; the search for soils took the Massachusetts men to Pennsylvania and to New York. As the eastern lands were taken up migration flowed across them to the west. Daniel Boone, the great backwoodsman, who combined the occupations of hunter, trader, cattle-raiser, farmer, and surveyor—learning, probably from the traders, of the fertility of the lands of the upper Yadkin, where the traders were wont to rest as they took their way to the Indians—left his Pennsylvania home with his father, and passed down the Great Valley road to that stream. Learning from a trader of the game and rich pastures of Kentucky, he pioneered the way for the farmers to that region. Thence he passed to the frontier of Missouri, where his settlement was long a landmark on the frontier. Here again he helped to open the way for civilization, finding salt licks, and trails, and land. His son was among the earliest trappers in the passes of the Rocky Mountains, and his party are said to have been the first to camp on the present site of Denver. His grandson, Col. A. J. Boone, of Colorado, was a power among the Indians of the Rocky Mountains, and was appointed an agent by the government. Kit Carson's mother was a Boone. Thus this family epitomizes the backwoodsman's advance across the continent.

The farmer's advance came in a distinct series of waves. In Peck's New Guide to the West, published in Boston in 1837, occurs this suggestive passage:

Generally, in all the western settlements, three classes, like the waves of the ocean, have rolled one after the other. First comes the pioneer, who depends for the subsistence of his family chiefly upon the natural growth of vegetation, called the "range," and the proceeds of hunting. His implements of agriculture are rude, chiefly of his own make, and his efforts directed mainly to a crop of corn and a "truck patch." The last is a rude garden for growing cabbage, beans, corn for roasting ears, cucumbers, and potatoes. A log cabin, and, occasionally, a stable and corn-crib, and a field of a dozen acres, the timber girdled or "deadened," and fenced, are enough for his occupancy. It is quite immaterial whether he ever becomes the owner of the soil. He is the occupant for the time being, pays no rent, and feels as independent as the "lord of the manor." With a horse, cow, and one or two breeders of swine, he strikes into the woods with his family, and becomes the founder of a new county, or perhaps state. He builds his cabin, gathers around him a few other families of similar tastes and habits, and occupies till the range is somewhat subdued, and hunting a little precarious, or, which is more frequently the case, till the neighbors crowd around, roads, bridges, and fields annoy him, and he lacks elbow room. The preemption law enables him to dispose of his cabin and cornfield to the next class of emigrants; and, to employ his own figures, he "breaks for the high timber," "clears out for the New Purchase," or migrates to Arkansas or Texas, to work the same process over.

The next class of emigrants purchase the lands, add field to field, clear out the roads, throw rough bridges over the streams, put up hewn log houses with glass windows and brick or stone chimneys, occasionally plant orchards, build mills, school-houses, court-houses, etc., and exhibit the picture and forms of plain, frugal, civilized life.

Another wave rolls on. The men of capital

and enterprise come. The settler is ready to sell out and take the advantage of the rise in property, push farther into the interior and become, himself, a man of capital and enterprise in turn. The small village rises to a spacious town or city; substantial edifices of brick, extensive fields, orchards, gardens, colleges, and churches are seen. Broadcloths, silks, leghorns, crapes, and all the refinements, luxuries, elegances, frivolities, and fashions are in vogue. Thus wave after wave is rolling westward; the real Eldorado is still farther on.

A portion of the two first classes remain stationary amidst the general movement, improve their habits and condition, and rise in the scale of society.

The writer has traveled much amongst the first class, the real pioneers. He has lived many years in connection with the second grade; and now the third wave is sweeping over large districts of Indiana, Illinois, and Missouri. Migration has become almost a habit in the West. Hundreds of men can be found, not over 50 years of age, who have settled for the fourth, fifth, or sixth time on a new spot. To sell out and remove only a few hundred miles makes up a portion of the variety of backwoods life and manners.

Omitting those of the pioneer farmers who move from the love of adventure, the advance of the more steady farmer is easy to understand. Obviously the immigrant was attracted by the cheap lands of the frontier, and even the native farmer felt their influence strongly. Year by year the farmers who lived on soil whose returns were diminished by unrotated crops were offered the virgin soil of the frontier at nominal prices. Their growing families demanded more lands, and these were dear. The competition of the unexhausted, cheap, and easily tilled prairie lands compelled the farmer either to go west and continue the exhaustion of the soil on a new frontier, or to adopt intensive culture. Thus the census of 1890 shows, in the Northwest, many counties in which there is an absolute or a relative decrease of population. These States have been sending farmers to advance the frontier on the plains, and have themselves begun to turn to intensive farming and to manufacture. A decade before this, Ohio had shown the same transition stage. Thus the demand for land and the love of wilderness freedom drew the frontier ever onward.

Having now roughly outlined the various kinds of frontiers, and their modes of advance, chiefly from the point of view of the frontier itself, we may next inquire what were the influences on the East and on the Old World. A rapid enumeration of some of the more noteworthy effects is all that I have time for.

First, we note that the frontier promoted the formation of a composite nationality for the American people. The coast was preponderantly English, but the later tides of continental immigration flowed across to the free lands. This was the case from the early colonial days. The Scotch-Irish and the Palatine Germans, or "Pennsylvania Dutch," furnished the dominant element in the stock of the colonial frontier. With these peoples were also the freed indented servants, or redemptioners, who at the expiration of their time of service passed to the frontier. Governor Spotswood of Virginia writes in 1717, "The inhabitants of our frontiers are composed generally of such as have been transported hither as servants, and, being out of their time, settle themselves where land is to be taken up and that will produce the necessarys of life with little labour." Very generally these redemptioners were of non-English stock. In the crucible of the frontier the immigrants were Americanized, liberated, and fused into a mixed race, English in neither nationality nor characteristics. The process has gone on from the early days to our own. Burke and other writers in the middle of the eighteenth century believed that Pennsylvania was "threatened with the danger of being wholly foreign in language, manners and perhaps even inclinations." The German and Scotch-Irish elements in the frontier of the South were only less great. In the middle of the present century the German element in Wisconsin was already so considerable that leading publicists looked to the creation of a German state out of the commonwealth by concentrating their colonization. Such examples teach us to beware of misinterpreting the fact that there is a common English speech in America into a belief that the stock is also English.

In another way the advance of the frontier decreased our dependence on England. The coast, particularly of the South, lacked diversified industries, and was dependent on England for the bulk of its supplies. In the South there was even a dependence on the Northern colonies for articles of food. Governor Glenn, of South Carolina, writes in the middle of the eighteenth century: "Our trade with New York and Philadelphia was of this sort, draining us of all the little money and bills we could gather from other places for their bread, flour, beer, hams, bacon, and other things of their produce, all which, except beer, our new townships begin to supply us with, which are settled with very industrious and thriving Germans. This no doubt diminishes the number of shipping and the appearance of our trade, but it is far from being a detriment to us." Before long the frontier created a demand for merchants. As it retreated from the coast it became less and less possible for England to bring her supplies directly to the consumer's wharfs, and carry away staple crops, and staple crops began to give way to diversified agriculture for a time. The effect of this phase of the frontier action upon the northern section is perceived when we realize how the advance of the frontier aroused seaboard cities like Boston, New York, and Baltimore to engage in rivalry for what Washington called "the extensive and valuable trade of a rising empire."

The legislation which most developed the powers of the national government, and played the largest part in its activity, was conditioned on the frontier. Writers have discussed the subjects of tariff, land, and internal improvement, as subsidiary to the slavery question. But when American history comes to be rightly viewed it will be seen that the slavery question is an incident. In the period from the end of the first half of the present century to the close of the Civil War slavery rose to primary, but far from exclusive, importance. But this does not justify Dr. von Holst (to take an example) in treating our constitutional history in its formative period down to 1828 in a single volume, giving six volumes chiefly to the history of slavery from 1828 to 1861, under the title "Constitutional History of the United States." The growth of nationalism and the evolution of American political institutions were dependent on the advance of the frontier. Even so recent a writer as Rhodes, in his "History of the United States since the Compromise of 1850," has treated the legislation called out by the western advance as incidental to the slavery struggle.

This is a wrong perspective. The pioneer needed the goods of the coast, and so the grand series of internal improvement and railroad legislation began, with potent nationalizing effects. Over internal improvements occurred great debates, in which grave constitutional questions were discussed. Sectional groupings appear in the votes, profoundly significant for the historian. Loose construction increased as the nation marched westward. But the West was not content with bringing the farm to the factory. Under the lead of Clay—"Harry of the West"—protective tariffs were passed, with the cry of bringing the factory to the farm. The disposition of the public lands was a third important subject of national legislation influenced by the frontier.

The public domain has been a force of profound importance in the nationalization and development of the government. The effects of the struggle of the landed and the landless States, and of the Ordinance of 1787, need no discussion. Administratively the frontier called out some of the highest and most vitalizing activities of the general government. The purchase of Louisiana was perhaps the constitutional turning point in the history of the Republic, inasmuch as it afforded both a new area for national legislation and the occasion of the downfall of the policy of strict construction. But the purchase of Louisiana was called out by frontier needs and demands. As frontier States accrued to the Union the national power grew. In a speech on the dedication of the Calhoun monument Mr. Lamar explained: "In 1789 the States were the creators of the Federal Government; in 1861 the Federal Government was the creator of a large majority of the States."

When we consider the public domain from the point of view of the sale and disposal of the public lands we are again brought face to face with the frontier. The policy of the United States in dealing with its lands is in sharp contrast with the European system of scientific administration. Efforts to make this domain a source of revenue, and to withhold it from emigrants in order that settlement might be compact, were in vain. The jealousy and the fears of the East were powerless in the face of the demands of the frontiersmen. John Quincy Adams was obliged to confess: "My own system of administration, which was to make the national domain the inexhaustible fund for progressive and unceasing internal improvement, has failed." The reason is obvious: a system of administration was not what the West demanded; it wanted land. Adams states the situation as follows: "The slaveholders of the South have bought the cooperation of the western country by the bribe of the western lands, abandoning to the new Western States their own proportion of the public property and aiding them in the design of grasping all the lands into their own hands. Thomas H. Benton was the author of this system, which he brought forward as a substitute for the American system of Mr. Clay, and to supplant him as the leading statesman of the West. Mr. Clay, by his tariff compromise with Mr. Calhoun, abandoned his own American system. At the same time he brought forward a plan for distributing among all the States of the Union the proceeds of the sales of the public lands. His bill for that purpose passed both Houses of Congress, but was vetoed by President Jackson, who, in his annual message of December, 1832, formally recommended that all public lands should be gratuitously given away to individual adventurers and to the States in which the lands are situated."

"No subject," said Henry Clay, "which has presented itself to the present, or perhaps any preceding Congress, is of greater magnitude than that of the public lands." When we consider the far-reaching effects of the government's land policy upon political, economic, and social aspects of

American life, we are disposed to agree with him. But this legislation was framed under frontier influences, and under the lead of Western statesmen like Benton and Jackson. Said Senator Scott of Indiana in 1841: "I consider the preemption law merely declaratory of the custom or common law of the settlers."

It is safe to say that the legislation with regard to land, tariff, and internal improvements—the American system of the nationalizing Whig party—was conditioned on frontier ideas and needs. But it was not merely in legislative action that the frontier worked against the sectionalism of the coast. The economic and social characteristics of the frontier worked against sectionalism. The men of the frontier had closer resemblances to the Middle region than to either of the other sections. Pennsylvania had been the seed-plot of frontier emigration, and, although she passed on her settlers along the Great Valley into the west of Virginia and the Carolinas, yet the industrial society of these Southern frontiersmen was always more like that of the Middle region than like that of the tide-water portion of the South, which later came to spread its industrial type throughout the South.

The Middle region, entered by New York harbor, was an open door to all Europe. The tide-water part of the South represented typical Englishmen, modified by a warm climate and servile labor, and living in baronial fashion on great plantations; New England stood for a special English movement—Puritanism. The Middle region was less English than the other sections. It had a wide mixture of nationalities, a varied society, the mixed town and county system of local government, a varied economic life, many religious sects. In short, it was a region mediating between New England and the South, and the East and the West. It represented that composite nationality which the contemporary United States exhibits, that juxtaposition of non-English groups, occupying a valley or a little settlement, and presenting reflections of the map of Europe in their variety. It was democratic and non-sectional, if not national; "easy, tolerant, and contented"; rooted strongly in material prosperity. It was typical of the modern United States. It was least sectional, not only because it lay between North and South, but also because with no barriers to shut out its frontiers from its settled region, and with a system of connecting waterways, the Middle region mediated between East and West as well as between North and South. Thus it became the typically American region. Even the New Englander, who was shut out from the frontier by the Middle region, tarrying in New York or Pennsylvania on his westward march, lost the acuteness of his sectionalism on the way.

The spread of cotton culture into the interior of the South finally broke down the contrast between the "tide-water" region and the rest of the State, and based Southern interests on slavery. Before this process revealed its results the western portion of the South, which was akin to Pennsylvania in stock, society, and industry, showed tendencies to fall away from the faith of the fathers into internal improvement legislation and nationalism. In the Virginia convention of 1829-30, called to revise the constitution, Mr. Leigh, of Chesterfield, one of the tide-water counties, declared:

One of the main causes of discontent which led to this convention, that which had the strongest influence in overcoming our veneration for the work of our fathers, which taught us to contemn the sentiments of Henry and Mason and Pendleton, which weaned us from our reverence for the constituted authorities of the State, was an overweening passion for internal improvement. I say this with perfect knowledge, for it has been avowed to me by gentlemen from the West over and over again. And let me tell the gentleman from Albemarle (Mr. Gordon) that it has been another principal object of those who set this ball of revolution in motion, to overturn the doctrine of State rights, of which Virginia has been the very pillar, and to remove the barrier she has interposed to the interference of the Federal Government in that same work of internal improvement, by so reorganizing the legislature that Virginia, too, may be hitched to the Federal car.

It was this nationalizing tendency of the West that transformed the democracy of Jefferson into the national republicanism of Monroe and the democracy of Andrew Jackson. The West of the War of 1812, the West of Clay, and Benton and Harrison, and Andrew Jackson, shut off by the Middle States and the mountains from the coast sections, had a solidarity of its own with national tendencies. On the tide of the Father of Waters, North and South met and mingled into a nation. Interstate migration went steadily on—a process of cross-fertilization of ideas and institutions. The fierce struggle of the sections over slavery on the western frontier does not diminish the truth of this statement; it proves the truth of it. Slavery was a sectional trait that would not down, but in the West it could not remain sectional. It was the greatest of frontiersmen who declared: "I believe this Government can not endure permanently half slave and half free. It will become all of one thing or all of the other." Nothing works for nationalism like intercourse within the nation. Mobility of population is death to localism, and the western frontier worked irresistibly in unsettling population. The effect reached back from the frontier and affected profoundly the Atlantic coast and even the Old World.

But the most important effect of the frontier has been in the promotion of democracy here and in Europe. As has been indicated, the frontier is productive of individualism. Complex society is precipitated by the wilderness into a kind of primitive organization based on the family. The tendency is anti-social. It produces antipathy to control, and particularly to any direct control. The tax-gatherer is viewed as a representative of oppression. Prof. Osgood, in an able article, has pointed out that the frontier conditions prevalent in the colonies are important factors in the explanation of the American Revolution, where individual liberty was sometimes confused with absence of all effective government. The same conditions aid in explaining the difficulty of instituting a strong government in the period of the confederacy. The frontier individualism has from the beginning promoted democracy.

The frontier States that came into the Union in the first quarter of a century of its existence came in with democratic suffrage provisions, and had reactive effects of the highest importance upon the older States whose peoples were being attracted there. An extension of the franchise became essential. It was *western* New York that forced an extension of suffrage in the constitutional convention of that State in 1821; and it was *western* Virginia that compelled the tide-water region to put a more liberal suffrage provision in the constitution framed in 1830, and to give to the frontier region a more nearly proportionate representation with the tide-water aristocracy. The rise of democracy as an effective force in the nation came in with western preponderance under Jackson and William Henry Harrison, and it meant the triumph of the frontier—with all of its good and with all of its evil elements. An interesting illustration of the tone of frontier democracy in 1830 comes from the same debates in the Virginia convention already referred to. A representative from western Virginia declared:

But, sir, it is not the increase of population in the West which this gentleman ought to fear. It is the energy which the mountain breeze and western habits impart to those emigrants. They are regenerated, politically I mean, sir. They soon become *working politicians;* and the difference, sir, between a *talking* and a *working* politician is immense. The Old Dominion has long been celebrated for producing great orators; the ablest metaphysicians in policy; men that can split hairs in all abstruse questions of political economy. But at home, or when they return from Congress, they have Negroes to fan them asleep. But a Pennsylvania, a New York, an Ohio, or a western Virginia statesman, though far inferior in logic, metaphysics, and rhetoric to an old Virginia statesman, has this advantage, that when he returns home he takes off his coat and takes hold of the plow. This gives him bone and muscle, sir, and preserves his republican principles pure and uncontaminated.

So long as free land exists, the opportunity for a competency exists, and economic power secures political power. But the democracy born of free land, strong in selfishness and individualism, intolerant of administrative experience and education, and pressing individual liberty beyond its proper bounds, has its dangers as well as its benefits. Individualism in America has allowed a laxity in regard to governmental affairs which has rendered possible the spoils system and all the manifest evils that follow from the lack of a highly developed civic spirit. In this connection may be noted also the influence of frontier conditions in permitting lax business honor, inflated paper currency and wild-cat banking. The colonial and revolutionary frontier was the region whence emanated many of the worst forms of an evil currency. The West in the War of 1812 repeated the phenomenon on the frontier of that day, while the speculation and wild-cat banking of the period of the crisis of 1837 occurred on the new frontier belt of the next tier of States. Thus each one of the periods of lax financial integrity coincides with periods when a new set of frontier communities had arisen, and coincides in area with these successive frontiers, for the most part. The recent Populist agitation is a case in point. Many a State that now declines any connection with the tenets of the Populists, itself adhered to such ideas in an earlier stage of the development of the State. A primitive society can hardly be expected to show the intelligent appreciation of the complexity of business interests in a developed society. The continual recurrence of these areas of paper-money agitation is another evidence that the frontier can be isolated and studied as a factor in American history of the highest importance.

The East has always feared the result of an unregulated advance of the frontier, and has tried to check and guide it. The English authorities would have checked settlement at the headwaters of the Atlantic tributaries and allowed the "savages to enjoy their deserts in quiet lest the peltry trade should decrease." This called out Burke's splendid protest:

If you stopped your grants, what would be the consequence? The people would occupy without grants. They have already so occupied in many places. You can not station garrisons in every part of these deserts. If you drive the people from one place, they will carry on their annual tillage and remove with their flocks and herds to another. Many of the people in the back settlements are already little attached to particular situations. Already they have topped the Appalachian Mountains. From thence they behold before them an immense plain, one vast, rich level meadow; a square of five hundred miles. Over this they would wander without a possibility of restraint; they would change their manners with their habits of life; would soon forget a government by which they were disowned; would become hordes of English Tartars; and, pouring down upon your unfortified frontiers a fierce and irresistible cavalry, become masters of your governors and your counselors, your collectors and comptrollers, and of all the slaves that adhered to them. Such would, and in no long time must, be the effect of attempting to forbid as a crime and to suppress as an evil the command and blessing of Providence, "Increase and multiply." Such would be the happy result of an endeavor to keep as a lair of wild beasts that earth which God, by an express charter, has given to the children of men.

But the English Government was not alone in its desire to limit the advance of the frontier and guide its destinies. Tidewater Virginia and South Carolina gerrymandered those colonies to insure the dominance of the coast in their legislatures. Washington desired to settle a State at a time in the Northwest; Jefferson would reserve from settlement the territory of his Louisiana Purchase north of the thirty-second parallel, in order to offer it to the Indians in exchange for their settlements east of the Mississippi. "When we shall be full on this side," he writes, "we may lay off a range of States on the western bank from the head to the mouth, and so range after range, advancing compactly as we multiply." Madison went so far as to argue to the French minister that the United States had no interest in seeing population extend itself on the right bank of the Mississippi, but should rather fear it. When the Oregon question was under debate, in 1824, Smyth, of Virginia, would draw an unchangeable line for the limits of the United States at the outer limit of two tiers of States beyond the Mississippi, complaining that the seaboard States were being drained of the flower of their population by the bringing of too much land into market. Even Thomas Benton, the man of widest views of the destiny of the West, at this stage of his career declared that along the ridge of the Rocky Mountains "the western limits of the Republic should be drawn, and the statue of the fabled god Terminus should be raised upon its highest peak, never to be thrown down." But the attempts to limit the boundaries, to restrict land sales and settlement, and to deprive the West of its share of political power were all in vain. Steadily the frontier of settlement advanced and carried with it individualism, democracy, and nationalism, and powerfully affected the East and the Old World.

The most effective efforts of the East to regulate the frontier came through its educational and religious activity, exerted by interstate migration and by organized societies. Speaking in 1835, Dr. Lyman Beecher declared: "It is equally plain that the religious and political destiny of our nation is to be decided in the West," and he pointed out that the population of the West "is assembled from all the States of the Union and from all the nations of Europe, and is rushing in like the waters of the flood, demanding for its moral preservation the immediate and universal action of those institutions which discipline the mind and arm the conscience and the heart. And so various are the opinions and habits, and so recent and imperfect is the acquaintance, and so sparse are the settlements of the West, that no homogeneous public sentiment can be formed to legislate immediately into being the requisite institutions. And yet they are all needed immediately in their utmost perfection and power. A nation is being 'born in a day.' . . . But what will become of the West if her prosperity rushes up to such a majesty of power, while those great institutions linger which are necessary to form the mind and the conscience and the heart of that vast world. It must not be permitted. . . . Let no man at the East quiet himself and dream of liberty, whatever may become of the West. . . . Her destiny is our destiny."

With the appeal to the conscience of New England, he adds appeals to her fears lest other religious sects anticipate her own. The New England preacher and school-teacher left their mark on the West. The dread of Western emancipation from New England's political and economic control was paralleled by her fears lest the West cut loose from her religion. Commenting in 1850 on reports that settlement was rapidly extending northward in Wisconsin, the editor of the *Home Missionary* writes: "We scarcely know whether to rejoice or mourn over this extension of our settlements. While we sympathize in whatever tends to increase the physical resources and prosperity of our country, we can not forget that with all these dispersions into remote and still remoter corners of the land the supply of the means of grace is becoming relatively less and less." Acting in accordance with such ideas, home missions were established and Western colleges were erected. As seaboard cities like Philadelphia, New York, and Baltimore strove for the mastery of Western trade, so the various denominations strove for the possession of the West. Thus an intellectual stream from New England sources fertilized the West. Other sections sent their missionaries; but the real struggle was between sects. The contest for power and the expansive tendency furnished to the various sects by the existence of a moving frontier must have had important results on the character of religious organization in the United States. The multiplication of rival churches in the little frontier towns had deep and lasting social effects. The religious aspects of the frontier make a chapter in our history which needs study.

From the conditions of frontier life came intellectual traits of profound importance. The works of travelers along each frontier from colonial days onward describe certain common traits, and these traits have, while softening down, still persisted as survivals in the place of their origin, even when a higher social organization succeeded. The result is that to the frontier the American intellect owes its striking characteristics. That coarseness and strength combined with acuteness and inquisitiveness; that practical, inventive turn of mind, quick to find expedients; that masterful grasp of material things, lacking in the artistic but powerful to effect great ends; that restless, nervous energy; that dominant individualism, working for good and for evil, and withal that buoyancy and exuberance which comes with freedom—these are traits of the frontier, or traits called out elsewhere because of the existence of the frontier. Since the days when the fleet of Columbus sailed into the waters of the New World, America has been another name for opportunity, and the people of the United States have taken their tone from the incessant expansion which has not only been open but has even been forced upon them. He would be a rash prophet who should assert that the expansive character of American life has now entirely ceased. Movement has been its dominant fact, and, unless this training has no effect upon a people, the American energy will continually demand a wider field for its exercise. But never again will such gifts of free land offer themselves. For a moment, at the frontier, the bonds of custom are broken and unrestraint is triumphant. There is not *tabula rasa*. The stubborn American environment is there with its imperious summons to accept its conditions; the inherited ways of doing things are also there; and yet, in spite of environment, and in spite of custom, each frontier did indeed furnish a new field of opportunity, a gate of escape from the bondage of the past; and freshness, and confidence, and scorn of older society, impatience of its restraints and its ideas, and indifference to its lessons, have accompanied the frontier. What the Mediterranean Sea was to the Greeks, breaking the bond of custom, offering new experiences, calling out new institutions and activities, that, and more, the ever retreating frontier has been to the United States directly, and to the nations of Europe more remotely. And now, four centuries from the discovery of America, at the end of a hundred years of life under the Constitution, the frontier has gone, and with its going has closed the first period of American history.

THE AMERICAN FRONTIER—FRONTIER OF WHAT?

by CARLTON J. H. HAYES

It is now over half a century since Frederick Jackson Turner assisted in Chicago at the international celebration of the discovery of America by reading his famous paper on "The Significance of the Frontier in American History." "Almost without critical test," as Professor Paxson has remarked, the frontier hypothesis in that paper met with prompt and well-nigh unanimous acceptance by historians of the United States.[1] And during succeeding years, we all know, it has inspired and been exploited in a multitude of tomes and monographs. Nowadays none of our university departments of history is complete without a frontier specialist, and no one, even a New Yorker, would essay a history of the United States, whether for the profession, the general reader, or the schools, without paying homage to the Turner hypothesis.

Our historical guild should have no illusion or pessimism about its ability, in the long run, to lodge in popular consciousness practically any interpretation or reconstruction of the past upon which it may concentrate. It can certainly perceive and rejoice that its concentration for a half century on the significance of the frontier in American history has been productive not only of caviar for seminars but of common fare for journalists and radio commentators. The hypothesis has become axiomatic that our democracy and

[1] Frederic L. Paxson, in *Encyclopedia of the Social Sciences*, XV (1935), 132-33.

From the *American Historical Review*, LI (January, 1946), by permission of the publisher.

social progress and national mores have been chiefly, if unconsciously, the creation of frontiersmen, as these, in an epic sweep westward across the continent, successively wrested new free lands from the wilderness and the Indians and there, "as nowhere else in recorded history, set up institutions relatively free from coercion by either law or habit."

I have neither the intention nor the competence to criticize this hypothesis. I can only bow, with respect and envy, to the numerous scholars in American history who, with extraordinary industry and enthusiasm, and in great detail, have applied and tested it during the last half century. I wonder, however, if the time has not come when our historians might profitably broaden their conception of the frontier and extend their researches and writing into a wider field. For granting that the frontier has been a major factor in the historical conditioning and development of what is distinctive in the United States, a large and now, I believe, most pertinent question remains about the American frontier. It is a frontier of what?

This would seem an obvious question, with an obvious answer. The answer was, indeed, clearly indicated several years ago by the late President Dixon Ryan Fox in a series of brilliant essays,[2] and likewise by the late Professor William R. Shepherd in his graduate lecture course and seminar on European expansion and in articles he published in the *Political Science Quarterly*.[3] Both those scholars, and a considerable number of others, including the California "school" of Professor Herbert Bolton, regarded the advancing frontier in North America, like similar frontiers in South America, Australasia, and South Africa, as a frontier of Europe. They were concerned with the transit of culture from Europe, or from already Europeanized oversea areas, to the frontier, as well as with the reverse cultural influences of the frontier.

Unfortunately, such broad vision was shared by relatively few specialists in American history, and it led to no appreciable lessening of their absorption in the frontier itself and in the one-way influences of the frontier upon purely American developments. One conventionally assumed that the frontier was a western frontier of the eastern United States. It was viewed as a peculiarly American phenomenon, determining the unique character of our own national society and culture.

2

The vogue of this restricted interpretation of the American frontier, and the concurrent neglect of broader and otherwise obvious considerations, have been, I submit, at once a result and a stimulant of growing intellectual isolationism in the United States. Our isolationism, of course, has many aspects, political and economic as well as intellectual, and many explanations. Before the days of steamships and airplanes we were, in truth, remote from the rest of the world; and our achievement of political independence naturally fostered an ambition for intellectual inde-

---

[2] Most notably, his "Civilization in Transit," "Culture in Knapsacks," and "Refuse Ideas and Their Disposal," conveniently assembled in D. R. Fox, *Ideas in Motion* (New York, 1935). The first of these appeared originally in the *American Historical Review*, XXXII (1927), 753-68.

[3] *Political Science Quarterly*, XXXII (1919), 43-60, 210-25, 392-412.

pendence. Moreover, a lurking suspicion of inferiority, which long lingered with us, has had the usual psychological compensation in strident assertion of superiority. And for utilitarian purposes, as well as under romantic influences, we have cultivated a lusty nationalism, the more intense because the more artificial. In Europe, everybody has been conscious of belonging to a particular nationality, with distinctive language and traditions, and nationalism has been a more or less natural flowering of the consciousness of nationality. In the United States, on the other hand, nationalism has been the fertilizer, rather than the flower. It has here been spread and utilized as the most effective means of producing in a population of very diverse origins—linguistic, religious, and racial—a common and luxuriant consciousness of belonging to a new and unique nationality. All this has inoculated us against Europe and built up an isolationist state of mind.

In all this, too, our historiography has played no inconsiderable part. It was marked, in the first generation of our political independence, by patriotic and panegyrical works, shelved now but influential then, such as David Ramsay's *History of the American Revolution,* Timothy Pitkin's *Political and Civil History of the United States of America,* and the biographies of Washington by Mason Weems and John Marshall. Afterwards, for two succeeding generations and well into the 1880's, its central monument was George Bancroft's elaborate presentation of American history as an unfolding of the Deity's grand design to enshrine in the New World and particularly in the United States the ark of the covenant of liberty and democracy.

Since the introduction, in the 1870's and 1880's, of professional university training, with its inculcation of scientific spirit and methods, American historiography has understandably reacted against the puerilities of a "Parson" Weems and the grandiose pietism of a Bancroft. Yet, if our historical writing has latterly become more critical in manner, it is not less American in subject matter and emphasis. Indeed, a striking general fact about it during the past seventy years has been the tendency to turn away from European themes and to concentrate upon strictly American. The seventy years mark a new and self-imposed sort of "Babylonian Captivity." There have been no real successors to Prescott, Motley, and Parkman; our recent literary historians write epics of the United States.

For every monograph or doctoral dissertation in European history during the past twenty years, there have been at least a dozen in American history. And whereas formerly every research worker in American history had had some basic training in medieval or modern European history, nowadays one can, and frequently does, produce a dissertation in a state of comparative innocence about what has occurred outside the geographical confines of the United States. This circumstance and the narrowing specialized training of our university seminars must explain why so many younger investigators of the American frontier have neglected its broader relationships and been indifferent to its comparative study. Even the growing number of economic determinists among us tend more and more to seek confirmation of their faith in exclusively American events.

Yet apparently the isolationist and nationalist trend in American historiography is not deemed fast or effective enough. In the columns of a leading metropolitan newspaper is alarmingly broadcast a series of embarrassing disclosures that there are "facts" of American history which high-school and college graduates have not learned, or do not remember. To remedy the sorry situation, state laws are being rapidly enacted by politicians addicted to Fourth of July oratory, and curriculums are being correspondingly refashioned by professional "educators." We are going to compel the next generation to have more American history—and, perforce, less of any other: the very generation which we expect to carry successfully the new and manifold international responsibilities we have assumed.

Of course the backbone of the schooling of our young people should be history—solid, vertebrate history—and not any of the amorphous jelly-like substitutes for it which were a fad with curriculum-makers between the first and second World Wars. But I, for one, do not see how we substantially improve matters by expanding a high-school course in American history from one year to two or three and telescoping all the rest of man's past and the history of all other nations into a single year or half year of fleeting elementary generalization quaintly described as "world history." Nor do I perceive how a college sequence or a university doctorate in "American civilization" is going to prepare our students and scholars for enlightened participation in the transcendent responsibilities of the United States as a world power, that is, unless "American civilization" is intimately and historically related to the original and widely ramifying civilization of which it is but a fragment.

The present trend, if unchecked, can only confirm the popular myths that the "American way of life" is something entirely indigenous, something wholly new, and something vastly superior to any other nation's. It is also likely to strengthen our people's missionary and messianic impulse, which will have far greater scope and far greater opportunity for expressing itself in the current aftermath of the second World War, and which, if unattended by realistic knowledge of other peoples and their historic cultures, may lead to the most dangerous consequences for the United States itself. Just when we are recognizing the futility of political isolation and joining at long last an international security organization, and when, through reciprocal trade agreements and acceptance of the Bretton Woods proposals, we are abandoning efforts at economic isolation, it is astonishing and paradoxical that at the same time we should keep alive and actually intensify an intellectual isolationism.

From the bitter experiences of recent years, we, as a nation, have derived surprisingly few lessons affecting our thinking. We have doubtless become a bit more aware of some kind of relationship between the United States and the world outside, and more inclined to wishful thoughts about a universal utopia which our sanguine publicists alluringly, though vaguely, picture as "the bright new world of tomorrow." Doubtless, too, certain patent strategic needs of the moment, coupled with a good deal of public advertising, have aroused a special interest in Latin America and popularized the concept of "hemispheric solidarity," which probably signifies, however, only a shift of isolationism from the nation to the hemisphere. At any rate, there can be no doubt that the bulk of Americans, including the bulk of our so-called intellectuals, continue to think, in essentially isolationist terms, of separate "Old World" and "New World," of detached Eastern and Western Hemispheres, of "Europe for the Europeans" and "America for the Americans."

This dichotomy in our thinking is the result, let me repeat, of ignorance, of self-centered absorption in local or sectional concerns, and of nationalist propaganda. It is unrealistic, contrary to basic historical facts, and highly dangerous for our country at the present and in the future.

3

We used to know that we were Europeans as well as Americans, that we were not Indians or a people miraculously sprung from virgin forests like the primitive Germans described by Tacitus, but modern Europeans living in America on a frontier of Europe. All our original white ancestors on this continent knew they came from Europe. They and their sons and grandsons knew they had ties with Englishmen, Spaniards, Portuguese, Hollanders, or Frenchmen, as the case might be, not only on this side of the ocean but on the other. And generation after generation of their descendants on this side, no matter on what segment of the frontier they chanced to be, and no matter how intent on clearing new lands, were concerned and found themselves participants in all the successive major wars of Europe from the sixteenth century to the twentieth: the English-Spanish wars, the English-Dutch wars, the War of the League of Augsburg, the War of the Spanish Succession, the War of the Austrian Succession, the Seven Years' War, the Revolutionary and Napoleonic Wars, the war of 1914, the war of 1939. From the first, moreover, it has been known or knowable, if latterly obscured, that our language, our religion, our culture are rooted in Europe, that our ideals of liberty and constitutional government are a heritage of Europe.

In paying tribute to the members of the Constitutional Convention of 1787, Charles A. Beard has remarked:

It is not merely patriotic pride that compels one to assert that never in the history of assemblies has there been a convention of men richer in political experience and in practical knowledge, or endowed with a profounder insight into the springs of human action and the intimate essence of government. It is indeed an astounding fact that at one time so many men skilled in statecraft could be found on the very frontiers of civilization among a population numbering about four million whites.[4]

It is not quite so astounding, I would add, if one bears in mind that those men "on the very frontiers of civilization" possessed lively contacts with, and solid knowledge of, the European civilization on whose frontiers they were. One has only to run through the numbers of the *Federalist* to recognize the sure and firm grasp of such men as Hamilton, Madison, and Jay on the history and political experience of ancient Greece and Rome and of the countries of medieval and modern Europe—Britain, Germany, France, Poland, the Netherlands, Switzerland.[5] The founding fathers may have

[4] Charles A. Beard, *The Supreme Court and the Constitution* (New York, 1912), pp. 86-87.
[5] See in particular Nos. 17-20, 34, 47, and 63 of the *Federalist,* in the convenient sesquicentennial reprint, edited by Edward Mead Earle (Washington, 1939).

been frontiersmen and greatly influenced by economic conditions in the New World, but they could readily have passed a searching examination for the doctorate in European history and European comparative government, which, I dare say, is more than the majority of our senators or even of our Ph.D.'s in American history could now do.

That the United States could become an independent nation and enjoy the freedom and opportunity to extend its frontiers and greatly to increase its population and prosperity and strength during the perilous fifty years of Revolutionary and Napoleonic Wars and Metternichean reaction, from 1775 to 1825, is attributable less to American aloofness from Europe than to the informed statecraft of Americans who were then in familiar touch with Europe and equipped to treat with it intelligently and realistically. Almost without exception, our presidents and secretaries of state and key diplomatists of that time had practical experience in European, as well as American, affairs— Franklin, Jefferson, Jay, Marshall, Madison, Monroe, John Adams, John Quincy Adams. Monroe, for example, served in diplomatic posts in France, England, and Spain for six years before he became Madison's Secretary of State, and his own Secretary of State, John Quincy Adams, had been a student at Paris and Leiden and had had twenty years' diplomatic experience in France, the Netherlands, Prussia, Russia, and Great Britain. The words which this qualified statesman put into Monroe's celebrated message of 1823 to the Congress expressed an enlightened realism in notable contrast with utterances and actions of certain American statesmen of a later date less in touch with the realities of Europe and more with ideological propaganda in America.

Said the message of 1823, without trace of a holier-than-thou attitude:

Our policy in regard to Europe . . . remains the same, which is, not to interfere in the internal affairs of any of its powers; to consider the Government *de facto* as the legitimate Government for us; to cultivate friendly relations with it, and to preserve those relations by a frank, firm, and manly policy; meeting, in all instances, the just claims of every power; submitting to injuries from none.

It was not only our statesmen of that time who knew and appreciated the relationship between Europe and America. Our colleges and academies, with their classical curriculum, and our literary men and publicists, with their extensive reading of British and French philosophers of the seventeenth and eighteenth centuries, possessed like knowledge and appreciation. Our commercial classes, including our cotton planters, had it, too. To protect our commerce with Europe, Jefferson dispatched to the Mediterranean an American armed expeditionary force which made landings in North Africa nearly a century and a half before the recent repetition of American campaigning in the Mediterranean. And what a reading public there was in the United States for those literary historians in our "middle period" —Irving, Prescott, Motley, and Parkman— who dwelt on exploits of Spanish, Dutch, and French. It might well be envied by any historian of the American frontier or even by the Book-of-the-Month Club. The Mediterranean Sea was not then so far off, or the Atlantic Ocean so wide, as our developing isolationist nationalism later made them.

Our successive American generations of

frontiersmen on the eastern seaboard, in the Piedmont, across the Alleghenies, along the Ohio, the Great Lakes, and the Mississippi, over the prairies, and into and beyond the Rockies, may have thought of themselves as Americans first. They may have adopted Indian dress and Indian usages in hunting and fishing and scalping. They may have exerted, and doubtless did exert, a profound and lasting influence on the nationalist evolution of the United States. But all this did not make them Indians or immunize them against the superior and eventually mastering civilization which emanated from Europe and relentlessly followed them. They remained Europeans and retained at least the rudiments of European civilization. After all, the American frontier, as Professor Turner so ably and perhaps regretfully showed, was an evanescent phenomenon, ever passing from primitiveness toward the social and intellectual pattern of the area in back of it. In other words, the abiding heritage of traditional civilization outweighed, in a relatively brief period, the novelties acquired from Indians and wilderness. Continuity proved stronger than change. The transit of culture was not so much *from* as *to* the frontier.

Differences admittedly obtain between Americans in the United States and the peoples in Europe from whom they are descended, but the differences are not greater in kind, and hardly greater in degree, than those obtaining between Englishmen and Spaniards or between Germans and Italians, or between the people of the United States and the peoples of Central and South America. True, the nationalism which has progressively infected all peoples of Europe and America during the last hundred and fifty years has grossly exaggerated the differences and given wide currency to the notion of distinctive and self-contained national cultures—a French culture, a Norwegian culture, a Spanish culture, an American culture. The result has been an obscuring and neglect of what these several national cultures have in common, a European or "Western" culture, the community of heritage and outlook and interests in Europe and its whole American frontier.

Actual differences are differences of emphasis and detail, associated with political sovereignty and independence, and arising from variant geographical and historical circumstances. Back of them all, however, is a unifying fact and force, which is describable as "European" or "Western," and which, now more than ever before, needs to be appreciated and applied. Actually and fundamentally, just as the European remains a European while thinking of himself first as an Englishman, a Frenchman, a German, or a Spaniard, so the descendants of Europeans in America remain European even while insisting that they are Americans first.

The frontier has undoubtedly been a very important source of what is distinctive and peculiar in the national evolution of the United States. But few European nations have been without a frontier in the American sense at some time in their history and without significant lasting effects of that frontier. Contemporary peculiarities in the life and customs of Spain, for instance, cannot be dissociated from the slow advance, during several centuries, of a frontier of conquest of Moorish lands; nor Germany's, from an analogous frontier in barbarous regions of north central Europe. In a larger way, all America is a frontier: Latin America, of Spain and Portugal; Quebec, of France; the United States, of Great Britain and Holland, Spain and France, Germany and Ireland, Scandinavia and Italy and Poland. Our Negroes and Indians, as these have been civilized, have been Europeanized as well as Americanized. The "melting pot" is no novelty in the history of Western civilization; it has latterly been doing in America, on a large scale, the same sort of fusing which at earlier dates produced the chief nations of modern Europe. Comparative study of frontiers in Europe and America, together with comparative study of melting pots and nationalisms in both, might serve to demonstrate that obvious differences between nations of European tradition are fewer and relatively less significant than their similarities.

4

"European," as I here use the term, does not refer merely to a detached piece of geography or to a continent by itself, and not to another "hemisphere" or a hoary and pitiable "Old World." Rather, it refers to a great historic culture, the "Western" civilization, which, taking its rise around the Mediterranean, has long since embraced the Atlantic, creating what Mr. Walter Lippmann has appropriately designated the "Atlantic Community."[6] As Professor Ross Hoffman says:

Every state of the North and South American continents originated from Western European Christendom which Voltaire, in the age before the independence movements, characterized so well as a "great republic." Englishmen, Frenchmen, Spaniards, Portuguese, Dutchmen and Danes in the early modern centuries made the Atlantic Ocean the inland sea of Western civilization; they made it an historical and geographical extension of the Mediterranean. . . . Many of these early-forged bonds still span the Atlantic, and the spread of British, French, and American ideals of liberty and constitutional government has made this oceanic region the citadel of what today is rather loosely called Democracy.[7]

Of such an Atlantic community and the European civilization basic to it, we Americans are co-heirs and co-developers, and probably in the future the leaders. If we are successfully to discharge our heavy and difficult postwar responsibilities, we shall not further weaken, but rather strengthen, the consciousness and bonds of this cultural community.

Against it, militate two current trends of quite contradictory character. One, which I have already indicated, is the nationalistic tendency to view each nation as *sui generis,* and to attribute to it an independent and distinctive culture all its own. The second is the hypothesizing of a "world civilization." This has already passed from the fictional titles of high-school textbooks to the solemn pronouncements of statesmen. It represents a leap from myopic nationalism to starry-eyed universalism. I, for one, have not the faintest idea what world civilization is. I know there are enduring and respectable civilizations in Moslem areas, in India, in China, and presumably in Japan. I also know there are considerable influences of such civilizations upon ours, and, especially in the material domain, heavy

[6] Walter Lippmann, *U. S. War Aims* (Boston, 1944), pp. 63-88.

[7] Ross Hoffman, "Europe and the Atlantic Community," *Thought,* XX (March, 1945), 25. See also his *The Great Republic* (New York, 1942) and *Durable Peace* (New York, 1944).

impacts by ours upon them. But the many existing civilizations still do not constitute a single "world civilization," and for a long time to come, I hazard, the common denominator among them is likely to be low—as low, I should suppose, as unadorned "human nature."

Neither devotion to one's nation nor idealization of the world at large should obscure the important cultural entities which lie between. These are the powerhouses of civilization for their constituent nationalities, and the units which must be brought into co-operation for any world order of the future. The one to which Americans belong is the "European" or "Western." It has conditioned our past. And whether we are aware of it, or not, it conditions our present and future.

In what does it consist? First, in the Greco-Roman tradition, with its rich heritage of literature and language, of philosophy, of architecture and art, of law and political concepts. Second, in the Judeo-Christian tradition, with its fructifying ethos and ethics, its abiding and permeating influence on personal and social behavior, its constant distinctions between the individual and the race, between liberty and authority, between mercy and justice, between what is Caesar's and what is God's. Third, proceeding from joint effects of the first two, it comprises traditions of individualism, of limitations on the state, of social responsibility, of revolt and revolution. Fourth, likewise proceeding from the others, particularly from the Christian tradition, it includes a tradition of expansiveness, of missionary and crusading zeal, which has inspired not merely a spasmodic but a steady pushing outward of European frontiers—from the Mediterranean to the Arctic and across the Atlantic, in turn over lands of Celts, Germans, Slavs, Magyars, and Scandinavians, over the full width of both American continents, and beyond to the Philippines and Australasia and into Africa.

In all these characteristics of European or Western civilization, every nationality of central and western Europe and of America shares. In measure as the frontier advances and is civilized, it is these characteristics which actuate and are embodied in the civilization. The United States is no exception.

One does not have to go to Athens and Rome to behold Greek and Roman architecture, or to Palestine and Europe to see Jewish synagogues and Christian churches. There are more churches and synagogues in the United States than in any other country in the world. There is more classical architecture in Leningrad or London than in Athens, and still more in Washington. It is indeed the practically official architecture of our American democracy from Jefferson to Hoover, and the favorite style for bank buildings, railway stations, and public schools, whether in Virginia or Illinois or the Far West. Our prevailing language continues to be transatlantic English, and distinctively American only in pronunciation and raciness of idiom. Shakespeare and Milton are as much ours as England's. Our juristic conceptions and legal usages are likewise transatlantic, and I know of no philosophical speculation on this continent, in the whole gamut from the pragmatic to the Thomistic, or on any subject from theological to scientific, including political and economic, which has not had its equivalent and usually its antecedent in Europe.

If we belonged to a Moslem or Confucian culture, or to a purely indigenous one, we would not have the mores which we have. We would not, for instance, be free on Sundays for church or golf or for surreptitious privacy in library or laboratory. Probably we would not use knives and forks, and we would wear different clothes. We might be more ceremonial and more externally polite. We might think, as well as behave, differently. Our sense of values and our frames of reference could not be quite the same. We are what we are only in part because of biological heredity and physical environment. In larger part it is because we are stamped from infancy with a historic culture of singularly educative and perduring potency. . . .

The student of the history of the United States, whether dealing with its political, economic, or cultural development, would be the better historian and the more enlightening if he was a specialist also in the history of a foreign country from which comparisons and contrasts could be drawn. Similarly, the student of the history of a foreign country could profitably extend his study beyond that country. Most of all, the historian of a particular phenomenon, such as nationalism, slavery, democracy, the frontier, etc., however specific in time or space may be his immediate work, must needs possess, if his work is to be informed and judicious, a wide background of acquaintance with other and comparable examples of the phenomenon.

In summary, the American frontier is a frontier of European or "Western" culture. This culture, however modified by or adapted to peculiar geographical and social conditions in America or elsewhere, is still, in essential respects, the culture and hence a continuous bond of the regional community of nations on both sides of the Atlantic. Like its predecessor and inspirer, the Mediterranean community of ancient times, the Atlantic community has been an outstanding fact and a prime factor of modern history. Despite the growth in latter years of an anarchical nationalism and isolationism on one hand, and of a utopian universalism on the other, the Atlantic community has lost none of its potential importance for us and for the world. We must look anew to it and strengthen our ties with it, if we are to escape the tragedy of another world war and ensure the blessings of liberty and democracy to future generations. To this end the historical guild in America can immeasurably contribute by extending the use of the comparative method, by emphasizing the continuity of history, and by stressing cultural and social, equally with political and economic, history.

WHAT'S AMERICAN ABOUT AMERICA?
by JOHN A. KOUWENHOVEN

THE DISCOVERY of America has never been a more popular pastime than it is today. Scarcely a week goes by without someone's publishing a new book of travels in the bright continent. The anthropologists, native and foreign, have discovered that

Copyright, John A. Kouwenhoven, reprinted by his permission.

the natives of Middletown and Plainville, U.S.A. are as amazing and as interesting as the natives of such better known communities as the Trobriand Islands and Samoa. Magazines here and abroad provide a steady flow of articles by journalists, historians, sociologists, and philosophers who want to explain America to itself, or to themselves, or to others.

The discoverers of America have, of course, been describing their experiences ever since Captain John Smith wrote his first book about America almost 350 years ago. But as Smith himself noted, not everyone "who hath bin at Virginia, understandeth or knowes what Virginia is." Indeed, just a couple of years ago the Carnegie Corporation, which supports a number of college programs in American Studies, entitled its Quarterly Report "Who Knows America?" and went on to imply that nobody does, not even "our lawmakers, journalists, civic leaders, diplomats, teachers, and others."

There is, of course, the possibility that some of the writers who have explored, vicariously or in person, this country's past and present may have come to understand or know what America really is. But how is the lay inquirer and the student to know which accounts to trust? Especially since most of the explorers seem to have found not one but two or more antipodal and irreconcilable Americas. The Americans, we are convincingly told, are the most materialistic of peoples, and, on the other hand, they are the most idealistic; the most revolutionary, and, conversely, the most conservative; the most rampantly individualistic, and, simultaneously, the most gregarious and herd-like; the most irreverent toward their elders, and, contrariwise, the most abject worshipers of "Mom." They have an unbridled admiration of everything big, from bulldozers to bosoms; and they are in love with everything diminutive, from the "small hotel" in the song to the little woman in the kitchen.

Maybe, as Henry James thought when he wrote *The American Scene,* it is simply that the country is "too large for any human convenience," too diverse in geography and in blood strains to make sense as any sort of unit. Whatever the reason, the conflicting evidence turns up wherever you look, and the observer has to content himself with some sort of pluralistic conception. The philosopher Santayana's way out was to say that the American mind was split in half, one half symbolized by the skyscraper, the other by neat reproductions of Colonial mansions (with surreptitious modern conveniences).

"The American will," he concluded, "inhabits the skyscraper; the American intellect inherits the Colonial mansion." Mark Twain also defined the split in architectural terms, but more succinctly: American houses, he said, had Queen Anne fronts and Mary Ann behinds.

And yet, for all the contrarieties, there remains something which I think we all feel to be distinctively American, some quality or characteristic underlying the polarities which—as Henry James himself went on to say—makes the American way of doing things differ more from any other nation's way than the ways of any two other Western nations differ from each other.

I am aware of the risks in generalizing. And yet it would be silly, I am convinced, to assert that there are not certain things which are more American than others. Take the New York City skyline, for example—that ragged manmade Sierra at the eastern edge of the continent. Clearly, in the minds of immigrants and returning travelers, in the iconography of the ad-men who use it as a backdrop for the bourbon and airplane luggage they are selling, in the eyes of poets and of military strategists, it is one of the prime American symbols.

Let me start, then, with the Manhattan skyline and list a few things which occur to me as distinctively American. Then, when we have the list, let us see what, if anything, these things have in common. Here are a dozen items to consider:

1. The Manhattan skyline
2. The gridiron town plan
3. The skyscraper
4. The Model-T Ford
5. Jazz
6. The Constitution
7. Mark Twain's writing
8. Whitman's *Leaves of Grass*
9. Comic strips
10. Soap operas
11. Assembly-line production
12. Chewing gum

Here we have a round dozen artifacts which are, it seems to me, recognizably American, not likely to have been produced elsewhere. Granted that some of us take more pleasure in some of them than in others—that many people prefer soap opera to *Leaves of Grass* while others think Mark Twain's storytelling is less offensive than chewing gum—all twelve items are, I believe, widely held to be indigenous to our culture. The fact that many people in other lands like them too, and that some of them are nearly as acceptable overseas as they are here at home, does not in any way detract from their obviously American character. It merely serves to remind us that to be American does not mean to be inhuman—a fact which, in certain moods of self-criticism, we are inclined to forget.

What, then, is the "American" quality which these dozen items share? And what can that quality tell us about the character of our culture, about the nature of our civilization?

Skylines and Skyscrapers

Those engaged in discovering America often begin by discovering the Manhattan skyline, and here as well as elsewhere they discover apparently irreconcilable opposites. They notice at once that it doesn't make any sense, in human or aesthetic terms. It is the product of insane politics, greed, competitive ostentation, megalomania, the worship of false gods. Its products, in turn, are traffic jams, bad ventilation, noise, and all the other ills that metropolitan flesh is heir to. And the net result is, illogically enough, one of the most exaltedly beautiful things man has ever made.

Perhaps this paradoxical result will be less bewildering if we look for a moment at the formal and structural principles which are involved in the skyline. It may be helpful to consider the skyline as we might consider a lyric poem, or a novel, if we were trying to analyze its aesthetic quality.

Looked at in this way, it is clear that the total effect which we call "the Manhattan skyline" is made up of almost innumerable buildings, each in competition (for height, or glamor, or efficiency, or respectability) with all of the others. Each goes its own way, as it were, in a carnival of rugged architectural individualism. And yet—as witness the universal feeling of exaltation and aspiration which the skyline as a whole evokes—out of this ir-

[844]

rational, unplanned, and often infuriating chaos, an unforeseen unity has evolved. No building ever built in New York was placed where it was, or shaped as it was, because it would contribute to the aesthetic effect of the skyline—lifting it here, giving it mass there, or lending a needed emphasis. Each was built, all those now under construction are being built, with no thought for their subordination to any over-all effect.

What, then, makes possible the fluid and ever-changing unity which does, in fact, exist? Quite simply, there are two things, both simple in themselves, which do the job. If they were not simple, they would not work; but they are, and they do.

One is the gridiron pattern of the city's streets—the same basic pattern which accounts for Denver, Houston, Little Rock, Birmingham, and almost any American town you can name, and the same pattern which, in the form of square townships, sections, and quarter sections, was imposed by the Ordinance of 1785 on an almost continental scale. Whatever its shortcomings when compared with the "discontinuous street patterns" of modern planned communities, this artificial geometric grid—imposed upon the land without regard to contours or any preconceived pattern of social zoning—had at least the quality of rational simplicity. And it is this simple gridiron street pattern which, horizontally, controls the spacing and arrangement of the rectangular shafts which go to make up the skyline.

The other thing which holds the skyline's diversity together is the structural principle of the skyscraper. When we think of individual buildings, we tend to think of details of texture, color, and form, of surface ornamentation or the lack of it. But as elements in Manhattan's skyline, these things are of little consequence. What matters there is the vertical thrust, the motion upward; and that is the product of cage, or skeleton, construction in steel—a system of construction which is, in effect, merely a three-dimensional variant of the gridiron street plan, extending vertically instead of horizontally.

The aesthetics of cage, or skeleton, construction have never been fully analyzed, nor am I equipped to analyze them. But as a lay observer, I am struck by fundamental differences between the effect created by height in the RCA building at Radio City, for example, and the effect created by height in Chartres cathedral or in Giotto's campanile. In both the latter (as in all the great architecture of the past) proportion and symmetry, the relation of height to width, are constituent to the effect. One can say of a Gothic cathedral, this tower is too high; of a Romanesque dome, this is top-heavy. But there is nothing inherent in cage construction which would invite such judgments. A true skyscraper like the RCA building could be eighteen or twenty stories taller, or ten or a dozen stories shorter without changing its essential aesthetic effect. Once steel cage construction has passed a certain height, the effect of transactive upward motion has been established; from there on, the point at which you cut it off is arbitrary and makes no difference.

Those who are familiar with the history of the skyscraper will remember how slowly this fact was realized. Even Louis Sullivan—greatest of the early skyscraper architects—thought in terms of having to close off and climax the upward motion of the tall building with an "attic" or cornice. His lesser contemporaries worked for years on the blind assumption that the proportion and symmetry of masonry architecture must be preserved in the new technique. If with the steel cage one could go higher than with load-bearing masonry walls, the old aesthetic effects could be counterfeited by dressing the façade as if one or more buildings had been piled on top of another—each retaining the illusion of being complete in itself. You can still see such buildings in New York: the first five stories perhaps a Greco-Roman temple, the next ten a neuter warehouse, and the final five or six an Aztec pyramid. And that Aztec pyramid is simply a cheap and thoughtless equivalent of the more subtle Sullivan cornice. Both structures attempt to close and climax the upward thrust, to provide something similar to the *Katharsis* in Greek tragedy.

But the logic of cage construction requires no such climax. It has less to do with the inner logic of masonry forms than with that of the old Globe-Wernicke sectional bookcases, whose interchangeable units (with glass-flap fronts) anticipated by fifty years the modular unit systems of so-called modern furniture. Those bookcases were advertised in the 'nineties as "always complete but never finished"—a phrase which could with equal propriety have been applied to the Model-T Ford. Many of us remember with affection that admirably simple mechanism, forever susceptible to added gadgets or improved parts, each of which was interchangeable with what you already had.

Here, then, are the two things which serve to tie together the otherwise irrelevant components of the Manhattan skyline: the gridiron ground plan and the three-dimensional vertical grid of steel cage construction. And both of these are closely related to one another. Both are composed of simple and infinitely repeatable units.

The Structure of Jazz

It was the French architect, Le Corbusier, who described New York's architecture as "hot jazz in stone and steel." At first glance this may sound as if it were merely a slick updating of Schelling's "Architecture . . . is frozen music," but it is more than that if one thinks in terms of the structural principles we have been discussing and the structural principles of jazz.

Let me begin by making clear that I am using the term jazz in its broadest significant application. There are circumstances in which it is important to define the term with considerable precision, as when you are involved in discussion with a disciple of one of the many cults, orthodox or progressive, which devote themselves to some particular subspecies of jazz. But in our present context we need to focus upon what all the subspecies (Dixieland, Bebop, Swing, or Cool Jazz) have in common; in other words, we must neglect the by no means uninteresting qualities which differentiate one from another, since it is what they have in common which can tell us most about the civilization which produced them.

There is no definition of jazz, academic or otherwise, which does not acknowledge that its essential ingredient is a particular kind of rhythm. Improvisation is also frequently mentioned as an essential; but even if it were true that jazz always involves improvisation, that would not distinguish it from a good deal of Western European music of the past. It is the distinctive rhythm which differentiates all

[846]

types of jazz from all other music and which gives to all of its types a basic family resemblance.

It is not easy to define that distinctive rhythm. Winthrop Sargeant has described it as the product of two superimposed devices: syncopation and polyrhythm, both of which have the effect of constantly upsetting rhythmical expectations. André Hodeir, in his recent analysis of *Jazz: Its Evolution and Essence,* speaks of "an unending alternation" of syncopations and of notes played *on* the beat, which "gives rise to a kind of expectation that is one of jazz's subtlest effects."

As you can readily hear, if you listen to any jazz performance (whether of the Louis Armstrong, Benny Goodman, or Charlie Parker variety), the rhythmical effect depends upon there being a clearly defined basic rhythmic pattern which enforces the expectations which are to be upset. That basic pattern is the 4/4 or 2/4 beat which underlies all jazz. Hence the importance of the percussive instruments in jazz: the drums, the guitar or banjo, the bull fiddle, the piano. Hence too the insistent thump, thump, thump, thump which is so boring when you only half-hear jazz—either because you are too far away, across the lake or in the next room, or simply because you will not listen attentively. But hence also the delight, the subtle effects, which good jazz provides as the melodic phrases evade, anticipate, and return to, and then again evade the steady basic four-beat pulse which persists, implicitly or explicitly, throughout the performance.

In other words, the structure of a jazz performance is, like that of the New York skyline, a tension of cross-purposes. In jazz at its characteristic best, each player seems to be—and has the sense of being—on his own. Each goes his own way, inventing rhythmic and melodic patterns which, superficially, seem to have as little relevance to one another as the United Nations building does to the Empire State. And yet the outcome is a dazzlingly precise creative unity.

In jazz that unity of effect is, of course, the result of the very thing which each of the players is flouting: namely, the basic 4/4 beat—that simple rhythmic gridiron of identical and infinitely extendible units which holds the performance together. As Louis Armstrong once wrote, you would expect that if every man in a band "had his own way and could play as he wanted, all you would get would be a lot of jumbled up, crazy noise." But, as he goes on to say, that does not happen, because the players know "by ear and sheer musical instinct" just when to leave the underlying pattern and when to get back on it.

What it adds up to, as I have argued elsewhere, is that jazz is the first art form to give full expression to Emerson's ideal of a union which is perfect only "when all the uniters are isolated." That Emerson's ideal is deeply rooted in our national experience need not be argued. Frederick Jackson Turner quotes a letter written by a frontier settler to friends back East, which in simple, unself-conscious words expresses the same reconciling of opposites. "It is a universal rule here," the frontiersman wrote, "to help one another, each one keeping an eye single to his own business."

One need only remember that the Constitution itself, by providing for a federation of separate units, became the infinitely extendible framework for the process of reconciling liberty and unity over vast areas and conflicting interests. Its seven brief articles, providing for checks and balances between interests, classes, and branches of the government establish, in effect, the underlying beat which gives momentum and direction to a political process which Richard Hofstadter has called "a harmonious system of mutual frustration"—a description which fits a jazz performance as well as it fits our politics.

The aesthetic effects of jazz, as Winthrop Sargeant long ago suggested, have as little to do with symmetry and proportion as have those of a skyscraper. Like the skyscraper, a jazz performance does not build to an organically required climax; it can simply cease. The "piece" which the musicians are playing may, and often does, have a rudimentary Aristotelian pattern of beginning, middle, and end; but the jazz performance need not. In traditional Western European music, themes are developed. In jazz they are toyed with and dismantled. There is no inherent reason why the jazz performance should not continue for another 12 or 16 or 24 or 32 measures (for these are the rhythmic cages which in jazz correspond to the cages of a steel skeleton in architecture). As in the skyscraper, the aesthetic effect is one of motion, in this case horizontal rather than vertical.

Jazz rhythms create what can only be called momentum. When the rhythm of one voice (say the trumpet, off on a rhythmic and melodic excursion) lags behind the underlying beat, its four-beat measure carries over beyond the end of the underlying beat's measure into the succeeding one, which has already begun. Conversely, when the trumpet anticipates the beat, it starts a new measure before the steady underlying beat has ended one. And the result is an exhilarating forward motion which the jazz trumpeter Wingy Manone once described as "feeling an increase in tempo though you're still playing at the same tempo." Hence the importance in jazz of timing, and hence the delight and amusement of the so-called "break," in which the basic 4/4 beat ceases and a soloist goes off on a flight of rhythmic and melodic fancy which nevertheless comes back surprisingly and unerringly to encounter the beat precisely where it would have been if it had kept going.

Once the momentum is established, it can continue until—after an interval dictated by some such external factor as the conventional length of phonograph records or the endurance of dancers—it stops. And as if to guard against any Aristotelian misconceptions about an end, it is likely to stop on an unresolved chord, so that harmonically as well as rhythmically everything is left up in the air. Even the various coda-like devices employed by jazz performers at dances, such as the corny old "without a shirt" phrase of blessed memory, are harmonically unresolved. They are merely conventional ways of saying "we quit," not, like Beethoven's insistent codas, ways of saying, "There now; that ties off all the loose ends; I'm going to stop now; done; finished; concluded; signed, sealed, delivered."

Twain and Whitman

Thus far, in our discussion of distinctively "American" things, we have focused chiefly upon twentieth-century items. But the references to the rectangular grid pattern of cities and townships and to the Constitution should remind us that the underlying structural principles with which we are concerned are deeply embedded in our civilization. To shift the emphasis, therefore, let us look at item number 7 on our list: Mark Twain's writing.

Mark's writing was, of course, very largely the product of oral influences. He was a born storyteller, and he always insisted that the oral form of the humorous story was high art. Its essential tool (or weapon), he said, is the pause—which is to say, timing. "If the pause is too long the impressive point is passed," he wrote, "and the audience have had time to divine that a surprise is intended—and then you can't surprise them, of course." In other words, he saw the pause as a device for upsetting expectations, like the jazz "break."

Mark, as you know, was by no means a formal perfectionist. In fact he took delight in being irreverent about literary form. Take, for example, his account of the way *Pudd'nhead Wilson* came into being. It started out to be a story called "Those Extraordinary Twins," about a youthful freak consisting, as he said, of "a combination of two heads and four arms joined to a single body and a single pair of legs—and I thought I would write an extravagantly fantastic little story with this freak of nature for hero—or heroes—a silly young miss [named Rowena] for heroine, and two old ladies and two boys for the minor parts."

But as he got writing the tale, it kept spreading along and other people began intruding themselves—among them Pudd'nhead, and a woman named Roxana, and a young fellow named Tom Driscoll, who—before the book was half finished —had taken things almost entirely into their own hands and were "working the whole tale as a private venture of their own."

From this point, I want to quote Mark directly, because in the process of making fun of fiction's formal conventions he employs a technique which is the verbal equivalent of the jazz "break"—a technique of which he was a master.

When the book was finished, and I came to look round to see what had become of the team I had originally started out with —Aunt Patsy Cooper, Aunt Betsy Hale, the two boys, and Rowena the light-weight heroine—they were nowhere to be seen; they had disappeared from the story some time or other. I hunted about and found them—found them stranded, idle, forgotten, and permanently useless. It was very awkward. It was awkward all around; but more particularly in the case of Rowena, because there was a love match on, between her and one of the twins that constituted the freak, and I had worked it up to a blistering heat and thrown in a quite dramatic love quarrel [now watch Mark take off like a jazz trumpeter flying off on his own in a fantastic break] wherein Rowena scathingly denounced her betrothed for getting drunk, and scoffed at his explanation of how it had happened, and wouldn't listen to it, and had driven him from her in the usual "forever" way; and now here she sat crying and brokenhearted; for she had found that he had spoken only the truth; that it was not he but the other half of the freak, that had drunk the liquor that made him drunk; that her half was a prohibitionist and had never drunk a drop in his life, and, although tight as a brick three days in the week, was wholly innocent of blame; and, indeed, when sober was constantly doing all he could to reform his brother, the other half, who never got any satisfaction out of drinking anyway, because liquor never affected him. [Now he's going to get back on the basic beat again.] Yes, here she was, stranded with that deep injustice of hers torturing her poor heart.

Now I shall have to summarize again. Mark didn't know what to do with her. He couldn't just leave her there, of course, after making such a to-do over her; he'd have to account to the reader for her somehow. So he finally decided that all he could do was "give her the grand bounce." It grieved him, because he'd come to like her after a fashion, "notwithstanding she was such an ass and said such stupid, irritating things and was so nauseatingly sentimental"; but it had to be done. So he started Chapter Seventeen with: "Rowena went out in the back yard after supper to see the fireworks and fell down the well and got drowned."

It seemed abrupt, [Mark went on] but I thought maybe the reader wouldn't notice it, because I changed the subject right away to something else. Anyway, it loosened up Rowena from where she was stuck and got her out of the way, and that was the main thing. It seemed a prompt good way of weeding out people that had got stalled, and a plenty good enough way for those others; so I hunted up the two boys and said they went out back one night to stone the cat and fell down the well and got drowned. Next I searched around and found Aunt Patsy Cooper and Aunt Betsy Hale where they were aground, and said they went out back one night to visit the sick and fell down the well and got drowned. I was going to drown some of the others, but I gave up the idea, partly because I believed that if I kept that up it would arouse attention, . . . and partly because it was not a large well and would not hold any more anyway.

That was a long excursion—but it makes the point: that Mark didn't have much reverence for conventional story structure. Even his greatest book, which is perhaps also the greatest book written on this continent—*Huckleberry Finn*—is troublesome. One can scarcely find a criticism of the book which does not object, for instance, to the final episodes, in which Tom rejoins Huck and they go through that burlesque business of "freeing" the old Negro Jim—who is, it turns out, already free. But, as T. S. Eliot was, I think, the first to observe, the real structure of *Huck Finn* has nothing to do with the traditional form of the novel—with exposition, climax, and resolution. Its structure is like that of the great river itself—without beginning and without end. Its structural units, or "cages," are the episodes of which it is composed. Its momentum is that of the tension between the river's steady flow and the eccentric superimposed rhythms of Huck's flights from, and near recapture by, the restricting forces of routine and convention.

It is not a novel of escape; if it were, it would be Jim's novel, not Huck's. Huck is free at the start, and still free at the end. Looked at in this way, it is clear that *Huckleberry Finn* has as little need of a "conclusion" as has a skyscraper or a jazz performance. Questions of proportion and symmetry are as irrelevant to its structure as they are to the total effect of the New York skyline.

There is not room here for more than brief reference to the other "literary" items on our list: Whitman's *Leaves of Grass*, comic strips, and soap opera. Perhaps it is enough to remind you that *Leaves of Grass* has discomfited many a critic by its lack of symmetry and proportion, and that Whitman himself insisted: "I round and finish little, if anything; and could not, consistently with my scheme." As for the words of true poems, Whitman said in the "Song of the Answerer"—

They bring none to his or her terminus or to be content and full,
Whom they take they take into space to behold the birth of stars, to learn one of the meanings,

To launch off with absolute faith, to sweep
 through the ceaseless rings and never be
 quiet again.

Although this is not the place for a detailed analysis of Whitman's verse techniques, it is worth noting in passing how the rhythm of these lines reinforces their logical meaning. The basic rhythmical unit, throughout, is a three-beat phrase of which there are two in the first line (accents falling on *none, his,* and *term . . . be, tent,* and *full*), three in the second and in the third. Superimposed upon the basic three-beat measure there is a flexible, nonmetrical rhythm of colloquial phrasing. That rhythm is controlled in part by the visual effect of the arrangement in long lines, to each of which the reader tends to give equal duration, and in part by the punctuation within the lines.

It is the tension between the flexible, superimposed rhythms of the rhetorical patterns and the basic three-beat measure of the underlying framework which unites with the imagery and the logical meaning of the words to give the passage its restless, sweeping movement. It is this tension, and other analogous aspects of the structure of *Leaves of Grass* which give to the book that "vista" which Whitman himself claimed for it. If I may apply to it T. S. Eliot's idea about *Huckleberry Finn,* the structure of the *Leaves* is open at the end. Its key poem may well be, as D. H. Lawrence believed, the "Song of the Open Road."

As for the comics and soap opera, they too—on their own frequently humdrum level—have devised structures which provide for no ultimate climax, which come to no end demanded by symmetry or proportion. In them both there is a shift in interest away from the "How does it come out?" of traditional story telling to "How are things going?" In a typical installment of Harold Gray's *Orphan Annie,* the final panel shows Annie walking purposefully down a path with her dog, Sandy, saying: "But if we're goin', why horse around? It's a fine night for walkin' . . . C'mon, Sandy . . . Let's go . . ." (It doesn't even end with a period, or full stop, but with the conventional three dots or suspension points, to indicate incompletion.) So too, in the soap operas, *Portia Faces Life,* in one form or another, day after day, over and over again. And the operative word is the verb *faces.* It is the process of facing that matters.

America Is Process

Here, I think, we are approaching the central quality which all the diverse items on our list have in common. That quality I would define as a concern with process rather than with product—or, to re-use Mark Twain's words, a concern with the manner of handling experience or materials rather than with the experience or materials themselves. Emerson, a century ago, was fascinated by the way "becoming somewhat else is the perpetual game of nature." And this preoccupation with process is, of course, basic to modern science. "Matter" itself is no longer to be thought of as something fixed, but fluid and ever-changing. Similarly, modern economic theory has abandoned the "static equilibrium" analysis of the neo-classic economists, and in philosophy John Dewey's instrumentalism abandoned the classic philosophical interest in final causes for a scientific interest in "the mechanism of occurrences"—that is, process.

It is obvious, I think, that the American system of industrial mass production reflects this same focus of interest in its concern with production rather than products. And it is the mass-production system, *not* machinery, which has been America's contribution to industry.

In that system there is an emphasis different from that which was characteristic of handicraft production or even of machine manufacture. In both of these there was an almost total disregard of the means of production. The aristocratic ideal inevitably relegated interest in the means exclusively to anonymous peasants and slaves; what mattered to those who controlled and administered production was, quite simply, the finished product. In a mass-production system, on the other hand, it is the process of production itself which becomes the center of interest, rather than the product.

If we are aware of this fact, we usually regard it as a misfortune. We hear a lot, for instance, of the notion that our system "dehumanizes" the worker, turning him into a machine and depriving him of the satisfactions of finishing anything, since he performs only some repetitive operation. It is true that the unit of work in mass production is not a product but an operation. But the development of the system, in contrast with Charlie Chaplin's wonderful but wild fantasy of the assembly line, has shown the intermediacy of the stage in which the worker is doomed to frustrating boredom. Merely repetitive work, in the logic of mass production, can and must be done by machine. It is unskilled work which is doomed by it, not the worker. More and more skilled workers are needed to design products, analyze jobs, cut patterns, attend complicated machines, and co-ordinate the processes which comprise the productive system.

The skills required for these jobs are different, of course, from those required to make hand-made boots or to carve stone ornament, but they are not in themselves less interesting or less human. Operating a crane in a steel mill, or a turret lathe, is an infinitely more varied and stimulating job than shaping boots day after day by hand. A recent study of a group of workers on an automobile assembly line makes it clear that many of the men object, for a variety of reasons, to those monotonous, repetitive jobs which (as we have already noted) should be—but in many cases are not yet—done by machine; but those who *like* such jobs like them because they enjoy the process. As one of them said: "Repeating the same thing you can catch up and keep ahead of yourself . . . you can get in the swing of it." The report of members of a team of British workers who visited twenty American steel foundries in 1949 includes this description of the technique of "snatching" a steel casting with a magnet, maneuvered by a gantry crane running on overhead rails:

In its operation, the crane approaches a pile of castings at high speed with the magnet hanging fairly near floor level. The crane comes to a stop somewhere short of the castings, while the magnet swings forward over the pile, is dropped on to it, current switched on, and the hoist begun, at the same moment as the crane starts on its return journey. [And then, in words which might equally be applied to a jazz musician, the report adds:] The whole operation requires timing of a high order, and the impression gained is that the crane drivers derive a good deal of satisfaction from the swinging rhythm of the process.

This fascination with process has possessed Americans ever since Oliver Evans in 1785 created the first wholly automatic factory: a flour mill in Delaware in which mechanical conveyors—belt conveyors, bucket conveyors, screw conveyors—are interlinked with machines in a continuous process of production. But even if there were no other visible sign of the national preoccupation with process, it would be enough to point out that it was an American who invented chewing gum (in 1869) and that it is the Americans who have spread it—in all senses of the verb—throughout the world. An absolutely non-consumable confection, its sole appeal is the process of chewing it.

The apprehensions which many people feel about a civilization absorbed with process—about its mobility and wastefulness as well as about the "dehumanizing" effects of its jobs—derive, I suppose, from old habit and the persistence of values and tastes which were indigenous to a very different social and economic system. Whitman pointed out in *Democratic Vistas* more than eighty years ago that America was a stranger in her own house, that many of our social institutions, like our theories of literature and art, had been taken over almost without change from a culture which was not, like ours, the product of political democracy and the machine. Those institutions and theories, and the values implicit in them, are still around, though some (like collegiate gothic, of both the architectural and intellectual variety) are less widely admired than formerly.

Change, or the process of consecutive occurrences, is, we tend to feel, a bewildering and confusing and lonely thing. All of us, in some moods, feel the "preference for the stable over the precarious and uncompleted" which, as John Dewey recognized, tempts philosophers to posit their absolutes. We talk fondly of the need for roots—as if man were a vegetable, not an animal with legs whose distinction it is that he can move and "get on with it." We would do well to make ourselves more familiar with the idea that the process of development is universal, that it is "the form and order of nature." As Lancelot Law Whyte has said, in *The Next Development in Man:*

Man shares the special form of the universal formative process which is common to all organisms, and herein lies the root of his unity with the rest of organic nature. While life is maintained, the component processes in man never attain the relative isolation and static perfection of inorganic processes. . . . The individual may seek, or believe that he seeks, independence, permanence, or perfection, but that is only through his failure to recognize and accept his actual situation.

As an "organic system" man cannot, of course, expect to achieve stability or permanent harmony, though he can create (and in the great arts of the past, has created) the illusion of them. What he can achieve is a continuing development in response to his environment. The factor which gives vitality to all the component processes in the individual and in society is "not permanence but development."

To say this is not to deny the past. It is simply to recognize that for a variety of reasons people living in America have, on the whole, been better able to relish process than those who have lived under the imposing shadow of the arts and institutions which Western man created in his tragic search for permanence and perfection—for a "closed system." They find it easy to understand what that very

American philosopher William James meant when he told his sister that his house in Chocorua, New Hampshire, was "the most delightful house you ever saw; it has fourteen doors, all opening outwards." They are used to living in grid-patterned cities and towns whose streets, as Jean-Paul Sartre observed, are not, like those of European cities, "closed at both ends." As Sartre says in his essay on New York, the long straight streets and avenues of a gridiron city do not permit the buildings to "cluster like sheep" and protect one against the sense of space. "They are not sober little walks closed in between houses, but national highways. The moment you set foot on one of them, you understand that it has to go on to Boston or Chicago."

So, too, the past of those who live in the United States, like their future, is open-ended. It does not, like the past of most other people, extend downward into the soil out of which their immediate community or neighborhood has grown. It extends laterally backward across the plains, the mountains, or the sea to somewhere else, just as their future may at any moment lead them down the open road, the endless-vistaed street.

Our history is the process of motion into and out of cities; of westering and the counter-process of return; of motion up and down the social ladder—a long, complex, and sometimes terrifyingly rapid sequence of consecutive change. And it is this sequence, and the attitudes and habits and forms which it has bred, to which the term "America" really refers.

"America" is not a synonym for the United States. It is not an artifact. It is not a fixed and immutable ideal toward which citizens of this nation strive. It has not order or proportion, but neither is it chaos except as that is chaotic whose components no single mind can comprehend or control. America is process. And in so far as people have been "American"—as distinguished from being (as most of us, in at least some of our activities, have been) mere carriers of transplanted cultural traditions—the concern with process has been reflected in the work of their heads and hearts and hands.

from THE FUTURE OF AMERICAN LIBERALISM
by Morris R. Cohen

Liberalism is too often misconceived as a new set of dogmas taught by a newer and better set of priests called "liberals." Liberalism is an attitude rather than a set of dogmas—an attitude that insists upon questioning all plausible and self-evident propositions, seeking not to reject them but to find out what evidence there is to support them rather than their possible alternatives. This open eye for possible alternatives which need to be scrutinized before we can determine which is the best

From Morris R. Cohen, *The Faith of a Liberal*. Copyright, 1946, by Henry Holt and Company, Inc.

grounded is profoundly disconcerting to all conservatives and to almost all revolutionaries. Conservatism clings to what has been established, fearing that, once we begin to question the beliefs that we have inherited, all the values of life will be destroyed. The revolutionary, impressed with the evil of the existing order or disorder, is prone to put his faith in some mighty-sounding principle without regard for the complications, compromises, dangers, and hardships that will be involved in the adjustment of this principle to other worthy principles. Revolutionaries and reactionaries alike are irritated and perhaps inwardly humiliated by the humane temper of liberalism, which reveals by contrast the common inhumanity of both violent parties to the social struggle. Liberalism, on the other hand, regards life as an adventure in which we must take risks in new situations, in which there is no guarantee that the new will always be the good or the true, in which progress is a precarious achievement rather than an inevitability.

OUR CHANGING CHARACTERISTICS
by JAMES TRUSLOW ADAMS

THERE ARE few things more difficult to generalize about without danger of valid objections than national character. The exceptions to any generalization at once begin to appear destructively numerous. A concept of a Frenchman must include not only such diverse types as the Gascon, the Parisian, and the Breton, but also the innumerable differences between individuals of these and other types in what is a rather small country which for long has been culturally and politically unified.

When we attempt the task in America it would seem to be hopeless. Who *is* an American? Is he the descendant of a Boston Brahman, of a Georgian cotton planter, or a newly arrived Armenian, Hungarian, or Italian? Is the typical American a clerk on the fifty-fourth story of a Wall Street office building or a farm hand of the machine age guiding in isolation a power plow along a furrow which stretches endlessly over the horizon? Is he a scientist working for pitiful pay and the love of science in some government bureau in Washington, or a one hundred per cent go-getter in a Chamber of Commerce whose ideas of progress are limited to increase of wealth and population? Is he Hamilton or Jefferson, Lincoln or Harding, Roosevelt or Coolidge, Emerson or Barnum?

The task of defining national character in such a conflicting welter of opposites is dismaying enough, and yet a fairly clear notion is of prime importance for any number of very practical purposes. The modern business man doing business on a national scale, making mass appeal to our whole hundred and twenty millions at once; the statesman, domestic or foreign, trying to forecast the success or failure of an idea or a policy; the genuine patriot interested in the highest development of his civilization—these and others must all take account of that real if vague concept which we call the national character. It is from the third point of view

From James Truslow Adams, *The Tempo of Modern Life,* Albert & Charles Boni, Inc., 1931.

that we are concerned with the topic in the present article.

There are many signs that our world is approaching a new and critical stage. Deeply embedded in the structure of the universe there is a power or force that is continually at work molding chaos into cosmos, formlessness into forms. These forms, or patterns, belong to the spiritual as well as to the physical plane of reality. A scale of values, an ethical system, a philosophy of life appear to be as "natural" and inevitable a part of the web and woof of that strange and inexplicable phantasmagoria that we call the universe as are crystals, corals, or living embodiments of the form-producing force in the plant or animal body.

For generations now we have been witnessing the gradual breakdown of old forms until we have reached the very nadir of formlessness in our whole spiritual life. But there are, as I have said, many indications that we are about to witness a new stage, the embryo stage of new forms.

For the most part this play of cosmic forces is independent of consciousness or will in individuals. The atoms know not and care not why or how they combine to make quartz crystals or a living cell of protoplasm. To a greater extent than we care to admit, perhaps, the higher forms —our scales of values, our philosophies— are also independent of conscious molding by ourselves. They are not wholly so, however, and if, as has recently been said, more and more of us here in America as elsewhere "are looking for a new set of controlling ideas capable of restoring value to human existence," it is evidence of the interplay between the blind form-making force of physical nature and the consciousness of man. What these ideas will be, will depend largely upon the soil in which they will be rooted, the soil of our national character.

It is also clear that the form in which life, either physical or spiritual, is embodied is of transcendent importance for the individual. If living cells are arranged in the form of a bird, both the powers and limitations of the individual are wholly different from those of the individual when they are arranged in the form of a fish. Similarly in the spiritual world, powers and limitations depend largely upon the forms within which the spirit has its being. Because they are so largely intangible, we are likely to lose sight of the fact that these forms—scales of values, systems of thought, philosophies of life— all afford the spirit peculiar powers and impose peculiar limits.

What of the new forms? Arising from and in large part molded by the national character, are they likely to afford wider scope for man's highest aspirations, to enlarge the powers of the spirit, or to place limits and bind them closer to the earth? What of the national character itself?

Let us for the present discussion avoid the more difficult problem of a complete analysis and seek to establish a trend, often a simpler task, in the spiritual as in the physical world. Are our characteristics changing, and, if so, in what direction? Can we, in the first place, establish any definite points of reference which will be tangible and certain? I think we can.

Man expresses himself in his arts, and among these none is more illuminating than the earliest and most practical, that of architecture. It is one, moreover, in which we as Americans excel.

We need not greatly concern ourselves with the inchoate beginnings of our nationality in the first few generations of early settlement in the wilderness of the Atlantic seaboard. The physical tasks were almost overwhelmingly hard and there was little opportunity for a distinctly American expression of either old or new spiritual life. By the time there was, we find that the spirit of the colonies had expressed itself in an architectural form, characteristic with minor variations throughout all of them.

When we speak of "colonial architecture," what at once comes to our mind is the home, the dwelling house of Georgian type, modeled on the English but with a delicacy and refinement surpassing most of the models overseas. From New England to the Far South these homes had outwardly a perfection of form and inwardly a proportion, a refinement of detail, a simplicity that all clearly sprang from the spirit of the time.

We may note quickly, in passing, several points in regard to them. The high point of the architecture was domestic. They were homes. They had an air of spaciousness, of dignity. They were aristocratic in the best sense. They were restrained and disciplined. Display or vulgarity were unthinkable in connection with them. They evidenced an ordered and stratified society. They held peace and rest. They were simple, unostentatious, and profoundly satisfying. They were shelters for a quiet life, alien from haste.

Let us, using the same architectural measure, pass from this first flowering of the American spirit to the very instant of today. The great contribution of twentieth century America to the art of building is the skyscraper, of which we may take the office building as both the earliest and most typical example. What are some of its usual characteristics?

The buildings are commercial, not domestic. Their very *raison d'être* is financial, the desire to get the most money possible from a given plot of ground. Their bulk is huge but they are not spacious, save perhaps for their entrance halls in some instances. They are democratic in the physical sense of herding within their walls thousands of persons of every possible sort. In their primary insistence upon mere size and height regardless of every other element, they are undisciplined and unrestrained. Peace or rest is unthinkable within their walls with the incessant movement of thousands of hurrying individuals, and elevators moving at incredible speed.

They are lavish in their ostentation of expense on the ground floor, bare and unsatisfying above. A "front" of vulgar cost is built to hide the emptiness of the countless floors beyond the reach of the first casual glance from the street. Yet every small and growing community cries for them, and we hold them to the world as our characteristic achievement in art, as our most significant contribution in that most telltale of all arts, the housing of man's chief interest.

II

Here, then, we have two points of reference tangible enough to be noted by all men, because they are physical in structure, yet full of spiritual implications for our task. When we turn to other means of establishing our trend, such as literature, newspapers, our methods of living, the wants we create and strive to satisfy, our social ways of contact, our national ideals as expressed in political campaigns and policies, and other means less obvious than the buildings in which we live or work or express our spiritual aspirations, what do we find? I think we find the same trends indicated above, amplified and emphasized.

It is, if I may repeat myself to prevent misunderstanding, only with these trends and not with the whole complex national character that I am here concerned. As a historian, and with no wish to make a case but only to report what I find, certain trends in the past century appear to me to be clearly indicated. Let me note them just as from time to time I have jotted them down, without at first trying either to order or explain them.

These trends are the substitution of self-expression for self-discipline; of the concept of prosperity for that of liberty; of restlessness for rest; of spending for saving; of show for solidity; of desire for the new or novel in place of affection for the old and tried; of dependence for self-reliance; of gregariousness for solitude; of luxury for simplicity; of ostentation for restraint; of success for integrity; of national for local; of easy generosity for wise giving; of preferring impressions to thought, facts to ideas; of democracy for aristocracy; of the mediocre for the excellent.

For the most part I do not think any observer would quarrel with the validity of most of the above list. Discipline, self or other, has almost completely vanished from our life. In earlier days it was amply provided by school, family, and social life, by ideals and religious beliefs. Today it is not only absent in all these quarters but is preached against by psychologists and sociologists, decried by the new pedagogy, and even legislated against in school and prison.

Nothing is imposed any longer, from learning one's ABC's to honoring one's parents. Everything is elective, from college courses to marital fidelity. The man or woman who casts all discipline to the winds for the sake of transient gratification of selfish desires, who denies obligations and duties, is no longer considered a libertine or a cad but merely a modernist pursuing the legitimate end of self-expression.

For a considerable time evidence has been accumulating that the national rallying cry has become an economic balance sheet. Perhaps one of the chief values of the whole prohibition muddle has been to serve as a mirror for the American soul. In the arguments advanced for and against, in the spiritual tone of the discussion, we can see all too well reflected the moving ideals of the American people, and the argument that carries most weight would clearly appear to be that of prosperity. Balanced against this, the questions of personal liberty, class legislation, or constitutional propriety are but as straw weighed against iron.

Prohibition is only one of the many mirrors that reflect the same truth. In innumerable cases of business practice and of legislation it has become evident that when personal freedom and initiative have to be balanced against the prosperity of the moment according to the business methods of the moment, prosperity wins. The one liberty that is still valued is the liberty to exploit and to acquire. That liberty will be defended to the death, but other liberties, such as freedom of thought and speech, have become pale and unreal ghosts, academic questions of no interest to the practical man.

Who cares in the slightest about the innumerable cases of encroachment on personal liberties on the part of both state and federal governments in the past ten years so long as business is good? Who cares about the methods employed by our police? Who is willing to give thought to the treatment frequently meted out to foreigners by our immigration officials—treatment that could hardly be surpassed by the old Russian régime at its worst, treatment that we could not stand a moment if accorded to *our* citizens by any foreign government? No, personal liberty as a rallying cry today receives no answer. But we will elect any man President who will promise us prosperity.

There is as little question of our growing restlessness. By rail, boat, automobile, or plane we are as restless as a swarm of gnats in a summer sunbeam. "We don't know where we're going but we're on our way" is the cry of all. Even the babies get their rest by traveling at forty miles an hour swung in cradles in Ford cars. That much of the movement is mere restlessness and does not spring from a desire to see and learn may easily be observed by watching the speed of our new tourists when they travel, and by listening to their comments when they have to stop to look at anything. As for the "nature" they claim to go to see, they are ruining our whole countryside with appalling indifference.

The home itself has yielded and has ceased to afford any sense of permanence and security. In the old days a home was expected to serve for generations. In the South, frequently property was entailed and the family was assured of a continuing center where it could cluster. A year ago, on October first, a hundred thousand families in New York City moved from one apartment to another, in many instances for no better reason than that they were bored with the one they had occupied a twelvemonth. Our multimillionaires build palaces, and in a few years abandon them to country clubs or office buildings.

As for thrift and saving, with the entire complex of spiritual satisfactions that go with an assured future, they have not only notoriously been thrown overboard but are vigorously denounced by advertising experts like Bruce Barton and great industrial leaders like Henry Ford. "We should use, not save," the latter teaches the American people while they mortgage their homes, if they own them, to buy his cars. On every side we are being taught not to save but to borrow. The self-respect and satisfaction of the man of a generation ago who did not owe a penny in the world is being replaced by the social-respect and deep dissatisfaction of the man who has borrowed to the limit to live on the most expensive scale that hard cash and bank credit will allow.

With this has naturally come a preference for show to solidity. A witty and observing foreigner has said that Americans put all their goods in the shop window. In every vein the insidious poison is at work. A man who toiled and saved to own his home would see to it that it was well built and substantial. The man who expects to move every year cares for nothing more than that the roof will not fall until he gets out, provided the appearance is attractive. In an advertisement of houses for sale in a New York suburb recently one of the great advantages pointed out was that the roofs were guaranteed for three years.

The first thing that every business firm thinks of is show. Its office or shop must look as if there were unlimited resources behind it. Even a savings bank, whose real solidity should be seen in its list of investments and whose object is to encourage thrift, will squander hugely on marbles and bronze in its banking room to impress the depositor.

The same motive is at work in our intellectual life. One has only to glance at the advertisements of the classics, of language courses, of "five foot shelves" and note the motives that are appealed to for desiring culture. Nor are our schools and colleges exempt from the same poison. The insistence on degrees after a teacher's name, the regulating of wage scales in accordance with them, the insistence on a professor's publishing something which can be listed, are as much part of the same trend as is the clerk's wanting to be cultured so as to pass from a grilled window to an assistant-assistant executive's desk.

III

We could expand the above examples almost indefinitely and continue through the remainder of the list. But it is all obvious enough to anyone who will observe with fresh eyes, and ponder. Both for those who may agree or disagree with me, let us pass to some of the other questions that arise in connection with the trends I have noted. Do they in any way hang together? Do they make a unified whole or are they self-contradictory and hence probably mistaken? Do they derive from any conditions in our history that would make them natural and probable, or are they opposed to those conditions? If they are real, do they represent a transient phase or a permanent alteration in our character?

As we study them carefully, it seems to me that they do hang together remarkably and ominously well. A person, for example, who is restless, rather than one who cares for rest and permanence, would naturally prefer the new to the old, the novel for the tried, impressions instead of difficult and sustained thought. Both these characteristics, again, naturally cohere with the desire for show rather than solidity, and for self-expression rather than self-discipline.

With these same qualities would go the love of gregariousness rather than solitude, of luxury rather than simplicity, and, easily belonging to the same type of character, we would find the desire to spend ousting the desire to save, and the substitution of prosperity for liberty and of success for integrity. With such a succession of substitutions, that of dependence for self-reliance is not only natural but inevitable, and so with the other items in the trend. They all fit into a psychological whole. There is no self-contradiction to be found among them.

But is there any connection to be found between them and our history? Are they qualities that might be found to have developed with more or less logical and psychological necessity from the conditions of American life which have separated the period of the colonial home from that of the seventy-story office building? I think here again we find confirmation rather than contradiction.

I have no intention to rival Mr. Coolidge by writing the history of America in five hundred words. All I can do in my limited space is to point to certain facts and influences.

Until well into the eighteenth century, there had been no very great change in the character of the American to mark him off from his English cousin. The wilderness and remoteness had, indeed, had some effect, but this was small compared with the later effects of what we have come to call "the West." Leaving out a few minor strains—such as the Dutch, Swedes, and the earlier Germans—the settlers were almost wholly British, who sought, in a somewhat freer atmosphere and with somewhat wider economic opportunity, to reproduce the life they had left.

The continent open to them was of limited extent. Beyond a comparatively narrow strip lay the long barrier of the Appalachians and the claims of the French. The strip itself contained no great natural resources to arouse cupidity or feverish activity. The character of the colonists had become a little more democratic, a little more pliant, a little more rebellious and self-reliant than that of their cousins of similar social ranks at home. That was all. They might differ with the majority of both Englishmen and Parliament over questions of politics and economics, but those were differences of interest and policy, not of character.

There lay ahead, however, the operation of two factors that were to prove of enormous influence—the exploitation of the American continent, and the immigration from Europe. We cannot here trace this influence step by step chronologically, but we must summarize it. "The West"—there were successively many of them—unlike the colonial America, was of almost limitless extent and wealth. There were whole empires of farm land and forest, mines that made fortunes for the lucky almost overnight, reservoirs of gas and oil that spawned cities and millionaires.

All did not happen in a day, but it did happen within what might almost be the span of one long life. In ages past an Oriental conqueror might sack the riches of a rival's state, a king of Spain might draw gold from a Peruvian hoard, but never before had such boundless opportunities for sudden wealth been opened to the fortunate among a whole population which could join in the race unhampered.

In the rush for opportunity, old ties and loyalties were broken. A restlessness entered the American blood that has remained in it ever since. In American legend, the frontier has become the Land of Romance and we are bid to think of the pioneers as empire-builders. A very few may have dreamed of the future glory of America rather than of private gain, but it is well not to gild too much the plain truth, which is that in the vast majority of instances, the rush was for riches to be made as quickly as might be. In the killing of a million buffaloes a year, in the total destruction of forests without replanting, in the whole of the story in all its aspects there were few thoughts for a national destiny not linked with immediate personal gain at any expense to the nation. In this orgy of exploitation it is not difficult to discover the soil in which some of the elements of the changed trend in American character had its roots.

Another factor was also at work which combined with the above in its effects. The racial homogeneity of our earlier colonial days was broken by the millions of immigrants who came to us of racial stocks other than our own. Our first character had been that of seventeenth and eighteenth century Englishmen, not greatly altered until the Revolution. It was unified and stable, but the West and Europe both operated to undermine its stability.

On the one hand, the influence of the West, with the loosening of old bonds, its peculiar population, and its opportunities of limitless expansion and wealth greatly altered old ideals and standards of value. On the other, the steady infusion in large numbers of Germans, Irish, Swedes, Norwegians, Jews, Russians, Italians, Greeks, and other races also bore a conspicuous part in making the national character less uniform and stable. I am not concerned with their several contributions of value, but merely with the fact that the introduction of such foreign swarms tended to destroy a unified national character.

By the latter part of the nineteenth century, two things had thus happened. In the first place, the real America had become the West, and its traits were becoming dominant. One of these was restlessness, not only a willingness but a desire to try any new place or thing and make a complete break with the old. Moreover, although the frontier may breed some fine qualities, it is a good deal like the farm in the respect that although it may be a fine place to come from, it is a soul-killing place in which to remain. It bred emotion rather than thought, and to a considerable extent substituted new material values for the spiritual ones of the older America.

In the rush for wealth—whether won from forests or mines; farms tilled, raped, and abandoned for fresher soil; real estate values from fast-growing cities; lands fraudulently obtained from a complaisant government—restraint, self-discipline, thought for the future ceased to be virtues. With all this came a vast optimism, a belief that everything would become bigger and better, and, because the standards of success were economic, better because bigger. Wealth was the goal, and the faster things got bigger—towns, cities, the piles of slain buffaloes, the area of forests destroyed—the quicker one's personal wealth accumulated. Statistics took on a new significance and spelled the letters of one's private fate.

At the same time, by the latter half of the nineteenth century another thing had happened, as we have said. Partly from the effects of the West and partly from immigration, the old, stable American-English character had become unstable, soft, pliant, something which could be easily molded by new influences. It could readily take the impress of an emotion, a leader, a new invention. It was full of possibility, both of good and evil.

Suddenly this new, unformed, malleable national character, already warped to a large degree toward material values, was called upon to feel the full force of the influences flowing from the fruition of the industrial revolution. Invention followed invention with startling rapidity. Life itself became infinitely more mobile. Scientists, engineers, manufacturers threw at the public contrivance after contrivance of the most far-reaching influence upon man's personal and social life without a thought of what that influence might be beyond the profit of the moment to the individual manufacturer.

Choice became bewildering in its complexity. The national character had become unstable. It was in a real sense unformed and immature, far more so than it had been a century earlier. It had also lost belief in the necessity of restraint and discipline. It had accepted material standards and ideals. It was in far more danger of being overwhelmed by the ideals of a new, raw, and crude machine age than was perhaps any other nation of the civilized group.

With an ingenuity that would have been fiendish had it not been so unthinking and ignorant, the leaders of the new era used every resource of modern psychology to warp the unformed character of the people, to provide the greatest possible profit to the individuals and corporations that made and purveyed the new "goods." Our best and worst qualities, our love of wife and children, our national pride, our self-respect, our snobbery, our fear of social opinion, our neglect of the future, our lack of self-restraint and discipline, our love of mere physical comfort have all been played upon to make mush of our characters in order that big business might thrive. Even our national government, whether wittingly or not, undertook to inflame our American love of gambling and our desire to "get rich quick" regardless of effect on character.

IV

Taking all the molding influences of the past century and more into account, it is little wonder, perhaps, that our national characteristics exhibit the trend noted. The situation, serious as it is, might be less so had it occurred at a time when the spiritual forms in the world at large—its scales of values, its ethical systems, its philosophies of life—were intact. But as we have noted, they have been largely destroyed; and at the very time when new forms are in process of arising, largely to be molded by the national characters of the peoples among whom they arise, our own is in the state pictured above. The question whether our new characteristics are temporary or permanent thus becomes of acute significance.

"Race" is a word of such vague and undefined content as to be of slight help to us, but if we take the whole history of the Western nations from which we derive, I think we may say that the characteristics noted above may be classed as acquired and not inherited. Biologists consider such not to be permanent and heritable, though the analogy with biology again is so vague as to afford little comfort.

More hopeful, I think, is the fact that these new characteristics appear to have derived directly from circumstances, and that these circumstances themselves have been in large part such as have passed and will not recur again. Immigration and "the West" have ceased to be continuing factors in our development. Their effects remain and must be dealt with, but neither factor will continue to intensify them. The tides of immigration have been shut off. There is significance in the fact that "the Wests" which won under Jefferson, Jackson, and Lincoln were defeated in 1896 under Bryan.

"The West" of today is a new West in which conditions, and to a large extent ideals, are different. Yet its greatest contribution to our national life and character remains that broadening and deepening of the dream of a better and a richer life for all of every class which was the cause of its earlier victories and which goes far to redeem its less noble influences. The nation as a whole is entering upon a new era in which all the conditions will be different from any experienced heretofore. Territory, resources, opportunities are none of them any longer unexploited and boundless. What the future may hold, we cannot tell, but in fundamental influences it will be different from the past. The menacing factor that remains is that of mass production and the machine.

Also, we have spoken thus far only of the trend in characteristics, not of our character as a whole. In that there are certain noble traits which remain unaltered, or have matured and strengthened. It is possible, now the warping influences of the past century have to some extent disappeared, that the national character may develop around them as a core, that we shall forget in manhood the wild oats sown in our youth.

But age acquires no value save through thought and discipline. If we cannot reinstate those, we are in danger of hampering rather than aiding in that reconstruction of the spiritual life of man that is the inevitable and most vital task now before the nations. We must either forward or retard it. We are too great to live aloof. We could not if we would, and upon the trend of our character depends to a great extent the future of the world.

Nor let us forget that although fortune has poured her favors in our lap, there is a Nemesis that dogs the steps of all, and we cannot lightly scorn the growing enmity of half the world. Are we to treat the machine age and mass production only as a new and different "West," or are we at last, in growing up, to learn wisdom and restraint? Are we going to change the trend in our character, or is it to become fixed in its present form, a danger to ourselves and a menace to mankind?

"Has anybody ever thought of winning the Communists over to *our* way of life?"

Permission The New Yorker. Copyright The F-R. Publishing Corporation

FAREWELL, MY LOVELY!

by Lee Strout White

I SEE by the new Sears Roebuck catalogue that it is still possible to buy an axle for a 1909 Model T Ford, but I am not deceived. The great days have faded, the end is in sight. Only one page in the current catalogue is devoted to parts and accessories for the Model T; yet everyone remembers springtimes when the Ford gadget section was larger than men's clothing, almost as large as household furnishings. The last Model T was built in 1927, and the car is fading from what scholars call the American scene—which is an understatement, because to a few million people who grew up with it, the old Ford practically *was* the American scene.

It was the miracle God had wrought. And it was patently the sort of thing that could only happen once. Mechanically uncanny, it was like nothing that had ever come to the world before. Flourishing industries rose and fell with it. As a vehicle, it was hard-working, commonplace, heroic; and it often seemed to transmit those qualities to the persons who rode in it. My own generation identifies it with Youth, with its gaudy, irretrievable excitements; before it fades into the mist, I would like to pay it the tribute of the sigh that is not a sob, and set down random entries in a shape somewhat less cumbersome than a Sears Roebuck catalogue.

The Model T was distinguished from all other makes of cars by the fact that its transmission was of a type known as planetary—which was half metaphysics, half sheer friction. Engineers accepted the word "planetary" in its epicyclic sense, but I was always conscious that it also meant "wandering," "erratic." Because of the peculiar nature of this planetary element, there was always, in Model T, a certain dull rapport between engine and wheels, and even when the car was in a state known as neutral, it trembled with a deep imperative and tended to inch forward. There was never a moment when the bands were not faintly egging the machine on. In this respect it was like a horse, rolling the bit on its tongue, and country people brought to it the same technique they used with draft animals.

Its most remarkable quality was its rate of acceleration. In its palmy days the Model T could take off faster than anything on the road. The reason was simple. To get under way, you simply hooked the third finger of the right hand around a lever on the steering column, pulled down hard, and shoved your left foot forcibly against the low-speed pedal. These were simple, positive motions; the car responded by lunging forward with a roar. After a few seconds of this turmoil, you took your toe off the pedal, eased up a mite on the throttle, and the car, possessed of only two forward speeds, catapulted directly into high with a series of ugly jerks and was off on its glorious errand. The abruptness of this departure was never equaled in other cars of the period. The human leg was (and still is) incapable of letting in a clutch with anything like the forthright abandon that used to send Model T on its way. Letting in a clutch is a negative, hesitant motion, depending on delicate nervous control; pushing down the Ford pedal was a simple, country mo-

From *The New Yorker*, May 16, 1936. Permission *The New Yorker*. Copyright, 1936, by the F-R. Publishing Corporation.

tion—an expansive act, which came as natural as kicking an old door to make it budge.

The driver of the old Model T was a man enthroned. The car, with top up, stood seven feet high. The driver sat on top of the gas tank, brooding it with his own body. When he wanted gasoline, he alighted, along with everything else in the front seat; the seat was pulled off, the metal cap unscrewed, and a wooden stick thrust down to sound the liquid in the well. There were always a couple of these sounding sticks kicking around in the ratty sub-cushion regions of a flivver. Refueling was more of a social function then, because the driver had to unbend, whether he wanted to or not. Directly in front of the driver was the windshield—high, uncompromisingly erect. Nobody talked about air resistance, and the four cylinders pushed the car through the atmosphere with a simple disregard of physical law.

There was this about a Model T: the purchaser never regarded his purchase as a complete, finished product. When you bought a Ford, you figured you had a start—a vibrant, spirited framework to which could be screwed an almost limitless assortment of decorative and functional hardware. Driving away from the agency, hugging the new wheel between your knees, you were already full of creative worry. A Ford was born naked as a baby, and a flourishing industry grew up out of correcting its rare deficiencies and combating its fascinating diseases. Those were the great days of lily-painting. I have been looking at some old Sears Roebuck catalogues, and they bring everything back so clear.

First you bought a Ruby Safety Reflector for the rear, so that your posterior would glow in another car's brilliance. Then you invested thirty-nine cents in some radiator Moto Wings, a popular ornament which gave the Pegasus touch to the machine and did something godlike to the owner. For nine cents you bought a fan-belt guide to keep the belt from slipping off the pulley.

You bought a radiator compound to stop leaks. This was as much a part of everybody's equipment as aspirin tablets are of a medicine cabinet. You bought special oil to prevent chattering, a clamp-on dash light, a patching outfit, a tool box which you bolted to the running board, a sun visor, a steering-column brace to keep the column rigid, and a set of emergency containers for gas, oil, and water—three thin, disc-like cans which reposed in a case on the running board during long, important journeys—red for gas, gray for water, green for oil. It was only a beginning. After the car was about a year old, steps were taken to check the alarming disintegration. (Model T was full of tumors, but they were benign.) A set of anti-rattlers (98c) was a popular panacea. You hooked them on to the gas and spark rods, to the brake pull rod, and to the steering-rod connections. Hood silencers, of black rubber, were applied to the fluttering hood. Shock-absorbers and snubbers gave "complete relaxation." Some people bought rubber pedal pads, to fit over the standard metal pedals. (I didn't like these, I remember.) Persons of a suspicious or pugnacious turn of mind bought a rear-view mirror; but most Model T owners weren't worried by what was coming from behind because they would soon enough see it out in front. They rode in a state of cheerful catalepsy. Quite a large mutinous clique among Ford owners went over to a foot accelerator (you could buy one and screw it to the floor board), but there was a certain madness in these people, because the Model T, just as she stood, had a choice of three foot pedals to push, and there were plenty of moments when both feet were occupied in the routine performance of duty and when the only way to speed up the engine was with the hand throttle.

Gadget bred gadget. Owners not only bought ready made gadgets, they invented gadgets to meet special needs. I myself drove my car directly from the agency to the blacksmith's, and had the smith affix two enormous iron brackets to the port running board to support an army trunk.

People who owned closed models builded along different lines: they bought ball grip handles for opening doors, window anti-rattlers, and deluxe flower vases of the cut-glass anti-splash type. People with delicate sensibilities garnished their car with a device called the Donna Lee Automobile Disseminator—a porous vase guaranteed, according to Sears, to fill the car with a "faint clean odor of lavender." The gap between open cars and closed cars was not as great then as it is now: for $11.95, Sears Roebuck converted your touring car into a sedan and you went forth renewed. One agreeable quality of the old Fords was that they had no bumpers, and their fenders softened and wilted with the years and permitted the driver to squeeze in and out of tight places.

Tires were 30 x 3½, cost about twelve dollars, and punctured readily. Everybody carried a Jiffy patching set, with a nutmeg grater to roughen the tube before the goo was spread on. Everybody was capable of putting on a patch, expected to have to, and did have to.

During my association with Model T's, self-starters were not a prevalent accessory. They were expensive and under suspicion. Your car came equipped with a serviceable crank, and the first thing you learned was how to Get Results. It was a special trick, and until you learned it (usually from another Ford owner, but sometimes by a period of appalling experimentation) you might as well have been winding up an awning. The trick was to leave the ignition switch off, proceed to the animal's head, pull the choke (which was a little wire protruding through the radiator), and give the crank two or three nonchalant upward lifts. Then, whistling as though thinking about something else, you would saunter back to the driver's cabin, turn the ignition on, return to the crank, and this time, catching it on the down stroke, give it a quick spin with plenty of That. If this procedure was followed, the engine almost always responded—first with a few scattered explosions, then with a tumultuous gunfire, which you checked by racing around to the driver's seat and retarding the throttle. Often, if the emergency brake hadn't been pulled all the way back, the car advanced on you the instant the first explosion occurred and you would hold it back by leaning your weight against it. I can still feel my old Ford nuzzling me at the curb, as though looking for an apple in my pocket.

The lore and legend that governed the Ford were boundless. Owners had their own theories about everything; they discussed mutual problems in that wise, infinitely resourceful way old women discuss rheumatism. Exact knowledge was pretty scarce, and often proved less effective than superstition. Dropping a camphor ball into the gas tank was a popular expedient; it seemed to have a tonic effect on both man and machine. There wasn't much to base exact knowledge on. The Ford driver flew blind. He didn't know the temperature of his engine, the speed of his car, the amount of his fuel, or the pressure of his oil (the old Ford lubricated itself by what was amiably described as the "splash system"). A speedometer cost money and was an extra, like a windshield-wiper. The dashboard of the early models was bare save for an ignition key; later models, grown effete, boasted an ammeter which pulsated alarmingly with the throbbing of the car. Under the dash was a box of coils, with vibrators which you adjusted, or thought you adjusted. Whatever the driver learned of his motor, he learned not through instruments but through sudden developments. I remember that the timer was one of the vital organs about which there was ample doctrine. When everything else had been checked, you "had a look" at the timer. It was an extravagantly odd little device, simple in construction, mysterious in function. It contained a roller, held by a spring, and there were four contact points on the inside of the case against which, many people believed, the roller rolled. I have had a timer apart on a sick Ford many times, but I never really knew what I was up to—I was just showing off before God. There were almost as many schools of thought as there were timers. Some people, when things went wrong, just clenched their teeth and gave the timer a smart crack with a wrench. Other people opened it up and blew on it. There was a school that held that the timer needed large amounts of oil; they fixed it by frequent baptism. And there was a school that was positive it was meant to run dry as a bone; these people were continually taking it off and wiping it. I remember once spitting into a timer; not in anger, but in a spirit of research. You see, the Model T driver moved in the realm of metaphysics. He believed his car could be hexed.

One reason the Ford anatomy was never reduced to an exact science was that, having "fixed" it, the owner couldn't honestly claim that the treatment had brought about the cure. There were too many authenticated cases of Fords fixing themselves—restored naturally to health after a short rest. Farmers soon discovered this, and it fitted nicely with their draft-horse philosophy: "Let 'er cool off and she'll snap into it again."

A Ford owner had Number One Bearing constantly in mind. This bearing, being at the front end of the motor, was the one that always burned out, because the oil didn't reach it when the car was climbing hills. (That's what I was always told, anyway.) The oil used to recede and leave Number One dry as a clam flat; you had to watch that bearing like a hawk. It was like a weak heart—you could hear it start knocking, and that was when you stopped and let her cool off. Try as you would to keep the oil supply right, in the end Number One always went out. "Number One Bearing burned out on me and I had to have her replaced," you would say, wisely; and your companions always had a lot to tell about how to protect and pamper Number One to keep her alive.

Sprinkled not too liberally among the millions of amateur witch doctors who drove Fords and applied their own abominable cures were the heaven-sent mechanics who could really make the car talk. These professionals turned up in undreamed-of spots. One time, on the banks of the Columbia River in Washington, I heard the rear end go out of my Model T when I was trying to whip it up a steep incline onto the deck of a ferry. Something snapped; the car slid backward into the mud. It seemed to me like the end of the trail. But the captain of the ferry, observing the withered remnant, spoke up.

"What's got her?" he asked.

"I guess it's the rear end," I replied, listlessly. The captain leaned over the rail and stared. Then I saw that there was a hunger in his eyes that set him off from other men.

"Tell you what," he said, carelessly, trying to cover up his eagerness, "let's pull the son of a bitch up onto the boat, and I'll help you fix her while we're going back and forth on the river."

We did just this. All that day I plied between the towns of Pasco and Kennewick, while the skipper (who had once worked in a Ford garage) directed the amazing work of resetting the bones of my car.

Springtime in the heyday of the Model T was a delirious season. Owning a car was still a major excitement, roads were still wonderful and bad. The Fords were obviously conceived in madness: any car which was capable of going from forward into reverse without any perceptible mechanical hiatus was bound to be a mighty challenging thing to the human imagination. Boys used to veer them off the highway into a level pasture and run wild with them, as though they were cutting up with a girl. Most everybody used the reverse pedal quite as much as the regular foot brake—it distributed the wear over the bands and wore them all down evenly. That was the big trick, to wear all the bands down evenly, so that the final chattering would be total and the whole unit scream for renewal.

The days were golden, the nights were dim and strange. I still recall with trembling those loud, nocturnal crises when you drew up to a signpost and raced the engine so the lights would be bright enough to read destinations by. I have never been really planetary since. I suppose it's time to say good-by. Farewell, my lovely!

WHITHER MANKIND?

by Charles A. Beard

What is called Western or modern civilization by way of contrast with the civilization of the Orient or medieval times is at bottom a civilization that rests upon machinery and science as distinguished from one founded on agriculture or handicraft commerce. It is in reality a technological civilization. It is only about two hundred years old, and, far from shrinking in its influence, is steadily extending its area into agriculture as well as handicrafts. If the records of patent offices, the statistics of production, and the reports of laboratories furnish evidence worthy of credence, technological civilization, instead of showing signs of contraction, threatens to overcome and transform the whole globe.

Considered with respect to its intrinsic nature, technological civilization presents certain precise characteristics. It rests fundamentally on power-driven machinery which transcends the physical limits of its human directors, multiplying indefinitely the capacity for the production of goods. Science in all its branches—physics, chemistry, biology, and psychology—is the servant and upholder of this system. The day of crude invention being almost over, continuous research in the natural sciences is absolutely necessary to the extension of the machine and its market, thus forcing continuously the creation of new goods, new processes, and new modes of life. As the money for learning comes in increasing proportions from taxes on industry and gifts by captains of capitalism, a steady growth in scientific endowments is to be expected, and the scientific curiosity thus aroused and stimulated will hardly fail to expand—and to invade all fields of thought with a technique of ever-refining subtlety. Affording the demand for the output of industry are the vast populations of the globe; hence mass production and marketing are inevitable concomitants of the machine routine.

For the present, machine civilization is associated with capitalism, under which large-scale production has risen to its present stage, but machine civilization is by no means synonymous with capitalism—that ever-changing scheme of exploitation. While the acquisitive instinct of the capitalist who builds factories and starts mass production is particularly emphasized by economists and is, no doubt, a factor of immense moment, it must not be forgotten that the acquisitive passion of the earth's multitudes for the goods, the comforts, and the securities of the classes is an equal, if not a more important, force, and in any case is likely to survive capitalism as we know it. Few choose nakedness when they can be clothed, the frosts of winter when they can be warm, or the misery of bacterial diseases when sanitation is offered to them. In fact, the ascetics and flagellants of the world belong nowhere in the main stream of civilization—and are of dubious utility and service in any civilization.

Though machine civilization has here been treated as if it were an order, it in fact differs from all others in that it is highly dynamic, containing within itself the seeds of constant reconstruction. Everywhere agricultural civilizations of the pre-

From Charles A. Beard, *Whither Mankind?*, Longmans, Green and Company, Inc.

machine age have changed only slowly with the fluctuations of markets, the fortunes of governments, and the vicissitudes of knowledge, keeping their basic institutions intact from century to century. Pre-machine urban civilizations have likewise retained their essential characteristics through long lapses of time. But machine civilization based on technology, science, invention, and expanding markets must of necessity change—and rapidly. The order of steam is hardly established before electricity invades it; electricity hardly gains a fair start before the internal combustion engine overtakes it. There has never been anywhere in the world any order comparable with it, and all analogies drawn from the Middle Ages, classical antiquity, and the Orient are utterly inapplicable to its potentialities, offering no revelations as to its future.

II

Granted that these essential characteristics of so-called Western civilization—namely, its mechanical and scientific foundations—are realistic, is it a mere "flash in the pan," an historical accident destined to give way to some other order based upon entirely different modes of life, lifting mankind "above the rudeness of the savage"? Now, if the term "decline" in this connection means anything concrete, it signifies the gradual or rapid abandonment of the material modes of production prevailing in any particular age and the habits and arts associated with them. Conceivably the Prussianism of the Hohenzollerns, described so well in Spengler's *Prussianism and Socialism,* may decline—is declining. It is highly probable that the petty tenure system of the French peasantry, the now sadly diluted aristocracy inherited from the eighteenth century, the church of little mysteries and miracles may decline, but these things are not the peculiar characteristics of the West. They are the remnants of the agricultural complex which the machine is everywhere steadily subduing. The real question is this: Can and will machine society "decline"?

It is generally agreed among historians that the decay of agriculture, owing to the lack of scientific management and fertilization, was one of the chief causes for the breakdown of the Roman state. Is it to be supposed that the drive of the masses of mankind for machine-made goods will fail, that large-scale production will be abandoned, that the huge literature of natural science will disappear in the same fashion as most of the literature of ancient Egypt, that the ranks of scientific men will cease in time to be recruited, that the scientific power to meet new situations will fail? An affirmative answer requires a great deal of hardihood. The scientific order is not recruited from a class, such as the patricians of ancient Rome; nor is scientific knowledge the monopoly of a caste likely to dissolve. Unless all visible signs deceive us, there is no reason for supposing that either machinery or science will disappear or even dwindle to insignificance. And they are the basis of the modern civilization.

If Western civilization does not break down from such internal causes, is there good reason for supposing that any of the races now inhabiting Asia or Africa could overcome the machine order of the West by any process, peaceful or warlike, without themselves adopting the technical apparatus of that order? No doubt, some of them are already borrowing various features of machine society, but slowly and with indifferent success. The most efficient of them, the Japanese, still rely largely upon the West for a substantial part of their mechanical outfit—for inventiveness and creative mechanical skill. Unless there is a material decline in Western technology—and no evidence of such a slump is now in sight—then it may be safely contended that none of the agricultural civilizations of Asia or Africa will ever catch up with the scientific development of the West. As things stand at present, none of them gives any promise of being able to overrun the West as the conquerors of Rome overran the provinces of that empire. Certainly there is not likely to be, in any future that we can foresee, such an equality of armaments as existed between the best of the Roman legions and the forces of their conquerors. Hence the downfall of the West through conquest may fairly be ruled out of the possibilities of the coming centuries. If, in due time, the East smashes the West on the battlefield, it will be because the East has completely taken over the technology of the West, gone it one better, and thus become Western in civilization. In that case machine civilization will not disappear but will make a geographical shift.

Defining civilization narrowly in terms of letters and art, are the probabilities of a "decline" more numerous? Here we approach a more debatable, more intangible, topic. With reference to letters, taking into account the evidence of the last fifty years, there is no sign of a decay—at all events, a decay like that which occurred between the first and the sixth century in Roman history. Indeed, there are many cautious critics who tell us that the writers of the past hundred years, with the machine system at a high pitch, may be compared in number, competence, and power without fear with the writers of any century since the appearance of the Roman grand style. Granted that we have no Horace, Shakespeare, or Goethe, we may reasonably answer that literature of their manner has little meaning for a civilization founded on a different basis. Considered in relation to their environment rather than some fictitious absolute, the best of modern writers, it may well be argued, rank with the best of the Middle Ages and antiquity. If poetry sinks in the scale and tragedy becomes comical, it may be because the mythology upon which they feed is simply foreign to the spirit of the machine age—not because there has been a dissolution of inherited mental powers. The imagination of an Einstein, a Bohr, or a Millikan may well transcend that of a Milton or a Virgil. Who is to decide?

The case of the arts is on a similar footing. For the sake of the argument, it may be conceded that the machine age has produced nothing comparable with the best of the painting, sculpture, and architecture of antiquity and the Middle Ages. What does that signify? Anything more than a decline in the arts appropriate to an agricultural and market-city era? The machine age is young. As yet it can hardly be said to have created an art of its own, although there are signs of great competence, if not genius, about us—signs of a new art appropriate to speed, mechanics, motion, railway stations, factories, office buildings, and public institutions. Using the lowest common denominator in the reckoning, there is no evidence of a decay in artistic power such as appears in the contrast between the Pantheon of Agrippa and the rude churches of Saxon England. To say that the modern age has produced no ecclesiastical architecture comparable with that of the Middle Ages is to utter a judgment as relevant to our situation as a statement that the medieval times can show no aqueducts or baths equal to the noblest structures of pagan Rome. It may be that the machine age will finally prove to be poor in artistic genius—a debatable point—but it can hardly be said that it has produced its typical art, from which a decline may be expected.

Passing to a more tangible subject, is it possible that machine civilization may be destroyed by internal revolutions or civil wars such as have often wrecked great states in the past? That such disturbances will probably arise in the future from time to time cannot be denied, and the recent Bolshevik Revolution in Russia is often cited as a warning to contemporary statesmen. If the revolutions of antiquity be taken as illustrations, it must be pointed out that the analogies are to be used with extreme care in all applications to the machine age. When the worst has been said about the condition of the industrial proletariat, it must be conceded that as regards material welfare, knowledge, social consideration, and political power, it is far removed from the proletariat of Rome or the slaves of a more remote antiquity. The kind of servile revolt that was so often ruinous in Greece and Rome is hardly possible in a machine civilization, even if economic distress were to pass anything yet experienced since the eighteenth century. The most radical of the modern proletariat want more of the good things of civilization—not a destruction of technology. If the example of Russia be pressed as relevant, the reply is that Russia possessed not a machine, but an agricultural civilization of the crudest sort; peasant soldiers supplied the storm troops of the November Revolution, and the Bolsheviki are straining every nerve to maintain their position by promising the peasants and urban dwellers that the benefits of a machine order will surely come. There will be upheavals in machine civilizations, no doubt, and occasional dictatorships like that in the United States between 1861 and 1865, but the triumph of a party dedicated to a deliberate return to pre-machine agriculture with its low standards of life, its diseases, and its illiteracy is beyond the imagination.

Finally, we must face the assertion that wars among the various nations of machine civilization may destroy the whole order. Probably terrible wars will arise and prove costly in blood and treasure, but it is a strain upon the speculative faculties to conceive of any conflict that could destroy the population and mechanical equipment of the Western world so extensively that human vitality and science could not restore economic prosperity and even improve upon the previous order. According to J. S. Mill, the whole mechanical outfit of a capitalistic country can be reproduced in about ten years. Hence the prospect of repeated and costly wars in the future need not lead us to the pessimistic view that suicide is to be the fate of machine civilization. We may admit the reality of the perils ahead without adopting the counsel of despair. If Europe and America were absolutely devastated, Japan with her present equipment in libraries, laboratories, and technology could begin the work of occupying the vacant areas, using the machine process in the operation.

For the reasons thus adduced it may be inferred: that modern civilization founded on science and the machine will not decline after the fashion of older agricultural civilizations; that analogies drawn from ages previous to technology are inapplicable; that according to signs on every hand technology promises to extend its area and intensify its characteristics; that it will afford the substance with which all who expect to lead and teach in the future must reckon.

III

Such appears to be the promise of the long future, if not the grand destiny of what we call modern civilization—the flexible framework in which the human spirit must operate during the coming centuries. Yet this view by no means precludes the idea that the machine system, as tested by its present results, presents shocking evils and indeed terrible menaces to the noblest faculties of the human race. By the use of material standards for measuring achievement, it is in danger of developing a kind of ignorant complacency that would make Phidias, Sophocles, Horace, St. Augustine, Dante, Michelangelo, Shakespeare, Lord Bacon, Newton, Goethe, Ruskin and Emerson appear to be mere trifling parasites as compared with Lord Beaverbrook, Hugo Stinnes, John Pierpont Morgan, and Henry Ford. To deny the peril that lies in any such numerical morality would be a work of supererogation. More perilous still is the concentration on the production of goods that will sell quickly at the best price the traffic will bear and fall to pieces quickly—mass production of cheap goods —rather than concentration on the manufacture and exchange of commodities with the finest intrinsic values capable of indefinite endurance. What the creed of "give as little as you can for as much as you can get" will do to the common honesty of mankind, if followed blindly for centuries, can readily be imagined. Finally, it must be admitted that the dedication of the engines of state, supported by a passionate and uninformed chauvinism, to the promotion and sale of machine-made goods is creating zones of international rivalry likely to flame up in wars more vast and destructive than any yet witnessed.

To consider for the moment merely the domestic aspects of the question, the machine civilization is particularly open to attack from three sides.

On esthetic grounds, it has been assailed for nearly a hundred years, England, the classical home of the industrial revolution, being naturally enough the mother of the severest critics—Ruskin, Carlyle, Kingsley, and Matthew Arnold. The chief article in their indictment, perhaps, is the contention that men who work with machinery are not creative, joyous, or free, but are slaves to the monotonous routine of the inexorable wheel. In a sense it is true that, in the pre-machine age, each craftsman had a certain leeway in shaping his materials with his tools and that many a common artisan produced articles of great beauty.

Yet the point can be easily overworked. Doubtless the vast majority of medieval artisans merely followed designs made by master workmen. This is certainly true of artisans in the Orient today. With respect to the mass of mankind, it is safe to assume that the level of monotony on which labor is conducted under the machine régime is by and large not lower but higher than in the handicraft, servile, or slave systems of the past. Let anyone who has doubts on this matter compare the life of laborers on the latifundia of Rome or in the cities of modern China with that of the workers in by far the major portion of machine industries. Those who are prepared to sacrifice the standard of living for the millions to provide conditions presumably favorable to the creative arts must assume a responsibility of the first magnitude.

Indeed, it is not certain, so primitive as yet are the beginnings of machine civilization, that there can be no substitute for the handicrafts as esthetic stimulants, assuming that mechanical industry is not favorable to the creative life. The machine régime does not do away with the necessity for designing or reduce the opportunities for the practice of that craft: it transfers the operation from the shop to the laboratory; and it remains to be seen whether great esthetic powers will not flourish after the first storm of capitalism has passed. In any case, it must be admitted that the "cheap and nasty" character of machine-made goods, so marked everywhere, may really be due to the profit-making lust and the desire of the multitude to have imitations of the gewgaws loved by the patricians, not to the inherent nature of machine industry. Possibly what is lost in the merits of individual objects of beauty may be more than offset by city and community planning, realizing new types of esthetic ideals on a vast, democratic basis. Certainly the worst of the esthetic offenses created by the machine—the hideous factory town—can be avoided by intelligent coöperative action, as the garden-city movement faintly foreshadows. In a hundred years the coal-consuming engine may be as obsolete as the Dodo, and the Birminghams, Pittsburghs, and Essens of the modern world live only in the records of the historians. However this may be, the esthetes of the future will have to work within the limitations and opportunities created by science and the machine, directed, it may be hoped, by a more intelligent economy and nobler concepts of human values.

Frequently affiliated with esthetic criticism of the machine and science is the religious attack. With endless reiteration, the charge is made that industrial civilization is materialistic. In reply, the scornful might say, "Well, what of it?" But the issue deserves consideration on its merits, in spite of its illusive nature. As generally used, the term "materialistic" has some of the qualities of moonshine; it is difficult to grasp. It is the fashion of certain Catholic writers to call Protestantism materialistic, on account of its emphasis on thrift and business enterprise—a fashion which some radicals have adopted: Max Weber in Germany and R. H. Tawney in England, for example. With something akin to the same discrimination, Oswald Spengler calls all England materialistic, governed by pecuniary standards—as contrasted with old Prussia where "duty," "honor," and "simple piety" reigned supreme. More recently, André Siegfried, following a hundred English critics, with Matthew Arnold in the lead, has found materialism to be one of the chief characteristics of the United States, as contrasted with the richer and older civilizations of Europe, particularly France. And Gandhi consigns every one of them—England, Prussia, France, and America—to the same bottomless pit of industrial materialism. When all this verbiage is sifted, it usually means that the charge arises from emotions that have little or no relation to religion or philosophy—from the quarrels of races, sects, and nations.

If religion is taken in a crude, anthropomorphic sense, filling the universe with gods, spirits, and miraculous feats, then beyond question the machine and science are the foes of religion. If it is materialistic to disclose the influence of technology and environment in general upon humanity, then perhaps the machine and science are materialistic. But it is one of the ironies of history that science has shown the shallowness of the old battle between materialist and spiritist and through the mouths of physicists has confessed that it does not know what matter and force are. Matter is motion; motion is matter; both elude us, we are told. Doubtless science does make short shrift of a thousand little mysteries once deemed as essential to Christianity as were the thousand minor gods to the religion of old Japan, but for these little mysteries it has substituted a higher and sublimer mystery.

To descend to the concrete, is the prevention of disease by sanitation more materialistic than curing it by touching saints' bones? Is feeding the multitude by mass production more materialistic than feeding it by a miracle? Is the elimination of famines by a better distribution of goods more materialistic than prevention by the placation of the rain gods? At any rate, it is not likely that science and machinery will be abandoned because the theologian (who seldom refuses to partake of their benefits) wrings his hands and cries out against materialism. After all, how can he consistently maintain that Omnipotent God ruled the world wisely and well until the dawn of the modern age and abandoned it to the Evil One because Henry VIII or Martin Luther quarreled with the Pope and James Watt invented the steam engine?

Arising, perhaps, from the same emotional source as esthetic and religious criticism is the attack on the machine civilization as lacking in humanitarianism. Without commenting on man's inhumanity to man as an essential characteristic of the race, we may fairly ask on what grounds can anyone argue that the masses were more humanely treated in the agricultural civilization of antiquity or the Middle Ages than in the machine order of modern times. Tested by the mildness of its laws (brutal as many of them are), by its institutions of care and benevolence, by its death rate (that telltale measurement of human welfare), by its standards of life, and by every conceivable measure of human values, machine civilization, even in its present primitive stage, need fear no comparison with any other order on the score of general well-being.

Under the machine and science, the love of beauty, the sense of mystery, and the motive of compassion—sources of esthetics, religion, and humanism—are not destroyed. They remain essential parts of our nature. But the conditions under which they must operate, the channels they must take, the potentialities of their action are all changed. These ancient forces will become powerful in the modern age just in the proportion that men and women accept the inevitability of science and the machine, understand the nature of the civilization in which they must work, and turn their faces resolutely to the future.

COMING ISSUES IN AMERICAN POLITICS
by Peter F. Drucker

We have reached a major watershed in American politics. Behind us are sixty years of great issues and constant change—the sixty years from Mark Hanna to Walter Reuther, from Booker T. Washington to the Supreme Court decision outlawing racial segregation in the schools, from Bryan's "Cross of Gold" speech to today's slogan of "People's Capitalism," from the electric streetcar to the hydrogen bomb. During these sixty years the United States has transmuted itself from an agrarian into an industrial society and from isolation into leadership as a world power.

The issues and slogans of these sixty years were still echoed, all but automatically, in last Fall's election campaign, seemed indeed at times to dominate it. But rarely in our history has campaign oratory fallen on deafer ears, sounded flatter, or meant less. For if the four years of the first Eisenhower Administration meant anything, they meant that the New Deal, in which all these issues of the past sixty years had culminated, finally passed into history, codified, consolidated, and accepted.

We have still to come to grips with the issues that are likely to dominate the decades ahead. One would have to go back to Franklin D. Roosevelt's First Hundred Days in 1933 to find anything comparable to the steady stream of proposals on major policy and requests for major legislation—on transportation, inflation, water use, medical care, education, tariff policy and so on—that President Eisenhower poured out in the early months of 1956. Every one of these proposals would have seemed radical, if not revolutionary, a few years ago. That only one of these proposals—the Highway Bill—became law, is therefore perhaps not too remarkable. But that none of them became a great issue, capable of arousing emotions, of organizing political alignments, or of being seriously debated in a campaign, indicates that we as a nation are still resting from the work of the past and not ready yet to tackle the jobs of tomorrow. Or rather we still—and that clearly goes for both parties—believe that these are the "jobs of tomorrow."

But "tomorrow," as the preceding chapters of this book have tried to show, is largely already accomplished fact. And tomorrow's issues in American politics can therefore already be identified, defined, and described by an analysis of the future that has already happened.

The New Migration

One starting point of this analysis, and one central fact, is, of course, the growth of our population and the changes in its structure. Equally important is its shift in geographic distribution. Twenty years ago, when it was commonly believed that America's population had ceased to grow, it was also widely held that our people had lost their traditional mobility. "The days of the frontier are forever gone," and so on. The past ten or fifteen years have proved this false. The largest migration in our history began during World War II; and it has continued ever since with undiminished momentum.

This is a migration both of people and

From *America's Next Twenty Years*, by Peter Drucker. Copyright, 1955, 1957, by Peter Drucker.

[878]

of industry. Three areas in particular have grown as fast as any on this continent ever did in the past: the Far West, the Southwest, and—just north of the border but intimately linked with the United States—Southern Ontario. To be sure, the spectacular growth of California—from fifth in size of population in 1940 to second in 1950—shows signs of slowing down. But even so, California will be the most populous state by 1965, if not by 1960. And Texas, New Mexico, Nevada, Oregon, and Florida are now growing at boom speed. Just across the border, Southern Ontario since the end of the war has become one of the major industrial areas of the world; and the opening of the St. Lawrence Seaway should bring another tremendous expansion to Canada's industrial center.

The new migration is an urban one. California is already one of the most highly urbanized states in the Union; and Southern Ontario is hardly less urban, despite all attempts by the Canadian government to direct into farming the "New Canadians" from Europe. Internal migration from the farm to the city is also changing the character of the Old South. Fifteen years ago the states that once formed the Confederacy were predominantly agricultural; only one out of every four people employed held a nonfarm job. Today half the Southern population makes its living away from the farm. And, significantly, the Southern Negro seems to have become urbanized even faster than the Southern white.

Already, in other words, the Americans are a *metropolitan* people. Almost two-thirds of us live and work in the 168 areas the Census recognizes as metropolitan. The country can in fact be best envisaged as a galaxy of urban solar systems. And while, within itself, every one of the metropolitan systems tends to decentralize—as people move to the suburbs—the country as a whole tends steadily to centralize. It is the push of people toward the metropolis that causes it to expand into the semi-urban countryside.

The basic issues of domestic policy in the next twenty years will therefore be those of a densely populated industrial country in which the metropolitan area is the basic unit. There will no longer be major regional differences in basic population patterns. Even in Colorado, Utah, and Arizona well over half the population is already metropolitan. Above all, the basic difference between the agrarian South and the industrial or commercial North—which has shaped so much of American history and culture—is bound to become increasingly just a memory.

These population developments by themselves are producing new basic issues of national policy, requiring broad national as well as local or regional resolution.

New Issue: Water

The geography textbooks have it that the United States is favored above all nations with natural resources. But there is one natural resource in which the United States, compared to Western Europe, has always been badly supplied. It is a basic one: *water*. Not only is rainfall over large parts of the country deficient, and abundant rainfall limited to small areas in the Northwest and Southeast; but because of geography, geology, or soil structure far too much of the rainfall we get seems to be lost in run-off rather than stored up in the subterranean water table for future use.

During the past fifteen years the signs

have multiplied that we are living off our water capital—running the risk of repeating with our water resources the orgy of destruction we indulged in with our soil. Water tables, once depleted, are even more difficult to restore than eroded and depleted soil. Yet we continuously pour new population and new industries into areas of marginal water supply, inviting disasters that we should have experience enough to forestall.

During the next twenty years the need for water will sharply increase, partly because of population growth, but mainly because the new and growing industries typically need water at an ever-increasing rate. A mad scramble for the *allocation* of water resources among metropolitan areas, states, and regions is already going full tilt—between New York and Philadelphia in the East, for example: between California, Oregon, Nevada, Arizona, New Mexico, and Colorado in the West. There will be so many of these fights for a larger share of an inadequate water supply—and they will be so bitter—that federal water allocation is certain to be demanded and heatedly discussed.

The conservation of water will be a more novel—and certainly a more intense—political issue. Twenty years hence, in many parts of the United States, the users of water (especially industrial ones) will have to re-use it and to return it, cleaned and cooled, to the underground water table—an expensive process. State laws or local ordinances on water conservation should therefore be the hottest of political hot potatoes nearly everywhere in the country from now on.

The same has already begun to apply to conservation of all kinds: soil and forests; grazing lands and petroleum; clean, unpolluted air and clean, unpolluted water; scenic beauty and open spaces. All of these will be continuously more desirable, more expensive, and more difficult to secure—and hence they will become even more prominent as political issues for national and local governments alike.

Power, Transportation, and Housing

The population pattern will also push into the foreground our national policies on all three of these basic facilities: power, transportation, and housing.

Our power needs will grow even faster than our water needs. Broadly speaking, technology is now moving from the age of mechanical industry into that of chemicals (where, for instance, atomic energy belongs). Electric power is the basic raw material of most chemical industries; and our present power supply, despite the tremendous building of new stations in the past ten years, is already inadequate. Need will continue to grow faster than supply. Most of the accessible sources of water-generated power have already been used up. From now on we will have to depend increasingly on thermal generation.

Already this has again raised the issue of the large governmental power system like TVA or Bonneville. They can only keep up with demand if they add thermal generating facilities. And whether they do this by building their own generating stations or by going into partnership with private companies, they are bound to arouse antagonism and debate. That much, at least, the Dixon-Yates contract can be said to have proved.

At the same time, however, as atomic power reactors are being developed, the basic technology of thermal power generation is changing. This will raise an even touchier political issue. The Atomic Energy Act of 1954, a major landmark in the relationship of government to private business, decided for the private development of the new resource. It did so, however, not merely by applying to atomic power the traditional and uniquely American principle of close regulation of private industry by public authority. It also for the first time established partnership between public bodies and private industry—and inevitably so, since atomic power cannot be wholly divorced from atomic war material. Even if the 1954 act were a clearer and less ambiguous document than it is, these twin features (regulation and partnership) would by themselves insure that the status of the power industry in relation to government will for years remain a source of contention.

Transportation needs, too, are fast outgrowing their facilities. During the past year we committed ourselves to making our highways adequate to the needs of an industrial continent. The program is certainly a giant step forward. Yet, though the Highway Bill of 1956 is the biggest and most ambitious program of "internal improvements" ever enacted in this country, it almost certainly will prove too little and too late within five years or so. As it stands it will give us, by 1970 or so, the highway system we already need today. And the attempt to shoehorn the program into the existing machinery of federal and state governments is unlikely to work; at the least it must seriously hamper the carrying out of the program within its limits of time and money.

Railroad regulation still assumes a transportation monopoly of the railroads, where the actual conditions of monopoly have long since disappeared. The Grand Canyon mid-air collision last summer showed dramatically how poorly equipped we are to organize tomorrow's air traffic. And there is no co-ordination of policy—even less, of regulating agencies—between rail, highway, and airway transportation. It has been obvious since the mid-thirties that the creation of a unified Department of Transportation at cabinet level would make good sense. Even more necessary—and more controversial—are national programs for building and maintaining a transport system adequate to our population and industry.

Housing will be a major political issue —nationally as well as locally. We are at present building in the new industrial areas some of the worst slums this country has ever seen—in and around Los Angeles, for example, and in the new industrial cities of the South. These new slums are expensive, but the fact that a tar-paper shack costs $14,000 does not make it any less of a shack.

The housing need, moreover, will grow mightily before it lessens. As every suburban home owner knows, we live today off the housing inheritance of our grandparents. Few middle-class families could afford to build the kind of house they are now able to live in, thanks to the lower building costs of thirty years ago. But these houses are rapidly deteriorating. Within the next twenty years most of them will have to be replaced. Together these older houses constitute the bulk of our available, and practically all of our good, housing. But they are rarely to be found, unfortunately, in the areas of maximum population growth. Here we will need large numbers of new houses. These had better be reasonably decent, reasonably cheap, and reasonably well built—and we will want to get them without state or federal entry, except for slum clearance, into the housing business.

Pressure on the Schools

Another area of constant concern, at all levels of government, will be education. Today we are at least 75,000 classrooms short of the minimum needs of our children in primary and secondary schools. This means that 1.5 million children cannot be properly educated—half of them are on double or triple sessions; half go to school in temporary barracks, unused garages, or church basements. Of the school buildings now in existence, one fifth are fire traps long past their maximum life span.

We are building 50,000 new classrooms a year, but that is less than we need to take care of the yearly growth in school population. The deficit is not being reduced; it grows by 10 or 20,000 classrooms a year. And in the mid-sixties another huge increase in school population will overtake us. And this is only the need in primary and secondary schools, to which must be added the needs of colleges and universities for additional facilities.

In the light of these needs President Eisenhower's school-building proposals of last year were indeed as inadequate as the harshest critics said they were. Even so, however, both parties in Congress were clearly only too happy to be able to use the segregation issue as a pretext for doing nothing about school construction.

At that they may have been wise. For physical facilities are but one aspect of the great education issue that looms on the American political horizon. They are the one aspect moreover that can be dealt with by paying out money. The others require something a good deal scarcer and more controversial: hard thinking about values, objectives, and policies.

There is first the need for teachers. Earlier in this book this was shown to be central to the problems higher education faces. But we also need teachers—many, many more—on all other levels, from kindergarten through senior high school. Yet, instead of training more teachers, we are training fewer today than we did twenty years ago.

Educational policy and curriculum also promise to become central issues. At present there is little left of the fervent interest in education that characterized the thirties; but now is the very moment when the pressure of numbers on the schools should force them into experiments with new methods, new subjects, and new educational policies. Moreover, the more going to college becomes the normal thing for the young American to do, the more crucial becomes the question of harmonizing academic freedom with education for citizenship—a problem by no means as easy to solve as it appears to either liberal or reactionary.

Medical Care For Everyone

During the next two decades we will also have to decide how to make medical and hospital care available to everyone. Already we have begun to tackle this problem through voluntary community co-operation; Blue Cross and Blue Shield are the obvious examples. We have yet to extend this system to the self-employed, the farmers, the very poor, and the aged. Above all, we have to extend it to cover major medical expenses or catastrophic illness expenses—the most serious medical costs for all but the very rich. The abortive proposal of the Eisenhower Administration to re-insure catastrophic illness insurance by co-operatives and private companies—and thus make it available to those who cannot be covered today—was thus a major step in the right direction.

There is also the question of providing for medical education. We do not train even enough doctors today to take care of an expanding population at our present standard. Any extension of medical cost insurance to make adequate medical care more easily available would create a *real* doctor shortage. Yet, medical education is so expensive that it puts medical school expansion beyond the reach of even the few rich universities. A good case can be made out for considering the cost of medical education as a long-term capital investment, which the doctor's higher earning power should enable him to repay over the years. Even such self-financing of medical education, however, might require some form of public re-insurance of the risk; and though the amounts would be fairly small, they are not going to be easy to find.

Decline of the Unions?

Nor are the next twenty years likely to be years of industrial peace. On the contrary, all signs point to labor ferment: the rapid rise of total population without an accompanying rise of working population; the major technological shifts which will change large numbers of jobs from unskilled work to highly skilled; the resulting need for radical change in concepts of seniority and training; and the rapid growth of industry in sparsely unionized areas. Unrest may arise not merely between management and labor but fully as much, perhaps even more, between labor and the public, and within labor itself.

There is today a large area of agreement on the rights and limitations of trade unions throughout the country—far larger than the shrill battle cries of small minorities on either side would lead you to suspect.

But there are four unresolved issues—each a basic one. There is the strike that imperils national welfare. There is the conflict between union security and the right to work. There are the union restrictions of access to a craft. And finally there is the fight over the unionization of employees who are not industrial workers—salaried employees, clerks, engineers, and so on. Since the work population will before long be dominated by white-collar employees, their acceptance or rejection of unionization will determine whether the labor union will continue to be a power in industrial society or become just another pressure group—and a rather insulated and rapidly aging one at that.

Demand For Equality

We can expect the status of the Negro minority, during the next two decades, to change fairly drastically. Twenty years hence, the rapid industrialization of the South—combined with the continuous emigration of Negroes from the South—should mean that the traditional Southern pattern of rural and small-town segregation, except for a few isolated areas, will be a thing of the past.

Indeed the Supreme Court decision on integration in the schools may, in the long run, prove to have been a rear-guard action—though an important and highly significant one—rather than the breakthrough. To be sure, half of our Negro population still lives in the South. But the proportion of young Negroes of school age still in the South is already very much less; and even fewer Negro children live in the rural areas where integration will be fought the hardest.

Increasingly, therefore, race relations will become problems of the industrial city, and especially of the Northern industrial city. For the future of race relations in this country what happens in Buffalo, Indianapolis, and Flint is already a great deal more important than what happens in Mississippi.

Increasingly, within the next twenty years, we can therefore expect the Negro's fight for equal opportunity and fair treatment to shift from a demand for equal employment opportunities to a demand for equal opportunities for advancement. While this would represent a tremendous achievement—nothing less than the attainment of economic equality for the American Negro—it would also encounter more resistance. Certainly a national policy focused on the steady and courageous pursuit of Negro equality—and based upon a firm insistence on the Negroes' civil and economic rights—will be badly needed during this period.

The economic forces which determine the employment of older workers—that is, over sixty-five—will pull in opposite directions. Wherever industry shifts to Automation, they will be under pressure to get out. This is not only the easiest way to take care of reductions in employment, it will also be more efficient; the old worker will have the greatest difficulty in re-learning and acquiring new skills. But elsewhere, in the absence of Automation, the shortage of labor will tend to force business to employ old people as long as they are able and willing to work. We will see pressure, therefore, toward better provisions and legislation to prevent discrimination against the older worker. Since the older people will continue, though slowly, to grow in numbers and proportion—at least 12 if not 15 percent of the population will be over sixty-five by 1975—they may well achieve highly organized and powerful pressure. It would certainly be no more than prudent for both management and union leaders to prepare immediately to determine which of the older people are capable of work, how to place them in jobs they can carry, and how to treat them with respect to lay-offs and promotion. In several states, unions are already clamoring for a Fair Employment Practices Act to forbid discrimination in both hiring and retirement on grounds of age.

New Ideas About Money

These are certainly not going to be years of low government spending—even if armaments expenditures, God willing, should become less necessary. There will be no "withering away of the state," whether Republicans or Democrats control the federal and state governments. Yet our notions of fiscal policy are still based largely on the assumption that high expenditure belongs only in an emergency. How, therefore, are we to combine the needs of the government for large revenue with the needs of an expanding economy for investment capital? Perhaps we may even have to give up the oldest principle of business taxation: the legal distinction between interest on fixed capital—which is considered a cost, and thus deductible from business profits—and the income on venture capital, which is profit and taxed. For under the present high corporation tax rates one dollar paid out in interest costs a company only fifty cents, while a dollar dividend to the stockholder actually requires two dollars in profit. The result of this disproportion is an increased dependence on fixed capital, a decreasing supply of venture capital, and a decreasing revenue therefrom—that is, both economic and fiscal decay.

Another unresolved conflict in fiscal policy lies between the realities of modern governmental life, which require planned long-term capital expenditures, and the constitutional requirement that Congress appropriate money on an annual basis. That no one Congress can commit a future Congress is sound doctrine. But much of the expenditure of modern government is meaningless unless it is considered in long-range terms. Actually, by refusing to accept the reality of a capital budget, Congress may well be sacrificing its control over expenditures. But how such problems as these should be resolved, let alone how they can be resolved, we are clearly not going to know for some time to come.

Footnote on Inflation

On one issue of fiscal policy, public opinion rather than government action may make the greatest difference. That is inflation.

Public opinion in economic matters is still deeply influenced by the depression psychology; it sees in unemployment the major threat and in full employment the earthly paradise. As a result, we have created defenses in depth against the last depression. We are committed to immediate government action the moment there is significant unemployment. And we have such a tremendous backlog of public works—not to mention armaments—that we could immediately mobilize the entire economy should the real threat of unemployment appear.

But the next depression is most unlikely to be an unemployment-depression. One of our greatest economists, the late Joseph Schumpeter of Harvard, pointed out in his last paper—read to the American Economic Association in December 1949, only a few days before his death—that it is inflation rather than unemployment that destroys society in the twentieth century. Schumpeter based his pessimistic appraisal of America's chances to survive as a free society on his belief that American public opinion did not understand the danger of inflation, and would not permit adequate safeguards against it.

Six years later, the keenest European student of the American economy, Felix Somary, the Swiss banker, who had correctly predicted every single economic development in this country from the mid-twenties on, echoed the warning. In a talk given at Harvard in June 1956 Somary was even more emphatic about the danger of inflation, yet even more pessimistic regarding America's will to avoid it.

Inflation is more than an impersonal and general danger to society—the breeder of class hatred and the destroyer of the middle class. In an economy where the great mass of people have become long-term creditors (through their insurance and pension holdings), and where as much as half of the employed population is on fixed salaries which do not readily adjust to changes in money values, inflation may cause more individual suffering than even widespread unemployment. This statement—obvious to any German, Frenchman, Italian, or Austrian (not to mention the people behind the Iron Curtain)—is still incomprehensible to most Americans. While we will not, and should not, forget the danger of an unemployment depression, we will have to learn that it is a major duty of government in our economy to safeguard monetary stability. And this requires, above all, a vigilant public opinion.

The first Eisenhower Administration did well by the country, therefore, in its willingness to brake incipient inflation twice, in 1953 and 1956. Yet quite clearly, public opinion neither understood nor supported these moves. And the administration itself did not dare to admit the obvious: that inflation cannot be prevented or stopped without temporary discomfort and unpleasantness. Yet, sooner or later, within the next decade or two the point will certainly be reached when these facts can no longer be hidden, and when the issue of inflation will have to be joined.

Whatever policies we adopt in these basic areas, their total impact on our national life will be enormous—greater even than that of the New Deal. Certainly—and deservedly—we will debate each one of them, will disagree about them, will engage in bitter partisan fights. But it is doubtful whether the answers adequate to our needs can be developed entirely through the give-and-take of political battle. What we should have are fundamental state papers on the economic and social policies of an industrial society—papers comparable, perhaps, to Jefferson's "Notes on the State of Virginia," Hamilton's "Report on Manufacturers," Henry Clay's "American System," or John Wesley Powell's papers on the management of the Western lands. President Truman made a start in this task by appointing commissions on Water Policy and on Raw Material Resources. The Eisenhower Administration tackled the job of highway modernization. It opened up for discussion government reinsurance against catastrophic illness, a national transportation policy, and federal aid to education. Its fiscal policy has revealed an awareness of the perils of inflation. But these are only beginnings.

Redrawing the Map

The federal government is the proper agency to develop broad policies in most of these areas. But the federal government simply cannot do the detailed job in any one of them. Much of the actual work will have to be done by local governments —municipal, state, regional. In most areas it will have to be done in close co-operation with private industry. It will have to take account of local or regional needs and circumstances, and the administration will have to be local. Yet existing local and state governments are patently unequal to the task.

The national population no longer corresponds to the traditional distinctions between local and state government. A metropolitan people cuts across the boundary lines of cities, counties, and states. And our political scientists increasingly believe that even the most "local" of these issues require a co-ordinated effort that embraces an entire "super-metropolis" such as the Eastern seaboard from Portland, Maine, to Norfolk, Virginia. The truly admirable system of parkways built by New Jersey, for instance, has only added to the traffic problems of New York, Pennsylvania, and Maryland. The best planning New Jersey can do has been largely nullified, in turn, by the lack of co-ordination with neighboring states. Similarly, Westchester County shows that schools can no longer be planned within the historical unit of the school district. One of the few communities in Westchester that planned ahead for tomorrow's school needs was Pleasantville. But the main effect of Pleasantville's foresight has been an influx of people from the surrounding towns, which has quickly rendered Pleasantville's careful plans inadequate.

Local and state governments, our oldest civic institutions, have remained basically unchanged since the Northwest Ordinance of 1787. But somehow we are going to have to invent and develop new ones that cut across existing jurisdictions. Leonard D. White of the University of Chicago has recently shown (in his three books *The Federalists, The Jeffersonians,* and *The Jacksonians*) how important the administrative foundations laid in the early years of the Republic were for the survival and growth of the United States, and how much courage and imagination went into their design. The creative skill required to build the regional institutions needed now will hardly be of a lesser order.

Our geographic ideas also need revision in the matter of atomic dispersal—a subject that has occasioned more confused talk than action. We now know, at last, that the largest theoretically possible bomb is limited both in its area of immediate danger and of total destruction. We know, too, that there is no defense against atomic attack; there is only early warning—and even this is problematical with guided intercontinental missiles. Finally we know —though it is highly secret information —what are the critical products and processes on which our ability to maintain an industrial economy really depends.

We know what we need to know, in other words, to escape paralysis from the first all-out attack. It should be emphasized that dispersal is not defense. It is only a safeguard against being knocked out in the first round. And it is not something we have actually achieved. In fact we may be more vulnerable today than we were ten years ago. Forty percent of the American population and 56 percent of all manufacturing are concentrated in forty metropolitan areas. The remaining 120 sizable cities contain only 16 percent of the population and 19 percent of the manufacturing facilities. In other words, we are so highly concentrated as to invite attack. If we had a national dispersal policy, we could use the internal migration of population and industry (which go on anyway) to change this pattern fairly rapidly and with a minimum of cost and dislocation. If we had only had such a policy during the past ten years we might by now be in a position to survive even a massive attack. The next ten years offer an equal opportunity. But we will have to do more about dispersal than we have done so far—which is chiefly to discuss it.

A HAVE-NOT COUNTRY

In international economics America has almost adjusted to the unfamiliar role of richest nation. During the past ten years we have successfully made the shift from debtor to creditor policies. But now, as the preceding chapter tried to show, we have to make an even greater one—from having enjoyed in all our history a raw-materials surplus, we will come to the new experience of a raw-materials shortage, becoming for the first time a "have-not" nation. The much-publicized dollar gap, the chronic and apparently incurable shortage of dollars in the outside world, may well be replaced by a shortage of foreign currency in American hands to cover the purchases we want to make abroad. America's economic health will increasingly depend on our ability to export enough manufactured goods to pay for our import needs.

Two conclusions follow that at first sight may appear both paradoxical and mutually exclusive. The first is that low American tariffs on manufactured goods are rapidly becoming obligatory. We are in a very exposed position precisely because of our high productivity. Every other country with a similar lead—France in the eighteenth century, Britain in the nineteenth—eventually became complacent; it is always harder to stay ahead than just to get ahead. And liberal tariff policy is the best—perhaps the only—safeguard of high productivity. Low tariffs are not primarily the means to live up to our obligations as world creditor and world leader. They are a domestic necessity, and are increasingly so recognized by many (though by no means by all) of our manufacturing industries. The fact that the low tariff fight is no longer led by Southern agrarians and New York bankers (the traditional free-trade groups) but by manufacturing leaders like Ford, Burroughs Adding Machine, and IBM is an indication of how drastically we have changed.

The second conclusion to be drawn from our becoming a "have-not" country is that we must lead in the rapid economic development of the underdeveloped areas in our own urgent self-interest.

We must conclude this book on America's domestic future in the recognition that events beyond this country's borders may play, whether we like it or not, the determining role. Not only does the shadow of atomic warfare darken all prediction, but even if we assume a relative amount of luck—immediate postponement of major conflict by fighting an indefinite number of little ones—we will have to recognize how many of our internal rewards depend on our international wisdom and leadership. In politics, as elsewhere, the two entwine—and offer the major parties a double opportunity to capture national leadership.

The demands that an expanding economy will make on public policy are clearly so great and so new that they will force drastic changes in political alignments, organizational structure, and voting patterns. Yet at the moment neither party seems adequate to the issues of tomorrow. The Republicans, with their vulnerability of futile nostalgia for a past that never was, and the Democrats, with their almost obsessive fear of depression unemployment, seem equally impervious to the future. Yet the very fact that the two congressional parties are so evenly balanced in popular appeal suggests that the first to produce imaginative, bold, and realistic economic leadership might thereby gain a twenty-year ascendancy.

But the same is true many times over of the demands—in fact, the absolute prerequisites—of our international position. Unless they are satisfied, none of the opportunities here sketched will ever see reality. And they can only be satisfied by a firm, determined, and long-sighted foreign policy—dedicated to the economic and social development, rapidly and peacefully, of the Free World. For the first time since the Louisiana Purchase and the War of 1812, that is, foreign affairs have returned to primacy in the national scene. This seems likely to be the most enduring fact—as it is certainly the most revolutionary one—of America's Next Twenty Years.

THE FOUR FREEDOMS
by Franklin D. Roosevelt

In the future days, which we seek to make secure, we look forward to a world founded upon four essential human freedoms.

The first is freedom of speech and expression—everywhere in the world.

The second is freedom of every person to worship God in his own way—everywhere in the world.

The third is freedom from want—which, translated into world terms, means economic understandings which will secure to every nation a healthy peace time life for its inhabitants—everywhere in the world.

The fourth is freedom from fear—which, translated into world terms, means a world-wide reduction of armaments to such a point and in such a thorough fashion that no nation will be in a position to commit an act of physical aggression against any neighbor—anywhere in the world.

That is no vision of a distant millennium. It is a definite basis for a kind of world attainable in our own time and generation.

—Franklin D. Roosevelt, January 6, 1941

THE RACES OF MANKIND
by Ruth Benedict *and* Gene Weltfish

Thirty-four nations are now united in a common cause—victory over Axis aggression, the military destruction of fascism. This is the greatest fighting alliance of nations in history. These United Nations include the most different physical types of men, the most unlike beliefs, the most varied ways of life. White men, yellow men, black men, and the so-called "red men" of America, peoples of the East and the West, of the tropics and the arctic, are fighting together against one enemy.

Every morning in the newspapers and on the bulletin boards we read of yester-

From *The Races of Mankind,* by Ruth Benedict and Gene Weltfish, published by the Public Affairs Committee, Inc., New York 20, N. Y.

day's battles in Russia, in China, in Italy, in the Solomon Islands, and in New Guinea. One day's hop in a plane can carry us across the oceans. Our supply ships go to every corner of the globe. On the radio we hear men reporting on the spot from Cairo and Australia. Burma is much closer to us today than New Orleans was to Washington at the time of the War of 1812. Distance then was a hard fact; it had not been scaled down by the triumphs of human invention.

This war, for the first time, has brought home to Americans the fact that the whole world has been made one neighborhood. All races of man are shoulder to shoulder. Our armed forces are in North Africa with its Negro, Berber, and Near-East peoples. They are in India. They are in China. They are in the Solomons with its dark-skinned, "strong"-haired Melanesians. Our neighbors now are peoples of all the races of the earth.

For Americans this is not so new an experience as it is to people of most nations. In our country men of different color, hair texture, and head shape have lived together since the founding of our nation. They are citizens of the United States. Negroes and whites, Indians, Mexicans, Chinese, and people from the European nations are all taxable, subject to the draft and to the other laws of the land. They are part of our great national community. History today is only bringing together on a world scale races which have been brought together on a smaller scale here in America.

Americans know better than most how much hard feeling there can be when people of different races and nationalities have to live together and be part of one community. They know that there is often conflict. Today, when what we all want more than anything else is to win this war, most Americans are confident that, whatever our origins, we shall be able to pull together to a final victory. Hitler, though, has always believed we were wrong; he has believed that hard feeling would break out and leave us defeated. He has been sure that he could "divide and conquer." He has believed that he could convince non-white races in Asia and Africa that this is a "white man's war." He has believed especially that America was a no man's land, where peoples of all origins were ready to fall to fighting among themselves. He believes that this is a front on which we are doomed to lose the battle. It is certainly a front no less important in this war than the Production Front and the Inflation Front.

In any great issue that concerns this war we turn to science. When we need new fuels, substitutes for rubber, lighter metals, or new plastics, we ask scientists to tell us what is possible and what is impossible. The chemists tell us how to make the plastics we need, and the physicists tell us how to detect and locate an approaching airplane, and the engineers tell us how to build a better fighting plane. When we are faced with war shortages, they tell us what essential materials we have been throwing out on the dump heap.

We need the scientist just as much on the race front. Scientists have studied race. Historians have studied the history of all nations and peoples. Sociologists have studied the way in which peoples band together. Biologists have studied how man's physical traits are passed down from one generation to the next. Anthropologists have studied man's bodily measurements and his cultural achievements. Psychologists have studied intelligence among different races. All that the scientists have learned is important to us at this crucial moment of history. They can tell us: "This is so," "This is not so," "This occurs under certain conditions," or "This occurs under opposite conditions."

This booklet cannot tell you all that science has learned about the races of mankind, but it states facts that have been learned and verified. We need them.

The Bible story of Adam and Eve, father and mother of the whole human race, told centuries ago the same truth that science has shown today: that all the peoples of the earth are a single family and have a common origin. Science describes the intricate make-up of the human body: all its different organs co-operating in keeping us alive, its curious anatomy that couldn't possibly have "just happened" to be the same in all men if they did not have a common origin. Take the structure of the human foot, for instance. When you list all the little bones and muscles and the joints of the toes, it is impossible to imagine that that would all have happened twice. Or take our teeth: so many front teeth, so many canines, so many molars. Who can imagine finding the same arrangements in two human species if they weren't one family?

The fact of the unity of the human race is proved, therefore, in its anatomy. It is proved also by the close similarity in what all races are physically fitted for. No difference among human races has affected limbs and teeth and relative strength so that one race is biologically outfitted like a lion and another biologically outfitted like a lamb. All races of men can either plow or fight, and all the racial differences among them are in non-essentials such as texture of head hair, amount of body hair, shape of the nose or head, or color of the eyes and the skin. The white race is the hairiest, but a white man's hair isn't thick enough to keep him warm in cold climates. The Negro's dark skin gives him some protection against strong sunlight in the tropics, and white men often have to take precautions against sunstroke. But the war has shown that white men can work and fight even in a tropical desert. Today white men in hot countries wear sun helmets and protect themselves with clothes and rub their skin with sun-tan oil. Very dark-skinned people in the North, too, can add cod-liver oil and orange juice to their diet, and, if they need to, take a vitamin pill or two. The shape of the head, too, is a racial trait; but whether it is round or long, it can house a good brain.

The races of mankind are what the Bible says they are—brothers. In their bodies is the record of their brotherhood.

What Are Race Differences?

The greatest adventure story in the history of the world is the spread of early man to all corners of the globe. With crude tools, without agriculture, without domesticated animals except the dog, he pressed on, from somewhere in Asia to the tip of Africa, to the British Isles, across Bering Strait into America and down to Cape Horn. He occupied the islands of the Pacific and the continent of Australia. The world had a small population then, and many of these pioneers were for centuries as separated from other peoples as if they lived on another planet. Slowly they developed physical differences.

Those who settled nearer the equator, whether in Europe, Asia, or in the Americas, developed a darker skin color than those who settled to the north of them. People's hair is often the same over great areas: frizzly hair, lank hair, wavy hair. Europeans remained quite hairy, but in some parts of the world body hair almost disappeared. Blue eyes appeared in the north. In some places in Asia a fold of skin developed over the inner corner of the eye and produced what we call a slant eye.

All these distinctive traits made it easy to recognize people as belonging to different parts of the world. In each place the people got used to looking at one another. They said, "Our men are really men. Our women are beautiful. This is the way people should look." Sometimes they liked the appearance of their close neighbors. But strangers seemed odd and queer. Strangers wore funny clothes and their manners were bad. Even more important, strangers did not look the way people should. Their noses were too flat or too pointed. Their skin was "a sickly white" or "a dirty black." They were too fat or too short. Everywhere in the world men and women used the standard of their own people to judge others and thought that people who differed from this standard looked funny or ugly.

After the discovery of America by Columbus, Europeans began traveling to every quarter of the globe, and all the new peoples they met were complete strangers to them. For one thing, the Europeans couldn't understand their languages. They looked and acted strange. Europeans thought they were different creatures and named a lot of different "races." Gradually the Europeans described each one as having a skin color, kind of hair, kind of lips, height, and head shape that was peculiar to that "race." Nowadays we know that this was a false impression.

Take height, for example. There are tall and short people almost everywhere in the world. Near the sources of the Nile the Shilluk Negroes are six feet two inches; their neighbors, the brown pygmies, are four feet eight inches. In Italy a six-footer and a five-footer could both be native Italians for generations back. Among the Arizona Indians the Hopi Pueblos are five feet four inches; their Mohave neighbors are nearly six feet.

A report of the Selective Service System of November 10, 1941, showed that registrants examined for the United States Army varied in height from four feet six inches to seven feet four inches. This represents the extremes of height anywhere in the world. The Army's limits for acceptance, from five feet to six feet six inches, would include most men the world over.

Take the shape of the head as another example. In West Africa there are more long heads; in the Congo, more round. Among the American Indians, as well as in the population of Europe, both the longest and the roundest heads are to be found, and in Asia Minor long heads and round heads appear among very close relatives.

Or let us take the brain itself. Because the brain is the thinking organ, some scientists have tried to find differences in the size and structure of the brain among different groups of people. In spite of these efforts, using the finest microscopes, the best scientists cannot tell from examining a brain to what group of people its owner belonged. The *average* size of the brain is different in different groups, but it has been proved over and over again that the size of the brain has nothing to do with intelligence. Some of the most brilliant men in the world have had very small brains. On the other hand, the world's largest brain belongs to an imbecile.

For ages men have spoken of "blood relations" as if different peoples had different blood. Some people have shouted that if we got into our veins the blood of someone with a different head shape, eye color, hair texture, or skin color, we should get some of that person's physical and mental characteristics.

Modern science has revealed this to be pure superstition. All human blood is the same, whether it is the blood of an Eskimo or a Frenchman, of the "purest" German "Aryan" or an African pygmy—except for one medically important difference. This medical difference was discovered when doctors first began to use blood transfusion in order to save life. In early attempts at transfusion it was discovered that "agglutination," or clumping together, of the red cells sometimes occurred and caused death. Gradually investigators learned that there are four types of blood, called O, A, B, and AB, and that although blood typed O can be mixed successfully with the other three, none of these can be mixed with one another without clumping.

These four types of blood are inherited by each child from its forebears. But whites, Negroes, Mongols, and all races of man have all these blood types. The color of their skin does not tell at all which blood type they have. You and an Australian bushman may have the same blood type. Because you inherit your bodily traits from your many different ancestors, you may have a different blood type from your mother or your father or your brothers and sisters. You may have eyes like your mother's, teeth and hair like your father's, feet like your grandfather's, and a blood type like your great-grandmother's.

Today doctors do not "type" blood for transfusion at all. The red and white cells or corpuscles are removed, and the remainder is the same whatever race it comes from. The Blood Bank calls it plasma. It is dried and kept indefinitely. When needed for emergency transfusions, it is mixed with water and can save the life of any man or woman in the world. The same blood plasma is used to restore any man of any color who has been wounded in battle.

Finally, let us take skin color, the most noticeable of the differences between peoples. Few traits have been used as widely to classify people. We all talk about black, white, and yellow races of man.

In the world today the darkest people are in West Africa, the lightest people in northwest Europe, while in southeast Asia are men with yellowish-tan skins. Most people in the world, however, are not of these extremes but are in-betweens. These in-betweens probably have the skin shades that were once most common, the white, yellow, and dark brown or black being extreme varieties.

Recently scientists found that skin color is determined by two special chemicals. One of these, *carotene,* gives a yellow tinge; the other, *melanin,* contributes the brown. These colors, along with the pinkish tinge that comes when the blood vessels show through, give various shades to the human skin. Every person, however light or dark his skin may appear, has some of each of these materials in his skin. The one exception is the albino, who lacks coloring substances—and albinos appear among dark- and light-skinned peoples alike. People of browner complexions simply have more *melanin* in their skin, people of yellowish color more *carotene.* It is not an all-or-nothing difference; it is a difference in proportion. Your skin color is due to the amount of these chemicals present in the skin.

[893]

How Are Races Classified?

The three primary races of the world are the Caucasian Race, the Mongoloid Race, and the Negroid Race.

The Caucasian Race inhabits Europe and a great part of the Near East and India. It is subdivided in broad bands that run east and west: Nordics (fair-skinned, blue-eyed, tall and long-headed) are most common in the north; Alpines (in-between skin color, often stocky, broad-headed) in the middle; Mediterraneans (slenderer, often darker than Alpines, long-headed) in the south. The distribution of racial subtypes is just about the same in Germany and in France; both are mostly Alpine and both have Nordics in their northern districts. Racially, France and Germany are made up of the same stocks in just about equal proportions.

American Indians are Mongoloid, though they differ physically both among themselves and from the Mongols of China.

The natives of Australia are sometimes called a fourth primary race. They are as hairy as Europeans, and yet they live in an area where other peoples have very little body hair.

Aryans, Jews, Italians are *not* races. Aryans are people who speak Indo-European, "Aryan" languages. Hitler uses the term in many ways—sometimes for blond Europeans, including the Scandinavians; sometimes for Germans, whether blond or brunet; sometimes for all who agree with him politically, including the Japanese. As Hitler uses it, the term "Aryan" has no meaning, racial, linguistic, or otherwise.

Jews are people who practice the Jewish religion. They are of all races, even Negro and Mongolian. European Jews are of many different biological types; physically they resemble the populations among whom they live. The so-called "Jewish type" is a Mediterranean type, and no more "Jewish" than the South Italian. Wherever Jews are persecuted or discriminated against, they cling to their old ways and keep apart from the rest of the population and develop so-called "Jewish" traits. But these are not racial or "Jewish"; they disappear under conditions where assimilation is easy.

Italians are a nationality. Italians are of many different racial strains; the "typical" South Italian is a Mediterranean, more like the Spaniard or the Greek or the Levantine Jew than the blond North Italian. The Germans, the Russians, and all other nations of Europe are *nations,* not races. They are bound together, not by their head shape and their coloring, but by their national pride, their love of their farms, their local customs, their language, and the like.

As far back in time as the scientist can go he finds proof that animals and men moved about in the world. There were different kinds of animals, and many of them went great distances. But wherever they went, the different kinds could not breed together. A tiger cannot mate with an elephant. Even a fox and a wolf cannot mate with each other. But whenever groups of people have traveled from one place to another and met other people, some of them have married and had children.

At first men had to travel by foot. It took them a long time, but they got almost all over the world that way. Long ago, when people knew only how to make tools out of stone, the Cro-Magnons lived in Europe. Waves of migration came in from the east and the southeast. These new people settled down, bred with the Cro-Magnons, and their children were the ancestors of modern Europeans. Since then there have been many migrations from Asia and northern Africa.

Later men tamed the horse. They built carts and rode horseback. They built great boats, which were rowed by hundreds of men. They could go faster and travel farther than ever before. The Phoenicians went on trading expeditions through the Mediterranean. The Romans went to Spain and up along the coast to the British Isles. Then the Huns swept in from Asia through central Europe and destroyed the Roman Empire. The Tartars came in from the east. They threatened to conquer all of Europe but were defeated in one of the greatest cavalry engagements of all time. The Mohammedans captured all of North Africa; they took Spain and went on up into France across the Pyrenees. Thousands of Negro slaves have been brought into Europe at various times. Where are they now? Peoples have come and gone in Europe for centuries. Wherever they went, some of them settled down and left children. Small groups were absorbed into the total population. Always the different races moved about and intermarried.

We are used to thinking of Americans as mixed. All of us have ancestors who came from regions far apart. But we think that the English are English and the French are French. This is true for their nationality, just as we are all Americans. But it is not true for their *race*. The Germans have claimed to be a pure German race, but no European is a pure anything. A country has a population. It does not have a race. If you go far enough back in the populations of Europe you are apt to find all kinds of ancestors: Cro-Magnons, Slavs, Mongols, Africans, Celts, Saxons, and Teutons.

It is true, though, that people who live closer together intermarry more frequently. This is why there are places like Alsace-Lorraine, where Germans and French have intermarried so much that the children cannot tell whether they are German or French and so call themselves Alsatians. Czechoslovakia included old Bohemia, which had a population of Nordics and semi-Asiatics and Slavs. After World War I the Germans and the Czechs along the border between the two countries intermarried so often that the Germans of this section got to look like Czechs and the Czechs began to speak German. But this did not make the two countries love each other.

People of every European nation have racial brothers in other countries, often ones with which they are at war. If at any one moment you could sort into one camp all the people in the world who were most Mediterranean, no mystic sense of brotherhood would unite them. Neither camp would have language or nationality or mode of life to unite them. The old fights would break out again unless social conditions were changed—the old hatred between national groups, the old antagonisms between ruler and ruled and between the exploiter and the exploited.

The movements of peoples over the face of the earth inevitably produce race mixture and have produced it since before history began. No one has been able to show that this is necessarily bad. It has sometimes been a social advantage, sometimes a running sore threatening the health of the whole society. It can obviously be made a social evil, and, where it is so, sensible people will avoid contributing to it by grieving if their children make such alliances. We must live in the world as it is. But, as far as we know, there are no immutable laws of nature that make racial intermixture harmful.

When they study racial differences, scientists investigate the way by which particular traits are passed on from parents to children. They measure head form and identify skin color on a color chart. They map out the distribution of different kinds of hair or noses in the world. Scientists recognize that these differences do not themselves show better or worse qualities in peoples, any more than bay horses are better than black ones. They knew that to prove that a bay horse is superior to a black one you have to do more than identify its skin color on a color chart; you have to test its abilities.

Science therefore treats human racial differences as facts to be studied and mapped. It treats racial superiorities as a separate field of investigation; it looks for evidence. When a Nazi says, "I am a blue-eyed Aryan and you are non-Aryan," he means, "I am superior and you are inferior." The scientist says: "Of course. You are a fair-haired, long-headed, tall North European (the anthropological term is Nordics, not Aryans), and I am a dark-haired, round-headed, less tall South European. But on what evidence do you base your claim to be superior? That is quite different."

Race prejudice turns on this point of inferiority and superiority. The man with race prejudice says of a man of another race, "No matter who he is, I don't have to compare myself with him. I'm superior anyway. I was born that way."

It is the study of racial superiorities and inferiorities, therefore, which is most important in race relations. This investigation, to have any meaning at all, must get evidence for and against the man who says, "I was *born* that way. My race is proof that I am the better man." It must be an investigation of what is better and what is worse in traits passed down by inheritance. Such traits are, by definition, racial. The first thing we want to know scientifically is what traits a man is born with and what things happen to him after he is born. If he is lucky after he is born, he will have good food, good care, good education, and a good start in life; these are not things of which he can boast: "I was *born* that way."

A man learns the language he speaks. If he'd been born of Nordic parents and brought up from infancy in China, he'd speak Chinese like a native and have as much difficulty learning Swedish when he was grown as if he'd been born of Chinese parents. He wasn't "born" to speak cockney English or to speak with a Brooklyn accent; he speaks the way people around him speak. It's not a racial trait; he didn't inherit it.

Differences in customs among peoples of the world are not a matter of race either. One race is not "born" to marry in church after a boy-and-girl courtship and another race to marry "blind" with a bride the groom has never seen carried veiled to his father's house. One race is not "born" equipped to build skyscrapers and put plumbing in their houses and another to run up flimsy shelters and carry their water from the river. All these things are "learned behavior," and even in the white race there are many millions who don't have our forms of courtship and marriage and who live in shacks. When a man boasts of his racial superiority and says that he was "born that way," perhaps what he's really saying is that he had a lot of luck after he was born. A man of another race might have been his equal if he'd had the same luck in his life. Science insists that race does not account for all human achievements.

The most careful investigations of intelligence have been made in America among Negroes and whites. The scientist realizes that every time he measures intelligence in any man, black or white, his results show the intelligence that man was born with *plus* what happened to him since he was born. The scientist has a lot of proof of this. For instance, in the First World War intelligence tests were given to the American Expeditionary Forces; they showed that Negroes made a lower score on intelligence tests than whites. But the tests also showed that Northerners, *black and white,* had higher scores than Southerners, *black and white.* Everyone knows that Southerners are inborn equals of Northerners, but in 1917 many Southern states' per capita expenditures for schools were only fractions of those in Northern states, and housing and diet and income were far below average too. Since the vast majority of Negroes lived in the South, their score on the intelligence test was a score they got not only as Negroes, but as Americans who had grown up under poor conditions in the South. Scientists therefore compared the scores of Southern whites and Northern Negroes.

MEDIAN SCORES ON A.E.F. INTELLIGENCE TESTS

Southern Whites:
Mississippi 41.25
Kentucky 41.50
Arkansas 41.55

Northern Negroes:
New York 45.02
Illinois 47.35
Ohio 49.50

Negroes with better luck after they were born got higher scores than whites with less luck. The white race did badly where economic conditions were bad and schooling was not provided, and Negroes living under better conditions surpassed them. The differences did not arise because people were from the North or the South, or because they were white or black, but because of differences in income, education, cultural advantages, and other opportunities.

Scientists then studied gifted children. They found that children with top scores turn up among Negroes, Mexicans, and Orientals. Then they went to European countries to study the intelligence of children in homelands from which our immigrants come. Children from some of these countries got poor scores in America, but in their homeland children got good scores. Evidently the poor scores here were due to being uprooted, speaking a foreign language, and living in tenements; the children were not unintelligent *by heredity.*

The second superiority which a man claims when he says, "I was born a member of a superior race," is that his race has better *character.* The Nazis boast of their racial soul. But when they wanted to make a whole new generation into Nazis they didn't trust to "racial soul"; they made certain kinds of teaching compulsory in the schools, they broke up homes where the parents were anti-Nazi, they required boys to join certain Nazi youth organizations. By these means they got the kind of national character they wanted. But it was a planned and deliberately trained character, not an inborn "racial soul." In just the same way the Japanese have bred a generation of ruthless fighters. Fifty years ago Europeans who lived in Japan used to describe them as "butterflies flitting from flower to flower," incapable of "the stern drives" of Western civilization. Since 1900 the "butterflies" have fought six times overseas, and they are desperate and ruthless fighters. In a generation the butterflies have become gamecocks. But their *race* has not changed. The same blood still flows in their veins. But spiritually they are more like the Germans than they are like their racial brothers, the peace-loving Chinese.

It can go the other way too. In 1520 the ancient Mexicans were like the Germans. They talked like Nazis, thought like them, in many ways felt like them. They, too, believed war to be man's highest mission. They, too, trained their children for it, placing their boys in great state schools where they learned little else but the glories of battle and the rituals of their caste. They, too, believed themselves invincible, and against small, defenseless villages they were. But they were defeated in battle by the Spaniards with the help of the peoples whom the Aztecs had oppressed; their leaders were killed, their temples destroyed, their wealth pillaged, and their power broken. The Mexican peasant, who still speaks the Aztec language and in whose veins still runs the blood of Aztec conquerors, no longer dreams of glorious death in battle and eternal life in an Indian Valhalla. He no longer goes on the warpath, no longer provokes war with peaceful villages. He is a humble peon, wishing only to be left in peace to cultivate his little field, go to church, dance, sing, and make love. These simple things endure.

Americans deny that the Nazis have produced a national character superior to that of Goethe's and Schiller's day, and that the ruthless Japanese of today are finer human beings than in those generations when they preferred to write poetry and paint pictures. Race prejudice is, after all, a determination to keep a people down, and it misuses the label "inferior" to justify unfairness and injustice. Race prejudice makes people ruthless; it invites violence. It is the opposite of "good character" as it is defined in the Christian religion—or in the Confucian religion, or in the Buddhist religion, or the Hindu religion, for that matter.

History proves that progress in civilization is not the monopoly of one race or subrace. When our white forebears in Europe were rude stone-age primitives, the civilizations of the Babylonians and the Egyptians had already flourished and been eclipsed. There were great Negro states in Africa when Europe was a sparsely settled forest. Negroes made iron tools and wove fine cloth for their clothing when fair-skinned Europeans wore skins and knew nothing of iron.

When Europe was just emerging from the Middle Ages, Marco Polo visited China and found there a great civilization, the like of which he had never imagined. Europe was a frontier country in those days compared with China.

Since the beginning of history an unusual collection of fortunate circumstances have been present among one race, sometimes among another. Up to now every great center of civilization has had its day and has given place to others. The proud rulers of yesterday become the simple peasants of another era. The crude people who once threatened the great cities become later the kings and emperors in the same country. The peoples change, but the old arts of life are, for the most part, not permanently lost. They pass into the common heritage of mankind.

Inventions pass, too, from one continent to another when people trade with each other. This has happened since the dawn of history. About five thousand years ago, when Europe was on the frontiers of the civilized world, Asiatics came to trade in Europe and North Africa in great caravans. They followed the main rivers—the Nile into North Africa, the Danube into Europe, and the Tigris and Euphrates rivers out of Asia. People from all over came in contact with one another and compared notes on what they knew. In this way they pooled their knowledge, and out of this combined knowledge came the great inventions of civilization—massive building and the arts of metallurgy, chemistry, writing, medicine, and mathematics; transportation on wheels. The idea of printing and the use of movable type is an old Chinese invention, and our power engines depend upon a knowledge of explosives that the Chinese worked out with firecrackers.

When Columbus discovered America, corn, "Irish" potatoes, tobacco, and "Boston" beans were unknown in Europe. They had been developed by American Indians. Within ten years corn was being planted in Central Asia and in the interior of Africa, and African tribes today think that corn was given them by their own gods "in the beginning."

All races have made their contributions to human knowledge. Those who have lived at the crossroads of the world have invented most; those who have lived isolated on islands or at the tip ends of continents have been content to earn their livelihoods by old traditional methods. There was, for them, no "necessity" to be "the mother of invention" after they had devised a way to live on the land.

Peoples who came into contact with strangers, however, gave what arts of life they had and took what the strangers had. These contributions to civilization accumulated over the centuries, and on this accumulation new discoveries are based. We are all the gainers.

The United States is the greatest crossroads of the world in all history. People have come here from every race and nation, and almost every race in the world is represented among our citizens. They have brought with them their own ways of cooking food, so that our "American" diet is indebted to a dozen peoples. Our turkey, corn, and cranberries come from the Indians. Our salads we borrowed from the French and Italians. Increasingly in recent years we have enriched our tables with soups from Russia, vegetables from Italy, appetizers from the Scandinavian countries, sea foods from the Mediterranean lands, chili and tortillas from Mexico, and so on almost endlessly. At the same time, everywhere we have gone in the world, we have popularized ice cream, beefsteak, breakfast cereals, corn on the cob, and other foods that are called "American."

Industry in the United States has taken the hand skills of our immigrants and made machines to do the work; without their skills we should not have known how. Our music, our buildings have developed from patterns brought to our shores or learned from every quarter of the world. Our country would be poorer in every phase of its culture if different cultures had not come together here, sharing and learning the special contributions each had to offer.

The Future of Race Prejudice

Nevertheless there is race prejudice in America and in the world. Race prejudice isn't an old universal "instinct." It is hardly a hundred years old. Before that, people persecuted Jews because of their religion—not their "blood"; they enslaved Negroes because they were pagans—not for being black.

Looking back now, moderns are horrified at all the blood that was shed for centuries in religious conflicts. It is not our custom any more to torture and kill a man because he has a different religion. The twenty-first century may well look back on our generation and be just as horrified. If that century builds its way of life on the Atlantic Charter—for the whole world—our era will seem a nightmare from which they have awakened. They will think we were crazy. "Why should race prejudice have swept the Western world," they will say, "where no nation was anything but a mixture of all kinds of racial groups? Why did nations just at that moment begin talking about 'the racial purity' of their blood? Why did they talk of their wars as racial wars? Why did they make people suffer, not because they were criminals or double-crossers, but because they were Jews or Negroes or non-Nordic?"

We who are living in these troubled times can tell them why. Today weak nations are afraid of the strong nations; the poor are afraid of the rich; the rich are afraid they will lose their riches. People are afraid of one another's political or economic power, they are afraid of revenge for past injuries, they are afraid of social rejection. Conflict grows fat on fear. And the slogans against "inferior races" lead us to pick on them as scapegoats. We pin on them the reason for all our fears.

Freedom from fear is the way to cure race prejudice. When aggressions like those of the Axis are made impossible by guarantees of collective security, those guarantees must cover countries of all races. Then Nazi race tactics will be outmoded. In any country every legal decision that upholds equal citizenship rights without regard to race or color, every labor decision that lessens the terror of being "laid off" and gives a man self-respect in his employment, every arrangement that secures the little farmer against losing his acres to the bank—all these and many more can free people from fear. They need not look for scapegoats.

The Russian nation has for a generation shown what can be done to outlaw race prejudice in a country with many kinds of people. They did not wait for people's minds to change. They made racial discrimination and persecution illegal. They welcomed and honored the different dress, different customs, different arts of the many tribes and countries that live as part of their nation. The more backward groups were given special aid to help them catch up with the more advanced. Each people was helped to develop its own cultural forms, its own written language, theater, music, dance, and so on. At the same time that each people was encouraged in its national self-development, the greatest possible interchange of customs was fostered, so that each group became more distinctively itself and at the same time more a part of the whole.

The Russians have welcomed cultural *differences* and they have refused to treat them as *inferiorities*. No part of the Russian program has had greater success than their racial program.

In the United States a considerable number of organizations are working for democratic race equality. To mention only a few: The East-West Association has done some splendid work in emphasizing the importance of racial understanding, especially between Asiatic and Western peoples. The China Institute is active in promoting the work of Chinese students in America, and the Phelps-Stokes Foundation has brought many African students here, cementing the relation between the two continents.

The Council Against Intolerance in America has a continuous program in the schools. The Council on Intercultural Relations has done much to emphasize the Negro's contribution to American culture. The Bureau for Intercultural Education interprets the contributions made to America by many different races and nationalities. The Rosenwald Foundation has sponsored Southern Negro schools, elementary, high school, and college, in order to make up for the deficiencies of Southern Negro education. They have also pressed for Negro housing and health projects in the North. The National Association for the Advancement of Colored People arranges publicity and fosters public education through periodicals, the radio, and special publications. It fights cases of discrimination in the courts and tries to get effective laws passed for the protection of Negro rights. The National Urban League helps Negroes who move from rural districts to the cities to find industrial work and proper living conditions.

Many church bodies have done much to help people realize that ideas of race superiority or inferiority are un-Christian. The Department of Race Relations of the Federal Council of the Churches of Christ in America and the National Conference of Christians and Jews have encouraged collaboration among church leaders interested in interracial co-operation. During World War II the Executive Committee of the Council called on all local churches to eliminate racial discrimination in their own practices. Church bodies of all faiths have encouraged education for tolerance.

For some twenty years white and Negro leaders of the South have co-operated actively through the Commission on Interracial Co-operation in establishing local committees of both whites and Negroes. This commission has promoted mutual respect and understanding. In many local areas small groups have worked patiently to increase interracial co-operation.

Among the unions we find that the National Maritime Union has fought and won the right of Negroes to serve as skilled workers instead of in menial jobs only. Today mixed crews on freighters, tankers, and merchant ships are doing a magnificent job without friction. The *Booker T. Washington,* with its Negro captain, Hugh Mulzac, is a notable example. The United Auto Workers has an interracial committee with Walter Hardin, a veteran Negro official, as its chairman. At first white workers resisted the right of Negroes to do more skilled kinds of work. For example, when Negroes were first placed on machines previously manned by white operators, a work stoppage shut down a whole section of the Packard plant. R. J. Thomas, the president of the union, ordered the white strikers to return to work or suffer loss of union membership and employment. Within a few hours the strikers were back, with the recently promoted Negroes still at their machines.

Besides the National Maritime Union and the Auto Workers, a number of other unions have taken the lead in promoting interracial understanding. They include the International Ladies Garment Workers, the Amalgamated Clothing Workers, the United Electrical Radio and Machine Workers, the Marine Shipbuilding Workers, and the United Rubber Workers. In the Birmingham, Alabama, area there are more than a hundred union locals with both white and Negro members, and the Southern Tenant Farmers Union has a mixed membership.

From the time of Lincoln's Emancipation Proclamation to the present day, the national and state governments have passed laws to carry forward the principles of our Declaration of Independence and our Constitution. In June 1941, President Roosevelt took direct action in his Executive Order No. 8802 toward eliminating discrimination in employment in plants with war contracts. The Fair Employment Practice Committee was set up and held public hearings in Los Angeles, Chicago, New York, and Birmingham. When an individual applied for a job in a plant doing war work and was refused for reasons of prejudice—because he was a Negro, a Jew, or a naturalized citizen—he could bring his case before the committee, who then called the company to a public hearing. This committee is now part of the War Manpower Commission.

The Negro Manpower Commission of this same body is headed by an able Negro economist and maintains a staff of Negro field representatives attached to the United States Employment Service. They also work through the regional offices of the Social Security Board to detect cases of racial discrimination.

The Bureau of Indian Affairs, under Commissioner Collier, should be mentioned here as a government bureau with a long record of successful effort for the adjustment of a racial minority.

But at best the government can act only as a policeman, finding a wrongdoer here and there. Only the people themselves can really end racial discrimination, through understanding, sympathy, and public action. But there is evidence that the American people as individuals are beginning to think and to act. One hundred thousand Americans have petitioned the War Department to have at least one division in the Army containing both Negroes and whites. A separate petition was signed by American white men of draft age who asked to be assigned to such a division—many of these were Southerners.

In Houston, Texas, the mayor and a group of prominent citizens advertised in the local papers that no disturbance would be tolerated that would blacken the reputation of Houston when the Negroes of that city celebrated Juneteenth Day in honor of the emancipation of the slaves. It began with the statement, "Don't do Hitler's work," and warned citizens not to repeat rumors. The celebration was peacefully carried out. It is unfortunate that in Beaumont, Texas, similar effective action was not undertaken and a serious riot occurred.

In the most disastrous of recent riots in Detroit, a number of obscure bystanders performed heroic actions.

A white passenger on a streetcar spoke to the mob and dissuaded them from searching the car.

Two women, a mother and daughter, realizing that the Negro passenger was in danger, sheltered him so that when the rioters looked into the car he was effectively hidden.

In a bus going South recently the white

passengers all remained standing rather than occupy the "white" seats of a Jim Crow bus.

During the recent disturbances in New York's Harlem, a group of Negroes stood in front of the restaurant of a white proprietor who had been their friend and in this way protected it from being broken into and destroyed by the mob.

In the last analysis these homely incidents tell the real story. They tell us that the conscience of America is aroused, that there is work to be done, and that some of us are already trying to do it.

With America's great tradition of democracy, the United States should clean its own house and get ready for a better twenty-first century. Then it could stand unashamed before the Nazis and condemn, without confusion, their doctrines of a Master Race. Then it could put its hand to the building of the United Nations, sure of support from all the yellow and the black races where the war is being fought, sure that victory in this war will be in the name, not of one race or of another, but of the universal Human Race.

from THE FAITH OF AN AMERICAN
by WALTER MILLIS

THE AMERICAN way of life has many faults and blemishes; it also has many things about it that one may hold up as worth fighting for and risking death for—its freedoms, its decencies, its strivings toward a better existence for greater numbers of its people, its effort to utilize as the springs of its social and political system the highest rather than the basest, the most advanced rather than the most primitive, instinctual drives in humanity. But great as these things are, and imminent though the present threat to them may be, I still do not think we can offer them as the sole, or even the primary, reason for again taking up the sword or again being prepared to do so. If our attitude is purely defensive, if we are merely sitting hoarding our liberties against threatened attack, those liberties are only too likely to atrophy anyway. If we try to make a bargain out of it, if we say to our countrymen, "you must be ready to fight in order to preserve your freedom, in order to enjoy this or that benefit of a democratic as opposed to a totalitarian system, in order to safeguard the nation against invasion," we may always find that the reasons do not particularly appeal. Men's values inevitably differ, and in the last analysis are always irrational, beyond assessment by any form of cost accounting in which such-and-such an amount of pain or death can be equated to such-and-such a quantity of human or social advance. It is not, really, that kind of calculation at all. But suppose we say: "You must be ready to fight; if you are that; if the society of which you are a part has that much cohesion, conviction and energy as a social whole, then perhaps you will have a chance to make good your freedoms, to avoid the crimes of totalitarian retrogression, really to preserve your nation and whatever of its values seem best to you from foreign invasion—and to do all these things probably with far less cost in life

From *Zero Hour: A Summons to the Free*, by Stephen Vincent Benét, Erika Mann, McGeorge Bundy, William L. White, Garrett Underhill and Walter Millis, copyright, 1940, by Rinehart & Company, Inc., and reprinted by their permission.

and suffering than if you confess your social organization to be a weak and spineless thing, a mere collection of individual selfishnesses." Suppose we say that. I think we are much closer to the facts both of war and of social organization as a whole; I think we are much nearer to putting our hands upon the primary levers that operate the world we live in. We are then moving with, and not in puny revolt against, the main stream of human existence. We are not then merely kicking against the machinery which drives it; we are not, with the totalitarians, developing all the crudest, most primitive and most wasteful elements of that machinery in order easily to establish a barren power; but we are utilizing the basic mechanisms to produce, in time, better machinery, better results, a better ultimate life.

from FAREWELL ADDRESS TO THE PEOPLE OF THE UNITED STATES, SEPTEMBER 17th, 1796

by George Washington

Towards the preservation of your Government and the permanency of your present happy state, it is requisite, not only that you steadily discountenance irregular oppositions to its acknowledged authority, but also that you resist with care the spirit of innovation upon its principles, however specious the pretexts.—One method of assault may be to effect, in the forms of the Constitution, alterations which will impair the energy of the system, and thus to undermine what cannot be directly overthrown.—In all the changes to which you may be invited, remember that time and habit are at least as necessary to fix the true character of Governments, as of other human institutions—that experience is the surest standard, by which to test the real tendency of the existing Constitution of a Country—that facility in changes upon the credit of mere hypothesis and opinion exposes to perpetual change, from the endless variety of hypothesis and opinion:—and remember, especially, that, for the efficient management of your common interests, in a country so extensive as ours, a Government of as much vigor as is consistent with the perfect security of Liberty is indispensable.—Liberty itself will find in such a Government, with powers properly distributed and adjusted, its surest Guardian.

THE UNIVERSE AND DR. EINSTEIN
by Lincoln Barnett
Part I

Carved in the white walls of the Riverside Church in New York, the figures of six hundred great men of the ages—saints, philosophers, kings—stand in limestone immortality, surveying space and time with blank imperishable eyes. One panel enshrines the geniuses of science, fourteen of them, spanning the centuries from Hippocrates, who died around 370 B.C., to Albert Einstein, who was sixty-nine years old this March. It is noteworthy that Einstein is the only living man in this whole sculptured gallery of the illustrious dead.

It is equally noteworthy that of the thousands of people who worship weekly at Manhattan's most spectacular Protestant church, probably ninety-nine per cent would be hard pressed to explain why Einstein's image is there. It is there because a generation ago, when the iconography of the church was being planned, Dr. Harry Emerson Fosdick wrote letters to a group of the nation's leading scientists asking them to submit lists of the fourteen greatest names in scientific history. Their ballots varied. Most of them included Archimedes, Euclid, Galileo, and Newton. But on every list appeared the name of Albert Einstein.

The vast gap that has persisted for more than forty years—since 1905, when the Theory of Special Relativity was first published—between Einstein's scientific eminence and public understanding of it is the measure of a gap in American education. Today most newspaper readers know vaguely that Einstein had something to do with the atomic bomb; beyond that his name is simply a synonym for the abstruse. While his theories form part of the body of modern science, they are not yet part of the modern curriculum. It is not surprising therefore that many a college graduate still thinks of Einstein as a kind of mathematical surrealist rather than as the discoverer of certain cosmic laws of immense importance in man's slow struggle to understand physical reality. He does not know that Relativity, over and above its scientific import, comprises a major philosophical system which augments and illumines the reflections of the great theorists of knowledge—Locke, Berkeley, and Hume. Consequently he has very little notion of the vast, arcane, and mysteriously ordered universe in which he dwells.

Dr. Einstein, now professor emeritus at the Institute for Advanced Study at Princeton, is currently hard at work on a problem that has stumped him for more than a quarter-century and which he intends to solve before he dies. His ambition is to complete his "unified field theory," setting forth in one series of equations the laws governing the two fundamental forces of the universe, gravitation and electromagnetism. The significance of this task can be appreciated only when one realizes that virtually all the phenomena of nature are produced by these two primordial forces. Until a hundred years ago electricity and magnetism—while known and studied since early Greek times—were regarded as separate quantities. But the experiments of Oersted and Faraday in the nineteenth century showed that a current

---

Copyright, 1948, by Harper & Brothers and Lincoln Barnett. Reprinted by permission of William Sloane Associates.

of electricity is always surrounded by a magnetic field, and conversely that under certain conditions magnetic forces can induce electrical currents. From these experiments came the discovery of the electromagnetic field which pervades all space and through which light waves, radio waves, and all other electromagnetic disturbances are propagated. Thus electricity and magnetism may be considered as a single force. Save for gravitation, nearly all other forces in the material universe—frictional forces, chemical forces which hold atoms together in molecules, cohesive forces which bind larger particles of matter, elastic forces which cause bodies to maintain their shape—are of electromagnetic origin; for all of these involve the interplay of matter, and all matter is composed of atoms which in turn are composed of electrical particles. Yet the similarities between gravitational and electromagnetic phenomena are very striking. The planets spin in the gravitational field of the sun; electrons swirl in the electromagnetic field of the atomic nucleus. The earth, moreover, is a big magnet—a peculiar fact which is apparent to anyone who has ever used a compass. The sun is also a magnet. And so are all the stars.

Although many attempts have been made to identify gravitational attraction as an electromagnetic effect, all have failed. Einstein himself thought he had succeeded in 1929 and published a unified field theory which he later scrapped as inadequate. His present objectives are more ambitious, for he is endeavoring now to formulate a set of universal laws that will encompass both the boundless gravitational and electromagnetic fields of interstellar space and the tiny, terrible field inside the atom. In this vast cosmic picture the abyss between macrocosmos and microcosmos—the very big and the very little—will be bridged, and the whole complex of the universe will resolve into a homogeneous fabric in which matter and energy are indistinguishable and all forms of motion from the slow wheeling of the galaxies to the wild flight of electrons become simply changes in the structure and concentration of the primordial field.

Since the aim of science is to describe and explain the world we live in, Einstein would, by thus defining the manifold of nature within the terms of a single harmonious theory, attain its loftiest goal. The meaning of the word "explain," however, suffers a contraction with man's every step in quest of reality. Science cannot yet really "explain" electricity, magnetism, and gravitation; their effects can be measured and predicted, but of their ultimate nature no more is known to the modern scientist than to Thales of Miletus, who first speculated on the electrification of amber around 585 B.C. Most contemporary physicists reject the notion that man can ever discover what these mysterious forces "really" are. Electricity, Bertrand Russell says, "is not a thing, like St. Paul's Cathedral; it is a way in which things behave. When we have told how things behave when they are electrified, and under what circumstances they are electrified, we have told all there is to tell." Until recently scientists would have scorned such a thesis. Aristotle, whose natural science dominated Western thought for two thousand years, believed that man could arrive at an understanding of ultimate reality by reasoning from *self-evident principles*. It is, for example, a self-evident principle that everything in the universe has its proper place, hence one can deduce that objects fall to the ground because that's where they belong, and smoke goes up because that's where *it* belongs. The goal of Aristotelian science was to explain *why* things happen. Modern science was born when Galileo began trying to explain *how* things happen and thus originated the method of controlled experiment which now forms the basis of scientific investigation.

Out of Galileo's discoveries and those of Newton in the next generation there evolved a mechanical universe of forces, pressures, tensions, oscillations, and waves. There seemed to be no process of nature which could not be described in terms of ordinary experience, illustrated by a concrete model or predicted by Newton's amazingly accurate laws of mechanics. But before the turn of the past century certain deviations from these laws became apparent; and though these deviations were slight, they were of such a fundamental nature that the whole edifice of Newton's machine-like universe began to topple. The certainty that science can explain "how" things happen began to dim about twenty years ago. And right now it is a question whether scientific man is in touch with reality at all—or can ever hope to be.

II

The factors which first led physicists to distrust their faith in a smoothly functioning mechanical universe loomed on the inner and outer horizons of knowledge—in the unseen realm of the atom and in the fathomless depths of intergalactic space. To describe these phenomena quantitatively, two great theoretical systems were developed between 1900 and 1927. One was the Quantum Theory, dealing with the fundamental units of matter and energy. The other was Relativity, dealing with space, time, and the structure of the universe as a whole.

Both are now accepted pillars of modern physical thought. Both explain phenomena in their fields in terms of consistent, mathematical relationships. They do not answer the Newtonian "how" any more than Newton's laws answered the Aristotelian "why." They provide equations, for example, that define with great accuracy the laws governing the radiation and propagation of light. But the actual mechanism by which the atom radiates light and by which light is propagated through space remains one of nature's supreme mysteries. Similarly the laws governing the phenomenon of radioactivity enable scientists to predict that in a given quantity of uranium a certain number of atoms will disintegrate in a certain length of time. But just which atoms will decay and how they are selected for doom are questions that man cannot yet answer.

In accepting a mathematical description of nature, physicists have been forced to abandon the ordinary world of our experience, the world of sense perceptions. To understand the significance of this retreat it is necessary to step across the thin line that divides physics from metaphysics. Questions involving the relationship between observer and reality, subject and object, have haunted philosophical thinkers since the dawn of reason. Twenty-three centuries ago the Greek philosopher Democritus wrote: "Sweet and bitter, cold and warm as well as all the colors, all these things exist but in opinion and not in reality; what really exists are unchangeable particles, atoms, and their motions in empty space." Galileo also was aware of the purely subjective character of sense qualities like color, taste, smell, and sound and pointed out that "they can no more be ascribed to the external objects than can the tickling or the pain caused sometimes by touching such objects."

The English philosopher John Locke tried to penetrate to the "real essence of substances" by drawing a distinction between what he termed the primary and secondary qualities of matter. Thus he considered that shape, motion, solidity, and all geometrical properties were real or primary qualities, inherent in the object itself; while secondary qualities, like colors, sounds, tastes, were simply projections upon the organs of sense. The artificiality of this distinction was obvious to later thinkers.

"I am able to prove," wrote the great German mathematician, Leibnitz, "that not only light, color, heat, and the like, but motion, shape, and extension too are mere apparent qualities." Just as our visual sense, for example, tells us that a golf ball is white, so vision abetted by our sense of touch tells us that it is also round, smooth, and small—qualities that have no more reality, independent of our senses, than the quality which we define by convention as white.

Thus gradually philosophers and scientists arrived at the startling conclusion that the whole objective universe of matter and energy, atoms and stars, does not exist except as a construction of the consciousness, an edifice of conventional symbols shaped by the senses of man. As Berkeley, the archenemy of materialism, phrased it: "All the choir of heaven and furniture of earth, in a word all those bodies which compose the mighty frame of the world, have not any substance without the mind. . . . So long as they are not actually perceived by me, or do not exist in my mind, or that of any other created spirit, they must either have no existence at all, or else subsist in the mind of some Eternal Spirit." Einstein carried this train of logic to its ultimate limits by showing that even space and time are forms of intuition, which can no more be divorced from consciousness than can our concepts of color, shape, or size. Space has no objective reality except as an order or arrangement of the objects we perceive in it, and time has no independent existence apart from the order of events by which we measure it.

These philosophical subtleties have a profound bearing on modern science. For with the philosophers' reduction of all objective reality to a shadow-world of perceptions, scientists became aware of the alarming limitations of man's senses. Anyone who has ever thrust a glass prism into a sunbeam and seen the rainbow colors of the solar spectrum refracted on a screen has looked upon the whole range of visible light. For the human eye is sensitive only to the narrow band of radiation that falls between the red and the violet. A difference of a few one hundred thousandths of a centimeter in wavelength makes the difference between visibility and invisibility. The wavelength of red light is .00007 cm. and that of violet light .00004 cm.

But the sun also emits other kinds of radiation. Infrared rays, for example, with a wavelength of .00008 to .032 cm. are just a little too long to excite the retina to an impression of light, though the skin detects their impact as heat. Similarly ultraviolet rays with a wavelength of .00003 to .000001 cm. are too short for the eye to perceive but can be recorded on a photographic plate. Photographs can also be made by the "light" of X-rays which are even shorter than ultraviolet rays. And there are other electromagnetic waves of lesser and greater frequency—the gamma rays of radium, radio waves, cosmic rays—which can be detected in various ways and differ from light only in wavelength. It is evident, therefore, that the human eye suppresses most of the "lights" in the world, and that what man can perceive of the reality around him is distorted and enfeebled by the limitations of his organ of vision. The world would appear far dif-

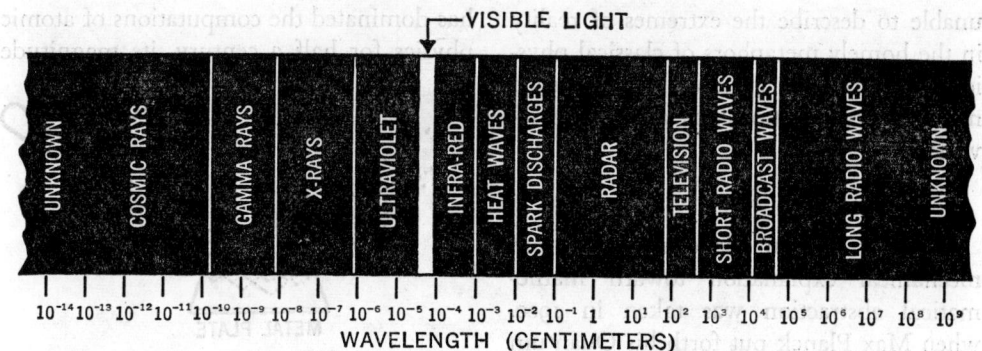

The electromagnetic spectrum reveals the narrow range of radiation visible to man's eye. From the standpoint of physics, the only difference between radio waves, visible light, and such high-frequency forms of radiation as X-rays and gamma rays lies in their wavelength. But out of this vast range of electromagnetic radiation, extending from cosmic rays with wavelengths of only one trillionth of a centimeter up to infinitely long radio waves, the human eye selects only the narrow band indicated in white on the above chart. Man's perceptions of the universe in which he dwells are thus restricted by the limitations of his visual sense. Wavelengths are indicated on the chart by the denary system; i.e. 10^3 centimeters equals $10 \times 10 \times 10$ equals 1,000; and 10^{-3} equals $1/10 \times 1/10 \times 1/10$ equals $1/1,000$.

ferent to him if his eye were sensitive, for example, to X-rays.

Realization that our whole knowledge of the universe is simply a residue of impressions clouded by our imperfect senses makes the quest for reality seem hopeless. If nothing has existence save in its being perceived, the world should dissolve into an anarchy of individual perceptions. But a curious order runs through our perceptions, as if indeed there might be an underlayer of objective reality which our senses translate. Although no man can ever know whether his sensation of red or of Middle C is the same as another man's, it is nevertheless possible to act on the assumption that everyone sees colors and hears tones more or less alike.

This functional harmony of nature Berkeley, Descartes, and Spinoza attributed to God. Modern physicists who prefer to solve their problems without recourse to God (although this seems to become more difficult all the time) emphasize that nature mysteriously operates on mathematical principles. It is the mathematical orthodoxy of the universe that enables theorists like Einstein to predict and discover natural laws simply by the solution of equations. But the paradox of physics today is that with every improvement in its mathematical apparatus the gulf between man the observer and the objective world of scientific description becomes more profound.

It is perhaps significant that in terms of simple magnitude man is the mean between macrocosm and microcosm. Stated crudely this means that a supergiant red star (the largest material body in the universe) is just as much bigger than man as an electron (tiniest of physical entities) is smaller. It is not surprising, therefore, that the prime mysteries of nature dwell in those realms farthest removed from sense-imprisoned man, nor that science, unable to describe the extremes of reality in the homely metaphors of classical physics should content itself with noting such mathematical relationships as may be revealed.

III

The first step in science's retreat from mechanical explanation toward mathematical abstraction was taken in 1900, when Max Planck put forth his Quantum Theory to meet certain problems that had arisen in studies of radiation. It is common knowledge that when heated bodies become incandescent they emit a red glow that turns to orange, then yellow, then white as the temperature increases. Painstaking efforts were made during the past century to formulate a law stating how the amount of radiant energy given off by such heated bodies varied with wavelength and temperature. All attempts failed until Planck found by mathematical means an equation that satisfied the results of experiment. The extraordinary feature of his equation was that it rested on the assumption that radiant energy is emitted, not in an unbroken stream but in discontinuous bits or portions which he termed *quanta*.

Planck had no evidence for such an assumption, for no one knew anything (then or now) of the actual mechanism of radiation. But on purely theoretical grounds he concluded that each quantum carries an amount of energy given by the equation, $E = h\nu$, where ν is the frequency of the radiation and h is Planck's Constant, a small but inexorable number (roughly .00000000000000000000000006624) which has since proved to be one of the most fundamental constants in nature. In any process of radiation the amount of emitted energy divided by the frequency is always equal to h. Although Planck's Constant has dominated the computations of atomic physics for half a century, its magnitude

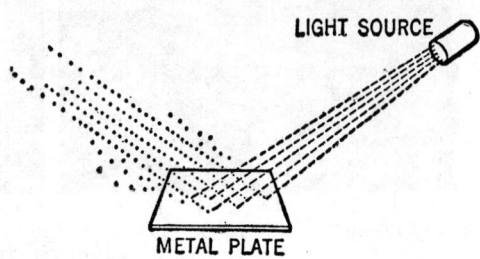

The photoelectric effect was interpreted by Einstein in 1905. When light falls on a metal plate, the plate ejects a shower of electrons. This phenomenon cannot be explained by the classic wave theory of light. Einstein deduced that light is not a continuous stream of energy but is composed of individual particles or bundles of energy which he called *photons*. When a photon strikes an electron the resulting action is analagous to the impact of billiard balls, as shown in the simplified conception above.

cannot be explained any more than the magnitude of the speed of light can be explained. Like other universal constants it is simply a mathematical fact for which no explanation can be given. Sir Arthur Eddington once observed that any true law of nature is likely to seem irrational to rational man; hence Planck's quantum principle, he thought, is one of the few real natural laws science has revealed.

The far-reaching implications of Planck's conjecture did not become apparent till 1905, when Einstein, who almost alone among contemporary physicists appreciated its significance, carried the quantum theory into a new domain. Planck had believed he was simply patching up the equations of radiation. But Einstein postulated that all forms of radiant energy—light, heat, X-rays—actually travel through space in separate and discontinuous quanta. Thus the sensation of warmth we experience when sitting in front of a fire results from the bombardment of our skin by innumerable quanta of radiant heat. Similarly sensations of color arise from the bombardment of our optic nerves by light quanta which differ from each other just as the frequency v varies in the equation $E = hv$.

Einstein substantiated this idea by working out a law accurately defining a puzzling phenomenon known as the photoelectric effect. Physicists had been at a loss to explain the fact that when a beam of pure violet light is allowed to shine upon a metal plate the plate ejects a shower of electrons. If light of lower frequency, say yellow or red, falls on the plate, electrons will again be ejected but at reduced velocities. The vehemence with which the electrons are torn from the metal depends only on the color of the light and not at all on its intensity. If the light source is removed to a considerable distance and dimmed to a faint glow the electrons that pop forth are fewer in number but their velocity is undiminished. The action is instantaneous even when the light fades to imperceptibility.

Einstein decided that these peculiar effects could be explained only by supposing that all light is composed of individual particles or grains of energy which he called *photons,* and that when one of them hits an electron the resulting action is comparable to the impact of two billiard balls. He reasoned further that photons of violet, ultraviolet, and other forms of high frequency radiation pack more energy than red and infrared photons, and that the velocity with which each electron flies from the metal plate is proportional to the energy content of the photon that strikes it. He expressed these principles in a series of historic equations which won him the Nobel Prize and profoundly influenced later work in quantum physics and spectroscopy. Television and other applications of the photoelectric cell owe their existence to Einstein's Photoelectric Law.

In thus adducing an important new physical principle Einstein uncovered at the same time one of the deepest and most troubling enigmas of nature. No one doubts today that all matter is made up of atoms which in turn are composed of even smaller building blocks called electrons, neutrons, and protons. But Einstein's notion that light too may consist of discontinuous particles clashed with a far more venerable theory that light is made up of waves.

There are indeed certain phenomena involving light that can only be explained by the wave theory. For example, the shadows of ordinary objects like buildings, trees, and telegraph poles appear sharply defined; but when a very fine wire or hair is held between a light source and a screen it casts no distinct shadow whatsoever, suggesting that light rays have bent around it just as waves of water bend around a small rock. Similarly a beam of light passing through a round aperture projects a sharply-defined disk upon a screen; but if the aperture is reduced to the size of a pinhole, then the disk becomes ribbed with alternating concentric bands of light and darkness, somewhat like those of a conventional target. This phenomenon is known as diffraction and has been compared with the tendency of ocean waves to bend and diverge on passing through the narrow mouth of a harbor. If instead of one pinhole, two pinholes are employed very close together and side by side, the diffraction patterns merge in a series of parallel stripes. Just as two wave systems meeting in a swimming pool will reinforce each other when crest coincides with crest and annul each other when the crest of one wave meets the trough of another, so in the case of the adjacent pinholes the bright stripes occur where two light waves reinforce each other and the dark stripes where two waves have interfered. These phenomena—diffraction and interference—are strictly wave characteristics and would not occur if light were made up of individual corpuscles. More than two centuries of experiment and theory assert that light *must* consist of waves. Yet Einstein's Photoelectric Law shows that light *must* consist of photons.

This fundamental question—is light waves or is it particles?—has never been answered. The dual character of light is, however, only one aspect of a deeper and more remarkable duality which pervades all nature.

The first hint of this strange dualism came in 1925, when a young French physicist named Louis de Broglie suggested that phenomena involving the interplay of matter and radiation could best be understood by regarding electrons not as individual particles but as systems of waves. This audacious concept flouted two decades of quantum research in which physicists had built up rather specific ideas about the elementary particles of matter. The atom had come to be pictured as a kind of miniature solar system composed of a central nucleus surrounded by varying numbers of electrons (one for hydrogen, 92 for uranium) revolving in circular or elliptical orbits. The electron was less vivid. Experiments showed that all electrons had exactly the same mass and the same electrical charge, so it was natural to regard them as the ultimate foundation stones of the universe. It also seemed logical at first to picture them simply as hard elastic spheres. But little by little, as investigation progressed, they became more capricious, defiant of observation and measurement. In many ways their behavior appeared too complex for any material particle. "The hard sphere," declared the British physicist, Sir James Jeans, "has always a definite position in space; the electron apparently has not. A hard sphere takes up a very definite amount of room; an electron—well it is probably as meaningless to discuss how much room an electron takes up as it is to discuss how much room a fear, an anxiety, or an uncertainty takes up."

Shortly after De Broglie had his vision of "matter waves" a Viennese physicist named Schrödinger developed the same idea in mathematical form, evolving a system that explained quantum phenomena by attributing specific wave functions to protons and electrons. This system, known as "wave mechanics," was corroborated in 1927 when two American scientists, Davisson and Germer, proved by experiment that electrons actually do exhibit wave characteristics. They directed a beam of electrons upon a metal crystal and obtained diffraction rings similar to those produced when light is passed through a pinhole. Their measurements indicated, moreover, that the wavelength of an electron is of the precise magnitude predicted by Schrödinger's equation, λ (lambda) $= h/mv$, where v is the velocity of the electron, m is its mass, and h is Planck's Constant. But further surprises were in store. For subsequent experiments showed that not only electrons but whole atoms and even molecules produce wave patterns when diffracted by a crystal surface, and that their wavelengths are exactly what de Broglie and Schrödinger forecast. And so all the basic units of matter—what J. Clerk Maxwell called "the imperishable foundation stones of the universe"—gradually shed their substance. The old-fashioned spherical electron was reduced to an undulating charge of electrical energy, the atom to a system of superimposed waves. One could only conclude that all matter is made of waves and we live in a universe of waves.

The paradox presented by waves of matter on the one hand and particles of light on the other was resolved by several developments in the decade before World War II. The German physicists, Heisenberg and Born, bridged the gap by developing a new mathematical apparatus that permitted accurate description of quantum phenomena either in terms of waves *or* in terms of particles as one wished. The idea behind their system had a profound influence on the philosophy of science. They maintained it is pointless for a physicist to worry about the properties of a single electron; in the laboratory he works with beams or showers of electrons, each containing billions of individual particles (or waves); he is concerned therefore only with mass behavior, with statistics and the laws of probability and chance. So it makes no practical difference whether individual electrons are particles or systems of waves—in aggregate they can be pictured either way. For example, if two physicists are at the seashore one may analyze a wave by saying, "Its properties and intensity are clearly indicated by the position of its crest and its trough"; while the other may observe with equal accuracy, "The section which you term a crest is significant simply because it contains more molecules of water than the area you call a trough." Analogously Heisenberg and Born took the mathematical expression used by Schrödinger in his equations to denote wave function and interpreted it as a "probability" in a statistical sense. That is to say they regarded the intensity of any part of a wave as a measure of the probable distribution of particles at that point. And so "waves of matter" were reduced to "waves of probability." It no longer matters how we visualize an electron or an atom or a probability wave. The equations of Heisenberg and Born fit any picture. And we can, if we choose, imagine ourselves living in a universe of waves, a universe of particles, or as one facetious scientist has phrased it, a universe of "wavicles."

IV

While quantum physics thus defines with great accuracy the mathematical relationships governing the basic units of radiation and matter, it further obscures the true nature of both. Most modern physicists, however, consider it rather naïve to speculate about the true nature of anything. They are "positivists" who contend that a scientist can do no more than report his observations. And so if he performs two experiments with different instruments and one seems to reveal that light is made up of particles and the other that light is made up of waves, he must accept both results, regarding them not as contradictory but as complementary. By itself neither concept suffices to explain light, but together they do. Both are necessary to describe reality and it is meaningless to ask which is really true. For in the abstract lexicon of quantum physics there is no such word as "really."

It is futile, moreover, to hope that the invention of more delicate tools may enable man to penetrate much farther into the microcosm. There is an indeterminacy about all the events of the atomic universe which refinements of measurement and observation can never dispel. The element of caprice in atomic behavior cannot be blamed on man's coarse-grained implements. It stems from the very nature of things, as shown by Heisenberg in 1927 in a famous statement of physical law known as the "Principle of Uncertainty." To illustrate his thesis Heisenberg pictured an imaginary experiment in which a physicist attempts to observe the position and velocity of a moving electron by using an immensely powerful supermicroscope. Inasmuch as an electron is smaller than a light wave, the physicist can "illuminate" his subject only by using radiation of shorter wavelength. Even X-rays are useless. The electron can be rendered visible only by the high-frequency gamma rays of radium. But the photoelectric effect, it will be recalled, showed that photons of ordinary light exert a violent force on electrons; and X-rays knock them about even more roughly. Hence the impact of a still more potent gamma ray would prove disastrous.

The Principle of Uncertainty asserts therefore that it is absolutely and forever impossible to determine the position and the velocity of an electron at the same time—to state confidently that an electron is "right here at this spot" and is moving at "such and such a speed." For by the very act of observing its position, its velocity is changed. And when the physicist computes the mathematical margin of uncertainty in his measurements of an electron's position and velocity he finds it is always a function of that mysterious quantity—Planck's Constant, h.

Quantum physics thus demolishes two more pillars of the old science, causality and determinism. For by dealing in terms of statistics and probabilities it abandons all idea that nature exhibits an inexorable sequence of cause and effect. And by its admission of margins of uncertainty it yields up the ancient hope that science, given the present condition and velocity of every material body in the universe, can forecast the history of the universe for all time. One byproduct of this surrender is a new argument for the existence of free will. For if physical events are indeterminate and the future is unpredictable, then perhaps the unknown quantity called "mind" may yet guide man's destiny among the infinite uncertainties of a capricious universe. But this notion invades a realm of thought with which the physicist is not concerned. Another conclusion of greater scientific importance is that in the evolution of quantum physics the barrier between man, peering dimly through the clouded windows of his senses, and whatever objective reality may exist has been rendered almost impassable. For whenever he attempts to penetrate and spy on the "real" objective world, he changes and distorts its workings by the very process of his observation. And when he tries to divorce this "real" world from his sense perceptions he is left with nothing but a mathematical scheme. He is indeed somewhat in the position of a blind man trying to discern the shape and texture of a snowflake. As soon as it touches his fingers or his tongue it dissolves. A wave electron, a photon, a wave of probability, cannot be visualized; they are simply symbols useful in expressing the mathematical relationships of the microcosm.

To the question, why does modern physics employ such abstract methods of description, the physicist answers: because the equations of quantum physics define more accurately than any mechanical model the fundamental phenomena beyond the range of vision. In short, *they work,* as the calculations which hatched the atomic bomb spectacularly proved. The aim of the practical physicist, therefore, is to enunciate the laws of nature in ever more precise mathematical terms. Where the nineteenth century physicist envisaged electricity as a fluid and, with this metaphor in mind, evolved the laws that generated our present electrical age, the twentieth century physicist tends to avoid metaphors. He knows that electricity is not a fluid, and he knows that such pictorial concepts as "waves" and "particles," while serving as guideposts to new discovery, must not be accepted as accurate representations of reality. In the abstract language of mathematics he can describe how things behave though he does not know—or need to know—what they are.

Yet there are present-day physicists for whom the void between science and reality presents a challenge. Einstein has more than once expressed the hope that the statistical method of quantum physics would prove a temporary expedient. "I cannot believe," he says, "that God plays dice with the world." He repudiates the positivist doctrine that science can only report and correlate the results of observation. He believes in a universe of order and harmony. And he believes that questing man may yet attain a knowledge of ultimate reality. To this end he has looked not within the atom, but outward to the stars, and beyond them to the vast drowned depths of empty space and time.

$$_{92}U^{238} + {_0}n^1 \longrightarrow {_{92}}U^{239} + \text{gamma rays}$$

$$_{92}U^{239} \xrightarrow[23 \text{ min.}]{} {_{93}}Np^{239} + {_{-1}}e^0$$

$$_{93}Np^{239} \xrightarrow[2.3 \text{ days}]{} {_{94}}Pu^{239} + {_{-1}}e^0 + \text{gamma rays}$$

U. S. Army A.A.F. photo

Nagasaki, Japan, under atomic bomb attack

[916]

UNITED STATES WAR DEPARTMENT RELEASE ON NEW MEXICO TEST, JULY 16, 1945

MANKIND'S SUCCESSFUL TRANSITION to a new age, the Atomic Age, was ushered in July 16, 1945, before the eyes of a tense group of renowned scientists and military men gathered in the desertlands of New Mexico to witness the first end results of their $2,000,000,000 effort. Here in a remote section of the Alamogordo Air Base 120 miles southeast of Albuquerque the first man-made atomic explosion, the outstanding achievement of nuclear science, was achieved at 5:30 A.M. of that day. Darkening heavens, pouring forth rain and lightning immediately up to the zero hour, heightened the drama.

Mounted on a steel tower, a revolutionary weapon destined to change war as we know it, or which may even be the instrumentality to end all wars, was set off with an impact which signaled man's entrance into a new physical world. Success was greater than the most ambitious estimates. A small amount of matter, the product of a chain of huge specially constructed industrial plants, was made to release the energy of the universe locked up within the atom from the beginning of time. A fabulous achievement had been reached. Speculative theory, barely established in pre-war laboratories, had been projected into practicality.

This phase of the Atomic Bomb Project, which is headed by Major General Leslie R. Groves, was under the direction of Dr. J. R. Oppenheimer, theoretical physicist of the University of California. He is to be credited with achieving the implementation of atomic energy for military purposes.

Tension before the actual detonation was at a tremendous pitch. Failure was an ever-present possibility. Too great a success, envisoned by some of those present, might have meant an uncontrollable, unusable weapon.

Final assembly of the atomic bomb began on the night of July 12 in an old ranch house. As various component assemblies arrived from distant points, tension among the scientists rose to an increasing pitch. Coolest of all was the man charged with the actual assembly of the vital core, Dr. R. F. Bacher, in normal times a professor at Cornell University.

The entire cost of the project, representing the erection of whole cities and radically new plants spread over many miles of countryside, plus unprecedented experimentation, was represented in the pilot bomb and its parts. Here was the focal point of the venture. No other country in the world had been capable of such an outlay in brains and technical effort.

The full significance of these closing moments before the final factual test was *not* lost on these men of science. They fully knew their position as pioneers into another age. They also knew that one false move would blast them and their entire effort into eternity. Before the assembly started a receipt for the vital matter was signed by Brigadier General Thomas F. Farrell, General Groves' deputy. This signaled the formal transfer of the irreplaceable material from the scientists to the Army.

During final preliminary assembly, a bad few minutes developed when the assembly of an important section of the bomb was delayed. The entire unit was machine-tooled to the finest measurement. The insertion was partially completed when it apparently wedged tightly and would go no farther. Dr. Bacher, however, was undismayed and reassured the group that time would solve the problem. In three minutes' time, Dr. Bacher's statement was verified and basic assembly was completed without further incident.

Specialty teams, comprised of the top men on specific phases of science, all of which were bound up in the whole, took over their specialized parts of the assembly. In each group was centralized months and even years of channelized endeavor.

On Saturday, July 14, the unit which was to determine the success or failure of the entire project was elevated to the top of the steel tower. All that day and the next, the job of preparation went on. In addition to the apparatus necessary to cause the detonation, complete instrumentation to determine the pulse beat and all reactions of the bomb was rigged on the tower.

The ominous weather which had dogged the assembly of the bomb had a very sobering effect on the assembled experts whose work was accomplished amid lightning flashes and peals of thunder. The weather, unusual and upsetting, blocked out aerial observation of the test. It even held up the actual explosion scheduled at 4:00 A.M. for an hour and a half. For many months the approximate date and time had been set and had been one of the high-level secrets of the best kept secret of the entire war.

Nearest observation point was set up 10,000 yards south of the tower where in a timber and earth shelter the controls for the test were located. At a point 17,000 yards from the tower at a point which would give the best observation the key figures in the atomic bomb project took their posts. These included General Groves, Dr. Vannevar Bush, head of the Office of Scientific Research and Development and Dr. James B. Conant, president of Harvard University.

Actual detonation was in charge of Dr. K. T. Bainbridge of Massachusetts Institute of Technology. He and Lieutenant Bush, in charge of the Military Police Detachment, were the last men to inspect the tower with its cosmic bomb.

At three o'clock in the morning the party moved forward to the control station. General Groves and Dr. Oppenheimer consulted with the weathermen. The decision was made to go ahead with the test despite the lack of assurance of favorable weather. The time was set for 5:30 A.M.

General Groves rejoined Dr. Conant and Dr. Bush, and just before the test time they joined the many scientists gathered at the Base Camp. Here all present were ordered to lie on the ground, face downward, heads away from the blast direction.

Tension reached a tremendous pitch in the control room as the deadline approached. The several observation points in the area were tied in to the control room by radio and with twenty minutes to go, Dr. S. K. Allison of Chicago University took over the radio net and made periodic time announcements.

The time signals, "minus 20 minutes, minus fifteen minutes," and on and on increased the tension to the breaking point as the group in the control room which included Dr. Oppenheimer and General Farrell held their breaths, all praying with the intensity of the moment which will live forever with each man who was there. At "minus 45 seconds," robot mechanism took over and from that point on the

United States War Department Release on New Mexico Test, July 16, 1945

whole great complicated mass of intricate mechanism was in operation without human control. Stationed at a reserve switch, however, was a soldier scientist ready to attempt to stop the explosion should the order be issued. The order never came.

At the appointed time there was a blinding flash lighting up the whole area brighter than the brightest daylight. A mountain range three miles from the observation point stood out in bold relief. Then came a tremendous sustained roar and a heavy pressure wave which knocked down two men outside the control center. Immediately thereafter, a huge multicolored surging cloud boiled to an altitude of over 40,000 feet. Clouds in its path disappeared. Soon the shifting substratosphere winds dispersed the now gray mass.

The test was over, the project a success.

The steel tower had been entirely vaporized. Where the tower had stood, there was a huge sloping crater. Dazed but relieved at the success of their tests, the scientists promptly marshaled their forces to estimate the strength of America's new weapon. To examine the nature of the crater, specially equipped tanks were wheeled into the area, one of which carried Dr. Enrico Fermi, noted nuclear scientist. Answer to their findings rests in the destruction effected in Japan today in the first military use of the atomic bomb.

Had it not been for the desolated area where the test was held and for the cooperation of the press in the area, it is certain that the test itself would have attracted far-reaching attention. As it was, many people in that area are still discussing the effect of the smash. A significant aspect, recorded by the press, was the experience of a blind girl near Albuquerque many miles from the scene, who, when the flash of the test lighted the sky before the explosion could be heard, exclaimed, "What was that?"

Interviews of General Groves and General Farrell give the following on-the-scene versions of the test. General Groves said: "My impressions of the night's high points follow: After about an hour's sleep I got up at 0100 and from that time on until about five I was with Dr. Oppenheimer constantly. Naturally he was tense, although his mind was working at its usual extraordinary efficiency. I attempted to shield him from the evident concern shown by many of his assistants who were disturbed by the uncertain weather conditions. By 0330 we decided that we could probably fire at 0530. By 0400 the rain had stopped but the sky was heavily overcast. Our decision became firmer as time went on.

"During most of these hours the two of us journeyed from the control house out into the darkness to look at the stars and to assure each other that the one or two visible stars were becoming brighter. At 0510 I left Dr. Oppenheimer and returned to the main observation point which was 17,000 yards from the point of explosion. In accordance with our orders I found all personnel not otherwise occupied massed on a bit of high ground.

"Two minutes before the scheduled firing time, all persons lay face down with their feet pointing towards the explosion. As the remaining time was called from the loud speaker from the 10,000-yard control station there was complete awesome silence. Dr. Conant said he had never imagined seconds could be so long. Most of the individuals in accordance with orders shielded their eyes in one way or another.

"First came the burst of light of a brilliance beyond any comparison. We all rolled over and looked through dark glasses at the ball of fire. About forty seconds later came the shock wave followed by the sound, neither of which seemed startling after our complete astonishment at the extraordinary lighting intensity.

"A massive cloud was formed which surged and billowed upward with tremendous power, reaching the substratosphere in about five minutes.

"Two supplementary explosions of minor effect other than the lighting occurred in the cloud shortly after the main explosion.

"The cloud traveled to a great height first in the form of a ball, then mushroomed, then changed into a long trailing chimney-shaped column and finally was sent in several directions by the variable winds at the different elevations.

"Dr. Conant reached over and we shook hands in mutual congratulations. Dr. Bush, who was on the other side of me, did likewise. The feeling of the entire assembly, even the uninitiated, was of profound awe. Drs. Conant and Bush and myself were struck by an even stronger feeling that the faith of those who had been responsible for the initiation and the carrying on of this Herculean project had been justified."

General Farrell's impressions are: "The scene inside the shelter was dramatic beyond words. In and around the shelter were some twenty-odd people concerned with last-minute arrangements. Included were Dr. Oppenheimer, the Director who had borne the great scientific burden of developing the weapon from the raw materials made in Tennessee and Washington, and a dozen of his key assistants, Dr. Kistiakowsky, Dr. Bainbridge, who supervised all the detailed arrangements for the test; the weather expert, and several others. Besides those, there were a handful of soldiers, two or three Army officers and one Naval officer. The shelter was filled with a great variety of instruments and radios.

"For some hectic two hours preceding the blast, General Groves stayed with the Director. Twenty minutes before the zero hour, General Groves left for his station at the base camp, first, because it provided a better observation point and, second, because of our rule that he and I must not be together in situations where there is an element of danger which existed at both points.

"Just after General Groves left, announcements began to be broadcast of the interval remaining before the blast to the other groups participating in and observing the test. As the time interval grew smaller and changed from minutes to seconds, the tension increased by leaps and bounds. Everyone in that room knew the awful potentialities of the thing that they thought was about to happen. The scientists felt that their figuring must be right and that the bomb had to go off but there was in everyone's mind a strong measure of doubt.

"We were reaching into the unknown and we did not know what might come of it. It can safely be said that most of those present were praying—and praying harder than they had ever prayed before. If the shot were successful, it was a justification of the several years of intensive effort of tens of thousands of people—statesmen, scientists, engineers, manufacturers, soldiers, and many others in every walk of life.

United States War Department Release on New Mexico Test, July 16, 1945

"In that brief instant in the remote New Mexico desert, the tremendous effort of the brains and brawn of all these people came suddenly and startlingly to the fullest fruition. Dr. Oppenheimer, on whom had rested a very heavy burden, grew tenser as the last seconds ticked off. He scarcely breathed. He held on to a post to steady himself. For the last few seconds, he stared directly ahead and then when the announcer shouted 'Now!' and there came this tremendous burst of light followed shortly thereafter by the deep growling roar of the explosion, his face relaxed into an expression of tremendous relief. Several of the observers standing back of the shelter to watch the lighting effects were knocked flat by the blast.

"The tension in the room let up and all started congratulating each other. Everyone sensed 'This is it!' No matter what might happen now all knew that the impossible scientific job had been done. Atomic fission would no longer be hidden in the cloisters of the theoretical physicists' dreams. It was almost full grown at birth. It was a great new force to be used for good or for evil. There was a feeling in that shelter that those concerned with its nativity should dedicate their lives to the mission that it would always be used for good and never for evil.

"Dr. Kistiakowsky threw his arms around Dr. Oppenheimer and embraced him with shouts of glee. Others were equally enthusiastic. All the pent-up emotions were released in those few minutes and all seemed to sense immediately that the explosion had far exceeded the most optimistic expectations and wildest hopes of the scientists. All seemed to feel that they had been present at the birth of a new age—The Age of Atomic Energy— and felt their profound responsibility to help in guiding into right channels the tremendous forces which had been unlocked for the first time in history.

"As to the present war, there was a feeling that no matter what else might happen, we now had the means to insure its speedy conclusion and save thousands of American lives. As to the future, there had been brought into being something big and something new that would prove to be immeasurably more important than the discovery of electricity or any of the other great discoveries which have so affected our existence.

"The effects could well be called unprecedented, magnificent, beautiful, stupendous and terrifying. No man-made phenomenon of such tremendous power had ever occurred before. The lighting effects beggared description. The whole country was lighted by a searing light with the intensity many times that of the midday sun. It was golden, purple, violet, gray and blue. It lighted every peak, crevasse and ridge of the near-by mountain range with a clarity and beauty that cannot be described but must be seen to be imagined. It was that beauty the great poets dream about but describe most poorly and inadequately. Thirty seconds after, the explosion came first, the air blast pressing hard against the people and things, to be followed almost immediately by the strong, sustained, awesome roar which warned of doomsday and made us feel that we puny things were blasphemous to dare tamper with the forces heretofore reserved to the Almighty. Words are inadequate tools for the job of acquainting those not present with the physical, mental and psychological effects. It had to be witnessed to be realized."

Drawing by Chas. Addams, © 1946 *The New Yorker Magazine*, Inc.

UNLOCKING THE STOREHOUSE OF ENERGY
by O. R. Frisch

In 1775 the French Academy of Sciences resolved no longer to receive any schemes for perpetual motion. With that, it shut its doors on a procession, stretching into the dim past, of men who had tried, by artful combining of pulleys, levers, water wheels, &c., to build a machine that would work for ever. None of them ever worked (except by fraud!), and gradually the belief arose that work could not be made from nothing but could merely be made to change from one form to another. But fundamental ideas are slow in taking shape. The steam engine had been in use for nearly a century before people fully realized (about 1850) that all it does is to turn heat into work. And it took even longer to understand what it was that changed into heat when coal was burned. This elusive something that could change from one form into another until it became work had to have a name, and the word "energy" (invented by Thomas Young about 1830 for a much more limited purpose) was pressed into use.

To give an exact definition of energy is not easy. "Capacity for doing work" might do, although work does not mean quite the same in physics as in everyday life. But let us look at some examples. If you wind a grandfather clock you do work: the weight is said to acquire "potential energy," which it gradually loses again during the week as it drives the clock. That energy is mostly turned into heat through friction inside the clock: a little goes into the sound of ticking (acoustic energy). If you cut the string the weight will drop, converting its potential energy into energy of motion or "kinetic energy," and this, in turn, will be converted into heat when the weight comes to rest on the floor. Heat, however, is energy of motion in disguise; it is nothing but the irregular motion of the atoms in a body, the more violent the hotter, and all energy tends eventually to be degraded into heat, through friction, inelastic impact, &c. It is also possible, however, as in the steam engine, to turn heat into work, but only part of the available heat can be converted.

With the rise of industry, energy became a commodity. Most of it has been obtained so far from fossil fuels (coal and oil): when we burn coal we merely liberate energy from the sun, stored for us by trees that grew and died millions of years ago. The sun also causes the air currents that drive our windmills: and hydro-electric power derives from the energy of water which the sun has raised by evaporation. So all our energy has come ultimately from the sun.

But in 1903 the French Academy once more marked the beginning of a new age by publishing an inconspicuous little note by P. Curie and A. Laborde in which they reported that the newly discovered metal, radium, was always a little warmer than its surroundings. Although they did not know it, this was the first observation of atomic energy. Not very much heat was produced—about as much in three days as could be got by burning the same weight of coal. But the heat from radium

From *The Times*, London, Calder Hall Supplement, and reprinted by permision of *The Times*.

is not exhausted as that from coal is, once burnt; it continues year after year without noticeable weakening.

Here was a miraculous storehouse of energy, a fuel many thousand times more concentrated than coal: if only one could make it "burn" more quickly! But all attempts were in vain. All kinds of chemical agents were tried, and heat and pressure as well; none had the slightest effect. Radium, uranium, polonium, and all the other radioactive substances continued to produce energy each at its own measured pace. Clearly this was a completely new kind of energy. What were those radioactive substances that had such miraculous properties?

Radioactivity was discovered in 1896 by the Belgian physicist Henri Becquerel. He had a hunch that certain chemicals might send out some of those X-rays that were the talk of the day, having just been discovered by Röntgen in Germany. So he placed a variety of chemicals on photographic plates wrapped in black paper. Some of the plates indeed showed blackening after a few days, and Becquerel soon saw that it was always those on which a compound containing uranium had been placed. A little later it was found that thorium had a similar effect, but much more weakly. But the blackening was feeble even after days of exposure, so the method was slow and inaccurate.

Now X-rays, as well as blackening photographic plates, had also been found to make an electroscope lose its electric charge, and by measuring the rate of loss one could measure X-rays quickly and accurately. With such an instrument Pierre and Marie Curie found to their surprise that uranium ores gave out more radiation than their uranium content would account for: yet none of the other elements which the chemists had found in those ores gave out radiation at all. So the Curies concluded that there must be a minute amount—too little to be found chemically—of some intensely radiating component; and they decided to search for it.

That search, on which the Curies embarked in 1897, became one of the great adventures of science. For over two years they toiled, groping their way through the dark, gradually discovering the chemical methods required. It was like one of those parlour games when you try to find a hidden object, guided by calls of "hot" and "cold" from the company: the Curies were guided by the electroscope to which they presented their various preparations to be told how much radiation they gave out. Soon it was clear that there was not one unknown substance but several, which made the search much more difficult. The first new element whose chemical properties they managed to clarify they called polonium, in honour of Marie Curie's native country, Poland. The second—of which there was much more—they called radium; but even of radium there were only a few grains in a ton of uranium ore. No wonder the chemists had missed it.

I said earlier that radium gives out energy year after year; actually the rate does drop, by about 4 per cent. in a century. This phenomenon of "decay" can be observed much more easily in polonium. Here the decay amounts to about 4 per cent. in a week, and after 138 days the radiation will be only half as strong. That is true of any sample of polonium, whether freshly prepared or quite old. It is usual to state this fact by saying that polonium has a half-life of 138 days. Of course, that does not mean that after twice 138 days its activity will be gone: it will merely be reduced by a factor, two times two or four. Every pure radioactive substance has its half-life, which can be anything from a fraction of a second to many million years. Radium has a half-life of 1,600 years; those of uranium and thorium are several thousand million years.

The radiation from radium was soon seen to be a mixture of different radiations, and it was analysed in a temporary fashion into three main components which were called alpha rays, beta rays, and gamma rays, pending the elucidation of their nature. Although their nature is now completely understood, those names are still in use.

To the layman the gamma rays may seem the most important: they can penetrate thick metal plates and are the ones most used in medicine and industry. But their nature posed no great problem: they were soon recognized as being of the same nature as X-rays, and indeed a mere by-product of radioactivity. Alpha rays, on the other hand, have very little penetrating power: they travel only a couple of inches in air, and a sheet of paper stops them. They are, therefore, of little practical importance now: but their historical importance is great because it was through their use that Ernest (later Lord) Rutherford discovered the atomic nucleus in 1911.

Atoms were known at that time, but very little about their structure. One common building brick of all atoms was known: the electron, a very light particle, about 2,000 times lighter than the lightest atom (that of hydrogen) and charged with one unit of negative electricity. There was reason to think that an average atom contained a few dozen electrons, but no more: hence most of the weight of the atom was not accounted for, and furthermore there had to be enough positive charge somewhere to neutralize the electrons, since an atom as a whole is electrically neutral. But nobody knew how those things were arranged inside the atom.

Rutherford realized that one might learn something about the inside of atoms by using alpha rays as very delicate probes. He had found that they were not true rays (like light, or X-rays) but really particles, positively charged helium atoms, shot out from the radium at very great speed. In his laboratory in Manchester, methods had been perfected for observing single alpha particles. He knew that they could go through thin metal foils and were usually slightly deflected in the process, and he suggested to Geiger and Marsden that they should study those deflections more closely, so that they might learn more about the electric forces acting on the alpha particles as they passed through the metal atoms. The result was surprising: a few particles were deflected much more strongly than the rest, and a very few—perhaps one in many thousand—bounced right back.

Rutherford alone realized how astounding that was: in his own words, it was like seeing an artillery shell bounce back from a sheet of tissue paper. For some months he would only say that there must be the most tremendous forces in the atom. And then one day he said that now he knew what the atom was like, and his bold guess was soon confirmed to the hilt. His guess was that all the positive charge and all the weight (except the small fraction to which the electrons amounted) were contained in a minute lump at the very centre, many thousand times smaller than the atom. That lump came to be called the atomic nucleus. Methods were soon discovered to determine the charge of each kind of nucleus; that tells us the number of electrons in the corresponding atom. Gold atoms have 79 electrons, helium atoms have only two. Alpha particles are just fast-moving helium nuclei. In going through a gold foil they will usually pass the gold nuclei at a safe distance, suffering only slight deflection from their electric repulsion: but occasionally an alpha particle, heading directly for a gold nucleus, will be turned sharply aside by an electric force which, close enough to a nucleus, is indeed tremendous.

From that day in 1911 our whole idea of matter has been changed. Its solid billiard-ball atoms have become transparent spheres of emptiness, thinly populated with electrons. The substance of the atom has shrunk to a core of unbelievable smallness: enlarged a thousand million times, an atom would be about the size of a football, but its nucleus would still be invisible, a mere speck of dust at the centre. Yet that nucleus radiates a powerful electric field which holds and controls the electrons around it and which—like a strong spring—pushes other nuclei away. That is why the radioactive decay cannot be speeded up by heat or chemical agents: because it is something that happens inside atomic nuclei, held apart by powerful "electric springs."

Rutherford saw that his alpha particles, although they were turned aside by gold nuclei, could probably break through the weaker electric barrier around lighter nuclei. But then the First World War broke out and he had to deal with the more urgent problem of detecting enemy submarines. It was 1917 before he could return to his experiments (this time at the Cavendish Laboratory, Cambridge), and 1919 before he published his great discovery: that alpha particles travelling through nitrogen would very occasionally enter a nitrogen nucleus and chip off a lighter particle, which he identified as the nucleus of a different element, hydrogen. For the first time an atomic nucleus had been split: man had at last succeeded in changing one chemical element into another.

Transmutation as such was no longer new: it occurs all the time spontaneously in radioactive substances, and this had been recognized as early as 1902, through the work of Rutherford and the chemist Frederick Soddy. Indeed, that is the explanation of radioactive decay. When a polonium nucleus shoots out an alpha particle—that is, a helium nucleus—the remainder is no longer a nucleus of polonium but of lead. Therefore the number of polonium nuclei in a given sample steadily decreases, and after 138 days only half the original number is left. But those left are still polonium nuclei, and although they are older they appear not to have aged: each of them has again a 50-50 chance of surviving a further 138 days. And so it is with all radioactive elements: their nuclei are unstable and tend to break up: that tendency is measured by the half-life, which is the time after which the chances are 50-50 that a given nucleus should be still unchanged, and hence the time after which half of a large number of such nuclei should have broken up.

The idea that chemical elements could change into one another was of course in conflict with the basic conviction of chemists that everything around us was made from combinations of chemical elements which were themselves immutable. But the evidence for transmutation among radioactive elements grew stronger as more chemists joined in the new field. And join they did, for here was a marvellous hunting ground: new elements were found at a great pace, with the electroscope acting like a divining rod. Indeed, soon there appeared to be more elements than could be reasonably expected, and some of them seemed to have the same chemical properties, yet different half-lives. For a time it seemed that the whole fabric of chemistry was going to pieces.

In 1912 Soddy put forward the new concept of "isotopes": substances with different radiations, half-life, and atomic weight, yet being the same chemical element. In other words, he suggested that a substance that the chemist could not decompose might yet be a mixture of different kinds of atoms. At the same time J. J. Thomson, already famous for having discovered the electron, found a way for sorting individual atoms according to weight. Again, that promising line was interrupted by the war, and not until 1919 did Aston build his first mass spectrograph, which recorded the masses of atoms directly on a photographic plate.

The mass spectrograph showed that isotopes occurred quite commonly, not only among the radioactive elements. For instance, copper turned out to have two isotopes, *i.e.*, to be a mixture of two kinds of atoms of different weights: nickel has five and tin holds the record with 10. In fact most elements turned out to be mixtures of isotopes, although some are not, for instance aluminium, phosphorus or gold. Another important result was that the weights of all atoms were almost exactly whole-number multiples of the customary chemical unit, which is the weight of one hydrogen atom (or more precisely, one sixteenth of the weight of one oxygen atom). That strongly suggested that they were all made out of hydrogen atoms; or, now that we knew about nuclei, that all nuclei were made of hydrogen nuclei.

That discovery gave the hydrogen nucleus a very important position as the fundamental unit of matter, and it was accordingly given the Greek name "proton" (the first one). But things were not quite so simple: the electric charge did not fit. An aluminium nucleus must contain 27 protons to account for its weight: but its charge is only that of 13 protons. One possible explanation, which used only known particles, was that there were electrons in the nucleus—14 in this case—since these were negatively charged. That would give the aluminium nucleus its correct charge ($27 - 14 = 13$), and would not appreciably affect its weight. This idea was for a time accepted but met with a good many difficulties.

Those difficulties disappeared in 1932 with the discovery of the neutron. In the intervening years most of the light nuclei (which are more vulnerable than the heavy ones) had been split by bombardment with alpha particles: but the beryllium nucleus was recalcitrant. It did not split off a proton like all the others, but instead gave some radiation which was more penetrating than any known gamma rays, and which furthermore had the power to set protons into rapid motion. That radiation was first noticed in Germany and studied further in France, but it was (Sir) James Chadwick at the Cavendish Laboratory who first realized that only a particle with no electric charge but weighing about as much as a proton could behave like that. Rutherford had previously speculated on the existence of such a "neutron": so this did not sound quite so fantastic in Cambridge as it might have done elsewhere.

Anyhow, by some very simple experiments Chadwick confirmed that the particles emitted from beryllium weighed indeed about as much as protons: later measurements showed the neutron to be slightly heavier, by one part in 1,200. After that, it was no longer necessary to postulate electrons inside atomic nuclei: they could now be constructed entirely from protons and neutrons, and a number of odd facts fell into place. We still do not completely understand how those particles are held together in the nucleus: but we have every reason to believe that protons and neutrons are the bricks from which all nuclei are made.

The mass spectrograph established yet another important fact: the masses are not accurately whole numbers; each nucleus weighs a little less than the protons and neutrons of which it is composed. The difference is small but can be measured quite accurately. If we could take 13 protons and 14 neutrons and put them together to form a nucleus of aluminium, a certain amount of mass—equivalent to about one-tenth of a proton—would disappear. What happens to that mass?

Mass and Energy

The answer is contained in a paper, written in 1905 by Albert Einstein, one of the papers from which the Relativity Theory was built. In that paper Einstein showed that whenever a body loses energy it also loses a proportionate amount of mass. If the change in energy is called E and the change in mass m, then they are related by the famous equation $E = mc^2$, where c^2 means "the speed of light multiplied by itself." That is a very large quantity, and therefore the change in mass is usually very small.

But when it comes to changes in atomic nuclei, then the mass changes become measurable. In putting 13 protons and 14 neutrons together enough energy is liberated in the form of radiation to account for the loss in mass. This has been checked quite accurately, not directly for this process, but for a great many other nuclear transformations. Conversely, we can now predict how much energy will be freed in a given process, once we know the weights of all the nuclei concerned, and that is very useful.

When Rutherford split the nitrogen nucleus in 1919, energy was not freed but consumed; the proton that was chipped off had less energy than the alpha particle that did the chipping. Other reactions that did liberate energy were soon discovered, but as practical energy sources were useless. In the first place, only a few nuclei a minute could be split, and the energy released could not have kept a wrist watch going. And to produce even that little power a much greater amount had to be wasted; only a few alpha particles in a million struck a nucleus, whereas all the others just frittered away their energy in scattering electrons along their brief path.

After 1932, much greater numbers of nuclei could be split. In that year (Sir) John D. Cockcroft and E. T. S. Walton built their first machine for accelerating protons to high speed, and almost simultaneously E. O. Lawrence, in the United States, built his first cyclotron. Those machines generated nuclear bullets in vastly greater numbers, and much more energy could now be liberated from nuclei; but the wastage still went up in the same proportion. The importance of these machines was rather that research could be speeded up enormously; but, oddly enough, all the fundamental discoveries that led to atomic energy were still made with fairly simple tools.

The next great step was taken by Irène Curie (daughter of Pierre and Marie) and her husband, Frédéric Joliot. They were studying the positive electrons which aluminium was sending out in small numbers under alpha ray bombardment, and they noticed that when the alpha source was removed the counter continued to record electrons, though at a decreasing rate. The rate dropped by a factor two every three minutes, so the indication was that the alpha bombardment had formed, from the aluminium, a minute amount of a radioactive substance with three minutes half-life. It was possible to separate that substance from the aluminium and to show that it had the chemical properties of phosphorus. Now the aluminium nucleus was known to emit a neutron when struck by an alpha particle, and that process would lead from aluminium-27 (there are no other isotopes) to phosphorus-30.

Charge Preserved

But why should phosphorus-30 be radioactive? Because it does not contain the right proportion of protons to neutrons, and whenever that happens the nucleus tends to adjust that proportion. So phosphorus-30 turns one of its protons into a neutron and becomes the stable isotope silicon-30. But the positive charge of the proton cannot just disappear, but is ejected from the nucleus in the form of a positive electron. In the opposite case, when a nucleus turns one of its neutrons into a proton, charge is preserved by the ejection of an ordinary negative electron. Those are the electrons which were found over 50 years ago among the radiations from radium and were then labelled beta rays.

When the elements we find on the earth came into existence several thousand million years ago—perhaps in the centre of an exploding star—a great variety of nuclei must have been formed. Some were stable and persisted to make our world. A few, like uranium and thorium nuclei, had a half-life of over a thousand million years; in consequence they still survive, and with them the less long-lived forms—like radium or polonium—through which they pass in their repeated transformations to a final, stable form. But most of them were unstable and disappeared within minutes, days, or centuries.

It was to that world of extinct radioactive isotopes that the discovery of the Curie-Joliots had opened the door. But it was only the back door, and it was Enrico Fermi who found the front door. Alpha particles, he argued, can penetrate into light nuclei, but around heavier ones the electric barrier is too strong; why not use Chadwick's neutrons as bullets? Having no charge, they would ignore the barrier. True, one only gets one neutron for many thousand alpha particles; but a neutron will not waste energy by scattering electrons left and right, but will carry on until it finds a nucleus straight on its path.

Fermi was already famous as a theoretical physicist; but when this idea occurred to him he decided to turn experimenter and to tackle the work with a few young men to all of whom this field was new. Their success was quick and astounding. Soon any physicist who could read Italian was in demand: he had to translate to his eager colleagues the latest news from the *Ricerca Scientifica,* the periodical in which the Rome group published their results. Within a few months they had produced a wealth of new radioisotopes, one or more for every element they tried. They discovered many astonishing phenomena; for instance, that neutrons could be slowed down by making them pass through water, and that their efficiency as bullets, far from being diminished thereby, was multiplied a thousandfold! Not since the discovery of radium had so much been discovered in such a short time, and with such simple tools.

Did this bring atomic energy nearer? Not directly. True, nearly every neutron would find its mark and then liberate an energy often many times its own; but to make one neutron one still had to waste many thousand charged particles. Thus as late as 1937 Lord Rutherford said there was little chance that nuclear energy would ever be utilized on a large scale.

Nuclear physics had by then become a broad stream in which big machines, special photographic emulsions, and many newly developed techniques all played their part in advancing knowledge on a wide front. But the development that led to the discovery of nuclear fission followed its own narrow and rather tortuous path. Fermi's imagination was fired by the thought of building up new elements beyond uranium, not found in Nature; new chemical elements, not just new isotopes. His attempts appeared to be successful: by bombarding uranium with neutrons, he found he could produce several radioactive bodies with chemical properties different from those of all neighbouring elements. As the work was followed up in Berlin and in Paris, more and more such substances were found, and the number and complex behavior of those presumably transuranic elements was quite unexpected and very puzzling.

I happened to be spending the Christmas vacation of 1938 in Sweden with Lise Meitner, who had worked with Otto Hahn in Berlin for many years but had gone to Sweden when the Nazis took over her native country, Austria. Her work with Hahn had been continued by him together with his fellow chemist Otto Strassmann, and they now reported a very strange result. One of the radioactive substances they had extracted from neutron-bombarded uranium had appeared to be an isotope of radium; but now Hahn and Strassmann had done further chemical tests and had come to the conclusion that it must be an isotope of barium. When Lise Meitner told me that, I would not listen at first; barium nuclei are only about half as heavy as uranium nuclei, and I could not see how half the uranium nucleus could have been chipped away by the impact of a neutron. But as we talked a new picture gradually took shape: the picture of a uranium nucleus stretching, forming a waist, and finally breaking in two. At first we thought the uranium nucleus would be too tough for that, but the mutual electric repulsion of its protons tends to tear it apart, and a short calculation convinced us that in such a heavy nucleus the forces must be balanced precariously, so that the impact of a neutron might be enough to cause break-up. This forming of a waist, followed by division, resembles the way that living cells divide, and the biologists call it fission; so when we published our interpretation of Hahn and Strassmann's result we introduced the term "nuclear fission."

Unlocking the Storehouse of Energy

Deeper Search

If barium nuclei could be formed from uranium, then the whole evidence for the formation of transuranic elements fell down; all those substances had never been compared, chemically, with elements much lighter than uranium. It must be said in fairness that one German chemist, Ida Noddack, had urged in 1934 that this ought to be done; but she had given no reason to think that such light elements might be formed, and so her advice had been disregarded. Those checks were now made, and all the so-called transuranic substances were found to be isotopes of well-known elements. To-day, a number of transuranic elements, with many isotopes, have been established beyond doubt, and one of them, plutonium, has risen to fame in a ball of fire. But all of them were discovered after 1938, although valid evidence that some must be formed was found earlier by Lise Meitner.

Did this bring atomic energy nearer? It did, but not for the obvious reason that the fission of a uranium nucleus liberates about 10 times more energy than any other nuclear transformation. The decisive point was this: when a uranium nucleus is torn in half, a few neutrons would probably be shaken loose, and those neutrons might strike other uranium nuclei and cause further fissions. In other words, there was the possibility of a chain reaction by which energy might be liberated on a large scale. Such a chain reaction had become possible because energy waste connected with the use of charged bullets was at last eliminated; this reaction would be carried exclusively by neutrons.

The next question was: Did any neutrons get shaken loose in the fission of a uranium nucleus, and—on an average—how many? That was a very difficult measurement to tackle, and it was several months before anybody dared tackle it. By then the War had broken out, and the military possibilities of an explosive nuclear chain reaction were soon apparent. Yet the first nuclear chain reaction established on the earth was not explosive but controlled, and the man who must have chief credit for it is once again Fermi. With his family he had left Italy in 1938 to escape life under Fascism; and in the United States this amazing man, already famous in both theoretical and experimental physics, turned engineer and organizer, and built the first atomic pile.

It was not just a matter of getting a sufficient amount of uranium together and then waiting until the first stray neutron (there are plenty in the cosmic radiation) should start off the chain reaction. The bulk of uranium is made from the isotope uranium-238 whose nuclei require fairly fast neutrons to make them undergo fission, faster than most of the neutrons that are shaken loose when fission occurs. Clearly such a material cannot support a chain reaction. There are two ways out of this difficulty. One is to separate off the other isotope, uranium-235, which is much "touchier." That way was taken by the scientists and engineers of the "Manhattan Project" and resulted in the atomic bomb that destroyed Nagasaki on August 9th, 1945. The other was to use ordinary uranium, combined with some substance which would slow down the neutrons. Slow neutrons are strongly attracted, as it were, to nuclei of uranium-235 and have a high likelihood of causing fission when they strike. Even so, there is 140 times as much uranium-238 in natural uranium, and some neutrons are bound to be swallowed up by it, as also by the "moderator," the material which is used to slow them down. The existing, rather inaccurate, measurements indicated that a chain reaction might be achieved, but only just.

That it was indeed achieved was not only a historic event, but also a scientific and engineering feat of the first order. The arrangement chosen was a regular array of uranium rods in a large pile of graphite; water is a more effective moderator but would have swallowed up too many neutrons. To calculate the best size and spacing for the uranium rods required delicate judgment and high mathematical skill. Metallic uranium, previously known as an impure powder, obtainable only in teaspoon quantities, had now to be manufactured by the ton, as solid metal of highest purity. Again, the best graphite was not pure enough; indeed, chemical tests were not sufficiently sensitive, and special tests, based on neutron absorption, had to be developed. And all this under conditions of extreme secrecy! When one evening a large party assembled at the Fermis' home in high spirits, his own wife did not know that they were celebrating the opening of the atomic age: that on December 2, 1942, in a disused squash court in Chicago, the first atomic pile had begun to operate.

THE PRIMITIVE AND THE TECHNICAL
by José Ortega y Gasset

IT IS MUCH to my purpose to recall that we are here engaged in the analysis of a situation—the actual one—which is of its essence ambiguous. Hence I suggested at the start that all the features of the present day, and in particular the rebellion of the masses, offer a double aspect. Any one of them not only admits of, but requires, a double interpretation, favorable and unfavorable. And this ambiguity lies, not in our minds, but in the reality itself. It is not that the present situation may appear to us good from one viewpoint, and evil from another, but that in itself it contains the twin potencies of triumph or of death.

There is no call to burden this essay with a complete philosophy of history. But it is evident that I am basing it on the underlying foundation of my own philosophical convictions. I do not believe in the absolute determinism of history. On the contrary, I believe that all life, and consequently the life of history, is made up of simple moments, each of them relatively undetermined in respect of the previous one, so that in it reality hesitates, walks up and down, and is uncertain whether to decide for one or other of various possibilities. It is this metaphysical hesitancy which gives to everything living its unmistakable character of tremulous vibration. The rebellion of the masses *may*, in fact, be the transition to some new, unexampled organization of humanity, but it *may* also be a catastrophe of human destiny. There is no reason to deny the reality of progress, but there is to correct the notion that believes this progress secure. It is more in accordance with facts to hold that there is no certain progress, no evolution, without

From *The Revolt of the Masses* by José Ortega y Gasset. Published by W. W. Norton & Company, Inc.

The Primitive and the Technical

the threat of "involution," of retrogression. Everything is possible in history; triumphant, indefinite progress equally with periodic retrogression. For life, individual or collective, personal or historic, is the one entity in the universe whose substance is compact of danger, of adventure. It is, in the strict sense of the word, drama.[1]

This, which is true in general, acquires greater force in "moments of crisis" such as the present. And so, the symptoms of new conduct which are appearing under the actual dominion of the masses, and which we have grouped under the term "direct action," *may* also announce future perfections. It is evident that every old civilization drags with it in its advance worn-out tissues and no small load of callous matter, which form an obstacle to life, mere toxic dregs. There are dead institutions, valuations and estimates which still survive, though now meaningless, unnecessarily complicated solutions, standards whose lack of substance has been proved. All these constituents of "indirect action," of civilization, demand a period of feverish simplification. The tall hat and frock-coat of the romantic period are avenged by means of present-day *déshabillé* and "shirt-sleeves." Here, the simplification means hygiene and better taste, consequently a more perfect solution, as always happens when more is obtained by smaller means. The tree of romantic love also was badly in need of pruning in order to shed the abundance of imitation magnolias tacked on to its branches and the riot of creepers, spirals, and tortuous ramifications which deprived it of the sun.

In general, public life and above all politics, urgently needed to be brought back to reality, and European humanity could not turn the somersault which the optimist demands of it, without first taking off its clothes, getting down to its bare essence, returning to its real self. The enthusiasm which I feel for this discipline of stripping oneself bare, of being one's real self, the belief that it is indispensable in order to clear the way to a worthy future, leads me to claim full liberty of thought with regard to everything in the past. It is the future which must prevail over the past, and from it we take our orders regarding our attitude towards what has been.[2]

But it is necessary to avoid the great sin

---

[1] Needless to say, hardly anyone will take seriously these expressions, and even the best-intentioned will understand them as mere metaphors, though perhaps striking ones. Only an odd reader, ingenuous enough not to believe that he already knows definitively what life is, or at least what it is not, will allow himself to be won over by the primary meaning of these phrases, and will be precisely the one who will *understand* them—be they true or false. Amongst the rest there will reign the most effusive unanimity, with this solitary difference: some will think that, *speaking seriously,* life is the process of existence of a soul, and others that it is a succession of chemical reactions. I do not conceive that it will improve my position with readers so hermetically sealed to resume my whole line of thought by saying that the *primary, radical* meaning of life appears when it is employed in the sense not of biology, but of biography. For the very strong reason that the whole of biology is quite definitely only a chapter in certain biographies, it is what biologists do in the portion of their lives open to biography. Anything else is abstraction, fantasy and myth.

[2] This freedom of attitude towards the past is not, then, a peevish revolt, but, on the contrary, an evident obligation, on the part of every "period of criticism." If I defend the liberalism of the XIXth Century against the masses which rudely attack it, this does not mean that I renounce my full freedom of opinion as regards that same liberalism. And vice versa, the primitivism which in this essay appears in its worst aspect is in a certain sense a condition of every great historic advance. Compare what, a few years ago, I said on this matter in the essay "Biología y Pedagogía" (*El Espectador,* III, *La paradoja del salvajismo*).

[933]

of those who directed the XIXth Century, the lack of recognition of their responsibilities which prevented them from keeping alert and on the watch. To let oneself slide down the easy slope offered by the course of events and to dull one's mind against the extent of the danger, the unpleasant features which characterize even the most joyous hour, that is precisely to fail in one's obligation of responsibility. Today it has become necessary to stir up an exaggerated sense of responsibility in those capable of feeling it, and it seems of supreme urgency to stress the evidently dangerous aspect of present-day symptoms.

There is no doubt that on striking a balance of our public life the adverse factors far outweigh the favorable ones, if the calculation be made not so much in regard to the present, as to what they announce and promise for the future.

All the increased material possibilities which life has experienced run the risk of being annulled when they are faced with the staggering problem that has come upon the destiny of Europe, and which I once more formulate: the direction of society has been taken over by a type of man who is not interested in the principles of civilization. Not of this or that civilization but—from what we can judge today—of any civilization. Of course, he is interested in anesthetics, motor-cars, and a few other things. But this fact merely confirms his fundamental lack of interest in civilization. For those things are merely its products, and the fervor with which he greets them only brings into stronger relief his indifference to the principles from which they spring. It is sufficient to bring forward this fact: since the *nuove scienze*, the natural sciences, came into being—from the Renaissance on, that is to say—the enthusiasm for them had gone on increasing through the course of time. To put it more concretely, the proportionate number of people who devoted themselves to pure scientific research was in each generation greater. The first case of retrogression—relative, I repeat—has occurred in the generation of those between twenty and thirty at the present time. It is becoming difficult to attract students to the laboratories of pure science. And this is happening when industry is reaching its highest stage of development, and when people in general are showing still greater appetite for the use of the apparatus and the medicines created by science. If we did not wish to avoid prolixity, similar incongruity could be shown in politics, art, morals, religion, and in the everyday activities of life.

What is the significance to us of so paradoxical a situation? This essay is an attempt to prepare the answer to that question. The meaning is that the type of man dominant today is a primitive one, a *Naturmensch* rising up in the midst of a civilized world. The world is a civilized one, its inhabitant is not: he does not see the civilization of the world around him, but he uses it as if it were a natural force. The new man wants his motor-car, and enjoys it, but he believes that it is the spontaneous fruit of an Edenic tree. In the depths of his soul he is unaware of the artificial, almost incredible, character of civilization, and does not extend his enthusiasm for the instruments to the principles which make them possible. When some pages back, by a transposition of the words of Rathenau, I said that we are witnessing the "vertical invasion of the barbarians" it might be thought (it generally is) that it was only a matter of a "phrase." It is now clear that the expression may enshrine a truth or an error, but that it is the very opposite of a "phrase," namely: a formal

The Primitive and the Technical

definition which sums up a whole complicated analysis. The actual mass-man is, in fact, a primitive who has slipped through the wings onto the age-old stage of civilization.

There is continual talk today of the fabulous progress of technical knowledge; but I see no signs in this talk, even amongst the best, of a sufficiently dramatic realization of its future. Spengler himself, so subtle and profound—though so subject to mania—appears to me in this matter far too optimistic. For he believes that "culture" is to be succeeded by an era of "civilization," by which word he understands more especially technical efficiency. The idea that Spengler has of "culture" and of history in general is so remote from that underlying this essay, that it is not easy, even for the purpose of correction, to comment here upon his conclusions. It is only by taking great leaps and neglecting exact details, in order to bring both viewpoints under a common denominator, that it is possible to indicate the difference between us. Spengler believes that "technicism" can go on living when interest in the principles underlying culture are dead. I cannot bring myself to believe any such thing. Technicism and science are consubstantial, and science no longer exists when it ceases to interest for itself alone, and it cannot so interest unless men continue to feel enthusiasm for the general principles of culture. If this fervor is deadened—as appears to be happening—technicism can only survive for a time, for the duration of the inertia of the cultural impulse which started it. We live with our technical requirements, but not *by* them. These give neither nourishment nor breath to themselves, they are not *causae sui*, but a useful, practical precipitate of superfluous, unpractical activities.[3] I proceed, then, to the position that the actual interest in technical accomplishment guarantees nothing, less than nothing, for the progress or the duration of such accomplishment. It is quite right that technicism should be considered one of the characteristic features of "modern culture," that is to say, of a culture which comprises a species of science which proves materially profitable. Hence, when describing the newest aspect of the existence implanted by the XIXth Century, I was left with these two features: liberal democracy and technicism. But I repeat that I am astonished at the ease with which when speaking of technicism it is forgotten that its vital center is pure science, and that the conditions for its continuance involve the same conditions that render possible pure scientific activity. Has any thought been given to the number of things that must remain active in men's souls in order that there may still continue to be "men of science" in real truth? Is it seriously thought that as long as there are dollars there will be science? This notion in which so many find rest is only a further proof of primitivism. As if there were not numberless ingredients, of most disparate nature, to be brought together and shaken up in order to obtain the cocktail of physico-chemical science! Under even the most perfunctory examination of this subject, the evident fact bursts into view that over the whole extent of space and time, phys-

[3] Hence, to my mind, a definition of North America by its "technicism" tells us nothing. One of the things that most seriously confuse the European mind is the mass of puerile judgments that one hears pronounced on North America even by the most cultured persons. This is one particular case of the disproportion which I indicate later on as existing between the complexity of present-day problems and the capacity of present-day minds.

ico-chemistry has succeeded in establishing itself completely only in the small quadrilateral enclosed by London, Berlin, Vienna, and Paris, and that only in the XIXth Century. This proves that experimental science is one of the most unlikely products of history. Seers, priests, warriors and shepherds have abounded in all times and places. But this fauna of experimental man apparently requires for its production a combination of circumstances more exceptional than those that engender the unicorn. Such a bare, sober fact should make us reflect a little on the supervolatile, evaporative character of scientific inspiration.[4] Blissful the man who believes that, were Europe to disappear, the North Amercians could *continue* science! It would be of great value to treat the matter thoroughly and to specify in detail what are the historical presuppositions, vital to experimental science and, consequently, to technical accomplishment. But let no one hope that, even when this point was made clear, the mass-man would understand. The mass-man has no attention to spare for reasoning, he learns only in his own flesh.

There is one observation which bars me from deceiving myself as to the efficacy of such preachments, which by the fact of being based on reason would necessarily be subtle. Is it not altogether absurd that, under actual circumstances, the average man does not feel spontaneously, and without being preached at, an ardent enthusiasm for those sciences and the related ones of biology? For, just consider what the actual situation is. While evidently all the other constituents of culture—politics, art, social standards, morality itself—have become problematic, there is one which increasingly demonstrates, in a manner most indisputable and most suitable to impress the mass-man, its marvelous efficiency: and that one is empirical science. Every day furnishes a new invention which this average man utilizes. Every day produces a new anesthetic or vaccine from which this average man benefits. Everyone knows that, if scientific inspiration does not weaken and the laboratories are multiplied three times or ten times, there will be an automatic multiplication of wealth, comfort, health, prosperity. Can any more formidable, more convincing propaganda be imagined in favor of a vital principle? How is it, nevertheless, that there is no sign of the masses imposing on themselves any sacrifice of money or attention in order to endow science more worthily? Far from this being the case, the post-war period has converted the man of science into a new social pariah. And note that I am referring to physicists, chemists, biologists, not to philosophers. Philosophy needs neither protection, attention nor sympathy from the masses. It maintains its character of complete inutility,[5] and thereby frees itself from all subservience to the average man. It recognizes itself as essentially problematic, and joyously accepts its free destiny as a bird of the air, without asking anybody to take it into account, without recommending or defending itself. If it does really turn out to the advantage of anyone, it rejoices from simple human sympathy; but does not live on the profit it brings to others, neither anticipating it nor hoping for it. How can it lay claim to

---

[4] This, without speaking of more internal questions. The majority of the investigators themselves have not today the slightest suspicion of the very grave and dangerous internal crisis through which their science is passing.

[5] Aristotle, *Metaphysics*, 893a. 10.

being taken seriously by anyone if it starts off by doubting its own existence, if it lives only in the measure in which it combats itself, deprives itself of life? Let us, then, leave out of the question philosophy, which is an adventure of another order. But the experimental sciences do need the co-operation of the mass-man, just as he needs them, under pain of dissolution, inasmuch as in a planet without physico-chemistry the number of beings existing today cannot be sustained.

What arguments can bring about something which has not been brought about by the motor-car in which those men come and go, and the pantopon injection which destroys, *miraculously*, their pains? The disproportion between the constant, evident benefit which science procures them and the interest they show in it is such that it is impossible today to deceive oneself with illusory hopes and to expect anything but barbarism from those who so behave. *Especially if, as we shall see, this disregard of science as such appears, with possibly more evidence than elsewhere, in the mass of technicians themselves—doctors, engineers, etc.,* who are in the habit of exercising their profession in a state of mind identical in all essentials to that of the man who is content to use his motor-car or buy his tube of aspirin—without the slightest intimate solidarity with the future of science, of civilization.

There may be those who feel more disturbed by other symptoms of emergent barbarism which, being positive in quality, results of action and not of omission, strike the attention more, materialize into a spectacle. For myself, this matter of the disproportion between the profit which the average man draws from science and the gratitude which he returns—or, rather, does not return—to it; this is much more terrifying.[6] I can only succeed in explaining to myself this absence of adequate recognition by recalling that in Central Africa the Negroes also ride in motor-cars and dose themselves with aspirin. The European who is beginning to predominate—so runs my hypothesis—must then be, *in relation to the complex civilization into which he has been born,* a primitive man, a barbarian appearing on the stage through the trap-door, a "vertical invader."

---

[6] The monstrosity is increased a hundredfold by the fact that, as I have indicated, all the other vital principles, politics, law, art, morals, religion, are actually passing through a crisis, are at least temporarily bankrupt. Science alone is not bankrupt; rather does it every day pay out, with fabulous interest, all and more than it promises. It is, then, without a competitor; it is impossible to excuse the average man's disregard of it by considering him distracted from it by some other cultural enthusiasm.

AN OUTLINE OF SCIENTISTS

by James Thurber

Having been laid up by a bumblebee for a couple of weeks, I ran through the few old novels there were in the cottage I had rented in Bermuda and finally was reduced to reading "The Outline of Science, a Plain Story Simply Told," in four volumes. These books were published by Putnam's fifteen years ago and were edited by J. Arthur Thomson, Regius Professor of Natural History at the University of Aberdeen. The volumes contained hundreds of articles written by various scientists and over eight hundred illustrations, forty of which, the editor bragged on the flyleaf, were in color. A plain story simply told with a lot of illustrations, many of them in color, seemed just about the right mental fare for a man who had been laid up by a bee. Human nature being what it is, I suppose the morbid reader is more interested in how I happened to be laid up by a bee than in what I found in my scientific research, so I will dismiss that unfortunate matter in a few words. The bee stung me in the foot and I got an infection (staphylococcus, for short). It was the first time in my life that anything smaller than a turtle had ever got the best of me, and naturally I don't like to dwell on it. I prefer to go on to my studies in "The Outline of Science," if everybody is satisfied.

I happened to pick up Volume IV first, and was presently in the midst of a plain and simple explanation of the Einstein theory, a theory about which in my time I have done as much talking as the next man, although I admit now that I never understood it very clearly. I understood it even less clearly after I had tackled a little problem about a man running a hundred-yard dash and an aviator in a plane above him. Everything, from the roundness of the earth to the immortality of the soul, has been demonstrated by the figures of men in action, but here was a new proposition. It seems that if the aviator were traveling as fast as light, the stop watch held by the track judge would not, from the aviator's viewpoint, move at all. (You've got to make believe that the aviator could see the watch, which is going to be just as hard for you as it was for me.) You might think that this phenomenon of the unmoving watch hand would enable the runner to make a hundred yards in nothing flat, but, if so, you are living in a fool's paradise. To an aviator going as fast as light, the hundred-yard track would shrink to nothing at all. If the aviator were going *twice* as fast as light, the report of the track judge's gun would wake up the track judge, who would still be in bed in his pajamas, not yet having got up to go to the track meet. This last is my own private extension of the general theory, but it seems to me as sound as the rest of it.

I finally gave up the stop watch and the airplane, and went deeper into the chapter till I came to the author's summary of a scientific romance called "Lumen," by the celebrated French astronomer, M. Flammarion (in my youth, the Hearst Sunday feature sections leaned heavily on M. Flammarion's discoveries). The great man's lurid little romance deals, it seems, with a man who died in 1864 and whose soul

From *Let Your Mind Alone*, by James Thurber. Harper & Brothers. Reprinted by permission of Mr. Thurber.

[938]

flew with the speed of thought to one of the stars in the constellation Capella. This star was so far from the earth that it took light rays seventy-two years to get there, hence the man's soul kept catching up with light rays from old historical events and passing them. Thus the man's soul was able to see the battle of Waterloo, fought backward. First the man's soul—oh, let's call him Mr. Lumen—first Mr. Lumen saw a lot of dead soldiers and then he saw them get up and start fighting. "Two hundred thousand corpses, come to life, marched off the field in perfect order," wrote M. Flammarion. Perfect order, I should think, only backward.

I kept going over and over this section of the chapter on the Einstein theory. I even tried reading it backward, twice as fast as light, to see if I could capture Napoleon at Waterloo while he was still home in bed. If you are interested in the profound mathematical theory of the distinguished German scientist, you may care to glance at a diagram I drew for my own guidance, as follows:

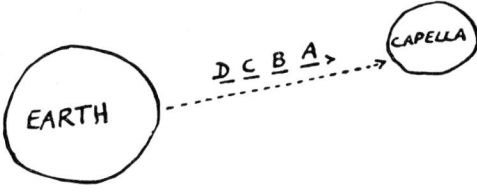

Now, A represents Napoleon entering the field at Waterloo and B represents his defeat there. The dotted line is, of course, Mr. Lumen, going hell-for-leather. C and D you need pay no particular attention to; the first represents the birth of Mr. George L. Snively, an obscure American engineer, in 1819, and the second the founding of the New England Glass Company, in 1826. I put them in to give the thing roundness and verisimilitude and to suggest that Mr. Lumen passed a lot of other events besides Waterloo.

In spite of my diagram and my careful reading and rereading of the chapter on the Einstein theory, I left it in the end with a feeling that my old grip on it, as weak as it may have been, was stronger than my new grip on it, and simpler, since it had not been mixed up with aviators, stop watches, Mr. Lumen, and Napoleon. The discouraging conviction crept over me that science was too much for me, that these brooding scientists, with their bewildering problems, many of which work backward, live on an intellectual level which I, who think of a hundred-yard dash as a hundred-yard dash, could never attain to. It was with relief that I drifted on to Chapter XXXVI, "The Story of Domesticated Animals." There wouldn't be anything in that going as fast as light or faster, and it was more the kind of thing that a man who has been put to bed by a bee should read for the alleviation of his humiliation. I picked out the section on dogs, and very shortly I came to this: "There are few dogs which do not inspire affection; many crave it. But there are some which seem to repel us, like the bloodhound. True, man has made him what he is. Terrible to look at and terrible to encounter, man has raised him up to hunt down his fellowman." Accompanying the article was a picture of a dignified and mournful-looking bloodhound, about as terrible to look at as Abraham Lincoln, about as terrible to encounter as Jimmy Durante.

Poor, frightened little scientist! I wondered who he was, this man whom Mr. J. Arthur Thomson, Regius Professor of Natural History at the University of Aberdeen, had selected to inform the world about dogs. Some of the chapters were signed, but this one wasn't, and neither was the one on the Einstein theory (you were given to understand that they had all been written by eminent scientists, however). I had the strange feeling that both of these articles had been written by the same man. I had the strange feeling that *all* scientists are the same man. Could it be possible that I had isolated here, as under a microscope, the true nature of the scientist? It pleased me to think so; it still pleases me to think so. I have never liked or trusted scientists very much, and I think now that I know why: they are afraid of bloodhounds. They must, therefore, be afraid of frogs, jack rabbits, and the larger pussycats. This must be the reason that most of them withdraw from the world and devote themselves to the study of the inanimate and the impalpable. Out of my analysis of those few sentences on the bloodhound, one of the gentlest of all breeds of dogs, I have arrived at what I call Thurber's Law, which is that scientists don't really know anything about anything. I doubt everything they have ever discovered. I don't think light has a speed of 7,000,000 miles per second at all (or whatever the legendary speed is). Scientists just think light is going that fast, because they are afraid of it. It's so terrible to look at. I have always suspected that light just plodded along, and now I am positive of it.

I can understand how that big baby dropped the subject of bloodhounds with those few shuddering sentences, but I propose to scare him and his fellow-scientists a little more about the huge and feral creatures. Bloodhounds are sometimes put on the trail of old lost ladies or little children who have wandered away from home. When a bloodhound finds an old lady or a little child, he instantly swallows the old lady or the little child whole, clothes and all. This is probably what happened to Charlie Ross, Judge Crater, Agnes Tufverson, and a man named Colonel Appel, who disappeared at the battle of Shiloh. God only knows how many thousands of people bloodhounds have swallowed, but it is probably twice as many as the Saint Bernards have swallowed. As everybody knows, the Saint Bernards, when they find travelers fainting in the snow, finish them off. Monks have notoriously little to eat and it stands to reason they couldn't feed a lot of big, full-grown Saint Bernards; hence they sick them on the lost travelers, who would never get anywhere, anyway. The brandy in the little kegs the dogs wear around their necks is used by the Saint Bernards in drunken orgies that follow the killings.

I guess that's all I have to say to the scientists right now, except *boo!*

from AN ANATOMIE OF THE WORLD:
"The First Anniversary"
by John Donne

And new Philosophy calls all in doubt,
The Element of fire is quite put out;
The Sun is lost, and th'earth, and no mans wit
Can well direct him where to looke for it.
And freely men confesse that this world's spent,
When in the Planets, and the Firmament
They seeke so many new; then see that this
Is crumbled out againe to his Atomies.
'Tis all in peeces, all cohaerence gone;
All just supply, and all Relation:
Prince, Subject, Father, Sonne, are things forgot,
For every man alone thinkes he hath got
To be a Phoenix, and that then can bee
None of that kinde, of which he is, but hee.

. . . .

We thinke the heavens enjoy their Sphericall,
Their round proportion embracing all.
But yet their various and perplexed course,
Observed in divers ages, doth enforce
Men to finde out so many Eccentrique parts,
Such divers downe-right lines, such overthwarts,
As disproportion that pure forme: It teares
The Firmament in eight and forty sheires,
And in these Constellations then arise
New starres, and old doe vanish from our eyes;

. . . .

Man hath weav'd out a net, and this net throwne
Upon the Heavens, and now they are his own.
Loth to goe up the hill, or labour thus
To goe to heaven, we make heaven come to us.

the Bright Young Men

[942]

From It's a long way to Heaven, *copyright, 1945, by Abner Dean, and reproduced by permission of Rinehart & Company, Inc., Publishers.*

THE VALUES OF SCIENCE
by J. W. N. Sullivan

I

SCIENCE is one of those human activities which has undergone a change of purpose or, at least, has come to serve different purposes, in the course of its development. The full wealth of values served by the major human activities are not apparent from the beginning. The cave drawings of primitive man, for example, are justly looked upon as the beginnings of pictorial art in the world. But it is very unlikely that primitive man conceived and executed them for purely artistic motives. They had, it is probable, a religious or magic significance. These representations of animals pierced with arrows were probably designed to secure a good kill on the morrow. And the early essays in science, as we have seen, were undertaken for purely practical reasons. Astronomy originated in the desire to construct a calendar for the benefit of an agricultural community, and the official reason given to-day for its support by civilized governments is that it aids navigation at sea.

Astronomy later developed into astrology, which had as its purpose the extremely practical one of foretelling human destiny. Biology began as medicine. Chemistry was for a long time alchemy, which was pursued chiefly because it was thought to hold the key to the discovery of the Philosopher's Stone and the Elixir of Life. Even mathematics was not always pursued for 'its own sake.' Certain mathematical relations were sought out for their supposed magical potencies, and others were valued for their usefulness in interpreting cabbalistic writings.

We have seen, however, that the sciences gradually lost their purely practical orientation and came to be pursued for the part they played in meeting man's curiosity about the external world. The 'search for truth' became the dominant motive in the prosecution of science. In the development of science it was often found, of course, that answers to questions of purely theoretic interest were also of great practical importance. But these practical applications were, very often, mere by-products of the scientific movement. Thus Maxwell's discovery of the electromagnetic theory of light was not prompted by the desire to provide every home with a wireless set.

Disinterested curiosity has been the great motive power of scientific research. Of the great 'Values' that condition our activities and make our lives worth living, Goodness, Beauty, Truth, science has been chiefly concerned with truth. But 'truth' does not seem to be a simple and unambiguous concept. We hear of 'higher' truths and 'deeper' truths. We may ask then, What sort of truth is science after? In what sense is a true scientific statement true?

This question, which the characteristically modern scientific researchers have raised to a position of supreme importance, has not yet received one clear, unequivocal answer. It will help us to understand the present position if we begin by

From *The Limitations of Science* by J. W. N. Sullivan. Copyright 1933 by The Viking Press, Inc. Reprinted by permission of The Viking Press, Inc., New York, N. Y.

considering what is meant by mathematical truth.

In the beginning, when man first became conscious of this curious mental power called mathematical reasoning, he regarded mathematical theorems as revelations of the fundamental principles on which the universe is constructed. And not only the exterior material universe, but also the universes of thought and emotion. Everything was regarded as being, essentially, an embodiment of number. Thus reason, whose great characteristic, according to the Pythagoreans, is its unchangeability, is a sort of embodiment of the number one. Mere opinion, as contrasted with reason, is an embodiment of the number two. The number two is also feminine, while three is masculine. Thus the essence of marriage is represented by the number five, which is a combination of the first feminine and the first masculine number. In this extreme form these ideas did not long survive. But, modified and debased, they persisted for centuries. We find traces of this outlook even in Kepler, and it persists to our own day, attenuated and incoherent, in superstitions about 'unlucky numbers.'

But even though Pythagorean extravagances had been abandoned, mathematics, until quite recent times, maintained the exalted position of acquainting us with 'necessary truths.' Descartes expresses this point of view in a famous passage from his Fifth Meditation:

I imagine a triangle, although perhaps such a figure does not exist and never has existed anywhere in the world outside my thought. Nevertheless this figure has a certain nature or form or determinate essence which is immutable and eternal, and which I have not invented, and which depends in no way on my mind. This is evident from the fact that I am able to demonstrate various properties of this triangle, for example, that its three interior angles are equal to two right angles, that the greatest angle is subtended by the greatest side, and so on. Whether I want to or not, I recognize very clearly and evidently that these properties are in the triangle although I have never thought about them before, and even if this is the first time I have imagined a triangle. Nevertheless, no one can say that I have invented or imagined them.

Thus the properties of a triangle, according to Descartes, in no way depend on the human mind. But the invention of the non-Euclidean geometries has taught us that these properties are necessary merely in the sense of being logical consequences of the axioms and postulates with which we start. And these axioms and postulates are arbitrary. They are not necessities of thought; they are matters of the mathematician's caprice. We can, if we like, start with the axioms assumed by Euclid, and then we get the properties that so impressed Descartes. Or we can start with Lobachevsky's axioms, and then we get quite different properties. Or we can start with Riemann's axioms, and get still different properties. And so on. None of these axioms are necessities of thought. Regarded logically, there is nothing to choose between them. Thus there is no reason to suppose that Descartes' triangle is a revelation of an eternally pre-existing truth—such as a thought in the mind of God. It is an arbitrary creation of the mathematician's mind, and did not exist until the mathematician thought of it.

Although the idea has been abandoned that mathematics gives us access to some external store of supersensible truths, there is still controversy as to its real nature. A school of Continental mathematicians holds that it is a sort of game, like noughts and crosses. Another school holds that it is a branch of formal logic. The arguments about this matter are extremely subtle and fatiguing, and the melancholy fact that they are not also convincing is sufficient testimony to the difficulty of the subject.

But the negative result of these investigations is sufficient for our present purpose; they have established the fact that mathematics has not the transcendental significance that was attributed to it by philosophers for about two thousand years. At the same time the precise nature of mathematical entities is still a difficult and controversial subject. Although the simple, primary mathematical ideas were doubtless originally suggested by experience, the mathematician's development of them has been very largely independent of the teachings of experience. He has been guided chiefly by considerations of form— a criterion which is probably, at bottom, aesthetic.

This development has, in fact, been so largely self-contained, so autonomous, that the fact that mathematical theorems can be applied to the happenings of the real world seems like a lucky accident. This lucky accident is so remarkable that it has led some modern speculators, as we have seen, to conclude that the universe had a mathematical designer. As against this we must remember the possibility that a mathematical web of some sort could be woven about any universe, and the extraordinary difficulties and incoherencies of modern mathematical physics suggest that, in spite of the extraordinary luxuriance of mathematical creation during the last few centuries, the universe is so odd an affair that we are not yet in a position to weave a satisfactory mathematical web about it. To sum up, we may say that even if mathematics be not purely subjective, it is not, in its nature, a body of truth about the objective, physical world. If it has an objective reference it is only in the sense that logic, according to some writers, has an objective reference.

When we come to science proper, as in the science of physics, we are obviously in a region where experience has played a much greater rôle. We have seen that all its primary concepts have been suggested by experience. In fact, to say that they have been 'suggested' by experience would seem to many an understatement. In their original intention, at any rate, the fundamental terms of physics were put forward as names for certain actual characteristics of nature. The physicist gave names to certain qualities that he observed just as Adam gave names to the animals in the Garden of Eden.

When Newton isolated the concept of 'mass,' for example, he thought he was singling out and naming an actual objective constituent of the external universe. Other properties of matter, such as size, shape, position, velocity, were also regarded as obviously objective existents. Force was a rather more mysterious notion. It was derived from our sensation of muscular effort. But it was not at all clear how we were to regard two distant bodies as pushing and pulling one another. It was hoped, however, to reduce all forces to impacts. It was hoped that, in the last analysis, all forces would reduce to the effects of little hard particles knocking against one another. Another way of dealing with the mystery was to declare the notion of force superfluous and attempts were made to construct systems of mechanics which would not employ this notion. Thus force came to be regarded as a semi-fictitious entity; it was a more abstract concept than the straightforward notions of mass, velocity, and so on. It became doubtful whether all these physical

The Values of Science

concepts are just names for objectively existing entities.

This doubt is heightened when we come to consider some of the entities that were later imported into physics. Thus the notion of energy is one of the most important of all physical concepts, and the principle of the Conservation of Energy one of its most important principles. But what is the precise status of this principle? Is it a fact of observation that there is some constituent of the external universe to which we have given the name Energy, and is it a fact of observation that this characteristic never increases and never diminishes?

Let us consider, for example, what happens when we let a stone fall from a height. The stone, on colliding with the ground, acquires heat, and the earth for a certain distance round the stone also acquires heat. Thus the universe, it appears, possesses more energy than it had at the moment before we let the stone fall. Where has this energy come from? It has come, we are told, from the energy of motion of the stone. Every moving body possesses energy in virtue of its motion. The stone has steadily been acquiring this sort of energy during its fall, and at the moment of impact, when its energy of motion is at its maximum, this energy is changed into heat energy.

But from what source has the stone been steadily acquiring its energy of motion? Here we come to the somewhat mysterious notion of 'potential' energy. A stone, or any other body, we are told, can possess energy purely in virtue of its position with respect to surrounding bodies. Thus a stone at the top of a mountain possesses more energy than an exactly similar stone at the foot of the mountain. Exactly similar stationary stones at different levels possess different energies. These energies are the potential energies of the stones. Potential energy, it must be admitted, is a somewhat mysterious notion. Other forms of energy, such as energy of motion and heat energy, are obviously 'energetic.' But potential energy is undetectable until it is transformed.

But it is only by importing this notion of potential energy that we can assert the conservation of energy. Otherwise, as in the case of the falling stone, we seem able to create energy. Similarly, by throwing a stone up in the air, we seem able to annihilate energy. At the moment of leaving the hand, the stone possesses energy of motion given to it by muscular exertion which has consumed energy from the body. But when the stone is at the top of its flight, its energy of motion, which has steadily been becoming less, becomes zero. It then begins again to acquire energy of motion, until it reaches the hand with the same energy with which it left it. The notion of potential energy comes in here to preserve the principle of the conservation of energy by saying that as the stone's energy of motion decreases in its upward flight its potential energy increases in such a way that, at the top of its flight, the potential energy is equal to the energy of motion with which the stone started.

Thus the notion of potential energy explains away apparent violations of the principle of the conservation of energy. But is not this the very reason for the importation of the notion of potential energy? Is it not a mathematical fiction, brought in for convenience? A quotation from a well-known Victorian text-book of physics [1] will show us the sort of attempts that were made to justify potential energy as a real physical quantity.

The question still remains, what becomes of the motion when the kinetic energy of a

[1] Preston's *Theory of Heat*.

[947]

system diminishes? Can motion ever be changed into anything else than motion? If we assume a fundamental medium whereby to explain all the phenomena of nature, then the properties of this medium ought to remain unchanged, and all other changes must be explained by motion of the medium. Such an assumption is quite philosophic, and the method of procedure is certainly scientific. An evident reply to the question of what becomes of the motion of a projectile rising upwards is that it passes into the ether. The first assumed property of the ether is that it can contain and convey energy. There is no *a priori* reason, then, why the energy of motion of a projectile as it rises upwards should not be stored up as energy of motion of the ether between the body and the earth, or elsewhere. The oscillation from kinetic to potential, and from potential to kinetic, in the case of the pendulum is then, from this point of view, merely an interchange of energy of motion going on between the mass of the pendulum and the ether around it. According to this view, all energy is energy of motion, and must be measured by the ordinary mechanical standard. The work we do in lifting a body from the earth is spent in generating motion in the ether, and as the body falls this motion passes from the ether to the body, which thus acquires velocity.

A rough mental picture of the process might be obtained as follows: We might suppose a body connected to the earth by vortex filaments in the ether, which would replace the lines of force. The ether is spinning round these lines, and when the body is lifted from the earth the work done is expended in increasing the length of the vortex filaments. The work is thus being stored up as energy of motion of the ether, and when the body falls to earth the vortex lines diminish in length, and their energy of motion passes into the body and is represented by the kinetic energy of the mass.

This quotation is sufficient to show that the author is uneasy at the apparently conventional character of potential energy, and accordingly invokes unknown properties of the ether in order to give it standing as a physical quantity. This line of reasoning raises the principle of the conservation of energy to a position where it can no longer be either verified or disproved. Thus the author in question goes on to say that if a material system is found to be losing energy in some way that we cannot account for, then we must assume that the system is radiating energy into the ether in some unknown manner. Similarly, if the system is found to be gaining energy, we must assume that the ether is somehow conveying energy to it.

Thus the conservation of energy becomes an article of faith. It is no longer an observed characteristic of nature, based upon experimental evidence, but becomes, at best, a metaphysical doctrine. We see how difficult it is, in practice, for science to remain faithful to Newton's criterion. In modern relativity theory the notion of potential energy is not used, and the principle of the conservation of energy is somewhat modified. We find that the notion of potential energy was not an arbitrary creation; it arose from a sound mathematical intuition, but the problem it was invented to answer was not correctly formulated. The art of putting correct questions to nature is learned only gradually, and there can be no doubt that some of our present difficulties arise from the fact that this art is not yet completely mastered.

2

The examples of force and potential energy suffice to show that the naïve view of science is not correct, and that science does not construct its mathematical formulation of the world wholly in terms of directly observable physical quantities. There is, in science, a certain amount of useful myth. But the myths are useful because they are, as it were, pegs on which the mathematical formulation can be hung. It is very seldom, however, that myths have been introduced in full consciousness of their mythical character. Thus it can hardly be doubted that Newton believed in the reality of forces. Potential energy, as our quotation shows, was regarded as more than a mathematical device. Bohr's theory of the atom, with its circulating electrons, was at first taken to be a faithful picture of the objective reality. It was only later that it came to be realized that any other picture will do equally well provided it leads to the same mathematical equations. And the modern Schrödinger atom, with its waves in multi-dimensional space, presents us with a picture which is frankly incredible. Again all that matters is the mathematical formulation.

The reason for this apparently curious unconsciousness of the true nature of their task, on the part of men of science, is very simple and obvious. It is that men try to explain the unfamiliar in terms of the familiar. Scientific concepts were suggested by ordinary daily experience. It was only gradually discovered that natural processes cannot be accurately described in terms of these concepts. Whether man will ever be able to evolve concepts which are entirely adequate to nature is obviously a question which cannot yet be decided. The materials out of which he has built his theories have hitherto shown themselves to be not quite suitable. It is as if one were given the task of constructing a map of a country out of little straight sticks. It was impossible, for instance, for Newton to give a perfectly accurate picture of the solar system with his apparatus of forces and Euclidean geometry, just as the Ptolemaic apparatus of circular motions *could* not be made to fit the observed heavenly motions. Similarly, the motion of a little hard particle, however much it may be refined, cannot be made to account for the behaviour of an electron. Even such guiding principles of thought as continuity and causality are being found inappropriate for the scientific description of nature.

It is evident, even from this brief survey of scientific ideas, that a true scientific theory merely means a successful working hypothesis. It is highly probable that all scientific theories are wrong. Those that we accept are verifiable within our present limits of observation. Truth, then, in science, is a pragmatic affair. A good scientific theory accounts for known facts and enables us to predict new ones which are then verified by observation. Thus Newton's theory of gravitation accounted, within the then limits of observation, for the heavenly motions. Subsequently, in the hands of Adams and Leverrier, it enabled the existence of a hitherto unknown planet, Neptune, to be predicted. It did, in fact, lead a very successful career, and is as good an example of a scientific theory as can be found. But sufficiently precise observation showed that it did not perfectly account for the motion of the planet Mercury, and it was then seen that its account of the motions of the other planets only seemed complete because, in those cases, departures from the predicted motions were below the limits of observation.

The way in which scientific men attempted to remedy the defects in Newton's theory is instructive. Their method was to tinker with the details. They tried the effect of making the law of attraction just a little different from the exact inverse square law. They tried the effect of giving gravitation a finite velocity of propagation.

But no advance was made in this way. The difficulties could not be met by any extension of the theory. It was not until Einstein introduced an entirely new theory based on entirely new concepts, that the difficulties were cleared up. We now know that the apparatus of ideas with which Newton started, however deftly used, cannot be made to perform the task for which it was invented. It would probably be impossible to find another instance of a change as fundamental as this in the history of the sciences. Here we have no step-by-step modification of a theory, but the complete sweeping away of the very foundations of a scientific outlook. The one feature of the Newtonian outlook that is left is the insistence on a mathematical formulation of nature.

Another instance, although rather less marked, of a radical change of outlook, is provided by the fate of the ether theory. The universal medium called the ether was postulated chiefly in order to account for the propagation of light. Light takes eight minutes to reach us from the sun. How is it transmitted? The hypothesis that it consists of little corpuscles shot out of the sun was found to be unsatisfactory, and the theory was developed that light is a wave motion of some kind. But a wave motion implies, of course, a medium in which the waves travel. Thus there naturally arose the question as to the constitution of the medium. It was at first conceived, on the basis of previous experience of extended and not readily perceptible media, as a sort of gas. Certain experiments showed that this theory was inadmissible, and the notion of the ether as a sort of huge jelly was then developed. This fitted the observed facts much better—but the accordance was not perfect. Attempts to perfect the ether theory led to the amazing developments that we have already described.

Then, by some obscure process of reason and intuition that cannot be clearly analysed, Maxwell developed his equations. He started with mechanical concepts not unlike those of his predecessors, but in developing them he made jumps—flashes of genius—that took him outside the mechanical scheme. He had arrived at the correct mathematical formulation of light-processes. He had thus, in a sense, reached the goal at which all the ether theorists had been aiming. But his mathematical formulation was not reducible to mechanical terms. Then what is Maxwell's Theory? Is it true, as Hertz said, that 'Maxwell's theory is Maxwell's system of equations'? In view of recent controversies this question conceals an ambiguity which it is desirable to make plain.

The issue raised divides physicists into two camps, and has an important bearing on our question as to what is meant by truth in science. The one group holds what is called the 'conventionalist' view, which has been expressed by a German writer as follows:

It has sometimes been supposed that a physical magnitude, such as time, for example, may have a meaning in itself, without any reference to the way in which it is to be measured, and that the method of measurement is a second question. As opposed to this view, it must be strongly emphasized that the meaning of every physical magnitude consists in certain numbers being ascribed to certain physical objects. Until it has been settled how this ascription is to take place, the magnitude itself is not settled and statements concerning it have no meaning.

Thus, on this view, there is no such thing as a physical quantity apart from a system of measurement. The other group holds that there are objective physical quantities which exist quite independently of our methods of measuring them. We may call this the 'realist' view. The conventionalist outlook is obviously an extension to physics of the outlook of the pure mathematician, for whom an entity exists purely in virtue of its definition. But the outlook seems to assign altogether too great a rôle to the subjective element in science. It may be true that the square root of 2 had no existence before the mathematician thought of it, but it certainly seems to be untrue that lapses of time, variations of light intensity, and so on, did not exist before the scientist devised ways of measuring them. We cannot say that the child and the savage have no knowledge whatever of such things simply because they cannot measure them. It seems, rather, that there are objective physical quantities of which they have a confused apprehension compared with the more precise apprehension of the scientific man.

And in the history of scientific measurement itself, the change from one system of measurement to another certainly does not appear to be a purely conventional change, but appears to be undertaken in the effort to obtain a more precise estimate of the magnitude of the physical quantity concerned. Thus, according to the conventionalist, the temperature of a body must be the reading on a thermometer. But scientific men, in their search for accuracy, have successively used different thermometers. Are there, then, as many temperatures as there are thermometers? Is there no objective physical quantity, *the* temperature of the body, that scientific men are trying to reach? According to the conventionalist it is meaningless to talk of any such quantity.

Another objection to the conventionalist outlook comes from the fact that, in the investigation of a physical quantity, entirely different methods, based on entirely different conventions, reach the same result. Unless it can be shown that the conventions have been specially designed so as to fit in with one another, we can explain the agreement only by supposing that there is an objective physical quantity that the measurements measure. But even if we assume that the world of physical quantities is a world that is investigated, but not created, by the physicist, it still remains true that the only knowledge of this world that science gives us is knowledge of its mathematical aspects.

The conventionalist view, we have given reason to suppose, goes too far. Nevertheless, there are physical quantities to which it can be plausibly applied. We have given instances in the notions of 'force' and 'potential energy.' These, it is evident, are not constituents of the external world in the sense that mass, temperature, electric charge, are constituents of the external world. But the basis of this difference is not to be found in our sense impressions. The earliest quantities isolated by physics are precisely those that directly affected our senses. Even 'heat' and 'cold,' as we have seen, were at one time regarded as distinct entities. But the degree of reality we now attach to a physical quantity seems to depend upon the part it plays in the coherent scheme of physics. And the history of physics shows that it is precisely in its search for reality that physics is led to its most abstract abstractions. And all that physics can tell us about these abstractions, we must repeat, is their mathematical specifications. Thus the 'real' world of physics is vastly different from the world of perception.

Owing to the lack of connection between quantum physics and field physics, it is impossible to say at present what are the fundamental physical quantities out of which physics proposes to build the world. Field physics, it is possible, can be based on 'point-events' and the relation called the 'interval.' This will not enable us to deduce quantum phenomena, which are at present based on different fundamental entities. But it is evident that, if we make an assumption similar to that of the old materialists, and regard the 'real' world of physics as the only objectively existing world, then it is not only the 'secondary qualities' of the old theorists that we must regard as illusory. Their fundamental realities must go too, for even space, time and matter are all derivative from more fundamental entities, according to the new physics.

The science of physics is concerned only with those aspects of the world which can be treated quantitatively. This imposes an immense restriction on the elements we select from the total elements of our experience. If we go further, and assume that only the elements of which physics treats are real, all the others being in some way illusory, then we are led to some such apparently fantastic conclusion as that 'point-events' are the only objective realities. But we may leave the philosophical issue involved here to the philosophers. Science itself does not assume that it alone is concerned with the real. The statements of science are true within the limited region it claims for itself—the region of mathematical structure. If you are curious about the mathematical structure of the material universe, then science can give you information on that point.

In pursuit of its aim science has shown itself to be accommodating and flexible. The science of physics has shown itself willing, at different times, to adopt quite different principles and concepts, provided they promised to be helpful in its one great aim of giving a mathematical description of nature. Where principles and concepts have persisted past their time of usefulness, this has been due to the inertia of mental habit. No scientific principles are sacrosanct; no scientific theory is held with religious conviction. Nevertheless, most scientific men believe that there is a final scientific truth about the universe to which successive scientific theories ever more closely approximate. But this is an article of faith. Science is still an adventure, and all its 'truths' are provisional.

3

This atmosphere of provisional hypothesis and practically verifiable statements constitutes what has been called the 'homely air' of science, and is one of its great charms. Science has adopted the pragmatic criterion of truth, namely, success, and as a result science has been successful. Indeed, it would not be too much to say that, judged by the criterion of general assent and practical efficacy, it is the most successful activity that man has yet hit upon. As Professor Levy[2] says:

Any such criterion of truth may not be one that commends itself to the professional philosopher. It may be that science ignores subtleties that appear vital to academic philosophy, that it skims easily over the surface of reality. The very principle that scientists must leave no differences behind may narrow the range to superficial agreement, and restrict the nature and number of the isolates it may form. Whether or not this be so, science can at any rate look upon itself as a united movement that has left in its wake a body of tested knowledge, while philosophy is still broken up into disunited schools of thought.

[2] *The Universe of Science.*

The Values of Science

The criticism has, indeed, been made that science pays for its success by its superficiality. All the deepest problems of mankind, it has been pointed out, lie outside science. If neither philosophy nor religion can present any such 'body of tested knowledge,' it is because they have not been content with such cheap victories. There is doubtless some truth in this criticism, and it is probably true that the problems with which science deals are intrinsically inferior in human interest to those dealt with by either philosophy or religion.

Nevertheless, the actual atmosphere of science, the manner in which it goes about its work, is quite exceptionally agreeable. It is in the scientific attitude, as much as in the scientific results, that the true value of science is to be found. If the man of science has not aimed high, according to the philosopher, he has at least aimed with a single heart, with a docility in face of the facts, with an impersonal purpose to serve which is not always found amongst our prophets and philosophers, and which it is almost impossible to find elsewhere.

There is probably no other period in history, since modern science began, when the particular values it incorporates were so rarely to be encountered in other human activities. The human tendencies to prize certitude and fear knowledge, to indulge emotion at the expense of reason, were probably always as strong as they are to-day, but the circumstances of the time did not show them up in so pitiless a light. The mass of men were probably always as impatient of that careful, honest verification that is the very essence of science as they are to-day, but there was no huge popular press to bear daily witness to the fact.

If we are to judge from what seems the overwhelming evidence provided by such activities as politics, business, finance, we must conclude that the attention and respect accorded to science is directed wholly to its results, and that its spirit is the most unpopular thing in the modern world. Yet it could very reasonably be claimed that it is in its spirit that the chief value of science resides. This can be asserted without abating anything of our claim for the values of its results. Knowledge for the sake of knowledge, as the history of science proves, is an aim with an irresistible fascination for mankind, and which needs no defence. The mere fact that science does, to a great extent, gratify our intellectual curiosity, is a sufficient reason for its existence.

But it must be pointed out that this value is inextricably intertwined with another value—the aesthetic value of science. If scientific knowledge consisted of a mere inventory of facts, it might still be interesting and even useful, but it would not be one of the major activities of the mind. It would not be pursued with passion. It could, at best, only exert a somewhat more intensified form of the attraction we feel for a time-table. Indeed, the greatest single testimonial to the fact-gathering power of science, resting, as it does, on centuries of labour and ingenuity, is probably the *Nautical Almanac*—useful, but not entrancing, reading.

For science to have inspired such ardour and devotion in men it is obvious that it must meet one of the deepest needs of human nature. This need manifests itself as the desire for beauty. It is in its aesthetic aspect that the chief charm of science resides. This is true, be it noted, for scientific men themselves. To the majority of laymen, science is valuable chiefly for its practical applications. But to all the greatest men of science practical applications have emerged incidentally, as a sort of by-product. This is, perhaps, most obviously true of the men who have created the mathematical sciences. In the work of mathematicians, in particular, the aesthetic motive is very apparent. Many mathematicians have written about their work in a sort of prose poetry, and the satisfactions they get from it seem indistinguishable from those of an artist. The language of aesthetics is never far to seek in the writings of mathematicians. In their frequent references to the 'elegance,' 'beauty,' and so on of mathematical theorems they evidently imagine themselves to be appealing to sensibilities that all mathematicians share. Nearly all mathematicians show themselves uneasy in presence of a proof which is inelegant, however convincing—one which 'merely commands assent,' as Lord Rayleigh said—and sooner, or later, endeavour to replace it by one which approaches closer to their aesthetic ideal. Some of them, as the late Henri Poincaré, have gone so far as to remark that the actual solution of a problem interests them much less than the beauty of the methods by which they found that solution.

There can be little doubt that it is the aesthetic element in mathematics that has been chiefly responsible for the attention it has received. If mathematics is to be ranked as a science, then it is, of all the sciences, the one most akin to the arts. The history of its development bears out this assertion, for this development, in the main, has been a formal development. Certain branches of mathematics, it is true, have been created to deal with some actual physical problem but, for the most part, mathematics has been a remarkably autonomous activity. In this respect it greatly resembles the art of music, whose development also has been so largely conditioned by considerations springing from its own ground, and owing nothing, or almost nothing, to the external world.

But if the aesthetic element is most prominent in mathematics it is certainly not lacking in the physical sciences. The search for universal laws and comprehensive theories is indubitably a manifestation of the aesthetic impulse. It is sometimes said that scientific men, in their choice of one of two theories that equally well cover the facts, always choose the simpler. But simplicity is, at bottom, an aesthetic criterion. Fresnel said 'Nature takes no account of analytical difficulties.' If we interpret this to mean that there is no *a priori* reason to suppose that nature is simple, then the remark is doubtless true. But if nature was not simple, it is very doubtful if science would ever have been pursued. It would still be possible for science, of a kind, to exist. It is within the resources of mathematics to construct a formula for almost any sequence of changes, however arbitrary, but if this formula is of a kind from which no further deductions can be drawn, the whole investigation is regarded as being in a very unsatisfactory state. Where such formulae are used, as they often are in engineering, for example, it is solely for their immediate practical value. The exclusive construction of such empirical formulae is not an object that any scientific man would propose for himself.

It is because nature does seem to exhibit an order we can understand, because diverse phenomena can be grouped under general laws, that the pursuit of science is worth while. If nature did not possess a harmony that was beautiful to contemplate, said Poincaré, science would not be worth pursuing, and life would not be worth living. Life would not be worth living, that is to say, for Poincaré. But although most scientific men would doubtless find a scientifically unaesthetic universe quite worth living in, we may be confident that they would not devote

The Values of Science

themselves to science. 'You are young, I am old,' wrote Faraday to Tyndall, 'but then our subjects are so glorious, that to work at them rejoices and encourages the feeblest; delights and enchants the strongest.' And Einstein, writing on Max Planck, reveals himself when he says:

> The longing to see this pre-established harmony is the source of the inexhaustible patience and persistence which we see in Planck's devotion to the most general problems of our science, undeflected by easier or more thankful tasks. I have often heard that colleagues sought to trace this characteristic to an extraordinary will-power; but I believe this to be wholly wrong. The emotional condition which renders possible such achievements is like that of the religious devotee or the lover; the daily striving is dictated by no principle or programme, but arises from an immediate personal need.

When we come to the sciences other than physics we find the same spirit. Whether it be Chemistry, Biology, or what not, we find that all the great advances have come from the desire to uncover what Einstein calls 'this pre-established harmony.' Science can, of course, content many appetites. It enables many more millions of lives to exist than would be possible without it. Also it enables many more millions of lives to be destroyed than was possible without it. It can give us marvels to gape at: the distance of the stars, the minuteness of the atom. It can stun us with figures. It can even help the dividend-hunter in his absorbing quest. But to the great man of science, science is an art, and he himself is an artist. And his creation is not the less a work of art because it is but a faint and imperfect copy of another—of the supreme work of art which is nature itself.

The aesthetic appeal of science is due to the fact that it bestows comprehension. Under the phrase 'aesthetic emotion' a number of elements are lumped together, and some only of them are present in any particular case. Our reaction to any great work of art is complex. But one of the most important of our reactions, in many cases, is that our desire for comprehension is gratified. To comprehend a thing is to see it in its relations, to see it in its place within a particular framework.

In the case of a work of literature this framework is provided by the artist's personal vision of life. This is, as it were, the unspoken context within which everything that the artist says acquires a meaning. And our lasting reaction to a work of art, the degree to which it works in us and modifies us when we have forgotten all its details, is dependent on the depth and comprehensiveness of this vision. This is the light which pervades the whole work, and bestows on it such harmony as it possesses, a harmony which lies much deeper than anything the artist may achieve by the technical dovetailing of the elements of his work. The chief function of art is to communicate this vision, and it is the mystery and miracle of art that it can do so.

The comprehension bestowed by a work of art is really the communication of the artist's personal vision. The comprehension bestowed by science is not so obviously personal. Indeed, it is generally supposed to be wholly impersonal. The frame of reference, or 'vision,' within which a scientific theory exists is the group of fundamental concepts and principles in terms of which that region of nature is to be described. These fundamental terms have often been regarded as necessary and unchangeable. We have seen that they are not. Theoretically they have alternatives, although their adoption at that particular time may seem to have been psychologically inevitable.

The Newtonian concepts, for instance, were the final formulation of ideas which, in a more or less vague state, had been 'in the air' for many years. Similarly, the biological theory of evolution has a long history. The Darwinian form of it, in fact, was independently hit upon by two different men. It was, as people say, 'bound to come.' Nevertheless, even if the impetus of the whole scientific movement was towards the Newtonian concepts, we see now that those concepts were not theoretically necessary. Einstein's utterly dissimilar way of looking at the same group of phenomena was a theoretically possible alternative. Not that Einstein could have produced his theory if he had lived at Newton's time. In the absence of the necessary mathematical technique that would have been impossible. In Newton's time it is probable that Einstein would either have developed Newton's theory or else have been the impotent prey of intuitions that he could not formulate. But this would have been merely an accident of history. Theoretically, the Newtonian concepts had alternatives. They were chosen although, as a mere matter of psychology, it may be, there was in fact no choice.

Einstein's theory is perhaps the clearest instance that can be given of our assertion that even a scientific theory may possess a personal element. Einstein's theory is so original that it is very difficult, even after the event, to provide it with an ancestry. It was not in the least a natural culmination of the ideas that preceded it. It was a bolt from the blue. The extraordinary lack of comprehension with which the scientific world at first greeted it was due not to its technical difficulties, but to the unfamiliarity of the outlook it assumed. It seemed to be the product of an alien mind.

We could say of this theory what Einstein said of some of the work of Gauss, that if its author had not thought of it, there is no reason to suppose that it would ever have been thought of. Science provides few instances of theories as original as this—indeed, perhaps there is no other scientific theory so intensely original as Einstein's theory. But there are other scientific theories which have a strong element of originality. Maxwell's electromagnetic theory, for example, was a very lonely achievement.

And it is precisely this quality of originality which is the personal element in science. The majority of men of science, including some of the greatest, impress us as journeying along the highroad. Newton, for instance, revealed nothing totally unsuspected by the best of his contemporaries. It is as if many converging lines of thought came to a focus in him. Newton's great quality was not a bewildering originality, but a bewildering and unequalled mastery of his material. Other men could see his problems; only Newton could solve them.

But the men who strike us as having branched away from the highroad, and having thereby given science an entirely new direction, have put to themselves entirely new problems. It is here, of course, that the personal element in the creation of a scientific theory is most clearly revealed. The history of science is not the history of some sort of automatic development. The actual course that science has pursued depends very largely on the types of mind which, as historical accidents, happen to have risen to the level of genius at favourable instants.

It is often said that the essential distinction between science and art consists in the fact that science makes appeal to universal assent, whereas art does not. A scientific statement, we are told, is open to verification by anybody, whereas a work of art appeals only to people with certain sensibilities. A work of music means nothing to a man who is stone-deaf. Science deals with a 'public' world, whereas art is concerned with a private world. A colour-blind man, for instance, would not appreciate painting, whereas a man born blind could master the whole theory of optics.

What are the primary judgments to which, according to this theory, science appeals? So far as the science of physics is concerned, they are judgments about the indications of measuring instruments. We have to say, for example, that a pointer coincides with a certain mark on a scale. We have to agree, also, about number judgments. We have to agree that an urn contains twelve balls, and not eleven or thirteen. These are the only judgments, we are told, that are involved in science, and about these we can secure unanimity. Two observers, with different colour perceptions, might disagree as to the colour of some particular bright line in the spectrum, but they would both agree as to its position on a numbered scale, that is, they would agree about its wave-length. And it is its wave-length, not its colour, that is dealt with by science. In any scientific statement where a colour is mentioned, the name of the colour could be deleted, and a figure for a wave-length substituted, without harming anything in the statement. The same is true about any scientific statement which seems to appeal to judgments about which men might differ. Two men might disagree as to whether one note was the octave of another, judging by sound only, but they would agree as to whether its rate of vibration, measured on a scale, was or was not double that of the other. And that, we are told, is all that is necessary for the purposes of science.

Now we may admit that universal agreement may be obtained about such things as the number of objects in a collection or coincidences in space without therefore concluding that science is potentially capable of securing universal assent. For science consists of a great deal more than such elementary judgments. <u>The chief thing about science is its theories</u>, and it is surely obvious that not all men are capable of assenting to its theories. A man may agree that a star crosses a wire in a transit telescope at the moment when the hands of a clock mark a certain time, but the theorem which enabled the astronomer to predict that occurrence may be for ever inaccessible to him. As a matter of fact, the upholders of this theory, which professes to be so realistic in the sense of dispensing with all 'subjective' elements, are not realistic at all.

A man may be blind, deaf, dumb, and paralysed—that, they cheerfully maintain, does not matter at all. But he must be a very fine reasoner. If we adopt this criterion that the truth of science is to be decided by an unanimous vote, then we must point out this unanimity, when it comes to actual science, and is not confined to such questions as the number of matches in a match-box, cannot be obtained. A large section of mankind, perhaps the majority, are congenitally incapable of understanding Einstein's theory, for example. If such people are to be ruled out as not affecting the unanimous vote, on what ground is the poet to be differentiated who rules out all those people who are insensitive to poetry? In both cases the claim could be made that *if* all people possessed the requisite sensibilities or faculties, the vote would be unanimous. And this is, in fact, the implied claim of those who preach the complete objectivity of science. For their criterion for objectivity is merely universal assent.

But even if we abandon the criterion of universal assent, and grant votes only to those capable of forming a judgment, we still do not get unanimity. It is notorious that theories that have been found convincing by some scientific men have been found unconvincing by others. Faraday, for instance, was opposed to the atomic theory at a time when, in the judgment of most of his contemporaries, it was well established.

At the present day we have an interesting example of the influence of purely 'subjective' factors in the creation of scientific theories in the methods adopted by Einstein and Eddington respectively in their attempts to reduce the laws of electromagnetism to geometry. Judged by the scientific criterion of accounting for phenomena, there seems nothing to choose between them. But Einstein has said that he dislikes Eddington's theory, although he is unable to disprove it, and Eddington has said of Einstein's theory that it is a matter of taste. Here we are in a region where the ordinary 'objective' criteria fail us. Our attitude towards these theories seems to depend on considerations which are, at bottom, aesthetic.

Other instances could be given, particularly from present-day quantum theory, where a chain of reasoning which is found quite convincing by one authority is found unconvincing by another. And the different judgments seem to depend on considerations which the authorities concerned find too elusive for expression. This dilemma sometimes becomes so acute, Professor Levy tells us, that a scientific society, in view of the conflicting reports of its referees, cannot decide whether to publish a certain paper or not. And Poincaré has told us that even in pure mathematics, where reason, one would think, is most pure and undefiled, a proof which is quite satisfactory to one mathematician is often not at all satisfactory to another. Indeed, Poincaré was led to divide mathematicians into psychological types, and to point out that a kind of reasoning which would convince one type would never convince another. These differences, in his opinion, are fundamental, and play a great part in the actual construction of science.

In view of these facts it is obviously misleading to present science as differing fundamentally from the arts by its 'impersonal' character. There is no absolute difference here, but only a difference of degree. Science is less personal than the arts, but it is a mistake to suppose that it is wholly impersonal. The reason for the difference lies in the fact that beauty and truth, in spite of Keats, are commonly distinguished. A work of art aims more consciously and deliberately at beauty than does a scientific theory. There are some works of art, indeed, where it is difficult to see that the criterion of truthfulness has any relevance at all. This is most obviously the case with some musical works. There are other works of art—e.g., in literature and painting—where truthfulness is relevant. And while it is probably true that no scientific theory has been constructed in complete independence of aesthetic considerations, it is nevertheless true that these alone are not sufficient.

Perhaps this is as far as the discussion can be carried on the common-sense level. A further analysis would have to distinguish between, for example, the 'truth' of mathematics and the 'truth' of physics. And we would have to question the complete independence of the quality called 'beauty.' We have already likened mathematics to music, and it could be objected that, since a mathematical development must be logical, any aesthetic charm it possesses must be incidental. But a musical development also obeys laws; it is not capricious. And although these laws are doubtless more various than those of logic and have not yet been isolated and given names, they nevertheless exist.

And in neither case is the beauty of the development some kind of extraneous quality mysteriously added on. It is in virtue of the fact that the development does obey laws that it is beautiful. Here, at any rate, we see some sense in Keats' remark that Truth is Beauty. When we come to an activity, such as physics, or a great part of literature, which is concerned with matters of fact, the notion of truth becomes somewhat different. Here we have the criterion of correspondence with an external world which need not have been as it is. But here, again, the truth is beautiful. Everywhere we encounter what Einstein calls 'pre-established harmonies,' and since the discovery and revelation of such harmonies is the concern, in their different regions, of both the artist and the man of science, we see once again that there is no essential distinction between the sciences and the arts.

In discussing the aesthetic aspect of science we have been discussing, perhaps at too great length, an aspect which appeals to the layman hardly at all. The layman is impressed, naturally enough, by the magnificent panorama of nature that science spreads before him, but the beauty of scientific theories is perhaps a consideration that appeals only to the scientific man.

The matter is different, however, when we come to what may be called the *moral* values incorporated in science. These have always been held, theoretically, in the greatest respect, especially the chief of them, namely, disinterested passion for the truth. But, as we have said, if we are to judge by its comparative rarity in the other activities of mankind, it is the most unpopular of virtues. How does it come about, then, that it plays so dominant a rôle in science? The first, and most obvious, reason is that science is an activity where success is not possible on any other terms. A business man, by concealment and misrepresentation, may become rich, that is, he may, by his standards, achieve success. A politician who was impatient with misleading catchwords, who really tried to think things out, would probably find his 'usefulness' destroyed, since he might become incapable even of stimulating that degree of conviction and moral fervour which is necessary to sway large audiences. And an advocate whose speeches should reflect the purely scientific attitude, giving every true fact its true weight, would not be likely to have a very successful career. Even those advocates who, we are told, never embrace a cause of whose justice they are not convinced, are hardly scientific, since they evidently have an extraordinary capacity for arriving at definite conclusions on matters which are obviously debatable.

Science is the activity where truthfulness is most obviously an essential condition for success. Its success, in fact, is measured by its truthfulness. Of hardly any other human activity can this be said. In nearly everything else truth is a means and not an end. And if it turns out to be an unsatisfactory means it is quite natural that it should be replaced by something else. But a scientific man who should misrepresent his observations, or deliberately concoct arguments in order to reach false conclusions, would merely be stultifying himself as a scientific man. He would not be prosecuting science. An advertisement may tell lies, but then telling the truth is not its object. Its object is to sell the stuff, which is an entirely different object. This is not to say, of course, that scientific men invariably tell the truth, or try to, even about their science. They have been known to lie, but they did not lie in order to serve science but, usually, religious or anti-religious prejudices. They were aiming at a different form of 'success.'

Such cases are, as it happens, very rare. Perhaps the reason is to be found in the fact that the success thereby achieved is very short-lived. Always the experiments are repeated, or the reasoning checked. The rigorous criticism, the complete lack of indulgence, that is shown by the scientific world, is one of its most agreeable characteristics. Its one simple but devastating criterion 'Is it true?' is perhaps the chief characteristic that makes it seem such an oasis for the spirit in the modern world.

One reason, then, for the embodiment of the disinterested passion for truth in science is that the activity is meaningless without it. But how did men come to pursue an object which can only be reached by what seems to be generally considered as a very painful discipline? The answer is that, owing to the nature of the subject-matter of science, the discipline was not felt to be painful. On all matters where their passions are strongly engaged, men prize certitude and fear knowledge. From certitude can come purpose and a feeling of strength. It breeds courage and action, and is a ready means of ensuring that most desired of all things, an increased sense of vitality. Only the man of strong convictions can be a popular leader of mankind. For most men in most matters, whether it be the justice of a war, the rightness of a political creed, the guilt of a criminal, the wholesomeness of apples, certitude, in the entire absence of adequate evidence, is easily arrived at and passionately welcomed.

The scientific insistence on evidence, and the scientific absence of generosity in drawing conclusions from evidence, are resented in these matters. The scientific attitude, it is felt, with its promise of a long and very probably inconclusive investigation, would merely dam up the emotions that are clamouring for an outlet. But the matters with which science has hitherto been chiefly concerned are comparatively indifferent to us. For that reason science has been so successful. When Galileo investigated the law governing the motion of falling bodies, we cannot imagine that he cared in the least what the law would turn out to be. He could search for the truth with a single mind because none of his emotions could be outraged by the result. Similarly Newton's demonstration of the law of inverse squares roused no horror anywhere. Nobody had a strong emotional preference for the law of inverse cubes.

Towards most of the results of science we are indifferent. Their charm lies in the fact that they illustrate a harmony, but the results, in themselves, are matters of indifference. Any other results would do, provided they illustrated an equally beautiful harmony. The empirical fact that the velocity of light is nearer to 186,000 miles per second than it is to double that figure, excites no particular interest. But the fact that there must be an unsurpassable critical velocity in the sort of non-

Euclidean universe we live in, is a matter of great interest.

Our reaction to most scientific facts is one of indifference, and our reaction to most scientific theories is one of purely aesthetic appreciation. But when a scientific theory has a philosophic, religious, or briefly, a 'human' interest, we find at once that we are no longer content with our rôle of the disinterested seeker after truth. The opposition encountered by the Copernican theory and the Darwinian theory gives sufficient evidence of this. The splendid moral integrity manifested in scientific work, therefore, is due very largely to the nature of scientific material. It shows us the height to which man can rise, provided that a part only of his nature is involved. Science is truthful because it has practically no temptation to be anything else. In his work the scientific man is an artist, and his moral standard is superb, but the value of his example to the rest of mankind is limited by the fact that, in his work, the scientific man is not completely a man.

Conversation—Earth and Sky

Painting by Charles Sheeler, reproduced by permission of the owner, the Downtown Gallery, and Fortune.

METAPHOR AND SOCIAL BELIEF
by Weller Embler

Grammarians have often busied themselves defining what a metaphor *is*. But it is more meaningful in our day to find out what a metaphor *does*. The little words "like" and "as" exert an enormous influence over our thoughts and our behavior; and there is vastly more to figurative language than the customary pedagogical distinctions between similes and metaphors. Our behavior is a function of the words we use. More often than not, our thoughts do not select the words we use; instead, words determine the thoughts we have. We can say with some assurance that language develops out of social conditions and in turn influences social behavior.

Modern rhetorics and grammar books insist that written and spoken English shall avoid the hackneyed figure of speech. Triteness, they say, is "evidence of a failure to attain animation and originality in expression." But the trite figure is worn-out not because it has been used often before, but because it cannot bear the burden of new attitudes. Consider the following extended figure of speech from the novel *Young Man with a Horn* by Dorothy Baker.

Fortune, in its workings, has something in common with a slot-machine. There are those who can bait it forever and never get more than an odd assortment of lemons for their pains; but once in a while there will come a man for whom all the grooves will line up, and when that happens there's no end to the showering down.

Fortune (or the more common "Fate") is a concept for which the only referent in the external world is a series of observable events without an assignable cause, and creative writers in all ages have sought analogies which will force the concept of fate, for the time being, at least, to accept a local habitation and a name. For instance, to the Elizabethans, it was quite believable that the capricious order of happenings should be governed by malicious creatures who looked like very old women. When the fantastical Witches appear before Macbeth and Banquo announcing Macbeth's ascendancy from Glamis to Cawdor to King, it appeared to Shakespeare's audience that the course of Macbeth's life was chargeable to the whims of the horrid sisters. What is important is not the originality of the metaphors "invented" by Dorothy Baker and William Shakespeare but the relationship which their figures of speech bear to their times. If we think of events of our lives as controlled by witches or even controlled by some force known only to witches, we shall behave in one way; if we think that the course of our experience is a matter of statistical probabilities, we shall behave in quite another way.

A whole philosophy of life is often implicit in the metaphors of creative writers, the philosophy of an entire generation, indeed, even of an entire civilization. In the great tradition of the western world, it has been common to liken (in some essential respects) men to gods. Classical

Reprinted by permission of the International Society for General Semantics.

man so loved the gods he had created that he wished to emulate them and to be like them. Ulysses was not a god, but he had many things in common with the classical divinities, and it was fair to call him god-like. In other words, it was important to the social attitudes of Homer's Greece to believe that some men at least were "like" gods; and it is common knowledge that this belief in the divinity of man was responsible for much that was fairest and best in the classical civilization. The statues of Phidias are metaphors inspired by this ideal; the temples and the great dramas and the noble philosophies all testify to the comparison.

By way of contrast to the Greek, consider the figurative language of a modern novelist. In one of John Steinbeck's short stories, "The Leader of the People," the old grandfather of the story had at one time been a man of the frontier world of Indians and buffalo. But it wasn't Indians that were important, he tells his grandson, Jody, "nor adventures, nor even getting out here. It was a whole bunch of people made into one big crawling beast. ... Every man wanted something for himself, but the big beast that was all of them wanted only westering." And while Jody thinks of "the wide plains and of the wagons moving across like centipedes," his grandfather continues, saying, "We carried life out here and set it down the way those ants carry eggs. And I was the leader."

We must remember that Steinbeck matured as a writer during the depression era and that his social philosophy grew out of the social problems of the 1930's. In his search for a social philosophy which could meet the problems of his day, he turned for assistance to the biological sciences. In these he found sound method, tested hypotheses, and, if it could be translated into language descriptive of human behavior, a body of usable information about subhuman life. Steinbeck was one of the first American novelists to think consistently and seriously, but not always clearly, and mostly with a political purpose in mind, of men as something other than men. And it became Steinbeck's habit to compare human beings with marine animals, with land animals, and with insects. It may be fairly said that Steinbeck's dramatic similarities between mice and men, between fish and men (*Sea of Cortez*), between centipedes and men, whether drawn from observation or embedded within the firm system of ecology, have changed the social thinking of many readers.

To future generations, an age may be known by the metaphors it chose to express its ideals. Between 1798 and 1859 a good deal happened to change men's minds about the world they lived in. Among other revolutions in thought not the least effective was the change in attitude toward nature. Wordsworth had said that nature was full of consolation, of joy, and of wisdom. Presently, however, as a result of geological and biological investigations, nature ceased to be regarded as "Wordsworthian" and came to be thought of as "Darwinian." The theory of natural selection brought about a new attitude toward nature that had perforce to be expressed and communicated in new figures of speech. Tennyson was not simply striving to attain animation and originality in expression when he described nature as "red in tooth and claw." The association of abstract nature with tigers was striking, but for the Victorians it was also to become "true." *In Memoriam* anticipated the *Origin of Species* by nearly a decade, but its representation of nature as a tiger was subsequently to assist in the firm entrenchment of the Darwinian hypothesis; in fact, I suspect that it did more to consolidate the philosophy of struggle than did the *Origin of Species* itself.

As a force behind nineteenth-century socialism, Edward Bellamy's famous stagecoach metaphor in his *Looking Backward* had an effect that was immense. Its pertinence to the social conditions of the time, and the "rightness" of its phrasing gave verbal form to many an inarticulated thought. The analogy of the watch in eighteenth-century Deism was so befitting the ideas of the scientists, poets, and philosophers of the age that the analogy became a "truth" and God a cosmic clockmaker. When an age abandons its attitudes, it will exile its figures to the limbo for clichés, and new metaphors will take the place of the old. T. S. Eliot inspired a whole generation with the image of the wasteland; and in 1935 Horace Gregory's poetic picture of a chorus of men joining hands to make a new world supplanted, for a time, the figure of the wasteland.

Metaphor as Statement of Fact

But it is here that we must observe an important linguistic and social phenomenon. It will be noted that Homer does not say that men *are* gods but only that in certain respects they resemble gods. Wordsworth does not say that nature *is* a teacher, but only that nature is like a teacher. Yet when metaphor is new, those who find their attitudes implicit in the metaphor construe the metaphor to be a statement of identity, that is, a statement of fact. Figures of speech, when they are fitting and felicitous, and especially when they occur in print, give poetic sanction, as it were, to hitherto dimly felt, inarticulated beliefs. When metaphor is new, and when the reader does not enjoy the perspective vouchsafed by time, the metaphor is taken literally, and its function is not that of rhetorical device, but of statement of fact, *prescribing* certain kinds of behavior. *Indeed, it may be said that the habit which sees the germane metaphor as a statement of identity is a habit which changes the character of civilizations.*

Iago is a villain, but a clever one, and he says many things which were pleasing to an Elizabethan ear. For instance:

'Tis in ourselves that we are thus or thus. Our bodies are our gardens, to which our wills are gardeners; so that if we will plant nettles, or sow lettuce, set hyssop and weed up thyme, supply it with one gender of herbs, or district it with many, either to have it sterile with idleness, or manured with industry, why, the power and corrigible authority of this lies in our wills.

We may find Shakespeare's figure entertainingly turned, and we may even agree with the sentiment expressed, but in the twentieth century we shall hardly be aware of more than a casual similarity between ourselves and gardens. But when my friend explains to me that life is like a pin-ball machine—that we are little balls shot out through an alley, kicked around from place to place, sometimes ringing a bell or flashing a light, and eventually falling into a trough and rolling out of sight—when he says this, I inquire whether his figure is not perhaps the perfect analogy. His figure has a lively meaning for us today because we believe in the laws of probability, and half suspect the aimlessness of our existence. For all practical purposes, I am well prepared to think of life and pin-ball machines as identities, of taking my friend's metaphor as a statement of fact about human experience.

When we read in Friedrich von Schelling that "architecture is frozen music," we are charmed with the originality and neatness of the analogy. But when James Johnson Sweeney in describing Piet Mondrian's painting *Victory Boogie-Woogie* says that "The eye is led from one group of color notes to another at varying speeds; at the same time contrasted with this endless change in the minor motives we have a constant repetition of the right angle theme like a persistent bass chord sounding through a sprinkle of running arpeggios and grace notes from the treble," we are convinced for the moment that the canvas *is* music.

The figure of Socrates as a gadfly is interesting but seldom taken literally. Yet when the villain in the cinema is called a "rat" and shot thrice in the abdomen forthwith, it is a nice question whether the villain was a man or a rat. We know that Grieg's music is not pink bonbons stuffed with snow, although we rather admire the aptness of the similarity and the sensuousness of the image. Yet when someone says of the music of Shostakovich that it is the "cacophonous scream of a communist manifesto," we wonder if that is not perhaps "true." We are delighted with the little girl who said that carbonated water tastes "like my foot's asleep," but when we say a dish we don't like is "garbage," it is indeed! When Byron says of poetry that it is the lava of the imagination which prevents an eruption, the metaphor strikes us as an amusing romantic definition of poetry; but when a contemporary writer (I have forgotten who) says that a poem is the sublimation of the social irritant which troubled the poet, just as a pearl is the "higher order" of the speck which irritated the oyster, we accept the metaphor as a statement of fact about all poetry.

The intricate and highly complex network making up the human nervous system has often been likened to a telephonic organization in which messages are sent out from central offices over the "wires" of the system to all areas of the organism. The analogy is a picturesque explanation of the way the human nervous system "seems to work." At the moment, the telephone metaphor is being supplanted by an electronic metaphor in a new system of efficiency called Cybernetics. In this system the mind is likened to a communication system which has its own "feedback," making possible automatic adjustments between what it imagines to be "out there" and what is really out there. But what the human nervous system will be likened to a century from now is unpredictable. New analogies will depend on future neurological theories and on future social, moral, and technological developments.

Most figurative language is not dangerous in its effects. It is when we take political and social metaphors literally, as statements of identities, that we must proceed with caution. Far more than we are aware, the way we use language determines what the social philosophy of our society shall be. When we take figurative language literally, we are in danger of behaving as if something were true which is manifestly not true *unless we proceed to make it so.* Orators disturbed with social conditions will see new relationships and will express them with vigor. The figure of the "brotherhood of man" arose out of the way the Age of Reason chose to look at its political situation; the figure was unusually far-reaching in its political effect.

Effect of Metaphor on Modern Behavior

Let us examine several current metaphors, stated or felt, which express "truths" of modern social beliefs and which, because they are often taken as identities, are in many ways responsible for modern social behavior.

1. Murray Schumach's extended figure of speech which appeared on the front page of The New York *Times* for February 26, 1946, is, to be sure, innocuous enough; moreover, it is an analogy which occurs to us as rather common, one which would seem to most people living in New York City to bear itself out in many exact ways:

Complete shutdown of the city's subways would be almost as disastrous to the city as a serious circulatory ailment to a human being. For New York's subways are her main veins and arteries, distributing her human corpuscles throughout the municipal body twenty-four hours a day.

Mr. Schumach had no ulterior motive, I am sure, in describing New York City in this fashion. I do not want to be misunderstood in what follows as saying that the authors of social metaphors are each and all conspirators against the public morale. Nor do I suggest that Mr. Schumach has caused the inhabitants of New York City to think of themselves as corpuscles. The idea had probably occurred to some people before. But I do suggest that the author of this figure has himself seen New York City in this way and that henceforth some of his readers will unconsciously identify *other* people in New York City as corpuscles. The effect of such metaphors is subtle. If the city is personified as a monstrous human being, and its inhabitants think of themselves as red and white corpuscles, presently, from their understanding of what red and white corpuscles do, they may be inclined to act as if they were, and that might or might not be a good thing; but if carried to extremes, the habit of behaving like a red corpuscle within a monstrous body will change the culture patterns of a society.

2. If it were not for the fact that a colleague of mine brought the following parallel to my attention, as a parallel that came spontaneously to his mind, I should consider it rather too far-fetched for inclusion in this essay. In the December 28, 1942 issue of *Life,* there is printed an extraordinary picture of Field Marshal Rommel's army retreating westward along the Mediterranean coast. The picture was photographed from a British plane, and it strongly resembles a slide of bacteria as seen under a microscope. New instruments, new inventions cause us to "see" things differently. In the *Life* picture we see thousands of men who look "exactly" *like* bacteria. The resemblance is so striking that for a moment we suspect an identity. If we say enough times that men are like or look like bacteria, and if we see enough pictures showing the resemblance, we shall soon begin to behave toward men as we behave toward bacteria. (One is reminded here, for example, of the rather widespread use of the phrase "to be immunized against totalitarian philos-

ophies.") Most important of all, from the social point of view, is the fact that our world is prepared in a great variety of ways to think of men as bacteria. Was it Robert Louis Stevenson who referred to humanity as a disease on the face of the earth? In any event, more than one sensitive person has taken Stevenson's metaphor literally and despaired.

3. I have often heard large cities referred to as jungles. The main characteristics of a jungle in darkest Africa, as I have read, are an amoral attitude toward all creatures outside the family, the need for alertness in order to survive, the constant feeling of insecurity, and the value of certain traits such as strength, cunning, and agility. Now it is quite possible that these are characteristics of modern city life, and in these respects, therefore, life in a city is like life in a jungle. This is, if true, and we suspect it is, unfortunate, for no one whom I know wants to live in a jungle. It is perfectly natural to think of a city as a jungle, perhaps, but the more we think of it in that way and the more we extend the analogy, the more likely it is that the city will *be* a jungle. At the moment, at any rate, a large city is not a "jungle," it is only in some respects like a jungle, and presumably the differences can be pointed out. When, therefore, we insist that the city *is* a jungle, we are no longer speaking figuratively, we are making a statement of moral fact; indeed, we are issuing (as did Upton Sinclair) a moral ultimatum.

4. Oswald Spengler was a master of intellectual analogy, perhaps the greatest of all time, certainly second to none in the modern world. *The Decline of the West* foretells the eventual demise of the western world, but the entire structure of Spengler's thesis rests on a metaphor. The organic theory of history is a figure of speech, which, simply put, says that a civilization is *like* a living creature—it is born, it grows, and it decays. But Spengler's book is no cause for pessimism, for a civilization is not identical with a living being, as will be seen when Spengler is as old as Homer. A civilization seems to be in some (pertinent, we admit) respects like a living being. But it should have occurred to someone long ago, and perhaps it did, that to take Spengler literally is to put all one's faith in the logic of "if." If one believes that the western world has entered upon a stage of decline, then what Spengler says about the western world is "true." If there were to take place an historical experience such as a "decline," it would perhaps happen as Spengler has described it. In fact, so long as we understand Spengler's analogies to be identities, so long shall we believe in, *and perhaps assist in,* the inevitable decline of the western world.[1]

5. One of the most pertinent of modern metaphors, one that seems to many young people to be an accurate description of our modern world is the analogy of the myth of Sisyphus with contemporary experience. Sisyphus was the mortal condemned by the gods for his sins to roll a stone to the top of a mountain from which the stone falls back down the mountain of its own weight, and Sisy-

---

[1] Talking about a "possible" future event will in itself tend to bring the event to pass. And the evidence selected to anticipate the event will direct the event to take the form foreseen. That people often behave according to the way they have expressed their expectations is brilliantly discussed by Robert K. Merton in his article "The Self-Fulfilling Prophecy," *Antioch Review*, 8.193ff (1948).

phus must again roll it to the top. The labor of Sisyphus goes on endlessly forever. Albert Camus, contemporary French novelist, and expositor of the "philosophy of the absurd," has written a philosophical work entitled *The Myth of Sisyphus,* and in this work he says, "The gods thought with some reason that there was no punishment more awful than useless and hopeless labor." Although Camus thinks of Sisyphus as a tragic hero, noble in his scorn of the gods, he also thinks of him as the absurd hero, and he likens the worker of today to Sisyphus. "The worker of today labors every day of his life at the same tasks and his destiny is no less absurd."

But the myth of Sisyphus is a story, as a moving picture is a story, as a ballad is a story, as an epic or a novel is a story. We often think of ourselves as "like" a character out of a novel or story. In fact, a whole nation of people (generally speaking) thought of themselves as "like" the Siegfried or Brunhild of Teutonic mythology. It is pleasant to some people to suspect that they have something in common with Siegfried, but if we say we *are* Siegfried, unless the whole world agrees with us, we are in trouble. We are not less in error if we take the myth of Sisyphus literally and say that we are Sisyphus, that we are absurd heroes engaged in "useless and hopeless labor." It is only too patently true that our world seems to be "like" the Hell of Sisyphus. But that our world *is* the Hell of Sisyphus and that we *are* doomed to hopeless labor is a fiction evolving out of an inferred identity which simply does not exist. Camus has used his parallel as a device for illuminating and criticizing the social world of today. If we take his figure literally, and especially if we take it without an understanding of its "tragic" implications, we are likely to be very unhappy if nothing more.

6. A good deal of theoretical discourse is diagrammatic in character. The Ptolemaic cosmology in the form of a diagram says only that as far as can be observed and inferred, the universe is "like" the diagram. Diagrammatic representations which are the results of inference and imaginative picturing forth of an idea cannot be tested empirically, and we must beware of seeing identities where they do not exist.[2]

To take the most illustrious modern example, I turn to the popularized psychology of Sigmund Freud. (But first I should like to point out that I have the greatest respect for Freud, and I should be the last to choose to discredit psychoanalysis. Only provincial prejudice finds Freud ridiculous and offensive.) Freud was a poet and a philosopher. Freud's work is one long extended figure of speech, as is the *Divine Comedy* of Dante. Both Dante and Freud have written allegories of the spiritual life. If there were a Hell, it might be "like" Dante's. I think it was Waldo Frank who said somewhere that if you believe in Hell, it makes a great deal of difference to you how many circles there "really are." If you take Freud literally, the true nature and character of "complexes" makes a great deal of difference; but what the analyst says in effect is that

[2] For an analysis of schematic, symbolic, and tropic "fictions" see Hans Vaihinger, *The Philosophy of "As if"* (London 1949), 24ff. In fact, Vaihinger's work is throughout a painstaking study of the consciously false assumptions which are implicit in most if not all metaphorical expressions. In many respects, my "Metaphor and Social Belief" is a kind of extended footnote to *The Philosophy of "As if."*

we act "as if" we had an Oepidus complex, supposing there were such a thing as an Oedipus complex, just as a physician might have said in the seventeenth century that his patient behaved as if he were a witch, supposing that there were such things as witches. But the "cure" for witches was different.

Freud was a philosopher whom many people have taken literally, assuming that the subconscious as Freud describes it is *identical* with some "part" of our "self." Freud's diagram of the Id, the Ego, and the Super-Ego is a schema which is metaphor useful merely in discussion. In *An Autobiographical Study* Freud warned against taking his schematic representations literally. "The subdivision of the unconscious is part of an attempt to picture the apparatus of the mind as being built up of a number of *functional systems* whose interrelations may be expressed in spatial terms, without reference, of course, to the actual anatomy of the brain." But many readers will take the image of the subconscious literally. We imagine the Id as a murky "depth" of turbulence somewhere at the bottom of the "mind," its poisonous fumes rising up from deep upon deep of mystery through the trap door of the censor at night when the censor is "asleep." The Ego, our every-day consciousness, lives on the first-floor of the mind, looks out of its windows, and conforms to the customs of the every-day world—the bewildered little man of the cartoon who always stands between two opposing forces. Above, at the "top" of our mind, is the Super-Ego, a kind of stern father who looks down upon our conscious behavior and issues commands.

Even professional analysts sometimes "think" in this manner; and amateur psychologists, as I have discovered, almost invariably do. It is impossible to know how much such a "metaphor" has affected the common reader in his attitudes toward life, but it is fairly certain that many have taken the figure of the subconscious literally, saying that this is the way the mind works. On the contrary, we should say that our inner life seems only in some respects to be *like* the Freudian description.

7. Drawing analogies between the subject-matter of zoology and biology and the subject-matter of the social sciences has been very popular in recent years among some social thinkers. It has been fashionable to think of men as animals and even as insects. One of the most common parallels drawn by fascist theorizers is the parallel between men and ants. I recall magazine articles describing Nazi scientists observing ant societies in order to discover how human society may most easily be converted into a society similar to (or identical with) that of the white ant of Africa.

The propagandistic use of the ant metaphor has been most vividly described by a character in Arthur Koestler's novel *Arrival and Departure*. In the enthusiasm with which Koestler's Nazi speaks, we see among other things that the language he uses has convinced him beyond any doubt of the desirability of understanding that ants and men are, for political purposes, identical. When, as in Nazi Germany, men are likened to ants, then beyond question men will be treated as though they were ants. Whatever is thinkable is also possible in the world of today.

Absolute conditioning must finally result in the creation of a collective consciousness in the full biological sense of the term. Nature has a perfect working model for it in the city-states of the African white ant. They each embrace several million members of the race, they cover areas up to fifty square miles and function with absolute expediency. They have perfect division of labor; they control highly complicated technical devices including a system of heating by vegetable fermentation which keeps the temperature in their vaults constant through all seasons; they enforce a mathematically perfect birthrate policy. And yet they have no planning body, no blue-prints, no governing administration, not even the means of written communication. How is this possible? The answer usually given is "by instinct"; but such a highly differentiated instinct which is shared by, and limited to, members of one city-state amounts to nothing less than a collective brain-function of the state organism. In a similar way, and probably helped by artificially-produced biological mutations, the individuals in the supra-state will become mere cells in an organism of a higher order—a million-legged, million-armed cyclopean colossus. . . .

8. It is apparent from the illustrations I have used that our contemporary social similitudes are often drawn from the biological sciences. The master metaphor of the modern world, however, is drawn from technology and is the identification of men with machines.

In our thinking we often, nay almost invariably, make the distinguished blunder of supposing that the human body is a machine, that it works as a machine works, according to the laws of mechanics. *Why* we prefer to "think" in this way about ourselves is open to speculation. In any event, that we should be unaware of the simple fact that men are only in a few unimportant respects like machines, but that machines are, *as far as they go,* in all respects like men is the supreme misunderstanding of our time and accounts almost exclusively for our lack, just when we need it most, of a real humanistic philosophy. The obvious fact is that machines are like men for the simple reason that man made the machine, as far as he could, *in his own image.* It would be unpleasing to some ears to have it said that man left out a soul when he made the machine, but that, or something very like that, is precisely what happened.

In recent years the machine has been perfected to perform uncanny tasks, the most striking being the calculation and solution of involved mathematical problems. The electronic brain has its place in the imaginations of men as the Most High. Presently we shall wish that our nerve cells were as clever as electron tubes, quite forgetting that it was our nerve cells that had the wit to create electron tubes.

Make no mistake about it, we think more highly of our machines than we do of ourselves. We try to live up to the machine, to learn from the machine, to be more nearly machines, because we think they are better than we are.[3] It appears that our dearest wish is to *be* machines and to function wholly as they do. This wish will strike future ages as the dominating feature of a lost society, of a deluded people who worshipped their engines more than their gods, to say nothing of themselves.

[3] While preparing this article for publication, the writer was introduced to *Dianetics* by L. Ronald Hubbard (New York 1950). In this "modern science of mental health" would appear to be the most appalling example yet of the identification of men with machines. Constructed in the name of efficiency, the central theme of *Dianetics* depends on the fiction that a human being is a calculating machine capable of functioning in a 100 per cent mechanical fashion.

But creative writers and some social philosophers have been saying all this for more than a hundred years. There is little excuse for me to labor the point. All I wish to insist upon is that the way we use language may account in part for our madness. The moment we say that the human being *is* a machine, at that moment we shall believe that the human being can be conditioned to behave in a perfectly predictable way with admirable regularity. Then it is that we shall have made of ourselves something less, ever so much less, than we are. But if we speak with caution to the effect that machines are *in some respects* like human beings, we can put the machine to its good use and still keep our self-respect and our humanity.

If ever we needed to think of man as man, as unique, identical with nothing else in the world, it is today. Contemporary imagery is blurred and confused. Our hardest intellectual task is to keep things apart, to separate out issues and ideas from one another. Our present efforts are to see all particulars as alike, and we tend to force identities where only similarities exist. No two things are identical, although we seem to want to think so. We have abandoned the exact and differentiated in favor of mingled associations and blurred relationships. The use of analogy in all branches of human thought is indispensable; but the making of nice distinctions is equally important and has ever been a leading characteristic of the human mind. The knowledge of subtle differences—as between people of different cultures, between one human being and another, or even between brands of coffee, kinds of perfumes, vintages in wines, spoiled food and edible food, poison and medicine, beauty and ugliness, justice and injustice—is a knowledge invaluable to mankind. What is more, the knowledge of differences leads to an understanding of relationships. We are more likely to be at home in our world not so much by striving to cut each particular to the same pattern, as by studying to understand the tenuous, the subtle, the often beautiful relationships which are the foundations of human society and to a great extent the joy of life. The knowledge of just and workable relationships among dissimilars is what every philosopher, every artist, and every statesman has longed to attain.

DOVER BEACH
by Matthew Arnold

The sea is calm to-night,
The tide is full, the moon lies fair
Upon the straits;—on the French coast the light
Gleams and is gone; the cliffs of England stand,
Glimmering and vast, out in the tranquil bay.
Come to the window, sweet is the night-air!
Only, from the long line of spray
Where the sea meets the moon-blanched land.
Listen! you hear the grating roar
Of pebbles which the waves draw back, and fling,
At their return, up the high strand,
Begin, and cease, and then again begin,
With tremulous cadence slow, and bring
The eternal note of sadness in.

Sophocles long ago
Heard it on the Aegaean, and it brought
Into his mind the turbid ebb and flow
Of human misery; we
Find also in the sound a thought,
Hearing it by this distant northern sea.

The Sea of Faith
Was once, too, at the full, and round earth's shore
Lay like the folds of a bright girdle furled.
But now I only hear
Its melancholy, long, withdrawing roar,
Retreating, to the breath
Of the night-wind, down the vast edges drear
And naked shingles of the world.
Ah, love, let us be true
To one another! for the world, which seems
To lie before us like a land of dreams,
So various, so beautiful, so new,
Hath really neither joy, nor love, nor light,
Nor certitude, nor peace, nor help for pain;
And we are here as on a darkling plain
Swept with confused alarms of struggle and flight,
Where ignorant armies clash by night.

THE PROBLEM OF UNBELIEF
by Walter Lippmann

1. Whirl Is King

AMONG THOSE who no longer believe in the religion of their fathers, some are proudly defiant, and many are indifferent. But there are also a few, perhaps an increasing number, who feel that there is a vacancy in their lives. This inquiry deals with their problem. It is not intended to disturb the serenity of those who are unshaken in the faith they hold, and it is not concerned with those who are still exhilarated by their escape from some stale orthodoxy. It is concerned with those who are perplexed by the consequences of their own irreligion. It deals with the

From Walter Lippmann, *A Preface to Morals*. By permission of The Macmillan Company, publishers.

problem of unbelief, not as believers are accustomed to deal with it, in the spirit of men confidently calling the lost sheep back into the fold, but as unbelievers themselves must, I think, face the problem if they face it candidly and without presumption.

When such men put their feelings into words they are likely to say that, having lost their faith, they have lost the certainty that their lives are significant, and that it matters what they do with their lives. If they deal with young people they are likely to say that they know of no compelling reason which certifies the moral code they adhere to, and that, therefore, their own preferences, when tested by the ruthless curiosity of their children, seem to have no sure foundation of any kind. They are likely to point to the world about them, and to ask whether the modern man possesses any criterion by which he can measure the value of his own desires, whether there is any standard he really believes in which permits him to put a term upon that pursuit of money, of power, and of excitement which has created so much of the turmoil and the squalor and the explosiveness of modern civilization.

These are, perhaps, merely the rationalizations of the modern man's discontent. At the heart of it there are likely to be moments of blank misgiving in which he finds that the civilization of which he is a part leaves a dusty taste in his mouth. He may be very busy with many things, but he discovers one day that he is no longer sure they are worth doing. He has been much preoccupied; but he is no longer sure he knows why. He has become involved in an elaborate routine of pleasures; and they do not seem to amuse him very much. He finds it hard to believe that doing any one thing is better than doing any other thing, or, in fact, that it is better than doing nothing at all. It occurs to him that it is a great deal of trouble to live, and that even in the best of lives the thrills are few and far between. He begins more or less consciously to seek satisfactions, because he is no longer satisfied, and all the while he realizes that the pursuit of happiness was always a most unhappy quest. In the later stages of his woe he not only loses his appetite, but becomes excessively miserable trying to recover it. And then, surveying the flux of events and the giddiness of his own soul, he comes to feel that Aristophanes must have been thinking of him when he declared that "Whirl is King, having driven out Zeus."

2. False Prophecies

The modern age has been rich both in prophecies that men would at last inherit the kingdoms of this world, and in complaints at the kind of world they inherited. Thus Petrarch, who was an early victim of modernity, came to feel that he would "have preferred to be born in any other period" than his own; he tells us that he sought an escape by imagining that he lived in some other age. The Nineteenth Century, which begat us, was forever blowing the trumpets of freedom and providing asylums in which its most sensitive children could take refuge. Wordsworth fled from mankind to rejoice in nature. Chateaubriand fled from man to rejoice in savages. Byron fled to an imaginary Greece, and William Morris to the Middle Ages. A few tried an imaginary India. A few an equally imaginary China. Many fled to Bohemia, to Utopia, to the Golden West, and to the Latin

Quarter, and some, like James Thomson, to hell where they were

> gratified to gain
> That positive eternity of pain
> Instead of this insufferable inane.

They had all been disappointed by the failure of a great prophecy. The theme of this prophecy had been that man is a beautiful soul who in the course of history had somehow become enslaved by

> Scepters, tiaras, swords, and chains, and tomes
> Of reasoned wrong, glozed on by ignorance,

and they believed with Shelley that when "the loathsome mask has fallen," man, exempt from awe, worship, degree, the king over himself, would then be "free from guilt or pain." This was the orthodox liberalism to which men turned when they had lost the religion of their fathers. But the promises of liberalism have not been fulfilled. We are living in the midst of that vast dissolution of ancient habits which the emancipators believed would restore our birthright of happiness. We know now that they did not see very clearly beyond the evils against which they were rebelling. It is evident to us that their prophecies were pleasant fantasies which concealed the greater difficulties that confront men, when having won the freedom to do what they wish—that wish, as Byron said:

> which ages have not yet subdued
> In man—to have no master save his mood,

they are full of contrary moods and do not know what they wish to do. We have come to see that Huxley was right when he said that "a man's worst difficulties begin when he is able to do as he likes."

The evidences of these greater difficulties lie all about us: in the brave and brilliant atheists who have defied the Methodist God, and have become very nervous; in the women who have emancipated themselves from the tyranny of fathers, husbands, and homes, and with the intermittent but expensive help of a psychoanalyst, are now enduring liberty as interior decorators; in the young men and women who are world-weary at twenty-two; in the multitudes who drug themselves with pleasure; in the crowds enfranchised by the blood of heroes who cannot be persuaded to take an interest in their destiny; in the millions, at last free to think without fear of priest or policeman, who have made the moving pictures and the popular newspapers what they are.

These are the prisoners who have been released. They ought to be very happy. They ought to be serene and composed. They are free to make their own lives. There are no conventions, no tabus, no gods, priests, princes, fathers, or revelations which they must accept. Yet the result is not so good as they thought it would be. The prison door is wide open. They stagger out into trackless space under a blinding sun. They find it nerve-racking. "My sensibility," said Flaubert, "is sharper than a razor's edge; the creaking of a door, the face of a bourgeois, an absurd statement set my heart to throbbing and completely upset me." They must find their own courage for battle and their own consolation in defeat. They complain, like Renan after he had broken with the Church, that the enchanted circle which embraced the whole of life is broken, and that they are left with a feeling of emptiness "like that which follows an attack of fever or an unhappy love affair." Where is my *home?* cried Nietzsche: "For it do I ask and seek, and have sought, but have not found it. O eternal everywhere, O eternal nowhere, O eternal in vain."

To more placid temperaments the pangs of freedom are no doubt less acute. It is possible for multitudes in time of peace and security to exist agreeably—somewhat incoherently, perhaps, but without convulsions—to dream a little and not unpleasantly, to have only now and then a nightmare, and only occasionally a rude awakening. It is possible to drift along not too discontentedly, somewhat nervously, somewhat anxiously, somewhat confusedly, hoping for the best, and believing in nothing very much. It is possible to be a passable citizen. But it is not possible to be wholly at peace. For serenity of soul requires some better organization of life than a man can attain by pursuing his casual ambitions, satisfying his hungers, and for the rest accepting destiny as an idiot's tale in which one dumb sensation succeeds another to no known end. And it is not possible for him to be wholly alive. For that depends upon his sense of being completely engaged with the world, with all his passions and all the faculties in rich harmonies with one other, and in deep rhythm with the nature of things.

These are the gifts of a vital religion which can bring the whole of a man into adjustment with the whole of his relevant experience. Our forefathers had such a religion. They quarreled a good deal about the details, but they had no doubt that there was an order in the universe which justified their lives because they were a part of it. The acids of modernity have dissolved that order for many of us, and there are some in consequence who think that the needs which religion fulfilled have also been dissolved. But however self-sufficient the eugenic and perfectly educated man of the distant future may be, our present experience is that the needs remain. In failing to meet them, it is plain that we have succeeded only in substituting trivial illusions for majestic faiths. For while the modern emancipated man may wonder how anyone ever believed that in this universe of stars and atoms and multitudinous life, there is a drama in progress of which the principal event was enacted in Palestine nineteen hundred years ago, it is not really a stranger fable than many which he so readily accepts. He does not believe the words of the Gospel but he believes the best-advertised notion. The older fable may be incredible today, but when it was credible it bound together the whole of experience upon a stately and dignified theme. The modern man has ceased to believe in it but he has not ceased to be credulous, and the need to believe haunts him. It is no wonder that his impulse is to turn back from his freedom, and to find someone who says he knows the truth and can tell him what to do, to find the shrine of some new god, of any cult however newfangled, where he can kneel and be comforted, put on manacles to keep his hands from trembling, ensconce himself in some citadel where it is safe and warm.

For the modern man who has ceased to believe, without ceasing to be credulous, hangs, as it were, between heaven and earth, and is at rest nowhere. There is no theory of the meaning and value of events which he is compelled to accept, but he is none the less compelled to accept the events. There is no moral authority to which he must turn now, but there is coercion in opinions, fashions and fads. There is for him no inevitable purpose in the universe, but there are elaborate necessities, physical, political, economic. He does not feel himself to be an actor in a great and dramatic destiny, but he is subject to the massive powers of our civilization, forced to adopt their pace, bound to their routine, entangled in their conflicts. He can believe what he chooses about this civilization. He cannot, however, escape the compulsion of modern events. They compel his body and his senses as ruthlessly as ever did king or priest. They do not compel his mind. They have all the force of natural events, but not their majesty, all the tyrannical power of ancient institutions, but none of their moral certainty. Events are there, and they overpower him. But they do not convince him that they have that dignity which inheres in that which is necessary and in the nature of things.

In the old order the compulsions were often painful, but there was sense in the pain that was inflicted by the will of an all-knowing God. In the new order the compulsions are painful and, as it were, accidental, unnecessary, wanton, and full of mockery. The modern man does not make his peace with them. For in effect he has replaced natural piety with a grudging endurance of a series of unsanctified compulsions. When he believed that the unfolding of events was a manifestation of the will of God, he could say: Thy will be done. . . . In His will is our peace. But when he believes that events are determined by the votes of a majority, the orders of his bosses, the opinions of his neighbors, the laws of supply and demand, and the decisions of quite selfish men, he yields because he has to yield. He is conquered but unconvinced.

3. Sorties and Retreats

It might seem as if, in all this, men were merely going through once again what they have often gone through before. This is not the first age in which the orthodox religion has been in conflict with the science of the day. Plato was born into such an age. For two centuries the philosophers of Greece had been critical of Homer and of the popular gods, and when Socrates faced his accusers, his answer to the accusation of heresy must certainly have sounded unresponsive. "I do believe," he said, "that there are gods, and in a higher sense than that in which my accusers believe in them." That is all very well. But to believe in a "higher sense" is also to believe in a different sense.

There is nothing new in the fact that men have ceased to believe in the religion of their fathers. In the history of Catholic Christianity, there has always existed a tradition, extending from the author of the Fourth Gospel through Origen to the neo-Platonists of modern times, which rejects the popular idea of God as a power acting upon events, and of immortality as everlasting life, and translates the popular theology into a symbolic statement of a purely spiritual experience. In every civilized age there have been educated and discerning men who could not accept literally and simply the traditions of the ancient faith. We are told that during the Periclean Age "among educated men everything was in dispute: political sanctions, literary values, moral standards, religious convictions, even the possibility of reaching any truth about anything." When the educated classes of the Roman world accepted Christianity they had ceased to believe in the pagan gods, and were much too critical to accept the primitive Hebraic theories of the creation, the redemption, and the Messianic Kingdom which were so central in the popular religion. They had to do what Socrates had done; they had to take the popular theology in a "higher" and therefore in a different sense before they could use it. Indeed, it is so unusual to find an age of active-minded men in which the most highly educated are genuinely orthodox in the popular sense, that the Thirteenth Century, the age of Dante and St. Thomas Aquinas, when this phenomenon is reputed to have occurred, is regarded as a unique and wonderful period in the history of the world. It is not at all unlikely that there never was such an age in the history of civilized men.

And yet, the position of modern men who have broken with the religion of their fathers is in certain profound ways different from that of other men in other ages. This is the first age, I think, in the history of mankind when the circumstances of life have conspired with the intellectual habits of the time to render any fixed and authoritative belief incredible to large masses of men. The dissolution of the old modes of thought has gone so far, and is so cumulative in its effect, that the modern man is not able to sink back after a period of prophesying into a new but stable orthodoxy. The irreligion of the modern world is radical to a degree for which there is, I think, no counterpart. For always in the past it has been possible for new conventions to crystallize, and for men to find rest and surcease of effort in accepting them.

We often assume, therefore, that a period of dissolution will necessarily be followed by one of conformity, that the heterodoxy of one age will become the orthodoxy of the next, and that when this orthodoxy decays a new period of prophesying will begin. Thus we say that by the time of Hosea and Isaiah the religion of the Jews had become a system of rules for transacting business with Jehovah. The Prophets then revivified it by thundering against the conventional belief that religion was mere burnt offering and sacrifice. A few centuries passed and the religion based on the Law and the Prophets had in its turn become a set of mechanical rites manipulated by the Scribes and the Pharisees. As against this system Jesus and Paul preached a religion of grace, and against the "letter" of the synagogues the "spirit" of Christ. But the inner light which can perceive the spirit is rare, and so shortly after the death of Paul, the teaching gradually ceased to appeal to direct inspiration in the minds of the believers and became a body of dogma, a "sacred deposit" of the faith "once for all delivered to the saints." In the succeeding ages there appeared again many prophets who thought they had within them the revealing spirit. Though some of the prophets were burnt, much of the prophesying was absorbed into the canon. In Luther this sense of revelation appeared once more in a most confident form. He rejected the authority not only of the Pope and the clergy, but even of the Bible itself, except where in his opinion the Bible confirmed his faith. But in the establishment of a Lutheran Church the old difficulty reappeared: the inner light which had burned so fiercely in Luther did not burn brightly or steadily in all Lutherans, and so the right of private judgment, even in Luther's restricted use of the term, led to all kinds of heresies and abominations. Very soon there came to be an authoritative teaching backed by the power of the police. And in Calvinism the revolt of the Reformation became stabilized to the last degree. "Everything," said Calvin, "pertaining to the perfect rule of a good life the Lord has so comprehended in His law that there remains nothing for man to add to that summary."

Men fully as intelligent as the most emancipated among us once believed that, and I have no doubt that the successors of Mr. Darrow and Mr. Mencken would come to believe something very much like it if conditions permitted them to obey the instinct to retreat from the chaos of modernity into order and certainty. It is all very well to talk about being the captain of your soul. It is hard, and only a few heroes, saints, and geniuses have been the captains of their souls for any extended period of their lives. Most men, after a little freedom, have preferred authority with the consoling assurances and the economy of effort which it brings. "If, outside of Christ, you wish by your own thoughts to know your relation to God, you will break your neck. Thunder strikes him who examines." Thus spoke Martin Luther, and there is every reason to suppose that the German people thought he was talking the plainest common sense. "He who is gifted with the heavenly knowledge of faith," said the Council of Trent, "is free from an inquisitive curiosity." These words are rasping to our modern ears, but there is no occasion to doubt that the men who uttered them had made a shrewd appraisal of average human nature. The record of experience is one of sorties and retreats. The search for moral guidance which shall not depend upon external authority has invariably ended in the acknowledgment of some new authority.

4. Deep Dissolution

This same tendency manifests itself in the midst of our modern uneasiness. We have had a profusion of new cults, of revivals, and of essays in reconstruction. But there is reason for thinking that a new crystallization of an enduring and popular religion is unlikely in the modern world. For analogy drawn from the experience of the past is misleading. When Luther, for example, rebelled against the authority of the Church, he did not suppose the way of life for the ordinary man would be radically altered. Luther supposed that men would continue to behave much as they had learned to behave under the Catholic discipline. The individual for whom he claimed the right of private judgment was one whose prejudgments had been well fixed in a Catholic society. The authority of the Pope was to be destroyed and certain evils abolished, but there was to remain that feeling for objective moral certainties which Catholicism had nurtured. When the Anabaptists carried the practice of his theory beyond this point, Luther denounced them violently. For what he believed in was Protestantism for good Catholics. The reformers of the Eighteenth Century made a similar assumption. They really believed in democracy for men who had an aristocratic training. Jefferson, for example, had an instinctive fear of the urban rabble, that most democratic part of the population. The society of free men which he dreamed about was composed of those who had the discipline, the standards of honor and the taste, without the privileges or the corruptions, that are to be found in a society of well-bred country gentlemen.

The more recent rebels frequently betray a somewhat similar inability to imagine the consequences of their own victories. For the smashing of idols is in itself such a preoccupation that it is almost impossible for the iconoclast to look clearly into a future when there will not be many idols left to smash. Yet that future is beginning to be our present, and it might be said that men are conscious of what modernity means insofar as they realize that they are confronted not so much with the necessity of promoting rebellion as of dealing with the consequences of it. The Nineteenth Century, roughly speaking the time between Voltaire and Mencken, was an age of terrific indictments and of feeble solutions. The Marxian indictment of capitalism is a case in point. The Nietzschean transvaluation of values is another; it is magnificent, but who can say, after he has shot his arrow of longing to the other shore, whether he will find Caesar Borgia, Henry Ford, or Isadora Duncan? Who knows, having read Mr. Mencken and Mr. Sinclair Lewis, what kind of world will be left when all the boobs and yokels have crawled back in their holes and have died of shame?

The rebel, while he is making his attack, is not likely to feel the need to answer such questions. For he moves in an unreal environment, one might almost say a parasitic environment. He goes forth to destroy Caesar, Mammon, George F. Babbitt, and Mrs. Grundy. As he wrestles with these demons, he leans upon them. By inversion they offer him much the same kind of support which the conformer enjoys. They provide him with an objective which enables him to know exactly what he thinks he wants to do. His energies are focused by his indignation. He does not suffer from emptiness, doubt, and division of soul. These are the maladies which come later when the struggle is over. While the rebel is in conflict with the established nuisances he has an aim in life which absorbs all his passions. He has his own sense of righteousness and his own feeling of communion with a grand purpose. For in attacking idols there is a kind of piety, in overthrowing tyrants a kind of loyalty, in ridiculing stupidities an imitation of wisdom. In the heat of battle the rebel is exalted by a wholehearted tension which is easily mistaken for a taste of the freedom that is to come. He is under the spell of an illusion. For what comes after the struggle is not the exaltation of freedom but a letting down of the tension that belongs solely to the struggle itself. The happiness of the rebel is as transient as the iconoclasm which produced it. When he has slain the dragon and rescued the beautiful maiden, there is usually nothing left for him to do but write his memoirs and dream of a time when the world was young.

What most distinguishes the generation who have approached maturity since the debacle of idealism at the end of the War is not their rebellion against the religion and the moral code of their parents, but their disillusionment with their own rebellion. It is common for young men and women to rebel, but that they should rebel sadly and without faith in their own rebellion, that they should distrust the new freedom no less than the old certainties—that is something of a novelty. As Mr. Canby once said, at the age of seven they saw through their parents and characterized them in a phrase. At fourteen they saw through education and dodged it. At eighteen they saw through morality and stepped over it. At twenty they lost respect for their home towns, and at twenty-one they discovered that our social system is ridiculous. At twenty-three the autobiography ends because the author has run through society to date and does not know what to do next. For, as Mr. Canby might have added, the idea of reforming that society makes no appeal to them. They have seen through all that. They cannot adopt any of the synthetic religions of the Nineteenth Century. They have seen through all of them.

They have seen through the religion of nature to which the early romantics turned for consolation. They have heard too much about the brutality of natural selection to feel, as Wordsworth did, that pleasant landscapes are divine. They have seen through the religion of beauty because, for one thing, they are too much oppressed by the ugliness of Main Street. They cannot take refuge in an ivory tower because the modern apartment house, with a radio loudspeaker on the floor above and on the floor below and just across the courtyard, will not permit it. They cannot, like Mazzini, make a religion of patriotism, because they have just been demobilized. They cannot make a religion of science like the post-Darwinians because they do not understand modern science. They never learned enough mathematics and physics. They do not like Bernard Shaw's religion of creative evolution because they have read enough to know that Mr. Shaw's biology is literary and evangelical. As for the religion of progress, that is pre-empted by George F. Babbitt and the Rotary Club, and the religion of humanity is utterly unacceptable to those who have to ride in the subways during the rush hour.

Yet the current attempts to modernize religious creeds are inspired by the hope that somehow it will be possible to construct a form of belief which will fit into this vacuum. It is evident that life soon becomes distracted and tiresome if it is not illuminated by communion with what William James called "a wider self through which saving experiences come." The eager search for new religions, the hasty adherence to cults, and the urgent appeals for a reconciliation between religion and science are confessions that to the modern man his activity seems to have no place in any rational order. His life seems mere restlessness and compulsion, rather than conduct lighted by luminous beliefs. He is possessed by a great deal of excitement amidst which, as Mr. Santayana once remarked, he redoubles his effort when he has forgotten his aim.

For in the modern age, at first imperceptibly with the rise of the towns, and then catastrophically since the mechanical revolution, there have gone into dissolution not only the current orthodoxy, but the social order and the ways of living which supported it. Thus rebellion and emancipation have come to mean something far more drastic than they have ever meant before. The earlier rebels summoned men from one allegiance to another, but the feeling for certainty in religion and for decorum in society persisted. In the modern world it is this very feeling of certainty itself which is dissolving. It is dissolving not merely for an educated minority but for everyone who comes within the orbit of modernity.

Yet there remain the wants which orthodoxy of some sort satisfies. The natural man, when he is released from restraints, and has no substitute for them, is at sixes and sevens with himself and the world. For in the free play of his uninhabited instincts he does not find any natural substitute for those accumulated convictions which, however badly they did it, nevertheless organized his soul, economized his effort, consoled him, and gave him dignity in his own eyes because he was part of some greater whole. The acids of modernity are so powerful that they do not tolerate a crystallization of ideas which will serve as a new orthodoxy into which men can retreat. And so the modern world is haunted by a realization, which it becomes constantly less easy to ignore, that it is impossible to reconstruct an enduring orthodoxy, and impossible to live well without the satisfactions which an orthodoxy would provide.

WHAT I BELIEVE

by E. M. Forster

I do not believe in belief. But this is an age of faith, in which one is surrounded by so many militant creeds that, in self-defense, one has to formulate a creed of one's own. Tolerance, good temper, and sympathy are no longer enough in a world which is rent by religious and racial persecution, in a world where ignorance rules, and science, which ought to have ruled, plays the subservient pimp. Tolerance, good temper, and sympathy—well, they are what matter really, and if the human race is not to collapse they must come to the front before long. But for the moment they don't seem enough; their action is no stronger than a flower battered beneath a military jack-boot. They want stiffening, even if the process coarsens them. Faith, to my mind, is a stiffening process, a sort of mental starch, which ought to be applied as sparingly as possible. I dislike the stuff. I do not believe in it, for its own sake, at all. My lawgivers are Erasmus and Montaigne, not Moses and St. Paul. My temple stands not upon Mount Moriah but in that Elysian Field where even the immoral are admitted.

I have, however, to live in an Age of Faith—the sort of thing I used to hear praised and recommended when I was a boy. It is damned unpleasant, really. It is bloody in every sense of the word. And I have to keep my end up in it. Where do I start?

With personal relationships. Here is something comparatively solid in a world full of violence and cruelty. Not absolutely solid, for psychology has split and shattered the idea of a "person" and has shown that there is something incalculable in each of us, which may at any moment rise to the surface and destroy our normal balance. We don't know what we're like. We can't know what we're like. We can't know what other people are like. How then can we put any trust in personal relationships, or cling to them in the gathering political storm? In theory we can't. But in practice we can and do. For the purpose of living one has to assume that the personality is solid, and the "self" is an entity, and to ignore all contrary evidence. And since to ignore evidence is one of the characteristics of faith, I certainly can proclaim that I believe in personal relationships.

Starting from them, I get a little order into the contemporary chaos. One must be fond of people and trust them if one isn't to make a mess of life, and it is therefore essential that they shouldn't let one down. They often do. The moral of which is that I must, myself, be as reliable as possible, and this I try to be. But reliability isn't a matter of contract. It is a matter for the heart, which signs no documents. In other words, reliability is impossible unless there is a natural warmth. Most men possess this warmth, though they often have bad luck and get chilled. Personal relationships are despised today. They are regarded as bourgeois luxuries, as products of a time of fair weather which has now passed, and we are urged to get rid of them, and to dedicate ourselves to some movement or cause instead. I hate the idea of dying for a cause, and if I had to choose between betraying my country

Copyright, 1939, by Simon and Schuster, Inc. Reprinted by permission of the publishers.

and betraying my friend, I hope I should have the guts to betray my country. Such a choice may scandalize the modern reader, and he may stretch out his patriotic hand to the telephone at once, and ring up the police. It wouldn't have shocked Dante, though. Dante placed Brutus and Cassius in the lowest circle of Hell because they had chosen to betray their friend Julius Caesar, rather than their country, Rome.

This brings me along to democracy, "even Love, the Beloved Republic, which feeds upon Freedom and lives." Democracy isn't a beloved republic really, and never will be. But it is less hateful than other contemporary forms of government, and to that extent it deserves our support. It does start from the assumption that the individual is important, and that all types are needed to make a civilization. It doesn't divide its citizens into the bossers and the bossed, as an efficiency-regime tends to do. The people I admire most are those who are sensitive and want to create something or discover something, and don't see life in terms of power, and such people get more of a chance under a democracy than elsewhere. They found religions, great or small, or they produce literature and art, or they do disinterested scientific research, or they may be what are called "ordinary people," who are creative in their private lives, bring up their children decently, for instance, or help their neighbors. All these people need to express themselves, they can't do so unless society allows them liberty to do so, and the society which allows them most liberty is a democracy.

Democracy has another merit. It allows criticism, and if there isn't public criticism there are bound to be hushed-up scandals.

That is why I believe in the press, despite all its lies and vulgarity, and why I believe in Parliament. The British Parliament is often sneered at because it's a talking-shop. Well, I believe in it *because* it is a talking-shop. I believe in the Private Member who makes himself a nuisance. He gets snubbed and is told that he is cranky or ill-informed, but he exposes abuses which would otherwise never have been mentioned, and very often an abuse gets put right just by being mentioned. Occasionally, too, in my country, a well-meaning public official loses his head in the cause of efficiency, and thinks himself God Almighty. Such officials are particularly frequent in the Home Office. Well, there will be questions about them in Parliament sooner or later, and then they'll have to mend their ways. Whether Parliament is either a representative body or an efficient one is very doubtful, but I value it because it criticizes and talks, and because its chatter gets widely reported.

So two cheers for democracy: one because it admits variety and one because it permits criticism. Two cheers are quite enough: there is no occasion to give three. Only Love, the Beloved Republic, deserves that.

What about force, though? While we are trying to be sensitive and advanced and affectionate and tolerant, an unpleasant question pops up; doesn't all society rest upon force? If a government can't count upon the police and the army how can it hope to rule? And if an individual gets knocked on the head or sent to a labor camp, of what significance are his opinions?

This dilemma doesn't worry me as much as it does some. I realize that all society rests upon force. But all the great creative actions, all the decent human relations, occur during the intervals when force has not managed to come to the front. These intervals are what matter. I want them to be as frequent and as lengthy as possible, and I call them "civilization." Some people idealize force and pull it into the foreground and worship it, instead of keeping it in the background as long as possible. I think they make a mistake, and I think that their opposites, the mystics, err even more when they declare that force doesn't exist. I believe that it does exist, and that one of our jobs is to prevent it from getting out of its box. It gets out sooner or later, and then it destroys us and all the lovely things which we have made. But it isn't out all the time, for the fortunate reason that the strong are so stupid. Consider their conduct for a moment in the Niebelungs' Ring. The giants there have the gold, or in other words the guns; but they do nothing with it, they do not realize that they are all-powerful, with the result that the catastrophe is delayed and the castle of Valhalla, insecure but glorious, fronts the storms for generations. Fafnir, coiled round his hoard, grumbles and grunts; we can hear him under Europe today; the leaves of the wood already tremble, and the Bird calls its warnings uselessly. Fafnir will destroy us, but by a blessed dispensation he is stupid and slow, and creation goes on just outside the poisonous blast of his breath. The Nietzschean would hurry the monster up, the mystic would say he didn't exist, but Wotan, wiser than either, hastens to create warriors before doom declares itself. The Valkyries are symbols not only of courage but of intelligence; they represent the human spirit snatching its opportunity while the going is good, and one of them even finds time to love. Brunhilde's last song hymns the recurrence of love, and since it is the privilege of art to exaggerate, she goes even further and proclaims the love which is eternally triumphant and feeds upon Freedom, and lives.

So that is what I feel about force and violence. I look the other way until fate strikes me. Whether this is due to courage or to cowardice in my own case I cannot be sure. But I know that if men hadn't looked the other way in the past nothing of any value would survive. The people I respect most behave as if they were immortal and as if society were eternal. Both assumptions are false: both of them must be accepted as true if we are to go on eating and working and loving, and are to keep open a few breathing holes for the human spirit. No millennium seems likely to descend upon humanity; no better and stronger League of Nations will be instituted; no form of Christianity and no alternative to Christianity will bring peace to the world or integrity to the individual; no "change of heart" will occur. And yet we needn't despair, indeed we cannot despair; the evidence of history shows us that men have always insisted on behaving creatively under the shadow of the sword, and that we had better follow their example under the shadow of the airplanes.

There is of course hero worship, fervently recommended as a panacea in some quarters. But here we shall get no help. Hero worship is a dangerous vice, and one of the minor merits of a democracy is that it does not encourage it, or produce that unmanageable type of citizen known as the Great Man. It produces instead different kinds of small men, and that's a much finer achievement. But people who can't get interested in the variety of life and can't make up their own minds get discontented over this, and they long for a hero to bow down before and to follow blindly. It's significant that a hero is an integral part of the authoritarian stock-in-trade today. An efficiency-regime can't be run without a few heroes stuck about to carry off the dullness—much as plums have to be put into a bad pudding to make it palatable. One hero at the top and a smaller one each side of him is a favorite arrangement, and the timid and the bored are comforted by such a trinity and, bowing down, feel exalted by it.

No, I distrust Great Men. They produce a desert of uniformity around them and often a pool of blood, too, and I always feel a little man's pleasure when they come a cropper. I believe in aristocracy though—if that's the right word, and if a democrat may use it. Not an aristocracy of power, based upon rank and influence, but an aristocracy of the sensitive, the considerate, and the plucky. Its members are to be found in all nations and classes, and all through the ages, and there is a secret understanding between them when they meet. They represent the true human tradition, the one permanent victory of our queer race over cruelty and chaos. Thousands of them perish in obscurity; a few are great names. They are sensitive for others as well as for themselves, they are considerate without being fussy, their pluck is not swankiness but the power to endure, and they can take a joke. I give no examples—it is risky to do that—but the reader may as well consider whether this is the type of person he would like to meet and to be, and whether (going further with me) he would prefer that the type should *not* be an ascetic one. I'm against asceticism myself. I'm with the old Scotchman who wanted less chastity and more delicacy. I don't feel that my aristocrats are a real aristocracy if they thwart their bodies, since bodies are the instruments through which we register and enjoy the world. Still, I don't insist here. This isn't a major point. It's clearly possible to be sensitive, considerate, and plucky and yet be an ascetic too, and if anyone possesses the first three qualities, I'll let him in! On they go—an invincible army, yet not a victorious one. The aristocrats, the elect, the chosen, the best people—all the words that describe them are false, and all attempts to organize them fail. Again and again authority, seeing their value, has tried to net them and to utilize them as the Egyptian priesthood or the Christian church or the Chinese civil service or the Group Movement, or some other worthy stunt. But they slip through the net and are gone; when the door is shut they are no longer in the room; their temple, as one of them remarked, is the holiness of the heart's imagination, and their kingdom, though they never possess it, is the wide-open world.

With this type of person knocking about, and constantly crossing one's path if one has eyes to see or hands to feel, the experiment of earthly life cannot be dismissed as a failure. But it may well be hailed as a tragedy, the tragedy being that no device has been found by which these private decencies can be transferred to public affairs. As soon as people have power they go crooked and sometimes dotty, too, because the possession of power lifts them into a region where normal honesty never pays. For instance, the man who is selling newspapers outside the House of Parliament can safely leave his papers to go for a drink, and his cap beside them:

anyone who takes a paper is sure to drop a copper into the cap. But the men who are inside the houses of Parliament—they can't trust one another like that; still less can the government they compose trust other governments. No caps upon the pavement here, but suspicion, treachery, and armaments. The more highly public life is organized the lower does its morality sink; the nations of today behave to each other worse than they ever did in the past; they cheat, rob, bully, and bluff, make war without notice, and kill as many women and children as possible; whereas primitive tribes were at all events restrained by taboos.

The Savior of the future—if ever he comes—will not preach a new gospel. He will merely utilize my aristocracy; he will make effective the good will and the good temper which are already existing. In other words he will introduce a new technique. In economics, we are told that if there was a new technique of distribution, there need be no poverty, and people would not starve in one place while crops were dug under in another. A similar change is needed in the sphere of morals and politics. The desire for it is by no means new; it was expressed, for example, in theological terms by Jacopone da Todi over six hundred years ago. "Ordina questo amore, O tu che mi ami," he said. ("O thou who lovest me, set this love in order.") His prayer was not granted and I do not myself believe that it ever will be, but here, and not through a change of heart, is our probable route. Not by becoming better, but by ordering and distributing his native goodness, will man shut up force into its box, and so gain time to explore the universe and to set his mark upon it worthily.

Such a change, claim the orthodox, can only be made by Christianity, and will be made by it in God's good time: man always has failed and always will fail to organize his own goodness, and it is presumptuous of him to try. This claim leaves me cold. I cannot believe that Christianity will ever cope with the present world-wide mess, and I think that such influence as it retains in modern society is due to its financial backing rather than to its spiritual appeal. It was a spiritual force once, but the indwelling spirit will have to be restated if it is to calm the waters again, and probably in a non-Christian form.

These are the reflections of an individualist and a liberal who has found his liberalism crumbling beneath him and at first felt ashamed. Then, looking around, he decided there was no special reason for shame, since other people, whatever they felt, were equally insecure. And as for individualism—there seems no way out of this, even if one wants to find one. The dictator-hero can grind down his citizens till they are all alike, but he can't melt them into a single man. He can order them to merge, he can incite them to mass-antics, but they are obliged to be born separately and to die separately and, owing to these unavoidable termini, will always be running off the totalitarian rails. The memory of birth and the expectation of death always lurk within the human being, making him separate from his fellows and consequently capable of intercourse with them. Naked I came into the world, naked I shall go out of it! And a very good thing, too, for it reminds me that I am naked under my shirt. Until psychologists and biologists have done much more tinkering than seems likely, the individual remains firm and each of us must consent to be one, and to make the best of the difficult job.

SOME MODERN NOVELS

AIKEN, CONRAD: *Blue Voyage* (1927), *King Coffin* (1935)
ALGREN, NELSON: *The Man with the Golden Arm* (1949), *A Walk on the Wild Side* (1956)
ANDERSON, SHERWOOD: *Winesburg, Ohio* (1919), *Poor White* (1920)
BENNETT, ARNOLD: *The Old Wives' Tale* (1908)
BOWEN, ELIZABETH: *The Death of the Heart* (1939), *The Heat of the Day* (1949)
BUCK, PEARL: *The Good Earth* (1931)
BURNS, JOHN HORNE: *The Gallery* (1947)
CABELL, JAMES BRANCH: *Jurgen* (1919)
CALDWELL, ERSKINE: *Tobacco Road* (1932)
CAMUS, ALBERT: *The Stranger* (1946), *The Plague* (1948), *The Fall* (1956)
CAPOTE, TRUMAN: *Other Voices, Other Rooms* (1948)
CATHER, WILLA: *My Ántonia* (1918), *A Lost Lady* (1923)
CLARK, WALTER VAN TILBURG: *The Ox-Bow Incident* (1940), *The Track of the Cat* (1949)
CONRAD, JOSEPH: *Lord Jim* (1900), *Victory* (1915), *Under Western Eyes* (1910)
COZZENS, JAMES GOULD: *Castaway* (1934), *The Just and the Unjust* (1942), *Guard of Honor* (1948), *By Love Possessed* (1957)
CUMMINGS, E. E.: *The Enormous Room* (1922)
DOS PASSOS, JOHN: *Three Soldiers* (1921), *Manhattan Transfer* (1925), *U.S.A.* (1937), *District of Columbia* (1952)
DOUGLAS, NORMAN: *South Wind* (1917)
DREISER, THEODORE: *Sister Carrie* (1900), *An American Tragedy* (1925).
FARRELL, JAMES T.: *Studs Lonigan* (1935)
FAULKNER, WILLIAM: *The Sound and the Fury* (1929), *As I Lay Dying* (1930), *Sanctuary* (1931), *Light in August* (1932), *Absalom! Absalom!* (1936), *Intruder in the Dust* (1948), *Requiem for a Nun* (1951)
FITZGERALD, F. SCOTT: *This Side of Paradise* (1920), *The Great Gatsby* (1925), *Tender is the Night* (1934), *The Last Tycoon* (1941)
FORD, FORD MADOX: *The Good Soldier* (1915), *Some Do Not* (1924), *The Last Post* (1928)
FORSTER, E. M.: *The Longest Journey* (1922), *A Passage to India* (1924)
GALSWORTHY, JOHN: *The Forsyte Saga* (1922), *A Modern Comedy* (1929)
GREEN, HENRY: *Living* (1925), *Party Going* (1939), *Loving* (1945), *Concluding* (1948)
GREENE, GRAHAM: *Brighton Rock* (1938), *The Power and the Glory* (1940), *The Heart of the Matter* (1948)
HEMINGWAY, ERNEST: *The Sun Also Rises* (1926), *A Farewell to Arms* (1929), *For Whom the Bell Tolls* (1940), *The Old Man and the Sea* (1952)
HERSEY, JOHN: *A Bell for Adano* (1944), *The Wall* (1950)
HEYWARD, DUBOSE: *Porgy* (1925)
HUDSON, W. H.: *Green Mansions* (1904)
HUXLEY, ALDOUS: *Antic Hay* (1923), *Point Counter Point* (1928), *Brave New World* (1932), *Time Must Have a Stop* (1944)
JOYCE, JAMES: *Portrait of the Artist as a Young Man* (1916), *Ulysses* (1922)
KAFKA, FRANZ: *The Trial* (1925), *The Castle* (1926)
KOESTLER, ARTHUR: *Darkness at Noon* (1942), *Arrival and Departure* (1943)
LAWRENCE, D. H.: *Sons and Lovers* (1913), *The Rainbow* (1915), *Women in Love* (1919), *Lady Chatterley's Lover* (1928)
LEWIS, SINCLAIR: *Main Street* (1920), *Babbitt* (1922), *Arrowsmith* (1925), *Dodsworth* (1929)
LOWRY, MALCOLM: *Under the Volcano* (1947)
MAILER, NORMAN: *The Naked and the Dead* (1948)
MALRAUX, ANDRÉ: *Man's Fate* (1934), *Man's Hope* (1938)
MANN, THOMAS: *Buddenbrooks* (1901), *The Magic Mountain* (1925), *Young Joseph* (1935), *The Transposed Heads* (1941), *The Holy Sinner* (1951), *Confessions of Felix Krull* (1955)

Appendices

MARQUAND, JOHN P.: *The Late George Apley* (1936), *So Little Time* (1943), *Point of No Return* (1949)
MAUGHAM, SOMERSET: *Of Human Bondage* (1915), *The Moon and Sixpence* (1919), *The Razor's Edge* (1945)
MCCULLERS, CARSON: *The Heart is a Lonely Hunter* (1940), *Reflections in a Golden Eye* (1941), *The Member of the Wedding* (1946)
MOTLEY, WILLARD: *Knock on Any Door* (1947)
NORRIS, FRANK: *The Octopus* (1901), *The Pit* (1903)
ORWELL, GEORGE: *Nineteen Eighty-four* (1949)
RICHARDSON, DOROTHY: *Pilgrimage* (1932)
SANTAYANA, GEORGE: *The Last Puritan* (1935)
SAROYAN, WILLIAM: *The Human Comedy* (1943)
SCHULBERG, BUDD: *What Makes Sammy Run?* (1941), *The Disenchanted* (1950)
SHAW, IRWIN: *The Young Lions* (1948), *The Troubled Air* (1952)
SINCLAIR, UPTON: *The Jungle* (1906)
STAFFORD, JEAN: *Boston Adventure* (1944), *The Mountain Lion* (1947)
STEIN, GERTRUDE: *Three Lives* (1909)
STEINBECK, JOHN: *Tortilla Flat* (1935), *Of Mice and Men* (1937), *The Grapes of Wrath* (1939), *Cannery Row* (1945), *The Wayward Bus* (1947), *The Pearl* (1948), *East of Eden* (1952)
UNDSET, SIGRID: *Kristin Lavransdatter* (1929)
WARREN, ROBERT PENN: *Night Rider* (1939), *All the King's Men* (1946), *World Enough and Time* (1950)
WAUGH, EVELYN: *Decline and Fall* (1928), *A Handful of Dust* (1934), *The Loved One* (1948)
WELLS, H. G.: *Tono-Bungay* (1909), *The Shape of Things to Come* (1933)
WEST, NATHANAEL: *Miss Lonelyhearts* (1933), *The Day of the Locust* (1939)
WESTCOTT, GLENWAY: *The Grandmothers* (1927), *The Pilgrim Hawk* (1940)
WHARTON, EDITH: *The House of Mirth* (1905), *Ethan Frome* (1911), *The Age of Innocence* (1920)
WILDER, THORNTON: *The Bridge of San Luis Rey* (1927), *The Woman of Andros* (1930), *Heaven's My Destination* (1935)
WOLFE, THOMAS: *Look Homeward, Angel* (1929), *Of Time and the River* (1935), *You Can't Go Home Again* (1940)
WOOLF, VIRGINIA: *Mrs. Dalloway* (1925), *To the Lighthouse* (1927)
WRIGHT, RICHARD: *Native Son* (1940)

RECORDINGS OF POEMS

A NUMBER of modern poets can be heard reading their own poems on records. Various companies and services can supply these records, among them Columbia, Decca, Erpi Classroom Films, Inc., Harvard, HBC, HMV, Library of Congress, Linguaphone, Musicraft, National Council of Teachers of English, Timely, Victor, and Caedmon.

Among the poets who have recorded their poems are:

Léonie Adams	Library of Congress
Conrad Aiken	Library of Congress
W. H. Auden	Linguaphone, NCTE, Columbia, Caedmon, Library of Congress
George Barker	Harvard

Recordings of Poems

S. V. Benét	NCTE
John Berryman	Library of Congress
Elizabeth Bishop	Columbia
J. P. Bishop	NCTE
Richard Blackmur	Library of Congress
Louise Bogan	Library of Congress
John M. Brinnin	Library of Congress
R. P. T. Coffin	Linguaphone, NCTE
E. E. Cummings	HBC, NCTE, Columbia, Caedmon, Library of Congress
Walter de la Mare	HMV
Richard Eberhart	Harvard, Library of Congress
T. S. Eliot	Harvard, Columbia, Library of Congress
William Empson	Library of Congress
Paul Engle	Library of Congress
J. G. Fletcher	Harvard, Library of Congress
Robert Frost	Erpi, NCTE, Library of Congress
Horace Gregory	Library of Congress
Robert Hillyer	Harvard
John Holmes	Harvard
Randall Jarrell	Library of Congress
Robinson Jeffers	Harvard, Library of Congress
Vachel Lindsay	Linguaphone, NCTE
Robert Lowell	Library of Congress
Edwin Markham	Timely
Archibald MacLeish	Linguaphone, NCTE, Caedmon
Edna St. V. Millay	Victor
Marianne Moore	Columbia, NCTE, Library of Congress
Ogden Nash	Columbia
J. C. Ransom	Library of Congress
Theodore Roethke	Library of Congress
Muriel Rukeyser	Library of Congress
Carl Sandburg	Decca, Musicraft
Delmore Schwartz	Library of Congress
Karl Shapiro	Library of Congress
Theodore Spencer	Library of Congress
Stephen Spender	Harvard, Library of Congress
Allen Tate	NCTE, Library of Congress
Dylan Thomas	Columbia, Caedmon
R. P. Warren	Library of Congress
W. C. Williams	Columbia, NCTE, Library of Congress
Yvor Winters	Library of Congress
Mark Van Doren	Library of Congress
Marya Zaturenska	Library of Congress

BIOGRAPHICAL NOTES

FURTHER INFORMATION on the authors can be found in *Who's Who, Twentieth Century Authors*, edited by Kunitz and Haycroft, *Webster's Biographical Dictionary*, and in *Contemporary American Authors* and *Contemporary British Literature*, revised editions, both edited by Fred B. Millett.

JAMES TRUSLOW ADAMS (1878-1949) was born in Brooklyn. He received his B.A. from the Brooklyn Polytechnic and his M.A. from Yale. He became a partner in a stock exchange firm in Wall Street and exercised his interests in banking, manufacturing and railroading. During World War I he was a captain in military intelligence, and was later on the Colonel House Commission to prepare data for the peace conference. For ten years he was on the advisory council of the *Yale Review*. Among his writings are *The Founding of New England*, 1921, *Our Business Civilization*, 1929, *The March of Democracy*, 1932, and *America's Progress in Civilization* (with G. E. Freeland), 1940.

CHARLES ADDAMS (1912-   ) was born in New Jersey and studied at Colgate University, the University of Pennsylvania, and the Grand Central School of Art in New York. He is a frequent contributor to *The New Yorker*, where his cartoons have been appearing regularly since 1935. He has exhibited at museums, including the Metropolitan Museum of Art in New York, and published three collections, *Drawn and Quartered*, 1942, *Addams and Evil*, 1947, and *Monster Rally*, 1950.

MAXWELL ANDERSON (1888-   ) was born in Pennsylvania. After graduating from the University of North Dakota, where he studied drama under Frederick H. Koch, he taught English in North Dakota and California. Several years' experience on newspapers in San Francisco and New York, during which time he wrote poetry and founded a poetry magazine, preceded his active work in drama. *White Desert* was a failure on the stage in 1923, but the success in 1924 of *What Price Glory?*, written with Laurence Stallings, turned him from editorial writing to the stage. His best known plays, besides *Winterset*, 1935, are *Elizabeth the Queen*, 1930, *Both Your Houses*, 1933, *Key Largo*, 1939, *The Eve of St. Mark*, 1942, *Joan of Lorraine*, 1946, and *Anne of the Thousand Days*, 1947.

KINGSLEY AMIS (1922-   ), whose poems *A Frame of Mind* appeared in 1953, is teaching at the University of Swansea, Swansea, Wales. His novel *Lucky Jim*, 1956, has aroused great interest in England.

MATTHEW ARNOLD (1822-1888) was a graduate of Balliol College, Oxford, winning the Newdigate prize in poetry in 1843. He was inspector of schools from 1851 to 1886 and professor of poetry at Oxford from 1857 to 1867. He lectured widely and was in America in 1883-1884 and 1886. His critical works include two series of *Essays in Criticism*, 1865, 1888, *Culture and Anarchy*, 1869, and *Literature and Dogma*, 1873; his poems were collected in 1890.

W. H. AUDEN (1907-   ) was born at York, England, and educated at Christ Church College, Oxford. He taught for a time. In 1937 he served as an ambulance driver for the Loyalist forces in the Spanish Civil War. In 1939 he came to the United States and took out citizenship papers. He has taught at the New School for Social Research, the University of Michigan, and Swarthmore. His *Collected Poems* appeared in 1945. Later volumes are *The Age of Anxiety*, 1947, and *Nones*, 1951.

MARCH AVERY (1932-   ), born in New York City, has studied art from an early age. She spent a year at William Smith College, then studied philosophy at and graduated from Barnard College. Besides an ambition to write and paint, she is interested in ballet and children's book illustration.

LINCOLN BARNETT (1909-   ) was born in New York and attended Horace Mann School and Princeton University. He received his master's degree from Columbia University School of Journalism in 1932, the year after he became a reporter on the city staff of the New York *Herald Tribune*. Later he joined *Life* as a staff writer and associate editor, where he remained until 1946. He now devotes all his time to writing.

PHILIP BARRY (1896-1949) was born in Rochester, New York, and educated at Yale. After graduation in 1919 he served as a clerk in embassy work in Washington and London, but resigned to enter the 47 Workshop at Harvard. For many years he wrote for both Broadway and Hollywood. His plays include *Hotel Universe,* 1930, *The Animal Kingdom*, 1932, and *The Philadelphia Story*, 1939.

CHARLES BEARD (1874-1948) was born in Indiana, and educated at DePauw, Oxford, Cornell and Columbia. He was professor of politics at Columbia from 1907 to 1917, after which he served for five years as director of the Training School for Public Service in New York. His later years have been devoted to writing and advisory work. His books include *Economic Interpretation of the Constitution*, 1913, *Economic Basis of Politics*, 1922, and, with his wife, *The Rise of American Civilization*, 1927, and *America in Midpassage*, 1939.

RUTH BENEDICT (1887-   ) was born in New York. After graduating from Vassar, she taught English, published poetry, and studied anthropology under Franz Boas at Columbia, where she later became a member of the department. She has done field work among the Pueblo, Apache and Blackfoot Indians. Her books include *Patterns of Culture*, 1934, and *Race: Science and Politics*, 1940.

PETER BLUME (1906-   ) was born in Russia and came to the United States as a child. He was naturalized as a citizen in 1921. After attending public schools in New York City, he studied at the Art Students' Educational Alliance and the Art Students' League. He has held a Guggenheim Fellowship twice, in 1932 and 1936. Prominent among his honors are a first prize at the Carnegie International in 1934 and a purchase award in the Artists for Victory Exhibition at the Metropolitan Museum of Art in 1942.

ROBERT CONQUEST (1917-   ) has published in English literary journals, and has edited an anthology of new British poets. His first volume of *Poems* appeared in 1955.

JOSEPH CONRAD (1857-1924) was born Jósef Teodor Konrad Korzeniowski in Russian Poland. He knew no English until he was twenty, learning it then laboriously from newspapers. At seventeen he shipped to sea on a French vessel, shifted later to English merchant ships and by 1880 had passed his examination as master. Failing health drove him from the sea in his late thirties, and settling in England, he became one of the greatest modern masters of prose fiction. His works include *Nigger of the Narcissus*, 1897,

Lord Jim, 1900, *Nostromo*, 1904, *Under Western Eyes*, 1911, and *Victory*, 1915.

E. E. CUMMINGS (1894-   ) was born in Cambridge, Massachusetts, and graduated from Harvard in 1915. He received his M.A. the following year. He was a volunteer ambulance driver in France before the entry of the United States into World War I. After the war he lived in Paris for a time, then returned to New York. He made a trip to Russia in 1930. His novel, *The Enormous Room*, was published in 1922. His poetry includes *Collected Poems*, 1938, *Fifty Poems*, 1940, *1 × 1*, 1934, and *XAIPE: seventy-one poems*, 1950.

ROBERT DAY (1900-   ) was born in California and studied at the Otis Art Institute. He began work as a cartoonist for the Los Angeles *Times* and was later in the art departments of the Los Angeles *Examiner* and the New York *Herald Tribune*. In addition to drawings for advertisements, he has published *All Out for the Sack Race!* and illustrated *We Shook the Family Tree*. He is a contributor to *The New Yorker* and *The Saturday Evening Post*.

ABNER DEAN (1910-   ) was born in New York. After graduating from Dartmouth in 1931, he experimented with various art forms, published for some years cartoons and covers for *The New Yorker*. His work gained a wider notice with the publication of seven of his drawings in *Life* magazine and the consequent recognition given to his collections, *It's a long way to Heaven*, 1945, and *What am I doing here?*, 1947.

EMILY DICKINSON (1830-1886) was born in Amherst, Mass., into the quiet life and religious atmosphere of a very conservative town. She studied at the Academy founded by her grandfather, and for one year at the Mount Holyoke Female Seminary. When she was twenty-three years old, she journeyed to Washington to visit her father who was serving in Congress. After 1856 she virtually isolated herself in the family home for the rest of her life, and there wrote the poems which were neither known nor published until after her death. There has been much speculation over the reasons for this self-imposed isolation. Her 1862 letter to T. W. Higginson may provide a clue.

When a little girl, I had a friend who taught me Immortality; but venturing too near, himself, he never returned. Soon after, my tutor died, and for several years my lexicon was my only companion. Then I found one more, but he was not contented I be his scholar, so he left the land.

The majority of her poems are found in *Poems*, 1890, Second Series, 1891, Third Series, 1896, *Poems*, 1930, *Bolts of Melody*, 1945.

BONAMY DOBRÉE (1891-   ), British literary critic and scholar, has been professor of English literature at Leeds University since 1936. He was educated at the Royal Military Academy in Woolwich and at Cambridge University. His chief critical volumes are *Restoration Comedy*, 1924, *Restoration Tragedy*, 1929, *The Lamp and the Lute*, 1929, *John Wesley*, 1933, and *Alexander Pope*, 1951. With Herbert Read he edited *The London Book of English Prose*, 1931, and *The London Book of English Verse*, 1949; the former is an anthology-companion to his *Modern Prose Style*.

JOHN DOS PASSOS (1896-   ) was born in Chicago and graduated from Harvard. He was in the ambulance and medical services during World War I. Later he traveled widely as a newspaper correspondent and free-lance writer. Among his novels are *Three Soldiers*, 1921, *Manhattan Transfer*, 1925, the two trilogies, *U.S.A.*, 1937, and *District of Columbia*, 1951, and *The Grand Design*, 1949. His volumes of discussion and reportage include *The Ground We Stand On*, 1941, and *Tour of Duty*, 1946.

Biographical Notes

PETER DRUCKER (1909-   ) was educated in Austria and England and received a degree in law from Frankfurt University in Germany. He has been a journalist and economic consultant in both Europe and the United States, and he has taught at Bennington College and New York University, where he now holds a professorship of Management in the Graduate School of Business. He has written widely for leading magazines and his published volumes include *The End of Economic Man*, 1939, *The Future of Industrial Man*, 1942, and *The New Society*, 1950.

HAROLD E. EDGERTON (1903-   ), electrical engineer and educator, was born in Fremont, Nebraska. After graduating from the University of Nebraska and employment with the Nebraska Light & Power Company and The General Electric Company, he studied at Massachusetts Institute of Technology for the degrees of Master and Doctor of Science. Now Professor of Electrical Engineering at M.I.T., he is the inventor of photographic apparatus for taking stroboscopic high-speed motion and still pictures. He is the winner of a medal from the Royal Photographic Society and author of *Flash!*, 1939.

T. S. ELIOT (1888-   ) was born in St. Louis, Missouri. He graduated with an M.A. in 1910 from Harvard, where his classmates included Heywood Broun, John Reed, Walter Lippmann and Stuart Chase. He has lived in England since 1915, and became a British subject in 1927. In 1928 he announced that he was "an Anglo-Catholic in religion, a classicist in literature, and a royalist in politics." His poetic works include *Collected Poems: 1909-1935*, *Four Quartets*, 1943, and the poetic plays, *Murder in the Cathedral*, 1935, *The Family Reunion*, 1939, *The Cocktail Party*, 1950, and *The Confidential Clerk*, 1954. Among his collections of essays are *Selected Essays: 1917-1932*, *Essays Ancient and Modern*, 1936, *The Idea of a Christian Society*, 1940, and *Notes towards the Definition of Culture*, 1949.

WELLER B. EMBLER (1906-   ) was educated at Syracuse and Yale Universities. He has taught at Syracuse and is now Head of the Department of Humanities at The Cooper Union, New York. His essays, in which he largely aims to show the relationship of the arts, literature, the sciences, and philosophy to each other, have appeared in *ETC.: A Review of General Semantics*, *Journal of Engineering Education*, *College Art Journal*, *College English*, and the *Virginia Quarterly Review*. In 1951 he was Director of the summer session of the Cummington School of the Arts in Cummington, Mass.

RALPH WALDO EMERSON (1803-1882) was born in Boston and educated at Harvard. Entering the ministry, he became pastor of the Second (Unitarian) Church of Boston, but personal and theological difficulties caused him to leave the ministry in 1832. Travel in America and Europe, where he met Coleridge, Wordsworth, Carlyle, and lecturing and writing occupied his later life. Edwin Arlington Robinson regarded Emerson as America's greatest 19th Century poet, but Emerson was modest about his poetry, writing, "I feel it a hardship that—with something of a lover's passion for what is to me the most precious thing in life, poetry —I have no gift of fluency in it, only a rude and stammering utterance." Among his important works are *Nature*, 1836, *Essays*, First Series, 1841, *Poems*, 1847, *The Conduct of Life*, 1860, and *Society and Solitude*, 1870.

WILLIAM FAULKNER (1897-   ) was born in New Albany, Mississippi, of a family that had been reduced to genteel poverty by the Civil War. After the fifth grade his schooling was desultory. During World War I he flew with the Canadian Air Force, had two planes shot down over France, and was wounded. He returned to live in Oxford, Mississippi, and to write novels and stories about the inhabitants of mythical Yoknapatawpha County. When asked he describes his profession as "farmer." In 1950 he was awarded the Nobel Prize for literature "for his forceful and independently artistic contribution to modern American fiction." Among his books are *The Sound and the Fury*, 1929, *As I Lay Dying*, 1930, *Sanctuary*, 1931, *Light in August*, 1932, *Absalom! Absalom!*, 1936, *Intruder in the Dust*, 1948, and *Collected Stories*, 1950. He prepared two versions of "The Bear": the shorter appears here, and the longer may be found in *Go Down, Moses, and Other Stories*, 1942.

KENNETH FEARING (1902-) was born in Oak Park, Illinois. He attended the University of Illinois, but transferred to and graduated from the University of Wisconsin in 1924. He worked at selling, free-lance writing, journalism, and for a time taught poetry at the League of American Writers in New York. He has said that poetry "must be exciting; otherwise it is valueless. . . . Besides being exciting, I think that poetry necessarily must be understandable." Among his books are *Collected Poems*, 1940, and *Afternoon of a Pawnbroker and Other Poems*, 1943.

F. SCOTT FITZGERALD (1896-1940) was born in St. Paul, Minnesota, and educated at Princeton. He left college in 1917 to serve as an infantry lieutenant and aide-de-camp until 1919. His first novel, *This Side of Paradise*, 1920, a reflection of the jazz age following World War I, was an instantaneous success. Thereafter he lived chiefly on Long Island or on the Riviera and in Rome. He spent his final three years in Hollywood and did some writing for motion pictures. Among his books are *The Great Gatsby*, 1925, *Tender Is the Night*, 1934, and the unfinished novel about Hollywood, *The Last Tycoon*, 1941.

IAIN FLETCHER (1920-) is a member of the English Department at the University of Reading, England. His poems have appeared in *Poetry, London*.

E. M. FORSTER (1879-) was born in England and educated at Cambridge. He has spent much time in traveling, and turned the experiences of two years in India into his famous novel, *A Passage to India*, 1924. His other books include *A Room with a View*, 1908, *Howards End*, 1910, and a series of lectures, *Aspects of the Novel*, 1927.

OTTO R. FRISCH (1904-) has been Jacksonian Professor of Natural Philosophy at Cavendish Laboratory, University of Cambridge, since 1947. Born and educated in Austria, he received the Dr. Phil. degree from the University of Vienna in 1926. He has conducted research in Berlin, London, Copenhagen, and Los Alamos. In addition to numerous papers on atomic and nuclear physics, he has published *Meet the Atoms*, 1947.

ROBERT FROST (1875-) was born in San Francisco. After the death of his father in 1885, his mother took her children to Lawrence, Massachusetts. Eventually, he attended Dartmouth for a few months, and Harvard for two years, but left college to teach and farm. He moved to England in 1912, where his first two books of poems were published—his first major recognition. In 1915 he returned to the United States. He has lectured and taught in various colleges, principally at Amherst. His work includes *Collected Poems*, 1939, *A Witness Tree*, 1942, *A Masque of Reason*, 1945, *A Masque of Mercy*, 1947, and *Steeple Bush*, 1947.

CHRISTOPHER FRY (1907-) was active in the theatre as actor and director for years before he turned to the writing of verse plays which, with *The Lady's Not for Burning*, 1948, brought him fame. Among his other plays are *The Boy with a Cart*, 1939, *A Phoenix Too Frequent*, 1946, *A Sleep of Prisoners*, 1951, *The Dark Is Light Enough*, 1955, and the translation of Jean Giraudoux's *Tiger at the Gates*, 1956.

Biographical Notes

JEAN GIRAUDOUX (1882-1944) was honored in France as a diplomat, novelist, short story writer, and dramatist. After a largely classical schooling, he spent five years in world travel before entering the French Diplomatic Service. At the age of forty-six he turned to drama with the production of *Amphitryon 38*. Among his plays are *Intermezzo*, 1933, *Ondine*, 1939, *The Madwoman of Chaillot*, which in an English version ran in New York in 1948, and *Tiger at the Gates* which in Christopher Fry's translation was produced in London in 1955, and in New York in 1956.

HERBERT GOLD (1924-   ) studied at Columbia and Cornell, holds an M.A. in Philosophy, and attended the Sorbonne on a Fulbright Fellowship. He visited Haiti on a grant from the International Institute of Education and teaches in the Writers' Workshop of the University of Iowa. His stories and essays have appeared in *The Hudson Review*, *New World Writing*, *Botteghe Oscure*, and *discovery*, and his novels include *Birth of a Hero*, 1951, and *The Prospect Before Us*, 1954.

DONALD HALL (1928-   ), after study and travel abroad, was awarded a Fellowship at Harvard. His volume *Exiles and Marriages* was the Lamont Poetry Selection for 1955. He is at present the Poetry Editor of *The Paris Review*.

THOMAS HARDY (1840-1928) was born in Dorsetshire. After brief schooling he served as an architect's apprentice for several years. He became increasingly interested in creative writing, particularly in poetry but "necessity" turned him to the writing of novels. The first of his many novels appeared in 1871. His brilliant career as novelist was brought to a close by the critical attack on *Tess of the D'Urbervilles* and *Jude the Obscure*. "Cured of all interest in novel-writing," as he said, at the age of 58 he returned to poetry. He gradually won over an at first apathetic public, and his *Collected Poems* in 1919 showed his power as a poet. He continued to write until his death at the age of 88. In addition to his novels, short stories, and poems, he completed in 1908 an epic drama of the Napoleonic Wars, *The Dynasts*.

MARSDEN HARTLEY (1877-1943), painter and poet, was born in Lewiston, Maine, and spent his early years in Cleveland, Ohio. After study at the National Academy in New York and in Europe, he settled in New York City to paint the strongly colored, often symbolic and almost abstract landscapes and figures now in many American collections and museums. His first work, shown by Alfred Stieglitz in 1908, caused some critical controversy, but he continued to hold one-man exhibits for 30 years. In 1930 he won a Guggenheim Fellowship for study in Mexico. His poems and reproductions of some of his paintings are in *Selected Poems*, 1945.

S. I. HAYAKAWA (1906-   ) was born in Canada, and educated at the University of Manitoba, McGill and the University of Wisconsin. At present he is a professor of English at the Illinois Institute of Technology. His book, *Language in Action*, 1941, which grew primarily out of his research in semantics with the Polish semanticist Korzybski, has been revised as *Language in Thought and Action*. He is editor of *ETC.*, a journal of semantics.

CARLTON J. H. HAYES (1882-   ), leading American historian, was born in New York City, and educated at Columbia, where he taught from 1907 to 1950, when he retired as emeritus professor. He served as a captain in Army Intelligence during the first World War. As the United States Ambassador to Spain from 1942 to 1945, he is credited with helping to keep that country out of active participation in World War II and with obtaining concessions helpful to the allies of the United States. He has received many honors and awards from universities, academies, and learned societies and has published textbooks and studies in European history. These include *Essays on Nationalism,* 1926, *A Generation of Materialism,* 1941, and *History of Europe,* 1949.

ERNEST HEMINGWAY (1898-   ) was born in Oak Park, Illinois, ended his formal education with high school and became a reporter in Kansas City. In World War I he served as volunteer ambulance driver in France and enlisted soldier in the Italian Army. While European correspondent for the Toronto *Star* and Paris correspondent for the Hearst newspapers, he began to write stories which brought him encouragement from Ezra Pound and Gertrude Stein. His subsequent writings have often been read less for their own qualities than for what they reveal about the skilled boxer, big-game hunter, ocean fisherman, and war correspondent who is their author. He reported on the Spanish Civil War, the Japanese invasion of northern China, and the Allied invasion of France in World War II, and he commanded his own yacht as a Q-boat hunting submarines off Cuba during the early years of World War II. *Death in the Afternoon,* 1932, and *Green Hills of Africa,* 1935, are stylized accounts of bullfighting and big-game hunting. His important novels are *The Sun Also Rises,* 1926, *A Farewell to Arms,* 1929, *For Whom the Bell Tolls,* 1940, *Across the River and into the Trees,* 1950, and *The Old Man and the Sea,* 1952. His stories are collected in *The Fifth Column and the First Forty-nine Stories,* 1938.

GEOFFREY HILL (1932-   ) is a member of the English Department at the University of Leeds, England. His first volume of poems is to be published in London early in 1958.

EDWARD HOPPER (1882-   ), American artist, has won many prizes and medals for his prints and paintings. He was born in Nyack, New York, and after attending public and private schools he studied at the New York School of Art under Chase and Henri. His works hang in a number of American museums, libraries, and private collections, and he is also a contributor to magazines.

A. E. HOUSMAN (1859-1936) was born in Worcestershire and attended St. John's College, Oxford. He failed his fourth-year honors examinations, but returned for one term of study to pass the degree. From 1882 to 1892 he was a clerk in the Government Patent Office in London. He continued his classical studies at night and won a reputation as a brilliant classical scholar. In 1892 he was appointed Professor of Latin in University College, London, and in 1911 received the same appointment in Trinity College, Cambridge, a position which he held until his death. He once said he was "not a pessimist but a pejorist." *A Shropshire Lad* was published in 1896, *Last Poems* in 1922. *More Poems,* a posthumous collection, appeared in 1936. His essay, *The Name and Nature of Poetry,* was printed in 1933.

ALDOUS HUXLEY (1894-   ) is the grandson of Thomas Henry Huxley and grand-nephew of Matthew Arnold. He was educated at Eton and Oxford. During 1919-1920 he was on the editorial staff of the *Athenaeum,* and during 1920-1921 served as dramatic critic on the *Westminster Gazette.* He has traveled widely and now lives in Hollywood, California. Among his novels are *Antic Hay,* 1923, *Point Counter Point,* 1928, *Brave New World,* 1932, *Eyeless in Gaza,* 1936, and *Time Must Have a Stop,* 1945. His other work includes *Proper Studies,* 1927, *Do What You Will,* 1929, *Texts and Pretexts,* 1932, *Ends and Means,* 1937, and *The Perennial Philosophy,* 1945.

RANDALL JARRELL (1914-   ) studied at Vanderbilt University, later taught at Kenyon College, the University of Texas, and Sarah Lawrence. He has been most re-

Biographical Notes

cently Consultant in Poetry at the Library of Congress. His works include *Poetry and the Age*, 1953, a novel, *Pictures from an Institution*, 1954, and *Selected Poems*, 1955.

ROBINSON JEFFERS (1887-   ) was born in Pittsburgh. He lived in Europe from 1899 until 1902. In 1905 he received his A.B. from Occidental College. He did some graduate work in forestry and medicine. In 1912 a legacy made him independent, and two years later he settled permanently at Carmel, California, where he built his famous stone tower. Among his books are *Selected Poetry*, 1938, *Be Angry at the Sun*, 1941, *Medea* (an adaptation of the Greek tragedy), 1946, and *The Double Axe*, 1948.

THOMAS JEFFERSON (1743-1826), third president of the United States, was born in Virginia and graduated from the College of William and Mary in 1762. Admitted to the bar in 1767, he was a member of Virginia's House of Burgesses from 1769 to 1774, and at that time began the work that was to lead to American independence. A member of the Continental Congress, he wrote and presented the first draft of the Declaration of Independence to the Congress in 1776. Before his election as President in 1801, he was Governor of Virginia, Minister to France, Secretary of State, and Vice President. His election to the Presidency was by the House of Representatives after a tie with Aaron Burr in the popular vote. After his retirement in 1809, he helped found the University of Virginia and pursued his studies in agriculture, architecture, and literature. His chief writings, official and personal, are collected by S. K. Padover in *The Complete Jefferson*, 1942.

JAMES JOYCE (1882-1941) was born in Dublin and educated, at first with the intention of entering the priesthood, at Clongowes Wood College and Belvedere College in Ireland, and at the Royal University, Dublin, where he studied languages and literature. In 1904 he left Ireland, to return briefly only twice during the rest of his life. He studied medicine and music in Paris, taught languages in Italy and Switzerland, was in Zurich during World War I, and moved soon after to Paris, where he spent the remainder of his life. His first book, *Dubliners*, a group of short stories intended to portray the "paralysis" of Western civilization, was ready for publication in 1907, but was suppressed for seven years because of references to Edward VII. *Ulysses* (1922) was at first banned in England and the United States, but was finally passed for publication in 1934. His last work, *Finnegans Wake*, an experiment in language and symbolism, was published in 1939.

JOHN A. KOUWENHOVEN (1909-   ), teacher, writer, and editor, was educated at Wesleyan University and Columbia University, where he received the Ph.D. degree in 1948. He has taught at Bennington College and Columbia and now holds a professorship at Barnard College. He has been associated with the editorial staff of *Harper's Magazine* since 1941. In addition to numerous articles for magazines, he has published *Made in America: The Arts in Modern Civilization*, 1948, and *The Columbia Historic Portrait of New York*, 1953.

D. H. LAWRENCE (1885-1930), British novelist and poet, struggled in his early years for an education and recognition of his gifts and in his later years against misunderstanding and prudish censorship of his work. Born in a small mining town in Nottinghamshire, he attended high school on a scholarship, worked as a clerk, and before he was twenty was an elementary school teacher. After two years in a Training College, he taught for five years until publication of some poems and his first novel gave him confidence in his talents. Rejected for war service because of his tubercular condition, he left England in 1919 in search of health and a simpler life than that allowed by what he considered the distorted values of modern civilization. Accompanied by his wife, the Baroness Frieda von Richtofen, he traveled in Australia, Sardinia, Sicily, and settled for longer periods in New Mexico and Mexico. When he died in 1930, at Vence, in southern France, he left nearly fifty volumes of novels, stories, plays, poems, essays and journals. Among his major novels are *Sons and Lovers*, 1913, *The Rainbow*, 1915, *Women in Love*, 1920, *The Plumed Serpent*, 1926, and *Lady Chatterley's Lover* 1928. His poems were collected in 1929, his stories in 1934, and his letters (with an introduction by Aldous Huxley) in 1932. His other works include *Studies in Classic American Literature*, 1923, *Apocalypse* (collected essays), 1931, and *Etruscan Places*, 1932.

WALTER LIPPMANN (1889-   ) was born in New York and graduated from Harvard in 1910. In his last year he was assistant to George Santayana. After college he worked with Lincoln Steffens on *Everybody's Magazine*. In 1914 he became one of the founding editors of the *New Republic*. For four months in 1917 he was assistant to Newton D. Baker, Secretary of War. He was a member of the American commission at the Versailles Conference. In 1929 he became editor of the New York *World*, and when that daily ceased publication he went to the *Herald Tribune*. In 1936 he reversed his political position, announcing himself a Republican. He made a tour of Germany in 1946. His many books include *A Preface to Politics*, 1913, *A Preface to Morals*, 1929, *The Good Society*, 1937, *U. S. Foreign Policy*, 1944, and *U. S. War Aims*, 1944.

LUIGI LUCIONI (1900-   ) was born in Italy and came to the United States in 1911. He studied at the Cooper Union Art School (1916-1920) and the National Academy of Design (1920-1925). His work is represented by many paintings and etchings in American galleries and collections. He won the Tiffany medal in 1928, the first popular prize at the Carnegie International Exhibition in 1939 and in the same year the first popular prize at the Biennial Exhibition in Washington, D. C.

THOMAS MACAULAY (1800-1859) was born in Leicestershire and educated at Cambridge. A member of Parliament for four terms between 1830 and 1856, he was Secretary of War in 1839-1841, and was made the first Baron Macaulay in 1857. He was a contributor to the *Edinburgh Review* from 1825 on, and wrote five volumes of a *History of England*, covering the reigns of James II and William III, as well as numerous speeches, biographical and literary essays and *The Lays of Ancient Rome*, 1842.

ARCHIBALD MacLEISH (1892-   ) was born in Glencoe, Illinois. He received his B.A. from Yale in 1915, and his LL.B. from Harvard in 1919. He enlisted in the Field Artillery in 1917 and was discharged as a captain. From 1923 to 1928 he traveled abroad. On his return he worked on *Fortune* magazine. In 1939 he was named Librarian of Congress, and in 1941 was appointed Director of Office of Facts and Figures (which later became the Office of War Information under Elmer Davis). For a while he served as Under-Secretary of State. Among his books are *Selected Poems: 1924-1933*, *Public Speech*, 1936, *America Was Promises*, 1939, the two radio plays, *The Fall of the City*, 1937, and *Air Raid*, 1938, and his essays, *The Irresponsibles*, 1940, *The American Cause*, 1941, and *A Time to Speak*, 1941. Since 1949 he has been Boylston Professor at Harvard University, and has contributed to many magazines. *Actfive and Other Poems* was published in 1948, and *Collected Poems* in 1952.

SOMERSET MAUGHAM (1874-   ) was born in Paris. Much of his early life is reflected in his novel, *Of Human Bondage*, 1915. He studied medicine, but never practiced, preferring writing instead. His first success came as a playwright in 1907. Since then he has traveled widely and lived in

[998]

many parts of the world. His fiction includes *The Moon and Sixpence*, 1919, *The Razor's Edge*, 1945, and such collections of short stories as *The Trembling of a Leaf*, 1921, and *The Mixture as Before*, 1940. Among his plays are *The Circle*, 1921, and *Our Betters*, 1923. *The Summing Up*, 1938, is autobiographical.

C. E. MONTAGUE (1867-1928), British journalist, essayist, and novelist, was educated at the City of London School and at Oxford University. He was a member of the staff of *The Manchester Guardian* for 35 years and published criticism, novels, and short stories. Among his works are *A Hind Let Loose*, 1910, *Disenchantment*, 1922, *Fiery Particles*, 1923, and *Rough Justice*, 1926.

EUGENE O'NEILL (1888-1953) was born in New York City. His father was a popular actor. After one year at Princeton, O'Neill prospected for gold in Honduras, shipped for a year as a seaman, acted in his father's company and reported for the New London *Telegraph*. Sent to a sanatorium at twenty-three for tuberculosis, he there decided to become a playwright. He enrolled in 1914 in the 47 Workshop at Harvard, and in 1916 became associated with the Provincetown Theatre. His first full-length play, *Beyond the Horizon*, 1920, won the Pulitzer Prize. He won it twice afterwards, with *Anna Christie*, 1922, and *Strange Interlude*, 1928. In 1936 he was awarded the Nobel Prize. Other important plays are *The Emperor Jones*, 1921, *Desire Under the Elms*, 1925, *Mourning Becomes Electra*, 1931, *Long Day's Journey into Night*, 1956. From 1935 to his death he was engaged in writing a cycle of nine plays tentatively titled *A Tale of Possessors Self-Dispossessed*, the saga of an American family, 1775-1932.

J. ORTEGA Y GASSET (1883-1955) was a Spanish philosopher, writer and statesman. A professor at the University of Madrid before the Spanish Civil War, he was also a member of the Cortes in 1931 and civil governor of Madrid. He lived in South America during the Spanish Civil War but later returned to Spain. He is the author of *Invertebrate Spain*, 1922, *The Revolt of the Masses*, 1932, *Concord and Liberty*, 1946, and *The Dehumanization of Art and Notes on the Novel*, 1948.

GEORGE ORWELL (1903-1950), whose real name was Eric Blair, was born in India of an Anglo-Indian family and attended Eton on scholarship. Five years of service with the India Imperial Police permanently injured his health and set his mind forever against the horrors of politics, particularly the imperialist kind, and he left India for Paris and England. Further political disillusionment came with the Spanish Civil War, in which he was wounded after four months of fighting for the Loyalists. He retired to a farm in England to become a prominent columnist and essayist for British and American periodicals, as well as to write the novels and personal accounts that have made him well known for insight into current affairs. Among his works are the satire on Russian Communism, *Animal Farm*, 1946, a novel of the future, *Nineteen Eighty-four*, 1949, a collection of essays, *Dickens, Dali, and Others*, 1946, and some volumes about his experiences in India, Paris, London, and Spain.

MARY PETTY lives in New York City and is married to Alan Dunn, the artist. In addition to drawing cartoons and covers for *The New Yorker*, she has illustrated *Goodbye, Mr. Chippendale* by T. H. Robsjohn-Gibbings and a new edition of Dickens' *Martin Chuzzlewit*. Of the people in her drawings she has said, "I'm afraid I am like the people I draw, of whom Harold Ross is reported to have once said, 'They look like something that lives under a rock.'"

Appendices

PABLO PICASSO (1881-   ) was born in Spain and studied at the academies of Barcelona and Madrid. By the age of 17 he was winning prizes for his paintings. In 1901 he went to Paris, where he studied the moderns and formed strong friendships among writers and other painters. After trying several styles, his work began to earn notice about 1905, when he painted Gertrude Stein's portrait. He has continued to experiment in cubist, classical, and surrealistic styles, and in many media, including stage settings for ballet, sculpture, collage, and ceramics. His "Guernica," a 250-foot-square mural, was intended as a protest against Franco's bombing of Spanish villages. His works are in the major collections of modern art all over the world, among them the Museum of Modern Art in New York.

EDWIN ARLINGTON ROBINSON (1869-1935) was born in Head Tide, Maine. He spent two years at Harvard, then went to New York, where he worked on new subway construction, lived very frugally and continued his writing. In 1905 President Theodore Roosevelt, who had read and been impressed by his poems, had him appointed to the New York Customs House. After 1911 Robinson spent his summers at the MacDowell Colony in Peterboro, New Hampshire, and his winters in New York. His *Collected Poems* was printed in 1937.

CARL SANDBURG (1878-   ) was born in Galesburg, Illinois. He left school at thirteen and worked at miscellaneous jobs for several years. During the Spanish-American War he enlisted and served in Puerto Rico for eight months. After his discharge he worked his way at Lombard College but did not graduate. He then engaged in newspaper work, and for a time was secretary to the Socialist mayor of Milwaukee. After 1914, his poetry began to win him wide recognition. His poetry includes *Selected Poems*, 1926, *The People, Yes*, 1936, and *Home Front Memo*, 1943. He has also published a biography: *Abraham Lincoln, the Prairie Years*, 1926, and *Abraham Lincoln, the War Years*, 1939.

MARK SCHORER (1908-   ), novelist and critic, was born in Sauk City, Wisconsin, and attended the University of Wisconsin, where he earned a Ph.D. degree. He began writing short stories in 1933 and published his first novel in 1935. He has taught at Dartmouth, Harvard, and the University of California at Berkeley, and has held a Guggenheim fellowship and a Fulbright Award. He is at present working on a biography of Sinclair Lewis, using the materials turned over to him by the executors of Lewis's estate. His novels include *The Hermit Place*, 1941, and *The Way of Love*, 1953; his short stories are collected in *The State of Mind*, 1947, and his chief critical work is *William Blake: The Politics of Vision*, 1946.

E. J. SCOVELL (1907-   ) has published her poems in *The River Steamer*, 1956.

GEORGE BERNARD SHAW (1856-1950) was born in Dublin. Largely self-educated, he started his literary career as a hack writer and author of five rejected novels before turning to political writing for the Fabian Society, and to the criticism of music, art, and drama which brought him a growing audience. His first plays, written in the mid-1890s, found little acceptance, but by 1910 he was recognized as one of the foremost dramatists of our century, and in 1925 he was awarded the Nobel Prize for Literature. In over fifty plays Shaw used the thesis form and the comedy of ideas to dramatize the free play of his mind over problems found in the individual, society, politics, art, science, history, and religion until—at the time of his death—he was described as "Headmaster to the Universe." Among his chief plays are *Candida*, 1898, *Caesar and Cleopatra*, 1900, *Man and Superman*, 1903, *Major Barbara*, 1905, *Pygmalion*, 1912, *Heartbreak*

Biographical Notes

House 1917, *Back to Methuselah*, 1921, *St. Joan*, 1923, and *The Apple Cart*, 1929.

BEN SHAHN (1898-   ) was born in Russia and came to the United States at the age of eight. After apprenticeship as a lithographer, attending high school at night, he studied at New York University and City College of New York. He then studied at the National Academy of Design and in several countries abroad. He first exhibited in 1929, was a member of the Public Works of Art Project, and worked for the Farm Security Administration from 1935 to 1938. He has painted a number of murals for public buildings, has had one-man shows at the Museum of Modern Art, 1947, and the Venice Biennale, 1954. His paintings hang in most of the major galleries in the United States.

CHARLES SHEELER (1883-   ) was born in Philadelphia and studied at the School of Industrial Art, Philadelphia, and at the Pennsylvania Academy of The Fine Arts. After painting trips to Europe, while he took up photography as a means of livelihood, he began to exhibit his paintings. He has exhibited in many galleries and museums, the most complete showing being at the Museum of Modern Art in 1939. His work in both painting and photography is based, to use his own words, on "the concept of a picture as having an underlying architectural structure to support the elements in nature which comprise the picture."

STANLEY SPENCER (1892-   ) was born in Cookham-on-Thames, Berkshire, England, and studied at the Slade School from 1910 to 1914. He served as Red Cross orderly and as a soldier in Macedonia throughout the first World War, after which he returned to live in his birthplace. His paintings are in many private collections as well as in American and British museums. His most famous series of works appears in the Memorial Chapel of Burghclere, completed in 1933.

STEPHEN SPENDER (1909-   ) was born in London. He attended University College, Oxford, where he met and worked with W. H. Auden and Louis MacNeice. In 1937 he went to Spain to attend the International Writers Congress, and remained there for several months during the Civil War. His sympathies were with the Loyalists. During World War II he was in or near London, and served as a fireman through the blitz. His work includes *Poems*, 1933, *The Still Centre*, 1939, *Ruins and Visions*, 1942, *Poems of Dedication*, 1947, *The Edge of Being*, 1949, and the prose volumes, *The Destructive Element*, 1934, *European Witness*, 1946, and an autobiography, *World within World*, 1951.

GERTRUDE STEIN (1874-1946) was born in Allegheny, Pennsylvania. Part of her early life was spent in Europe, and after her college course at Radcliffe, where she studied under William James, and several years at the Johns Hopkins Medical School, she returned to France for residence. During World War I she drove an ambulance and increased the circle of her friends, which already included Picasso and Matisse. After the war she gave guidance and encouragement to many young writers, such as Ernest Hemingway, Glenway Westcott and F. Scott Fitzgerald. Her own writings include *Three Lives*, 1908, *Tender Buttons*, 1915, *The Making of Americans*, 1925, *The Autobiography of Alice B. Toklas*, 1933, *Four Saints in Three Acts* (with music by Virgil Thomson), 1934, *Lectures in America*, 1935, and *Picasso*, 1938. Her experiences during World War II were dealt with in *Wars I Have Seen*, 1945, and *Brewsie and Willie*, 1946.

JOHN STEINBECK (1902-   ) was born in Salinas, California, the scene of some of his fiction. He spent four years as a special student at Stanford, where his chief interest was in biology. Later he worked at many odd jobs. His first three books were failures. In 1935 *Tortilla Flat* was well received and was followed by *In Dubious Battle*, 1936, *Of Mice and Men*, 1937, and *The Long Valley* (short stories), 1938. His *The Grapes of Wrath*, 1939, was a best-seller and was awarded the Pulitzer Prize in 1940. He also published *Sea of Cortez* (with E. F. Ricketts), 1941, *The Moon Is Down*, 1942, *Cannery Row*, 1945, *The Wayward Bus*, 1947, *The Pearl*, 1948, *Burning Bright*, 1950, and *East of Eden*, 1952.

SAUL STEINBERG (1914-   ), illustrator and cartoonist, was born in Rumania and studied in Italy. He has contributed to *Fortune, The New Yorker,* and other leading magazines, and his work may be found in the Museum of Modern Art. His drawings are collected in *All in Line*, 1945.

J. W. N. SULLIVAN (1886-1937), British mathematician, physicist, and philosopher, pursued his aptitude for mathematics at University College, London, and then turned to writing. Well known in England as an interpreter of modern science, he also wrote on philosophy and music and occasionally turned to fiction. Among his works are *Aspects of Science, Beethoven: His Spiritual Development, Three Men Discuss Relativity,* and *But for the Grace of God.*

DYLAN THOMAS (1914-1953) was born in Wales. After an early career in journalism and film scripting, he published *18 Poems* in 1934, saying that the poems were, "the record of my individual struggle from darkness towards some measure of light . . . My poetry is or should be useful to others for its individual recording of that same struggle with which they are necessarily acquainted." During the war he worked for the BBC. In 1950-52 he traveled in the United States reading his poems at many colleges. His important collections are *The World I Breathe,* 1939, *Selected Writings,* 1946, *In Country Sleep,* 1952, and *Collected Poems,* 1953.

JAMES THURBER (1894-   ) was born in Columbus, Ohio, and educated at Ohio State University. For a time he was a reporter and writer on the Paris edition of the Chicago *Tribune*. He returned to New York in 1926, and began contributing humorous sketches, stories and drawings to *The New Yorker*. His books include *The Owl in the Attic and Other Perplexities,* 1931, *My Life and Hard Times,* 1933, *My World—and Welcome to It,* 1942, *The Thurber Carnival,* 1945, and *The Thurber Album,* 1952.

GEORGE TOOKER (1920-   ), American painter, was born in Brooklyn and attended Phillips Academy, Andover. After receiving the A.B. degree at Harvard University, he studied at the Art Students' League with Reginald Marsh. He has exhibited his work at the Whitney Museum of American Art since 1947, at the Institute of Contemporary Art, London, and was represented at the Venice Biennale in 1956.

LIONEL TRILLING (1905-   ) was born and educated in New York City. His graduate study was at Columbia University, where he is now Professor of English. His editorial service on *The Kenyon Review* and *The Partisan Review* and for "The American Men of Letters Series" has made him well known among students of literature. Besides stories and criticism for leading magazines, he has published two critical biographies, *Matthew Arnold,* 1939, and *E. M. Forster,* 1943, a novel, *The Middle of the Journey,* 1949, and a collection of essays, *The Liberal Imagination,* 1950.

FREDERICK J. TURNER (1861-1932), American historian, was born in Portage, Wisconsin. He taught at the University of Wisconsin (1889-1910), as described here in Carl L. Becker's essay, and at Harvard University (1910-1924). His essay here, read be-

Biographical Notes

fore the American Historical Association in 1893, inaugurated a new theory concerning the influence of the West in American experience and has become a landmark for later historians. It was first included in *The Frontier in American History*, 1920. For his *The Significance of Sections in American History*, 1932, he was posthumously awarded the Pulitzer Prize.

GENE WELTFISH (1902-   ) studied at Barnard College, Columbia University. She has been an instructor in the Department of Anthropology at Columbia.

EUDORA WELTY (1909-   ) has lived all her life in her native Jackson, Mississippi, except for excursions to the University of Wisconsin, where she received a bachelor's degree in 1929, and to the School of Advertising at Columbia University. She has done publicity work—writing feature stories and radio scripts and taking photographs. Her stories have won a number of awards, the O. Henry Memorial Prize in 1942 and 1943 and the American Academy award, for "her artistry in the subtle portrayal of character," in 1944. Her first collection of short stories, *A Curtain of Green*, was introduced by Katherine Anne Porter in 1941. Other collections are *The Wide Net*, 1943, and *The Golden Apples*, 1949; her novels are *The Robber Bridegroom*, 1942, and *Delta Wedding*, 1946.

WALT WHITMAN (1819-1892), was born on Long Island. Brief schooling followed the family's removal to Brooklyn, and young Whitman went to work as a "printer's devil" and typesetter. Years of hack-work as a printer-journalist led to his editorship of the *Brooklyn Eagle*. After two years he left, and there followed years of unsuccessful journalism, of carpentry with his father, of lecturing. In 1855 his publication of *Leaves of Grass* brought high praise from Emerson, but abuse and incomprehension from others. He continued his poetry, and the third edition of *Leaves of Grass* in 1860 contained 157 poems. During the Civil War he worked as a volunteer nurse in army hospitals, and for some years after the War as a government clerk. In 1873 he suffered a paralytic stroke which forced him to leave Washington. He settled in Camden, N. J., where he remained, a semi-invalid, for the rest of his life. In 1891 he was able to attend a dinner where he received the congratulations of some of the most distinguished Americans and Englishmen for his writing. His other works were *Drum Taps*, 1865, and *Democratic Vistas*, 1871.

RICHARD WILBUR (1921-   ), after study at Amherst and Harvard, taught at Harvard and at Wellesley. His volume *Things of This World* won the National Book Award for poetry in 1956.

TENNESSEE WILLIAMS (1914-   ) was born in Columbus, Mississippi, and attended the University of Missouri, Washington University, and the University of Iowa. He has said that seeing a performance of Ibsen's *Ghosts* made him want to write for the theatre. By 1939 his one-act plays had attracted attention. Scholarship awards from Theresa Helburn and John Gassner of the Theatre Guild, and awards from the American Academy and the Rockefeller Fellowship encouraged his writing. *The Glass Menagerie* in 1945 and *A Streetcar Named Desire* in 1947 established him as one of our finest dramatists. *Summer and Smoke* in 1948 and *The Rose Tattoo* in 1951, while not so widely praised, show further development of his sensitive artistry.

THOMAS WOLFE (1900-1938) was born in Asheville, North Carolina. He graduated from the University of North Carolina in 1920, went on to Harvard, and after receiving his M.A. there was appointed instructor in English at Washington Square College, New York University. During the next six years he taught, traveled in Europe and worked at his writing. "A man must use the material and experience of his own life," he said, "if he is to create anything that has substantial value." The editor, Maxwell Perkins, helped him put his writing in publishable form, and in 1929 *Look Homeward, Angel* appeared. Its success was immediate. Among his other books are *Of Time and the River*, 1935, *From Death to Morning*, 1935, *The Story of a Novel*, 1936, and *You Can't Go Home Again*, 1940.

ANDREW WYETH (1917-   ), painter, was born in Chadds Ford, Pennsylvania, and studied under his father, the noted illustrator N. C. Wyeth. He has won many prizes for his paintings, including a medal from the American Academy of Arts and Letters in 1947. He has exhibited his work at the Art Institute of Chicago and the Museum of Modern Art in New York, as well as in England.

WILLIAM BUTLER YEATS (1865-1939) was born in Dublin. He first studied art, then turned to writing. He worked to encourage an Irish literary renaissance. For four years he was a Senator of the Irish Free State. He was awarded the Nobel Prize in 1923. His books include *Collected Poems*, 1933, *Collected Plays*, 1934, and *Last Poems and Plays*, 1940.

INDEX OF AUTHORS, TITLES, AND FIRST LINES

A

"About suffering they were never wrong," 766
"A broken flower-stem, a broken vase," 796
"A cold coming we had of it," 704
Acquainted with the Night, 682
"Across the long-curved bight or bay," 790
Adams, James Truslow, 855
Addams, Charles, 922
"A father sees his son nearing manhood," 82
"A flying word from here and there," 667
"After the first powerful plain manifesto," 755
Afterwards, 655
"Against the burly air I strode," 793
Age of Happy Problems, The, 85
"Ah, are you digging on my grave?" 652
"Although I put away his life," 637
"Ambassador Puser the ambassador," 736
American Frontier—Frontier of What?, The, 833
American Letter, 725
American Rhapsody (4), 751
America Was Promises, 730
Amis, Kingsley, 796
"Among the smoke and fog of a December afternoon," 700
"An ant on the table cloth," 674
Anatomie of the World, An (excerpt), 941
Anderson, Maxwell, 153
"And here face down beneath the sun," 723
"And new Philosophy calls all in doubt," 941
"And summer mornings the mute child, rebellious," 4
"And these few precepts in thy memory," 79
Animula, 694
Answer, The, 720
Any Man's Advice to His Son, 83
"anyone lived in a pretty how town," 744
Appreciations (excerpt), 168
Araby, 46
"Ares at last has quit the field," 772
Arnold, Matthew, 973
"A sudden blow: the great wings beating still," 688
As You Like It (excerpt), 3
Auden, W. H., 760
"Autumn's attrition, Then this world laid waste," 789
Avery, March, 126

B

Barnett, Lincoln, 905
Barry, Philip, 464

Bear, The, 295
Beard, Charles A., 871
Benedict, Ruth, 889
Bloodhound and the Bug, The (picture), 714-715
Blume, Peter, 215
Brahma, 634
"Breathe not, hid Heart: cease silently," 653
Bright Young Men, The (picture), 942-943
"But it could never be true," 754
Byron, George Gordon, Lord, 93
Byzantium, 689

C

Campers at Kitty Hawk, The, 180
Casino, 768
Child Waking, 791
Childe Harold's Pilgrimage (excerpt), 93
Chinese vase (picture), 634
Christina's World (picture), 585
"Christmas Eve, and twelve of the clock," 654
Cohen, Morris R., 854
Coleridge, S. T., 125
"Coming around a corner of the dark trail . . . what was wrong with the valley?" 721
Coming Issues in American Politics, 878
Conquest, Robert, 789
Conrad, Joseph, 110, 322
Credo, 662
Cummings, E. E., 3, 740

D

"Daughters of Time, the hypocritic Days," 633
Day, Robert, 742
Days, 633
Day the Dam Broke, The, 211
Dean, Abner, 94-95, 748, 942-943
Death of a Traveling Salesman, 228
Departmental, 674
Devil's Dream, 754
Dickinson, Emily, 635
Discoveries (excerpt), 110
Dobrée, Bonamy, 158
Donne, John, 941
"Do not go gentle into that good night," 788
Dos Passos, John, 180, 183
Dover Beach, 973
Dream of Fair Women, A, 796

[1005]

Index of Authors, Titles, and First Lines

Drucker, Peter, 878
Drumlin Woodchuck, A, 676

E

Earth and Sky (picture), 962
East Coker, 706
Edgerton, Harold E., 168
Education in the World State, 185
Eleven, 4
Eliot, T. S., 693
"Elysium is as far as to," 635
Embler, Weller, 963
Emerson, Ralph Waldo, 631
Epistemology of Poetry, 790
Epistle to be Left in the Earth, 738
Essence of Tragedy, The, 153
Express, The, 75
Extraordinary Little Cough, 50

F

Face Within the Face, The, 220
Faith of an American, The (excerpt), 903
Farewell Address (excerpt), 904
Farewell, My Lovely, 866
Faulkner, William, 295, 803
Fearing, Kenneth, 83, 747
Figure a Poem Makes, The (excerpt), 669
Fire and Ice, 679
"First you bite your fingernails," 751
Fitzgerald, F. Scott, 80, 271
"Five soldiers fixed by Matthew Brady's eye," 799
Flammonde, 665
Fletcher, Iain, 794
Foreword to *The Selected Poetry of Robinson Jeffers* (excerpt), 716
Foreword to *The Still Centre* (excerpt), 755
Forster, E. M., 190, 982
Four Freedoms, The, 889
"Fred, where is north?" 677
Friar, Kimon, 691
Frisch, O. R., 923
Frost, Robert, 669
Fry, Christopher, 586
Future of American Liberalism, The (excerpt), 854

G

Genesis, 793
Geography of This Time, 739
Giraudoux, Jean, 586
Girl in the Snow, A, 789
"Give all to love," 633
Glass Menagerie, The, 543
Gold, Herbert, 85
Guernica mural (detail), 168
Guided Missiles Experimental Range, 789

H

"Hairy Ape, The," 515
Hall, Donald, 797
Hamlet of A. MacLeish, The (excerpt), 723
Handball (picture), 23
Hand That Signed the Paper Felled a City, The, 777
Hap, 650
Hardy, Thomas, 649
Harris, Eugene, 792
Hartley, Marsden, 668
"Has anybody ever thought . . . "(picture), 865
Hayakawa, S. I., 127
Hayes, Carlton J. H., 833
Heart of Darkness, 322
Hemingway, Ernest, 307
Hill, Geoffrey, 793
Hollow Men, The, 702
Home (picture), 219
Hopper, Edward, 682
Housman, A. E., 656
How Writing Is Written, 169
Humanities, 791
Hurt Hawks, 717
Huxley, Aldous, 24, 185
"Hypnotized and told they're seeing red," 791

I

"I am that witness through whom the whole," 758
"I cannot find my way: there is no star," 662
"I celebrate myself, and sing myself," 639
"If but some vengeful god would call to me," 650
"If the red slayer thinks he slays," 634
"If tired of trees I seek again mankind," 675
"If you can't eat you got to," 744
"If you have lost the radio beam, then guide yourself by the sun or the stars," 83
"I have been one acquainted with the night," 682
Impercipient, The, 651
"I never saw a moor," 635
"in Just-spring," 3
"In May, when sea-winds pierced our solitudes," 631
"In my beginning is my end. In succession," 706
"In my craft or sullen art," 777
Inquisitors, The, 721
Inspiration (picture), 94-95
In Tenebris, II, 652
"In the mustardseed sun," 782
In the White Giant's Thigh, 780
"Issues from the hand of God, the simple soul," 694
"I think continually of those who were truly great," 759
"It is a winter's tale," 784
"It is colder now," 738
"It is not—I swear by every fiery omen," 752
"It was my thirtieth year to heaven," 778
"It went many years," 671

Index of Authors, Titles, and First Lines

J

Jarrell, Randall, 113
Jeffers, Robinson, 716
Jefferson, Thomas, 804
Jonson, Ben, 110
Journey of the Magi, 704
Joyce, James, 46
"Just lost when I was saved!" 638

K

Kouwenhoven, John A., 842

L

Landscape Near an Aerodrome, The, 757
Language of Reports, The, 127
Law Like Love, 767
Lawrence, D. H., 236
"Law, say the gardeners, is the sun," 767
Leda and the Swan, 688
Letter to a Correspondent in America, 807
Letter to his daughter (Fitzgerald), 80
Letter to Lord Byron, Part IV, 761
"Let us go then, you and I," 695
Level of Abstraction, A, 790
Life, 150
"Lincoln?" 683
Lippmann, Walter, 973
Lockless Door, The, 671
Looking into History, 799
Lost Boy, The, 57
Love Calls Us to the Things of This World, 798
"love is more thicker than forget," 746
"Loveliest of trees, the cherry now," 661
Love Song of J. Alfred Prufrock, The, 695
Lucioni, Luigi, 630

M

Macaulay, Thomas Babington, 807
"Macavity's a Mystery Cat: he's called the Hidden Paw—," 712
Macavity: The Mystery Cat, 712
Machine Stops, The, 190
MacLeish, Archibald, 4, 723
Major Barbara, 403
Master, The, 667
Masters, 796
Maugham, W. Somerset, 100
McFee, William, 126
Memorial Rain, 736
Men, 728
Mending Wall, 680
Metaphor and Social Belief, 963
Mill, The, 664
Millis, Walter, 903
Montague, C. E., 96

"More beautiful and soft than any moth," 757
Mr. Flood's Party, 663
Mt. Kilimanjaro, photograph of, 306
"Much madness is divinest sense," 635
Musée des Beaux Arts, 766
"My life closed twice before its close," 638

N

Nagasaki, Japan, under bomb attack (picture), 916
Name and Nature of Poetry, The (excerpt), 656
Neither Out Far Nor In Deep, 677
"Never until our souls are strong enough," 664
New Way of Writing, The, 158
"Night after night I lie like this listening," 723
Nighthawks (picture), 682
"nobody loses all the time," 743
No Credit, 750
Nones, 770
Note on "Byzantium," A, 691
"Not palaces, an era's crown," 756
"Now, at a particular spot on the radio dial,— 'in this corner, wearing purple trunks,'" 749
"Now through night's caressing grip," 761
Nursery, The (picture), 84

O

Obscurity of the Poet, The, 113
Ode . . . to Channing, 631
Of This Time, Of That Place, 246
"Old Eben Flood, climbing alone one night," 663
On Natural Aristocracy, 804
"On no work of words now for three lean months in the bloody," 782
On Style (excerpt), 125
"Once more the storm is howling, and half hid," 81
O'Neill, Eugene, 515
One's-Self I Sing, 639
"One's-self I sing, a simple separate person," 639
"One thing has a shelving bank," 676
"Only the hands are living; to the wheel attracted," 768
Ortega y Gasset, José, 932
Orwell, George, 135
"O sweet spontaneous," 741
Our Changing Characteristics, 855
"Our history is grave noble and tragic," 728
"Our sardine fishermen work at night in the dark of the moon; daylight or moonlight," 719
Outline of Scientists, An, 938
"Out of the mud two strangers came," 669
Oxen, The, 654

P

Parade (picture), 215
Pattern-Makers, The (excerpt), 126
People Yes, The (Parts 9, 57), 82, 683
Petty, Mary, 699, 865

Index of Authors, Titles, and First Lines

Philadelphia Story, The, 464
Picasso, Pablo, 5, 168
Piper (photograph), 792
Poem in October, 778
Poem On His Birthday, 782
Politics and the English Language, 135
Polonius to Laertes, 79
Portrait (2), 750
Portrait of a Lady, 700
Prayer for My Daughter, A, 81
Preface to *Late Lyrics and Earlier*, 649
Preface to *Leaves of Grass* (excerpt), 809
Preface to *Major Barbara*, 384
Preface to *Nigger of the Narcissus*, 110
Prime, 769
Primitive and the Technical, The, 932
Problem of Unbelief, The, 973
"Promise you'll wait for me" (picture), 699
Proteus, 183
Purse-Seine, The, 719

R

Races of Mankind, The, 889
Readings, Forecasts, Personal Guidance, 752
Reception Good, 749
Red Pony, The, Part I, 5
Release on New Mexico Test, U. S. War Department, 917
Remarks upon Receiving the Nobel Prize, 803
Return to Normal (picture), 748
Reveille, 661
Rhodora, The, 631
Richard Cory, 665
Rich Boy, The, 271
Robinson, Edwin Arlington, 662
Rocking-Horse Winner, The, 236
Roosevelt, Franklin D., 889
Rose of the World, The, 687

S

Sailing to Byzantium, 668
Sandburg, Carl, 82, 683
Schorer, Mark, 220
Scovell, E. J., 791
Second Coming, The, 687
Secret Life of Walter Mitty, The, 215
Selected Essays (excerpt), 693
Selected Letters, E. A. Robinson (excerpt), 662
Selected Writings, Dylan Thomas (excerpt), 777
Shahn, Ben, 23
Shakespeare, 3, 79
Shaw, George Bernard, 384, 403
Sheeler, Charles, 962
Shine, Perishing Republic, 718
Significance of the Frontier in American History, The, 816
"Simultaneously, as soundlessly," 769

"since feeling is first," 744
Snows of Kilimanjaro, The, 307
"Soft sounds and odours brim up through the night," 789
"Soldier from the wars returning," 657
"Some say the world will end in fire," 679
"Something there is that doesn't love a wall," 680
Song of Myself (Parts 1, 3, 30, 52), 639
Sonnet; 664
Sources of the Past, The, 796
"Space being (don't forget to remember) curved," 740
Speech to Those Who Say Comrade, 729
Speed photograph of tennis player, 168
Spencer, Stanley, 84
Spender, Stephen, 755
Spiritual Explorations (excerpt), 758
Squares and Oblongs (excerpt), 760
Star-Splitter, The, 671
Stein, Gertrude, 169
Stein, Leo, 168
Steinbeck, John, 5
Steinberg, Saul, 176-177
"Stone, bronze, stone, steel, stone, oakleaves horses' heels, 705
"Stonecutters fighting time with marble, you foredefeated," 718
Stopping by Woods on a Snowy Evening, 676
Story of a Novel, The (excerpt), 144
Subway, The (picture), 190
"Success is counted sweetest," 636
Sullivan, J. W. N., 944
"Summer, stream and stillness," 790

T

"Terence, this is stupid stuff," 659
"That horse whose rider fears to jump will fall," 795
"That is no country for old men. The young," 688
"That with this bright believing band," 651
"The broken pillar of the wing jags from the clotted shoulder," 717
"The brotherhood is not by the blood certainly," 729
"The chestnut casts his flambeaux, and the flowers," 658
"The child sleeps in the daytime," 792
"The clear brown eyes, kindly and alert," 750
"The door still swinging to, and girls revive," 796
"The eyes open to a cry of pulleys," 798
"The Great War had begun: but masters' scrutiny," 761
"The guns spell money's ultimate reason," 758
"The habit of these years is constant choice," 797
"The half-moon westers low, my love," 657
"The last step taken found your heft," 674
"The laws of God, the laws of man," 658
"The man Flammonde, from God knows where," 665
"The miller's wife had waited long," 664
"Then what is the answer?—Not to be deluded by dreams," 720

[1008]

Index of Authors, Titles, and First Lines

"The people along the sand," 677
"There is a jungle, there is a jungle, there is a vast, vivid, wild, wild, marvelous, marvelous, marvelous jungle," 747
"There's a certain slant of light," 636
"The sea is calm tonight," 973
There Are Roughly Zones, 681
"these children singing in stone a," 745
"The soul selects her own society," 636
"The unpurged images of day recede," 689
"The wind is east but the hot weather continues," 725
"Think no more, lad; laugh, be jolly," 658
"This is my letter to the world," 635
Thomas, Dylan, 50, 777
"Though loath to grieve," 631
"Through throats where many rivers meet, the curlews cry," 780
Thurber, James, 211, 215, 219, 714-715, 938
Tiger at the Gates, 586
Time and Motion Study, 794
To an Unborn Pauper Child, 653
To a Thinker, 674
"To fight aloud is very brave," 637
Tooker, George, 190
To the Stone-Cutters, 718
Travelogue in a Shooting-Gallery, 747
Trilling, Lionel, 246
Triumphal March, 705
Turner, Frederick Jackson, 816
"Turning and turning in the widening gyre," 687
Two Tramps in Mud Time, 669

U

Ultima Ratio Regum, 758
Under Which Lyre, 772
Universe and Dr. Einstein, The, Part I, 905
Unlocking the Storehouse of Energy, 923
Untragic America, 150

V

Values of Science, The, 944
Vantage Point, The, 675

W

"Wake: the silver dusk returning," 661
Washington, George, 904
"We are the hollow men," 702
Weary of the Truth (picture), 668
"Well, it looks like a buttercup to me" (picture), 742
Weltfish, Gene, 889
Welty, Eudora, 228
"We sit indoors and talk of the cold outside," 681
West-running Brook, 677
"What are they? Why, only qualities of light," 794
What I Believe, 982
"What is required of us is the recognition," 715
What's American about America? 842
"What we know to be not possible," 770
"Whenever Richard Cory went down town," 665
"When I heard the learn'd astronomer," 649
"When I was one-and-twenty," 661
"When lilacs last in the dooryard bloom'd," 642
"when serpents bargain for the right to squirm," 746
"When the clouds' swoln bosoms echo back the shouts of the many and strong," 652
"When the Present has latched its postern behind my tremulous stay," 655
"Whether dinner was pleasant, with the windows lit by gunfire," 750
"While this America settles in the mould of its vulgarity, heavily thickening to empire," 718
White, Lee Strout, 866
Whither Mankind? 871
Whitman, Walt, 2, 639, 809
"Who dreamed that beauty passes like a dream?" 687
"Who is the voyager in these leaves?" 730
"Whose woods these are I think I know," 676
Wilbur, Richard, 798
Williams, Tennessee, 543
Winter's Tale, A, 784
Wolfe, Thomas, 57, 144
Words, Words, Words, 96
World, the Times, The, 797
Writing Prose, 100
Wyeth, Andrew, 585

Y

"Years of the modern! years of the unperform'd!" 2
Yeats, William Butler, 81, 687
You, Andrew Marvell, 723
"You know Orion always comes up sideways," 671
Young Archimedes, 24
Youth (picture), 5

found out after upon to settle to the scheduling
sometime in etc.
middle age - age of industrial
8th century - age of reason
Middle age - Renaissance age
including reproducing divine power eg to create
religion, reason. Reason is not
what is demanded of that particular time is what
gives this age its name.

Day 90's - Gay 90's
1920 - Jazz age
1930 - depression
1940 - conflict
1950 - Frustration of world war.

Scotland - Everyone was convinced that we were
making false idols and worshiping.
Robes, no arms so robes must have a
highly significant and they deep altogether
of the mainland nature had thought that the
Scotsmen were so odd so they said it was.
They wouldn't even have clothes to wait about
in coming - that 3/4 of Scotland demanded by the
Gentiles Textiles.

United Textiles created the standard leathers
Believed in socially closed. Perfumed religion
fact. Religion were hymn class demanded by
church (Christian).

Post to groups - a quickening of their ideas, but
they have not up by God, or Bothered to read
Neither prophesying what came to be reality!
Merely fixed order - unless trying to record
what they should do, his nothing what was
English is American freedom and Roman in
some time.

People began to do quite spiritual, after W.W.I
a revolt of mind, and he couldn't a
divergi of our time,
has come ridiculousness.

Later came novels to attack the wasteland idea.

19th century - advising people to change themselves the laboring class must change so things are better.

20th century - advising society to change itself so that the people can be happier.

An American Tragedy = novel by Dreiser. Story of a young man caught by the physiological hinder of sex, the other of ambition.
  Man is born with free will to make free choices.
  Calvinists denied the freedom of will. (not very good theologians). If you see man only as a reacting organism, then man can not change himself.

New belief that man is a reacting organism, grown from Freudism, and Darwinism, and implied in Marxism.

Every reaction that man makes is a reaction of ———.
  The physicists reject the idea that every reaction results in another. That man is left with the ability to make choices. If man is only a reaction mechanism, makes no difference if he survives or perishes, perhaps better if he perished, at least for society.

In our age -

Poetry becoming a bitter, satirical attack in our age.

Universe looked to as being started by the creator, thrown down and forgot completely about.

Using logic impossible to confirm the concept of the freedom of the will. As though he can't make choices. Logically all determined.

In Mohammedanism - everything was set in action and every motion to the end of time was determined.

Return to religion - Kreider + my thesis - Huxley.
To a vision of a new earth.
An attack on personal problems in writings of Wolfe, Lewis, Richardson,
Auden, Spender, a